DATA ANALYSIS FOR BUSINESS, EC~~~~~~~~, ~~~ ~~~~~

This textbook provides future data analysts with the tools, methods, and skills needed to answer data-focused, real-life questions; to carry out data analysis; and to visualize and interpret results to support better decisions in business, economics, and public policy.

Data wrangling and exploration, regression analysis, machine learning, and causal analysis are comprehensively covered, as well as when, why, and how the methods work, and how they relate to each other.

As the most effective way to communicate data analysis, running case studies play a central role in this textbook. Each case starts with an industry-relevant question and answers it by using real-world data and applying the tools and methods covered in the textbook. Learning is then consolidated by 360 practice questions and 120 data exercises.

Extensive online resources, including raw and cleaned data and codes for all analysis in Stata, R, and Python, can be found at `http://www.gabors-data-analysis.com`.

Gábor Békés is an assistant professor at the Department of Economics and Business of the Central European University, and Director of the Business Analytics Program. He is a senior fellow at KRTK and a research affiliate at the Center for Economic Policy Research (CEPR). He has published in top economics journals on multinational firm activities and productivity, business clusters, and innovation spillovers. He has managed international data collection projects on firm performance and supply chains. He has done policy-advising (the European Commission, ECB) as well as private-sector consultancy (in finance, business intelligence, and real estate). He has taught graduate-level data analysis and economic geography courses since 2012.

Gábor Kézdi is a research associate professor at the University of Michigan's Institute for Social Research. He has published in top journals in economics, statistics, and political science on topics including household finances, health, education, demography, and ethnic disadvantages and prejudice. He has managed several data collection projects in Europe; currently, he is co-investigator of the Health and Retirement Study in the USA. He has consulted for various governmental and non-governmental institutions on the disadvantage of the Roma minority and the evaluation of social interventions. He has taught data analysis, econometrics, and labor economics from undergraduate to PhD levels since 2002, and supervised a number of MA and PhD students.

"This exciting new text covers everything today's aspiring data scientist needs to know, managing to be comprehensive as well as accessible. Like a good confidence interval, the Gabors have got you almost completely covered!"

Professor Joshua Angrist, Massachusetts Institute of Technology

"This is an excellent book for students learning the art of modern data analytics. It combines the latest techniques with practical applications, replicating the implementation side of classroom teaching that is typically missing in textbooks. For example, they used the World Management Survey data to generate exercises on firm performance for students to gain experience in handling real data, with all its quirks, problems, and issues. For students looking to learn data analysis from one textbook, this is a great way to proceed."

Professor Nicholas Bloom, Department of Economics and Stanford Business School, Stanford University

"I know of few books about data analysis and visualization that are as comprehensive, deep, practical, and current as this one; and I know of almost none that are as fun to read. Gábor Békés and Gábor Kézdi have created a most unusual and most compelling beast: a textbook that teaches you the subject matter well and that, at the same time, you can enjoy reading cover to cover."

Professor Alberto Cairo, University of Miami

"A beautiful integration of econometrics and data science that provides a direct path from data collection and exploratory analysis to conventional regression modeling, then on to prediction and causal modeling. Exactly what is needed to equip the next generation of students with the tools and insights from the two fields."

Professor David Card, University of California–Berkeley

"This textbook is excellent at dissecting and explaining the underlying process of data analysis. Békés and Kézdi have masterfully woven into their instruction a comprehensive range of case studies. The result is a rigorous textbook grounded in real-world learning, at once accessible and engaging to novice scholars and advanced practitioners alike. I have every confidence it will be valued by future generations."

Professor Kerwin K. Charles, Yale School of Management

"This book takes you by the hand in a journey that will bring you to understand the core value of data in the fields of machine learning and economics. The large amount of accessible examples combined with the intuitive explanation of foundational concepts is an ideal mix for anyone who wants to do data analysis. It is highly recommended to anyone interested in the new way in which data will be analyzed in the social sciences in the next years."

Professor Christian Fons-Rosen, Barcelona Graduate School of Economics

"This sophisticatedly simple book is ideal for undergraduate- or Master's-level Data Analytics courses with a broad audience. The authors discuss the key aspects of examining data, regression analysis, prediction, Lasso, random forests, and more, using elegant prose instead of algebra. Using well-chosen case studies, they illustrate the techniques and discuss all of them patiently and thoroughly."

Professor Carter Hill, Louisiana State University

"This is not an econometrics textbook. It is a data analysis textbook. And a highly unusual one - written in plain English, based on simplified notation, and full of case studies. An excellent starting point for future data analysts or anyone interested in finding out what data can tell us."

Professor Beata Javorcik, University of Oxford

"A multifaceted book that considers many sides of data analysis, all of them important for the contemporary student and practitioner. It brings together classical statistics, regression, and causal inference, sending the message that awareness of all three aspects is important for success in this field. Many 'best practices' are discussed in accessible language, and illustrated using interesting datasets."

Professor Ilya Ryzhov, University of Maryland

"This is a fantastic book to have. Strong data skills are critical for modern business and economic research, and this text provides a thorough and practical guide to acquiring them. Highly recommended."

Professor John van Reenen, MIT Sloan

"Energy and climate change is a major public policy challenge, where high-quality data analysis is the foundation of solid policy. This textbook will make an important contribution to this with its innovative approach. In addition to the comprehensive treatment of modern econometric techniques, the book also covers the less glamorous but crucial aspects of procuring and cleaning data, and drawing useful inferences from less-than-perfect datasets. An important and practical combination for both academic and policy professionals."

Laszlo Varro, Chief Economist, International Energy Agency

DATA ANALYSIS FOR BUSINESS, ECONOMICS, AND POLICY

Gábor Békés

Central European University, Vienna and Budapest

Gábor Kézdi

University of Michigan, Ann Arbor

CAMBRIDGE
UNIVERSITY PRESS

University Printing House, Cambridge CB2 8BS, United Kingdom

One Liberty Plaza, 20th Floor, New York, NY 10006, USA

477 Williamstown Road, Port Melbourne, VIC 3207, Australia

314–321, 3rd Floor, Plot 3, Splendor Forum, Jasola District Centre, New Delhi – 110025, India

79 Anson Road, #06–04/06, Singapore 079906

Cambridge University Press is part of the University of Cambridge.

It furthers the University's mission by disseminating knowledge in the pursuit of education, learning, and research at the highest international levels of excellence.

www.cambridge.org
Information on this title: www.cambridge.org/9781108483018
DOI: 10.1017/9781108591102

© Gábor Békés and Gábor Kézdi 2021

First published 2021

Printed in Singapore by Markono Print Media Pte Ltd 2021

A catalogue record for this publication is available from the British Library.

ISBN 978-1-108-48301-8 Hardback
ISBN 978-1-108-71620-8 Paperback

Additional resources for this publication at www.cambridge.org/bekeskezdi and www.gabors-data-analysis.com

BRIEF CONTENTS

CONTENTS

WHY USE THIS BOOK

An applied data analysis textbook for future professionals

Data analysis is a process. It starts with formulating a question and collecting appropriate data, or assessing whether the available data can help answer the question. Then comes cleaning and organizing the data, tedious but essential tasks that affect the results of the analysis as much as any other step in the process. Exploratory data analysis gives context to the eventual results and helps deciding the details of the analytical method to be applied. The main analysis consists of choosing and implementing the method to answer the question, with potential robustness checks. Along the way, correct interpretation and effective presentation of the results are crucial. Carefully crafted data visualization help summarize our findings and convey key messages. The final task is to answer the original question, with potential qualifications and directions for future inquiries.

Our textbook **equips future data analysts with the most important tools, methods, and skills** they need through the entire process of data analysis to answer data focused, real-life questions. We cover all the fundamental methods that help along the process of data analysis. The textbook is divided into four parts covering **data wrangling and exploration, regression analysis, prediction with machine learning, and causal analysis**. We explain when, why, and how the various methods work, and how they are related to each other.

Our approach has a **different focus compared to the typical textbooks** in econometrics and data science. They are often excellent in teaching many econometric and machine learning methods. But they don't give much guidance about how to carry out an actual data analysis project from beginning to end. Instead, students have to learn all of that when they work through individual projects, guided by their teachers, advisors, and peers – but not their textbooks.

To cover all of the steps that are necessary to carry out an actual data analysis project, we **built a large number of fully developed case studies**. While each case study focuses on the particular method discussed in the chapter, they illustrate all elements of the process from question through analysis to conclusion. We facilitate individual work by **sharing all data and code in Stata, R, and Python**.

Curated content and focus for the modern data analyst

Our textbook focuses on the most relevant tools and methods. Instead of dumping many methods on the students, we selected the most widely used methods that tend to work well in many situations. That choice allowed us to discuss each method in detail so students can gain a deep understanding of when, why, and how those methods work. It also allows us to compare the different methods both in general and in the course of our case studies.

The textbook is divided into four parts. The first part starts with data collection and data quality, followed by organizing and cleaning data, **exploratory data analysis** and data visualization, generalizing from the data, and hypothesis testing. The second part gives a thorough introduction to **regression analysis**, including probability models and time series regressions. The third part covers **predictive analytics** and introduces cross-validation, LASSO, tree-based machine learning methods such as random forest, probability prediction, classification, and forecasting from time series data. The fourth part covers **causal analysis**, starting with the potential outcomes framework and causal maps, then discussing experiments, difference-in-differences analysis, various panel data methods, and the event study approach.

When deciding on which methods to discuss and in what depth, we drew on our own experience as well as the advice of many people. We have taught Data Analysis and Econometrics to students in Master's programs for years in Europe and the USA, and trained experts in business analytics, economics, and economic policy. We used earlier versions of this textbook in many courses with students who differed in background, interest, and career plans. In addition, we talked to many experts both in academia and in industry: teachers, researchers, analysts, and users of data analysis results. As a result, this textbook offers **a curated content that reflects the views of data analysts with a wide range of experiences**.

Real-life case studies in a central role

A cornerstone of this textbook are 43 case studies spreading over one-third of our material. This reflects our view that working through case studies is the best way to learn data analysis. Each of our case studies starts with a relevant question and answers it in the end, using real-life data and applying the tools and methods covered in the particular chapter.

Similarly to other textbooks, our case studies illustrate the methods covered in the textbook. In contrast with other textbooks, though, they are much more than that.

Each of our case studies is a fully developed story linking business or policy questions to decisions in data selection, application of methods and discussion of results. Each case study uses **real-life data** that is messy and often complicated, and it discusses data quality issues and the steps of data cleaning and organization along the way. Then, each case study includes **exploratory data analysis** to clarify the context and help choose the methods for the subsequent analysis. After carrying out the main **analysis**, each case study emphasizes the correct **interpretation** of the results, effective ways to present and visualize the results, and many include robustness checks. Finally, each case study **answers the question** it started with, usually with the necessary qualifications, discussing internal and external validity, and often raising additional questions and directions for further investigation.

Our case studies cover a wide range of topics, with a potential appeal to a wide range of students. They cover **consumer decision, economic and social policy, finance, business and management, health, and sport**. Their regional coverage is also wider than usual: one third are from the USA, one third are from Europe and the UK, and one third are from other countries or includes all countries from Australia to Thailand.

Support material with data and code shared

We offer a truly comprehensive material with data, code for all case studies, 360 **practice questions**, 120 **data exercises**, derivations for advanced materials, and reading suggestions. Each chapter ends with practice questions that help revise the material. They are followed by data exercises that invite students to carry out analysis on their own, in the form of robustness checks or replicating the analysis using other data.

We share all raw and cleaned data we use in the case studies. We also share the codes that clean the data and produce all results, tables, and graphs in **Stata, R, and Python** so students can tinker with our code and compare the solutions in the different software.

All data and code are available on the textbook website:

`http://gabors-data-analysis.com`

Who is this book for?

This textbook was written to be a **complete course** in data analysis. It introduces and discusses the most important concepts and methods in exploratory data analysis, regression analysis, machine learning and causal analysis. Thus, readers don't need to have a background in those areas.

The textbook includes formulae to define methods and tools, but it **explains all formulae in plain English**, both when a formula is introduced and, then, when it is used in a case study. Thus, understanding formulae is not necessary to learn data analysis from this textbook. They are of great help, though, and we encourage all students and practitioners to work with formulae whenever possible. The mathematics background required to understand these formulae is quite low, at the the level of basic calculus.

This textbook could be useful for university students in graduate programs as **core text** in applied statistics and econometrics, quantitative methods, or data analysis. The textbook is best used as core text for non-research degree Masters programs or part of the curriculum in a PhD or research Masters programs. It may also **complement online courses** that teach specific methods to give more context and explanation. Undergraduate courses can also make use of this textbook, even though the workload on students exceeds the typical undergraduate workload. Finally, the textbook can serve as a **handbook for practitioners** to guide them through all steps of real-life data analysis.

SIMPLIFIED NOTATION

A note for the instructors who plan to use our textbook.

We introduced some new notation in this textbook, to make the formulae simpler and more focused. In particular, our **formula for regressions is slightly different** from the traditional formula. In line with other textbooks, we think that it is good practice to write out the formula for each regression that is analyzed. For this reason, it important to use a notation for the regression formula that is as simple as possible and focuses only on what we care about. Our notation is intuitive, but it's slightly different from traditional practice. Let us explain our reasons.

Our approach starts with the definition of the regression: it is a model for the conditional mean. The formulaic definition of the simple linear regression is $E[y|x] = \alpha + \beta x$. The formulaic definition of a linear regression with three right-hand-side variables is $E[y|x_1, x_2, x_3] = \beta_0 + \beta_1 x_1 + \beta_2 x_2 + \beta_3 x_3$.

The regression formula we use in the textbook is a simplified version of this formulaic definition. In particular, we have y^E on the left-hand side instead of $E[y|...]$. y^E is just a shorthand for the expected value of y conditional on whatever is on the right-hand side of the regression.

Thus, the formula for the simple linear regression is $y^E = \alpha + \beta x$, and y^E is the expected value of y conditional on x. The formula for the linear regression with three right-hand-side variables is $y^E = \beta_0 + \beta_1 x_1 + \beta_2 x_2 + \beta_3 x_3$, and here y^E is the expected value of y conditional on x_1, x_2, and x_3. Having y^E on the left-hand side makes notation much simpler than writing out the conditional expectation formula $E[y|...]$, especially when we have many right-hand-side variables.

In contrast, the traditional regression formula has the variable y itself on the left-hand side, not its conditional mean. Thus, it has to involve an additional element, the error term. For example, the traditional formula for the linear regression with three right-hand-side variables is $y = \beta_0 + \beta_1 x_1 + \beta_2 x_2 + \beta_3 x_3 + e$.

Our notation is simpler, because it has fewer elements. More importantly, our notation makes it explicit that the regression is a model for the conditional mean. It focuses on the data that analysts care about (the right-hand-side variables and their coefficients), without adding anything else.

ACKNOWLEDGMENTS

Let us first thank our students at the Central European University, at the University of Michigan, and at the University of Reading. The idea of writing a textbook was born out of teaching and mentoring them. We have learned a lot from teaching them, and many of them helped us writing code, collecting data, reading papers, and hunting for ideas.

Many colleagues helped us with their extremely valuable comments and suggestions. We thank Eduardo Arino de la Rubia, Emily Blanchard, Imre Boda, Alberto Cairo, Gergely Daróczi, János Divényi, Christian Fons-Rosen, Bonnie Kavoussi, Olivér Kiss, Miklós Koren, Mike Luca, Róbert Lieli, László Mátyás, Tímea Laura Molnár, Arieda Muço, Jenő Pál, and Ádám Szeidl and anonymous reviewers of the first draft of the textbook.

We have received help with our case studies from Alberto Cavallo, Daniella Scur, Nick Bloom, John van Reenen, Anikó Kristof, József Keleti, Emily Oster, and MyChelle Andrews. We have learned a lot from them.

Several people helped us a great deal with our manuscript. At Cambridge University Press, our commissioning editor, Phil Good, encouraged us from the day we met. Our editors, Heather Brolly, Jane Adams, and Nicola Chapman, guided us with kindness and steadfastness from first draft to proofs. We are not native English speakers, and support from Chris Cartwrigh and Jon Billam was very useful. We are grateful for Sarolta Rózsás, who read and edited endless versions of chapters, checking consistency and clarity, and pushed us to make the text more coherent and accessible.

Creating the code base in Stata, R and Python was a massive endeavour. Both of us are primarily Stata users, and we needed R code that would be fairly consistent with Stata code. Plus, all graphs were produced in R. So we needed help to have all our Stata codes replicated in R, and a great deal of code writing from scratch. Zsuzsa Holler and Kinga Ritter have provided enormous development support, spearheading this effort for years. Additional code and refactoring in R was created by Máté Tóth, János Bíró, and Eszter Pázmándi. János and Máté also created the first version of Python notebooks. Additional coding, data collection, visualization, and editing were done by Viktória Kónya, Zsófia Kőműves, Dániel Bánki, Abuzar Ali, Endre Borza, Imola Csóka, and Ahmed Al Shaibani.

The wonderful cover design is based on the work by Ágoston Nagy, his first but surely not his last.

Collaborating with many talented people, including our former students, and bringing them together was one of the joys of writing this book.

Let us also shout out to the fantastic R user community – both online and offline – from whom we learned tremendously. Special thanks to the Rstats and Econ Twitter community – we received wonderful suggestions from tons of people we have never met.

We thank the Central European University for professional and financial support. Julius Horvath and Miklós Koren as department heads provided massive support from the day we shared our plans.

Finally, let us thank those who were with us throughout the long, and often stressful, process of writing a textbook. Békés thanks Saci; Kézdi thanks Zsuzsanna. We would not have been able to do it without their love and support.

PART I Data Exploration

1 Origins of Data

What data is, how to collect it, and how to assess its quality

> **Motivation**
>
> You want to understand whether and by how much online and offline prices differ. To that end you need data on the online and offline prices of the same products. How would you collect such data? In particular, how would you select for which products to collect the data, and how could you make sure that the online and offline prices are for the same products?
>
> The quality of management of companies may be an important determinant of their performance, and it may be affected by a host of important factors, such as ownership or the characteristics of the managers. How would you collect data on the management practices of companies, and how would you measure the quality of those practices? In addition, how would you collect data on other features of the companies?

Part I of our textbook introduces how to think about what kind of data would help answer a question, how to collect such data, and how to start working with data. It also includes chapters that introduce important concepts and tools that are fundamental building blocks of methods that we'll introduce in the rest of the textbook.

We start our textbook by discussing how data is collected, what the most important aspects of data quality are, and how we can assess those aspects. First we introduce data collection methods and data quality because of their prime importance. Data doesn't grow on trees but needs to be collected with a lot of effort, and it's essential to have high-quality data to get meaningful answers to our questions. In the end, data quality is determined by how the data was collected. Thus, it's fundamental for data analysts to understand various data collection methods, how they affect data quality in general, and what the details of the actual collection of their data imply for its quality.

The chapter starts by introducing key concepts of data. It then describes the most important methods of data collection used in business, economics, and policy analysis, such as web scraping, using administrative sources, and conducting surveys. We introduce aspects of data quality, such as validity and reliability of variables and coverage of observations. We discuss how to assess and link data quality to how the data was collected. We devote a section to Big Data to understand what it is and how it may differ from more traditional data. This chapter also covers sampling, ethical issues, and some good practices in data collection.

This chapter includes three case studies. The case study **Finding a good deal among hotels: data collection** looks at hotel prices in a European city, using data collected from a price comparison website, to help find a good deal: a hotel that is inexpensive relative to its features. It describes the collection of the `hotels-vienna` dataset. This case study illustrates data collection from online information by web scraping. The second case study, **Comparing online and**

offline prices: data collection, describes the `billion-prices` dataset. The ultimate goal of this case study is comparing online prices and offline prices of the same products, and we'll return to that question later in the textbook. In this chapter we discuss how the data was collected, with an emphasis on what products it covered and how it measured prices. The third case study, **Management quality and firm size: data collection**, is about measuring the quality of management in many organizations in many countries. It describes the `wms-management-survey` dataset. We'll use this data in subsequent case studies, too. In this chapter we describe this survey, focusing on sampling and the measurement of the abstract concept of management quality. The three case studies illustrate the choices and trade-offs data collection involves, practical issues that may arise during implementation, and how all that may affect data quality.

Learning outcomes
After working through this chapter, you should be able to:
- understand the basic aspects of data;
- understand the most important data collection methods;
- assess various aspects of data quality based on how the data was collected;
- understand some of the trade-offs in the design and implementation of data collection;
- carry out a small-scale data collection exercise from the web or through a survey.

1.1   What Is Data?

A good definition of data is "factual information (such as measurements or statistics) used as a basis for reasoning, discussion, or calculation" (Merriam-Webster dictionary). According to this definition, information is considered data if its content is based on some measurement ("factual") and if it may be used to support some "reasoning or discussion" either by itself or after structuring, cleaning, and analysis. There is a lot of data out there, and the amount of data, or information that can be turned into data, is growing rapidly. Some of it is easier to get and use for meaningful analysis, some of it requires a lot of work, and some of it may turn out to be useless for answering interesting questions.

An almost universal feature of data is that it rarely comes in a form that can directly help answer our questions. Instead, data analysts need to work a lot with data: structuring, cleaning, and analyzing it. Even after a lot of work, the information and the quality of information contained in the original data determines what conclusions analysts can draw in the end. That's why in this chapter, after introducing the most important elements of data, we focus on data quality and methods of data collection.

Data is most straightforward to analyze if it forms a single **data table**. A data table consists of **observations** and **variables**. Observations are also known as cases. Variables are also called features. When using the mathematical name for tables, the data table is called the data matrix. A **dataset** is a broader concept that includes, potentially, multiple data tables with different kinds of information to be used in the same analysis. We'll return to working with multiple data tables in Chapter 2.

In a data table, the rows are the observations: each row is a different observation, and whatever is in a row is information about that specific observation. Columns are variables, so that column one is variable one, column two is another variable, and so on.

A common file format for data tables is the **csv file** (for "comma separated values"). csv files are text files of a data table, with rows and columns. Rows are separated by end of line signs; columns are separated by a character called a delimiter (often a comma or a semicolon). csv files can be imported in all statistical software.

Variables are identified by names. The data table may have variable names already, and analysts are free to use those names or rename the variables. Personal taste plays a role here: some prefer short names that are easier to work with in code; others prefer long names that are more informative; yet others prefer variable names that refer to something other than their content (such as the question number in a survey questionnaire). It is good practice to include the names of the variables in the first row of a csv data table. The observations start with the second row and go on until the end of the file.

Observations are identified by **identifier** or **ID variables**. An observation is identified by a single ID variable, or by a combination of multiple ID variables. ID variables, or their combinations, should uniquely identify each observation. They may be numeric or text containing letters or other characters. They are usually contained in the first column of data tables.

We use the notation x_i to refer to the value of variable x for observation i, where i typically refers to the position of the observation in the dataset. This way i starts with 1 and goes up to the number of observations in the dataset (often denoted as n or N). In a dataset with n observations, $i = 1, 2, \ldots, n$. (Note that in some programming languages, indexing may start from 0.)

1.2 Data Structures

Observations can have a cross-sectional, time series, or a multi-dimensional structure.

Observations in **cross-sectional data**, often abbreviated as **xsec** data, come from the same time, and they refer to different units such as different individuals, families, firms, and countries. Ideally, all observations in a cross-sectional dataset are observed at the exact same time. In practice this often means a particular time interval. When that interval is narrow, data analysts treat it as if it were a single point in time.

In most cross-sectional data, the ordering of observations in the dataset does not matter: the first data row may be switched with the second data row, and the information content of the data would be the same. Cross-sectional data has the simplest structure. Therefore we introduce most methods and tools of data analysis using cross-sectional data and turn to other data structures later.

Observations in **time series data** refer to a single unit observed multiple times, such as a shop's monthly sales values. In time series data, there is a natural ordering of the observations, which is typically important for the analysis. A common abbreviation used for time series data is **tseries** data. We shall discuss the specific features of time series data in Chapter 12, where we introduce time series analysis.

Multi-dimensional data, as its name suggests, has more than one dimension. It is also called **panel data**. A common type of panel data has many units, each observed multiple times. Such data is called **longitudinal data**, or cross-section time series data, abbreviated as **xt data**. Examples include countries observed repeatedly for several years, data on employees of a firm on a monthly basis, or prices of several company stocks observed on many days.

Multi-dimensional datasets can be represented in table formats in various ways. For xt data, the most convenient format has one observation representing one unit observed at one time (country–year observations, person–month observations, company-day observations) so that one unit (country, employee, company) is represented by multiple observations. In xt data tables, observations are identified by two ID variables: one for the cross-sectional units and one for time. xt data is called **balanced** if all cross-sectional units have observations for the very same time periods. It is called unbalanced if some cross-sectional units are observed more times than others. We shall discuss other specific features of multi-dimensional data in Chapter 23 where we discuss the analysis of panel data in detail.

Another important feature of data is the level of aggregation of observations. Data with information on people may have observations at different levels: age is at the individual level, home location is at the family level, and real estate prices may be available as averages for zip code areas. Data with information on manufacturing firms may have observations at the level of plants, firms as legal entities (possibly with multiple plants), industries with multiple firms, and so on. Time series data on transactions may have observations for each transaction or for transactions aggregated over some time period.

Chapter 2, Section 2.5 will discuss how to structure data that comes with multiple levels of aggregation and how to prepare such data for analysis. As a guiding principle, the analysis is best done using data aggregated at a level that makes most sense for the decisions examined: if we wish to analyze patterns in customer choices, it is best to use customer-level data; if we are analyzing the effect of firms' decisions, it is best to use firm-level data.

Sometimes data is available at a level of aggregation that is different from the ideal level. If data is too disaggregated (i.e., by establishments within firms when decisions are made at the firm level), we may want to aggregate all variables to the preferred level. If, however, the data is too aggregated (i.e., industry-level data when we want firm-level data), there isn't much that can be done. Such data misses potentially important information. Analyzing such data may uncover interesting patterns, but the discrepancy between the ideal level of aggregation and the available level of aggregation may have important consequences for the results and has to be kept in mind throughout the analysis.

Review Box 1.1 Structure and elements of data

- Most datasets are best contained in a data table, or several data tables.
- In a data table, observations are the rows; variables are its columns.
- Notation: x_i refers to the value of variable x for observation i. In a dataset with n observations, $i = 1, 2, \ldots, n$.
- Cross-sectional (xsec) data has information on many units observed at the same time.
- Time series (tseries) data has information on a single unit observed many times.
- Panel data has multiple dimensions – often, many cross-sectional units observed many times (this is also called longitudinal or xt data).

1.A1 CASE STUDY – Finding a Good Deal among Hotels: Data Collection

Introducing the hotels-vienna dataset

The ultimate goal of our first case study is to use data on all hotels in a city to find good deals: hotels that are underpriced relative to their location and quality. We'll come back to this question and data in subsequent chapters. In the case study of this chapter, our question is how to collect data that we can then use to answer our question.

Comprehensive data on hotel prices is not available ready made, so we have to collect the data ourselves. The data we'll use was collected from a price comparison website using a web scraping algorithm (see more in Section 1.5).

The `hotels-vienna` dataset contains information on hotels, hostels, and other types of accommodation in one city, Vienna, and one weekday night, November 2017. For each accommodation, the data includes information on the name and address, the price on the night in focus, in US dollars (USD), average customer rating from two sources plus the corresponding number of such ratings, stars, distance to the city center, and distance to the main railway station.

The data includes $N = 428$ accommodations in Vienna. Each row refers to a separate accommodation. All prices refer to the same weekday night in November 2017, and the data was downloaded at the same time (within one minute). Both are important: the price for different nights may be different, and the price for the same night at the same hotel may change if looked up at a different time. Our dataset has both of these time points fixed. It is therefore a cross-section of hotels – the variables with index i denote individual accommodations, and $i = 1...428$.

The data comes in a single data table, in csv format. The data table has 429 rows: the top row for variable names and 428 hotels. After some data cleaning (to be discussed in Chapter 2, Section 2.10), the data table has 25 columns corresponding to 25 variables.

The first column is a hotel_id uniquely identifying the hotel, hostel, or other accommodation in the dataset. This is a technical number without actual meaning. We created this variable to replace names, for confidentiality reasons (see more on this in Section 1.11). Uniqueness of the identifying number is key here: every hotel has a different number. See more about such identifiers in Chapter 2, Section 2.3.

The second column is a variable that describes the type of the accommodation (i.e., hotel, hostel, or bed-and-breakfast), and the following columns are variables with the name of the city (two versions), distance to the city center, stars of the hotel, average customer rating collected by the price comparison website, the number of ratings used for that average, and price. Other variables contain information regarding the night of stay such as a weekday flag, month, and year, and the size of promotional offer if any. The file VARIABLES.xls has all the information on variables.

Table 1.1 shows what the data table looks like. The variables have short names that are meant to convey their content.

Table 1.1   List of observations

hotel_id	accom_type	country	city	city_actual	dist	stars	rating	price
21894	Apartment	Austria	Vienna	Vienna	2.7	4	4.4	81
21897	Hotel	Austria	Vienna	Vienna	1.7	4	3.9	81
21901	Hotel	Austria	Vienna	Vienna	1.4	4	3.7	85
21902	Hotel	Austria	Vienna	Vienna	1.7	3	4	83
21903	Hotel	Austria	Vienna	Vienna	1.2	4	3.9	82

Note: List of five observations with variable values. accom_type is the type of accommodation. city is the city based on the search; city_actual is the municipality.

Source: `hotels-vienna` dataset. Vienna, for a November 2017 weekday. N=428.

1.3   Data Quality

Data analysts should know their data. They should know how the data was born, with all details of measurement that may be relevant for their analysis. They should know their data better than their audience. Few things have more devastating consequences for a data analyst's reputation than someone in the audience pointing out serious measurement issues the analyst didn't consider.

Garbage in – garbage out. This summarizes the prime importance of data quality. The results of an analysis cannot be better than the data it uses. If our data is useless to answer our question, the results of our analysis are bound to be useless, no matter how fancy a method we apply to it. Conversely, with excellent data even the simplest methods may deliver very useful results. Sophisticated data analysis may uncover patterns from complicated and messy data but only if the information is there.

We list specific aspects of data quality in Table 1.2. Good data collection pays attention to these as much as possible. This list should guide data analysts on what they should know about the data they use. This is our checklist. Other people may add more items, define specific items in different ways, or de-emphasize some items. We think that our version includes the most important aspects of data quality organized in a meaningful way. We shall illustrate the use of this list by applying it in the context of the data collection methods and case studies in this book.

Table 1.2 Key aspects of data quality	
Aspect	**Explanation**
Content	The content of a variable is determined by how it was measured, not by what it was meant to measure. As a consequence, just because a variable is given a particular name, it does not necessarily measure that.
Validity	The content of a variable (actual content) should be as close as possible to what it is meant to measure (intended content).
Reliability	Measurement of a variable should be stable, leading to the same value if measured the same way again.
Comparability	A variable should be measured the same way for all observations.
Coverage	Ideally, observations in the collected dataset should include all of those that were intended to be covered (complete coverage). In practice, they may not (incomplete coverage).
Unbiased selection	If coverage is incomplete, the observations that are included should be similar to all observations that were intended to be covered (and, thus, to those that are left uncovered).

We should note that in real life, there are problems with even the highest-quality datasets. But the existence of data problems should not deter someone from using a dataset. Nothing is perfect. It will be our job to understand the possible problems and how they affect our analysis and the conclusions we can draw from our analysis.

The following two case studies illustrate how data collection may affect data quality. In both cases, analysts carried out the data collection with specific questions in mind. After introducing the data collection projects, we shall, in subsequent sections, discuss the data collection in detail and how its various features may affect data quality. Here we start by describing the aim of each project and discussing the most important questions of data quality it had to address.

A final point on quality: as we would expect, high-quality data may well be costly to gather. These case study projects were initiated by analysts who wanted answers to questions that required collecting new data. As data analysts, we often find ourselves in such a situation. Whether collecting our own data is feasible depends on its costs, difficulty, and the resources available to us. Collecting data on hotels from a website is relatively inexpensive and simple (especially for someone with the necessary coding skills). Collecting online and offline prices and collecting data on the quality of management practices are expensive and highly complex projects that required teams of experts to work together for many years. It takes a lot of effort, resources, and luck to be able to collect such complex data; but, as these examples show, it's not impossible.

Review Box 1.2 Data quality

Important aspects of data quality include:

- content of variables: what they truly measure;
- validity of variables: whether they measure what they are supposed to;
- reliability of variables: whether they would lead to the same value if measured the same way again;
- comparability of variables: the extent to which they are measured the same way across different observations;
- coverage is complete if all observations that were intended to be included are in the data;
- data with incomplete coverage may or may not have the problem of selection bias; selection bias means that the observations in the data are systematically different from the total.

1.B1 CASE STUDY – Comparing Online and Offline Prices: Data Collection

Introducing the billion-prices dataset

The second case study is about comparing online prices and offline prices of the same products. Potential differences between online and offline prices are interesting for many reasons, including making better purchase choices, understanding the business practices of retailers, and using online data in approximating offline prices for policy analysis.

The main question is how to collect data that would allow us to compare online and offline (i.e., in-store) prices for the very same product. The hard task is to ensure that we capture many products and that they are actually the same product in both sources.

The data was collected as part of the Billion Prices Project (BPP; www.thebillionprices project.com), an umbrella of multiple projects that collect price data for various purposes using various methods. The online–offline project combines several data collection methods, including data collected from the web and data collected "offline" by visiting physical stores.

BPP is about measuring prices for the same products sold through different channels. The two main issues are identifying products (are they really the same?) and recording their prices. The actual content of the price variable is the price as recorded for the product that was identified.

Errors in product identification or in entering the price would lower the validity of the price measures. Recording the prices of two similar products that are not the same would be an issue, and so would be recording the wrong price (e.g., do recorded prices include taxes or temporary sales?).

The reliability of the price variable also depends on these issues (would a different measurement pick the same product and measure its price the same way?) as well as inherent variability in prices. If prices change very frequently, any particular measurement would have imperfect reliability. The extent to which the price data are comparable across observations is influenced by the extent to which the products are identified the same way and the prices are recorded the same way.

Coverage of products is an important decision of the price comparison project. Conclusions from any analysis would refer to the kinds of products the data covers.

1.C1   CASE STUDY – Management Quality and Firm Performance: Data Collection

Introducing the wms-management-survey dataset

The third case study is about measuring the quality of management in organizations. The quality of management practices are understood to be an important determinant of the success of firms, hospitals, schools, and many other organizations. Yet there is little comparable evidence of such practices across firms, organizations, sectors, or countries.

There are two research questions here: how to collect data on management quality of a firm and how to measure management practices themselves. Similarly to previous case studies, no such dataset existed before the project although management consultancies have had experience in studying management quality at firms they have advised.

The data for this case study is from a large-scale research project aiming to fill this gap. The World Management Survey (WMS; http://worldmanagementsurvey.org) collects data on management practices from many firms and other organizations across various industries and countries. This is a major international survey that combines a traditional survey methodology with other methods; see Sections 1.5 and 1.6 below on data collection methods.

The most important variables in the WMS are the management practice "scores." Eighteen such scores are in the data, each measuring the quality of management practices in an important area, such as tracking and reviewing performance, the time horizon and breadth of targets, or attracting and retaining human capital. The scores range from 1 through 5, with 1 indicating worst practice and 5 indicating best practice. Importantly, this is the intended content of the variable. The actual content is determined by how it is measured: what information is used to construct the score, where that information comes from, how the scores are constructed from that information, whether there is room for error in that process, and so on.

Having a good understanding of the actual content of these measures will inform us about their validity: how close actual content is to intended content. The details of measurement will help us assess their reliability, too: if measured again, would we get the same score or maybe a different one? Similarly, those details would inform us about the extent to which the scores are comparable – i.e., they measure the same thing, across organizations, sectors, and countries.

The goal of the WMS is to measure and compare the quality of management practices across organizations in various sectors and countries. In principle the WMS could have collected data from all organizations in all sectors and countries it targeted. Such complete coverage would have been prohibitively expensive. Instead, the survey covers a sample: a small subset of all organizations. Therefore, we need to assess whether this sample gives a good picture of the management practices of all organizations – or, in other words, if selection is unbiased. For this we need to learn how the organizations covered were selected, a question we'll return to in Section 1.8 below.

1.4 How Data Is Born: The Big Picture

Data can be collected for the purpose of the analysis, or it can be derived from information collected for other purposes.

The structure and content of data purposely collected for the analysis are usually better suited to analysis. Such data is more likely to include variables that are the focus of the analysis, measured in a way that best suits the analysis, and structured in a way that is convenient for the analysis. Frequent methods to collect data include scraping the Web for information (web scraping) or conducting a survey (see Section 1.5 and Section 1.6).

Data collected for other purposes can be also very useful to answer our inquiries. Data collected for the purpose of administering, monitoring, or controlling processes in business, public administration, or other environments are called administrative data ("admin" data). If they are related to transactions, they are also called transaction data. Examples include payment, promotion, and training data of employees of a firm; transactions using credit cards issued by a bank; and personal income tax forms submitted in a country.

Admin data usually cover a complete population: all employees in a firm, all customers of a bank, or all tax filers in a country. A special case is Big Data, to be discussed in more detail in Section 1.9, which may have its specific promises and issues due to its size and other characteristics.

Often, data collected for other purposes is available at low cost for many observations. At the same time, the structure and content of such data are usually further away from the needs of the analysis compared to purposely collected data. This trade-off has consequences that vary across data, methods, and questions to be answered.

Data quality is determined by how the data was born, and data collection affects various aspects of data quality in different ways. For example, validity of the most important variables tends to be higher in purposely collected data, while coverage tends to be more complete in admin data. However, that's not always the case, and even when it is, we shouldn't think in terms of extremes. Instead, it is best to think of these issues as part of a continuum. For example, we rarely have the variables we ideally want even if we collected the data for the purpose of the analysis, and admin data may have variables with high validity for our purposes. Or, purposely collected data may have incomplete coverage but without much selection bias, whereas admin data may be closer to complete coverage but may have severe selection bias.

However the data was born, its value may increase if it can be used together with information collected elsewhere. Linking data from different sources can result in very valuable datasets. The purpose of linking data is to leverage the advantages of each while compensating for some of their disadvantages. Different datasets may include different variables that may offer excellent opportunities for analysis when combined even if they would be less valuable on their own.

Data may be linked at the level of observations, for the same firms, individuals, or countries. Alternatively, data may be linked at different levels of aggregation: industry-level information linked to firms, zip-code-level information linked to individuals, and so on. We shall discuss the technical details of linking data tables in Chapter 2, Section 2.6. In the end, linkages are rarely perfect: there are usually observations that cannot be linked. Therefore, when working with linked data, data analysts should worry about coverage and selection bias: how many observations are missed by imperfect linking, and whether the included and missing observations are different in important ways.

A promising case of data linkage is a large administrative dataset complemented with data collected for the purpose of the analysis, perhaps at a smaller scale. The variables in the large but inexpensive data may allow uncovering some important patterns, but they may not be enough to gain a deeper understanding of those patterns. Collecting additional data for a subset of the observations may provide valuable insights at extra cost, but keeping this additional data collection small can keep those costs contained.

For example, gender differences in earnings at a company may be best analyzed by linking two kinds of data. Admin data may provide variables describing current and previous earnings and job titles for all employees. But it may not have information on previous jobs, skill qualifications, or family circumstances, all of which may be relevant for gender differences in what kind of jobs employees have and how much they earn. If we are lucky, we may be able to collect such information through a survey that we administer to all employees, or to some of them (called a sample, see Section 1.7). To answer some questions, such as the extent of gender differences, analyzing the admin data may suffice. To answer other questions, such as potential drivers of such differences, we may need to analyze the survey data linked to the admin data.

1.5   Collecting Data from Existing Sources

Data collected from existing sources, for a purpose other than our analysis, may come in many forms. Analysis of such data is called secondary analysis of data. One type of such data is purposely collected to do some other analysis, and we are re-using it for our own purposes. Another type is collected with a general research purpose to facilitate many kinds of data analysis. These kinds of data are usually close to what we would collect for our purposes.

Some international organizations, governments, central banks, and some other organizations collect and store data to be used for analysis. Often, such data is available free of charge. For example, the World Bank collects many time series of government finances, business activity, health, and many others, for all countries. We shall use some of that data in our case studies. Another example is FRED, collected and stored by the US Federal Reserve system, which includes economic time series data on the USA and some other countries.

One way to gather information from such providers is to visit their website and download a data table – say, on GDP for countries in a year, or population for countries for many years. Then we import that data table into our software. However, some of these data providers allow direct computer access to their data. Instead of clicking and downloading, data analysts may use an Application Programming Interface, or **API**, to directly load data into a statistical software package. An API is a software intermediary, or an interface, that allows programs, or scripts, to talk to each other. Using an API, data analysts may load these datasets into their statistical software as part of the code they write for that software.

Besides data collected and provided for the purposes of analysis, there is a lot of information out there that can be turned into useful data even though it is not collected for the purpose of analysis. Here we discuss the two most important such sources: information on the web and administrative data. The emergence of Big Data (see Section 1.9) is due to the availability and use of more and more such information.

Collecting data from the web can yield useful data for many kinds of analysis as more and more economic and social activity takes place on the web or leaves an information trace there. Examples include collecting price data from classified ads or price comparison websites, collecting data on the results of sports tournaments, and collecting data on the frequency of online web search for certain words.

In principle we can collect data from the web manually, by creating a data table and entering relevant information by hand. Manual data collection may make sense when the number of observations is very small. Whenever possible, though, automated data collection is superior. It involves writing code that collects all relevant data and puts it into an appropriate data table. Collecting data from the web using code is called **web scraping**. Well-written web scraping code can load and extract data from multiple web pages. Some websites are easier to scrape than others, depending on how they structure and present information. There are many web scraping software solutions available, and there is a lot of help available online. In the end, scraping is writing code so it requires both general experience in coding and learning the specifics of scraping.

Collecting **data from administrative sources** is another important case. As we discussed briefly in Section 1.4, a lot of information, often in digital format, is collected for administrative purposes in business organizations and governments.

Important advantages of most administrative data include high reliability of the variables they measure, and high, often complete, coverage, which also leads to large size in most cases. Data on employees in a firm tends to include all employees, typically going back in time for many years. Such data may contain many variables with respect to their performance and pay at the firm. Credit card transactions may cover all customers of a financial firm and include all of their transactions, including the identity of the sellers. Individual tax data usually covers all tax filers in a country with all income information entered on the tax form, and perhaps some characteristics of the individual tax filers such as their age and location of residence.

Admin data tends to have two disadvantages, First, typically, it includes few variables and misses many that may be useful for analysis. Second, important variables may have low validity: their content may be quite different from what analysts would want to measure. Employee records in firms contain little information on other jobs, previous employment, or family characteristics. Credit card transaction data has no information on the income, wealth, and other expenditures of the customer. The income variable in individual tax records may be very different from total family income because the tax records of spouses and other family members may not be linked, and some income sources may not be reported.

All advantages and disadvantages of admin data stem from the original purpose of administrative data: facilitating administration in an organization as opposed to lending itself to analysis to answer the specific questions analysts might ask. Data analysts should pay special attention to the content and validity of variables in admin data.

> **Review Box 1.3 Collecting data from existing sources**
>
> - Web scraping is using code to retrieve information available on the web.
> - Administrative sources of data collect information for goals other than data analysis.
> - Frequent advantages of data collected from existing sources: low costs (especially low marginal costs), many observations.
> - Frequent disadvantages: fewer variables, lower validity of variables.

1.A2 CASE STUDY – Finding a Good Deal among Hotels: Data Collection

How the data was born

The dataset on hotels in Vienna was collected from a price comparison website, by web scraping. The purpose of the website is not facilitating data analysis. It is to offer a list of hotels, hostels, and other accommodation with prices and other features to customers and induce them to choose one of their offerings. Customers are requested to enter a date for check-in, a date for check-out, number of visitors, and, optionally, other information on their planned stay.

The price the website lists is the price that customers pay if they choose to make a reservation right away. The website lists all hotels from its registry that have vacancies and meet the criteria. Not all hotels in Vienna may be covered by the website, and not all that are covered may have rooms available for the date in question. When listing hotels, the website shows not only the variables we collected but also photos and other information that our data does not include.

Many of these features have important consequences for the analysis. The dataset was collected on a specific date. The analysis may take time and results will be available on some later date. Prices are valid on the date of data collection; they may change by the time the results of the analysis are available. That may decrease the validity of the price variable for the purpose of the analysis. The data does not contain all information available on the website. Most importantly, it does not use the photos even though those are likely important determinants of the decision. If the analysis is carried out to help find a good price, we should not let the analysis result in a single choice: what looks best in the data may not be the best if prices change or the photos are examined. Instead, it is probably best to produce a shortlist with several candidates and do manual checking of those options to find the best deal from among them.

Coverage of hotels in Vienna is not complete. First, the data contains only hotels with rooms available on the night asked. That is fine if we are analyzing the data to choose a hotel for that night. It may be less fine for other purposes, such as understanding the pricing practices of hotels. Another concern is that not all hotels in the city are covered by the website. That may be an issue as other hotels may offer better deals: that's what selection bias would mean in this case. The only way to check this is to use data from other sources. This case study is restricted to this particular data source. We would need to collect data from other sources to assess how incomplete the coverage is and whether that affects the conclusions of our analysis.

The hotel data looks rather useful and offers a great many options to study hotel features that would affect the room price. It is good quality and rather reliable, and we did manage to capture prices at a given moment. However, it unfortunately does not include detailed descriptions of hotel quality, services, or what the room looks like.

1.B2 CASE STUDY – Comparing Online and Offline Prices: Data Collection

How the data was born

The BPP online–offline price project collected data, in ten countries, from retailers that sold their products both online and offline (in physical stores). (We'll discuss the selection of stores and products later.) Only those retailers were selected that had a unique product identificaion number both online and in their stores. The unique identifiers ensured that online and offline price data was collected on the same products.

The project was managed by a team of researchers and research assistants (the "BPP team"). They hired data collectors in each country using online crowdsourcing platforms (Mechanical Turk, Elane) to carry out the offline data collection. Data collectors were responsible for selecting products in the physical stores they were assigned to (more on selection later). They received a mobile phone app designed to scan prices in physical stores in a quick and standardized fashion. With the help of this mobile app, the data collectors scanned the barcode of products, marked whether the product was on promotion or this was a regular price, and took a photo of the price tag. The data entered in the mobile app was synchronized with a central server and was verified by a member of the BPP team. Once the offline price data was collected, the BPP team searched for and entered the online price of the same product.

Online prices were collected on, or shortly after, the day when the corresponding offline prices were entered. Whether taxes were included or not was determined by how prices were presented in offline stores (without sales taxes in the USA; with value-added tax and, potentially, sales tax in most other countries).

The unique product identifiers ensured that offline and online prices were collected for the exact same products. The manual entry of prices might have left room for error, but the price tag photos ensured that those errors were rare. The data collection harmonized online and offline prices in terms of whether the products were on promotion and whether taxes were included. Shipping costs were not included, and neither were transportation costs for visiting physical stores.

This data collection procedure ensures high validity and high reliability for the price data collected. Comparability of the price data across products and stores is likely high, too. Frequent changes of prices may make measurement result in different prices if carried out at different times, but online and offline data were collected on the same date, or very soon before or after, so the effect of such changes were minimal for the comparison of online and offline prices. Note that the time difference between recording the online and offline price of a product may be informative about the reliability of these variables. Similarly, institutional differences across countries may make the content of price differ (e.g., whether taxes are included), but those differences affect online and offline prices the same way.

1.6 | Surveys

Surveys collect data by asking people questions and recording their answers. Typically, the answers are short and easily transformed into variables, either qualitative (factor) or quantitative (numerical; see Chapter 2, Section 2.1 for information about variable types). The people answering questions are called respondents. The set of questions presented to respondents is called a questionnaire. There are two major kinds of surveys: self-administered surveys and interviews.

In self-administered surveys, respondents are left on their own to answer questions. Typically, the questions are presented to them in writing. Web surveys are the most important example. Respondents see the questions on the screen of a web-connected device, and they tap, click, or enter text to answer the questions. The answers are immediately recorded and transformed into an appropriate data table. This feature is an important advantage of web surveys: there is no need for anyone else to enter the data or put it into an appropriate structure. That means lower costs and less room for error.

Respondents need to be recruited to participate in web surveys just like in any other survey. Apart from that, however, web surveys have low marginal costs: once the web questionnaire is up and running, having more respondents answer them incurs practically no extra cost. Before the web, self-administered surveys were done on paper, and respondents were most often required to mail the filled out questionnaires. That method entailed higher costs and, arguably, more burden on respondents.

Besides low costs and quick access to data, web surveys have other advantages. They can present questions with visual aids and interactive tools, and they can embed videos and sound. They may be programmed to adapt the list and content of questions based on what respondents entered previously. Web surveys can include checks to ensure cleaner data. For example, they can give alerts to respondents if their answers do not seem to make sense or are inconsistent with information given earlier.

A disadvantage of self-administered questionnaires is that they leave little room for clarifying what the questions are after. This may affect the validity of measurement: respondents may answer questions thinking that some questions are about something different from what was intended. Web surveys have an advantage over traditional paper-based surveys in that they can accommodate explanations or help. However, it is up to the respondents to invoke such help, and there is little room to follow up if the help received is not enough.

Another disadvantage of some self-administered surveys is a high risk of incomplete and biased coverage. Potential respondents are left on their own to decide whether to participate, and those that can and choose to participate may be different from everyone else. People without access to the Internet can't answer web surveys. People who can't read well can't answer self-administered surveys that are presented in writing. The coverage issue is more severe in some cases (e.g., surveys of children, of the elderly, or in developing countries) than in others (e.g., surveys of university students). Moreover, when respondents are left on their own, they may be less likely to participate in surveys than when someone is there to talk them into it. With ingenuity and investment these issues may be mitigated (offering web connection, presenting questions in voice, offering compensation). Nevertheless, incomplete and biased coverage need special attention in the case of self-administered surveys.

Interviews are the other main way to conduct surveys besides self-administration. They create a survey situation with two participants: an interviewer and a respondent. During survey interviews, interviewers ask the questions of the survey and nothing else. In a broader sense, interviews may include freer conversations, but here we focus on surveys.

Interviews may be conducted in-person or over the telephone. Modern interviews are often done with the help of a laptop, tablet, or other device. Such computer-aided interviews share some advantages with web surveys. They allow for checks on admissible answers and consistency across answers, and, sometimes, the use of visualization, videos, and voice. With answers entered into such devices, they can then produce data tables that are ready to use.

An advantage of interviewers is the potential for high validity. Interviewers can, and are often instructed to, help respondents understand questions as they are intended to be understood. Interviewers may also help convince respondents to participate in surveys thus leading to better coverage.

At the same time, comparability of answers may be an issue with interviews. Different interviewers may ask the same survey question in different ways, add different details, may help in different ways, or record answers differently. All this may result in interviewer effects: systematic differences between answers recorded by different interviewers even if the underlying variables have no such differences. It is good practice to mitigate these interviewer effects during data collection by precise instructions to interviewers and thorough training.

The main disadvantage of interviews is their cost. Interviewers need to be compensated for the time they spend recruiting respondents, interviewing them, and, in the case of personal interviews, traveling to meet them. Interviews are thus substantially more expensive than self-administered surveys, especially if they invest in insuring high data quality by using computer-aided techniques and intensive training.

Mixed-mode surveys use different methods within the same survey: telephone for some and web for others; in-person for some and telephone for others, and so on. Sometimes the same person is asked to answer different questions in different survey modes. Sometimes different people are asked to participate in different modes. Usually, the idea behind mixed mode surveys is saving on costs while maintaining appropriate coverage. They allow for data to be collected at lower costs for some variables, or some observations, using the more costly survey mode only when needed. Comparability may be an issue in mixed-mode surveys when different people answer the same question in different modes. Extensive research shows that answers to many kinds of questions compare well across survey modes but that some kinds of questions tend to produce less comparable answers.

Review Box 1.4   Collecting data by surveys

- Surveys ask people (respondents) and record their answers.
- In self-administered surveys, such as web surveys, respondents answer questions on their own.
- Interviews (personal, telephone) involve interviewers as well as respondents.
- Mixed-mode surveys use multiple ways for different respondents or different parts of the survey for the same respondents.

<table>
<tr><td>**1.C2**</td><td># CASE STUDY – Management Quality and Firm Size: Data Collection</td></tr>
</table>

How the data was born

The World Management Survey is a telephone interview survey conducted in multiple countries. The interviewers were graduate students in management. All participated in a lengthy and intensive training. An important task for interviewers was to select the respondents within each firm that were knowledgeable about management practices. To make this selection comparable, interviewers had to follow instructions. How to apply those rules in particular situations was practiced during the training sessions.

The key variables of the survey are the 18 management practice scores. The scores were assigned by the interviewers after collecting information on each area. For each of the 18 areas, interviewers were instructed to ask a series of questions. Each interviewer had to read out the exact same questions. Then they recorded the answers and assigned scores based on those answers. The assignment of scores for each area was laid out by the survey in detail with examples (e.g., for tracking performance, score 1 has to be assigned if "measures tracked do not indicate directly if overall business objectives are being met"). Interviewers practiced applying these rules during the training sessions.

The content of each score is therefore based on information that the interviewers gathered in a standardized way and translated to scores using standardized rules. Their validity, reliability, and comparability is difficult to assess without further investigation. Nevertheless, it is safe to say that they have substantially higher validity and are more comparable across observations than an alternative measure: asking each respondent to score their own management practices.

<table>
<tr><td>**1.7**</td><td># Sampling</td></tr>
</table>

Sometimes data is collected on all possible observations, attempting complete coverage. This makes sense when we are targeting few observations (e.g., employees of a medium-sized firm) or the marginal cost of data collection is negligible (as with web scraping). Often, though, finding more observations may be costly (e.g., recruiting respondents for surveys), and collecting data on new observations may also have high costs (e.g., additional personal interviews). In such cases it makes sense to gather information on only a subset of all potential observations. Data collection here is preceded by **sampling**: selecting observations for which data should be collected. The set of observations on which data is collected in the end is called the **sample**. The larger set of observations from which a sample is selected is called the **population** or universe.

Samples have to represent the population. A sample is **representative** if the distribution of all variables in the sample are the same as, or very close to, their corresponding distribution in the population. (The distribution of variables is the frequency of their values, e.g., fraction female, percent with income within a certain range. Chapter 3, Under the Hood section 3.A, will discuss distributions in more detail.) A representative sample of products in a supermarket has the same distribution of prices, sales, and frequency of purchase as all products in the supermarket. A representative sample of transactions in a financial institution has the same distribution of value, volume, and so on, as when all transactions are considered. A representative sample of workers in an economy has the same distribution of demographic characteristics, skills, wages, and so on, as all workers in the economy. Representative samples do not cover all observations in the population, but they are free from selection bias.

Whether a sample is representative is impossible to tell directly. We don't know the value of all variables for all observations in the population, otherwise we would not need to collect data from a sample in the first place. There are two ways of assessing whether a sample is representative: evaluating the data collection process and, if possible, **benchmarking** the few variables for which we know the distribution in the population.

Benchmarking looks at variables for which we know something in the population. We can benchmark our sample by comparing the distribution of those variables in the sample to those in the population. One example could be comparing the share of various industries in a sample of companies to the share of industries published by the government, based on data that includes the population of companies.

If this kind of benchmarking reveals substantial differences then the sample is not representative. If it shows similar distributions then the sample is representative for the variable, or variables, used in the comparison. It may or may not be representative for other variables. A successful benchmarking is necessary but not sufficient for a sample to be representative.

The other way to establish whether a sample is representative, besides benchmarking, is evaluating the sampling process. That means understanding how exactly the observations were selected, what rules were supposed to be followed, and to what extent those rules were followed. To understand what good sampling methods are, the next section introduces the concept of random sampling, argues why it leads to representative samples, and provides examples of random samples.

1.8 Random Sampling

Random sampling is the process that most likely leads to representative samples. With the simplest ideal random sampling, all observations in the population have the same chance of being selected into the sample. In practice that chance can vary. Which observations are selected is determined by a random rule. For the purpose of getting representative samples, selection rules are random if they are not related to the distribution of the variables in the data. Textbook examples of random rules include throwing dice or drawing balls from urns.

In practice, most random samples are selected with the help of random numbers generated by computers. These numbers are parts of a sequence of numbers that is built into the computer. The sequence produces numbers without a recognizable pattern. Where the sequence starts is either specified by someone or determined by the date and time the process is launched. In a sense these numbers are not truly random as they always come up the same if started from the same point, in contrast with repeatedly throwing dice or drawing balls from urns. Nevertheless, that is not a real concern here because this selection rule is unrelated to the distribution of variables in any real-life data.

Other methods of random sampling include fixed rules that are unrelated to the distribution of variables in the data. Good examples are selecting people with odd-numbered birth dates (a 50% sample), or people with birthdays on the 15th of every month (approx. 3% sample). Again, these rules may not be viewed as "truly random" in a stricter sense, but that's not a concern for representation as long as the rules are not related to the variables used in the analysis.

In contrast, non-random sampling methods may lead to selection bias. Non-random sampling methods are related to important variables. In other words, they have a higher or lower likelihood of selecting observations that are different in some important variables. As a result, the selected observations tend to be systematically different from the population they are drawn from.

Consider two examples of non-random sampling methods. Selecting people from the first half of an alphabetic order is likely to lead to selection bias because people with different names may belong to different groups of society. Selecting the most recently established 10% of firms is surely not random for many reasons. One reason is called survivor bias: newly established firms include those that would fail within a short time after their establishment while such firms are not present among older firms. The practice questions will invite you to evaluate particular sampling methods and come up with other good and not-so-good methods.

Random sampling works very well if the sample is large enough. In small samples, it is possible that by chance, we pick observations that are not representative of the population. Consider for instance whether samples represent the age distribution of the population of a city. By picking a sample of two people, the share of young and older people may very well be different from their shares in the entire population. Thus, there is a considerable chance that this sample ends up being not representative even though it's a random sample. However, in a random sample of a thousand people, the share of young and old people is likely to be very similar to their shares in the population, leading to a representative sample. The larger the sample, the larger the chance of picking a representative sample.

An important, although not necessarily intuitive, fact is that it is the size of the sample that matters and not its size as a proportion of the entire population. A sample of five thousand observations may equally well represent populations of fifty thousand, ten million, or three hundred million.

Quite naturally, the larger the random sample, the better. But real life raises other considerations such as costs and time of data collection. How large a random sample is large enough depends on many things. We shall return to this question when we first discuss inference from samples to populations, in Chapter 5.

Random sampling is the best method of producing representative samples. True, it is not bullet-proof, with a tiny chance a sample may be way off. But that tiny chance is really tiny, especially for large samples. Nevertheless, the fact that it is not literally bullet-proof makes some people uncomfortable when they first encounter it. In fact, it took a lot of evidence to convince most data users of the merits of random sampling.

In practice, sampling often starts with a sampling frame: the list of all observations from which the sample is to be drawn. Incomplete and biased coverage may arise at this stage: the sampling frame may not include the entire population or may include observations that are not part of the population to be represented.

Ideally, data is collected from all members of a sample. Often, however, that is not possible. Surveys need respondents who are willing to participate and answer the questions. The fraction of people that were successfully contacted and who answered the questionnaire is called the response rate. A low response rate increases the chance of selection bias. That is, of course, not necessarily true: a sample with an 80% response rate may be more biased than another sample with a 40% response rate. It is good practice to report response rates with the data description and, if possible, to benchmark variables available in the population.

Review Box 1.5   Basic concepts of sampling

- The set of all observations relevant for the analysis is called the population.
- The subset for which data is collected is called a sample.
- A representative sample has very similar distributions of all variables to that of the population.

- To assess if a sample is representative we can benchmark statistics available both in the sample and the population. It is a good sign if they are similar, but it's not a guarantee.
- Random sampling means selecting observations by a rule that is unrelated to any variable in the data.
- Random sampling is the best way to get a representative sample.
- Incomplete sampling frames and nonresponse are frequent issues; whether they affect the representative nature of the sample needs to be assessed.

1.B3 CASE STUDY – Comparing Online and Offline Prices: Data Collection

The process of sampling

The BPP online–offline prices project carried out data collection in ten countries. In each country, it selected the largest retailers that sold their products both online and offline and were in the top twenty in terms of market share in their respective countries. The set of all products in these stores is the sampling frame. Sampling of products was done in the physical stores by the data collectors. The number of products to include was kept small to ensure a smooth process (e.g., to avoid conflicts with store personnel).

   The sample of products selected by data collectors may not have been representative of all products in the store. For example, products in more eye-catching displays may have been more likely to be sampled. At the same time, we have no reason to suspect that the online–offline price differences of these products were different from the rest. Thus, the sample of products may very well be representative of the online–offline price differences of the entire population, even though it may not be representative of the products themselves.

   This case study asked how to collect data so that we could compare online and offline prices. With careful sampling, and a massive effort to ensure that the very same products are compared, the project did a good job in data collection. A potential shortcoming is the fact that the products collected may not be fully representative of the consumption basket.

1.C3 CASE STUDY – Management Quality and Firm Size: Data Collection

The process of sampling

The WMS is an ongoing data collection project. By 2019, it has collected data from samples of organizations in 35 countries, using sampling methods that have varied by country. Initially, in 2004, it carried out surveys in the USA and three large European countries. The starting point for the sampling frame was a list of all firms maintained by data providers Compustat in the

USA and the Bureau van Dijk's Orbis/Amadeus in the European countries. The sampling frame was then adjusted by keeping only firms in selected sectors and of medium size (50 to 10 000 employees). The survey took a random sample. The response rate was 54%. This is considered a relatively high rate provided that participation was voluntary and respondents received no compensation.

The data collectors benchmarked many variables and concluded that there were two deviations: response rate was smaller in one country than the rest, and it was usually higher in larger firms. The distribution of other variables were similar in the sampling frame and the sample.

The project aimed to collect systematic data on management quality that could be compared across firms and countries. The way it was set up created a unified data collection process across countries. Systematic checks were introduced to avoid bias in collecting answers. A possible shortcoming is biased selection due to nonresponse: firms that answered the survey may not fully represent all firms in the surveyed countries.

1.9 Big Data

Data, or less structured information that can be turned into data, became ubiquitous in the twenty-first century as websites, apps, machines, sensors, and other sources, collect and store it in increasing and unfathomable amounts. The resulting information from each source is often massive to an unprecedented scale. For example, scanned barcodes at retail stores can lead to millions of observations for a retail chain in a single day. For another example, Twitter, a social media site, generates 500 million tweets per day that can be turned into data to analyze many questions. The commonly used term for such data is **Big Data**. It is a fairly fluid concept, and there are several definitions around. Nevertheless, most data analysts agree that Big Data provides unique opportunities but also specific challenges that often need extra care and specific tools.

A frequently used definition of Big Data is **the four Vs**: volume (scale of data), variety (different forms), velocity (real-time data collection), and veracity (accuracy). The fourth v is actually a question of data quality that we think is better left out from the definition. Rephrasing the first three of the Vs, Big Data refers to data that is:

- massive: contains many observations and/or variables;
- complex: does not fit into a single data table;
- continuous: often automatically and continuously collected and stored.

Big Data is massive. Sometimes that means datasets whose size is beyond the ability of typical hardware and software to store, manage, and analyze it. A simpler, and more popular version, is that Big Data is data that we cannot store on our laptop computer.

Big Data often has a complex structure, making it rather difficult to convert into data tables. A variety of new types of data have appeared that require special analytical tools. For example, networks have observations that are linked to each other, which may be stored in various forms. Maps are multidimensional objects with spatial relationship between observations. Text, pictures, or video content may be transformed into data, but its structure is often complex. In particular, text mining has become an important source of information both for social scientists and business data scientists.

Big Data is often automatically and continuously collected. Apps and sensors collect data as part of their routine, continuously updating and storing information. As part of the functioning of social media or the operation of machines such as airplane turbines, all the data is stored.

Big Data almost always arises from existing information as opposed to being collected purposely by analysts. That existing information typically comes from administrative sources, transactions, and as other by-products of day-to-day operations. Thus Big Data may be thought of as admin data with additional characteristics. As a result, it tends to share the advantages and disadvantages of admin data.

A main advantage of Big Data, shared with other kinds of admin data, is that it can be collected from existing sources, which often leads to low costs. The volume, complexity, or continuous updating of information may make Big Data collection more challenging, but there are usually appropriate methods and new technology to help there.

Coverage of Big Data is often high, sometimes complete. Complete coverage is a major advantage. When coverage is incomplete, though, the left-out observations are typically different from the included ones, leading to selection bias. In other words, Big Data with incomplete coverage is rarely a random sample of the population we'd like to cover. To re-iterate a point we made earlier with respect to non-coverage: higher coverage does not necessarily mean better representation. In fact a relatively small random sample may be more representative of a population than Big Data that covers a large but selected subset of, say, 80 %. Thus, if its coverage is incomplete, Big Data may be susceptible to selection bias – something that data analysts need to address.

Another common feature of Big Data, shared with admin data, is that it may very well miss important variables, and the ones included may not have high validity for the purpose of our analysis. That can be a major disadvantage. At the same time, because of the automatic process of information gathering, the variables tend to be measured with high reliability and in comparable ways.

The specific characteristics of Big Data have additional implications for data management and analysis as well as data quality.

The massive size of Big Data can offer new opportunities, but it typically requires advanced technical solutions to collect, structure, store, and work with the data. Size may have implications for what data analysis methods are best to use and how to interpret their results. We'll discuss these implications as we go along. Here we just note that sometimes when the data is big because there are many observations, all analysis can be done on a random sample of the observations. Sometimes, going from a massive number of observations (say, billions or trillions) to a large but manageable number of observations (say, a few millions) can make the analysis possible without making any difference to the results. This is not always an option, but when it is, it's one to consider.

We'll see an example for such massive data when we analyze the effect of a merger between two airlines on prices in Chapter 22. The original data is all tickets issued for routes in the USA. A 10 % sample of the data is made available for public use (without personal information). Even this sample data is available in multiple data files. We'll have to select parts of the data and aggregate it to apply the methods we'll cover in the textbook.

If Big Data is of a complex nature, this has consequences for the management and structuring of the data. Sometimes, with thorough re-structuring, even complex data can be transformed into a single data table that we can work with. For example, connections in a network may be represented in panel data, or features of texts may be summarized by variables, such as the frequency of specific words, that can be stored as a data table. Other times, though, complexity calls for methods that are beyond what we cover in this textbook and may also be beyond the traditional toolkit of statistical analysis.

For example, the features of routes on maps or the sound of the human voice are less straightforward to transform into data tables.

With Big Data that is continuously collected and updated, the process of data work and analysis is different from the more traditional way of doing data analysis that we'll focus on in this textbook. For example, instead of having a final data table ready for analysis, such cases require constant updating of the data and with it, updating all analysis as new data comes in. This approach implies some fundamental differences to data analysis that are beyond the scope of this textbook.

In the remainder of this textbook, we will focus on the most common kind of Big Data: very large numbers of observations. In addition, we'll note some issues with data that has a massive number of variables. We'll ignore complexity and continuous data collection. And we won't discuss technical issues such as the need for additional computational power or specific data management tools to store and manipulate data with billions of observations. Our focus will be on what the massive number of observations, or sometimes variables, implies for the substantive conclusions of data analysis.

A final comment: most of the traditional, "small data" issues and solutions we will discuss in this textbook will remain relevant for Big Data as well. We shall always note when that is not the case. Similarly, when relevant, we shall always discuss the additional issues Big Data may imply for the methods and tools we cover.

> **Review Box 1.6   Big Data**
>
> - Big Data is characterized by a massive number of observations or variables.
> - Sometimes Big Data is also complex in its structure and/or continuously updated.
> - Typically, Big Data is collected for purposes other than analysis. Thus it shares all the advantages and disadvantages of other kinds of admin data.
> - Its size, complexity, and continuous updating present additional challenges for its collection, structuring, storage, and analysis.

1.10   Good Practices in Data Collection

Several good practices in data collection are recognized to increase or help assess data quality. Some are general across many methods; others are specific.

Carrying out one or more pilot studies before data collection is general advice. To pilot a data collection method means to try it out in microcosm before doing the whole thing. Piloting is more powerful the more features of the final data collection are included. In web scraping this may mean small-scale collection of data from all websites across all kinds of items that will be relevant. In web surveys it may include recruiting a few respondents as well as asking them to fill out the entire questionnaire. With complex data collection, piloting may come in several steps, such as identifying the sampling frame, drawing a sample, identifying observations or recruiting respondents, and collecting the data itself by scraping, interviewing. Sometimes these steps are given different names as they get to include more and more parts of the entire data collection process (pilot, pretest, field rehearsal, and so on).

When people are involved in data collection, it is good practice to give them precise instructions to follow. An important objective of these is to get the actual content of measured variables as close as possible to their intended contents, thus increasing their validity. These practices also help with comparability and reliability by inducing different people to measure similar things in similar ways. For example, in interview-based surveys, precise instructions usually include questions to be read out (as opposed to letting interviewers ask questions using their own words), when and exactly how to clarify things, and how to translate answers into what is to be recorded. Instructions need to be easy to follow, so a balance needs to be found in how detailed and how accessible instructions are.

Another good practice is training people that participate in data collection in how to follow those instructions and how to make other kinds of decisions. Good training involves many hands-on exercises with examples that are likely to come up during data collection. Training of interviewers for complex surveys may take several days and is often very costly. Nevertheless, it is important to give thorough training to people involved in the data collection in order to ensure high data quality.

Less frequent but very useful practices aim at assessing data quality as part of the data collection. For example, the validity of measures in surveys may be assessed with the help of cognitive interviews. These ask respondents to explain why they answered a survey question the way they did. Another technique is asking a survey question in slightly different ways for different respondents (or the same respondents) to see if differences in wording that should not matter make a difference in the answers.

A useful practice to evaluate reliability is test–retest measurement: measuring the same thing more than once within the same data collection process. For example, the price of the same product in the same store may be recorded by two people, independent of each other. Or the same question may be asked of the same respondent twice within the same questionnaire, preferably with many questions in-between. Such a test–retest measurement took place within the World Management Survey: it re-interviewed several hundred firms to assess the reliability of the management quality scores.

There are good practices that help assess coverage issues, too. Whether **nonresponse** in a survey leads to severe biases may be assessed by giving some of the would-be respondents higher incentives to participate. If that results in a higher response rate, we may compare the distributions of variables across respondents with and without the extra incentives to see if different response rates lead to different distributions.

There are many other techniques and practices that data collection may include to assess various dimensions of data quality. Making use of all is practically impossible. Nevertheless, it can be very useful to include one or two of them if data collectors are concerned with one or two issues in particular. The results of these techniques can not only shed light on the extent of particular issues but they may be used to mitigate their consequences in the course of the analysis.

Very often, data collection is a complex task. Teamwork here is especially useful as designing and implementing data collection may require a wide range of expertise. The more complex the process, the larger the benefits of advice and collaboration. However, even seemingly simple data collection tasks may have issues that inexperienced researchers are not aware of and can result in inferior data quality. Thus, we think it always makes sense to seek advice and, if needed, mentoring during all stages of data collection. Garbage in, garbage out: if the data we collect ends up having crucial flaws, our analysis will not be able to answer our question. It's better to minimize that possibility if we can.

> **Review Box 1.7   Some good practices for data collection**
>
> - Piloting data collection.
> - Assessing the validity and reliability of the most important variables by, for example, cognitive interviews or test–retest measurement – when feasible and economical.
> - Examining sources of imperfect coverage to assess potential selection bias.
> - Working in teams with experts to design data collection.

1.11   Ethical and Legal Issues of Data Collection

Observations in data analyzed in business, economics, or policy most often concern people or firms. Collecting and using such data is subject to strong legal and ethical constraints and rules. These constraints and rules are meant to protect the subjects of data collection: the business interests of firms, the physical and mental health, safety, and integrity of people. Observing these constraints and rules is extremely important: breaching them can have severe consequences for the ongoing data collection and beyond. When the rules are not observed, firms or people may decline participation or take legal action during or after data collection. These, in turn, may affect not only the ongoing data collection but also the general attitude of potential respondents toward data collection in society.

One general principle is confidentiality. In general, data users should not be able to learn sensitive information about identifiable subjects of the data collection. Sensitive information includes, but is not restricted to, information that may harm firms or individuals. When the data contains sensitive information, the principle of confidentiality implies that respondents should be impossible to identify. At a minimum that means that data needs to be de-identified: names and addresses should not be part of the dataset. But it is more than that. Some variables, or combinations of variables, may help identify firms or persons even without names and addresses. Ensuring confidentiality also means ensuring that no such combination allows respondents to be identified from observations.

The collection of data on people, or, as sometimes referred to, human subjects, is subject to a large body of regulation at both international and national levels. The regulation originates from medical research, but it has been adapted for data collection for non-medical purposes, too. The most important guiding principles include respect for persons (people should be treated as autonomous human beings), their protection from harm, and their equal treatment during data collection. It is good practice to obtain informed consent from people for collecting data on them. This means not only data collected here and now but also potential linkages to other data sources. In fact, when data collection is supported by research grants from government or non-governmental foundations, these, and many more, principles are required to be observed.

Another general principle is ownership of information. A lot of information and a lot of data is available on the web or offline. However, availability does not imply the right to analyze that data for any purpose. Who owns that information and what the owner permits to be done with that information is not always easy to find out. Nevertheless, we should always aim to understand the details of ownership and usage rights to make sure it is ethical and legal to collect and use the data.

The rules of data collection are complex. One seemingly good way to think about these issues is to consider ourselves to be a subject of the data collection and think about what protection we would need to feel safe and be willing to participate. Another seemingly good starting point is to consider whether similar data was collected recently. But these are not enough. Practices may not be OK just because we, as data analysts, would feel comfortable with them, or a recent data collection project got away with them. Instead, it is strongly advised to consult experts in the legal and ethical aspects of data collection.

> **Review Box 1.8   Ethical and legal principles**
>
> • Ethical and legal rules need to be fully observed; consulting experts is good practice before collecting data.
> • Important rules include ensuring confidentiality and observing ownership rights.

1.12 Main Takeaways

Know your data: how it was born and what its major advantages and disadvantages are to answer your question.

- Data quality is determined by how the data was born.
- Data is stored in data tables, with observations in rows and variables in columns.

PRACTICE QUESTIONS

1. What are in the rows and columns of a data table? What are ID variables?
2. What are xsec, tseries, and xt panel data? What's an observation in each? Give an example for each.
3. What's the validity and what's the reliability of a variable? Give an example of a variable with high validity and one with low validity.
4. What's selection bias? Give an example of data with selection bias and are without.
5. List two common advantages of admin data and two potential disadvantages.
6. How can we tell if a sample is representative of a population?
7. List two sampling rules that likely lead to a representative sample and two sampling rules that don't.
8. List three common features of Big Data. Why does each feature make data analysis difficult?
9. An important principle for research is maintaining confidentiality. How can we achieve that when we collect survey data?
10. You want to collect data on the learning habits of students in your data analysis class. List two survey methods that you may use and highlight their advantages and disadvantages.
11. You want to collect data on the friendship network of students in a class. You consider two options: (1) collect their networks of Facebook users using data there (80% of them are on Facebook), or (2) conduct an online survey where they are asked to mark their friends from a list of all students. List arguments for each option, paying attention to representation, costs, and ethical issues.
12. You consider surveying a sample of employees at a large firm. List four selection methods and assess whether each would result in a representative sample.

13. You want to examine the growth of manufacturing firms in a country. You have data on all firms that are listed on the stock exchange. Discuss the potential issues of coverage and its consequences. Does it matter which country it is?

14. 1000 firms are randomly selected from all the SMEs (small and medium enterprises) in a country. What is the population, what is the sample, and is the sample representative?

15. You are doing a survey about the smoking habits of the students of your university and want to reach a 20% sample. Here are some potential sampling rules. Would each lead to a representative sample? Why or why not? (1) Stand at the main entrance and select every fifth entering student. (2) Get the students' email list from the administration and select every fifth person in alphabetic order. (3) The same, but select the first fifth of the students in alphabetic order. (4) The same, but now sort the students according to a random number generated by a computer and select the first fifth of them.

DATA EXERCISES

Easier and/or shorter exercises are denoted by [*]; harder and/or longer exercises are denoted by [**].

1. Take the `hotels-vienna` dataset used in this chapter and use your computer to pick samples of size 25, 50, and 200. Calculate the simple average of hotel price in each sample and compare them to those in the entire dataset. Repeat this exercise three times and record the results. Comment on how the average varies across samples of different sizes. [*]

2. Choose a course that you take, and design a short survey to measure how much time your classmates spend on this course, broken down by activities (lectures, practice sessions, study groups, individual study time, and so on). Carry out a web survey (e.g., using Survey Monkey, Google Forms) among your classmates. Report the response rate and average of the main variables. Comment on your results. Write a short report on the challenges of designing and executing the survey. [**]

3. Choose two products that are sold in most supermarkets and gas stations. Visit ten retailers and record the price of each product. What difficulties, if any, did you encounter during this data collection? Are there differences in the prices you collected? Do you see an interesting pattern there? [**]

4. Collect data on used cars of a specific make and model (e.g., Ford Focus) in a city, from the Web, using a classified ads website or a used cars website as a source. Use web scraping to collect all available data on these cars. (Alternatively, collect the most important variables by hand from the 100 most recently advertised cars.) Write a short report on what you did, how many cars you ended up with in the data, and what difficulties you encountered, if any. [**]

5. Download country–year panel data on three variables ("indicators") of your choice from the World Bank website. Write a short report on what you did, how many countries and years you ended up with in the data, and what difficulties you encountered, if any. [*]

REFERENCES AND FURTHER READING

On surveys, we recommend Tourangeau et al. (2000). On sampling, a classic book is Kish (1965). A more recent overview is Bethlehem (2009).

On Big Data and data collection in marketing, Faro & Ohana (2018) is an informative discussion.

Regarding technical issues, there is more on the World Bank API at http://datahelpdesk .worldbank.org

The first surveys collected by the World Management Survey are summarized by Bloom et al. (2007). See also https://worldmanagementsurvey.org/

The online versus offline price data collection of the Billion Prices Project is described by Cavallo (2017). See also www.thebillionpricesproject.com/

2 Preparing Data for Analysis

How to organize, manage, and clean data

Motivation

What are the benefits of immunization of infants against measles? In particular, does immunization save lives? To answer that question you can use data on immunization rates and mortality in various countries in various years. International organizations collect such data on many countries for many years. The data is free to download, but it's complex. How should you import, store, organize, and use the data to have all relevant information in an accessible format that lends itself to meaningful analysis? And what problems should you look for in the data, how can you identify those problems, and how should you address them?

You want to know who the most successful managers (as coaches are also called in football, or soccer) are in the top English football league. To investigate this question, you have downloaded data on all games played in the league, as well as data on managers, including which team they worked at and when. How should you combine this data to investigate your question? Moreover, how would you uncover whether there are issues with the data that prevent linking the data and investigating it, and how would you address those issues?

Before analyzing their data, data analysts spend a lot of time on organizing, managing, and cleaning it to prepare it for analysis. This is called data wrangling or data munging. It is often said that 80% of data analysis time is spent on these tasks. Data wrangling is an iterative process: we usually start by organizing and cleaning our data, then start doing the analysis, and then go back to the cleaning process as problems emerge during analysis.

This chapter is about preparing data for analysis: how to start working with data. First, we clarify some concepts: types of variables, types of observations, data tables, and datasets. We then turn to the concept of tidy data: data tables with data on the same kinds of observations. We discuss potential issues with observations and variables, and how to deal with those issues. We describe good practices for the process of data cleaning and discuss the additional challenges of working with Big Data.

This chapter includes three case studies. The first one, **Finding a good deal among hotels: data preparation**, continues to work towards finding hotels that are underpriced relative to their location and quality. In this chapter, the case study illustrates how to find problems with observations and variables and how to solve those problems. It uses the `hotels-vienna` dataset. The second case study, **Identifying successful football managers**, combines information on English football (soccer) games and managers, using the `football` dataset. We'll use this data in a case study in Chapter 24 to uncover whether replacing football managers improves team performance. This case study illustrates linking data tables with different kinds of observations, problems that may arise with such linkages, and their solutions. The third case study, **Displaying immunization rates across countries**, illustrates how to store multi-dimensional data. It uses the `world-bank-immunization` dataset. We'll use this data in a case study to investigate whether immunization saves lives, in Chapter 23.

Learning outcomes

After working through this chapter, you should be able to:

- understand types of variables and observations;
- organize data in a tidy way;
- clean the data: identify and address problems with observations and variables;
- create a reproducible workflow to clean and organize data;
- document data cleaning and understand such documentation.

2.1 Types of Variables

Data is made up of observations and variables. Observations are the units for which the information is collected (customers, countries, days when an asset is traded). Variables contain the information (income, size, price). Variables take on specific values. The name variable comes from the fact that they have more than one value: the values vary across observations.

   We first discuss the various kinds of variables, and the following sections will discuss the various kinds of observations. We describe types of variables by what kind of information they capture and how the values of the variable are stored in the data. It is useful to understand the variable types as they help explain what we can do with the variables. Sometimes statistical software also asks data analysts to specify the type of each variable.

   Quantitative variables are born as numbers, and they are stored as numbers, in numeric format. Typically, they can take many values. Examples include prices, numbers of countries, costs, revenues, age, distance. Date and time are special cases of quantitative variable. They are often measured in specific scales and stored in a specific date/time format.

   Qualitative variables, also called **categorical variables** or **factor variables**, are not born as numbers. Instead, their values have a specific interpretation, typically denoting that the observation belongs to a category. Types or brands of products, name of countries, highest levels of education of individuals are examples. Most often, qualitative variables have few values, but sometimes they have many values. A special type of qualitative variable has the sole purpose of identifying observations – they are identifiers, or ID variables. With many observations, an ID variable has many values. (We introduced ID variables earlier in Chapter 1, Section 1.1.)

   Finally, quantitative variables are also called **continuous** and qualitative variables are also called **discrete** variables. These names come from mathematics, where a continuous variable have values without gaps, while a discrete variable can have specific values only, with gaps in-between. These labels are a little misleading for real data where few variables are measured in a truly continuous way because of integer units of measurement (dollars, thousand dollars, kilometers, and so on).

   The values of qualitative variables are sometimes stored as text, describing the categories. Text in data is also called a **string**. Most data analysts prefer storing qualitative variables as numbers. In that case each number should correspond to a category, and value labels show this correspondence, giving the meaning of each number value. For example, the brand of chocolate chosen by a chocolate customer, a qualitative variable, may be stored as string with the name or abbreviation of the brand, or as a number with appropriate labels (e.g., 1 = Lindt, 2 = Godiva).

Binary variables are a special case of qualitative variable: they can take on two values. Most often the information represented by binary variables is a yes/no answer to whether the observation belongs to some group. Examples include whether the respondent to a survey is female or not, whether a firm is in the manufacturing sector or not. For the purpose of data analysis it is best to have them take values 0 or 1: 0 for no, 1 for yes. Binary variables with 0/1 values are also called **dummy variables** or **indicator variables**.

In terms of measurement scale, data analysts often distinguish four types of data: nominal, ordinal, interval, and ratio. These may be thought as refinements of the qualitative/quantitative classification.

- **Nominal variables** are qualitative variables with values that cannot be unambiguously ordered. Examples include the chocolate brand names a costumer purchased or headquarter cities for chocolate makers. Individual decision makers may have some ordering of these options, but there is no universally agreed ranking of all options for these types of variables.
- **Ordinal** or **ordered variables** take on values that are unambiguously ordered. All quantitative variables can be ordered; some qualitative variables can be ordered, too. Examples include subjective health measures (whether someone rates their health as poor, fair, good, very good, or excellent) or the strength of an opinion (e.g., whether one strongly agrees, agrees, disagrees, or strongly disagrees with a statement).
- **Interval variables** have the property that a difference between values means the same thing regardless of the magnitudes. All quantitative variables have this property, but qualitative variables don't have this property. A one degree Celsius difference in temperature is the same when 20 is compared with 21 or 30 is compared with 31. A one dollar price difference of $3 versus $4 is the same as $10 versus $11.
- **Ratio variables**, also known as **scale variables**, are interval variables with the additional property that their ratios mean the same regardless of the magnitudes. This additional property also implies a meaningful zero in the scale. Many but not all quantitative variables have this property. Measures of length, elapsed time, age, value, or size are typically ratio variables. Zero distance is unambiguous, and a 10 km run is twice as long as a 5 km run. A used car sold for zero dollars costs nothing unambiguously, and a used car sold for 8000 dollars is twice as expensive as one sold for 4000 dollars. An example of an interval variable that is not a ratio variable is temperature: 20 degrees is not twice as warm as 10 degrees, be it Celsius or Fahrenheit.

Often, the raw data already has variables that fall into the groups described above, and they are ready for cleaning and then analysis. Sometimes, though, variables need to be created from the information we access. That may be challenging. Such difficult cases include texts, pictures, voice, and videos. For example, variables that we may want to create from text are the frequency of specific words or the proportion of positive or negative adjectives. Working with such information is a fast developing branch of data science, but it's beyond the scope of our textbook.

> **Review Box 2.1 Types of variables**
>
> - Qualitative (factor, categorical) variables have few values, often denoting a category to which the observation belongs. They may be nominal or ordered.

- Binary (dummy) variables are a special case of qualitative variable, with only two values; it's best to have those as 0 and 1.
- Quantitative (numeric) variables are born as numbers and can take many values that are meaningful in themselves. They are always interval variables with meaningful differences, and sometimes they are ratio variables.

2.2 Stock Variables, Flow Variables

Before turning to observations, let's consider one more way we can distinguish quantitative variables. In business, economics, and policy analysis we often work with quantities that could measure a flow or capture a stock.

Flow variables are results of processes during some time. Typically, they are the result of activities over time. The textbook example of a flow variable is the amount of water in a river that flowed through a reservoir gate yesterday; economic examples include sales of chocolate last month and government deficit last year.

Stock variables refer to quantities at a given point in time. Often, they are a snapshot of a business, a market, an economy, or a society. The textbook example is the amount of water in a reservoir at 8 a.m. this morning. Economic examples include the inventory of chocolate in a shop at the end of last month, or the amount of government debt at the end of last year.

The importance of distinguishing flow and stock variables comes from how we typically work with them. For example, their meaningful aggregation differs: often, flow variables are summed (monthly sales to annual sales); stock variables are averaged (average inventory at the end of each month last year). But flow and stock variables may be related: the difference between stocks at different points in time are often related to flow variables. For example, the difference between inventories of a chocolate factory at the end of this month and the end of last month is the difference between chocolate production and chocolate sales during last month, two flow variables.

Not every quantitative variable is either flow or stock: counterexamples include price and distance. But when a variable is either a flow or a stock, it may be important to keep that in mind.

2.3 Types of Observations

Just as it makes life easier to distinguish various kinds of variables, it makes sense to introduce concepts for types of observations. Recall that observations are the rows of a data table (Chapter 1, Section 1.1). But in different data tables observations may mean very different things. Those "things" are related to the actual physical or legal entities, or dimensions, our data is about, such as companies, individuals, days, or transactions. There are two main entity types in economic data analysis: cross-sectional entities and time series entities. These may result in data with cross-sectional observations, time series observations, or observations that have both a cross-sectional and a time series dimension (Table 2.1).

In **cross-sectional data (xsec data)**, observations are cross-sectional entities, such as people, firms, or countries. Such entities are also called cross-sectional units. In xsec data, each variable refers to the same time across units (same month, same year). Cross-sectional units are denoted by index i, so that x_i refers to variable x for cross-sectional unit i. The ID variable in cross-sectional data tables should identify each cross-sectional unit.

In **time series data** (**tseries data**), observations are different points or intervals in time, such as closing time of the stock market, or the duration of a calendar year. These time series entities are also called time periods. In tseries data, all observations refer to the same entity (person, firm, country), and they are different in terms of the time period of observation. Time series observations are denoted by index t. The ID variables in time series data denote the time period of observation.

Time periods are characterized by their **time series frequency**, also called periodicity. Time series frequency is the time difference between observations. Time series frequency may be yearly, monthly, weekly, daily, hourly, and so on. Time series frequency is lower if observations are less frequent; time series frequency is higher if the observations are more frequent. For example, yearly data is of lower frequency than monthly data; weekly data is of higher frequency than monthly data.

Time series frequency may also be irregular. For example, adjacent observations may refer to times of transactions, separated by as much time as happens to pass between the transactions. In fact most frequencies have some irregularities: years and months may have different numbers of days, or the effective time relevant for the variable may be different (such as the number of working days in a year to produce GDP in a country or the number of working hours in a month to produce output at a company). Whether and how one should address such irregularities is to be decided on a case by case basis.

Multi-dimensional data have observations across multiple dimensions. The most common multi-dimensional data is **cross-section time series data** – also called **xt data**, **longitudinal data**, or **panel data**. xt data include multiple cross-sectional units observed multiple times. Examples include yearly financial data on all companies in a country, weekly sales at various retail stores, or quarterly macroeconomic data on various countries.

Observations in xt data are one unit observed in one time period. Typically, observations in xt data are referred to using two indices – i for the cross-section and t for the time series – so that x_{it} denotes variable x for xsec unit i at time t.

Table 2.1 Types of observation

Observation type	Observations	ID variable	Example
Cross-sectional (xsec)	x_i: different cross-sectional units observed at same time	Identifies each cross-sectional unit	People, companies, countries observed in the same year/month
Time series (tseries)	x_t: same cross-sectional unit observed at different time periods	Identifies each time period	A single person/company/country observed at different times
Cross-section time series (xt, longitudinal, or panel)	x_{it} multiple cross-sectional units observed across multiple time periods	One ID identifies cross-sectional units; one ID identifies time periods	Retailer stores observed weekly, countries observed yearly

2.4 **Tidy Data**

After learning about types of variables and observations, let's introduce some concepts on how data is, or should be, organized. A useful guide to organize and storing data is the **tidy data** approach. In this section we'll introduce the principles of tidy data organization.

Data is stored in one or more **data tables**, each consisting of rows of observations and columns of variables. A **dataset** may consist of a single data table or multiple data tables that are related. In short, the tidy data approach prescribes that:

1. In a data table, each observation forms a row.
2. In a data table, each variable forms a column.
3. Each kind of observation forms a data table.

The last point means that when the dataset has information on different kinds of observations made up of different kinds of entities, the information on them should be stored in different data tables. For example, a dataset on customer purchases of various products may include a data table on customers (their age, income, and so on), a data table on products (type, brand, price, quality indicators), and a data table on purchase events (which customer purchased which product when).

We introduced ID variables earlier, in Section 2.1. They are especially important for datasets with multiple data tables. To keep track of entities within and across data tables, each kind of entity should have its own ID variable, and that should be stored in each data table with information on that kind of entity. The purpose of an ID variable is to uniquely and unambiguously identify each entity in the data table as well as across data tables in a dataset.

Consider our example of a dataset with three data tables, the first one on customers and their characteristics, the second one on products and their characteristics, and the third one on purchase events. Customers need to have their ID that identifies them in the first and the third data table; products need to have their ID that identifies them in the second and the third data table; the third data table should have yet one more ID variable that identifies the event of purchase.

The tidy data approach prescribes that data tables should have one observation in one and only one row. It's a simple principle, but various issues may arise in practice. Sometimes there are non-observation rows in the data table. These should be erased. If such rows contain important information they should be stored in some other way, e.g., in the data documentation. One potential exception is the header row that contains the names of the variables. In spreadsheet and text format, the header occupies the first row in the data table. When read into statistical software, this header row becomes a separate object so that when we look at the data table, the first row is the first observation.

The tidy data approach has many advantages. It offers a simple guiding principle to organize all kinds of data, including complicated datasets with many data tables. Working with data, such as coding and recoding variable types or generally resolving issues with observations and variables, is easier with **tidy data tables**. Tidy data tables are also transparent, which helps other users to understand them and work with them. Moreover, tidy data can be extended easily. New observations are added as new rows; new variables as new columns.

Data tables are a fundamental unit of data analysis. All processes of cleaning and analyzing are best done within tidy data tables. For the actual analysis, data analysts create a new data table from those tidy data tables. This new data table is called a **workfile**. With a tidy dataset including multiple data tables, this requires combining variables from those multiple data tables, with the help of appropriate ID variables. We will discuss the details of this process in the next few sections.

2.A1 CASE STUDY – Finding a Good Deal among Hotels: Data Preparation

Types of variables, tidy data table

Let us continue our case study from the previous chapter. Recall that the question of the case study is to find a good deal among hotels in a particular European city on a particular night. We collected the data from the web, which we call the `hotels-vienna` dataset. The dataset consists of information on hotels that have an available room for a weekday night in November 2017. We have 428 observations in the dataset. In this chapter we'll learn how to start working with this data. Before doing so, let's consider its most important variables.

The first variable is a number that denotes each hotel. We created these numbers to replace the names of the hotels for confidentiality reasons. It is a qualitative and nominal variable stored in numeric format. A particular value has no meaning besides identifying a particular hotel. This variable is our identifier (ID).

The type of accommodation is another qualitative and nominal variable. It denotes whether the hotel is in fact a hotel, or a hostel, an apartment-hotel, and so on.

Important quantitative variables are the hotel's price and its distance from the city center. Both are stored as numeric variables and are measured in a ratio scale.

Stars is a qualitative variable, and an ordinal one. To earn stars, hotels need to satisfy certain criteria. More stars mean more criteria checked. Stars have values of 1, 2, …, 5, and there are some in-between values, too (2.5, 3.5, 4.5).

Customer rating was originally collected as an ordered qualitative variable, 1 through 5. This allowed the price comparison site to compute the average customer rating. The variable in our data is the average of those individual ratings. It is a number with many values, so we treat it as a quantitative variable. However, we need to keep in mind that its source is an ordered qualitative variable, thus the same difference may mean different things at different levels (4.2 versus 4.0 is not the same as 3.2 versus 3.0).

The number of ratings that were used for this average is a quantitative variable, and a ratio variable with a meaningful zero.

Table 2.2 summarizes the types of these variables and gives an example of each from the actual data.

Table 2.2 List of the variables in the `hotels-vienna` dataset

Variable name	Type	Example value
ID (hotel identifier)	qualitative, nominal	21897
accommodation type	qualitative, nominal	hotel
price	quantitative	81
distance	quantitative	1.7
star	qualitative, ordered	4
average customer rating	assumed quantitative, based on a qualitative, ordered variable	3.9
number of customer ratings	quantitative	189

The data is stored as tidy data. Its rows are observations, its columns are the variables, and this table contains one kind of observations, hotels. The data table in Table 2.3 shows a few rows and columns of a data table, using the `hotels-vienna` dataset.

Table 2.3 A simple tidy data table

	Variables/columns		
	hotel_id	price	distance
	21897	81	1.7
Observations/rows	21901	85	1.4
	21902	83	1.7

Source: `hotels-vienna` dataset. Vienna, November 2017 weekday. N=428, of which 264 are hotels.

2.5 Tidy Approach for Multi-dimensional Data

Multi-dimensional data may be stored in more than one way in data tables. Let us focus on xt data (cross-section time series data).

The tidy approach recommends storing xt data in a data table with each row referring to one cross-sectional unit (i) observed in one time period (t). Thus, one row is one observation (it). This is called the **long format for xt data**. The first row is the first time period of the first cross-sectional unit. The next row is the same cross-sectional unit observed in the next time period. After the last time period observed for this cross-sectional unit, the next row in the data table is the first time period for the next cross-sectional unit. Correspondingly, observations in xt data are identified by two ID variables, one for each cross-sectional unit and one for each time period.

An alternative, but not tidy, way of storing multi-dimensional data is called the **wide format for xt data**. Here one row would refer to one cross-sectional unit, and different time periods are represented in different columns. Thus, there are as many columns for each variable as the number of time periods in the data. Here each observation is a different cross-sectional unit to be identified by the cross-sectional identifier i. Time should be "identified" in the names of the variables.

Sometimes doing analysis is easier with wide format, especially if there are only a few time periods. However, it is good practice not to store data in wide format. Instead, the tidy approach prescribes storing multi-dimensional data in long format and transforming it for analysis when necessary. The advantages to the long format for xt data are transparency and ease of management. It is straightforward to add new observations to long format tables, be those new cross-sectional units or new time periods, and it is easier to transform and clean variables.

2.B1 CASE STUDY – Displaying Immunization Rates across Countries

Tidy tables

As an example, consider an xt panel of countries with yearly observations, downloaded from the World Development Indicators data website maintained by the World Bank. We'll use this `world-bank-immunization` dataset in Chapter 23, Section 23.B1 where we'll try to uncover the extent to which measles immunization saves the lives of children. Here we illustrate the data structure focusing on the two ID variables (country and year) and two other variables, immunization rate and GDP per capita.

Table 2.4 shows parts of this xt panel data table in long format. Table 2.5 shows the same part of this xt panel data table, but now in wide format. We can see the main difference: in the long format we have multiple rows for a country, as each country is shown three times for the three years we cover. We can also see the advantage of the long and tidy format: if we were to add a new variable such as population, it would be simply adding a new column.

Table 2.4 Country–year panel on immunization and GDP per capita – tidy, long data table

Country	Year	imm	gdppc
India	2015	87	5743
India	2016	88	6145
India	2017	88	6516
Pakistan	2015	75	4459
Pakistan	2016	75	4608
Pakistan	2017	76	4771

Note: Tidy (long) format of country–year panel data, each row is one country in one year. imm: rate of immunization against measles among 12–23-month-old infants. gdppc: GDP per capita, PPP, constant 2011 USD.

Source: `world-bank-immunization` dataset. 2015–17. N=573.

Table 2.5 Country–year panel on immunization and GDP per capita – wide data table

Country	imm2015	imm2016	imm2017	gdppc2015	gdppc2016	gdppc2017
India	87	88	88	5743	6145	6516
Pakistan	75	75	76	4459	4608	4771

Note: Wide format of country–year panel data, each row is one country, different years are different variables. imm: rate of immunization against measles among 12–23-month-old infants. gdppc: GDP per capita, PPP, constant 2011 USD.

Source: `world-bank-immunization` dataset. 2015–17. N=191.

2.6 Relational Data and Linking Data Tables

After discussing how to organize and store data in tidy data tables with appropriate ID variables, we turn to how to combine such tables into a workfile. Sometimes, with complex data, that can be challenging. We may have macroeconomic data on many countries in many years, geographic information on the same countries for continents with many countries that is the same across time, and variables describing the global economy in each year that are the same for all countries. As another example, we may have data on companies and their managers, with some variables describing companies that may change through time, other variables describing the characteristics of managers that don't change, and data that tell us which manager worked for which company and when.

Relational data (or relational database) is the term often used for such datasets: they have various kinds of observations that are linked to each other through various relations.

Data analysts clean and describe the data tables one by one in a tidy relational dataset. Then, to actually work with such data, they combine the variables they need from the various data tables to form a single data table, their workfile. Sometimes they use all variables from all data tables to create the workfile. More often, they pick certain variables from each data table and work with those only. In either case, data analysts need appropriate ID variables to find the same entities across data tables.

The process of pulling different variables from different data tables for well-identified entities to create a new data table is called **linking**, **joining**, **merging**, or **matching** data tables.

To do so, data analysts start with one data table, and they merge with it observations from another data table. The most straightforward linkage is one-to-one (1:1) matching: merging tables with the same type of observations. For example, a data table with customers as observations with their age and income as variables may be merged with another data table on customers with a variable describing how they rated their last visit to the retail store. As another example, a country–year data table with population as a variable may be merged with another country–year data table with GDP per capita as a variable.

Other times we may want to do many-to-one (m:1) matching. For example, we may want to link average family income in zip code locations, a data table with observations on zip codes, to a data table with customers as observations whose zip code of residence is a variable. In the customer-level data table multiple customers may live in the same zip code area, thus the same zip code information may be merged with many customers. As another example, a data table with country–year observations with macro data may be merged with a data table with countries as observations and area as a variable. Here many country–year observations on the same country are merged with the same country observation.

An alternative is one-to-many (1:m) matching. One-to-many matching can be thought of as the same as many-to-one (m:1) matching but changing the order of the data tables: starting with the data table with the more aggregated observations (zip codes, countries) and merging with it the observations from the other dataset (customers, country–year observations).

The most complex case is many-to-many (m:m) matching: one observation in the first table may be matched with many observations in the second table, and an observation in the second data table may be matched with many observations in the first data table. In such an instance, we may need to have a separate table that connects IDs. For example we may want to link information on companies and information on managers. Each company may have had more than one manager during the time span of our data; each manager may have worked for more than one company. In such complicated cases, we often need to think a bit and rephrase the problem as a set of 1:m and m:1 matching problems.

When merging two data tables, be that 1:1, 1:m, m:1, or m:m matching, data analysts may be able to link all observations or only some of them. The latter may happen in two ways: observations in the first data table have no matching observations in the second data table, or observations in the second data table have no matching observations in the first data table. Depending on their goals, data analysts may keep all observations whether matched and unmatched, or they may keep matched observations only.

> **Review Box 2.2   Tidy data tables**
>
> 1. In tidy data tables, each observation is a row and each column is a variable.
> 2. Multi-dimensional data may need to be reformatted to a tidy data version, with ID variables for each dimension (such as country and year).
> 3. In relational datasets, a set of tidy data tables can be linked via appropriate ID variables.

2.C1   CASE STUDY – Identifying Successful Football Managers

Question and data

In this case study, we are interested to identify the most successful football managers in England. We'll extend this case study to focus on the impact of replacing managers later, in Chapter 24. We combine data from two sources for this analysis, one on teams and games, and one on managers. Our focus in this chapter is how to combine the two data sources and what problems may arise while doing so.

Before we start, let us introduce some concepts. We will talk about football, called soccer in the USA and a few other countries. In England and some other countries, coaches are called managers – as they take on managerial duties beyond coaching. We will focus on the English Premier League (EPL, for short) – the top football division in England. A season runs for about 9 months, from mid-August to mid-May, and the league consists of 20 teams each season.

Our data cover 11 seasons of EPL games – 2008/2009 to 2018/2019 – and come from the publicly available Football-Data.co.uk website. At the end of every season, some teams are relegated to the second division, while some are promoted to join the EPL from the second division. In this 11-season long period, some teams feature in all seasons (such as Arsenal, Chelsea, or Manchester United), while others play in the EPL just once (such as Cardiff).

Each observation in the data table is a single game. Key variables are the date of the game, the name of the home team, the name of the away team, the goals scored by the home team, and the goals scored by the away team. Each team features 19 times as "home team" and 19 times as "away team." We have 380 rows for each season. With 11 seasons, the total number of observations is 4180. A small snippet of the data is presented in Table 2.6.

Is this a tidy data table? It is; each observation is a game, and each game is a separate row in the data table. Three ID variables identify each observation: date, home team, away team. The

Table 2.6 Football game results – game-level data				
Date	**Home team**	**Away team**	**Home goals**	**Away goals**
2018-08-19	Brighton	Man United	3	2
2018-08-19	Burnley	Watford	1	3
2018-08-19	Man City	Huddersfield	6	1
2018-08-20	Crystal Palace	Liverpool	0	2

Table 2.6   (cont.)

Date	Home team	Away team	Home goals	Away goals
2018-08-25	Arsenal	West Ham	3	1
2018-08-25	Bournemouth	Everton	2	2
2018-08-25	Huddersfield	Cardiff	0	0

Note: One observation is one game.

Source: `football` dataset. English Premier League, all games, 11 seasons from 2008/9 through 2018/9. N=4180.

other variables describe the result of the game. From the two scores we know who won, by what margin, how many goals they scored, and how many goals they conceded.

But there is an alternative way to structure the same data table, which will serve our analysis better – in this data table, each row is a game played by a team. It includes variables from the perspective of that team: when they played, who the opponent was, and what the score was. That is also a tidy data table, albeit a different one. It has twice as many rows as the original data table: 38 weeks x 20 teams = 760 observations per season, 8360 observations in total.

Table 2.7 shows a small part of this tidy data table. Each game appears twice in this data table, once for each of the playing team's perspectives. For each row here we had to introduce a new variable to denote whether the team at that game was the home team or the away team. Now we have two ID variables, one denoting the team, and one denoting the date of the game. The identity of the opponent team is a qualitative variable.

Table 2.7   Football game results – team–game-level data

Date	Team	Opponent team	Goals	Opponent goals	Home/ away	Points
2018-08-19	Brighton	Man United	3	2	home	3
2018-08-19	Burnley	Watford	1	3	home	0
2018-08-19	Man City	Huddersfield	6	1	home	3
2018-08-19	Man United	Brighton	2	3	away	0
2018-08-19	Watford	Burnley	3	1	away	3
2018-08-19	Huddersfield	Man City	1	6	away	0

Note: One observation is one game for one team.

Source: `football` dataset. English Premier League, all games, 11 seasons from 2008/9 through 2018/9. N=8360.

Our second data table is on managers. We collected data on the managers from Wikipedia. One row is one manager–team relationship: a job spell by a manager at a team. So each manager may feature more than once in this data table if they worked for multiple teams. For each observation, we have the name of the manager, their nationality, the name of the team (club), the start time of the manager's work at the team, and the end time. Table 2.8 lists a few rows.

Table 2.8	Football managers - spells at teams			
Name	**Nat.**	**Club**	**From**	**Until**
Arsene Wenger	France	Arsenal	1 Oct 1996	13 May 2018
Unai Emery	Spain	Arsenal	23 May 2018	Present*
Ron Atkinson	England	Aston Villa	7 June 1991	10 Nov 1994
Brian Little	England	Aston Villa	25 Nov 1995	24 Feb 1998
John Gregory	England	Aston Villa	25 Feb 1998	24 Jan 2002
Dean Smith	England	Aston Villa	10 Oct 2018	Present*
Alan Pardew	England	Crystal Palace	2 Jan 2015	22 Dec 2016
Alan Pardew	England	Newcastle	9 Dec 2010	2 Jan 2015

Note: Managers in EPL. One observation is a job spell by a manager at a team. * As of September 2019.
Source: `football` dataset. N=395.

As we can see, some managers had a long spell, others a shorter spell at teams. Some managers coached more than one team: Alan Pardew, for instance, worked for both Crystal Palace and Newcastle. We have 395 observations for 241 managers.

So we have a relational dataset. It has one data table with team–game observations, and one data table with manager–team observations. The first data table contains dates for the games; the second data table contains the start dates and end dates for the time each manager worked for each team. To work with the information in the two data tables together, we need to create a workfile, which is a single data table that is at the team–game level with the additional variable of who the manager was at the time of that game.

We have all the information to link managers to team–games: which manager was in charge at the time a team played a game. But creating that linkage is not straightforward. We discuss some of the problems and its solutions in the next section, and we'll return to our case study afterwards.

2.7 Entity Resolution: Duplicates, Ambiguous Identification, and Non-entity Rows

In many data tables that we start working with, we may observe strange things: the ID variable is not unique when it should be, we appear to have multiple observations with different ID variables for entities that should be the same, or we may have rows that are not for the kinds of entities we want. These are issues with the entities in the data table. Before doing any meaningful analysis, such issues need to be resolved, to the extent it is possible. That process is called **entity resolution**.

One potential issue is having **duplicate observations**, or, simply, **duplicates**, in the data table. Duplicates appear when some entities that should be a single observation appear more than once in the data table. While the name suggests two appearances, it may refer to three or more appearances as well. Duplicates may be the result of human error (when data is entered by hand), or the features of the data source (e.g., data scraped from classified ads with some items posted more than once). When possible, duplicates need to be reduced to a single observation.

In the simplest case, duplicates are perfect: the value of all variables is the same. In such cases we have to delete the duplicates and leave one data row for each observation only. In more difficult cases, the value of one or more variables is different across data rows that appear to correspond to the same observation. Then, we have to make a decision about whether to keep all observations or select one, and if the latter, which value to keep – or maybe create a new value, such as the average.

A related, but conceptually different issue is to have **ambiguous identification**: the same entity having different IDs across different data tables. The task here is to make sure that each entity has the same ID across data tables. That is necessary to link them properly. Entities are frequently identified by names. Unfortunately, though, names may cause issues for two main reasons: they are not unique (more than one person may be called John Smith), and different data tables may have different versions of the same name (e.g., middle names sometimes used, sometimes not: Ronald Fisher, Ronald A. Fisher, and Sir Ronald Aylmer Fisher is the same person, a famous statistician). This task is called **disambiguation**: making identification of entities not ambiguous.

Yet another issue is having non-entity observations: rows that do not belong to an entity we want in the data table. Examples include a summary row in a table that adds up variables across some entities. For example, a data table downloaded from the World Bank on countries often includes observations on larger regions, such as Sub-Saharan Africa, or the entire World, and they are included just like other rows in the data table together with the rows for individual countries. Before any meaningful analysis can be done, we need to erase such rows from the data table.

The important message is this: assigning unique IDs is important. As a ground rule, we should avoid names as ID since people or firm names are not unique (remember, even the two authors have the same first name) and can be frequently misspelled. Using numerical ID variables is good practice.

Finally, note that, very often, there is no single best solution to entity resolution. We may not be 100% certain if different rows in the data table belong to the same real-life observation or not. Moreover, often it is not evident what to do when different values of a variable show up for the same real-life observation. As a result, our clean data table may end up not really 100 percent clean. But that is all right for the purpose of data analysis. Data analysts have to learn to live with such imperfections. When the magnitude of the problem is small, it is unlikely to have a substantial effect on the results of our subsequent analysis. When the magnitude of the problem is large, we may have to try different versions of solving it, and see if they have an effect on the results of our analysis.

2.C2   CASE STUDY – Identifying Successful Football Managers

Entity resolution

Let us look at data issues for the football manager case study and see if we need to resolve entities. Indeed, the data does have ambiguous entities that we need to deal with. For instance, consider Manchester City and Manchester United, the two major football teams from the city of Manchester. When we looked through official sites, news reports, and datasets, we could find many different versions of how teams were named, as summarized in Table 2.9. Entity resolution here is defining unique IDs and deciding which names do actually belong to the same team.

Table 2.9	Different names of football teams in Manchester, UK	
Team ID	**Unified name**	**Original name**
19	Man City	Manchester City
19	Man City	Man City
19	Man City	Man. City
19	Man City	Manchester City F.C.
20	Man United	Manchester United
20	Man United	Manchester United F.C.
20	Man United	Manchester United Football Club
20	Man United	Man United

Source: Various sources including source for the football dataset.

For the manager names, we sometimes see one or more space characters in the name, and sometimes we don't see them. Another issue is whether and how accents are included in names, such as "Arsène Wenger", a former manager of Arsenal. On a very few occasions, the manager's name may be missing. One example is that there are no records for the team Reading for mid-March 2013. In our case this comes from a caretaker manager who somehow was not recorded. In such cases we can create a separate ID, with the name missing.

Having made these corrections and combined the datasets, we can create unambiguous ID variables for teams in the first data table and managers and teams in the second data table. With these ID variables and the dates of the games and the date for the managers' job spells, we can create a workfile by joining the managers data table to the team–games data table of the appropriate date. This procedure is not straightforward, and it can be done in multiple ways. You are invited to check our code on the textbook website to see one way to do it.

With the workfile at hand, we can describe it. The workfile has 8360 team–game observations: in each of the 11 seasons, 20 teams playing 38 games (19 opponent teams twice; $11 \times 20 \times 19 \times 2 = 8360$). For these 11 seasons, we have 124 managers in the data.

From this case study, we learned that entity resolution, having the data structured right, and having proper ID variables are essential when working with relational data. Only with clearly identified teams and managers can we hope to match managers to teams and the games they play.

2.8 Discovering Missing Values

With tidy data and no issues with entities to resolve, we can turn our attention to the actual content of variables. And there may be issues there, too. A frequent and important issue with variables is **missing values**. Missing values mean that the value of a variable is not available for some observations. They present an important problem, for three main reasons.

First, missing values are not always straightforward to identify, and they may be mistakenly interpreted as some valid value. That is not a problem when missing values are represented by a specific character in the data, such as "NA" (for "not available"), a dot ".", or an empty space "". Statistical software recognizes missing values if stored appropriately. Sometimes, however, missing values are recorded with number values, outside the range (e.g., 0 for no, 1 for yes, 9 for missing). Such values need to be replaced with a value that the software recognizes as missing. Identifying missing values and storing them in formats recognizable by the statistical software is always a must. It should be the first step for dealing with missing values, and it needs to be done even if it affects one single observation.

The second issue with missing values is that they mean fewer observations in the data with valid information. As we shall see in subsequent chapters, the number of observations is an important determinant of how confidently we can generalize our results from the particular dataset to the situation we truly care about. When a large fraction of the observations is missing for an important variable in the analysis, we have a lot fewer observations to work with than the size of the original dataset.

The magnitude of the problem matters in two ways: what fraction of the observations is affected, and how many variables are affected. The problem is small if values are missing for one or two variables and only a few percent of the observations for each variable. The problem is bigger the larger fraction is missing and/or the more variables affected. For an example with small missing rates of many variables, consider a dataset on 1000 people with 50 variables that aim to capture personality characteristics. For each of these variables, 2% of the observations have missing values – i.e., we do not have information on a given characteristic for 20 of the 1000 people. Suppose, moreover, that for each variable on personal characteristics, the occurrence of missing values is independent across variables. In this case we end up with as few as 360 people with valid values for all 50 variables, which is 36% of the original number of observations (0.98 raised to the power of 50 = 0.36). This is a large drop even though each missing rate is tiny in itself.

The third issue is potential **selection bias**. One way to think about missing values is that they lead to a dataset used for the analysis that covers fewer observations than the entire dataset. We discussed coverage earlier in Chapter 1, Section 1.3. As always, when coverage is incomplete, an important question is whether this smaller sample represents the larger dataset. When the missing observations are very similar to the included ones, thus there is no selection bias, we say that the observations are **missing at random**.

How can we tell whether values are missing at random or there is selection bias? The two approaches that work for assessing whether a sample represents a population work here as well: benchmarking and understanding the selection process.

Benchmarking means comparing the distribution of variables that are available for all observations. Think of missing values of a variable y. Then benchmarking involves comparing some statistics, such as the mean or median (see more in Chapter 3, Section 3.6) of variables x, z, ..., each of which is thought to be related to variable y, in two groups: observations with missing y and observations with non-missing y. If these statistics are different, we know there is a problem.

Understanding the selection process requires knowing how the data was born and a good understanding of the content of the variables. In some other cases, missing is really just that: no information. Then we should understand why it is so – e.g., why some respondents refused to answer the survey question, or why some companies failed to report a value. However, in some cases missing doesn't really mean missing but zero, only the value zero was not filled in for the relevant observations. For example, a variable for export revenues in company-level data may be left missing for companies that do not have such revenue. But it means zero. When missing values can be replaced with meaningful ones, we should do so. In other cases, missing values decrease the quality of data, just like incomplete coverage.

2.9 Managing Missing Values

Having missing values for some variables is a frequent problem. Whatever the magnitude, we need to do something about them. But what can we do about them?

There are two main options. First, we can work with observations that have non-missing values for all variables used in the analysis. This is the most natural and most common approach. It is usually a reasonable choice if the fraction of missing values is not too high, there are few variables affected, and selection bias is not too severe. One version of this approach is to work with observations that make up a well-defined subsample, in which the missing data problem is a lot less severe. For example, if missing values are a lot more prevalent among small firms in administrative data on firms, we may exclude all small firms from the data. The advantage of such a choice is transparency: the results of the analysis will refer to medium and large firms.

The second option is filling in some value for the missing values, such as the average value. This is called **imputation**. Imputation may make sense in some cases but not in others. In any case, imputation does not add information to the data. For that reason, it is usually not advised to do imputation for the most important variables in the analysis. When data analysts use many variables, imputation may make sense for some of them. There are sophisticated methods of imputation, but those are beyond the scope of this textbook. Partly for that reason, we advise against imputing missing values in general.

Let us offer three practical pieces of advice regarding managing missing observations.

First, when possible, focus on more fully filled variables. Sometimes the variable that best captures the information we need has many missing values, but a less perfect variable is available with few missing variables. For instance, working with data on customers, we may have a variable describing family income for each customer, but that information may be missing for most customers. Instead, we may have information on the zip code of their residence available for virtually all customers. In this case it makes sense not to use the family income variable at all, and instead use a variable on the average family income in zip code locations available from another source. Importantly, when missing values are replaced with some other value, it is good practice to create a binary variable that indicates that the original value was missing. Such a variable is called a **flag**.

Second, imputation for qualitative variables should be done differently: these variables have no average value. Instead, we should add an additional category for missing values. For instance, consider the district of a hotel within a city. We would need to add "missing" as a new district value. For ordinal variables, we may also impute the median category and add a new variable denoting that the original value was missing.

Third, whatever we choose to do with missing values, we should make a conscious choice and document that choice. Some choices are more reasonable than others, depending on the situation. But all choices have consequences for the analysis.

As with other steps of **data cleaning**, there may not be an obviously best solution to deal with missing values. Such imperfections are a fact of life for data analysts. Magnitudes matter: small issues are likely to have small effects on the results of our analysis; issues that affect many observations may have substantial effects. In the latter case, data analysts often try alternative decisions during the cleaning process and see whether and how they affect their results in the end.

Review Box 2.3   Missing values

- Missing values of variables may be an issue for several reasons:
  - they may be interpreted as values, often as extreme values;
  - they yield fewer observations to analyze;
  - observations with missing values may be different, which could cause selection bias.
- There are several options to deal with missing values:
  - drop variables with too many missing values;
  - drop observations with missing values if there aren't many;
  - replace missing values with some other value (imputation) and add a binary variable to indicate missing values (a flag).

2.A2 | CASE STUDY – Finding a Good Deal among Hotels: Data Preparation

Duplicates and missing values

We illustrate the above data problems with the raw `hotels-vienna` dataset with observations on hotels in Vienna for a weekday in November 2017.

Recall that we replaced hotel names with a numerical ID variable for confidentiality reasons. The way we did that ensured that each hotel name corresponds to a single number. Thus, duplicates with hotel names would show up as duplicates in the ID variable, too. And there are duplicates. There are 430 observations in the raw data, yet there are only 428 different ID values. It turns out that the reason for this difference is that there are two hotels that are featured twice in the raw data table. They are listed in Table 2.10, together with the most important variables.

Table 2.10   Duplicates in the `hotels-vienna` dataset

ID	Accommodation type	Price	Distance to center	Stars	Avg. rating	Number of ratings
22050	hotel	242	0.0	4	4.8	404
22050	hotel	242	0.0	4	4.8	404
22185	hotel	84	0.8	3	2.2	3
22185	hotel	84	0.8	3	2.2	3

Source: `hotels-vienna` dataset. Vienna, November 2017 weekday. N=428.

The table shows that these duplicates are of the simple kind: all variables have the same value. To resolve the issue we need to drop one of each of the duplicates. The result is 428 hotels in the data table (this is the number of observations we described in Chapter 1, Section 1.A1).

Next let's turn to missing values. The most important variables have no missing values except for average customer rating, which is missing for 35 of the 428 observations. This is an 8% missing rate. When we dig deeper into the data, we can see that the type of accommodation is strongly related to whether average customer rating is missing. In particular, 34 of the 35 observations with missing values are for apartments, guest houses, or vacation homes. Of the 264 regular hotels in the data, only 1 has a missing value for average customer rating. It's a hotel with 2.5 stars, 0.7 miles from the city center, charging 106 dollars. Later, when we analyze the data to find a good deal, we'll restrict the data to regular hotels with 3 to 4 stars; this hotel would not be in that data (see Chapter 7, Section 7.A1).

2.10   The Process of Cleaning Data

The **data cleaning process** starts with the raw data and results in clean and tidy data. It involves making sure the observations are structured in an appropriate way and variables are in appropriate formats.

Data cleaning may involve many steps, and it's good practice to document every step.

An important step of data cleaning is to make sure all important variables are stored in an appropriate format. Binary variables are best stored as 0 or 1. Qualitative variables with several values may be stored as text or number. It is usually good practice to store them as numbers, in which case there should be a correspondence to say what number means what: this is called **value labeling** . Cleaning variables may include slicing up text, extracting numerical information, or transforming text into numbers.

Another important step is identifying missing values and making appropriate decisions on them. As we have described above, we have several options. We may opt to leave them as missing; then missing values need to be stored in a way that the statistical software recognizes.

Data cleaning also involves making sure that values of each variable are within their admissible range. Values outside the range are best replaced as missing unless it is obvious what the value was meant to be (e.g., an obvious misplacement of digits). Sometimes we need to change the units of measurement, such as prices in another currency or replace very large numbers with measures in thousands or millions. Units of measurement should always be indicated with the variables. Sometimes it makes sense to keep both the original and the new, generated variable to be able to cross-check them later in the analysis.

As part of data cleaning, variable description (also called **variable labels**) should be prepared showing the content of variables with all the important details. Similarly, when qualitative variables are stored as numbers, value labels that show the correspondence between values and the content of the categories need to be stored as well. In a spreadsheet, those labels should be stored in a separate sheet or document. Some software can include such labels together with the data table.

In any case, it is important to be economical with one's time. Often, there are variables in the data that we think we won't use for our analysis. Most of the time it does not make sense to invest time and energy to clean such variables. It is good practice to make the tidy data file leaner, containing the variables we need, and work with that data file. As the raw data is stored anyway, we can always go back and add and clean additional variables if necessary.

Data wrangling is part of a larger process. Data analysts start with structuring and cleaning the data, then turn to data description and analysis. They almost always find errors and problems in those latter stages, and they go back to structuring and cleaning. For instance, in some cases, missing values tell us that there is a problem in the data management and cleaning process, and in some cases we can improve the process and reduce the number of missing values. Maybe we actually made some coding mistakes causing errors, such as mishandled joining of two data tables.

Data analysts make many choices during the process of data wrangling. Those choices need to be the results of conscious decisions and have to be properly documented. Often, there are multiple ways to address the same issue, and there may not be a single best solution available. We have seen examples of this for handling apparent duplicates in the data with different values of the same variable, or handling missing values. When the issue in question affects few observations, that ambiguity is unlikely to be a problem. When it affects many observations, it may have effects on the results of our analysis. In such a case it is good practice to try different solutions to the problem and see whether and how that affects the results of the analysis. This process is called **robustness checking**.

2.11 Reproducible Workflow: Write Code and Document Your Steps

Data wrangling should be executed in a way that is easy to repeat and reproduce. This means documenting what we do and writing code so that steps can be repeated.

Documentation is very important. It is good practice to produce a short document, called README, that describes the most important information about the data used in any analysis. This document may be helpful during the analysis to recall important features of the data.

Another, often longer, document can describe all data management and cleaning steps we have done. It is also essential to enable other analysts to check your work, replicate your analysis, or build on your analysis in the future (including the future version of yourself). Such a document should allow recalling the steps as well as communicating them. It is important to cite the data source, too.

Table 2.11 offers a checklist to guide describing datasets.

Table 2.11 Describing data	
Topic	**Content to include**
Birth of data	When, how, for what purpose it was collected
	By whom, and how is the data available
	Whether it's the result of an experiment
Observations	Type: cross-sectional, time series, and so on
	What an observation is, how it is identified, number of observations
Variables	List of variables to be used, their type, their content, range of values
	Number or percentage of missing values
	If a generated variable, how it was created
Data cleaning	Steps of the process

It is also useful to write code for for all data wrangling steps. Yes, writing code takes more time than making edits in a spreadsheet or clicking through commands in software. However, investing some time can be rewarding. In most cases, we have to redo data cleaning after new issues emerge or the raw data changes. There the benefits of code tend to massively outweigh its costs:

1. It makes it easy to modify part of the data wrangling and cleaning procedure and re-do the entire procedure from the beginning to the end.
2. An automated process can be repeated when needed, perhaps due to a slight change in the underlying raw data.
3. It makes it easy for anyone else to reproduce the procedure thus increasing the credibility of the subsequent analysis.
4. Code becomes the skeleton for documentation: it shows the steps in the procedure itself.
5. Many existing platforms, such as GitHub, assist and promote collaboration.

Of course, there are trade-offs between all those benefits and the work needed to write code, especially for short tasks, small datasets, and for novice data analysts. Yes, it's OK to use a spreadsheet to make some quick changes in order to save time. However, we think that it makes sense to write code all the time, or very frequently, even if it seems too big an effort at first sight. We typically don't know in advance what data cleaning decisions we'll have to make and what their consequences will be. Thus, it is quite possible that we would have to re-do the whole process when things change, or for a robustness check, even for a straightforward-looking data cleaning process. Moreover, writing code all the time helps in mastering the coding required for data cleaning and thus helps in future projects.

As we have emphasized many times, data cleaning is an iterative process. We start by cleaning and creating a tidy data version and then a workfile. Then, while describing the data and working on the analysis, it is very common to discover further issues that require going back to the data cleaning step. This is yet one more reason to work with code: repeating everything and adding new elements to data cleaning is a lot easier and a lot less time consuming if written in code.

Review Box 2.4   Data wrangling: common steps

1. Write code – it can be repeated and improved later.
2. Understand the types of observations and what actual entities make an observation.
3. Understand the types of variables and select the ones you'll need.
4. Store data in tidy data tables.
5. Resolve entities: find and deal with duplicates, ambiguous entities, non-entity rows.
6. Get each variable in an appropriate format; give variable and value labels when necessary.
7. Make sure values are in meaningful ranges; correct non-admissible values or set them as missing.
8. Identify missing values and store them in an appropriate format; make edits if needed.
9. Make a habit of looking into the actual data tables to spot issues you didn't think of.
10. Have a description of variables.
11. Document every step of data cleaning.

2.12   Organizing Data Tables for a Project

After having discussed how to detect issues with observations and variables in a data table and what to do with such issues, let's turn to how the various data tables should be organized. It is good practice to organize and store the data at three levels. These are:

- Raw data tables
- Clean and tidy data tables
- Workfile(s) for analysis.

Raw data, the data as it was obtained in the first place, should always be stored. Raw data may come in a single file or in multiple files. It should be stored in the original format before anything is done to it. This way we can always go back and modify steps of data cleaning if necessary. And, most often it is necessary: something may go wrong, or we may uncover new issues during the process of data cleaning or data analysis. Having the raw data is also key for replicating our analysis. That becomes especially important if similar analyses are to be done in the future.

The next step is producing clean and tidy data from raw data. That's the process of data cleaning. It involves making sure each observation is in one row, each variable is in one column, and variables are ready for analysis. This is the long and tedious process of data cleaning that we have discussed in the larger part of this chapter.

Often tidy data means multiple data tables. It often makes sense to create different data tables for data coming from different sources. That makes the process of creating tidy data from raw data transparent. We should always create different data tables for data with different kinds of observations.

In cross-sectional data this means potentially different kinds of entities, such as individuals, families, neighborhoods, schools of children, employers of workers. In time series data this means potentially different time periods, such as daily observation of prices but weekly observations of quantities. For multi-dimensional data this may mean all of the above, plus different data tables for information at different levels of observations.

In cross-sectional time series data we may have data tables with one row for each cross-sectional unit i without any change in time, data tables with aggregate time series with observations t (that are the same for all cross-sectional units), and some data tables with observations i, t – in the long format of course.

The last of the three levels of the file structure is the workfile. This is the one file on which the analysis is to be done. The rows of workfiles are observations that form the basis of the analysis. Typically, they contain only a subset of all available variables, and, with more than one tidy data file, they may use data from all or only a subset of those files. Workfiles may or may not be in tidy data format.

Let us emphasize the advantage of having tidy data before turning them into a workfile for the analysis. Tidy data files tend to be more transparent. Thus they are better suited to identifying problems in the data, addressing those problems and producing clean data, and adding or taking away observations and variables. With tidy data we can add new variables to be included in the analysis, and we can produce various kinds of workfiles for various kinds of analyses.

Consider the organization of files for this textbook. For all case studies, we stored raw files as they were collected. The clean folder contains cleaned tidy data tables as well as the code that produces these clean files from the raw ones. The folder for each case study includes the code that creates the workfile and performs the analysis itself. It may also include the workfile as well. We also added an output folder for storing graphs and tables.

2.C3   CASE STUDY – Identifying Successful Football Managers

Organizing files

As always, we produced three kinds of files during the process of cleaning the football managers data: data files, code, and documentation files. We have three kinds of data files: raw data files (the original ones without any modification), tidy data files, and a workfile for our analysis.

We have two raw data files here, one on every game from 11 seasons of the English Premier League, and one on football managers who worked for any of the teams that appeared in the English Premier League during those 11 years. In fact, the data on games from those 11 years are 11 separate data files that we downloaded. We then combined these 11 files to form a single data file.

From these raw data files, we created three tidy data files, one with games as an observation (epl_games), one with one team playing one game as an observation (epl_teams_games), and one with one spell for a manager working for a team as an observation (epl_managers). Then, for our analysis, we combined the second and third tidy data tables to form a workfile, with one team playing one game as an observation, together with the information of who the manager was then. That's our workfile for this chapter (football_managers_workfile).

Table 2.12 shows these data files together with the file name of the R, Python, and Stata code that produces them (.R, .py and .do). Besides data and code, the file list includes a README file that contains the most important information on the data and our code.

Table 2.12   Structure of storing data and code files

path	folder	files
da_data_repo	football	README
	football/raw	fdata_pl_2008.csv - fdata_pl_2018.csv
		managers_epl.xls
	football/clean	epl_games.csv
		epl_teams_games.csv
		epl_managers.csv
		football_managers_workfile.dta
		football_managers_workfile.csv
		football-epl-maker.do
		football-epl-maker.R
		VARIABLES.xls
da_case_studies	ch02-football-manager-success	ch02-football-manager-success.do
		ch02-football-manager-success.py
		ch02-football-manager-success.R

2.C4 CASE STUDY – Identifying Successful Football Managers

Finding the most successful managers

Having compiled the data we need, we can answer our question: which managers have been the most successful ones over the 11 seasons of EPL. We continue considering managerial spells at teams: if a manager worked for two teams, we consider it two cases. First, we need to define success. Let us consider average points per game as a measure of success.

To calculate it, we simply add up both the points earned over a career at a team and the number of games he managed, and divide total points by the number of games. We rank them, and take a look at those with at least 2 points per game – we have eleven such manager–team combinations.

Figure 2.1 shows the top managers. We can see some well-known names in European football, like Alex Ferguson (Manchester United), Pep Guardiola (Manchester City), or Carlo Ancelotti (Chelsea) among top managers.

One interesting aspect is the presence of a few lesser known names, starting with Michael Appleton topping the chart with a perfect 3/3 ratio. The reason behind that is that some managers were only sitting in on a few games, and if lucky, they could get a high win ratio. To make this clear, we used a different color for manager–team spells that lasted less than 18 games, such as in the case of caretakers.

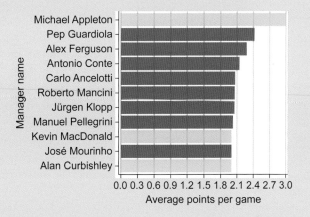

Figure 2.1 The most successful managers

Note: Manager–team spells. Yellow denotes spells less than 18 games (caretakers).
Source: `football` dataset. English Premier League, 11 seasons. N=177.

Once we discount caretakers, we have the most successful managers. In terms of average points per game, Pep Guardiola tops our league of managers, with 2.42 points per game for his entire spell of 3 years (114 games) at Manchester City followed by Alex Ferguson (2.28 points) having managed Manchester United for 190 games in this 11-year period.

| 2.13 | **Main Takeaways** |

You'll have to spend a lot of time on data wrangling, and you'll have to make many decisions.

- Your data wrangling decisions may affect the conclusions of your analysis.
- Write code to repeat, reproduce, or change your decisions.
- Document everything you do.
- Tidy structure helps all subsequent work with data.

PRACTICE QUESTIONS

1. What's the difference between a dataset and a data table, and which do we use for actual analysis?
2. What is panel (multi-dimensional) data, and what is xt panel data? Give one example of xt panel data and one of non-xt panel data.
3. What's a binary variable? Give two examples.
4. What are nominal and ordinal qualitative variables? Give two examples for each.
5. What are interval and ratio quantitative variables? Give two examples for each.
6. What are stock and flow variables? Give two examples for each.
7. What's the difference between long and wide format xt panel data? Which one would you prefer and why?
8. What are missing values and how can we discover them? What options do we have to work with variables that have missing data, and which should we choose when?
9. What's entity resolution? Give an example.
10. List four topics that data cleaning documentation should address.
11. What are the benefits of writing code for cleaning data?
12. What does merging two data tables mean, and how do we do it? Give an example.
13. Decide what types of variables the following are. Are they qualitative or quantitative? Are they binary variables? Also think about whether they are measured on a nominal, ordinal, interval, or ratio scale.
    (a) IQ
    (b) Country of origin
    (c) Number of years spent in higher education
    (d) The answer to the question in a survey that says: "Indicate on the scale below how much you agree with the following statement: Everyone has to learn data analysis for at least two semesters." with options "5 – Fully agree" "4 – Somewhat agree" "3 – Indifferent" "2 – Somewhat disagree" "1 – Fully disagree"
    (e) A variable that is 1 if an individual bought a car in a given month
    (f) Eye color
14. Consider the following data tables. Data table 1 includes countries in its rows; its columns are the name of the country, its area, and whether it has access to the sea. Data table 2 includes countries in its rows; its columns are GDP and population for various years, each year in a

different column. Is this a tidy dataset? If yes, why? If not, why not, and how can you transform it into a tidy dataset?

15. Consider the following data tables. Data table 1 includes single-plant manufacturing companies in its rows; its columns are the name of the company, the zip code of its plant, its industry, and the average wage the company pays in 2019. Data table 2 includes zip codes in its rows; its columns are total population, population density, and average house prices in 2019 in the zip code area. You want to analyze how the average wage paid by companies is related to the average house prices. How would you create a workfile from these data tables for that analysis?

DATA EXERCISES

Easier and/or shorter exercises are denoted by [*]; harder and/or longer exercises are denoted by [**].

1. Use the `hotels-europe` data for another city (not Vienna). Load and clean the data, document the cleaning, and describe the clean dataset. In particular, look at the raw data and make it into tidy data. [*]

2. Use a classified ads site and get data on the price and some of the most important characteristics of used cars. Pick a city and a make and type of car (e.g., Ford Fusion). Load and clean the data, document the cleaning, and describe the clean dataset. Discuss any decisions you may have made. [**]

3. Consider a department that uses this textbook for a sequence of four courses: DA1, DA2, DA3, and DA4. Below you will find textual descriptions of the organization of teaching. Create a tidy table with this info in any spreadsheet (Excel, Google Sheets, etc). [*]
   (courses and programs) The department has five programs running some courses: EC1, EC2, EC3, BA, FIN. A course may be core or elective. Courses DA1 and DA2 are core for all programs. DA3 is core for BA and elective for FIN. DA4 is core for EC1 and elective for all other programs.
   (lectures and seminars) Each course is composed of a lecture and a seminar. For FIN, there is one lecture for DA1 and DA2, and another lecture for all other programs. For all relevant programs there is one shared lecture in DA3 and DA4. In courses DA1 and DA2, there is one seminar for BA, one for EC1, EC2 and EC3 together, and one for FIN. In DA3 there is a single seminar for relevant programs. In DA4, there is a joint seminar for BA and FIN, and another one for EC1, EC2, EC3.
   (professors) For FIN, lectures and seminars in DA1 and DA2 are taught by Prof X. All other lectures are taught by Prof Y. Seminars with students from BA are taught by Prof W. Remaining seminars are taught by Prof Z.

4. Consider the `world-bank-immunization` dataset based on World Bank data. Generate a new variable for the growth rate of GDP per capita, in percentage terms, $(gdppc_{it}/gdppc_{i,t-1} - 1) * 100$. Add this variable to the long and wide format of the data and to Tables 2.4 and 2.5. [*]

5. Consider the `football` dataset we used. Create a table counting the number of seasons each team spent in the Premier League. List the teams that featured in all 11 seasons. List the teams that were in the League for only one season. [*]

REFERENCES AND FURTHER READING

On tidy data, the original paper is Wickham (2014).
A similar set of suggestions to ours for spreadsheet users may be found in Broman & Woo (2018).
The discussion on naming conventions and quite a few points come from Brian (2015).

2.U1 UNDER THE HOOD: NAMING FILES

Many seemingly mundane issues can make a big difference when working with data and code. Naming files is one of them.

Good names are easy to understand and informative for other people who may want to work with our files. That includes our future selves: we shouldn't count on remembering all the details that are not documented.

There are three useful criteria for naming files: names should be machine readable, human readable, and work well with default ordering.

Machine readable means it will be easy to extract information by splitting bits of text; for searching files, or narrowing the list of files by terms such as "graph", "table", "chapter05", "cleaner".

It also means to keep it plain and simple so that a variety of software could read it. In particular, it means having **no**:

- spaces
- punctuation(.,;)
- accented characters
- capitalized letters.

Human readable means that the name should also contain information on content – so that it is easy to figure out what a particular program or document is about. We may add a word or two on the purpose or the topic of the file (such as data-cleaner, financials-merger) as well as adding the type of the file (draft, presentation, conf-talk).

We suggest a deliberate use of "_" and "-", which allows us to recover meta-data from the file names. One approach is to use only "_" or "-"; another one is to use both in a systematic way, such as:

- "_" underscore used to delimit units to use for search, differentiate between parts of information. These parts will be easy to search on later. E.g., "firms_financials_2012."
- "-" hyphen used to delimit words for easy readability such as "compare-means-age."

Works well with default ordering as the computer default sorting already makes some sense.

For cases where we have several similar files, put something numeric first (or early on). This will help natural ordering (01, 02 or ch01, ch02). The date can be at the beginning, if it is crucial, or it can go at the end of a file name.

A useful little trick is to **left pad** other numbers with zeros, i.e. have 01 and not 1. Otherwise 10 will be before 2.

Finally, use the **ISO 8601 standard for dates:** "YYYY-MM-DD" – for example, "2018-06-01." While this order may look strange in some countries this is indeed the global standard.

These are not essential to data science, but they are easy to implement, and the payoffs will accumulate as your skills evolve and projects get more complex.

Below are some examples of file names that we like:

* "bekes-kezdi_textbook-presentation_2018-06-01.pdf" – it uses "-" and "_" deliberately, has a date in ISO format, all is in lower case, no special characters, and accents on names are gone.
* "ch02_organizing-data_world-bank-download_2017-06-01.tex" – it starts with a number early on, can be ordered, has left padding (02 and not 2), combines title (organizing data) and type (draft-text), all lower case.

Examples of file names we do not like include: thesis.pdf, mytext.doc, calculations1112018.xls, Gábor's-01.nov.19_work.pdf.

3 Exploratory Data Analysis

How to describe the information contained in variables

Motivation

You want to identify hotels in a city that are underpriced for their location and quality. You have scraped the web for data on all hotels in the city, including prices for a particular date, and many features of the hotels. How can you check whether the data you have is clean enough for further analysis? And how should you start the analysis itself?

You want to learn the extent of home advantage in football (soccer): how much more likely it is that a team wins if it plays in its home stadium, and how many more goals it scores. You have data from all games from a league, including who won, the score difference, and which team played in their home stadium. How should you summarize the data in a graph or a number that best describes the extent of home advantage? What additional graphs or numbers could help you understand this phenomenon?

After collecting the data, assessing its quality, cleaning it, and structuring it, the next step is exploratory data analysis (EDA). Exploratory data analysis aims to describe variables in a dataset. EDA is important for understanding potential problems with the data and making analysts and their audiences familiar with the most important variables. The results of EDA help additional data cleaning, decisions for further steps of the analysis, and giving context to the results of subsequent analysis.

The chapter starts with why we use exploratory data analysis. It then discusses some basic concepts such as frequencies, probabilities, distributions, and extreme values. It includes guidelines for producing informative graphs and tables for presentation and describes the most important summary statistics. The chapter, and its appendix, also cover some of the most important theoretical distributions and their uses.

There are four case studies in this chapter. The first one, **Finding a good deal among hotels: data exploration**, continues using the `hotels-vienna` dataset to illustrate the description of distributions and their use in identifying problems in the data. The second case study, **Comparing hotel prices in Europe: Vienna vs. London**, uses the `hotels-europe` dataset which contains hotels from several European cities, to illustrate the comparison of distributions. The third case study, **Measuring home team advantage in football**, examines whether and to what extent football (soccer) teams tend to perform better if they play in their home stadium, using the `football` dataset. It illustrates the use of exploratory data analysis to answer a substantive question. The last one, **Distributions of body height and income**, uses data from a large survey to illustrate theoretical distributions, using the `height-income-distributions` dataset.

Learning outcomes

After working through this chapter, you should be able to:

• understand the importance and uses of exploratory data analysis;
• understand distributions, visualize them, and describe their most important features;
• identify situations when extreme values matter and make conscious decisions about extreme values;
• produce graphs and tables of presentation that are focused, informative, and easy to read;
• know the main features of the most important theoretical distributions and assess whether they are good approximations of distributions of variables in actual data.

3.1 Why Do Exploratory Data Analysis?

Informative description of variables is an essential first step of data analysis. It is called **exploratory data analysis**, abbreviated as **EDA**, also called **descriptive analysis**. There are five important reasons to do EDA.

First, to know if our data is clean and ready for analysis. EDA is part of the iterative process of data cleaning that we discussed previously, in Chapter 2. Informative description of variables tells us about problems that we need to address in the data cleaning process. Results of EDA may show too few observations because we discarded too many by mistake; they may suggest that the true units of measurement are different from what we thought; or they may tell us that there are values that a variable should not have because of mistakes or because such values are used to signify missing data. These are mundane but surprisingly common issues that could result in the nonsensical outcome of an analysis if not addressed. Therefore, the results of EDA may make data analysts go back to the cleaning process and start over.

Second, to guide subsequent analysis. Some features of variables, such as how spread the values are or whether there are extreme values, have important consequences for further analysis. They may suggest that data analysts transform a variable, or what method may be best suited to analyze patterns related to a variable. This is a little cryptic for now, but we'll see many instances of this in the subsequent chapters. The results of EDA may also help in getting a sense of what we can expect from future analysis. For example, we can't expect to understand what may cause differences in a variable if that variable has little spread in the data – i.e., if most observations have the same value.

Third, to give context. Describing the most important variables in our data is an important part of presenting the results of data analysis. Decision makers who will use those results need to know what is contained in key variables and how their characteristics affect the interpretation of the main results. For example, when our results show the effect of one variable on another variable, we want to know if that effect is large or small. Exploratory data analysis helps in answering that question by uncovering typical values, or typical differences, in variables, which we can use as benchmarks to compare our results to.

Fourth, sometimes, we can answer our question with very simple tools that are used as parts of exploratory data analysis. That's quite rare, but when that's the case, EDA is the end of our analysis.

Fifth, to ask more questions. Quite often, exploratory data analysis uncovers an interesting phenomenon for a variable of interest. This should lead to asking questions that further analysis with more data and more sophisticated methods may answer.

In the remainder of this chapter we discuss what features of variables data analysts need to uncover, what methods they have to do that, and how they can produce graphs and tables that summarize the most important information in an accessible way.

> **Review Box 3.1 The use of exploratory data analysis (EDA)**
>
> - Exploratory data analysis (EDA) describes the features of the most important variables in the data.
> - We may use EDA for five purposes:
>   - To check data cleaning
>   - To guide subsequent analysis
>   - To give context of the results of subsequent analysis
>   - To answer simple questions
>   - To ask additional questions.

3.2 Frequencies and Probabilities

Let's start with the most basic property of variables: what values they can take and how often they take each of those values. We first introduce the concept of frequency that makes sense from the viewpoint of the data we have. Then we generalize frequencies to the concept of probability that makes sense in more abstract settings.

The **absolute frequency**, or count, of a value of a variable is simply the number of observations with that particular value in the data. The **relative frequency** is the frequency expressed in relative, or percentage, terms: the proportion of observations with that particular value among all observations in the data. If a variable has missing values, this proportion can be relative to all observations including the missing values or only to observations with non-missing values. Most often we express proportions excluding observations with missing values. When our goal is to check the data cleaning process, absolute frequencies including missing values is the better option.

Probability is a general concept that is closely related to relative frequency. Probability is a measure of the likelihood of an event. An event is something that may or may not happen.

In the context of data, an event is the occurrence of a particular value of a variable. For example, an event in a data table is that the manager of the firm is female. This event may occur various times in the data. The probability of the event is its relative frequency: the proportion of firms with a female manager among all firms in the data. Considering a more abstract example, whether there is pasta for lunch at the canteen today is an event, and the probability of pasta for lunch today is a measure of its likelihood.

Probabilities are always between zero and one. We denote the probability of an event as $P(event)$, so that $0 \leq P(event) \leq 1$. Sometimes they are expressed in percentage terms so they are between 0% and 100%: $0\% \leq P(event) \leq 100\%$.

Considering a single event, it either happens or does not. These two are mutually exclusive: the probability of an event happening and it also not happening is zero. We denote an event not happening as $\sim event$ so $P(event \& \sim event) = 0$.

Probabilities are more general than relative frequencies as they can describe events without data. However, with some creative thinking, we can often think of potential data that contains the event so that its probability is a proportion. Data on what's for lunch at our canteen for many days is an example. If we had such data, the frequency of the event (pasta served for lunch) would give its probability.

But not always. Sometimes probabilities may be defined for events for which no data can be imagined. These include **subjective probabilities** that describe the degree of uncertainty an individual feels about events that may happen in the future but have no precedents. Examples include the probability that you, the reader, will like this textbook enough to keep it for future reference, or the probability that rising sea levels will flood the underground system of Singapore within 20 years.

Abstract probabilities are interesting and important from various points of view. But data analysts work with actual data. For most of them, probabilities and frequencies are closely related. Thus, most data analysts tend to think of probabilities as relative frequencies in actual data or data they can imagine.

Review Box 3.2   Frequencies and probabilities

- Frequencies describe the occurrence of specific values (or groups of values) of a variable.
  - ○ Absolute frequency is the number of observations (count).
  - ○ Relative frequency is the percentage, or proportion.
- Probability is a measure of the likelihood of an event; its value is always between 0 and 1 $(0 \leq P(event) \leq 1)$.
- In data, probabilities are relative frequencies; the "events" are the specific values of the variable.

3.3   Visualizing Distributions

Frequencies are summarized by distributions. The **distribution** of a variable gives the frequency of each value of the variable in the data, either in terms of absolute frequency (number of observations), or relative frequency (proportion or percent). The distribution of a variable completely describes the variable as it occurs in the data. It does so focusing on the variable itself, without considering the values of other variables in the data.

It is good practice to examine distributions of all important variables as the first step of exploratory data analysis.

The simplest and most popular way to visualize a distribution is the **histogram**. The histogram is a bar chart that shows the frequency (absolute or relative) of each value. The bars can be presented horizontally; that's more common in business presentations and when there are few bars. The more traditional presentation is vertical bars.

For binary variables, the distribution is the frequency of the two possible values and thus the histogram consists of two bars. For variables that take on a few values, the histogram shows as many bars as the number of possible values.

For variables with many potential values, showing bars for each value is usually uninformative. Instead, it's better to group the many values in fewer groupings or bins. The histogram with binned variables shows bars with the number or percentage of observations within each bin. It is good practice to create bins of equal width so each bin covers the same range of values. As the case study will illustrate, the size of bins can have important consequences for how histograms look and how much they reveal about the properties of distributions.

For any histogram, we need to decide on the bin size, either by setting the number of bins or the bin width. (Letting our statistical software set the bin size is also one such decision.) Very wide bins may lump together multiple modes. But very narrow bins may show a lot of ups and downs for random reasons and thus can blur important properties of a distribution. It is good practice to experiment with a few alternative bin sizes to make sure that important features of the distribution don't remain hidden.

Visual inspection of a histogram reveals many important properties of a distribution. It can inform us about the number and location of **modes**: these are the peaks in the distribution that stand out from their immediate neighborhood. Most distributions with many values have a center and tails, and the histogram shows the approximate regions for the center and the tails. Some distributions are more symmetric than others. Asymmetric distributions, also called **skewed distributions**, have a long left tail or a long right tail; histograms visualize those. Histograms also show if there are **extreme values** in a distribution: values that are very different from the rest. We'll discuss extreme values in detail in Section 3.5.

Density plots – also called **kernel density estimates** – are an alternative to histograms for variables with many values. Instead of bars, density plots show continuous curves. We may think of them as curves that wrap around the corresponding histograms. Similarly to histograms, there are details to set for density plots, and those details may make them look very different. The most important detail to specify is the bandwidth, the closest thing to bin size for histograms. Density plots are less precise than histograms, and hence we advise you to rely on histograms when possible.

Review Box 3.3 Distributions and their visualization

- A distribution of a variable shows the frequency, absolute or relative, of each potential value of the variable in the data.
- The histogram is a bar graph showing the frequency of each value of a variable if the variable has few potential values.
- Density plots (also known as kernel density estimates) are continuous curves; they can be viewed as wrapped around corresponding histograms.

3.A1   ## CASE STUDY – Finding a Good Deal among Hotels: Data Exploration

Describing distributions

The broader question on hotels we will be discussing in chapters to come is how to find a good deal among hotels. Here, we explore the most important variables we'll use in that analysis, with a focus on location – asking where hotels are located and what is the share of hotels close to the city center. Describing the distribution of hotels in quality or distance can help business decisions on hotel development.

This case study uses the `hotels-vienna` dataset. We introduced this data in Chapter 1, Section 1.A1. We will keep focusing on the data from Vienna for a particular night. The data we work with contains proper hotels only, without apartment houses, and so on. We have $N = 264$ hotels.

Let us start with stars, a measure of hotel quality. Stars are determined by the services hotels offer, according to detailed criteria. Hotel stars can take on a few distinct values; thus a histogram becomes a set of bars – one for each value.

Figures 3.1a and 3.1b show the histogram of stars in our data. The horizontal axis shows the potential values of this variable such as 3 stars, 4 stars, and also 3.5 stars (3 stars plus). In Figure 3.1b, the vertical axis shows absolute frequencies: the number of observations corresponding to each value. In Figure 3.1a, we show relative frequency (percent).

According to the histogram, there are 88 hotels with 3 stars, 14 with 3.5 stars, and 116 hotels with 4 stars. In relative terms this means 33% (88/264 = 0.33) with 3 stars, 5% with 3.5 stars, and 44% with 4 stars. Indeed, most properties are either 3 or 4 star hotels.

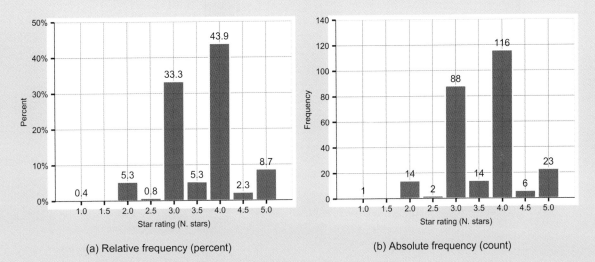

(a) Relative frequency (percent)   (b) Absolute frequency (count)

Figure 3.1   Histogram of hotel stars

Note: Histogram for a qualitative variable.
Source: `hotels-vienna` dataset. Vienna, hotels only, for a November 2017 weekday. N=264.

From now on we will focus on proper hotels and the mid-quality segment: our data will consist of hotels in Vienna with three to four stars. This is a subset of the `hotels-vienna` dataset described in Chapter 1, excluding non-hotel accommodation, hotels with fewer than three stars or more than four stars. We have $N = 218$ such hotels in Vienna.

The next variable we explore is hotel room price. The distribution of prices may be visualized in multiple ways. In this data, prices range from 50 dollars to 383 dollars plus a single hotel offering a room for 1012 dollars. Let us disregard that extreme value for the rest of the section; we'll come back to that decision soon. We will work with $N = 217$ observations in this section.

A histogram with a bar for each value is not a particularly informative visualization, but we show it for educational purposes in Figure 3.2a. Most values occur once, with some values (like 110 dollars) occurring several times. This histogram shows more bars, thus more hotels, with room price below 200 dollars, with most values between 80 and 150 dollars.

Figure 3.2b shows a histogram with 10-dollar bins. This graph is far more informative. Most of the distribution is between 60 and 180 dollars, with few observations above 180 dollars. It suggests a distribution with a mode at 80 dollars. The distribution is skewed, with a long right tail. A long right tail means that there are several values on the right end of the histogram that are a lot further away from its center than the values on the left end of the histogram. There is one extreme value at 380 dollars.

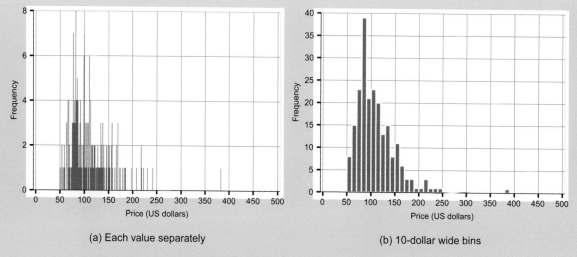

(a) Each value separately   (b) 10-dollar wide bins

Figure 3.2   Histogram of hotel price

Note: Panel (a): bars at each value; panel (b): bars for 10-dollar bins; excluding extreme value.
Source: `hotels-vienna` dataset. Vienna, 3–4 stars hotels only, for a November 2017 weekday. N=217.

We can increase bin width further, lumping together more values in a bin and thus reducing the number of bars. Figure 3.3 shows histograms of the same price distribution with wider bins, first of 40 dollars, second of 80 dollars. The wider the bin, the fewer details of the distribution are revealed by the histogram. All show the same long right tail, but the 80-dollar bin puts the mode in the leftmost bin, whereas it was in the second bin earlier. The histograms with the wider bins suggest a more gradual decline in frequency.

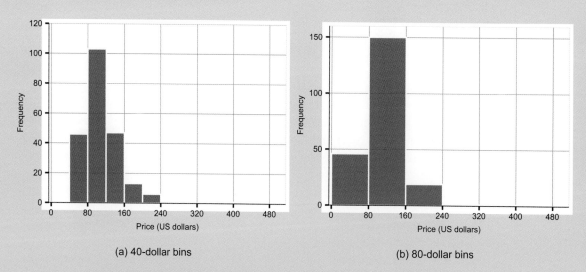

(a) 40-dollar bins   (b) 80-dollar bins

Figure 3.3   The distribution of hotel price: Histograms with wide bins

Note: Panel (a): 40-dollar bins; panel (b): 80-dollar bins; excluding extreme value.
Source: `hotels-vienna` dataset. Vienna, 3-4 stars hotels only, for a November 2017 weekday. N=217.

These graphs (Figures 3.2a, 3.2b, 3.3a, and 3.3b) taken together suggest a trade-off. Narrower bins give you a more detailed view but make it harder to focus on the really important properties of the distribution. Finding a good compromise may depend on the purpose. To design further analytic work, a 20-dollar bin is very useful. For presenting to a more generalist audience, a 40-dollar bin may be better. Designing bin size is a necessary task, and requires practice.

3.4 Extreme Values

Some quantitative variables have **extreme values**: substantially larger or smaller values for one or a handful of observations than the rest.

Sometimes extreme values don't belong in the distribution because they are errors. Most frequently, such errors are due to mistakes in digits or units of measurement, such as company revenues in dollars instead of millions of dollars or number of visits to a supermarket per year instead of per week. In addition, extreme values may not belong in the distribution because they represent patterns that we aren't interested in.

But other times extreme values are an integral part of the distribution. Indeed, they may be the most important observations. For example, in investment decisions extreme future returns and their frequencies are among the most important things to know as they may lead to huge losses or huge gains. The overall gain or loss of such an investment may be determined by a few extreme events as opposed to the cumulative result of many small gains or losses. Similarly, when the question is about what damages to expect from floods or earthquakes, it's the largest of damages that we should care about.

Some data analysts call extreme values **outliers**. We prefer not using that term as it implies that they do not belong in the distribution, which may or may not be the case.

The most worrying problem with extreme values is that they may not show up in a dataset even if they are an inherent characteristic of a variable. Extreme values, by nature, are indeed rare. For example, data spanning a few years may not have instances of the most extreme losses on an asset that may come in the future.

When extreme values are included in our data, we need to identify them. Visualizing the distribution via a histogram is a good way to catch extreme values. What to do, if anything, with extreme values is a more difficult question. It depends both on why extreme values occur and what the ultimate question of the analysis is.

Extreme values that occur due to error should be replaced by a missing value marker or, in the rare case when one can infer the correct value, by that correct value. Error-caused extreme values are rare but are often straightforward to catch. For example, earnings a thousand times higher than the average in low-skilled occupations are surely an error and so are more than 168 working hours a week.

More often, extreme values are an inherent part of the distribution. The size of the largest countries or firms, the salaries of chief executives in a firm, the best-paid actors among all actors, or a large drop in asset prices on the day of a stock-market crash are not errors in the data. What we do in such cases depends on the question of our analysis.

If the question is more relevant for the rest of the observations, we may discard the observations with extreme values and restrict the analysis to the rest. When we look into how salaries and other incentives may keep employees at a firm, it makes sense not to focus on chief executives but restrict the analysis to the other employees. When we want to know how distance to main highways affects the price of commercial real estate, we may discard the largest cities and focus on smaller towns. It is good practice to be explicit about such decisions when presenting the results of the analysis, saying that the analysis is relevant for some kinds of observations but not for others.

In fact, what, if anything, we should do with observations with extreme values of a variable depends also on the role of the variable in our analysis. Starting with Chapter 4, Section 3.U1, we will distinguish a y variable and one or more x variables in the analysis. Typically, our analysis will aim to uncover patterns in how values of y tend to differ for observations that have different values of x: hotel price differences by how far they are from the city center, differences in the quality of management by firm size, and so on.

Data analysts tend to be conservative when discarding observations with extreme y values: they usually keep them unless they are errors. However, data analysts tend to be less conservative when discarding observations with extreme x values: they often discard them even if they are parts of the distribution. The reason is in the different roles y and x play in the analysis.

Discarding observations with extreme x values narrows the scope of the comparisons. That's a transparent decision, because it defines what kinds of comparisons we want to make. In contrast, discarding observations with extreme y values changes the result of the comparisons. The consequences of this decision are not straightforward, and it's often safer to avoid those consequences. We'll discuss this issue in more detail in Chapter 8, Section 7.U1.

Review Box 3.4   Extreme values

- Some variables have extreme values: substantially larger or smaller values for a few observations than the values for the rest of the observations.
- Extreme values may be genuine or they may be an error.
  - When errors, extreme values should be corrected or treated as missing values.
  - When genuine, extreme values should be kept, unless we have a substantive reason to restrict the analysis to the subset of observations without extreme values.

3.A2   CASE STUDY – Finding a Good Deal among Hotels: Data Exploration

Identifying and managing extreme values

Both price and distance to the city center have extreme values in the `hotels-vienna` dataset. In subsequent chapters, we will use this data to find hotels that are underpriced for their location and quality. Hotel price will be our y variable, and so we drop extreme values only if they are errors. In contrast, distance will be an x variable, so we can drop extreme values even if they are parts of the distribution if we want to narrow our analysis.

We first look at distance. The data here includes all hotels in Vienna with 3 to 4 stars, regardless of their distance to the city center. Figure 3.4 shows the histogram of distance.

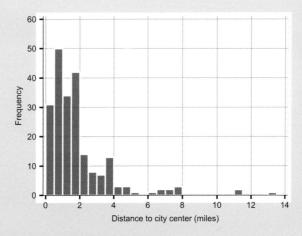

Figure 3.4   Histogram of distance to the city center.

Source: `hotels-vienna` dataset. Vienna, all hotels with 3 to 4 stars. N=217.

For this histogram we used 0.5-mile-wide bins. This way we can see the extreme values in more detail even though the rest of the histogram looks a bit less nice (too uneven). The y axis shows the frequency. The histogram shows three hotels above 8 miles: two at around 11 miles and one at close to 13 miles. We see another group of hotels between 6 and 8 miles that are a little separated from the rest of the distribution (no value between 8 and 11 miles).

We decided to drop the three hotels that are more than 8 miles away from the city center and keep the ones at 6 to 8 miles. The extreme values we dropped are not errors. But they are values that would not be relevant for the main question of the analysis: finding hotels that are underpriced relative to their distance to the city center (and their quality). Eleven and 13 miles are far enough from the city center that we think we wouldn't choose these hotels if our aim was to stay in Vienna to explore the city. At the same time we didn't discard the hotels at 6 to 8 miles, thinking that maybe some of them are so inexpensive that they could be good deals even factoring in their distance. Note that this decision is arbitrary, but one such decision is necessary. In a thorough analysis, we would see if including the 8+ miles hotels, or excluding the 6–8 miles hotels, changes the answer to our question.

To better understand the features of hotels far from the center, we investigated our "city_actual" variable. It turns out that even within the 8-mile radius, a few hotels are in villages (such as Voesendorf) that are related to Vienna but are not Vienna proper. Hence, we decided to drop these hotels, too. The result is a sample of 208 hotels.

Next we looked at prices, using the data of the 208 hotels that are within 8 miles from the city center and are in Vienna proper. Earlier, we pointed out a single observation with a price of 1012 dollars. This is an extreme value indeed. We dropped it because we decided that it is almost surely an error. It's a room in a 3 star hotel and is unlikely to cost over a thousand dollars. Moreover, in the `hotels-europe` dataset that contains prices for several dates for these same hotels, and many more, the price of this hotel is around 100 dollars on all other dates not 1000 dollars.

We have identified, in Figure 3.2b, an additional observation with an extreme value, close to 400 dollars. We decided to keep this observation. This is a high price for this kind of a hotel (3 stars). At the same time, inspecting the `hotels-europe` dataset reveals another date with a similarly high price, and the prices on the rest of the dates, while considerably lower, are not lower by an order of magnitude that would indicate a digit error. Thus, we can't conclude that this extreme value is an error.

To summarize, our exploratory analysis led us to focus our sample. Our key steps were:

1. We started with full data, $N = 428$.
2. We inspected the histograms of the qualitative variables.
   - Accommodation type – could be apartment, house and so on; kept hotels only, $N = 264$.
   - Stars – kept only: 3, 3.5, 4 stars, $N = 218$.
3. We looked at quantitative variables, focusing on extreme values.
   - Price: the extreme value of 1012 dollars is a likely error, dropped it; kept all others, $N = 217$.
   - Distance: some hotels are far away; defined cutoff; dropped beyond 8 miles, $N = 214$.
   - Distance, one more step: looked at variable city_actual, realized that some hotels are not in Vienna proper; dropped them, $N = 207$.
4. The final sample is hotels with 3 to 4 stars, below 400 dollars, less than 8 miles from center, in Vienna proper, $N = 207$.

3.5   Good Graphs: Guidelines for Data Visualization

Now that we have introduced visualization of distributions, let's pause and spend some time on how to produce good graphs in general. These thoughts are meant to guide all decisions that go into producing graphs. They correspond to the practice of data visualization professionals; see some important references at the end of the chapter.

Before we begin, let us point out that our principles and suggestions are aimed at data analysts not visual designers. Typically, data analysts want to spend less time designing graphs than visual designers. As a result, they are more likely to use ready-made graph types and templates, and they benefit more from following a few simple rules instead of engaging in a creative process each and every time. Just like with any of our advice, this is not a must do list. Instead it shows how to think about decisions data analysts must take. You may take other decisions, of course. But those decisions should be conscious instead of letting default settings determine the look of your graphs.

The starting principle is that all of our decisions should be guided by the usage of the graph. The **usage of a graph** is a summary concept to capture what we want to show and to whom. Its main elements are purpose, focus, and audience. Table 3.1 explains these concepts and gives some examples. Note that some of the examples use graphs that we haven't introduced yet; this is because we want the advice to serve as reference later on.

Once usage is clear, the first set of decisions to make are about how we convey information: how to show what we want to show. For those decisions it is helpful to understand the entire graph as the overlay of three graphical objects:

1. Geometric object: the geometric visualization of the information we want to convey, such as a set of bars, a set of points, a line; multiple geometric objects may be combined.
2. Scaffolding: elements that support understanding the geometric object, such as axes, labels, and legends.
3. Annotation: adding anything else to emphasize specific values or explain more detail.

Table 3.1 Usage of a graph			
Concept	Explanation	Typical cases	Examples
Purpose	The message that the graph should convey	Main conclusion of the analysis An important feature of the data Documenting many features of a variable	y and x are positively associated There are extreme values of y at the right tail of the distribution All potentially important properties of the distribution of y
Focus	One graph, one message	Multiple related graphs for multiple messages	A histogram of y that identifies extreme values, plus a box plot of y that summarizes many other features of its distribution
Audience	To whom the graph wants to convey its message	Wide audience Non-data-analysts with domain knowledge Analysts	Journalists Decision makers Fellow data analysts, or our future selves when we want to reproduce the analysis

When we design a graph, there are many decisions to make. In particular, we need to decide how the information is conveyed: we need to choose a **geometric object**, which is the main object of our graph that visualizes the information we want to show. The geometric object is often abbreviated as a geom. The same information may be conveyed with the help of different geometric objects, such as bar charts for a histogram or a curved line for a density plot. In practice, a graph may contain more than one geometric object, such as a set of points together with a line, or multiple lines.

Choosing the details of the geometric object, or objects, is called **encoding**. Encoding is about how we convey the information we want using the data we have, and it means choosing elements such as height, position, color shade. For a graph with a set of bars as the geometric object, the information may be encoded in the height of these bars. But we need to make additional choices, too. These include general ones such as color and shade as well as choices specific to the geometric object, such as width of the bars or lines, or size of the dots.

In principle, a graph can be built up freely from all kinds of graphical objects. Data visualization experts and designers tend to follow this bottom-up approach. In contrast, most data analysts start with choosing a predefined **type of graph**: a single geometric object or a set of some geometric objects and a scaffolding, possibly some annotation. One graph type is the histogram that we introduced earlier in this chapter. Histograms are made of a set of bars as a geometric object, with the information in the data (frequency) encoded in the height of the bar. The scaffolding includes an x axis with information on the bins, and a y axis denoting either the absolute (count) or relative frequency (percent). We'll introduce many more graph types in this chapter and subsequent chapters of the textbook. Table 3.2 offers some details and advice.

The next step is **scaffolding**: deciding on the supporting features of the graph such as axes, labels, and titles. This decision includes content as well as format, such as font type and size. Table 3.3 summarizes and explains the most important elements of scaffolding.

Table 3.2 The geometric object, its encoding, and graph types

Concept	General advice	Examples
Geometric object	Pick an object suitable for the information to be conveyed	Set of bars comparing quantity A line showing value over time
One or more geoms	May combine more than one geom to support message or add context	Dots for the values of a time series variable over time, together with a trend line
Encoding	Pick one encoding only	Histogram: height of bars encodes information (frequency) Don't apply different colors or shades
Graph type	Can pick a standard object to convey information	Histogram: bars to show frequency Scatterplot: values of two variables shown as a set of dots

Table 3.3 Scaffolding

Element	General advice	Examples
Graph title	Title should be part of the text; it should be short emphasizing main message	Swimming pool ticket sales and temperature Swimming pool sales fluctuate with weather
Axis title	Each axis should have a title, with the name of the actual variable and unit of measurement	Distance to city center (miles) Household income (thousand US dollars)
Axis labels	Value numbers on each axis, next to tics, should be easy to read	0, 2, 4, 6, 8, 10, 12 14 miles for distance to city center
Gridlines	Add horizontal and, if applicable, vertical gridlines to help reading off numbers	Vertical gridlines for histogram Both horizontal and vertical gridlines for scatterplots
Legends	Add legend to explain different elements of the geometric object Legends are best if next to the element they explain	Two groups, such as "male" and "female" Time series graphs for two variables; it's best to put legends next to each line
Fonts	Large enough size so the audience can read them	Font size "10"

Lastly, we may add **annotation** – if there is something else we want to add or emphasize. Such additional information can help put the graph into context, emphasize some part of it. The two main elements of annotation are notes and visual emphasis, see Table 3.4 for some advice.

Table 3.4 Annotation		
Concept	**General advice**	**Examples**
Graph notes	Add notes to describe all important details about how the graph was produced and using what data	Lowess non-parametric regression with scatterplot `Hotels-vienna` dataset. Vienna, all hotels with 3 to 4 stars. N=217
Added emphasis	May add extra annotation to graph to emphasize main message	A vertical line or circle showing extreme values on a histogram An arrow pointing to a specific observation on a scatterplot

3.A3 CASE STUDY – Finding a Good Deal among Hotels: Data Exploration

The anatomy of a graph

Let us use a previous graph here, to illustrate the most important parts of a good graph. Recall that we should should keep in mind usage, encoding, scaffolding, annotation. We use a previous graph with the histogram of hotel distance to the city center (Figure 3.4), but here we added some annotation (Figure 3.5).

Usage. We use this graph to search for extreme values and document them. The main message is that the three hotels that are located more than 8 miles away from the city center are separate from the rest. The target audience is a specialized one: fellow data analysts. The figure may serve to document the reasons of our decisions, again a special usage.

Encoding. The graph shows the distribution in enough detail to spot extreme values, but it also shows the main part of the distribution to put those extreme values in context. Our encoding choice was a histogram with a 0.5-mile bin. Alternative choices would have been a density plot or wider or narrower bins for the histogram. Choosing the histogram with a 0.5-mile bin led to a balance for the usage of the graph: showing the main part distribution and the extreme values. One message, one encoding: we use a single color as bar height is enough to help compare through distance bins.

Scaffolding. The x axis denotes distance to city center. Although bins are every 0.5 mile, the labels are at 2-mile intervals to help readability. The y axis denotes the number of hotels per bin. It is absolute frequency here not percentage, because our focus is on counting observations with extreme values. Notice the labels on the y axis: they are in increments of 10. The scaffolding includes horizontal and vertical gridlines to help reading off numbers.

Annotation. We point out the main message of the graph: the three hotels beyond 8 miles from the center appear to form their own cluster. We used a colored rectangle, but we could have circled them, or had an arrow pointed at them. For a scientific audience we could have skipped that annotation because that audience would understand the issue anyway and may appreciate a clean histogram.

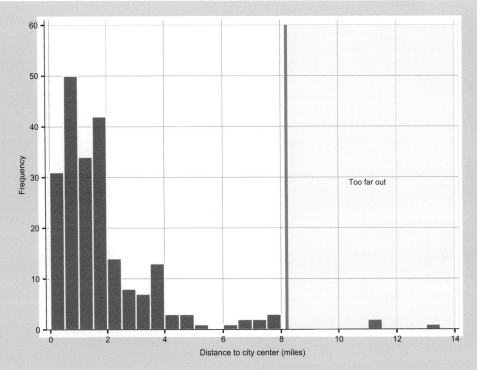

Figure 3.5 Histogram of distance to the city center

Source: `hotels-vienna` dataset. Vienna, all hotels with 3 to 4 stars. N=217.

3.6 Summary Statistics for Quantitative Variables

A histogram of a quantitative variable can inform us about the shape of the distribution, whether it has extreme values, or where its center is approximately. But visual displays don't produce the numbers that are often important to answer our questions. How far are hotels from the city center in general? What's the spread of prices? How skewed is the distribution of customer ratings? To answer such questions we need numerical summaries of variables. They are called statistics, and this section covers the most important ones.

A **statistic** of a variable is a meaningful number that we can compute from the data. Examples include mean income or the range of prices. Basic **summary statistics** are numbers that describe the most important features of the distribution of a variable. Summary statistics can answer questions about variables in our data, and they often lead to further questions to examine.

Most readers are probably well acquainted with many summary statistics, including the **mean**, the **median** (the middle value), various **quantiles** (terciles, quartiles, **percentiles**), and the **mode** (the value with the highest frequency in the data). The mean, median, and mode are also called measures of central tendency, because they give an answer to where the center of the distribution is. Those answers may be the same (the mean, median, and mode may be equal, or very close to each other), or they may be different.

Importantly, we use the terms mean, average, and expected value as synonyms, and we use the notation $E[x]$ as well as $\bar{x}$.

The mean of a quantitative variable is the value that we can expect for a randomly chosen observation. The mean of a 0/1 binary variable is the proportion of observations with value 1. No observation would have the expected value as it is between 0 and 1 since the value of the binary variable can be only 0 or 1.

Similarly, most readers know the most important measures of spread, such as the **range** (the difference between the largest and smallest value), **inter-quantile ranges** (e.g., the 90–10 percentile range, or the **inter-quartile range**), the **standard deviation**, and the **variance**. The standard deviation captures the typical difference between a randomly chosen observation and the mean. The variance is the square of the standard deviation. The variance is a less intuitive measure, but it is easier to work with because it is a mean value itself. The formulae are:

$$Var[x] = \frac{\sum(x_i - \bar{x})^2}{n} \tag{3.1}$$

$$Std[x] = \sqrt{\frac{\sum(x_i - \bar{x})^2}{n}} \tag{3.2}$$

Note that alternative formulae for the variance and the standard deviation divide by $n - 1$ not n. Most data are large enough that this makes no practical difference. It turns out that dividing by $n - 1$ is the correct formula if we use the statistic in the data to infer the standard deviation in the population that our data represents (see more details in Chapter 5, Section 5.12). Since it makes little difference in practice, and dividing by n is easier to remember, we will continue to divide by n in this textbook.

The standard deviation is often used to re-calculate differences between values of a quantitative variable, in order to express those values relative to what a typical difference would be. In a formula, this amounts to dividing the difference by the standard deviation. Such measures are called **standardized differences**. A widely used standardized difference is from the mean value; it is called the **standardized value of a variable** or the **z-score** of the variable.

$$x_{standardized} = \frac{(x - \bar{x})}{Std[x]} \tag{3.3}$$

While measures of central value (such as mean, median) and spread (such as range, standard deviation) are usually well known, summary statistics that measure **skewness** are less frequently used. At the same time skewness can be an important feature of a distribution, showing whether a few observations are responsible for much of the spread. Moreover, there is a very intuitive measure for skewness (which exists in a few variants).

Recall that a distribution is **skewed** if it isn't symmetric. A distribution may be skewed in two ways, having a long left tail or having a long right tail. A long left tail means having a few observations with small values with most observations having larger values. A long right tail means having a few observations with large values with most observations having smaller values. Earlier we showed that the hotel price distributions has a long right tail – such as in Figure 3.4. That is quite typical: skewness with a long right tail is frequent among variables in business, economics, and policy, such as with prices, incomes, and population.

The statistic of skewness compares the mean and the median and is called the **mean–median measure of skewness**. When the distribution is symmetric, its mean and median are the same. When it is skewed with a long right tail, the mean is larger than the median: the few very large values in the right tail tilt the mean further to the right. Conversely, when a distribution is skewed with a long left tail, the mean is smaller than the median: the few very small values in the left tail tilt the mean further to the left. The mean–median measure of skewness captures this intuition. In order to make this measure comparable across various distributions, we use a standardized measure, dividing the difference by the standard deviation. (Sometimes this measure is multiplied by 3, and then it's called Pearson's second measure of skewness. Yet other times the difference is divided by the mean, median, or some other statistic.)

$$Skewness = \frac{\bar{x} - median[x]}{Std[x]} \tag{3.4}$$

Table 3.5 summarizes the most important descriptive statistics we discussed.

Table 3.5 Summary table of descriptive statistics

Type of statistic	Name of statistic	Formula	Intuitive content
Central value	Mean	$\bar{x} = \frac{1}{n}\sum x_i$	The value we expect from a randomly chosen observation
	Median	-	The value of the observation in the middle
	Mode	-	The value (bin) with the highest frequency
Spread	Range	$max[x] - min[x]$	Width of the interval of possible values
	Inter-quantile range	$q_{upper}[x] - q_{lower}[x]$	Distance between the upper quantile and the lower quantile
	Variance	$Var[x] = \frac{\sum(x_i-\bar{x})^2}{n}$	-
	Standard deviation	$Std[x] = \sqrt{\frac{\sum(x_i-\bar{x})^2}{n}}$	Typical distance between observations and the mean
Skewness	Mean–median skewness	$Skewness = \frac{\bar{x}-median(x)}{Std[x]}$	The extent to which values in the tail pull the mean

3.B1   CASE STUDY – Comparing Hotel Prices in Europe: Vienna vs. London

Comparing distributions over two groups

We are interested in comparing the hotel markets over Europe, and would like to learn about characteristics of hotel prices. To do that, let us focus on comparing the distribution of prices in Vienna to another city, London.

The data we use is an extended version of the dataset we used so far. The `hotels-europe` dataset includes the same information we saw, for 46 cities and 10 different dates. We will explore it more in Chapter 9. For this case study, we consider the same date as earlier (weekday in November 2017) for Vienna and London.

We focus on hotels with 3 to 4 stars that are in the actual city of Vienna or London. We have no extreme value of price in London, so we need to drop the single, above 1000 dollars priced hotel in Vienna. In our sample, there are $N = 435$ hotels in the London dataset compared to the $N = 207$ hotels in Vienna.

Figure 3.6 shows two histograms side by side. To make them comparable, they have the same bin size (20 dollars), the same range of axes, and each histogram shows relative frequencies. The same range of axes means that the x axis goes up to 500 dollars both Vienna and London because the maximum price is close to 500 dollars in London.

The histograms reveal many important features. Here is a selected set of observations we can make:

- The range is around 50 dollars in both cities but it ends below 400 dollars in Vienna while it goes close to 500 dollars in London.
- The London distribution of prices covers more of the higher values, and it is more spread out (i.e. has a larger difference between the minimum and maximum price).
- Hotel prices tend to be higher in London.
- Both distributions have a single mode, but their location differs. The bin with the highest frequency (the mode) in Vienna is the 80–100-dollar bin, and it is the 120–140-dollar bin in London.

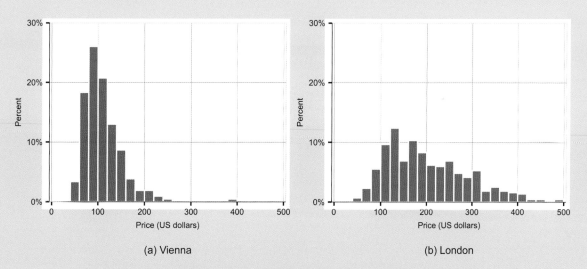

(a) Vienna   (b) London

Figure 3.6 The distribution of hotel price in Vienna and London

Source: `hotels-europe` dataset. Vienna and London, 3-4 stars hotels only, for a November 2017 weekday. Vienna: N=207, London: N=435.

The same price distributions can be visualized with the help of density plots. Figure 3.7 shows the Vienna and London distributions laid on top of each other. The density plots do not convey more information than the histograms. In fact, they are less specific in showing the exact range or the prevalence of extreme values. But comparing density plots on a single graph is just easier – we can see immediately where the mass of hotels are in Vienna and in London.

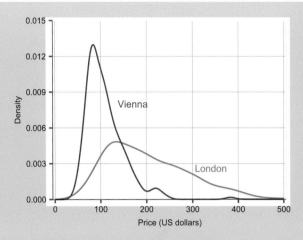

Figure 3.7   Density plots of hotel prices: Vienna and London

Note: Kernel density estimates with Epanechnikov smoothing method.

Source: `hotels-europe` dataset. Vienna and London, 3–4 stars hotels only, for a November 2017 weekday. Vienna: N=207, London: N=435.

We can quantify some aspects of the distributions, too. Table 3.6 contains some important summary statistics in the two datasets.

Table 3.6   Descriptive statistics for hotel prices in two cities

City	N	Mean	Median	Min	Max	Std	Skew
London	435	202.36	186	49	491	88.13	0.186
Vienna	207	109.98	100	50	383	42.22	0.236

Source: `hotels-europe` dataset. Vienna and London, November 2017, weekday.

Average price is 110 dollars in Vienna and 202 dollars in London. The difference is 92 dollars, which is almost an extra 90 % relative to the Vienna average. The mean is higher than the median in both cities, indicating a somewhat skewed distribution with a long right tail. Indeed, we can calculate the standardized mean–median measures of skewness, and it is more positive in Vienna ((110 − 100)/42 = 0.236) than in London ((202 − 186) / 88 = 0.186).

The range of prices is substantially wider in London (491 − 49 = 442) than in Vienna (383 − 50 = 343), and the standard deviation shows a substantially larger spread in London (88 versus 42). The first column shows that the London dataset has about twice as many observations (435 versus 207).

These summary statistics are in line with the conclusions we drew by inspecting the visualized distributions. Hotel prices in London tend to be substantially higher on average. They are also more spread, with a minimum close to the Vienna minimum, but many hotels above 200 dollars. These together imply that there are many hotels in London with a price comparable to hotel prices in Vienna, but there are also many hotels with substantially higher prices.

3.7 Visualizing Summary Statistics

The summary statistics we discussed are often presented in table format. But there are creative ways to combine some of them in graphs. We consider two such graphs.

The more traditional visualization is the **box plot**, also called the box and whiskers plot shown in Figure 3.8a. The box plot is really a one-dimensional vertical graph, only it is shown with some width so it looks better. The center of a box plot is a horizontal line at the median value of the variable, placed within a box. The upper side of the box is the third quartile (the 75th percentile) and the lower side is the first quartile (the 25th percentile). Vertical line segments on both the upper and lower side of the box capture most of the rest of the distribution. The ends of these line segments are usually drawn at 1.5 times the inter-quartile range added to the third quartile and subtracted from the first quartile. These endpoints are called **adjacent values** in the box plot. The lines between the lower (upper) adjacent value and the 25th (75th) per-centile range are called **whiskers**. Observations with values not contained within those values are usually added to the box plot as dots with their respective values. The box plot conveys many important features of distributions such as their skewness and shows some of the quantiles in an explicit way.

A smarter-looking alternative is the **violin plot** shown in Figure 3.8b. In essence, the violin plot adds a twist to the box plot by overlaying a density plot on it. Violin plots show the density plot on both sides of the vertical line, but there is no difference between the two sides. In a sense, as with a box plot, we have two sides here purely to achieve a better look. Compared to the traditional box

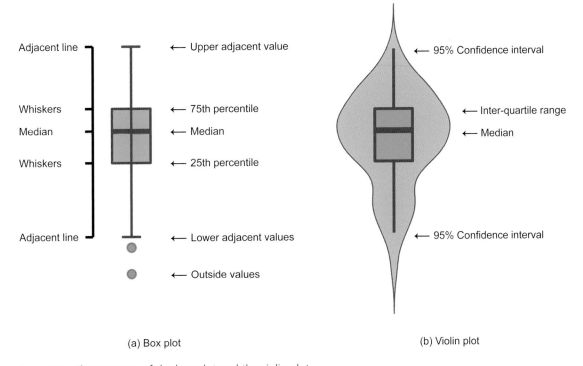

(a) Box plot

(b) Violin plot

Figure 3.8 The structure of the box plot and the violin plot

plot, the basic violin plot shows fewer statistics and does not show the extreme values. In exchange, it gives a better feel for the shape of the distribution. As there are many complementing features of box plots and violin plots, we advise you to consider both.

Review Box 3.5   Summary statistics and their visualization

- Measures of central value: Mean (average), median, other quantiles (percentiles), mode.
- Measures of spread: Range, inter-quantile range, variance, standard deviation.
- Measure of skewness: The mean–median difference.
- The box plot is a visual representation of many quantiles and extreme values.
- The violin plot mixes elements of a box plot and a density plot.

3.C1   CASE STUDY – Measuring Home Team Advantage in Football

Distribution and summary statistics

The idea of home team advantage is that teams that play on their home turf are more likely to play better and win compared to the same game played at the other team's stadium (the other team is also called the "away" team). In particular, this case study asks whether professional football (soccer) teams playing in their home stadium have an advantage and what is the extent of that advantage.

These questions are interesting in order for fans to know what to expect from a game, but also for professional managers of football teams who want to maximize the number of wins and the support of fans. If home team advantage is important, managers need to know its magnitude to benchmark the performance of their teams.

Here we use data from the English Premier League, with the same data we started with in Chapter 2. Here we focus on games in the 2016/7 season. In each season, each pair of teams plays twice, once in the home stadium of one team, and once in the home stadium of the other team. This gives 380 games total (20 × 19: each of the 20 teams plays once at home against each of the other 19 teams). The observations in the data table we use here are the games; there are N = 380 observations.

The most important variables are the names of the home team and the away team and the goals scored by each team. From these two quantitative variables we created a goal difference variable: home team goals – away team goals. Examining the distribution of this goal difference can directly answer our question of whether there is a home team advantage and how large it is.

Let's look at the distribution of the home team – away team goal difference first. Figure 3.9 shows the histogram. While the goal difference is a quantitative variable, it doesn't have too many values so we show a histogram that shows the percentage of each value instead of bins.

The mode is zero: 22.1% of the games end with a zero goal difference (a draw). All other goal differences are of smaller percentage – the larger the difference, the smaller their frequency. This gives an approximately bell-shaped curve, except it is skewed with more observations (taller bars) to the right of zero. That suggests home team advantage already. But let's look more closely into this histogram.

The most striking feature of the histogram is that for each absolute goal difference, the positive value is more frequent than the negative value. The home team – away team goal difference is +1 in 20.8% of the games while it is −1 in 13.2% of the games; it's +2 in 17.1% of the games and −2 in only 8.2% of the games, and so on. This clearly shows that home teams score more goals so there is a home team advantage. It also seems pretty large. But how large is it? To answer that we need to provide a number and put it into context.

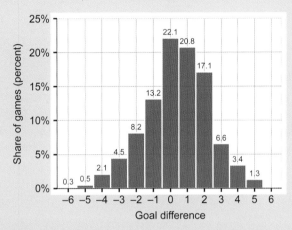

Figure 3.9 The distribution of home team – away team goal difference

Source: `football` dataset. English Premier League, season 2016–2017, all games. N=380.

To that end, we calculated the mean and the standard deviation of the goal difference as shown in Table 3.7. Moreover, we calculated the relative frequency of games in which the home team wins (positive goal difference), games in which the away team wins (negative goal difference), and games that end with a draw (zero goal difference: we know their proportion is 22%). Table 3.7 shows the results.

Table 3.7 Describing the home team – away team goal difference	
Statistic	**Value**
Mean	0.4
Standard deviation	1.9
Percent positive	49
Percent zero	22
Percent negative	29
Number of observations	380

Source: `football` dataset. English Premier League, season 2016–2017, all games. N=380.

The average goal difference is 0.4: on a randomly chosen game in the 2016/7 season of the English Premier League, the home team is expected to score 0.4 more goals.

Is this a large difference? We can answer that in two ways. First, 0.4 goals appears to be a sizeable difference: it's almost one goal every two games. Second, we can put it into the context of the spread of the goal difference across games, with the help of the standard deviation. The standard deviation is 1.9, showing the typical deviation from the average. The average goal difference, 0.4, is thus about one fifth of the typical deviation. Viewed this way, the average goal difference is not negligible but not huge, either.

While football is played for goals, what truly matters is who wins a game. From this point of view, the home team advantage looks large again. Forty-nine percent of the games are won by the home team, and only 29% are won by the away team. That's two thirds more.

To conclude, we have uncovered a sizeable home team advantage in the English Premier League. Home teams score 0.4 goals more on average, and they win almost 50% of the time but lose only about 30% of the time. This should serve as a useful benchmark for what to expect from each game. It also shows the importance of the phenomenon. So anyone who cares about the home team advantage should do more analysis to try to learn about its cause, or causes.

What did we learn from this exercise? The simple tools of exploratory analysis revealed something interesting and important. The histogram showed clear evidence for the home team advantage. The mean goal difference summarized the extent of the home team advantage in a single number that we could interpret on its own and in comparison with the standard deviation. Finally, we use the goal difference variable to compute the relative frequency of home wins versus away wins that showed the magnitude of home team advantage from a different, and arguably more relevant, point of view.

3.8   Good Tables

In Section 3.5 we gave advice on how to produce good graphs. Here we do the same for tables. While graphs show visual representation of some results from the data, tables present statistics: meaningful numbers computed from the data. Despite these differences, the structured thinking that helps produce good graphs works just the same here. To produce a good table, data analysts need to think about its **usage**, choose **encoding** and **scaffolding** accordingly, and may add **annotation**.

First, usage: what's the purpose and who's the target audience. One important type wants to communicate the main result, or results, of the analysis to people who would use those results. A table of this type is called a **results table**, or a communication table. Just like good graphs, good communication tables are focused on one message. The other main table type is the **documentation table**. Its aim is to document exploratory data analysis. Documentation tables describe the structure of the data, one or more variables, or some other features such as missing values or extreme values. Such tables are also used to summarize the results of data cleaning and restructuring processes – e.g., by showing numbers of observations and statistics of important variables for the original data and the data we chose to work with in the end. Documentation tables are produced for other analysts who may want to have a deep understanding of the data, possibly to carry out their own analysis by reproducing or modifying what we did. As usual, those other analysts may include our future selves: documentation tables help us remember certain details of the data that may prove to be important during our analysis.

Usage of tables should guide all subsequent decisions. Encoding here means what numbers to present in the table, and in what detail. The numbers may be averages, counts, standard deviations, or other statistics – for the entire data table or for subsets of observations. Documentation tables tend to be large and include everything that is, or may become, important. In contrast, communication tables should be simple and focused. For example, when analyzing company data to understand churn (why some employees quit while others stay), a communication table on churn rates may show the percent who quit within, say, one year of entry, by a handful of major categories of job rank. A documentation table, on the other hand, may include more job categories, present numbers by year, and show numbers of employees that quit and stayed together with their ratio. The additional detail in the documentation table helps other analysts reproduce our analysis in the future, and it helps us catch potential anomalies in the data.

A good practice of encoding is to show totals together with components. Even though showing totals is often redundant, it can be very informative as it helps grasp what the components mean, by highlighting what they should add up to. For example, when a table shows the percent of sales by day of the week in the rows of a table, it is good practice to show the total of 100 percent in the bottom row. Similarly, in a documentation table with numbers of observations in subgroups in the data, the total number of observations is usually included, too.

Another good practice is to include the number of observations in all tables. This helps the audience have a rough idea about the extent to which the results may generalize beyond the data (see Chapter 5). It may also help remind them whether the statistics refer to all observations or a group of them.

The second question of encoding is how much detail the numbers should have in the table. Here, too, usage should be our guide. Communication tables should have no more detail than necessary. For example, a table on churn percentages should include few, if any, decimal digits. If 123 employees leave the firm within six months in a dataset of 1234 employees, this proportion is 9.967 585%, to six decimal digits. We find it ridiculous to present this number to such a precision. 9.97% is better; and, for a general audience, 10% is even better. Usually, documentation tables have numbers in more detail. When reproducing steps of analysis, we want to see, step by step, whether we get the same numbers as the first analysis did. But, there too, many decimals of percentages can be confusing. Instead, it's more helpful to include the numbers of observations that make up a percentage.

Third, scaffolding. Tables should have titles that say what's in the table. They need to have row headings and column headings that say what's in each row and column. And they need to have notes to give all the important detail. The main message is often a good choice for a title (e.g., "Churn is twice as high in sales than in other job roles"). A more conservative choice is to describe what kind of comparison the table does (e.g., "Churn by job rank"). It is good practice to keep the title short and focused. Similarly, row and column headings should be short. The notes then should contain all detailed information, including the longer description of row and column headings, source of data, if the statistics are computed from a subsample, and so on.

Finally, we may want to add annotation to our table to highlight specific numbers. We may circle a number, or use color or bold typeface. One frequent annotation is to put asterisks next to certain statistics, something that we'll see from

Chapter 9 on for regression tables.

As with all of our advice, these principles should be viewed as starting points. You should keep to them or deviate from them if you have reasons to. The important thing is to make decisions in conscious ways. Table 3.8 summarizes this section.

Table 3.8 Good tables

Layer	What that means here	Specifics	Examples
Usage	Purpose and audience	Presentation table	Average in groups; percent of observations in groups
		Documentation table	Summary statistics of important variables
Encoding	What numbers	Include totals; include number of observations	Have row/column totals; include 100% in table with percentages
	In what detail	Few details for presentation; more for documentation	Few or no decimals for percentages; exact numbers of observations for documentation
Scaffolding	Title	Focused titles	What statistics, in what groups
	Row and column heading	All rows and columns should have short and informative headings	
	Notes	All necessary information in notes	How variables and/or groups are constructed; source of data
Annotation	Optional: may highlight specific numbers	Circle, use different color, boldface	

3.C2   CASE STUDY – Measuring Home Team Advantage in Football

The anatomy of a table

Let us return to our football case study that investigates home team advantage, and let's review the table that shows some statistics of the home versus away goal difference. To ease the discussion, let us repeat Table 3.7 above as Table 3.9 below.

Let's start with the usage of this table. Its purpose is showing that there is home team advantage in this data, and it's not small. It's a presentation table: its target audience is people who want to learn about home team advantage in football but may not be data analysts. Thus, we kept the table simple. It has a single column and six rows, presenting six numbers altogether.

Usage dictates encoding: what numbers to present in the table. The first number we present is the mean of the home versus away goal difference. It's positive, showing that, on average, there is a home team advantage in this data. Its magnitude is 0.4, which can be appreciated in comparison with the standard deviation (1.9) shown in the next row. The next three rows show the percent of games with a positive home–away difference (when the home team won), the percent with zero difference (draws), and the percent with negative difference (the home team lost). Note that here we didn't put a total row, going against our own advice. That's because we decided that it would make the table look odd. Thus, we made a conscious decision. Finally, the last row shows the number of observations, adhering to our other general advice.

Table 3.9 Describing the home team – away team goal difference

Statistic	Value
Mean	0.4
Standard deviation	1.9
Percent positive	49
Percent zero	22
Percent negative	29
Number of observations	380

Note: Repeating Table 3.7

Source: football dataset. English Premier League, season 2016–2017, all games. N=380.

The title of the table is relatively short and meaningful. Note that it is about the variable (goal difference), not the concept it is meant to measure (home advantage). The table has column and row headings that are relatively short and to the point. The notes say what the data is about (games from a league in one season) and the name of the data source (so you can look for it in our data repository).

We could have made other choices with encoding and scaffolding to serve the same usage. Among the data exercises, you'll be invited to create your own version of this table with possibly other numbers and text, and you'll be invited to explain your choices.

3.9 Theoretical Distributions

Before closing our chapter by reviewing the process of exploratory data analysis, let's take a detour on theoretical distributions. Theoretical distributions are distributions of variables with idealized properties. Instead of showing frequencies in data, they show more abstract probabilities: the likelihood of each value (or each interval of values) in a more abstract setting. That more abstract setting is a hypothetical "data" or "population," or the abstract space of the possible realizations of events.

But why should we care about theoretical distributions? The main reason is that they can be of great help when we want to understand important characteristics of variables in our data. Theoretical distributions are usually simple to describe and have a few well-established properties. If a variable in our data is well approximated by a theoretical distribution, we can simply attribute those properties to the variable without having to check those properties over and over. It turns out that there are surprisingly many real-world variables whose distributions are quite well approximated by one of the theoretical distributions.

Another reason to know about theoretical distributions is that some of them are useful in understanding what happens when we want to generalize from the data we have. This second reason may sound very cryptic for now, but it should be much clearer after having read Chapters 5 and 6.

Many theoretical distributions are known in statistics. We focus on two in this section and discuss a few more in Under the Hood section 3.U1.

Before we review these two, let's note something about language. When describing variables in the abstract, statisticians also call them random variables. The idea behind that terminology is that there is randomness in their value: we don't know what the value is before looking at it. While this terminology certainly makes sense, we do not use that expression in this textbook. Instead we simply call variables variables, without the qualifier "random," whether in a very abstract setting or in a particular dataset. Besides simplicity, our choice of terminology helps reserve the term "random" for events and things without pattern, as in random sampling or values missing at random.

The **normal distribution** is the best known and most widely used theoretical distribution of quantitative variables. It is a pure theoretical construct in the sense that it was derived mathematically from another distribution, the **binomial** (see Under the Hood section 3.U1). Variables with a normal distribution can in principle take on any value from negative infinity to positive infinity. The histogram of the normal distribution is bell shaped. For that reason the popular name for the normal distribution is the bell curve. It is also called the Gaussian distribution after the German mathematician who played a role in popularizing it (it was the French mathematician Laplace who first derived it).

The normal distribution is characterized by two **parameters**, usually denoted as μ and σ. They refer to the mean (μ) and the standard deviation (σ). The variance is the square of the standard deviation, σ^2.

A special case of the normal distribution is the **standard normal distribution**. It is a normal distribution with parameters $\mu = 0$ and $\sigma = 1$: its mean is zero and its standard deviation is one (and thus its variance is also one). If a variable x is normally distributed with mean μ and standard deviation σ, its transformed version is distributed standard normal if we take out the mean and divide this difference by the standard deviation: $\frac{(x-\mu)}{\sigma}$.

It turns out that when we transform a normally distributed variable by adding or multiplying by a number, the result is another normally distributed variable, with appropriately transformed mean and standard deviation. It also turns out that when we add two normally distributed variables, the resulting new variable is also normally distributed, and its mean is the sum of the means of the two original variables. (The standard deviation is a function of the original standard deviations and the correlation of the two variables.)

Some variables in real life are well approximated by the normal distribution. The height of people in a population is usually approximately normal, and so is their IQ, a measure of intelligence (although that is in part because the tests behind the IQ measure are constructed that way). Variables in real life are well approximated by the normal distribution if they are a result of adding up many small things. We discuss this in detail in Under the Hood section 3.U1.

The normal is a bad approximation to real-life variables with extreme values. Extreme values are very unlikely in the normal distribution. For example, the normal distribution formula (see Under the Hood section 3.U1) suggests that only 0.3% of the values of a normally distributed variable should be more than three standard deviations above the mean; only 0.000 000 2% should be higher than six standard deviations above the mean.

Besides the absence of extreme values, symmetry is another feature of the normal distribution that makes it a bad approximation to many economic variables. Earnings, income, wealth, and firm productivity are usually asymmetrically distributed with long right tails. One theoretical distribution that may be a better approximation to such variables is the lognormal distribution.

The **lognormal distribution** is very asymmetric, with a long right tail, potentially including many extreme values at the positive end (but not at the other end). The lognormal distribution is derived from the normal distribution. If we take a variable that is distributed normally (x) and raise e to its power (e^x), the resulting variable is distributed lognormally. The old variable is the **natural logarithm** of the new variable, hence the name of the new distribution (the log of which is normal). Because we raised e to the power of the original variable, the values of the resulting lognormal variable are always positive. They range between zero and positive infinity (never reaching either). By convention, the parameters of the lognormal are the mean μ and standard deviation σ of the original, normally distributed variable, which is the logarithm of the new variable. Thus the mean and the standard deviation of the lognormal are complicated functions of these parameters. They are: $e^{\mu + \frac{\sigma^2}{2}}$ and $\sqrt{e^{\mu + \frac{\sigma^2}{2}} e^{\sigma^2 - 1}}$.

There are real-life variables that are approximately lognormally distributed. These include distributions of price, income, and firm size. Variables are well approximated by the lognormal if they are the result of many things multiplied together (the natural log of them is thus a sum). Another way to think about lognormal variables is that their percentage differences are normally distributed. Thus, they do not have many extreme values in terms of percentage differences. (Note that normally distributed percentage differences translate into quite extreme differences in terms of absolute values.)

3.D1	**CASE STUDY – Distributions of Body Height and Income**

Data and describing distributions

Let us consider two examples using population data from the USA. For this purpose, we use the `height-income-distributions` dataset from 2014.

Our first example is adult height, which is well approximated by the normal distribution for the vast part of the distribution, but not for extreme values. Average height among adult women in the USA population is around 163 cm (5'4"), with standard deviation 7.1 cm (2.5"). Thus, for example, women shorter than 145 cm (4'8") should be around 0.1 percent in the population. Yet there are more than 0.1 percent American women that short (over 1 percent in our sample). Similarly to height, many real-life variables with some extreme values are still well approximated by the normal for the larger middle part of the distribution, often as much as over 99 percent of the distribution. Whether that makes the normal a good approximation or not for the purpose of data analysis depends on whether we are interested in extreme values or not.

Figure 3.10 shows an example: the histogram of the height of American women aged 55–59. We have overlaid the density plot of the bell-shaped theoretical normal distribution that has the same mean and standard deviation as height in the data (1.63, 0.07).

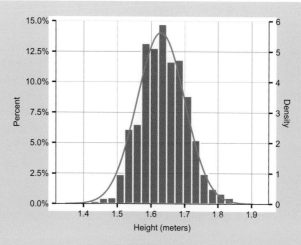

Figure 3.10 Example for approximately normal distribution: women's height

Note: Histogram of the height of women. Overlaid with bell curve of the normal distribution.
Source: height-income-distributions dataset, Health and Retirement Study 2014, females of age 55–59.
N=1991.

Second, let us consider a variable that has a few large values: household income. Figure 3.11 shows the distribution of household income among households of women age 55 to 59 in the USA. Figure 3.11a shows the histogram of household income (in 1000 US dollars, without incomes below 1 thousand or above 1 million US dollars). Figure 3.11b shows the histogram of the log of household income, overlaid with the density plot of the normal distribution with the same mean and standard deviation.

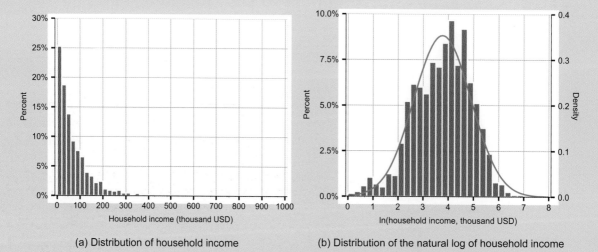

(a) Distribution of household income   (b) Distribution of the natural log of household income

Figure 3.11 An example for an approximately lognormal variable: Household income

Source: height-income-distributions dataset, Health and Retirement Study 2014, females of age 55–59. N=2012.

3.10 Steps of Exploratory Data Analysis

At the end of this chapter let us review the steps of exploratory data analysis (EDA). With clean and tidy data we can start our analysis. EDA is the first step of analysis: we should describe variables on their own before doing anything else. EDA helps data analysts "know their data," which is one of our most important pieces of advice. Getting familiar with the details of the data is important. Results of EDA may feed back into data wrangling (cleaning and restructuring data) if they uncover further issues. Moreover, these results should influence the next steps of analysis and may lead to transforming or changing the data. They are also essential for putting results in context. Finally, the results of EDA may lead to asking new questions that we previously haven't thought of.

Exploratory data analysis and data wrangling form an iterative process. EDA may uncover issues that call for additional data cleaning, stepping back again. Then, further steps of data analysis may raise additional questions or issues that call for additional EDA and, possibly, additional data wrangling. For example, when exploring employee churn at our company (whether and why some employees quit within a short time), we may uncover a 100 % churn rate in one department (everybody seems to have quit). That may be true churn that we would explore in detail. Or, it may be something else – e.g., an error in the data or closing of a department. Those cases would call for fixing the error or modifying the data for the analysis by excluding employees of that department from the analysis.

Exploratory data analysis should start by focusing on the variables that are the most important for the analysis. If other variables turn out to be important, we can always come back to explore those variables later.

For each variable, it is good practice to start by describing its entire distribution. For qualitative variables with a few values, that is best done by listing the frequencies and producing simple bar charts. For quantitative variables we usually produce histograms to visualize the distributions.

An important first question is whether the distribution has extreme values. If yes, we need to decide what to do with them: if they are obvious errors, we replace them with missing values (or, less frequently, correct them). Similarly, if extreme values are not relevant for the question of the analysis, it makes sense to drop those observations. If they are not obvious errors and may be relevant for the question of the analysis, it is good practice to keep them. We may also decide to transform variables with extreme values.

Examining the distribution of a variable can answer other important questions such as whether the distribution is symmetric or skewed, or how many modes it has. We can also go further and see if it is well approximated by one of the theoretical distributions we considered.

The next step is looking at descriptive statistics. These summarize some important features of distributions in more precise ways. Having numeric values is necessary to appreciate the magnitude of subsequent results, understand the amount of variation in each variable, see if some values are very rare, and so on. Summary statistics may call for data transformations. Examples include changing units of measurement (e.g., expressing values in thousand dollars) and creating relative measures (e.g., GDP per capita). It usually makes sense to look at minimum, maximum, mean, and median values, standard deviation, and the number of valid observations. Other measures of spread may also be informative, and we may compute the mean–median measure of skewness, standardized by the standard deviation or the mean.

Exploratory data analysis may go substantially further, comparing variables or comparing distributions across groups of observations. As in all cases, our advice should be considered as a starting point.

Data analysts should make conscious decisions at many points of the analysis, including the focus and details of exploratory data analysis.

Review Box 3.6 Recommended steps of exploratory data analysis

1. First focus on the most important variables. Go back to look at others if subsequent analysis suggests to.
2. For qualitative variables, list relative frequencies.
3. For quantitative variables, look at histograms.
4. Check for extreme values. Decide what to do with them.
5. Look at summary statistics.
6. Do further exploration if necessary (time series data, comparisons across groups of observations, and so on).

3.11   Main Takeaways

Start all data analysis with exploratory data analysis (EDA).

- Results from EDA will be important for data cleaning, reality checks, understanding context, or asking further questions.
- Explore all aspects of the distribution of your most important variables, including potential extreme values.
- Produce visualization and tables guided by their usage.

PRACTICE QUESTIONS

1. The distribution of quantitative variables may be visualized by a histogram or a density plot (kernel density estimate). What's the difference between the two and which one would you use? List at least one advantage for each. How about qualitative variables with a few values?
2. The mean, median, and mode are statistics of central tendency. Explain what they are precisely.
3. The standard deviation, variance, and inter-quartile range are statistics of spread. Explain what they are and give the formula for each.
4. What are percentiles, quartiles, and quintiles? Is the median equal to a percentile?
5. Why do we take the sum of squared deviations from the mean as a measure of spread, not the sum of the deviations themselves?
6. A distribution with a mean higher than the median is skewed. In what direction? Why? Give an intuitive explanation.
7. Extreme values are a challenge to data analysis if they are relevant for the question of the analysis. List two reasons why.
8. What kind of real-life variables are likely to be well approximated by the normal distribution? What are well approximated by the lognormal distribution? Give an example for each.

9. What is a box plot, what is a violin plot, and what are they used for?
10. Based on what you have learnt about measurement scales and descriptive statistics, decide if it is possible to calculate the mean, mode, and median of the following variables that tell us information about the employees at a company:
    (a) number of years spent in higher education
    (b) the level of education (high school, undergraduate, graduate, doctoral school)
    (c) field of education (e.g., IT, engineering, business administration)
    (d) binary variable that shows whether someone has a university degree.
11. Take Figure 3.9 in Case Study 3.C1. Describe its usage, its main geometric object and how it encodes information, and scaffolding. Would you want to add annotation to it? What and why?
12. Take Table 3.6 in Case Study 3.B1, **Comparing hotel prices in Europe: Vienna vs. London** Describe its usage, encoding, and scaffolding. Would you do some things differently? What and why?
13. What kind of real-life variables are likely to be well approximated by the Bernoulli distribution? Give two examples.
14. What kind of real-life variables are likely to be well approximated by the binomial distribution? Give two examples.
15. What kind of real-life variables are likely to be well approximated by the power-law distribution? Give two examples.

DATA EXERCISES

Easier and/or shorter exercises are denoted by [*]; harder and/or longer exercises are denoted by [**].

1. Pick another city beyond Vienna from the `hotels-vienna` dataset, and create a data table comparable to the one used in our case study. Visualize the distribution of distance and the distribution of price and compute their summary statistics. Are there extreme values? What would you do with them? Describe the two distributions in a few sentences. [*]
2. Use the data on used cars collected from a classified ads site (according to the Chapter 1 data exercise). Visualize the distribution of price and the distribution of age, and compute their summary statistics. Are there extreme values? What would you do with them? Describe the two distributions in a few sentences. [*]
3. Pick another season from the `football` dataset and examine the extent of home team advantage in ways similar to our case study. Compare the results and discuss what you find. [*]
4. Choose the same 2016/7 season from the `football` dataset as in our data exercise and produce a different table with possibly different statistics to show the extent of home team advantage. Compare the results and discuss what you find. [*]
5. Choose a large country (e.g., China, Japan, the United Kingdom) and find data on the population of its largest cities. Plot the histogram of the distribution and create a table with the most important summary statistics. Plot the histogram of log population as well. Finally, create a log rank–log population plot. Is the normal, the lognormal, or the power-law distribution a good approximation of the distribution? Why? [*]

REFERENCES AND FURTHER READING

There are quite a few papers on the phenomenon of home advantage (Pollard, 2006), and two excellent books on many aspects of soccer and data – Sally & Anderson (2013) and Kuper & Szymanski (2012).

On the idea of extreme values and their potentially large role, an interesting book is Nassim Nicholas Taleb: *The Black Swan* (Taleb, 2007).

A great book on the emergence of statistics is (Salsburg, 2001). It offers a non-technically demanding yet precise discussion of how key concepts such as distribution, random sampling, or correlation emerged.

An early apostle of good graphs is Ronald A. Fisher. In his 1925 book (Fisher, 1925) the first chapter after the introduction is called Diagrams.

Data visualization has now a robust literature as well as a large variety of online resources. In particular, our section on graphs has been shaped by the approach of Alberto Cairo, see for instance *The Functional Art: An Introduction to Information Graphics and Visualization* (Cairo, 2012) and *How Charts Lie* (Cairo, 2019).

There are many great books on data visualization. Edward Tufte, *Visual Explanations: Images and Quantities, Evidence and Narrative* (Tufte, 1997) or any other Tufte book are classics. Two recent wonderful books, both with R code, are Kieran Healy, *Data Visualization – A Practical Introduction* (Healy, 2019) and Claus O. Wilke, *Fundamentals of Data Visualization* (Wilke, 2019). Another great resource is Chapter 03 in the book *R for Data Science* by Garrett Grolemund and Hadley Wickham (Grolemund & Wickham, 2017).

3.U1 UNDER THE HOOD: MORE ON THEORETICAL DISTRIBUTIONS

Let's introduce a few more useful concepts that theoretical statisticians use to describe theoretical distributions. We will rarely use these concepts in this textbook. However, they are frequently used in more traditional and more advanced statistical textbooks as well as in statistically more sophisticated analyses.

The first concept is the **probability distribution function**, or *pdf*. In essence, the pdf is the theoretical generalization of the histogram and its smoother cousin, the density plot. The pdf of qualitative (also called discrete) variables, including binary variables, shows the probability of each value in the distribution. The pdf of quantitative (continuous) variables, such as normal or lognormal variables, shows the probability of each value and the values in its close neighborhood in the distribution. The pdf is expressed in a formula as a function of the parameters of the distribution, and it is often represented graphically as a bar chart like the histogram (for qualitative variables) or as a continuous curve like a density plot (for continuous variables).

A variation on the pdf is the *cdf*, the **cumulative distribution function**. For each value in the distribution, the cdf shows the probability that the variable is equal to that value or a lower value. Thus, at each value of the distribution, the cdf equals the pdf plus the sum of all pdf below that value.

Hence the name "cumulative": the cdf accumulates the pdf up to that point. Similarly to the pdf, the cdf is expressed as a function of the parameters of the theoretical distribution and is often represented graphically.

The third advanced concept that is good to know about is the **moments** of distributions. Moments are a more general name for statistics like the mean and the variance for theoretical distributions. These are the expected value of the variable or the expected value of the square, cube, ..., of the variable, or, like the variance, the expected value of the square, cube, ..., of the variable minus its mean. Moments are numbered according to the power they take, so that the first moment is $E[x]$, the second moment is $E[x^2]$, and so on. The variance is a second moment of the variable minus its mean so it is also called the second centered moment: $E[(x - E[x])^2]$.

Theoretical distributions are fully captured by a few parameters: these are statistics that determine the distributions. For each distribution we introduce their parameters, establish the range of possible values, show the shape of the histogram, and describe how the mean and standard deviation are related to the parameters of the distribution.

Bernoulli distribution

The distribution of a zero–one binary variable is called **Bernoulli**. The name comes from Jacob Bernoulli, the mathematician from the 1600s who first examined it. The Bernoulli distribution is one of those rare theoretical distributions that we observe over and over: all zero–one variables are distributed Bernoulli. (Note the use of words: if the distribution of a variable is Bernoulli, we say "it is distributed Bernoulli"; we'll use this expression for other theoretical distributions, too.) Examples include whether a customer makes a purchase, whether the CEO of a firm is young, whether a portfolio produces a large negative loss, or whether the online price of a product is lower than its offline price. The Bernoulli distribution has one parameter: p, the probability of observing value one (instead of value zero).

With only two possible values, zero and one, the range of the Bernoulli distribution is zero to one, and its histogram consists of two bars: the frequency of observations with value zero, and the frequency of observations with value one. If, instead of frequency, the histogram shows the proportion of each value, the height of the bar at value one is equal to p, and the height of the bar at zero equals $1 - p$. The mean of a Bernoulli variable is simply p, the proportion of ones. (To verify this try $p = 0$ or $p = 1$ or $p = 0.5$.) Its variance is $p(1 - p)$ so its standard deviation is $\sqrt{p(1 - p)}$.

Binomial distribution

The binomial distribution is based on the Bernoulli distribution. A variable has a binomial distribution if it is the sum of independent Bernoulli variables with the same p parameter. Some actual variables that may have a binomial distribution include the number of car accidents, the number of times our portfolio experiences a large loss, or the number of times an expert correctly predicts if a new movie will be profitable. Binomial variables have two parameters: p, the probability of one for each Bernoulli variable and n, the number of Bernoulli variables that are added up.

The possible values of a binomial variable are zero, one, and all other integer numbers up to n. Its range is therefore 0 through n. The histogram of a binomial variable has $n + 1$ bars (zero, one, through n) if not grouped in bins. The binomial distribution has one mode in the middle, and it is symmetric so its median, mean, and mode are the same. With large n the histogram of a binomial variable is bell shaped. The mean of a binomial variable is np, and its variance is $np(1 - p)$, so its standard deviation is $\sqrt{np(1 - p)}$.

The other distributions we cover in this section may approximate *quantitative variables* (as defined in Chapter 2, Section 2.1). These theoretical distributions are for continuous variables that include fractions as well as irrational numbers such as π or the square root of two. In real data few variables can take on such values. Even variables that may in principle be continuous such as distance or time are almost always recorded with countable values such as integers or fractions rounded to a few decimal places. The continuous distributions are best seen as potential *approximations* of the distribution of real-life quantitative variables.

Uniform distribution

The uniform distribution characterizes continuous variables with values that are equally likely to occur within a range spanned by a minimum value and a maximum value. Examples of real-life variables that may be approximately uniformly distributed are rare; the day of birth of people is an example. The uniform distribution is more often used as a benchmark to which other distributions may be compared. The uniform distribution has two parameters, the minimum value a and the maximum value b. The histogram of the uniform distribution is completely flat between a and b with zero frequency below a and above b. It is therefore symmetric. It has no mode: any value is just as frequent as any other value. The mean of a uniformly distributed variable is $\frac{a+b}{2}$, the variance is $\frac{(b-a)^2}{12}$, the standard deviation is $\sqrt{\frac{(b-a)^2}{12}}$.

Power-law distribution

While the lognormal distribution may well approximate the distribution of variables with skewness and some extreme values, it is usually a bad approximation when those extreme values are very extreme. Distributions with very large extreme values may be better approximated by the power-law distribution.

The **power-law distribution** is also known as the **scale-free distribution** or the **Pareto distribution**, and it is closely related to **Zipf's law**.

The power-law distribution is a very specific distribution with large extreme values. Its specificity is perhaps best captured by its scale invariance property (hence the name scale-free distribution). Let's take two values in the distribution and their ratio (say, 2:1). Let's compute the number of observations with one value (or within its neighborhood) relative to the number of observations with the other value (its neighborhood). For example, there may be 0.6 times as many cities with a population around 200 thousand than around 100 thousand in a country. If the variable has a power-law distribution, this proportion is the same for all value-pairs with the same ratio through the entire distribution. In the city population example, this means that there should be 0.6 times as many cities with 600 thousand inhabitants than 300 thousand, 2 million than 1 million, and so on. This is the scale invariance property.

A related, though less intuitive, property, of the power-law distribution is that a scatterplot of the log of the rank of each observation against the log of the value of the variable yields a straight line. The log of the rank of the observation with the largest value is $ln(1) = 0$, the log of the rank of the second largest observation is $ln(2)$, and so on. Figure 3.12 shows an example using the population of the 159 largest Japanese cities in 2015 (those larger than 150 000 inhabitants). You will be asked to produce similar plots using other data as data exercises.

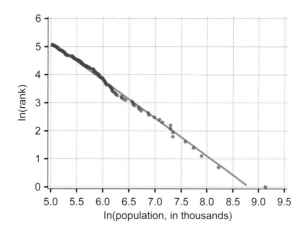

Figure 3.12 Log rank–log value plot. Size of Japanese cities

Note: The natural log of the rank in the distribution (1st largest, 2nd largest, ...) and the natural log of population.
Source: `city-size-japan` dataset. N=159.

This latter property of the power-law distribution is the consequence of the fact that the probability of values in the close neighborhood of any value x is proportional to $x^{-\alpha}$: the value to a negative power, therefore the name power-law. Larger values are less likely than smaller values, and how much less likely depends only on the parameter α. The larger the α, the smaller the likelihood of large values. This α is the only parameter of the power-law distribution.

The range of the power-law distribution is zero to infinity (neither included). The power-law distribution is similar to the lognormal in that it is very asymmetric with a long right tail and thus allows for very extreme values. It is different from the lognormal by having a substantially larger likelihood of very extreme large values and thus a substantially fatter right tail.

The left part of the power-law distribution is also very different from the lognormal: its histogram continuously decreases in contrast with the up-then-down histogram of the lognormal.

There are many variables in real life that are well approximated by a power-law distribution. To be more precise, this is usually true for the upper part of the distribution of such real-life variables. In other words, they are well approximated by power-law above certain values but not below. Examples include the population of cities, the size of firms, individuals' wealth, the magnitude of earthquakes, or the frequency of words in texts (ranking word frequency "the" would be most frequent, followed by "be," and so on). Indeed, the idea that the frequency of a word is inversely proportional to its rank in the frequency table is often referred to as the original version of Zipf's law. These variables have extremely large values with low proportion but still a much higher proportion than what a lognormal distribution would imply.

An informative statistic of power-law distributions is the share of the values that is attributed to the top x percent of the distribution. One example is that in the USA, the richest 1% own 40% of the total wealth. Another example is the so-called 80–20 "rule" that posits that 80% of total sales for a product will be concentrated among 20% of customers. Of course, 80–20 is not so much a rule as an empirical observation that holds in some cases but not necessarily in others. The point is that the fraction of wealth (or population in cities, workers in firms, energy released by earthquakes in the top 20%, top 5%, or top 1% characterizes the power-law distribution.

Review Box 3.7   Important theoretical distributions

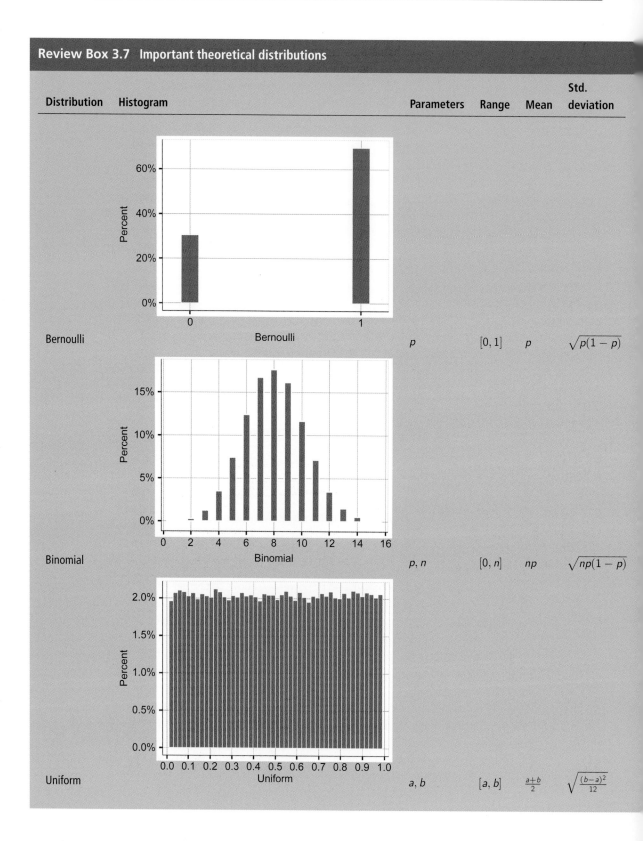

Distribution	Histogram	Parameters	Range	Mean	Std. deviation
Bernoulli		p	$[0, 1]$	p	$\sqrt{p(1-p)}$
Binomial		p, n	$[0, n]$	np	$\sqrt{np(1-p)}$
Uniform		a, b	$[a, b]$	$\frac{a+b}{2}$	$\sqrt{\frac{(b-a)^2}{12}}$

Review Box 3.7 (cont.)

Distribution	Histogram	Parameters	Range	Mean	Std. deviation

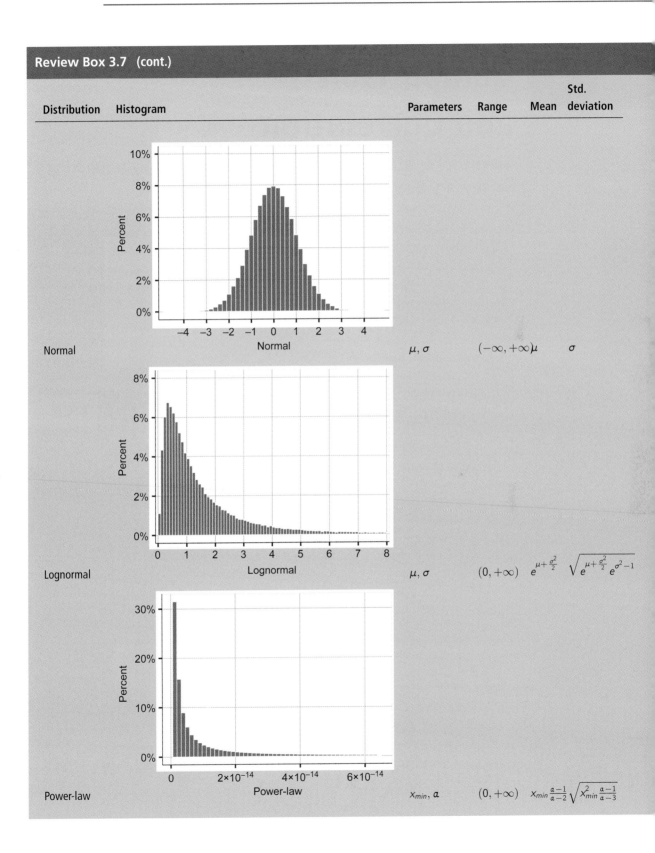

Normal		μ, σ	$(-\infty, +\infty)$	μ	σ
Lognormal		μ, σ	$(0, +\infty)$	$e^{\mu + \frac{\sigma^2}{2}}$	$\sqrt{e^{\mu + \frac{\sigma^2}{2}} e^{\sigma^2} - 1}$
Power-law		x_{min}, a	$(0, +\infty)$	$x_{min}\frac{a-1}{a-2}$	$\sqrt{x_{min}^2 \frac{a-1}{a-3}}$

4 Comparison and Correlation

Simple tools to uncover patterns of association by comparing values of *y* by values of *x*

Motivation

Are larger companies better managed? To answer this question, you downloaded data from the World Management Survey. How should you describe the relationship between firm size and the quality of management? In particular, can you describe that with the help of a single number, or an informative graph?

To answer the previous question, you have to use the variables in the data to measure the quality of management. In particular, you can use the quality of the many kinds of management practices separately, or you can use a summary measure. What are the advantages and disadvantages of each approach? If you want to use a summary measure, what's the best way to create it, and how should you interpret its magnitude?

Many questions that data analysis can answer are based on comparing values of one variable, *y*, against values of another variable, *x*, and often other variables. Such comparisons are the basis of uncovering the effect of *x*: if *x* affects *y*, the value of *y* should be different if we were to change the value of *x*. Uncovering differences in *y* for different values of one or more *x* variables is also essential for prediction: to arrive at a good guess of the value of *y* when we don't know it but we know the value of *x*.

We start by emphasizing that we need to measure both *y* and *x* well for meaningful comparisons. We introduce conditioning, which is the statistical term for uncovering information related to one variable for different values of another variable. We discuss conditional comparisons, or further conditioning, which takes values of other variables into account as well. We discuss conditional probabilities, conditional distributions, and conditional means. We introduce the related concepts of dependence, mean-dependence, and correlation. Throughout the chapter, we discuss informative visualizations of the various kinds of comparisons.

In this chapter, we use the **Management quality and firm size: describing patterns of association** case study, which uses the `wms-management-survey` dataset. The question is to what extent the quality of management tends to be different when comparing larger firms to smaller firms. We illustrate conditional probabilities, conditional means, and various aspects of conditional distributions with this case study.

Learning outcomes

After working through this chapter, you should be able to:

- define the *y* and *x* variables (or *x* variables) and identify them in the data;
- understand the concepts of conditional probability, conditional distribution, conditional mean;
- create informative figures to visualize conditional means (bin scatter), other conditional statistics (box plots), and joint distributions of quantitative variables (scatterplots);
- understand the concepts of dependence, mean-dependence, and correlation, and produce and interpret correlation coefficients.

4.1　The *y* and the *x*

Much of data analysis is built on comparing values of a *y* variable by values of an *x* variable, or more *x* variables. Such a comparison can uncover the **patterns of association** between the two variables: whether and how observations with particular values of one variable (*x*) tend to have particular values of the other variable (*y*). The *y* and *x* notation for these variables is as common in data analysis as it is for the axes of the Cartesian coordinate system in calculus.

The role of *y* is different from the role of *x*. It's the values of *y* we are interested in, and we compare observations that are different in their *x* values. This asymmetry comes from the goal of our analysis.

One goal of data analysis is predicting the value of a *y* variable with the help of other variables. The prediction itself takes place when we know the values of those other variables but not the *y* variable. To predict *y* based on the other variables we need a rule that tells us what the predicted *y* value is as a function of the values of the other variables. Such a rule can be devised by analyzing data where we know the *y* values, too.

Those other variables are best thought of as many *x* variables, such as x_1, x_2, ... We use the same letter, *x*, for these variables and distinguish them by subscripts only because their role in the prediction is similar. For instance, to predict the price of Airbnb rentals, we need *x* variables that matter for that price, such as number of rooms and beds, and location (we will investigate this in Chapters 14 and 16). To predict whether applicants for unsecured loans will repay their loans, we need variables that matter for that repayment probability, such as applicants' income, occupation, age, and family status.

The other most frequent goal of data analysis is to learn about the effect of a **causal variable** *x* on an **outcome variable** *y*. Here, we typically are interested in what the value of *y* would be if we could change *x*: how sales would change if we raised prices; whether the proportion of people getting sick in a group would decrease if they received vaccination (we will investigate this in Chapter 23); how the employment chances of unemployed people would increase if they participated in a training program.

Data analysis can help uncover such effects by examining data with both *y* and *x* and comparing values of *y* between observations with different values of *x*. Examples of observations with different *x* values indicate weeks with different prices, groups with different vaccination rates, or people who participated in a training program versus people who didn't. Often, when trying to uncover the effect of *x* on *y*, data analysts consider other variables, too. For example, they want to compare weeks in which the price of the product is different but the price of competing products is the same; groups with different vaccination rates but of the same size and living conditions; people who participate and don't participate in the training program but have the same level of skills and motivation. We often denote these other variables by another letter, z (or $z_1, z_2, \ldots$), to emphasize that their role is different from the role of the x variable.

In sum, deciding on what's y and what's x in the data is the first step before doing any meaningful analysis. In this chapter we discuss some general concepts of comparisons and introduce some simple and intuitive methods.

Review Box 4.1 y and x in data analysis

Most of data analysis is based on comparing values of a y variable for different values of an x variable (or more variables).

- For prediction we want to know what value of y to expect for different values of various x variables, such as $x_1, x_2, \ldots$
- For causal analysis we want to know what value of y to expect if we changed the value of x, often comparing observations that are similar in other variables ($z_1, z_2, \ldots$).

4.A1 CASE STUDY – Management Quality and Firm Size: Describing Patterns of Association

Question and data

In this case study we explore whether, and to what extent, larger firms are better managed.

Answering this question can help benchmarking management practices in a specific company. It can also help understand why some firms are better managed than others. Size may be a cause in itself as achieving better management may require fixed costs that are independent of firm size with benefits that are larger for larger firms. Whether firm size is an important determinant of better management can help in answering questions such as the potential benefits of company mergers (merged companies are larger than their component companies), or what kinds of firms are more likely to implement changes that require good management.

We use data from the World Management Survey to investigate our question. We introduced the survey in Chapter 1. In this case study we analyze a cross-section of Mexican firms from the 2013 wave of the survey.

Mexico is a medium-income and medium-sized open economy with a substantial heterogeneity of its firms along many dimensions. Thus, Mexican firms provide a good example to study the quality of management. We excluded 33 firms with fewer than 100 employees and 2 firms with more than 5000 employees. There are 300 firms in the data, all surveyed in 2013. (Among the Data Exercises, you'll be invited to carry out an analogous analysis of firms from a different country.)

The y variable in this case study should be a measure of the quality of management. The x variable should be a measure of firm size.

Recall that the main purpose of this data collection was to measure the quality of management in each firm. The survey included 18 "score" variables. Each score is an assessment by the survey interviewers of management practices in a particular domain (tracking and reviewing performance or time horizon and of targets) measured on a scale of 1 (worst practice) to 5 (best practice).

Our measure of the quality of management is the simple average of these 18 scores. We – following the researchers who collected the data – call it "the" management score. By construction, the range of the management score is between 1 and 5 because that's the range of all 18 items within the average. The mean is 2.9, the median is also 2.9, and the standard deviation is 0.6. The histogram (Figure 4.1) shows a more-or-less symmetric distribution with the vast majority of the firms having an average score between 2 and 4.

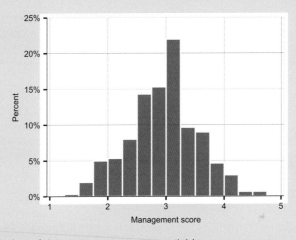

Figure 4.1 Distribution of the management score variable

Note: Histogram, bin width set to 0.25.
Source: `wms-management-survey` dataset. Mexican firms with 100–5000 employees. N=300.

We measure firm size by employment: the number of workers employed by the firm. The range of employment we kept in the Mexican data is 100 to 5000. The mean is 760 and the median is 350, signaling substantial skewness with a long right tail. The histogram (Figure 4.2a) shows this skewness. It also shows two extreme values: the largest four firms have 5000 employees, followed by two firms with about 4500 employees and three with 4000 employees. Recall from Chapter 3, Section 3.9 that distributions with long right tails may be well approximated by the lognormal distribution. To check this, we also show the histogram of the natural log of employment (Figure 4.2b). That histogram is still skewed with a longer right tail, but it is substantially more symmetric. Also note that the extreme values are not so extreme anymore with log employment. Thus, we can conclude that the distribution of employment in this data is skewed, it is closer to lognormal than normal, but even the lognormal is not the best approximation.

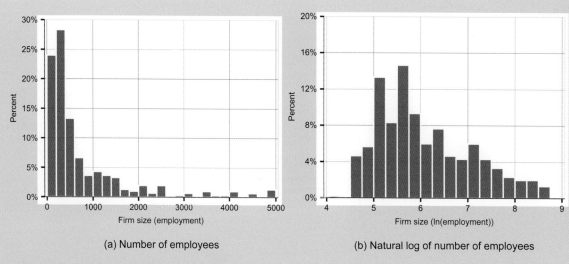

(a) Number of employees   (b) Natural log of number of employees

Figure 4.2   The distribution of employment

Note: Histograms.
Source: `wms-management-survey` dataset. Mexican firms with 100–5000 employees. N=300.

4.2   Conditioning

The word statisticians use for comparison is **conditioning**. When we compare the values of *y* by the values of *x*, we condition *y* on *x*. *y* is also called the **outcome variable**; *x* is also called the **conditioning variable**. Most of the time, we will simply call them *y* and *x*.

When data analysts want to uncover values of *y* for observations that are different in *x* but similar in *z*, they do one more step of conditioning: they compare *y* by *x* conditional on *z*. That is called **further conditioning** or a **conditional comparison**. Thus the word conditioning can be confusing if used without more context. It may mean a simple comparison – uncovering values of *y* for different values of *x* – or it may mean a conditional comparison – uncovering values of *y* for observations that are different in *x* but the same in *z*. Therefore we will try to be more specific and always add the necessary context.

Conditioning is an abstract concept. In practice we explore conditional probabilities, conditional means, and conditional distributions. The next sections discuss these in detail.

> **Review Box 4.2   Conditioning**
>
> - Conditioning is the statistical term used for comparing values, or statistics, of *y* by values of *x*.
> - Going one more step, we can further condition on *z*: compare *y* by values of *x* among observations with similar value for *z*.

Conditional Probabilities

In Section 3.2 of the previous chapter, we introduced probability as the generalization of relative frequency. The probability of a value of a variable in a dataset is its relative frequency (percentage). In more abstract settings, the probability of an event is the likelihood that it occurs. In this section we discuss comparing the probability of events, or the probability of values of variables, by another event, or by values of another variable.

Conditional probability is the probability of one event if another event happens. The event the conditional probability is about is called the **conditional event**; the other event is called the **conditioning event**. Conditional probabilities are denoted as $P(event_1 \mid event_2)$: the probability of $event_1$ conditional on $event_2$.

Note that the conditional probability is not symmetrical: $P(event_1 \mid event_2) \neq P(event_2 \mid event_1)$ in general. Pairs of probabilities of this sort are called **inverse conditional probabilities**. Thus, inverse conditional probabilities are not equal in general. In fact, they are related to each other in a somewhat complicated way. Understanding their relation can be important to understand a lot of real-life problems, such as understanding the probability of having a condition after receiving a test result. It is also useful to understand the logic of generalizing results from the data that we'll discuss in Chapter 5. We discuss inverse conditional probabilities and their relationship in more detail in Under the Hood section 4.U1.

Joint probabilities are related to conditional probabilities. The **joint probability** of two events is the probability that both occur: $P(event_1 \ \& \ event_2)$. When two events are mutually exclusive, their joint probability is zero (the two never happen together).

Another probability related to two events denotes the likelihood that one event or the other happens. This is the sum of the two probabilities minus their joint probability: $P(event_1 \ OR \ event_2) = P(event_1) + P(event_2) - P(event_1 \ \& \ event_2)$. If the two events are mutually exclusive, we subtract zero from the sum of the two probabilities.

The conditional probability can be expressed as the corresponding joint probability divided by the probability of the conditioning event:

$$P(event_1 \mid event_2) = \frac{P(event_1 \ \& \ event_2)}{P(event_2)} \tag{4.1}$$

Two events are **independent** if the probability of one of the events is the same regardless of whether or not the other event occurs. In the language of conditional probabilities this means that the conditional probabilities are the same as the unconditional probabilities: $P(event_1 \mid event_2) = P(event_1)$ and $P(event_2 \mid event_1) = P(event_2)$.

Less intuitive, but also true is that the joint probability of independent events equals the product of their individual probabilities: $P(event_1 \ \& \ event_2) = P(event_1) \times P(event_2)$. (You can see this after plugging it into the formula that relates conditional and joint probabilities.)

In data, the events refer to values of variables. Often, the conditional variable, y, is a binary variable: $y = 0$ or $y = 1$. Then the conditional probability is the probability that $y = 1$ if x has some value: $P(y = 1 \mid x = value)$. Since y is binary, we know the probability of $y = 0$ if we know the probability of $y = 1$, be it a conditional or unconditional probability; e.g., $P(y = 0 \mid x = value) = 1 - P(y = 1 \mid x = value)$. When x is binary too, there are two conditional probabilities:

$$P(y = 1 \mid x = 1) \tag{4.2}$$

$$P(y = 1 \mid x = 0) \tag{4.3}$$

With more values for either of the two variables (y, x), we have more numbers to compare: $P(y = value|x = value)$. With relatively few values, visualization often helps. There are many options for using standard graphs as well as creating individualized graphs. A good solution is the **stacked bar chart** . It presents the relative frequencies within bars that are on top of each other and thus always add up to a height of 100 %. To visualize conditional probabilities if both y and x have few values, a good visualization is to show stacked bar charts of y for the values of x.

Review Box 4.3   Conditional probability

- Conditional probability of an event: the probability of an event if another event (the conditioning event) happens:
  $P(event_1 \mid event_2)$
- Two events are independent if the probability of one of the events is the same regardless of whether the other event occurs or not:
  $P(event_1 \mid event_2) = P(event_1)$ and $P(event_2 \mid event_1) = P(event_2)$.
- The joint probability of two events is the probability that both happen at the same time:
  $P(event_1 \,\&\, event_2)$

4.A2   **CASE STUDY – Management Quality and Firm Size: Describing Patterns of Association**

Conditional probabilities

Both the management score and employment are quantitative variables with many values. They do not lend themselves to investigating conditional probabilities, at least not without transforming them. Thus, to illustrate conditional probabilities, we consider the individual score variables as y – recall that there are 18 of them, each with five potential values, 1 to 5. For x, we created a qualitative variable by creating three bins of employment: small, medium, large. These three bins are obviously arbitrary. We have chosen them to be bounded by round numbers: 100–199, 200–999, and 1000+ (with 72, 156, and 72 firms, respectively). Thus, for each score variable we have 15 conditional probabilities: the probability of each of the 5 values of y by each of the three values of x – e.g., $P(y = 1|x = small)$.

Listing 15 conditional probabilities in a table is not a very good way to present them. But stacked bar charts are a great way to visualize them. Figure 4.3 shows two examples, one for lean management and one for performance tracking (each with values 1,2,..,5), each separately by small, medium, and large as firm size bins.

For both lean management and performance tracking, the figures show the same pattern of association between the quality of management and firm size. Small firms are more likely to have low scores and less likely to have high scores than medium-sized firms, and, in turn, medium-sized firms are more likely to have low scores and less likely to have high scores than large firms. For lean management, scores 4 and 5 together take up 11% of small firms (only score 4, actually), 27% of medium-sized ones, and 36% of large ones. For performance tracking, the corresponding percentages are 40%, 57%, and 68%. These results suggest that larger firms are more likely to be better managed. As a data exercise, you will be invited to produce similar stacked bar charts to confirm that the patterns for other management variables are the same.

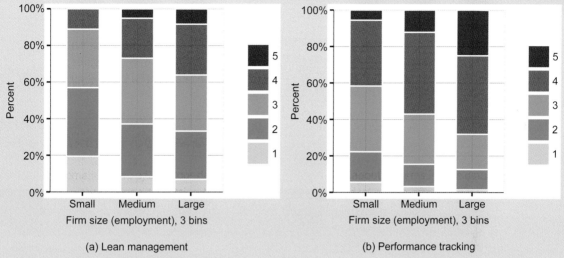

Figure 4.3 Quality of specific management practices by three bins of firm size: conditional probabilities

Note: Firm size as defined by number of employees. Stacked bar charts by firm size bins (bins are 100–199, 200–999, 1000+, with 72, 156, and 72 firms, respectively).

Source: `wms-management-survey` dataset. Mexican firms with 100–5000 employees., N=300.

4.4 Conditional Distribution, Conditional Expectation

Just as all variables have a distribution (Chapter 3, Section 3.2), all *y* variables have a **conditional distribution** if conditioned on an *x* variable. This is a straightforward concept if the *x* variable has few values. The simplest case is a binary *x* when the conditional distribution of *y* is two distributions, one for each of the two *x* values.

Conditional distributions with few *x* values are best presented by visualization: for each *x* value we show stacked bar charts if *y* has few values or histograms if *y* is a quantitative variable with many values. The previous section covered conditional stacked bar charts. Here we discuss conditional histograms. Whatever we said about histograms in Chapter 3, Section 3.3 applies here: the look of the histograms are affected by our choice of bin size; density plots may be an alternative but are more sensitive to parameter settings. Our additional advice here is to make sure that the histograms are fully comparable across the *x* values: most importantly, they have the same bins of *y*, and they have the same scale on the vertical axis.

Comparing histograms can reveal qualitative differences in the distributions. We can tell which distribution tends to be to the left or right of the other, how their modes compare, which one looks more spread out, which one looks more skewed. To make quantitative comparisons, however, we need to compare statistics that summarize the important features of distributions.

The most important conditional statistic is the **conditional mean**, also known as the **conditional expectation**, which shows the mean (average, expected value) of y for each value of x. The abstract formula for the conditional mean is

$$E[y|x] \qquad\qquad (4.4)$$

From a mathematical point of view this is a function: if we feed in a number value for variable x, the conditional expectation gives us the number that is the mean of y for observations that have that particular x value. Note that while the overall mean of y, $E[y]$, is a single number in a data table, the conditional mean $E[y|x]$ varies in the data, because it can be different for different values of x.

Analogously, we can look at conditional medians, other conditional quantiles, conditional standard deviations, and so on. Comparing box plots and violin plots is a great way to visualize conditional statistics of y when x has few values.

Review Box 4.4   Conditional distribution and conditional mean – quantitative y, few values of x

- Conditional distribution of y by x is the distribution of y among observations with specific values of x.
- $E[y|x]$ denotes the conditional mean (conditional expectation) of y for various values of x.
- If x has few values, it is straightforward to visualize conditional distributions and calculate conditional means and other conditional statistics.

4.5   Conditional Distribution, Conditional Expectation with Quantitative x

When the x is quantitative with many values, things are more complicated. It is usually impossible or impractical to plot histograms or compute the conditional mean for each and every value of x. First, there are too many values of x and, typically, too few observations for each value. Second, even if we had enough observations, the resulting statistics or pictures would typically be too complex to make sense of.

We have two approaches to deal with these problems. The first approach circumvents the problem of too many x values by reducing them through creating bins. With few bins and thus many observations within each bin, we can calculate conditional means, plot histograms, box plots, and so on, in ways that are easy to interpret. Creating bins from x is not only the simplest approach, but it often produces powerful results. Usually with just three bins of x – small, medium, large – we can capture the most important patterns of association between a quantitative y and a quantitative x.

Visualization of conditional means of y for bins of x is called a **bin scatter**. A bin scatter is a figure with the values of the binned x on the horizontal axis and the corresponding conditional mean values of y on the vertical axis. It is good practice to visualize bin scatters with meaningful x values for the x bins, such as their midpoint or the median value of observations within the bin.

The second approach keeps x as it is. The most widely used tool is the **scatterplot**, which is a visualization of the **joint distribution** of two variables. The joint distribution of two variables is the frequency of each value combination of the two variables. A scatterplot is a two-dimensional graph with the x and y values on its two axes, and dots or other markers entered for each observation in the data with the corresponding x and y values. With small or moderately large datasets, scatterplots can reveal interesting things. With a very large number of observations, scatterplots can look like a big cloud and allow us to infer less information.

Starting with Chapter 7, we'll consider the most widely used method to uncover $E[y|x]$: regression analysis. This is a natural continuation of the methods considered in this chapter. But we don't discuss regression here as it requires more time and space. And, before moving on to regression analysis, we consider a few more topics within this chapter and the next two chapters.

Review Box 4.5   Joint and conditional distributions of two quantitative variables

- The joint distribution of two variables shows the frequency of each value combination of the two variables.
- The scatterplot is a good way to visualize joint distributions.
- Conditional expectations may be computed and visualized in bins created from the conditioning variable.

4.A3   CASE STUDY – Management Quality and Firm Size: Describing Patterns of Association

Conditional mean and joint distribution

Let's return to our case study on management quality and firm size, using our data of Mexican firms. y is the management score, and x is employment. Recall that this data contains firms with 100 to 5000 employees, and the distribution of employment is skewed with a long right tail (Figure 4.2a).

The next two charts (Figures 4.4a and 4.4b) show two bin scatters with mean y conditional on three x bins and ten x bins. We created the three bins in the same way as earlier, 100–199, 200–999, and 1000+ employees, with 72, 156, and 72 firms in the bins, respectively. Our approach to create the ten bins was different: instead of looking for round numbers to separate them, we simply split the data into ten equal-sized subsamples by the number of employees. Most statistical software can create such bins in a straightforward way. On both bin scatter graphs, we show the average management score as a point corresponding to the midpoint in the employment bin (e.g., 150 for the 100–199 bin).

The bin scatter with three bins implies a clear positive association: larger firms are better managed, on average. In particular, the mean management score is 2.68 for small firms, 2.94 for medium-sized ones, and it is 3.19 for large firms. The bin scatter with ten bins shows a less straight linear relationship, with a very similar mean in bins 4 through 8. But, overall, that picture too shows higher means in bins of larger firm size. The magnitude of the difference in mean management quality between large and small firms is moderate (about 0.5 for the 1–5 scale).

Finally, note that the bin scatters reflect the very skewed distribution of employment by having larger distances between bin midpoints at larger sizes. We could have presented the bin scatters with the same bins but showing log employment on the *x* axis instead of employment; that would have shown a more even distribution of the bins and a more linear pattern. Such figures would show the exact same association: management tends to be of higher quality for larger firms, and that difference is smaller, in terms of absolute employment, at higher levels of employment. You'll be invited to do this as a data exercise.

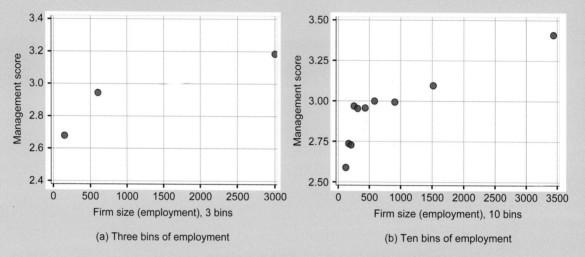

(a) Three bins of employment   (b) Ten bins of employment

Figure 4.4   Mean management quality score and firm size

Note: Bin scatters.
Source: `wms-management-survey` dataset. Mexican firms with 100–5000 employees. N=300.

The bin scatters show a positive pattern of association on average. But does that mean that all larger firms are better managed in this data? Not at all. To appreciate the distribution of the management score around its conditional mean values, we look at the scatterplot.

On the left panel (Figure 4.5a) we see the consequences of the very skewed employment distribution: most observations are clustered in the leftmost part of the figure. We can see a positive slope on this graph among larger firms, but it's hard to see any pattern among smaller firms.

To make the patterns more visible, the right panel (Figure 4.5b) shows the same scatterplot with the natural log of employment on the *x* axis instead of employment itself. This amounts to stretching the employment differences between firms at lower levels of employment and compressing those differences at higher levels. (We'll spend a lot more time on what such a transformation does to variables and comparisons of variables later, in Chapter 8.) This scatterplot leads to a more spread out picture, reflecting the more symmetric distribution of the *x* variable. Here the positive association between mean management score and (log) employment is more visible.

In any case, we also see a lot of variation of the management score at every level of employment. Thus, there is a lot of spread of the management score among firms with the same size. As for other features of the distribution, the scatterplot doesn't show a clear pattern between employment (or log employment) and either spread or skewness of the distributions. But that may be because such features are not always easy to read off a scatterplot.

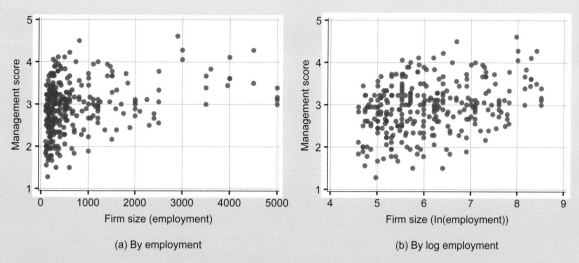

(a) By employment   (b) By log employment

Figure 4.5   The joint distribution of the management quality score and firm size

Note: Scatterplots.
Source: `wms-management-survey` dataset. Mexican firms with 100–5000 employees. N=300.

To gain yet more insight into whether, and to what extent, the spread or skewness of the management score distribution differ at different levels of employment, we produced box plots and violin plots of the management score for three employment bins (Figure 4.6).

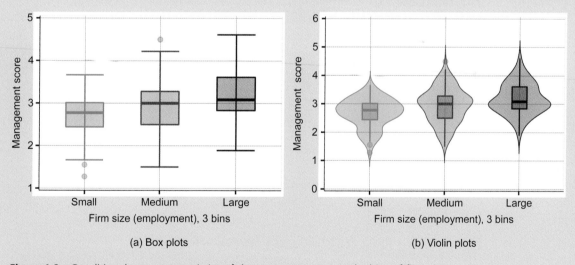

(a) Box plots   (b) Violin plots

Figure 4.6   Conditional summary statistics of the management score by bins of firm size

Note: Visuals of the conditional summary statistics: box plot and violin plot.
Source: `wms-management-survey` dataset. Mexican firms with 100–5000 employees. N=300.

Both the box plots and the violin plots reveal that the median management score is higher in larger firms, reflecting the same positive association as the bin scatters and the scatterplot. That positive pattern is true when we compare almost any statistic of the management score: median, upper and lower quartiles, minimum and maximum. These figures also show that the spread of management score is somewhat smaller in smaller firms. That means that small firms are more similar to each other in their management scores, besides having lower scores on average. In contrast, larger firms differ more from each other in terms of their management score.

4.6 Dependence, Covariance, Correlation

After discussing the conditional mean and the conditional distribution and their visualizations, let's introduce a few related concepts that are often used in data analysis.

Dependence of two variables, also called **statistical dependence** means that the conditional distributions of one variable (y) are not the same when conditional on different values of the other variable (x). In contrast, **independence of variables** means that the distribution of one conditional on the other is the same, regardless of the value of the conditioning variable. These concepts may be viewed as generalizations of independent events (see Section 4.3).

Dependence of y and x may take many forms. For example y may be more spread out or more skewed for some x values. But the most important form of dependence is **mean-dependence**: the mean of y is different when the value of x is different. In other words, the conditional expectation $E[y|x]$ is not always the same but varies with the value of x.

The **covariance** and the **correlation coefficient** are measures of this mean-dependence. To be a bit more precise, they measure mean dependence in an average sense. $E[y|x]$ may have ups and downs by the value of x, and the covariance and correlation coefficient are average measures of those ups and downs. When y and x are positively correlated, $E[y|x]$ tends to be higher when the value of x is higher. When y and x are negatively correlated, $E[y|x]$ tends to be lower when the value of x is higher. The two measures are very closely related: the correlation coefficient is the standardized version of the covariance.

The formula for the covariance between two variables x and y in a dataset with n observations is

$$Cov[x, y] = \frac{\sum_i (x_i - \bar{x})(y_i - \bar{y})}{n} \qquad (4.5)$$

The correlation coefficient divides this by the product of the two standard deviations:

$$Corr[x, y] = \frac{Cov[x, y]}{Std[x]\,Std[y]} \qquad (4.6)$$

$$-1 \leq Corr[x, y] \leq 1 \qquad (4.7)$$

The covariance may be any positive or negative number, while the correlation coefficient is bound to be between negative one and positive one. But their sign is always the same: the covariance is zero when the correlation coefficient is zero; the covariance is positive when the correlation coefficient is positive; the covariance is negative when the correlation coefficient is negative.

When the correlation coefficient is zero we say that y and x are **uncorrelated**. With positive correlation, y and x are **positively correlated**. With negative covariance and correlation we say that y and x are **negatively correlated**. The magnitude of the correlation coefficient shows the strength of the association: the larger the magnitude, the stronger the mean-dependence between the two variables. Data analysts tend to consider a correlation of 0.2 or less (in absolute value) weak, and a correlation above 0.7 in absolute value is usually considered strong.

If two variables are independent, they are also mean-independent and thus the conditional expectations are all the same: $E[y|x] = E[y]$ for any value of x. The covariance and the correlation coefficient are both zero in this case. In short, we say that independence implies mean independence and zero correlation. But the reverse is not true. We can have zero correlation but mean-dependence (e.g., a symmetrical U-shaped conditional expectation has an average of zero), and we can have zero correlation and zero mean-dependence without complete independence (e.g., the spread of y may be different for different values of x).

Spending a little time with its formula can help understand how the covariance is an average measure of mean-dependence. The product within the sum in the numerator multiplies the deviation of x from its mean $(x_i - \bar{x})$ with the deviation of y from its mean $(y_i - \bar{y})$, for each observation i. The entire formula is the average of these products across all observations. If a positive deviation of x from its mean goes along with a positive deviation of y from its mean, the product is positive. Thus, the average of this product across all observations is positive. The more often a positive $x_i - \bar{x}$ goes together with a positive $y_i - \bar{y}$, the more positive is the covariance. Or, the larger are the positive deviations that go together the larger the covariance.

If, on the other hand, a positive $x_i - \bar{x}$ goes along with a negative $y_i - \bar{y}$, the product tends to be negative. Thus the average of this product is negative. The more often a positive $x_i - \bar{x}$ goes together with a negative $y_i - \bar{y}$, the more negative the covariance.

Finally, if a positive $x_i - \bar{x}$ goes along with a positive $y_i - \bar{y}$ some of the time and a negative $y_i - \bar{y}$ at other times, and these two balance each other out, the positive values of the product and the negative values of the product cancel out. In this case the average is zero. Exact zero covariance rarely happens in real data because that would require an exact balancing out. The more balanced the positive deviation in x_i and positive deviation in y_i instances are with the positive deviation in x_i and negative deviation in y_i instances, the closer the covariance is to zero.

Also note that the formulae of the covariance or the correlation coefficient allow for all kinds of variables, including binary variables and ordered qualitative variables as well as quantitative variables. The covariance and the correlation coefficient will always be zero if the two variables are mean-independent, positive if positively mean-dependent, and negative if negatively mean-dependent. Thus, they give a quick and not completely meaningless picture about mean-dependence among binary and ordered qualitative variables. However, they are more appropriate measures for qualitative variables. That's because the differences $y_i - \bar{y}$ and $x_i - \bar{x}$ make less sense when y and x are qualitative variables. For that reason, data analysts use other correlation-like measures for qualitative variables, but those measures are beyond the scope of our textbook.

Review Box 4.6 Covariance and correlation

- The covariance measures the mean-dependence of two variables: $Cov[x, y] = \frac{\sum_i (x_i - \bar{x})(y_i - \bar{y})}{n}$
- The correlation coefficient is a standardized version of the covariance and ranges between -1 and 1: $Corr[x, y] = \frac{Cov[x,y]}{Std[x]\,Std[y]}$
- The covariance and the correlation are both zero if the variables are independent, positive if the variables are positively associated, and negative if they are negatively associated.

4.7 From Latent Variables to Observed Variables

Before closing the chapter, let's discuss two more topics briefly. The first one is the concept of latent variables.

Often, the *y* or *x* variables we have in question are abstract concepts: the quality of management of a firm, skills of an employee, risk tolerance of an investor, health of a person, wealth of a country. Typically, such variables are not parts of an actual dataset, and they can't be because they are too abstract. Such variables are called **latent variables**.

Data analysis can help answer questions involving latent variables only by substituting observed variables for them. Those observed variables are called **proxy variables**, where "proxy" means substitute (the word proxy is used as noun, adjective, and verb). The quality of management may be proxied by answers to survey questions on management practices, as in our case study; employee skills may be proxied by qualifications or measures of past performance; and so on.

The most important thing to keep in mind here is that data analysis compares values of measured variables. Even if those variables are supposed to measure abstract concepts, it's never the abstract concepts themselves that we have in our data. Thus we can never examine things such as skills or attitudes or health; instead, we examine proxies such as measures of performance, answers to survey questions, or results of doctors' diagnoses. This is simply re-iterating the point we made earlier in Chapter 1, Section 1.3: the content of a variable is determined by how it is measured – not by what name somebody attached to it.

A specific issue arises when our data contains not one but more variables that could serve as proxies to the latent variable we want to examine. The question here is how to combine multiple observed variables. Data analysts use one of three main approaches:

* Use one of the observed variables
* Take the average (or sum) of the observed variables
* Use principal component analysis (PCA) to combine the observed variables.

Using one measured variable and excluding the rest has the advantage of easy interpretation. It has the disadvantage of discarding potentially useful information contained in the other measured variables.

Taking the average of all measured variables makes use of all information in a simple way. When all of those variables are measured using the same scale, this approach yields a combined measure with a natural interpretation. When the variables are measured at different scales, we need to bring the observed variables to the same scale. Usually, we do that by standardizing them: subtracting the mean and dividing by the standard deviation (see Chapter 3, Section 3.6). This standardized measure is also called a **z-score**.

By taking a simple average of all these variables we give them equal weight. This may be a disadvantage if some of the variables are better measures of the latent variable than others. The third approach remedies that problem. **Principal component analysis** (**PCA**) is a method to give higher weights to the observable variables that are better measures. PCA finds those weights by examining how strongly they would be related with the weighted average. The logic is an iterative process: create an average, examine how each variable is related to it by looking at their correlations, give higher weights to those with stronger correlation, start over. The actual technique takes an ingenious approach to do the whole thing in one step.

Of the three approaches, we recommend the second one: taking a simple average of the observed variables after making sure that they are measured at the same scale. This is the simplest way to combine all variables in a meaningful way. In principle, PCA produces a better combined measure, but it is more complicated to produce and harder to present to non-expert audiences. Moreover, it often gives similar results to a simple average. Thus we recommend that PCA is used as a robustness check, if at all. If the results of our analysis are very different with a simple average and with a PCA measure, some of our observed variables are very differently related to the average measure than others. It is good practice then to go back and understand the content of those variables and, perhaps, discard some of them from the analysis.

Review Box 4.7   Latent and proxy variables

- Latent variables are abstract concepts that are not actual variables in the data.
- Proxy variables (proxies) are variables in the data that measure latent variables.
- When more proxy variables are available for a single latent variable it is good practice to take their average, after making sure that they are measured on the same scale (for example, by standardizing them).

4.A4   CASE STUDY – Management Quality and Firm Size: Describing Patterns of Association

Correlation and latent variable

The covariance between firm size and the management score in the Mexican sample we use is 177. The standard deviation of firm size is 977; the standard deviation of management score is 0.6. The correlation coefficient is 0.30 (177/(977 * 0.6) =0.30).

This result shows a positive association: firms with more employees tend to have a higher management score. The magnitude of the correlation is moderate, presumably because many other things matter for the quality of management besides the size of a firm.

Table 4.1 shows the correlation coefficient in seven broad categories of industrial classification (plus one "other" category with the industries with very few firms, combined).

Table 4.1   Management score and employment: correlation and average management score by industry

Industry	Management–employment correlation	Observations
Auto	0.50	26
Chemicals	0.05	69
Electronics, equipment, machinery	0.28	36

Table 4.1 *(cont.)*		
	Management–employment	
Industry	**correlation**	**Observations**
Food, drinks, tobacco	0.05	34
Materials, metals	0.32	50
Textile, apparel, leather	0.36	38
Wood, furniture, paper	0.28	37
Other	0.63	10
All	0.30	300

Source: `wms-management-survey` dataset. Mexican firms with 100–5000 employees. N=300.

The table reveals that the management quality–firm size correlation varies considerably across industries. The correlation is strongest in the auto and "other" industries. At the same time, we see hardly any correlation among firms in the chemicals and food industries.

Before concluding our case study, note that it illustrates the measurement issues related to latent variables, too. From a conceptual point of view, the y variable in our case study is management quality, a latent variable. We have 18 measures for this latent variable in the data; those are the 18 score variables on the quality of various aspects of management. Each of these 18 variables is measured by the survey (as we discussed in Chapter 1, Section 1.C1), and each is measured on the same 1-to-5 scale.

For the measure of the overall quality of management, we used two of the three strategies we recommended in Section 4.7. To illustrate conditional probabilities, visualized by the stacked bar charts in Figures 4.3a and 4.3b, we used 2 of the 18 score variables. Each one is an imperfect measure of the overall quality of management, but each has a clear interpretation: the rating of the particular aspect of management quality by the interviewer. For most of the case study, we used the average score: the simple average of the 18 scores. We could use this simple average because each of the 18 variables aimed to measure an aspect of the same thing, management quality, and each was measured on the same scale (1 to 5).

As a data exercise you are invited to try the third option we recommended in Section 4.7, and create a principal component from the 18 scores instead of their simple average. When analyzing the relationship between firm size and management quality, using this principal component measure turns out to give very similar results to what we have uncovered using the average score measure.

This concludes our case study. What did we learn from it about the association between firm size and management quality? We found that, among Mexican manufacturing firms, larger firms tend to be better managed. Large firms (with 1000–5000 employees) have an average score of 3.19, compared to 2.94 for medium-sized firms (with 200–999 employees), and 2.68 for small ones (with 100–199 employees).

We also found that the correlation, while positive, is not very strong, perhaps because other things matter for the quality of management besides firm size. When disaggregating the results into smaller industry groups, we found that the strength of the management–size correlation differs in some industries from the rest, but we haven't seen any clear pattern that would tell us why. Finally, we have seen that management quality is not only better, on average, among larger firms, but it is also somewhat more spread among larger firms.

These results inform the business or policy questions we may be interested in. When considering the management practices of a specific firm, we should have firms of similar size as a benchmark. And, better management of a larger firm may be a potential benefit of increased firm size – e.g., through a merger between companies.

As for the methods discussed in this chapter, this case study illustrated what we can do to uncover patterns of associations and conditional distributions when both *y* and *x* are quantitative variables. We have seen that creating bins from *x* can lead to informative visualizations, such as a bin scatter or box plots of *y* by bins of *x*. Three bins (small, medium, large) appeared a good choice in our case. For example, the bin scatter with ten bins did not give much more information than the bin scatter with three bins. We have also seen that the correlation coefficient is a useful statistic to summarize mean-dependence between *y* and *x*, and it allows us to dig a little deeper by showing whether and how the correlation differs across groups by a third variable (here industry). Finally, we have seen that, with rich enough data, we can use an average score variable calculated from many (here 18) variables to measure a latent variable, management quality in our case study.

4.8 Sources of Variation in *x*

Our final section in this chapter is a note on variation in *x*, the variable (or variables) we condition on to make comparisons in *y*. The first thing to note is that we need variation in *x*, and the more variation we have the better in general. In data with no variation in *x*, all observations have the same values and it's impossible to make comparisons. This may sound trivial, but it's essential to keep in mind. Similarly, the more variation in *x*, the better the chances for comparison.

For example, when data analysts want to uncover the effect of price changes on sales, they need many observations with different price values. If prices don't change at all, there is no way to learn how they may affect sales. If prices change very rarely or the changes are negligible in magnitude, there isn't much room for comparison and thus there isn't much to learn.

The second question is where that variation in *x* comes from. As we shall see in subsequent chapters (e.g., Chapters 19 through 24), data analysts need to understand the **sources of variation** in *x*. This is a somewhat fancy way of saying that data analysts should have a good understanding of why values of *x* may differ across observations. From this perspective, there are two main types of data: experimental data and observational data.

In **experimental data**, the value of *x* differs across observations because somebody made them different. In a medical experiment assessing the effects of a drug, some patients receive the drug while others receive a placebo, and who receives what is determined by a rule designed by the experimenter, such as a coin flip or a computer generated sequence of numbers. Here *x* is the binary variable indicating whether the person received the drug, instead of the placebo. Such variation is called **controlled variation**. Uncovering the effect of an experiment amounts to comparing *y* (such as whether a subject recovers from the illness or not) across the various values of *x* (whether a subject received the drug or not).

In contrast, in **observational data**, no variable is fully controlled by an experimenter or any other person. Most data used in business, economics, and policy analysis are observational. Typical variables in such data are the results of the decisions of many people with diverging goals and circumstances, such as customers, managers of firms, administrators in a government, or members of the board of the monetary authority. Thus, typically, variation in these variables has multiple sources.

Whether the variation in conditioning variables is controlled (experimental) or not (observational) is extremely important for causal analysis. Learning the effects of a variable x is a lot easier when we have data from an experiment, in which variation in x is controlled. With observational variation, of the many other things that affect an intervention variable, some may affect the outcome variable in a direct way, too. Disentangling those effects requires data analysts to further condition on many variables at the same time, using methods that we'll cover later in this textbook. Even with the best methods, conditioning on variables is possible only if those variables are measured in the data, which typically is not the case. We'll return to these questions in Chapter 10 and, in more detail, in Chapters 19 through 24.

For example, the price of a product (x) sold by a retailer may vary across time. In a sense that variation has one source, the decisions of people in charge at the retail company. But that decision, in turn, is likely affected by many things, including costs, predicted customer demand, and the pricing decisions of competitors, all of which may change through time and thus lead to variation in prices. Here a data analyst may want to uncover what would happen if the retailer increased its price (x) on sales (y), using observational data. That requires conditioning on price: looking at differences in sales across observations with different prices. But the results of this comparison won't tell us what would happen if the retailer increased the price. That's because the question is about changing x as an autonomous decision, whereas, in the data, x tends to change together with some other things. The data analyst then may go on to try to further condition on those other things that are sources of variation, such as the price charged by the competitors, or seasonal variation in demand. If lucky, the data analyst may be able to measure all those variables. But that's a tall order in most cases. The power of experimental data is that there is no need to measure anything else.

The other frequent goal of data analysis, making predictions about y, poses somewhat different requirements for variation in x. Understanding the sources of variation in x or, more realistically, the many x_1, x_2,..., variables, is still useful, although not in the way it is in causal analysis. Here the main question is stability: whether the patterns of association between y and all those x variables are the same in our data as in the situation for which we make the prediction. Controlled variation in x helps only in the rare case when x would also be controlled in the situation we care about. But uncovering cause and effect relationships can be helpful in prediction in general. We shall discuss these issues in more detail in Part III, from Chapter 13 through Chapter 18.

This chapter introduced some fundamental concepts and methods of conditioning y on x, the statistical concept of comparing values of y by values of x (or more x variables). We'll return to conditioning y on x in Chapter 7 where we introduce regression analysis. Before doing so, we discuss some general principles and methods in the next chapter that help draw conclusions from our data about the situation we are really interested in.

4.9   Main Takeaways

Data analysis answers most questions by comparing values of y by values of x.

- Be explicit about what y and x are in your data and how they are related to the question of your analysis.
- $E[y|x]$ is mean y conditional on x.

- Often many x variables are used for prediction and we may further condition on many other variables for causal analysis.

PRACTICE QUESTIONS

1. Give an example with two independent events. Can independent events happen at the same time?
2. Give an example of two mutually exclusive events. Can mutually exclusive events happen at the same time?
3. What's the conditional probability of an event? Give an example.
4. What's the conditional mean of a variable? Give an example.
5. How is the correlation coefficient related to the covariance? What is the sign of each when two variables are negatively associated, positively associated, or independent?
6. Describe in words what it means that hotel prices and distance to the city center are negatively correlated.
7. When we want to compare the mean of one variable for values of another variable, we need variation in the conditioning variable. Explain this.
8. What's the difference between the sources of variation in x in experimental data and observational data?
9. What's the joint distribution of two variables, and how can we visualize it?
10. What's a scatterplot? What does it look like for two quantitative variables, each of which can be positive only, if the two variables are positively correlated?
11. What's a bin scatter, and what is it used for?
12. What's a latent variable, and how can we use latent variables in data analysis? Give an example.
13. List two ways to combine multiple measures of the same latent variable in your data for further analysis, and list an advantage and a disadvantage of each way.
14. You want to know if working on case studies in groups or working on them independently is a better way to learn coding in R. What would be your y and x variables here and how would you measure them?
15. Can you tell from the shape of a bin scatter if y and x are positively correlated? Can you tell from it how strong their correlation is?

DATA EXERCISES

Easier and/or shorter exercises are denoted by [*]; harder and/or longer exercises are denoted by [**].

1. Are central hotels better? To answer this, using the `hotels-vienna` dataset (as discussed in Chapter 3, Section 3.A1), create two categories by the distance from center: close and far (by picking a cutoff of your choice). Show summary statistics, compare stars and ratings and prices for close and far hotels. Create stacked bar charts, box plots, and violin plots. Summarize your findings. [*]
2. Using the `wms-management-survey` dataset, pick a country different from Mexico, reproduce all figures and tables of our case study, and compare your results to what we found for Mexico. [*]
3. Use the `wms-management-survey` dataset from a country of your choice, and create a management score from a meaningful subset of the 18 items (e.g. managing talent). Carry out

an analysis to uncover the patterns of association with employment. Summarize what you find, and comment on which visualization you find the most useful. [*]

4. Use the `wms-management-survey` dataset from a country of your choice, and produce a principal component using all 18 items to form an alternative management score variable. Use this principal component and the simple average management score to produce bin scatters, scatterplots, and calculate conditional statistics to uncover the patterns of their association with employment. Compare your results and comment on which *y* measure you would use in presenting them. [*]

5. Use the `football` dataset and pick a season. Create three groups of teams, based on their performance in the previous season (new teams come from the lower division, and you may put them in the lowest bin). Examine the extent of home team advantage (as in Chapter 3, Section 3.C1) by comparing it across these three groups of teams. Produce bin scatters and scatterplots, and calculate conditional statistics. Discuss what you find, and comment on which visualization you find the most useful. [**]

REFERENCES AND FURTHER READING

Regarding the World Management Survey, you will find plenty of reading at the survey website at `https://worldmanagementsurvey.org/academic-research/manufacturing-2/` – with links to papers. For a business perspective, you could have a look at the *Harvard Business Review* article by Bloom et al. (2017). For a more detailed review of the project, consider reading Bloom et al. (2014).

4.U1   UNDER THE HOOD: INVERSE CONDITIONAL PROBABILITIES, BAYES' RULE

As we introduced in Section 4.3, inverse conditional probabilities are two conditional probabilities, in which the role of the conditioning event and the conditional event are switched: $P(event_1 \mid event_2)$ and $P(event_2 \mid event_1)$. In this section we discuss their relationship to each other.

Suppose that we want to know if an athlete used an illegal substance (doping). For this case we collect lab tests. Does the positive result of the test indicate that there is illegal substance in the body of the athlete? In other words, we are interested in whether the athlete has doped given the positive test result. But tests are imperfect so a test result will not reveal doping for sure. Instead, what we may hope for is a probability: the likelihood that someone doped, or not doped, given the result of the test. These are conditional probabilities: $P(doped \mid positive)$ and $P(not\ doped \mid positive)$. (Knowing one of these two gives the other one as the two sum up to one.) Imperfection of tests mean that they may give positive results even if athletes don't dope: $P(positive \mid not\ doped) > 0$.

Tests that are used in real life are usually validated so the level of their imperfection is known. Thus we typically know $P(positive \mid not\ doped)$. What we are interested is the inverse probability: $P(not\ doped \mid positive)$. The relation of inverse conditional probabilities tells us how the imperfect nature of a doping test determines how confident we can be concluding that an athlete doped if the result of the test is positive.

The two inverse conditional probabilities are related although their relation might seem complicated. We can derive one from the other using the formula that links conditional probabilities and joint probabilities as both are related to the same joint probability, the probability of both $event_1$ and $event_2$ occurring. The relation is called Bayes' rule after the Reverend Bayes who was the first to express this formula, in the seventeenth century.

$$P(event_2 \mid event_1) = \frac{P(event_1 \mid event_2)P(event_2)}{P(event_1)} \tag{4.8}$$

Which in turn, can be rewritten as

$$P(event_2 \mid event_1) = \frac{P(event_1 \mid event_2)P(event_2)}{P(event_1 \mid event_2)P(event_2) + P(event_1 \mid \sim event_2)P(\sim event_2)} \tag{4.9}$$

The most important message of this formula is that inverse conditional probabilities are not the same in general. The formula is also complicated. Instead of memorizing the formula we suggest using a different approach. This approach amounts to thinking in terms of frequencies and proportions in place of abstract probabilities.

Consider our doping example: what's the likelihood that an athlete is a doper (or a non-doper) if they receive a positive test result? Start with assuming that a fifth of the athletes dope. Out of, say, 1000 athletes that means 200 doping and 800 not doping. Consider a test that is imperfect but not bad: it always shows a positive result when the athlete dopes, but it also shows positive results 10% of the times if an athlete does not dope. The former means that the test will be positive for all 200 dopers.

The latter means that the test will also be positive for 10% of the non-dopers, which would be 80 out of the 800. In total we have 280 positive tests out of 1000. Of these 280 positives 200 are dopers and 80 non-dopers. We don't know which 200 are dopers and which 80 are non-dopers, but we can use these figures to calculate probabilities. The probability that an athlete is a doper if their test is positive is 200/280 = 71% approximately. The probability that an athlete is not a doper if their test is positive is 80/280 = 29% approximately. This may look surprising: a relatively small imperfection (10% of positive results for non-dopers) results in a much larger drop in our confidence: the chance that a positive tester did not dope in fact is 29%. (Working through the formulae gives the same result.) The inverse conditional probability is larger because we started with the assumption that only 20% of athletes dope.

This example highlights several important things. First, working through the frequencies is not super-easy, but it is doable. Second, however we carry out the calculation we need the probability that the test comes out positive for each of the groups, dopers and non-dopers (these are $P(event_1 \mid event_2)$ and $P(event_1 \mid \sim event_2)$).

Third, we need the overall fraction of athletes that dope. That is $P(event_2)$ in the formulae above. This proportion is sometimes called the **base rate**. Without the base rate we can't compute the inverse probability. Unfortunately, we may not know the base rate. A good practice in such cases is to use several plausible values and give a range of inverse conditional probabilities.

In our example, we assumed a base rate of 20%: 200 out of 1000 athletes use doping. If, instead we assumed a 5% base rate (50 out of 1000 doped) a test with a 10% positive rate for non-dopers (and 100% positive rate for dopers) would result in 50 dopers among the positively tested and 95 non-dopers (10% of 950). Thus the likelihood of doping conditional on a positive test is only 34% ($= 50/(50 + 95)$. On the other hand, if we assumed a 50% base rate (500 out of 1000 doped) the same test would result in 500 dopers among the positively tested and 50 non-dopers. In this case the likelihood of doping conditional on a positive test is a high 91% ($= 500/(500 + 50)$. The base rate has a substantial effect on the result. With few dopers an imperfect test would give more misleading results than the same imperfect test with many dopers.

5 Generalizing from Data

How to generalize the results of analysis of your data and how to assess the validity and the limits of such generalizations

Motivation

How likely is it that you will experience a large loss on your investment portfolio of company stocks? To answer this, you have collected data on past returns of your portfolio and calculated the frequency of large losses. Based on this frequency, how can you tell what likelihood to expect in the coming calendar year? And can you quantify the uncertainty about that expectation in a meaningful way?

How is the quality of management among manufacturing firms related to how much they export to foreign markets? You have data on a sample of manufacturing firms, and you can calculate various measures of association in your data. But you are interested in that association among all firms, not just this sample, and you are interested in how that may look like in the near future. Can you generalize the findings in the sample to all firms and to the future? And can you assess the quality, and uncertainty, of such generalization?

Most often, we analyze the data we have to help a decision in a situation that's not included in the data. To do so, we need to generalize the results of our analysis from the data we have to the situation we care about. The most important questions are whether we can generalize the results, and whether we can quantify the uncertainty brought about by such a generalization.

We start this chapter by discussing the two steps of the process of generalization: generalizing from the data to a general pattern it represents, such as a population, and assessing how the situation we care about relates to the general pattern our data represents. The first task is statistical inference. We introduce the conceptual framework of repeated samples. We introduce the standard error and the confidence interval that quantify the uncertainty of this step of generalization. We introduce two methods to estimate the standard error, the bootstrap and the standard error formula. We then discuss external validity of the results of an analysis, which is the second step of generalization: from the general pattern our data represents to the general pattern behind the situation we care about. While there are no readily available methods to quantify the uncertainty this step brings to the results, we discuss how we can think about it and how we can use the results of additional data analysis to assess it.

The case study **What likelihood of loss to expect on a stock portfolio?** examines the probability of large negative returns on financial assets and how to infer that probability in future investment situations using the data at hand. It uses the sp500 dataset. This case study illustrates not only how statistical inference works but also its limitations.

Learning outcomes

After working through this chapter, you should be able to:

- think about generalization beyond the actual data;
- understand the concept and logic of statistical inference and external validity;
- understand the concepts of repeated samples and bootstrap;
- compute and use standard errors to create confidence intervals and use those for statistical inference;
- understand whether and how additional data analysis can help assess external validity.

5.1 When to Generalize and to What?

Sometimes we analyze our data with the goal of learning about patterns in that data itself, among the observations it contains. When we search for a good deal among offers of hotels or used cars, all we care about are the hotels, or cars, in our data. In such cases there is no need to generalize our findings to any other situation. More often, though, we analyze a dataset in order to learn about patterns that are likely to be true in other situations.

Examples for the need to generalize are plentiful. We may analyze data on used cars to determine what price we may get for a similar car that we own. Or, we may use data on a sample of working people from a country in certain occupations to assess what wage current students studying for such occupations may expect. Or, we may analyze data on the history of returns on an investment portfolio to assess the probability of losses of a certain magnitude in the future.

In all of these latter cases we want to infer something from the data at hand for a situation we care about, but which is not contained in the data. The data on used cars does not include our car. The sample of working people includes only a subset of all working people in the country, and it is about the past not about the future we care about. The data on the history of portfolio returns covers the past, whereas we are interested in the likelihood of losses in the future.

This chapter focuses on how to generalize the results from a dataset to other situations. The act of generalization is called **inference**: we infer something from our data about a more general phenomenon because we want to use that knowledge in some other situation. Inference is best broken down into two steps: generalizing from the data to the general pattern it represents, and generalizing from that general pattern to the general pattern that is behind the situation we truly care about. These may sound a little cryptic at first, so let's discuss them in detail.

The first step is **statistical inference**, which aims at generalizing to the situation that our data represents, using statistical methods. Our data may represent a population if it's a representative sample (see Chapter 1, Section 1.8). More generally, it may represent a general pattern. To be able to generalize to it, that general pattern needs to exist, and it needs to be stable over time and space.

The simplest case here is a random sample that represents a well-defined **population**. As we defined it earlier (see Chapter 1, Section 1.8), a sample is representative of a population if the distribution of all variables is very similar in both. Having learned more about distributions of many variables in Chapter 4, we can be more specific now: the joint distribution of all variables needs to be similar. That includes conditional distributions and correlations, too. For example, a dataset on market analysts in your country from last year with variables age, gender, and salary represents the population of all market analysts in your country last year if the distribution of gender, age, and salary is very similar in the data and the population, including conditional statistics such as average salary by age and gender.

The **general pattern** is a more abstract concept, but, often it can also be something rather specific. Examples include the probability of a large loss on our portfolio, or how much more likely better managed firms in medium-sized medium-income countries are to export to foreign markets. For our data to represent this general pattern, it is not necessary that all variables have the same distribution. Instead, we require that the specific pattern (a likelihood, a conditional probability, a conditional mean) is the same. But we want that similarity not purely for a well-defined population but reflecting something more general that's behind our data. Examples include what determined the history of asset returns, or all the things that influenced the relationship between management quality and exporting in medium-sized medium-income economies during the time our data was collected.

Generalizing to a general pattern that our data represents can make sense even when our data covers an entire population. For example, our data may include all companies in India that were in business in 2016. Thus, the management quality–exporting association in the data is what it is in the population of firms in 2016. However, we rarely carry out data analysis to learn about a specific population at a specific time in the past. Instead, we want to learn about something more general: in India at other times, or in other countries like India.

When making statistical inference, we can use readily available tools to learn about the general pattern our data represents. Those tools can quantify the uncertainty about this step of generalization. We'll introduce the toolbox of statistical inference in the subsequent sections of this chapter.

The second step is assessing the **external validity** of the results. External validity is about whether the general pattern our data represents is the same as the general pattern that would be relevant for the situation we truly care about. Whatever lies behind gender differences in earnings in the population that our data represents may or may not be similar to whatever will determine gender differences five years from now in our country, or in a different country. Whatever made large losses likely during the time that our data is from may or may not be similar to what would make large losses possible in the future we care about.

If the general pattern behind the situation we care about and the data we have is the same, what we uncover from our data has high external validity for the situation we care about. If, on the other hand, the general pattern behind the situation we care about is different from the general pattern that our data represents, whatever we uncover from our data would have low external validity. External validity is best thought of as a continuum, from very high (our data represents the same general pattern we are interested in) through medium (the two general patterns are similar but not the same) to very low (the two general patterns are very different). Assessing external validity requires thinking and knowledge about the situations; statistical methods can help in indirect ways only. We shall return to external validity and challenges to it later in this chapter.

In contrast with statistical inference, we don't have statistical methods that give direct answers to the degree of external validity. And there are no methods that can quantify the extra degree of uncertainty (although one branch of advanced statistics, called **Bayesian statistics**, makes an attempt at this, but that's beyond the scope of our textbook). Instead, assessing external validity is a thinking exercise that requires knowledge about the patterns themselves, and it usually results in qualitative statements about how high or low external validity is in our case.

In practice, the goal of most analyses is a quantitative summary of patterns: in the simplest case, it is a **statistic**. A statistic, as we discussed, is a number that we can calculate from the data. Examples include uncovering a probability, a correlation coefficient, or a difference between two groups. Using a somewhat simplistic but useful terminology, we want to infer the **true value** of the statistic after having computed its **estimated value** from actual data. The true value is a shorthand for the value in a population or a general pattern. Using this terminology, external validity is about the extent to which the true value of the statistic is similar in the general pattern our data represents and the general pattern that's behind the situation we care about. The goal of statistical inference is to uncover the true value of the statistic in the general pattern, or population, that our data represents. The starting point of statistical inference is the estimated value of the statistic that we calculate from our data. It is called an estimated value because the reason for calculating it is to uncover (estimate) the true value.

Review Box 5.1 Generalization from a dataset

- Inference is the act of generalizing from the data to some more general pattern.
- In practice it amounts to conjecturing the true value of a statistic given its estimated value.
- The true value of the statistic is its value in a population, or general pattern.
- It is good practice to split the inference process into two parts:
  - Use statistical inference to uncover what the true value may be in the population, or general pattern, the data represents.
  - Assess external validity: define the population, or general pattern, you are interested in; define the population, or general pattern, the data represents; compare the two.

5.A1 CASE STUDY – What Likelihood of Loss to Expect on a Stock Portfolio?

Question and data

The case study in this chapter aims to assess the likelihood of experiencing a loss of a certain magnitude on an investment portfolio from one day to the next day. The goal is to guess the frequency of such a loss for the coming calendar year. This is an inference problem: we use data from the past to learn something about a different situation, the future. First, let's think about external validity. The general pattern we care about is the pattern that determines the probability of large losses in the coming year. That may or may not be the same general pattern that determined the frequency of large losses in our data, covering past years. For now, let's proceed assuming that the general pattern remains the same, and let's return to this question at the end of our case study. The main part of the analysis will be statistical inference: assessing the likelihood of a large loss in the general pattern represented by our data.

The investment portfolio in this case study is the S&P500, a stock market index based on company shares listed on the New York Stock Exchange and Nasdaq. It is the weighted average of the price of 500 company shares and thus it is an investment portfolio with 500 company shares, each with its appropriate proportion.

The data includes day-to-day returns on the S&P500, defined as percentage changes in the closing price of the index between two consecutive days. It covers 11 years starting with August 25, 2006 and ending with August 26, 2016. It includes 2519 days. This is time series data at daily frequency. The original data has gaps as there are no observations for the days the markets are closed, such as weekends and holidays. The data used in this case study ignores those gaps and simply takes returns between two consecutive days the markets were open. Figure 5.1 shows the histogram of daily returns.

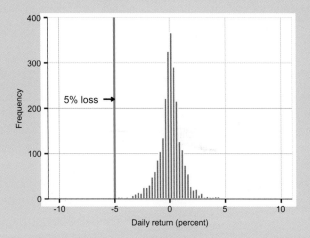

Figure 5.1   Histogram of daily returns in the entire data

Note: Day-to-day (gaps ignored) changes, as percentages. From August 25, 2006 to August 26, 2016.
Source: sp500 dataset. S&P500 market index. N=2519.

To define large loss, we take a day-to-day loss exceeding 5%. That is a rare event, but it's not extremely rare. The histogram shows that −5% cutoff with a vertical line. We define large loss as a binary variable, taking the value one when the day-to-day loss exceeds 5% and zero otherwise. The statistic in the data is the proportion of days with such losses. It is 0.5% in this data: the S&P500 portfolio lost more than 5% of its value on 13 out of the 2519 market days between August 25, 2006 and August 26, 2016. What can we infer from this 0.5% chance for the next calendar year?

Note a limitation to our question: it is about the likelihood of a 5% or larger loss. It is not about the probability of a very large loss of, say, 20%. Nor is it about the expected value of losses. That's not because these other questions are less interesting. It's because our data does not allow for answering them. The largest loss on the S&P500 is 9% in our data, so the likelihood of larger losses is impossible to infer from our data, even though they are not impossible of course.

5.2   Repeated Samples, Sampling Distribution, Standard Error

The conceptual background to statistical inference is **repeated samples**. The basic idea is that the data we observe is one example of many datasets that could have been observed. Each of those potentially observed datasets can be viewed as a sample drawn from the population, or the more abstract general pattern. When our data is in fact a sample from a well-defined population, it is easy to see that many other samples could have turned out instead of what we have.

That would be the case with data on the earnings of market analysts. We have data from a sample taken from the population of all market analysts from the USA last year; another random draw would have resulted in a different sample of individuals.

When the data is representative of a more abstract general pattern, the concept of repeated samples is more abstract, too. The data of returns on an investment portfolio is an example: our data is best thought of as a particular realization of the history of returns that could have turned out differently. Another example is when our data consists of a population, such as all firms in India that were in business in 2016. Here the management practices and performance of those firms are just one realization of what could have happened in a country like India in a year like 2016.

The goal of statistical inference is learning the value of a statistic in the population, or general pattern, represented by our data. With repeated samples, the statistic has a distribution: its value may differ from sample to sample. Within each sample the calculated value of the statistic is called an **estimate** of the statistic. The distribution of the statistic is called its **sampling distribution**. The difference between female and male market analysts could have turned out differently in a different sample. The distribution of the quality of management may have been different if we chose a different sample of firms. The proportion of days with a 5% or larger loss on an investment portfolio may have turned out different if we could re-run history.

The sampling distribution of a statistic shows the values that the estimated statistic takes across repeated samples. The most important aspect of this sampling distribution is its standard deviation: how much spread there is across repeated samples. The standard deviation of the sampling distribution has a specific name: it is the **standard error**, abbreviated as **SE**, of the statistic. The name originates from the fact that any particular estimate is likely to be an erroneous estimate of the true value. The magnitude of that typical error is one SE.

Review Box 5.2   Sampling distribution

- The sampling distribution is the distribution of the estimates of the statistic across many repeated samples of the same size.
- The standard deviation of the sampling distribution is called the standard error (SE) of the estimated statistic.

5.A2   CASE STUDY – What Likelihood of Loss to Expect on a Stock Portfolio?

Repeated samples, standard error

The situation we care about in our case study is returns on the S&P500 portfolio next year. The data we have is returns on the S&P500 portfolio for a period of 11 years. The statistic of interest to us is the proportion of days with 5% or larger losses. This is a single number in our data: 0.5%. Statistical inference answers the question of what the proportion of such days could be in the general pattern that governed the observed history of returns.

The fraction of 5%+ losses could have turned out different in those 11 years if history played out differently. That history could have turned out differently is an assumption, but one that sounds reasonable, and we'll maintain that assumption throughout this case study. This is the main idea behind the concept of repeated samples.

Ideally, we would like to analyze many repeated samples of that 11-year history: alternative series of daily returns that could have happened instead of the one that did happen. We cannot re-run history, of course. In the following sections we'll learn methods that help make an educated guess of what could have happened had we been able to re-run history. For now, let's consider an artificial but educational example.

In this artificial example we carry out a **simulation exercise** to illustrate the concept of the sampling distribution. Simulation exercises are used often in statistics. The main idea behind simulation exercises is to create an artificial world where we know the true value of the statistic and see whether and how a particular method can uncover it. In our case that means knowing the true fraction of 5%+ losses in the general pattern that is behind what we observe in the data we have, and see what its estimated value looks like across repeated samples from that general pattern.

Of course we don't know the true value of the general pattern behind the 11-year history we observe. Instead, in this exercise we replace the question with one to which we know the answer. Suppose, for the sake of this artificial example, that the 11-year data is all there is. It is the population, with the general pattern: the fraction of days with 5%+ losses is 0.5% in the entire 11 years' data. That's the true value. The question is how we could uncover this true value if we had data not on all 11 years but only a part of it.

So, in the next step of the simulation exercise let's forget that we know this true value. Assume, instead, that we have only four years' worth of daily returns in our data. Our task is then to estimate the true value (in the entire 11-year period) from the data we have (4 years). In the course of this exercise we can directly look at repeated samples because we can draw many random samples of 4-year time series from the 11-year time series we have. Those 4-year time series may be different from each other, thus the fraction of days with 5%+ losses may vary across them.

There are many ways to draw a sample of four years. For simplicity let's define four years of stock market data as 1000 days of data (there are approximately 250 workdays in a year). We could start with the first 1000 days, then the next 1000 days and so on – but that would yield only two whole samples. Alternatively, we could start with the first 1000 days, then the 1000 days starting with the second day, and so on. Instead, we opt for a third approach: simple random sampling. We start with the 11-year data, consider each day in it, one after the other, and we select or don't select each day in an independent random fashion.

(Note that this kind of sampling destroys the time series nature of our original data as the observations in the samples are not necessarily days next to each other. That is fine if the variable of interest, daily returns, is independent across days in the original data: whatever the return is on one day has nothing to do with whatever it is on any other day, including the previous day or the subsequent day. It turns out that there is some dependence across daily returns, but it's very weak and we'll ignore it in this exercise.)

So that's what we did. We took many random samples of 1000 days and computed the percentage share of days with 5%+ loss in each sample. The power of this exercise lies in the fact that we can do this many times, creating many repeated samples from the same population.

Figure 5.2 shows the histogram created from the 10 000 random samples, each with 1000 observations, drawn from the entire data. For each of these 10 000 samples, we have calculated the percentage of days with losses of 5% or more; those are the estimates of the statistics. The histogram shows the absolute frequency (out of 10 000) of the various values of the estimates across the repeated samples.

The histogram shows a distribution that has quite some spread: in some of the samples none of the days experienced such losses (0%); in other samples as many as 2% of the days did. Most values are closer to 0.5%. In fact, the average of these values across the repeated samples is 0.5%, very close to the true value in the entire 11-year dataset that we aim to estimate (the difference is in the second decimal point).

The standard deviation of this sampling distribution is 0.2. That means that in a particular sample, we can expect to be 0.2% off from the mean across samples, which, as we have seen, is also equal to the true value. This is the standard error of the statistic of interest (the fraction of 5%+ losses).

The third thing to note about this sampling distribution is its shape. The histogram shows a bell-shaped, or approximately normal, distribution (see Chapter 3, Under the Hood section 3.U1.)

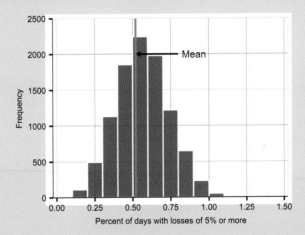

Figure 5.2 Histogram of simulated number of days with big losses

Note: Histogram of the proportion of days with losses of 5% or more, across repeated samples of size N=1000. 10 000 random samples.
Source: sp500 dataset. Daily closing values of the S&P500 stock market index.

5.3 Properties of the Sampling Distribution

As we introduced in the previous section, the sampling distribution of a statistic is the distribution of this statistic across repeated samples. The sampling distribution has three important properties that are true in general. (To be more precise, they are true whenever the statistic is an average.) These properties are:

1. The average of the values in repeated samples is approximately equal to its true value (the value in the entire population, or general pattern, represented by our data).
2. The sampling distribution is approximately normal.
3. The standard error (the standard deviation of the sampling distribution) is smaller the larger the sample, with a proportionality factor of the square root of the sample size.

The first property is called **unbiasedness**: the average computed from a representative sample is an unbiased estimate of the average in the entire population.

The second property is called **asymptotic normality**, or **approximate normality**. The "approximate" adjective means that the distribution is close to normal. The "asymptotic" adjective means that the larger the sample, the closer the distribution is to normal. Looking at larger and larger samples, the closer and closer the sampling distribution is to normal.

The third property is called **root-n convergence**: the standard error (the standard deviation of the sampling distribution) is inversely proportional to the square root of the sample size. As we look at larger and larger samples, the standard deviation is smaller and smaller by the square root of the sample size.

One consequence of root-n convergence is that the standard deviation is very small in very large samples. Taking this to its mathematical extreme, as we look at samples that are infinitely large, the standard deviation shrinks to zero. In that hypothetical extreme case, the sampling distribution is not really a distribution but yields the same value in virtually all of the repeated samples.

Because the sampling distribution is approximately normal, we know that the measured values fall within plus or minus two standard errors (SE) of the truth approximately 95% of the time. Similarly, we know that they fall within plus or minus 1.6 SE of the truth with a 90% chance, and within 2.6 SE with a 99% chance.

In reality, we don't get to observe the sampling distribution. If we did, we would know what the true value was: it would be just its center, the mean of the sampling distribution. Instead, we observe data that is one of the many potential samples that could have been drawn from the population, or general pattern. However, it turns out that we can get a very good idea of what the sampling distribution would look like even from a single sample. We won't be able to locate its center. But, with appropriate tools, we'll get a pretty good estimate of the standard error. And with that, we'll be able to come up with a range of where the true value may be, using our knowledge that the sampling distribution is approximately normal.

Review Box 5.3   Properties of the sampling distribution

- The sampling distribution of a statistic that can be expressed as an average has three properties:

    1. Its mean approximately equals the true value.
    2. It is approximately normal.
    3. Its standard deviation is inversely proportional to the square root of the size of the sample.

- These properties are approximate; the approximation is better, the larger the sample.

5.A3 CASE STUDY – What Likelihood of Loss to Expect on a Stock Portfolio?

Sampling distribution with different sample sizes

We can carry out similar simulation exercises with different sample sizes. For example, let's look at samples of 500 days, half as many as we had earlier. The distribution of the fraction of days with 5% or larger losses are summarized by the two histograms shown together in Figure 5.3. The histograms have the same bins; within each bin, they show the number of draws (out of 10 000) for which the estimate (the proportion of days with large losses) falls within the bin. For example, in the bin (0.8, 1), we have 512 cases for the $N = 1000$ exercise and 1250 cases for the $N = 500$ exercise with values of 0.8 or 1.

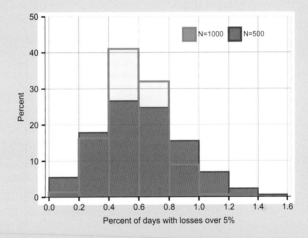

Figure 5.3   Histograms of big loss simulations with $N = 500$ and $N = 1000$

Note: Histogram of the proportion of days with losses of 5% or more, across 10,000 repeated samples in two simulation exercises, with $N = 500$ and $N = 1000$.
Source: sp500 dataset. Daily closing values of the S&P500 stock market index.

The figures show that, with 500 observations, more of the estimates are in the smallest and the largest bins, and fewer of the estimates are in the middle bins, than with 1000 observations. The mean of the two sampling distributions is very similar, around 0.5%, but the distribution that corresponds to the smaller sample is more spread out. The standard deviation of the fraction estimates across the repeated samples is 0.3 for 500 observations, and it is 0.2 for 1000 observations. Both distributions are approximately bell shaped, with some skewness with a longer right tail. The distribution of the smaller sample (500 observations) is more skewed.

Recall that the main properties of the sampling distribution are unbiasedness, approximate (asymptotic) normality, and root-n convergence. The results in this simulation exercise are in line with those properties. Recall also that the properties hold if the statistic is an average. Our statistic turns out to fit that criterion. The proportion of days with a 5%+ loss is the average of a binary indicator variable with a value of one on all days with a 5%+ loss and a value of zero on all other days (the average is 0.5% or 0.005 in our data).

A side note: how can then the fraction of 5%+ losses be normally distributed across repeated samples when it can never be negative? The answer is that the normal distribution is never literally true. Instead, it is always an approximation. Taken literally, the normal distribution would allow not only for negative values but also irrational values such as pi or the square root of two. Returns on portfolios don't take these values either, at least not the way that we define them. The question is how close the distribution is to this ideal normal distribution. Going back to the histogram of the sampling distribution with $N = 1000$, we can see that it's fairly close. So saying that the distribution is approximately normal may make sense even if it can't be literally normal.

5.4   The Confidence Interval

The **confidence interval (CI)** is the most important measure of statistical inference. Recall that we use statistical inference when we analyze a dataset to infer the true value of a statistic: its value in the population, or general pattern, represented by our data. The idea of a CI is to tell us a range where we can expect the true value in the population, or the general pattern, to lie. More than that: the idea of the CI is to give us a range, in which we can expect the true value to lie with a certain probability. That probability is something data analysts need to pick. Typical probability picks are 95% or 90%. The "95% CI" gives the range of values where we think that the true value falls with a 95% likelihood. It also says that we think that with 5% likelihood, the true value will fall outside the confidence interval. Well this is at least what we would like the CI to tell us. Things are a little more complicated, but we'll discuss those complications in Section 5.5.

The confidence interval is constructed as a symmetric range around the estimated value of the statistic in our data. We first calculate the estimated value of the statistic in our data. Then we specify the length of the CI on the two sides of the estimated value. But how do we know the length of the appropriate CI? It turns out that the key is the standard error (SE): the SE is the general unit of measurement when constructing confidence intervals. The appropriate 95% CI is the ± 2 SE or, more precisely, 1.96 SE interval around the estimate from the data. The appropriate 90% CI is the ± 1.6 SE interval around the estimate from the data; and the appropriate 99% CI is the ± 2.6 SE interval around it.

In practice we don't know the sampling distribution so we don't know the appropriate standard error. So we need to estimate it somehow: come up with a good guess using the data we have. The next two sections describe two approaches that give good estimates of the SE. Before discussing them, let's spend some time understanding why the CI constructed this way may tell us where to expect the true value.

Here is an intuitive argument. Assume that you know the sampling distribution. The histogram of the sampling distribution shows the frequency of particular values of the estimates across repeated samples from the same population (or general pattern). Ninety-five percent of all estimates are within two standard errors of its center (± 2 SE). Now take any value within that range. Measure the 95% confidence interval around this value: it is ± 2 SE. The center of the sampling distribution will be within this interval. Recall that the center of the sampling distribution is the true value. Thus, the true value will be within the interval as long as we measure it around a point within ± 2 SE of the center. If we were to measure the same interval around points outside that range, the true value would not be contained in it. The fraction of the samples for which this interval contains the true value is 95%; the fraction of the samples for which this interval does not contain the true value is 5%. That's why this is the 95% CI we are looking for: this interval contains the truth in 95% of the times among repeated samples. Viewed from the perspective of a single sample, the chance that the truth is within the CI measured around the value estimated from that single sample is 95%.

5.A4 CASE STUDY – What Likelihood of Loss to Expect on a Stock Portfolio?

Repeated samples and confidence interval

Let's return to our simulation example of repeated samples of 1000 days where the statistic is the proportion of days with losses of 5% or more. If we know the sampling distribution of this proportion, we know its standard deviation. That's the standard error (SE), and its value is 0.2 here. The mean of the sampling distribution is 0.5. Thus, the fraction of days with losses of 5% or more is within 0.1 and 0.9% in 95% of the samples ($0.5 \pm 2 \times 0.2$).

Recall that this sampling distribution is from 1000-day samples. If, instead of 1000 days, we measured the fraction of 5%+ loss days in samples of 500 days, the SE would be 0.3; the fraction of days with losses of 5% or more would be within 0 and 1.1% in 95% of the samples ($0.5 \pm 2 \times 0.3$ and recognizing that the fraction can't be negative so the lower bound is zero).

5.5 Discussion of the CI: Confidence or Probability?

Having introduced the confidence interval and how we can compute it if we know the SE, let us discuss a bit more what we exactly mean by a CI. It turns out that there are two major leaps in the intuitive reasoning we presented in the previous section.

The first one is conceptual. The 95% probability that a statistic is within a range in a particular sample is the 95% frequency that it would occur in repeated samples. This probability is thus a relative frequency. In contrast, our "95% confidence" that the true value is within a range has no corresponding frequency to consider. The population, or general pattern, is not repeated. Rather, this 95% confidence characterizes our personal feeling of uncertainty. That's why we call it "confidence" and not probability. But for the argument to work, that confidence needs to be a probability, even if it cannot be defined through frequencies. It is a "subjective probability," a concept that we mentioned when we first discussed probabilities in Chapter 3, Section 3.2.

The second leap builds on the first one and takes the 95% confidence as a probability. If so, it is a conditional probability: the probability that the true value is within an interval conditional on the estimated value. This conditional probability is the inverse of the probability that the estimated value falls in an interval conditional on the true value. It is this latter probability that we can derive from the approximately normal sampling distribution. And, as we discussed in the Under the Hood section 4.U1 of Chapter 4, inverse conditional probabilities are not equal in general. Here, for the two to be equal, we need to assume that, without the data, we would have no idea what the true value could be. In particular, we have no prior knowledge, or even a guess, of the true value. Note that, more often than not, we do have some idea about the true value: the average price of cars like ours cannot be anything, the fraction of days with large losses is unlikely to be very high, and so on. Nevertheless, we usually go ahead and interpret the confidence interval as if we had no prior idea.

Bayesian statistics, a branch of statistics that we mentioned earlier in Section 5.1, takes these issues seriously. It works with the assumption that analysts can quantify their prior ideas and takes those into account for inference. We don't cover Bayesian statistics in this book. Instead, we construct and interpret confidence intervals the way most data analysts do, maintaining the assumption of classical statistical inference: as analysts we approach every inference problem with a completely open mind about what the true value may be.

So far all this is just theory. We can't come up with a CI in practice unless we know the standard error, but we can't know it by looking at the distribution of repeated samples as we only observe a single one of those repeated samples. However, statistics offers not one but two solutions to make a good guess of the SE from that single sample. Both solutions are quite ingenious, but neither is simple to understand. Some of us would argue that these solutions are among the things that make statistics exciting – you could say, beautiful.

5.6 Estimating the Standard Error with the Bootstrap Method

Recall our simulation study: we took many samples of the same size from the original data to construct the sampling distribution of the statistic we were after. We introduced three important properties of the sampling distribution: unbiasedness, root-n convergence, and approximate (asymptotic) normality. We illustrated how to get a sampling distribution with the help of an artificial example: the true value of a statistic to figure out was actually its value in the entire dataset. We wanted to see the sampling distribution of this true value's estimates from data with fewer observations.

But that was an artificial situation. In practice we examine all the data we have, and we would like to uncover the sampling distribution of a statistic in samples similar to that data. In particular, we want the sampling distribution of samples of the same size as the original data, all of which represent the same population or, more generally, the same general pattern.

The **bootstrap** is a method to achieve just that: it creates the sampling distribution across repeated samples that are representative of the same population, or general pattern, as the original data and also have the same size. The bootstrap method stretches the logic of the simulation exercise to draw samples using the data we have, and those samples have the same size as the original data yet are different from it. We might think that this should be impossible just like it is impossible to pull yourself out of the swamp by your bootstraps. Hence the name of the method. It turns out, however, that the trick is possible here.

The bootstrap method takes the original data and draws many repeated samples of the size of that data. The trick is that the samples are drawn with replacement. The observations are drawn randomly one by one from the original data; once an observation is drawn it is "replaced" into the pool so that it can be drawn again, with the same probability as any other observation. The drawing stops when the sample reaches the size of the original data. The result is a sample of the same size as the original data, yielding a single **bootstrap sample**. This bootstrap sample includes some of the original observations multiple times, and it does not include some of the other original observations. Perhaps surprisingly, in data that are moderately large, more than one third of the original observations in the data don't end up in a typical bootstrap sample.

Repeating this sampling many times, the bootstrap method creates many repeated samples that are different from each other, but each has the same size as the original data. The miracle of the bootstrap is that the distribution of a statistic across these repeated bootstrap samples is a good approximation to the sampling distribution we are after: what the distribution would look like across samples similar to the original data.

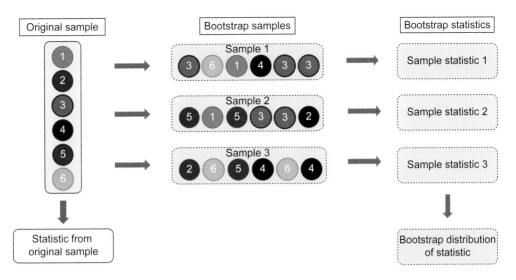

Figure 5.4 Bootstrap samples

Note: Illustration of the bootstrap method of uncovering the sampling distribution of the estimates of a statistic. Three bootstrap samples drawn from the original sample; in each bootstrap sample some observations from the original sample are included more than once and some observations are not included.

The bootstrap method works if the variable we consider is independent across observations: its value is not related to its previous values or subsequent values. By sampling observations one by one and then replacing them into the pool to be possibly drawn again, we destroy the before–after relationships in the original data. That is not a problem if there is no relationship across observations, which is true in most cross-sectional data. If there is an important relationship, as in many kinds of time series data, this bootstrap method does not work. (Some time series variables may be independent across observations, as we had in our case study.) Note that there are more sophisticated bootstrap methods that work with time series data by preserving relationships across observations, but we don't consider those in this textbook.

Since the distribution of a statistic across bootstrap samples is a good approximation of the sampling distribution, it gives a good approximation of the standard error, too. The **bootstrap estimate of the standard error** is the standard deviation of the estimated values of the statistic across the bootstrap samples.

Once we have the standard error, we have everything we need for constructing the confidence interval of our choice. First, we take the value of the statistic estimated from the original data. Second, we take the standard error computed with the bootstrap. Using these two numbers, we calculate the confidence interval, for instance taking the ± 2 SE for the 95% CI.

The bootstrap is based on a clever yet conceptually simple idea. It is computationally intensive: the computer has to take many random draws, calculate the estimated value of the statistic across many samples, store those results, and then calculate the standard deviation. All this is done by the machine, so it may take some time, but it is not the data analyst's time.

If the bootstrap sounds like a miracle, something too good to be true, it is because there is something to that. The bootstrap does indeed have its limitations, on top of the independence we discussed above. For example, it tends to provide very poor standard error estimates in the presence of extreme values. In fact, if the data has very extreme values, such as in the power-law distribution, the standard error estimates are way too small and very misleading. Moreover, the bootstrap may produce poor standard error estimates in small samples if the statistic is not the mean but the median or some other quantile. At the same time, there are many extensions of the bootstrap that can deal with some of its problems. In this textbook we focus on the average and related statistics of variables that are independent across observations: situations that are well suited for bootstrap standard error estimation.

It turns out that the largest advantage to SE estimation by the bootstrap method is that, in large datasets, it allows us to estimate confidence intervals for statistics other than averages. This includes quantiles or nonlinear functions of averages. This is a big advantage as the other method, which we'll discuss in the next section, is not available for many of those statistics.

Review Box 5.4   The bootstrap method

- The bootstrap is a method to generate samples that represent the same population, or general pattern, as our original data and also have the same size.
- Each bootstrap sample is a random sample from the original data with replacement. The bootstrap procedure generates many such samples, approximating the sampling distribution of a statistic.
- We use the bootstrap method to get the standard error (SE) of the estimate of a statistic: it is the standard deviation of the estimated value of the statistic across the bootstrap samples.

5.A5   CASE STUDY – What Likelihood of Loss to Expect on a Stock Portfolio?

Bootstrap standard error estimation

Going back to our example, the task is to estimate the confidence interval for the proportion of days with large negative returns. First, we estimate that proportion from the data: we have already done that, it is 0.5%. The second step is estimating its standard error. The third step is measuring plus and minus two standard errors around that 0.5% value. The result will be the 95% CI that tells us where to expect the majority of days with large negative returns in the general pattern represented by our data.

We estimate the standard error by bootstrap. We apply the bootstrap procedure we studied that is applicable for variables that are independent across observations. As we noted earlier, there appears to be some dependence in this data but it's weak and we ignore it.

Then the procedure is as follows. Take the original data and draw a bootstrap sample. Calculate the proportions of days with 5%+ loss in that sample. Save that value. Then go back to the original data and take another bootstrap sample. Calculate the proportion of days with 5%+ loss and save that value, too. And so on, repeated many times. In the end, we end up with a new data table, in which one observation stands for one bootstrap sample, and the only variable contained in it is the estimated proportion for each bootstrap sample. The standard error we are after is simply the standard deviation of those estimated values in this new data.

We created 10 000 bootstrap samples from the original data. Each bootstrap sample had 2519 observations just like the original data. We calculated the estimate of the statistic in each: the proportion of days with 5%+ loss. Its value varied across the bootstrap samples, from as low as

0.1% to as high as 1.2%. On average, the value of the statistic was 0.5, equal to its value in the original data. The median is equal to the mean, indicating a symmetric distribution.

Figure 5.5 shows the bootstrap distribution: the sampling distribution of the fraction of days with 5%+ losses across the 10 000 bootstrap samples. The histogram shows a bell-shaped distribution, as it should.

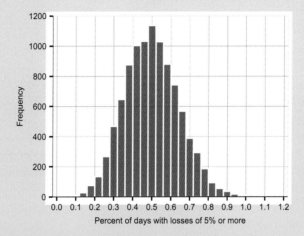

Figure 5.5   Bootstrap distribution of the proportion of days with losses of 5% or more

Note: 10 000 bootstrap samples from the original data; each had 2519 observations just like the original data.
Source: sp500 dataset. Daily closing values of the S&P500 stock market index.

The goal of this exercise was to get the standard error of the statistic, which is the standard deviation across the bootstrap samples. Here that value is 0.14: this is the bootstrap SE estimate. With the standard error estimate at hand, we are ready to construct the confidence interval. The 95% CI is 0.5% ± 2 × 0.14%, which is [0.22%, 0.78%] using values rounded to the second decimal. Its interpretation: in the general pattern represented by the 11-year history of returns in our data, we can be 95% confident that the chance of daily losses of more than 5% is somewhere between 0.22% and 0.78%.

5.7   The Standard Error Formula

The bootstrap method reconstructs the entire sampling distribution and calculates the standard error directly from that distribution. In this section we show an alternative approach: using a formula for the standard error, without the need to simulate the entire sampling distribution by bootstrap or any other method.

The case we consider is a variable whose value is independent across observations in the data, just like for the bootstrap. The statistic we consider is the average. In this case we know that the sampling distribution is approximately normal, with the true value as its mean. We have seen that the standard error, which is the standard deviation of the sampling distribution, depends on the size of the sample.

We called that dependence root-n convergence, as the standard error decreases by the square root of the sample size.

There is a relatively simple formula for the standard error (SE) of the average ($\bar{x}$). The formula includes the root-n factor and just one other element. $\bar{x}$ is the mean value of x in the sample; it is the estimate of the true mean value of x in the general pattern (or the population).

The **standard error formula** for $\bar{x}$ is

$$SE(\bar{x}) = \frac{1}{\sqrt{n}} Std[x] \tag{5.1}$$

where $Std[x]$ is the standard deviation of the variable in the data (the square root of its variance), and n is the number of observations in the data. We emphasize again that this formula is valid if the values of x are independent across observations in the data. There are corresponding SE formulae for variables with dependence across observations. We'll consider some of them in Chapters 9, 12, and 23 in this textbook.

The standard error is larger, the smaller the sample and the larger the standard deviation of the variable. The first of these we know already, it's root-n convergence. The second one is new. The relation of $SE(\bar{x})$ to $Std[x]$ is not an obvious one, but it makes intuitive sense. Recall that the standard error of $\bar{x}$ is the standard deviation of the various $\bar{x}$ estimates across repeated samples. The larger the standard deviation of x itself, the more variation we can expect in $\bar{x}$ across repeated samples. At the extreme, if x is always the same so that $Std[x] = 0$, its average value estimated in various repeated samples should be the same, too, so that $SE(\bar{x}) = 0$.

The standard error formula is built into all statistical packages. Therefore, we rarely compute it using the formula ourselves. Nevertheless, we think it is instructive to memorize this simple formula for the intuition it contains.

Review Box 5.5 The standard error formula

- The standard error formula of the estimate of an average is

$$SE(\bar{x}) = \frac{1}{\sqrt{n}} Std[x] \tag{5.2}$$

- This formula gives a good estimate of the standard error if the values of x are independent across observations in the data.
- $SE(\bar{x})$ is larger if:
  - the number of observations, n, is smaller;
  - the standard deviation of the variable, $Std[x]$, is larger.

5.A6 CASE STUDY – What Likelihood of Loss to Expect on a Stock Portfolio?

The standard error formula

Let's consider our example of 11 years' data on daily returns of the S&P500 portfolio. The size of the sample is n = 2519 so that $\sqrt{(1/n)} = 0.02$. The standard deviation of the fraction of 5%+

losses is 0.07. Multiplying 0.07 by 0.02 results in 0.0014, or 0.14%. This is the same number that we got from the bootstrap exercise.

With the same SE as in the bootstrap, the CI and its interpretation are the same, too: the 95% CI is [0.22, 0.78]. This means that in the general pattern represented by the 11-year history of returns in our data, we can be 95% confident that daily losses of more than 5% occur with a 0.2% to 0.8% chance.

5.8 External Validity

The confidence interval summarizes uncertainty about the true value of the statistic in the population, or the general pattern, that our data represents. An important part in inference is defining the population, or general pattern, we care about, and assessing how close it is to the population, or general pattern, our data represents. As we introduced earlier in Section 5.1, **external validity** is the concept that captures the similarity of those two general patterns. We say that the external validity is high when the two are the same. When the two general patterns are very different, we say that the external validity is low.

With high external validity, the confidence interval captures all uncertainty about our estimate. With low external validity, it does not. With low external validity, our estimate of the statistic is likely to be off with a larger likelihood than is suggested by the confidence interval. How much larger is very difficult to quantify. Therefore, we usually describe that extra uncertainty in qualitative terms only. For example, we may say that the CI captures all or most of the uncertainty when we believe that external validity is high. In contrast, when we believe that external validity is low, we say that the estimated value may be off with a higher likelihood than the CI suggests.

External validity is as important as statistical inference. However, it is not a statistical question. By that we mean that the methods of data analysis and statistics cannot be used to assess it in a direct fashion. Instead, we need substantive knowledge of the situations. Some data analysis may help in that assessment, such as benchmarking variables for which we have some information in the population we care about (benchmarking was introduced in Chapter 1, Section 1.7). But those methods can never fully assess external validity.

The most important challenges to external validity may be collected in three groups: time, space, and sub-groups. Viewed from a more abstract perspective, all three concern the stability of the general pattern, between the one our data represents and the one we care about.

First, stability in time. The data we analyze is always from the past, whereas the situation we care about is almost always in the future. Thus, in order to generalize from the data, we need to assume that the general pattern that was relevant in the past will remain relevant for the future.

In many applications, there is a great deal of stability. The impact of rain and temperature on crops is pretty stable from one year to another (even if the patterns of weather may change). At the same time, whatever predicts the success of businesses in an industry in the past may be different from what will predict their success in the future (regulations, trade relations, technology, and the entire business climate may change.

A specific issue with time is the occurrence of extreme values. Our data may be free of extreme values because some very rare extreme events may not have happened in the historic period that our data represents. However, this does not imply that such a rare extreme event could not happen in the future we care about.

Second, stability through space. The data we analyze may come from a different country, region, or city than the situation we care about. Taste and behavior of people may vary and so does historic background or the transport infrastructure. Whether that means that the general pattern of interest varies through space is an important question. For example, gender differences in earnings may differ from country to country; the extent to which better management is associated with exporting to foreign markets may be more stable across countries.

Third, stability across subgroups. A pattern may be strong among one group of people, but it may not be there for people in different professional, age, gender, cultural, or income groups. For example, an experiment may show that working from home makes employees more productive and less likely to quit a company in the service industry in China (this will be our case study in Chapter 20). Would working from home have similar effects on accountants or programmers at a Chinese IT company?

Review Box 5.6   External validity of the results of data analysis

- External validity of the results of data analysis is about how those results generalize to the population, or general pattern, we care about, from the population, or general pattern, our data represents.
- When the results are close in the general pattern our data represents and in the general pattern we care about, we say the external validity of the analysis is high. When the two are far, we say its external validity is low.

5.A7   CASE STUDY – What Likelihood of Loss to Expect on a Stock Portfolio?

External validity

The 95% confidence interval of the probability of a daily loss greater than 5% was [0.2, 0.8] percent in our example. This is where the probability of such losses is likely to be found in the general pattern that our data represents.

The general pattern represented by our data is how things worked in the 11 years covered by our data; the general pattern we care about represents how things will work in the coming year. External validity of the 95% confidence interval is high if the future year will be like the past 11 years in terms of the general pattern that determines returns on our investment portfolio. With high external validity, this confidence interval would tell us where to expect the probability of 5%+ loss in the coming year.

However, external validity may not be that high in our case. Whether the next year will be like the past 11 years is difficult to tell. Even if we have no particular reason to expect the future to be systematically different, we can't rule that out. For instance, our 2006–2016 data includes the financial crisis and great recession of 2008–2009. It does not include the dotcom boom and bust of 2000–2001. We have no way to know which boom and which crisis is representative of future booms and crises to come.

Therefore, it makes sense to consider a wider interval for 5%+ loss in the general pattern in the future. How much wider is impossible to determine by data analysis. This is quite common, as we can't, in general, put numbers on uncertainty coming from low external validity. At the very least it is good practice to consider the 95% CI of [0.2, 0.8] to be too narrow. Sound investment decisions based on our analysis should acknowledge that daily losses of more than 5% may have a higher probability than 0.8%, the upper end of this interval.

This concludes our case study. Our question was the frequency of a large loss we can expect for the coming calender year on a portfolio of company stocks that is represented by the S&P500 index. This case study illustrated how to make statistical inference in two ways, using the bootstrap and using a formula for the standard error. The two methods gave the same result, which is how it should be, and is almost always the case when the distribution of the variable is not very skewed and has no extreme values, the statistic is an average and the sample is large enough. Then we used this SE to construct a 95% confidence interval to quantify the degree of uncertainty about the true value of the statistic: where we can expect the probability of a 5% or larger loss may be in the general pattern that determined the 11-year history of our data. Before carrying out that statistical inference, we used the data of this case study for a simulation exercise to illustrate the concept of repeated samples. Finally, we illustrated the way to think about inference in general: start thinking external validity, go ahead with statistical inference if there is a chance that external validity is high, and then return to the question when the analysis is done, to qualify its results in case external validity is not that high.

5.9 Big Data, Statistical Inference, External Validity

Big Data and the advance of computing have changed the way we conduct statistical inference in several important ways. Recall that Big Data means a great many observations, or, less often, a great many variables. The case of many variables can pose a unique challenge for inference, and we'll discuss that in Chapter 6, Sections 6.8 and 6.10. Here we focus on Big Data with very many observations.

With very many observations, confidence intervals are typically very narrow. That should be obvious by now, from the more abstract concept of root-n convergence and the more tangible role of the number of observations in the SE formula. Whatever statistic we estimate from our Big Data, it will be very close to its true value in the population, or general pattern, our data represents. Thus, statistical inference is just not very important with such Big Data.

In case we still wanted to carry out statistical inference, the advances in computing makes it a lot easier to use computationally intensive methods, such as the bootstrap, instead of formulae. This is actually more important with not-so-big data. With very big data, the bootstrap process may take a lot of time.

Importantly, however, Big Data in itself does not change the need to assess external validity or the way to do that. In particular, our analysis does not have higher external validity just because we have many observations. External validity is not affected by the size of the dataset or the ability to carry out better statistical inference by computationally intensive methods. From the viewpoint of external validity, having very many observations that poorly represent the general pattern that we are after is just as problematic as having few such observations. Indeed, a smaller representative dataset may be highly superior to a huge non-representative dataset.

This concludes our chapter that introduces the conceptual questions of generalizing from data, and the methods to carry out statistical inference. The next chapter introduces testing hypotheses, a way to look at the same question from a more specific angle.

| 5.10 | **Main Takeaways** |

Generalizing results of an analysis from our data usually means guessing the value of a statistic in the population, or general pattern, that we care about.

- First step is computing the confidence interval that can tell what the value of the statistic may be in the population, or general pattern, our data represents.
- Second step is assessing external validity: how close the population, or general pattern, we care about is to the population, or general pattern our data represents.
- With Big Data (large N), statistical inference is often not interesting but external validity remains important.

PRACTICE QUESTIONS

1. When do we call a sample representative and is it connected to random sampling?
2. What are the two parts of the inference process? List them, explain them, and give an example with the two parts.
3. When do we say that results from analyzing our data have high external validity? Low external validity? Give an example for each.
4. What's the population, or general pattern, represented by the monthly time series of unemployment rates in Chile between 2000 and 2018?
5. What's the population, or general pattern, that represents the time series of GDP in Vietnam between 1990 and 2020?
6. Does it make sense to create a confidence interval for a statistic that you calculated using cross-country data with all countries in the world? If not, why not? If yes, what's the interpretation of that CI?
7. What does the confidence interval show? What are the typical likelihoods used for them?
8. The proportion of daily losses of more than 2% on an investment portfolio is 5% in the data. Its confidence interval is [4,6] percent. Interpret these numbers.
9. In the data that is a random sample of the population of your country from last year, 30-year-old market analysts earn 30% more than 25-year-old market analysts, on average. The 95% CI of this difference is [25,35] percent. Interpret these numbers.
10. In the example above, what can you conclude about the expected wage difference between 30 and 25 year-old market analysts in your country five years from now? In a different country five years from now?
11. How would you estimate the bootstrap standard error of the average of a variable from cross-sectional data?
12. What's the standard error formula for an average, and what does it imply about what makes the SE larger or smaller? Under what assumption does this formula work?
13. How do you create the 95% CI of a statistic if you know its SE? How do you create the 90% CI?
14. Name two kinds of stability that are important challenges to external validity. Give an example for each when they are likely to result in low external validity.
15. You downloaded data from the World Development Indicators database on GDP per capita and CO_2 emission per capita, and find that their correlation coefficient is 0.7, with SE = 0.05. Create a 95% CI and interpret it.

DATA EXERCISES

Easier and/or shorter exercises are denoted by [*]; harder and/or longer exercises are denoted by [**].

1. Download ten years of daily data on the price of a financial asset, such as an individual stock, or another stock market index. Document the main features of the data, create daily percentage returns, and create a binary variable indicating large losses by choosing your own cutoff. Estimate the standard error of the estimated likelihood of large daily losses by bootstrap and using the SE formula; compare the two, and create 95% confidence intervals. Conclude by giving advice on how to use these results in future investment decisions. [*]

2. Download ten years of daily data on the price of a financial asset, such as an individual stock, or another stock market index. Create daily percentage returns, and create a binary variable indicating large losses by choosing your own cutoff. Carry out a simulation exercise pretending that the truth is contained in your entire data and you want to infer that from a sample of 300 days. Take repeated samples, visualize the distribution of large daily losses, and describe that distribution. Repeat the simulation with samples of 900 days instead of 300 days, and compare the results. [**]

3. Use the `hotels-europe` dataset and pick two cities and the same date. In each city, take hotels with three stars and calculate the average price. Estimate the standard error of the estimated average price by bootstrap and using the SE formula, and create 95% confidence intervals. Compare the average price and the confidence intervals across the two cities, and explain why you have a narrower CI for one city than the other. [*]

4. Use the `wms-management-survey` dataset and pick two countries. Estimate the average management quality score in each. Estimate their standard errors by bootstrap and using the SE formula, and create 95% confidence intervals. Compare the average prices and the confidence intervals across the two countries, and explain why you may have a narrower CI for one country than the other. Discuss the external validity of your results for the quality of management in your country of origin in the current year. [*]

5. Download the most recent data from the World Development Indicators website on GDP per capita and CO_2 emission per capita. Divide countries into two groups by their GDP per capita and calculate the average difference in CO_2 emission per capita between the two groups. Use bootstrap to estimate its standard error, create the appropriate 95% CI, and interpret it. [**]

REFERENCES AND FURTHER READING

A classic but still relevant introduction to the logic of statistical inference is the introductory chapter of Ronald A. Fisher's 1925 book (Fisher, 1925).

On the central role that the confidence interval should play in statistical inference in economic applications see Romer (2020).

The way statistics represents uncertainty and potential issues with this approach is discussed in a historical context by Salsburg (2001).

A related, but broader question is examined in great detail by Manski (2020): why should results of data analysis try to quantify the degree of uncertainty when data analysts want to influence decisions?

On Bayesian analysis, a comprehensive text is Gelman et al. (2018). Andrew Gelman also has a great blog on statistics and causal analysis in social sciences at `http://statmodeling.stat.columbia.edu/`.

5.U1   UNDER THE HOOD: THE LAW OF LARGE NUMBERS AND THE CENTRAL LIMIT THEOREM

The **Law of Large Numbers** (LLN) and the **Central Limit Theorem** (CLT) are the two most important tools to assess how an estimate in a dataset compares to its true value: its value in the population, or general pattern, represented by the data. The LLN and the CLT are true when our estimates are averages.

In a nutshell,

- the LLN tells us that the estimated average ($\bar{x}$) is likely to be very close to the true mean if our sample is large enough, while
- the CLT tells us in what range $\bar{x}$ is around the true mean and helps to estimate that range from the sample we have.

The results of the LLN and the CLT are mathematically correct when the samples are infinitely large. Of course, in practice they never are. We use these results to describe how things look like in samples that are "large enough." What "large enough" means is not defined by the theorems.

There are, however, many simulation studies that give us some guidance. If the variable is close to normally distributed, it seems that these theorems give surprisingly good approximation for samples as small as 40 or even smaller. The further away the variable is from normality, the larger the sample needs to be. A few hundred observations almost always justify the use of the LLN and CLT results. There are special cases, though, with large extreme values, when even hundreds of observations may not be enough, so some alertness is helpful.

The LLN and CLT we present below are derived for **i.i.d. variables**: identical and independently distributed variables. For such variables, the value of this variable in one observation conveys no information about its value in another observation, and knowing nothing more than the position of an observation in the data, we should expect that it is just like any other observation. The LLN is true for many other kinds of variables, too. There are versions of the CLT that are true for other kinds of variables; they differ from the version we present by the standard deviation of the normal distribution. We do not consider those other LLN and CLT results here.

The LLN tells us that in large enough samples, our estimates of the average will be very close to their population value. The larger the sample, the closer to that value our estimate will be.

The theorem itself tells us that the sample average of a variable gets very close to the population mean of that variable if the sample is large.

The most straightforward version is derived for i.i.d. variables. As a formula, LLN says that

$$\bar{x} = \frac{1}{n} \sum_{i=1}^{n} x_i \to E[x] \text{ in probability} \tag{5.3}$$

where $E[x]$ means the true expected value of x, and $\to$ in probability means that the left-hand side of the formula approaches the right-hand side, with probability 1 if n goes to infinity. Somewhat more precisely this means the following: tell me how close you want to be to the population value and I can give you a large enough sample size that will get you that close with as high a probability as you want: 90%, 99%, or 99.99%. Another notation of the same thing is that the probability limit, abbreviation plim, of the sample average is the expected value:

$$plim \, \bar{x} = E[x] \tag{5.4}$$

The LLN assures us that the estimated value is likely close to the true value, but it does not tell us how close it is. This is where the CLT can help.

The CLT states that, in large enough data, the estimated average will be distributed normally around the true expected value, and the variance of this normal distribution is related to the variance of the original variable that makes up the average.

The CLT we discuss here is derived for i.i.d. variables. The CLT states the following:

$$\sqrt{n}(\bar{x} - E[x]) \overset{A}{\sim} N(0, Var[x]) \tag{5.5}$$

In English, the sample average minus the expected value, multiplied by the square root of the sample size, is distributed approximately normally (the wiggle with letter A on top means approximate distribution) with mean zero and variance that equals the variance of the variable itself.

Of course we rarely are interested in the distribution of things like $\sqrt{n}(\bar{x} - E[x])$. Instead, we are usually interested in the distribution of $\bar{x}$ itself. The question is how we can get that from the CLT. The formula is relatively straightforward:

$$\bar{x} \overset{A}{\sim} N\left(E[x], \frac{1}{n}Var[x]\right) \tag{5.6}$$

In large samples, the sample average is distributed approximately normally around the population mean, and the variance of that distribution equals the variance of the variable itself divided by the sample size.

One may wonder why we state the CLT in the first form at all instead of proceeding right away with this second form. The reason is that the theorem is literally true as n goes to infinity; but then the variance in the second formula would go to zero (as it should, otherwise it would not be consistent with the LLN, which says that sample mean should go to the population mean with probability one). In practice, there is of course no such thing as an infinitely large sample. Instead, we want to interpret these theoretical results as approximations in large samples. So we can use the second formula in practice.

In order to understand the main messages of the CLT, let's go back to the theoretically derived first formulation. It is instructive to break down the message of the CLT into three pieces:

1. In large enough samples, the estimated average minus the true expected value, multiplied by the square root of the sample size, falls within a range around zero. Technically, it is a variable, which means that we can't tell its value for sure but we can tell its distribution. This means that for any probability, we can find a range within which the variable falls with that particular probability. If you think about it, this is already a remarkable result. As the sample size goes to infinity, $\sqrt{n}$ goes to infinity. At the same time, $\bar{x}$, the sample average, goes to the expected value $E[x]$ with probability one (by the LLN), so that their difference $\bar{x} - E[x]$ goes to zero with probability one. And here is the interesting thing: the product of the two goes neither to infinity nor to zero. Actually, we know more: it will fall within certain ranges around zero with certain probabilities.

2. The distribution of this thing, the sample average minus the expected value multiplied by the square root of the sample size, is normal. This is true regardless of the distribution of the variable

itself. This is a remarkable result, too. Whatever the distribution of x, the distribution of $\sqrt{n}(\bar{x} - E[x])$ will be normal. That's right: whatever the distribution of x is! In fact, you can think of the normal distribution as defined by the CLT, so that we can expect something to be distributed normally if it is the average of many independent things.

3. The mean and the variance of that distribution equal the mean and the variance of the original variable itself. Thus, if we know the sample size n, the mean of x, and the variance of x, we know everything about the distribution. That is, of course, if the sample is large enough. The great thing is that we have pretty good estimates for these: the LLN guarantees that we can substitute the sample average and the within-sample variance for the population mean and variance, respectively. Why? The LLN tells us that the sample mean x is close to the population mean $E[x]$. But the LLN also tells us that the within-sample variance is close to the population variance because the latter is a kind of a mean, too: $Var[x] = E[(x_i - E[x])^2]$. So the variance within the sample, $\frac{1}{n}\sum_{i=1}^{n}(x_i - x)^2$, is close to the population variance in large samples.

6 Testing Hypotheses

How to formulate a hypothesis, and how to use evidence in the data to help decide if we can maintain or reject it

Motivation

You want to know whether online and offline prices differ in your country for products that are sold in both ways. You have access to data on a sample of products with their online and offline prices. How would you use this data to establish whether prices tend to be different or the same for all products?

You have conducted an experiment to see whether a new design for the online ad of your product would yield more customers purchasing your product. In your experiment, customers were randomly chosen to see one of the two versions of the ad. You have data on whether each customer followed up and made a purchase decision. You see more follow-ups for those who saw the new version in your data, but the follow-up rates are very small to begin with, and their difference is not very large. How can you tell from this evidence whether to expect the new version to result in more follow-ups in the future?

Generalizing the results of our analysis from the data we have to the situation we care about can be carried out in a more focused way than we discussed in the previous chapter. One such focused approach uses a statistic (e.g., a difference in two means) computed from our data to see whether its true value is equal to something we assume (e.g., the difference is zero). This is called hypothesis testing: using results in the data to see if we have enough evidence to tell whether a hypothesis (the two means are equal) is wrong (they are not equal) or whether we don't have enough evidence (they may be equal).

This chapter introduces the logic and practice of testing hypotheses. We describe the steps of hypothesis testing and discuss two alternative ways to carry it out: one with the help of a test statistic and a critical value, and another one with the help of a p-value. We discuss how decision rules are derived from our desire to control the likelihood of making erroneous decisions, and how significance levels, power, and p-values are related to the likelihood of those errors. We focus on testing hypotheses about averages, but, as we show in one of our case studies, this focus is less restrictive than it may appear. The chapter covers one-sided versus two-sided alternatives, issues with testing multiple hypotheses, the perils of p-hacking, and some issues with testing on Big Data.

The main case study in this chapter, **Comparing online and offline prices: testing the difference**, is based on the `billion-prices` dataset we described in Chapter 1, Section 1.B1. This data includes online and offline prices of selected products sold by selected retailers. The data we analyze in this case study is for retailers in the United States. The question we test is whether online and offline prices are the same, on average. In addition, we continue the case study called

Testing the likelihood of loss on a stock portfolio we started in Chapter 5. In this case study we ask about the probability of a large loss on an investment portfolio, using the sp500 dataset. Here our question is whether such losses are likely to occur more frequently than a threshold frequency that we can tolerate.

Learning outcomes

After working through this chapter, you should be able to:

- formulate a null and an alternative hypothesis that correspond to the question you want to answer;
- think in terms of false positives and false negatives;
- understand the logic of hypothesis testing with the help of a test statistic and a critical value;
- carry out hypothesis testing with the help of a p-value;
- interpret the result of a hypothesis test;
- understand the additional issues that arise with testing multiple hypotheses from the same data.

6.1   The Logic of Testing Hypotheses

A hypothesis is a statement about a population, or general pattern. Testing a hypothesis amounts to gathering information from a dataset and, based on that information, deciding whether that hypothesis is false or true in the population, or general pattern.

Thus, **hypothesis testing** means analyzing the data at hand to make a decision about the hypothesis. Two decisions are possible: rejecting the hypothesis or not rejecting it. We reject the hypothesis if there is enough evidence against it. We don't reject it if there isn't enough evidence against it. We may have insufficient evidence against a hypothesis either if the hypothesis is true or if it is not true but the evidence is weak. Rejecting a hypothesis is a more conclusive decision than not rejecting it; we'll discuss this asymmetry more in the next section.

Testing a hypothesis is a way of making an inference, with a focus on a specific statement. As with any kind of inference, we have to assess external validity, too: the extent to which the population, or general pattern, represented by our data is the same as the population, or general pattern, we are truly interested in.

Hypothesis testing is a formal procedure. It is educational to break that procedure into specific steps. In what follows, we'll describe the steps we suggest to follow.

The first step is defining the statistic that would answer our question. Recall that a statistic is anything whose value can be computed from data. Often the statistic that would answer our question is an average, or the difference between two average values. In fact, we'll focus on averages in this chapter.

For convenience, let's call this statistic s. We are interested in the true value of s, which is its value in the population, or general pattern, our data represents. Let's denote this true value by s_{true}. The value of the statistic in our data is its estimated value, denoted by a hat on top, $\hat{s}$.

For example, we may look at data from an **experiment** that presented some of the potential customers of a company the old version of an online ad and other potential customers a new version. Our question is whether the new version is different in terms of how many people follow up and visit the website of the company after being presented one of the two versions of the ad. Here the statistic is the difference in the follow-up frequency in the two groups of people. If we denote the follow-up rate among customers who saw the old version as r_{old} and among customers who saw the new version as r_{new}, the statistic we are interested in is $s = r_{new} - r_{old}$

Or, we may use company data on firm growth rates (e.g., in terms of sales), and the age of their managers, to learn if firms with a young manager tend to grow at a different rate than firms with an old manager. Here the statistic is the difference in average growth between firms with older managers and firms with younger managers: $s = \overline{growth}_{youngmanager} - \overline{growth}_{oldmanager}$.

It is good practice to pause at this point and, as a second step, think about external validity. Having defined the statistic that translates our question into something we can compute from our data, we should get a sense of whether, and to what extent, that statistic in the data is generalizable to the situation we care about. This amounts to defining the population, or general pattern, our data represents, and making sure we understand how it compares to the population, or general pattern we are interested in. Fortunately, we don't need the two to be similar in every respect. The question is whether the value of the statistic is the same in the two. If there is very little chance that the two are similar it makes little sense to continue with the analysis.

If our data on firms with growth rates and the age of their managers was collected in a country that has very different cultural norms about age than our country, whatever age-related differences we may find in our data would have low external validity for our country. In that case we may decide not to use that data to learn about whether firms with younger versus older managers grow at the same rate in our country. Or, we may uncover that the firms in our data are all very small, whereas we are interested in the growth of medium-sized firms. Here, too, external validity of our findings may be low for the kinds of firms we care about, and we may decide not to go ahead with the analysis using this particular data. On the other hand, we may conclude that external validity may be high enough from the viewpoint of the patterns of association between manager age and firm growth rate, thus the general pattern represented by the firms in our data and what we care about may be similar. In this case we should go ahead with our analysis. As we'll see, it makes sense to return to external validity at the end of the process, to qualify the results if necessary.

In our example of testing the new versus old version of an online ad, we are interested in whether the new version would result in more follow-ups among customers in the future. Thus, we need to think about whether the customers in our experiment are a representative sample of our future customers, and whether the circumstances during the experiment are similar to what future customers would face. To be more precise, the sample and the circumstances need to be similar in the experiment and the future roll-out of the ad in terms of the new versus old follow-up rate difference.

We shall discuss the other steps in detail in the following sections of this chapter.

6.A1 CASE STUDY – Comparing Online and Offline Prices: Testing the Difference

Question, data, statistics, external validity

The general question of this case study is whether online and offline prices of the same products tend to be different. We use the `billion-prices` dataset from the Billion Prices project. We introduced this data earlier, in Chapter 1. It contains the online and offline price of the same product measured, ideally, at the same time, in various countries over various years. In this case study we use data from the United States, and we include products with their regular prices recorded (as opposed to sales or discounted prices). This data was collected in 2015 and 2016; it includes the online and offline prices of 6439 products (after dropping three products with extreme values that are likely errors).

The general question of the case study is whether online and offline prices of the same products tend to be different. The "tend to be" part of the question is vague. We can turn this into various statistics. We choose the average, both because it's an intuitive statistic of central value (Chapter 3, Section 3.6), and because the tools of statistical inference are best used for the average. Alternatives to the mean of the price differences may be the median or the mode of the online and offline price distributions, but we don't consider those statistics in this chapter.

Thus, our statistic is the average of the difference of the online versus offline price. Each product i has both an online and an offline price in the data, $p_{i,online}$ and $p_{i,offline}$. Let the variable $pdiff$ denote their difference:

$$pdiff_i = p_{i,online} - p_{i,offline} \tag{6.1}$$

Then, the statistic with n observations (products) in the data, is

$$\hat{s} = \overline{pdiff} = \frac{1}{n}\sum_{i=1}^{n}\left(p_{i,online} - p_{i,offline}\right) \tag{6.2}$$

Note that the average of the price differences is equal to the difference of the average prices; thus this s statistic also measures the difference between the average of online prices and the average of offline prices among products with both kinds of price: $\frac{1}{n}\sum_{i=1}^{n}\left(p_{i,online} - p_{i,offline}\right) = \frac{1}{n}\sum_{i=1}^{n}p_{i,online} - \frac{1}{n}\sum_{i=1}^{n}p_{i,offline}$.

The mean difference is -0.05 US dollars: online prices are, on average, 5 cents lower in this data.

$$\hat{s} = -0.05 \tag{6.3}$$

There is substantial spread around this average: the standard deviation of the price differences is 10 US dollars. But that larger spread is due to a few very large price differences, in both directions. The minimum price difference is -380 US dollars, the maximum is $+415$ US dollars. At the same time, 5593 (87%) of the 6439 products in this data have the difference within ± 1 dollars. Furthermore, 4112 (64%) have the exact same online and offline price.

To get a sense of how the distribution looks, let's look at the histogram. Figures 6.1a and 6.1b show the histograms of the same distribution, except the first one has all observations and shows the distribution over its entire range, while the second one includes observations within a ± 5 dollar price difference. Except for how large the range is, the first histogram shows little of the features of the distribution; the second one is more informative. It shows the large spike at zero, which corresponds to the fact that 64% of the products in this data have the exact same online and offline price. In addition, this histogram suggests that the distribution is not perfectly symmetrical. Indeed, 25% of the products have a lower online price and 11% have a higher online price. This asymmetry shows up in another way: the distribution is slightly skewed with a longer left tail (the median is zero, so the mean–median difference is negative).

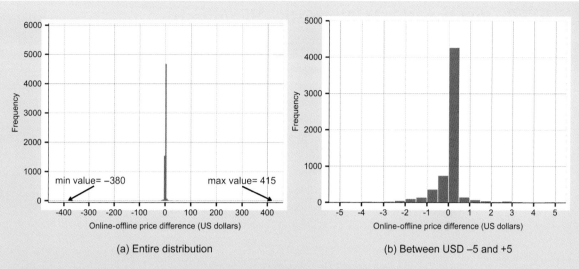

(a) Entire distribution   (b) Between USD –5 and +5

Figure 6.1   The distribution of online–offline price differences

Note: The distribution of the difference of the online and offline prices of the same products. Mean = −0.05, Std.Dev. = 10.0, Median = 0.
Source: `billion-prices` dataset. US retailers in 2015–2016, sales and promotions excluded. N=6439.

After having defined the statistic of interest and calculated its value from the data, let's review what we know about the source of this data so we can get some sense of whether we can generalize the average price difference in this data to a situation we care about. As we discussed in Chapter 1 this data includes 10 to 50 products in each retail store included in the survey (which are the largest retailers in the USA that sell their products both online and offline). The products were selected by the data collectors in offline stores, and they were matched to the same products the same stores sold online. The products in the data may not represent all products sold at these stores. While there is no particular reason to suspect that online offline price differences are different for other kinds of products, we can't rule out that possibility. Thus, strictly speaking, the general pattern of the statistic represented by this data is the average online–offline price differences in large retail store chains for the population of the kinds of products that data collectors would select with a high likelihood.

That's a rather narrow population. Instead, we would want to further generalize the findings to another general pattern of interest, such as the online–offline price differences among all products in the USA sold both online and offline by the same retailers. This extra step of generalization is best thought of as a question of external validity. External validity is high if the distribution of price differences among the products represented in our data is similar to that more general pattern among all products that are sold both online and offline in the USA.

Of course, we may care about the online–offline price difference in another country or a different year (the data was collected in the USA in 2015–2016). For that additional step of generalization, the question is whether the general patterns that determine the average price difference in the country and the year of interest are similar to the USA in 2015–2016. For now, we assume that that's the case and continue with our analysis. We shall return to the external validity of our findings at the end of the case study.

6.2 Null Hypothesis, Alternative Hypothesis

After specifying the statistic that helps answer our question, and after convincing ourselves that the statistic computed from our data may help answer the question in the situation we truly care about, the next step is formally stating the question in hypotheses. More specifically, we need to state two competing hypotheses, of which only one can be true. The first one is the **null hypothesis**, denoted as H_0, and also simply called the null. The second one is the **alternative hypothesis**, denoted as H_A, and called the alternative for short. These hypotheses are formulated in terms of the unknown **true value** of the statistic. This is statistical inference (Chapter 5), so the true value means the value in the population, or general pattern represented by our data. The null specifies a specific value or a range of values, while the alternative specifies other possible values. Together, the null and the alternative should cover all possibilities we are interested in.

With our definition of statistic s, the most widely examined null and alternative hypotheses are the following:

$$H_0: s_{true} = 0 \tag{6.4}$$

$$H_A: s_{true} \neq 0 \tag{6.5}$$

The null says that the true value of the statistic is zero; the alternative says that it's not zero. Together, these cover all logical possibilities for the true value of the statistic.

It may seem odd to have $H_0: s_{true} = 0$ when, presumably, we analyze the data because we suspect that the true value of s is not zero (online and offline prices may differ on average; companies with younger managers may grow at a different rate, on average). This seemingly twisted logic comes from the fact that testing a hypothesis amounts to seeing if there is enough evidence in our data to reject the null. It is sometimes said that the null is protected: it should not be too easy to reject it otherwise the conclusions of hypothesis testing would not be strong.

As we introduce the concept of hypothesis testing, it is helpful to relate its logic to the logic of a criminal court procedure. At court the task is to decide whether an accused person is guilty or innocent of a certain crime. In most modern societies the starting point is the assumption of innocence: the accused person should be judged guilty only if there is enough evidence against their innocence. This is so even though the accused person was brought before court presumably because there was a suspicion of their guilt. To translate this procedure to the language of hypothesis testing, H_0 is that the person is innocent, and H_A is that the person is guilty.

Medical tests are another instructive example. When testing whether a person has a certain medical condition, the null is that the person does not have the condition (healthy), and the alternative is that they have it (sick). The testing procedure amounts to gathering information to see if there is evidence to decide that the person has the condition.

The case when we test if $H_A: s_{true} \neq 0$ is called a **two-sided alternative** as it allows for s_{true} to be either greater than zero or less than zero. For instance, we focus on the difference in online and offline prices, with H_0 being the equality. In such a case we are not really interested if the difference is positive or not, or whether it is negative or not.

The other case is working with a **one-sided alternative**, when we are indeed interested if a statistic is positive. The null and the alternative should be set up so that the hypothesis we are truly interested in is in the alternative set. So when we want to know if s_{true} is positive, we want to put $s_{true} > 0$ in the alternative thus, making the null $s_{true} \leq 0$:

$$H_0: s_{true} \leq 0 \tag{6.6}$$

$$H_A: s_{true} > 0 \tag{6.7}$$

For reasons that we'll see later, the null needs to contain the equality sign, and the alternative should contain the strict inequality.

An example where a one-sided alternative would make sense is the likelihood of large losses on a portfolio in the **Testing the likelihood of loss on a stock portfolio** case study. There we want to know if this likelihood is greater than a threshold value. In other words, we want to know if the difference of the likelihood and the threshold value is greater than zero.

Review Box 6.1   Null hypothesis, alternative hypothesis

- To carry out a test we need to have a clearly stated null hypothesis ("the null," H_0) and a clearly stated alternative hypothesis ("the alternative," H_A).
- H_0 and H_A are statements about the true value of the statistic (the value in the population, or general pattern, represented by our data).
- A typical null–alternative pair with a two-sided alternative is $H_0: s_{true} = 0$, $H_A: s_{true} \neq 0$.
- A typical null–alternative pair with a one-sided alternative is $H_0: s_{true} \leq 0$, $H_A: s_{true} > 0$.
- Together, the null and the alternative cover all possibilities (or all interesting possibilities).
- Statistical testing amounts to producing evidence from the data and seeing if it's strong enough so we can reject the null.

6.3   The t-Test

After introducing the logic of hypothesis testing, let's dive into the actual process. In this chapter we focus on one specific test, called the **t-test**. This testing procedure is based on the **t-statistic** that we'll introduce in this section.

Following the logic of hypothesis testing, we start from the assumption that the null is true and thus $s_{true} = 0$. Then we look at the evidence to see if we want to reject this null or maintain our assumption that it's true. Intuitively, the evidence we look for is how far the estimated value of the statistic, $\hat{s}$, is from zero, its hypothesized value. We reject the null if the distance is large – i.e., if the estimate is far from its hypothesized value. Conversely, we do not reject the null if the estimate is not very far – i.e., when there is not enough evidence against it. How far is far enough for rejecting requires a measure of the distance. That measure is the t-statistic that we'll introduce here.

More generally, the t-statistic is a **test statistic**. A test statistic is a measure of the distance of the estimated value of the statistic from what its true value would be if H_0 were true.

Consider $H_0: s_{true} = 0$, $H_A: s_{true} \neq 0$, where s is an average, or the difference of that average from a number, or a difference of two averages. The null and alternative are about the true value of the statistic: s_{true}. Our data contains information to compute the estimated value of the statistic: $\hat{s}$. The t-statistic for this hypotheses uses the estimated value $\hat{s}$ and its standard error:

$$t = \frac{\hat{s}}{SE(\hat{s})} \tag{6.8}$$

When $\hat{s}$ is the average of a variable x, the t-statistic is simply

$$t = \frac{\bar{x}}{SE(\bar{x})} \tag{6.9}$$

When $\hat{s}$ is the average of a variable x minus a number, the t-statistic is

$$t = \frac{\bar{x} - number}{SE(\bar{x})} \tag{6.10}$$

When $\hat{s}$ is the difference between two averages, say, $\bar{x}_A$ and $\bar{x}_B$, the t-statistic is

$$t = \frac{\bar{x}_A - \bar{x}_B}{SE(\bar{x}_A - \bar{x}_B)} \tag{6.11}$$

In the first two formulae, the denominator is the SE of average x, something that we know how to estimate in two ways, by bootstrap or by formula (Chapter 5, Sections 5.6 and 5.7). In the last formula we have something different: the SE of the difference of two averages. We haven't discussed ways to estimate it, although the intuition behind the bootstrap suggests that that may be an appropriate method. Moreover, there is a formula for it as well that makes use of the potentially different standard deviations of x in the two groups. Fortunately, we don't need to learn that formula as all statistical software we use has it built in and uses it when carrying out such a test.

The sign of the t-statistic is the same as the sign of $\hat{s}$. If $\hat{s}$ is positive, the t-statistic is positive; if $\hat{s}$ is negative, the t-statistic is negative. The magnitude of the t-statistic measures the distance of $\hat{s}$ from what s_{true} would be if the null were true. The unit of distance is the standard error. For example, the t-statistic is one (or negative one) if $\hat{s}$ is exactly one standard error away from zero.

Review Box 6.2   The t-test

- The t-test is a procedure to decide whether we can reject the null.
- The t-test is designed to test hypotheses about the mean of a variable.
- The t-statistic transforms the original statistic of interest into a standardized version.
- When the question is whether the mean of a variable is equal to zero, the t-statistic is
$t = \frac{\bar{x}}{SE(\bar{x})}$
- When the question is whether the mean of a variable is the same in group A and group B, the t-statistic is
$t = \frac{\bar{x}_A - \bar{x}_B}{SE(\bar{x}_A - \bar{x}_B)}$

6.4   Making a Decision; False Negatives, False Positives

The following step is making a decision: either rejecting the null or not rejecting it. In hypothesis testing this decision is based on a clear rule specified in advance. Having such a decision rule makes the decision straightforward.

A clear rule also makes the decision transparent, which helps avoid biases in the decision. That's important because biases may occur, sometimes unconsciously. Unfortunately, we humans are often tempted to use evidence to support our pre-existing views or prejudices. If, for example, we think that firms with younger managers tend to grow faster, we may pay more attention to the evidence that supports that belief than to the evidence against it. In particular, we may be tempted to say that the estimated growth rate difference $\hat{s}$ is large enough to reject the null, because we believe that the null isn't true. Clear decision rules are designed to minimize the room for such temptations.

To be specific, the decision rule in statistical testing is comparing the test statistic to a **critical value**. The critical value thus tells us whether the test statistic is large enough to reject the null. The null is to be rejected if the test statistic is larger than the critical value; the null is not to be rejected if the test statistic isn't larger than the critical value. To be transparent, we need to set the critical value before looking at the test statistic. As that is impossible to document, the practice is to use a commonly accepted critical value.

But how to select the critical value? Or, more to the point, why is a particular critical value commonly used for a test?

To answer that question, we first need to understand that the critical value reflects a preference for how conservative we want to be with the evidence. If we set the critical value high, we require that far means very, very far. That makes rejecting the null hard. We often say that a choice for such a critical value is a conservative choice. If we set the value low, we consider not-so-far as far, too. That makes rejecting the null easier. That would be a lenient choice. The process of setting the critical value involves a trade-off between being too conservative or too lenient. To explore that trade-off we need to dig a little deeper into the consequences of the decision.

We can make one of two decisions with hypothesis testing: we reject the null or we don't reject the null. That decision may be right or wrong. There is no way to know if we are right or wrong when we make the decision. Nevertheless, we can think about these possibilities. We can be right in our decision in two ways: we reject the null when it is not true, or we do not reject the null when it is true. We can be wrong in our decision in two ways, too: we reject the null even though it is true, or we do not reject the null even though it is not true. Let's focus on the two ways of being wrong.

We say that our decision is a **false positive** if we reject the null when it is true. The decision is "false" because it is erroneous. It is "positive" because we take the active decision to reject the protected null. The language may seem familiar from medical testing: a result is "positive" if it suggests that the person has the condition that they were tested against (rather negative news in most cases ...).

We say that our decision is a **false negative** if we do not reject the null even though it's not true. This decision is "negative" because we do not take the active decision and, instead, leave the null not rejected. In medical testing a result is "negative" if it suggests that the person does not have the condition that they were tested against (which often is rather good news ...).

In formal statistical language, a false positive decision is called a **Type-I error** and a false negative decision is called a **Type-II error**.

Table 6.1 summarizes these possibilities.

Table 6.1 Two ways to be right, and two ways to be wrong when testing a null hypothesis

	Null hypothesis is true	Null hypothesis is false
Don't reject the null	True negative (TN) Correct	False negative (FN) Type- II error
Reject the null	False positive (FP) Type- I error	True positive (TP) Correct

False positives and false negatives are both wrong, but they are not equally wrong. The way we set up the null and the alternative, wrongly rejecting the null (a false positive) is a bigger mistake than wrongly accepting it (a false negative). Thus, the testing procedure needs to protect the null: we want to reject it only if the evidence is strong. Therefore, the critical value is to be chosen in a way that makes false positives rare. But that is a balancing act. It would be easy to completely avoid false positives just by never making a positive decision: if we never reject the null we could not possibly reject it wrongly. That is, of course, not a useful procedure. Otherwise, false positives are always a possibility. The usual solution is to go for a very small chance for false positives.

Let's focus on a t-test for a null with a two-sided alternative, $H_0: s_{true} = 0$, $H_A: s_{true} \neq 0$. (We shall return to cases with a one-sided alternative later, in Section 6.7.) A commonly applied critical value for a t-statistic is ± 2: reject the null if the t-statistic is smaller than -2 or larger than $+2$; don't reject the null if the t-statistic is between -2 and $+2$ (The precise critical value is 1.96, but for all practical purpose we can use the rounded value 2. To calculate precise estimates, we'll use 1.96.) That way the probability of a false positive is 5%.

Why? Answering this question is not easy, but we know everything already to do so. We can calculate the likelihood of a false positive because we know what the sampling distribution of the test statistic would be if the null were true. Recall, from Chapter 5, Section 5.2, that the sampling distribution of a statistic is its distribution across repeated samples of the same size from the same population. The sampling distribution of an average is approximately normal, its mean is equal to the true mean, and its standard deviation is called the standard error. The t-statistic has the average in its numerator, so that its distribution is also approximately normal, but its standard deviation is one because the denominator is the SE of $\hat{s}$. (It turns out that with fewer than 30 observations, the normal approximation to the distribution of the t-statistic is not very good. Instead, under some specific circumstances, the distribution is closer to something called a t-distribution – hence the name of the t-statistic.)

Here we ask how the sampling distribution would look if the null hypothesis were true. In that case the distribution of the t-statistic would be standard normal: a normal distribution with mean zero and standard deviation of one. The mean would be zero because $s_{true} = 0$ if the null were true. The standard deviation would be one because the t-statistic is standardized (Chapter 3, Section 3.6): it has the SE in the denominator.

By the properties of the standard normal distribution, the probability that the t-statistic is less than -2 is approximately 2.5%, and the probability that it is greater than $+2$ is also about 2.5%. Therefore the probability that the t-statistic is either below -2 or above $+2$ is 5% if the null is true. And that 5% is the probability of false positives if we apply the critical values of ± 2 because that's the probability that we would reject the null if it was true. Figure 6.2 illustrates these probabilities.

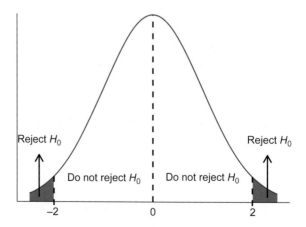

Figure 6.2   The probability of a false positive

Note: The sampling distribution of the test statistic when the null is true. The probability of a false positive is the sum of the areas marked blue. This false positive probability refers to the decision to reject the null if the t-statistic is larger than +2 or smaller than −2.

Based on the same argument, we can set other critical values that correspond to different probabilities of a false positive. If we make the critical values −2.6 and +2.6, the chance of a false positive is 1%. With critical values −1.6 and +1.6 it is 10%. While these other critical values are also used sometimes, the ±2 critical value and the corresponding 5% chance is the conventional choice. That choice means that we tolerate a 5% chance for being wrong when rejecting the null.

So this is how data analysts avoid biases in their decision when testing hypotheses. They use the same ±2 critical value of the t-test regardless of the data and hypothesis they are testing. That gives a 5% chance of a false positive decision.

After the probability of a false positive, let's turn to false negatives. Fixing the chance of false positives affects the chance of false negatives at the same time. Recall that a false negative arises when we don't reject the null even though it's not true. We don't reject the null when the t-statistic is within the critical values. Can we tell how likely it is that we make a mistake by not rejecting it?

It shows what happens when, instead of what's stated in the null, the true value of the statistic is something else, contained in the alternative. In this case the distribution of the t-statistic is different from what it would be if the null were true. If the null were true, it would be centered around zero, shown by the bell curve on the left of Figure 6.3 for comparison. However, in reality, now the distribution is centered around a different value, which is 2.6 here. This is the bell curve on the right of Figure 6.3. The figure shows what happens when we apply the usual decision rule to reject the null if the test statistic falls outside the ±2 range but not otherwise. For comparison, the figure also shows what the distribution of the t-statistic would be if the null were true. The teal shaded area is the case when we reject the null, and we should (TP). The shaded purple area shows the probability that this decision would suggest not to reject the null, which would be a mistake here (FN).

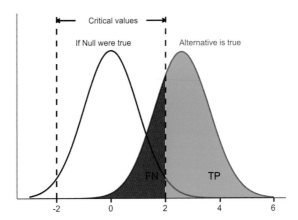

Figure 6.3 The probabilities of a true positive and a false negative

Note: The left bell-shaped curve shows the sampling distribution of the t-statistic if the null were true. The right curve shows the sampling distribution when, instead, the true value of the test statistic is something else, here 2.6. TP, true positive; FN, false negative.

It turns out that the chance of a false negative depends on two things: how far the true value is from the value defined in the null hypothesis, and how large the sample is. We can see that if we think how Figure 6.3 would change under various scenarios. First, the further away the true value is from zero, the smaller the purple region. Thus the smaller the probability of a false negative. Second, the larger the sample, the smaller the purple region, again. So the probability of a false negative is smaller.

In the next section we'll build on all this and introduce an alternative way to make the decision – one that is easier in practice and involves fewer steps. Before that, let's introduce a few more concepts that are often used when testing hypotheses.

The probability of a false positive is called the **size of the test**. The maximum probability that we tolerate is the **level of significance**. When we fix the level of significance at 5% and end up rejecting the null, we say that the statistic we tested is significant at 5%. The probability of avoiding a false negative is the **power of the test**. Thus, we usually fix the level of significance at 5% and hope for a high power (i.e., a high probability of avoiding a false negative), which is more likely the larger the sample and the further away the true value is from what's in the null.

As we have seen, the power of the test is larger the further away the truth is from what we stated in the null and the more observations we have in our data. The power of the test means our ability to tell if the null is in fact not true. With high power (e.g., because of many observations) we have a good chance that we can reject the null if it's not true. In contrast, with low power (e.g., because of too few observations), we don't have a good chance to reject the null if it's not true.

Let's consider the example of the experiment that shows some potential customers the old version of an online ad and other potential customers the new version of the ad. Here the question is whether the new ad has a different effect. The statistic, as we discussed earlier, is the difference between the fraction of people who follow up to the product website after being presented the ad in the two groups. Translating the question into a null and a two-sided alternative, the null here is no difference, and the alternative is a difference. A false negative would be to decide that the follow-up rates are the same in the two versions when in fact they are different. If we have many subjects, a well-designed experiment has high power and would reject the null of no difference if there is indeed a difference. However, with too few subjects, even an otherwise well-designed experiment has low power. Thus, it would not reject the null even if the two versions are different in the follow-up rates. What's too few and what's many depend on a lot of things. We'll return to this question when we discuss the design of experiments in Chapter 20.

Review Box 6.3   False positives, false negatives, size, significance, and power

- A false positive is a decision to reject the null hypothesis when it is in fact true.
- A false negative is a decision not to reject the null hypothesis when it is in fact not true.
- The level of significance is the maximum probability of a false positive that we tolerate.
- The power of the test is the probability of avoiding a false negative.
- In statistical testing we fix the level of significance of the test to be small (5%, 1%).
- Tests with more observations have more power in general.

6.5   The p-Value

The **p-value** makes testing substantially easier. In effect it saves us from the need to calculate test statistics and specify critical values. Instead, we can make an informed decision based on the p-value only.

The p-value informs us about the probability of a false positive. To be more precise, the p-value is the probability that the test statistic will be as large as, or larger than, what we calculate from the data, if the null hypothesis is true. Thus, the p-value is the smallest significance level at which we can reject H_0 given the value of the test statistic in the data. It is sometimes denoted by lowercase p or $P >$ test statistic, as in "$P > |t|$" for a two-sided t-test. Because the p-value tells us the smallest level of significance at which we can reject the null, it summarizes all the information we need to make the decision. The p-value depends on the test statistic and the sampling distribution of the test statistic.

Let's say that we get a p-value of 0.04. That means that the smallest level of significance at which we can reject the null is 4%. In this case we should reject if our initially set target was 5% or higher. If, on the other hand, our initially set target was 1%, we shouldn't reject the null if we get a p-value of 0.04. If, instead, we get a tiny p-value of, say, 0.0001, we should reject the null if our initial target level is 10%, 5%, 1%, or even 0.1%.

To be transparent, we should set the level of significance before carrying out the test, as we explained earlier in Section 6.4. In practice, that means applying the convention of 5% or 1%.

The great thing about the p-value is that statistical software calculates it for us. Of course, to do so, we have to define the statistic and the null and alternative hypotheses. Then we just look at the p-value and reject the null if the p-value is below the pre-set level of significance (5% or 1%), and we don't reject it otherwise.

Review Box 6.4 The p-value

- The p-value is the smallest significance level at which we can reject H_0 given the value of the test statistic in the sample.
- More intuitively, it is the probability that the test statistic will be as large as, or larger than, what we calculate from the data, if the null hypothesis is true.
- The p-value summarizes all the information in the data we need to make a decision when testing a hypothesis.
- Reject the null if the p-value is less than the level of significance we set for ourselves (say, 5%). Don't reject the null otherwise.

6.A2 CASE STUDY – Comparing Online and Offline Prices: Testing the Difference

In our case study, the hypotheses are about whether the online versus offline price difference is zero on average in the population of products represented by the data:

$$H_0: s_{true} = \overline{pdiff}_{true} = 0 \tag{6.12}$$

$$H_A: s_{true} = \overline{pdiff}_{true} \neq 0 \tag{6.13}$$

Following usual practice, let's fix the level of significance at 5%. By doing so, we tolerate a 5% chance for a false positive. That is, we allow ourselves a 5% chance to be wrong if we reject the null hypothesis of zero average price difference. A 5% level of significance translates to ± 2 bounds for the t-statistic.

The value of the statistic in the data is -0.054. Its standard error is 0.124. Thus the t-statistic is

$$t = \frac{-0.054}{0.124} = -0.44 \tag{6.14}$$

This is well within ± 2. Thus we don't reject the null hypothesis of zero difference. Doing so would be inconsistent with our goal to keep the probability of false positive below 5%. Thus we can't reject the hypothesis that the average price difference is zero in the population of products represented by the data.

So our decision is not to reject the null. That can be the result of two things. One: the null is true indeed, and online and offline prices are equal, on average, in the population of products represented by the data. Two: the null is not true, only we didn't have enough evidence against it in this data. While we can't tell which of these two is the case, we have evidence to help. Notably, note that our dataset is large, with over six thousand observations. Thus, the power of the test is likely high. A caveat is that the power may be low against very small alternatives: if the true average price difference was not zero but very close to zero. Taking these together, we got a small test statistic, and we couldn't reject the null hypothesis of no price difference. Thus either the null is true or, if it isn't true, the true price difference is tiny. That means that we can be quite certain that the average online–offline price difference is zero or very small in the population of products represented by our data.

We arrive at the same conclusion with the help of the p-value. The software calculated that the p-value of the test is 0.66. That means that there is a 66% chance that we could observe a price difference of this magnitude (or a larger one) if the null is true. It also means that the smallest level of significance at which we could reject the null is 66%. So we don't reject the null as this 66% is well over the 5% level of significance we have chosen. This is of course the same decision that we made with the t-statistic and the critical value.

Finally, note that we would arrive to a similar conclusion if, instead of carrying out a test, we just looked at the 95% confidence interval of the average price difference. We have all the ingredients to calculate that CI: average price difference in the data is -0.054, with SE $= 0.124$. Thus the 95% CI is

$$CI_{95\%} = [-0.054 - 2SE, -0.054 + 2SE] = [-0.30, +0.19] \tag{6.15}$$

This CI contains zero. So the value of the true average price difference (the average price difference in the population of products represented by our data) may very well be zero.

In fact, the CI has more information than a p-value or a t-statistic. It also shows that it's very unlikely that the true average price difference is more than -30 cents or $+20$ cents.

This concludes our case study. From it, we learned that online and offline prices are, on average, very similar among the products represented by our data. Indeed, we can't reject our hypothesis that they are the same on average.

What does that imply for products we are interested in? For example, we can conclude that differences between online and offline prices of the same products are likely zero on average among all products in the USA that were sold by large retailers in the USA in 2015–2016. For this step of generalization, we need to assume that the products sampled in this dataset represent all products in those stores, at least in terms of the average online–offline price difference. Also, keeping in mind that we restricted our data to regular prices (without sales or promotions), we would need to assume that the average zero difference holds for sales and promotions if we wanted to generalize to them. Moreover, we need to assume that the retailers sampled in this data represent all larger retailers in the USA, at least in terms of the difference of their online versus offline prices. Finally, if we are interested in another year, say this year, then we would need to assume that the pattern is stable enough from 2015–2016 to this year. If we want to make further generalizations, we would need to assume more. For example, these results may have a lower external validity if we wanted to compare online and offline prices of the same products sold by different retailers. Similarly, they may have low external validity for other countries.

This case study illustrated how to carry out a hypothesis test. First, we translated a question (do online and offline prices tend to be the same?) into a statistic (the average of the difference of online and offline prices of the same products). Then we formed a null hypothesis and an alternative hypothesis; here that was a two-sided alternative. We calculated the statistic from the data, together with its standard error, and divided the two to calculate the t-statistic. We compared the value of this t-statistic to the critical values and decided that we couldn't reject the null. We repeated this decision with the help of the p-value that we calculated directly using the software. We also looked at the 95% CI and arrived at the same decision. We then thought about what that decision really meant, and then, the extent to which we could generalize that decision from the population of products represented by the data to the population of products we were interested in.

Perhaps the most important take-away from this case study is that carrying out hypothesis testing is actually not that hard. We had to follow some steps, but most of the work was done by the computer. A harder task is to define the statistic of interest, the null, and the alternative. And the even harder task is to understand what rejecting or not rejecting the null really means, and whether we could generalize that decision to the situation we really care about.

6.6 Steps of Hypothesis Testing

The previous sections described all the ingredients to carry out a hypothesis test. We have illustrated how to do that in our case study. But there are specific cases that call for doing things a bit differently. Before moving to those, let us summarize the steps of hypothesis testing.

Review Box 6.5   Steps of hypothesis testing

1. Define the statistic that corresponds to your question.
2. Initial assessment of external validity: general pattern of interest, general pattern represented by the data, does it make sense to continue?
3. State the null and alternative hypotheses.
4. Choose a critical value. In practice, that should correspond to 5%, but present an argument if you want to choose some other value.
5. Calculate the test statistic from the data.
6. Make a decision based on the calculated test statistic and the critical value.

7. Alternatively to the previous three steps, calculate the p-value and make a decision by comparing it to a pre-set level of significance that in practice will usually be 5%. Again, make an argument if you want to choose some other value.
8. Interpret the results.
9. Final assessment of external validity. Would the same decision be fine for the population, or general pattern, of interest?

6.7   One-Sided Alternatives

When we discussed false positives and false negatives we focused on two-sided hypotheses, with $H_0: s_{true} = 0$ against $H_A: s_{true} \neq 0$. And that's what we had in our case study, too. However, as we mentioned earlier in Section 6.2, sometimes we want to do a one-sided test instead.

Testing a null hypothesis against a one-sided alternative means having an inequality in H_A. Most often, it goes with having an inequality in the null hypothesis instead of an equality. The two most frequent examples are $H_0: s_{true} \leq 0$ against $H_A: s_{true} > 0$ and $H_0: s_{true} \geq 0$ against $H_A: s_{true} < 0$.

In order to reject the null $s_{true} \leq 0$, we need to reject each and every possible value in the hypothesized interval in favor of $s > 0$. The hardest of those possible values to reject would be $s = 0$. This is because if we can reject $s = 0$ against $s > 0$, we can reject all $s < 0$ values, too. For that reason we need the equality to be always part of the null. Therefore, in practice, testing $H_0: s_{true} \leq 0$ against $H_A: s_{true} > 0$ is the same as testing $H_0: s_{true} = 0$ against $H_A: s_{true} > 0$. Similarly, testing $H_0: s_{true} \geq 0$ against $H_A: s_{true} < 0$ is the same as testing $H_0: s_{true} = 0$ against $H_A: s_{true} < 0$.

Having only one of the inequalities in the alternative leads to focusing on one side of the test statistic only. Here we don't care how far the estimate is from the hypothesized value in one direction; we only care about the deviation in the other direction. Focusing on deviations in one direction means that we care about one half of the sampling distribution of the test statistic. The question therefore is the probability that the test statistic would fall outside the critical value in the "wrong direction," given that it deviates from the hypothesized value in that "wrong direction." With $H_0: s_{true} \leq 0$ against $H_A: s_{true} > 0$, we care about whether $\hat{s}$ is large positive enough in order to reject the null; if it is negative, we don't reject the null whatever its size.

The probability of a false positive is smaller in this case. We don't reject the null if the test statistic falls in the region that is specified in the null hypothesis – we may reject it only if it falls in the other region. Thus, we make a false positive decision only half of the time. The probability of a false positive decision here is therefore half of the probability of a false positive in the corresponding two-sided test.

Therefore, the practical way to test a one-sided hypothesis is a two-step procedure.

1. If the test statistic is in the region of the null, don't reject the null. This happens if $\hat{s}$ is in the region of the null (e.g., $\hat{s} < 0$ for $H_0: s_{true} \leq 0$ against $H_A: s_{true} > 0$).
2. If the test statistic is in the region of the alternative, proceed with testing the usual way with some modification. Ask the software to calculate the p-value of the null hypothesis of the equality (for example, $H_0: s_{true} = 0$ if the true null is $H_0: s_{true} \leq 0$) and divide the p-value by two.

In practice, we almost never go through these steps. Most software carries out a test against a one-sided alternative and calculates the appropriate p-value.

CASE STUDY – Testing the Likelihood of Loss on a Stock Portfolio

One-sided test of a probability

To illustrate how to carry out a one-sided hypothesis test, let's go back to our case study in Chapter 5, on stock market returns. The question there was the probability of a loss on our portfolio of at least 5% from one day to another. Our portfolio was the company stocks contained in the S&P500 index in the USA. We used the `sp500` dataset on the daily value of the S&P500 stock market index in 11 years, from 2006 through 2016, with 2519 observations. Recall from Chapter 5, Section 5.A6, that the proportion of such losses was 0.5% of the days in the data.

For this illustrative example, let's say that we can tolerate such losses as long as they are not more frequent than 1% of the days. That 1% chance is larger than the 0.5% chance we see in our data. Thus, we would want to know if we can safely reject that larger chance. And we are interested in what would happen next year. Assume for the sake of this illustrative example that external validity is high, and let's focus on the general pattern represented by our 11 years of data.

The statistic is the proportion of days with a loss of 5% or more. This is a relative frequency or, in a more abstract sense, a probability. Up to this point we looked at averages: we introduced the t-test for averages, and we used our knowledge of the sampling distribution of averages. Can we use that knowledge to test a probability?

The answer is yes. In fact, we already answered this question earlier in Chapter 5, Section 5.A3. The proportion of days with a 5%+ loss is nothing else than the average of a binary indicator variable. This binary indicator variable, which we may call *lossof5*, is one on days with a loss of 5% or more, and it is zero on other days. The average of this variable is the proportion of the times it has the value one. In our data, that average is 0.005, which corresponds to a frequency of 0.5% of the days.

We want to see its difference from the 1% frequency that we can tolerate. So our s here is the proportion of days with such a loss in our data minus 0.01: $s = \overline{lossof5} - 0.01$ where *lossof5* is our binary variable.

Here the tricky part is translating our question into an appropriate null hypothesis and an appropriate alternative hypothesis. We want to make sure that the proportion of large losses is less than 1%. So this should go into the alternative: $H_A: s_{true} < 0$. The null should cover all other possibilities, including the equality sign: $H_0: s_{true} \geq 0$. This is one-sided testing.

In our data, we found a proportion of days of such losses to be 0.005, so $\overline{lossof5} = 0.005$. Then the statistic calculated from our data is $\hat{s} = 0.005 - 0.01 = -0.005$. The proportion of days with large losses is half of a percent in our data. It's smaller than the threshold value of one percent, so the test statistic is less than zero.

Following the decision rules we outlined, first note that the test statistic is outside the region of the null. The region of the null is positive numbers and zero; the test statistic is negative. Then, the next step is to make the software calculate the p-value for the corresponding two-sided test ($H_0: s_{true} = 0$; $H_A: s_{true} \neq 0$). That p-value is shown to be 0.0000, which means that it's less than 0.000 05. According to step 2 above, we can further divide this by two, and that would lead to an even smaller p-value.

In any case, the p-value is very small so we reject the null. The conclusion: we can safely say that large losses occur less frequently than one percent of the days. This is true for the general pattern behind the 11-year-old history of the S&P500 in our data. It is true for the general pattern behind next year, too, if external validity is high. But the p-value is very small, so we can draw the same conclusion even if we allow for some extra uncertainty due to potentially not-super-high external validity.

Note, finally, that the 95% CI would have given us a similar conclusion. The SE we calculated to be 0.0014 so the 95% CI of large losses is [0.22%, 0.78%]. This CI doesn't contain the threshold value of 1% we are concerned about. So, with high confidence we can say that we can expect daily losses of 5% or more to occur on less than 1% of the days. Of course, whether the same general pattern will prevail in the future is an open question, so we may qualify this decision.

6.8 Testing Multiple Hypotheses

Our last technical topic in this already pretty technical chapter deals with how to interpret the results of tests when we carry out many of them using the same data. That situation is called **testing multiple hypotheses**.

The simplest decision rule to testing a hypothesis consists of calculating a p-value from the data and comparing it to a pre-set level of significance. So far we have considered cases with one pair of hypotheses: a null and an alternative. Often, though, data analysis involves testing multiple null hypotheses, each with its corresponding alternative. For example, we may be interested in the correlation of firm size and various dimensions of the quality of management, using the 18 different scores in the World Management Survey, or we may want to see if that correlation is positive in each industry separately (see our case study in Chapter 4, Section 4.A4). Or we may be interested in losses on a portfolio of multiple magnitudes: 2%, 3%, 4%, 5%, and so on. Or we may be interested in whether online and offline prices are the same, on average, in various groups of products. So, by asking slightly more detailed questions that correspond to our original question, we can easily end up with dozens of hypotheses to test.

Testing multiple hypotheses is an issue because the statistical theory of testing, and the corresponding tools, have been developed for testing a single null hypothesis. The way the p-value is calculated makes it capture the likelihood of the observed or larger value of a statistic for a single null hypothesis. When testing multiple hypotheses, we may be tempted to use these tools, such as the p-value, for each hypothesis. But that would lead to misleading results.

To understand why using a decision rule, which is designed for a single test, would lead to misleading conclusions when applied to multiple tests, consider a situation in which we are testing 20 hypotheses. An example is whether the online–offline price differential is zero in each of 20 groups of products. Assume that all of those 20 null hypotheses are true. If we set the level of significance for a single hypothesis, we allow for a 5% chance to be wrong when rejecting the null. That means that we are allowed to be wrong 5% of the time by rejecting the null. Thus, we can expect that, following that rule, we would reject the null about once when we test our 20 null hypotheses. In practice, that would mean that we can expect to see a p-value less than 0.05 in 1 out of the 20 tests. Naively we may pick that one null hypothesis and say that there is enough evidence to reject it, and say that we can't reject the other 19. But that would be a mistake: we started out assuming that all 20 nulls are true. Yes, rejecting the null when it's true is a risk we always have. But at the heart of the procedure is to make sure that happens rarely – here 5% of the time. And, yet, here we can expect that to happen with a much higher chance.

That is because the p-value for a single null hypothesis is designed to calculate the likelihood that we were wrong to reject that particular null hypothesis if tested by itself. In multiple hypothesis testing, the question is the likelihood that any one of the true nulls will be wrongfully rejected. These are just two different probabilities.

There are various ways to deal with probabilities of false positives when testing multiple hypotheses. Multiple testing is a rather complicated part of statistics, and its tools are beyond the scope of this textbook. In any case, it is good practice to be especially cautious and conservative when testing multiple hypotheses and to use conservative criteria. One option is to use a 1%, or even lower, level of significance instead of the customary 5% for rejecting null hypotheses.

6.A3 CASE STUDY – Comparing Online and Offline Prices: Testing the Difference

Testing multiple hypotheses

To illustrate the issues with testing multiple hypotheses, let's go back to our case study of online and offline prices of the same products. Besides pooling all products as we did so far, we may be interested in whether online and offline prices are the same, on average, for each retailer in the data. This sample has 16 retailers. Thus testing whether the average price difference is zero in each is testing multiple hypotheses – 16 of them. One way to express these 16 hypotheses in a condensed format is denoting each store by index j:

$$H_0: s_{j,true} = \overline{pdiff}_{j,true} = 0 \tag{6.16}$$

$$H_A: s_{j,true} = \overline{pdiff}_{j,true} \neq 0 \tag{6.17}$$

Table 6.2 shows the 16 p-values that we get if we carry out each test one by one.

Table 6.2 Multiple testing of price differences

Retailer ID:	44	45	46	47	48	49	50	51
Diff	3.74	−1.2	−0.43	0.05	0.42	2.41	0.61	0.28
p-value	0.04	0.22	0.00	0.10	0.04	0.20	0.10	0.06
Retailer ID:	53	54	56	57	58	59	60	62
Diff	−0.97	−0.03	−0.49	0.93	−0.17	−0.53	−0.14	1.36
p-value	0.01	0.80	0.04	0.00	0.00	0.00	0.70	0.12

Note: The table reports 16 tests – one for each retailer. The columns refer to each retailer, identified by an ID number. The first row is the average online–offline price difference for the particular retailer in the data; the p-value refers to the p-value of a single null hypothesis that the online–offline price difference at that particular retailer is zero.
Source: `billion-prices` dataset. US retailers in 2015–2016, sales and promotions excluded. N=6439.

If the null hypothesis were true for each retailer, we would expect about one of the p-values to be below 0.05 (5% of 16 is slightly less than 1). However, the p-value is less than 0.05 in 8 of the 16 hypotheses. This is more than what we would expect if there was zero price difference in each store.

As an alternative way to assess multiple hypotheses, let's apply a more conservative criterion for rejection, say, a 1% level of significance. That would mean that we would reject four of the nulls here.

Thus, we may conclude that the average online–offline price difference is not zero in some of the retail chains in the data, even if we factor in the fact that we are testing multiple hypotheses.

How come, then, that we could not reject the assertion that it's zero when averaged over all retailers? Mechanically, this is because the average price difference is negative in some retailers and positive in others. Of the eight retailers with a p-value that is less than 0.05, five have a negative price difference and three a positive difference.

To make sense of what we see, let's ask why would some retailers charge higher prices online while other stores charge higher prices offline. A likely answer is that they don't in fact do that. More likely, what we see is that there are errors in the data, or differences for some products due to specific reasons. Those errors or deviations are sometimes positive, sometimes negative, and their magnitude is large for some retailers and small for others. And, crucially, they appear to average out when considering all 16 retailers, but not so much for some of the retailers when they are considered separately.

One such source of error could be a time lag in data collection from retailers. As we dig deeper in the data collection process, we learn that in our data, 25% of the products had their online price collected on the same day; the remaining 75% were collected within two to eight days. As prices may change over time, the larger the time lag between the registration of the two prices, the more likely their difference is due to an error.

It turns out that the proportion of products with online prices registered later is larger among the retailers with p-values below 0.05 in the previous table. Thus their measured price differences are more likely to be due to error. As a data exercise, you will be invited to re-do the analysis including products whose offline and online prices were evaluated on the same day.

Going back to the main story, what do these findings imply for our original question of whether online and offline prices are the same, on average? Our question is about the general pattern represented by the data that includes all 16 retailers. Averaging over the retailers may reduce potential errors in data collection. In principle, the hypothesis would also allow for some retailers charging higher prices online while others do the reverse. Thus the conclusions of the two kinds of tests (single test on the full set vs. multiple tests on individual retailers) are not in conflict. The multiple tests either reveal artificial features of the data (measurement error), or they may add new information on differences in pricing by retailer. In this case study the former is more likely.

6.9 p-Hacking

Earlier, we discussed why it is good practice to use a conventional level of significance (5% or 1%) when making a decision. This rule eliminates a potentially arbitrary decision of how large a likelihood we would tolerate for the false positive decision. And, as we argued, that's good because allowing for an arbitrary decision may compel data analysts to make testing decisions that are biased towards their preconceptions. For example, if we think that firms with younger managers tend to grow at equal rates, and we test the null of no difference and arrive at a p-value of 0.04, we may decide that we can't tolerate a 4% chance for the false positive and decide not to reject the null. That decision would reinforce our belief of no difference. In contrast, if we believed that the firms with younger managers tend to grow at different rates than firms with older managers, and we see the same p-value of 0.04, we may decide that this 4% chance is something we can live with and reject the null, reinforcing our belief of differences in growth rates. All that controversy can be avoided if we adopt a conventional 5% threshold. That would make us reject the null and say the growth rates are different, regardless of what our prior belief was.

Unfortunately, however, data analysts can make other decisions during their analysis to arrive at test results that would reinforce their prior beliefs. For example, we may face some issues during data cleaning – e.g., what to do with extreme values (see Chapters 2 and 3). For example, when analyzing growth rates of firms by the age of their managers, some firms may have unusually large positive growth in the data. Suppose, moreover, that it's not obvious whether those observations with extreme values should be kept or discarded. Then, suppose that we end up rejecting the null of equal average growth rates if we decide to keep the observations with extreme values, but we end up not rejecting the same null if we discard those observations. Then, we, as humans, may prefer the version that reinforces our prior beliefs, and go ahead with the data cleaning decision that produces the test results that are in line with those beliefs. A specific, but apparently frequent, case is when a data analyst prefers to show "significant" results – i.e., results when the null is rejected. Recall that rejecting the null is the stronger, more informative decision. Thus, a data analyst may prefer to show the results of tests that lead to rejecting the null, because those are "more conclusive."

These are examples of **p-hacking**. In a narrower sense, p-hacking refers to showing only results of hypothesis tests that suggest one decision, when different choices in the process of data wrangling or data analysis would lead to a different decision for those hypotheses. Often, this means presenting positive decisions, where the null is rejected, and not presenting negative results, where the null isn't rejected. Hence the name p-hacking: carrying out tests with different versions of the data and the analysis, and presenting only the positive results. In a broader sense, p-hacking refers to presenting results of any analysis that reinforce prior beliefs even though other results may be similarly meaningful, but they are not presented.

p-hacking is bad because it deceives our audience, and it can deceive us, too. It's a particularly dangerous way to lie with statistics because the methods are fine, only not everything is presented. The seemingly obvious way to avoid it would be to present all results, including those that would lead to a conflicting, or less strong, conclusion. Unfortunately, that goes against our other general advice to stay focused and show few results that the audience can digest. Thus, a good practice is to produce many robustness checks, and report their results next to the main results, sometimes only as a qualifier. For example, we may say that including extreme values would lead to a less strong conclusion.

Another consequence of p-hacking is that we can't fully trust the results of previous research. As an extreme example, suppose that there is a medical intervention that turns out not to have any effect. (Think of your favorite hoax here.) But it was tested in 100 well-designed experiments. In five of the 100 experiments, the researchers found that they can reject the null that it has no effect. So these five are false positives. That's actually what we would expect if all experiments used a 5% level of significance for their test. This is all very well, but now suppose that only those five positive results are published, the other 95 are not. Looking through the published results, we would see only five experiments, all of which with a positive result, concluding that the intervention had an effect.

While p-hacking is in reality probably not as extreme as we have described it here, it surely exists. Because much published research shows something that may not always be true, the phenomenon is also called **publication bias**: answers to a question that end up being published may be a biased sample of all answers to the question that were produced during analyzing available data. There are some ingenious methods to detect p-hacking and publication bias and correct results for those biases. Discussing those is beyond the scope of our textbook. Instead, we advise treating published evidence with some healthy skepticism. Yes, there is usually a lot to learn about a question from reading previous research. But no, the answer that emerges from all that reading is not always the final and only true answer.

6.10 Testing Hypotheses with Big Data

As we discussed in Chapter 5, Section 5.9, generalizing to the population, or general pattern, represented by the data is not really an issue with Big Data that has a lot of observations. The CI produced from such big data would be so narrow that it would be practically the same as our estimated value. However, generalizing from the population, or general pattern, represented by the data to the population, or general pattern, we care about, is a different question. Here it does not help if the data is big, with very many observations. By the same logic, the process of testing hypotheses with Big Data is not usually a big deal: if the statistic computed from the data is not literally equal to the value in the null, we would always reject the null. But whether that decision is readily generalizable to the situation we care about is a matter of external validity, where Big Data doesn't help.

One caveat here is that Big Data with very many observations may not be so big if we examine very rare phenomena. Consider our example of presenting two versions of the same online ad to two groups of people, and examining whether the follow-up rate in the two groups is the same. In many experiments of this kind, the actual follow-up rates are tiny. Suppose, for example, that of 1 million people that were shown the old version of the ad, 100 followed up to visit the company's website. Of the other 1 million people that were shown the new version, 130 followed up. There is a difference in the follow-up rates in this data, but that doesn't necessarily mean that the difference is there in the general pattern represented by this data. That's even though we have 2 million observations, which is a lot. However, the follow-up rates are tiny. Thus, the test statistic that tells us whether that difference of 30 people is large enough is not that tiny in the end. Thus, small differences need to be properly tested even with Big Data. You will be invited to carry out this test among the practice questions.

Some Big Data has a lot of variables instead of, or on top of, a lot of observations. Examples include data from DNA sequencing, or detailed data on credit card transactions. In some cases the number of variables exceeds the number of observations – sometimes by orders of magnitude. The issues with testing multiple hypotheses are especially relevant in such data. When, for example, we want to see which parts of the DNA are associated with a certain medical condition, the number of hypotheses to test may be in the millions. Applying conventional 5% or even 1% levels of significance would yield many false positives. Instead, it becomes critically important to apply appropriate methods to handle this issue in an explicit manner – e.g., by applying very conservative levels of significance such as one millionth of a percent. Testing multiple hypotheses with that many variables is at the frontier of statistical research on using Big Data. Thus we just describe the issue; solutions to it are beyond the scope of our textbook.

| 6.11 | **Main Takeaways** |

Testing in statistics means making a decision about the value of a statistic in the general pattern represented by the data.

- Hypothesis starts with explicitly stating H_0 and H_A.
- A statistical test rejects H_0 if there is enough evidence against it; otherwise it doesn't reject it.
- Testing multiple hypotheses at the same time is a tricky business; it pays to be very conservative with rejecting the null.

PRACTICE QUESTIONS

1. Write down an example for a null and a two-sided alternative hypothesis.
2. Write down an example for a null and a one-sided alternative hypothesis.
3. What is false positive? What is false negative? Give an example of a test, and explain what a false positive and a false negative would look like.
4. What is the level of significance or size of a test, and what is the power of a test? Give an example of a test, and explain the concept of size, significance, and power in the context of this example.
5. Tests on larger datasets have more power in general. Why?
6. What is the p-value? The p-value of a test is 0.01. What does that mean and what can you do with that information?
7. Why is testing multiple hypotheses problematic?
8. What is p-hacking, and how can you minimize its perils when presenting the results of your analysis? Give an example.
9. What is the effect of p-hacking on published results that examine the same question? What does that imply for the usefulness of reading through the literature of published results? Give an example.
10. You examine the wages of recent college graduates, and you want to test whether the starting wage of women is the same, on average, as the starting wage of men. Define the statistic you want to test. Define the population for which you can carry out the test if your data is a random sample of college graduates from your country surveyed in 2015. Write down the appropriate null and alternative hypotheses, and describe how you would carry out the test. What would be a false negative in this case? What would be a false positive?
11. You are testing whether an online advertising campaign had an effect on sales by comparing the average spending by customers who were exposed to the campaign with the average spending of customers who were not exposed. Define the statistic you want to test. What is the null and the alternative if your question is whether the campaign had a positive effect? What would be a false negative in this case? What would be a false positive? Which of the two do you think would have more severe business consequences?
12. Consider the null hypothesis that there is no difference between the likelihood of bankruptcy of firms that were established more than three years ago and firms that were established less than

three years ago. You carry out a test using data on all firms from a country in 2015, and the test produces a p-value of 0.001. What is your conclusion? What if the p-value was 0.20?

13. A randomly selected half of the employees of a customer service firm participated in a training program, while the other half didn't. How would you test whether the training had an effect on the satisfaction of the customers they serve? Describe all steps of the test procedure.

14. Consider our example of online ads in Section 6.10, in which two versions of the same ad were shown to 1 million people each, and 100 followed up from the group that was shown the old version, while 130 followed through from the other group. Write down the test statistic, the null, and the alternative (go for two-sided alternative). Carry out the test using the t-statistic with the help of the following statistics: the follow-up rate for the new version is 0.000 13; for the old version 0.000 10; their difference is 0.000 03; the SE of that difference is 0.000 021. Interpret your decision.

15. Consider the same online ad example as in the previous question, but now go for a one-sided alternative. Write down the test statistic, the null, and the alternative, and argue why you did it that way. Carry out the test using the information that the p-value of the two-sided test would be 0.07.

DATA EXERCISES

Easier and/or shorter exercises are denoted by [*]; harder and/or longer exercises are denoted by [**].

1. Use the same `billion-prices` dataset as in the case study. Pick another country, exclude sales and promotions, and test whether online and offline prices are the same, on average. Compare your results to the case study. [*]

2. Use the same `billion-prices` dataset as in the case study. Pick the same country, but now include sales and promotions, and test whether online and offline prices are the same, on average. Compare your results to the case study. [*]

3. Use the same `billion-prices` dataset as in the case study. Pick the same country, exclude sales and promotions, and keep only products whose offline and online prices were assessed on the same day. Test whether online and offline prices are the same, on average. Also test the multiple hypotheses of whether they are the same in each store. Compare your results to the case study. [*]

4. Use the same `sp500` dataset as in the case study. Pick a different definition for a large loss, and/or a different threshold for its frequency. Test whether the frequency of large losses is larger or smaller than that threshold frequency. Carry out the test and interpret its results, including what to expect for a similar investment portfolio next year. [*]

5. Consider the `hotels-europe` dataset. Pick a city and two different dates. Test if prices are the same, on average, on those two days. Watch out for potential differences in the included hotels for those two dates. One way to see if the two groups are different is comparing their average customer ratings – so test if their average ratings are the same. Discuss your findings. [*]

REFERENCES AND FURTHER READING

On p-hacking and publication bias, an informative article is Franco et al. (2014).

An advanced treatment of testing multiple hypotheses is Anderson (2008), which considers some of the most influential experiments on the long-run effects of early childhood education.

PART II Regression Analysis

7 Simple Regression

Why and how to carry out simple regression analysis, and how to interpret its results

Motivation

You want to identify hotels in a city that are good deals: underpriced for their location and quality. You have scraped the web for data on all hotels in the city, and you have cleaned the data. You have carried out exploratory data analysis that revealed that hotels closer to the city center tend to be more expensive, but there is a lot of variation in prices between hotels at the same distance. How should you identify hotels that are underpriced relative to their distance to the city center? In particular, how should you capture the average price–distance relationship that would provide you a benchmark, to which you can compare actual price to find good deals?

The analysis of hotel prices and distance to the city center reveals that hotels further away from the center are less expensive by a certain amount, on average. Can you use this result to estimate how much more revenue a hotel developer could expect if it were to build a hotel closer to the center rather than farther away?

Part II of our textbook is about regression analysis, the most widely used method in data analysis. Regression is a model for the conditional mean: the mean of y for different values of one or more x variables. Regression is used to uncover patterns of association. That, in turn, is used in causal analysis, to uncover the effect of x on y, and in predictions, to arrive at a good guess of what the value of y is it we don't know it, but we know the value of x.

Simple regression analysis uncovers patterns of association between two variables: y and a single x variable. We spend this chapter, and the next two chapters, on simple regression. We turn to multiple regression, which includes more x variables, in Chapter 10. While simple regression is rarely used as the only method in actual data analysis, we spend a lot of time to understand it in detail. We do so because simple regression is a good starting point to most analyses, it is the building block of more complicated methods, and what we learn about it will carry over to multiple regression with appropriate, and usually small, modifications.

In this chapter, we introduce simple non-parametric regression and simple linear regression, and we show how to visualize their results. We then discuss simple linear regression in detail. We introduce the regression equation, how its coefficients are uncovered (estimated) in actual data, and we emphasize how to interpret the coefficients. We introduce the concepts of predicted value and residual and of goodness of fit, and we discuss the relationship between regression and correlation. We end with a note on the relationship between causation and regression.

The case study in this chapter, **Finding a good deal among hotels with simple regression**, uncovers the pattern of association between hotel prices in a European city and the distance of the hotel to the city center. We use the same data as in Chapters 1 and 2, the `hotels-vienna` dataset.

In this chapter we use this case study to illustrate simple non-parametric and linear regression, and we will develop this study further in subsequent chapters.

Learning outcomes

After working through this chapter, you should be able to:

- identify problems that call for and lend themselves to regression analysis;
- estimate simple non-parametric regression and simple linear regression using standard statistical software;
- interpret the results of simple linear regression analysis in a precise yet useful and accessible way;
- visualize patterns uncovered by regression analysis.

7.1   When and Why Do Simple Regression Analysis?

In Chapter 4 we introduced several tools to uncover patterns of association between two variables: whether and how the values of y differ when the values of x differ. In this chapter we focus on the most important pattern of association, mean-dependence. Recall that mean-dependence tells whether, and to what extent, the mean of y is different when the value of x is different.

The method we introduce in this chapter is **regression analysis**, often abbreviated simply to **regression**. Regression is the most widely used method of comparison in data analysis. **Simple regression analysis** uncovers mean-dependence between two variables. It amounts to comparing average values of one variable, called the dependent variable (y) for observations that are different in the other variable, the explanatory variable (x). This and the following chapters provide a thorough introduction and discuss many details, issues, and generalizations of the method. **Multiple regression analysis**, to be introduced in Chapter 10, involves more variables.

Discovering patterns of association between variables is often a good starting point even if our question is more ambitious. We are often interested in causal analysis: uncovering the effect of one variable on another variable. Examples include how sales would change as a result of more or different kinds of advertising, or how the educated workforce of a city would change in the future if the city were to spend more on education. Or, we may be interested in predictive analysis: what to expect of a variable (long-run polls, hotel prices) for various values of another variable (immediate polls, distance to the city center). In both causal analysis and predictions we are often concerned with other variables that may exert influence. Simple regression is a good starting point to answering the main question even if we want to consider more variables, too. Simple regression is also a major building block for more complicated methods.

7.2   Regression: Definition

Regression analysis is a method that uncovers the average value of a variable y for different values of variable x. (In this textbook we use expected value, average, and mean as synonyms.) Regression is a **model** for the **conditional mean**, or, in other words, the **conditional expectation**. Introduced in Chapter 4, Section 4.4, the conditional mean shows the mean value of y for various values of x. The model for the conditional mean gives a rule that takes x values and tells what the mean value of y is.

The precise way to formulate this idea is

$$E[y|x] = f(x) \tag{7.1}$$

This should be read as follows: the expected value of y conditional on x is given by the function f. That function f is the model, which we call regression. For most of the textbook, we use a simpler shorthand notation:

$$y^E = f(x) \tag{7.2}$$

The shorthand y^E here stands for $E[y|x]$. It is less precise because it does not say what variable the function is conditional on (here x). Instead, we should infer this from the context (here the dependence is on x because it equals $f(x)$).

There is another often used notation for the regression. This different notation acknowledges the fact that the actual value of y is equal to its expected value plus a deviation from it. That deviation is called the **error term** of the regression:

$$y = f(x) + e \tag{7.3}$$

We are not going to use this notation in this textbook. Instead, we'll denote a regression as the conditional mean: $y^E = f(x)$. Later, in Chapter 21, Sections 21.3 and 21.12, we'll discuss why a version of the error term notation may be helpful in causal analysis.

Some more conventions in notation: written as $y^E = f(x)$, the expression is a general statement of the model: the relationship between the expected value of y and different values of x. Alternatively, written as $y^E = f(x = x_0)$ means the expected value of y if the variable x equals a particular value x_0 (substitute a suitable number for x_0). It shows the result of plugging a specific x value into the model.

The y and x variables in the $y^E = f(x)$ regression are labeled using various names. Throughout this text, we shall use the following names: **dependent variable** or **left-hand-side variable**, or simply the y variable, and **explanatory variable**, **right-hand-side variable**, or simply the x variable. The box below lists a few more names that are often used. We sometimes say that we "regress y on x," or "run a regression of y on x." By these we mean that we do simple regression analysis with y as the dependent variable and x as the explanatory variable.

Regression analysis finds patterns in the data by comparing observations with different values of the x variable to see whether and how the mean value of the y variable differs across them. Thus, we need data with variation in x. Usually, the more variation in x, the better because it allows for more comparisons.

Regression analysis may reveal that average y tends to be higher at higher values of x. That would be a pattern of positive mean-dependence, or positive association. Or, it may reveal a negative association, or negative mean-dependence, with average y being lower at higher values of x. However, the pattern of association may be non-monotonic, in which average y tends to be higher for higher values of x in a certain range of the x variable and lower for higher values of x in another range of the x variable. Regression analysis may also reveal no association between average y and x, when average y tends to be the same regardless of the value of x. The goal of regression analysis is to uncover this pattern and characterize it in a useful way, by visualizing it or summarizing it in one or more numbers.

> ### Review Box 7.1   Regression and regression analysis
>
> - Regression analysis finds patterns of association between variables.
> - Simple regression shows the average value of the variable y for different values of variable x.
> - As a formula, $y^E = f(x)$, where y^E is a shorthand for the conditional expectation $E[y|x]$.
> - Naming the variables in the regression:
>   - y, dependent variable or left-hand-side variable, also explained variable, regressand, outcome variable, predicted variable;
>   - x, explanatory variable or right-hand-side variable, also independent variable, regressor, feature variable, predictor variable.

7.3   Non-parametric Regression

Non-parametric regressions describe the $y^E = f(x)$ pattern without imposing a specific **functional form** on f. They let the data dictate what that function looks like, at least approximately. In contrast, **parametric regressions** impose a functional form on f. Parametric examples include linear functions: $f(x) = a + bx$; exponential functions: $f(x) = ax^b$; quadratic functions: $f(x) = a + bx + cx^2$. These are called parametric because the functions have parameters a, b, c. As we shall see, parametric regressions are restrictive, but they produce readily interpretable numbers. In contrast, non-parametric regressions can spot patterns that restrictive parametric functions may miss, but that comes at a price: they do not produce readily interpretable numbers.

Non-parametric regressions come in various forms. When x has few values and there are many observations in the data, the best and most intuitive non-parametric regression for $y^E = f(x)$ shows average y for each and every value of x. There is no functional form imposed on f here. For example, the hotels in our data have 3 stars, 3.5 stars, or 4 stars. If we calculate the average price of hotels with the same numbers of stars and compare these averages across 3, 3.5, and 4 stars, we are carrying out a non-parametric regression analysis.

With many x values, things become more complicated, especially when the data has few observations for some, or all, x values. In such cases, there are two ways to do non-parametric regression analysis: **bins** and **smoothing**.

The first and more straightforward way is based on grouped values of x: bins. Bins are disjoint categories (no overlap) that span the entire range of x (no gaps). How exactly to create bins and how many such bins should be created are decisions for the analyst, similarly to the case of creating a histogram.

In fact, we have already seen such non-parametric regressions in Chapter 4 where we introduced their visualization: **bin scatters**. Bin scatters show the average value of y that corresponds to each bin created from the values of x, in an x–y coordinate system. An alternative visualization of the same non-parametric regression is the **step function**. A step function shows average y over the entire range of the bins. The case study will show some examples.

The second method produces a "smooth" graph that is both continuous and has no kink at any point. There are many ways of smoothing and thus many ways of producing such graphs. In data science these types of graphs are called smoothed conditional means plots. Indeed, non-parametric regression of this kind shows conditional means, smoothed to get a better image. Of the various methods available we consider one, called lowess.

Lowess is one of the most widely used non-parametric regression methods that produces a smooth graph. The name is an abbreviation of locally weighted scatterplot smoothing (sometimes abbreviated as "loess"). A lowess may be thought of as a smooth curve fit around a bin scatter. It may help to relate this method to density plots (introduced in Chapter 3, Section 3.3). Similarly to density plots, we have to set the bandwidth for smoothing, a choice that affects the results. In general, a wider bandwidth results in a smoother graph but may miss important details of the pattern. In contrast, a narrower bandwidth produces a more rugged-looking graph but may uncover more details of the pattern. Producing a lowess graph with default software settings is usually a meaningful way to visualize the patterns of association between two variables.

Smooth non-parametric regression methods, including lowess, do not produce numbers that would summarize the $y^E = f(x)$ pattern. Instead, they provide a value y^E for each of the particular x values that occur in the data, as well as for all x values in-between. The typical way to show the results of non-parametric regressions is via a graph. We interpret these graphs in qualitative, not quantitative ways. They can show interesting shapes in the pattern, such as non-monotonic parts, steeper and flatter parts.

In any case, if we want to visualize a regression, such as a lowess, it is good practice to plot it **together with the scatterplot** of y versus x. As we introduced in Chapter 4, Section 4.5, scatterplots visualize the joint distribution of two variables in the data in an $x-y$ coordinate system. Together with the scatterplot, visualization of a regression shows not only the extent to which the mean of y tends to differ across observations with different values of x, but it also shows how the actual values of y are scattered around those mean y values. That helps in putting the slope of the regression in context.

7.A1 CASE STUDY – Finding a Good Deal among Hotels with Simple Regression

Question, data, non-parametric regression

In this case study we use simple regression analysis to find a good deal among hotels. In particular, we want to find hotels that are underpriced relative to their distance to the city center. The use of regression analysis is to find what the hotel price "should be" for various levels of distance to the city center, and then compare that price to the actual price of each hotel to identify the especially low values.

We look at Vienna hotels for a November 2017 weekday. Based on our investigations in Chapters 2 and 3, we focus on hotels that are located in Vienna actual, are not too far from the center, are classified as hotels, and have 3, 3.5, or 4 stars. We excluded extremely high priced hotels that we had classified as error. In the original dataset, there are 428 hotels for that weekday in Vienna; our focused sample has N = 207 observations.

To learn about the average price of hotels with differing distances to the city center, the simplest comparison is to split the data into two parts, or, as we say, two bins: one with hotels that are close to the city center and one with hotels that are further away. At what distance to split the data is, of course, arbitrary. Let's say that the couple is fine walking two miles, so let's put the distance threshold at two miles. The "close" bin contains 157 hotels, with an average distance of 1 mile (minimum 0.1 miles, maximum 1.9 miles); the "far" bin contains 50 hotels, with an average distance of 3.2 miles (minimum 2.0 miles, maximum 6.6 miles).

The average price of the hotels close to the city center is 116 US dollars; the average price of the hotels far from the city center is 90 dollars. The average price difference is therefore −26 dollars. Simple as it may be, this comparison of average prices between "close" and "far" hotels is actually an example of regression analysis. Indeed, as we indicated earlier, regression may be thought of as generalizing this approach of comparing means.

We can create more refined bins, splitting each of the previous close and far bins into two. The four bins we have created have ranges [0,1], [1,2], [2,3], and [3,7] – all expressed in miles. This produces a different non-parametric regression from the previous one. It has the same dependent variable but different bins for the explanatory variable.

The results of the two regressions are visualized in Figures 7.1a and 7.1b. These are bin scatters. The x axis of Figure 7.1a has only two points, close and far. We put these two points at arbitrary places in terms of the x axis. In contrast, on Figure 7.1b we chose to have the continuous distance on the x axis. Here we put the regression points at specific values of distance within the bins. We chose the midpoint of each bin, which is usually good practice.

Both regressions show that hotels that are closer to the city center are, on average, more expensive. In other words, both suggest a negative pattern of association between hotel price and distance to the center. Whether the relationship is linear, convex, concave, or none of these, cannot be established with two values of x only (Figure 7.1a). With four distance categories, we can say more (Figure 7.1b). The relationship appears to be monotonic but nonlinear: the differences in average y between the adjacent bins are not always the same. We see a larger negative difference between the [0,1] miles and the [1,2] miles bins than between adjacent bins at higher distances.

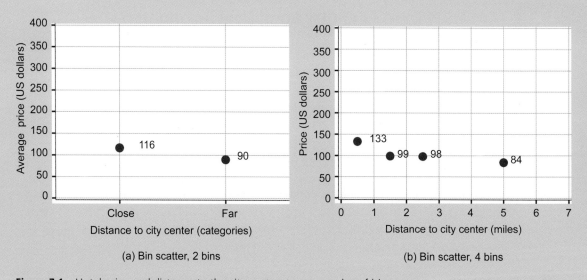

Figure 7.1   Hotel price and distance to the city center: two examples of bin scatters

Note: Bin scatter non-parametric regression. 2 bins: close if 0–1.9 miles, far if 2–7 miles. 4 bins: [0,1], [1,2], [2,3], [3,7] miles; average price visualized at the midpoint of each distance bin.
Source: `hotels-vienna` dataset. Vienna, November 2017, weekday. N=207.

Figure 7.2a visualizes the same four-bin non-parametric regression in a different way. Instead of a bin scatter, it shows a step function: horizontal line segments spanning the entire range of each bin. The figure includes the scatterplot as well, with the prices and distances of all 207 hotels. Having the regression results together with the scatterplot puts the regression in perspective. The average pattern is downward sloping, but there is a lot of variation of prices around that average pattern. Also, the scatterplot suggests that the negative pattern may not be valid beyond five miles, although there are only two hotels there.

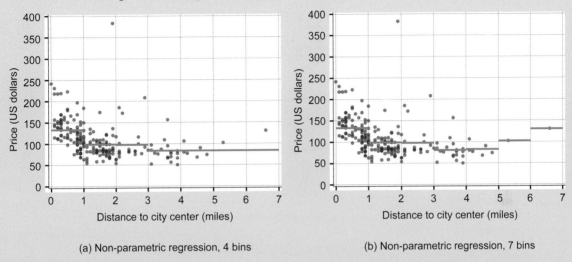

(a) Non-parametric regression, 4 bins   (b) Non-parametric regression, 7 bins

Figure 7.2 Hotel price and distance to the city center: non-parametric regression and scatterplot

Note: Bin scatter non-parametric regression with 4 bins and 7 bins.
Source: `hotels-vienna` dataset. Vienna, November 2017, weekday. N=207.

A non-parametric regression with even more bins is visualized in Figure 7.2b. There are seven bins here, each of width of one mile. This regression looks non-monotonic, with flat parts in the middle and positive slope at the end. If we take a closer look, there is more variation around the step function in the middle than towards the end. At the same time there are very few observations in some of these bins: only one hotel in the [6,7] bin, one in the [5,6] bin, and six in the [4,5] bin. It also turns out that defining the bins in different ways, such as bins with equal numbers of hotels instead of equal-length distances produces a somewhat different shape. You are invited to produce non-parametric regressions with alternative bin definitions as a data exercise.

We can already draw an important conclusion from this analysis: when using bins, the number and size of bins may affect the patterns suggested by the non-parametric regressions.

After bin scatters, let's look at a smooth non-parametric regression. Figure 7.3 shows the lowess non-parametric regression, together with the scatterplot. The default bandwidth selected by statistical software is 0.8 miles. This is very close to the 1 mile bin width of the bin scatter with seven bins shown in Figure 7.2b. The smooth non-parametric regression retains some aspects of that figure but not all. In particular, it, too, is steeper at small distances and flatter at longer distances, and it turns positive at the longest distances. At the same time it has fewer rugged features. It is what it is supposed to be: a smoother version of the corresponding non-parametric regression with disjoint bins of similar width.

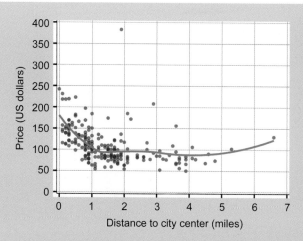

Figure 7.3 Hotel price and distance to the city center: lowess regression and scatterplot

Note: Lowess non-parametric regression, bandwidth=0.8.
Source: `hotels-vienna` dataset. Vienna, November 2017, weekday. N=207.

The most robust pattern we uncovered across these various non-parametric regressions is a negative slope in general. Yes, there are two hotels at large distance that do not fit this pattern. But the other more than 200 hotels do. Thus, hotels further away from the city center are, on average, less expensive. But how much less expensive are they? In particular, if we compare two hotels, one of which is one mile further away from the city center than the other, what price difference should we expect between the two? This is a quantitative question that is not easy to answer with the non-parametric regression results at hand. That would be a lot easier to do with a regression that produces readily interpretable quantitative answers. Linear regression does that; we shall discuss it in the next section.

Review Box 7.2 Non-parametric regression

- Non-parametric regressions show the average of the dependent variable as a function of the explanatory variable without imposing a particular functional form.
- The three most frequent types of non-parametric regressions show the average of the dependent variable computed:
  - for each and every value of the explanatory variable;
  - for bins (disjoint intervals) created from the explanatory variable;
  - as a smooth curve making use of overlapping intervals of the explanatory variable (lowess being the most widely used method).

7.4 ## Linear Regression: Introduction

Linear regression is the most widely used method in data analysis. It is the simplest regression method, and it is also the major building block of many more complicated regression models. Simple linear regression imposes linearity of the function f in $y^E = f(x)$. Linear functions have two parameters, also called coefficients: the **intercept coefficient** and the **slope coefficient**. By convention, we use Greek letters for these coefficients so that a linear regression has the form

$$y^E = \alpha + \beta x \tag{7.4}$$

To be more precise, linear regression imposes linearity in terms of its coefficients. We can have any function, including any nonlinear function, of the original variables themselves. It's still a linear regression as long as it consists of an intercept plus a slope coefficient, whether that slope multiplies x or any function of x (think of logarithm, square, and so on). Indeed, in Chapter 8 we will discuss several ways we can use linear regression to capture nonlinear, and potentially non-monotonic, patterns of associations between the original y and x variables. For the remainder of this chapter, we focus on linear regressions with y and x, not their functions. Or, alternatively, whatever we say should be understood for regressions with a left-hand-side variable and a right-hand-side variable, be those the original variables in the data or their transformations.

With y on its left-hand side and x on its right-hand side, linear regression is a line through the $x-y$ scatterplot. With the usual method of calculating the coefficients, to be discussed below in Section 7.7, this line is the best-fitting line one can draw through the scatterplot. It is the best fit in the sense that it is the line that is closest to all points of the scatterplot. We shall discuss the fit of the linear regression in more detail later, in Section 7.9.

One way to look at the linearity in linear regression is as an assumption: by doing linear regression analysis we assume that the regression function is linear in its coefficients. While, as we shall see, this can accommodate various **nonlinear patterns**, it cannot capture all kinds of nonlinear patterns. The linearity assumption may or may not be true, and, unfortunately, that often cannot be established within the framework of linear regression.

Another, more useful way to look at linearity is to treat it as an approximation. Whatever the form of the $y^E = f(x)$ relationship, the $y^E = \alpha + \beta x$ regression fits a line through it. By fitting a line, linear regression approximates the average slope of the $y^E = f(x)$ curve. The average slope has an important interpretation: it is the difference in average y that corresponds to different values of x, averaged across the entire range of x in the data.

7.5 Linear Regression: Coefficient Interpretation

What makes linear regression very powerful is that its coefficients have a clear interpretation based on the idea of comparing conditional means. The linear regression $y^E = \alpha + \beta x$ has two coefficients.

Less important is the **intercept**: α. It is the average value of y when x is zero. Formally: $E[y|x = 0] = \alpha + \beta \times 0 = \alpha$.

The more important coefficient is the **slope**: β. It shows the expected difference in y corresponding to a one unit difference in x. y is higher, on average, by β for observations with a one-unit higher value of x. Or, in a longer version that is sometimes more helpful: comparing two observations that differ in x by one unit, we expect y to be β higher for the observation with one unit higher x. Formally: $E[y|x = x_0 + 1] - E[y|x_0] = (\alpha + \beta \times (x_0 + 1)) - (\alpha + \beta \times x_0) = \beta$.

Sometimes the slope of linear regression is given more ambitious interpretations. One such ambitious interpretation talks about increases or decreases, e.g., saying that "β shows how much y increases, on average, when x is increased." This interpretation may be correct if the data is a time series where a change in y is regressed on a change in x. However, it is not correct in general.

In fact, it can be very misleading for cross-sectional data where we are comparing different observations instead of comparing changes for the same observation. Another, even more ambitious interpretation is calling the slope the "effect" of x on y. Attributing a cause and effect relationship to differences uncovered by regression analysis is a conclusion that may or may not be correct. Typically, it is not correct in observational data – a question that we'll return to at the end of this chapter and in Chapters 19 and 21.

Importantly, the interpretation based on comparing conditional means is always true whether or not the more ambitious interpretations are true. It is good practice to always state this interpretation explicitly. If we want to go further to a more ambitious interpretation, we should state that more ambitious interpretation after this one, adding the additional assumptions behind it and the evidence that substantiates those assumptions.

Review Box 7.3   Simple linear regression

- Simple linear regression shows the average of the dependent variable as a linear function of the explanatory variable:

$$y^E = a + \beta x$$

- This line is best thought of as a linear approximation of an underlying $y^E = f(x)$ pattern of any form.
- The parameters, or coefficients, of the linear regression are:
  - a is the intercept: it is the average value of y when x is zero.
  - β is the slope: y is β units higher, on average, for observations with one unit higher value of x.

7.6   Linear Regression with a Binary Explanatory Variable

An important special case of linear regression is when x is a binary variable, zero or one. The regression formula is the same:

$$y^E = a + \beta x \tag{7.5}$$

The parameters of this regression are interpreted as follows: a is the average value of y when x is zero; β is the difference in average y between observations with $x = 1$ and observations with $x = 0$; and the average value of y when $x = 1$ is $a + \beta$. In formulae:

$$E[y|x = 0] = a \tag{7.6}$$

$$E[y|x = 1] - E[y|x = 0] = \beta \tag{7.7}$$

$$E[y|x = 1] = a + \beta \tag{7.8}$$

In the case of a binary explanatory variable, linear regression is also the only non-parametric regression. The results of non-parametric regression with a binary x are two values: average y when x is zero and average y when x is one. We can get these two numbers with the help of the two parameters of the linear regression. Graphically, the regression line of linear regression goes through two points: average y when x is zero (a) and average y when x is one ($a + \beta$).

> ### Review Box 7.4 Simple linear regression with binary right-hand-side variable
>
> Consider a binary variable x, where $x = 0$ or 1. In this case, the simple linear regression, $y^E = a + \beta x$, has the following interpretations:
>
> - a (intercept): the average value of y is a when x is zero.
> - β (slope): average y is β higher among observations with $x = 1$ than among observations with $x = 0$.
> - When $x = 1$, the average value of y is $a + \beta$.

7.7 Coefficient Formula

One of the advantages of linear regression is that there are ready formulae for its coefficients. These formulae can help us understand how linear regression works. At a practical level, we simply have to plug in appropriate values in the data in these formulae to get the coefficients. In practice, statistical software does the plugging in. This is an advantage compared to methods that don't have such formulae, which instead require computers to execute long iterative algorithms (we'll discuss such methods in Chapter 11). With the advance of computing, this advantage has lost its appeal for small and moderate-sized data. But it still matters with very big data.

a and β denote the coefficients of linear regression in the abstract. In a particular dataset, the calculated values are denoted by putting a hat on top of the Greek letters of the parameters, such as $\hat{a}$ and $\hat{\beta}$. These calculated values $\hat{a}$ and $\hat{\beta}$ are called **estimates** of the coefficients a and β. This distinction becomes important when we want to generalize the patterns uncovered in a particular dataset to other situations, a question we shall address in Chapter 9. The formulae are called **estimators** as they give the estimates once data is plugged into them.

The slope coefficient is calculated by first calculating the covariance of the dependent variable and the explanatory variable in the data and then dividing that by the variance of the explanatory variable in the data. The slope coefficient formula is

$$\hat{\beta} = \frac{Cov[x, y]}{Var[x]} = \frac{\frac{1}{n}\sum_{i=1}^{n}(x_i - \bar{x})(y_i - \bar{y})}{\frac{1}{n}\sum_{i=1}^{n}(x_i - \bar{x})^2}$$

One way to understand the slope coefficient formula is to view it as a normalized version of the covariance between x and y. Recall from Chapter 4 that the covariance measures the degree of association between the two variables, but it returns values that are hard to interpret. The slope measures the covariance relative to the variation in x. That is why the slope can be interpreted as differences in average y corresponding to differences in x.

The intercept is calculated after the slope is calculated. It is average y minus average x multiplied by the estimated slope $\hat{\beta}$:

$$\hat{a} = \bar{y} - \hat{\beta}\bar{x} \tag{7.9}$$

The formula of the intercept reveals that the regression line always goes through the point of average x and average y. To see that formally, just rearrange the formula to get $\bar{y} = \hat{a} + \hat{\beta}\bar{x}$. In linear regressions, the expected value of y for average x is indeed average y.

The derivation of the formulae is called **ordinary least squares** and is abbreviated as **OLS**. In Under the Hood section 7.U1, we present the derivation in detail. The idea underlying OLS is to find the values of the intercept and slope parameters that make the regression line fit the scatterplot best.

Data analysts sometimes use the name OLS for the linear regression with coefficients estimated by ordinary least squares. The frequent usage of this name reflects the fact that the simple linear regression is a line fitted on the scatterplot, and OLS finds the best fit.

Figure 7.4 shows the idea: it is a scatterplot with the best-fitting linear regression found by OLS. The figure is based on artificial data with two variables, x and y, that we created for illustration purposes. Besides the best-fitting OLS regression line it shows a vertical dashed line at the average value of x and a horizontal dashed line at the average value of y. The regression line goes through the point of average x and average y.

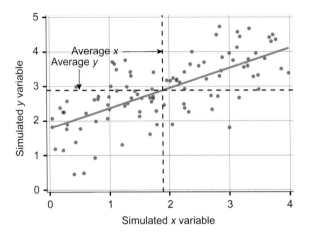

Figure 7.4   Scatterplot and best-fitting linear regression found by OLS

Note: Artificial data with 100 observations. Dashed lines at average x and average y.

Mathematically, the OLS method finds the values of the coefficients of the linear regression that minimize the sum of squares of the difference between actual y values and their values implied by the regression, $\hat{a} + \hat{\beta}x$. In the next section we'll discuss these differences: they are called regression residuals.

$$min_{a,\beta} \sum_{i=1}^{n}(y_i - a - \beta x_i)^2 \tag{7.10}$$

For this minimization problem, we can use calculus to give $\hat{a}$ and $\hat{\beta}$, the values for a and β that give the minimum. Under the Hood section 7.U1 gives the details.

Review Box 7.5   The OLS coefficients of simple linear regression

$$y^E = a + \beta x$$

- The formula for β, the slope: $\hat{\beta} = \dfrac{Cov[x, y]}{Var[x]} = \dfrac{\dfrac{1}{n}\sum_{i=1}^{n}(x_i - \bar{x})(y_i - \bar{y})}{\dfrac{1}{n}\sum_{i=1}^{n}(x_i - \bar{x})^2}$

- The formula for a, the intercept: $\hat{a} = \bar{y} - \hat{\beta}\bar{x}$

- The calculated values are called estimates.
- The formulae used for calculating the values are called estimators.
- The method to calculate the estimates is called OLS (for ordinary least squares).
- The estimates, and estimators, are also called OLS estimates or OLS estimators. Sometimes linear regression with OLS estimation is simply called OLS, too.
- The linear regression is the best-fitting line through the scatterplot when its coefficients are estimated with OLS.

7.A2 CASE STUDY – Finding a Good Deal among Hotels with Simple Regression

Linear regression

The linear regression of hotel prices (in dollars) on distance (in miles) produces an intercept of 133 and a slope of −14. Figure 7.5 shows the regression line together with the scatterplot.

The intercept is 133, suggesting that the average price of hotels right in the city center is 133 US dollars. Note that there is no such hotel right in the city center because that is the middle of a square containing a church: the hotel closest to the city center is a few steps away from it.

The slope of the linear regression is −14. Hotels that are 1 mile further away from the city center are, on average, 14 US dollars cheaper in our data.

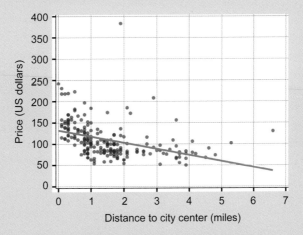

Figure 7.5 Hotel price by distance to the city center: linear regression and scatterplot

Source: `hotels-vienna` dataset. Vienna, November 2017, weekday. N=207.

Simple regressions fit a straight line. Therefore, by design, our simple regression cannot reproduce the convex nonlinear pattern suggested by the non-parametric regressions, i.e., that the same difference in distance is associated with larger price differences closer to the city center.

We can assess how good the linear regression is in approximating the nonlinear relationship between average price and distance we uncovered earlier. The slope of the linear regression is −14; if it gave a perfect approximation to the average slope, it would be close to the average of the many slopes calculated in a non-parametric regression with many distance bins. Take our non-parametric regression with four non-overlapping bins in distance, shown earlier in Figure 7.2a.

The distance of the midpoints of the first and second bins is 1 mile, the distance between the midpoints of the second and the third bin is 1 mile again, and for the third and fourth bins it's 2.5 miles. The corresponding slopes are between the consecutive values: $99 - 133 = -34$, $98 - 99 = -1$, and $84 - 98 = -14$. Let's divide these by the distance between midpoints: 1, 1, and 2.5, and get -34, -1, and -6 (rounded). Their unweighted average is -14. But that's not really the right way of calculating the average, as the different bins have different numbers of hotels. A weighted average of the differences is -20.

This average slope of -20 that we have calculated from the four-point bin scatter is one approximation of the average slope of the $f(x)$ function. The slope of the linear regression, -14 (coincidentally the same as the unweighted average), is another approximation. These two numbers are different but not very different.

7.8 Predicted Dependent Variable and Regression Residual

The **predicted value** of the dependent variable is our best guess for its average value if we know the value of the explanatory variable. The predicted value can be calculated from the regression: it is the calculated value of y^E using $f(x)$ for a particular value of x. As the name suggests, the primary use of the predicted value is in predictive analysis.

The predicted value of dependent variable y for observation i is denoted as $\hat{y}_i$. The predicted value is straightforward to compute in a linear regression: $\hat{y}_i$ for observation i, making use of a simple linear regression, is calculated by plugging in the value of the explanatory variable (x_i) and the estimated values of the coefficients to get

$$\hat{y}_i = \hat{a} + \hat{\beta} x_i \tag{7.11}$$

Predicted dependent variables exist in non-parametric regressions, too. They cannot be computed by plugging in values into a formula as there is no formula for non-parametric regressions. Instead, the result of a non-parametric regression is the complete list of predicted values of the dependent variable for each value of the explanatory variable in the data.

The **residual** is another important measure that we can compute from a regression. It is the difference between the actual value of the dependent variable for an observation and its predicted value:

$$e_i = y_i - \hat{y}_i. \tag{7.12}$$

The concept of the residual is general for all regressions, not only linear regression. The residual is always the difference between the actual dependent variable and the value implied by the regression: $y_i - \hat{y}_i$. The residual may be important in its own right. Indeed, we may be interested in identifying observations that are special in that they have a dependent variable that is much higher or much lower than "it should be" as predicted by the regression. That is in fact the case in our case study, as we'll explain below.

The scatterplot with the regression line helps visualizing both concepts. The predicted values of the dependent variable are the points of the regression line itself. The residual for a particular observation is a difference of two y values: the value of y for the observation (the y value of the scatterplot point) minus its predicted value $\hat{y}$ (the y value of the regression line for the corresponding x value). Thus, the residual is the vertical distance between the scatterplot point and the regression line. For points above the regression line the residual is positive. For points below the regression line the residual is negative. For points right on the regression line the residual is zero.

It turns out that the residuals sum to zero if a linear regression is fitted by OLS. As their sum is zero, the average of the residuals is zero, too. A related fact is that the predicted average is equal to the actual average of the left-hand-side variable: average $\hat{y}$ equals average y. These are all consequences of the way OLS calculates coefficients $\hat{a}$ and $\hat{\beta}$. The derivations are included in Under the Hood section 7.U1.

With estimated $\hat{a}$ and $\hat{\beta}$, the predicted value of y can be computed for any value of x. This is possible for any x value: not only those that correspond to an observation in our data but other values for x, too.

Computing the predicted value of the dependent variable for non-existing values of the explanatory variable in-between existing values in the data is **interpolation**. Computing it for values of the explanatory variable that are outside its range (below the smallest existing value in the data or above the largest existing value) is called **extrapolation**. Usually, interpolation is viewed as a relatively benign exercise. Extrapolation, on the other hand, is often viewed as adventurous. It works fine if the patterns are similar outside the range but not otherwise. However, this is an assumption that we cannot check using the existing data. Hence, we suggest caution with extrapolation.

In contrast with predicted y values, residuals can be computed for existing observations only. That's because a residual is the difference between the actual value of y for an observation and its predicted value. While we can have predicted values for any x, actual y values are only available for the observations in our data.

Review Box 7.6 Predicted dependent variable and residual in simple linear regression

- The predicted value of the dependent variable for observation i is $\hat{y}_i = \hat{a} + \hat{\beta}x_i$, where $\hat{a}$ and $\hat{\beta}$ are the OLS estimates for the coefficients of the linear regression $y^E = \alpha + \beta x$.
- The residual for observation i is $e_i = y_i - \hat{y}_i$.
- Predicted values ($\hat{y}$) can be computed for any x value even if it's not in the data:
  - interpolation means predicting $\hat{y}$ for x not in the data but in-between x values in the data;
  - extrapolation means predicting $\hat{y}$ for x not in the data and outside the range of x in the data.
- Residuals can only be computed for observations in the data.

7.A3   CASE STUDY – Finding a Good Deal among Hotels with Simple Regression

Predicted price and regression residual

Figure 7.6a illustrates the predicted values and residuals of the linear regression of hotel prices as the dependent variable and distance to the city center as the explanatory variable. It is an exact replica of Figure 7.5 with added notes. The regression line shows the predicted values. The vertical distance of each point in the scatterplot from the regression line is the residual corresponding to that observation.

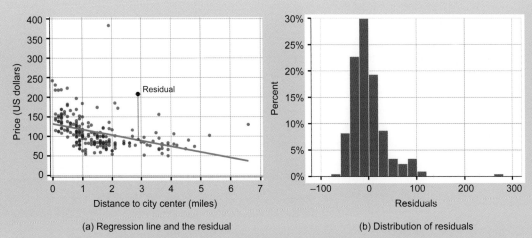

(a) Regression line and the residual   (b) Distribution of residuals

Figure 7.6   Hotel price by distance to the city center: linear regression and residuals

Source: `hotels-vienna` dataset. Vienna, November 2017, weekday. N=207.

Figure 7.6b shows the distribution of the residuals. The distribution has mean zero, but it is skewed with a longer right-hand tail. There are more hotels with a negative residual, but those residuals tend to be smaller than the positive residuals.

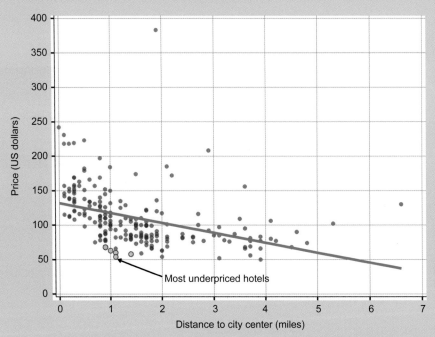

Figure 7.7   Underpriced hotels

Note: Scatterplot, regression line, and hotels with the five lowest values of the residual. Underpriced hotels are below the regression line; overpriced hotels are above the regression line.
Source: `hotels-vienna` dataset. Vienna, November 2017, weekday. N=207.

The residuals help find an answer to the question of the case study: how to find a good deal. Candidates for a good deal are hotels that are underpriced relative to their location. These are hotels that come with a lower price than is expected for their location. Regression residuals show the difference of actual price from what's expected based on the regression. The most underpriced hotels are the ones with the lowest, most negative residuals, as shown in Figure 7.7.

Table 7.1 shows a list of the hotels with the five lowest values of the residual.

Table 7.1	Most underpriced hotels				
No.	Hotel_id	Distance	Price	Predicted price	Residual
1	22080	1.1	54	116.17	−62.17
2	21912	1.1	60	116.17	−56.17
3	22152	1	63	117.61	−54.61
4	22408	1.4	58	111.85	−53.85
5	22090	0.9	68	119.05	−51.05

Note: List of the five hotels with the largest negative residual from the linear regression of hotel price on distance.
Source: `hotels-vienna` dataset. Vienna, November 2017, weekday. N=207.

If we thought that the simple linear regression we estimated gave good prediction and good residuals, we would be done. Then this list would offer five good candidates for the couple to consider and investigate more carefully to choose a hotel that is underpriced for its location.

Unfortunately, this simple linear regression may not produce the best possible predictions and residuals. Indeed, it's a little suspicious that this particular list includes hotels that are all around 1 mile from the center. The reason can be seen in Figure 7.6: there is a bunching of large negative-residual observations around 1 mile. But that appears to be a consequence of fitting a line on a nonlinear pattern.

The regression line does not capture the nonlinear pattern suggested by the non-parametric regressions and, indeed, by the scatterplot (steeper slope at shorter distances). In Chapters 8 and 10 we shall further develop this study to get a better list, using residuals from regressions that accommodate the nonlinear pattern and that add other features of hotels besides their distance to the city center.

Finally, let us discuss the data visualization aspect of the graph in Figure 7.7. In particular, let's discuss the visual layers we introduced in Chapter 3, Section 3.5: graph type, encoding, scaffolding, and annotation.

In the graph, we used a plain scatterplot as the number of observations is not very large, and we had several information encoded. First, it is a scatterplot, so each observation is denoted by a dot. Second, the five most underpriced hotels are denoted with a different color. Third, a regression line is shown, drawn with a different color.

For scaffolding: as x and y are quantitative, we used grid lines, as they help read off approximate values. We have prices and distance values along both axes.

Finally, regarding annotations, we used a different color and added an arrow and a textbox to draw attention to the five dots depicting best deals.

7.9   Goodness of Fit, R-Squared

An important property of regression is how well it fits the data, called **goodness of fit**. One result of an estimated regression are the predicted values of y for all values of x in the data. The **fit of a regression** captures how these predicted values compare to the actual values.

The most commonly used measure of the fit of a regression is the **R-squared** (R^2). R-squared captures how close the predicted y values are to the actual values. It does so by measuring how much of the variation in y is captured by the regression, and how much is left for residual variation. R-squared may be defined as how much of the overall variation in y is captured by variation predicted by the regression, that is, the variation in $\hat{y}$. Another way of looking at the same thing considers how much is there that is not residual variation. In formulae:

$$R^2 = \frac{Var[\hat{y}]}{Var[y]} = 1 - \frac{Var[e]}{Var[y]} \tag{7.13}$$

where $Var[y] = \frac{1}{n}\sum_{i=1}^{n}(y_i - \bar{y})^2$, $Var[\hat{y}] = \frac{1}{n}\sum_{i=1}^{n}(\hat{y}_i - \bar{y})^2$, and $Var[e] = \frac{1}{n}\sum_{i=1}^{n}(e_i)^2$. Note that $\bar{\hat{y}} = \bar{y}$, and $\bar{e} = 0$.

This is based on the decomposition of the overall variation in the dependent variable into variation in predicted values (variation "explained by the regression") and the remaining, residual variation (variation "not explained by the regression"):

$$Var[y] = Var[\hat{y}] + Var[e] \tag{7.14}$$

R-squared (or R^2) can be defined for both parametric and non-parametric regressions. Any kind of regression produces predicted $\hat{y}$ values, and all we need to compute R^2 is its variance compared to the variance of y.

The value of R-squared is always between zero and one. R-squared is one if the regression fits the data perfectly. In this case each and every data point is equal to its predicted value from regression, and all residuals are zero. In a linear regression it means that all data points lie exactly on the regression line. The other polar case is an R-squared of zero. In this case all of the predicted $\hat{y}$ values are equal to the overall average value $\bar{y}$ in the data regardless of the value of the explanatory variable x. This corresponds to a slope of zero: the regression line is completely flat.

The fit of a regression depends on two factors: (1) how well the particular version of the regression captures the actual function f in $y^F = f(x)$, and (2) how far actual values of y are spread around what would be predicted using the actual function f. The decisions of the analyst can affect the first: for example, a non-parametric regression almost always gives a better fit than a linear regression. The second factor is beyond the control of the analyst and is determined by the nature of the data. In some data actual y values are close to some $f(x)$; in other data they are widely spread around it. In the second case, even the best-fitting regressions may achieve low R-squared.

When our goal is prediction, R-squared may help in choosing between different versions of regression for the same data. Besides giving information on the fit of a particular regression R-squared is used to compare alternative regressions that use different x variables to predict the same y variable. Comparing two regressions, the one with a higher R-squared does a better job at predicting y in the data.

> **Review Box 7.7 The fit of a regression**
>
> - The fit of a regression captures how close the predicted y values are to the actual values.
> - R-squared is a measure of fit of a regression.
> - R-squared measures the fit by calculating how much of the variation in y is captured by the regression, and how much is left for residual variation:
> $$R^2 = \frac{Var[\hat{y}]}{Var[y]} = 1 - \frac{Var[e]}{Var[y]}$$
> - R-squared is based on the fact that $Var[y] = Var[\hat{y}] + Var[e]$.

7.10 Correlation and Linear Regression

Linear regression is closely related to correlation. As we introduced in Chapter 4, the correlation coefficient measures the degree of association between two variables. It is a normalized version of the covariance, dividing it by the standard deviations of the two variables: $Corr[x, y] = \frac{Cov[y,x]}{Std[y]\,Std[x]}$. The correlation coefficient is between -1 and $+1$, and the measure is symmetric in that x and y are interchangeable.

The OLS formula for the slope estimate of the linear regression $y^E = a + \beta x$ is also a normalized version of the covariance, only here it is divided by the variance of the x variable: $\hat{\beta} = \frac{Cov[y,x]}{Var[x]}$. In contrast with the correlation coefficient, its values can be anything, and y and x are not interchangeable.

Despite their differences, the covariance, the correlation coefficient, and the slope of a linear regression capture similar information: the degree of association between the two variables. Formally, we can express the correlation coefficient in terms of the slope coefficient and vice versa (recall that $Var[x] = (Std[x])^2$):

$$\ddot{\beta} = Corr[x, y]\frac{Std[y]}{Std[x]} \quad \text{or} \quad Corr[x, y] - \hat{\beta}\frac{Std[x]}{Std[y]} \tag{7.15}$$

As a side note, let's consider yet one more way to normalize the covariance: dividing it by the variance of y not x. Actually, that would be the OLS estimator for the slope coefficient of the **reverse regression**: switching the role of y and x in the linear regression. Using different Greek letters to avoid confusion, the reverse regression formula is

$$x^E = \gamma + \delta y \tag{7.16}$$

The OLS estimator for the slope coefficient here is $\hat{\delta} = \frac{Cov[y,x]}{Var[y]}$. Again, this captures very similar information to the covariance, the correlation coefficient, and the OLS estimator of the slope of the original linear regression, $\hat{\beta}$. The OLS slopes of the original regression and the reverse regression are related as $\hat{\beta} = \hat{\delta}\frac{Var[y]}{Var[x]}$. The two are different unless $Var[x] = Var[y]$, but they always have the same sign, and both are larger in magnitude the larger the covariance.

It also turns out that R-squared of the simple linear regression is the square of the correlation coefficient. So the R-squared is yet another measure of the association between the two variables. This is harder to see right away, but it comes from the fact that the numerator of R-squared, $Var[\hat{y}]$, can be written out as $Var[\hat{a} + \hat{\beta}x] = \hat{\beta}^2 Var[x]$, and thus $R^2 = \hat{\beta}^2 Var[x]/Var[y] = (\hat{\beta}\,Std[x]/Std[y])^2$.

> **Review Box 7.8   Correlation and linear regression**
>
> Consider the OLS estimators for the coefficients of the linear regression $y^E = \alpha + \beta x$.
>
> - The slope of a simple linear regression and the correlation coefficient are closely related as
>
> $$\hat{\beta} = Corr[x, y]\frac{Std[y]}{Std[x]} \quad \text{or} \quad Corr[x, y] = \hat{\beta}\frac{Std[x]}{Std[y]}$$
>
> - The R-squared is the square of the correlation coefficient:
>
> $$R^2 = (Corr[x, y])^2$$

7.11   Regression Analysis, Regression toward the Mean, Mean Reversion

The relationship between the slope coefficient of the simple linear regression and the correlation coefficient helps explain the somewhat strange name for the method itself: regression. The concept of the linear regression, and its name, originated with Francis Galton in the second half of the nineteenth century. Galton analyzed the association between the height of parents (x) and the height of their children (y) and estimated the regression line using this data. He found a slope coefficient that was less than one. We now understand why: the standard deviation of y and x were the same in his data, and thus the regression coefficient was also the correlation coefficient (that name was invented somewhat later), which is naturally between -1 and 1.

From this Galton concluded that height exhibits a **regression toward the mean**: parents with height away from the mean tend to have children who also have height away from the mean but less so. This substantive conclusion about a particular phenomenon then stuck to the name of the method of linear regression, and, more generally, regression analysis. To separate the method from the substantive phenomenon, we use the term **mean reversion** instead of the term regression toward the mean to describe the substantive phenomenon: events further away from the mean tend to be followed by events closer to the mean. We reserve the name regression to the method of regression analysis.

7.12   Regression and Causation

Correlation does not imply causation – a warning we can find in every introduction to statistics. The slope of a simple regression describes the same association as correlation, so this message is equivalent to saying that the slope of a simple regression does not imply causation. By that we mean that, in general, the slope coefficient of a linear regression does not show the effect of the explanatory variable on the dependent variable.

Causality is a concept that is not that easy to define. One intuitive approach postulates that x causes y if we could expect y to change if we were to change x. We shall define the cause and effect relationship in a more systematic way in Chapter 19.

Regression does not imply causation because, in general, we cannot infer a cause and effect relationship from differences we see in data. Regression is a method of comparison: it compares observations that are different in x and shows corresponding average differences in y. It is a way to find patterns of association by comparisons. The fact that we can't, in general, infer causation from regression analysis is not the fault of the method. It is a consequence of the nature of the data. In particular, whether we can or cannot infer causation depends on the source of variation in the right-hand-side variable, a concept we introduced in Chapter 4, Section 4.2 and we'll discuss in more detail in Chapter 19.

Regression analysis cannot in general uncover the effect of x on y in observational data because there variation in x is not controlled. In observational data we compare observations that may be different in terms of x for many reasons. As a result, the data does not necessarily inform us of what would happen to y if we were to change x. For example, using observational data to uncover the effect of advertising on sales, we may regress sales on the amount of advertising and see a strong positive coefficient. But that may not show an effect at all. For example, both advertising and sales may be above average in the holiday season. That in itself would lead to a positive slope coefficient without any effect of advertising.

In contrast, the same regression analysis can uncover the effect of x on y in experimental data where variation in x is controlled. In well-designed experiments (to be discussed in Chapter 20), an experimenter induces controlled variation in x: they manipulate the value of x in a way that rules out the influence of other effects and observe differences in the expected value of y as a result. For example, a firm may consciously experiment by allocating varying resources to advertising, in a random fashion, and keep track of sales. A regression of sales on the amount of advertising can uncover the effect of advertising here.

This is why proper interpretation of the slope of a regression is important. Comparing observations that are different in x and seeing the extent to which y differs among them on average is what regression analysis does. The proper interpretation of the slope is necessary whether the data is observational or comes from a controlled experiment. A positive slope in a regression of sales on advertising means that sales tend to be higher when advertising time is higher. This interpretation is true both in observational and experimental data. It may or may not imply that we have learned how we could expect y to change if we were to change x.

Instead of saying that the correlation, or regression, does not imply causation, we should rather say that we should not infer cause and effect from comparisons, especially when the data is observational. That's not as catchy and short. But it has the advantage of being both true and useful.

In any case, when the slope of the $y^E = \alpha + \beta x$ regression is not zero in our data ($\beta \neq 0$) and the linear regression captures the y–x association reasonably well, one of three things – which are not mutually exclusive – may be true:

1. x causes y. If this is the single one thing behind the slope, it means that we can expect y to increase by β units if we were to increase x by one unit.
2. y causes x. If this is the single one thing behind the slope, it means that we can expect x to increase if we were to increase y.
3. A third variable causes both x and y (or many such variables do). If this is the single one thing behind the slope it means that we cannot expect y to increase if we were to increase x.

7.A4 CASE STUDY – Finding a Good Deal among Hotels with Simple Regression

Fit and causation

In our example of linear regression of hotel prices on their distance to the city center, the R-squared of the regression is 0.16 = 16%. This means that of the overall variation in hotel prices, 16% is explained by the linear regression with distance to the city center; the remaining 84% is left unexplained. 16% may not seem much, but it is actually a rather good fit for a cross-sectional regression with a single explanatory variable. In any case it is the fit of the best-fitting line.

In our case study, the slope of the linear regression in question tells us that hotels that are one mile further away from the city center are, on average, 14 US dollars cheaper. The model fits the data decently. Does that mean that a longer distance causes hotels to be cheaper by that amount? Maybe. Our calculations are certainly consistent with such an interpretation. But this is observational data so our result does not imply causality. It is consistent with other interpretations, too.

If we think about it, a causal relationship is not that simple here. One way to think about causality is that it would imply that we would see the price of a hotel decrease by 14 US dollars if we could somehow move that hotel one mile further away from the city center. That's clearly impossible. Perhaps a better way to think about causality is what would happen if we built a very similar hotel one mile further away. How does this effect compare to what we actually do when we calculate the slope coefficient in our regression in our data?

The regression slope coefficient estimate is based on comparing many different hotels that are in different locations. However, these hotels are likely to be different in other features as well. That's clearly not the same as building a very similar hotel one mile further away. The hotels in the data are not identical to each other, and those differences likely affect their price. As we shall see in subsequent chapters, what matters is whether location and differences in those other features are related to each other. In other words, whether hotels that are further away tend to be different from hotels closer to the city center. They may very well be. It may make sense to build higher quality hotels closer to the city center. And that would mean that hotels further away tend to have lower quality, which may explain all or part of the negative association our regression uncovered.

Regression does not imply cause and effect in this data. There may be a third variable, quality, that may explain the negative slope on distance. As we discussed above, this is not the fault of the method. It is a consequence of the nature of our data. It is observational data – a cross-section of different hotels. In Chapter 10 we'll learn how to incorporate variables that measure quality in the regression so we can compare hotels that are similar in quality – at least according to our measures. However, whatever statistical method we use, we are bound to compare the prices of different hotels in the end.

7.13 Main Takeaways

Regression is a method to compare average y across observations with different values of x; it models the conditional mean $E[y|x]$.

- Non-parametric regressions (bin scatter, lowess) can visualize any form of $E[y|x]$, but they don't produce a single interpretable number.
- Linear regression is an approximation of $E[y|x]$.

- In the linear regression $y^E = \alpha + \beta x$, β shows how much larger y is, on average, for observations with a one-unit larger x.
- When β is not zero, one of three things (or any combination of them) may be true:
  - x causes y
  - y causes x
  - a third variable causes both x and y.

PRACTICE QUESTIONS

1. How can you calculate $y^E = f(x)$ in the data if x is a binary variable?
2. What's lowess and what is it good for?
3. How can you get the intercept and slope parameter of a linear regression by OLS? Write down the formulae and explain how in practice you get these numbers using the statistical software of your choice.
4. How do you interpret the parameters of the linear regression $y^E = \alpha + \beta x$ if x is a binary variable?
5. Does it make sense to estimate a simple linear regression between y and x when the pattern of association between them is nonlinear? Why or why not?
6. How is an R-squared computed and what does it show?
7. What are the features of the residuals of a linear regression if $y^E = f(x)$ follows a nonlinear pattern? You may draw a graph, or simply use Figure 7.5.
8. What's the relationship between the covariance, the correlation coefficient, and the slope coefficient of a simple linear regression? Do they measure the same thing?
9. The R-squared of a simple linear regression $y^E = \alpha + \beta x$ is 0.5. Interpret this number. What is the correlation coefficient between x and y (approximately)? What are your answers if the R-squared is 0.8? If the R-squared is 0.01?
10. The estimated slope coefficient on x is positive in a simple linear regression. List the three kinds of causal relations that may be behind this coefficient estimate.
11. The phrase "Correlation doesn't mean causation" is often stated. Argue why this statement should not be about the method to measure association but the kind of data it is applied to.
12. The slope parameter of a simple linear regression $y^E = \alpha + \beta x$ is +2. Interpret this number.
13. The intercept parameter of a simple linear regression $y^E = \alpha + \beta x$ is –2. Interpret this number.
14. An analysis relates the age of used cars (in years) to their price (in USD), using data on a specific type of car. In a linear regression of the price on age, the slope parameter is –700. Interpret this number.
15. An analysis relates the size of apartments (in square meters) to their price (in USD), using data from one city. In a linear regression of price on size, the slope parameter is +600. Interpret this number.

DATA EXERCISES

Easier and/or shorter exercises are denoted by [*]; harder and/or longer exercises are denoted by [**].

1. Use the same `hotels-vienna` dataset that we used for the case study. Analyze the pattern of association between hotel price and average customer rating. First estimate a bin scatter with

two bins, then one with four bins, and then estimate a lowess regression. Visualize the results and summarize the most important findings from these non-parametric regressions. Then move on to estimate a simple linear regression and interpret its coefficients. [*]

2. Use the same `hotels-vienna` dataset that we used for the case study. Analyze the pattern of association between hotel price and stars. First estimate the non-parametric regression. Visualize its results and summarize the most important findings from this non-parametric regression. Then move on to estimate a simple linear regression as if stars were a quantitative variable and interpret its coefficients. [*]

3. Analyze the hotel price–distance to the center pattern for another city. Select a city from the large `hotels-europe` dataset. Keep hotels only, those with 3 to 4 stars, for a November 2017 weekday. Examine the distribution of the distance variable and drop observations if you think you should. First estimate a bin scatter with four bins and then a lowess regression. Visualize the results and summarize the most important findings from these non-parametric regressions. Then move on to estimate a simple linear regression and interpret its coefficients. Compare your results to what we found for Vienna. [**]

4. Collect data on used cars of a specific brand and type, and analyze price and age of the car. First estimate a bin scatter with two bins, then one with four bins, and then estimate a lowess regression. Visualize the results and summarize the most important findings from these non-parametric regressions. Then move on to estimate a simple linear regression and interpret its coefficients. Finally, use the results from the simple linear regression to list candidate cars for the best deal using the residuals of the linear regression. [**]

5. Analyze the pattern of association between how easy it is to do business in a country and how much income the country generates. Download data from the World Bank on GDP per capita in PPP (y) and the time required to start a business (x) for a recent year. Estimate a non-parametric regression, visualize its results, and summarize its main findings. Then estimate a simple linear regression and interpret its results. Do you think the results show the effect of the business-friendliness of a country on how much income it generates? [**]

REFERENCES AND FURTHER READING

There are many econometric textbooks that discuss regression analysis, typically with more technical detail than us. Of them, we especially recommend Cameron & Trivedi (2005), Hansen (2019), Stock & Watson (2015), and Wooldridge (2001, 2012).

On non-parametric regression, see Takezawa (2006).

On the early history of regression analysis, two interesting books are Stigler (1986) and Stigler (2016).

7.U1   UNDER THE HOOD: DERIVATION OF THE OLS FORMULAE FOR THE INTERCEPT AND SLOPE COEFFICIENTS

In this subsection, we'll derive the formulae of the intercept and slope coefficients using ordinary least squares (OLS).

The goal is to find values for a and β that minimize the sum of squared deviations from the regression line:

$$min_{a,\beta} \sum_{i=1}^{n}(y_i - a - \beta x_i)^2 \qquad (7.17)$$

The values for a and β that minimize this formula are $\hat{a}$ and $\hat{\beta}$. For them to minimize the formula, they need to satisfy the first-order conditions: the first derivatives should be zero. (That's a necessary condition; we'll check second-order conditions later.)

Let's start with the first-order condition with respect to a:

$$\frac{\partial}{\partial a}\sum_{i=1}^{n}(y_i - \hat{a} - \hat{\beta}x_i)^2 = \sum_{i=1}^{n}\left[2(y_i - \hat{a} - \hat{\beta}x_i)(-1)\right] = 0$$

Divide by two and then by -1 and expand to get

$$\sum_{i=1}^{n}(y_i - \hat{a} - \hat{\beta}x_i) = 0$$

Collect terms, realizing that both $\hat{a}$ and $\hat{\beta}$ are the same for all i so we can move them outside the sum:

$$\sum_{i=1}^{n}y_i - \hat{a}\sum_{i=1}^{n}1 - \hat{\beta}\sum_{i=1}^{n}x_i = 0$$

Now multiply both sides of the equation by $\frac{1}{n}$ (and realize that $\sum_{i=1}^{n}1 = n$):

$$\frac{1}{n}\sum_{i=1}^{n}y_i - \hat{a}\frac{1}{n}n - \hat{\beta}\frac{1}{n}\sum_{i=1}^{n}x_i = 0$$

Realize that these are averages for y and x:

$$\bar{y} - \hat{a} - \hat{\beta}\bar{x} = 0$$

Finally, rearrange this to get the OLS formula for $\hat{a}$:

$$\hat{a} = \bar{y} - \hat{\beta}\bar{x}$$

Now consider the first-order condition for β:

$$\frac{\partial}{\partial\beta}\sum_{i=1}^{n}(y_i - \hat{a} - \hat{\beta}x_i)^2 = \sum_{i=1}^{n}\left[2(y_i - \hat{a} - \hat{\beta}x_i)(-x_i)\right] = 0$$

Divide by two and expand to get

$$\sum_{i=1}^{n}(-y_i x_i + \hat{a}x_i + \hat{\beta}x_i^2) = 0$$

Now substitute in $\hat{a} = \bar{y} - \hat{\beta}\bar{x}$:

$$\sum_{i=1}^{n}(-y_i x_i + (\bar{y} - \hat{\beta}\bar{x})x_i + \hat{\beta}x_i^2) = 0$$

Collect terms:

$$\sum_{i=1}^{n}(-y_i x_i) + \sum_{i=1}^{n}(\bar{y}x_i) + \sum_{i=1}^{n}(-\hat{\beta}\bar{x}x_i) + \sum_{i=1}^{n}(\hat{\beta}x_i^2) = 0$$

Realize that $\bar{y}$, $\bar{x}$, and $\hat{\beta}$ are the same for all i and can be moved outside of the respective sums:

$$\sum_{i=1}^{n}(-y_i x_i) + \bar{y}\sum_{i=1}^{n}(x_i) + \hat{\beta}\bar{x}\sum_{i=1}^{n}(-x_i) + \hat{\beta}\sum_{i=1}^{n}(x_i^2) = 0$$

Multiply by $\frac{1}{n}$:

$$\frac{1}{n}\sum_{i=1}^{n}(-y_i x_i) + \bar{y}\frac{1}{n}\sum_{i=1}^{n}(x_i) + \hat{\beta}\bar{x}\frac{1}{n}\sum_{i=1}^{n}(-x_i) + \hat{\beta}\frac{1}{n}\sum_{i=1}^{n}(x_i^2) = 0$$

Now realize that what is left in the second and third term is average x. So:

$$\frac{1}{n}\sum_{i=1}^{n}(-y_i x_i) + \bar{y}\bar{x} + -\hat{\beta}\bar{x}^2 + \hat{\beta}\frac{1}{n}\sum_{i=1}^{n}(x_i^2) = 0$$

Now let's put back those averages into the sums:

$$-\frac{1}{n}\sum_{i=1}^{n}(y_i x_i - \bar{y}\bar{x}) + \hat{\beta}\frac{1}{n}\sum_{i=1}^{n}(x_i^2 - \bar{x}^2) = 0$$

And now the hard part. We can verify that

$$\frac{1}{n}\sum_{i=1}^{n}(y_i x_i - \bar{y}\bar{x}) = \frac{1}{n}\sum_{i=1}^{n}(y_i - \bar{y})(x_i - \bar{x})$$

and

$$\frac{1}{n}\sum_{i=1}^{n}(x_i^2 - \bar{x}^2) = \frac{1}{n}\sum_{i=1}^{n}(x_i - \bar{x})^2$$

Applying these we get that

$$-\frac{1}{n}\sum_{i=1}^{n}(y_i - \bar{y})(x_i - \bar{x}) + \hat{\beta}\frac{1}{n}\sum_{i=1}^{n}(x_i - \bar{x})^2 = 0$$

So that

$$\hat{\beta}\frac{1}{n}\sum_{i=1}^{n}(x_i - \bar{x})^2 = \frac{1}{n}\sum_{i=1}^{n}(y_i - \bar{y})(x_i - \bar{x})$$

Which gives us the OLS formula for $\hat{\beta}$:

$$\hat{\beta} = \frac{\frac{1}{n}\sum_{i=1}^{n}(y_i - \bar{y}_i)(x_i - \bar{x}_i)}{\frac{1}{n}\sum_{i=1}^{n}(x_i - \bar{x})^2}$$

The first-order conditions are necessary conditions but not sufficient in themselves. In principle, they may identify a maximum as well as a minimum (or an inflection point). To verify that these indeed give a minimum, let's look at the second-order conditions. For a minimum, a sufficient condition is to have the matrix of the second-order conditions to be positive definite (its determinant should be positive). There are four second-order conditions: differentiating twice by a, differentiating twice by β, and differentiating once by a and once by β – this third one takes care of the remaining two conditions, because by symmetry it is the same as differentiating in the other order.

The second derivatives are

$$\frac{\partial^2}{\partial a^2}\sum_{i=1}^{n}(y_i - \hat{a} - \hat{\beta}x_i)^2 = \frac{\partial}{\partial a}\sum_{i=1}^{n}\left[2(y_i - \hat{a} - \hat{\beta}x_i)(-1)\right] = 2$$

$$\frac{\partial^2}{\partial \beta^2}\sum_{i=1}^{n}(y_i - \hat{a} - \hat{\beta}x_i)^2 = \frac{\partial}{\partial \beta}\sum_{i=1}^{n}\left[2(y_i - \hat{a} - \hat{\beta}x_i)(-x_i)\right] = \sum_{i-1}^{n}2x_i^2$$

$$\frac{\partial^2}{\partial a \partial \beta}\sum_{i=1}^{n}(y_i - \hat{a} - \hat{\beta}x_i)^2 = \frac{\partial}{\partial \beta}\sum_{i=1}^{n}\left[2(y_i - \hat{a} - \hat{\beta}x_i)(-1)\right] = 2\sum_{i=1}^{n}x_i = 2\sum_{i=1}^{n}\bar{x}$$

The determinant of the matrix of the second-order conditions is positive:

$$det = 4\sum_{i=1}^{n}x_i^2 - 4\sum_{i=1}^{n}\bar{x}\sum_{i=1}^{n}\bar{x} = 4\sum_{i=1}^{n}(x_i^2 - \bar{x}) = 4nVar[x] > 0$$

So $\hat{a}$ and $\hat{\beta}$ do indeed give minimum values.

7.U2 UNDER THE HOOD: MORE ON RESIDUALS AND PREDICTED VALUES WITH OLS

In this subsection we show that with OLS, the sum and the average of the residuals are zero, and average predicted y equals average y.

Recall that the regression residual for observation i in the data is

$$y_i - \hat{a} - \hat{\beta} x_i$$

The sum of residuals is

$$\sum_{i=1}^{n} (y_i - \hat{a} - \hat{\beta} x_i)$$

Plug in the formula for the intercept $\hat{a} = \bar{y} - \hat{\beta} \bar{x}$ to get

$$\sum_{i=1}^{n} \left(y_i - (\bar{y} - \hat{\beta} \bar{x}) - \hat{\beta} x_i \right) = \sum_{i=1}^{n} \left(y_i - \bar{y} + \hat{\beta} \bar{x} - \hat{\beta} x_i \right)$$

Rewrite this by putting the sum in front of each term:

$$\sum_{i=1}^{n} y_i - \sum_{i=1}^{n} \bar{y} + \sum_{i=1}^{n} \hat{\beta} \bar{x} - \sum_{i=1}^{n} \hat{\beta} x_i$$

Realize that $\sum_{i=1}^{n} y_i = n\bar{y}$, also $\sum_{i=1}^{n} \bar{y} = n\bar{y}$, take $\hat{\beta}$ outside the sum, and use $\sum_{i=1}^{n} x_i = n\bar{x}$ and $\sum_{i=1}^{n} \bar{x} = n\bar{x}$ to get

$$n\bar{y} - n\bar{y} + \hat{\beta} n\bar{x} - \hat{\beta} n\bar{x} = 0$$

So the sum of residuals is zero.

If the sum is zero then the average is zero, too: it's the sum divided by n.

Now let's show that, for a linear regression estimated by OLS, the average of the predicted dependent variable in the data is equal to the average of the dependent variable itself: $\bar{\hat{y}} = \bar{y}$.

Let's start with the OLS predicted value for observation i:

$$\hat{y}_i = \hat{a} + \hat{\beta} x_i$$

Its average in the data is

$$\frac{1}{n} \sum_{i=1}^{n} \hat{y}_i = \frac{1}{n} \sum_{i=1}^{n} \hat{a} + \frac{1}{n} \sum_{i=1}^{n} (\hat{\beta} x_i)$$

Plug in the formula for $\hat{a} = \bar{y} - \hat{\beta} \bar{x}$:

$$\frac{1}{n} \sum_{i=1}^{n} (\bar{y} - \hat{\beta} \bar{x}) + \frac{1}{n} \sum_{i=1}^{n} (\hat{\beta} x_i)$$

Expand this and move $\hat{\beta}$ outside the sum:

$$\frac{1}{n}\sum_{i=1}^{n}\bar{y} - \hat{\beta}\frac{1}{n}\sum_{i=1}^{n}\bar{x} + \hat{\beta}\frac{1}{n}\sum_{i=1}^{n}x_i$$

Realize that $\frac{1}{n}\sum_{i=1}^{n}\bar{y} = \bar{y}$ and $\frac{1}{n}\sum_{i=1}^{n}\bar{x} = \bar{x}$ so that

$$\bar{y} - \hat{\beta}\bar{x} + \hat{\beta}\bar{x} = \bar{y}$$

So $\bar{\hat{y}} = \bar{y}$.

8 Complicated Patterns and Messy Data

How to uncover nonlinear patterns with linear regression, and how to deal with influential observations and measurement error in regression analysis

Motivation

Life expectancy at birth shows how long residents of a country live; it is a summary measure of their health. Residents of richer countries tend to live longer, but you want to know the strength of that pattern. You also want to identify countries where people live especially long for the income level of their country, to start thinking about what may cause their exceptional health. You download cross-country data on life expectancy and GDP per capita, and you want to uncover the pattern of association between them. How would you do that in a way that accommodates potentially nonlinear patterns and, at the same time, produces results that you can interpret?

Continuing with your investigation to find underpriced hotels, you want to examine the association between hotel price and hotel quality. Your data includes averages of customer ratings, which may be a good measure of hotel quality. However, the number of customers whose ratings are used to calculate this measure varies across hotels, from a few dozen ratings to many hundreds. Arguably, average ratings that are based on the ratings of a few customers are a less reliable measure of quality. Should you worry about this for your analysis? In particular, would a regression of price on average ratings be different, and less informative, if the average of ratings is based on too few customers? If yes, what can you do about it?

Linear regression gives a meaningful approximation to the patterns of association, but real-life data can be messy, and the patterns may be nonlinear. What those mean for regression analysis and what we can do about them is important to understand. There are several tools that we can apply to make linear regression approximate nonlinear patterns of association, but whether we want to do so depends on the goal of the analysis. The fact that real-life data tends to be messy, with errors and extreme values, poses other challenges for regression analysis.

The first part of this chapter covers how linear regression analysis can accommodate nonlinear patterns. We discuss transforming either or both the dependent variable and the explanatory variable, such as taking the log; piecewise linear spline of the explanatory variable; and quadratic and higher-order polynomials of the explanatory variable. We discuss whether and when to apply each technique, and emphasize the correct interpretation of the coefficients of these regressions. The second half of the chapter discusses potential issues with regression analysis using influential observations and variables that are measured with error. We outline potential consequences of these issues and, when needed, ways to deal with them. The chapter closes by discussing whether and how to use weights in regression analysis.

There are three case studies in this chapter. The first one, **Finding a good deal among hotels with nonlinear function**, is a continuation of the study in the previous chapters: hotel prices in a European city and the distance of the hotel to the city center, using the `hotels-vienna` dataset. It illustrates the use of logarithms in linear regression. The case study **Hotel ratings and measurement error** uses the same data to illustrate the effect of measurement error in ratings on the regression of hotel price on ratings. The case study **How is life expectancy related to the average income of a country?** uses the `worldbank-lifeexpectancy` dataset on all countries to characterize the shape and strength of the association between life expectancy and GDP. This case study illustrates the transformations of variables (logs, per capita measures) and nonlinear functional forms.

Learning outcomes
After working through this chapter, you should be able to:

• identify situations that call for uncovering nonlinear patterns in regression analysis;
• estimate linear regressions using transformed variables, piecewise linear spline of the explanatory variable, or polynomials of the explanatory variable;
• interpret the parameters of such regressions and visualize the uncovered patterns;
• identify influential observations in linear regression and decide on whether and how to deal with them;
• assess the consequences of measurement error in variables of linear regression;
• identify the need for weights in linear regression analysis and estimate models using weights if necessary.

8.1 When and Why Care about the Shape of the Association between y and x?

The previous chapter introduced linear regression as the major tool to uncover the average association between y and x. The best way to think about linear regression is a linear approximation of a conditional mean of unknown shape: $y^E = f(x)$. Sometimes the pattern is close to linear. But often it isn't. In such cases we may or may not want to get that nonlinear pattern right. Typically, we want to get the regression to better characterize the nonlinear pattern:

• when we want to make a prediction or analyze residuals;
• when we want to go beyond the average pattern of association;
• when all we care about is the average pattern of association, but the linear regression gives a bad approximation to that.

In contrast, we may ignore nonlinear patterns if all we care about is the average pattern of association, and the linear regression gives a reasonable approximation to that average pattern.

This is an important point. How closely we want our regression to approximate a nonlinear pattern is a matter of choice. This choice should be guided by the benefits and the costs of the alternatives. In general, non-monotonic or highly nonlinear patterns may be more important to capture, but such patterns often are more difficult to include in regression. And, even if we choose to accommodate a nonlinear pattern in a regression, we should aim at a simple solution. Simpler models are easier to interpret and communicate, and they tend to be more robust across datasets that represent the same population or general pattern.

If we want to capture a potentially complicated pattern, non-parametric regression seems to be the best option. Unfortunately, non-parametric regressions do not provide statistics or other numbers that summarize the most important aspects of a pattern. They are also difficult to generalize for multiple regressions – something that we'll show may be important.

Instead, when they want to capture nonlinear patterns of association in regressions, data analysts use relatively simple techniques to approximate those patterns. The next sections discuss several approaches for doing so.

Review Box 8.1   When and why care about the shape of the association between *y* and *x*?

- Whether the shape of a regression is linear or nonlinear matters if:
  - our goal is prediction;
  - our goal is uncovering the patterns of association and we want to uncover more than the average association;
  - all we want to uncover is the average association, but that average is badly estimated due to nonlinearities (most often due to strong skewness or extreme values).
- Potential nonlinear shapes don't matter if all we want to uncover is the average association, and we can get a good estimate of that average.

8.2   Taking Relative Differences or Log

Some frequent nonlinear patterns are better approximated by linear regressions if *y* or *x*, or both, are transformed by taking **relative differences**, or **percentage differences**. In a time series of GDP it makes sense to transform the variable to have year-to-year growth rates. In a time series of the prices of a company stock, it makes sense to transform the price variable into percentage change from the previous time period. This transformation is possible when there is a previous observation that could serve as the natural base for comparison. The case study in Chapter 12, Section 12. A1 will show an example. But doing so is impossible in cross-sectional data where there is no previous observation that could serve as a natural base for comparison. Taking the **natural logarithm** of a variable is often a good solution in such cases. When transformed by taking the natural logarithm, differences in variable values approximate relative differences.

The natural logarithm of a variable x is denoted as $\ln(x)$ or $\ln x$. Sometimes the notation $\log(x)$ is also used, but we prefer ln to log as log may refer to logarithm of another base, such as 10, while ln is reserved for the natural log. While we keep the notation ln in formulae, we shall often refer to the natural logarithm simply as **log** in the text. When we want to differentiate variables that are not in logs, we often say that they are in **level**, or levels.

Examining log differences works because differences in natural logs approximate percentage differences. For example, if x_2 is 10% larger than x_1, that is, $x_2 = 1.1 \times x_1$, then $\ln x_2 - \ln x_1 \approx 0.1$. Or, if x_2 is 10% smaller than x_1, that is, $x_2 = 0.9 \times x_1$, then $\ln x_2 - \ln x_1 \approx -0.1$.

Log differences are approximations of percentage differences that work well for small differences of 30% or less. For larger positive differences, the log difference is smaller (for example, a log difference of +1.0 corresponds to a +170% difference). For larger negative differences, the log difference is larger in absolute value (for example, a log difference of -1.0 corresponds to a -63% difference). The Under the Hood section 8.U1 provides more detail on why **log approximation** works and how bad it becomes with large relative differences.

To use precise language, we also call differences in logs **log point** differences. For example, if $\ln x_2 - \ln x_1 = 0.1$, we say that x_2 is 10 log points greater than x_1. If $\ln x_2 - \ln x_1 = -0.1$, we say that x_2 is 10 log points less than x_1. Most of the time the rationale for talking about log points is to avoid the difficulties of the approximation, especially with larger log differences. But, however precise this language, looking at log differences is most useful when they approximate relative differences well. As a result we'll talk about relative differences, or percentage differences, whenever we can, instead of using the more precise, but less useful, language of log point differences.

Measuring differences in relative terms is often a good choice with many variables analyzed in business, economics, and policy, including prices, incomes, sales, or measures of size. First, relative comparisons are free from measures of the variables that are often different across time and space and are arbitrary to begin with (counting in dollars or thousand dollars). Second, differences in relative terms are likely to be more stable across time and space than absolute differences, partly because causes behind these variables, such as trends in time or regional differences, tend to be more stable in relative terms. Third, many economic decisions are based on differences in relative terms, such as GDP growth or profit margins.

There is a related, statistical reason to take relative differences or logs. The distribution of variables in relative terms, including after taking the log, is often less skewed than distributions of levels (where level refers to the values as they are, as opposed to their logs). The distribution of many important economic variables is skewed with a long right tail and are reasonably well approximated by a **lognormal distribution** (see Chapter 3, Section 3.9). Examples include hourly wages or hotel prices. Thus, the natural log of such variables are close to normally distributed with all of the associated nice statistical properties such as symmetry and low frequency of extreme values.

Having variables with such nice properties is a good thing in linear regression analysis. Recall from Chapter 7 that the slope in a linear regression is an approximation of the average slope of an underlying conditional expectation that may be nonlinear. It turns out that the closer the distribution of variables is to normal, the better the approximation. Thus, even if we are interested in average associations only, taking relative differences, or logs, is often a good choice when the variables are skewed.

Taking relative differences or logs keeps some aspects of the variables the same but changes other aspects. Moreover, these transformations are not always feasible. Let us review the key features of the log transformation.

First, relative differences and log differences between two observations are not affected by the original units of measurement. Thus, relative, or log, differences in prices, wages, incomes, and other variables with a money dimension are the same whatever monetary unit is applied. Note that all of this is true for units of measurements that are multiples of each other, such as currencies or measures of distance. A 10% difference or a 10 log points difference is the same whether the underlying measurement is in dollars, million dollars, or euros. The same is not true for additive transformations $(x+c)$ – units that differ by an additive factor, potentially on top of a multiplying one. Thus, for example, a 10% difference in Fahrenheit is different from a 10% difference in Celsius. Indeed, it makes most sense to take relative differences or logs of ratio variables only (see Chapter 2, Section 2.1).

Second, when we take the log of a variable, we do a monotonic transformation: the ordering of observations in terms of a transformed variable is the same as their ordering in terms of the original variable. Thus, the observation with the smallest value also has the smallest log value, and observations with larger values also have larger log values.

Third, taking relative, or log differences is tricky with averages. In general, the average of many relative, or log differences, is not equal to the relative, or log difference, of average variables. A related fact is that the average of the log value is not the same as the log of the average value: $\overline{\ln(x)} \neq \ln(\bar{x})$. Technically this is because the log is a nonlinear function. That nonlinearity does not affect ordering and thus quantiles, but it matters for averages. This affects all statistics that are based on some kind of average. Importantly, it also affects prediction from regression analysis with log y variables. Regressions with $\ln y$ predict the expected value of $\ln y$. Most often, we are interested in predicting y itself. But getting $\hat{y}$ from $\widehat{\ln y}$ is not straightforward, and we shall discuss this in detail in Chapter 14, Section 14.3.

Summing up: taking relative differences, or logs, of variables with money or size dimensions is usually a good idea, and it may make sense to do so with other variables too. There are two related reasons to do so. The substantive reason is to consider differences in relative terms that are free from arbitrary units of measurement and represent how decision makers think about them. The statistical reason is to transform variables that are skewed with a long right tail to variables that are more symmetric and closer to being normally distributed. However, logs and relative differences are problematic when values are zero or negative. We explore that issue in the next section.

8.3 Log Transformation and Non-positive Values

An important constraint on taking relative differences or logs is that they are possible for positive values only. And that can be a problem, because we may encounter variables that we want to analyze in relative terms yet they have non-positive values. Examples of variables that may have zero values as well as positive values include a company's sales, earnings, expenditures. The relative change of sales from last year is impossible to calculate if sales were zero last year. It is also impossible to take the log of that zero number. Similarly problematic are variables that can take negative values, too, such as corporate profits or a family's net assets. The relative change in profits from last year is impossible to take if last year's profit was negative, and taking the log of that negative number is also impossible.

In such cases, relative difference or log cannot be taken of all of the observations. Yet, sometimes, we would like to analyze relative differences with such variables, too. Is there anything we can do in such cases? Let us briefly review some specific cases and potential solutions. We focus on taking logs here, but the discussion applies to taking relative differences in time series data, too, with appropriate modifications.

First, the reason for zero, or negative, values may matter. In particular, the variable may have only positive values in principle, but the data has zeros because of rounding. If the reason is rounding, the zeros are not really zeros but small positive values. In this case the problem is that we don't know what those positive values are.

When zeros are the results of rounding, it's good practice to replace those apparently zero values with what may be the average non-rounded value for them, such as 0.25 (if values below 0.5 are rounded to zero and the distribution of the variable is likely close to uniform in that region). This is in fact the most straightforward case of variables with positive and zero values. In what follows, we consider all other cases, when the non-positive values are real zeros or negative values.

Second, the magnitude of the problem matters. If only 1 percent of the observations have zero value, we may simply drop them from the data. If, in contrast, 60 percent, or 90 percent, have zero value, we have a very different problem: whether a value is zero or positive is important information, so much so that we may convert this variable into a binary one, showing whether it's positive or zero. It's the cases in-between that we'll focus on below: when a non-negligible minority of the variables have non-positive value.

Third, the available options are different for the y and x variables in the regression, and whether the non-positive values are all zero, or there are negative values, too.

Let's start with an x variable that is positive for most observations and zero for a non-negligible minority of the observations. In this case it is good practice to create a binary variable denoting whether $x = 0$. Then we make $\ln x = 0$ when $x = 0$, and enter both the binary variable and this modified $\ln x$ in the regression (see later in this chapter and in Chapter 10 of using more variables on the right-hand side of the regression). The interpretation of the first coefficient is expected y when $x = 0$ versus $x > 0$, and the interpretation of the second coefficient is the usual one with $\ln x$, given that $x > 0$ (see the next section for the interpretation of the coefficients of regressions with logs).

We can follow the same logic with an x variable that is positive for some observations but zero or negative for a non-negligible minority of the observations. Here we can define the binary variable denoting whether $x \leq 0$. Alternatively, we can create two binary variables, one for whether $x = 0$, and one for whether $x < 0$. Either way, we replace $\ln x = 0$ for all $x \leq 0$ observations, enter the binary variable, or variables, together with $\ln x$, and interpret their coefficients accordingly.

Unfortunately, the same options are not available for the y variable in the regression. But all is not lost here, either.

Data analysts often use involved nonlinear models that can deal with this case, but those are beyond the scope of our textbook. Another possibility is transforming y in a way that allows for examining relative differences and is feasible with non-positive values. One such transformation is $y/(y - \bar{y})$. This is a relative difference, with some of the nice features of logs, including being a monotonic transformation and yielding the same result regardless of the unit of measurement. Its interpretation is different from a relative or log difference, because the measurement scale of this transformed variable is different.

In summary, when some of the values are non-positive, various alternative options exist to make relative comparisons. Which option to use depends on the source of non-positive values, the prevalence of such values, and whether the variable is on the left-hand side of a regression or on the right-hand side. Moreover, not all options are equally good. Thus, data analysts can't simply use a one-fits-all tool but have to think and make a conscious decision.

Review Box 8.2 Taking relative differences and logs

- For many variables, differences in relative terms (e.g., percent difference) make more sense for the analysis.
- We can take relative change in time series data where the previous period's value is a natural basis for comparison.
- Taking the natural log of a variable approximates relative differences; this option is available in cross-sectional data, too.
- The difference in natural logs approximates the relative difference. If x_2 is D% larger than x_1, and $d = D/100$ so that $x_2 = (1 + d) \times x_1$, then $\ln x_2 - \ln x_1 \approx d$.

- This approximation works well for small relative differences of 30% or less (either positive or negative).
- Relative differences and logs can be taken of positive nonzero variables only. For non-positive values, various alternative options exist to make relative comparisons.

8.4 Interpreting Log Values in a Regression

When y, or x, or both are relative changes in time series data, the interpretation of the regression coefficients is straightforward, and we'll discuss it in Chapter 12. When, instead, the variables are log transformations, things are less straightforward. There are three possible simple regressions with log variables: both y and x are in log, only y is in log, only x is in log. In one sense, the interpretation of the coefficients of these regressions is the same as usual, using the language of log points (see the previous section). However, the fact that one or both of the variables is in logs makes another, more meaningful interpretation possible. The three kinds of regressions are as follows.

log–log regression: $(\ln y)^E = \alpha + \beta \ln x$. α here is average $\ln y$ when $\ln x$ is zero. This is rarely meaningful as average $\ln y$ is difficult to interpret. In contrast, the slope of a log–log regression has a nice interpretation. y is β percent higher on average for observations with one percent higher x. Note that the usual interpretation is still true, here with log points as units of measurement: y is β log points higher, on average, for observations one log point higher x. β in this regression is sometimes interpreted as an **elasticity**: the expected percent difference in y related to a one percent difference in x.

log–level regression: $(\ln y)^E = \alpha + \beta x$. α here is average $\ln y$ when x is zero – rarely meaningful again. The slope of a log–level regression has a nice interpretation although it is a bit complicated. y is $\beta \times 100\%$ higher on average for observations having one unit higher x. ($\ln y$ is β units higher, on average, for observations with one unit higher x, which translates into β times one hundred percent higher y.)

level–log regression: $y^E = \alpha + \beta \ln x$. α here is average y when $\ln x$ is zero, which happens when x is one. The slope, again, is a little complicated. y is $\beta/100$ units higher on average for observations having one percent higher x. (y is β units higher, on average, for observations with one unit higher $\ln x$; for observations with one hundredth of a unit higher $\ln x$, which is also one percent higher value for x, y is $\beta/100$ units higher.)

Review Box 8.3 Interpreting the slope of simple regressions with log variables

- log–log regression: $(\ln y)^E = \alpha + \beta \ln x$
  β: y is β percent higher on average for observations having one percent higher x.
- log–level regression: $(\ln y)^E = \alpha + \beta x$
  β: y is $\beta \times 100$ percent higher on average for observations having one unit higher x.
- level–log regression: $y^E = \alpha + \beta \ln x$
  β: y is $\beta/100$ units higher on average for observations having one percent higher x.

8.A1 CASE STUDY – Finding a Good Deal among Hotels with Nonlinear Function

Regression with logs

Recall our study that analyzes hotel prices to find a good deal for a couple that wants to spend a night in a European city. The analysis aims to identify hotels that are underpriced relative to their distance to the city center. Capturing the shape of the pattern is important here. If the pattern is well captured by the regression, the lowest prices are well captured by the smallest (most negative) regression residuals. If, however, the pattern is poorly captured, the calculated residuals will be off, too.

The case study uses data downloaded from a price comparison website. We narrowed the data to hotels that are within eight miles of the city center. In the previous chapter, we estimated a linear regression of $price^E = \alpha + \beta \times distance$, and listed the hotels with the lowest residuals to identify hotels with the lowest price for their distance (Table 7.1).

Our analysis in the previous chapter uncovered problems with the linear regression $price^E = \alpha + \beta \times distance$. Looking back at Figure 7.5, we see that the regression line does not fully reproduce the pattern suggested by the non-parametric regression (Figure 7.3): the same difference in distance is associated with larger price differences closer to the city center. That implies that the true shape of the $y^E = f(x)$ relationship is nonlinear: it is steeper close to the city center, flatter farther away, and may have positive slope for the farthest hotels in the data.

But does that nonlinearity matter? Our question is based on prediction: we want to identify hotels with the lowest price compared to what's predicted for them given their distance. So yes, this nonlinear pattern does matter here. Thus, we need to find a better regression that can accommodate it.

The distribution of hotel prices is skewed with a long right tail (see, e.g., the histogram in Figure 3.4 in Chapter 3, Section 3.A2). This gives a statistical reason to transform it to measure differences in relative terms instead of dollars. This is cross-sectional data so we can't take percent differences from a natural basis. Instead, we can make the regression approximate relative price differences by taking the natural log of the hotel price variable. Let's call this transformed variable ln *price*. Price is always positive so we can take the log for every observation. The range of ln *price* is [3.9, 5.9], mean is 4.6, the median is also 4.6. The distribution of ln *price* is rather symmetric, unlike the distribution of price. Recall that the average price is 110 US dollars. The natural log of 110 is 4.7, slightly more than the average of ln *price*.

We compare two simple linear regressions, one with price as the dependent variable, measured in dollars, and another with the natural logarithm of price as the dependent variable. Figures 8.1a and 8.2b show the scatterplots with the regression lines.

The R-squared of the log–level regression is higher, suggesting a better fit. However, we are comparing the R-squared of two regressions here that have different dependent variables. That comparison is unfair as it compares fit in different units. Thus, we usually avoid comparing R-squares of regressions with different dependent variables.

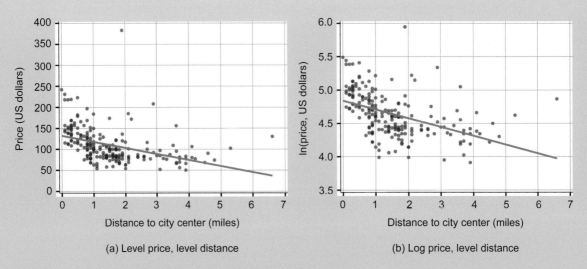

(a) Level price, level distance   (b) Log price, level distance

Figure 8.1   Regressions of hotel price and distance to the city center

Source: `hotels-vienna` dataset. Vienna, November 2017, weekday. N=207.

But, setting measures of fit aside, we have a good reason to prefer the log–level regression: it gives a better approximation to the average slope of the pattern. That is because the distribution of log price is closer to normal than the distribution of price itself. We can see the consequence in Figures 8.1a and 8.1b: the scatterplot is more symmetrically distributed around the regression line in Figure 8.1b.

We may also have a substantive reason to examine relative differences, but that depends on the goal of the analysis. Here we are after a good deal on a single night. So, perhaps, absolute price differences are meaningful, as they tell us how much money we can save. However, if we were to generalize the findings to, say, another time, relative differences would be better. Percentage differences in price may remain valid if inflation and seasonal fluctuations affect prices proportionately.

Note, however, that the log–level regression still doesn't appear to capture the nonlinear pattern. Even just eyeballing Figure 8.1b suggests that the negative log price–distance association is steeper at lower levels of distance. As a consequence, we still have the hotels with the most negative residuals at around 1 mile, just as earlier with the level–level regression (Table 7.1). But, as in that case, this may very well be an artifact of our regression line not fitting the nonlinear pattern. As we shall see in the following sections, we can do a much better job of fitting to the nonlinear pattern by an extension of this log–level regression.

For comparison purposes, we can add two additional simple linear regressions, with the natural logarithm of distance as the explanatory variable. Of the 207 hotels in the data there is one with zero distance. Note that distance is rounded to 0.1 mile, and it is measured from the center of the main square. This hotel is on the main square, but not at its center, so this zero is in fact a rounded number that is less than 0.1. We'll replace its value by 0.05. Figures 8.2a and 8.2b show the scatterplots with the regression lines.

Recall that the results of the level–level regression are: intercept 133, slope −14, R-squared 0.157. The slope of the level–level regression implies that hotels that are 1 mile farther away from

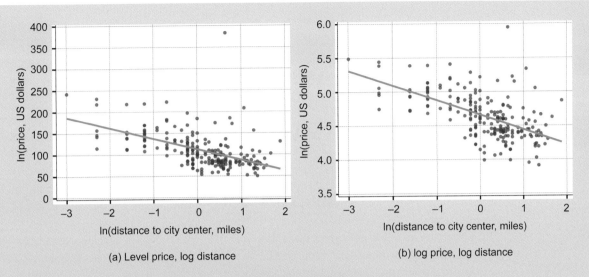

(a) Level price, log distance

(b) log price, log distance

Figure 8.2 Regressions of hotel price and distance to the city center

Source: `hotels-vienna` dataset. Vienna, November 2017, weekday. N=207.

the city center are 14 dollars less expensive, on average. The results of the log–level regression are: intercept 4.84, slope −0.13, R-squared 0.205. The slope of the log–level regression implies that hotels that are 1 mile farther away from the city center are 13 percent less expensive, on average.

All results are summarized in Table 8.1. Let us now interpret the additional two regressions with log distance as explanatory variable. The results of the level–log regression are: intercept 112.42 ≈ 112, slope −24.77 ≈ −25, R-squared 0.280. The intercept implies that hotels that are 1 mile from the center (for which ln *dist* = 0) cost 112 dollars, on average. The slope coefficient implies that hotels that are 10 percent farther away from the city center are 2.5 dollars less expensive, on average. Finally, the results of the log–log regression are: intercept 4.66, slope −0.225, R-squared 0.334. We don't interpret the intercept because the left-hand-side variable is in log. The slope coefficient implies that hotels that are 1 percent farther away from the city center are 0.22 percent less expensive, on average.

Table 8.1 Hotel price and distance regressions

VARIABLES	(1) price	(2) ln(price)	(3) price	(4) ln(price)
Distance to city center, miles	−14.41	−0.13		
ln(distance to city center)			−24.77	-0.22
Constant	132.02	4.84	112.42	4.66
Observations	207	207	207	207
R-squared	0.157	0.205	0.280	0.334

Source: `hotels-vienna` dataset. Prices in US dollars, distance in miles.

Which regression should we prefer from these four? The fit, in terms of the R-squared, is best for the log–log regression. Nevertheless, our choice is the log–level regression. The reasons for having log price are its better interpretation and skewed distribution. The reason for having distance in level and not log is better interpretation. Our question (how a visitor should pick a hotel) implies thinking about time or money spent on traveling, which are likely linear in terms of distance.

8.5   Other Transformations of Variables

Sometimes we need transformations of y or x for the linear regression to make more sense and/or give a better approximation to the underlying nonlinear conditional expectation. In this section we cover one of many such transformations: ratios of variables – most notably, per capita measures of aggregate variables.

It is typically useful to use **per capita measures** rather than total measures of aggregate variables for cross-country comparisons. Take, for example, the pattern of association between CO_2 emission and GDP across countries. If we have both variables as totals, we have an issue: size. Small countries have low levels of total CO_2 emission and low levels of total GDP at the same time. Large countries have large levels of both. Thus, the pattern of association between totals mixes in size differences. In fact, even if there were no substantive association between CO_2 emission and GDP, we would have a strong positive association of the totals. But all this would show is that, for example, China is large and Singapore is small. Per capita measures both for GDP and CO_2 emission solve this issue. Similar arguments work for many sum-like variables in aggregate data, such as imports, exports, and number of internet users.

Per capita measures are the most frequent normalization of totals; they divide by population. Sometimes other variables are used to normalize totals, such as area, GDP, or labor force. All of these produce ratios, either in their own units (e.g., percent of area covered by forests, or debt over GDP) or dividing different units (e.g., GDP per capita).

We can take the log of a ratio just like any other variable to express differences in relative terms. Technically, we could consider it as a difference of two variables, because the log of a ratio equals the difference of the two logs: $\ln(GDP/Pop) = \ln(GDP) - \ln(Pop)$. Usually, however, it makes more intuitive sense to treat it as a single variable that approximates percentage differences in something that happens to be a ratio. For example, a difference of 0.1 in $\ln(GDP/Pop)$ between two countries is a 10 percent difference in average income produced in the two countries for each of their residents.

8.B1   CASE STUDY – How is Life Expectancy Related to the Average Income of a Country?

Per capita measure and logs

Our second case study examines the pattern of association between how long people live in a country and how rich people in that country are, on average. Uncovering that pattern may be interesting for many reasons. One may be to identify countries where people live longer than what we would expect based on their average income, or countries where people live shorter lives.

That would require analyzing regression residuals, similarly to our hotel price case study. For this purpose, getting a good approximation of the $y^E = f(x)$ function is important.

Life expectancy at birth in a given year is a measure of how long people live in a country on average. It is the average age at which people die in the given year. If newborn children were to live to the same age as the current population, this would be the expected length of their lives – hence the name of the variable. GDP per capita is a commonly used measure of average income in a country. It is a flow variable, measuring the total income generated within a country over a year. It is also a per capita measure, dividing by country population, the transformation we discussed in the previous section. At the end of this section we will illustrate why dividing by population is important.

We use data from the publicly available World Development Indicators website, maintained by the World Bank. This is a panel data, and we only look at data referring to 2017. There are 217 countries in this data table, but GDP and life expectancy is available for only 182 of them. Most of the 35 countries with missing values are very small, but a few are medium-sized countries with missing GDP data that are affected by conflict or a collapse of the state (Syria or Venezuela) or do not collect reliable data to assess their GDP (Cuba, North Korea).

Average life expectancy across the 182 countries is 72 years, with a range of 52 to 85. Thus, there is substantial variation in the average length of life across countries. Countries with the lowest life expectancy are from sub-Saharan Africa, including Chad and Nigeria. Countries with the highest life expectancy are a mixture of East Asian countries (Hong Kong, Japan) and Western European ones (Switzerland, Spain).

The distribution of GDP per capita is skewed with a long right tail; Figure 8.3a shows its histogram. There are four countries with extremely high GDP per capita values: Luxembourg, Singapore, Macao, and Qatar. Average GDP per capita is 19 000 US dollars in this data; the median is 12 000 US dollars, which also shows the skewness of the distribution. The standard deviation is 20 000 US dollars, suggesting substantial spread.

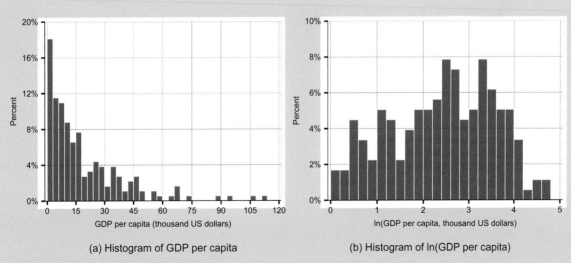

(a) Histogram of GDP per capita   (b) Histogram of ln(GDP per capita)

Figure 8.3   The distribution of GDP per capita

Note: Histograms. GDP measured at Purchasing Power Parity.
Source: `worldbank-lifeexpectancy` dataset. World Development Indicators 2017. N=182.

When we take the natural log of GDP per capita, the distribution is close to symmetric (Figure 8.3b). There are four countries with less than one thousand dollars of GDP per capita (Burundi, the Central African Republic, the Democratic Republic of Congo, and Niger); their log GDP per capita value is less than zero. The average of log GDP per capita is 2.4 in this data; its median is 2.5, suggesting a fairly symmetric distribution. The standard deviation is 1.2.

Figure 8.4 shows the results of a linear regression with life expectancy as the y variable, and GDP per capita as the x variable. This regression shows a positive slope, but the scatterplot implies that there are strong nonlinearities in the association that the linear regression doesn't capture. In particular, the slope appears a lot steeper at lower levels of GDP per capita and a lot flatter at higher levels. Thus, the linear regression does not capture the shape of the pattern, and, because of the skewed distribution of the x variable, it is not a very good approximation of the average of that nonlinear pattern either. The R-squared of this regression is 0.44.

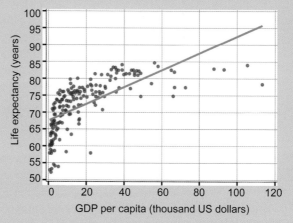

Figure 8.4   Life expectancy and GDP per capita

Note: Regression line and scatterplot. GDP measured at Purchasing Power Parity.
Source: `worldbank-lifeexpectancy` dataset. World Development Indicators 2017. N=182.

Figure 8.5a shows the same regression with the natural log of GDP per capita as the x variable. In contrast with the regression without taking logs, the scatterplot with log GDP per capita suggests a remarkably linear pattern – except maybe at the highest levels, a question we'll return to later. Indeed, for most of the range of log GDP per capita, the linear fit appears to be a good approximation of the conditional expectation. The R-squared is higher than without taking logs, 0.68.

Before we move on to quantify and interpret the results of this regression, let's spend a little time on the details of visualizing regressions with variables in logs. One way to visualize them is what we did for Figure 8.5a: measure the units of the log variable on the appropriate axis (here the x axis). That's the usual choice of visualization for expert audiences. However, those numbers don't mean much for most people. Thus, an alternative way to visualize the same regression is to put natural units as axis labels instead of the log values. Figure 8.5b shows this solution. It's the exact same figure, with different units for the x labels. To alert users of the graph that the labels are in natural units but the regression is in logs, the axis title adds "**ln scale.**"

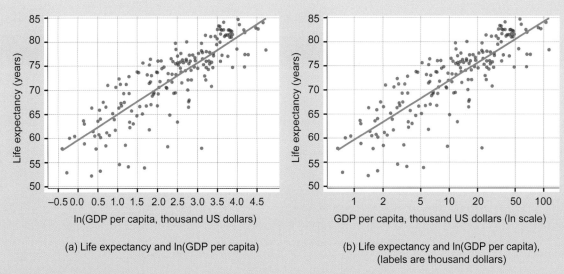

(a) Life expectancy and ln(GDP per capita)   **(b)** Life expectancy and ln(GDP per capita),
                                                              (labels are thousand dollars)

Figure 8.5 Life expectancy and GDP per capita

Note: Life expectancy regressed on the natural log of GDP per capita. Two visualizations of the same regression, with different labels on the *x* axis. Scatterplots and regression lines. GDP measured at Purchasing Power Parity.
Source: `worldbank-lifeexpectancy` dataset. World Development Indicators 2017. N=182.

We can conclude, therefore, that the association between life expectancy and average GDP is best captured with a regression that has log GDP per capita as the *x* variable. The slope of this regression is 5.3. This is a level–log regression, so the interpretation of the slope is a bit tricky. It shows that countries with a 1 percent higher GDP per capita have life expectancy higher by 0.053 years, on average. Note that 1-percent differences in GDP per capita are very small. Recall that the standard deviation of log GDP per capita is more than 1 so that typical cross-country differences are in the order of hundred percents not one percents. At the same time, the log approximation becomes quite bad at such high levels. As a middle ground, let's interpret the slope coefficient by looking at 10-percent differences. Countries with a 10 percent higher GDP per capita have a half (0.53) year higher life expectancy on average.

One purpose of the exercise is identifying countries where people live especially long or especially short lives for their average income. With the level–log linear regression, the countries with the shortest lives given their average income include Equatorial Guinea, Nigeria, and Cote d'Ivoire, where the average age at death is 18, 15, and 12 years shorter than what we could expect given their GDP per capita. The countries with the longest lives given their income include Vietnam, Nicaragua, and Lebanon where the average age at death is a little more than seven years longer than what we could expect given their GDP per capita. Other interesting results include that lives are more than two years shorter than expected in the USA, two years longer than expected in China, and five years longer than expected in Japan. Looking at the richest countries, lives are six years shorter than expected in Qatar, 0.5 years shorter than expected in Macao and Singapore, and one year shorter than expected in Luxembourg.

In fact, the eight countries with the highest levels of GDP per capita have lower life expectancy than predicted by the linear regression. These countries are a mix of city-states (Macao, Singapore), oil-rich countries (Brunei, United Arab Emirates, Qatar), and well-off small Western European countries (Ireland, Luxembourg). This may mean that these particular countries have specific reasons for falling behind what's expected, maybe including mismeasurement of income due to GDP accounted for that does not enrich local people. But, maybe, this result shows that we just can't expect life expectancy to be proportionately higher with higher (log) GDP per capita among countries with the highest levels of GDP per capita. We'll try to do some more analysis to shed light on this question.

Before turning to investigate functional forms, let's examine what would have happened if, instead of per capita GDP, we had used total GDP for comparison. Total GDP varies even more than GDP per capita, from 0.2 billion to 20 trillion, reflecting variation both in size (number of people) and average income (GDP per capita). The distribution of total GDP is also very skewed with a long right tail: the mean is 630 billion and the median is 74 billion. There are two countries with extreme values, China and the USA.

Figures 8.6a and 8.6b show two regression lines, each with the corresponding scatterplot. Like earlier, the dependent variable is life expectancy in each regression. Different from what we had earlier, the explanatory variable is total GDP and its natural log, not GDP per capita and its natural log.

Figure 8.6a shows that something is obviously wrong with the regression on total GDP. Most of the observations are very close to each other at the bottom of the distribution of total GDP, and the regression line fits the few observations with very high values. The R-squared of this regression is 0.02, which is very low, due mainly to the fact that there is a lot of variation around the regression line at lower levels of total GDP. This picture illustrates why it's a good idea to include the scatterplot together with the regression line, as that in itself can reveal serious problems with the variables in the regression.

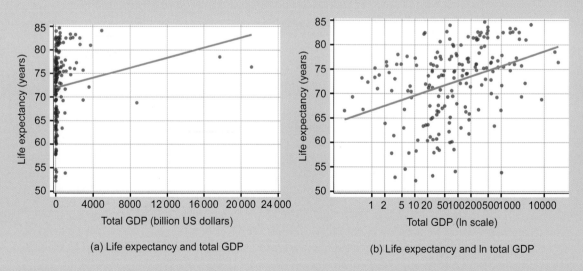

(a) Life expectancy and total GDP   (b) Life expectancy and ln total GDP

Figure 8.6   Life expectancy and total GDP

Note: Life expectancy regressed on total GDP. Level (panel a) and natural log (panel b). Scatterplot and regression line. GDP measured at Purchasing Power Parity.
Source: `worldbank-lifeexpectancy` dataset. World Development Indicators 2017. N=182.

More disturbing is the fact that Figure 8.6b doesn't show that something is necessarily wrong. In fact, it shows a linear regression that fits the scatterplot rather well. The R-squared of this regression is 0.14, which is low, but not as low as it was before taking logs of total GDP. However, this regression is misleading, too. It mixes two associations: the association of life expectancy with average income (GDP per capita) and with country size (population). Since our question is about the association with average income, we should get rid of the second one. Having GDP per capita as our *x* variable ensures that; having its log value ensures that we get a much better approximation of the functional form of the association.

8.6 Regression with a Piecewise Linear Spline

Data analysts use two main tools to approximate nonlinear patterns in the framework of linear regression besides transforming variables: piecewise linear splines and polynomials. Both tools involve specifying a nonlinear functional form for f in $y^E = f(x)$.

Although they allow for nonlinearities in the functional form, both tools specify regressions that are estimated within the framework of linear regression. This may sound strange, but recall from Chapter 7, Section 7.4 that a linear regression is linear in its coefficients. Technically, these two tools have more than one right-hand-side variable, as a multivariate linear function. Thus, technically, they are multiple regressions, which we'll cover in Chapter 10. Substantively, however, they have one right-hand-side variable, only entered in a more complicated way.

A **piecewise linear spline** allows the slope to differ for different sections (values) of the explanatory variable. It is a set of connected line segments instead of a single line with a single slope. The points at which the different line segments are connected are called knots. With two line segments we have one knot. With three line segments we have two knots. With m line segments we have $m-1$ knots.

Importantly, piecewise linear splines are not the same thing as separate linear regressions for different ranges of the explanatory variable. Both methods allow for a different slope for the different intervals of the explanatory variable. However, piecewise linear spline regressions produce connected line segments while separate regressions produce line segments that are typically not connected.

It is the job of the analyst to specify the number and the place of the knots of the piecewise linear spline – i.e., at what values of the explanatory variable x the knots are. Then, the regression uncovers the slopes of the different line segments. Whether their slopes are different indeed is determined by the data. The decision of where to allow for knots is not an easy one. We may start with a nonparametric regression and allow for knots where the shape appears to change. We should aim for many observations within each x segment, and, in any event, simplicity is a virtue, so the fewer line segments the better.

The formula for a piecewise linear spline with two segments connected at knot k is

$$y^E = a_1 + \beta_1 x[\text{if } x < k] + (a_2 + \beta_2 x)[\text{if } x \geq k] \tag{8.1}$$

The interpretation of the coefficients of this regression are straightforward generalizations of the coefficients of a simple linear regression:

a_1: Average y for observations with value zero for x.

β_1: Among observations with x values less than k, y is β_1 units higher, on average, for observations with one unit higher x value.

β_2: Among observations with x values greater than k, y is β_2 units higher, on average, for observations with one unit higher x value.

Note that when we estimate a spline, a_2 is automatically calculated as $a_2 = a_1 + \beta_1 k$.

The formula for a piecewise linear spline with m line segments connected at knots $k_1, k_2, \ldots, k_{m-1}$ is

$$y^E = a_1 + \beta_1 x[\text{if } x < k_1] + (a_2 + \beta_2 x)[\text{if } k_1 \leq x \leq k_2] + \cdots + (a_m + \beta_m x)[\text{if } x \geq k_{m-1}] \qquad (8.2)$$

The interpretations of the coefficients in this regression are similar: each line segment has its own slope coefficient. Once again $a_2, \ldots, a_m$ are calculated automatically. Software will publish the estimated a_1 and $\beta_1, \beta_2, \ldots, \beta_m$ coefficients.

Specifying a regression with piecewise linear splines is relatively straightforward in most statistical software as they have built-in routines to do that. The analyst just needs to define the knots.

Note that there is an alternative way to present the results of a regression with a piecewise linear spline: selecting a line segment as a reference and showing the slope of each of the other line segments in terms of its difference from the reference slope. The interpretation of the coefficients is different, and the underlying formula for this representation is different, too. However, taken together, the information content of the coefficients is the same. Usually, statistical software allows for presenting the results in both ways, and they have one, and not always the same one, as their default setting. Data analysts need to choose the version they prefer and understand the default settings.

Review Box 8.4   Regression with piecewise linear spline of x

- A piecewise linear spline regression results in connected line segments, each line segment corresponding to a specific interval of x.
- The formula for a piecewise linear spline regression with m line segments (and $m - 1$ knots in-between) is

$$y^E = a_1 + \beta_1 x[\text{if } x < k_1] + (a_2 + \beta_2 x)[\text{if } k_1 \leq x \leq k_2] + \cdots + (a_m + \beta_m x)[\text{if } x \geq k_{m-1}]$$

  - a_1: Average y when x is zero.
  - β_1: Among observations with x values less than k_1, y is β_1 units higher, on average, for observations with one unit higher x value.
  - β_2: Among observations with x values between k_1 and k_2, y is β_2 units higher, on average, for observations with one unit higher x value.
  - β_m: Among observations with x values greater than k_{m-1}, y is β_m units higher, on average, for observations with one unit higher x value.

8.7   Regression with Polynomial

An alternative to piecewise linear splines are **polynomials**, having squared, cubed, or higher-order terms of the explanatory variable together with the linear term. The simplest and most widely used is the **quadratic function** of x that adds a square term:

$$y^E = a + \beta_1 x + \beta_2 x^2 \qquad (8.3)$$

Graphically, a quadratic function of x replaces the regression line with a regression parabola. A cubic functional form adds a third power term: $y^E = a + \beta_1 x + \beta_2 x^2 + \beta_3 x^3$. Higher-order polynomials have more terms: 4th term, 5th term, and so on, allowing for even more complicated curves. The highest power in the polynomial is called its order. The order of the regression equation determines the number of potential points at which the curve may twist (turning steeper, flatter, up, or down).

Compared to piecewise linear splines, quadratic or higher-order polynomial specifications have both advantages and disadvantages. Polynomials do not require the analyst to specify where the pattern may change. The only thing to decide is the order of the polynomial; where and how the curve would twist is determined by the data. That comes at a cost: polynomials are rigid functional forms. Quadratic polynomials result in a parabola so that the pattern is bound to be U-shaped: negative slope for low levels of x and positive slope for high levels (or an upside-down U with positive slope first and negative slope next). Moreover, the pattern is bound to be steeper farther away from the middle of the parabola. Higher-order polynomials specify curves with fixed features too.

In practice, the limitation of a fixed curve may or may not be important. For example, while a quadratic always results in a parabola if extended to the entire x line, it is possible that the range of x in the data shows only a part of the parabola. Therefore it is possible that with a quadratic model, the curve that best fits the data may be increasing over the entire range of x in the data, or decreasing over the entire range. The eventually unavoidable turn would occur outside the range of the data, which, in most cases, has no practical consequence for the analyzed patterns.

For example, the pattern of association between the (log) wage of employees and their age is often well captured by a quadratic. This quadratic is increasing over most of the age range in most economies. But it's a nonlinear increase, being a lot steeper at younger ages and flat at old age. We usually don't want to extrapolate that pattern to very old ages with no employees so it doesn't matter that the quadratic would imply a steeper and steeper decline in wages.

Another disadvantage of having polynomials in the regression is that their coefficients are hard to interpret. In a regression with a quadratic function of x $y^E = a + \beta_1 x + \beta_2 x^2$, a is average y when $x = 0$, but β_1 has no interpretation, and β_2 only shows whether the parabola is U-shaped, in other words, convex (if $\beta_2 > 0$) or inverted U-shaped, or concave (if $\beta_2 < 0$).

Sometimes we are interested in the slope of the curve. With a quadratic or a higher-order poly-nomial the slope is different for different values of x, and getting the slope requires work. In the regression with a quadratic $y^E = a + \beta_1 x + \beta_2 x^2$, the slope is $\beta_1 + 2\beta_2 x$ (the first derivative of the quadratic function). We can compare two observations, denoted by j and k, that are different in x, by one unit so that $x_k = x_j + 1$. y is higher by $\beta_1 + 2\beta_2 x_j$ units for observation k than for observation j.

Review Box 8.5 Regression with quadratic or higher-order polynomial in x

$$y^E = a + \beta_1 x + \beta_2 x^2$$

- The result is a parabola that is either U-shaped (convex) or upside-down U-shaped (concave).
- Interpretation of the coefficients:
  - a: average y when x is zero;
  - β_1: no meaningful interpretation;
  - β_2: signals whether the relationship is convex (if β_2 is positive) or concave (if β_2 is negative).

- Regression with higher-order polynomial of the explanatory variable:

$$y^E = \alpha + \beta_1 x + \beta_2 x^2 + \cdots + \beta_k x^k$$

8.8 Choosing a Functional Form in a Regression

The choice of functional form for the regression analysis is rarely straightforward. The most important guiding principle should be the ultimate goal of the analysis. The importance of functional form is different if the question is prediction, uncovering an average effect, or learning how an effect varies. Statistical tools can help make this choice but should never substitute for thinking about the substantive goals of the analysis.

To recap, we may want to ignore nonlinear patterns if all we care about is an average association and the linear regression gives a reasonable approximation to that average association. If that approximation is not good, we may want to transform variables, for example by taking logs, but only if the interpretation of the transformed variables makes more sense for the substantive question of the analysis. However, if our goal is prediction, identifying observations with large residuals, or learning about how an association varies with x, nonlinear patterns are important. In such cases we should uncover the shape of the pattern. As simplicity is a virtue for many reasons, it's often best to approximate such a shape within the framework of the linear regression.

As we have seen, we may have more options to uncover nonlinear patterns and incorporate them in linear regression analysis: transforming variables, piecewise linear spline, quadratic or other polynomials. Statistics can help choosing the best, or a good enough, method, but it never substitutes for thinking. In the subsequent chapters of the book (for example in Chapters 13 and 14) we'll cover some more systematic methods and more systematic ways of thinking for choosing the best regression to answer the question of the analysis. These are sometimes referred to as methods for model selection.

Even before learning those more systematic methods, we can often make good enough choices. Here is a roadmap that we think is useful to follow. We'll apply this roadmap for our case study below.

- Start by deciding whether you care about nonlinear patterns.
  - We usually are fine with a linear approximation if our focus is on an average association.
  - Even then we often transform variables if that makes for a better interpretation of the results and makes linear regression better approximate the average association.
  - In contrast, we usually want our regression to accommodate a nonlinear pattern if our focus is:
    * on prediction;
    * the analysis of residuals;
    * about how an association varies with x.
- If we want to uncover and include a potentially nonlinear pattern in the regression analysis we should:
  - uncover the most important features of the pattern of association by examining a scatterplot or a graph produced by a non-parametric regression such as lowess;
  - choose one or more ways to incorporate those features into a linear regression (transformed variables, piecewise linear spline, quadratic, and so on);
  - compare the results across various regression approaches that appear to be good choices.

In social sciences, the last point is referred to as **robustness checks**. Doing robustness checks basically means running several different regressions and comparing results. In other words, it amounts to checking the extent to which the most important conclusions of the analysis are robust to our choices. Here the choice is of functional form. This is an important step because, most often, all we can aspire to is a good enough approximation. Thus, there is rarely a single best choice. Robustness checks focus our attention on what's really important in our analysis: whether and how much our choices during the analysis affect the answer to the ultimate question of the analysis.

8.B2   CASE STUDY – How is Life Expectancy Related to the Average Income of a Country?

Piecewise linear spline and polynomials

Our reason for analyzing the pattern of association between life expectancy and GDP per capita is to identify countries that do especially well on this health measure relative to how much income they generate. This calls for an analysis of the residuals. Thus, getting the shape of the pattern is important here.

We want to have a regression that fits the pattern of association between life expectancy and log GDP per capita. The scatterplot reveals that the association may be flatter for countries with the highest levels of GDP per capita. Recall from Figure 8.4b that life expectancy is below the simple linear regression line for all of the eight highest-GDP countries, with GDP per capita over 50 000 dollars.

One choice is thus a piecewise linear spline regression with a knot at GDP per capita of 50 000 dollars, which translates to 3.9 in natural logs. It produces the results shown in Figure 8.7a.

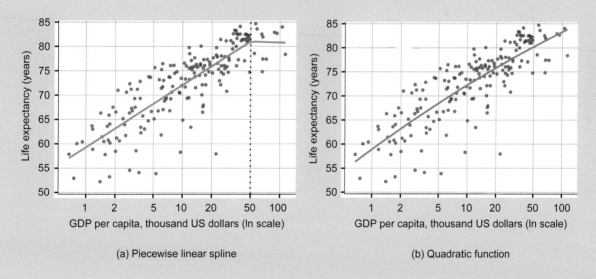

(a) Piecewise linear spline   (b) Quadratic function

Figure 8.7   Life expectancy and GDP per capita: scatterplot and nonlinear regression

Note: Piecewise linear spline with one knot at 50 000 dollars per capita. GDP measured at Purchasing Power Parity.
Source: `worldbank-lifeexpectancy` dataset. World Development Indicators 2017. N=182.

The slope of the first, long, line segment is 5.5, just a little steeper than with a single log GDP per capita right-hand-side variable. The slope of the other line segment is −0.3. Comparing countries with GDP per capita below 50 thousand dollars, life expectancy is higher, on average, by approximately 0.55 years in countries with 10% higher GDP per capita. But, comparing countries with GDP per capita above 50 thousand dollars, life expectancy is lower, on average, by approximately 0.03 years in countries with 10% higher GDP per capita. This is a very small difference, and we can safely treat it as if it were zero: no difference in life expectancy by GDP per capita above 50 thousand dollars.

The R-squared is 0.69 here. The R-squared of the previous linear regression, with a single regression line, was 0.68. This is an improvement, but only a small one. A linear regression that allows for slopes to differ for different values of the explanatory variable must produce at least as good a fit as a linear regression that does not allow for different slopes. However, the improvement on the fit is very small in this case. That should not be surprising as the new regression provides a substantially better fit for only a few observations.

Let's see if an alternative way to capture the nonlinear pattern leads to a similar conclusion. One such way may be to fit a quadratic. Figure 8.7b shows that the quadratic fit settles for slight nonlinearity. The pattern is a positive association through the range of observed ln GDP per capita, with less positive association at higher levels than at lower levels of GDP per capita. The model fit is once again just marginally improved with R-squared of 0.69.

Note that a quadratic function always fits a parabola (Section 8.7). This time it is an upside-down parabola. But we don't see it on the graph. Why? That's because the estimated segment of the parabola is very close to linear. The turning point of the parabola would be at levels of GDP per capita way above what's observed in the data.

The two slope parameters are 6.3 and −0.22, with no clear interpretation except the second, negative, number showing that the parabola is concave (upside-down). The slope of the curve varies with the value of the x variable: it is $6.3 - 0.44 \times \ln(GDPpercapita)$. A quick calculation shows that this slope would be zero for ln GDP per capita around 14.3, corresponding to GDP per capita over 1 600 000 measured in thousand dollars, which is USD 1.6 trillion. That would be the turning point above which the implied pattern would be negative. Of course, that value is stratospherically high, so the main message of the quadratic is that the pattern is always positive, only it is a tiny bit flatter at higher levels of income. Whether that aspect of the pattern is stable, whether it reflects anything causal, and whether it's generalizable from this data are questions that we shall address in the subsequent chapters.

Looking at specific countries with unusually low or unusually high life expectancy given their level of income, we see very similar groups as for the models without the spline or quadratic on the right-hand side. The countries with the shortest lives given their income include Equatorial Guinea, Nigeria, and Cote d'Ivoire, and the countries with the longest lives given their income include Vietnam, Nicaragua, and Lebanon again. The ranking of the top and bottom lists are similar across these various regressions, although the magnitudes of the residuals differ slightly. The fact that these results don't change much is not surprising, as neither the piecewise linear spline nor the quadratic specification lead to strong nonlinear shapes in the estimated regression line.

What can we conclude from this case study? We'll estimate one more kind of regression later in Section 8.B3, but its results will not change the conclusions we can draw. The cross-sectional relationship between life expectancy and (log) GDP per capita is strong positive throughout almost the entire range of observable GDP per capita. For most of the range, a 10 percent difference in GDP per capita is associated with a higher life expectancy by one half of a year on average. Life expectancy in the richest countries is lower than the average pattern would suggest. That can be viewed in various ways; maybe, the association at very high income levels is flat, or maybe it is attributable to country-specific factors.

Given the pattern of association between life expectancy and GDP per capita, we identified countries with unexpectedly low life expectancy and unexpectedly high life expectancy. The former include the sub-Saharan African countries of Equatorial Guinea, Nigeria, and Cote d'Ivoire. The latter group includes, perhaps surprisingly, countries such as Nicaragua and Lebanon next to some less surprising ones such as Vietnam.

In terms of methods, this case study illustrated that we may want to transform a variable, here the x variable, in more than one way. We took GDP per capita instead of total GDP in order to focus on the association with the level of income without the association with size. And we took the log of GDP per capita in order to have a more symmetric distribution of the x variable, which gave a substantially better fit of the regression. It also made the regression very close to linear. We have also learned how to apply the piecewise linear spline and the quadratic specifications. In this example, those more complicated specifications didn't lead to very different conclusions because the pattern of association turned out to be fairly linear overall. Finally, we have illustrated that we can identify countries with unusually high and unusually low life expectancy in a way that is robust to how we specify the regression.

8.9 Extreme Values and Influential Observations

After the overall functional form of the regression, let's spend some time on a potential issue that may have consequences for the shape, as well as the slope, of the regression. This issue arises when patterns are driven by a few observations. Typically, these observations have unusually large or small values for y and x. For example, nonlinear patterns may be largely due to a few observations with low or high values of x. Such extreme values are rare, by definition. Whether to do something with them, and what to do, are important questions in data analysis – unfortunately, without an easy answer.

As we discussed in Chapter 3, **extreme values** are simply values of a variable that are very small or very large and are somewhat separated from the rest of the values. For example, distributions with long right tails have extreme large values.

However, not all extreme values matter for regression analysis. Observations with extreme values that influence the results of regression analysis are called **influential observations**. Influential observations tilt regression lines: the slope of the regression is different when we include them in the data from the slope when we exclude them from the data. Extreme values with little effect on the results of regression analysis are not really an issue: they just don't make a difference. It is influential observations that matter.

Influential observations are often called "outliers." We prefer not using this term because it suggests that such observations do not belong in the analysis. Instead of making such a judgment right away, data analysts need to think about what to do with those influential observations.

Whether influential observations belong in the analysis is an important decision that should be based on thinking. Two issues need to be considered: (1) why the values are extreme for the influential observations, and (2) what the question of the analysis is.

Influential observations should be excluded from the data if they are due to errors. Spotting whether extreme values are due to errors is an important goal of exploratory data analysis, as we discussed in Chapter 3. Observations with erroneous extreme values are best discarded at the exploratory phase of data analysis, even before they could show up as influential observations for regression analysis.

If not due to errors, extreme values belong to the distribution of variables. As a general rule, we should keep such observations in the data even if they prove to be influential observations.

An exception to this rule is when we decide that we don't want our analysis to say anything about certain kinds of observations. That is usually fine if the decision is made based on the value of the x variable. Indeed, that is the decision we made when we discarded hotels from our data with less than 3 stars or more than 4 stars or that were more than 8 miles away from the city center. In contrast, it is usually not fine to discard observations based on the y variable. That's because we want our analysis to explain variation in y. If we were to discard some y values we would "explain" some of the variation in y without an analysis by saying that those values are the result of a fundamentally different pattern.

Indeed, observations with extreme values may be the most valuable observations. For example, the pattern of association between prices and sales is difficult to uncover unless there is enough difference in prices. When comparing markets with very similar prices, the few instances of large price difference may be the only source of variation that can help uncover the pattern.

Moreover, it turns out that observations that are influential in some kinds of regressions are not influential in others. Taking the log of variables with long right tails often takes care of extremely large values and thus influential observations. Similarly, expressing variables as ratios (GDP per capita, stock price per earnings, and so on) makes otherwise extreme values not extreme. Dropping such extreme values before transforming them would be a mistake.

Sometimes, our decision is clear (drop if error), sometimes it is debatable (is it part of the pattern we are interested in?). Hence, on some occasions, there is no clearly superior decision. Importantly, we should be transparent in what we decide and document every step of data manipulation. When no obvious single best solution exists, it is good practice to carry out robustness checks, just like when choosing a functional form (Section 8.8): examine whether and how key results change if we make different decisions.

Review Box 8.6 Extreme values and influential observations

- Observations with extreme values may or may not influence the results of the regression analysis; if they do they are called influential observations.
- It is not good practice to drop observations with extreme values without thinking.

8.10   Measurement Error in Variables

Measurement error in variables may have severe consequences for regression analysis beyond producing extreme values and potentially influential observations. Such errors may arise due to technical or fundamental reasons.

Technical sources of measurement error include reporting errors when the source of variables is a survey; recording errors in data recorded by humans as well as machines; and coding errors that are introduced during transforming raw data into analysis data, or data cleaning. Unfortunately, both humans and machines tend to make errors when they have the opportunity. Another technical source of measurement error is frequent in aggregate variables that are calculated from a sample of observations (average wage in firms, total sales summed over stores). As we have seen in Chapter 5, the number of observations used to produce averages matters: with fewer observations, those numbers may fluctuate more for statistical reasons.

Fundamental sources of error occur when the variable we would like to include in the analysis is not contained in the data; instead, we use another variable, or variables, that are related. Such fundamentally unobserved variables are called **latent variables**, a concept we introduced earlier in Chapter 4, Section 4.7. Observed variables that we use in analyses instead of latent variables are called **proxy variables**. As we discussed in Chapter 4, we often have more than one observed variable to measure a latent concept. When we combine those, most often into an average score, this generated variable can be thought of as a proxy variable, too.

Proxy variables are erroneous measures of latent variables. When we want to measure the relationship of earnings and skills, skills is a fundamentally latent variable. Skills may be measured by scores on a test. But scores are not the same as skills; they can be thought of as erroneous measures of skills. When we want to measure the relationship of firm productivity and worker turnover, productivity is a latent variable. Sales per staff member may be used as a proxy variable for firm productivity. It would be an erroneous measure: productivity is output conditional on many inputs besides staff numbers.

Regardless of whether being due to fundamental or technical reasons, measurement errors in variables affect the results of regression analysis. The effect depends on properties and magnitude of the errors, as well as whether they affect a dependent variable or an explanatory variable in a regression. Consider simple linear regressions of the form $y^E = \alpha + \beta x$. The questions to consider are (1) whether the error leads to a bias in the slope coefficient – i.e., whether it is expected to lead to a different slope coefficient from what it would be without an error; (2) whether the error has other consequences, such as worse fit. As we shall see, the answer to the first question may be very different depending on the properties of the error and whether it affects y or x. As for the second question, measurement error almost always results in worse fit of the regression.

8.11 Classical Measurement Error

We first consider the simplest kind of error: **classical measurement error**. Classical measurement error is an error that is zero on average and is independent of all other relevant variables, including the error-free variable. To be more specific, classical measurement error, denoted by e, is added to the error-free value of a variable y^* or x^*, resulting in an observed variable y or x. Classical measurement error is also called noise.

Technical errors are often close to being classical errors. These include recording errors, such as errors in surveys (wrong values entered) or in automatic measurements (noise in recording). Variables in aggregate data are often estimates from samples, and such estimates are often well represented as variables measured with classical error (estimations have error reflecting the fact that other, equally representative samples may result in different values, as discussed in Chapter 5).

An example is using county-level data to analyze how the local unemployment rate may affect local support for a political party. Typically, both the unemployment rate and the party support variables are estimated from individual-level surveys from samples of respondents. Thus, each variable contains error: the true unemployment rate plus error, and true party support rate plus error.

If measurement error is classical, the average of the error is zero, so the average of the observed variable is the same as the average of the error-free variable, which would be: $\bar{x} = \overline{x^*}$. At the same time classical measurement error makes the spread of the measured variable larger than what the spread of the error-free variable would be. In fact, the variance of an error-ridden variable is the sum of the variance of the error-free variable and the variance of the error.

For example, if x is measured with classical error e:

$$Var[x] = Var[x^*] + Var[e] \qquad (8.4)$$

The variance of the sum of two variables is the sum of the variance of the two variables plus twice their covariance; the covariance here is zero because classical measurement error is independent of the error-free values.

The importance of measurement error is captured by the **noise-to-signal ratio**: the ratio of error variance to what the variance of the error-free variable would be. When a variable x includes classical measurement error so that $x = x^* + e$, the noise-to-signal ratio is $Var[e]/Var[x^*]$. When the noise-to-signal ratio is small, we may safely ignore the problem. This occurs when we are confident that coding errors are not important or when our data has an aggregate variable estimated from very large samples. When the noise-to-signal ratio is substantial, we may be better off assessing its consequences.

In our example of county-level estimates, we can expect a larger error, and thus a larger noise-to-signal ratio, when the original sample is smaller. The original sample here is the sample of individuals who participated in a labor force survey to measure the unemployment rate, and the sample of individuals who participated in a political poll to measure party support. The sizes of the two samples may be different in each county.

What are the consequences of classical measurement error for regression analysis? We focus on linear regressions of the form $y^E = \alpha + \beta x$, and examine what happens to the fit of the regression and the slope coefficients when either y or x is measured with classical error. It turns out that the consequences are different for the two variables.

Classical measurement error leads to worse fit of a regression when the error affects the dependent variable, $y = y^* + e$, but it does not affect estimates of the regression coefficients. It's quite intuitive to see why the fit is worse. Regressions fit the variation in observed y. But when y is measured with classical error, part of that variation is just noise, independent of everything. Regressions do not fit noise: they find patterns of association between variables, and noise due to classical measurement error is not associated with anything relevant. It also makes sense that regressions are expected to produce the same slope (and intercept) when the dependent variable is measured with classical error as if they were free from error. That is because classical error in y averages to zero for all values of x, so when the regression looks at average y for different values of x, it is expected to find the same value as for average y^*. (See Under the Hood section 8.U2, for a more technical derivation.)

In contrast, when the explanatory variable is measured with classical measurement error, the regression coefficients are off. That is less intuitive at first, but it also makes sense. The problem is due to the fact that the error conflates comparisons between different x values. When comparing observations, their typical distance in measured x is inflated by noise: part of it is error-free x^*, but part of it is error e. Thus, if a unit difference in x^* would go with an average difference of, say, β^* in y, a unit difference in measured x would go with a smaller average difference in y. Technically, this is all due to the fact that the noise inflates the variance ($Var[x] = Var[x^*] + Var[e]$), and this variance is in the denominator of the slope coefficient estimate ($\hat{\beta} = Cov[y, x]/Var[x]$).

Notice the difference between the role of error in the dependent variable and the explanatory variable. Noise-induced extra variance in the dependent variable leads to worse fit but does not affect the coefficients. Noise-induced extra variance in the explanatory variable affects the coefficients.

In our county-level example, we would run a regression in which y is the percent of supporters of the political party in the county and x is the unemployment rate in the county. Suppose that the estimated slope is $\hat{\beta} = 0.1$. That means that in counties with one percentage point higher unemployment rate, support for the party tends to be higher by one tenth of a percentage point. But there is measurement error in both y and x here. The former has no effect on the estimated slope; the latter makes the estimated slope smaller than it truly is. If the noise-to-signal ratio is small, the estimated slope is close to what it would be without the error. With large noise-to-signal ratio, the difference is larger. If, for example, the samples are smaller in rural counties than in urban ones, then we would see a smaller slope in rural counties even if the true slope were the same.

The effect of classical measurement error in the explanatory variable is called the **attenuation bias**. The slope of a simple linear regression is flatter if the explanatory variable is measured with classical error. The larger the noise-to-signal ratio, the larger the attenuation. A flatter line means smaller slope coefficient in absolute value. If the slope with error-free x^* was positive, we would expect the slope with the error-ridden x to be positive, too, but smaller. If the slope with error-free x^* was negative, we would expect the slope with the error-ridden x to be negative, too, but less negative. An additional consequence of this extra flatness is that the intercept is biased in the other direction: if the slope is biased in the negative direction, the intercept is biased in a positive direction, and vice versa. (See Under the Hood section 8.U2, for a more technical derivation.) We'll see these features in our hotels case study (Section 8.C1).

Review Box 8.7   Classical measurement error in simple linear regression

- Classical measurement error is pure noise, independent of everything of interest.
- If y is measured with classical error: $y = y^* + e$
  - the fit of the regression is worse;
  - but the slope of the regression is expected to be the same as it would be with an error-free y^*.
- If x is measured with classical error: $x = x^* + e$
  - this leads to an estimated slope coefficient that is closer to zero (attenuation bias).
- Often, errors in variables are not classical. Such errors affect regression coefficients in different ways.

8.C1   CASE STUDY – Hotel Ratings and Measurement Error

Regression and measurement error in average customer ratings

Measurement error is not something we may know – if we did, we would correct it and it would not be a problem anymore. However, we can explore our data to get a better understanding of its magnitude. To do that we would need a variable in the dataset that is a good indicator of the magnitude of the measurement error, and use that to map out the impact of measurement error on regression estimates.

Going back to the case study of hotel prices, let's investigate another association: price and customer rating. The price comparison website publishes the averages of ratings customers gave to each hotel. Ratings vary between 1 and 5, with 5 being excellent. The website collects such ratings and shows their average value for each hotel. Customer ratings are a measure of quality: hotels with higher ratings provide an experience that was valued higher by their customers. Thus a regression of hotel price on rating may show an association between price and quality. Large negative residuals from this regression may help identify hotels that are underpriced relative to their quality.

However, the measure of customer rating is an average calculated from individual evaluations. That is a noisy measure of hotel quality, for at least two reasons.

First, a fundamental reason. Ratings may be influenced by factors other than quality. For example, they may be influenced by the price itself as customers may give higher ratings to cheaper hotels of the same quality. That is an error that is certainly not classical as it is related to an important variable: price. We can't investigate this source here, in part because we don't have the statistical tools, but also because it's a fundamentally difficult question.

Second, a technical reason. Average ratings are based on a number of individual ratings, and few ratings provide noisier averages than many ratings. That is simply due to larger variation of estimates from small samples than from large samples, as covered in Chapter 5. This is typical classical measurement error: observed average customer ratings are a noisy measure because they are averages from a sample of all customers. The noise is more important if fewer customers provide ratings that go into the average measure. That is, the noise-to-signal ratio is larger, the fewer the ratings.

The data includes the number of ratings that were used to calculate average customer ratings. If classical measurement error plays a role, it should play a larger role for hotels with few ratings than for hotels with many ratings. To investigate this possibility, we divided our data into three subsamples of roughly equal size: hotels with few ratings, hotels with a medium number of ratings, and hotels with many ratings.

We labeled hotels as having few ratings if they had less than 100 ratings (77 hotels, with 57 ratings each on average). We labeled hotels as having many ratings if they had more than 200 ratings (72 hotels, with 417 ratings each on average). In-between are hotels with a medium amount of ratings (58 hotels, with 147 ratings each on average). Average customer rating is rather similar across these three groups (3.94, 4.03, and 4.20). But the standard deviation of the average customer ratings across hotels is a lot larger among hotels with few ratings (0.42 versus 0.26). Thus, there is more spread across hotels in terms of average customer ratings when we compare hotels in which those ratings were given by fewer customers. That may be due to many reasons, but it is also in line with more noise among hotels with fewer ratings.

We regressed log hotel price on average ratings separately for hotels with few ratings (less than 100) and hotels with many ratings (more than 200). If there is classical measurement error in average ratings, the error should be more prevalent among hotels with few ratings, and so the regression line should be flatter there.

That is indeed what we find. Figure 8.8 shows two regression lines, one for hotels with few ratings (< 100) and one for hotels with many ratings (> 200). The first slope coefficient is 0.35; the second one is 0.55 (we don't show the regression line for hotels in-between; its slope is 0.45). The corresponding intercepts are ordered in the opposite way: 3.14 for the first regression and

2.39 for the second. The figure visualizes those differences: flatter, less positive slope and higher intercept among hotels with few ratings.

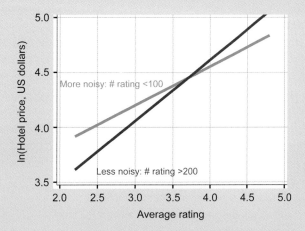

Figure 8.8　Log hotel price and average customer ratings: samples by noisiness

Note: Log hotel price and average customer ratings. Hotels with noisier measure of ratings (number of ratings < 100) versus hotels with less noisy measure (number of ratings > 200).
Source: `hotels-vienna` dataset. Vienna, November 2017, weekday. N=207.

The take-away from this analysis is that there appears to be substantial measurement error in average customer ratings among hotels where that average rating is based on a few customers' reports. Thus, we can expect a regression with average customer ratings on the right-hand side to produce an attenuated slope. Should we do anything about that? And if yes, what?

If we are interested in the effect of ratings on prices, this is clearly an issue. In such an analysis we may want to discard hotels with less than a minimum number of reviews (maybe 10 or 20 or 50 or 100). This is hard, as there is no clear threshold here, so we may try various thresholds. Another approach would be to keep all data but acknowledge that the slope estimate is attenuated due to measurement error. In fact, we could assess the magnitude of the error and adjust the estimates with it. That would require more sophisticated analysis that is beyond the scope of this textbook.

8.12

Non-classical Measurement Error and General Advice

Not all errors in variables are classical in nature. In fact, most errors in variables in real data are not classical. For example, when asked about their earnings or income, survey respondents tend to report values that vary less than their earnings, or income measured in tax records or other administrative sources. Survey responses here are erroneous measures of the values from administrative sources, but they are actually less dispersed, not more dispersed as classical errors should be.

Errors due to misreporting or omission of elements that should be included can lead to biased estimates, too. The consequences of such errors for regression analysis are typically different from the consequences of classical error. Discussing them is beyond the scope of this textbook. Nevertheless, when we suspect substantive errors in variables, it pays to understand the sources and features of error and its consequences for the analysis.

Most variables in economic and social data are measured with noise. So what is the practical consequence of knowing the potential bias? The first take-away is that we should have a good idea about the magnitude of the problem. Noisy measures may be a problem if the noise-to-signal ratio is high. Second, if the ratio is high, we need to have a good idea of the source of the error. If that source makes the measurement error classical, we know what to expect: error in x is a bigger problem for inference than error in y. If non-classical error, we need to think more and, possibly, ask for more advice.

Ultimately, the potentially severe consequences of errors in variables highlight the importance of data quality. A variable that is better measured is more useful for analysis. By "better" we mean both high validity (intended content close to actual content) and high reliability (repeated measurement would lead to similar values). For example, the quality of management of firms is measured with higher validity if based on a scoring system (as in the World Management Survey, see Chapter 1) than on what the firms' managers would say. And answers to difficult survey questions on, for example, household savings or the value of one's home, are more reliable the more background information respondents have available to them.

Thus, assessing the magnitude and properties of measurement error in the most important variables is important. Measurement error may have substantial, and sometimes surprising, consequences. When possible, it pays to work with variables with less error. When error in variables is unavoidable, we need to document it and think about its potential effects.

8.13   Using Weights in Regression Analysis

In the last section of this chapter we discuss whether, when, and how to use **weights in regression analysis**. Using weights makes some observations count more than others in the analysis. We consider two cases for using weights: samples that represent populations, and aggregate data that represent smaller units.

Datasets that are samples of a population often have weights to tell us the number of population items each observation represents (see Chapter 1 for more detail). Such weights may compensate for unequal sampling probabilities, or they may be meant to compensate for some of the biases in the sample due to differences in coverage or response rates.

Using weights in regression analysis is one way to compensate for unequal sampling and biased coverage. Weights in regressions $y^E = f(x)$ produce weighted average values for y^E instead of an unweighted average. In weighted averages, observations with higher weights count more than observations with lower weights.

In practice, weights that compensate for unequal sampling or unequal coverage rarely make a big difference in regression results, especially in multiple regression analysis (to be covered in Chapter 10). Nevertheless, it is good practice to do the analysis both with and without such weights and show whether the results are robust. If they are not, that is if results with and without these kinds of weights differ a lot, there usually is some problem in the background. It is advised to dig deeper in such cases and perhaps incorporate variables that may explain the discrepancies in multiple regression analysis (see later in Chapter 10).

The second potential case for weighting arises with aggregate data. Observations in aggregate data may be units of different size (countries, firms, families). Analyzing aggregate data without weights treats each aggregate unit equally. Analyzing aggregate data with weights makes larger units more important.

Whether to use the size of each observation as weight in analysis of aggregate data should be guided by the substantive question of the analysis. Without weights, a regression using aggregate data compares the aggregate units (e.g., countries). With weights, a regression using aggregated data is best interpreted as approximate comparisons of the smaller units that make up the aggregate ones (e.g., people living in various countries).

For example, we may not want to use weights when interested in how certain policies affect aggregate economic measures (say, the effect of tax policy on income inequality). In this case each country is as important an observation as another country. In contrast, we may want to use weights if we use aggregate data to uncover how certain conditions of people are related to their outcomes (say, the association between vaccination rate and disease prevalence). Here we use aggregate measures but the outcome (disease) makes sense for individuals.

Sometimes whether to use weights or not to use weights is a difficult question. Without a clear best answer we should carry out robustness checks, as usual. If the most important results are similar, we're fine – weights just don't matter. If, however, they turn out to be different, we need to understand the difference and make a choice accordingly.

Review Box 8.8   Using weights in regression analysis

- Different observations may have different weights for two reasons:
  - to compensate for unequal representation of the population (e.g., due to unequal sampling probabilities);
  - to denote different size of larger units when those larger units are the observations in the data (e.g., population of countries).
- It is good practice to use weights in regression analysis if those weights compensate for unequal representation. (This rarely matters, so it can be part of robustness checks.)
- Weights of size should be used if we want to uncover the patterns of association for the individuals who make up the larger units (e.g., people in countries), but not if we want to uncover the patterns of association between the larger units (e.g., countries).

8.B3   CASE STUDY – How is Life Expectancy Related to the Average Income of a Country?

Weights in the regression

Let's go back to cross-country association between GDP per capita and life expectancy. Recall that, when life expectancy (in years) is regressed on log GDP per capita, the slope coefficient is 5.3. This shows that life expectancy is around half a year higher on average in countries with 10% higher GDP per capita.

The same linear regression using population as weight gives a slope of 5.8. This shows that people who live in countries with 10% higher GDP per capita live, on average, 0.6 years longer. This interpretation is similar to the previous one but it is not quite the same. Whereas the unweighted regression compares countries, the regression weighted by population compares people living in different countries. Thus people in larger countries are compared more often to other people than those in smaller countries.

Figures 8.9a and 8.9b show the two regression lines with the corresponding scatterplots. The scatterplot for the weighted regression shows the size of each country: the area of the circles is proportionate to their population.

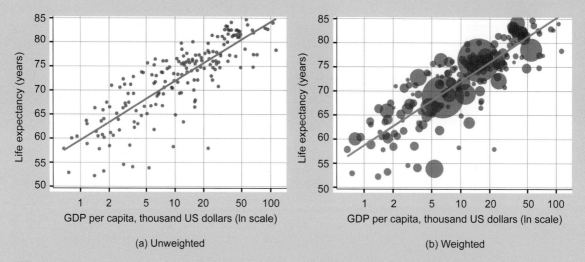

(a) Unweighted   (b) Weighted

Figure 8.9   Life expectancy and log GDP per capita: unweighted and weighted regressions

Note: Life expectancy regressed on log GDP per capita. Regression without weights (panel a); regression weighted by population (panel b). GDP measured at Purchasing Power Parity.
Source: `worldbank-lifeexpectancy` dataset. World Development Indicators 2017. N=182.

The differences in principle notwithstanding, the actual slope estimates turn out to be similar. The R-squared values are similar, too, with 0.68 in the unweighted regression and 0.66 in the weighted regression. The two regressions show similar results because larger countries do not tilt the regression line much. For example, India and China are in the middle of the GDP per capita distribution so they do not affect the slope much when they are counted with their huge weights. As the weighted regression produces results that are similar to the unweighted regression, the conclusions that we drew at the end of Section 8.B2 remain the same.

8.14   Main Takeaways

Nonlinear functional forms may or may not be important for regression analysis.

- They are usually important for prediction.
- They are usually less important for causal analysis.
- When important, we have multiple options, such as taking logs or specifying linear splines or polynomials such as a quadratic.

Influential observations and other extreme values are usually best analyzed with the rest of the data; we should discard them only if we have a good reason.

PRACTICE QUESTIONS

1. When and why may it make sense to take the natural log of a variable to be used in a regression?

2. The slope parameter of a linear regression $(\ln y)^E = \alpha + \beta \ln x$ is 0.5. Interpret this number.

3. The slope parameter of a linear regression $(\ln y)^E = \alpha + \beta x$ is 0.2. Interpret this number.

4. The slope parameter of a linear regression $y^E = \alpha + \beta \ln x$ is 5. Interpret this number.

5. What kind of pattern could be captured by a regression with a single explanatory variable entered as a piecewise linear spline with one knot? Give an example.

6. The slope parameters of a linear regression $y^E = \alpha_1 + \beta_1 x [if\ x < 5] + (\alpha_2 + \beta_2 x)[if\ x > 5]$ are $\beta_1 = 2$, $\beta_2 = 1$. Interpret these numbers.

7. The slope parameters of a quadratic regression $y^E = \alpha + \beta x + \gamma x^2$ are $\beta = 2$, $\gamma = -0.1$. Interpret these numbers. Is the relationship positive between y and x?

8. A piecewise linear spline regression of y on x shows a steeper positive slope in the lower 90% of the range of the x variable and a flatter, but still positive slope, for the remaining 10%. What shape do you expect from a quadratic fitted on the same data? What are the advantages and disadvantages of these two specifications?

9. Observations with extreme values are also called outliers and are often discarded from the data before analysis. Is this good practice? If yes, why? If not, why not and what would be a better approach?

10. When interviewed for a household survey, people who drink large amounts of alcohol often tend to understate the frequency and quantity of their alcohol consumption. Can you think of the frequency of alcohol consumption variable in such data as a variable measured with error? Is it a classical error?

11. When interviewed for a household survey, people give rough and approximate answers to the question of how much time they spend commuting to work. However, those with longer commuting times are not more likely to understate or overstate their time than those with shorter times. Can you think of the commuting variable in such data as one measured with error? Is it a classical error?

12. You are interested in whether more educated people are different in terms of their commuting time to work than less educated people. Time to commute to work is measured with classical error in the data. What is the effect of this measurement error on the slope coefficient in a regression of commuting time on education?

13. You are interested in whether people who need to commute a lot to work earn more. Time to commute to work is measured with classical error in the data. The slope coefficient of a regression of log earnings on commuting time (in hours) is 0.01. Interpret this coefficient. Would it be smaller, larger, or the same if commuting time were measured without any error?

14. In a dataset on firms, the percentage of employees leaving a firm within a year is regressed on the average number of paid holidays employees receive. The slope coefficient is -0.1 in a regression without weights; it is -0.2 in a regression weighted by the number of employees. Interpret each number.

15. The amount of credit card debt is regressed on (log) household income. Compare the slope coefficient you expect if income is measured with substantial classical error to the slope coefficient you expect if income is measured without any error.

DATA EXERCISES

Easier and/or shorter exercises are denoted by [*]; harder and/or longer exercises are denoted by [**].

1. Continue the hotel price vs. distance to the city center regression analysis with log dependent variable but allowing for a piecewise linear spline in the explanatory variable, then a quadratic, and then a cubic. Compare the five best deals from the four specifications (linear, linear spline, quadratic, cubic). What do you conclude from this analysis? [*]
2. Re-do the hotel vs. distance to the city center regression analysis in a log–log specification. How do you interpret the coefficients of the simple linear regression? Then estimate corresponding regressions allowing for a piecewise linear spline in the explanatory variable, then a quadratic. Compare the five best deals from these specifications (linear, linear spline, quadratic). What do you conclude from this analysis? [*]
3. Re-do the cross-country regression analysis of life expectancy and ln GDP per capita for a different year. Use weights if you think that's a good choice, and use a functional form that allows for nonlinearity if you think that's a good choice. Compare your results to what's in our case study. [*]
4. Your task is to understand the pattern of association between how easy it is to do business in a country and how much income the country generates. Download data from the World Bank on GDP per capita in PPP (y) and the time required to start a business (x) for a recent year. Besides an average association, you are also asked to uncover if the association is linear or it is different at higher numbers of days. Estimate a regression that would measure such a potentially nonlinear pattern of association, interpret its coefficients. and draw conclusions. (During your analysis you may want to consider taking logs, inspecting and dealing with influential observations, experimenting with functional forms, using weights, and so on.) [**]
5. Download data on used cars of a specific brand and type, and analyze price vs. age of cars in order to find a good deal. Estimate a regression that fits the pattern of association well enough. Use the results from the best linear regression to list candidate cars for the best deal using the residuals of the regression. (During your analysis you may want to consider taking logs, inspecting and dealing with influential observations, experimenting with functional forms, and so on.) [**]

REFERENCES AND FURTHER READING

The influential study Preston (1975) analyzed the relationship between per capita GDP and life expectancy and the changes of this association with time.

8.U1 UNDER THE HOOD: DETAILS OF THE LOG APPROXIMATION

In this subsection we dig deeper into why and how log differences approximate relative, or percentage differences. Understanding these details helps appreciate the approximate nature of log differences and why they are better with small differences than larger differences.

For a number d that is small enough (say, 0.1 or –0.1), it is true that $\ln(1 + d) \approx d$, then

$$(x_1 - x_0)/x_0 = d \approx \ln(1 + d) = \ln(1 + (x_1 - x_0)/x_0) = \ln(1 + x_1/x_0 - 1) = \ln(x_1/x_0) = \ln(x_1) - \ln(x_0).$$

The exact difference, using the exponential function is

$$(x_1 - x_0)/x_0 = x_1/x_0 - 1 = \exp(\ln(x_1/x_0)) - 1 = \exp(\ln(x_1) - \ln(x_0)) - 1.$$

Table 8.2 shows selected exact values for $(x_1 - x_0)/x_0$ and $\ln(x_1) - \ln(x_0)$.

Table 8.2 Tabulating log approximation

in the negative range		in the positive range		in the positive range, continued	
$(x_1 - x_0)/x_0$	$\ln(x_1) - \ln(x_0)$	$(x_1 - x_0)/x_0$	$\ln(x_1) - \ln(x_0)$	$(x_1 - x_0)/x_0$	$\ln(x_1) - \ln(x_0)$
−1.00	n.a.	0.00	0.00	1.00	0.69
−0.95	−3.00	0.05	0.05	1.05	0.72
−0.90	−2.30	0.10	0.10	1.10	0.74
−0.85	−1.90	0.15	0.14	1.15	0.77
−0.80	−1.61	0.20	0.18	1.20	0.79
−0.75	−1.39	0.25	0.22	1.25	0.81
−0.70	−1.20	0.30	0.26	1.30	0.83
−0.65	−1.05	0.35	0.30	1.35	0.85
−0.60	−0.92	0.40	0.34	1.40	0.88
−0.55	−0.80	0.45	0.37	1.45	0.90
−0.50	−0.69	0.50	0.41	1.50	0.92
−0.45	−0.60	0.55	0.44	1.55	0.94
−0.40	−0.51	0.60	0.47	1.60	0.96
−0.35	−0.43	0.65	0.50	1.65	0.97
−0.30	−0.36	0.70	0.53	1.70	0.99
−0.25	−0.29	0.75	0.56	1.75	1.01
−0.20	−0.22	0.80	0.59	1.80	1.03
−0.15	−0.16	0.85	0.62	1.85	1.05
−0.10	−0.11	0.90	0.64	1.90	1.06
−0.05	−0.05	0.95	0.67	1.95	1.08
0.00	0.00	1.00	0.69	2.00	1.10

UNDER THE HOOD: DERIVING THE CONSEQUENCES OF CLASSICAL MEASUREMENT ERROR

In this subsection we formally derive the consequences of classical measurement error in variables for the OLS estimates of the slope and intercept parameters of the simple linear regression.

Classical measurement error in the dependent variable does not affect the regression coefficients. To see this, compare the slope of a simple linear regression with an error-free dependent variable y^* to the slope of the same regression in which the dependent variable y is measured with classical error:

$$y = y^* + e \tag{8.5}$$
$$y^{*E} = a^* + \beta^* x \tag{8.6}$$
$$y^E = a + \beta x \tag{8.7}$$

The slope coefficient in the first regression with error-free dependent variable is

$$\beta^* = \frac{Cov[y^*, x]}{Var[x]} \tag{8.8}$$

The coefficient in the second regression with a dependent variable measured with classical error is

$$\beta = \frac{Cov[y, x]}{Var[x]} \tag{8.9}$$

The two are equal because the measurement error e is uncorrelated with all relevant variables, including x, so that $Cov[e, x] = 0$.

$$\beta = \frac{Cov[y, x]}{Var[x]} = \frac{Cov[(y^* + e), x]}{Var[x]} = \frac{Cov[y^*, x] + Cov[e, x]}{Var[x]} = \frac{Cov[y^*, x]}{Var[x]} = \beta^* \tag{8.10}$$

Classical measurement error in the left-hand-side variable makes the slope coefficient unchanged because the expected value of the error-ridden y is the same as the expected value of the error-free y.

In contrast, classical measurement error in a right-hand-side variable makes the regression coefficient estimates different. Here we need to compare the slope of a simple linear regression with an error-free right-hand-side variable x^* to the slope of the same regression in which the right-hand-side variable x is measured with classical error:

$$x = x^* + e \tag{8.11}$$
$$y^E = a^* + \beta^* x^* \tag{8.12}$$
$$y^E = a + \beta x \tag{8.13}$$

The slope coefficient in the first regression with error-free dependent variable is

$$\beta^* = \frac{Cov[y, x^*]}{Var[x^*]} \tag{8.14}$$

The coefficient in the second regression with a dependent variable measured with classical error is

$$\beta = \frac{Cov[y, x]}{Var[x]} \tag{8.15}$$

These two are different in the presence of classical measurement error. The slope coefficient in the regression with an error-ridden right-hand-side variable is smaller in absolute value than the slope coefficient in the corresponding regression with an error-free right-hand-side variable:

$$\beta = \beta^* \frac{Var[x^*]}{Var[x^*] + Var[e]} \tag{8.16}$$

The derivation follows:

$$\beta = \frac{Cov[y, x]}{Var[x]} = \frac{Cov[y, (x^* + e)]}{Var[x^* + e]} = \frac{Cov[y, x^*] + Cov[y, e]}{Var[x^*] + Var[e]} = \frac{Cov[y, x^*]}{Var[x^*] + Var[e]}$$

$$= \frac{Cov[y, x^*]}{Var[x^*]} \frac{Var[x^*]}{Var[x^*] + Var[e]}$$

$$= \beta^* \frac{Var[x^*]}{Var[x^*] + Var[e]}$$

Technically, attenuation bias occurs because the error inflates the variance in the right-hand-side variable and the slope coefficient normalizes the (unaffected and thus unbiased) covariance with this inflated variance.

If the slope is attenuated towards zero, the intercept is tilted away from zero. Recall that the intercept equals average y minus average x multiplied by the slope coefficient. Without measurement error,

$$a^* = \bar{y} - \beta^* \overline{x^*} \tag{8.17}$$

With measurement error,

$$a = \bar{y} - \beta \bar{x} \tag{8.18}$$

Classical measurement error leaves expected values unchanged so we can expect

$$\bar{x} = \overline{x^*} \tag{8.19}$$

The regression line on error-free variables with slope β^* and the regression line on erroneous variables with slope β go through the same $(\bar{x}, \bar{y})$ point. Classical measurement error in x makes β attenuated relative to β^*. That means a flatter regression line. With x and y positive only (and thus the $(\bar{x}, \bar{y})$ point in the upper right quadrant of the coordinate system) and a positive slope, an attenuated slope leads to an upward biased intercept. Depending on where the point is and whether the slope is negative or positive, the intercept with an error-ridden x can be higher or lower than the intercept with an error-free x.

We can derive that the difference in the two intercepts depends on the sign of the slope as well as the sign of average x:

$$a = \bar{y} - \beta \bar{x} = \bar{y} - \beta \overline{x^*} = \bar{y} - \beta \overline{x^*} + \beta^* \overline{x^*} - \beta^* \overline{x^*} = a^* + (\beta^* - \beta)\overline{x^*}$$

$$= a^* + \left(\beta^* - \beta^* \frac{Var[x^*]}{Var[x^*] + Var[e]} \right) \overline{x^*} = a^* + \beta^* \frac{Var[e]}{Var[x^*] + Var[e]} \overline{x^*}$$

9 Generalizing Results of a Regression

How to construct confidence intervals, prediction intervals, and tests in linear regression analysis to uncover general patterns represented by the data, and how to think about external validity

---

Motivation

You want to find out if the earnings of women and men tend to be different in your country in the occupation you are considering: market analysts. Analyzing data from a random sample of market analysts in the USA, you find that women earn less, by 11 percent on average. How much gender difference can you expect among all market analysts in the USA? In particular, is there a difference in the population, or is it just a chance event true in your data? And can you generalize these results to the future or to other countries?

Using the same data, you uncover that earnings tend to be higher for older market analysts than younger ones, but the association is not linear. In particular, the age differences are large and positive between older versus younger employees if both are below age 30; they are smaller but still positive if both are between 30 and 40; they are zero or slightly negative if comparing employees over age 40. How can you tell whether, and by how much, the nonlinear association you estimated in your sample generalizes to the population of all market analysts? How could you visualize the shape of the expected association in the population based on the shape you estimated in your data? And, can you generalize these results to learn what earnings trajectory you could expect in the future among market analysts?

Most often, we want to generalize the results of a regression from the data we are analyzing to a decision situation we care about. We introduced the relevant conceptual framework in Chapters 5 and 6 for simpler statistics. The same framework applies to regression coefficients, and we can build on the methods we introduced there. In particular, we can use methods to quantify the uncertainty brought about by generalizing to the general pattern represented by the data (statistical inference), and we can have guidelines to assess whether the general pattern represented by the data is likely close to the general pattern behind the situation we care about (external validity).

We start by describing the two steps of generalization in the context of regression analysis: statistical inference and external validity. Then we turn to quantifying uncertainty brought about by generalizing to the general pattern represented by our data. We discuss how to estimate the standard errors and confidence intervals of the estimates of the regression coefficients, how to estimate prediction intervals, and how to test hypotheses about regression coefficients. We introduce ways to visualize the confidence interval and the prediction interval together with the regression line, and we introduce the standard way to present the results of regression analysis in tables.

The first, and main, case study in this chapter, **Estimating gender and age differences in earnings**, uncovers earnings differences by gender and age among people employed as market analysts, using standard survey data from the United States. Learning such differences may help young adults predict what kinds of differences in earnings they can expect. This case study uses the `cps-earnings` dataset. The second case study, **How stable is the hotel price–distance to center relationship?**, is a short illustration of potential issues with external validity. It uses the `hotels-europe` dataset to explore how the coefficients of the price–distance regression in one city for one day compare to the estimates on other days and in other cities.

Learning outcomes

After working through this chapter, you should be able to:

- estimate standard errors of regression coefficients in an appropriate way;
- construct and interpret confidence intervals of regression coefficients;
- construct and interpret prediction intervals;
- carry out and interpret tests of hypotheses about regression coefficients;
- present results of regression analysis in standard and easily interpretable ways;
- think about the external validity of a regression analysis.

9.1 Generalizing Linear Regression Coefficients

With the help of a simple linear regression $y^E = \alpha + \beta x$, we can uncover $\hat{\beta}$, the average difference of y corresponding to unit differences in x in the data. The regression coefficients calculated within the data allow for constructing predicted values. $\hat{y}_i$ is our best guess for expected y for an observation i with value x_i – based on the regression coefficients that characterize patterns in the data.

Sometimes all we care about are patterns, predicted values, or residuals in the data we have. An example is our case study of finding a good deal among hotels in the data. Most often, though, we are interested in patterns and predicted values in situations that are not contained in the data we can analyze. That's true for all other case studies in this textbook. There the question is whether and to what extent predictions and patterns uncovered in the data generalize to a situation we care about. This is the question of generalization that we covered in Chapter 5 earlier, applied to regression analysis.

As we argued there, answering this question is best broken down into two steps. One step is **statistical inference**: generalizing from the data to the population, or general pattern, it represents. Our best tool here is the confidence interval (Chapter 5, Section 5.4), but sometimes we carry out more formal hypothesis testing (Chapter 6). The other step is about **external validity**. We have to define the population, or general pattern, we are interested in and compare it to the population, or general pattern, that the data represents. If we conclude that external validity is high, the confidence interval is the end of the story. If external validity is not that high, then the confidence interval we estimated does not capture all uncertainty, and we may consider wider ranges – how much wider is hard to tell, unfortunately. If external validity is very low, we may not learn anything meaningful from our data for the situation we care about. It's perhaps best to see if our case is that bad early in the analysis so we don't do the entire analysis for nothing.

Applying these principles to the results of regression analysis is straightforward conceptually, but it involves some new techniques. Typically, there are two statistics we want to generalize from regression analysis: the slope coefficient β that summarizes the pattern of differences in average y corresponding to differences in x and the predicted value of $\hat{y}$ for specific values of x. Often, we want to test hypotheses about the coefficients. All of these questions are discussed in this chapter.

9.2   Statistical Inference: CI and SE of Regression Coefficients

With a simple linear regression $y^E = \alpha + \beta x$, the estimate $\hat{\beta}$ shows the average difference in y corresponding to one unit difference in x in the data. The question of statistical inference is the true value of β. The **true value** means its value in the population, or general pattern, represented by the data. The **confidence interval of the regression coefficient** can answer that question with the caveats we discussed in Chapter 5, Section 5.5. The 95% CI of β can tell us where its true value is with 95% likelihood. Its 99% CI can tell us where its true value is with 99% likelihood. And so on, with confidence intervals for different percentage likelihood.

Estimating the 95% CI of the slope coefficient β of a linear regression is similar to estimating a 95% CI of any other statistic. We take the value of the statistic estimated from the data and measure twice its standard error around it. To be precise, the 95% CI value is 1.96. However, as all of this is an approximation, we prefer the round number 2. For the slope of the linear regression, the 95% CI is

$$CI(\hat{\beta})_{95\%} = [\hat{\beta} - 2SE(\hat{\beta}), \hat{\beta} + 2SE(\hat{\beta})] \tag{9.1}$$

As always, the CI is narrower the smaller the SE, in which case we also say that the estimate of the regression coefficient is **more precise**. A larger SE and thus a less precise estimate leads to a wider CI.

The standard error (SE) of the slope coefficient is conceptually the same as the SE of any statistic. It measures the spread of the values of the statistic across hypothetical repeated samples drawn from the same population, or general pattern, that our data represents – as discussed in detail in Chapter 5, Section 5.2. Just as with the standard error of an average, there are two ways to get the standard error of the slope of a linear regression: bootstrap and formula.

Recall that the bootstrap is an intuitive method to get standard errors. It generates samples that represent the same population, or general pattern, as our original data and have the same size, too. Each bootstrap sample is a random sample from the original data with replacement. After estimating the slope coefficient $\hat{\beta}$ in each sample, we can look at its distribution. The standard deviation of this distribution is the bootstrap estimate of the standard error (SE) of the slope coefficient. The simple bootstrap procedure we discussed in Chapter 5 works here as well.

There are various versions of the SE formula for the slope of the linear regression, and they are not equally good. Here we show what is called the **simple SE formula**. The simple SE formula assumes that variables are independent across observations, which is likely true in most cross-sectional data. However, the formula assumes something else, too, called homoskedasticity, which may not be a good assumption in many cases. We'll discuss this second assumption later. Thus, this formula is not correct in many applications. So the simple SE formula turns out to be not a good formula in general. We discuss it, nevertheless, because it is the simplest formula that contains the most important elements of other, more complicated SE formulae for a slope coefficient. The simple SE formula of the slope is

$$SE(\hat{\beta}) = \frac{Std[e]}{\sqrt{n}Std[x]} \tag{9.2}$$

The formula contains three elements:

1. $Std[e]$, the standard deviation of the regression residual ($e = y - \hat{a} - \hat{\beta}x$);
2. $Std[x]$, the standard deviation of the explanatory variable;
3. $\sqrt{n}$, the square root of the number of observations in the data.

A smaller standard error translates into a narrower confidence interval, which pins down the true value of the slope coefficient with more precision. The simple SE formula shows that the SE is smaller, the smaller the standard deviation of the residual, the larger the standard deviation of the explanatory variable, and the more observations there are in the data. There is a corresponding formula for the intercept; see Under the Hood section 9.U1 for the details.

As we indicated, the simple SE formula is not correct in general. It relies on the assumption that the fit of the regression line is the same across the entire range of the x variable, an assumption called **homoskedasticity**. In general, though, the fit may differ at different values of x, in which case the spread of actual y around the regression line is different for different values of x, a phenomenon called **heteroskedasticity**.

There is a SE formula that is correct whether the situation is one of homoskedasticity or of heteroskedasticity. That is called the **robust SE formula**, also known as the "White" or "Huber" formula (for the two statisticians who uncovered it independently), or the heteroskedasticity-robust SE formula. This formula shares the same properties as the simple formula in that it is smaller the smaller $Std[e]$, the larger $Std[x]$, and the larger $\sqrt{n}$.

Most statistical software can calculate both the simple and the robust SE of the regression coefficients. Typically, the default choice of statistical software is to show the simple SE estimate. However, this is not the best default. The robust SE is correct both under heteroskedasticiy and homoskedasticity; the simple SE is correct only under homoskedasticity. (In small samples, the robust SE may be worse.) Therefore, in reasonably large samples, it is good practice to consider the robust SE as a default choice. Note that, most often, this choice does not make much of a difference, as the simple and robust SE estimates tend to be very similar. But sometimes it does, and then the robust SE tends to be the better choice.

Review Box 9.1 Statistical inference for regression coefficients

- Consider the simple linear regression: $y^E = a + \beta x$ with coefficient estimates in the data $\hat{a}$ and $\hat{\beta}$.
- We are interested in the value of β in the population, or general pattern, of interest.
- The question is best broken down into two parts:

  1. Statistical inference: what is the value of β in the general pattern represented by the data if we know its estimated value $\hat{\beta}$?
  2. External validity: how close is the general pattern of interest to the general pattern represented by the data?

- The most useful tool of statistical inference is the confidence interval (CI). The 95% CI around $\hat{\beta}$ gives a range in which we can expect β to lie with a 95% confidence in the general pattern represented by our data.
- The 95% CI around $\hat{\beta}$ is $\hat{\beta} \pm 2SE(\hat{\beta})$.
- We can estimate $SE(\hat{\beta})$ by bootstrap or a formula.
- The simple SE formula for the slope estimate is

$$SE(\hat{\beta}) = \frac{Std[e]}{\sqrt{n}Std[x]}$$

- Accordingly, the SE of the slope estimate is smaller the better the fit of the regression, the larger the sample, and the larger the spread of the x variable.
- In practice, we should use the robust SE formula, not the simple SE formula.

9.A1   CASE STUDY – Estimating Gender and Age Differences in Earnings

Question, data, confidence interval

Do women earn the same as or less than men in jobs that many students consider taking after their studies in data analysis? And how much more do older employees earn than younger employees? Answering these questions helps set the expectations of students about their future salaries. It also helps answer a bigger question: are there systematic differences in earnings by gender and age of employees in the same occupation? And, if yes, why?

The case study in this chapter examines patterns of earnings by gender and age. We will first uncover patterns in the data. But our question relates to a situation outside our data: what to expect in the future? This generalization involves both of the usual steps: do statistical inference to learn what the average difference may be in the population represented by the data, and assess external validity to understand how that average difference may look like in the future situation we care about.

In this chapter we focus on employees in a particular occupation category: "market research analysts and marketing specialists". We use the `cps-earnings` dataset. It is part of the Current Population Survey (CPS) of the USA, a major survey that provides federal statistics on employment, unemployment, and earnings and allows for in-depth research on many related topics. The so-called morg sample of the CPS has earnings data. The CPS is a sample, although a large one. It is a random sample aimed at representing the adult population of the USA. The data we use is from 2014.

The 2014 CPS earnings data has 317 056 observations, each observation being an individual of age 16 through 85. We kept all respondents between age 16 and 64 who were employed but not self-employed, reported a wage that was more than zero, and reported working more than zero hours in the previous week.

Out of the 317 056 in the 2014 survey, there are 254 904 working age individuals, 175 661 of whom were in employment. 367 individuals reported zero wage or zero hours worked, and 26 345 had missing or zero earnings and/or worked hours in the data. That's 15% of all observations. It turns out that whether earnings or hours are missing (or zero) is weakly associated with some demographic variables (gender, race), but it's not associated with education. Thus, while this is not a completely random phenomenon, it doesn't appear to lead to a strong selection bias, so we decided to simply exclude the observations missing data for our analysis. The size of this sample is 149 316 individuals.

In this sample, 281 individuals are in the "market research analyst and marketing specialist" occupation, 61% of whom are women. The dependent variable of the analysis is the natural logarithm of earnings per hour, which we denote as ln w. We calculated this by dividing weekly earnings by usual hours worked. 63% of the sample reports 40 hours per week, and an additional 17% reports 41–50 hours. It turns out that weekly earnings are capped in the CPS: if its value is above a threshold level, the data shows the threshold level for earnings and not the true higher value. This is due to confidentiality reasons, to prevent potential identification of very high-earning respondents. The threshold value was USD 2 285 in 2014, and it affects only 5% of the sample of market analysts. We'll ignore this issue for our analysis and take the capped values as actual earnings. The distribution of earnings per hour is distributed with a long right tail; the distribution of its natural log is more symmetric and quite close to normal.

We regressed log earnings per hour on a binary variable that is one if the individual is female and zero if male:

$$(\ln w)^E = \alpha + \beta \times female \tag{9.3}$$

This is a log–level regression. The slope shows average differences in relative wages by gender in the data: women earn $\beta \times 100$ percent more than men, on average. The regression estimate is -0.11: female market analysts earn 11 percent less, on average, than male market analysts in this data.

Based on these estimates, what can university students expect about the gender gap in pay if they choose to become market analysts?

First, statistical inference. Our data is a random sample of all market analysts working in the USA in 2014. The CPS is a high-quality sample with careful random sampling and high response rates in general. Earnings or hours are missing for 15% of the respondents, but that's not strongly related to variables that matter for earnings. Thus, we treat it as missing at random, and so we treat the part of the data with valid earnings and hours measures as a random sample of the original sample. We can therefore use the standard tools of statistical inference to estimate the standard error and then the confidence interval for the estimated slope coefficient of -0.11. We computed three alternatives for the standard error and the corresponding confidence interval. First by bootstrap, second using the simple standard error formula, and third using the robust standard error formula. Of these three, the second, the simple formula, may be wrong, while the bootstrap and the robust SE should both be fine.

Second, external validity. Students are interested in the future not the past. Whether gender differences will follow the same general pattern in the future as in the recent past is impossible to know. However, a more thorough analysis may shed light on this question. For example, we may analyze gender differences in earnings in many years in the past. Such analysis would reveal that gender differences in earnings have been relatively stable over those years. Therefore, we may assume that they will be similar in the future as well, at least in the near future. Students outside the USA should also ask if gender differences in the USA are close to what they would be in their countries. Again, some research may help assess this question. We may not have access to average earnings by gender and occupation to make direct comparisons among market analysts across countries, but average earnings by gender among all employees are available in most countries (typically, estimated from surveys). If, for example, earnings differences by gender are similar, in general, in our country to those surveyed in the USA, we may assume that they are likely similar among market analysts, too.

Figure 9.1 shows the histogram of the slope estimates from the 1000 bootstrap samples we took, with a vertical line denoting −0.11. The bootstrap SE is 0.06, and the 95% CI is [−0.23,0.01]. The simple SE and the robust SE estimates are also 0.06, implying the same 95% CI, [−0.23,0.01] (there are minor differences in the third digit). Thus, the two estimates that should be similar (bootstrap and robust SE) are similar indeed. The simple SE is similar, too; while it may be off in principle, it turns out just fine here.

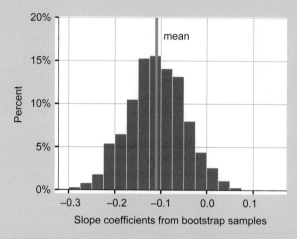

Figure 9.1   Bootstrap distribution of the average female–male wage difference among market analysts

Note: Histogram of 1000 bootstrap sample estimates of the slope in $(\ln w)^E = \alpha + \beta \times female$.
Source: `cps-earnings` dataset. USA, 2014. Employees in "market research analyst and marketing specialist" occupations, N=281.

Interpreting the 95% CI, we can say that in 2014 in the USA (the population represented by the data), we can be 95% confident that the average difference between hourly earnings of female market analysts versus male market analysts was −23% to +1%. This confidence interval includes zero. Thus we can't rule out with 95% confidence that their average earnings are the same. More likely, though, female market analysts earn less in the population as a large part of the CI is negative.

Note that in the case study, our confidence interval is rather wide. As we discussed, the sample size affects the standard error, and in the case study we had 281 observations only. If, instead of market research, we considered computer science occupations with 4740 observations, our slope coefficient estimate would be −0.15 with a smaller standard error of 0.018 and narrower 95% CI of $[-0.185, -0.115]$. As a data exercise you will be asked to reproduce the whole case study for an occupation other than market research analysts.

9.3 Intervals for Predicted Values

One of the two main goals of regression analysis is prediction. There the task is predicting the value of y for observations outside the data, for which only the value of x is known. To predict y with the help of x using linear regression, we need to know the coefficients α and β. To be more precise, we need to know their values in the general pattern that is relevant for the situation where we want to predict y. This is the usual problem of generalizing statistics from a dataset, with its two steps: statistical inference and external validity.

Using our data we can estimate the regression coefficients. Then, with their help, we can calculate the predicted value of y for a particular observation with known x. For an observation j with known value x_j this is $\hat{y}_j = \hat{\alpha} + \hat{\beta} x_j$. The question we ask here is how we can quantify and present the uncertainty corresponding to this specific predicted value, $\hat{y}_j$. The answer is producing an interval around it, with some level of confidence.

It turns out that there are two kinds of intervals to consider for predicted values. The first one is the **confidence interval (CI) of the predicted value**, also called the **CI of the regression line**. The second one is called the **prediction interval** for an observation, y_j. Let's start with the first one.

The predicted value $\hat{y}$ combines the estimated values $\hat{\alpha}$ and $\hat{\beta}$. Thus the CI of the predicted value combines the CI for $\hat{\alpha}$ and the CI for $\hat{\beta}$. It answers the question of where we can expect y^E to lie if we know the value of x and we have estimates of coefficients $\hat{\alpha}$ and $\hat{\beta}$ from the data. Similarly to the CI formulae discussed earlier, the 95% CI of the predicted value is the value estimated from the sample plus and minus its standard error. We call this estimate the **standard error of the predicted value** y and denote it by $SE(\hat{y}_j)$:

$$95\% \, CI(\hat{y}_j) = \hat{y}_j \pm 2SE(\hat{y}_j) \tag{9.4}$$

$SE(\hat{y}_j)$ can be estimated using bootstrap or an appropriate formula. As usual, we need the robust SE formula in practice. However, as usual, that robust formula is quite complicated and difficult to understand. Therefore, we continue to show the simple formula, because it contains the most important ingredients of the more complicated robust formula and thus helps understand the intuition behind it. The simple formula for the SE of the predicted value from a simple linear regression is

$$SE(\hat{y}_j) = Std[e] \sqrt{\frac{1}{n} + \frac{(x_j - \bar{x})^2}{n \, Var[x]}} \tag{9.5}$$

One way of making sense of what's in this formula is to recognize that it has elements from the standard error of the slope estimate: $Std[e]$, n, and $Std[x]$ ($Std[x] = \sqrt{Var[x]}$). Thus, $SE(\hat{y}_j)$ is smaller, the smaller $Std[e]$, the larger n, and the larger $Std[x]$. These are the same things that make $SE(\hat{\beta})$ small. Thus, not surprisingly, the standard error of the predicted value is small if the standard error of $\hat{\beta}$ is small. There are two additional elements here, under the square root. The factor $\frac{1}{n}$ within the square root amplifies the role of the sample size: the larger n is, the smaller the SE. This extra element comes from the SE formula of the intercept $\hat{a}$. The second element is new: $(x_j - \bar{x})^2$. It says that the standard error of predicted y_j depends on the corresponding value x_j. The closer that x value is to $\bar{x}$, the smaller the SE of the predicted value.

To summarize: the SE of the predicted value for a particular observation is small if the SEs of the coefficient estimates are small and the particular observation has an x value close to its average. The second part means that predictions for observations with more extreme x values are bound to have larger standard errors and thus wider confidence intervals.

The CI of the predicted value may be estimated for all kinds of regressions, not just for simple linear regression. That includes regressions with piecewise linear spline, quadratic or other polynomial, as well as non-parametric regressions including lowess. The general idea is the same: it is an interval that tells us where to expect average y given the value of x in the population, or general pattern, represented by the data. The way it is computed is different for different kinds of regressions, but it is always true that the CI is narrower, the smaller the $Std[e]$, the larger the n, and the larger the $Std[x]$.

The best way to use the CI of the predicted value is visualizing it, together with the regression line (or curve). The CI of the predicted value shows up as a band around the regression line, telling us where else the regression line could be besides where it is in the data, with 95% (or some other) chance, in the population, or general pattern represented by the data.

A frequent use of the CI of the predicted value is choosing the functional form for the $y^E = f(x)$ regression. We may compare two regressions that apply a different functional form for f, say a quadratic and a piecewise linear spline. Visualizing the estimated regressions together with their 95% confidence intervals is very informative. This visualization may show that the confidence intervals overlap over the entire range of x. That would imply that the quadratic is indistinguishable from the piecewise linear spline with a 95% chance in the population, or general pattern, represented by the data. Thus, the quadratic and the piecewise linear spline are very similar in capturing the unknown f function. Conversely, we may find that the two CIs don't overlap for a substantial part of the range. That would imply that the quadratic and the piecewise linear splines are different approximations for the pattern in the population, or general pattern, represented by the data.

Let's turn to the second kind of interval now, the one around predicted values: the prediction interval for y_j. This interval answers a different question: where to expect the particular y_j value if we know the corresponding x_j value and the estimates of the regression coefficients. Note the difference. The CI of the predicted value is about $\hat{y}_j$: the expected value if we know x_j. The prediction interval is about y_j itself: the actual value of y_j if we know x_j.

The prediction interval for y_j starts from the CI for $\hat{y}_j$ and adds the extra uncertainty due to the fact that the actual y_j will be somewhere around $\hat{y}_j$. To distinguish it from the confidence interval around $\hat{y}_j$, we denote the **prediction interval** for y_j as $PI(\hat{y}_j)$ and the corresponding standard error as the **standard prediction error**, $SPE(\hat{y}_j)$.

The formula for the 95% prediction interval is

$$95\% PI(\hat{y}_j) = \hat{y}_j \pm 2SPE(\hat{y}_j) \tag{9.6}$$

The simple formula for $SPE(\hat{y}_j)$ is instructive to look at for the same reason as the simple formulae earlier: it only contains the most important ingredients.

$$SPE(\hat{y}_j) = Std[e]\sqrt{1 + \frac{1}{n} + \frac{(x_j - \bar{x})^2}{nVar[x]}} \tag{9.7}$$

The formula has one, seemingly minor, additional element to $SE(\hat{y}_j)$: the plus one under the square root. It is as if we added $Std[e]$ to the previous formula. This additional part summarizes the additional uncertainty here: the actual y_j value is expected to be spread around its average value. The magnitude of this spread is best estimated by the standard deviation of the residual. In very large samples, the standard error for average y is very small. In contrast, no matter how large the sample, we can always expect actual y values to be spread around their average values. In the formula, all elements get very small if n gets large, except for this new element. We shall discuss the prediction error in more detail in Chapter 13.

Note that the additional assumption of homoskedasticity is explicit in the simple formula: it assumes that the spread of actual y around the regression line is $Std[e]$, the same everywhere. If this assumption fails, and the fit of the regression is not the same at different x values, the additional standard deviation will be different, too. (Appropriate robust formulae are difficult to obtain and standard statistical software do not contain such a formula in a simple fashion.) Thus, when the fit of the regression is very different across the range of x, we do not have a general formula to capture the prediction interval.

Review Box 9.2   Intervals for predicted values

Consider the simple linear regression estimates $\hat{y} = \hat{\alpha} + \hat{\beta}x$:

- The confidence interval (CI) of the predicted value (CI of the regression line)
  - tells us about where y^E is in the general pattern represented by the data if we know the value of x and we have estimates of coefficients $\hat{\alpha}$ and $\hat{\beta}$;
  - is narrower, the narrower the CIs of the regression coefficient (their SEs are small);
  - is narrower, the closer the value of x is to its average $\bar{x}$.
- The prediction interval
  - tells us about where the actual value of y_j is in the general pattern represented by the data if we know the value of x_j and we have estimates of coefficients $\hat{\alpha}$ and $\hat{\beta}$;
  - adds uncertainty to the CI of the predicted value: the actual y values are expected to be spread around the regression line.

9.A2 ## CASE STUDY – Estimating Gender and Age Differences in Earnings

Visualizing confidence and prediction intervals

Let's now turn to the pattern of association between earnings and age in our sample of 281 market analysts. Learning this age pattern may help early-career market analysts predict how they can expect their earnings to change throughout their career. How much we can learn about this question from uncovering the age–average earnings pattern in the data depends on the usual issues plus an additional one here. The usual steps of generalization are statistical inference and external validity (the data is from the USA in 2014; students are interested in the future, possibly in another country). The additional issue is what we can learn from cross-sectional differences in age about what to expect about changes in earnings as individuals advance in age.

For illustration purposes, let us start by showing the confidence interval and the prediction interval for the simple linear model. Figure 9.2a shows the confidence interval. It's fairly narrow overall, but wider farther away from the sample mean. Figure 9.2b depicts the prediction interval, it is rather wide showing how hard indeed it is to make predictions for single observations.

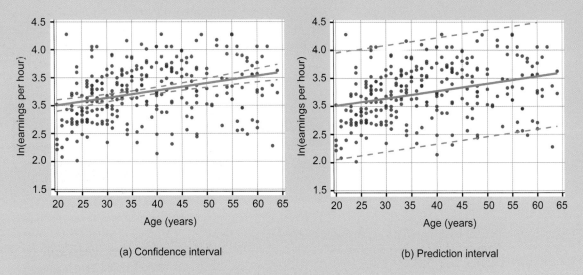

(a) Confidence interval   (b) Prediction interval

Figure 9.2 Log hourly wage and age: regression line, confidence interval, prediction interval.

Note: Market analysts. 95% confidence and prediction intervals.
Source: `cps-earnings` dataset. USA 2014. Employees in "market research and marketing specialist" occupations, N=281.

Using the same data on 281 market analysts, let's now turn to uncovering the actual shape of the $(\ln w)^E = f(age)$ pattern. To begin with, we estimated a lowess regression; the result is visualized in Figure 9.3a, together with the scatterplot. According to the pattern uncovered by lowess, earnings are substantially higher for older ages among young adults. Average log earnings is about 0.4 log unit (or 50%) higher for 25-year-old market analysts than for 20-year-old market analysts. The age differences are positive but get smaller and smaller as we compare older people: around 0.2 log units between age 25 and 30, 0.1 between age 30 and 35. There is little if any difference by age between 40 and 60, and those older than 60 earn less on average. The pattern is, thus, increasing in young age, flat in middle age, and slightly decreasing in old age, and concave throughout. It is an asymmetric upside-down U curve that is steeper in its positive part and a lot flatter in its negative part.

Figure 9.3b shows the same lowess curve as in Figure 9.3a together with two parametric regressions approximating it: a piecewise linear spline with knots at ages 30 and 40 and a quadratic model. To better see differences, we applied a different scale on the y axis.

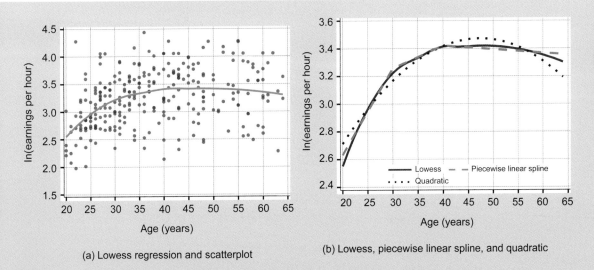

(a) Lowess regression and scatterplot

(b) Lowess, piecewise linear spline, and quadratic

Figure 9.3   Log hourly wage and age: regressions that capture nonlinearity

Source: `cps-earnings` dataset. USA 2014. Employees in "market research analyst and marketing specialist" occupations, N=281.

Both the piecewise linear spline and the quadratic capture the increasing-then-decreasing concave pattern shown by the lowess, but they do that differently. The piecewise linear spline does not capture the smooth transition from steep to flat, and it shows a little higher average earnings than the lowess around age 30. But it does a good job of capturing the average slopes between the knots (not surprisingly as this is what splines are for). Moreover, it captures the very flat part above age 40. The quadratic captures the smooth change in slopes, and it is close to the lowess curve below age 35. But it is a little too steep between 35 and 45, and it is way too steep in the declining range above age 50. This is the result of the rigid upside-down U functional form of the quadratic: it has to be symmetric and thus as steep in the negative part as in the positive part, whereas the lowess suggests an asymmetric curve.

But how seriously should we take these differences across the regressions? That depends on whether we expect these regression lines or curves to be different in the population represented by the data. The best way to answer that question is comparing the CI of the predicted values, also known as the CI of the regression line.

Figure 9.4 shows the same three regressions as the previous one, but it adds the 95% confidence bounds to the piecewise linear regression and the quadratic regression. These confidence bounds show up with the same color and line pattern on the graph as the corresponding regression, only with a thin line.

The graph is a bit hard to read: it has three regression lines plus two CI bounds for two of the regressions. But its two main messages are not that hard to see. First, and most importantly, the lowess regression line is within the CI bounds of both the piecewise linear spline and the quadratic regression. Second, the quadratic is within the CI bounds of the piecewise linear spline, and, vice versa, the piecewise linear spline is within the CI bounds of the quadratic. (Well, almost: the kink of the piecewise linear spline at age 30 is just above the upper CI bound of the quadratic, but that one blip we ignore as the rest of the regression is very much inside.) Moreover, the confidence bounds around the quadratic and the piecewise linear spline overlap over the entire age range in the data.

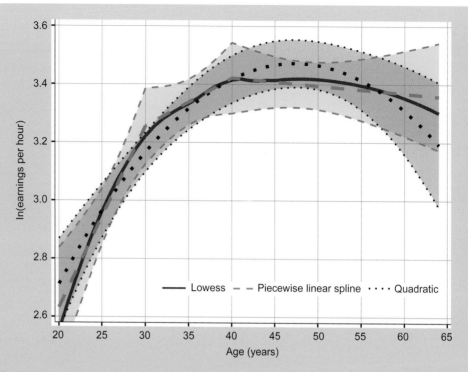

Figure 9.4   Average log earnings and age: regressions with CI

Note: Lowess regression; piecewise linear spline in age and its 95% CI; quadratic in age and its 95% CI. The CI are shown as dashed curves of the same color as their respective regressions.
Source: `cps-earnings` dataset. USA, 2014. Employees in "market research analyst and marketing specialist" occupations, N=281.

What should we conclude from these figures? The most important conclusion is that both the piecewise linear spline and the quadratic are pretty good at capturing the general pattern in the population represented by our data. If we wanted to represent the pattern in a parametric regression, both are equally good choices. They are, as is sometimes said, "statistically indistinguishable" from each other.

That conclusion may be due to the fact that we have relatively few observations: 281 people. The confidence bounds are wide. Many other kinds of patterns may fit into them. But all such patterns should be steep in younger ages and flat above age 40. These are the most important characteristics of the pattern anyway. With this much data, we simply cannot pin down the pattern more precisely.

Returning to the original question: what can students expect about how their earnings may change through their career if they choose to be market analysts? High external validity requires that the general patterns that determine age differences in earnings in 2014 remain stable for the coming decades. But even that is not sufficient to conclude that these cross-sectional age differences show how earnings are expected to change as individuals age; for that we need to assume that those cross-sectional differences show the effects of aging only, as opposed to mixing in how the content of education or initial labor market conditions differed for different birth cohorts of people. These are big ifs, and thus external validity is unlikely to be very high. For that reason it makes more sense to take away the qualitative findings as opposed to the numerical estimates themselves. Even if external validity is not super high, we can expect earnings of market analysts to rise fast until age 30 and then more slowly until age 40 or 45. But above age 45 they aren't expected to increase as much, or at all, in this profession.

Analyzing additional data won't resolve all the issues with external validity, but it may help a little. We could, for example, look for panel data in which we can examine how earnings change as people age, instead of looking at the cross-section. It turns out that most analyses of such data reveal similar patterns between age and average earnings: concave shape with steep upward part and a mostly flat part afterwards. Of course, no data from the past can tell us if the future is going to be similar or very different. But, with those caveats, the results of this simple analysis are informative.

9.4 Testing Hypotheses about Regression Coefficients

Recall from Chapter 6 that testing hypotheses means making a statement about a general pattern and deciding whether we can reject it using information in the data. Such statements are called hypotheses, and in statistical testing hypotheses are about values of statistics. We specify a **null hypothesis** H_0 ("the null") and an **alternative hypothesis** H_A ("the alternative").

The logic remains the same when testing hypotheses about regression coefficients. An important question in regression analysis is whether y and x are mean-dependent. In the context of the linear regression $y^E = \alpha + \beta x$, this question is whether the true value of β is zero, which means its value in the population, or general pattern represented by the data. The null and alternative hypotheses are

$$H_0: \beta_{true} = 0 \qquad (9.8)$$

$$H_A: \beta_{true} \neq 0 \qquad (9.9)$$

The test is carried out with the help of the **t-statistic**. As we discussed in Chapter 6, Section 6.3, the t-statistic is best viewed as a measure of distance: how far the value of the statistic in the data ($\hat{\beta}$) is from its value hypothesized by the null (zero). The distance is measured in terms of the standard error (SE). A value 0 of the t-statistic means that the value of $\hat{\beta}$ is exactly what's in the null hypothesis (zero distance). A t-statistic of 1 means that the value of $\hat{\beta}$ is exactly one SE larger than the value in the null hypothesis. A t-statistic of -1 means that the value of $\hat{\beta}$ is exactly one SE smaller than the value in the null hypothesis. And so on.

With the null $H_0: \beta_{true} = 0$ and the alternative $H_A: \beta_{true} \neq 0$, the t-statistic is

$$t = \frac{\hat{\beta}}{SE(\hat{\beta})} \qquad (9.10)$$

Another often investigated null states that the slope is of a particular value c, $H_0: \beta_{true} = c$ and the alternative $H_A: \beta_{true} \neq c$. Simply rewriting these hypotheses to $H_0: \beta_{true} - c = 0$ and the alternative $H_A: \beta_{true} - c \neq 0$, we can derive the t-statistic to be

$$t = \frac{\hat{\beta} - c}{SE(\hat{\beta})} \qquad (9.11)$$

The t-statistic for the intercept coefficient is analogous.

To make a decision we apply the usual **critical value** to the t-statistic: ±2. We reject the null if the t-statistic is larger than 2 or smaller than −2, and we don't reject the null if it's in-between.

Alternatively, we can make a decision with the help of the appropriate **p-value**. This saves us from calculating t-statistics and thinking about critical values. As we have discussed in Chapter 6, Section 6.5, the p-value is the smallest significance level at which we can reject the null. Thus, for example, a p-value of 0.001 means that we are safe to reject the null if we can tolerate a 0.001 (0.1%) or larger chance of a false positive. We have to simply look at the p-value and decide if it is larger or smaller than the level of significance that we set for ourselves in advance. Following common practice, we set a 5% level of significance, and then we reject the null if the p-value is less than 0.05.

Most often, the hypothesis we test is $H_0: \beta_{true} = 0$. This amounts to the hypothesis that average y does not differ according to the value of x, which also means that y and x are uncorrelated. If this null is rejected at the 5% level of significance, x is said to be **statistically significant** at 5% in the regression. Statistical software shows the result of this among the default set of regression results. Sometimes we put a star next to the coefficients (or their SE) that are significant at 5%, and an additional star if significant at 1%.

As we explained in Chapter 6, Section 6.6, the general practice is to set a 5% critical value to avoid making biased decisions. But there may be very legitimate reasons to deviate from this rule, in either way, to require a more lenient criterion (higher level of significance) or a more conservative criterion (lower level of significance).

We may want to set a more lenient criterion if the purpose of our analysis is exploration or a **proof of concept**. Examples include when we use cross-country data to explore how various policies may affect CO_2 emission, or when we use time series data from our company to see if changes in marketing mix may affect sales. In many such instances, the size of the data is small, and there may be a great amount of noise in measurement. Thus, we are unlikely to get precise estimates, and we may not reject the null of no association at the 5% level (and the 95% CI of the slope coefficient would contain zero). But then we would risk missing something potentially important. If, instead, we adopt a more lenient criterion of a 10% or 15% level of significance, we are more likely to find a positive result and thus avoid a false negative. Of course we should acknowledge that our level of significance is higher than is conventional, with all of its potential consequences.

In contrast, we may want to have a more conservative criterion if we are looking for a **proof beyond reasonable doubt**. For example, if a firm is sued for violating gender equality rules, the judge would need convincing evidence that wages are indeed different from one another. In this scenario, we typically aim for a conservative critical value of 1%. If multiple testing is taking place, we should take an ever lower critical value. Once again, being explicit about the details of statistical inference and our assumptions is critical.

Review Box 9.3 Steps of testing hypotheses about regression coefficients

- Select the statistic to test. Most often it is β, the slope coefficient.
- State the null and alternative hypotheses. They are about the "true" value: the value of the coefficient in the population, or general pattern, represented by the data. Often: $H_0: \beta_{true} = 0$, $H_A: \beta_{true} \neq 0$.
- Calculate or read the appropriate t-statistic. With $H_0: \beta_{true} = 0$ it is $\frac{\hat{\beta}}{SE(\hat{\beta})}$.
- Choose a critical value (or values). Reject the null if the absolute value of the t-statistic is outside the range defined by the critical value(s); don't reject otherwise. Often, we choose ±2 for critical

values, corresponding to a 5% level of significance. But this choice may depend on the purpose of the work.
- Instead of the last two steps, we may look at the appropriate p-value. Reject the null if the p-value is smaller than the level of significance (say, 5%); don't reject if it is larger.
- Think external validity. (Compare the general pattern you are interested in to the general pattern your data represents.)

9.5 Testing More Complex Hypotheses

Some hypotheses are more complex than H_0: $\beta_{true} = 0$, H_A: $\beta_{true} \neq 0$. We consider three cases.

The first case is testing against a **one-sided alternative**. We do that when we are interested in whether the slope is negative or positive. The corresponding hypotheses here would be H_0: $\beta_{true} \geq 0$, H_A: $\beta_{true} < 0$. As discussed in Chapter 6, Section 6.7, the question that we are truly interested in should be in the alternative (e.g., whether women earn less on average), and the equality sign should be in the null. In practice, testing these hypotheses is similar to testing H_0: $\beta_{true} = 0$, H_A: $\beta_{true} \neq 0$, with two modifications. First, don't reject the null if the coefficient falls in the region that is specified in the null hypothesis (here $\hat{\beta} > 0$). Second, divide the p-value of the H_0: $\beta_{true} = 0$, H_A: $\beta_{true} \neq 0$ test by two and apply it for the decision if the coefficient falls in the direction of the alternative (here $\hat{\beta} \leq 0$).

The second case is hypotheses that involve more than one coefficient. An important example is whether two slope coefficients are the same. That question can be asked about slope coefficients in the same regression. For example, we may want to know if there is a difference in slopes between two parts of a piecewise linear spline. Alternatively, the question may be asked about slope coefficients in different regressions estimated on different data. Whether the slopes of, say, earnings on age are the same in different occupations may be asked after estimating the slopes in two regressions on two samples.

The intuition and principles of testing hypotheses that involve more than one regression coefficient are the same as the principles of testing hypotheses about a single regression coefficient. We have to set null and alternative hypotheses in such a way that the null has the form of "something equals zero." For example, when interested in whether $\beta_{1true} = \beta_{2true}$, the corresponding null should be

$$H_0: \beta_{1true} - \beta_{2true} = 0 \tag{9.12}$$

$$H_A: \beta_{1true} - \beta_{2true} \neq 0 \tag{9.13}$$

Then we have to estimate the SE of the estimated version of the statistic in the null: $\hat{\beta}_1 - \hat{\beta}_2$. With the SE in hand, we can calculate the appropriate t-statistic, say $\frac{\hat{\beta}_1 - \hat{\beta}_2}{SE[\hat{\beta}_1 - \hat{\beta}_2]}$. With the appropriate SE estimates, all follows as usual: reject the null if the t-statistic is outside the range specified by appropriate critical values, say ± 2. Of course, if we have the appropriate p-value, the decision is even easier. Estimating the appropriate SE may be tricky, but sophisticated statistical software can do that for us and can also report appropriate p-values.

In the third case the null is more than one statement; these are called **joint hypotheses**. One example of joint hypotheses is that all slope coefficients are zero in a piecewise linear spline regression.

With two such slopes, these hypotheses have the form

$$H_0: \beta_{1true} = 0 \ \& \ \beta_{2true} = 0 \tag{9.14}$$

$$H_A: \beta_{1true} \neq 0 \ or \ \beta_{2true} \neq 0 \tag{9.15}$$

Testing joint hypotheses has the same overall principle as before: estimate the test statistic, and compare the test statistic against the critical value that corresponds to a pre-specified level of significance. In practice, though, all this is more complicated for testing joint hypotheses. Luckily, we do not carry out the test this way. Instead, we make use of the p-value that statistical software produces. We estimate the regression with the appropriate standard errors, specify the null hypothesis to test, and ask the software to return the appropriate p-value.

9.A3 | **CASE STUDY – Estimating Gender and Age Differences in Earnings**

Testing hypotheses about regression coefficients

We return to our question of whether women earn the same, on average, as men among market analysts, using our data on 281 market analysts from the USA in 2014 (the `cps-earnings` dataset). We regressed log hourly earnings on a binary variable that is one if the person is female and zero if male: $(\ln w)^E = \alpha + \beta \times female$. Recall that the coefficient estimate was -0.11, implying that women earn 11 percent less, on average, than men in this sample. The SE of the coefficient was 0.06, and the 95% CI was $[-0.23, +0.01]$ implying that we can be 95% confident that the difference in average earnings between women and men was between -23% and $+1\%$ among all market analysts in the USA in 2014. Notably, this interval contains zero. Thus, we cannot rule out with 95% confidence that average earnings are the same among women and men in this occupation (in the USA in 2014).

To formally test whether average earnings are the same by gender, we simply test if the coefficient on the binary variable is zero, against the alternative that it is not zero: $H_0: \beta_{true} = 0$ against $H_A: \beta_{true} \neq 0$. The regression output from software will typically show coefficient estimates together with their standard errors, as well as t-statistic and p-values for testing whether each coefficient is zero (against the alternative that it isn't zero). In our case, the corresponding t-statistic is -1.8. The critical values for a 5% significance level are ± 2, and -1.8 falls within the critical values not outside of them. Thus, we cannot reject the null of equal average earnings at a 5% level of significance. The same conclusion is implied by the p-value that the software presents: it is 0.07, which is greater than 0.05 that would correspond to a 5% level of significance.

After testing whether gender differences in earnings are zero in the population represented by our data, let's turn to a more complex hypothesis: whether the age–earnings pattern is the same between ages 20 and 30 versus 30 and 40. To answer this question, we consider the regression with piecewise linear spline in age. If the slopes of the first two splines are the same, the pattern is the same; if they are different, the pattern is different. This can be formulated as a hypothesis that involves two regression coefficients.

The results of the piecewise linear estimates give a slope coefficient of 0.06 for the first line segment (age 20 to 30) and 0.02 for the second line segment (age 30 to 40). These are different in the data. Do we have enough evidence to tell if they are different in the population as well?

One way to approach this question is by looking at the confidence intervals. The 95% CI around the first coefficient is [0.035,0.089]; the 95% CI around the second coefficient is [−0.003, +0.036]. The point estimates of the coefficients (0.06 and 0.02) are each outside of the CI of the other coefficient. At the same time, the two CIs overlap, if only barely. What should we conclude? Apparently, the CIs can't tell us that here.

We should carry out a formal test to decide. We asked the software to test whether the two coefficients are the same, after having estimated a regression with robust standard errors. The software returned a p-value of 0.03. That implies that we are safe to reject the null at a 5% level of significance. Thus we decide that the patterns are different in the population represented by the data. By doing so, we allow ourselves to be wrong with less than a 5% chance.

Unlike formal tests, confidence intervals are not always informative when testing hypotheses that compare regression coefficients. Checking whether each point estimate is within the other coefficient's confidence interval is too harsh: even if they fall outside, we may not want to reject the null that they are the same in the general pattern. Checking whether the confidence intervals overlap is too lenient: even if they overlap, we may want to reject the null that they are the same in the general pattern. We need to carry out formal tests in such cases.

Nevertheless, there are more straightforward situations when looking at the confidence intervals is enough. If the confidence intervals do not overlap, we can always conclude that the two coefficients are different. Conversely, if the point estimates are both within the CI of the other coefficients, we can always conclude that we cannot reject the null of equal coefficients. It is the occasions similar to our case study that are difficult: when the point estimates are outside each other's CI but the CIs overlap. In any case, carrying out formal tests is always a good solution.

9.6 Presenting Regression Results

The standard way to present the results of linear regression is in a table format, with coefficients and corresponding standard errors listed in one column. Usually, the standard errors are below the coefficient estimates, in parentheses or brackets. Typically, two lines at the bottom of the table show the number of observations and the R-squared of the regression. Column headings show the name of the dependent variable, or some information that differentiates the regressions in the same table.

In addition, stars are sometimes put as superscripts to the coefficients to indicate whether the coefficients are significant: that is, whether we can reject the hypothesis that each one is zero. Usually, one star is attached to coefficients that are significant at 5% (we can reject that they are zero at the 5% level), and two stars are attached to coefficients that are significant at 1%.

Some data analysts have strong views about whether and how such stars should be included in **regression tables**. Many argue that stars are misleading: they focus attention on whether a particular coefficient is zero or not in the population, even though that is not always the most important question. (In R, one package that creates regression tables with stars is called stargazer.) We do not take a firm stand on this issue. Most software that produces standard regression tables includes stars by default; analysts should keep them or erase them according to their preference.

It is good practice to include notes at the bottom of regression tables that clarify things. If the table contains stars for levels of significance, then the notes should explain what they mean. The notes should also clarify what is shown in the parentheses: e.g., are they **robust standard error** estimates, or simple standard error estimates? Sometimes values of t-statistics are shown instead of standard errors (i.e., values of t-statistics that test whether the coefficient is zero). Yet other times the CI are shown instead of, or in addition to, the SE or the t-statistic. The information content of the two is the same since we can get one from the other. We prefer showing standard errors because they are easy to use to construct t-statistics for testing H_0: $\hat{\beta} = 0$ or H_0: $\hat{\beta} = c$ for any c value. It is also straightforward to use them to construct confidence intervals for any level of confidence (95%, 90%, 99%).

9.A4 CASE STUDY – Estimating Gender and Age Differences in Earnings

Presenting regression results

The standard regression table of the regression $(\ln w)^E = a + \beta \times female$ from our data on 281 market analysts is presented in Table 9.1

Table 9.1	Wage and gender gap baseline regression
Variables	**ln wage**
Female	−0.11
	(0.062)
Constant	3.31**
	(0.049)
Observations	281
R-squared	0.012

Note: Robust standard error estimates in parentheses.
** p<0.01, * p<0.05.

Source: `cps-earnings` dataset. USA, 2014. Employees in "market research analyst and marketing specialist" occupations.

The leftmost column has the variable names, also indicated by its header. The column with numbers shows the results of the regression analysis. The header of the column contains the name of the dependent variable. Then we have the slope estimate of the variable of the regression ("female"), followed by its standard error in parentheses. The next pair of numbers is the intercept estimate and its standard error (variable name "**Constant**"). The bottom of the table shows the number of observations in the regression and the R-squared. Stars denote levels of significance at 5% and 1% levels. This table summarizes the results we discussed earlier: a −11% difference in average earnings in the data, with SE of 0.6 implying a confidence interval [−0.23, +0.01] and a test that we cannot reject the null of $\beta = 0$ at 5% or 1% because the p-value is greater than 0.05 (it's 0.07, not shown in the table).

Note that we set the table to show coefficient estimates up to two digits; standard error esti-mates are up to three digits. We show two digits for the coefficient estimates as more digits would convey a false impression of precision. Showing one more digit would tell us that the slope coeffi-cient is −0.114 in the data. But that is not really informative. The confidence interval [−0.23, +0.01] swamps such differences. Even if the confidence interval was super narrow, it wouldn't make any meaningful difference to know that the average earnings difference is 11.4% not 11%. We show one more digit for the SE estimates because that third digit can be helpful when constructing confidence intervals of various confidence (95%, 90%, 99%).

This standard table format allows showing results of more than one regression at the same time. Table 9.2 shows results from three regressions using the same data, each specifying a different functional form to the $(\ln w)^E = f(age)$ regression. The first column is a linear specification, the second a quadratic, the third a piecewise linear spline with two knots, at ages 30 and 40. With smaller coefficients, we now use three digits.

Table 9.2 Wage and age – different specifications

Variables	(1) ln wage	(2) ln wage	(3) ln wage
age	0.014** (0.003)	0.096** (0.018)	
age squared		−0.001** (0.000)	
age spline <30			0.062** (0.014)
age spline 30–40			0.017 (0.010)
age spline 40<			−0.003 (0.006)
Constant	2.732** (0.101)	1.193** (0.341)	1.383** (0.369)
Observations	281	281	281
R-squared	0.098	0.168	0.173

Note: Robust standard error estimates in parentheses. ** $p<0.01$, * $p<0.05$.
Source: `cps-earnings` dataset. USA, 2014. Employees in "market research analyst and marketing specialist" occupations.

The first column shows that a line fit on the scatterplot would have a slope of 0.014: market analysts that are one year older earn 1.4% more, on average, in this sample. We know that the pattern is nonlinear: increasing in a concave way up to middle age and flat, or even decreasing, above that. This average slope combines the steep slope at young age with the flat slope in middle and older ages. The average difference of 1.4% is what it is: the average difference. It may be informative for some purpose; it is not very informative for students if they want to uncover the age pattern of earnings to learn about what to expect during their career. That's why we estimated two alternatives that capture the nonlinear pattern.

The second column shows the results of the quadratic specification. The coefficient of the linear term ("age") has no interpretation in itself; the coefficient of the quadratic term ("age square") is negative, indicating a concave pattern. This term is statistically significant, meaning that the concave pattern is very likely true in the population.

The third column shows the estimates of the piecewise linear spline with two knots, resulting in three line segments. The slope estimate of the first one ("age spline <30") is 0.06: among market analysts of age 20 to 30, those that are one year older earn 6% higher, on average. Its standard error implies a 95% confidence interval $[0.03, 0.09]$. It is significant at 1%: age and earnings are very likely correlated in the population (all market analysts in the USA in 2014 younger than 30). The slope estimate of the second line segment is 0.017, but its 95% CI includes zero $[-0.003, 0.037]$. The estimated slope of the third line segment ("age spline >40") is -0.003, practically zero. The slopes of the second and third line segments are not statistically different from zero: they may very well be zero in the population.

9.7   Data Analysis to Help Assess External Validity

As external validity is about generalizing beyond what our data represents, we can't assess it using our data. But analyzing other data may help. The most important question usually is β, the slope coefficient on x. As emphasized in Chapter 5, Section 5.8, the three common dimensions of generalization are time, space, and other groups.

If we want to generalize for our country but we have data from other countries only, we can estimate β from several countries and see if they differ substantially, or whether their differences have some systematic pattern. For example, we may want to know how much domestic prices change if the exchange rate changes substantially. We may not have enough data for the particular country we are interested in, but we may have estimates using data from several countries with various degrees of openness. Then, if the country we are interested in is among the more open ones, the coefficient estimates for such countries are more likely to be valid for this country.

Similarly, if we are worried about the fact that β may change in the future, we can try to estimate it for many years and see if it's stable or, if not, if its changes show a particular pattern. The same goes for groups: gender differences in earnings may be different for different occupations, and while we may not have enough data for market analysts, estimating the difference for some other occupations may shed light on how stable that difference is or, if not, whether there is a pattern in its variation.

9.B1   CASE STUDY – How Stable is the Hotel Price–Distance to Center Relationship?

External validity, other cities and time periods, beyond hotels

Let's go back to our example of hotel prices and distance to the city center. The goal of the analysis in the previous chapters was to find a good deal from among the hotels for the date contained in the data. External validity was not an issue there.

Here we ask a different question: whether we can infer something about the price–distance pattern for situations outside the data: different time, different city, or different kinds of hotels. Such a speculation may be relevant if we want to expand development services we offer for relatively low priced hotels. Or maybe we simply want to find a good deal in the future without estimating a new regression but taking the results of this regression and computing residuals accordingly.

Recall that our data is collected from a price comparison website. So far we have used the data we collected for Vienna for a particular autumn weekday. In the `hotels-europe` dataset, we have similar data for other dates and other European cities, too. We collected data for various dates. In the present analysis, we restricted our data to hotels with 3 to 4 stars for the analysis.

Let's start with generalizing to the future. Although all the price data were collected at a single point in time, we can use data on prices shown for a variety of future dates to assess how stable the price–distance pattern may be. The pattern we examine is linear regression of log price with a piecewise linear spline in distance with knot at 2 miles.

Table 9.3 shows results for four dates: November 2017 weekday (the date we used in our baseline example in Chapters 7 and 8); a November 2017 weekend; December 2017 holidays; June 2018 weekend. The coefficient estimates for the spline regressions show the slope separately for 0–2 miles and 2–7 miles.

Table 9.3 External validity – comparing dates

Variables	(1) 2017-NOV-weekday	(2) 2017-NOV-weekend	(3) 2017-DEC-holiday	(4) 2018-JUNE-weekend
Distance spline <2	-0.31**	-0.44**	-0.36**	-0.31**
	(0.038)	(0.052)	(0.041)	(0.037)
Distance spline 2–7	0.02	-0.00	0.07	0.04
	(0.033)	(0.036)	(0.050)	(0.039)
Constant	5.02**	5.51**	5.13**	5.16**
	(0.042)	(0.067)	(0.048)	(0.050)
Observations	207	125	189	181
R-squared	0.314	0.430	0.382	0.306

Note: Dependent variable is log price, distance is entered as spline with a knot at 2 miles. Robust standard error estimates in parentheses. ** $p<0.01$, * $p<0.05$.

Source: `hotels-europe` dataset. Vienna, reservation price for November and December 2017, June 2018.

Among hotels in the data that are within 2 miles from the city center, prices are 0.31 log units or 36% ($\exp(0.31)-1$) cheaper, on average, for hotels that are 1 mile farther away from the city center both for the November weekday and the June weekend. The coefficient estimate is similar for December (-0.36) and June (-0.31). The coefficient is -0.44 for the November weekend, which suggests a stronger negative association with distance. The corresponding 95% confidence intervals overlap somewhat: they are $[-0.39, -0.23]$ and $[-0.54, -0.34]$, so they don't help in deciding whether price–distance patterns are different during the weekday and weekend in November. However, a test of equal coefficients produces a p value of 0.035, which tells us that we can reject that they are equal at a 5% level.

The second part of the piecewise linear spline has an estimated slope that is close to zero with CI including zero, for all dates. Thus, among hotels that are 2 miles or farther away from the city center, average prices are essentially the same regardless of how far away the hotels are. This holds for all dates.

The regression constants show the intercept estimates, which don't have a good interpretation because this is a log–level regression. But we can compare them across regressions, which tells us differences in expected hotel price in the very center of the city. The results suggest that prices are almost 50 log points (60%) higher during the November weekend than on the November weekday, and they are 15% higher during the June weekend.

So it seems that guests are more willing to pay extra to be close to the city center during the November weekend, and perhaps also during the December holidays. Why do we see these differences? We can only speculate. Perhaps the weekend makes distance from the city center more undesirable for tourists when the weather is cold.

Before we conclude from the comparisons across time, let's pause for an important technical issue. When comparing regression results across time, we should always be careful with the observations we actually compare. Here the question is whether the regressions for the different dates are estimated for the same hotels. Looking at the number of observations, we see that there must be some differences: there are more hotels for the November weekday in the data than for the November weekend. (Even if the number of observations was the same, the hotels themselves may be different.)

This difference could be important: hotels with available rooms at a weekend or during a holiday could be different in a non-random way. Variation in demand for hotel rooms makes available hotels vary by dates. This is an illustration of potential selection bias due to a non-random sampling, a concept we introduced in Chapter 1, Sections 1.7 and 1.8.

To compare apples to apples, we re-estimated the same three regressions with hotels that are observed at all four times. Table 9.4 shows the results.

Table 9.4 External validity – comparing dates 2

Variables	(1) 2017-NOV- weekday	(2) 2017-NOV- weekend	(3) 2017-DEC- holiday	(4) 2018-JUNE- weekend
Distance spline <2	−0.28**	−0.44**	−0.40**	−0.28**
	(0.058)	(0.055)	(0.045)	(0.053)
Distance spline 2–7	−0.03	−0.02	−0.01	−0.03
	(0.049)	(0.041)	(0.031)	(0.039)
Constant	5.02**	5.52**	5.19**	5.12**
	(0.068)	(0.069)	(0.067)	(0.078)
Observations	98	98	98	98
R-squared	0.291	0.434	0.609	0.332

Note: Hotels available for all four dates only. Dependent variable is log price, distance is entered as spline with a knot at 2 miles. Robust standard error estimates in parentheses. ** $p<0.01$, * $p<0.05$.

Source: `hotels-europe` dataset. Vienna, reservation price for November and December 2017, June 2018.

First note the number of observations: we now have the same 98 hotels for all four dates, and so selection is not an issue anymore. The results turn out be rather similar: weekend patterns in November and December look a bit different now with a stronger price slope (−0.44 and −0.40 versus −0.28 log units).

What can we conclude from these results about the external validity of our findings? While we can't tell how the price–distance pattern would look like in the future in Vienna, we saw some instability in the pattern from weekdays to weekends. If we want to generalize the pattern into some future situation, we now know that we need to pay attention to dates. More generally, the instability in the pattern we uncovered highlights the fact that the pattern may very well change in other future situations. As important as differences in the price–distance pattern were differences in the intercept. Those differences reflect the fact that prices at weekends and during the holiday season tend to be higher overall. This is important if we want to use coefficients from one day to predict prices on another day: such predictions may be off by a large amount.

External validity across space is another potential question we may be interested in. To show some examples, we estimated the same regression for the same date (November 2017 weekday) in two more cities, Amsterdam and Barcelona. Table 9.5 shows the results.

Table 9.5 External validity – comparing cities

Variables	(1) Vienna	(2) Amsterdam	(3) Barcelona
Distance spline <2	−0.31**	−0.27**	−0.06
	(0.038)	(0.040)	(0.034)
Distance spline 2–7	0.02	0.03	-0.05
	(0.033)	(0.037)	(0.058)
Constant	5.02**	5.24**	4.67**
	(0.042)	(0.041)	(0.041)
Observations	207	195	249
R-squared	0.314	0.236	0.023

Note: Dependent variable is log price, distance is entered as spline with a knot at 2 miles. Robust standard error estimates in parentheses. ** $p < 0.01$, * $p < 0.05$.

Source: `hotels-europe` dataset. November 2017, weekday.

The slope coefficients are quite similar from Vienna to Amsterdam. Among hotels within 2 miles from the city centers, those that are 1 mile further away from the center are, on average, 35 percent (around 30 log points) less expensive. However, Barcelona is very different: there seems to be no difference in prices by distance from the city center. Confidence intervals do not overlap. Prices in Barcelona decline little as we consider hotels further away from the center (around the famous Las Ramblas). This could come from different city structure, or a variety of other reasons.

In terms of space, external validity seems weak. Patterns found in Vienna may work out fine in some, but not all, other cities. Hence the external validity of Vienna results is much weaker regarding space than it is regarding time.

Finally, we can compare hotels with another type of accommodation, apartments, that were also advertised on the price comparison website we used to collect our data. The data are from the same city (Vienna) for the same date (November weekday). Similarly to hotels, we restricted apartments to those with 3 to 4 stars. Table 9.6 shows the results.

Table 9.6 External validity – accommodation types

Variables	(1) Hotels	(2) Apartments
Distance spline <2	-0.31**	-0.26**
	(0.035)	(0.069)
Distance spline 2–7	0.02	0.12
	(0.032)	(0.061)
Constant	5.02**	5.15**
	(0.044)	(0.091)
Observations	207	92
R-squared	0.314	0.134

Note: Dependent variable is log price, distance is entered as spline with a knot at 2 miles. Robust standard error estimates in parentheses. ** p<0.01, * p<0.05.

Source: hotels-europe dataset. Vienna, November 2017, weekday.

Again, the patterns are quite similar across the two groups, which here differ by accommodation type. Among hotels and apartments within 2 miles of the city center, those that are 1 mile further away tend to be around 30 percent (26 vs. 31 log points) less expensive. The 95% confidence intervals overlap to a great extent. Among apartments that are more than 2 miles away from the center, those that are 1 mile further away are not less expensive; in this data they are actually slightly more expensive, although the 95% confidence intervals contain zero.

Let us summarize how we now think about external validity. We started by showing a pattern for a particular lodging type, time, and city. We then continued and looked for evidence of the same pattern for other dates, locations, and types. We found some additional variation to what is suggested by statistical inference. In particular, external validity across dates and types seems fairly solid, but across space seems moderate: the patterns in our data may not transfer to other cities.

9.8 Main Takeaways

The confidence interval (CI) is the most useful tool for statistical inference of regression coefficients.

- The standard error of a slope coefficient estimate is smaller (its CI is narrower) the more observations we have, the larger the spread (standard deviation) of x, and the larger the R-squared (smaller residual standard deviation).
- We should use heteroskedasticity-robust standard errors unless we have a good reason to do otherwise.

PRACTICE QUESTIONS

1. The SE of $\hat{\beta}$ in the simple regression is larger, the smaller the standard deviation of x. Why?
2. The SE of $\hat{\beta}$ in the simple regression is larger, the smaller the R-squared of the regression. Why?
3. The 95% CI for $\hat{\beta}$ in the simple regression is narrower, the more observations we have in the data. Why?
4. Which one is narrower – the 95% CI for $\hat{\beta}$ or the 90% CI for $\hat{\beta}$? Why?
5. The 95% CI for $\hat{y}$ in the simple regression is narrower, the closer x is to its average. Why?
6. What additional uncertainty do we have when we want to predict y_j instead of $\hat{y}_j$ in the simple linear regression?
7. What's a false positive for $H_0: \beta = 0$ in the regression $y^E = \alpha + \beta x$? Give an example.
8. What's a false negative for $H_0: \beta = 0$ in the regression $y^E = \alpha + \beta x$? Give an example.
9. Which is a more conservative rule for rejecting $H_0: \beta = 0$: a 5% level of significance or a 1% level of significance? Why?
10. When exploring potential associations in the data, we often allow a more lenient criterion for rejecting $H_0: \beta = 0$ than when we want to prove beyond reasonable doubt that an association exists. Give an example and argue why the difference in the rules makes sense.
11. We estimate a regression of log hourly wage on a binary "female" variable on a random sample of employees in computer science occupations in the USA in 2014. The slope coefficient estimate is -0.15; its 95% CI is $[-0.18, -0.12]$. Interpret these results.
12. In the previous regression, the software reports a p-value of 0.000 next to the slope coefficient. What does this mean?
13. Interpret the coefficient estimate on the first piecewise linear spline and the confidence interval you create around it in Table 9.5 in our **How stable is the hotel price–distance to center relationship?** case study.
14. In Table 9.5 in our **How stable is the hotel price–distance to center relationship?** case study, the coefficient estimates on the first piecewise linear spline are different for Vienna and Amsterdam in the data. Can you reject the hypothesis that they are the same in the general pattern represented by the data?
15. In Table 9.5 in our **How stable is the hotel price–distance to center relationship?** case study, the coefficient estimates on the first piecewise linear spline are different for Vienna and Barcelona in the data. Can you reject the hypothesis that they are the same in the general pattern represented by the data?

DATA EXERCISES

Easier and/or shorter exercises are denoted by [*]; harder and/or longer exercises are denoted by [**].

1. Replicate the case study of patterns of earnings by gender and age using data on employees in the same occupation (market research analysts and marketing specialists) for another year. Use another CPS Morg file (`www.nber.org/data/morg.html`) to pick another year in the USA. Carry out the analysis and compare your results to what we found for the USA in 2014. [*]
2. Replicate the case study of patterns of earnings by gender and age using data on employees in the same occupation in another country. For a different country find and use survey data on

earnings, hours, and occupations that represent the population of interest. If possible, pick an occupation close to market research analysts and marketing specialists. Carry out the analysis and compare your results to what we found for the USA in 2014. [**]

3. Replicate the case study of patterns of earnings by gender and age using data on employees in another occupation. Use the same 2014 USA CPS Morg file, carry out the same sample selection steps, and create the same variables, but select another occupation group. Go on the USA Census website to see which codes refer to which occupations. Carry out the analysis and compare your results to what we found for market research analysts. [*]

4. Use the `hotels-europe` dataset and pick a European city (not Vienna). Select a sample that is appropriate for a couple searching for a good deal among 3-to-4-star hotels not very far from the center. Show a lowess regression for the pattern between log hotel price and ratings. Estimate a simple linear regression and alternative regressions that better fit the nonlinear pattern. Visualize the confidence interval around the regression lines together with the lowess regression, and decide which specification is the best approximation. [*]

5. Use the `wms-management-survey` dataset and pick a country. Estimate a linear regression with the management quality score and employment. Interpret the slope coefficient, create its 95% CI, and interpret that, too. Explore potential nonlinearities in the patterns of association by lowess. Estimate a regression that can capture those nonlinearities, and carry out a test to see if you can reject that the linear approximation was good enough for the population of firms represented by the data. [**]

REFERENCE AND FURTHER READING

For a recent review on the extent and potential causes of gender differences in earnings, see Bertrand (2018).

9.U1 UNDER THE HOOD: THE SIMPLE SE FORMULA FOR REGRESSION INTERCEPT

The simple formula for the SE for the intercept of a simple linear regression $y^E = \alpha + \beta x$ is

$$SE(\hat{a}) = Std[e]\sqrt{\frac{1}{n} + \frac{(\bar{x})^2}{nVar[x]}} \tag{9.16}$$

This is similar to the standard error of the slope coefficient with two differences: the additional $\frac{1}{n}$ term and the $(\bar{x})^2$ in the numerator (note that $\sqrt{Var[x]} = Std[x]$). The first of these two new elements makes the relation of the standard error to the number of observations stronger. The larger n, the smaller $SE(\hat{a})$ because of both n in the denominator and this new $\frac{1}{n}$ term. The second element makes the standard error depend on the mean value of x. One way to understand its role is to acknowledge that the intercept is estimated for y^E when $x = 0$. The larger $(\bar{x})^2$, the further away it is from zero, in any direction. The further away zero is from typical x values in the data, the larger is the uncertainty as to where the intercept could be in the population, or general pattern, represented by the data.

As always, the simple formula is not the right formula in general. In cross-sectional regressions we should use the robust formula instead. We don't show that formula here; standard statistical software packages have it and compute it easily.

9.U2   UNDER THE HOOD: THE LAW OF LARGE NUMBERS FOR $\hat{\beta}$

Recall from Under the Hood section 5.U1 that the Law of Large Numbers tells us that the sample average of a variable is very close to its mean in the population (or general pattern) the data represents if the sample is large; the larger the sample, the closer they are.

$$\bar{x} = \frac{1}{n}\sum_{i=1}^{n} x_i \rightarrow E[x] \text{ in probability} \tag{9.17}$$

where $E[x]$ means the expected value of x (its mean value in the population), and $\rightarrow$ in probability ("convergence in probability") means that the left-hand side of the formula approaches the right-hand side, with probability 1 if n goes to infinity. Another notation of the same thing is that the "probability limit," abbreviation *plim*, of the sample average is the expected value:

$$plim(\bar{x}) = E[x] \tag{9.18}$$

Considering the simple linear regression $y^E = \alpha + \beta x$, the corresponding Law of Large Numbers for $\hat{\beta}$ tells us that $\hat{\beta}$ is very close to β in the population (or general pattern) the data represents if the sample is large; the larger the sample, the closer they are.

$$plim(\hat{\beta}) = \beta \tag{9.19}$$

The OLS formula for $\hat{\beta}$ is

$$\hat{\beta} = \frac{\frac{1}{n}\sum_{i=1}^{n}(x_i - \bar{x})(y_i - \bar{y})}{\frac{1}{n}\sum_{i=1}^{n}(x_i - \bar{x})^2} \tag{9.20}$$

The important insight is that this is the ratio of two averages. The Law of Large Numbers applies to both the numerator and the denominator:

$$plim\left(\frac{1}{n}\sum_{i=1}^{n}(x_i - \bar{x})(y_i - \bar{y})\right) = Cov[x, y] \tag{9.21}$$

where $Cov[x, y]$ is the covariance in the population. (Note the specific meaning of Cov here: in the text it could refer to the covariance in the data; here it is reserved to refer to the covariance in the population.)

Similarly,

$$plim\left(\frac{1}{n}\sum_{i=1}^{n}(x_i - \bar{x})^2\right) = Var[x] \tag{9.22}$$

where $Var[x]$ is the variance in the population (again, note that $Var[x]$ here means the variance in the population).

There is one more result to use: if both the numerator and the denominator converge in probability to some number, their ratio converges in probability to the ratio of those two numbers. This is called the Slutsky theorem (named after the Russian statistician–mathematician–economist Evgeny Slutksy). Thus,

$$plim\hat{\beta} = \frac{Cov[y, x]}{Var[x]} = \beta, \tag{9.23}$$

9.U3   UNDER THE HOOD: DERIVING $SE(\hat{\beta})$ WITH THE CENTRAL LIMIT THEOREM

Recall from Chapter 5, Under the Hood section 5.U1 that the Central Limit Theorem (CLT) states that, in large enough samples, the average is distributed normally around its expected value, and the variance of this normal distribution is related to the variance of the original variable that makes up the average.

Formally, the CLT states that

$$\bar{x} \overset{A}{\sim} N\left(E[x], \frac{1}{n}Var[x]\right) \tag{9.24}$$

Recall that the normal distribution result holds regardless of the distribution of those original variables. The variance of this normal distribution, which is the square of its standard deviation across repeated samples, is equal to the variance of x itself divided by n. Thus we can estimate it from the data. That's why we can have a formula for the SE of $\bar{x}$: all of its elements can be estimated from the data we have.

$$SE(\bar{x}) = \sqrt{\frac{Var[x]}{n}} = \frac{Std[x]}{\sqrt{n}} \tag{9.25}$$

The CLT for regression coefficients follows the same logic. The estimated slope coefficient follows a normal distribution around its value in the population; this distribution is across many repeated samples if those samples are large. Thus the standard error of the regression coefficient is the standard deviation of this distribution, which is the square root of the variance.

It turns out that the general formula for the distribution is

$$\hat{\beta} \overset{A}{\sim} N\left(\beta, \frac{E[e^2(x - E[x])^2]}{n(Var[x])^2}\right) \tag{9.26}$$

where e denotes the regression residual. This is actually the robust formula for the standard error that we need to use in regressions using cross-sectional data. It is complicated and thus we don't interpret it. But we can recognize the three elements in it that we emphasized: the spread of the residuals is embedded in the formula in the numerator, and the number of observations and the variance of x is in the denominator.

The general formula simplifies to the simple formula we show in the text if $E[e^2(x - E[x])^2] = E[e^2]E[(x - E[x])^2]$, which is nothing else than $Var[e]Var[x]$, where $Var[e]$ is the variance of the regression residuals:

$$\hat{\beta} \overset{A}{\sim} N\left(\beta, \frac{Var[e]}{nVar[x]}\right) \tag{9.27}$$

That additional assumption is one of homoskedasticity. The formula $E[e^2(x - E[x])^2]$ is the expected value of the product of e^2 and $(x - E[x])^2$. e^2 is the square of the residual, measuring how far it is from the regression line. If the spread of the residuals around the regression line is the same for all values of x (the assumption of homoskedasticity), the squared value of the residual is expected to be the same for all values of x. This is expected to be the same for all values of $(x - E[x])^2$, too. And then the expected value of the product of the two is equal to the product of the two expected values: $E[e^2(x - E[x])^2] = E[e^2]E[(x - E[x])^2]$.

From this we get the simple formula of the standard error by taking the square root of the variance in the normal distribution:

$$SE(\hat{\beta}) = \frac{Std[e]}{\sqrt{n}Std[x]} \tag{9.28}$$

9.U4 UNDER THE HOOD: DEGREES OF FREEDOM ADJUSTMENT FOR THE SE FORMULA

As we introduced in Chapter 5, the simple standard error formula for the estimated $\bar{x}$ is

$$SE(\bar{x}) = \frac{Std[x]}{\sqrt{n}} \qquad (9.29)$$

Here we introduced the simple standard error formula for $\hat{\beta}$ in a simple regression:

$$SE(\hat{\beta}) = \frac{Std[e]}{\sqrt{n}Std[x]} \qquad (9.30)$$

Both have $\sqrt{n}$ in the denominator. However, statistical software packages don't divide by $\sqrt{n}$. For $SE(\bar{x})$ the correct formula uses $\sqrt{n-1}$ instead of $\sqrt{n}$. For $SE(\hat{a})$ and $SE(\hat{\beta})$ the correct formula uses $\sqrt{n-2}$. Why, and how much does this matter?

The number less than n that is used in the denominator is called the **degrees of freedom**, abbreviated as **df**. Thus, the degrees of freedom for $SE(\bar{x})$ is $df = n-1$; the degrees of freedom for both $SE(\hat{a})$ and $SE(\hat{\beta})$ is $df = n-2$.

The idea is that we need some data to use for estimates that are included in the standard error formula, and thus we are left with less data once we have estimated those. Degrees of freedom means the number of "free" observations we are left with after considering the fact that we need to estimate those other things. For example, we need $\bar{x}$ in the formula for $SE(\bar{x})$. If we didn't have to estimate $\bar{x}$ but knew it somehow, we would have more information in n observations to calculate $SE(\bar{x})$. But we don't know it, so we need to use data to estimate it. Degrees of freedom acknowledges this and takes out one for each and every object within the SE formulae that needs to be estimated.

For $SE(\bar{x})$ we need one thing: $\bar{x}$, because we have $Std[x]$ that in turn needs $\bar{x}$: $Std[x]$ has $\sum(x_i - \bar{x})^2$ in its numerator.

For $SE(\hat{\beta})$ we need $Cov[y, x]$ and $Var[x]$, and they need $\bar{x}$ and $\bar{y}$. That's two things to calculate from the data ($Var[x]$ has $\sum(x_i - \bar{x})^2$ in its numerator and $Cov[y, x]$ has $\sum(y_i - \bar{y})(x_i - \bar{x})$ in its numerator).

How much does this matter? Not much for simple regressions. Dividing by $\sqrt{n}$ or $\sqrt{n-1}$ or $\sqrt{n-2}$ is practically the same for the data we use. In very small datasets this may matter, but in very small datasets the standard error formulae are likely to be wrong anyway. At the same time, the degrees of freedom correction may matter in methods that have many objects estimated at the same time; we will start discussing such models in the next chapter.

10 Multiple Linear Regression

Why and how to carry out multiple linear regression analysis, and how to interpret its results

Motivation

There is a substantial difference in the average earnings of women and men in all countries. You want to understand more about the potential origins of that difference, focusing on employees with a graduate degree in your country. You have data on a large sample of employees with a graduate degree, with their earnings and some of their characteristics, such as age and the kind of graduate degree they have. Women and men differ in those characteristics, which may affect their earnings. How should you use this data to uncover gender difference that are not due to differences in those other characteristics? And can you use regression analysis to uncover patterns of associations between earnings and those other characteristics that may help understand the origins of gender differences in earnings?

You have analyzed your data on hotel prices in a particular city to find hotels that are underpriced relative to how close they are to the city center. But you have also uncovered differences in terms of other features of the hotels that measure quality and are related to price. How would you use this data to find hotels that are underpriced relative to all of their features? And how can you visualize the distribution of hotel prices relative to what price you would expect for their features in a way that helps identify underpriced hotels?

After understanding simple linear regression, we can turn to multiple linear regression, which has more than one explanatory variable. Multiple linear regression is the most used method to uncover patterns of associations between variables. There are multiple reasons to include more explanatory variables in a regression. We may be interested in uncovering patterns of association between y and several explanatory variables, which may help uncover patterns of association that could be investigated in subsequent analysis. Or, we may be interested in the effect of an x variable, but we want to compare observations that are different in x but similar in other variables. Finally, we may want to predict y, and we want to use more x variables to arrive at better predictions.

We discuss why and when we should estimate multiple regression, how to interpret its coefficients, and how to construct and interpret confidence intervals and test the coefficients. We discuss the relationship between multiple regression and simple regression. We explain that piecewise linear splines and polynomial regressions are technically multiple linear regressions without the same interpretation of the coefficients. We discuss how to include categorical explanatory variables as well as interactions that help uncover different slopes for groups. We include an informal discussion on how to decide what explanatory variables to include and in what functional form. Finally, we discuss why a typical multiple regression with observational data can get us closer to causal interpretation without fully uncovering it.

The first case study in this chapter, **Understanding the gender difference in earnings**, uses the `cps-earnings` dataset to illustrate the use of multiple regression to understand potential sources of gender differences in earnings. We also go back to our question on finding underpriced hotels relative to their location and quality in the case study **Finding a good deal among hotels with multiple regression**, using the `hotels-vienna` dataset, to illustrate the use of multiple regression in prediction and residual analysis.

Learning outcomes

After working through this chapter, you should be able to

- identify questions that are best answered with the help of multiple regression from available data;
- estimate multiple linear regression coefficients and present and interpret them;
- estimate appropriate standard errors, create confidence intervals and tests of regression coefficients, and interpret those;
- select the variables to include in a multiple regression guided by the purpose of the analysis;
- understand the relationship between the results of a multiple regression and causal effects when using observational data.

10.1 Multiple Regression: Why and When?

There are three broad reasons to carry out multiple regression analysis instead of simple regression. The first is exploratory data analysis: we may want to uncover more patterns of association, typically to generate questions for subsequent analysis. The other two reasons are the two ultimate aims of data analysis: making a better prediction by explaining more of the variation, and getting closer to establishing cause and effect in observational data by comparing observations that are more comparable.

The first example of the introduction is about understanding the reasons for a difference. It's a causal question of sorts: we are interested in what causes women to earn less than men. The second example is one of prediction: we want to capture average price related to hotel features that customers value in order to identify hotels that are inexpensive compared to what their price "should be."

10.2 Multiple Linear Regression with Two Explanatory Variables

Multiple regression analysis uncovers average y as a function of more than one x variable: $y^E = f(x_1, x_2, ...)$. It can lead to better predictions of $\hat{y}$ by considering more explanatory variables. It may improve the interpretation of slope coefficients by comparing observations that are different in terms of one of the x variables but similar in terms of all other x variables.

Multiple linear regression specifies a linear function of the explanatory variables for the average y. Let's start with the simplest version with two explanatory variables:

$$y^E = \beta_0 + \beta_1 x_1 + \beta_2 x_2 \tag{10.1}$$

This is the standard notation for a multiple regression: all coefficients are denoted by the Greek letter β, but they have subscripts. The intercept has subscript 0, the first explanatory variable and its coefficient have subscript 1, and the second explanatory variable and its coefficient have subscript 2.

Having another right-hand-side variable in the regression means that we further condition on that other variable when we compare observations. The slope coefficient on x_1 shows the difference in average y across observations with different values of x_1 but with the same value of x_2. Symmetrically, the slope coefficient on x_2 shows difference in average y across observations with different values of x_2 but with the same value of x_1. This way, multiple regression with two explanatory variables compares observations that are similar in one explanatory variable to see the differences related to the other explanatory variable.

The interpretation of the slope coefficients takes this into account. β_1 shows how much larger y is on average for observations in the data with one unit larger value of x_1 but the same value of x_2. β_2 shows how much larger y is on average for observations in the data with one unit larger value of x_2 but with the same value of x_1.

Review Box 10.1   Multiple linear regression

Multiple linear regression with two explanatory variables:

$$y^E = \beta_0 + \beta_1 x_1 + \beta_2 x_2$$

Interpretation of the coefficients:

- β_0 (intercept): average y for observations if both x_1 and x_2 are zero in the data.
- β_1 (slope of x_1): on average, y is β_1 units larger in the data for observations with one unit larger x_1 but with the same x_2.
- β_2 (slope of x_2): on average, y is β_2 units larger in the data for observations with one unit larger x_2 but with the same x_1.

10.3   Multiple Regression and Simple Regression: Omitted Variable Bias

It is instructive to examine the difference in the slope coefficient of an explanatory variable x_1 when it is the only variable on the right-hand side of a regression compared to when another explanatory variable, x_2, is included as well. In notation, the question is the difference between β in the simple linear regression

$$y^E = \alpha + \beta x_1 \tag{10.2}$$

and β_1 in the multiple linear regression

$$y^E = \beta_0 + \beta_1 x_1 + \beta_2 x_2 \tag{10.3}$$

For example, we may use time series data on sales and prices of the main product of our company, and regress month-to-month change in log quantity sold (y) on month-to-month change in log price (x_1). Then β shows the average percentage change in sales when our price increases by 1%.

For example, $\hat{\beta} = -0.5$ would show that sales tend to decrease by 0.5% when our price increases by 1%.

But we would like to know what happens to sales when we change our price but competitors don't. The second regression has change in the log of the average price charged by our competitors (x_2) next to x_1. Here β_1 would answer our question: average percentage change in our sales in months when we increase our price by 1%, but competitors don't change their price. Suppose that in that regression, we estimate $\hat{\beta}_1 = -3$. That is, our sales tend to drop by 3% when we increase our price by 1% and our competitors don't change their prices. Also suppose that the coefficient on x_2 is positive, $\hat{\beta}_2 = 3$. That means that our sales tend to increase by 3% when our competitors increase their prices by 1% and our price doesn't change.

As we'll see, whether the answer to the two questions is the same will depend on whether x_1 and x_2 are related. To understand that relationship, let us introduce the regression of x_2 on x_1, called the **x–x regression**, where δ is the slope parameter:

$$x_2^E = \gamma + \delta x_1 \tag{10.4}$$

In our own price–competitor price example, δ would tell us how much the two prices tend to move together. In particular, it tells us about the average percentage change in competitor price in months when our own price increases by 1%. Let's suppose that we estimate it to be $\hat{\delta} = 0.83$: competitors tend to increase their price by 0.83% when our company increases its price by 1%. The two prices tend to move together, in the same direction.

To link the two original regressions, plug this x–x regression back in the multiple regression (this step is fine even though that may not be obvious; see Under the Hood section 10.U1):

$$y^E = \beta_0 + \beta_1 x_1 + \beta_2(\gamma + \delta x_1) = \beta_0 + \beta_2\gamma + (\beta_1 + \beta_2\delta)x_1 \tag{10.5}$$

Importantly, we find that with regards to x_1, the slope coefficients in the simple (β) and multiple regression (β_1) are different:

$$\beta - \beta_1 - \delta\beta_2 \tag{10.6}$$

The slope of x_1 in a simple regression is different from its slope in the multiple regression, the difference being the product of its slope in the regression of x_2 on x_1 and the slope of x_2 in the multiple regression. Or, put simply, the slope in simple regression is different from the slope in multiple regression by the slope in the x–x regression times the slope of the other x in the multiple regression.

This difference is called the **omitted variable bias**. If we are interested in the coefficient on x_1 with x_2 in the regression, too, it's the second regression that we need; the first regression is an incorrect regression as it omits x_2. Thus, the results from that first regression are biased, and the bias is caused by omitting x_2. We will discuss omitted variables bias in detail when discussing causal effects in Chapter 21, Section 21.3.

In our example, we had that $\hat{\beta} = -0.5$ and $\hat{\beta}_1 = -3$, so that $\hat{\beta} - \hat{\beta}_1 = -0.5 - (-3) = +2.5$. In this case our simple regression gives a biased estimate of the slope coefficient on x_1 compared to the multiple regression, and the bias is positive (the simple regression estimate is less negative). Recall that we had $\hat{\delta} = 0.83$ and $\hat{\beta}_2 = 3$. Their product is approximately 2.5. This positive bias is the result of two things: a positive association between the two price changes (δ) and a positive association between competitor price and our own sales (β_2).

In general, the slope coefficient on x_1 in the two regressions is different unless x_1 and x_2 are uncorrelated ($\delta = 0$) or the coefficient on x_2 is zero in the multiple regression ($\beta_2 = 0$). The slope in the simple regression is more positive or less negative if the correlation between x_2 and x_1 has the same sign as β_2 (both are positive or both are negative).

The intuition is the following. In the simple regression $y^E = \alpha + \beta x_1$, we compare observations that are different in x_1 without considering whether they are different in x_2. If x_1 and x_2 are uncorrelated this does not matter. In this case observations that are different in x_1 are, on average, the same in x_2, and, symmetrically, observations that are different in x_2 are, on average, the same in x_1. Thus the extra step we take with the multiple regression to compare observations that are different in x_1 but similar in x_2 does not matter here.

If, however, x_1 and x_2 are correlated, comparing observations with or without the same x_2 value makes a difference. If they are positively correlated, observations with higher x_2 tend to have higher x_1. In the simple regression we ignore differences in x_2 and compare observations with different values of x_1. But higher x_1 values mean higher x_2 values, too. Corresponding differences in y may be due to differences in x_1 but also due to differences in x_2.

In our sales–own price–competitors' price example, the drop in sales when our own price increases (and competitors do what they tend to do) is smaller than the drop in sales when our own price increases but competitor prices don't change. That's because when our own price increases, competitors tend to increase their prices, too, which in itself would push up our sales. The two work against each other: the increase in our price makes sales decrease, but the increase in competitors' prices that tends to happen at the same time makes sales increase.

> **Review Box 10.2   Multiple linear regression and simple linear regression**
>
> - The difference of slope β in $y^E = \alpha + \beta x_1$ and the slope β_1 in $y^E = \beta_0 + \beta_1 x_1 + \beta_2 x_2$ is
> $$\beta - \beta_1 = \delta\beta_2$$
> where δ is the slope in the regression of x_2 on x_1: $x_2^E = \gamma + \delta x_1$
> - In words, briefly: slope in the simple regression differs from the slope in the multiple regression by the product of the slope in x–x regression and slope of other x in multiple regression.

10.A1   CASE STUDY – Understanding the Gender Difference in Earnings

Multiple linear regression

We continue investigating patterns in earnings, gender, and age. The data is the same cps-earnings dataset that we used earlier in Chapter 9, Section 9.A1: it is a representative sample of all people of age 15 to 85 in the USA in 2014.

Compared to Chapter 9, Section 9.A1, where we focused on a single occupation, we broaden the scope of our investigation here to all employees with a graduate degree – that is, a degree higher than a four-year college degree: these include professional, master's, and doctoral degrees.

We use data on people of age 24 to 65 (to reflect the typical working age of people with these kinds of graduate degrees). We excluded the self-employed (their earnings is difficult to measure) and included those who reported 20 hours or more as their usual weekly time worked. We have 18 241 observations.

The dependent variable is log hourly earnings (ln wage). Table 10.1 shows the results from three regressions: (1) is a simple regression of *ln wage* on a binary *female* variable; (2) is a multiple regression that includes age as well, in a linear fashion; and (3) is a simple regression with *age* as the dependent variable and the *female* binary variable.

Table 10.1	Gender differences in earnings – log earnings and gender		
	(1)	**(2)**	**(3)**
Variables	ln wage	ln wage	age
female	−0.195**	−0.185**	−1.484**
	(0.008)	(0.008)	(0.159)
age		0.007**	
		(0.000)	
Constant	3.514**	3.198**	44.630**
	(0.006)	(0.018)	(0.116)
Observations	18 241	18 241	18 241
R-squared	0.028	0.046	0.005

Note: Robust standard error estimates in parentheses. ** $p < 0.01$, * $p < 0.05$.

Source: cps-earnings dataset. 2014, USA. Employees of age 24–65 with a graduate degree and 20 or more work hours per week.

According to column (1), women in this sample earn 19.5 log points (around 21%) less than men, on average. Column (2) suggests that when we compare employees of the same age, women in this sample earn 18.5 log points (around 20%) less than men, on average. This is a slightly smaller gender difference than in column (1). While the log approximation is not perfect at these magnitudes, from now on, we will ignore the difference between log units and percent. For example, we will interpret a 0.195 coefficient as a 19.5% difference.

The estimated coefficients differ, and we know where the difference should come from: average difference in age. Let's use the formula for the difference between the coefficient on *female* in the simple regression and in the multiple regression. Their difference is $-0.195 - (-0.185) = -0.01$. This should be equal to the product of the coefficient of *female* in the regression of *age* on *female* (our column (3)) and the coefficient on *age* in column (2): $-1.48 \times 0.007 \approx -0.01$. These two are indeed equal.

Intuitively, we can see that women of the same age have a slightly smaller earnings disadvantage in this data because they are somewhat younger, on average, and employees who are younger tend to earn less. Part of the earnings disadvantage of women is thus due to the fact that they are younger. This is a small part, though: around one percentage point of the 19.5% difference, which is a 5% share of the entire difference.

But why are women employees younger, on average, in the data? It's because there are fewer female employees with graduate degrees over age 45 than below. Figure 10.1 shows two density plots overlaid: the age distributions of male and female employees with graduate degrees. There are relatively few below age 30. From age 30 and up, the age distribution is close to uniform for men. But not for women: the proportion of female employees with graduate degrees drops above age 45, and again above age 55.

In principle, this could be due to two things: either there are fewer women with graduate degrees in the 45+ generation than among the younger ones, or fewer of them are employed (i.e., employed for 20 hours or more for pay, which is the criterion to be in our subsample). Further investigation reveals that it is the former: women are less likely to have a graduate degree if they were born before 1970 (those 45+ in 2014) in the USA. The proportion of women working for pay for more than 20 hours is very similar among those below age 45 and above.

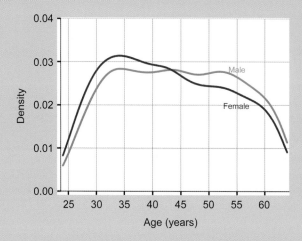

Figure 10.1   Age distribution of employees with graduate degree by gender

Note: Kernel density estimates of the age distribution of employees with a graduate degree; female and male employees separately.

Source: `cps-earnings` dataset. 2014, USA. Employees of age 24–65 with a graduate degree and 20 or more work hours per week. N=18 241.

10.4   Multiple Linear Regression Terminology

Multiple regression with two explanatory variables (x_1 and x_2) allows for assessing the differences in expected y across observations that differ in x_1 but are similar in terms of x_2. This difference is called **conditional** on that other explanatory variable x_2: difference in y by x_1, conditional on x_2. It is also called the controlled difference: difference in y by x_1, controlling for x_2. We often say that we condition on x_2, or control for x_2, when we include it in a multiple regression that focuses on average differences in y by x_1.

When we focus on x_1 in the multiple regression, the other right-hand-side variable, x_2, is called a **covariate**. In some cases, it is also called a **confounder**: if omitting x_2 makes the slope on x_1 different, it is said to confound the association of y and x_1 (we'll discuss confounders in Chapter 19, Section 19.14).

> **Review Box 10.3   Multiple linear regression terminology**
>
> In a regression $y^E = \beta_0 + \beta_1 x_1 + \beta_2 x_2$ that focuses on β_1,
>
> - if we estimate a multiple regression $y^E = \beta_0 + \beta_1 x_1 + \beta_2 x_2$, and we are interested in β_1, x_2 is a covariate, and we say that we condition on x_2 or control for x_2;
> - if, instead, we estimate $y^E = \alpha + \beta x_1$, we say x_2 is an omitted variable.

10.5   Standard Errors and Confidence Intervals in Multiple Linear Regression

The concept of statistical inference and the interpretation of confidence intervals in multiple regressions is similar to that in simple regressions. For example, the 95% confidence interval of the slope coefficient of x_1 in a multiple linear regression shows where we can expect the coefficient in the population, or general pattern, represented by the data.

Similarly to the coefficients in the simple regression, the 95% CI of a slope in a multiple regression is the coefficient value estimated from the data plus-or-minus two standard errors. Again similarly to the simple regression case, we can get the standard error either by bootstrap or using an appropriate formula. And, as usual, the simple SE formula is not a good approximation in general: it assumes homoskedasticity (same fit of the regression over the range of the explanatory variables). There is a robust SE formula for multiple regression, too, that works in general, both under homoskedasticity and heteroskedasticity . Thus, just as with simple regressions we should make the software calculate **robust SE** as default.

While not correct in general, the simple formula is good to examine because it shows what makes the SE larger in a simpler more intuitive way than the robust formula. The simple SE formula for the slope $\hat{\beta}_1$ is

$$SE(\hat{\beta}_1) = \frac{Std[e]}{\sqrt{n} Std(x_1) \sqrt{1 - R_1^2}} \tag{10.7}$$

Similarly to the simple SE formula for the simple linear regression in Chapter 9, Section 9.2, this formula has $\sqrt{n}$ in its denominator. But, similarly again to the simple linear regression, the correct number to divide with would be slightly different: the degrees of freedom instead of the number of the observations (see Under the Hood section 9.U4). Here that would be $\sqrt{n - k - 1}$, where k is the number of right-hand-side variables in the regression. Similarly to the simple regression, this makes little practical difference in most cases. However, in contrast with the simple regression case, it may make a difference not only when we have too few observations, but also when we have many right-hand-side variables relative to the number of observations. We'll ignore that issue for most of this textbook, but it will come back in Chapter 21, Section 21.4.

This formula is very similar to what we have for simple regressions in other details, too, except for that new $\sqrt{1 - R_1^2}$ term in the denominator. R_1^2 is the R-squared of the regression of x_1 on x_2. Recall that the R-squared of a simple regression is the square of the correlation between the two variables in the regression. Thus, R_1^2 is the square of the correlation between x_1 and x_2. The stronger this correlation, the larger R_1^2, the smaller $\sqrt{1 - R_1^2}$, but then the larger $1/\sqrt{1 - R_1^2}$ ($\sqrt{1 - R_1^2}$ is in the denominator). So, the stronger the correlation between x_1 and x_2, the larger the SE of $\hat{\beta}_1$. Note the symmetry: the same would apply to the SE of $\hat{\beta}_2$. As for the familiar terms in the formula: the SE is smaller, the smaller the standard deviation of the residuals (the better the fit of the regression), the larger the sample, and the larger the standard deviation of x_1.

At the polar case of a correlation of one (or negative one) that corresponds to $R_1^2 = 1$, the SE of the two coefficients does not exist. A correlation of one means that x_1 and x_2 are linear functions of each other. It is not only the SE formulae that cannot be computed in this case; the regression coefficients cannot be computed either. In this case the explanatory variables are said to be **perfectly collinear**.

Strong but imperfect correlation between explanatory variables is called **multicollinearity**. It allows for calculating the slope coefficients and their standard errors, but it makes the standard errors large. Intuitively, this is because we would like to compare observations that are different in one of the variables but similar in the other. But strong correlation between the two implies that there are not many observations that are the same in one variable but different in the other variable. Indeed, the problem of multicollinearity is very similar to the problem of having too few observations in general. We can see it in the formula as well: the role of $(1 - R^2)$ and n are the same.

Consider our example of using monthly data to estimate how sales of the main product of our company tend to change when our price changes but the prices of competitors do not. In that example our own price and the competitors' prices tended to move together. One consequence of this is that omitting the change in the competitors' price would lead to omitted variable bias; thus we need to include that in our regression. But here we see that it has another consequence. Including both price variables in the regression makes the SE of the coefficient of our own price larger, and its confidence interval wider, too. Intuitively, that's because there are fewer months when our price changes but the competitors' prices don't change, and it is changes in sales in those months that contain the valuable information for estimating the coefficient on our own price. Months when our own and competitors' prices change the same way don't help. So the reason why we want competitors' price in our regression (strong co-movement) is exactly the reason for having imprecise estimates with wide confidence intervals.

That's true in general, too. Unfortunately, there is not much we can do about multicollinearity in the data we have, just as there is not much we can do about having too few observations. More data helps both, of course, but that is not much help when we have to work with the data that's available. Alternatively, we may decide to change the specification of the regression and drop one of the strongly correlated explanatory variables. However, that results in a different regression. Whether we want a different regression or not needs to be evaluated keeping the substantive question of the analysis in mind.

Review Box 10.4   Inference in multiple regression

- In the linear regression $y^E = \beta_0 + \beta_1 x_1 + \beta_2 x_2$, the 95% confidence interval (CI) of $\hat{\beta}_1$ tells us about the range in which we can expect, with 95% confidence, the difference in y to fall in the general pattern, or population, that our data represents, when comparing observations with the same x_2 but differing in x_1 by one unit.

- In the linear regression $y^E = \beta_0 + \beta_1 x_1 + \beta_2 x_2$, the simple SE formula of $\hat{\beta}_1$ is

$$SE(\hat{\beta}_1) = \frac{Std[e]}{\sqrt{n}\,Std(x_1)\sqrt{1 - R_1^2}}$$

> where e is the residual $e = y - \hat{\beta}_0 + \hat{\beta}_1 x_1 + \hat{\beta}_2 x_2$ and R_1^2 is the R-squared in the simple linear regression of x_1 on x_2.
> - The standard error of $\hat{\beta}_1$ is smaller:
>   - the smaller the standard deviation of the residual (the better the fit of the regression);
>   - the larger the sample;
>   - the larger the variance of x_1;
>   - the smaller the correlation between x_1 and x_2 (the smaller R_1^2).

10.6   Hypothesis Testing in Multiple Linear Regression

Testing hypotheses about coefficients in a multiple regression is also very similar to that in a simple regression. The standard errors are estimated in a different way but with the appropriate SE, all works just the same. For example, testing whether $H_0: \beta_1 = 0$ against $H_A: \beta_1 \neq 0$, we need the p-value or the t-statistic. Standard regression output produced by most statistical software shows those statistics. If our level of significance is 0.05, we reject H_0 if the p-value is less than 0.05, or – which is the same information in a different form – the t-statistic is less than -2 or greater than $+2$.

Besides testing a hypothesis that involves a single coefficient, we sometimes test a hypothesis that involves more coefficients. As we explained in Chapter 9, Section 9.5, these come in two forms: a single null hypothesis about two or more coefficients (e.g., if they are equal), or a list of null hypotheses (e.g., that several slope coefficients are zero). The latter is called testing joint hypotheses .

Testing joint hypotheses are based on a test statistic called the F-statistic, and the related test is called the **F-test**. The underlying logic of hypothesis testing is the same here: reject the null if the test statistic is larger than a critical value, which shows that the estimated coefficients are too far from what's in the null. The technical details are different. But the meaning of the p-value is the same as always. Thus, we advise getting the p-value when testing a joint hypothesis.

In fact, the test that asks whether all slope coefficients are zero in the regression has its own name: the **global F-test**, or simply "the" F-test. Its results are often shown by statistical software by default. More frequently, we use joint testing of joint hypotheses to decide whether a subset of the coefficients (such as the coeffients on all geographical variables) are all zero.

Similarly to testing hypotheses about single coefficients, the F-test needs appropriate standard error estimates. In cross-sectional data, those appropriate estimates are usually the robust SE estimates.

10.A2   CASE STUDY – Understanding the Gender Difference in Earnings

Statistical inference

Let's revisit the results in Table 10.1, taking statistical inference into account. The data represents employees with a graduate degree in the USA in 2014. According to the estimate in column (1), women in this sample earn 19.5 percent less than men, on average. The appropriately estimated (robust) standard error is 0.008, implying a 95% CI of approximately $[-0.21, -0.18]$. We can be

95% confident that women earned 18 to 21 percent less, on average, than men among employees with graduate degrees in the USA in 2014.

Column (2) suggests that when we compare employees of the same age, women in this sample earn approximately 18.5 percent less than men, on average. The 95% CI is approximately $[-0.20, -0.17]$. It turns out that the estimated -0.195 in column (1) is within this CI, and the two CIs overlap. Thus it is very possible that there is no difference between these two coefficients in the population. We uncovered a difference in the data between the unconditional gender wage gap and the gender gap conditional on age. However, that difference is small. Moreover, it may not exist in the population. These two facts tend to go together: small differences are harder to pin down in the population, or general pattern, represented by the data. Often, that's all right. Small differences are rarely very important. When they are, we need more precise estimates, which may come with larger sample size.

10.7   Multiple Linear Regression with Three or More Explanatory Variables

We spent a lot of time on multiple regression with two right-hand-side variables. That's because that regression shows all the important differences between simple regression and multiple regression in intuitive ways. In practice, however, we rarely estimate regressions with exactly two right-hand-side variables. The number of right-hand-side variables in a multiple regression varies from case to case, but it's typically more than two. In this section we describe multiple regressions with three or more right-hand-side variables. Their general form is

$$y^E = \beta_0 + \beta_1 x_1 + \beta_2 x_2 + \beta_3 x_3 + \cdots \tag{10.8}$$

All of the results, language, and interpretations discussed so far carry forward to multiple linear regressions with three or more explanatory variables. Interpreting the slope of x_1: on average, y is β_1 units larger in the data for observations with one unit larger x_1 but with the same value for all other x variables. The interpretation of the other slope coefficients is analogous. The language of multiple regression is the same, including the concepts of **conditioning**, **controlling**, **omitted**, or **confounder variables**.

The standard error of coefficients may be estimated by bootstrap or a formula. As always, the appropriate formula is the robust SE formula. But the simple formula contains the things that make even the robust SE larger or smaller. For any slope coefficient $\hat{\beta}_k$ the simple SE formula is

$$SE(\hat{\beta}_k) = \frac{Std[e]}{\sqrt{n} Std[x_k] \sqrt{1 - R_k^2}} \tag{10.9}$$

Almost all is the same as with two right-hand-side variables. In particular, the SE is smaller, the smaller the standard deviation of the residuals (the better the fit of the regression), the larger the sample, and the larger the standard deviation of x_k. The new-looking thing is R_k^2. But that's simply the generalization of R_1^2 in the previous formula. It is the R-squared of the regression of x_k on all other x variables. The smaller that R-squared, the smaller the SE.

> **Review Box 10.5 Multiple linear regression with three or more explanatory variables**
>
> - Equation: $y^E = \beta_0 + \beta_1 x_1 + \beta_2 x_2 + \beta_3 x_3 + \cdots$
> - Interpretation of β_k (slope of x_k):
>   - On average, y is β_k units larger in the data for observations with one unit larger x_k but with the same value for all other x variables.
>   - $SE(\hat{\beta}_k) = \dfrac{Std[e]}{\sqrt{n}Std[x_k]\sqrt{1-R_k^2}}$ where e is the regression residual and R_k^2 is the R-squared of the regression of x_k on all other x variables.

10.8 Nonlinear Patterns and Multiple Linear Regression

In Chapter 8 we introduced piecewise linear splines, quadratics, and other polynomials to approximate a nonlinear $y^E = f(x)$ regression.

From a substantive point of view, piecewise linear splines and polynomials of a single explanatory variable are not multiple regressions. They do not uncover differences with respect to one right-hand-side variable conditional on one or more other right-hand-side variables. Their slope coefficients cannot be interpreted as the coefficients of multiple regressions: it does not make sense to compare observations that have the same x but a different x^2. But such regressions are multiple linear regressions from a technical point of view. This means that the way their coefficients are calculated is the exact same way the coefficients of multiple linear regressions are calculated. Their standard errors are calculated the same way, too and so are their confidence intervals, test statistics, and p-values.

Testing hypotheses can be especially useful here, as it can help choose the functional form. With a piecewise linear spline, we can test whether the slopes are the same in adjacent line segments. If we can't reject the null that they are the same, we may as well join them instead of having separate line segments. Testing hypotheses helps in choosing a polynomial, too. Here an additional complication is that the coefficients don't have an easy interpretation in themselves. At the same time, testing if all nonlinear coefficients are zero may help decide whether to include them at all.

However, testing hypotheses to decide whether to include a higher-order polynomial has its issues. Recall that a multiple linear regression requires that the right-hand-side variables are not perfectly collinear. In other words, they cannot be linear functions of each other. With a polynomial on the right-hand side, those variables are exact functions of each other: x^2 is the square of x. But they are not a linear function of each other, so, technically, they are not perfectly collinear. That's why we can include both x and x^2 and, if needed, its higher-order terms, in a linear regression. While they are not perfectly collinear, explanatory variables in a polynomial are often highly correlated. That multicollinearity results in high standard errors, wide confidence intervals, and high p-values . As with all kinds of multicollinearity, there isn't anything we can do about that once we have settled on a functional form.

Importantly, when thinking about functional form, we should always keep in mind the substantive focus of our analysis. As we emphasized in Chapter 8, Section 8.1, we should go back to that original focus when deciding whether we want to include a piecewise linear spline or a polynomial to approximate a nonlinear pattern. There we said that we want our regression to have a good approximation to a nonlinear pattern in x if our goal is prediction or analyzing residuals. We may not want that if all we care about is the average association between x and y, except if that nonlinearity messes up the average association. This last point is a bit subtle, but usually means that we may want to transform variables to relative changes or take logs if the distribution of x or y is very skewed.

Here we have multiple x variables. Should we care about whether each is related to average y in a nonlinear fashion? The answer is the same as earlier: yes, if we want to do prediction or analyze residuals; no, if we care about average associations (except we may want to have transformed variables here, too). In addition, when we focus on a single average association (with, say, x_1) and all the other variables (x_2, x_3, ...) are covariates to condition on, the only thing that matters is the coefficient on x_1. Even if nonlinearities matter for x_2 and x_3 themselves, they only matter for us if they make a difference in the estimated coefficient on x_1. Sometimes they do; very often they don't.

10.A3   CASE STUDY – Understanding the Gender Difference in Earnings

Nonlinear patterns and multiple linear regression

This step in our case study illustrates the point we made in the previous section. The regressions in Table 10.2 enter age in linear ways. Using part of the same data, in Chapter 9, Section 9.A2 we found that log earnings and age follow a nonlinear pattern. In particular, there we found that average log earnings are a positive and steep function of age for younger people, but the pattern becomes gradually flatter for the middle-aged and may become completely flat, or even negative, among older employees.

Should we worry about the nonlinear age–earnings pattern when our question is the average earnings difference between men and women? We investigated the gender gap conditional on age. Table 10.2 shows the results for multiple ways of doing it. Column (1) shows the regression with the unconditional difference that we showed in Table 10.1, for reference. Column (2) enters age in linear form. Column (3) enters it as quadratic. Column (4) enters it as a fourth-order polynomial.

The unconditional difference is -19.5%; the conditional difference is -18.5% according to column (2), and -18.3% according to columns (3) and (4). The various estimates of the conditional difference are very close to each other, and all of them are within each others' confidence intervals. Thus, apparently, the functional form for age does not really matter if we are interested in the average gender gap.

At the same time, all coefficient estimates of the high order polynomials are statistically significant, meaning that the nonlinear pattern is very likely true in the population and not just a chance event in the particular dataset. The R-squared of the more complicated regressions are larger. These indicate that the complicated polynomial specifications are better at capturing the patterns. That would certainly matter if our goal was to predict earnings. But it does not matter for uncovering the average gender difference in earnings.

	(1)	(2)	(3)	(4)
Table 10.2 Gender differences in earnings – log earnings and age, various functional forms				
Variables	ln wage	ln wage	ln wage	ln wage
female	−0.195**	−0.185**	−0.183**	−0.183**
	(0.008)	(0.008)	(0.008)	(0.008)
age		0.007**	0.063**	0.572**
		(0.000)	(0.003)	(0.116)
age^2			−0.001**	−0.017**
			(0.000)	(0.004)
age^3				0.000**
				(0.000)
age^4				−0.000**
				(0.000)
Constant	3.514**	3.198**	2.027**	−3.606**
	(0.006)	(0.018)	(0.073)	(1.178)
Observations	18 241	18 241	18 241	18 241
R-squared	0.028	0.046	0.060	0.062

Note: Robust standard error estimates in parentheses. ** $p<0.01$, * $p<0.05$.

Source: cps-earnings dataset. 2014 USA. Employees of age 24–65 with a graduate degree and 20 or more work hours per week.

10.9 Qualitative Right-Hand-Side Variables

A great advantage of multiple linear regression is that it can deal with binary and other qualitative explanatory variables (also called categories, factor variables), together with quantitative variables, on the right-hand side.

To include such variables in the regression, we need to have them as binary, zero–one variables – also called **dummy variables** in the regression context. That's straightforward for variables that are binary to begin with: assign values zero and one (as we did with *female* in the case study). We need to transform other kinds of qualitative variables into binary ones, too, each denoting whether the observation belongs to that category (one) or not (zero). Then we need to include all those binary variables in the regression. Well, all except one.

We should select one binary variable denoting one category as a **reference category**, or **reference group** – also known as the "left-out category." Then we have to include the binary variables for all other categories but not the reference category. That way the slope coefficient of a binary variable created from a qualitative variable shows the difference between observations in the category captured by the binary variable and the reference category. If we condition on other explanatory variables, too, the interpretation changes in the usual way: we compare observations that are similar in those other explanatory variables.

As an example, suppose that *x* is a categorical variable measuring the level of education with three values *x* = *low*, *medium*, *high*. We need to create binary variables and include two of the three in the regression. Let the binary variable x_{med} denote if $x = medium$, and let the binary x_{high} variable denote if $x = high$. Include x_{med} and x_{high} in the regression. The third potential variable for $x = low$ is not included. It is the reference category.

$$y^E = \beta_0 + \beta_1 x_{med} + \beta_2 x_{high} \tag{10.10}$$

Let us start with the constant, β_0; this shows average y in the reference category. Here, β_0 is average y when both $x_{med} = 0$ and $x_{high} = 0$: this is when $x = low$. β_1 is the difference in average y between observations that are different in x_{med} but the same in x_{high}. Thus β_1 shows the difference of average y between observations with $x = medium$ and $x = low$, the reference category. Similarly, β_2 shows the difference of average y between observations with $x = high$ and $x = low$, the reference category.

Which category to choose for the reference? In principle that should not matter: choose a category and all others are compared to that, but we can easily compute other comparisons from those. For example, the difference in y^E between observations with $x = high$ and $x = medium$ in the example above is simply $\beta_2 - \beta_1$ (both coefficients compare to $x = low$, and that drops out of their difference). But the choice may matter for practical purposes. Two guiding principles may help this choice, one substantive, one statistical. The substantive guide is simple: we should choose the category to which we want to compare the rest. Examples include the home country, the capital city, the lowest or highest value group. The statistical guide is to choose a category with a large number of observations. That is relevant when we want to infer differences from the data for the population, or general pattern, it represents. If the reference category has very few observations, the coefficients that compare to it will have large standard errors, wide confidence intervals, and large p-values.

Review Box 10.6   Qualitative right-hand-side variables in multiple linear regression

- We should include qualitative right-hand-side variables with more categories as a series of binary ("dummy") variables.
- For a qualitative right-hand-side variable with k categories, we should enter $k-1$ binary variables; the category not represented by those binary variables is the reference category.
- Coefficients on each of the $k - 1$ binary variables show average differences in y compared to the reference category.

10.A4   CASE STUDY – Understanding the Gender Difference in Earnings

Qualitative variables

Let's use our case study to illustrate qualitative variables as we examine earnings differences by categories of educational degree. Recall that our data contains employees with graduate degrees. The dataset differentiates three such degrees: master's (including graduate teaching degrees, MAs, MScs, MBAs), professional (including MDs), and PhDs.

Table 10.3 shows the results from three regressions. As a starting point, column (1) repeats the results of the simple regression with *female* on the right-hand side; column (2) includes two education categories *ed_Profess* and *ed_PhD*; and column (3) includes another set of education categories, *ed_Profess* and *ed_MA*. The reference category is MA degree in column (2) and PhD in column (3).

Table 10.3   Gender differences in earnings – log earnings, gender and education

Variables	(1) ln wage	(2) ln wage	(3) ln wage
female	−0.195**	−0.182**	−0.182**
	(0.008)	(0.009)	(0.009)
ed_Profess		0.134**	−0.002
		(0.015)	(0.018)
ed_PhD		0.136**	
		(0.013)	
ed_MA			−0.136**
			(0.013)
Constant	3.514**	3.473**	3.609**
	(0.006)	(0.007)	(0.013)
Observations	18 241	18 241	18 241
R-squared	0.028	0.038	0.038

Note: MA, Professional, and PhD are three categories of graduate degree. Column (2): MA is the reference category. Column (3): the reference category is Professional or PhD. Robust standard error estimates in parentheses. ** $p<0.01$, * $p<0.05$.

Source: `cps-earnings` dataset. USA, 2014. Employees of age 24–65 with a graduate degree and 20 or more work hours per week.

The coefficients in column (2) of Table 10.3 show that comparing employees of the same gender, those with a professional degree earn, on average, 13.4% more than employees with an MA degree, and those with a PhD degree earn, on average, 13.6% more than employees with an MA degree. The coefficients in column (3) show that, among employees of the same gender, those with an MA degree earn, on average, 13.6% less than those with a PhD degree, and those with a professional degree earn about the same on average as those with a PhD degree. These differences are consistent with each other.

This is a large dataset so confidence intervals are rather narrow whichever group we choose as a reference category. Note that the coefficient on *female* is smaller, −0.182, when education is included in the regression. This suggests that part of the gender difference is due to the fact that women are somewhat more likely to be in the lower-earner MA group than in the higher-earner professional or PhD groups. But only a small part. We shall return to this finding later when we try to understand the causes of gender differences in earnings.

10.10 Interactions: Uncovering Different Slopes across Groups

Including binary variables for various categories of a qualitative variable uncovers average differences in y. But sometimes we want to know something more: whether and how much the slope with respect to a third variable differs by those categories. Multiple linear regression can uncover that too, with appropriate definition of the variables.

More generally, we can use the method of linear regression analysis to uncover how association between y and x varies by values of a third variable z. Such variation is called an **interaction**, as it shows how x and z interact in shaping average y. In medicine, when estimating the effect of x on y, if that effect varies by a third variable z, that z is called a **moderator variable**. Examples include whether malnutrition, immune deficiency, or smoking can decrease the effect of a drug to treat an illness. Non-medical examples of interactions include whether and how the effect of monetary policy differs by the openness of a country, or whether and how the way customer ratings are related to hotel prices differs by hotel stars.

Multiple regression offers the possibility to uncover such differences in patterns. For the simplest case, consider a regression with two explanatory variables: x_1 is quantitative; x_2 is binary. We wonder if the relationship between average y and x_1 is different for observations with $x_2 = 1$ than for $x_2 = 0$. How shall we uncover that difference?

A multiple regression that includes x_1 and x_2 estimates two parallel lines for the y–x_1 pattern: one for those with $x_2 = 0$ and one for those with $x_2 = 1$.

$$y^E = \beta_0 + \beta_1 x_1 + \beta_2 x_2 \tag{10.11}$$

The slope of x_1 is β_1 and is the same in this regression for observations in the $x_2 = 0$ group and observations in the $x_2 = 1$ group. β_2 shows the average difference in y between observations that are different in x_2 but have the same x_1. Since the slope of x_1 is the same for the two x_2 groups, this β_2 difference is the same across the range of x_1. This regression does not allow for the slope in x_1 to be different for the two groups. Thus, this regression cannot uncover whether the y–x_1 pattern differs in the two groups.

Denote the expected y conditional on x_1 in the $x_2 = 0$ group as y_0^E, and denote the expected y conditional on x_1 in the $x_2 = 1$ group as y_1^E. Then, the regression above implies that the intercept is different (higher by β_2 in the $x_2 = 1$ group) but the slopes are the same:
First group, $x_2 = 0$

$$y_0^E = \beta_0 + \beta_1 x_1 \tag{10.12}$$

Second group, $x_2 = 1$

$$y_1^E = \beta_0 + \beta_2 \times 1 + \beta_1 x_1 \tag{10.13}$$

If we want to allow for different slopes in the two x_2 groups, we have to do something different. That difference is including the interaction term. An **interaction term** is a new variable that is created from two other variables, by multiplying one by the other. In our case:

$$y^E = \beta_0 + \beta_1 x_1 + \beta_2 x_2 + \beta_3 x_1 x_2 \tag{10.14}$$

Not only are the intercepts different; the slopes are different, too:

$$y_0^E = \beta_0 + \beta_1 x_1 \qquad (10.15)$$

$$y_1^E = \beta_0 + \beta_2 + (\beta_1 + \beta_3)x_1 \qquad (10.16)$$

It turns out that the coefficients of this regression can be related to the coefficients of two simple regressions of y on x_1, estimated separately in the two x_2 groups:

$$y_0^E = \gamma_0 + \gamma_1 x_1 \qquad (10.17)$$

$$y_1^E = \gamma_2 + \gamma_3 x_1 \qquad (10.18)$$

What we have is $\gamma_0 = \beta_0$; $\gamma_1 = \beta_1$; $\gamma_2 = \beta_0 + \beta_2$; and $\gamma_3 = \beta_1 + \beta_3$.

   In other words, the separate regressions in the two groups and the regression that pools observations but includes an interaction term yield exactly the same coefficient estimates. The coefficients of the separate regressions are easier to interpret. But the pooled regression with interaction allows for a direct test of whether the slopes are the same. $H_0 : \beta_3 = 0$ is the null hypothesis for that test; thus the simple t-test answers this question.

   We can mix these tools to build ever more complicated multiple regressions. Binary variables can be interacted with other binary variables . Binary variables created from qualitative explanatory variables with multiple categories can all be interacted with other variables. Piecewise linear splines or polynomials may be interacted with binary variables. More than two variables may be interacted as well. Furthermore, quantitative variables can also be interacted with each other, although the interpretation of such interactions is more complicated.

Review Box 10.7   Interactions of right-hand-side variables in multiple linear regression

- Interactions between right-hand-side variables in a linear regression allow for the slope coefficient of a variable to differ by values of another variable.
- Interactions between two right-hand-side variables are modeled in a linear regression as $y^E = \beta_0 + \beta_1 x_1 + \beta_2 x_2 + \beta_3 x_1 x_2$.
- β_1 shows average differences in y corresponding to a one-unit difference in x_1 when $x_2 = 0$.
- β_2 shows average differences in y corresponding to a one-unit difference in x_2 when $x_1 = 0$.
- β_3 is the coefficient on the interaction term. It shows the additional average differences in y corresponding to a one-unit difference in x_1 when x_2 is one unit larger, too. (It's symmetrical in x_1 and x_2 so it also shows the additional average differences in y corresponding to a one-unit difference in x_2 when x_1 is one unit larger, too.)
- When one of the two right-hand-side variables is binary, a simpler interpretation is also true. Say, $x_2 = 0$ or 1. Then,
  - ○ β_1 shows the average difference in y corresponding to a one-unit difference in x_1 when $x_2 = 0$;
  - ○ $\beta_1 + \beta_3$ shows the average difference in y corresponding to a one-unit difference in x_1 when $x_2 = 1$;
  - ○ the coefficients of the regression are the same as the coefficients of two separate regressions on two parts of the data, one with $x_2 = 0$ and one with $x_2 = 1$:
    if $x_2 = 0$: $y^E = \beta_0 + \beta_1 x_1$
    if $x_2 = 1$: $y^E = (\beta_0 + \beta_2) + (\beta_1 + \beta_3)x_1$

10.A5   CASE STUDY – Understanding the Gender Difference in Earnings

Interactions

We turn to illustrating the use of interactions as we consider the question of whether the patterns with age are similar or different for men versus women. As we discussed, we can investigate this in two ways that should lead to the same result: estimating regressions separately for men and women and estimating a regression that includes age interacted with gender. This regression model with an interaction is

$$(\ln w)^E = \beta_0 + \beta_1 \times age + \beta_2 \times female + \beta_3 \times age * female \qquad (10.19)$$

Table 10.4 shows the results with age entered in a linear fashion. Column (1) shows the results for women, column (2) for men, column (3) for women and men pooled, with interactions. To have a better sense of the differences, which are often small, the table shows coefficients up to three digits.

Table 10.4	Gender differences in earnings – log earnings, gender, age, and their interaction		
Variables	**(1)** Women	**(2)** Men	**(3)** All
female			−0.036
			(0.035)
age	0.006**	0.009**	0.009**
	(0.001)	(0.001)	(0.001)
female × age			−0.003**
			(0.001)
Constant	3.081**	3.117**	3.117**
	(0.023)	(0.026)	(0.026)
Observations	9 685	8 556	18 241
R-squared	0.011	0.028	0.047

Note: Column (1) is women only; column (2) is men only; column (3) includes all employees. Robust standard error estimates in parentheses. ** $p<0.01$, * $p<0.05$.

Source: `cps-earnings` dataset. USA, 2014. Employees of age 24–65 with a graduate degree and 20 or more work hours per week.

According to column (1) of Table 10.4, women who are one year older earn 0.6% more, on average. According to column (2), men who are one year older earn 0.9% more, on average. Column (3) repeats the age coefficient for men. Then it shows that the slope of the log earnings–age pattern is, on average, 0.003 less positive for women, meaning that the earnings advantage of women who are one year older is 0.3 percentage points smaller than the earnings advantage of men who are one year older.

The advantage of the pooled regression, is its ability to allow for direct inference about gender differences. The 95% CI of the gender difference in the average pattern of ln wages and age is [−0.005, −0.001]. Among employees with a post-graduate degree in the USA in 2014, the wage difference corresponding to a one year difference in age was 0.1 to 0.5 percentage points less for women than for men. This confidence interval does not include zero. Accordingly, the t-test of whether the difference is zero rejects its null at the 5% level, suggesting that we can safely consider the difference as real in the population (as opposed to a chance event in the particular dataset); we are less than 5% likely to make a mistake by doing so.

The coefficient on the *female* variable in the pooled regression is −0.036. This is equal to the difference of the two regression constants: 3.081 for women and 3.117 for men. Those regression constants do not have a clear interpretation here (average log earnings when age is zero are practically meaningless). Their difference, which is actually the coefficient on *female* in the pooled regression, shows the average gender difference between employees with zero age. Similarly to the constants in the separate regressions, the coefficient is meaningless for any substantive purpose. Nevertheless, the regression needs it to have an intercept with the ln *w* axis.

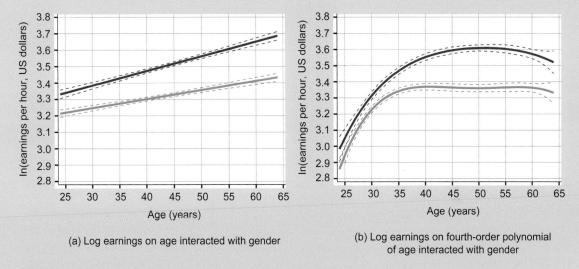

(a) Log earnings on age interacted with gender

(b) Log earnings on fourth-order polynomial of age interacted with gender

Figure 10.2 Earning differences by gender as function of age

Note: Regression lines (curves) and 95% confidence intervals from regression of log earnings on age interacted with gender. **Source:** `cps-earnings` dataset. USA, 2014. Employees of age 24–65 with a graduate degree and 20 or more work hours per week. N=18 241.

Taking the coefficients on *female*, *age*, and *female × age* together, the regression allows us to calculate the average gender difference by age. This exercise takes the linear functional form seriously, an assumption we know is false. We shall repeat this exercise with a better approximation of the nonlinear patterns. For now, let's stick to the linear specification, for educational purposes. The youngest people in our sample are 25 years old. Starting with the separate regressions, the predicted log wage for women of age 25 is $3.081 + 25 \times 0.006 \approx 3.231$. For men, $3.117 + 25 \times 0.009 \approx 3.342$. The difference is −0.11. We get the same number from the pooled regression: the gender difference at age 25 should be the gender difference at age zero implied by the coefficient on *female* plus 25 times the difference in the slope by age, the coefficient on the interaction term *female* × *age*: $-0.036 + 25 \times -0.003 \approx -0.11$. Carrying out the same calculations for age 45 yields a difference of -0.17. These results imply that the gender difference in average earnings is wider for older ages.

Figure 10.2a shows the relationship graphically. It includes two lines with a growing gap: earnings difference is higher for older age. Remember, our regression can capture this growing gap because it includes the interaction. Without the interaction, we would not be able to see this, as that specification would force two parallel lines at constant distance.

However, we know that the pattern on age and (log) earnings is not linear. Our earlier results indicate that a fourth-order polynomial is a better approximation to that pattern. To explore whether the shapes of the age–earnings profiles are different between women and men, we re-estimated the regression with age in a fourth-order polynomial interacted with gender:

$$(\ln w)^E = \beta_0 + \beta_1 age + \beta_2 age^2 + \beta_3 age^3 + \beta_4 age^4 + \beta_5 female + \beta_6 female \times age$$
$$+ \beta_7 female \times age^2 + \beta_8 female \times age^3 + \beta_9 female \times age^4 \tag{10.20}$$

This is a complicated regression with coefficients that are practically impossible to interpret. We don't show the coefficient estimates here. Instead we visualize the results. The graph in Figure 10.2b shows the predicted pattern (the regression curves) for women and men, together with the confidence intervals of the regression lines (curves here), as introduced in Chapter 9, Section 9.3.

Figure 10.2a suggests that the average earnings difference is a little less than 10% between ages 25 and 30, increases to around 15% by age 40, and reaches 22% by age 50, from where it decreases slightly to age 60 and more by age 65. These differences are likely similar in the population represented by the data as the confidence intervals around the regression curves are rather narrow, except at the two ends.

These results are very informative. Many factors may cause women with a graduate degree to earn less than men. Some of those factors are present at young age, but either they are more important in middle age, or additional factors start playing a role by then.

What can students infer from these results about the gender differences they may experience through their careers? Statistical inference established that the patterns are very likely present in the population represented by the data: employees with graduate degrees in the USA in 2014. The first question of external validity is whether similar patterns are likely to be true in the future as well and, if we are interested in another country, whether the patterns are similar there. The second question is the extent to which differences by age in the cross-section are informative about what we can expect to happen through time as people age. As we discussed earlier, those questions are impossible to answer with this data. Analyzing more data may help some but will never give a definitive answer to all questions. Nevertheless, the information produced by our analysis is a good starting point.

10.11 Multiple Regression and Causal Analysis

When interpreting regression coefficients, we advise being careful with the language, talking about differences and associations not effects and causation. But, can we say anything regarding the extent to which our results may indicate a causal link?

This question is all the more relevant because one main reason to estimate multiple regressions is to get closer to a causal interpretation. By conditioning on other observable variables, we can get closer to comparing similar objects – "apples to apples" – even in observational data. But getting closer is not the same as getting there.

For example, estimating the effect of a training program at a firm on the performance of employees would require comparing participants to non-participants who would perform similarly to how participants would without the program. A randomized experiment ensures such comparability. By randomly deciding who participates and who does not participate, we get two groups that are very similar in everything that is relevant, including what their future performance would be without the program. If, instead of a random rule, employees decided for themselves whether they participate in the program, a simple comparison of participants to non-participants would not measure the effect of the program because participants may have achieved different performance without the training.

The difference is between data from controlled experiments and observational data . Simple comparisons don't uncover causal relations in observational data. In principle, we may improve this by conditioning on every potential confounder: variables that would affect y and the causal variable x_1 at the same time. (In the training example, these are variables that would make participants and non-participants achieve different performance without the training, such as skills and motivation.) Such a comparison is called **ceteris paribus**.

But, importantly, conditioning on everything is impossible in general. Ceteris paribus prescribes what we want to condition on; a multiple regression can condition on what's in the data the way it is measured.

One more caveat. Not all variables should be included as covariates even if correlated both with the causal variable and the dependent variable. Such variables are called **bad conditioning variables**, or bad control variables. Examples include variables that are actually part of the **causal mechanism**, for example, how much participants in the training program actually learn.

What variables to include in a multiple regression and what variables not to include when aiming to estimate the effect of x on y is a difficult question. Chapter 19 will discuss this question along with the more general question of whether and when conditioning on other variables can lead to a good estimate of the effect of x on y, and what we mean by such an effect in the first place.

10.A6 CASE STUDY – Understanding the Gender Difference in Earnings

Thinking about cause and effect and getting closer to estimating it via multiple regression

Figure 10.2a showed a large and relatively stable average gender difference in earnings between ages 40 and 60 in the data and the population it represents (employees with a graduate degree in the USA in 2014). What might cause that difference?

One potential explanation is labor market discrimination. Labor market discrimination means that members of a group (women, minorities) earn systematically less per hour than members of another group (men, the majority) even if they have the same marginal product. Marginal product simply means their contribution to the sales of their employer by working one additional hour.

If one hour of work by women brings as much for the employer as one hour of work by men, they should earn the same, at least on average. There may be individual deviations for various reasons due to mistakes and special circumstances, but there should not be systematic differences in earnings per hour.

Note that this concept of labor market discrimination is quite narrow. For example, women may earn less on average because they are less frequently promoted to positions in which their work could have a higher effect on company sales. That would not count as labor market discrimination according to this narrow definition. A broader notion of discrimination would want to take that into account. An even broader concept of social inequality may recognize that women may choose occupations with flexible or shorter hours of work due to social norms about division of labor in the family. That may result in the over-representation of women in jobs that offer lower wages in return for more flexible hours.

Let's use our data to shed some light on these issues. Starting with the narrow definition of labor market discrimination, we have a clear steer as to what ceteris paribus analysis would be: condition on marginal product, or everything that matters for marginal product (and may possibly differ by gender). These may include cognitive skills, motivation, the ability to work efficiently in teams, and so on. Real-life data does not include all those variables. Indeed, our data has very little on skills: three broad categories of graduate degree and age. We may add race, ethnicity, and whether a person was born in the USA that may be related to the quality of education as well as other potential sources of discrimination.

To shed light on broader concepts of discrimination, we may want to enrich our regression by including more covariates. One example is occupation. Women may choose occupations that offer shorter and more flexible hours in exchange for lower wages. For the narrow concept of discrimination, we would like to condition on occupation, because we would want to compare women and men with the same work tasks. For the broad concept, we would not want to condition on it, because choice of occupation is affected by social norms about gender. Similar variables are industry, union status, hours worked, or whether the employer is private, nonprofit, or government.

Table 10.5 shows the results of those regressions. Some regressions have many explanatory variables. Instead of showing the coefficients of all, we show the coefficient and standard error of the variable of focus: *female*. The subsequent rows of the table indicate which variables are included as covariates. This is in fact a standard way of presenting results of large multiple regressions that focus on a single coefficient.

The data used for these regressions in Table 10.5 is a subset of the data used previously: it contains employees of age 40 to 60 with a graduate degree who work 20 hours per week or more. We focus on this age group because, as we have seen, this group has the largest average gender difference in earnings. We have 9816 such employees in our data.

Column (1) shows that women earn 22.4% less than men, on average, in the data (employees of age 40 to 60 with a graduate degree who work 20 hours or more). When we condition on age and the two binary variables of education, the difference is only slightly less, 21.2% (column (2)). This small difference appears to suggest that differences in age and education do not contribute to gender differences in earnings. However, our measures of education are only two binary variables of degree level, and more detailed data may imply a larger role of educational differences.

Table 10.5 Gender differences in earnings – regression with many covariates on a narrower sample

Variables	(1) ln wage	(2) ln wage	(3) ln wage	(4) ln wage
female	−0.224**	−0.212**	−0.151**	−0.141**
	(0.012)	(0.012)	(0.012)	(0.012)
Age and education		YES	YES	YES
Family circumstances			YES	YES
Demographic background			YES	YES
Job characteristics			YES	YES
Age in polynomial				YES
Hours in polynomial				YES
Observations	9816	9816	9816	9816
R-squared	0.036	0.043	0.182	0.195

Note: Education: professional, PhD. Family circumstances: marital status and number of children. Demographic background: race, ethnicity, whether US-born. Job characteristics: hours worked, whether employer is federal, state, local government, or nonprofit; union membership, two-digit industry, and two-digit occupation codes. Age and hours polynomials are fourth-order. Robust standard error estimates in parentheses. ** $p<0.01$, * $p<0.05$.

Source: `cps-earnings` dataset. USA, 2014. All employees of age 40–60 with a graduate degree and 20 or more work hours per week.

Column (3) includes all other covariates. The gender difference is 15.1%. When we compare people with the same personal and family characteristics and job features as measured in the data, women earn 15.1% less than men. Some of these variables are meant to measure job flexibility, but they are imperfect. Omitted variables include flexibility of hours and commuting time. Column (4) includes the same variables but pays attention to the potentially nonlinear relations with the two continuous variables, age and hours worked. The gender difference is very similar, 14.1%. The confidence intervals are reasonably narrow around these coefficients ($\pm 2\%$). They suggest that the average gender difference in the data, unconditional or conditional on the covariates, is of similar magnitude in the population represented by our data to what's in the data.

What did we learn from this exercise? We certainly could not safely pin down the role of labor market discrimination versus other reasons in driving the gender inequality in pay. Even their relative role is hard to assess from these results as the productivity measures are few, and the other covariates may be related to discrimination as well as preferences or other aspects of productivity. Thus, we cannot be sure that the 14.1% in column (4) is due to discrimination, and we can't even be sure if the role of discrimination is larger or smaller than that.

Nevertheless, our analysis provided some useful facts. The most important of them is that the gender difference is quite small below age 30, and it's the largest among employees between ages 40 and 60. Thus, gender differences, whether due to discrimination or other reasons, tend to be small among younger employees. In contrast, the disadvantages of women are large among middle-aged employees who also tend to be the highest earning employees. This is consistent with many potential explanations, such as the difficulty of women to advance their careers relative to men due to "glass ceiling effects" (discrimination at promotion to high job ranks), or differences in preferences for job flexibility versus career advancement, which, in turn, may be due to differences in preferences or differences in the constraints the division of labor in families put on women versus men.

On the methods side, this case study illustrated how to estimate multiple linear regressions, and how to interpret and generalize their results. It showed how we can estimate and visualize different patterns of association, including nonlinear patterns, between different groups. It highlighted the difficulty of drawing causal conclusions from regression estimates using cross-sectional data. Nevertheless, it also illustrated that, even in the absence of clear causal conclusions, multiple regression analysis can advance our understanding of the sources of a difference uncovered by a simple regression.

10.12   Multiple Regression and Prediction

One frequent reason to estimate a multiple regression is to make a **prediction**: find the best guess for the dependent variable, or target variable y_j for a particular target observation j, for which we know the right-hand-side variables x but not y. Multiple regression offers a better prediction than a simple regression because it includes more x variables.

The predicted value of the dependent variable in a multiple regression for an observation j with known values for the explanatory variables $x_{1j}, x_{2j}, \ldots$ is simply

$$\hat{y}_j = \hat{\beta}_0 + \hat{\beta}_1 x_{1j} + \hat{\beta}_2 x_{2j} + \cdots \tag{10.21}$$

When the goal is prediction, we want the regression to produce as good a fit as possible. More precisely, we want as good a fit as possible to the general pattern that is representative of the target observation j. Good fit in a dataset is a good starting point – that is, of course, if our data is representative of that general pattern. But it's not necessarily the same. A regression with a very good fit in our data may not produce a similarly good fit in the general pattern. A common danger is **overfitting** the data: finding patterns in the data that are not true in the general pattern. Thus, when using multiple regression for prediction, we want a regression that provides good fit without overfitting the data. Finding a multiple regression means selecting right-hand-side variables and functional forms for those variables. We'll discuss this issue in more detail when we introduce the framework for prediction in Chapter 13.

But how can we assess the fit of multiple regressions? Just like with simple regressions, the most commonly used measure is the R-squared. The R-squared in a multiple regression is conceptually the same as in a simple regression that we introduced in Chapter 7:

$$R^2 = \frac{Var[\hat{y}]}{Var[y]} = 1 - \frac{Var[e]}{Var[y]} \tag{10.22}$$

where $Var[y] = \frac{1}{n}\sum_{i=1}^{n}(y_i - \bar{y})^2$, $Var[\hat{y}] = \frac{1}{n}\sum_{i=1}^{n}(\hat{y}_i - \bar{y})^2$, and $Var[e] = \sum_{i=1}^{n}(e_i)^2$. Note that $\bar{\hat{y}} = \bar{y}$, and $\bar{e} = 0$.

The R-squared is a useful statistic to describe the fit of regressions. For that reason, it is common practice to report the R-squared in standard tables of regression results.

Unfortunately, the R-squared is an imperfect measure for selecting the best multiple regression for prediction purposes. The reason is that regressions with the highest R-squared tend to overfit the data.

When we compare two regressions, and one of them includes all the right-hand-side variables in the other one plus some more, the regression with more variables always produces a higher R-squared. Thus, regressions with more right-hand-side variables tend to produce higher R-squared. But that's not always good: regressions with more variables have a larger risk of overfitting the data. To see this, consider an extreme example. A regression with a binary indicator variable for each of the observations in the data (minus one for the reference category) produces a perfect fit with an R-squared of one. But such a regression would be completely useless to predict values outside the data. Thus, for variable selection, alternative measures are used, as we shall discuss it in Chapter 14.

Until we learn about more systematic methods to select the right-hand-side variables in the regression for prediction, all we can do is to use our intuition. The goal is to have a regression that captures patterns that are likely to be true for the general pattern for our target observations. Often, that means including variables that capture substantial differences in y, and not including variables whose coefficients imply tiny differences. That implies leaving out variables that capture detailed categories of qualitative variables or complicated interactions. To do really well, we will need the systematic tools we'll cover in Chapters 13 and 14.

The last topic in prediction is how we can visualize the fit of our regression. The purpose of such a graph is to compare values of y to the regression line. We visualized the fit of a simple regression with a scatterplot and the regression line in the x–y coordinate system. We did something similar with the age–gender interaction, too. However, with a multiple regression with more variables, we can't produce such a visualization because we have too many right-hand-side variables.

Instead, we can visualize the fit of a multiple regression by the **$\hat{y}$–y plot**. This plot has $\hat{y}$ on the horizontal axis and y on the vertical axis. The plot features the 45 degree line and the scatterplot around it. The 45 degree line is also the regression line of y regressed on $\hat{y}$. To see this consider that the regression of y on $\hat{y}$ shows the expected value of y for values of $\hat{y}$. But $\hat{y}$ is already the expected value of y conditional on the right-hand-side variables, so the expected value of y conditional on $\hat{y}$ is the same as $\hat{y}$. Therefore this line connects points where $\hat{y} = y$, so it is the 45 degree line.

The scatterplot around this line shows how actual values of y differ from their predicted value $\hat{y}$. The better the fit of the regression, the closer this scatterplot is to the 45 degree line (and the closer R-squared is to one). This visualization is more informative than the R-squared. For example, we can use the $\hat{y}$–y plot to identify observations with especially large positive or negative residuals. In this sense, it generalizes the scatterplot with a regression line when we only had a single x.

Review Box 10.8   Prediction with multiple linear regression

- The predicted value of the y variable from a multiple regression is

$$\hat{y} = \hat{\beta}_0 + \hat{\beta}_1 x1 + \hat{\beta}_2 x_2 + \cdots$$

- The $\hat{y}$–y plot is a good way to visualize the fit of a prediction. It's a scatterplot with $\hat{y}$ on the horizontal axis and y on the vertical axis, together with the 45 degree line, which is the regression line of y on $\hat{y}$.
  - observations to the right of the 45 degree line show overpredictions ($\hat{y} > y$).
  - observations to the left of the 45 degree line show underpredictions ($\hat{y} < y$).

CASE STUDY – Finding a Good Deal among Hotels with Multiple Regression

Prediction with multiple regression

Let's return once more to our example of hotel prices and distance to the city center. Recall that the goal of the analysis is to find a good deal from among the hotels for the date contained in the data. A good deal is a hotel that is inexpensive relative to its characteristics. Of those characteristics two are especially important: the distance of the hotel to the city center and the quality of the hotel. In the earlier chapters we considered simple regressions with the distance to the city center as the only explanatory variable. Here we add measures of quality and consider a multiple regression. Those measures of quality are stars (3, 3.5, or 4) and rating (average customer rating, ranging from 2 to 5).

With prediction, capturing the functional form is often important. Based on earlier explorations of the price–distance relationship and similar explorations of the price–stars and price–ratings relationships, we arrived at the following specification. The regression has log price as the dependent variable, a piecewise linear spline in distance (knots at 1 and 4 miles), a piecewise linear spline in rating (one knot at 3.5), and binary indicators for stars (one for 3.5 stars, one for 4 stars; 3 stars is the reference category).

From a statistical point of view, this is prediction analysis. The goal is to find the best predicted (log) price that corresponds to distance, stars, and ratings of hotels. Then we focus on the difference of actual (log) price from its predicted value.

Good deals are hotels with large negative residuals from this regression. They have a (log) price that is below what's expected given their distance, stars, and rating. The more negative the residual, the lower their log price, and thus their price, compared to what's expected for them. Of course, our measures of quality are imperfect. The regression does not consider information on room size, view, details of location, or features that only photos can show. Therefore the result of this analysis should be a shortlist of hotels that the decision maker should look into in more detail.

Table 10.6 shows the five best deals: these are the hotels with the five most negative residuals. We may compare this list with the list in Chapter 7, Section 4.U1, that was based on the residuals of a simple linear regression of hotel price on distance. Only two hotels "21912" and "22080" featured on both lists; hotel "21912" is the best deal now, there it was the second best deal. The rest of the hotels from Chapter 7 did not make it to the list here. When considering stars and rating, they do not appear to be such good deals anymore because their ratings and stars are low. Instead, we have three other hotels that have good measures of quality and are not very far yet they have relatively low price. This list is a good shortlist to find the best deal after looking into specific details and photos on the price comparison website.

How good is the fit of this regression? Its R-squared is 0.55: 55 percent in the variation in log price is explained by the regression. In comparison, a regression with log price and piecewise linear spline in distance would produce an R-squared of 0.37. Including stars and ratings improved the fit by 18 percentage points.

The $\hat{y}$–y plot in Figure 10.3 visualizes the fit of this regression. The plot features the 45 degree line. Dots above the line correspond to observations with a positive residual: hotels that have

Table 10.6   Good deals for hotels: the five hotels with the most negative residuals

Hotel name	Price	Residual in ln(price)	Distance	Stars	Rating
21912	60	−0.565	1.1	4	4.1
21975	115	−0.405	0.1	4	4.3
22344	50	−0.385	3.9	3	3.9
22080	54	−0.338	1.1	3	3.2
22184	75	−0.335	0.7	3	4.1

Note: List of the five observations with the smallest (most negative) residuals from the multiple regression with
log *price* on the left-hand side; right-hand-side variables are distance to the city center (piecewise linear spline
with knots at 1 and 4 miles), average customer rating (piecewise linear spline with knot at 3.5), binary variables
for 3.5 stars and 4 stars (reference category is 3 stars).

Source: `hotels-vienna` dataset. Vienna, November 2017, weekday. Hotels with 3 to 4 stars within 8 miles of
the city center, N= 217.

higher price than expected based on the right-hand-side variables. Dots below the line correspond
to observations with a negative residual: hotels that have lower price than expected. The dots that
are furthest down from the line are the candidates for a good deal.

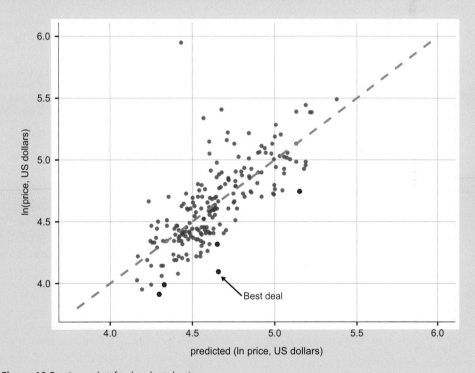

Figure 10.3 $\hat{y}-y$ plot for log hotel price

Note: Results from a regression of ln price on distance to the city center (piecewise linear spline with knots at
1 and 4 miles), average customer rating (piecewise linear spline with knot at 3.5), binary variables for 3.5
stars and 4 stars (reference category is 3 stars). *y* is ln *price*; $\hat{y}$ is predicted ln *price* from the regression. Five
best deals denoted with purple.
Source: `hotels-vienna` dataset. Vienna, November 2017, weekday. Hotels with 3 to 4 stars within 8 miles of
the city center; N=207.

This concludes the series of case studies using the `hotels-vienna` dataset to identify the hotels that are the best deals. We produced a shortlist of hotels that are the least expensive relative to their distance to the city center and their quality, measured by average customer ratings and stars.

10.13   Main Takeaways

Multiple regression allows for comparing mean y for different values of x for observations with the same values for the other variables.

- Doing so leads to better predictions and estimates of the slope on x that are usually closer to its true effect.
- Qualitative variables should be entered as binary variables on the right-hand side of multiple regressions.
- Interactions can uncover different slopes of one variable by values of another variable (e.g., denoting different groups).

PRACTICE QUESTIONS

1. The 95% CI of a slope coefficient in a multiple regression is narrower, the larger the R-squared of the regression. Why?
2. The 95% CI of a slope coefficient in a multiple regression is wider, the more the variable is correlated with the other right-hand-side variables. Why?
3. What's the difference between β in $y^E = \alpha + \beta x_1$ and β_1 in $y^E = \beta_0 + \beta_1 x_1 + \beta_2 x_2$? Why is this difference called omitted variable bias?
4. You want to estimate differences in spending on cigarettes by family income, and you are also interested how this difference in spending varies by the level of education of the adults in the family. Write down a regression that can uncover those differences, and interpret the coefficients of that regression. (Hint: you may define education as a binary variable, high versus low.)
5. Give an example of a multiple regression with two binary right-hand-side variables and their interaction. Write down the regression and interpret its coefficients.
6. What's a $\hat{y}-y$ plot, and what is it good for? Give an example.
7. You want to predict y with the help of ten x variables using multiple linear regression. A regression that includes the ten variables produces an R-squared of 0.4. A regression that includes those ten variables together with many of their interactions has 100 variables altogether, and it produces an R-squared of 0.43. List pros and cons for choosing each of the two regressions for your prediction.
8. You want to estimate the effect of x on y with the help of a multiple regression. You have 10 z variables that you want to condition on to get closer to causality. A regression that includes the ten variables produces a coefficient on x that is 0.40, $SE = 0.05$. A regression that includes those

ten variables together with many of their interactions gives a coefficient estimate of 0.35 and $SE = 0.10$. List pros and cons for choosing each of the two regressions for your causal analysis.

9. True or false? Why? Multiple regression analysis of observational data shows expected differences in the dependent variable corresponding to differences of an explanatory variable, ceteris paribus.

10. In a dataset of a cross-section of cars advertised on an online platform, log price is regressed on a binary variable that is one if the ad comes from a dealer and zero if it comes from the owner of the car. The slope coefficient is 0.1. When we add the age of the car to the regression, the slope coefficient on the same binary variable is 0.05. Interpret both numbers.

11. In the previous example the coefficient on the age of the car is -0.1. Are dealer-advertised cars older or younger on average? By how much?

12. Log hotel price is regressed on distance to the city center, average customer rating, and number of stars in a linear regression, using data on a cross-section of hotels in a city. The slope coefficient on stars is 0.2. Interpret this number.

13. The standard error on the slope coefficient in the previous question is 0.05. What's its 95% CI and what does that mean?

14. We are interested in how airline prices are related to the distance traveled and the size of the market (number of passengers). The data consists of average prices on the most popular markets (routes) of the USA (e.g., Boston–Chicago) for the year 2018. OLS estimates of our regression are the following:

$$(\ln price)^E = 4.4 + 0.3 distance - 0.06 passengers \qquad (10.23)$$

where $\ln price$ is log price, *distance* is measured in thousand miles, and *passengers* is the number of passengers per day (thousands). Interpret the two slope coefficient estimates.

15. We include the interaction of distance and passengers in the same regression and get a coefficient estimate of -0.002. Interpret this number. What can we conclude from its inclusion about the interaction of distance and passengers if the SE is 0.002?

DATA EXERCISES

Easier and/or shorter exercises are denoted by [*]; harder and/or longer exercises are denoted by [**].

1. Re-do the case study on gender difference in earnings by age – using a different group of employees or a different year in the USA, a different educational group, or a different country. Compare your results to those in the text and try to explain what you see. [*]

2. Use the `hotels-europe` dataset and pick a different city or a different date than used in the case study. Estimate a regression to predict hotel prices (or their log) using stars of the hotel, average customer ratings, and distance to the city center. Pay attention to functional forms. Argue for the best regression specification, and use its results to create a shortlist of five hotels that are underpriced. [**]

3. Use the same data as in the previous exercise and consider adding other variables in the data in an appropriate functional form. Argue for the best regression specification. Use the results to create a shortlist of five hotels that are underpriced, and compare this list to the list you produced in the previous exercise. [**]

4. Use the `worldbank-lifeexpectancy` dataset on a cross-section of countries. Pick a year. Regress life expectancy on log GDP per capita separately for different groups of countries (e.g., by continent). Then estimate a regression with the group dummies and their interactions with log GDP per capita. Interpret the coefficients and their 95% CI, and visualize the regression lines. What do you conclude from this exercise? [**]

5. Football is a global sport; FIFA, its governing body has 211 countries. There is plenty of evidence that countries' success in football is correlated with many socio-economic variables. Collect data on the results of all international games in a recent year, and pick a few socio-economic variables such as GDP/capita (pick three or more variables). Build a linear regression model to see which variables are correlated with the goal difference between teams. Create a $\hat{y}-y$ graph to see which countries perform better or worse than expected. [**]

REFERENCES AND FURTHER READING

A great reading on the role of regressions in arguing social change is Golbeck (2017).

One example of multivariate regression used in real life is the widespread use of the hedonic price index. For more on price indexes and hedonic regression, a great resource is Eurostat's *Handbook on Residential Property Prices Indices (RPPIs)* (Eurostat, 2013).

10.U1 UNDER THE HOOD: A TWO-STEP PROCEDURE TO GET THE MULTIPLE REGRESSION COEFFICIENT

We can get β_1 in the multiple regression from a two-step procedure that involves two simple regressions. There is no practical use for this two-step procedure: we get the exact coefficient we need by running multiple regression in software. In fact, this procedure is inferior because it produces standard errors that are wrong. Nevertheless, this procedure may highlight the intuition of how multiple regression works and how we should interpret its results. Moreover, the procedure, or its underlying logic, may become useful in substantially more complicated models.

We can get coefficient $\hat{\beta}_1$ in

$$y^E = \beta_0 + \beta_1 x_1 + \beta_2 x_2 \tag{10.24}$$

by (1) regressing x_1 on x_2:

$$x_1^E = \kappa + \lambda x_2 \tag{10.25}$$

and saving the residual $e = x_1 - \hat{\kappa} - \hat{\lambda} x_2$ and then (2) regressing y on this residual:

$$y^E = \pi + \rho e \tag{10.26}$$

The estimated slope coefficients are exactly the same:

$$\hat{\beta}_1 = \hat{\rho} \tag{10.27}$$

The procedure is analogous with more right-hand-side variables, only we have to regress x_1 on all other right-hand-side variables in step (1).

11 Modeling Probabilities

When and how to use regression to analyze conditional probabilities, and when and how to use alternative methods for this purpose

Motivation

Does smoking make you sick? And can smoking make you sick in late middle age even if you stopped years earlier? You have data on many healthy people in their fifties from various countries, and you know whether they stayed healthy four years later. You have variables on their smoking habits, their age, income, and many other characteristics. How can you use this data to estimate how much more likely non-smokers are to stay healthy? How can you uncover if that depends on whether they never smoked or are former smokers? And how can you tell if that association is the result of smoking itself or, instead, underlying differences in smoking by education, income, and other factors?

You are tasked to understand what drives employee churn: the fact that some employees leave the company shortly after they're hired while other employees stay with the firm. You have access to data from the company on all employees that were hired in the past five years, and you know a lot about them. How can you use this data to uncover important predictors of employee churn? How should you define your y variable here? How should you specify and estimate a model that can uncover patterns of association between y and those right-hand-side variables?

This chapter discusses probability models: regressions with binary y variables. In a sense, we can treat a binary y variable just like any other variable and use regression analysis as we would otherwise. But the fact that y is binary allows for a different interpretation of the results of such regressions, and it may make us use alternative ways to evaluate its fit. Moreover, with a binary y variable, we can estimate nonlinear probability models instead of the linear one. Data analysts need to have a good understanding of when to use these different probability models, and how to interpret and evaluate their results.

This chapter starts with the linear probability model, and we discuss the interpretation of its coefficients. Linear probability models are usually fine to uncover average associations, but they may be less good for prediction. The chapter introduces the two commonly used alternative models, the logit and the probit. Their coefficients are hard to interpret; we introduce marginal differences that are transformations of the coefficients and have interpretations similar to the coefficients of linear regressions. We argue that linear probability, logit, and probit models often produce very similar results in terms of the associations with explanatory variables, but they may lead to different predictions. We end by explaining how data analysts can analyze more complicated y variables, such as ordinal qualitative variables or duration variables, by turning them into binary ones and estimating probability models.

The case study **Does smoking pose a health risk?** examines the difference between how likely smokers and non-smokers are to remain healthy among 50- to 60-year-old Europeans. This case study uses the `share-health` dataset and illustrates the use of the linear probability model, the logit, and the probit. We show their applications when our goal is to uncover the average difference in the probability conditional on other variables, and when our goal is predicting the probability. In a short case study, **Are Australian weather forecasts well calibrated?**, we look at a way to evaluate probability predictions.

Learning outcomes

After working through this chapter, you should be able to:

- identify problems that call for and lend themselves to analysis by probability models;
- estimate linear probability models as well as logit and probit models;
- interpret the coefficients of linear probability models;
- estimate marginal differences from logit and probit models and interpret them;
- estimate predicted probabilities and conduct simple evaluation of models based on those predictions.

11.1 The Linear Probability Model

Often, the y variable of our analysis denotes an event: whether something happens or not. Examples include whether an internet user follows up on an online ad, whether an employee stays with the company for two years or more, or whether a debtor defaults on their debt. **Conditional probabilities**, introduced in Chapter 4, Section 4.3, capture how the probability of such an event depends on the value of the conditioning variable, or variables. Events are represented by binary variables in data: $y = 0$ or 1. Thus, when we are interested in how the probability of the occurrence of the event depends on the values of x, we want to know $P[y = 1|x]$.

Recall that the expected value of a 0–1 binary variable is also the probability that it is one. In other words, the average of a 0–1 variable is equal to the relative frequency of the value 1 among all observations. For example, an average of 0.5 corresponds to 50% of the observations being one; an average of 0.1 corresponds to 10% of ones. This is true whether the expectation, and thus the probability, is unconditional or conditional on some x variable(s). In notation, when $y = 0$ or 1, then

$$E[y] = P[y = 1] \tag{11.1}$$

$$E[y|x] = P[y = 1|x] \tag{11.2}$$

For this reason the linear regressions with binary dependent variables show not only differences in expected y by x, but also differences in the probability of $y = 1$ by x. Because of this additional interpretation, a linear regression with a binary y is also called a **linear probability model** (LPM). A linear probability model with two or more explanatory variables is

$$y^P = \beta_0 + \beta_1 x_1 + \beta_2 x_2 + \cdots \tag{11.3}$$

where we use the shorthand

$$y^P = P[y = 1|...] \tag{11.4}$$

In other words, y^P denotes the probability that the dependent variable is one, conditional on the right-hand-side variables of the model. In effect, y^P is a shorthand replacing y^E. y^E would be fine here, too, but y^P conveys the message that y^E is not only a conditional expectation but also a conditional probability.

In this model β_1 shows the difference in the probability that $y = 1$ for observations that are different in x_1 but are the same in terms of x_2 and all other right-hand-side variables. This interpretation is in addition to what's still true: average difference in y corresponding to differences in x_1 with the other right-hand-side variables being the same.

Just like any multiple linear regression, linear probability models allow for explanatory variables in logs, piecewise linear splines, polynomials, interactions, and so on. The interpretation of coefficients in such more complex models remains the same, with the added feature that differences in average y are also differences in the probability that $y = 1$. Similarly, all formulae and interpretations for standard errors, confidence intervals, hypotheses, and p-values of tests are the same. Linear probability models are not really different models: they are the same old linear regressions, only they allow for a specific interpretation beyond what's usual.

However, because of the binary nature of y, the linear probability model has some issues. Less importantly, it is always heteroskedastic. Therefore, we should always estimate robust standard errors. The more important issue will concern the range of predicted values in an LPM, as we will discuss in the next section.

11.2 Predicted Probabilities in the Linear Probability Model

Predicted values from linear probability models are **predicted probabilities**. Their interpretation is the estimated probability that $y = 1$ for observations with the particular value of the right-hand-side variables. Let's denote the predicted probability by $\hat{y}^P$. In the linear probability model with two or more explanatory variables, it is

$$\hat{y}^P = \hat{\beta}_0 + \hat{\beta}_1 x_1 + \hat{\beta}_2 x_2 + \cdots \tag{11.5}$$

Let's pause a little bit to consider this terminology and notation. $\hat{y}^P$ is of course the usual predicted value from the linear regression. And, thus, it is the predicted mean of y, conditional on the values of the x variables. With quantitative y, this mean is what we would expect for an observation with those x values. However, y is binary here, so we can never expect its mean value for any observation. The mean value of y is a probability between zero and one; for any particular observation, the value of y is never between zero and one but is either zero or one. Hence the new term (predicted probability) and notation ($\hat{y}^P$).

So predicted values from the linear probability model are predicted probabilities. And, therefore, they need to be between zero and one; they cannot be negative, and they cannot be greater than 1. The problem is that, in some linear probability models, $\hat{y}^P$ may be less than zero or more than one. The problem follows from the linear relation between the x variables and y^P.

This is an issue for some linear probability models but not for others. $\hat{y}^P$ likely goes below 0 or above 1 if the model includes an x variable that is not bounded in the sense that it can take any value, including large positive values or large negative values. Many quantitative variables are not bounded, including income or wealth of individuals, sales of companies, GDP of countries. A line fitted with such an x variable would sooner or later go above $\hat{y}^P = 1$ or below $\hat{y}^P = 0$, unless, of course, its slope is zero, but that's rare. On the other hand, $\hat{y}^P$ may stay between zero and one for linear probability models if all x variables are bounded. Some regression models have a combination of binary right-hand-side variables that makes them free of this problem. They are called **saturated models**; we'll discuss them in a little more detail in Under the Hood section 11.U1.

When the goal is to predict probabilities, linear probability models that produce $\hat{y}^P < 0$ or $\hat{y}^P > 1$ are clearly a problem. Note that the issue is whether the model may yield such predictions for observations not only in the particular data used for estimation but also in the data we would use for prediction. A linear probability model with unbounded x variables that happens not to produce such $\hat{y}^P$ values in our data may still be problematic later on as observations used for prediction may have such x values.

At the same time, the fact that predicted probabilities may go below zero or above one is not an issue when the goal is to uncover patterns of association. Predicted probabilities do not play a direct role in uncovering differences in the probability of the $y = 1$ event corresponding to differences in the x variables. In fact, as we shall see at the end of this chapter, more complex models that deal with the prediction issue often produce very similar patterns of association to linear probability models. Thus, however imperfect, linear probability models are very useful. They are not only the simplest way to uncover associations with binary dependent variables, but they tend to be just as good as more complicated models for that purpose.

Before illustrating predicting probabilities with our case study and moving on to other kinds of probability models, let's introduce the concept of **classification**. Classification is another kind of prediction with binary y variables. Instead of predicting the probability of $y = 1$ for target observations, the goal of classification is to put target observations into the $y = 1$ or $y = 0$ category. We can do that once a predicted probability is available: we can put the observation in the $y = 1$ category if the predicted probability of $y = 1$ is high, and we can put it in the $y = 0$ category if the predicted probability is low. What constitutes high and low is a decision to be made, with important consequences for the classification. For this and other related reasons, classification has its own problems and solutions. We restrict our attention to predicting probabilities in this chapter; we'll discuss classification in Chapter 17.

Review Box 11.1 Linear probability model

- Linear probability models (LPM) are linear regressions with binary dependent variables: $y = 0$ or 1.
- The LPM specifies the conditional probability of $y = 1$, denoted as y^P, as a linear function:

$$y^P = \beta_0 + \beta_1 x_1 + \beta_2 x_2 + \cdots$$

- β_0 shows the probability that $y = 1$ for observations with all explanatory variables zero.
- β_1 shows how much higher the probability of $y = 1$ is for observations with one unit higher x_1 and the same value for all other explanatory variables $x_2, \ldots$
- Linear probability models predict the probability of $y = 1$ for values of the x variables:

$$\hat{y}^P = \hat{\beta}_0 + \hat{\beta}_1 x_1 + \hat{\beta}_2 x_2 + \cdots$$

- The predicted probability from an LPM may be less than zero or larger than one, which is a problem for prediction but not for uncovering associations.

11.A1   CASE STUDY – Does Smoking Pose a Health Risk?

Question, data, linear probability model estimates

The question of the case study is whether and by how much smokers are less likely to stay healthy than non-smokers. We focus on people of age 50 to 60 who consider themselves healthy, and four years later we look at which of them are still considered healthy and which changed their answer to "not healthy." Ultimately, we would like to uncover the extent to which smoking leads to deteriorating health. This is observational data, so uncovering that effect is difficult. Even if we can't unambiguously estimate the effect of smoking, we may be able to uncover associations that can get us closer to learn about the effect.

This case study uses the `share-health` dataset, from the SHARE survey (Survey for Health, Aging and Retirement in Europe; www.share-project.org). SHARE is a longitudinal survey studying the process of aging on a large sample of individuals across many European countries. It is a harmonized survey: questions were asked the same way in each country. It has interviewed individuals every two years since 2004. The design of the SHARE survey is similar to longitudinal surveys of aging in other countries, including the Health and Retirement Study that we used for illustration in Chapter 3, Section 3.D1.

SHARE is a complicated dataset to work with. Luckily, some of its most important variables are accessible in a simpler dataset called easySHARE. easySHARE contains basic demographic information on all individuals, their perceived health, whether they smoked at the time of the interview, whether they smoked earlier, and a few other interesting variables.

Our data contains all individuals in the SHARE dataset who participated both in 2011 ("wave 4") and in 2015 ("wave 6"), were 50 to 60 years old in 2011, and said that they were in good health in 2011. We define the binary variable staying healthy by considering whether the same individual reported to be in good health in 2015 too; $y = 1$ if the individual remained in good health, and $y = 0$ if not. To be precise, respondents rate their health on a scale with 5 options, from excellent to poor. We defined an individual to be of good health if reported health was excellent or very good.

The data has 3272 individuals who reported to be in good health in 2011 and participated in the 2015 survey. Of those, body weight is missing for 163 people, and we will use that information in one of our regressions, so we restrict our data to the 3109 people with valid information for all variables. The individuals are from 14 European countries. Thus the population represented by this data are 50- to 60-year-old individuals from these 14 European countries who consider themselves healthy. 60% of individuals stayed healthy according to our definition. 22% were smokers in 2011; 49% reported to have ever smoked.

First, we estimated a linear probability model with being healthy in 2015 as the binary dependent variable and whether the individual is a current smoker in 2011 as the only explanatory variable – also a binary variable. The linear probability model has the following form:

$$stayshealthy^P = \alpha + \beta \times currentsmoker \quad (11.6)$$

Second, we included another binary variable in the regression – whether the individual ever smoked:

$$stayshealthy^P = \beta_0 + \beta_1 \times currentsmoker + \beta_2 \times eversmoked \quad (11.7)$$

Table 11.1 shows the results.

Table 11.1   Probability of staying healthy

Variables	(1) Stays healthy	(2) Stays healthy
Current smoker	−0.070**	−0.079**
	(0.021)	(0.025)
Ever smoked		0.014
		(0.020)
Constant	0.620**	0.615**
	(0.010)	(0.012)
Observations	3109	3109

Note: Linear probability model. Robust standard error estimates in parentheses.
** $p<0.01$, * $p<0.05$.

Source: `share-health` dataset. People of age 50 to 60 from 14 European countries who reported to be healthy in 2011.

According to column (1), 62% of non-smokers stayed healthy (the constant); smokers were 7 percentage points less likely to stay healthy (the slope), which means that 55% of them stayed healthy. The 95% confidence interval around the slope parameter is $[-0.11, -0.03]$ implying that we can be 95% confident that smokers in the population represented by our dataset stay healthy with a lower probability of 3 to 11 percentage points. This is a relatively wide confidence interval. Nevertheless, it does not contain zero so we can be quite confident that smokers are less likely to stay healthy in the population represented by this dataset (50–60-year-old people from 14 European countries who consider themselves healthy).

We show the scatterplot and the regression line that correspond to this simple regression in Figure 11.1, primarily for educational purposes. The scatterplot looks funny: all data points are in one of the four corners. That is because both the dependent variable and the explanatory variable are binary; thus any observation can have one of only four combinations of two zero–one values. To visualize the distribution of observations across these four value-combinations, the size of the four dots is proportional to their frequency in the data. The regression line looks funny, too: it connects two points that are the two predicted probabilities: the fraction that stayed healthy among non-smokers and the 7-percentage-points lower fraction among smokers. The slope of the line is the difference between these two probabilities as the difference in the two x values is one (one minus zero).

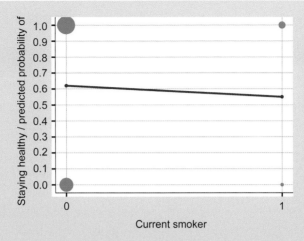

Figure 11.1   Staying healthy and smoking – scatterplot and regression line

Note: Linear probability model with a single binary right-hand-side variable (whether current smoker).
Source: `share-health` dataset. People of age 50 to 60 from 14 European countries who reported to be healthy in 2011. N=3109.

The regression in column (2) of Table 11.1 adds whether people ever smoked. Interpreting the coefficients of this regression is a little tricky. The coefficient on *current smoker* shows the difference in the probability of staying healthy comparing current smokers and current non-smokers who have the same value of the *ever smoked* variable. But note that among those who never smoked (*ever smoked* = 0) we cannot make this comparison because this group does not include current smokers. It is only among those that ever smoked (*ever smoked* = 1) that we can find both current smokers and current non-smokers. The current non-smokers in this group used to smoke but quit by the time we observe them (aged 50–60). Thus, the slope on *current smoker* in regression (2) shows that current smokers are 7.9 percentage points less likely to stay healthy than those that used to smoke but quit.

The coefficient on *ever smoked* in this regression compares people with the same current smoking status but with a different past smoking status. That comparison is possible only among current non-smokers. Thus this coefficient compares those who used to smoke but quit with those who have never smoked. The coefficient on *ever smoked* turns out to be positive, implying that in this dataset those who used to smoke but quit are 1.4 percentage points more likely to stay healthy than those who have never smoked. But the confidence interval contains zero, suggesting that in the population represented by the data, there may be no difference in staying healthy between those who have never smoked and those who used to smoke but quit.

To what extent is the difference between smokers and non-smokers due to smoking itself? Smokers and non-smokers may be different in many other behaviors and conditions, including how much they exercise, how much income they have, or in which of the 14 countries they live. Those behaviors and conditions may affect whether they stay in good health and thus make smoking and health appear related on top of the effect of smoking itself.

In order to get closer to uncovering the effect of smoking, we conditioned on observable characteristics in the regression. These variables are gender, age, years of education, income (measured as in which of the 10 income groups individuals belong within their country), body mass index (BMI, a measure of weight relative to height), whether the person exercises regularly, and, finally, the country in which they live. Gender, exercising, and country are qualitative variables and are entered as binary indicators. Age, years of education, income, and BMI are quantitative variables with many values. Age, years of education, and income are bounded quantitative variables here; BMI is not bounded, at least in principle (although we don't expect it to go to infinity).

We examined lowess regressions with staying healthy in order to decide in what functional form to include each of them in the regression. We show two of them below: lowess regressions with years of education (Figure 11.2a) and income (Figure 11.2b). To capture nonlinearity, we included education as a piecewise linear spline with knots at 8 and 18 years; while we included income in a linear way. As for additional variables, we entered age linearly, too, and body mass index (BMI) as a piecewise linear spline with knot at 35 (a high value showing obesity).

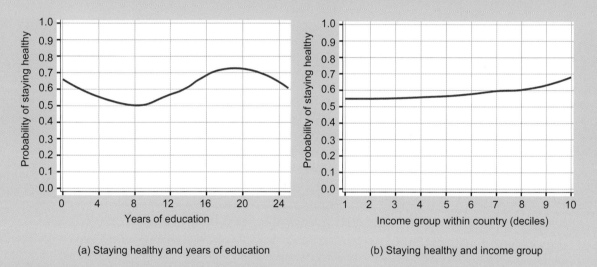

(a) Staying healthy and years of education   (b) Staying healthy and income group

Figure 11.2   Education, income, and the probability of staying healthy – non-parametric regressions

Note: Non-parametric lowess regressions to investigate functional forms.
Source: `share-health` dataset. People of age 50 to 60 from 14 European countries who reported to be healthy in 2011. N=3109.

Table 11.2 shows the regression results. The table does not show the coefficients on the countries; they show important differences in the probability of staying healthy (conditional on the other right-hand-side variables), with the highest probabilities for Denmark, Austria, and Switzerland and lowest probabilities for Poland, Portugal, and Estonia. We don't show the constant, either, as it is not informative (it would refer to age zero, for example). Note that, similarly to the previous table we don't show the R-squared. In contrast with the standard way of presenting regression results with quantitative y variables, the R-squared is usually not shown with linear probability models. The reason is that the interpretation of the R-squared is not straightforward with a binary y variable; we'll return to this issue in Section 11.5.

Variables	(1) Staying healthy
Current smoker	−0.061*
	(0.024)
Ever smoked	0.015
	(0.020)
Female	0.033
	(0.018)
Age	−0.003
	(0.003)
Years of education (if < 8)	−0.001
	(0.007)
Years of education (if ≥ 8 and < 18)	0.017**
	(0.003)
Years of education (if ≥ 18)	−0.010
	(0.012)
Income group	0.008*
	(0.003)
BMI (if < 35)	−0.012**
	(0.003)
BMI (if ≥ 35)	0.006
	(0.017)
Exercises regularly	0.053**
	(0.017)
Country indicators	YES
Observations	3109

Table 11.2 Smoking and the probability of staying healthy – rich LPM

Note: Linear probability model. For BMI and education, coefficients are slopes of the spline. Robust standard error estimates in parentheses. ** $p<0.01$, * $p<0.05$.

Source: `share-health` dataset. People of age 50 to 60 from 14 European countries who reported to be healthy in 2011.

In the regression in Table 11.2, the coefficient on currently smoking is –0.061. Comparing people who live in the same country, have the same gender, age, years of education, body mass index, and exercising habits, and belong to the same income group, those who smoke are 6 percentage points less likely to stay healthy. The 95% confidence interval is relatively wide [–0.108,–0.014], but it does not contain zero, suggesting that smoking is negatively related to staying healthy in the population represented by the data, even conditional on these other variables. Similarly to the simple regression results, there are no significant differences in staying healthy when comparing those who never smoked to those who used to smoke but quit.

The other coefficients are interesting, too. Conditional on their other characteristics included in the regression, women are 3.3 percentage points more likely to stay in good health, while age does not seem to matter in this relatively narrow age range of 50 to 60 years. Differences in years of education do not matter if we compare people with less than 8 years or more than 18 years, but it matters a lot in-between, with a one-year difference corresponding to 1.7 percentage points difference in the likelihood of staying healthy. Someone with 18 years of education is 17 percentage points more likely to stay healthy than someone with 8 years of education and the same gender, age, income, BMI, smoking, exercising, and country.

Income matters somewhat less, with a coefficient of 0.008. Someone with a top 10% income is thus 8 percentage points more likely to stay healthy than someone with the bottom 10% of income and the same gender, age, years of education, BMI, smoking, exercising, and country. Body mass index is related to staying healthy, with a coefficient of −0.012 below value 35. Thus someone with a BMI value of 25 (the upper value for normal weight) is 12 percentage points more likely to stay healthy than someone with a value of 35 (obese), with the other variables in the regression being the same. Finally, those who exercise regularly are 5.3 percentage points more likely to stay healthy, a difference similar to smoking (of opposite sign of course).

Figure 11.3 shows the histogram of the predicted probabilities. The predicted probability of staying healthy from this linear probability model ranges between 0.036 and 1.011. It thus does not stay between zero and one, surpassing 1, if only just marginally.

Differences in predicted probabilities of staying healthy come from differences in the values of the x variables in the regression. One by one the x variables are related to moderate differences in staying healthy. But they add up to make people very different in terms of the predicted probability. At the extremes, some people are predicted to stay healthy with a 98% or higher chance; other people are predicted to stay healthy with a 20% or lower chance. Looking at the composition of people in low and high predicted probability groups helps understand how this happens.

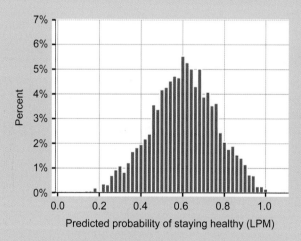

Figure 11.3   Histogram of the predicted probabilities

Note: Predicted probabilities are calculated from the rich linear probability model.
Source: `share-health` dataset. People of age 50 to 60 from 14 European countries who reported to be healthy in 2011. N=3109.

In our case, people with the top 1% predicted probability in the data have no current smokers among them, are all women, have 17.3 years of education, on average, a BMI of 20.7, on average, tend to come from higher income groups, and 90% of them exercise. For these 31 individuals in the top 1%, predicted probabilities range between 0.942 and 1.011.

In contrast, people with the bottom 1% predicted probability in the data have 37.5% current smokers, 37.5% of them are women, have 7.6 years of education, on average, a BMI of 30.5, on average, tend to come from lower income groups, and only 19% of them exercise. For these 32 individuals in the bottom 1%, predicted probabilities range between 0.036 and 0.245.

11.3   Logit and Probit

To circumvent the problem of predicting probabilities that are less than zero or greater than one, data analysts use two models as alternatives to the linear probability model: these are called **logit** and **probit**. Both may be thought of as putting their own twist on top of a linear probability model. The linear probability model relates the probability of the $y = 1$ event to a linear combination of the explanatory variables. Logit and probit models relate the probability of the $y = 1$ event to a nonlinear function – called the **link function** – of the linear combination of the explanatory variables. The logit and the probit differ in the link function; however, both make sure that, in the end, the resulting probability is always strictly between zero and one.

The logit model has the following form:

$$y^P = \Lambda(\beta_0 + \beta_1 x_1 + \beta_2 x_2 + \cdots) = \frac{\exp(\beta_0 + \beta_1 x_1 + \beta_2 x_2 + \cdots)}{1 + \exp(\beta_0 + \beta_1 x_1 + \beta_2 x_2 + \cdots)} \qquad (11.8)$$

where the link function $\Lambda(z) = \frac{\exp(z)}{1+\exp(z)}$ is called the logistic function.

The probit model has the following form:

$$y^P - \Phi(\beta_0 \mid \beta_1 x_1 + \beta_2 x_2 + \cdots) \qquad (11.9)$$

where the link function $\Phi(z) = \int_{-\infty}^{z} \frac{1}{\sqrt{2\pi}} \exp\left(-\frac{t^2}{2}\right) dt$ is the cumulative distribution function (cdf) of the standard normal distribution.

Both Λ and Φ are increasing S-shaped curves. Figure 11.4 shows the two curves overlaid on each other; the blue curve is the logit, the green curve is the probit.

The two curves in Figure 11.4 are virtually indistinguishable from each other when they are plotted against their respective "z" values (the linear combination they produce with their respective β coefficients, which are typically different in the two models). Both curves are steepest when the probability is around 0.5 and the argument in the link function is zero. It is not really visible here, but the logit is a little less steep close to zero and one and thus has somewhat thicker tails than the probit. But those differences are very small. Predicted probabilities from logit or probit models are computed using the appropriate link function and the estimated coefficients:

$$\hat{y}^P_{logit} = \Lambda(\hat{\beta}_0 + \hat{\beta}_1 x_1 + \hat{\beta}_2 x_2 + \cdots) \qquad (11.10)$$

$$\hat{y}^P_{probit} = \Phi(\hat{\beta}_0 + \hat{\beta}_1 x_1 + \hat{\beta}_2 x_2 + \cdots) \qquad (11.11)$$

It would be a little involved to calculate these by hand. Fortunately, all statistical software will calculate the predicted probabilities for us.

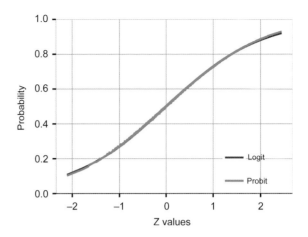

Figure 11.4   The logit and probit link functions

Note: The logit and probit link functions as a function of their respective z values (the linear combination of the x variables using their coefficients).
Source: `share-health` dataset. People of age 50 to 60 from 14 European countries who reported to be healthy in 2011. N=3109.

Review Box 11.2   Logit and probit

- Logit and probit are nonlinear probability models.
- Logit: $y^P = \Lambda(\beta_0 + \beta_1 x_1, \beta_2 x_2 + \cdots)$, where the function Λ is called the logistic function.
- Probit: $y^P = \Phi(\beta_0 + \beta_1 x_1, \beta_2 x_2 + \cdots)$, where the function Φ is called the cumulative distribution function (cdf) of the standard normal distribution.
- The predicted probabilities from logit and probit models are always between zero and one.
- In most cases logit and probit models produce very similar predictions. They may be different from the predicted probabilities from corresponding linear probability models, especially if the probability is close to zero or one.

11.A2   CASE STUDY – Does Smoking Pose a Health Risk?

Predicted probabilities

We estimated logit and probit models for the probability of staying healthy in the same data with the same right-hand-side variables as our last linear probability model. The predicted probabilities from the logit and the probit are practically the same. Their range is between 0.06 and 0.99, which is somewhat narrower than the predicted probabilities from the LPM (their range is 0.04 to 1.01 there). The narrower ranges are the results of the S-shaped curves of the logit and the probit that approach zero and one slowly, in contrast with the straight line produced by the LPM.

Figure 11.5 shows how the predicted probabilities compare across the three models. It plots the predicted probabilities from the logit and the probit on the y axis against the predicted probability from the LPM on the x axis. The figure includes the 45 degree line, which is just the predicted probability of the LPM measured again on the y axis so we can compare it to the logit and probit probabilities.

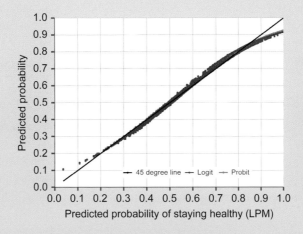

Figure 11.5   Predicted probabilities from three different models

Note: Predicted probabilities from linear probability, logit, and probit models with the same right-hand-side variables. y variable: staying healthy.
Source: `share-health` dataset. People of age 50 to 60 from 14 European countries who reported to be healthy in 2011. N=3109.

The logit and probit probability predictions are indistinguishable from each other in Figure 11.5. They are also all very close to the 45 degree line except at the tails, where the logit and probit predicted probabilities are less extreme (less close to zero; less close to one).

Two important conclusions emerge from this exercise. First, logit and probit models produce almost exactly the same predicted probabilities. That is true in most cases. Thus, choosing between logit and probit models for binary dependent variables is not an important choice: we can go with either of the two. Second, the linear probability model predicts very similar probabilities to the logit and the probit, except for the lowest and highest probabilities. That is also a general phenomenon: as long as the predicted probabilities are in the middle range, the linear probability model tends to produce predictions that are very similar to the logit and the probit. For probabilities closer to zero or one, the LPM produces different predictions. Indeed, LPM may predict probabilities that are greater than one or less than zero. The logit and the probit predictions are always within zero and one.

11.4 Marginal Differences

Both the probit and the logit transform the $\beta_0 + \beta_1 x_1 + \cdots$ linear combination using a link function that shows an S-shaped curve. Because of its shape, the slope of this link function is different at different places, depending on whatever is inside the link function. The slope is steepest when $y^P = 0.5$; it is flatter further away; and it becomes very flat if y^P is close to zero or one. All this implies that the difference in y^P that corresponds to a unit difference in any explanatory variable is not the same: it varies with the values of the x variables. This is in contrast with the linear probability model. For the logit and probit, the same difference in an explanatory variable corresponds to a larger difference in y^P, the closer y^P is to 0.5. The same difference in an explanatory variable corresponds to a smaller difference in y^P, the closer y^P is to 0 or 1. All of this is a natural consequence of the S-shaped link function that ensures that predicted probabilities are always between zero and one.

In a linear probability model, the coefficients have the usual interpretations. In logit and probit models the coefficients do not have the same interpretation. In fact, we do not interpret those coefficients. Instead, we transform them to arrive at an interpretation that is similar to what we have in linear probability models. (It turns out that the logit, but not the probit, coefficients do have some interpretation, but we don't consider that in this textbook.)

To evaluate the magnitude of association between explanatory variables and y^P in logit and probit models, we compute and interpret **marginal differences**. The marginal difference corresponding to an explanatory variable is the average difference in y^P that corresponds to a one unit difference in that explanatory variable (for observations that are the same in the other explanatory variables). Thus, marginal differences have the same interpretation as the coefficients of linear probability models.

Computing the marginal differences is complicated. They are functions of all coefficients and the values of all explanatory variables. The logit and probit coefficients themselves are also complicated to estimate, and so are their standard errors. We provide some details on the estimation of the coefficients and the computation of marginal differences in Under the Hood sections 11.U2 and 11.U3.

The typical output of logit and probit models in statistical software is similar to the output of linear regressions: it includes the coefficient estimates and their standard errors. As we do not interpret logit and probit coefficients, such tables are not very informative. Luckily, most statistical software packages can calculate marginal differences corresponding to the explanatory variables in logit and probit. (They may call them "marginal effects," "**average marginal effects**," or "average partial effects.") Typically, they can also produce an output that is similar to regression outputs but includes the marginal differences and the standard errors corresponding to the marginal differences.

Review Box 11.3   Marginal differences, LPM versus logit and probit models

- The coefficients of logit and probit models are hard to interpret. It is better to transform them into marginal differences.
- A marginal difference is the average difference in the probability of $y = 1$ corresponding to a one-unit difference in the explanatory variable if all other explanatory variables are the same.
- The sign (positive, negative, zero) of marginal differences are the same as the corresponding coefficients. Thus, for example, if a coefficient is zero, the corresponding marginal difference is also zero.
- The marginal differences computed from logit and probit models are usually very similar to each other, and they are often very similar to the corresponding coefficients of linear probability models.

| 11.A3 | CASE STUDY – Does Smoking Pose a Health Risk? |

Marginal differences

Table 11.3 Smoking and the probability of staying healthy – LPM, logit and probit models

Variables	(1) LPM	(2) logit coeffs	(3) logit marginals	(4) probit coeffs	(5) probit marginals
Current smoker	−0.061*	−0.284**	−0.061**	−0.171*	−0.060*
	(0.024)	(0.109)	(0.023)	(0.066)	(0.023)
Ever smoked	0.015	0.078	0.017	0.044	0.016
	(0.020)	(0.092)	(0.020)	(0.056)	(0.020)
Female	0.033	0.161*	0.034*	0.097	0.034
	(0.018)	(0.082)	(0.018)	(0.050)	(0.018)
Age	−0.003	−0.012	−0.003	−0.008	−0.003
	(0.003)	(0.014)	(0.003)	(0.009)	(0.003)
Years of education (if < 8)	−0.001	−0.003	−0.001	−0.002	−0.001
	(0.007)	(0.033)	(0.007)	(0.020)	(0.007)
Years of education (if ≥ 8 and < 18)	0.017**	0.079**	0.017**	0.048**	0.017**
	(0.003)	(0.016)	(0.003)	(0.010)	(0.003)
Years of education (if ≥ 18)	−0.010	−0.046	−0.010	−0.029	−0.010
	(0.012)	(0.055)	(0.012)	(0.033)	(0.012)
Income group	0.008*	0.036*	0.008*	0.022*	0.008*
	(0.003)	(0.015)	(0.003)	(0.009)	(0.003)
BMI (if < 35)	−0.012**	−0.057**	−0.012**	−0.035**	−0.012**
	(0.003)	(0.011)	(0.002)	(0.007)	(0.002)
BMI (if ≥ 35)	0.006	0.031	0.007	0.017	0.006
	(0.017)	(0.071)	(0.015)	(0.044)	(0.015)
Exercises regularly	0.053**	0.255**	0.055**	0.151**	0.053**
	(0.017)	(0.079)	(0.017)	(0.048)	(0.017)
Observations	3109	3109	3109	3109	3109
Country indicators	YES	YES	YES	YES	YES

Note: Linear probability model, logit and probit, dependent variable staying healthy. For BMI and education, coefficients are slopes of the spline. For logit and probit, average marginal differences reported in the columns next to the corresponding coefficient estimates. Appropriate standard error estimates in parentheses.
** $p < 0.01$, * $p < 0.05$.

Source: `share-health` dataset. People of age 50 to 60 from 14 European countries who reported to be healthy in 2011.

Let's look at the logit and probit estimates for the model that associates the probability of staying healthy to current smoking and ever smoking, conditional on gender, age, years of education, income group within country, body mass index, exercising, and country. All of the variables are entered in the same way as in the linear probability model above (linear in age and income, piecewise linear spline in years of education and BMI).

Table 11.3 has five columns: LPM coefficients, logit coefficients, logit marginal differences, probit coefficients, probit marginal differences.

The logit coefficients are almost five times the size of the corresponding marginal differences; the probit coefficients are about three times their size. We do not want to interpret the coefficients themselves. Instead, we interpret the marginal differences.

The marginal differences are essentially the same across the logit and the probit, and they are essentially the same as the corresponding LPM coefficients. This is true for all explanatory variables. To focus on our main question, these results imply that comparing people who ever smoked, have the same gender, age, years of education, income group, BMI, exercising habits, and live in the same country, current smokers have a 6 percentage points lower chance of staying healthy than those who do not smoke.

In this example, all the extra work didn't pay off. We estimated logit and probit models and obtained their marginal differences only to discover that they are essentially the same as the LPM coefficients. It turns out that this is a rather common finding. Except for models for very rare or very common events (with probabilities close to zero or one), the marginal differences from logit and probit are usually very close to the LPM coefficients.

11.5   Goodness of Fit: R-Squared and Alternatives

Probability models predict probabilities, which we denote by $\hat{y}^P$. This is true for the linear probability model as well as for logit and probit models. Typically, these predicted probabilities take many values, somewhere between zero and one (or, for the linear probability model, sometimes beyond zero or one). In contrast, the dependent variable itself does not take on many values – just two: zero or one. As a result, probability models cannot fit zero–one dependent variables perfectly. And they don't need to: their task is to predict probabilities or uncover patterns of association between probabilities and the right-hand-side variables. As we described in Section 11.2, predicting values of a binary y would be a different task, called classification, which we'll discuss in detail in Chapter 17.

Recall from Chapter 7, Section 4.U1, that goodness of fit of a regression tells us how good the estimated regression is in producing a prediction within the data. It is based on comparing actual y values with the predictions of an estimated model, and this comparison is done within the same dataset that we used for the estimation. When y is quantitative, we directly compare values of y to their predicted values from a regression. R-squared, the most widely used measure of fit for regressions, is the result of such a comparison, and so is the $\hat{y}-y$ plot, a good visualization of that fit (see Chapter 10, Section 10.12).

While the R-squared is a less natural measure of fit for probability models, we can calculate it just the same. Then we can use that R-squared to rank different models. That's one statistic to look at. We introduce three alternatives here that are more widely used in the context of probability models. At the end of the section we will give advice on which measure to choose when.

For historical reasons, when evaluating the fit of predictions and ranking various models, many data analysts use a statistic that is very closely related to the R-squared but is not the same. It is called the **Brier score** (named after statistician Glenn W. Brier). With n observations, its formula is

$$Brier = \frac{1}{n} \sum_{i=1}^{n} (\hat{y}_i^P - y_i)^2 \tag{11.12}$$

The Brier score is the average squared distance between predicted probabilities and the actual value of y. Thus, the smaller the Brier score, the better. When comparing two predictions, the one with the larger Brier score is the worse prediction because it produces more error.

Just like the R-squared, the Brier score measures how close the predicted probabilities are to the actual values of y. Only it shows it with the opposite sign. In fact, the R-squared and the Brier score are very closely related. Recall (from Chapter 7, Section 7.9) that we can write out the R-squared equation in a way that has the variance of the residual: $R^2 = 1 - \frac{Var[e]}{Var[y]}$. For probability models, residual variance is nothing else than the Brier score: $Var[e] = Brier$. Thus, whenever the Brier score is smaller, the R-squared is larger, both indicating a better fit.

The second alternate measure is the **pseudo R-squared**. It turns out that there are various versions of this measure. The most widely used version is called McFadden's R-squared (named after economist and statistician Daniel McFadden), and can be computed for the logit and the probit but not for the linear probability model. It is similar to the R-squared in that it, too, measures how much better the fit is compared to what it would be if we were not using any of the right-hand-side variables for prediction. (In that case the R-squared would be zero.) At the same time, the pseudo R-squared is computed differently, and it is based on the nonlinear way the logit and the probit are estimated. Some statistical software show the pseudo R-squared together with logit or probit estimates by default. While the pseudo R-squared has an interpretation for a single estimated model (how much better it is than not using the right-hand-side variables), it is more often used to compare different estimated models and rank them.

Another related alternative is called the **log-loss**. Its name is derived from the loss function, a general way of evaluating estimated models that we will introduce in detail in Chapter 13. The log-loss is a negative number. We want the log-loss to be as small as possible in absolute value: better fit means smaller (less negative) log-loss. It turns out that when comparing the fit of logit models, the log-loss and the pseudo R-squared (of McFadden's) give the same result. The same is not necessarily true for the probit.

Thus, we have four summary measures of the goodness of fit for probability models. None of them is perfect or easily interpretable on its own. Some are easier to compute than others, but that's not a major deal as all statistical software can be asked to compute all. One caveat is that the pseudo R-squared is reserved for logit and probit models and not calculated for linear probability models. But, when computed, all four can be used to compare and rank estimated probability models by how well their predicted probabilities fit the actual y variables in the data.

Most often, the four give the same ranking. Indeed, the R-squared and the Brier score always give the same ranking, and the pseudo R-squared and the log-loss give the same ranking with logit models. Thus, the choice between the four measures is not a very important choice in practice. We prefer the Brier score and have shown its formula because that's the simplest one, and it is the one used by many analysts who specialize in predictions.

> **Review Box 11.4 Measures of fit of probability models**
>
> There are several measures of fit used for estimated probability models:
>
> - We can compute and use the R-squared for comparing probability models, but it no longer has the interpretation we had with quantitative dependent variables.
> - The pseudo R-squared may be used to rank logit and probit models.
> - The Brier score measures the average distance between probability predictions and actual outcomes. It can be computed for all models.
> - The different measures often give the same ranking of models.

11.6 The Distribution of Predicted Probabilities

Beyond single numbers, we can evaluate the fit of estimated probability models with the help of informative visualizations. Recall that the $\hat{y}$–y plot is a good visualization tool for evaluating predictions of quantitative outcomes (Chapter 10, Section 10.12). It shows how predicted values are distributed around the line that represents the regression, and we can produce this graph for regressions with many right-hand-side variables.

With probability models, the $\hat{y}$–y plot is in fact the $\hat{y}^P$–y plot: the predicted values are predicted probabilities. The $\hat{y}^P$–y plot looks funny because y is binary: it is a picture with two rows of points. With a binary y we just have two values on the vertical axis, 0 and 1. The horizontal axis measures $\hat{y}^P$ so the picture shows all observations and their different $\hat{y}^P$ values for $y = 0$ in one row of points, and all $\hat{y}^P$ values for $y = 1$ in another row. In principle, those two rows show the two distributions of $\hat{y}^P$. But it's hard to see those distributions this way.

Instead, we can examine the two distributions of $\hat{y}^P$ in a more standard way, by looking at the two histograms: one histogram for observations with $y = 0$ and one histogram for observations with $y = 1$. And that is an informative comparison indeed. We'll see an illustration of this in our case study below.

But why should we compare these two distributions? Reasonable probability models should predict higher probabilities among the $y = 1$ observations. The larger the difference between the $y = 1$ and $y = 0$ groups in terms of predicted probabilities, the better the fit of a model. Perfect fit would be achieved when all $y = 1$ observations have higher predicted probabilities than all $y = 0$ observations. That would mean that the distributions of the predicted probabilities don't overlap across the two groups. Real-life predictions do not produce such perfect fits. But, intuitively, we could measure their fit by how little the two distributions (for the $y = 1$ and the $y = 0$ groups) overlap, or how far apart their means or medians are.

11.7 Bias and Calibration

Another tool for visualizing the fit of estimated probability models has a more specific goal: evaluating the **bias of the prediction**. Probability predictions are **unbiased** if they are right on average. Unbiasedness means that the average of predicted probabilities is equal to the actual probability of the outcome. If, in our data, 20% of observations have $y = 0$ and 80% have $y = 1$, and we predict the probability to be 80%, then our prediction is unbiased. Formally, with n observations, the bias is simply the difference between average predicted probability and average outcome:

$$Bias = \frac{1}{n}\sum_{i=1}^{n}\left(\hat{y}_i^P - y_i\right) = \overline{\hat{y}^P} - \overline{y} \tag{11.13}$$

If the prediction is unbiased, the bias is zero. A larger value of bias indicates a greater tendency to underestimate or overestimate the chance of an event. If a model predicts that the probability of defaulting on consumer loans is 20%, and we see that the proportion of defaults in the data is just 10%, then the prediction is biased upwards, predicting too many defaults.

Unbiasedness can be applied to conditional probabilities as well: the probability prediction for any value of x should be equal to the actual probability for that value of x. That is called **calibration**. A probability prediction is called well calibrated if the actual probability of the outcome is equal to the predicted probability for each and every value of the predicted probability.

Calibration is about how unbiased probability predictions are for each prediction. It requires comparing the actual proportion of observations with $y = 1$ with their predicted probabilities, for each predicted probability separately. If a probability model predicts 10% for some observations and 30% for other observations, calibration looks at the proportion for those with 10% predictions and those with 30% predictions separately. The prediction is well calibrated if the proportion of observations with $y = 1$ is indeed 10% among the observations for which the prediction is 10%, and the proportion of observations with $y = 1$ is indeed 30% among the observations for which the prediction is 30%.

A **calibration curve** is a visualization of these calculations. Its horizontal axis shows the values of all predicted probabilities $(\hat{y}^P)$. Its vertical axis shows the fraction of $y = 1$ observations for all observations with the corresponding predicted probability. Thus, in a well-calibrated case, the calibration curve is close to the 45 degree line. In a poorly calibrated case, the calibration curve deviates from the 45 degree line. Note that a model may be unbiased on average but not well calibrated. For instance, it may underestimate the probability when it's high and underestimate it when it's low.

When we want to produce a calibration curve, we often encounter a practical problem. Probability models often predict a variety of probability values. With many values for the predicted probabilities, we may have few observations to look at for each value. To circumvent this problem, a good practice is to group observations that are close to each other in terms of predicted probabilities, creating a few bins. For instance, we can create 10 bins, such as $[0, 0.1], \ldots, [0.9, 1]$. Then we can compute the calibration curve as the proportion of $y = 1$ observations within each bin. The more observations we have, the more bins we can allow. With millions of observations, we may be able to create bins of percentiles. For a few hundred observations, a handful of bins would be better. We'll show an example for a calibration curve with bins in our case study below.

11.B1 CASE STUDY – Are Australian Weather Forecasts Well Calibrated?

Data and calibration curve

This short case study illustrates when calibration is important and informative. We consider predictions of rain for the day following the prediction. In some countries, such predictions come as probabilities, in percentages, such as 0% chance of rain tomorrow, 10%, 20% chance of rain tomorrow, and so on. Thus, we can evaluate how well calibrated they are because they are probability predictions. To do so, we need data on predictions and actual rain. Using such data, we have to calculate the proportion of days with rain for all days for which the prediction was 0%, then do the same for all days for which the prediction was 10%, and so on. Perfect calibration would mean that when the prediction was 0%, people should never see rain, and when the prediction was 20%, they should see rain on one in every five days.

Note that weather forecasts are not produced by simple statistical probability models. They use data, but they feed the data into a more complex model that is a physical representation of how weather should change. Being well calibrated is essential for weather forecasts. Good calibration is important for gaining trust in those predictions.

To illustrate calibration, we collected data on rain forecast and actual rain for the Northern Australian city of Darwin, from the `australia-weather-forecasts` dataset. The data covers one year (350 days between May 3, 2015 to April 30, 2016), and for each day, a binary variable captures if it rained that day at Darwin airport. A rainy day is defined as a day when at least 1 mm rain had fallen. The forecast was made 39 hours before the start of each day. The probability forecasts were given in percentages, such as 0%, 1%, …; their range in the data is 0% to 88%. The average predicted probability is 21.5%, and it actually rained on 20% of days.

Figure 11.6 shows the results of the exercise. It's a calibration curve that summarizes all this information. Its horizontal axis shows the values of all predicted probabilities, in bins of probabilities with width of 0.1 (10%), with each point drawn at the average of predicted probabilities within the bin. We added an extra bin for the exact 0% prediction due to its special importance, and the last bin [0.9, 1] has no observations. Its vertical axis shows the percent of $y = 1$ observations (rainy days) for all observations with the corresponding predicted probability bin.

The figure suggests that prediction of rain in Australia is fairly well calibrated. The calibration curve lies close to the 45 degree line or somewhat below for low and medium probabilities, and

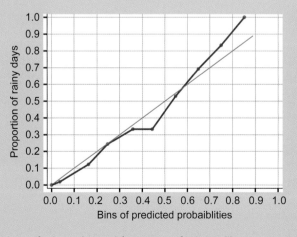

Figure 11.6   Predictions of rain and actual frequency of rain. Calibration curve

Note: Proportion of days with rain (vertical axis) for days with particular predicted probabilities of rain.
Source: `australia-weather-forecasts` dataset. Forecasts of rain 39 hours before start of day, Darwin, Australia, 2005/06. N=350.

somewhat above for higher ones. The results mean that people of Darwin, Australia can trust these forecasts in the sense that a 20% prediction of rain means they expect one in five such days to have at least 1 mm of rain. Only 15% of days have a higher probability of rain than 50%, and that part is not very well calibrated.

11.8 Refinement

For a prediction to be well calibrated is important, but it's not everything. Two predictions that are equally well calibrated may be very different in how useful they are for making decisions. Suppose, for example, that it rains about 20% of the days in a city in a year. Then, a prediction of 20% for each and every day of the year may be well calibrated. Yet such a prediction would not be very useful. In contrast, a well-calibrated prediction that predicts 0% of rain for some days, 10% for some days, and so on, is a lot more useful. Moreover, even if this latter kind of prediction is not as well calibrated, it can be a lot more useful than the well-calibrated simple average probability.

The point here is that we need variation in predicted probabilities besides calibration. Such variation is called **refinement** or **discrimination**. The larger the differences across observations in terms of predicted probabilities, the higher the refinement. A refined model may or may not be well calibrated. It's a different feature of predictions.

Comparing two predictions that are equally well calibrated, the one with greater refinement is always more useful. But sometimes there is a trade-off between calibration and refinement: a slightly less well calibrated but much more refined prediction is likely better, and, analogously, a much better calibrated but slightly less refined prediction is also likely better. What we need, therefore, is a measure that combines calibration and refinement.

It turns out that we have that measure already. The Brier score, introduced earlier, does just that. It can be decomposed into the sum of two terms, the square of the bias and a term measuring the lack of refinement (which we call nonrefinement here):

$$Brier = Bias^2 + NonRefinement \qquad (11.14)$$

Recall that the smaller the Brier score, the better. A Brier score is larger, indicating a worse prediction, if it is more biased or less refined. A Brier score is smaller, indicating a better prediction, if it is less biased or more refined. Comparing two predictions, one of which is more biased but also more refined, the Brier score combines these two and ranks the two predictions by balancing bias and refinement.

The calibration curve is a very useful visualization of how well probabilistic predictions do on average. It is also informative about refinement (how different the predicted values are), as it shows the range of predicted values on its horizontal axis. However, to produce a clear ranking of predictions, we advise using the Brier score or the other summary measures of probability predictions that we considered in Section 11.5.

Review Box 11.5 Bias, calibration, refinement

- Probability predictions are unbiased if they are right on average.
- The calibration curve is a useful visualization of how probability predictions are biased, or unbiased, for various values of those predictions.
- Comparing two predictions that are equally well calibrated, the one with greater refinement (more variation in predicted probabilities) is always better.

11.A4   CASE STUDY – Does Smoking Pose a Health risk?

Evaluating predicted probabilities

In the last part of our case study, we illustrate the various measures of fit for probability predictions, focusing on what they mean and how we can use them to rank various models.

Let's start with comparing the distributions of predicted probabilities by actual y values. Figures 11.7a and 11.7b show the distributions for the simple linear probability model and the rich linear probability model. Each graph shows two histograms laid over each other: one for observations with actual $y = 0$ (did not stay healthy) and one for observations with actual $y = 1$ (stayed healthy). In what follows, we will compare a simple and a complex (or rich) model, as well as look at various functional forms.

The simple LPM has one binary right-hand-side variable: current smoker. This model has two values of predicted probability: the probability of staying healthy for smokers (0.55) and the probability of staying healthy for non-smokers (0.62). Accordingly, the histograms have two bars, at these two predicted values, shown in Figure 11.7a. The height of each bar shows the proportion of individuals with the corresponding predicted probability. The full bars show these for those who stayed healthy in fact. The empty bars show these for those who did not. The proportion of individuals with prediction 0.62 is larger among those who stayed healthy, and that is how it should be as 0.62 is the larger predicted value. This model predicts higher probability of staying healthy for those who do stay healthy. But the difference between the two groups is small.

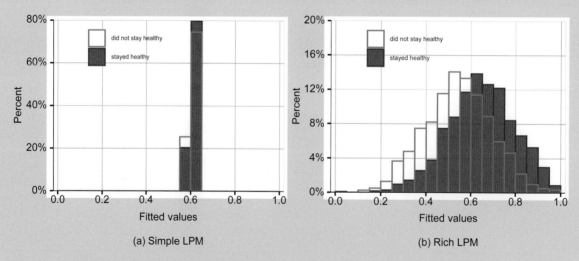

(a) Simple LPM   (b) Rich LPM

Figure 11.7   Staying healthy and the distribution of the predicted probability of staying healthy. Two linear probability models

Note: Linear probability models. The rich model includes several explanatory variables, see Table 11.2.
Source: `share-health` dataset. People of age 50 to 60 from 14 European countries who reported to be healthy in 2011. N=3109.

The rich LPM, the one with the many right-hand-side variables we examined in Table 11.2, has a range of predicted probabilities from close to zero to slightly over one. Figure 11.7b shows the histogram of the distribution of predicted values among those who stayed healthy (full bars) and those who did not. A larger part of the distribution covers higher predicted values among individuals who stayed healthy, as it should. But the two distributions overlap to a large extent. So this prediction is very far from producing a perfect fit, which would correspond to no overlap between the two distributions. However, the distributions have smaller overlap here than for the simple LPM. Not surprisingly, these two figures suggest that the richer model fits the dependent variable better.

The corresponding distributions for the logit and the probit models are similar to the LPM (you are invited to produce them as data exercises). The distribution of predicted probabilities among individuals who stayed healthy is more to the right but there is a large overlap. Based on those histograms, it is difficult to tell which of the three models fits the dependent variable better.

Table 11.4 shows the means and medians of these distributions. The more different these statistics are between the $y = 0$ and $y = 1$ groups, the better the fit of the probability models.

Table 11.4	Comparing probability models – mean and median			
	(1) Simple LPM	(2) Rich LPM	(3) Logit	(4) Probit
Mean if didn't stay healthy ($y = 0$)	0.603	0.543	0.542	0.542
Mean if stayed healthy ($y = 1$)	0.606	0.645	0.646	0.646
Median if didn't stay healthy ($y = 0$)	0.620	0.543	0.544	0.545
Median if stayed healthy ($y = 1$)	0.620	0.647	0.655	0.653

Note: Rich LPM includes several variable, see Table 11.2.

Source: `share-health` dataset. People of age 50 to 60 from 14 European countries who reported to be healthy in 2011. N=3109.

Both the mean and the median predicted probabilities are very close across the two groups for the simple LPM. As for the rich probability models, the difference between the two groups is larger, and it is very similar across the linear probability, logit, and probit models. Both for means and medians it is about 0.1, or 10 percentage points. These statistics suggest that the richer model provides a better fit than the simple LPM, but the three rich models produce very similar fits.

Next, let's turn to calibration. We compare two predictions: the rich linear probability model and the logit model with the same right-hand-side variables. For each, we created bins of their predicted probabilities. The bins are of width 0.05, except the first bin that covers 0 to 0.20 and the last bin that covers 0.85 to 1.05 (a few predictions of the LPM go beyond 1). So, our bins are 0–0.20, 0.20–0.25,..., 0.80–0.85, 0.85–1.05. Then, within each bin, we calculated the proportion of people who actually stayed healthy. To plot the calibration curve, we need to assign a value to each bin so we can fix its place on the horizontal axis. We assigned the value of the average prediction within each bin to represent the bin. Figure 11.8 shows the calibration curves.

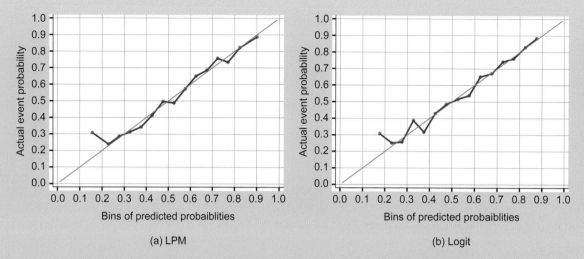

(a) LPM   **(b) Logit**

Figure 11.8   Calibration curves for the predictions of the linear probability and logit models

Note: Proportion of people who stayed healthy (vertical axis) in bins of predicted probability of staying healthy. Rich models, for details, see Table 11.2.
Source: `share-health` dataset. People of age 50 to 60 from 14 European countries who reported to be healthy in 2011. N=3109.

Both the linear probability and the logit predictions are well calibrated. Both calibration curves stay close to the 45 degree line. Thus, comparing these graphs suggests that the predictions of the different models are almost equally well calibrated.

Finally, let's turn to the four summary measures of goodness of fit: R-squared, Brier score, pseudo R-squared, and log-loss. Table 11.5 shows the four statistics for the three models (LPM, logit, probit) that include the rich set of right-hand-side variables.

Table 11.5   Statistics of goodness of fit for the probability predictions of three models

Statistic	LPM	Logit	Probit
R-squared	0.103	0.104	0.104
Brier score	0.215	0.214	0.214
Pseudo R-squared	n.a.	0.080	0.080
Log-loss	−0.621	−0.617	−0.617

Note: Rich linear probability model, logit and probit. See Table 11.2. for details.
Source: `share-health` dataset. People of age 50 to 60 from 14 European countries who reported to be healthy in 2011. N=3109.

The main message of Table 11.5 is that the ranking of the three models is the same whichever statistic we look at. Recall that better predictions have a higher R-squared and pseudo R-squared and a lower Brier score and a smaller log-loss in absolute values. The predictions from both the logit and the probit are of the same quality, and both are better than the predictions from the linear probability model. The differences are small, so we probably wouldn't make a huge mistake with linear probability either. But, if we care about prediction, it's better to use the logit or the probit.

Which one of the two doesn't really matter. This is in fact what we expected. We know that the logit and the probit should be better at prediction, and we know that the two are usually equally good with binary dependent variables.

This concludes our case study. What did we learn from it? Most importantly, we learned that 50- to 60-year-old healthy smokers are less likely to stay healthy than non-smokers of the same gender, age, education, income, and body weight, whether they exercise or not. The difference is 6 percentage points, which is about 10% lower than the same probability for non-smokers. We also learned that there is little difference in this between those who never smoked and those who quit smoking. These results are from 14 European countries in 2015. They probably generalize to other rich countries and for the near future.

Did we show that smoking makes people less healthy? Not really. To do so we should have done a ceteris paribus comparison, conditioning on all variables that may affect smoking and health at the same time, such as diet and other aspects of lifestyle. It is possible that smokers tend to live less healthy lives in general, which makes them less likely to stay healthy. We did condition on some indicators of healthy life (exercising, BMI), but we didn't have much more in the data. At the same time, our results are consistent with the harmful effect of smoking.

What did we learn about probability models? Most importantly, we saw that the linear probability model produced coefficient estimates that were just fine. The more complicated logit and probit marginal difference estimates were virtually the same as the linear probability estimates. In terms of predicted probabilities, all three models produced well-calibrated results. The logit and the probit performed equally well, and both performed a little better than the linear probability model, although that difference is very small.

11.9 Using Probability Models for Other Kinds of y Variables

Probability models can uncover patterns of association with a binary y variable. There are many variables of great importance that are naturally defined as binary variables: whether an online ad induces a customer to make a purchase, whether a debtor repays their debt, whether a political candidate gets elected, and so on.

But there are other kinds of y variables that are not born binary but are not quantitative either, or have other issues that may make the linear regression not necessarily a good choice to analyze them – at least not as they are, without transforming them. Such variables include nominal variables or ordinal variables (see Chapter 2, Section 2.1), or duration variables (e.g., for how long did an employee stay with the company?).

Quite often, we can transform such y variables into binary ones and apply all we learned in this chapter to analyze them. Typically, such a transformation results in loss of information in the original variable. But, in exchange, the probability model applied to the binary version can reveal something important and interesting in a transparent way. There are many sophisticated statistical models that can deal with such variables, but learning them requires more training, and many such models work only under specific circumstances. The other alternative – applying regression analysis to the original y variable – often makes less sense than a probability model, and it may even produce biased results. We briefly discuss three cases.

First, **nominal variables**, also called **multinomial variables** for having several categories. These are qualitative variables with more than two categories, and there is no clear ordering between the categories. Examples include brand of product, name of political party, city of location. Nominal variables may be stored as text or number, but the numbers in themselves don't have any meaning. So, even if stored as numbers, treating them as a quantitative y variable in a regression would produce results that make no sense. Instead, what we can do is to create a series of binary variables from them and analyze these one by one. For example, when analyzing which brand of chocolate a customer chose, a 0–1 variable may denote Lindt, another 0–1 variable may denote Godiva, and so on, and perhaps a last 0–1 variable may denote if the customer chose not to buy any chocolate. Then, we can estimate separate probability models for each of the 0–1 variables.

The second type are **ordinal variables**, also called **ordered categorical variables**. Ordinal variables are qualitative variables, too, but with a ranking. Their categories are ordered in an unambiguous way, such as whether someone doesn't agree, agrees, or strongly agrees with a statement, or the degree to which somebody likes a product (not at all, neutral, somewhat, very much). We often assign numbers to these categories (e.g., 1 for doesn't agree, ..., 4 for agrees a lot).

Running regressions with such numbers as the y variable is not meaningless at all. If an x variable (say, age) has a positive coefficient, it shows that observations with higher x values (older people) tend to have a higher ranked y variable (agree more). However, such linear regressions assume that differences between values of y are equally important for the estimated patterns of associations. But they may not be; for example, the difference between agreeing and agreeing a lot to a political statement may be less important than agreeing or being neutral.

Here is where converting an ordered qualitative y variable into a binary one may make more sense. Doing so we join some categories into the same value, focusing the question on the difference between two sets of values. Indeed, this is how we created our "healthy" and "staying healthy" variables in our case study. We took the 5-valued ordinal self-rated health variable (poor, fair, good, very good, excellent) and created a binary healthy variable (1 if very good or excellent, 0 if poor, fair or good). This decision was motivated by the fact that most respondents with no severe medical conditions rated themselves as very good or excellent.

The third type of variable we consider here is different. **Duration variables**, also called **survival time variables** are quantitative variables that measure duration in time. Examples include the length of life, for how long employees stay with a company, or how long it takes for a child with measles to recover. Linear regressions would be fine to analyze such y variables, although there are more complicated alternatives, too. The issue with such variables is that their analysis is often plagued by data censoring.

In general, **data censoring** means that, for some of the observations, we don't know the value of the y variable, only that it's greater or less than some value. For duration data, censoring means that, for some observations, we don't get to see how long the duration is, only that it's longer than some value. Data on how long people live after a medical intervention usually stops after some time, with some people still alive whose length of life thus remains unknown. For these people we know that they lived to be at least some age. Similarly, data that follows employees from their hiring can tell how long some of them stayed with the company if they left already. But employees still with the company are known to have stayed at least as long as the time since they were hired, not how much more they will stay.

With censored data on y, we may still run a linear regression, and it would not be meaningless. The sign of the coefficient estimates would be informative, but the magnitudes would not be straightforward to interpret. That's because they mix two things: associations with the expected duration y and associations with whether that duration is greater than the censoring threshold. A seemingly better alternative, restricting the analysis to not censored observations only, is actually a worse solution, as here even the signs of the coefficients may not be informative.

A better alternative is to create a binary variable, indicating whether the duration is at least as long as a threshold value. With some ingenuity and luck, we may be able to set the threshold in such a way that censoring of the original duration is not an issue anymore.

For example, we may analyze data on employees who were hired two or more years ago by the company. Then, we would create a binary y indicating whether the employee stayed with the company for two years or not. This way we would lose information: we wouldn't distinguish between those who left within a few months versus almost two years. In exchange, we have a y variable that is not affected by data censoring and which we can put on the left-hand side of a probability model and get nicely interpretable estimates. In a sense, this is what we did in our case study. The big question there was health and smoking, and we translated this into the question of whether non-smokers stay healthy for a longer time. Instead of a quantitative duration y variable measuring how long people stay in good health (after reducing the 5-scale ordered health variable into good health or not), we examined a binary variable: whether people stayed healthy for four years.

Thus, probability models are a powerful method. They are relatively straightforward to estimate, and their coefficients (or the marginal differences) are straightforward to interpret. There are various tools to evaluate how well predicted probabilities fit the actual y variables, and those tools tend to agree on ranking the various models. Moreover, as we discussed here, many y variables that would be problematic to put into linear regressions can be transformed to binary ones and put into probability models. That's often a good solution – complementing, or even substituting, more sophisticated models that are designed to deal with such y variables.

11.10 Main Takeaways

Probability models have a binary y; they capture differences in the probability of $y = 1$ for different values of the x variables.

- To uncover patterns of association, the linear probability model (linear regression) is usually a good method.
- For logit and probit models, instead of the estimated coefficients, it's better to interpret the marginal differences computed from them.
- For prediction, logit and probit are usually better choices than the linear probability model.

PRACTICE QUESTIONS

1. The linear probability model is a linear regression. Linear regressions are designed to analyze conditional expectations. Why do they work here?
2. The linear probability model may produce predicted values that are less than zero or more than one. How can that happen and when is it a problem?
3. What is a logit model, what is a probit model, and why would we want to estimate them instead of linear probability?

4. Does a unit difference in x translate into a difference in the conditional probability $P[y = 1|x]$ the same way across the values of x for a linear probability model? For a logit model?

5. What are marginal differences and why are we interested in them?

6. List two measures of fit of probability predictions and explain their intuitive content and what we expect from each for a better prediction.

7. When do we say that a probability prediction is unbiased? Give an example.

8. When do we say that a probability prediction is well calibrated? Give an example.

9. When do we say that a probability prediction is more refined than another probability prediction, and why is that a good thing?

10. Whether a family purchased a car last year (1 if yes, 0 if no) is regressed on whether the family had an unemployed member last year (1 if yes, 0 if no). The intercept is 0.05, the slope is −0.04. Write down the regression and interpret its coefficients.

11. Whether a family purchased a car last year (1 if yes, 0 if no) is regressed on log family income last year. The intercept is −0.15, the slope is 0.05. Write down the regression and interpret its coefficients.

12. In a logit model the dependent variable is whether a family purchased a car last year (1 if yes, 0 if no), and the explanatory variable is log family income last year. The intercept is −1.60, the slope is 0.45. The marginal difference corresponding to log family income is 0.05. Write down the model and interpret these numbers.

13. Can you compute the R-squared from a linear probability model? How? Does it have the same interpretation as in a linear regression with a quantitative left-hand-side variable? Can you use the R-squared to compare the fit of linear probability models or would you rather use the Brier score?

14. You are examining whether family structure is related to whether young men smoke, using data on men from 2018 from your country. In a linear probability model with smoking (0–1) as the y variable and age, education, whether the person lives with a spouse or partner, and whether the person lives with children as x variables, you find that the coefficient on living with children is −0.2, $SE = 0.05$. Interpret this coefficient, create a 95% CI, and interpret that, too.

15. In the previous example (young men's smoking and whether they have children), can you infer from the results that having children makes men quit smoking? Why or why not?

DATA EXERCISES

Easier and/or shorter exercises are denoted by [*]; harder and/or longer exercises are denoted by [**].

1. Use the `share-health` dataset and pick two countries. Carry out an appropriate analysis to answer the question of our case study in the two countries separately. Compare and discuss your results. [*]

2. Use the `share-health` dataset and pick two countries. Carry out an appropriate analysis to see how the probability of staying healthy is related to gender in the two countries separately. You may or may not want to condition on other covariates; argue for your choices. Compare and discuss your results. [*]

3. Use the `share-health` dataset to examine how exercising is related to income and family factors. In the data, the variable "br015" denotes the frequency of sport and exercise activities.

Using this categorical variable, create a binary one using the threshold of your choice, and argue for your choice. Estimate a probability model of your choice with age, income, and family circumstances as explanatory variables. Argue for your choices and discuss your results. [*]

4. Use the `hotels-europe` dataset and pick a city. Use hotel rating to create a binary variable: highly_rated=1 if rating $\geq$ 4, 0 otherwise. Examine how high rating is related to the other hotel features in the data. Estimate linear probability, logit, and probit models with distance and stars as explanatory variables. Compare coefficients, marginal differences, and predicted probabilities, and discuss your results. [*]

5. Use the `wms-management-survey` dataset and pick a country. Choose one from the 18 score variables on the quality of various aspects of management and create a binary variable for values 4 or greater to denote high management quality in that area. Are firms that export a larger share of their products more likely to have higher quality management in the area you picked? Estimate a linear probability model, a logit and a probit model, and compare their results. Do the same after conditioning on employment and industry. Discuss your results and conclude whether the linear probability model is good enough to answer your question. [*]

REFERENCES AND FURTHER READING

On probability predictions, a nice non-technical book is Silver (2012).

There is a very large literature on the effects of smoking. Cornfield et al. (1959) is a classic study; a more recent study, using probability models, is Sloan et al. (2006).

11.U1   UNDER THE HOOD: SATURATED MODELS

Saturated models are linear regressions that are non-parametric regressions at the same time. That can happen if there is only one possible functional form for each right-hand-side variable. An important example of a saturated model is a regression that has only one binary variable on the right-hand side. For example, a simple linear regression of staying healthy on smoking (a binary variable) is a non-parametric regression at the same time: the constant is the probability of staying healthy among non-smokers in the dataset, and the slope is the probability difference between smokers and non-smokers in the dataset. The same probabilities would be predicted by a logit or probit model with smoking on the right-hand side.

Regressions with more binary right-hand-side variables are saturated if those variables are all interacted so that they cover all possible combinations. For example, a linear regression of staying healthy on smoking and being female (two binary variables) is a saturated model if it includes smoking, female, and smoking interacted with female on the right-hand side. These three explanatory variables cover all four possibilities of gender and smoking. A regression with three binary explanatory variables is saturated if it has all three interacted with each other. For example, with smoking, being female, and exercising we need four additional variables: their pairwise interactions and their three-way interaction. Those variables together would cover all combinations of smoking, gender, and exercising (e.g., a non-smoker exercising woman, a smoker exercising man, and other combinations).

Predicted probabilities from saturated models are always between zero and one. This is because they are equal to the observed relative frequencies in the data. Thus, if saturated, the linear probability model is as good as, and essentially the same as, any other probability model, including the logit or the probit.

11.U2

UNDER THE HOOD: MAXIMUM LIKELIHOOD ESTIMATION AND SEARCH ALGORITHMS

Recall that we (or, more accurately, statistical software packages) calculate the coefficients of linear regressions using the method of OLS (ordinary least squares). When applying OLS, we obtain coefficients that lead to the smallest possible (squared) deviations of the predicted values from the actual values. OLS gives formulae for the estimated coefficients, into which we can plug the values of variables in the dataset.

The estimated coefficients of logit and probit models are obtained using a different method, called **maximum likelihood estimation**. We can think of maximum likelihood estimation as another way to get coefficients that give the best fit to the data. It is a more widely applicable method than OLS, but it requires more assumptions to work.

Maximum likelihood estimation starts with assuming a theoretical distribution for the dependent variable (y) conditional on the explanatory variables ($x_1, x_2, ...$). That theoretical distribution is called the likelihood function. It is a conditional distribution so it tells how likely certain values of y are if we observe specific values of $x_1, x_2, ...$ Hence the name likelihood. The principle of maximum likelihood estimation is that it produces coefficient values that make the theoretical distribution the most likely distribution for the observed data.

The likelihood is first specified for each observation separately, and then for the entire dataset. Consider a logit model with two explanatory variables, x_1 and x_2. The likelihood of observing a particular value y_i for observations i with particular values x_{1i} and x_{2i} is the probability that we observe that particular y value conditional on observing those particular x values. It is $P[y = 1|x_{1i}, x_{2i}] = \Lambda(\beta_0 + \beta_1 x_{1i} + \beta_2 x_{2i})$ if y_i happens to be one; it is $P[y = 0|x_{1i}, x_{2i}] = 1 - P[y = 1|x_{1i}, x_{2i}] = 1 - \Lambda(\beta_0 + \beta_1 x_{1i} + \beta_2 x_{2i})$ if y_i happens to be zero.

To write down the likelihood for an observation in a single formula, we can apply a little trick that combines these two probabilities. This trick makes use of the fact that y is a binary variable with values 0 or 1, and thus $1 - y = 1$ when $y = 0$. Written this way, the likelihood of observing a particular value of y_i is

$$\ell_i = P[y = 1|x_{1i}, x_{2i}]^{y_i} (1 - P[y = 1|x_{1i}, x_{2i}])^{(1-y_i)} \tag{11.15}$$

This formula simply says that the likelihood of observing the particular value for y_i is equal to:

- the probability that y is one if y_i is one (the first part is raised to the power of one, the second part to the power of zero, so the second part equals one);
- the probability that y is zero if y_i happens to be zero (the first part is raised to the power of zero and is thus equal to one, the second part to the power of one).

From the likelihood of a particular observation, we can get to the likelihood of all observations in the data by realizing that the latter is the joint probability of each individual probability. If observations are independent, as we assume they are in cross-sectional data, then the joint probability is simply the product of all individual probabilities. So the likelihood of observing the particular y values in the dataset conditional on having the particular x values is

$$L = \prod \ell_i = \prod \left(P[y = 1 | x_{1i}, x_{2i}]^{y_i} (1 - P[y = 1 | x_{1i}, x_{2i}])^{(1 - y_i)} \right) \tag{11.16}$$

where the symbol $\prod$ means multiplying the things after it (similar to summing, only here it's multiplication).

The goal is to find the coefficients inside those $P[y = 1 | x_{1i}, x_{2i}] = \Lambda(\beta_0 + \beta_1 x_{1i} + \beta_2 x_{2i})$ that give the highest value of this L. It turns out that this goal is easier if we try to find the coefficients that make the log of this L the largest (as the log is a monotonic function, whatever makes log L the largest, makes L the largest, too):

$$\log L = \sum \log \ell_i = \sum \left(y_i \log P[y = 1 | x_{1i}, x_{2i}] + (1 - y_i) \log(1 - P[y = 1 | x_{1i}, x_{2i}]) \right) \tag{11.17}$$

It turns out that this maximum likelihood problem does not yield a solution that is a formula, unlike the OLS problem. Instead, iterative algorithms are used to find the coefficients that make the likelihood the largest. These are called search algorithms as they search for the best values of the coefficients. We'll introduce algorithms more generally in Chapter 13, Section 13.12.

There are various search algorithms we can use. The most intuitive but often least practical is grid search that tries every possible value combination of the coefficients (or, to be more precise, divides the range of potential coefficient values into intervals, called grids, and tries values in each grid). Other algorithms start with a starting value for the coefficients and examine whether the likelihood increases if the values are changed in one direction or the other. We do not discuss the details of search algorithms; statistical software applies methods that are well suited to the estimation problem at hand.

Fortunately, both the logit and the probit are "well behaved" for maximum likelihood estimation so that good search algorithms always find the best coefficients. It also turns out that OLS is also a maximum likelihood estimation, and also a well-behaved one, if the theoretical distribution of y conditional on $x_1, x_2, \ldots$ is normal; in that case the maximum likelihood estimates are exactly the same as the OLS estimates of the coefficients.

Besides coefficient estimates, maximum likelihood gives estimates for standard errors as well. It does not in general give an intuitive measure of fit such as R-squared. There are likelihood-based measures of fit that are somewhat more difficult to interpret; of them, we briefly discussed pseudo R-squared.

The important things to recall from this rather technical section is that the logit and probit coefficients and their appropriate standard errors are straightforward to obtain using statistical software. The underlying method is quite complicated, but modern computers can easily deal with it. The method is called maximum likelihood, and the solution to the method is found by appropriate search algorithms.

11.U3 UNDER THE HOOD: FROM LOGIT AND PROBIT COEFFICIENTS TO MARGINAL DIFFERENCES

Marginal differences show how, on average, a unit difference in a right-hand-side variable is associated with a difference in the probability of the left-hand-side variable (conditional on all other right-hand-side variables included in the model). They are analogous to the interpretation of linear regression coefficients. Here we give some detail on how we can obtain marginal differences once the coefficients of a logit model or a probit model are obtained (via maximum likelihood estimation, see the previous subsection).

Consider again a probability model with two right-hand-side variables, x_1 and x_2, each of which is continuous. With some calculus we can derive the marginal difference associated with x_1. Let's start with differences in the probability associated with unit differences in x_1, which is the partial derivative of the conditional probability:

$$\frac{\partial P[y = 1 | x_1, x_2]}{\partial x_1} \tag{11.18}$$

In the logit model that translates to

$$\frac{\partial P[y = 1 | x_1, x_2]}{\partial x_1} = \frac{\partial \Lambda(\beta_0 + \beta_1 x_1 + \beta_2 x_2)}{\partial x_1} = \beta_1 \lambda(\beta_0 + \beta_1 x_1 + \beta_2 x_2) \tag{11.19}$$

where $\lambda(.)$ is the first derivative of the logistic function $\Lambda(z) = \frac{exp(z)}{1+exp(z)}$, and it turns out to equal $\lambda(z) = \frac{1}{1+exp(z)}$.

The way that the probability of $y = 1$ is associated with a unit difference in x_1 is the logit coefficient of the variable times a number that comes from a function that contains all other coefficients and variables as well. This number is less than one so the marginal difference is smaller than the coefficient, but how much smaller depends on the value of the variable as well as all other variables.

The marginal difference is the average of all these differences in the dataset. To emphasize that this average is across all observations in the data, we add the i subscript to the variables:

$$MargDiff(x_1) = \frac{1}{n} \sum \frac{\partial P[y = 1 | x_{1i}, x_{2i}]}{\partial x_{1i}} = \beta_1 \frac{1}{n} \sum \lambda(\beta_0 + \beta_1 x_{1i} + \beta_2 x_{2i}) \tag{11.20}$$

where we moved β_1 in front of the sum because it is the same for all observations, and to highlight that we can think of marginal differences as the respective coefficients multiplied by the average of a complicated function that involves all coefficients and all variables in the model.

Marginal differences in probit models are derived in an analogous way, with the partial derivatives taken with respect to the appropriate Φ function. Recall that $\Phi(.)$ is the cumulative standard normal distribution function; its first derivative is $\varphi(.)$, the standard normal density function.

$$\frac{\partial P[y = 1 | x_1, x_2]}{\partial x_1} = \frac{\partial \Phi(\beta_0 + \beta_1 x_1 + \beta_2 x_2)}{\partial x_1} = \beta_1 \varphi(\beta_0 + \beta_1 x_1 + \beta_2 x_2) \tag{11.21}$$

Similarly to the logit case, this derivative depends not only on the corresponding probit coefficient β_1 but also on the value of x_1 and all other coefficients and variables on the right-hand side. It, too, varies across observations with different values of x_1 and x_2. The marginal difference is, again, the average of these partial derivatives,

$$MargDiff(x_1) = \frac{1}{n} \sum \frac{\partial P[y - 1 | x_{1i}, x_{2i}]}{\partial x_{1i}} = \beta_1 \frac{1}{n} \sum \varphi(\beta_0 + \beta_1 x_{1i} + \beta_2 x_{2i}) \tag{11.22}$$

Note that with binary right-hand-side variables we cannot take derivatives. In their case differences are computed: $P[y = 1 | x_1 = 1, x_2] - P[y = 1 | x_1 = 0, x_2]$. These differences, again, depend on all coefficients and variables. The corresponding marginal difference is the average of these differences.

The standard errors of marginal differences are hard to compute as there are complicated nonlinear functions involved, with many coefficients. The most straightforward method is to do bootstrap: estimate models and calculate marginal differences in bootstrap subsamples and take their standard deviation across the subsamples. Statistical software that produces marginal differences with logit and probit models also computes the corresponding bootstrap standard errors.

12 Regression with Time Series Data

How to carry out regression analysis with time series data, what special problems it may have, and how to address those problems

Motivation

You are considering investing in a company stock, and you want to know how risky that investment is. In finance, a relevant measure of risk relates returns on a company stock to market returns: a company stock is considered risky if it tends to move in the direction of the market, and the more it moves in that direction, the riskier it is. You have downloaded data on daily stock prices for many years. How should you define returns? How should you assess whether and to what extent returns on the company stock move together with market returns?

Heating and cooling are potentially important uses of electricity. To investigate how weather conditions affect electricity consumption, you have collected data on temperature and residential electricity consumption in a hot region. How should you estimate the association between temperature and electricity consumption? How should you define the variables of interest, and how should you prepare the data, which has daily observations on temperature and monthly observations on electricity consumption? Should you worry about the fact that both electricity consumption and temperature vary a lot across months within years, and if yes, what should you do about it?

Time series data is often used to analyze business, economic, and policy questions. Time series data presents additional opportunities as well as additional challenges for regression analysis. Unlike cross-sectional data, it enables examining how y changes when x changes, and it also allows us to examine what happens to y right away or with a delay. However, variables in time series data come with some special features that affect how we should estimate regressions, and how we can interpret their coefficients.

   In this chapter we discuss the most important features of time series variables, such as trends, seasonality, random walk, and serial correlation. We explain why those features make regression analysis challenging and what we can do about them. In particular, we discuss why it's usually a good idea to transform both y and x variables into differences, or relative differences. We introduce two methods to get appropriate standard error estimates in time series regressions: the Newey–West standard error estimator and including the lagged y variable on the right-hand side. We also discuss how we can estimate delayed associations by adding lags of x to a time series regression, and how we can directly estimate cumulative, or long run, associations in such a regression. We also discuss how to present time series data graphically, especially when interested in comparing multiple variables.

The first case study, **Returns on a company stock and market returns**, uses the `stocks-sp500` dataset to estimate the extent to which monthly returns on a technology company stock in the USA move together with the Standard and Poor's 500 stock market index. This case study illustrates simple time series regression with relative changes as variables. The second case study in this chapter, **Electricity consumption and temperature**, uses the `arizona-electricity` dataset to examine residential electricity consumption and temperature in a particularly hot city: Phoenix, Arizona, in the United States. This case study illustrates how to handle and interpret seasonality and lagged associations, and how to estimate standard errors in time series regressions.

Learning outcomes

After working through this chapter, you should be able to:

- identify questions and data that call for and lend themselves to time series regression analysis;
- identify issues in time series data that may affect regression analysis;
- specify and estimate regressions that address the issues of time series data;
- present the results of time series regression analysis in an informative way;
- interpret the results of time series regressions and their relationship to the questions of the analysis.

12.1 Preparation of Time Series Data

As introduced in Chapter 1, time series data has observations that refer to the same unit but different points in time. Variables in time series data show measurements at those different points in time. Examples include the daily price of company stock; monthly price and quantity sold of a single product on a single market; and quarterly observations of inflation, GDP, and other macroeconomic variables of a single economy.

Before estimating a regression with time series data, we need to understand some concepts specific to time series data. We also need to address problems with time series data on top of the usual issues we discussed in Chapter 2.

Observations in time series data are usually denoted by t, and are typically numbered from 1 through T. The notation of a variable y in a time series is usually $y_t, t = 1, 2, ..., T$. The difference between time series observations is the **frequency of the time series**; it can vary from seconds to years. Time series with more frequent observations are said to have higher frequency: monthly frequency is higher than yearly frequency, but it is lower than daily frequency.

Time series frequency may also be irregular with gaps in-between. **Gaps in time series data** can be viewed as missing values of variables. But they tend to have specific causes. Data from the stock market is not available for weekends and other days when the market is closed; sales of a retail store are not available for days when the store is closed. Often, we can ignore such gaps and pretend that the time series has no gaps so that, for example, Monday is the day after Friday, just like Tuesday is the day after Monday. When we want to explore whether gaps make a difference, it's good practice to create one or more binary variables denoting the changes that occur over gap periods.

To run a regression of y on x in time series data, the two variables need to be at the same time series frequency. When the time series frequencies of y and x are different, we need to adjust one of them. Most often that means aggregating the variable at higher frequency (e.g., from weekly to monthly). With flow variables, such as sales, aggregation means adding up; with stock variables and other kinds of variables, such as prices, it is often taking an average (recall our discussion of flow and stock variables in Chapter 2, Section 2.1).

Consider an example of a retailer that wants to examine sales of a product at various prices. That comparison involves two variables: sales, which is a flow variable and price, which is not a flow variable. If sales are measured per week and price is measured per day, the time series frequencies are not the same, and we need to do something. Here we need to aggregate price to weekly frequency, and the best choice is to take the average price. If, on the other hand, sales are at daily frequency and price is at weekly frequency, it is sales that we need to aggregate to weekly frequency, and this means creating total weekly sales by adding up the daily values within each week.

Once variables are at the same time series frequency, the next step is to plot the time series. With two time series variables y and x, we may show the two on the same graph. That may require using two different vertical axes with different scales.

Plotting the time series of variables helps assess whether they have **extreme values**. Just as we can see extreme values on a histogram, a time series graph shows them too, here as a spike (or trench). Indeed, many time series may have a few extreme values. As we saw in Chapter 5, Section 5.A1, it is very rare to have the S&P500 stock market price index change by more than 5% a day. Yet, on October 19, 1987, the S&P500 fell 20.5%.

As usual, whether to do anything to extreme values and, if yes, what to do with them, is a choice we have to make. Let's re-iterate our advice that we gave earlier in Chapter 3, Section 3.4. We should keep observations with extreme values in the data unless we are sure they are an error, or we decide that it's better to analyze the data without extreme values because that's a better way to answer our question.

In practice, we make that second choice more often if it's about the x variable. Excluding observations with non-erroneous extreme values of the y variable is rarely a good choice. In any case, we should make conscious choices about extreme values, document such choices, and carry out robustness checks with other alternatives if our choice is not evidently the best one.

For example, we may analyze the daily sales of an ice cream parlour together with weather forecast data from the preceding days, to help predict the next day's sales based on today's weather forecasts. Eventually, we want to run a regression, in which y is sales and x is the forecast of highest temperature. Suppose that, after plotting the two time series, we realize that on one summer day, our data shows unusually low sales. Further investigation reveals that there was a power outage at noon that day that led to shutting down sales for the rest of the day. This is not an error, and it is our y variable, so the general advice is to keep this observation. Yet we may also argue that it doesn't belong in the data. What to do is not obvious. One choice here is to carry out the analysis in two ways: with or without this observation. Most likely that decision won't make any difference in our main result of how weather forecasts help predict next day's sales. Including a separate right-hand-side variable for special time periods such as a power outage is a good solution; but it helps prediction only if we know when they would occur.

Review Box 12.1 Time series data preparation

- Figuring out the right frequency is essential. Sometimes, aggregation is necessary.
- Gaps in time series are frequent. We often ignore them or create binary variables to denote them.
- Extreme values are easy to spot on time series graphs. As usual a good solution is to keep them in the data; we may include binary variables to denote them.

12.2   Trend and Seasonality

There are several features of time series data that have consequences for regression analysis. In this section, we introduce those features. We'll discuss their consequences for regressions in Section 12.5.

A fundamental feature of time series data is that variables evolve with time. They may hover around a stable average value, or they may drift upwards or downwards. A variable in time series data follows a **trend** if it tends to change in one direction; in other words, it has a tendency to increase or decrease. Because of such systematic changes, later observations of trending variables tend to be different from earlier observations.

A time series variable follows a positive trend if its change is positive on average. It follows a negative trend if its change is negative on average. A change in a variable, also called the first difference (FD) of the variable, is denoted by Δ ($\Delta y_t = y_t - y_{t-1}$). A positive trend and a negative trend are defined as follows:

$$\text{Positive trend: } E[\Delta y_t] > 0 \tag{12.1}$$

$$\text{Negative trend: } E[\Delta y_t] < 0 \tag{12.2}$$

We say that the trend is **linear** if the change is the same on average as time passes. We say the trend is **exponential** if the relative change in the variable is the same on average as time passes. As usual, we can calculate such relative changes directly, in percentage changes, or approximate them as log changes. In terms of the variable itself, an exponential trend means larger and larger increases as time passes.

$$\text{Linear trend: } E[\Delta y_t] \approx \textit{constant over time} \tag{12.3}$$

$$\text{Exponential trend: } E[\frac{\Delta y_t}{y_{t-1}}] \approx \textit{constant over time} \tag{12.4}$$

Variables in business and economics often follow an exponential trend due to the multiplicative nature of the mechanisms behind them. Typical examples include prices (price changes are often in percentages, be they temporary sales or permanent increases due to inflation) or national income (growth rates in GDP tend to be relatively stable percentages).

Besides a potential trend, another important property of many time series variables is **seasonality**. Seasonality means that the value of the variable is expected to follow a cyclical pattern, tracking the seasons of the year, days of the week, or hours of the day.

Similarly to trends, seasonality may be linear, when the seasonal differences are constant. Seasonality may also be exponential, if relative differences (that may be approximated by log differences) are constant. Many economic activities follow seasonal variation over the year, and through the week or day. Seasonality in most economic variables is relative: gasoline sales may tend to be higher by, say, 20% in summer months; CO_2 emission in a European economy may be lower, on average, by 30% in spring months.

A time series variable y follows a trend if it changes on average: its later values tend to be different from its earlier values.

- Linear trend: $E[\Delta y_t] \approx constant\ over\ time$
- Exponential trend: $E[\frac{\Delta y_t}{y_t}] \approx constant\ over\ time$

A time series variable y has seasonality if it tends to follow a cyclical pattern (varying with seasons of the year, days of the week, hours of the day).

12.3 Stationarity, Non-stationarity, Random Walk

Understanding trends and seasonality is important because they make regression analysis challenging. They are examples of a broader concept, non-stationarity. **Stationarity** means stability; non-stationarity means the lack of stability. Stationary time series variables have the same expected value and the same distribution at all times. Trends and seasonality violate stationarity because the expected value is different at different times. With a positive trend, the expected value increases over time; with a negative trend, the expected value decreases over time; with seasonality, the expected value follows a regular cycle.

Another common kind of non-stationarity is the **random walk**. Time series variables that follow a random walk change in random, unpredictable ways. Whatever the current value of the variable and whatever its previous change was, the next change may be anything: positive or negative, small or large. As a formula, y_t follows a random walk if its value at time t equals its previous value plus a completely random term, which we denote by e_t:

$$y_t = y_{t-1} + e_t \tag{12.5}$$

The random term (e_t) is independent across time: its value next time is independent of what it was this time. But the random walk variable itself, y_t, is not independent across time. Its value next time is heavily dependent on its value last time.

Because at each time period a new random term is added, a random walk variable may end up anywhere after a long time, wherever it started. Another, related result of these random changes is that the spread of the variable increases through time. The name random walk describes the intuition. As a two-dimensional analogy, imagine a drunken sailor leaving a bar in an unknown port town. Each of his steps is completely random. Initially, he will be around his starting point. We can't predict where exactly he will be, but he won't be very far away in the first few instances. However, as time passes, his location could be farther and farther away. After a long time, a random walker may end up being very far, but may actually be close if randomly returned toward the point of origin. We just don't know. Random walks are non-stationary as they violate another aspect of stability: their spread increases with time.

Figure 12.1 shows five random walk series starting from the same point. These are simulated time series: we generated them to illustrate the concept. Each random walk series wanders around randomly. Some start diverging upwards or downwards and then continue in either direction after such deviations. Others don't experience large falls or increases and hover more closely to their starting values. As time passes, the different random walks tend to be farther away from each other. This illustrates the non-stationary nature of random walks: the standard deviation calculated over an interval increases with time.

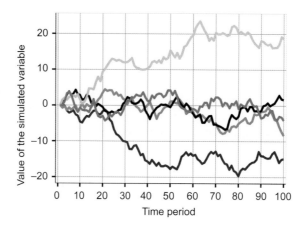

Figure 12.1   Five artificially generated random walk series

Source: Randomly generated.

Random walks may have trends, which are called drifts. A **random walk with drift** is non-stationary on two counts: both its expected value and its spread change with time. It turns out many real-life variables are well approximated by random walks, with or without drifts. These include the price of stocks and stock-market indices, exchange rates, and measures of technological progress. An important feature of random walk series is that they are impossible to predict (apart from their potential drift). As each step is completely random, independent of all previous steps, there is no way to use information from the past to predict the next steps. Another of their important features is that, after a change, they don't revert back to some value or trend line but continue their journey from that point.

In general, time series variables that have this random walk-like property are called variables with a **unit root**. In Under the Hood section 12.U1, we briefly discuss how we can detect unit root in a time series variable. The important message about such variables is that it's usually best to analyze their changes not their levels; we'll discuss this in more detail in Section 12.5.

Review Box 12.3 Non-stationarity in time series variables

Variables in time series data may be non-stationary in several ways. The most common forms of non-stationarity are:

- Trend: expected value increases or decreases with time.
- Seasonality: expected value is different in periodically recurring time periods.
- Random walk and other unit-root series: variance increases with time.

12.A1 CASE STUDY – Returns on a Company Stock and Market Returns

Question and data; preparation and exploration; visualization of time series

Our first case study asks how changes in the price of a company's stock are related to changes in market prices. Relative changes in prices are called returns: for example, an increase in price of 2% is a 2% return. Thus our question is how the returns on one company stock are related to market returns. This question is a frequent one asked in financial analysis. Answering it helps investors decide whether, and to what extent, the risks of investing in the company stock are related to the market risks. A company stock is riskier than the market if returns on the company stock tend to be even more positive when the market return is positive and even more negative when the market return is negative. The more so, the riskier the company stock. A core insight of finance is that investing in riskier stocks should be compensated by higher expected returns.

In this case study we examine how returns on the Microsoft company stock are related to the market returns. For market returns, we use returns on the Standard and Poor's 500 index (S&P500), which is a (weighted) average of 500 company stock prices listed on the New York Stock Exchange and Nasdaq.

When analyzing returns, we need to choose the time window for which the returns are calculated. That choice should be driven by the decision situation that will use the results of our analysis. In finance, portfolio managers often focus on monthly returns. Hence, we choose monthly returns to analyze. For comparison, we'll show results for daily returns, too; as a data exercise you are invited to analyze returns defined for other time windows.

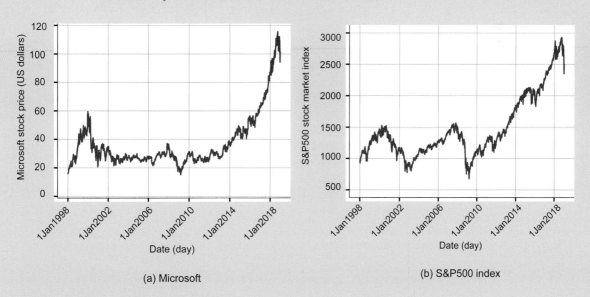

(a) Microsoft   (b) S&P500 index

Figure 12.2 Stock prices, daily time series

Note: Daily closing price of the Microsoft company stock and the S&P500 stock market index.
Source: `stocks-sp500` dataset. December 31, 1997 to December 31, 2018. N=5284.

We use the `stocks-sp500` dataset. It consists of daily data on the closing price of one company stock, Microsoft, and the S&P500. The data covers 21 years starting with December 31, 1997 and ending with December 31, 2018. This is time series data at daily frequency. The data has gaps as there are no observations for the days the markets are closed, such as weekends and holidays. The frequency of the Microsoft time series and the S&P500 time series is the same, including the gaps. We ignore those gaps for this case study and simply take returns between two consecutive days the markets were open. Both time series include 5284 days.

We'll analyze monthly returns, but let's start with visualizing the original time series of daily prices. Figure 12.2 shows the daily time series of the Microsoft stock price and the S&P500 index over this 21-year-long period.

There are ups and downs in each series, and the overall trend is positive in each. This is good to know, but our analysis requires monthly data as opposed to daily data. We now turn our attention to the monthly time series. We have defined the monthly time series of prices as the closing price on the last day of each month. Figure 12.3 shows the monthly time series of prices.

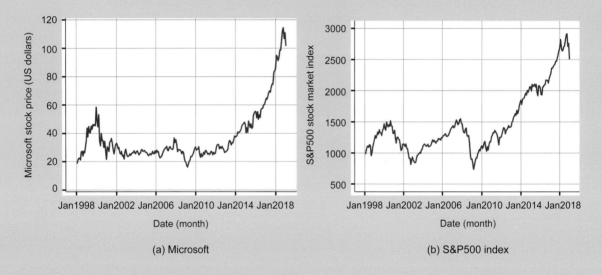

(a) Microsoft   (b) S&P500 index

Figure 12.3   Stock prices, monthly time series

Note: Closing price on the last day of the month of the Microsoft company stock and the S&P500 stock market index.
Source: `stocks-sp500` dataset. December 31, 1997 to December 31, 2018. N=253.

The monthly price time series look similar to the corresponding daily series, without the ups-and-downs within months. The trends are positive overall, mostly driven by the second half of the time period. In addition, both time series follow a random walk. The results of Phillips–Perron unit root tests are p-values of 0.99 (Microsoft) and 0.95 (S&P500), telling us not to reject the null hypothesis of a unit root (random walk) in either case (i.e., there may very well be a random walk in these series). As we will discuss later in Section 12.5, trends and random walks pose problems for regression. This is one reason why we only focus on returns instead of prices.

The question of our analysis is about returns: percent changes of prices. Monthly returns are the percent changes of prices between the last days of each month. With the 253 last-day-of-month observations, we calculated 252 monthly returns. Figure 12.4 shows the monthly time series of the percent returns.

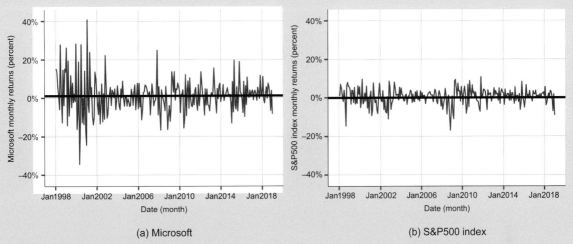

(a) Microsoft   (b) S&P500 index

Figure 12.4   Monthly returns time series

Note: Percent change of closing price between last days of the month of the Microsoft company stock and the S&P500 stock market index.
Source: `stocks-sp500` dataset. December 31, 1997 to December 31, 2018, monthly frequency. N=252.

These figures show no trends. The Phillips–Perron test rejects its null hypothesis for both time series, with p-values less than 0.001. Thus the time series of monthly returns don't follow random walks, either. Monthly returns appear to fluctuate around zero, and the fluctuations tend to be larger for the return on the Microsoft stock than on the S&P500 index. In fact, the fluctuations are around the average return, which is small but positive for both, as displayed in Table 12.1.

Table 12.1 summarizes the most important statistics of the two monthly returns variables. The range is [-34.4,40.8] for Microsoft; it's less than half as wide, [-16.9,10.8], for the S&P500. We could see the same on Figure 12.4. The mean of the Microsoft monthly returns is 1.1%: it's 0.5% for the S&P500. The standard deviation is more than twice as large for returns on Microsoft: 9.1% versus 4.3%.

Table 12.1   Descriptive statistics on monthly returns

Variables	Min	Max	Mean	Std. dev.	N
Monthly returns on Microsoft (%)	−34.4	40.8	1.1	9.1	252
Monthly returns on the S&P500 (%)	−16.9	10.8	0.5	4.3	252

Note: Monthly percentage returns on the Microsoft stock and the S&P500 index.
Source: `stocks-sp500` dataset. December 31, 1997 to December 31, 2018, monthly frequency N=252.

The most important conclusion of the exploratory analysis is that the time series of monthly returns don't follow trends or random walks. Monthly returns are higher, on average, for Microsoft than for the S&P500 index, and they vary more. That also means that prices themselves follow a positive trend (hence their average change is positive), which is steeper for Microsoft. Returns on the Microsoft company stock are not only higher on average, but they also vary in a wider range, with a larger standard deviation. In a sense, that shows higher risk for the Microsoft company stock. However, recall that finance theory tells us that what matters is not simply how much returns vary, but how they vary in relation to market returns. To uncover that, we need to run a regression.

12.4 Time Series Regression

Regression with time series data is defined and estimated the same way as with other data. But we add something to our usual notation here: the **time index** of the variables, such as y_t and x_t. This additional notation serves two purposes. First, it reminds us that the regression is on time series data, which will allow for additional interpretation of its coefficients. Second, later we'll add observations from other time periods to the regression, and there it's essential to record the time period to know what's what. With this new notation, a linear regression with one explanatory variable on time series data is the following:

$$y_t^E = \alpha + \beta x_t \tag{12.6}$$

Instead of levels of y and x, we can regress the change in y on the change in x. A change in a variable is also called **first difference**, as it is a difference between time t and time $t - 1$, the first preceding time period. (A second difference would be between t and $t - 2$, and so on.) We use the Δ notation to denote a first difference:

$$\Delta y_t = y_t - y_{t-1} \tag{12.7}$$

A linear regression in differences is the following:

$$\Delta y_t^E = \alpha + \beta \Delta x_t \tag{12.8}$$

At a basic level, the coefficients have the same interpretation as before, except we can use the "when" word to refer to observations: α is the average left-hand-side variable when all right-hand-side variables are zero, and β shows the difference in the average left-hand-side variable for observations with different Δx_t.

But the regression coefficients have another, more informative, interpretation when the variables denote changes. Starting with the intercept: α is the average change in y when x doesn't change. The slope coefficient on Δx_t shows how much more y is expected to change when x changes by one more unit. Note the word "more" before how much y is expected to change in the interpretation of the slope. It is required there because we expect y to change anyway, by α, when x doesn't change. The slope shows how y is expected to change when x changes, in addition to α.

Besides first differences, we often have **relative changes** in regressions denoting how the value changed relative to its previous value. Often, we express such relative changes in percentages, which are then **percentage changes** so that a value of +1 means a 1 percent increase, and a value of −1 means a 1 percent decrease. With percentage differences in y or x, or both, the interpretation of the regression coefficients is a straightforward modification to first differences. A linear regression in percentage changes is the following:

$$pctchange(y_t)^E = \alpha + \beta \, pctchange(x_t) \tag{12.9}$$

where

$$pctchange(y_t) = 100\% \frac{y_t - y_{t-1}}{y_{t-1}} \qquad (12.10)$$

Here α shows the expected percentage change in x when x doesn't change, and β shows how much more y is expected to change, in percentage points, when x increases by one more percent.

Finally, just as with cross-sectional regressions, we can approximate relative differences by log differences, which are here **log change**: first taking logs of the variables and then taking the first difference, for example, $\Delta \ln(y_t) = \ln(y_t) - \ln(y_{t-1})$. With time series data, we don't actually have to make use of the **log approximation** because we can directly compute relative, and percentage changes (in contrast with cross-sectional data, see Chapter 8, Section 8.2). Nevertheless, data analysts often use log differences in time series regressions – it is easy to carry out and is often a good approximation.

> **Review Box 12.4 Linear regression with changes in time series data**
>
> - With time series data, we often estimate regressions in changes.
> - We use the Δ notation for changes:
>
> $$\Delta x_t = x_t - x_{t-1} \qquad (12.11)$$
>
> - The regression in changes is
>
> $$\Delta y_t^E = \alpha + \beta \Delta x_t \qquad (12.12)$$
>
>   - α : y is expected to change by α when x doesn't change.
>   - β : y is expected to change by β more when x increases by one unit more.
> - We often have variables in relative or percentage changes, or log differences that approximate such relative changes.

12.A2 CASE STUDY – Returns on a Company Stock and Market Returns

Time series regression with monthly returns

The main question of this case study is how returns on a company stock are related to market returns. To answer that question, we have estimated a simple regression with the percentage monthly returns on the Microsoft stock (*MSFT*) on the percentage monthly returns on the S&P500 index *(SP500)*:

$$pctchange(MSFT_t)^E = \alpha + \beta pctchange(SP500_t) \qquad (12.13)$$

The result of this regression is presented in Table 12.2.

The intercept estimate shows that returns on the Microsoft stock tend to be 0.54 percent when the S&P500 index doesn't change. Its 95% confidence interval is [−0.34,1.44], which contains zero. This intercept estimate shows that, on average, the returns on Microsoft were 0.5% when the S&P500 didn't change during the 21-year period we examined. That can be interpreted as 0.5% extra returns on the Microsoft stock, compared to the market returns. But the confidence interval is wide and contains zero, so we can't say with high confidence that the Microsoft stock has positive extra returns in the general pattern represented by our data of 1998–2018.

Table 12.2   Returns on Microsoft and market returns: Simple regression results

Variables	(1) Microsoft returns
S&P500 returns	1.26**
	(0.10)
Constant	0.54
	(0.45)
Observations	252
R-squared	0.36

Note: Dependent variable: monthly percentage returns on the Microsoft stock; explanatory variable: monthly percentage returns on the S&P500 index. Robust standard errors in parentheses.
** $p < 0.01$, * $p < 0.05$.
Source: `stocks-sp500` dataset. December 31, 1997 to December 31, 2018, monthly frequency.

The slope estimate shows that returns on the Microsoft stock tend to be 1.26% higher when the returns on the S&P500 index are 1% higher. The 95% confidence interval is [1.06,1.46]. This interval doesn't include one, thus we can be more than 95% confident that the slope coefficient is larger than one in the general pattern represented by our data. Note that asterisks next to the coefficients show the p-values for testing whether the coefficient is zero. That's what statistical software test by default. Instead, the more interesting question here is whether the coefficient is larger than one. Even without carrying out that test in a formal way, the 95% CI helped answer this question.

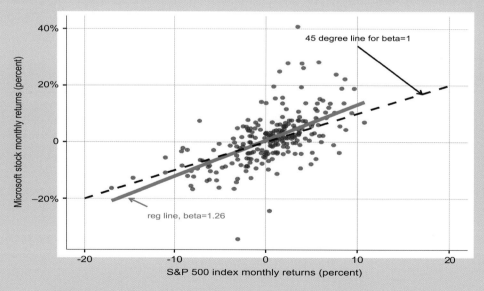

Figure 12.5   Returns on Microsoft and market returns: scatterplot and regression line

Note: Monthly percentage returns on the Microsoft stock and the S&P500 index. Scatterplot, regression line and the 45 degree line for comparison.
Source: `stocks-sp500` dataset. December 31, 1997 to December 31, 2018, monthly frequency. N=252.

Finally, note that the R-squared is 0.36, which is a lot less than one. Thus, it's not that the Microsoft price increases by 1.26% whenever the S&P500 increases by 1%. That happens on average, but sometimes the Microsoft price change is even larger, it is sometimes smaller, and it is sometimes in the opposite direction. Apparently, there are a lot of ups and downs in the Microsoft stock price that are independent of how the market moves.

We can visualize this time series regression in two ways. The first one is the usual scatterplot with the regression line; Figure 12.5 shows them, together with the 45 degree line.

The regression line shows a strong positive association. The slope of the line is more than 45 degrees. The scatterplot also shows the wider range and larger standard deviation for returns on Microsoft than returns on the S&P500.

The second visualization of the regression makes use of the time series nature of the data; it overlays the two time series on each other. In principle, this second visualization can show directly whether, in what direction, and by how much the two time series move together. A positive slope coefficient would mean that the two series tend to have ups and downs in the same direction; a negative slope coefficient would mean that the ups and downs tend to be in opposite directions. Figure 12.6 shows the two time series together, both for the entire 1998–2018 time period and the last two years, 2017–2018. Note that these figures show two time series on the same graph, which raises the question of whether to plot them on the same scale, with a single y axis, or on two different scales, with a separate y axis for each (shown on the left and right side of the figure). Here we opted for a single y axis, because the magnitudes of the two time series are directly comparable: both are percentage changes. Moreover, the magnitudes are not only comparable, but our question is about comparing them directly.

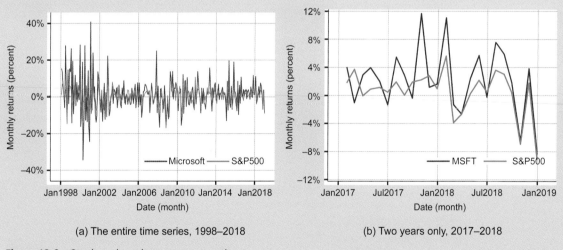

(a) The entire time series, 1998–2018   (b) Two years only, 2017–2018

Figure 12.6 Stock and market returns over time

Note: Monthly percentage returns on the Microsoft stock and the S&P500 index.
Source: `stocks-sp500` dataset. December 31, 1997 to December 31, 2018, monthly frequency. N=252.

The regression slope coefficient estimate is 1.26, so these figures should show that ups and downs tend to go together. But that is hard to see for the entire 1998–2018 time period, because it shows too many ups and downs on the same figure (252 of them). It's a lot more visible on the figure that zooms in on the last two years. That figure also shows that, while the ups and downs tend to be in the same direction, that's not always the case. Moreover, when they move in the same direction, the Microsoft ups and downs tend to be larger, but that's not always the case, either. These facts are in line with a slope coefficient estimate that is greater than one, together with an R-squared that is a lot less than one.

Before concluding our case study, let's carry out some robustness checks and examine two more questions: whether the results are robust to how we measure changes, and whether we get similar results if we examine a different time series frequency. Table 12.3 shows the benchmark regression results, with monthly percent returns in column (1); column (2) shows the results when returns are monthly log changes, while columns (3) and (4) show the same regressions with returns calculated at daily frequency. Because the log changes are two orders of magnitude smaller than the corresponding percentage changes, and this may be important for the intercept estimates, we show four digits on this table.

Table 12.3 Returns on Microsoft and market returns: alternative measurements

Variables	(1) Monthly pct change	(2) Monthly log change	(3) Daily pct change	(4) Daily log change
S&P500 returns	1.2636**	1.2403**	1.1000**	1.0951**
	(0.1030)	(0.1003)	(0.0243)	(0.0236)
Constant	0.5396	0.0026	0.0266	0.0002
	(0.4529)	(0.0045)	(0.0202)	(0.0002)
Observations	252	252	5283	5283
R-squared	0.3573	0.3627	0.4492	0.4465

Note: Dependent variable: returns on the Microsoft stock; explanatory variable: returns on the S&P500 index. The returns are defined differently for the four regressions: monthly percentage changes for (1); monthly log changes for (2); daily percentage changes for (3); daily log changes for (4). Robust standard errors in parentheses.
$**p<0.01$, $*p<0.05$.
Source: `stocks-sp500` dataset. December 31, 1997 to December 31, 2018.

Comparing columns (1) and (2) reveals that using log differences instead of percentage changes makes little difference in terms of the slope coefficient: it's 1.24 instead of 1.26, and the standard error estimates are similar, too. At the same time, the intercept estimates are different. Our benchmark results, repeated in column (1), suggest excess returns of 0.5% (with a very wide confidence interval). The intercept with log changes, in column (2), suggests half as large excess returns, of 0.26 percent (corresponding to a log change of 0.0026). While the point estimates are different, the confidence intervals are wide, so the conclusion about excess returns that we can infer from both regressions is very uncertain.

When estimating the regression using daily returns, we get a smaller slope coefficient, 1.1 instead of 1.26 (columns 3 and 1). The 95% confidence interval doesn't contain one, even with the smaller point estimate in column (3), so we can be quite confident that the Microsoft stock is risky in the general patterns represented by the data in terms of daily returns as well as in terms of monthly returns. Naturally, the intercept estimate is a lot smaller for daily returns, and its confidence interval, too, contains zero. Finally, when using log changes for measuring returns, we get very similar results for the slope and also for the intercept, using daily frequency data (columns 3 and 4). These findings are very similar to what we have seen for monthly returns.

Taken together, the results of these robustness checks suggest that defining returns in terms of percent changes or log changes makes little difference for our main question, the slope coefficient in the regression. It matters somewhat for the intercept estimates, but those are very imprecisely estimated anyway. At the same time, choosing the time series frequency is important for the slope coefficient. In our case, a higher time series frequency led to a smaller coefficient estimate, although it, too, is above one, and its 95% CI is entirely above one, too.

This concludes our case study. Our question was how returns on the Microsoft company stock move together with market returns, measured by returns on the S&P500 index. Using data on monthly percentage returns from 21 years, we have estimated a slope coefficient of 1.26 (95% CI [1.04,1.48]). This means that returns on the Microsoft stock tend to be larger than average by 1.26% in months when returns on the S&P500 is larger than average by 1%. This estimate is larger than one, suggesting that the Microsoft stock is risky: its price tends to move in the same direction as the market, only even more so. Along the way we also estimated that the returns on Microsoft tend to be larger than the market returns, but that conclusion, based on the intercept estimate, is less certain to hold in the general pattern.

Note that what we estimated is very close to what is known as the **"beta" of an asset** in finance. That beta is the **slope coefficient** of a regression almost like ours, except that returns there are measured above the risk-free rate. That may make a difference, because the risk-free rate tends to change through time, too. In any case, the finance "beta" is the slope coefficient in a simple regression of time series data. Hence its name. Similarly, the **intercept coefficient** of the relevant regression is known as "alpha" in finance, measuring extra return, also called excess return. We, as all data analysts, denote the intercept and slope coefficients of a simple regression by the Greek letters α and β, regardless of the content of the variables. But it's good to remember that the finance usage of these Greek letters is more specific.

This case study illustrated some of the important questions we need to address for time series regressions. The first task was to determine the time series frequency for the regression. We opted for monthly frequency because that conforms to the decision frequency of many investors. Our results with daily frequency showed that this decision mattered for the regression estimates. The second task was to define returns. We chose percentage changes, a quite natural choice, because percentage returns are the unit of interest for investments. Our additional results have shown that an alternative measure, log changes, yields very similar results, at least in terms of the slope coefficient estimates. It turns out that using changes in the regression made sure that the time series don't have trends and are not random walks, even though the original time series of prices had both trend and followed a random walk. And that was important to get good estimates, a topic that we'll discuss in the next section.

12.5   Trends, Seasonality, Random Walks in a Regression

Trends, seasonality, and random walks can present serious threats to uncovering meaningful patterns in time series data. Fortunately, we know how to detect them. In this section we also discuss what to do about them.

Consider a simple time series regression in levels and not changes, $y_t^E = \alpha + \beta x_t$. If both y and x have a positive trend, the slope coefficient β will be positive whether the two variables are related or not. That is simply because in later time periods both tend to have higher values than in earlier time periods.

Associations between variables only because of the effect of trends are said to be **spurious**, also called **spurious regression** or **spurious correlation**.

For example, a regression of the price of college education in the USA on global cocoa production over the past few decades would result in a positive slope coefficient even though these two may not be related in any fundamental way. Similarly, two variables with trends of opposite signs produce negative slope coefficients, even if the variables are not related. For example, the revenues of the print industry have a negative trend over the past years, while the revenues of the wine industry have a positive trend. Regressing one on the other would yield a negative slope coefficient whether the two are related or not.

A good solution to trends is replacing variables in the regression with their changes: first differences in case of linear trends and relative changes, or their approximation, log differences, if the trend is exponential. The first difference of a variable with a linear trend has no trend; the relative change of a variable with an exponential trend has no trend. In fact, that's what we did in our **Returns on a company stock and market returns** case study. Instead of stock prices, which have an exponential trend, we included percentage returns, which are their relative changes, in the regressions.

Similarly to trends, seasonality in both y and x in a regression introduces a spurious association. For example, monthly expenditures on ice cream and beer are positively correlated because both are higher in summer months, yet the consumption of the two is unlikely to be related in any fundamental way (one is rarely consumed together with the other).

What can we do with seasonality in a regression? Unlike with trends, transforming variables into first differences doesn't help here. For example, if y tends to be higher in the summer months, it is also expected to increase from spring to summer. Thus, seasonality in y would show up in seasonality in Δy, too. Instead, we can do one of two things.

Often, a good solution to seasonality is including binary season variables in the regression; these are called **season dummies**. With monthly data that would mean including 11 binary variables for each of 11 of the 12 months, leaving one out as the reference category. Often, that takes care of linear seasonality if y is in levels or first differences, and it takes care of exponential seasonality if y is in logs, relative changes, or log differences.

Another good solution to handle seasonality is transforming variables into differences between time periods that are at the same point of the seasonal cycle. With seasonality within a year, these are called **year-over-year differences**. With monthly data, year-over-year differences would mean changes between the same month in the previous year (say, last November) to the current month (this November). Taking such differences takes care of trends, too. However, they introduce overlaps into the time series; for example, a November-to-November change would be followed by a December-to-December change in the data, and the two would differ by one month only and would have 11 months in common. Such overlaps introduce additional problems with regressions, which we would have to deal with. Coefficients on such variables are also a little tricky to interpret. Therefore, we don't do such transformations in this textbook. Instead, we deal with seasonality by including season dummies in regressions.

Note that the reason why trends and seasonality in both y and x introduce a spurious association is often some common cause behind y and x, even if that common cause is quite distant sometimes. Using the terminology of Chapter 10, Section 10.4, these common cause variables confound the relationship. The negative association between the number of printed newspapers (decreasing) and the number of people using ride-sharing to travel within cities (increasing) is most likely spurious in the sense that there is no direct mechanism of causation between them. But technological progress is behind each trend. Similarly, the positive association between ice cream consumption and beer consumption across months of the year in moderate climates is spurious in the sense that most people don't consume the two together, and few think to substitute one with the other. But consumption of both is related to the weather. Whether or not we can identify such common causes, having trend or seasonality in variables on both sides of the regression affects the coefficient estimates.

In contrast with trends and seasonality, when both y and x follow a random walk without drift or seasonality, the regression coefficient estimates are expected to be the same as what they would be without random walks. However, with random walks, the usual standard error estimates are off by a large margin. Typically, the SE estimates are too small, which may suggest a statistically significant association where there isn't one. Moreover, there is no easy fix to that problem to get good SE estimates.

So what can we do about random walks? It turns out that taking first differences is a good solution here, too. When y_t follows a random walk, Δy_t is stationary. To see this, just look at the formula of the random walk: when we subtract y_{t-1}, we end up with $y_t - y_{t-1} = e_t$. By the definition of the random walk, that e_t term is completely random, independent across time, so it is stationary. Moreover, taking a first difference solves the problem of a trend at the same time, so the difference is stationary even if the original variable is a random walk with drift.

Thus, it is good practice to have variables as changes (relative changes, percentage changes, log changes) in time series when we want to estimate average associations or effects (levels may be fine for prediction, as we'll explain in Chapter 18). Analyzing changes saves us from spurious regressions because of trends, and it saves us from biased standard error estimates because of random walks. Moreover, time series regressions in changes produce readily interpretable results. That is true even if the variables have no trend or random walk.

Analyzing percentage returns instead of prices in our **Returns on a company stock and market returns** case study took care of the random walk properties of the time series variables besides their trends. The variables didn't have any seasonality to begin with. Thus, the regressions we estimated were free from the problems we covered in this section.

Review Box 12.5 Trends, seasonality, and random walks in time series regressions: problems and solutions

Problems:
- If both y and x follow trends, a regression in levels, $y_t^E = \alpha + \beta x_t$, produces spurious results, showing an association even if there isn't one.
- If both y and x have seasonality, a regression in levels or changes produces spurious results, showing an association even if there isn't one.
- If both y and x follow a random walk, the usual standard error and confidence interval estimates in a regression in levels, $y_t^E = \alpha + \beta x_t$, are biased.

Solutions:
- Estimating regressions in changes, or relative or log changes, tends to solve the problems with trends and random walks.
- To address seasonality, we include season dummies. Less frequently, we analyze year-over-year changes.

12.B1   ## CASE STUDY – Electricity Consumption and Temperature

Question and data

The second case study in this chapter examines residential electricity consumption in the state of Arizona in the USA, and its association with the weather, more precisely, temperature. Most of Arizona has a hot and dry, desert-like climate. Our question is how monthly energy consumption is related to monthly temperature. Answering this question can help in making long-run predictions of electricity consumption for various scenarios of monthly temperature. It can also help understand what drives electricity consumption: to what extent electricity consumption is related to temperature, presumably through air-conditioning and heating.

The data has two sources. We downloaded residential electricity consumption data for Arizona from the US Energy Information Administration (EIA) website. This is monthly time series data of total electricity usage in all states of the USA from 2001 through 2018. We downloaded temperature data from the National Oceanic and Atmospheric Administration (NOAA). That source has monthly aggregates of temperature data (more on the variables later) for individual weather stations across the USA. In Arizona alone, more than 100 stations are included in the data. A few stations have measurements from 1989 through 2018, but most stations have substantially shorter time coverage, starting in later years or ending in earlier years. We use data from a single weather station, Phoenix Airport.

All of our variables are in monthly frequency. However, note the discrepancy between the level of spatial aggregation in the two data sources: electricity consumption is for the entire state of Arizona, while weather data is for Phoenix only. Luckily for our analysis, 60% of the state population lives in the Phoenix metropolitan area. Thus, while weather in Phoenix may not be representative of all electricity consumers in Arizona, it covers at least 60% of them. Moreover, the second and third largest cities of Arizona are quite close to Phoenix, covering yet more population.

This is typical of a decision that data analysts have to make very often. By using weather data from more locations, we could get better measurement of the average weather exposure of the entire state of Arizona. But given the population concentration in and around Phoenix, it is probably good enough to work with the weather in Phoenix.

The weather data includes "cooling degree days" and "heating degree days" per month. These aim at measuring the number of days when most residents would use energy for cooling or heating, in a way that captures how hot or how cold those days are. The cooling degree days measure takes the average temperature within each day, subtracts a reference temperature (65 °F, or 18 °C), and adds up these daily values. If the average temperature in a day is, say, 75 °F (24 °C), the cooling degree is 10 °F (6 °C). This would be the value for one day. Then we would calculate the corresponding values for each of the days in the month and add them up. Days when the average temperature is below 65 °F have zero values. For heating degree days it's the opposite: zero for days with 65 °F or warmer, and the difference between the daily average temperature and 65 °F when lower. For example, with 45 °F (7 °C), the heating degree is 20 °F (11 °C). In essence, cooling degree days and heating degree days are daily temperatures transformed in a simple way and then added up within a month.

All variables are at monthly frequency. The electricity data starts at 2001 and ends in the early months of 2018, while the weather data starts at 1989 and ends in early 2018. The combined data starts at January 2001 and ends in December 2017. There are altogether 204 months.

Figures 12.7a and 12.7b show the time series of electricity consumption, first in levels and then in logs. There is an upward trend until 2008 but no trend afterwards. Together with the upward trend, the spread of electricity consumption appears to increase, too, but less so in logs. This suggests that the trend is closer to an exponential trend than a linear trend. Most visible is the strong seasonality: electricity consumption is much higher in the summer months than in the spring and the fall, and there is a smaller peak in the winter months, too. The magnitude of the seasonal variation increases with time in terms of levels, but it's similar over time in terms of logs.

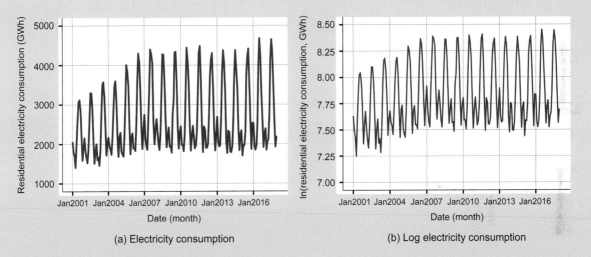

(a) Electricity consumption (b) Log electricity consumption

Figure 12.7 Residential electricity consumption in Arizona

Note: Monthly residential electricity consumption, state of Arizona, USA.
Source: `arizona-electricity` dataset. January 2001–December 2017. N=204.

We'll have two right-hand-side variables in our regression: the monthly sum of cooling degree days and the monthly sum of heating degree days. For better interpretation in the regressions, we transformed the sums into monthly averages. Formally, let F_i be the average temperature for a given day of the month, and M is the number of days in the month:

$$CD = \sum_i \frac{max(F_i - 65, 0)}{M} \tag{12.14}$$

$$HD = \sum_i \frac{min(65 - F_i, 0)}{M} \tag{12.15}$$

Figures 12.8a and 12.8b show the two time series. The graphs don't suggest any trend or increased spread in these variables. At the same time, both show strong seasonality, with average cooling degree values of 30 in July and August (meaning 95 °F daily average temperatures) and low, practically zero, values in December and January. Heating degrees are zero from May through September, and their peak in December and January is only at around 10 degrees (referring to 55 °F daily average temperature). Summers are very hot in Phoenix, Arizona, and winters are cool but mild.

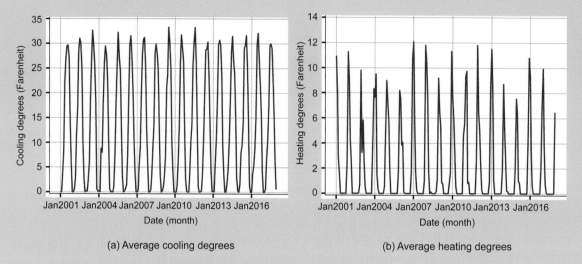

(a) Average cooling degrees   (b) Average heating degrees

Figure 12.8   Arizona monthly cooling and heating degree day averages

Note: Degree days averaged per month, Phoenix, Arizona, USA.
Source: `arizona-electricity` dataset. January 2001–December 2017. N=204.

This exploratory data analysis revealed the following. Electricity consumption has a positive trend, especially in the first few years, and the trend is better approximated as exponential as opposed to linear. We haven't detected trend or increased spread in cooling degrees or heating degrees. All variables have strong seasonality.

Based on these findings, what kind of a time series regression should we estimate? Recall that our advice is to estimate time series regressions in changes, as a default choice. In what follows, we'll proceed accordingly. The left-hand-side variable of the regression will be log changes of electricity consumption. The right-hand-side variables will be heating and cooling degrees as changes from the previous month. Note that the right-hand-side variables don't follow any trend, so there is no obvious need to estimate the regression in changes. You will be invited to carry out the analysis without taking differences as a data exercise (regressing ln Q on the temperature variables). As it turns out, the results of that regression are very similar to the results of the regression in changes that we'll estimate.

In contrast to trends, we have strong seasonality in all variables. When estimating our regression, we'll have to address that seasonality. Following our advice, that will mean including month dummies in the regression. As we'll see, the regression estimates with and without season dummies are different, and we'll have to think about what those differences mean for the question of our analysis.

12.6 | # Serial Correlation

After trend and seasonality, the third property of many times series we consider in this chapter is **serial correlation**. Serial correlation means correlation of a variable observed at some time with the previous values of the same variable. Previous observations of a time series variable are called its **lagged values**, or simply its **lags**. Thus, serial correlation is correlation between the observation of a variable and a lagged observation of the same variable.

Serial correlation does not violate stationarity. It is perfectly possible for a time series to have serial correlation but have no trend, seasonality, or any other kind of non-stationary feature.

Most often, serial correlation involves correlation between adjacent observations in the time series. That is called **first-order serial correlation**. Second-order serial correlation means correlation between observations that are two time periods away from each other. Third- and higher-order serial correlations are defined analogously. Serial correlation is characterized by the correlation coefficient. The first-order serial correlation coefficient of variable y is the correlation between its value at time t, y_t, and its first lag, y_{t-1}:

$$\rho_1 = Corr[y_t, y_{t-1}] \tag{12.16}$$

The second- and higher-order serial correlation coefficients are defined analogously, $\rho_2 = Corr[y_t, y_{t-2}]$, $\rho_3 = Corr[y_t, y_{t-3}]$, and so on.

Note that, while the broader concept of serial correlation makes sense both for stationary and nonstationary time series, we focus on stationary time series. Without stationarity, the ingredients of correlation coefficients (covariance, standard deviation) may change over time. This means that, if a time series variable is non-stationary, its first-order, second-order, and higher-order correlation coefficients may change with time. In contrast, if a time series variable is stationary, its first-order correlation is the same across time, its second-order correlation is also the same across time, and so on. In stationary time series variables, serial correlation depends only on how far the observations are from each other, not on where they are in the time series. So, for example, $\rho_1 = Corr[y_t, y_{t-1}] = Corr[y_{t-1}, y_{t-2}] = Corr[y_{t-2}, y_{t-3}]$, ..., and $\rho_2 = Corr[y_t, y_{t-2}] = Corr[y_{t-1}, y_{t-3}] = Corr[y_{t-2}, y_{t-4}]$, ... More generally, a stable pattern of serial correlation (which includes no serial correlation at all) is also necessary for stationarity. A time series variable whose serial correlation changes with time would be non-stationary even if it had neither trend, nor seasonality, nor a random walk-like increase in spread.

Figures 12.9a and 12.9b show two stationary time series variables – both are simulated data. Both are stationary, with mean zero. The left panel has no serial correlation ($\rho_1 = 0$); the right panel has strong serial correlation ($\rho_1 = 0.8$). Each time series fluctuates around its mean. In Figure 12.9a the serially uncorrelated variable does not spend much time on one side of the average: a positive deviation is not particularly likely to be followed by another positive deviation. In contrast, the serially correlated variable in Figure 12.9b spends more time on one side of the average before returning to it. Here, a positive deviation is likely to be followed by another positive deviation, and a negative deviation is likely to be followed by another negative deviation.

For a positively serially correlated variable, if its value is above average this time, it is more likely that it will be above average next time, too. For a negatively serially correlated variable, if its value is above average this time, it is less likely that it will be above average next time.

A time series variable without any serial correlation is called serially uncorrelated. For a serially uncorrelated variable, its value this time has no information about what to expect for its value the

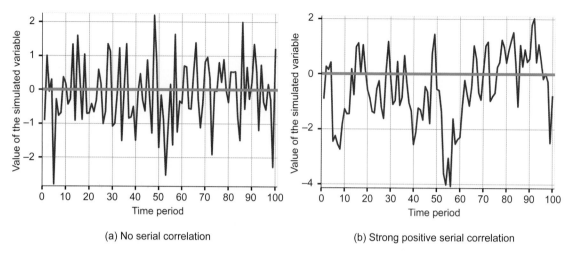

(a) No serial correlation   (b) Strong positive serial correlation

Figure 12.9   Two simulated time series variables with different serial correlation

Note: Two simulated time series variables, both stationary – one serially uncorrelated, the other strongly serially correlated, with $\rho_1 = 0.8$. N=100.

next time. It turns out that returns on the stocks of large companies are serially uncorrelated, and so are market indices such as the S&P500.

But why should we care about serial correlation in variables? First, when a variable is serially corre-lated, its present value may help predict its value in the near future. Here serial correlation can be very useful. We'll return to that use of serial correlation in Chapter 18, which discusses forecasting with time series data. Second, serial correlation creates issues with regressions whatever we use them for. That makes serial correlation an issue. What kind of an issue and what we can do with that issue is the subject of the next section.

12.7   **Dealing with Serial Correlation in Time Series Regressions**

Serial correlation of variables in time series data does not lead to biased regression coefficients. But it makes the usual standard error estimates wrong. When the dependent variable is serially corre-lated, both the simple SE and the heteroskedasticity robust SE are wrong – sometimes very wrong, with a large bias. To be more precise, it is serial correlation in the residual of the regression that is problematic. Note that the residual is nothing other than the dependent variable after its conditional expectation is subtracted. Thus, we will loosely – although not correctly – talk about serial correlation in the dependent variable instead of serial correlation in the residuals. As we'll see in our case study, the two aren't necessarily equal. However, focusing on the dependent variable makes us err on the safe side, as serial correlation tends to be stronger, or similar, in the dependent variable than in the residual.

Let us think back to our **Returns on a company stock and market returns** case study. Why did we not worry about all this? The answer is simple: because daily returns have very lit-tle serial correlation. Neither y_t, nor x_t have substantial serial correlation in the regression, and thus the residual has no serial correlation either. As a result, the usual standard error estimates are fine.

Estimating a regression in differences, or relative (percentage, log) differences often reduces the problem of serial correlation. Our stock price example was an extreme case, in which both the single stock price and the market index time series had random walk (with drift), and random walks are extreme in terms of serial dependence. The time series of the (percentage) difference of both time series had no serial correlation at all. With less extreme serial dependence, taking a difference may mitigate, but not eliminate serial correlation. In fact, with no serial correlation in the time series in levels, taking a difference can introduce some extra serial correlation. But that extra serial correlation is rarely very severe.

When we do worry about serial correlation, we have several solutions to get good standard error estimates. In this chapter we discuss two of them.

The first solution is to estimate standard errors that are robust to serial correlation. **Newey–West standard errors** are a good solution. Their practical use is similar to the White robust standard error estimates we considered for cross-sectional regressions: all coefficients are the same, only the standard errors are different.

The Newey–West procedure incorporates the structure of serial correlation of the regression residuals into the calculation of the standard errors. This is in contrast to the simple SE and the heteroskedasticity-robust SE estimates that we considered earlier as those assume zero serial correlation. Newey–West standard errors are fine in the presence of serial correlation as well as without it. They are also fine with heteroskedasticity as well as without it. We may think of them as one step beyond the previously considered robust SE estimation: they are robust not only to heteroskedasticity but serial correlation as well.

For a technical reason, the Newey–West standard error estimation process requires that we define how many "lags" it should consider. These lags refer to a way of modeling the structure of serial correlation in the dependent variable. Usually a few lags are fine. To be on the safe side, we may experiment with many lags – especially if the time series is long enough – and pick the most conservative (i.e., largest) standard error. How many lags are enough is hard to tell, but we might consider a full period of seasonal variation (e.g., 4 for quarterly data, 12 for monthly data).

The second solution is including the **lagged dependent variable** in the right-hand side of the regression. The idea is to specify a regression that incorporates all serial correlation of the left-hand-side variable in the regression and produces residuals that are serially uncorrelated. For example, if y has nonzero first-order serial correlation, $Corr[y_t, y_{t-1}], \neq 0$ and we are interested in the regression $y_t^E = \alpha + \beta x_t$, we instead estimate the regression $y_t^E = \alpha + \beta x_t + \gamma y_{t-1}$. The correlation of y_t and y_{t-1} is included in the regression so it is not in the residual anymore.

In contrast with estimating Newey–West SE, this procedure makes the coefficient estimates different. In principle, then, the coefficient estimates with the lagged dependent variable are better. But they are very different only if serial correlation in y is very strong. That is rare when our variables are in differences. Thus, when having changes in the regression, as we advised earlier, we usually have similar coefficient estimates with or without having lagged y in the regression. But the standard errors are better with that lag.

Usually, including one lag of the dependent variable takes care of the problem. But sometimes it doesn't, and we may need to include more lags of y in the regression, such as y_{t-2}, y_{t-3}, and so on.

One way to proceed is first including many lags (such as three or four), look at their p-values, and then include only the ones with significant coefficients. That procedure turns out not to be ideal. There are more systematic procedures, known as lag order selection, but those are beyond the scope of our textbook.

Review Box 12.6   Serial correlation

A time series variable is serially correlated if its values from different time periods are correlated. Most common is first-order serial correlation: $Corr[y_t, y_{t-1}]$.

Problem and solution:

- If y is serially correlated, the usual standard errors of regressions are wrong.
- One solution is to estimate Newey–West standard errors instead; they are robust to serial correlation (and heteroskedasticity).
- Another solution is to model serial correlation within the regression and include lagged y on the right-hand side: $y_t^E = \alpha + \beta x_t + \gamma y_{t-1}$.

12.B2   CASE STUDY – Electricity Consumption and Temperature

Time series regression, seasonality, serial correlation

Let's turn to estimating the regression that can answer our question in this case study. We denote electricity consumption by Q (for quantity), the monthly average of cooling degrees as CD, and the monthly average of heating degrees as HD. We will estimate the regression in changes; as we noted after exploring the data, that's our default choice with time series regressions, even if, here, it makes little difference because there is trend only in the left-hand-side variable. Here $\Delta \ln Q_t$ will denote the first difference of the log of consumption. We will estimate two regressions, one without season dummies and one with season dummies. The regression without the season dummies has the following formula:

$$(\Delta \ln Q_t)^E = \beta_0 + \beta_1 \Delta CD_t + \beta_2 \Delta HD_t \tag{12.17}$$

The regression with season dummies adds 11 binary variables for each month (we left out January as the reference category):

$$(\Delta \ln Q_t)^E = \beta_0 + \beta_1 \Delta CD_t + \beta_2 \Delta HD_t + \gamma_1 Feb_t + \cdots + \gamma_{11} Dec_t \tag{12.18}$$

To handle possible serial correlation and heteroskedasticity, the regressions have Newey–West standard error estimates. Table 12.4 shows the results.

Table 12.4 Electricity consumption and temperature – baseline regression

Variables	(1) $\Delta \ln Q$	(2) $\Delta \ln Q$
ΔCD	0.031**	0.017**
	(0.001)	(0.002)
ΔHD	0.037**	0.014**
	(0.003)	(0.003)
month = 2, February		−0.274**
		(0.020)
month = 3, March		−0.122**
		(0.023)
month = 4, April		−0.184**
		(0.026)
month = 5, May		0.033*
		(0.014)
month = 6, June		0.081**
		(0.030)
month = 7, July		0.058**
		(0.014)
month = 8, August		−0.085**
		(0.015)
month = 9, September		−0.176**
		(0.016)
month = 10, October		−0.246**
		(0.028)
month = 11, November		−0.242**
		(0.031)
month = 12, December		0.067**
		(0.025)
Constant	0.001	0.092**
	(0.002)	(0.013)
Observations	203	203

Note: Q is electricity consumption, CD and HD are daily average cooling and heating degrees. Δ denotes first difference. Newey–West standard error estimates in parentheses. ** $p<0.01$, * $p<0.05$.

Source: `arizona-electricity` dataset. January 2001–December 2017.

There are 203 observations in each regression: these are the changes calculated using data for 204 months.

The slope coefficient estimates are different across the two regressions. Let's start with the first one, without season dummies. When cooling degrees increase by one degree from the previous month and heating degrees do not change, electricity consumption increases by 3.1%, on average. When heating degrees increase by one degree and cooling degrees do not change, electricity consumption increases by 3.7% on average. The 95% confidence interval is tight around both coefficients: $3.1\% \pm 0.2\%$ and $3.7\% \pm 0.6\%$. The regression constant is practically zero, implying no trend in electricity consumption through this time period.

Let's turn to the results with season dummies. First, let's interpret the coefficients on the season dummies. They show the average difference in the y variable in a month compared to the reference month when all other variables are the same in the regression. That's a little tricky here, because the y variable is a log change. The reference month is January; the regression constant shows that, when cooling and heating degrees stay the same, electricity consumption increases by about 9% from December to January. The other season coefficients compare to this change. Thus, for example, the coefficient on the February variable suggests that the January to February change is approximately 28% lower than in the reference month, December to January. That was +9%, so electricity consumption decreases by about 19% on average to February from January when cooling and heating degrees stay the same.

The seasonal pattern is quite clear: residential electricity consumption tends to increase in December and January (being the reference month, the change estimate for January is the regression constant) as well as May, June, and July; it tends to decrease in other months; and all this is when cooling and heating degrees don't change. This suggests that the month-to-month changes in residential electricity consumption are not fully captured by our measures of cooling and heating degrees. There are many potential reasons, including other uses of electricity or cooling and heating needs not fully captured by our temperature measures.

Now let's turn to interpreting the coefficients in the cooling and heating degree variables. Comparing the same months across years in Arizona, electricity consumption tends to increase by 1.7% more when average monthly cooling degrees increase by one degree Fahrenheit more (and heating degrees change the same way). Comparing the same months across years in Arizona, electricity consumption tends to increase by 1.4% more when average monthly heating degrees increase by one degree Fahrenheit more (and cooling degrees change the same way).

Why are the coefficients about half as large when we include the month dummies, and what does that mean? Mechanically, the difference is due to the fact that both electricity consumption and temperature are strongly seasonal across the year in Arizona. Thus, apparently, part of the association between electricity consumption and our measures of temperature is attributable to months. But does that mean that month-to-month changes in residential electricity consumption are due to factors other than changes in temperature? Maybe, but not necessarily. As we indicated above, the strong season coefficients may show changes in electricity consumption due to other uses of electricity (lighting, entertainment). That can lead to smaller coefficient estimates on cooling and heating degrees if those extra uses happen to increase in months when heating and cooling needs increase too, e.g., in holiday seasons.

But it is also possible that the season coefficients pick up cooling and heating uses of electricity that our measures of cooling and heating degrees don't capture. That may happen if there are strong nonlinearities: a large increase of cooling or heating degrees associated with disproportionately large increases in electricity consumption. You will be invited to explore this possibility among the data exercises. And let's not forget that in our data the temperature is measured at the airport of Phoenix, while electricity consumption is for the entire state of Arizona. Month dummies may capture changes in temperature elsewhere.

Before moving on, let's spend some time on how we estimated standard errors. The SEs in Table 12.4 are Newey–West estimates; thus, they are correct whether there is serial correlation or not and whether there is heteroskedasticity or not. For educational purposes, let's look at two other ways to estimate SE. Column (1) in Table 12.5 shows the simple SE estimates that are wrong if there is serial correlation or heteroskedasticity. Column (2) shows the Newey–West SE estimates that are correct either way. Column (3) shows the other solution to serial correlation: including lagged *y* on the right-hand side of the regression. This solution is correct whether there is serial correlation or not. All three regressions include the 11 season dummies and a constant, but we don't show their coefficient estimates for simplicity.

Table 12.5 Electricity consumption and temperature – different SE estimates

Variables	(1) Simple SE $\Delta \ln Q$	(2) Newey–West SE $\Delta \ln Q$	(3) Lagged dep. var $\Delta \ln Q$
ΔCD	0.017**	0.017**	0.017**
	(0.002)	(0.002)	(0.002)
ΔHD	0.014**	0.014**	0.014**
	(0.002)	(0.003)	(0.002)
Lagged $\Delta \ln Q$			−0.002
			(0.062)
Month dummies	Yes	Yes	Yes
Observations	203	203	202
R-squared	0.951		0.951

Note: *CD* and *HD* are daily average cooling and heating degrees. Month dummies included but not shown; standard error estimates in parentheses. (1) Simple SE estimates, (2) Newey–West SE estimates, (3) simple SE estimates with lagged dependent variable. ** $p < 0.01$, * $p < 0.05$.

Source: `arizona-electricity` dataset. January 2001–December 2017.

The estimated coefficients should be the same in columns (1) and (2), and they are. The SE estimates should be different if there is serial correlation, but they, too, are very similar. In column (3), where we include the lagged dependent variable to deal with serial correlation, neither the coefficient estimates, nor the SE estimates need to be the same as before, but they are, again, very close. In column (3) we see why that's so: conditional on the change in cooling degrees and heating degrees (and the season dummies), the lagged change in monthly electricity consumption is not related to its current change.

Thus, serial correlation turns out not to be an issue with our regression. But we didn't know this when we started the analysis. In fact, the serial correlation in the log change of electricity consumption is not zero: $Corr(\Delta \ln Q_t, \Delta \ln Q_{t-1} = 0.4)$. However, when we condition on all the right-hand-side variables, that serial correlation disappears and doesn't cause any problems with estimating the standard errors.

12.8 Lags of *x* in a Time Series Regression

An important advantage of regression analysis using time series data is its ability to uncover associations across time. For example, we may ask what we can expect to happen for a dependent variable one or two time periods after an explanatory variable changes. These are called **lagged associations**, or if they show true effects, **lagged effects**.

Having lags is very useful when it takes time for an effect to materialize. A technology investment may take years to elevate profitability. A jump in oil prices will take months or years to influence economic activity. A change in social policy may take years to affect unemployment or health outcomes.

The time series regression in first differences with a single right-hand-side variable x and its two lags has the form

$$\Delta y_t^E = \alpha + \beta_0 \Delta x_t + \beta_1 \Delta x_{t-1} + \beta_2 \Delta x_{t-2} \tag{12.19}$$

Note the change in notation. β_0 does not denote the intercept anymore; α does. β_0 is the coefficient on Δx_t. The reason is that, when it is included in the regression, this Δx_t can be thought of as lag zero. Then, the explanatory variable lagged by one time period, Δx_{t-1}, has coefficient β_1 because it's the first lag, and so on. Regressions with lags are one reason why we show the t subscript for the variables. Here the expected change in y at time t is conditional on the change in x measured at the same time t as well as at one time period earlier, at $t-1$, and at two time periods earlier, at $t-2$.

The coefficients in this regression can tell us how y is expected to change after a one-time change in x, i.e., when x changes in one time period but not afterwards. β_0 shows the contemporaneous association: what to expect in the same time period. β_1 shows the once-lagged association: what to expect in the next time period. Finally, β_2 shows the twice-lagged association: what to expect two time periods later.

More precisely, β_0 shows how many units more y is expected to change within the same time period when x changes by one more unit (and it didn't change in the previous two time periods). β_1 shows how much more y is expected to change in the next time period after x changed by one more unit – provided that it didn't change at other times. Finally, β_2 shows how much more y is expected to change two time periods after x changed by one more unit – provided that it didn't change at other times.

The same coefficients can tell us how much y is expected to change in total as the result of a one-time change in x. After a change in x by one unit, we expect y to change by β_0, then by β_1, and then by β_2. The **cumulative association** or **long-run association** with a one-time change in x is

$$\beta_{cumul} = \beta_0 + \beta_1 + \beta_2 \tag{12.20}$$

We can easily compute this from the estimated coefficients. However, computing its standard error would be difficult. Primarily for this reason, it often makes sense to use a trick that allows us to get the sum of the coefficients directly. This trick involves transforming the right-hand-side variables by taking more differences and adding these transformed variables into the regression:

$$\Delta y_t^E = \alpha + \beta_{cumul} \Delta x_{t-2} + \delta_0 \Delta(\Delta x_t) + \delta_1 \Delta(\Delta x_{t-1}) \tag{12.21}$$

It turns out that β_{cumul} in this regression is exactly the same as β_{cumul} in the previous regression. You'll be invited to show that in a practice question.

The other two right-hand-side variables are quite strange: they are differences of variables that are already in differences. Their coefficients are hard to interpret. But that's OK because the goal of the whole exercise is to get an estimate of β_{cumul}, together with its standard error. If we are interested in the exact pattern of the lagged effects, we should go back and estimate the original regression. In practice we often estimate both, which also helps check if we transformed the variables correctly to get the cumulative effect. Note that this trick also generalizes to having more lags as well as more right-hand-side variables.

Review Box 12.7   Lags of x in a time series regression

- Including lagged values of x in a time series regression helps uncover what tends to happen to y after x changes, with lags.
- A time series regression with a single x variable and its two lags is

$$\Delta y_t^E = a + \beta_0 \Delta x_t + \beta_1 \Delta x_{t-1} + \beta_2 \Delta x_{t-2}$$

  o β_0 shows the average change in y (in addition to its potential trend) when x increases by one unit;
  o β_1 shows the average change in y (in addition to its potential trend) one time period after x increases by one unit;
  o β_2 shows the average change in y (in addition to its potential trend) two time periods after x increases by one unit.
- The cumulative association, or cumulative coefficient, shows the average change in y adding up all the changes:

$$\beta_{cumul} = \beta_0 + \beta_1 + \beta_2$$

  o To get the estimated β_{cumul}, we can simply add up the estimated slope coefficients.
  o Or, with a trick, we can estimate this β_{cumul} and its standard error directly.

12.B3   CASE STUDY – Electricity Consumption and Temperature

Lagged associations

To explore potential lagged associations, we estimated the regression with up to two lags of each of the two temperature variables. Table 12.6 shows two displays of the regression. Column (1) shows the coefficient estimates of each lagged x variable. Column (2) shows the cumulative coefficient.

The regression conditions on month dummies, too but we don't show the month coefficients to save space, and we don't show the regression constant either. Note that the regression in column (2) also includes the necessary further differenced variables, but we don't show their coefficients because we won't interpret them.

Table 12.6   Electricity consumption and temperature – lagged associations

Variables	(1) $\Delta \ln Q$	(2) $\Delta \ln Q$
ΔCD	0.020**	
	(0.002)	
ΔCD 1st lag	0.006**	
	(0.002)	
ΔCD 2nd lag	0.001	
	(0.002)	
ΔHD	0.019**	
	(0.003)	
ΔHD 1st lag	0.011**	
	(0.003)	
ΔHD 2nd lag	0.000	
	(0.003)	
ΔCD cumulative coeff		0.027**
		(0.005)
ΔHD cumulative coeff		0.030**
		(0.007)
Observations	201	201
R-squared	0.957	0.957
Month binary variables	Yes	Yes

Note: The regressions include month dummies. For the content of the variables see Table 12.4. Standard error estimates in parentheses; ** $p<0.01$, * $p<0.05$.

Source: `arizona-electricity` dataset. January 2001–December 2017.

Perhaps surprisingly, we find some positive lagged association for both cooling and heating degrees. Why would there be lagged associations here? They may show the actual effect of temperature from the month before: some people may respond to a temperature increase by increasing air-conditioning more if temperature increased in the previous month, on top of its increase this month. Alternatively, these lagged associations may capture something about temperature that our measures miss. They may show the effect of changes in temperature elsewhere in the state that are preceded by changes in temperature in Phoenix. Or, perhaps, the electricity needs of, say, cooling, are nonlinear and disproportionally higher when the temperature is really high. Such high-temperature days tend to happen in the summer, in months that follow months that were also warmer than average. That may make it look as if the past month mattered for electricity consumption this month, whereas we see that only because we don't incorporate nonlinearity in our measure of cooling and heating degrees. You are invited to explore potential nonlinear associations as a data exercise.

This concludes our case study. From a substantive viewpoint, it established that temperature is strongly associated with residential electricity consumption in Arizona. Electricity consumption is substantially higher in summer months that are hotter than average and in winter months that are cooler than average.

Some of our results are puzzling. Besides the strong seasonal effects, we found lagged associations. Most likely, more refined data would help uncover the effect of temperature on residential electricity consumption and solve those puzzles. It may be better to analyze data from smaller regional aggregates with closer geographic match of the temperature and electricity data. Perhaps it would be more important to use data on daily, or even hourly, frequency of electricity use and temperature. Nevertheless, even this relatively simple analysis provides useful information about how temperature may affect residential electricity consumption.

On the methods side, we saw that the trend in electricity consumption is unlikely to cause trouble because it's only in the dependent variable but not in the explanatory variables. Nevertheless, we analyzed the data in changes, and that saved us from the trouble of thinking about potential trends in temperature. (As a data exercise, you will be invited to carry out the analysis in levels as opposed to changes and confirm that the conclusions are similar.) We have uncovered strong seasonality in all variables, and when we included binary month variables, we obtained smaller coefficient estimates on the temperature variables. While we couldn't fully explain that difference in the estimates, this result showed that seasonality can greatly affect our results. Finally, this case study illustrated the many things we need to address when performing regression analysis with time series data.

12.9 The Process of Time Series Regression Analysis

Time series analysis shares a great deal of tasks and tools with the analysis of cross-sectional data, such as data preparation and cleaning or variable selection. There are, however, additional issues, and these affect the process of work and the scope of decisions to make. In this final section, let us review the most important steps, issues, and solutions.

First, we need to understand the time series frequency of each variable we'll work with. We need to deal with gaps if necessary, and we need to make sure that all variables have the same time series frequency. This may require aggregating variables to a lower frequency (e.g., daily to monthly, quarterly to yearly). When aggregating variables, we need to sum flow variables such as daily sales to get monthly sales. For stock variables, such as population or price, we need to take a single value, such as the period average or the last value. We need to make sure the length of the time series is the same for all variables.

The second step is exploratory data analysis, the results of which often send us back to data cleaning. Here it is good practice to start with plotting all time series variables in time series graphs with time on the horizontal axis, using the original time series frequency of the data. Typically, this means plotting each time series separately. Plotting the series helps identify the most important features of each time series variable, such as trends, seasonality, changing spread, or extreme values. We can perform simple tests to see if the variable has trend (is its difference, or relative difference zero?) or random walk (e.g., with the help of a Phillips–Perron unit root test).

It is often a good choice to transform the variables to changes (first differences) or relative or percentage changes; the latter we may approximate by taking the log and then the difference. It is always a good choice to work with changes (or relative changes) if our key variables have trend or random walk.

The next step is to specify the regression. If we have seasonality in the y and x variables, we need to handle that; including seasonal dummies in the regression usually does the trick. The other aspect of specifying regressions is whether to include lags of the explanatory variables or not. It is good practice to try including lags and see if they matter. If they do, keep lags in the regression. If they do not, drop them. With lags in the regression we can use the trick we learned above to directly estimate cumulative (long-run) associations and their standard errors.

Finally, when estimating a regression, we have to get the standard errors right. In time series data that means handling serial correlation on top of heteroskedasticity. Detecting serial correlation is not that straightforward; we haven't covered the necessary tools in this chapter. Instead, we suggest to do things in a way that works anyway: estimating regressions with Newey–West SE, or including a lagged dependent variable and estimate the usual robust SE.

Finally, when interpreting the results of a time series regression, we have to pay attention to all estimates that matter. If it has trend or seasonality, y is expected to change accordingly even if x doesn't change. Thus, the slope coefficient estimates that measure what happens when x changes, estimate change in y in addition to what we would expect due to a trend or seasonality.

Review Box 12.8 Time series regressions step by step

- Decide on the time series frequency; deal with gaps if necessary.
- Plot the series. Identify features and issues.
- Handle trends by transforming variables (levels, changes, relative changes).
- Specify a regression that handles seasonality, usually by including season dummies.
- Include or don't include lags of the right-hand-side variable(s).
- Handle serial correlation.
- Interpret coefficients in a way that pays attention to potential trend and seasonality.

12.10 Main Takeaways

Regressions with time series data allow for additional opportunities, but they pose additional challenges, too.

- Regressions with time series data help uncover associations from changes and associations across time.
- Trend, seasonality, and random walk-like non-stationarity are additional challenges.
- Do not regress variables that have trend or seasonality; without dealing with them they produce spurious results.

PRACTICE QUESTIONS

1. Interpret the intercept and the slope coefficient of the time series regression $y_t^E = \alpha + \beta x_t$.
2. Interpret the intercept and the slope coefficient of the time series regression $\Delta y_t^E = \alpha + \beta \Delta x_t$.
3. Interpret the intercept and the slope coefficient of the time series regression
   $(\Delta \ln(y_t))^E = \alpha + \beta \Delta \ln(x_t)$.
4. When do we say that a time series variable has a trend? Give an example.

5. When do we say that a time series variable has seasonality? Give an example.
6. When do we say that a time series variable follows a random walk? Give an example.
7. You are regressing y on x in time series data, and both variables have positive trends. What problem does that cause? What can you do about it? Give an example.
8. You are regressing y on x in time series data, and both variables have seasonality. What problem does that cause? What can you do about it? Give an example.
9. Consider a time series regression in levels and with one lag. Write down this regression, then the corresponding regression with the cumulative coefficient, and show the correspondence between the coefficients of the two regressions.
10. Using weekly national time series data on the log change of gasoline sold and the log change of gasoline price, estimate a regression with one lag of the price variable (the right-hand-side variable). The estimated slope coefficients are -0.4 and -0.2. Write down the regression and interpret its coefficients.
11. Using the same data and regression as in the previous question, calculate the cumulative (long-run) coefficient of association. Interpret this coefficient. Does it tell you the long-run effect of increasing gasoline prices on gasoline consumption?
12. In daily time series data, the maximum temperature in London is regressed on the number of British tourists in Rome, Italy. The slope coefficient is positive. Interpret this coefficient and try to make sense of it. In particular, can you conclude that British tourists escape the heat in London?
13. Yearly time series of the value of housing stock in a city is regressed on yearly time series of income per capita in the city, with both variables in log differences. How would you estimate the standard error of the regression coefficients and why?
14. In a yearly time series, the log change of total cigarette consumption is regressed on the log change in the average price of cigarettes in a country. The slope coefficient is -0.2. Interpret this number. Is it a good estimate of the price elasticity of demand?
15. The number of observations is not the same in all regressions of the case study. Explain why.

DATA EXERCISES

Easier and/or shorter exercises are denoted by [*]; harder and/or longer exercises are denoted by [**].

1. Use the `stocks-sp500` dataset and reproduce the analysis of the **Returns on a company stock and market returns** case study with another stock. Compare your findings with the case study findings. [*]
2. In finance, "beta" is the measured regression return above the risk-free rate. Download the risk-free rate as treasury yield from `https://finance.yahoo.com/quote/%5EIRX?p=%5EIRX` or `https://fred.stlouisfed.org/series/TB3MS`. Calculate the excess return for each month as return − risk-free rate. Regress the excess return of MSFT on excess return of the index. Compare your results with the case study results. [*]
3. Using the `arizona-electricity` dataset, investigate nonlinearity in the associations. Discuss your results. [*]
4. Using the `arizona-electricity` dataset, look at the proportion of days with more than 90 degrees Fahrenheit of highest temperature and the proportion of days with less than 70

Fahrenheit. Estimate regressions that are analogous to the case study, interpret and discuss your results, and compare them with the case study results. [*]

5. Using the `arizona-electricity` dataset, reproduce the analysis of electricity consumption and temperature using levels as opposed to differences of the variables (you may take the log of Q). Interpret and discuss your results. Compare your results with the case study results. [*]

REFERENCES AND FURTHER READING

A nice textbook on applied time series analysis with a focus on forecasting is Hyndman & Athanasopoulos (2019). An advanced text with applications is Shumway & Stoffer (2017). For more on financial econometrics, see Tsay (2010).

12.U1   UNDER THE HOOD: TESTING FOR UNIT ROOT

In this section we briefly introduce how we can tell if a time series variable has a unit root; for example, whether it follows a random walk. There are tests developed for this purpose; they are called **unit root tests**. There are several tests, of which we recommend to use the most widely applied test, the **Phillips–Perron test**. Its simplest form is based on the following model:

$$x_t = a + \rho x_{t-1} + e_t \tag{12.22}$$

This model represents a random walk if $a = 0$ and $\rho = 1$. It's a random walk with drift if $a \neq 0$ and $\rho = 1$. The Phillips–Perron test has hypothesis $H_0: \rho = 1$ against the alternative $H_A: \rho < 1$.

Statistical software calculate the p-value for this test. When the p-value is large (e.g., larger than 0.05), we don't reject the null, concluding that the time series variable may follow a random walk (perhaps with drift).

PART III Prediction

13 A Framework for Prediction

How to carry out a prediction, and how to find the best predicting model

Motivation

You have a car that you want to sell in the near future. You want to know what price you can expect if you were to sell it. You may also want to know what you could expect if you were to wait one more year and sell your car then. You have data on used cars with their age and other features, and you can predict price with several kinds of regression models with different right-hand-side variables in different functional forms. How should you select the regression model that would give the best prediction?

You want to predict sales at an ice cream shop for the next few days. You have data from the recent past on daily sales and temperature, and you have good weather forecasts for the next few days. How should you use this data to make sales predictions that will be as close to actual sales as possible? What issues should you consider to make sure that the prediction from your data will be as good as possible for the future situation you are interested in?

Part III of our textbook introduces the logic of predictive data analysis and its most widely used methods. We focus on predicting a target variable y with the help of predictor variables x. The basic logic of prediction is estimating a model for the patterns of association between y and x in existing data (the original data), and then using that model to predict y for observations in the prediction situation (in the live data), in which we observe x but not y. The task of predictive analytics is to find the model that would give the best prediction in the live data by using information from the original data.

This chapter introduces a framework for prediction. We discuss the distinction between various types of prediction, such as quantitative predictions, probability predictions, and classification, and we focus on the first of these. We introduce point prediction versus interval prediction; we discuss the components of prediction error and how to find the best prediction model that will likely produce the best fit (smallest prediction error) in the live data, using observations in the original data. We introduce loss functions in general, and mean squared error (MSE) and its square root (RMSE) in particular, to evaluate predictions. We discuss three ways of finding the best predictor model: using all data and the Bayesian Information Criterion (BIC) as the measure of fit, using training–test splitting of the data, and using k-fold cross-validation, which is an improvement on the training–test split. We discuss how to assess and, if possible, improve the external validity of predictions. We close the chapter by discussing what machine learning means.

The case study in this chapter is **Predicting used car value with linear regressions**, which uses the `used-cars` dataset on used cars of a specific model advertised in a single city. We use this case study to illustrate the main issues we need to address in predictive data analysis and the logic of model selection.

Learning outcomes

After working through this chapter, you should be able to:

- identify situations where you want to, and can, predict y with the help of x;
- understand the concept of prediction error and its components;
- carry out point predictions and interval predictions of quantitative outcomes with linear regression;
- understand the role of model complexity in overfitting the original data;
- use BIC and k-fold cross-validation to find the model that best fits the population, or general pattern, behind the original data;
- assess external validity with the help of domain knowledge, and, if possible, with additional analysis of the original data.

13.1 Prediction Basics

In data analysis, prediction means assigning a value to y, the **target variable**, or **outcome variable**, for a **target observation** or more **target observations**. The value of y is not known for the target observations, but the value of one or more x variables is known. Those x variables are called **predictor variables** in this context. Data analysis with the aim of prediction is called **predictive data analysis** or **predictive analytics**.

The basic logic of prediction is as follows. We have data with observations on both y and x. We call this data the **original data**. The original data doesn't include the target observations for which we want to make the prediction. We use the original data to uncover patterns of association between y and x that we'll use in our prediction. To uncover those patterns, we specify and estimate a model. With the help of that model, we then predict the value of y for the target observations, for which we can observe x but not y. We call data that includes the target observations the **live data**. Thus, in short, we uncover patterns in the original data that we use for prediction in the live data.

Mathematically, those patterns of association are expressed as a function. Recall that a function is a rule that gives a value for y if we plug in values for x. For a target observation j in the live data, we observe the values of the predictor variables x_j. If we know the function, all we need to do is feed those x_j values into it. The abstract notation for the variable and observation we want to predict is y_j. The specific predicted value we call $\hat{y}_j$. The abstract notation for the function we use for the prediction is f; the notation for the specific function we use is $\hat{f}$:

$$\hat{y}_j = \hat{f}(x_j) \tag{13.1}$$

In data analysis, such functions are called **predictive models**. Typically, we can have many different predictive models that give some value of y if we feed in values of x, but we need the model that gives the best prediction. To be more precise, we use the original data to find the model that will then give the best prediction in the live data.

An example for a predictive model is the linear regression with a specific choice of functional forms (e.g., with interactions or without interactions). In the abstract, the linear regression with y, x_1, x_2, is a model for the conditional expected value of y, and it has coefficients β. We need estimated coefficients ($\hat{\beta}$) and actual x values (x_j) to predict an actual value $\hat{y}$:

$$y^E = \beta_0 + \beta_1 x_1 + \beta_2 x_2 + \cdots \tag{13.2}$$

$$\hat{y}_j = \hat{\beta}_0 + \hat{\beta}_1 x_{1j} + \hat{\beta}_2 x_{2j} + \cdots \tag{13.3}$$

Here the function, or model, is $f(x_1, x_2, \ldots) = \beta_0 + \beta_1 x_1 + \beta_2 x_2 + \cdots$, and its estimated version, with specific values for its coefficients, is $\hat{f}(x_{1j}, x_{2j}, \ldots) = \hat{\beta}_0 + \hat{\beta}_1 x_{1j} + \hat{\beta}_2 x_{2j} + \cdots$.

For example, we may want to predict sales of ice cream in our ice cream shop for a specific summer day. We know what day of the week that is, what month of the year, and we have a good forecast for the highest temperature on that day: Wednesday, August, and 30 degrees Celsius (88 degrees Fahrenheit). y is sales, j is the target day, the x are binary variables for day of the week and the month of the year, and temperature. We have access to daily data from three years with the sales, temperature, day of the week, and month variables. That's our original data.

One way to carry out the prediction is the following. We estimate a linear regression using all observations in our original data. That gives us the $\hat{\beta}$ coefficient values. Then we plug in the x_j values and multiply them by the estimated $\hat{\beta}$ coefficient values. The results are our $\hat{y}_j$.

In practice, we'll carry out additional steps when making a prediction. The reason is that there may be other possible models using the same data, and some of those other models could give better predictions. For example, we could have a linear regression with piecewise linear spline for temperature, or we could include interactions of temperature and day of the week, and so on. Or, we may have a model that is not a linear regression at all – we'll introduce such models in subsequent chapters. Some of those models may be better at predicting y using the same data, others less good. Finding the best of such models accounts for many additional steps in predictive analytics.

The fundamental task of predictive analytics is finding the best model. We have the original data that we can use for that. But the best model is best in the sense that it gives the best prediction in the live data, not in the original data. What exactly we mean by the best model, and whether and how we can find it using the original data, are difficult questions.

Review Box 13.1   The logic of prediction

- Prediction means finding a value for y with the help of x for observations with observed x but unobserved y.
- Data analysts use patterns of association between y and x in their original data to predict y in the live data.
- Patterns of association between y and x are captured by a model.
- The fundamental task of prediction is to find the model using the original data that gives the best prediction in the live data.

13.2   Various Kinds of Prediction

Before we move on to finding the best model, let's introduce some more concepts that help describe what kind of prediction we want.

Sometimes we want to predict the value of a quantitative outcome y: that would be a **quantitative prediction**. Sometimes our y is binary, and we want to predict the probability of $y = 1$; that would be a **probability prediction**. Yet other times, when we have a binary y, we want to predict whether the outcome is 0 or 1, not the probability. That's called **classification**. In principle, probability predictions and classifications can be applied not only to binary y variables but to qualitative y variables with more categories, too.

Our example of predicting sales in an ice cream shop is a quantitative prediction. An example for a probability prediction is the probability of whether a loan applicant will repay their loan. Here we have a binary y variable (1 if repays, 0 if defaults); the prediction would be based on the probability that an applicant would repay their loan as a function of various predictor variables that we know about the applicant when they apply for the loan. For a classification example, consider the same question of whether a loan applicant would repay their loan, but here we want to classify each applicant into one of two groups: whether they'll repay their loan or not.

With quantitative predictions, and with probability predictions, we can predict a single value $\hat{y}_j$. That is called **point prediction**, to distinguish it from **interval prediction**. An interval prediction produces a **prediction interval**, or **PI**, that tells where to find the value of y_j with a certain likelihood (e.g., a 95% prediction interval or an 80% prediction interval).

In the context of the simple linear regression, we have already introduced the prediction interval, in Chapter 9, Section 9.3: the point prediction plus or minus the standard prediction error (SPE), multiplied by a number. That multiplying number reflects the likelihood that we want for the prediction interval for covering the actual values. For a 95% PI this number is 2: $95\% PI(\hat{y}_j) = \hat{y}_j \pm 2SPE(\hat{y}_j)$; for an 80% PI it would be 1.3: $80\% PI(\hat{y}_j) = \hat{y}_j \pm 1.3SPE(\hat{y}_j)$; for a 67% PI it would be 1: $67\% PI(\hat{y}_j) = \hat{y}_j \pm SPE(\hat{y}_j)$. Recall the formula for the standard prediction error in a linear regression with a single x variable is:

$$SPE(\hat{y}_j) = Std[e]\sqrt{1 + \frac{1}{n} + \frac{(x_j - \bar{x})^2}{nVar[x]}} \tag{13.4}$$

With more x variables the formula is more complicated, but the intuition is similar. The SPE is smaller the larger the sample, the smaller the residual standard deviation, the closer the observation to the average of the x variable(s), and the larger the spread of the x variable(s). In subsequent chapters we'll consider alternative models for prediction. The concept of prediction interval, and the intuition behind its components, will be similar for those alternative models, too.

For example, a point prediction of ice cream sales is a single number, such as 1462 dollars. An example for an interval prediction would be [1299; 1625] with an 80% likelihood. When we want to predict the probability of whether a loan applicant will repay their loan, a point prediction may be 0.82. We may have a corresponding interval prediction, say [0.74; 0.90] with an 80% likelihood.

In this chapter and the following few chapters, we'll focus on quantitative predictions. We'll discuss probability prediction and classification in Chapter 17.

Finally, we will use the term **forecasting** for making predictions about future values of y when the original data is a time series. True, most of the time the original data is from the past and the live data, with the target observation(s), is in the future. So most predictions are about future values, and thus distinguishing forecasting from other kinds of predictions is a little arbitrary. For historical reasons, in business and economics, the term forecasting is used when the original data is a time series itself. We'll discuss forecasting in Chapter 18.

> **Review Box 13.2 Types of predictions**
>
> - Quantitative predictions predict the value of a quantitative y; probability predictions predict the probability of $y = 1$ for a binary variable; classifications predict whether $y = 1$ or $y = 0$ for a binary variable.
> - Quantitative predictions provide a single value (point prediction) or a range of values (interval prediction).
> - Forecasts are predictions that use time series data.

13.A1 CASE STUDY – Predicting Used Car Value with Linear Regressions

Question and data

The goal of this case study is to predict the price for cars with particular features. Suppose that we have a car that we want to sell in the near future. It is a regular gas-fueled Toyota Camry LE sedan that is 10 years old with 120 000 miles on it and a 4-cylinder engine, and our car is in an excellent condition. We live in the Chicago area in the United States, so we will look at the Chicago used car market. We want to predict the future selling price of the car. To make this prediction, we use data on ad prices of similar cars. Our main interest is in predicting the price we can expect to get for our car. But we may also be interested in how we can expect the price to change if we were to wait one more year, which would increase age and miles.

Predicting the price of a used car is a quantitative prediction exercise. The goal is to assign a price (point prediction) or a range of prices to cars with certain features.

In this case study, we use the `used-cars` dataset, which we collected in early 2018 from offers in Chicago. To match the car of interest, our data is on a single model, the Toyota Camry. The features include the more specific type of the car (LE, Hybrid), when it was made, how many miles it has, whether it's in good condition, and so on.

First, as usual, we started with data cleaning. We identified variable values in the data that are obvious errors and dropped those observations. Second, we created a data table with cars that are not fundamentally different from the car whose price we want to predict. We dropped cars that are found erroneously in the data (e.g. trucks) as well as hybrid cars. Our variables are price, age, miles, type, whether in good condition, whether 4 cylinders or 6 cylinders, and whether advertised by the owner or a dealer.

13.3 The Prediction Error and Its Components

The goal of a prediction is getting as close to the value of y for the target observation as possible. With a quantitative prediction, the point prediction is $\hat{y}_j$. The difference between the two is the **prediction error**:

$$e_j = \hat{y}_j - y_j \tag{13.5}$$

The actual value, y_j, is not known when the prediction is made; hence the need to predict it. Thus, the prediction error is not known, either, until we observe y_j itself. But arriving at a good prediction requires thinking about the prediction error before we get to observe it.

The ideal prediction error, e_j, is zero: our predicted value is right on target. The prediction error is positive if we over-predict the value: we predict a higher value than the actual value. It is negative if we under-predict the value: our prediction is too low. The prediction error is larger in absolute value the further away our prediction is from the actual value. It is smaller the closer we are. Whether positive versus negative errors matter more, or they are equally bad, depends on the decision problem for which we are using the prediction. We shall return to this question in the next section.

Our definition is valid for quantitative predictions. We can define the prediction error for probability predictions in a very similar way, too. For classification, the prediction error still makes sense, but it can be of few values only (classified right or classified wrong). As indicated earlier, we'll focus on quantitative predictions in this chapter.

Often we want to make predictions for more than one target observation. Then the goal is to arrive at predicted values with as small an error as possible for all of them. We shall return later to the question of how we should combine prediction errors for many observations.

The prediction error can be decomposed into three components: **estimation error, model error, and irreducible error** – also called **idiosyncratic error** or **genuine error**.

The estimation error comes from the fact that, with a model f, we use our original data to find $\hat{f}$. When using a linear regression for prediction, this error is due to the fact that we don't know the values of the coefficients of the regression (β), only their estimated values ($\hat{\beta}$). This error is captured by the SE of the regression line (Chapter 9, Section 9.3). The smaller the SE of the regression line, the smaller estimation error we can expect, which tends to happen the larger the sample, the smaller the residual standard deviation (the better the fit), the closer the target observation to the average of the x variables, and the more spread the x variables are.

The model error reflects the fact that we may not have selected the best model for our prediction. More specifically, instead of model f, there may be a better model, g, which uses the same predictor variables x or different predictor variables from the same original data. For example, when using a linear regression for prediction, we should have included interactions that we didn't, or we included interactions that we shouldn't have included. Or, maybe, the best model to predict y is not a linear regression but something else.

The last component, irreducible error, is due to the fact that we are not able to make a perfect prediction for y_j with the help of the x_j variables even if we find the best model and we can estimate it without any estimation error. Maybe, if we had data with more x variables, we could have a better prediction using those additional variables. But, with the variables we have, we can't do anything about this error. That's why its name is irreducible error.

Recall that we use the prediction interval (PI) for interval predictions, and the PI depends on the standard prediction error (SPE) (Section 13.2). It turns out that this SPE includes two of the three components of the prediction error: estimation error and irreducible error. It includes model error within the irreducible error component. It is computed using the results from a specific model, so it measures uncertainty in the context of that specific model.

For practical purposes, we shall try to reduce the estimation error and the model error, and we'll acknowledge that there is some, often large, irreducible part of the prediction error. To reduce the estimation error, we'll try to use as many observations as possible. To reduce model error, we have to find the best possible model. That is the topic of the rest of this chapter.

Review Box 13.3 Prediction error and its components

- The prediction error is the difference between the predicted value of the target variable and its actual (yet unknown) value y_j for the target observation: $e_j = \hat{y}_j - y_j$.
- The prediction error can be decomposed into three parts:

  1. Estimation error: the difference between the prediction from the estimated model and the model that would be true in the population, or general pattern, represented by the data.
  2. Model error: the difference between the prediction from the model we use and the best model.
  3. Irreducible error (idiosyncratic or genuine error): the difference between the predicted value from the best possible model and the actual value.

- The prediction interval from a linear regression includes uncertainty due to estimation error and the mix of irreducible error and model error.

13.A2 CASE STUDY – Predicting Used Car Value with Linear Regressions

Five regression models

Let's consider the predictor variables in the analysis. To model nonlinearity in age for a regression with price as the dependent variable, we may try a quadratic approximation.

Table 13.1 Versions of regression models for predicting used car price

Model No.	Used variables
Model 1	age, age squared
Model 2	age, age squared, odometer, odometer squared
Model 3	age, age squared, odometer, odometer squared, LE, condition like new, excellent condition, good condition, dealer
Model 4	age, age squared, odometer, odometer squared, LE, condition like new, excellent condition, good condition, dealer, SE, XLE, cylinder
Model 5	same as Model 4 but with all variables interacted with age

The odometer, measuring miles the car traveled (in 10 thousand mile units), is a likely strong predictor of price. We also include the more specific type of the car: LE, XLE, SE (this information is missing in about 30 percent of the observations). We also include if the ad says that the car is in good condition, excellent condition, or it is like new (this is missing for about one third of the ads). We have a binary variable capturing if the ad was posted by a dealer rather than a private person. Finally, we include whether the car's engine has 6 cylinders (20 percent of ads say this; 43

percent say 4 cylinders, and the rest have no information on this characteristic). Our data has 281 observations.

Using the data, we build various prediction models described in Table 13.1. We start by adding age and odometer reading (mileage) and then gradually add more variables.

Table 13.2 shows the results from the first four regressions. The fifth regression includes inter-actions with age and has many coefficients; we don't include those estimates in the table for simplicity. The table shows the regression coefficients but not the standard errors or stars for significance. This is a prediction exercise and thus statistical inference of the coefficients is not interesting – our goal is not to generalize the coefficients to the population represented by the data.

Table 13.2 Regression models for predicting used car price

Variables	(1) Model 1	(2) Model 2	(3) Model 3	(4) Model 4
age	−1, 530.09	−1, 149.22	−873.47	−836.64
age squared	35.05	27.65	18.21	17.63
odometer		−303.84	−779.90	−788.70
odometer squared			18.81	19.20
type: LE			28.11	−20.48
type: XLE				301.69
type: SE				1, 338.79
condition: like new				558.67
condition: excellent			176.49	190.40
condition: good			293.36	321.56
cylinder_6				−370.27
dealer			572.98	822.65
Constant	18 365.45	18 860.20	19 431.89	18 963.35
Observations	281	281	281	281
R-squared	0.847	0.898	0.913	0.919

Note: Coefficient estimates for four regression models. Standard errors not shown.

Source: used-cars dataset Used Toyota Camry cars, Chicago area.

We can interpret the coefficients, mostly to check if the model makes sense. Age is negatively related to price, in a convex fashion, which means the left half of a U-shaped curve. The same is true for odometer reading. Cars that are advertised as being like new, in good condition, or in excellent condition, have higher prices than others.

To illustrate a point prediction, take Model 3 and values of the predictor variables for our car: age 10, odometer 12×10 thousand miles, type LE, and in excellent condition. To compute the predicted value, we use the coefficient estimates from model (3):

$$19431.89 + 10*(-873.47) + 100*(18.21) + 12*(-779.9) + 144*(18.81) + 1*(28.11) + 1*176.49 = 6072.63$$

Hence the predicted price for a car like ours is 6073 dollars.

As summarized in Table 13.3, this point prediction has the 95% prediction interval (PI) of PI[3382–8763]. Ads for cars just like ours may ask a price ranging from 3382 to 8763 dollars with a 95% chance. That's a very wide range of over 5000 dollars. The 80% prediction interval is narrower by almost 2000 dollars. Note that the first, simplest model has a point prediction of 6569 dollars, with an even wider prediction interval.

Table 13.3 Point predictions and interval predictions for a specific car, using models 1 and 3		
	Model 1	**Model 3**
Point prediction	6569	6073
Prediction Interval (80%)	[4,296–8,843]	[4,317–7,829]
Prediction Interval (95%)	[3,085–10,053]	[3,382–8,763]

Source: used-cars dataset. Used Toyota Camry cars, Chicago area, N=281.

Even though our Model 3 captures a large part of the variation in prices (with an R-squared of 91.8%), there remains a large uncertainty in any given prediction. This example is instructive: despite having a great fit within the sample, predicting a single value with great confidence is hard.

If we want to sell fast or think that other features of our car make it less valuable, we may want to advertise it at a price closer to the lower end. Conversely, if we think that other features of our car make it more valuable and we have time, we may want to pick a price closer to the high end. Or, we may go for the best prediction of 6073 dollars.

13.4 The Loss Function

When making a prediction we want as small a prediction error as possible. The prediction error forms the basis of measuring the quality of our prediction. As we discussed it, it's something we can think about but not measure, as one of its components is the unknown y_j. Let's keep putting that aside, and let's think about how we can build on the prediction error to evaluate a prediction.

We certainly care about the magnitude of the prediction error: a larger error is always worse than, or at least as bad as, a smaller error. In fact, a larger error may be disproportionately worse than a smaller error. But we may also care about the direction of the error. Underpredicting the value by the same amount as overpredicting it may be equally bad, but it may be better, or it may be worse.

Ultimately, both magnitude and the direction of the error matter because predictions lead to decisions that have consequences. Thus, an error in the prediction has consequences, too. For example, when we want to predict sales of ice cream in our ice cream shop, underprediction may make us prepare less ice cream and run out of it. That's bad both because we forgo profits on that day, but also because it would hurt our reputation. If, in contrast, we overpredict sales, we may produce too much ice cream and end up with a lot of unsold ice cream. That's bad because we incur costs without revenues for unsold ice cream; ice cream is perishable, especially if it's in the display area.

To help decisions, we would attach a value to the consequences of the prediction error: a loss that we incur due to decisions we make because of a bad prediction. This idea is formulated in a **loss function**. A loss function translates the prediction errors into a number that makes more sense for the decisions and their consequences. Typically, we have more than one target observation. The loss function takes the prediction error for each of them and produces a single number. The loss function helps to rank predictions. Of course, we could simply rank the predictions based on adding up prediction errors: that would be a linear loss function. But a loss function may be a nonlinear function of the errors.

However nice it would be, specifying a loss function can be very hard in practice. It would involve quantifying all of the consequences of all of the decisions that are made based on the predictions. But some general properties of a loss function may be established without fully specifying it. Of those, the two most important are symmetry versus asymmetry, and linearity versus convexity.

Symmetric loss functions attach the same value to positive and negative errors of the same magnitude. **Asymmetric** loss functions attach different values to errors of the same magnitude if they are on different sides. Linearity versus convexity is about the magnitudes of error in quantitative predictions (or probability predictions). **Linear** loss functions attach proportionally larger loss to an error, regardless of its magnitude. In contrast, **convex** loss functions attach a disproportionately larger loss to an error that is larger.

For example, if our ice cream shop has a lot of competition, we may be more worried about damaged reputation than incurring more costs, and so our loss function would be asymmetric, with larger loss attached to a negative prediction error than to a positive prediction error of the same size. Most likely, our loss function would be convex in both directions: a larger prediction error would have disproportionately larger consequences than a smaller prediction error.

Or consider the inflation forecasts used by central banks to decide on monetary policy. The loss function of central banks should describe the social costs of wrong decisions based on erroneous predictions. The larger the prediction error, the larger the chances of wrong decisions and thus the larger the social costs. It is not straightforward to assess whether social costs are symmetric and how large they are. Arguably, however, larger errors may induce costs that are disproportionately larger: small prediction errors may not divert monetary policy from the best choice at all, or they may divert it only to a small extent that is relatively easy to reverse. Therefore, the loss function may or may not be symmetric, and it is likely to be convex.

Figure 13.1 shows some examples for the various shapes of loss functions. One loss function is linear, one is convex and symmetric, and one is convex and asymmetric, assigning smaller losses to negative errors than to positive errors.

As we discussed, ideally we would attach a loss function to the prediction error based on the actual consequences of that error in our decision situation. That's very difficult in practice, and very often it is simply impossible. Instead, we often use a generic loss function that we think represents the most important properties of our situation.

By far the most widely used generic loss function is the **squared loss**. It defines the loss as the square of the error. It is therefore a symmetric and convex loss function.

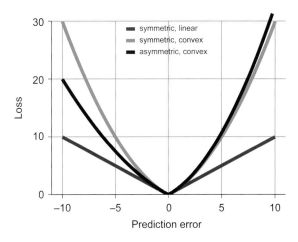

Figure 13.1   The shape of three loss functions: linear and symmetric, convex and symmetric, convex and asymmetric

---

Review Box 13.4   Loss functions

- A loss function translates the prediction error into losses due to such predictions.
- A loss function is necessary to evaluate the quality of a prediction.
- Two key characteristics of loss functions are symmetry and convexity.

13.5 Mean Squared Error (MSE) and Root Mean Squared Error (RMSE)

The most frequently used loss function is squared loss. When we have a prediction for multiple observations, we aggregate those squared losses across them. The most widely used aggregation is the mean, and it's called the **mean squared error**, or **MSE**. Often, we use its square root, the **root mean squared error**, or **RMSE**. Comparisons using RMSE lead to the same results as comparisons based on MSE, but the magnitude of RMSE is easier to interpret: it's the typical error we are expected to make (similar to standard deviation versus variance). In the formula, J observations are used; each is labeled with index j:

$$MSE = \frac{1}{J}\sum_{j=1}^{J}(\hat{y}_j - y_j)^2 \tag{13.6}$$

$$RMSE = \sqrt{MSE} = \sqrt{\frac{1}{J}\sum_{j=1}^{J}(\hat{y}_j - y_j)^2} \tag{13.7}$$

The MSE formula should look familiar, because it's like the numerator of the R-squared formula for the linear regression; see Chapter 7, Section 7.9. The difference is that the R-squared is calculated using predicted values in the original data used for the regression, while the MSE as a loss function is defined for the live data, although it can be computed for the original data as well.

Review Box 13.5   Squared loss, MSE, RMSE

- The most widely used loss function is squared loss: $L(e_j) = e_j^2 = (\hat{y}_j - y_j)^2$. It's symmetric and convex.
- Mean squared error (MSE) is the average squared loss across several target observations:

$$MSE = \frac{1}{J} \sum_{j=1}^{J} (\hat{y}_j - y_j)^2$$

- Root mean squared error (RMSE) is its square root:

$$RMSE = \sqrt{MSE}$$

13.6   Bias and Variance of Predictions

Earlier, we discussed the three components of the prediction error in Section 13.3: estimation error, model error, and irreducible error. Analogously, the MSE can be decomposed into these three parts, too: estimation mean squared error, model mean squared error, and irreducible mean squared error. This decomposition is useful because it helps guide our thinking of how to find the best model: the model should give as precise estimates as possible, and it should be as close to the theoretically best model as possible. With the data we have, we can't do anything with the third component. Moreover, these two can be traded off: having a model that is close to, but not exactly, the theoretically best model may be fine if it buys us substantially smaller estimation MSE. Or, the other way around, a little more estimation error may be fine if it's more than compensated by a smaller model error.

There is another way to decompose the MSE, and that can also help thinking about the best model and potential trade-offs in finding it. That is the bias–variance decomposition.

The **bias of a prediction** is the average of its prediction error. An unbiased prediction produces zero error on average across multiple predictions. A biased prediction produces nonzero error on average; the bias can be positive or negative.

The **variance of a prediction** describes how it varies around its average value when multiple predictions are made. It's the variance of the prediction error around its average value. That average value can be zero or not, so the prediction may be unbiased or biased. The variance is zero if the prediction error is the same for all predictions. The variance is higher the larger the spread of specific predictions around the average prediction.

It turns out that the MSE is the sum of the squared bias and the prediction variance:

$$MSE = \frac{1}{J} \sum_{j=1}^{J} (\hat{y}_j - y_j)^2$$

$$= \left(\frac{1}{J} \sum_{j=1}^{J} (\hat{y}_j - y_j) \right)^2 + \frac{1}{J} \sum_{j=1}^{J} (y_j - \bar{y})^2 \tag{13.8}$$

$$= Bias^2 + PredictionVariance$$

This decomposition helps appreciate a trade-off: a biased prediction with small variance may be better than an unbiased prediction with a large variance. Of course, a prediction with both smaller bias and smaller variance is always better.

A metaphor that is often invoked in this context is target shooting. Unbiased shooters hit the target on average. But they can do that in various ways: they can be very close to the target all the time; or they can shoot over a very wide range, but the errors average to zero. The first example is one of low variance, the second is one of high variance. Moreover, when comparing an unbiased but high-variance shooter with a biased but low-variance shooter, we may prefer the latter. That's because the first one is prone to make big mistakes, while the second one is known to make small mistakes, even if those mistakes don't average to zero.

The linear regression, estimated by OLS, gives an unbiased prediction. Thus, the ranking of linear regression models by their MSE means ranking them by their prediction variance. But there are other models that are a little biased but produce a smaller prediction variance and achieve a better MSE that way.

13.7 The Task of Finding the Best Model

After introducing the theoretical basis for comparing the predictions of various models, we can now discuss how to do that in practice. The fundamental difficulty stems from the fact that what we have is the original data. Thus, we can compare the predictions of various models using the original data only. However, what we want is the best prediction in terms of the live data, not the original data.

An important dimension along which various models may differ is **model complexity**. For example, in a linear regression, a more complex model has more coefficients. That may be because it has more right-hand-side variables. Of two linear regressions that make use of the same x variables in the data, a more complex model has more coefficients because of more complicated functional forms (more variables squared terms, higher-order polynomial terms, more knots for splines, and so on), or more interactions. In our case study of predicting used car value, the five models we considered were five linear regressions of increasing level of complexity. Finding the best model involves finding the right degree of complexity. That turns out to be a balancing act.

Using the language we introduced in the context of regression (Chapter 7, Section 7.9), the best model is the one that fits the live data best. But there is no way to tell how predictions would fit the live data. Instead, we have to choose the best model using the original data. The fit of a regression model to the original data can be measured by the R-squared. Recall that the R-squared is just like the MSE, except it is computed using predictions within the original data, and it is divided by the variance of y and subtracted from one:

$$R^2 = 1 - \frac{\frac{1}{n}\sum_{i=1}^{n}(y_i - \hat{y}_i)^2}{\frac{1}{n}\sum_{i=1}^{n}(y_i - \bar{y})^2} \tag{13.9}$$

So we can rank models by their R-squared in the original data. This ranking is the same as ranking by their MSE would be if it were computed using the original data.

Unfortunately, though, the best R-squared in the original data may not give the best MSE in the live data. In fact, it never does. That's because a more complex model always gives a better R-squared. But that complexity may reflect patterns that are specific to the original data but would not be there in the live data.

In fact, comparing two models, Model 1 can give a worse fit in the live data than Model 2 in two ways. First, Model 1 may give a worse fit both in the original data and the live data. In this case, we say that Model 1 **underfits** the original data. This is quite straightforward. Second, however, Model 1 may actually give a better fit in the original data, but a worse fit in the live data. In this case, we say that Model 1 **overfits** the original data. This is less straightforward, but it's just as important.

Overfitting is a serious threat, because all we have is the original data to find the best model. The possibility of overfitting the original data means that the model that gives the best fit in the original data may not be the one that gives the best prediction in the live data. A more complex model always gives a higher R-squared in the original data. That's because a more complex model tends to find more detailed patterns in the original data. But some of those more detailed patterns will be there for the original data only; they will not be present in the live data. Thus, a very complex model would produce a very good fit in the original data, but, with a high chance, it would in fact overfit the original data.

Consider our example of predicting sales in our ice cream shop. Suppose that we have daily time series data on temperature and sales for three years, with about 1000 observations in total. Model 1 may be a linear regression with month dummies (11 variables), day of the week dummies (6 variables), and temperature in a quadratic function. These are 20 coefficients, including the intercept. Model 2 may add interactions of month with temperature (in quadratic). These are 22 additional variables, with a total of 42 coefficients to estimate. Model 3 includes interactions of month, day of week, and temperature. This means 12×7 month–day interactions (minus the reference group), twice as many temperature coefficients (in quadratic), plus day of the week–temperature interactions for the reference month category, with close to 300 coefficients to estimate in total.

In this example, Model 1 may underfit the original data compared to Model 2: the temperature–sales pattern may differ by months both in the original data and the live data, which is captured in Model 2 but not in Model 1. In contrast, Model 3 may overfit the original data. One way to understand Model 3 is that it fits a regression of sales and temperature in a quadratic form for each month and day of the week separately. Consider Wednesdays in August, with around 12 to 15 such observations in the data (three years means three Augusts, each with 4 or 5 Wednesdays). That's a very small sample. We fit a quadratic in temperature on this data. A lot of other things affect sales that may have happened on August Wednesdays during these three years that won't necessarily happen in the live data (one of our competitors ran a price discount, one of our refrigerators was out for a few hours, and so on). And some of those other things may have happened on days with unusually high or unusually low temperatures. This is a small sample, so one or two such events could tilt the regression curve to a large degree in some way. But that's not how the sales–temperature pattern will play out in the live data. Our very complex model is bound to fit some of these patterns in the original data. But that's overfitting.

Figure 13.2 illustrates underfitting and overfitting and its relation to model complexity. It shows many hypothetical models. The horizontal axis shows their complexity: more complex models are to the right. The vertical axis shows the RMSE of each model: higher values show worse fit. The blue curve shows RMSE in the original data; the green curve shows RMSE in the live data. Models with very low complexity give a bad fit to both the original data and the live data. Looking at more and more complex models, the fit in the original data keeps getting better and better. However, the same is not true for fit in the live data: after a point, fit starts to become worse as model complexity increases. Too complex models overfit the original data: they tend to give much worse fits in the live data than in the original data.

Finding the best model requires using the original data to infer something about the live data. Similarly to what we did when we discussed inference earlier in Chapter 5, it makes sense to split this problem into two. The first problem is the original data versus the population, or general pattern, it represents. The second problem is the two worlds: the population, or general pattern, that is relevant

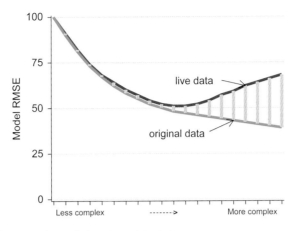

Figure 13.2   Underfitting and overfitting the original data

Note: RMSE on artificial original and live data; the grey bars indicate the difference.

for the original data, and the other world that will be relevant for the live data. Thus, the problem of overfitting the original data is best split into two problems, too: fitting patterns in the original data that are not there in the population, or general pattern, it represents; and fitting patterns in the world of the original data that will not be there in the world of the live data.

In the following three sections we'll introduce three methods that can help with the first problem: selecting the model that is the best in terms of prediction in the general pattern represented by the original data. We'll turn to the second problem, external validity, afterwards.

> **Review Box 13.6   Main concepts of prediction**
>
> - The best model gives the best prediction in the live data.
> - The only data we can use to find the best model is the original data.
> - The model that gives the best prediction (best fit) in the original data may not give the best prediction (best fit) in the live data.
> - Overfitting means achieving a good fit in the original data by finding patterns that are specific to the original data only and would not achieve a good fit in the live data.

13.8   Finding the Best Model by Best Fit and Penalty: The BIC

One solution to finding the best model is using all of the original data for estimation and finding the model that fits the original data best, but measuring fit in a way that discourages overfitting. In effect, that means using a measure of fit that has a **penalty for model complexity**. In essence, a measure of fit with a penalty term has two parts: one part measuring fit, and another part measuring complexity. The final measure is better, the better the fit if the complexity is the same, or if the complexity is less but the fit is the same. Comparing models with different fits and different complexities at the same time, the two properties are traded off to rank the models.

There are several measures of fit that include a penalty term for model complexity. They differ in how they trade off fit with complexity. We mention three measures: **adjusted R-squared**, **AIC**

(Akaike's information criterion), and **BIC** (the Bayesian information criterion). Most statistical software shows these measures by default when reporting the results of regression models.

Of the three, we suggest using BIC because many data analysts have found it to be the best of these similar measures. It is also called the Schwarz criterion. The BIC is a statistic measuring how far the predicted values are from actual values so the lower the BIC value, the better the expected fit. Thus, a lower BIC implies a better fit, a less complex model, or both.

It turns out that the BIC is derived from a set of complicated assumptions regarding the data. Most of those assumptions are hard, or impossible, to check. For that reason, the BIC is not necessarily an ideal way to select the model that would provide the best fit to the live data. In particular, the BIC is sometimes too harsh on model complexity, giving a lower ranking to models that are more complex even when those end up being better at prediction in the live data.

Despite its shortcomings, in many cases the BIC can help avoid severe overfitting and pick the best model, or at least one of the best of models. It is easy to calculate, and it often gives a good enough answer.

The most important caveat to keep in mind is that the BIC is calculated using the original data. If external validity is high and the patterns in the live data are likely similar to the patterns in the original data, that's fine. However, if external validity is low, we have a problem. The BIC is not tuned to appreciate whether external validity is high or low. It is tuned to measure fit in the original data and penalize complexity.

Review Box 13.7   The BIC

- The BIC is a measure of the fit of a model using all the original data.
- The BIC penalizes model complexity and thus helps avoid overfitting the original data.

13.9   Finding the Best Model by Training and Test Samples

An alternative to using all the original data and a measure of fit that penalizes model complexity is imitating the original versus live data problem in a more direct way. All we have is the original data. But we can split the original data into two, and use one part for estimation and the other part for measuring fit.

The first part of the data is called the **training set**, or **training sample**. We use this part of the data as if it were all the original data we had. In particular, we do exploratory data analysis that we use to specify regression models, and then we estimate the regression models using the training set only.

The second part of the data is called the **test set** or **test sample**. This is the part we use to evaluate the predictions. In particular, we pretend that we can observe x in this data but not y, and we use the model estimates from the training set to predict $\hat{y}$ for each observation in the test set. Then, we compare those predictions with the actual y values to calculate the prediction error and then the measure of fit, such as MSE, RMSE, or something else if we have a different loss function. The model that gives the best fit to the test set is the best model.

Finally, once the best model is found, we re-estimate that model using the entire original data. We use this estimated model for prediction.

Let's spend a little more time on related language that is used broadly in predictive analytics. In the prediction setup, **training a model** means all the steps of data analysis that lead to a prediction:

selecting the *x* variables, maybe transforming the *y* and/or some of the *x* variables, specifying the model, and estimating it. In predictive analytics, **testing** means predicting *y* values using a model (that was "trained" previously) and evaluating that prediction. Importantly, this kind of testing is a different thing from testing hypotheses that we discussed in Chapter 6. The method itself is called the **train–test method**, or the **training–test split**, to evaluate predictions.

All of this sounds quite intuitive, indeed: the proof of the pudding is in the eating. If we want to find a model that best fits data that is similar to, but not the same as, the data used for the estimation, let's do just that: let's find the best fit on data that is similar to, but not the same as, the data we use for estimation. However, there are some details that we need to decide on, and those details may matter. And, as we'll see, there are issues with this approach, no matter how we decide on those details.

The details to be decided for the training–test split are how many observations to allocate to the training set and the test set and how to select those observations. In general, data analysts choose more observations to be in the training set than the test set. Typical choices for the size of the training sample are 80% or 90% of the full original data, with corresponding test sample sizes of 20% and 10%.

How to select the observations is the other decision to make. The guiding principle is to have the test set as similar to the live data as possible. Unfortunately, however, we know little about what the live data will look like. In particular, we don't know whether and how the patterns of association between predictors and the outcome will differ from the original data. For this reason, the usual choice is a random sample. The training set is a random subsample of the original data; the test set is the remaining part that is thus also a random sample.

Three issues makes the training–test split a less-than-ideal method for choosing the best prediction method.

First, this method uses fewer observations for model estimation than are available, at least when trying to find the best model. The training set is a subsample of the original data. Recall that the prediction error tends to be larger when the estimation error is larger, and the estimation error is larger the fewer observations are used. This actually is the reason why, once the best model is found, we go back and use all observations in the original data to estimate the model for the actual prediction. So we avoid the issue for the prediction itself. But higher estimation error may still matter for our ability to find the best model. We try to minimize the issue by having the training sample contain more observations than the test sample, such as 80% versus 20%.

The second of the three issues is that the training–test method doesn't really avoid overfitting the original data. True, it avoids overfitting the training sample, as the predictions are evaluated without using observations from that sample. But it may very well overfit the test sample. In fact, the test sample may have patterns in it that are specific to it and not present in the live data, just as the training sample would have such patterns. Thus, overfitting the test sample is a likely problem.

The third issue is common across the training–test method and the BIC and the similar measures. It's the fundamental issue with external validity. All we have is the original data. Thus, with a clever method, we may be able to find the best model for the population, or general pattern, represented by the original data. That way we can avoid overfitting patterns that are there in the original data but would not be there in the population represented by the original data. Whether the model that we find this way is also the best model for the live data requires a leap of faith: external validity. As we'll see later, we can sometimes find some guidance for that leap even in the original data, but that requires thinking instead of using a method off the shelves.

Before turning to external validity, we discuss an improvement on the train–test method, which helps a lot with the second issue we listed (overfitting the test sample).

13.10   Finding the Best Model by Cross-Validation

Using a test set to evaluate predictions rewards models that fit patterns that are in the test set and penalizes models that fit other patterns which are not in the test set. This way, the procedure avoids overfitting in the training data. At the same time, we may fit a model on patterns that are specific to the test set. An improved version of splitting the data is called k-fold cross-validation, and it remedies this problem.

Cross-validation (**CV**), also known by a more precise name, **k-fold cross-validation**, is a method of sample splitting that involves taking more than one split of the original data into training and test sets, and then looking at the average fit across all test sets. Each observation will appear exactly once in a test set and $k - 1$ times in the training sets. A training set–test set combination is called a **fold**. A k-fold cross-validation works with k folds.

For example, with 10-fold cross-validation, we split the original data into ten subsets in a random way, so each subset consists of 10% of the observations. Then we take each of the ten 10% samples as a test set and define the corresponding training set as the other 90%. There are ten folds: ten training–test combinations. The test sets do not overlap with each other, and they cover all observations in the original data. The training–test method described above is hence carried out ten times. We can calculate the loss function, such as the MSE, ten times: $MSE_1 \dots MSE_k$. The overall fit of the model is measured by the average of the ten MSE values, or the RMSE, which is the square root of this average:

$$MSE_{cv(k)} = \frac{1}{k} \sum_{i=1}^{k} MSE_i \qquad (13.10)$$

$$RMSE_{cv(k)} = \sqrt{\frac{1}{k} \sum_{i=1}^{k} MSE_i} \qquad (13.11)$$

This approach decreases the role of a particular test set in determining the MSE and thus the risk of overfitting the patterns of a particular test set.

A further improvement would repeat cross-validation many times, each for a different random partition of the dataset, and compute the overall average MSE. This approach further decreases the problem of overfitting a particular test set by selecting a larger number of different test sets. In most cases, this refinement offers little further improvement.

Thus, k-fold cross-validation helps greatly with what we listed as the second issue with the training–test method: overfitting the test sample. Thus, k-fold cross-validation is a better method to find the best model than a single training–test split.

In addition, k-fold cross-validation has a clear advantage over BIC, too. While BIC can be applied to regression models, k-fold cross-validation is a method that can be applied to any prediction model. As a result, k-fold cross-validation is the most widely used method to find the best model in predictive analytics. It requires a lot of work, but that work is done by the computer, not the analyst. k-fold cross-validation is a built-in feature of most statistical software.

> **Review Box 13.8   Training–test split and k-fold cross-validation**
>
> - The training–test split partitions the original data into two sets in a random way. All analysis and estimation takes place using observations in the training set. The evaluation of prediction takes place using observations in the test set.
> - The training–test split avoids overfitting the training set; however, it may overfit the test set.
> - k-fold cross-validation improves on the single training–test split by repeating it *k* times. Each split is called a fold. The prediction of a model is evaluated across the folds, such as the average MSE.
> - k-fold cross-validation is a good way to find the model that would give the best prediction for the population, or general pattern, represented by the original data.

13.A3   CASE STUDY – Predicting Used Car Value with Linear Regressions

Finding the best model

Let us go back to our case study and find the best of the five predictive models using the tools we have just covered.

Table 13.4   Car price models estimated using all original data and measures of fit using all original data

Model	N vars	N coeff	R-squared	RMSE	BIC
Model 1	1	3	0.85	1755	5018
Model 2	2	5	0.90	1433	4910
Model 3	5	9	0.91	1322	4893
Model 4	6	12	0.92	1273	4894
Model 5	6	22	0.92	1239	4935

Note: Five linear regression models; see Table 13.1 for details. Here N vars is the number of variables; and N coeff is the number of all coefficients including the intercept.

Source: `used-cars` dataset. Used Toyota Camry cars, Chicago area, N=281.

The loss function for predicting the value of our used car may or may not be symmetric, depending, among other things, on how we value money and how we value how much time it takes to sell our car. Too low a prediction may lead to selling our car cheap but fast; too high a prediction may make us wait a long time and, possibly, require us to revise the sales price downwards before selling our car. The loss function may be linear or convex, again, depending on how we value money and time. We will consider a symmetric and convex loss function, the one captured by RMSE.

We have 281 observations, and our regression models have few variables, but the most complex models include many interactions. For several categories such as car types, we have a few dozen observations driving results. Hence, we may indeed overfit the data, especially with models that include many interactions. To find the best predictive model, we first look at BIC values along with R-squared and the RMSE in Table 13.4.

Second, we cross-validate using k-fold cross-validation. We set $k = 4$, given the small sample (a few hundred observations is a small sample for prediction). This means splitting the data into four in a random fashion to define the four test sets. Thus, each fold has 1/4 of the observations in the test set and 3/4 of the observations in the training set. For each fold, we estimate ("train") all five models using the training set and calculate MSE on the corresponding test sample. We then average out MSE values over the four test samples for each model. The results are shown in Table 13.5.

Table 13.5   Car price models estimated and evaluated using 4-fold cross-validation and RMSE

Fold No.	Model 1	Model 2	Model 3	Model 4	Model 5
Fold1	1734	1428	1331	1395	1391
Fold2	2010	1781	1692	1638	1693
Fold3	1465	1251	1256	1253	1436
Fold4	1823	1325	1250	1246	1307
Average	1769	1460	1394	1392	1464

Note: Five linear regression models; for details see Table 13.1. Cross-validated RMSE values.

Source: used-cars dataset. Used Toyota Camry cars, Chicago area, N=281.

Both approaches suggest that Model 3 and Model 4 are the ones that have the best prediction properties. They have the lowest BIC (4893 and 4894), and they have the lowest average cross-validated RMSE (1394 and 1392). The ranking of Model 3 and Model 4 is different, but the actual difference between the two models is very small in terms of both of the performance measures. So here BIC and cross-validation found the same two models to be the best. From our experience, that turns out to be a common outcome when we compare regression models.

As a final point on model selection in the case of a range of less and more complicated models, note that choosing a simple model can be valuable as it may help us avoid overfitting the live data. Whenever simple and complicated models have RMSE values that are very close, we suggest picking a simple one. Here that implies choosing Model 3.

13.11   External Validity and Stable Patterns

With the help of the BIC or k-fold cross-validation, we can find the model that is best in predicting y in the population, or general pattern, represented by the original data. But that's just the first of the two steps of finding the model that will give the best prediction in the live data. We now turn to external validity, the second step and perhaps the biggest – certainly the hardest – of all problems with prediction.

In the abstract, external validity is about whether, and to what extent, we can generalize findings in the population, or general pattern, represented by our data to the population, or general pattern, we are truly interested in (Chapter 5, Section 5.8). In predictive analytics, external validity means the extent to which the prediction errors are similar in the live data and in the population, or general patterns, represented by the original data. Thus the external validity of a prediction is high if the model that produces the best prediction in the population, or general pattern, represented by the original data is also the model that produces the best prediction in the population, or general pattern, that is behind the live data. Moreover, external validity of a prediction is high if the fit (e.g., RMSE) is similar in the two.

For high external validity, we require that the patterns of association between y and x are similar in the two worlds: the population, or general pattern, behind the original data, and the population, or general pattern, behind the live data. All models make use of those patterns of association to make a prediction. Thus, for a model to be best in both worlds, those patterns of association must be similar in the two worlds. This requirement is one of **stability**: the patterns of association between y and x should be stable across the two worlds. Because the original data is from the past and prediction is usually about the future, this also requires **stationarity**, which is a statistical concept describing stability across time (Chapter 12, Section 12.3). But stability may require more than that. Recall from Chapter 5, Section 5.8, that other frequent threats to external validity are differences across space or groups of observations. We need stability along those dimensions, too.

In our ice cream shop example the main issue is stability over time. We have data from three recent years, and we uncovered the patterns of association between sales, temperature, and monthly and daily seasonality in the data. The question of external validity is to what extent those patterns are going to be the same in the near future we want to predict. We may worry about changes in demand for many reasons, including changes in the structure of competition, changes in income and tastes of potential customers, or changes in the size of the customer pool.

Or take our other example, predicting default of people on personal loans. Suppose that our data covers applicants from one geographic region. However, the way the default probability is related to personal characteristics may be different in other regions. For example, some industries may be expanding in our region but contracting in other regions, thus employment in those industries is associated with lower loan default in our region but less so in the other regions. That leads to low external validity of a prediction that uses the industry of employment as a predictor variable.

Being able to list our worries is fine, but how can we tell whether they make external validity of a prediction high or low? And can we do anything to select a model with higher external validity?

Here is where **domain knowledge** and thinking can help. Domain knowledge means knowledge of the mechanisms behind the patterns of association of y and x. For example, the best-predicting model we find may make use of some patterns of association that are surprising. Then we need to think about whether those associations are likely true in the live data, too, or if they are specific to the original data. Often, surprising patterns are surprising because they are not generally true.

When external validity is not perfect, we may want to reflect that in our prediction in some way. Intuitively, less-than-perfect external validity adds to the uncertainty of our prediction. Recall that one way to represent that uncertainty is giving an interval prediction instead of, or complementing, a point prediction. Worries about external validity could be reflected in a wider prediction interval for the same level of confidence or by attaching a lower level of confidence to a prediction interval. Unfortunately, it's very hard to quantify external validity or lack of it, so these modifications are most often ad-hoc.

In our ice cream example, we may know of a few things that should affect demand. Four new large office buildings just opened within a few blocks, increasing the pool of potential customers. At the same time, a new ice cream shop opened further down the road, increasing competition. Doing some math, we calculate that the two may just balance out each other, so, as a result, we may face the same amount of demand. Thus, we may conclude that the predictions from our data have high external validity for the near future. But those developments increase uncertainty. Thus, we should probably attach more uncertainty to our predictions, either in a formal way, by making the prediction interval wider, or by making business decisions with the consideration that our prediction may be off by a wider margin than what the prediction interval suggests.

Analyzing our original data can also help. For example, when the original data is from the same geographic area, covering the same groups of observations, as what the live data will be, we have more reason to assume stability. Or, if our data covers many geographic areas, we can check if the patterns of association are similar across them. Similarly, we can check stability in time if our original data is from different points in time. Of course, all we can find is evidence for stability in the past, which doesn't guarantee stability in the future. But patterns of associations that were stable in the past are more likely to remain stable in the future, too. As a flipside, if we find that the patterns of association changed substantially from year to year in the past, we have less hope of using historic data to produce good predictions for the future.

Review Box 13.9   External validity of a prediction

- A prediction has high external validity if the best model for the population, or general pattern, behind the original data is also the best model for the population, or general pattern, behind the live data.
- High external validity of a prediction requires that the patterns of association between y and x are stable, so that they are very similar in the original data and the live data.
- Domain knowledge, thinking, and data from multiple time periods can help assess external validity.

13.A4   CASE STUDY – Predicting Used Car Value with Linear Regressions

External validity

This case study offered our first insight into prediction. We started with data cleaning, and we specified five different linear regressions to predict used car prices. To find the best of the five models we considered two methods: using all data to estimate the models and calculate their BIC, and using 4-fold cross-validation to calculate cross-validated RMSE. In the end, both methods suggested that we choose Model 3 or 4, which had many, but not all, of the predictor variables in the data, and which didn't have any interactions. More complex models were found to overfit the data. Out of Models 3 and 4 with equal fit, we pick the simpler one, Model 3.

We motivated this exercise by focusing on a single car with specific characteristics. Yet the model selection criteria we used looked at all predictions, including cars that were different from that car in terms of age, odometer reading, and other characteristics. We had two reasons to do so. First, we wanted a model that is expected to perform well. Looking at the average of predictions (or squared prediction errors) across many cars was one way to assess that expectation. Second, another motivation for the analysis was to see what price we could predict if we were to wait a year or two and sell a car with higher age, more miles, and so on. Thus we wanted a model that produces good predictions not only for the particular car we have but for the cars with other characteristics, too.

Using Model 3, our point prediction for the type of car we want to sell was 6073 dollars with a wide 80% prediction interval, of 4317 to 7829 dollars.

How confident can we be that in the case we need to predict the price of a similar car, we can rely on this estimate? Estimation error and irreducible error make the PI wide, reflecting a high level of uncertainty. Still, these results can help us advertise our car. If we want to sell quickly and know of some unmeasured negative features about our car, we may go towards the lower end of the interval. If our car is in a truly excellent condition for its age and miles and we have time, we may go for the upper end.

Finally, let's think about external validity. Shall we expect the patterns of association between y and x to be the same in the original data (from 2018) and the live data (now)? The data is from the same geographic area, covering very similar kinds of cars. Thus, what we have to worry about is stability in time. Are car prices related to age, mileage, and car type the same way now as in 2018? To evaluate that, we need to think about inflation, changes in income conditions in the area, and perhaps changes in the demand for combustion-engined cars. If we are close to 2018, then with all likelihood these factors will have changed little. As we move further away from 2018, external validity likely decreases. We could reflect this by making the PI even wider. Or, we'd perhaps be better to collect new data from the more recent past to carry out a predictive analysis.

From a methodological point of view, two main conclusions emerge. First, the best prediction model was the one with a medium level of complexity. Some models were too simple and led to underfitting the data; other models were too complex and led to overfitting the data. Second, we have used two ways to select the best prediction model: using all data and BIC, and using cross-validation. Here, the two methods ended up selecting the same two models that have very similar performance. In such a case, we argued that the best choice is to pick the simpler model.

13.12 Machine Learning and the Role of Algorithms

We close this chapter with a note on terminology often used both by data analysts and the general public. As we introduced earlier, the term **predictive analytics** is often used for data analysis whose goal is prediction. But a more popular, and related, term is **machine learning**.

In essence, **machine learning** is an umbrella concept for methods that use algorithms to find patterns in data and use them for prediction purposes.

In the context of predictive analytics, an **algorithm** is a set of rules and steps that defines how to generate an output (predicted values) using various inputs (variables, observations in the original data). A **formula** is an example of an algorithm – one that can be formulated in terms of an equation. For example, the OLS formula for estimating the coefficients of a linear regression is an algorithm. It's an equation that specifies the rules to follow to arrive at the OLS estimate of a coefficient using observations and variables in actual data.

But not all algorithms can be translated into a formula. The bootstrap estimation of a standard error (Chapter 5, Section 5.6) is an example. It starts with random sampling, continues with estimation, repeating this across all bootstrap samples, storing the estimates from each bootstrap sample, and then combining those to calculate the standard error. Here the estimation part may be translated into a single formula, and how we combine the various estimates may have a formula, too (the standard deviation). But other steps are verbal descriptions without a mathematical formula. Yet another example is k-fold cross-validation. It starts with creating the k random partitions of the original data, followed by all the steps of data analysis to get an estimate of a model using the training set, then using the test set to carry out and evaluate the prediction, repeating this for all k folds, and then combining these evaluations across each fold.

An important aspect of the algorithms in machine learning methods is their heavy use of machines, that is computers. Computers are used to plug data into formulae. But computers are used for all other parts of the algorithm, too. The main feature of algorithms is that they specify each and every step to follow in a clear way. Those steps can therefore be translated into computer code and make the computer follow those steps.

Besides machines, the other important part of machine learning is, well, learning. Algorithms in machine learning are used to learn something from the data. We may use the data and an algorithm to learn what the predicted value of y is if we combine the x variables using a particular model. But, in a narrower sense, learning here means learning which model is best for predicting y as well as what that predicted value is.

Not all data analysts agree on what methods constitute machine learning and what methods don't. Calculating the mean of y in the data and using that mean to predict a future value $\hat{y}_j$ can be viewed as machine learning, but many data analysts wouldn't call it that. We use the computer and an algorithm (a formula) to learn something about the future predicted value. But what we learn is the predicted value only, not whether it's a prediction that is better than some other prediction. It's perhaps too simple, too, to qualify for such a fancy name. In contrast, many data analysts would be comfortable using the term machine learning for using 10-fold cross-validation to compare that prediction to another one.

In a sense, machine learning is an approach to predictive data analysis. This approach is derived from the focus on achieving the best possible prediction from available data. That has two broad implications.

First, understanding the patterns of associations between y and x is of secondary importance in machine learning. To be more precise, these patterns are important in the sense that they should be stable across time and other dimensions that make the original data and the live data differ from each other. But beyond that stability, why y and x are associated with each other is not interesting for making a prediction.

Second, the machine learning attitude includes a preference for evaluating methods based on data as opposed to abstract principles. That's because we want to make a prediction here and now, from the original data we have to the live data we'll face. We don't want to devise a prediction rule that will be fine for every possible scenario with potentially different original data or live data.

One example of the preference for data-driven methods is finding the best prediction model using cross-validation. In principle, the BIC can be used for the same purpose for an estimated model using the entire original data. But the BIC is derived as a best measure of fit if some assumptions are true about the data. Thus, using cross-validation better conforms to the machine learning attitude. In the end, the BIC and 10-fold cross-validation may lead to the same conclusion, as they did in our case study. When they don't, the machine learning approach trusts cross-validation.

The following chapters will introduce new methods that show the real power of the machine learning approach to prediction. Some of these methods will help find the best linear regression model. Others will be alternatives to linear regression using more complex algorithms making heavy use of the computer, to arrive at better predictions than linear regression.

13.13 Main Takeaways

Prediction uses the original data with y and x to predict the value of y for observations in the live data, in which x is observed but y is not.

- Prediction uses a model that describes the patterns of association between y and x in the original data.
- Cross-validation can help find the best model in the population, or general pattern, represented by the original data.
- Stability of the patterns of association is needed for a prediction with high external validity.

PRACTICE QUESTIONS

1. Give one example for quantitative predictions, one for probabilistic predictions and one for classification.
2. What's a prediction error, and what are its three components?
3. What's a loss function? When do we say that the loss function is symmetric? Asymmetric? Convex?
4. What's the role of the loss function in finding the best predictive model? Give an example.
5. How is model complexity related to its propensity to underfit/overfit the original data? Give an example.
6. The MSE can be decomposed into bias and variance. What do these terms mean? Give an example for two predictions with similar bias but different variance.
7. What's the role of the penalty term in the BIC, and why is it useful?
8. What's a training–test split, and how may we use it to find the best model?
9. Based on clients' daily history of balances and transactions on their bank accounts, a bank wants to predict the daily average of the amount of money held on the bank account by each client, on each day of a year. What kind of a prediction problem is this; what's the original data, what's the live data, and what is are potential x variables?
10. You specified five linear regression models for prediction in the previous example. How would you find the best of them by cross-validation? Explain each step of the procedure.
11. List two potential threats to external validity in the example of a bank predicting its customers' daily balances. How can you assess each of them?
12. Can k-fold cross-validation help to improve your prediction for live data that is characterized by the same patterns of association as your original data? Why or why not?
13. Can k-fold cross-validation help to improve your prediction for live data that is characterized by different patterns of association than your original data? Why or why not?

14. Consider the case of forecasting if it will rain tomorrow. Is it likely that people will have the same loss function? Give two different kinds of loss function, and argue why each may make sense for some people.

15. What's an algorithm? Give an example of an algorithm that can be summarized by a formula, and give an example of an algorithm for which there is no formula.

DATA EXERCISES

Easier and/or shorter exercises are denoted by, [*]; harder and/or longer exercises are denoted by [**].

1. Consider the case study on used cars. Instead of 4-fold cross-validation, use cross-validation with a different number of folds. Find the best model, and carry out the prediction, including a prediction interval. Discuss what you find and compare with the findings in our case study. [*]

2. Consider the case study on used cars. Instead of the 281 cars in the data, keep only LE types and cars that are at least 5 years old. Consider five regression models that are analogous to the ones we used in the case study, find the best model by cross-validation and carry out the prediction, including a prediction interval. Discuss what you find and compare it with the findings in our case study. [*]

3. Collect data on used cars for a different city, different time, or different make to what we used in our used car case study. Consider five linear regression models of increasing complexity, find the best model by cross-validation, and carry out the prediction, including a prediction interval. Discuss your findings. [**]

4. Using the `hotels-vienna` dataset, specify five regression models with price as the y variable, find the best model by cross-validation, and carry out the prediction, including a prediction interval. Discuss your findings. [**]

5. Consider the `cps-earnings` dataset we used in Chapters 9 and 10 with a starting sample size of 149 316 individuals. Build five predictive models using linear regression for earnings per hour. Compare model performance of these five models using BIC and cross-validated RMSE. Discuss the relationship between model complexity and performance. [**]

REFERENCES AND FURTHER READING

There are many more advanced textbooks on predictive analytics. We especially recommend James et al. (2014) and Hastie & Tibshirani (2016).

There are several books discussing business applications of prediction. Two popular books are Ajay et al. (2018) and Siegel (2013).

Breiman et al. (1984) is a classic book suggesting the choice of simple models; Breiman (2001) is a seminal article on the essence and practice of the machine learning approach.

14 Model Building for Prediction

How to build a regression model for prediction; how to use LASSO to help with variable selection and functional forms; and how to evaluate a prediction on a holdout sample

Motivation

You want to predict rental prices of apartments in a big city using their location, size, amenities, and other features. You have access to data on many apartments with many variables. You know how to select the best regression model for prediction from several candidate models. But how should you specify those candidate models to begin with? In particular, which of the many variables should they include, in what functional forms, and in what interactions? More generally, how can you make sure that the candidates include the truly good predictive models?

You want to predict hourly sales for a new shop that your company is about to open. You have data from an existing shop that sells similar products. How should you define your *y* variable, and how should you select your predictor variables for regression models that you can choose from to find the best model? And how can you evaluate the prediction in the end in a way that also informs decision makers about the uncertainty of your prediction?

We have learned to use BIC or cross-validation to select the best regression model for prediction, and we have learned how to think about its external validity. But how should we specify the regression models? In particular, when we have many candidate predictor variables, how should we select from them, and how should we decide on their functional forms?

This chapter discusses how to build regression models for prediction and how to evaluate the predictions they produce. With respect to model building, we discuss whether and when it's a good idea to take logs of the *y* variable and what to do with such a prediction, how to select variables out of a large pool of candidate *x* variables, and how to decide on their functional forms. We introduce LASSO, an algorithm that can help with variable selection. With respect to evaluating predictions, we discuss why we need a holdout sample for evaluation that is separate from all of the rest of the data we use for model building and selection. We close this chapter with a discussion on the additional opportunities and challenges Big Data brings for predictive analytics.

We have two case studies in this chapter. First, we continue looking at used cars with the **Predicting used car value: log prices** case study, using the `used-cars` dataset. We use this case study to discuss whether to take logs of *y* and, if yes, what to do with such a prediction. The main case study in this chapter is **Predicting Airbnb apartment prices: selecting a regression model**; it aims to predict the price of Airbnb apartments in London, UK, based on their many characteristics using the `airbnb` dataset. This case study illustrates the use of a holdout sample and the various methods of building regression models.

Learning outcomes

After working through this chapter, you should be able to:

- understand the process of building regression models for prediction;
- carry out predictions of *y* using models with ln *y*;
- use LASSO to specify a regression model for prediction and understand how this leads to a selected set of the candidate *x* variables;
- define and use a holdout sample to evaluate a prediction using various diagnostic tools.

14.1 Steps of Prediction

In the previous chapter we overviewed the conceptual framework for prediction, focusing on the task of selecting the best prediction model. In this chapter we discuss more details of the process of prediction. Similarly to the previous chapter, we'll focus on quantitative predictions using linear regression. Some of what we discuss in this chapter is more general and is applicable to other prediction methods, which we'll cover in subsequent chapters. Other topics are specific to regressions. We'll be clear about this distinction along the way.

Before discussing specific topics, let's summarize the main steps of the prediction process. All data analysts go through all of these steps, even if sometimes resorting to default options, leaving things as they are. As always, we recommend making conscious decisions: thinking through each step in an explicit way even if, in the end, we may opt for a default option.

Figure 14.1 summarizes the most important steps.

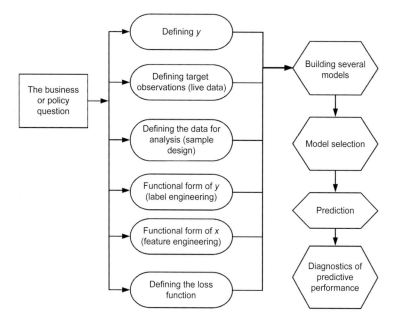

Figure 14.1 The process of prediction

The starting point is the business or policy question we seek to answer. What do we want to predict, and for what kinds of observations? What decisions would that prediction support? Answering this question is necessary to make good decisions in subsequent steps.

Based on the question, we need to define y, the target variable. In some cases, this requires no action – the business question defines it: the price of our used car is one such case. However, for other instances, it requires thinking and decision making. If interested in predicting the probability of survival of companies, we need to define what we mean by survival (filing tax forms? having employees? reporting nonzero sales? all three?), and what time horizon we have in mind (one year from now? two years?). Similarly, we need to define live data: what the target observations are for which we want to predict y.

The following steps are selecting the observations to use (sample design), deciding whether to transform y (label engineering), and how to select the predictor variables, their functional form and potential interactions (feature engineering). The subsequent sections of this chapter provide more details about these steps.

Using the data that results from the previous steps, we can start building our models; we will discuss several tools for building linear regressions in this chapter. The next step is model selection, which was the topic of Chapter 13, Section 13.7. The final steps are making the actual prediction by using the selected model, and then evaluating its performance by applying diagnostic tools.

14.2   Sample Design

Sample design means selecting observations from the raw data (the dataset we got or collected) to create the data we'll use for predictive analysis. The data we use for analysis is what we called the original data. Well, that original data may actually be a selected part of all of the data we could use. The reason is simple: we want to have the data used for the analysis as close to the live data as possible. Sometimes selecting observations helps in that, and our original data will contain only a subset of observations from the raw data. In other cases, the original data will contain all observations from the raw data.

The main task of a prediction is to use patterns of association between y and x in the original data to predict y in the live data. To achieve high external validity, we need the original data and the live data to be as close as possible in terms of those patterns. Of course, we can't ensure that: we cannot observe y in the live data. But we may be able to compare the distribution of the x variables. Whether we want the range and distribution of x in the original data close to that in the live data is a decision we have to make. There is a trade-off here: we want the patterns of association between y and x to be the same, but we also want many observations in the original data. With Big Data with millions or billions of observations, that tends to be less of an issue. With smaller datasets we may decide either way.

For example, when we want to predict sales in a newly opened store using seasonality of sales in existing stores, the x variables are hours of the day, days of the week, months of the year. These x variables are always observable: we know their values for all observations both in the original data and the live data. Thus, if we want, we can make sure their distribution is the same in the two data. If we want to predict sales in March, our live data has the month of March and not from other months. We can also choose to make the original data for the analysis consist of observations from March only. We would do so if we thought that the patterns of seasonality by day of the week and hour of the day were very different in March than in other months. Alternatively, we can include all months in the original data if we think the patterns of daily and hourly seasonality are not that different across months. This way we would gain 12 times as many observations, which would reduce estimation error by a factor of more than 3. Or we could include February, March, and April, if we think they are similar enough but the rest of the months are different.

Sometimes, as in the examples above, we have more x values in the original data than in the live data (more months, more industries, more countries, and so on). Other times the opposite problem is true: we have fewer x values in the original data than in the live data. For example, we may want to predict the survival chances of many kinds of companies, but we only have data on companies of a certain size. In such cases we can't give a prediction for all kinds of observations in the live data. Thus, the best we can do is be explicit about the parts of the live data for which we can carry out a prediction.

A second issue that sample design should deal with is observations with missing y values. Such observations should be dropped from the data: we can't use them for predicting y. If a large fraction of our observations have missing y, we had better understand why they are missing. If, moreover, we uncover systematic patterns in missing y values, we may have a problem. At a minimum we should acknowledge this problem and be transparent about it when presenting the results of our prediction. At best, we may want to carry out another prediction together with our main one, predicting the probability of missing y. The results of that prediction can help understand for which observations we have a better chance to predict y and for which observations we have a worse chance.

Yet one more question is what to do with extreme values. As always, this decision should be guided by whether the patterns we are interested in should be valid for extreme values. In particular, here we should keep extreme values of y or x if they may be part of the live data. In contrast, we should exclude them if we know they would not be part of the live data. As we tend to know more about the distribution of x in the live data than the distribution of y, we should be more conservative with extreme y values. In particular, we shouldn't discard observations with extreme y values except in the – extremely rare – case when we know for sure that those extreme y values won't occur in the live data.

For example, when predicting sales, we may have some days in the original data with unusually low y values. After some digging we may find out that those happened because of severe weather conditions that kept customers from coming into the stores. In this case it's probably not a good idea to discard those observations from the original data. Severe weather conditions may affect sales in the live data, too. In contrast, if we find out that some extreme sales values in the data are due to recording errors, we should probably discard those observations from the original data. True, if recording errors occurred in the past, they may occur in the live data, too. But our task is to predict sales, not how sales are recorded.

14.3   Label Engineering and Predicting Log y

The next step in our list is label engineering: deciding on the functional form of y. Most of the time that means leaving y as it is in the original data. Sometimes, though, we may want to transform it. An example is when we have a quantitative y, but most of its values are concentrated at two values. In this case we may want to transform the original y into a binary one, transforming all values to one of the two frequent values and carrying out a probability prediction or classification instead of a quantitative prediction. For example, our data is about ads shown and number of clicks by people: 80% did not click, 18% clicked once, and 2% clicked more than once. Here, a binary click or no-click would be better to predict than the original count of clicks.

The most frequent example of transforming y is taking the log. As we discussed it in Chapter 8, Section 8.2, taking the natural log of the y variable can make modeling easier, at least for linear regressions. For example, when price is the target variable, its relation to predictor variables is often closer to linear when expressed as log price. This tends to have both substantive and technical reasons. Log differences approximate relative, or percentage differences, and relative price differences are often more stable. The related technical advantage is that the distribution of log prices is often close to normal, which makes linear regressions give a better approximation to average differences.

Whether we should transform y into a log value for prediction is an important modeling choice, but one that is not straightforward. Very often, we will try both options and then select the one that gives a better prediction, for example, by cross-validation.

Importantly, regardless of whether y is in logs or not, we want to predict the original y variable, not its log. Thus, when we have $\ln y$ in the prediction model, we want to transform its predicted value back to y. In other words, we want $\hat{y}$ not $\widehat{\ln y}$. As $y = e^{\ln y}$, it seems reasonable to think that all it takes is simply to raise e to the power of $(\widehat{\ln y})$ to get $\hat{y}$. It turns out, however, that this is not the best solution. Instead, we have to adjust this power by a function of the standard deviation of the residual $\hat{\sigma}$ of the regression model with $\ln y$ on its left-hand side:

$$\hat{y}_j = e^{\widehat{\ln y_j}} e^{\hat{\sigma}^2/2} \tag{14.1}$$

The reason behind the **log correction** is a little complicated. It has to do with two things: first, the exponential function is not linear, and second, the regression and most other predictions are models of the expected value. The regression predicts the expected value (mean) of $\ln y$, while we need the expected value (mean) of y. But the mean of $e^{\ln y}$ is not the same as the mean of y since the log function is not linear. The correction term serves to remedy this. Actually, this correction is an approximation: it is correct only when y is lognormally distributed conditional on the x variables (see the expected value of the lognormal distribution in Chapter 3, Section 3.9). The closer the distribution of y (conditional on x) is to lognormal, the better the approximation.

Review Box 14.1 Predicting log versus level target variables

- When using linear regression for prediction, taking log of y may be a good option.
- Even when our model is about $\ln y$, we want to predict y not $\ln y$. To do so we need to work more; the log correction formula is often a good approximation:

$$\hat{y}_j = e^{\widehat{\ln y_j}} e^{\hat{\sigma}^2/2}$$

where $\hat{\sigma}$ is the standard deviation of the regression residual.

14.A1   CASE STUDY – Predicting Used Car Value: Log Prices

Levels or logs

In the case study **Predicting used car value with linear regressions** that we introduced in Chapter 13, the question was pricing a certain type of car. To that aim we used the used-cars dataset on used cars of the same type collected from classified ads. In this case study we work with the same dataset.

The question we investigate here is whether to transform y into ln y. y is price, and we argued earlier, e.g., in Chapter 8, Section 8.2, that we should always consider transforming prices to log prices in regression analysis.

To get a sense for why log transformation of the price variable may make sense, let's look at its relationship with the age of the car. The non-parametric lowess regression estimates provide the predicted values. Both figures show a strong negative association but also some variation around the regression line. The log model of Figure 14.2b shows a simple linear pattern, while the one of Figure 14.2a shows a nonlinear one.

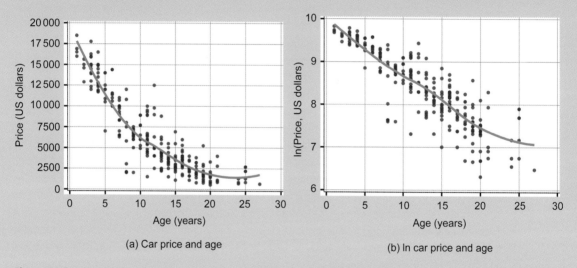

Figure 14.2   Car price, or ln car price, and age. Lowess non-parametric regressions
Source: used-cars dataset. Used Toyota Camry cars, Chicago area, N=281.

Hence, to model the price–age relationship we should either use log price as the target variable or have a polynomial function of age. The first one has fewer coefficients and allows for a simpler interpretation. Recall, however, that our goal is not to have a simpler functional form or a nicer picture or an easier interpretation of the patterns of association. Instead, we want to predict price. Thus, we want the model that is best at predicting price, and that model may have price itself or log price as the dependent variable.

Table 14.1 shows the predicted values from Model 3 (Chapter 13, Section 13.A2) that has age, odometer reading, whether the car is an LE, and in excellent or good condition. The table shows the predictions from both the level and log model (i.e., the models with both price and log price as the predicted variable). The predictions from the log model are transformed back to price using the log correction formula in Equation (14.1).

The point prediction from the log model is similar to the level model. The predicted price is 6000 dollars when price is in logs, very close to the predicted value from the level model.

Table 14.1 Prediction with the model in log of y			
	Model in logs	**Recalculated to level**	**Model in levels**
Point prediction	8.63	5932	6073
80% PI: upper bound	8.18	3783	4317
80% PI: lower bound	9.08	9301	7829

Note: Predictions based on Model 3 – for details see Chapter 13, Table 13.1. Point predictions and 80% prediction intervals (lower bound and upper bound). Second column is level predictions from the log model with correction. Third column repeats prediction results from level model; it has squared age and odometer.

Source: used-cars dataset. Used Toyota Camry cars, Chicago area. N=281.

But the prediction intervals differ. To get the PI for the log model, we simply calculated the PI for log price and converted the endpoints to predicted price values using the appropriate correction term. The result is [3783, 9301]. While the 80% prediction interval is symmetric for level regression, it is asymmetric for the log based regression with an upper bound further out. That is because the PI in log prices is symmetric by design, but when we undo the log transformation, we expand deviations in the positive direction. This leads to a wider prediction interval, primarily because of a higher upper bound. This is a disadvantage of the log model: its prediction can become more uncertain.

14.4 Feature Engineering: Dealing with Missing Values

Feature engineering is the part when we take the variables as recorded in the raw data and create the x variables that we'll include in a predictive model. Those x variables are called **features** in predictive analytics.

The first part of feature engineering is data cleaning, something we always do with the variables we want to use. As discussed in Chapter 2, Section 2.9, this includes discovering and handling missing values. In a prediction context, dealing with missing values is an especially relevant task: with any missing value, an observation may not be used for prediction. This is also called the need for complete input data: a set of observations with all predictors x and the target variable y need to be non-missing.

We should start by describing the missing value problem, variable by variable, listing the percent of missing values for each. Then, for each variable, we have to decide what to do.

Our first option is to keep observations with missing values and replace the missing values with something else. Recall, from Chapter 2, Section 2.9, that for qualitative variables we may simply create another category, missing value, and a corresponding binary variable. For quantitative variables, we may replace it with an imputed value, such as the overall average, but here, too, it is good practice to create a binary variable indicating that the original value was missing. Note that this binary (flag) variable's value will not matter for prediction if randomly missing, but it may matter if it's a result of some selection. Also, we need to check the source of why values are missing; in some cases missing means zero, and hence, imputation should also be zero.

The second option is to drop the x variable in question from the analysis. When a large fraction of the observations have missing values, that is often the best choice. This way we lose a predictor variable only. Dropping this variable makes sense especially if we expect it to have a lot of missing values in the live data, too.

Our third option is dropping the observations with missing values. We recommend using this option only if there are very few missing values for a few variables. Otherwise, we can end up with dropping many observations altogether.

14.5 Feature Engineering: What x Variables to Have and in What Functional Form

The second part of feature engineering is **variable selection**: what variables to have in the model and in what functional forms, including potential interactions.

We should start with what variables we want to consider for the prediction. The aim is to build several prediction models, from which we'll select the best one, for example, by cross-validation. Thus, a good practice is to select a broader set of candidate x variables, clean them, and specify models of varying complexity using them. Less complex models would have fewer x variables and in simpler functional forms; more complex models would have more x variables and/or more complicated nonlinear functions and more interactions.

Specifying the functional form of the x variables is another difficult aspect of feature engineering. That includes capturing nonlinear relationships with quantitative x variables (quadratic, other polynomial, piecewise linear spline), deciding on the number of categories for qualitative variables (joining rare categories into fewer ones), and deciding on interactions. The emphasis is on getting the best fit without overfitting the data.

But how should we decide on these questions? How should we specify what x variables should go in the models that we'll evaluate, and in what functional forms?

Domain knowledge is important: knowledge from previous analyses, and/or theory, about what tends to make y different. Domain knowledge can help answer what x variables are likely to be more important versus less important, what interactions are likely important, and where should we be most worried about nonlinearity. For instance, professional weather forecasts use computational models that use the laws of physics to relate many variables and feed in measured values of those variables from data. Or, many central banks complement purely data-driven inflation forecasts with predictions from general equilibrium models that are simplified representations of how the economy works.

The other source of information is, of course, the data itself. Exploratory data analysis (EDA) is a key part of all predictive analytics. We do EDA to make sure we understand the content of each x variable, to make sure they are as clean as possible, and to understand their distribution. Besides exploring the variables themselves, we need to investigate the patterns of association with the y variable, making use of the tools we covered in Chapters 4 and 8. In addition, we may look at how the x variables are correlated with each other, to make sure that we don't include variables together that are extremely closely related to each other (e.g., that have a correlation coefficient of 0.95), unless we have a very good reason to do so.

This work is tedious and time consuming. Some of it is unavoidable. We need to know our data: we should never build models with x variables whose content we don't understand. That's because we cannot assess, or even think about, stability of the patterns of association between y and x if we don't know what those variables are, what their content is, and how they are measured. And assessing stability is necessary for assessing external validity, which is a key aspect of a good prediction. Thus, we can play around with data and train and test models without knowing what's in them, but that won't necessarily help with the true goal of our analysis: predicting *y* in the live data.

However, some parts of this long and tedious work can be made more efficient. Later in this chapter we'll learn about algorithms that can select variables, functional forms, and interactions, to build one or more candidate models that we can then evaluate by cross-validation. Before doing so, let us introduce our second case study.

Review Box 14.2   Feature engineering

Feature engineering typically includes:

- deciding on what predictor variables to include;
- exploring and addressing potential missing values and extreme values;
- deciding about function forms of the predictor variables;
- designing possible interactions of the predictor variables.

14.B1   CASE STUDY – Predicting Airbnb Apartment Prices: Selecting a Regression Model

Question and data

Our second, and longer, case study in this chapter is **Predicting Airbnb apartment prices: selecting a regression model**. This case study is about predicting the rental price for an apartment offered by Airbnb in London.

The goal is to predict the price that may be appropriate for an apartment with certain features. This prediction can help answer various business questions. One such question is what revenue we could expect if we invested in an apartment in London and rented it via Airbnb. Another question is finding a good deal for one night in a specific neighborhood. We narrowed down the question to predict prices for apartments in Hackney, a London borough. To plan for that, we have to know what rental price we can expect to receive for various kinds of apartment at various locations of the city.

This is a quantitative prediction exercise and a cross-sectional prediction. We want to predict prices for many types of apartments in Hackney, London. For external validity we have to worry about the extent to which the patterns of association between price and apartment characteristics and location remain stable between the time our data is collected and the future date of our inquiry. We'll return to this question at the end of the case study.

The case study uses the `airbnb` dataset. The dataset has a single data table that includes 4499 observations. The data refer to rental prices for one night in March 2017. The target variable is price per night per person, expressed in US dollars, because it was US dollars in the raw data.

Similarly to the used cars case study earlier, we are predicting price. Thus, we should ask whether we should leave the price variable as it is or take its log. The two histograms in Figure 14.3 show the distribution of price and log price.

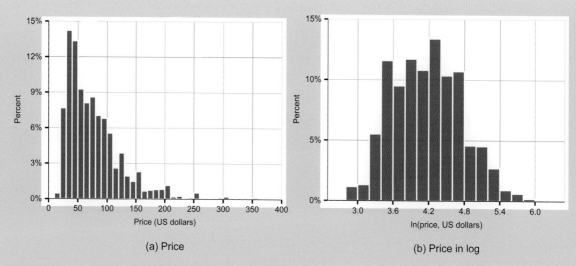

Figure 14.3   Airbnb apartment price and ln price distributions.

Note: Price for one night in US dollars. Histograms without extreme values (price < 400 US dollars).
Source: `airbnb` dataset, Hackney, borough of London, March 2017. Observations with 7 or fewer guests accommodated.
N=4393.

As usual with price data, the distribution of Airbnb apartment prices is strongly skewed with a long right tail. Log price is close to normally distributed. Here we don't take log of price but carry out the prediction with price as the *y* variable for all models. You will be invited to carry out the prediction with log price as a data exercise.

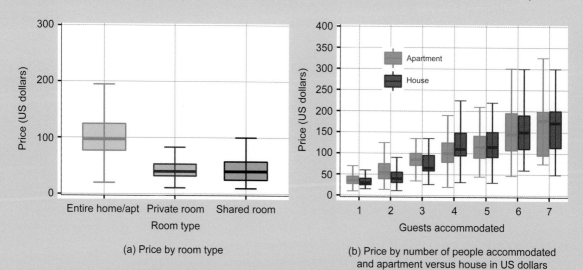

Figure 14.4   Airbnb apartment price distribution by important features

Note: Box plots for price; the graphs don't show the extreme values.
Source: `airbnb` dataset, Hackney, borough of London, March 2017. Observations with 7 or fewer guests accommodated.
N=4393.

Of the other important predictor variables, some are related to size: the number of guests the apartment can accommodate, number of rooms, number of beds. There are some variables related to reviews: average review score, the number of reviews, the date of the first review (to indicate for how long this apartment was in business). The number of apartments or rooms is left as it is, and treated as continuous.

The number of guests to accommodate, the number of beds, the average review score, the number of reviews, and the days since the first review are quantitative variables. These quantitative variables may be better converted into categories (such as number of reviews: 0, 1 to 50, 50+) or have few values to begin with (guests to accommodate goes up to 16, but most apartments accommodate 1 through 7 guests). The two box plots in Figures 14.4a and 14.4b (both without values outside whiskers) show average price by room type and size of the apartment. Single or shared rooms are cheaper, typically below 70 dollars, while whole apartments are centered around 100 dollars. About one-third of observations had no review. For them, we replaced review-related variables with the sample mean and added a binary variable (flag) to capture being a missing value.

With regards to these quantitative x variables, we made one key decision on sample design: we dropped very large apartments.

Our final original data has 4393 observations.

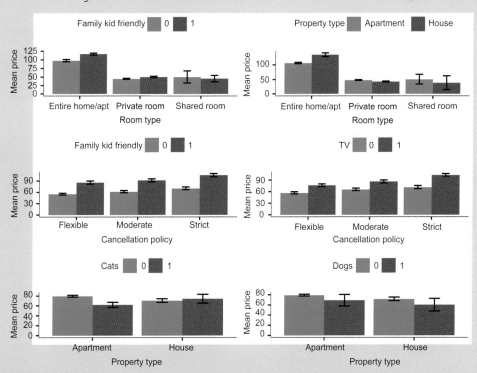

Figure 14.5 Graphical way of finding interactions

Note: Conditional mean price by selected variables. 95% confidence intervals on top of bars.
Source: `airbnb` dataset, Hackney, borough of London, March 2017. N=4393.

Regarding other predictors, we have several binary variables, which we kept as they were: type of bed, type of property (apartment, house, room), cancellation policy. Furthermore, there is a variable, called amenities that includes various words such as air conditioning, cable tv, hairdryer, and wi-fi. These words were parsed out of text variables, and we created 60 binary indicator variables to correspond to each amenity. (For the process, see Under the Hood section 14.U1.)

As for interactions, one simple option is to graphically look at conditional means of y by different values of the categorical variables. We may use domain knowledge to pick some candidates. In Figure 14.5, we show six small graphs doing just that. This suggested *room_type* × *property_type* and *room_type* × *familykidfriendly* as interactions. After exploring other potential interactions, we decided to include some of those in our more complex models.

14.6 We Can't Try Out All Possible Models

As we have seen, feature engineering is a long and tedious task. Some of it is unavoidable in order to know our data. But other parts may be replaced by some algorithm, at least in principle. In particular, when we are interested in which variables to include, in what functional forms, and in which interactions, we may get help from algorithms.

In principle, one such algorithm could specify all possible models and make the computer choose from them. To do so, we would have to consider all potential x variables in the data and specify all possible models with various combinations of them. Unfortunately, however, that's impossible to carry out. Except for the simplest of cases, such as a handful of binary variables and many observations, we would have way too many models to consider. In real life we will never be able to try out all models. In computer science, problems of this sort that are too hard to solve in practice because of computational complexity are called **np-hard** problems.

As an example, consider the case with $p = 10$ potential x variables to include in a regression model: $x_1, \ldots, x_{10}$. First, let's just think about which of the ten variables to include in the model. If we wanted to try out all possible combinations, that in itself would be over 1000 models. Then, we should think about interactions. Just consider all pairwise interactions: there are $10 \times 9/25 = 45$ of them. Just like with the ten original variables, we want to try out models that include various combinations of interactions. But the number of models with all possible combinations of the two-way interactions is in the millions. And then there are potential three-way interactions, and, for quantitative x variables, various ways to approximate potential nonlinearities. This number of possible combinations is orders of magnitudes more models than what our computer could evaluate during the time we would have or, indeed, our lifetime.

Of course, using our domain knowledge, we may not want to try out all models but only a subset of them. But even then, thinking about the many possible models is impossible in practice.

Thus, we can't hope to specify all possible models ourselves and then pick the best one from them. Moreover, we can't design an algorithm that would do that. Instead, the best we can hope for is an algorithm that can help specify a model that is likely to be among the best possible models without actually considering all possible models.

This may sound a little mysterious for now, but is in fact where machine learning methods can be extremely helpful (see our introduction of what machine learning means in Chapter 13, Section 13.12).

Later in this chapter, in Section 14.8, we'll consider one such algorithm that helps find the best candidate model from the regression models. In Chapters 15 and 16 we'll discuss other algorithms that may outperform the regression models we have considered so far.

14.7 Evaluating the Prediction Using a Holdout Set

Before turning to how to specify a regression model that likely outperforms other ones, let's take a detour. In Chapter 13, we argued for selecting the best model using cross-validation, which is an improved version of the training–test method. The basic idea is to use one part of the data (the training set) for model building, and another part for looking at how good the resulting model is at predicting y (the test set). The best model should fit the test sets the best (k-fold cross-validation would have k test sets). The reason for this split is to avoid overfitting the data that we use for model building. Once we have picked the best model, we advised going back and using the entire original data for the final estimate and to make a prediction.

That's all fine, but what part of the data should we use to evaluate that final prediction? What data do we use to measure its error (say, RMSE), construct a prediction interval (PI), or look at the $\hat{y}-y$ graph? If we use all data to make the prediction, its coefficient estimates are going to be computed in a way to ensure the best fit: the smallest RMSE, the narrowest PI, the best-looking $\hat{y}-y$ graph. Yet what we are interested in is not how good a model is at predicting y when we can estimate its coefficients in a way that ensures the best fit. Instead, we are interested in how good that model would be at predicting y in the live data.

One issue, of course, is external validity. We discussed how to think about this and what we might do about it in Chapter 13, Section 13.11. Here we ask another, easier but still important, question: how can we evaluate the prediction ability of the model in the population, or general pattern, represented by the original data? To answer this, we need data to evaluate the prediction on that is just like our original data, but which we haven't used for estimation.

The solution is similar in spirit to the training–test split. We do all of the work using one part of the data: model building, selecting the best model by, say, cross-validation, and then making the prediction itself – e.g., by estimating the coefficients of the linear regression that we picked as the best. We call this part the **work set**. It includes the training sets and the test sets. But we use another part of the data for evaluating the prediction itself. That part is called the **holdout set**. The splitting of the original data into a work set and a holdout set needs to be random, because we need both sets to represent the same population, or general pattern.

We illustrate this data splitting in Figure 14.6. We start with the entire **original data**. First, we select the observations in the holdout set, by random sampling. That's usually a small part of the original data, such as 20%. The remaining part of our data is our work set. We further divide the work set k-times for training-test splits. We build the models on the training sets, and pick the best model by how they fit the test sets – e.g., by picking the one with the smallest average MSE. Then, we take that model and re-estimate it on the entire work set (the original data less the holdout set). Finally, we use that estimated model on the holdout set to see how it predicts y there.

Review Box 14.3 Cross-validation and holdout set procedure

Use various subsamples of the original data for various steps of predictive analysis.

1. Starting with the original data, split it into a larger work set and a smaller holdout set.
2. Further split the work set into training sets and test sets for k-fold cross-validation.
3. Build models and select the best model using k-fold cross-validation.
4. Re-estimate the best model using all observations in the work set.

5. Take the estimated best model and apply it to the holdout set.
6. Evaluate the prediction using the holdout set.

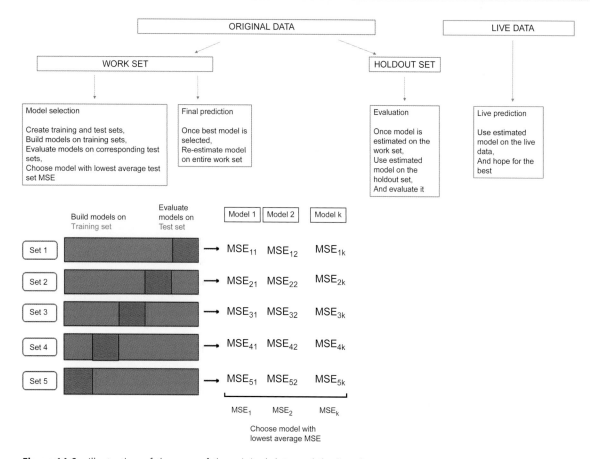

Figure 14.6   Illustration of the uses of the original data and the live data

CASE STUDY – Predicting Airbnb Apartment Prices: Selecting a Regression Model

Building regression models and finding the best of them

We have specified eight linear regression models for predicting price. All have price as the target variable. They differ in the predictor variables included. The models are ordered by increasing complexity. The predictor variables included in the eight regression models are shown in Table 14.2.

Model complexity is related to the number of variables used. For regression models, model complexity is best measured by the number of regression coefficients to be estimated. This is not the same as the number of variables: we always have an intercept, and for the same variables we can have different functional forms (piecewise linear spline, polynomial) that involve several coefficients. Moreover, for qualitative variables with more than two values, we include a set of binary variables in regressions (for example, room type has three values, so it leads to two coefficient estimates). For this reason, when we define models, we list the number of variables they use as well as the number of coefficients they estimate.

Table 14.2 Versions of the Airbnb apartment price prediction models

Model	Predictor variables	N var	N coeff
M1	guests accommodated as a quantitative variable, entered linearly	1	2
M2	= M1 + number of beds (linear), number of days since first review (linear), property type, room type, bed type	6	8
M3	= M2 + bathroom, cancellation policy, average review score (linear), number reviews (three categories), missing score flag	11	16
M4	= M3 + square term for guests, square and cubic terms for days since first review	11	17
M5	= M4 + room type and number of reviews interacted with property type	11	25
M6	= M5 + air conditioning and whether pets are allowed interacted with property type	13	30
M7	= M6 + all other amenities	70	87
M8	= M7 + all other amenities interacted with property type as well as bed type	70	315

As we review these models, we can observe that regression model M1 has one x variable and the OLS estimates two coefficients, while M8 has 315 coefficients for 70 variables.

We looked at patterns of association between price and each of the quantitative x variables: maximum number of guests and review score. We found that average price is approximately linearly related to the number of guests to accommodate, with some potential convexity for large numbers of guests: hence, the quadratic specification in M4. We also found that average price is very weakly related to the review score, but this association may be nonlinear with a flat section at the start, then increasing, and then decreasing: hence, we included a cubic specification in M4.

Recall, that after sample design, our data has 4393 observations. This is our original data. Of this, we selected a random 20% holdout set with 878 observations. The remaining random 80% is our work set (3515 observations). We will use this work set for cross-validation with several folds of training and test sets.

Table 14.3 shows the number of coefficients, R-squared, BIC, and cross-validated training set and test set RMSE for the eight regressions. First, we estimated all regressions using all observations in the work set. The table shows two statistics for the entire work set: R-squared and BIC. Then, we estimated the models again using 5-fold cross-validation: for each fold, we estimated the regression using the training set, and used it for prediction not only in the training set but also in the corresponding test set. The last two columns of the table show the training and test RMSE for each model, calculated as the square root of the average MSE on the five training sets and the five test sets.

Table 14.3   Comparing model fit measures

Model	Coefficients	R-squared	BIC	Training RMSE	Test RMSE
M1	2	0.38	36 356	42.46	42.23
M2	8	0.46	35 941	39.74	39.61
M3	16	0.48	35 827	38.78	38.68
M4	17	0.49	35 824	38.63	38.53
M5	25	0.49	35 846	38.52	38.47
M6	30	0.49	35 877	38.41	38.42
M7	87	0.53	36 025	37.12	37.78
M8	315	0.56	37 679	35.24	42.19

Note: Model descriptions: Table 14.2. BIC and R-squared are calculated on the work set (training+test samples). Training RMSE and Test RMSE is based on 5-fold CV; the average RMSE (square root of the average MSE) is reported.

Source: `airbnb` dataset. Hackney, borough of London, March 2017, price per night. N=4393 (work set, N=3515).

R-squared in the work set keeps improving as more and more predictor variables are added, as it should. The most complex model explains 56% of the variation in prices.

In contrast, the BIC stops improving after a while (recall that smaller values of BIC indicate better performance). According to the BIC, the best model is regression M4: this model has relatively few variables. According to the BIC, the more complex models have a high risk of overfitting the data. The disagreement between R-squared and BIC is most noticeable for the most complex M8. Compared to M7, R-squared improves from 0.53 to 0.56 while BIC deteriorates from 37 679 to 36 025.

RMSE in the training sets keeps improving with model complexity, as it should. The test set RMSE improves too, until M7, but it is substantially worse for the more complex M8. Thus, M7 produces the lowest test RMSE, with a value of 37.78. This suggests that the best predictor model is the one that has all features included, as well as polynomials for number of guests and review score and interactions of a few features with property type. This model is much more complex than M4 that BIC picked as the best.

The RMSE suggests that the typical size of the prediction error in the test sets is 37.78 dollars for the model M7. It is 38.53 dollars for M4, which is not much higher. In fact models M3 through M6 produce almost identical RMSE, and all are pretty close to the best M7. In the event that building model M3 or M4 is much cheaper, we can use these as we'd only lose a tiny bit of predictive power. Figure 14.7 visualizes the training and test set RMSE for the various models. It shows the two are close for less complex models but diverge a lot for the most complex models.

What should we conclude from this exercise? When BIC and cross-validation produce conflicting results, we may want to choose the model picked by cross-validation. That's because cross-validation is not based on auxiliary assumptions. This picks model M7. At the same time, the improvement from M3 (the one picked by BIC measure) to M7 is rather small, so we probably wouldn't have made a huge mistake if we were to pick M3 instead.

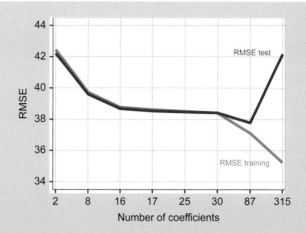

Figure 14.7 Training and test set RMSE for the eight regression models

Note: Average training set RMSE and average test set RMSE from 5-fold cross-validation for the eight regression models.
Source: `airbnb` dataset, Hackney, borough of London, March 2017. N=4393 (work set, N=3515).

14.8 | Selecting Variables in Regressions by LASSO

This section introduces the most widely used algorithm that helps select variables in a linear regression to arrive at the model with the best prediction. One way to think about it is that it's an add-on to linear regression models. Another way to think about it is that it's an alternative way of estimating the coefficients of the same old linear regression.

So far we have used ordinary least squares (OLS) models to fit regressions on the data. As we have been arguing in previous chapters, OLS is an intuitive method that tends to give a good approximation to average differences in y related to differences in x. It turns out, however, that we can get better predictions from regression if we do things differently.

One approach that tends to give better prediction is called **shrinkage**. The approach starts with a regression with many right-hand-side variables: p of them, where p is a large number. These right-hand-side variables can contain squares and higher-order polynomials of the original x variables, piecewise linear splines of them with many knots, and interactions between these. Thus, even if the number of original variables is not very large, we can have a regression with a large number of right-hand-side variables.

In this textbook, we focus on **LASSO**, the most widely used shrinkage method. LASSO (the acronym of Least Absolute Shrinkage and Selection Operator) is an algorithm that fits a model by shrinking coefficients and, importantly, shrinking some of them to zero. Hence, it does two things at the same time. It selects a subset of the right-hand-side variables fed into it to stay in the regression, while dropping the other variables. It also shrinks coefficients (compared to OLS) for some variables that it keeps in the regression. The output of LASSO are a list of variables and their estimated coefficients.

The way LASSO does this is by adding a **penalty term** to the usual OLS estimation algorithm. This term penalizes the sum of the absolute value of the coefficients. Thus the closer the coefficients are to zero, the smaller the penalty term. In particular, coefficients with a value of zero don't add to the penalty term and are thus the best from that point of view. On the other hand, LASSO still wants to fit the data similarly to OLS, so it won't simply set all coefficients to zero. Instead, it will set those coefficients to zero that make the smallest reduction in the fit. Similarly, it will decrease the value of those remaining coefficients the most that lead to the smallest reduction in the fit.

Consider a linear regression with n observations, each labeled with i, and p variables, each labeled with j:

$$y^E = \beta_0 + \beta_1 x_1 + \cdots + \beta_p x_p = \beta_0 + \sum_{j=1}^{p} \beta_j x_j \tag{14.2}$$

Recall that the usual way to estimate the coefficients of such a regression is by ordinary least squares (OLS). OLS minimizes the sum of squared residuals:

$$\underset{\beta}{\text{minimize}} \sum_{i=1}^{n} \left(y_i - \left(\beta_0 + \sum_{j=1}^{p} \beta_j x_{ij} \right) \right)^2 \tag{14.3}$$

LASSO modifies this minimization by adding a penalty term:

$$\underset{\beta}{\text{minimize}} \sum_{i=1}^{n} \left(y_i - \left(\beta_0 + \sum_{j=1}^{p} \beta_j x_{ij} \right) \right)^2 + \lambda \sum_{j=1}^{p} |\beta_j| \tag{14.4}$$

This penalty term makes LASSO want to reduce the OLS coefficients' absolute value. An effect of this particular functional form for the penalty term is that LASSO tends to reduce many coefficients to zero, effectively dropping those x variables from the regression.

Unlike OLS, the minimization problem of LASSO cannot be solved with the help of a formula. Instead, the computer finds the solution via an algorithm. The output of the LASSO algorithm is the values of the $\hat{\beta}$ coefficients. In particular, some coefficients will be shrunk to zero, so the corresponding predictor variable is dropped from the regression.

λ in the formula above is called the **tuning parameter**. It serves as a weight for the penalty term versus the OLS fit. Thus, it drives the strength of the variable selection. If λ is zero, we get back the OLS model. As λ increases, it leads to more aggressive selection and thus fewer variables left in the regression, with smaller coefficients. But what values should λ have?

The solution is to have our computer try out many values for λ, and to pick the one that gives the best prediction in the end using k-fold cross-validation. First, a LASSO algorithm is run on the training set with a specific value of λ. It finds its estimated coefficients (some of which will be zero), gives a prediction of the corresponding test set, calculates the MSE, and then repeats the whole thing for the other training–test splits. When all of this is done, it saves the average MSE across the test sets. Then it starts again, doing the same thing for another value of λ. And so on, for many possible lambda values. In fact, the LASSO algorithm is embedded in another algorithm that searches for the best λ; that other algorithm is called a **search algorithm**. Where to start the search (at what value of λ), when to stop, and the size of steps to consider when moving from one λ value to another λ value are details of the search algorithm that are beyond the scope of this textbook. Luckily, statistical packages have built-in search algorithms for cross-validated search for λ as part of their LASSO packages. These statistical packages tend to have sensible default options for the algorithm so we can run them without more detailed knowledge of how the algorithm works.

The only thing we need to decide for LASSO is the initial set of right-hand-side variables. Unfortunately, that turns out to be not such a simple choice after all. It is good practice to start with a wide set that may include many interactions and functions that can approximate nonlinearity if warranted (e.g., polynomials or piecewise linear splines with several knots). Disappointingly, it's usually impossible to feed in all possible interactions and extremely detailed functional forms, so LASSO drops the unnecessary variables and the unnecessary terms. But, using our domain knowledge and what we learned about the variables during the exploratory data analysis, we can usually come up with a meaningful but broad set of potential right-hand-side variables including interactions and nonlinear forms.

Finally, note that LASSO tinkers with the OLS estimates, and those OLS estimates were known to produce unbiased predictions. The result of the LASSO modification is that the predictions become biased. The larger λ, the larger the difference between LASSO and OLS and the larger the bias of LASSO. Recall, however, that a biased prediction is not necessarily a worse prediction (Chapter 13, Section 13.6). The total loss due to the prediction error (e.g., MSE) has two parts: bias and variance. We can get a smaller total loss with larger bias if the variance is smaller. And that's exactly what LASSO achieves. The search for the best λ finds the prediction with the smallest total loss, thus finding an optimal way to trade off bias and variance.

Review Box 14.4   LASSO

- LASSO is a method for estimating a linear regression with a large set of candidate x variables, typically including nonlinear functional forms and interactions to arrive at a good prediction.
- LASSO selects some of the candidate x variables to remain in the regression and drops the rest.
- We need to specify the set of candidate x variables; it's good practice to specify a large set including potentially meaningful interactions and nonlinear functional forms.
- The LASSO algorithm finds the best predictor by shrinking coefficients, some to zero.

14.B3   CASE STUDY – Predicting Airbnb Apartment Prices: Selecting a Regression Model

LASSO

The LASSO algorithm is completely automated in most satistical software, with sensible default options for the details of the algorithm. All we have to do is specify a regression with a large set of starting predictor variables, and let the algorithm run. At the end, LASSO returns with an estimated regression that has fewer coefficients: it chooses zero for some of the coefficients, which practically means dropping the corresponding variables from the regression. For the variables that it retains, it gives estimated coefficients.

Thus, the most important task is specifying the set of candidate x variables. Here we start with the variables in our Model 8. This set includes all of the variables we extracted from the ads, including the 60 amenities, each interacted with property type as well as bed type. The set also includes polynomials for the number of guests accommodated and the average review score. In total, these are more than 300 candidate variables in the regression.

We ran the LASSO algorithm with 5-fold cross-validation for selecting the optimal value for λ. In the end, the algorithm picked a regression with 81 variables. This number is very close to the number of variables in our model M7 that cross-validation picked as the best from the eight models we specified earlier. M7 had all the variables and polynomials, but it did not have most of the interactions included in M8. There is a large overlap in the predictor variables included in M7 and the model LASSO picked, and the estimated coefficients of these variables are similar, too. There are some differences, though, with some of the more detailed interactions included in the LASSO regression and some amenities dropped.

The overall RMSE across the five test sets for the LASSO regression is 37.60. It is 37.78 for M7, suggesting that our hand-picked M7 is almost as good as the LASSO regression. But again, the LASSO is automatic, a great advantage. Our decision is to have the model M7 as our preferred model, because it may be easier to explain which variables are included.

14.9   Diagnostics

The last step of the prediction process is to evaluate the actual prediction. At this point we have a best model that we selected by cross-validation. To make the final prediction, we estimate it using all of the work data. And now we use the holdout set of the observations from the original data to evaluate that prediction. Recall that we haven't done anything to this holdout set, except for cleaning it. All exploratory data analysis, model building, and model selection was done using the work set. We retain the holdout set for evaluating the final prediction.

The process of evaluating the prediction is called **post-prediction diagnostics**. We may want to do three kinds of things here.

Firstly, and most obviously, we want to evaluate the fit of the prediction. We can use MSE or RMSE, or another loss function, to summarize the goodness of fit. And we can use a $\hat{y}-y$ graph to visualize it. Secondly, we use the holdout set to create the prediction interval around the prediction.

Third, and perhaps most importantly, we can zoom in to the kinds of observations we care about the most. Even if we are interested in predicting y for a specific value of x (our car or its older self; sales in a particular month; and so on), we tend to use a broader set of observations for the prediction. Here we can look at what the prediction looks like for the observations in the holdout set that are most similar to the specific x values we want to predict for.

Alternatively, when we want to predict for a wide range of x values, we can look at the fit in various subsamples of the data. For example, we may want to predict the survival of many kinds of firms in an economy. Here, we can use the holdout set to see whether and how the quality of our prediction varies across firms with different sizes, in different industries, or in different financial situations.

Finally, as we emphasized in Chapter 13, Section 13.11, data analysts should assess external validity and be explicit about that assessment when presenting the results of a prediction. Having a holdout set makes sure that the prediction model is selected and estimated using a different part of the original data than the part used for diagnostics. That way the diagnostics show the fit and the uncertainty of the prediction not in the data we have but more generally in the population, or general pattern, represented by the original data. But, eventually, we want to predict y in the live data. That additional step, external validity, is just as important a step as the previous one. Typically, we can say a lot less about this step than the previous one, and we certainly can't run any fancy, or less fancy, algorithm to assess it. But analyzing the prediction in various subsets of the holdout set can provide some guidance about the additional uncertainty it brings.

14.B4 CASE STUDY – Predicting Airbnb Apartment Prices: Selecting a Regression Model

Diagnostics and summary

Let us first summarize our modeling results. A 5-fold cross-validation of eight candidate linear regression models and LASSO (with tuning parameter selected by 5-fold cross-validation) both suggest a prediction model with as many as 70–80 predictor variables. The particular regression LASSO estimated is a little different from, but very close to model M7 that we specified using exploratory data analysis and domain knowledge. In particular, not only the set of x variables and their coefficients are similar, but also their test set RMSE. Thus, we may choose either of the two.

Note that we also estimated our model M7 with the target variable defined in logs. The cross-validated RMSE is 37.9, basically the same, so we stuck to levels. You are invited to carry out the prediction with log price as a data exercise.

Thus, we chose the OLS estimated M7. What can we say about model performance? After estimating the model on all observations in the work sample, we calculated its RMSE in the holdout sample. The RMSE for M7 is 31.9. The holdout set RMSE is smaller than the cross-validated RMSE. That's a common finding, because the sample size that we use for the prediction is larger than for cross-validation.

We can show how predicted prices compare to actual prices in Figure 14.8a, on a $\hat{y}-y$ graph as introduced in Chapter 10, Section 10.12. We can see that the prediction does a somewhat better job for lower than for higher prices. Indeed, the range of actual prices is wider than the range of predicted prices as we never predict a price greater than 200 US dollars. This is not a rare phenomenon; regression models often have a hard time predicting extreme values, unless there are many of them in a very large dataset.

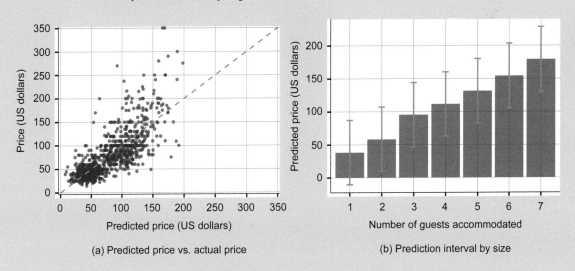

(a) Predicted price vs. actual price

(b) Prediction interval by size

Figure 14.8 Airbnb prediction – model diagnostics

Note: Linear regression M7. See model details in text. PI is 80% prediction interval.
Source: airbnb dataset, Hackney, borough of London, March 2017. N=4393 (holdout sample, N=878).

The model generates a very wide 80% prediction interval. For the average apartment we predict a 77 dollar price. We face a great deal of uncertainty despite having a good model; prices may vary between 28.5 and 126.5 dollars.

We also show the prediction interval (at the 80% level) by the number of guests the apartment can accommodate (Figure 14.8b).

The conclusion from these diagnostics is that our prediction has substantial uncertainty. That uncertainty is present in all subgroups; for a four-person apartment, the 80% PI is between 60 and 150 dollars. One way to reduce the prediction error is to have a larger sample size. Indeed, we can improve our model, by not limiting ourselves to Hackney and using the full London dataset (we will also do that in Chapter 16). As a data exercise, you are invited to reproduce the prediction and the diagnostics for the full London dataset.

This concludes our case study. Our goal was to produce the best prediction of Airbnb apartment prices for the Hackney borough of London, using linear regression that makes use of the many apartment features available in the data. We carried out extensive feature engineering. Of the original data, we selected a random 80% to be our work set and set aside the remaining 20% as the holdout set for diagnosis in the end. With a lot of work, we specified eight regression models, and used cross-validation to find our model M7 to be the best. Then we used LASSO, which selected a linear regression model that was very similar to our model M7. Finally, using the holdout sample, we evaluated the predictive performance of model M7. We found that its prediction error is similar across various variables, which suggests that its quality is similar across all kinds of observations, but we also found that the prediction interval is quite wide. Thus, we found that our best model could make large errors when predicting the price for any particular apartment.

14.10   Prediction with Big Data

We close this chapter with a note on Big Data and the additional opportunities and challenges it brings to predictive analytics. As we noted earlier in Chapter 1, Section 1.9, Big Data can denote data with many observations, many variables, and data that is continuously updated. As in most of the textbook, we focus on the first kind of Big Data here: data with many observations.

Consider the problem of using sales and inventory system data to make predictions about sales in many stores of a large retailer. This could be Big Data indeed: point of sale and inventory management systems collect data on each sales transaction for each store. The data is continuously updated as sales take place. Suppose that our aim is to predict sales for each item at a weekly level, as inventories are refreshed once a week. To make a prediction for the first week of March, our data includes observations till the end of February for all the stores in the chain, for all products. An observation is a product code, sales price, date, and location (we will see a similar data in Chapter 18). The data could easily have millions of observations. Predictors could include prices, weather conditions, advertising, as well as features of inventory – i.e., what similar products (such as other brands) were available at the time of sale.

In principle, having a great many observations doesn't change the logic of predictive analytics. We need a work set for model building and selection, and a holdout set for diagnostics. To select models, we use k-fold cross-validation and an appropriate loss function. To build models, we may use LASSO. But all of this may take a lot of time with Big Data that has a massive number of observations, and little time is available for the analysis of Big Data that is updated regularly.

The most obvious advantage of having a great many observations is that estimation error plays little role in the prediction error. For this reason Big Data likely produces better predictions than smaller data with the same variables. More observations help in picking the best model, too, because they allow for smaller estimation error in the training sets and a more accurate way to evaluate predictions in the test sets. Thus, model error tends to be smaller with Big Data, too.

The magnitude of the third source of error, irreducible error, doesn't depend on the number of observations. Instead, it depends on how good our predictor variables are. In practice, most Big Data comes from administrative sources (Chapter 1, Section 1.4). That may result in fewer x variables and larger irreducible error. Sometimes, though, admin data contains variables that we would not have in purposely collected data because data collectors wouldn't be able to collect them, and such variables may turn out to help prediction. That is especially true if different data sources are combined to add more variables.

At the same time, the sheer number of observations poses a challenge for predictive analytics. With a great many observations, it would take way too much time to run all of the algorithms we want to use. Recall that k-fold cross-validation means estimating and evaluating various models many times, and LASSO itself is an algorithm that takes time, especially if it's embedded in a search for its optimal λ parameter using another layer of cross-validation.

Often, the best solution is to take a modest random sample from our Big Data on which our algorithms can run in a reasonable time. This is a balancing act: we should aim for the largest sample that we can feasibly analyze to preserve the advantages of size.

Finally, external validity of predictions is not affected by the number of observations. The size of the original data does not matter for whether, and to what extent, the prediction in the population, or general pattern, represented by the original data is similar to the prediction in the population, or general pattern, that is behind the live data. For that reason, we should do the same kinds of things to assess and, potentially, improve external validity of our prediction, regardless of the size of the data. In particular, Big Data does not substitute for domain knowledge and the need to know our data and, thus, carry out exploratory data analysis.

In sum, Big Data brings important advantages to predictive analytics while posing some challenges, and it leaves some issues the same. In particular, Big Data can be a great help for prediction by minimizing estimation error and decreasing model error. But Big Data may be too big for the necessary algorithms to run quickly enough, in which case we should take a random sample to arrive at a "big enough but not too big" dataset. Finally, some of the most important aspects of predictive analytics remain the same regardless of the number of observations, including uncertainty of predictions due to irreducible error and potential issues with external validity.

Review Box 14.5 Prediction with Big Data

- The principles of prediction are the same with Big Data as with moderate-sized data.
- Big Data leads to smaller estimation error. This reduction makes the total prediction error smaller.
- The magnitude of irreducible error, and problems with external validity, remain the same with Big Data.
- When N is too large, we can take a random sample and select the best model with the help of usual cross-validation using that random sample.

14.11   Main Takeaways

We can never evaluate all possible models to find the best one.

- Model building is important to specify models that are likely among the best.
- LASSO is an algorithm that can help in model building, by selecting the x variables and their functional forms.
- Exploratory data analysis and domain knowledge remain important alongside powerful algorithms, for assessing and improving the external validity of predictions.

PRACTICE QUESTIONS

1. When might we want to select a specific subset of the observations from our original data for predictive analytics? Give an example.
2. We don't want to use the same data to evaluate predictions and build, estimate, and select the prediction models. Why?
3. What's a holdout sample, and what do we use it for?
4. Give two reasons why exploratory data analysis is important for predictive analytics even when using an algorithm to build the best model.
5. How would you predict y from a regression with ln y as its left-hand-side variable?
6. What's sample design, what's label engineering, and what's feature engineering?
7. What does LASSO do to the OLS estimates? Give an intuitive explanation.
8. What's the role of λ in LASSO, and how do we find the appropriate value for it?
9. Does LASSO give unbiased predictions? If yes, why? If not, why not, and why do we use it anyway?
10. What steps of model building does LASSO substitute, and what steps remain the same with it?
11. What's the advantage of Big Data in predictive analytics? What's its disadvantage, and what can we do about that?
12. You want to predict the price of used cars of a certain make and type based on their age and other characteristics. You find that one of the regression models you built achieves practically the same cross-validated RMSE as a LASSO. Which model would you choose for prediction and why?
13. You want to predict the price of used cars of a certain make and type based on their age and other characteristics. You find that even your best prediction model produces a very wide prediction interval on the holdout set. What would you need to make a prediction with a narrower prediction interval?
14. You want to predict daily sales in your shop using monthly and daily seasonality. Give an example for how the two types of seasonality may interact with each other. How would you capture such interactions in a model with the help of LASSO?
15. You want to predict the two-year growth rate of medium-sized firms in your country with the help of many variables. The data includes ten thousand firms for a ten-year period. Give an example of why external validity could be low with this prediction. How could you use diagnostic tools to asses this problem?

DATA EXERCISES

Easier and/or shorter exercises are denoted by [*]; harder and/or longer exercises are denoted by [**].

1. Assume you have p predictors, $x_1 \ldots x_p$. Let us consider four scenarios:
   (a) Only linear form of variables.
   (b) Linear and quadratic form of each variable (if you have the x_i squared, you will also have x_i in the model, but of course, you can have x_i alone).
   (c) Linear form, but also have all the pairwise interactions possible.
   (d) Linear and quadratic forms, and you also have all the pairwise interactions possible (i.e., for two variables, $x_i x_j$ and $x_i^2 x_j$ and $x_i^2 x_j$ and $x_j^2 x_j^2$).
   There are two questions for each case: (i) How many different models can we have? (ii) What is the maximum number of predictors? Please submit a formula and two graphs showing how increasing p from 2 to 10 raises the total number of features and the number of possible models. [**]

2. Consider the Airbnb case study. Repeat the model building and selection exercise with log target variable instead of levels. Compare the results to those in this chapter. [**]

3. Consider the Airbnb case study. Repeat the model building and selection exercise using a 5-fold CV rather than a 10-fold CV. Compare results. Calculate the PI and compare with the PI for the 10-fold case. [*].

4. Repeat the whole exercise on the full London dataset without LASSO, but add a set of binary variables for boroughs. Discuss the results and compare them to our case study. Include prediction interval graphs, by, e.g., the number of people accommodated, and compare them with our case study. [**]

5. Consider the `cps-earnings` dataset we used in Chapters 9 and 10 with a starting sample size of 149 316 individuals. Take 30% of observations for the holdout set. Build four predictive models using linear regression: a simple and a complicated model for earnings per hour; and a simple and a complicated model for log earnings per hour. Compare the model performance of these four models on the holdout set. Discuss your findings. [**]

REFERENCES AND FURTHER READING

On LASSO and other general sparsity models, see the book Hastie et al. (2015). A classic computer science paper on feature selection is Guyon & Elisseeff (2003). A comprehensive book on applied modeling decisions is Kuhn & Johnson (2019).

14.U1 UNDER THE HOOD: TEXT PARSING

Texts, such as descriptions, quotes, and reviews, are often used to record information that could be useful for prediction. This work is part of natural language processing, the process of understanding and analyzing textual information.

The simplest example is a text variable that could be used as a categorical variable, such as the name of a brand or a country. A slightly more complex situation is when we have a sentence or a paragraph and want to extract information from it. The difficulty comes from the fact that any word may be in the text and that furthermore, it will include useless information. Getting out useful information (e.g. a set of variables) from text is called **text parsing**. Text parsing can make use of sophisticated methods that are beyond the scope of this textbook.

Consider the case where we have text describing features of a product, maybe formed in sentences like "The apartment has TV, cable, wifi, with a kitchen equipped with microwave oven and dishwasher." The simplest option is collecting all the words in such descriptions; this is called a **bag of words**, a vector of words collected from text without ordering or grammatical information. From the bag of words we can discard what we do not need such as "the" or "with," or even "the apartment," and keep the rest. Then we can simply create a binary variable for each word: wifi-bin would be 1 if the word "wifi" features in the text. This is the process we used in the **Predicting Airbnb apartment prices: selecting a regression model** case study for this chapter.

14.U2 UNDER THE HOOD: LOG CORRECTION

Recall that it's good practice to transform predicted $\ln y$ to predicted y with the help of a correction factor:

$$\hat{y}_j = e^{\widehat{\ln y_j}} e^{\hat{\sigma}^2/2} \qquad (14.5)$$

The rationale behind the correction comes from the lognormal distribution. Recall from Chapter 2 that a variable follows a lognormal distribution if its natural logarithm is normally distributed. In other words, y is lognormally distributed if $\ln y$ is normally distributed. Denoting the mean and standard deviation of that normally distributed ($\ln y$) variable by μ and σ, the mean of the lognormally distributed variable $y = e^{\ln y}$ is $\bar{y} = e^{\mu+\sigma^2/2}$.

The correction factor is based not on the distribution of the target variable y but its distribution conditional on the predictor variable (or predictor variables). This distribution is centered around the regression line (that shows the predicted values corresponding to the values of the predictor variables). Its standard deviation is best approximated by the standard deviation of the regression residuals. That's why the the correction factor is a function of the standard deviation of the regression residuals, which we denote as $\hat{\sigma}$.

This argument highlights that the correction is based on an assumption: that the distribution of the log target variable is normal conditional on the predictor variables. If this assumption is true, the correction factor is exact. If the assumption is not true, the correction factor is an approximation. The closer the distribution to normal, the better the approximation. We can check how good the approximation is by examining the distribution of the regression residuals. The closer it is to normal, the better the approximation.

In our case study, the adjustment factor makes the prediction from the log price model often rather close to the other prediction. But that is no proof that it works how it should. Instead, we have to check the assumption behind it: that log prices conditional on age are distributed normally. That translates to looking at the distribution of the residuals. The closer their distribution is to normal, the better the correction factor.

15 Regression Trees

How to build a regression tree to predict a quantitative y variable

> **Motivation**
>
> You want to predict the price of used cars as a function of their age and other features. You want to specify a model that includes the most important interactions and nonlinearities of those features, but you don't know how to start. In particular, you are worried that you can't start with a very complex regression model and use LASSO or some other method to simplify it, because there are way too many potential interactions. Is there an alternative approach to regression that includes the most important interactions without you having to specify them?
>
> To carry out the prediction of used car prices, you have learned to use the regression tree, an alternative to linear regressions that is designed to build a model with the most important interactions and nonlinearities for a prediction. However, the regression tree you build appears to overfit your original data. How can you build a regression tree model that is less prone to overfitting the original data and can thus give a better prediction in the live data?

We know that, when trying to predict y with the help of many x variables, we can't specify all possible models that we can select from. We also know that we can use LASSO to get to a less complex linear regression model from a more complex linear regression model, which helps avoid overfitting the original data. However, when we have many variables with many potential interactions and nonlinearities, we may not be able to specify one very complex model and thus would not be able to start the LASSO algorithm. Instead, we would need a method that finds the most important variables, interactions, and nonlinearities in a different way.

This chapter introduces the regression tree, an alternative to linear regression for prediction purposes that can find the most important predictor variables and their interactions and can approximate any functional form automatically. Regression trees split the data into small bins (subsamples) by the value of the x variables. For a quantitative y, they use the average y value in those small sets to predict $\hat{y}$. We introduce the regression tree model and the most widely used algorithm to build a regression tree model. Somewhat confusingly, both the model and the algorithm are called CART (for classification and regression trees), but we reserve this name for the algorithm. We show that a regression tree is an intuitively appealing method to model nonlinearities and interactions among the x variables, but it is rarely used for prediction in itself because it is prone to overfit the original data. Instead, the regression tree forms the basic element of very powerful prediction methods that we'll cover in the next chapter.

The case study **Predicting used car value with regression trees** in this chapter illustrates how we can build a regression tree model with the help of a CART algorithm and how such a model would overfit the original data. This case study uses the `used-cars` dataset.

Learning outcomes

After working through this chapter, you should be able to:

- build regression trees with the CART algorithm to predict y with the help of x variables;
- understand how the CART algorithm approximates nonlinear functional forms and finds important interactions;
- understand why regression trees likely overfit the data;
- understand how pruning works and why it reduces overfitting;
- understand the similarities and differences between using the CART algorithm to grow a regression tree and building a linear regression.

15.1 The Case for Regression Trees

In the previous chapter we saw that it's impossible to specify all possible regression models to predict y using the data we have. Therefore, we can't be sure to find the best regression model for prediction by trying all models and evaluating their performance by, for example, cross-validation. Our evaluation tools allow us to find the best one from the regression models we try, but there may be an even better one among the regression models that we did not try. To help with that situation, we introduced LASSO, an algorithm that helps select x variables from a large candidate set of x variables to arrive at a good prediction.

As we also discussed, selecting the x variables means deciding on which original variables from our data to include as well as in what functional forms and with what interactions with each other. In fact, the latter are far more difficult tasks, because the number of variables that can approximate functional forms and the number of possible interactions is huge even with a small number of original x variables. The logic of LASSO is to start with a large set of them (complicated functional forms, many interactions) and narrow the set down. However, it's our decision to define that original set, and we simply can't include in it every possible interaction and every flexible functional form. LASSO cannot find variables and interactions that we don't include in the candidate set of variables.

In this chapter, we'll introduce regression trees that follow a different approach. A regression tree is designed to capture the most important x variables, approximate the functional forms of the $x-y$ relationships whether they are linear or not, and identify the most important interactions among the x variables to predict y. A regression tree creates the prediction using a step-by-step process, first including the most important x variable, then going forward to include other variables, approximating nonlinearities and creating interactions among x variables in the process. The end of the process is a prediction that assigns $\hat{y}$ values to all observations depending on the values of the x variables included in the tree.

As we'll see, building a regression tree is an intuitive procedure, but it, too, requires some shortcuts compared to what would be a theoretically optimal way. Nevertheless, a regression tree can arrive at very good predictions of y from a given set of x variables. Unfortunately, that is true for the training sample fit; regression trees tend to severely overfit the training data and thus produce poor fits in test samples. And that implies that they tend to overfit the original data and would produce inferior predictions in the live data.

There are ways to improve upon this shortcoming of regression trees, and we'll introduce them in this chapter. However, in most cases, those tools don't do a good enough job. For that reason, regression trees are rarely used in themselves for prediction. Instead, they are the building blocks of much more successful prediction models that tend to outperform most other prediction methods, including regressions with or without LASSO. Those more successful prediction models will be the subject of the next chapter.

15.2 Regression Tree Basics

A **regression tree** is a model that produces predicted values $\hat{y}$ for observations with particular values of the x variables. The basic idea of a regression tree is **splitting** the data into small **bins** by the values of the x variables, and predicting y as the average value of y within those bins. That is, at least, how things work for a quantitative y variable, which will continue to be the focus in this chapter. When y is a binary variable, we can use a similar algorithm to build a classification tree – we'll return to the prediction of binary y variables in Chapter 17.

Regression trees are also called **CART**, standing for Classification And Regression Trees. However, CART is used not only for the tree models themselves but also for the specific algorithm that is used to create them. In this textbook, we will reserve the CART name for the algorithm that is used to build a regression tree (or a classification tree).

Creating a regression tree model is called **building** or **growing** a tree. Trees are built by the **CART algorithm**, which has no formula. The goal of the algorithm is to arrive at a set of bins, defined by the values of the various x variables, in such a way that the average value of y in these bins comprises the best prediction of y. By doing so, the bins are defined so that they best represent the patterns of association between x and y that leads to the best prediction of y. As we'll see, the CART algorithm doesn't exactly target that goal explicitly. Instead, it approximates that goal by going step by step, setting intermediate goals for each successive step that are easier to achieve than the ultimate goal of a best final prediction. Each step of the CART algorithm consists of splitting the sample into smaller and smaller bins.

Let's describe the CART algorithm with a single x variable. The algorithm starts with the entire sample (the entire training sample in the case of cross-validation). This first step is called the **top node** of the tree. It consists of splitting the sample into two parts.

When x is binary, there is only one way to split the sample along its values: one part has all observations with $x = 0$, the other part has all observations with $x = 1$. And that would be the end of the process with a single x variable. When x is not binary, there are multiple ways to do the splitting. Of those, the algorithm finds the split that makes the best prediction of y from among all potential splits, using some criterion. This is done with a **search algorithm**. The result of the search algorithm is the x value, along with the split that improves the prediction the most. The value at which the split happens is the **cutoff point** for that particular x variable.

The first split produces two **branches** going from the top node. At the end of each branch is one new **node**, corresponding to two respective bins (subsamples). Then the algorithm re-starts for each bin and considers a subsequent split for each, following the same approach as it did in the previous step. Naturally, when the algorithm continues from a node, it considers observations that are in the relevant bin. The result of the second step is one split from each of the two nodes, which results in four new subsamples, represented by four new nodes, at the end of two branches from each previous node. And so on.

The process stops when a pre-defined **stopping rule** tells it to stop. We'll discuss how to set stopping rules in the next section. The set of nodes after the algorithm stops are called **terminal nodes**; the collection of terminal nodes is also called the **bucket**. Each and every observation in the data corresponds to one bin in the bucket. The bucket is the set of bins that produces the prediction of y. The predicted $\hat{y}$ values are the average y values within each bin.

The process may stop after a different number of steps on the different branches of the tree, depending on when it arrives at a subsample where no further splits can improve the prediction. Thus, the number of splits may differ for different branches. The size of the tree is often expressed as the number of **levels**: the largest number of splits it took to get to a terminal node, plus one.

The tree itself is a visualization of all of the steps of the procedure. It's a funny tree, because it's upside down. The first node is at the top of the tree, that's why it's also called the top node. The nodes after the first split are one level below, and so on, until we reach the terminal nodes that are at the bottom of the tree. Different branches may have different terminal nodes at their ends.

However, with a single quantitative x variable, we can visualize the regression tree in a different, and perhaps more intuitive, way. The regression tree creates bins from the x variable, which are intervals that cover its entire range. The regression tree then assigns the same average y value to each observation within the same bin as the prediction. That's nothing other than a visualization of the conditional mean, covered in Chapter 4, Section 4.5 and again in Chapter 7, Section 4.U1. It's a **step function**. In a step function, the values (here $\hat{y}$, the predicted y values) are the same for all x values within an interval, then jump to another value in the next interval, and so on. We'll see examples for visualized step functions in the case study below. Before that, let's spend a little time on measures of fit and stopping rules.

15.3   Measuring Fit and Stopping Rules

The fit of the prediction from a regression tree can be measured in the same way as the fit of any prediction model. The end of the algorithm gives a predicted value $\hat{y}$ that corresponds to particular x values. To measure the fit we compare these $\hat{y}$ values to the actual y values. The best tree is found via cross-validation.

One measure of fit often used for regression trees is called the **relative error**. It is calculated as the ratio of the sum of squared errors of the prediction and the total sum of squared deviation of y from its overall mean. This is, of course, simply $1 - R^2$ (recall the R-squared formula from Chapter 7, Section 4.U1). Lower relative error means a higher R-squared, which implies better model fit. Alternatively, we can use MSE or its square root, RMSE. MSE is nothing else than the numerator of relative error. Thus, whether we use MSE, RMSE, R-squared, or relative error, we arrive at the same ranking of different predictions.

However, just as with any other prediction model, we should keep in mind that we could end up with a model so complex that it overfits the data. That's a very real possibility with a regression tree because it is built by successive steps, each step designed to improve the fit. In fact, left alone, the algorithm would go on as long as splits are possible. In principle, this could go on until all observations in the bin have the exact same value for the x variable. That bin cannot be split further. So a fully grown regression tree would have final bins with observations having the same x values, with a corresponding average y as the predicted value $\hat{y}$. At the extreme, we may end up with only one observation in some of the bins, or all of the bins, with the corresponding y value as the prediction. That would obviously produce an overfitted model.

To decrease the likelihood of overfitting, the splitting algorithm stops at some point, as prompted by a rule. The **stopping rule** is a condition, or a set of conditions, that defines when the algorithm stops, based on results from the most recent step. Data analysts use various stopping rules when growing a regression tree, such as the minimum number of observations in a bin for further splitting or the number of observations in any terminal node. One widely used stopping rule requires that a split is made only if it improves the fit of the by a minimum amount. Such a minimum improvement on the fit prediction is called the **complexity parameter**, often abbreviated as cp. One example is that the split needs to improve the R-squared by at least 0.001. That would correspond to a complexity parameter $cp = 0.001$. Thus, this rule tells the algorithm to stop and make the bin a terminal node if splitting it would improve the R-squared by less than 0.001.

> **Review Box 15.1   Regression trees with one x variable**
>
> - A regression tree is the result of a series of binary splits of the sample.
> - The subsamples that result from splits are called bins and are represented as nodes of the tree.
> - With a single binary x, there is only one split possible; thus the tree has two levels with two terminal nodes.
> - With a single non-binary x, the algorithm starts with one split that improves the fit the most, and carries on to further splits within each bin.
> - The splitting algorithm stops as dictated by a stopping rule.
> - The result of the algorithm is a set of bins (the terminal nodes) that cover the entire sample. The predicted $\hat{y}$ values are the average y value within each bin.

15.A1   CASE STUDY – Predicting Used Car Value with a Regression Tree

One quantitative x variable

The question of this case study is how to find the best price of a used car, or multiple used cars, that we want to sell. To that aim we need to know how the various features of used cars are related to their sales price. One observation in the dataset is one advertisement. All observations are Toyota Camry ads. This is the same question as in our case study in Chapter 13, using the same data source, but while there we used ads from Chicago only, here we add ads from Los Angeles, too, to be able to consider more complex models with more observations. In total, the number of observations is 477. The y variable to predict is price; average price is 5844 US dollars in the data.

For the sake of this case study, we grossly simplify the prediction process. In particular, we don't leave out a holdout sample, and we use a single training–test split instead of k-fold cross-validation. Our training set is a random 70 percent of the original data ($N = 333$). We made these decisions in order to keep the example simple and illustrate the most important aspects of, and issues with, building a regression tree. You are invited to reproduce the analysis with k-fold cross-validation as a data exercise.

First, let us use the age of the car as the only predictor variable. The average age in the training set is 12.4 years. In the CART M1 model, the first split in the regression tree finds the age value that divides cars into two groups with the largest difference in average price. The algorithm finds the split at the age of 8: is the car age greater or equal to 8 years (yes or no). The left branch will include cars at least 8 years old; the right branch below 8 (i.e., 7 or less).

There are 77 cars below the age cutoff (age 0–7 years), with average price 11 771 dollars. There are 256 cars above the cutoff (age 8 or older), with average price 3788 dollars. Figures 15.1a and 15.1b show two visualizations of this single-split tree: the tree form and the step function form – the latter together with the scatterplot.

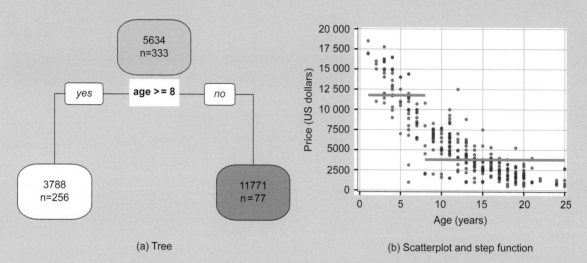

(a) Tree   (b) Scatterplot and step function

Figure 15.1   Two visualizations of a regression tree with two levels: price and age of used cars

Note: CART M1: Regression tree grown by CART, allowing for two levels (a single split).
Source: `used-cars` dataset. Used Toyota Camry cars, Chicago and Los Angeles areas, N=477 (training set, N=333).

Going forward, in the next step the CART algorithm starts from each of the two bins and considers further splits. In the CART M2 model we see that in the 0–7 age bin it splits creating a bin for cars of 5–7 years and another for 0–4 years. For the age bin of 8 years and older, it creates two groups: 8–12 and 13+. Thus, we have four groups as shown in Table 15.1.

Table 15.1   CART M2 output summary

Category	Number of observations	Average_price
Age 0–4	38	14194.84
Age 5–7	39	9408.56
Age 8–12	86	5870.52
Age 13 or more	170	2734.54

Note: The predicted y values from CART M2, a regression tree grown by CART allowing for three levels.

Source: `used-cars` dataset. Used Toyota Camry cars, Chicago and Los Angeles areas, N=477 (training set, N=333).

We can see how price falls with age. Also, we can see that the different bins have different numbers of observations: in the youngest age bin there are 38 observations, and there are 170 observations in the oldest age bin. Figures 15.2a and 15.2b show the corresponding tree visualization and step function visualization.

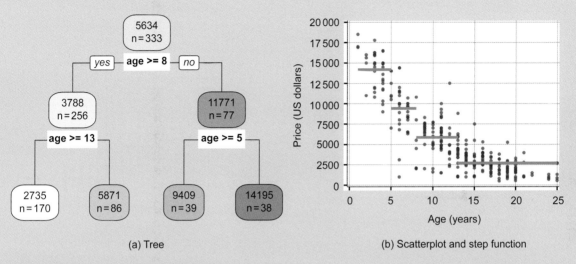

(a) Tree   (b) Scatterplot and step function

Figure 15.2   Two visualizations of CART M2, a three-level regression tree: price and age of used cars

Note: The predicted y values from a regression tree grown by CART, allowing for three levels.
Source: used-cars dataset. Used Toyota Camry cars, Chicago and Los Angeles areas, N=477(training set, N=333).

We can let the algorithm go on with a decision rule to stop. In the previous model with four terminal nodes, we used a stopping rule defining the level to be three. Now, instead of setting the stopping rule in terms of the number of splits, we set it in terms of the minimum improvement on the fit, requiring a minimum $cp = 0.001$. Figures 15.3a and 15.3b show this CART M3 model: the tree and step function visualizations.

We can compare the predictive performance of this tree with two alternative prediction models. The simple model OLS M1 is a linear regression estimated by OLS with a single predictor: age (Figure 15.4a). The scatterplot with the lowess regression in Figure 15.4b shows that the pattern is clearly nonlinear. The CART can capture nonlinear patterns but produces a non-smooth step-function. The simple linear regression cannot capture nonlinear patterns but fits a smooth line.

Table 15.2 compares the performance of these models. Recall that the models were estimated in a training set. We evaluated their fit by the RMSE of their predictions using the single test set we set aside. In particular, we compare the three regression trees we have grown and the linear regression we estimated. We do not include the lowess results here. The reason is that the lowess is practically useless for prediction purposes, because it doesn't allow to include more predictor variables. Instead, we used it as an illustration benchmark for capturing the nonlinearity in terms of a single predictor variable (age here).

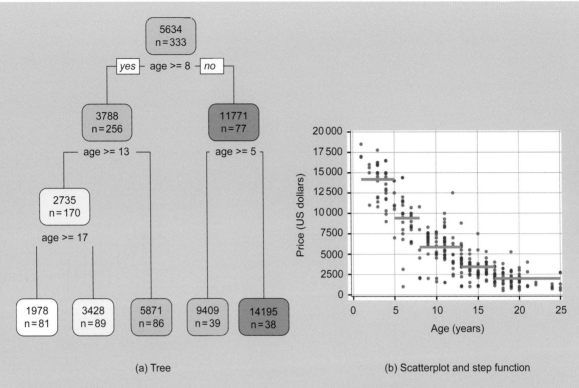

(a) Tree   (b) Scatterplot and step function

Figure 15.3 Two visualizations of CART M3: a regression tree grown with a stopping rule: price and age of used cars

Note: A regression tree grown by CART, with stopping rule of $cp = 0.001$.

Source: `used-cars` dataset. Used Toyota Camry cars, Chicago and Los Angeles areas, N=477 (training set, N=333).

The results show that, as we add additional splits, the test set RMSE falls with each level of added splits. Already with four terminal nodes, the regression tree does better than a simple regression that is linear in age. The most complex regression tree we have here, the one that is grown with a stopping rule of $cp = 0.001$, improves further on that, but only by very little.

Model	Description	RMSE
Table 15.2	Predicting price with age: a comparison of CART and OLS models	
CART M1	2 term. nodes	2781.06
CART M2	4 term. nodes	2074.46
CART M3	5 term. nodes	1969.52
OLS M1	1 variable only	2357.01

Note: Age is the only predictor. RMSE from single 30% test set.

Source: `used-cars` dataset. Used Toyota Camry cars, Chicago and Los Angeles areas, N=477 (training set, N=333; test set, N=144).

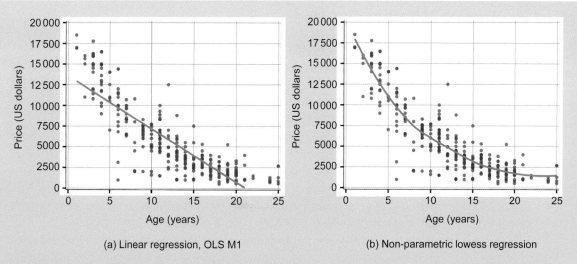

(a) Linear regression, OLS M1   (b) Non-parametric lowess regression

Figure 15.4 Linear and non-parametric lowess regressions

Note: Price regressed on age.
Source: `used-cars` dataset. Used Toyota Camry cars, Chicago and Los Angeles areas, N=477 (training set, N=333).

15.4 Regression Tree with Multiple Predictor Variables

Having discussed the simplest case with a single predictor variable x, we can move on to include more x variables. The idea of building a regression tree is the same as before: finding the best split at each and every step. The new thing is that, here, the algorithm compares splits according to many variables, in addition to comparing splits along different values of the same variable. At each node, the algorithm finds the best potential split for each x variable, which includes finding the best cutoff value for each non-binary x, and then selects the x variable that produces the best split. This procedure is repeated for each and every node.

Consider, for example, predicting the spending of customers of the loyalty program of a clothing store based on their age and gender. Age is a quantitative variable, and, for simplicity of the analysis, assume that gender is binary. Suppose that, in its first step, the algorithm finds that the largest improvement in RMSE of the prediction (compared to prediction without any x, which is using average spending for all observations) is splitting at age 30. That is, from among all possible values, age 30 is the cutoff that results in the best prediction using age. Also suppose that the improvement of the prediction by using this age cutoff is larger than using gender as a predictor in the first step. Thus, the first split results in two bins, one with people below 30 years of age, and one with people above 30 years of age. Then, moving forward, the algorithm looks for the split that gives the best prediction separately in the two bins. Suppose that, among the below-30 customers, the best split is differentiating customers below 25 and above 25. And, suppose that, among customers above 30, the best split is differentiating men and women. Although it's very unlikely to happen in real life, suppose that the algorithm stops after these splits.

The tree we have grown here has three levels: initial sample, first split, second and final split. The tree has four final terminal nodes: customers younger than 25, customers between 25 and 30 years of age, female customers older than 30, and male customers older than 30.

15.5 Pruning a Regression Tree

As it turns out, the stopping rule we introduced earlier tends not to produce the best prediction. With a very strict rule (e.g., requiring a big improvement in the fit with a large *cp* value), we tend to underfit the data: we could get better predictions with more variables, more interactions, or more refined step function approximations to the quantitative variables. With a more lenient stopping rule (a smaller *cp* value), we tend to overfit the data. Even worse, it's not simply that we can't know what the best stopping rule is – that we could remedy with the help of a search algorithm to find which *cp* value would give the best fit in the test sets by cross-validation, similarly to the way we find the best value of the tuning parameter for a LASSO (Chapter 14, Section 14.8). The real problem is that even with the best such value, our prediction is usually not the best.

A better solution is called **pruning** the tree. The name of this process is another example for a word taken from gardening. When we grow a plant, pruning is the process of cutting back branches. The purpose of pruning is to make the plant more robust and healthy in the long run. That is the idea here, too: grow a large regression tree first, with a stopping rule that lets it grow big, and prune it afterwards by deleting some of the splits, with the goal of arriving at a better prediction. We will use one type of pruning, called **cost complexity pruning**.

A CART with pruning is a complicated procedure. First we grow a large tree by applying a lenient stopping rule (such as a very small complexity parameter). Then, starting from that large tree, we start deleting splits at the end of the tree, one by one. As we do not know which final split is the least useful, we try deleting one split at a time at the last level, and re-evaluate the model fit in the test sample (or test samples for k-fold cross-validation). We try this with all such splits, and, in this way, we eventually compare many trees that are smaller by just one node. The result is a tree that is one node smaller, and this tree has a new set of terminal nodes (because one terminal node disappeared from the previous tree, and its observations are assigned to a different node, according to the previous level). Then we carry on, and delete one more split at the new terminal level using the same approach, and so on. We use cross-validation to evaluate the fit after each deletion. The process goes on until the fit is improved, and it stops when we can't improve the fit by deleting any of the nodes.

Pruning turns out to produce a better fit than simply stopping before growing a large tree. However, it can still lead to overfitting the data – something that we can remedy using the more complicated methods we'll cover in the next chapter.

15.6 A Regression Tree is a Non-parametric Regression

A regression tree is a non-parametric regression. It is a regression, because it calculates average *y* as a function of the *x* variables. Recall that a regression is a model of average *y* as a function of *x*: $y^E = f(x)$ (Chapter 7).

The regression tree is non-parametric because there are no intercept or slope coefficients or other parameters that would characterize how average *y* depends on the values of the *x* variables. Or, in other words, there is no formula that would link average *y* to the *x* variables. Instead, the result is the set of the bins that make up the terminal nodes, the values of the *x* variables that define those bins, and the corresponding *ŷ* values. For example, with a single quantitative *x* variable, the regression tree approximates the $y^E = f(x)$ function by a step function, whatever the true form of that *f* function is.

Consider our previous example, predicting how much customers of the loyalty program of a clothing store spend, based on their age and gender. Recall that the result of our small tree is four terminal nodes (bins): customers younger than 25 years of age, customers between 25 and 30 years of age, female customers older than 30, and male customers older than 30. This can be viewed as a non-parametric function of age, interacted with gender. From the quantitative age variable we created three categories, we assigned average y to all observations within the same category, and we have gender interacted for one age bin.

Importantly, gender and age are not fully interacted in this example. We could specify a linear regression that would give the exact same $\hat{y}$ values. This regression would have three binary variables for the age categories instead of the quantitative age variable, and it would interact the oldest age category with gender. But we wouldn't specify such a regression if we started model building ourselves. Instead, following the advice we gave in Chapter 10, Section 10.10, we would interact all age categories with gender. Yet the CART algorithm doesn't do that here: gender is interacted with only one of the age categories. This is of course a very artificial example, with a very small tree. But the fact that not all interactions are included is a feature of almost all regression trees. In fact, it's a very important feature of them: regression trees tend to include only a few of the many possible interactions – the ones that are the most important for predicting y.

Viewing the regression tree as a non-parametric regression helps appreciate the power of the CART algorithm in selecting x variables, functional forms, and interactions. With many x variables, we could not possibly specify all possible ways to model nonlinearity, and we couldn't possibly include all interactions, and thus we couldn't rely on model selection or LASSO to find the ones that matter. Instead, the CART algorithm builds such a model for us, making use of a simple approximation to any functional form and considering the most important interactions.

> **Review Box 15.2 Regression tree with multiple x variables, pruning, and regression trees as non-parametric regressions**
>
> - A regression tree with multiple x variables considers all splits across all x variables and chooses the split that improves the fit the most.
> - The regression tree is a non-parametric regression, one which approximates any functional form with a step function and includes interactions.
> - A regression tree grown with CART includes only the most important interactions and the most important steps of a step function.
> - Pruning means first growing a large regression tree with a lenient stopping rule, and then erasing final splits one by one to improve fit in the test set (or cross-validated test sets).
> - Pruning tends to produce a better fit in the test sets than a strict stopping rule, but even pruning tends to leave regression trees overfitting the original data.

15.A2   CASE STUDY – Predicting Used Car Value with a Regression Tree

Multiple x variables and pruning

We now further develop the used car price prediction exercise. Besides age, we consider all other available predictor variables. We show two regression trees that we have built using two different stopping rules. With a new CART M4 model, we grew a smaller tree based on setting the complexity parameter as stopping rule, with $cp = 0.01$. That is, we stopped the regression tree when the subsequent split would have improved the R-squared in the test sample by less than 0.01.

Then, we grew a larger tree with a combined stopping rule. For CART M5, the minimum improvement in complexity parameter was set to be $cp = 0.002$ and the minimum number of observations at a node was set at 20. The smaller tree has 4 levels and 7 terminal nodes; the larger tree has 7 levels and 17 terminal nodes. Figure 15.5a shows the smaller tree; Figure 15.5b shows the larger tree. Despite the fact that we have many potential predictor variables in the data, the smaller regression tree uses age and odometer reading only. In the larger tree of Figure 15.5b, the binary variables, dealer, car type, and excellent condition become predictors by which a split happens. Thus, the larger regression tree captures many interactions between age, odometer, and the dealer binary variable.

Table 15.3	CART M4 output as model is being fitted		
	cp	**N split**	**Rel error**
1	0.62976	0	1.0000
2	0.09376	1	0.3702
3	0.07500	2	0.2764
4	0.01660	3	0.2014
5	0.01507	4	0.1848
6	0.01478	5	0.1697
7	0.01000	6	0.1549

Note: Relative error. Regression tree grown with CART M4, using multiple predictors and a stopping rule of $cp=0.01$.

Source: used-cars dataset. Used Toyota Camry cars, Chicago and Los Angeles areas, N=477 (training set, N=333).

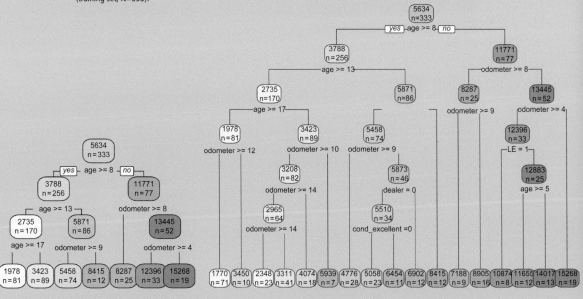

(a) Multiple predictors, CART M4 (4 levels)   (b) Multiple predictors, CART M5 (7 levels)

Figure 15.5   Regression trees grown with many predictors

Note: Regression trees grown with CART. Predictors: age, odometer reading, condition, type, city, dealer, cylinders.
Source: used-cars dataset. Used Toyota Camry cars, Chicago and Los Angeles areas, N=477 (training set, N=333).

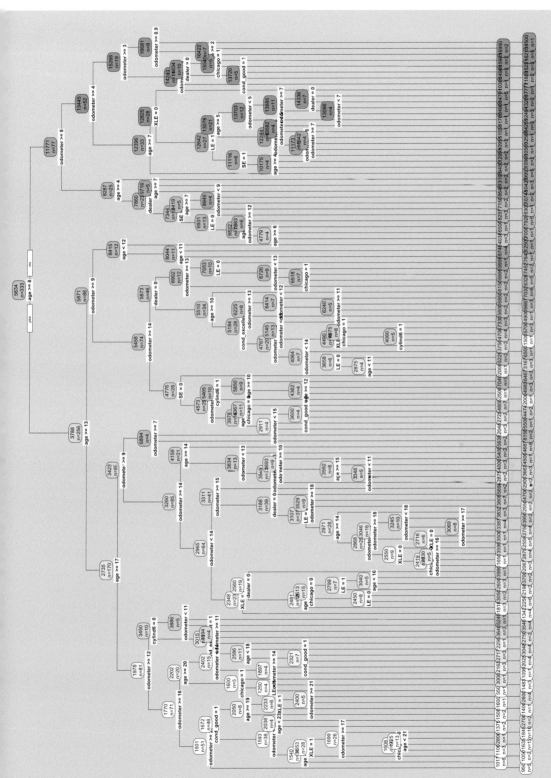

(a) CART M6, *cp* = 0.0001 before pruning (CART M6)

Figure 15.6a Regression trees grown by CART before pruning.

Note: Graphs are drawn on the training data. Predictors: age, odometer reading, condition, type, city, dealer, cylinders.

Source: used-cars dataset. Used Toyota Camry cars, Chicago and Los Angeles areas, N=477 (training set, N=333).

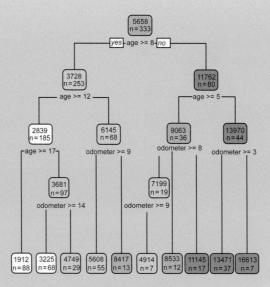

(b) CART M7, the pruned tree

Figure 15.6b   Regression trees grown by CART after pruning (CART M7)

Note: Graphs are drawn on the training data. Predictors: age, odometer reading, condition, type, city, dealer, cylinders.
Source: used-cars dataset. Used Toyota Camry cars, Chicago and Los Angeles areas, N=477 (training set, N=333).

Table 15.3 shows details of the smaller tree of CART M4 (Figure 15.5a). It shows how the relative error $(1 - R^2)$ is reduced as we add splits. We can see how every new split yields an improvement, but that improvement gets smaller and smaller. The first split (by age) already yields a very large increase in explanatory power, as the relative error falls to 0.37. As the process continues, it picks the best way to improve the fit, and thus picks the next largest improvement. This goes on until no improvement could be made that would increase the fit by at least 0.01. In the end, the relative error is 0.155, which corresponds to $R^2 = 0.845$.

Finally, we illustrate how we can use pruning to arrive at an even better prediction. We start by growing a large tree (Figure 15.6a) with the complexity parameter set at 0.0001 (CART M6). Then we can apply pruning to yield a second tree (Figure 15.6b, CART M7). We will examine the test set fit of the pruned regression tree and compare it to other models in the concluding section of our case study.

15.7   Variable Importance

The result of a regression tree is the set of terminal nodes with the corresponding x values and average y values. We can also visualize how we got there by drawing the tree itself. Regression trees are non-parametric regressions. Thus, they do not have coefficient estimates that would tell us how each x variable, or each interaction of x variables, is related to y. That is not a problem for the prediction itself, because the result of a regression tree completely describes what $\hat{y}$ should be for each and every x value in the data. Moreover, we don't need to know more about the $y-x$ relationship to use cross-validation so we can find the best regression tree to predict y. That prediction would be the best one in the population, or general pattern, our original data represents. However, what we do care about is prediction in the live data, not our original data or the population, or general pattern, our original data represents. As we have emphasized many times (first in Chapter 13, Section 13.11), that additional step requires high external validity: that the patterns of association between y and x are similar in the two. In order to assess whether, and to what extent, that's true, we need to know about the patterns of associations that drive our prediction in the first place.

Thus, after all, we do need to understand which x variables are the most important for our prediction, and how those x variables affect $\hat{y}$. With a few x variables and a single regression tree, we assess that by examining the tree itself. However, with many x variables, that approach is challenging.

The most widely used measure data analysts use to assess the important of each x variable in the regression tree is called **variable importance**. It measures how much the fit of the prediction is improved when a particular x variable is used for splitting, summed across all splits in which that variable occurs. Variable importance is expressed as the share of fit improvement (MSE reduction) due to the particular x variable relative to the overall improvement of fit achieved by the regression tree (as opposed to a prediction that doesn't use any x variables). The graph expresses variable importance in relative terms – as percent of total reduction in MSE.

Variable importance is a post-prediction diagnostic tool (see Chapter 14, Section 14.9). Therefore, it should be performed on the holdout set.

High variable importance means that the given variable plays an important role in prediction; low variable importance means it doesn't play an important role. The graphical representation of the variable importance of all x variables is called the variable importance plot. Most CART packages compute variable importance for all x variables and show the variable importance plot among their outputs.

Review Box 15.3 Variable importance

- For a regression tree, variable importance summarizes the relative contribution of a predictor variable x to the prediction.
- Variable importance shows the reduction in the test set MSE (or the average cross-validated test set MSE) when a particular x variable is used for splitting.
- Variable importance sums across all splits in which that variable occurs, relative to the overall improvement of fit achieved by the regression tree.
- The variable importance plot is a visualization of the importance of the predictor variables used in the regression tree.

15.8 Pros and Cons of Using a Regression Tree for Prediction

The promise of regression trees and the CART algorithm is that they can find the best prediction of y using only the most important x variables, their most important interactions, and the most important aspects of potential nonlinear associations. The algorithm builds the regression tree by successively adding the next most important split at each node. For this reason, CART is also called a top-down algorithm because it begins at the top of the tree, although this name is based on the upside-down tree visualization and can be misleading. In any case, this approach has the important advantage that it considers all variables and all of their potential interactions. This is in contrast with the approach of LASSO, which starts with a model with a candidate set of many x variables and interactions and selects the most important ones from them. LASSO doesn't consider all variables and potential interactions, only those that are in the candidate set. However, the CART approach has its issues, too.

The algorithm itself is sometimes characterized as a **greedy algorithm**. To understand what this means, let's first recall what the algorithm does. At each and every step, it looks at the consequences of the upcoming split: which variable and what cutoff value to use for that split. It does not consider how that upcoming split will affect the possibilities for all subsequent splits. In that sense, this algorithm is myopic. That may or may not matter. It may matter for strategic splits that would generate advantageous split options in the future, even if the splitting itself would not improve fit that much. The greedy algorithm does not make such strategic splits and can thus result in a less good prediction in the end. A less myopic algorithm would also consider strategic splits, by evaluating how a specific split would affect the set of possible subsequent splits and how doing so would affect the fit of the final prediction.

CART applies a greedy algorithm because a less myopic algorithm would be a lot more complex, and it would take a lot of time to run. In fact, an optimal non-myopic algorithm would amount to considering all possible combinations of the x variables with all possible cutoff values and all possible interactions. However, as we explained earlier in Chapter 14, it's impossible to consider all such models – this is another example of np-hard problems.

Thus, the CART algorithm offers a solution to the problem by another imperfect method. The question then is which of the various imperfect methods produce a better prediction: a linear regression with hand-picked variables, a linear regression that is the result of regularization such as LASSO, or a regression tree. In the spirit of machine learning, that question should be answered by comparing the predictive performance of each approach instead of some theoretical consideration. And we can do that, at least with respect to the population, or general pattern, represented by the data. It turns out that a regression tree can, but not always does, outperform those alternative approaches.

The reason why a regression tree can do better is because the CART algorithm performs **automatic pattern detection**. We do not need to decide which variables to include or on a functional form. For this reason, we cannot make mistakes by omitting something that would be important. As a bonus, the CART algorithm saves human work: the model building is completely automated.

But the specific features of the CART algorithm have several disadvantages, too.

We have already covered the first disadvantage: deciding on where to stop the algorithm is not easy. We have argued that growing a large tree and then pruning it tends to give better predictions than tinkering with the stopping rule. It turns out, however, that even pruning can leave us with a model that overfits the original data.

The second disadvantage is that the algorithm is rather sensitive to extreme values and, thus, errors in the data. The presence or absence of an extreme value in y or one of the x variables can determine which x variable is used for a particular split, and with what cutoff value it is used. But that has far-reaching consequences for the tree, because it affects all subsequent splits. Thus, small changes in the data, such as including or excluding an observation with an extreme value, can lead to very different regression trees and thus very different predictions.

The third disadvantage is the black box nature of the regression tree. As we argued earlier, we need to know the most important aspects of the patterns of association between y and x, because we need to use that knowledge to assess the external validity of our prediction. Variable importance, a measure we introduced above, can rank the x variables by how important they are in predicting y. But that measure doesn't tell us how exactly an important x variable is associated with y, in what functional form, or through what interactions.

To appreciate the advantages and disadvantages of regression trees grown with a CART algorithm, let's compare its main features with the corresponding features of the linear regression estimated by OLS. Table 15.4 summarizes these features.

Table 15.4 OLS linear regression versus CART regression tree: a comparison

Feature	Linear regression (OLS)	Regression tree (CART)
Solution method	Formula	Algorithm without a formula
Solution goal	Minimize loss (MSE)	Minimize loss (MSE)
Solution optimality	Finds best possible linear regression, but only given the included x variables	Greedy algorithm; does not find best possible tree
Variable selection	Pre-defined list of x variables	No pre-defined list
Main results	Set of coefficient estimates; prediction by plugging into formula	Set of terminal nodes; prediction by specifying values of x variables
Predicted y value and x values	Different $\hat{y}$ for different x values	May have same $\hat{y}$ for different x values if in the same bin
Linear relationship between x and average y	Captures a linear relationship	Approximates linearity by step function
Nonlinear relationship between x and average y	Need to pre-specify functional form to approximate nonlinearity	Approximates nonlinearity by step function

15.A3 CASE STUDY – Predicting Used Car Value with a Regression Tree

Regression tree (CART) summary and discussion

In this case study, we built several regression tree models with CART. As our last model, we grew a large tree using several predictors and then pruned it to a smaller one to avoid overfitting.

In Figure 15.7, we can look at variable importance for a regression tree on the holdout set. Note that the role of the holdout set is played by the single test set of 144 observations in this over-simplified case study. Here we see that odometer and age are about equally important predictors while other variables help substantially less.

Finally, we evaluate the predictive performance of all regression tree models by the test set RMSE. Recall that, for simplicity, we have a single training–test split in the case study. Table 15.5 shows the results. For comparison purposes we estimated two more linear regressions, too. OLS M2 linearly includes all seven variables we used for the CART, which also means that both age and odometer reading are included linearly. OLS M3 then adds quadratic terms for age and odometer reading.

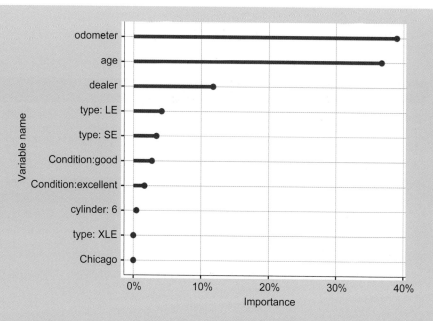

Figure 15.7   Variable importance plot of a regression tree

Note: Regression tree grown with CART Model 4 with *cp* set at 0.01.
Source: used-cars dataset. Used Toyota Camry cars, Chicago and Los Angeles areas, N=477 (holdout set, N=144).

Table 15.5   A comparison of prediction models: regression trees and linear regressions

Model	Number of variables	Model details	RMSE
CART M1	1	2 levels	2781.06
CART M2	1	3 levels	2074.46
CART M3	1	4 levels	1969.52
CART M4	7	$cp = 0.01$	1892.96
CART M5	7	$cp = 0.002$	1892.35
CART M6	7	$cp = 0.0001$	2072.60
CART M7	7	pruned	1818.09
OLS M1	1	linear	2357.01
OLS M2	7	linear	1905.85
OLS M3	7	w/ polynomial terms	1636.50

Note: *cp* is complexity parameter; all RMSE on the 30% test sample.
Source: used-cars dataset. Used Toyota Camry cars, Chicago and Los Angeles areas; N=477 (test set, N = 144).

When comparing the regression trees, we can see how the test set RMSE falls as we build more and more complicated trees. However, at some point we overfit, and the test set RMSE rises. This is where pruning helps – the last model RMSE is the lowest. At the same time, the linear regression model that includes quadratic terms for age and odometer reading outperforms the best regression tree.

This concludes our case study. We saw how the regression tree fits a step function to approximate the $y-x$ pattern of association with a quantitative x variable. Perhaps surprisingly, even a relatively simple model, with a few steps of the step function, can give a reasonably good prediction. When we considered more predictor variables, we saw more complex trees, with better fit in the test set. The best regression tree was the one that we grew large and applied pruning to it.

The comparison with linear regression nevertheless highlights the often unremarkable performance of a single regression tree in prediction. It is the key reason we need something better for actual work. In Chapter 16, we will introduce a more complicated method that builds on, but improves upon, the single regression tree. The result will be a method that is robust and tends to work very well, especially with large datasets.

15.9 Main Takeaways

A regression tree is a method for predicting y based on x variables using an automated algorithm that approximates any functional form and any interaction between the x variables.

- A regression tree splits the sample into many bins according to values of the x variables and predicts y as the average within those bins.
- Regression trees can be thought of as non-parametric regressions.
- A regression tree is prone to overfitting the data even after pruning. For this reason, it is rarely used for prediction in itself.

PRACTICE QUESTIONS

1. The regression tree produces bins from the original sample. How does it predict y using those bins?
2. What are the terminal nodes of a regression tree?
3. We say that the regression tree can be thought of as a non-parametric regression. Why?
4. What's a step function?
5. The regression tree with a quantitative y and a single quantitative x approximates $y^E = f(x)$, whatever the form of f is, by a step function. How?
6. Without a stopping rule or pruning but many x variables, a regression tree would likely overfit the data. Why?
7. The CART algorithm is greedy. What does this mean, and why is it an important feature of the algorithm?
8. Give an example for a stopping rule when growing a regression tree.
9. What does "pruning a regression tree" mean, and why would we want to do it?
10. You want to predict the percentage of votes for a political candidate (y) using polling data from two weeks before the election with the percentage of respondents supporting the candidate (x). Observations in your data are elections; you have the results of many elections (y), and for each election, you have the polling data from two weeks before (x). You grow a regression tree for prediction. What would be the first step of the CART algorithm when growing that tree?

11. In the same example of predicting the percentage of votes using polling data, you observe not only the support in the polls but also whether the candidate was an incumbent. Explain how a regression tree can capture the interaction between those variables to predict y.

12. You want to predict the GPA (grade point average, y) of university students using data on which program they are enrolled in and in which year of that program, what country they come from, and whether they participated in various activities at their university such as sports, clubs. Explain what kinds of x variables these are, and how a regression tree would use these variables to predict y. Give a hypothetical example for the first two levels of a regression tree using these variables.

13. In the same example of predicting GPA (y) using many variables on program, year, and activities, explain how a regression tree would capture interactions. Give an example.

14. You want to predict the number of medals in the next summer Olympic games. You have data on all countries that participated in the past five games, with the number of their medals, their population, GDP per capita, and whether they were the hosts of the games. Explain how a regression tree would capture potential interactions between the three predictor variables, and give a hypothetical example.

15. Using the same prediction exercise (Olympic medals), give an example of how a fully grown regression tree without pruning could overfit the data.

DATA EXERCISES

Easier and/or shorter exercises are denoted by [*]; harder and/or longer exercises are denoted by [**].

1. Consider the `used-cars` dataset. Build a linear regression model that would do better than the ones in the case study by way of feature engineering. Use a single training set (of, say, 70%) and a single test set (the remaining 30%). Compare its fit to the CART results and discuss your finding. [*]

2. Consider again the `used-cars` dataset, a single training set and a test set, and build a linear regression model with the help of LASSO. Compare its fit to the CART results and discuss your finding. [**]

3. All predictions in this chapter were produced with a single train–test cut. Reproduce all results with k-fold cross-validation. Choose k and explain your pick. Compare model performance metrics to what we have in the text and discuss your findings. [**]

4. Use the `hotels-vienna` dataset to predict hotel price with hotel characteristics employing a regression tree with pruning. Use k-fold cross-validation. Describe each step of your analysis, and describe the tree you obtain. Find the five best deals in the entire original data and compare them to the list from Chapter 10. [**]

5. Consider the `cps-earnings` dataset we used in Chapter 10 and focus on employees of age 40–60 with a graduate degree and 20 or more work hours per week. Take a single test set of 30% of the observations. Build a CART regression tree predictive model for the log earnings per hour. Compare the model performance of this model on the test set to the OLS models (2) and (4) in Table 10.5 of Chapter 10. Repeat the same exercise with the plain earnings per hour. Discuss your findings. [**]

REFERENCES AND FURTHER READING

For more on decision trees, see Chapter 8 of James et al. (2014) and Chapter 8 in Kuhn & Johnson (2019).

Athey & Imbens (2016) developed an alternative to the CART algorithm that is less sensitive to extreme values.

16 Random Forest and Boosting

How to use random forest and boosting to combine many regression trees to get a good prediction

Motivation

You need to predict rental prices of apartments using various features. You don't know that the various features may interact with each other in determining price, so you would like to use a regression tree. But you want to build a model that gives the best possible prediction, better than a single tree. What methods are available that keep the advantage of regression trees but give a better prediction? How should you choose from those methods?

How can you grow a random forest, the most widely used tree-based method, to carry out the prediction of apartment rental prices? What details do you have to decide on, how should you decide on them, and how can you evaluate the results?

A regression tree can capture complicated interactions and nonlinearities for predicting a quantitative *y* variable, but it is prone to overfit the original data, even after appropriate pruning. It turns out, however, that combining multiple regression trees grown on the same data can yield a much better prediction. Such methods are called ensemble methods. There are many ensemble methods based on regression trees, and some are known to produce very good predictions. But these methods are rather complex and some of them are not straightforward to use.

This chapter introduces two ensemble methods based on regression trees: the random forest and boosting. We start by introducing the main idea of ensemble methods: combining results from many imperfect models can lead to a much better prediction than a single model that we try to build to perfection. Of the two methods, we discuss the random forest (RF) in more detail. The random forest is perhaps the most frequently used method to predict a quantitative *y* variable, both because of its excellent predictive performance and because it is relatively simple to use. Even more than with a single tree, it is hard to understand the underlying patterns of association between *y* and *x* that drive the predictions of ensemble methods. We discuss some diagnostic tools that can help with that: variable importance plots, partial dependence plots, and examining the quality of predictions in subgroups. Finally, we briefly introduce the idea of boosting, an alternative approach to make predictions based on an ensemble of regression trees. There are various boosting methods, and they can produce even better predictions. However, it is hard to choose from the various methods, and none of them are easy to understand or to use. We illustrate the power of boosting through the performance of the gradient boosting machine (GBM) method.

The case study in this chapter, **Predicting apartment prices with random forest**, uses the `airbnb` dataset to illustrate prediction with random forest and boosting and evaluate such predictions.

Learning outcomes

After working through this chapter, you should be able to:

- understand the basic idea of ensemble models;
- understand the most important elements of the random forest algorithm, including bagging and decorrelating trees;
- carry out prediction of a quantitative y variable using random forest;
- use diagnostics to understand how various predictors contribute to the prediction in a random forest model;
- understand the basic idea behind boosting, and how it differs from bagging.

16.1   From a Tree to a Forest: Ensemble Methods

In Chapter 15, we introduced the regression tree, which predicts y by splitting the data into many small bins according to the values of the x variables, and the CART algorithm, which builds that model in an automatic way, approximating any kind of function and including the most important interactions. We have also seen that, unfortunately, a regression tree built by the CART algorithm has some important weaknesses. The tree tends to overfit the data despite pruning. It is also sensitive to extreme values and small changes in the data. Thus, a single regression tree built by the CART algorithm is best viewed as an intuitive way to find complicated patterns of association between y and x and use them for prediction, but a single regression tree is rarely the best model to predict y.

In this chapter we will introduce two new methods that keep the advantages of regression trees but greatly improve upon their predictive performance. Both use many trees instead of a single tree. They are examples of **ensemble methods**. Ensemble methods use the results of many predictive models and combine those results to generate a final prediction. They are based on the idea that a combination of many imperfect models can generate a much better prediction than a single predictive model that we try to build to perfection.

The idea behind ensemble methods is related to another idea, known as the **wisdom of crowds**. The wisdom of crowds posits that a combination of many predictions tends to generate a much better prediction than any individual prediction, even one that uses the best methods. This is of course not always true: counterexamples include groupthink, when one prediction influences all the rest, or homogeneity, when all predictions are based on the same information and method. In fact, it is generally thought that the wisdom of crowds works under some specific conditions. These conditions include that the individual predictions are made independently, using different parts of the relevant information or using different methods that are not biased in the same way. There are several institutional solutions to combining predictions by humans and harnessing the wisdom of crowds, including prediction markets that operate as betting markets on whether an event will occur.

Ensemble methods use data and combine predictive models to produce a prediction of y using x. Different ensemble methods do that in different ways. We introduce two such methods in this chapter. The first one, **random forest**, combines many independently grown trees from random parts of the data to produce a prediction. In spirit, the random forest is close to the wisdom of crowds: it combines many imperfect predictions. It is perhaps the most widely used predictive model for quantitative outcomes. Its basic idea is relatively easy to understand, and it is really easy to use.

After discussing the random forest and associated diagnostic tools to understand which are the most important *x* variables to drive the prediction, we give a short introduction to the basic idea behind a set of other ensemble methods: **boosting**. Instead of combining many independent models, boosting builds better and better trees using the results of previous ones and combines the results of them in the end. Of the many models that use boosting, we show results from **gradient boosting**, abbreviated as **GBM** for gradient boosting machine. In practice, both random forest and boosting methods tend to work well, with small difference in predictive performance.

Review Box 16.1   Ensemble methods

- Ensemble methods combine the results of many imperfect models to produce a prediction.
- Compared to a single model built to perfection, ensemble methods tend to produce much better predictions.

16.2   Random Forest

The random forest is an ensemble prediction method in that it uses many regression trees that are grown to predict *y* with the help of variables *x*. The basic idea is to use the same data to grow many trees, each of which is very imperfect, and then combine those many imperfect trees into one prediction. The method that implements that basic idea is called **Bootstrap aggregation**, abbreviated as **bagging** ("bagg" for bootstrap aggregation).

To understand bagging, let's refresh our memory on bootstrap, an algorithm we introduced in Chapter 5, Section 5.6. The algorithm takes the original data (or the training set if cross-validated), and draws many repeated samples, each of which is a different sample but has the same size as the original data. For each bootstrap sample, the algorithm takes a random sample with replacement from the observations in the original data. As a result, a bootstrap sample includes some of the original observations multiple times, and it does not include some of the original observations. In fact, a typical bootstrap includes about two thirds of the observations of the original sample – some of them just once and some of them multiple times.

The result of the bootstrap algorithm is many different samples. The set of observations included in the different bootstrap samples overlap to some degree, but they are not the same. At the same time, all of them are representative of the same population, or general pattern, as the original data. And they contain the same *y* and *x* variables.

The bagging algorithm starts by taking bootstrap samples from the original data, say *K* of them, where *K* is a large number, usually in the hundreds (more on this later). Then, within each bootstrap sample, it grows a large tree, without pruning. Each tree is used to generate its own predictions. Then the algorithm takes these *K* prediction rules and combines them. In a training–test setup, it makes *K* predictions for each observation in the test sample, according to the terminal nodes of each of the *K* trees. The final step is aggregation: the final predicted *y* value is the simple mean of the *K* predicted *y* values for each observation.

Bagging keeps the advantages of trees: each tree is built from scratch, and each approximates any function and selects the most important interactions. At the same time, the procedure helps avoid the disadvantages of a single tree. Although each individual prediction overfits the data of its own bootstrap sample, the average prediction is a lot less prone to overfitting the entire original data.

Moreover, the average prediction is less sensitive to including or excluding observations with specific values, such as extreme values, because the different bootstrap samples include and exclude different observations.

It turns out that the prediction can be further improved by an additional modification. This modification affects the way each tree is grown. It is based on an ingenious idea, which makes a lot of difference, but it is not easy to understand why. Let's give it a try anyway.

The additional procedure built into a random forest is growing **decorrelated trees**. When growing a decorrelated tree on a bootstrap sample, we don't use all x variables. Instead, at each splitting decision within the same tree, we select only a few of the x variables and use only those few for the splitting. These x variables we choose randomly from the set of all x variables, and we set the number of variables to choose in advance, for all splits. In practice, the number of variables to choose is about the square root of the number of all x variables (4 is often used as minimum). At the end of this procedure, there is one tree for each bootstrap sample, which is K trees in total. From these K trees we produce the final prediction as described above.

Why does this modified way to grow trees make sense? By using only a few of the x variables for each split, we use less information in the data. That, in itself, would make each tree underfit the data. However, we use different x variables at each splitting when growing a tree. That decreases the risk of underfitting. What it buys is giving more chance to all x variables to predict y.

Suppose, for example, that we have a very strong predictor in the data, along with a number of weaker predictors. That means that the values of y differ a lot with respect to the values of the strong predictor, while the values of y differ only a little with respect to the values of each weaker predictor. But there are lot of those weaker predictors, and, combined, they would be important for the prediction. It is possible, for example, that y is very different for some value combinations of those weaker predictors. Without decorrelating the trees, all trees grown with the bagging procedure would use the strong predictor for the first few splits. As a result, all bagged trees would look similar, and each would give less chance for those value combinations of the weaker predictor to make a difference. That would make the predictions from the bagged trees highly correlated. And recall that ensemble methods work best if they aggregate independent predictions.

Decorrelating trees fits with the basic idea of ensemble methods: it can be good to make each individual prediction work by making them use less information, if doing so makes them more independent of each other. We can make up for the inferiority of each prediction by making a lot of them and aggregating their results. Both bootstrapping and decorrelating trees mean using random sets of the information (observations, x variables). By taking many of them we end up using all the information in the end. What's important is to make each prediction use the same data in different ways to make a prediction.

A random forest tends to better predict a quantitative y variable than any other method we have considered so far, including single trees or linear regressions estimated with LASSO. But that better performance comes at a cost. Even more than before, it's hard to tell what patterns of association between y and x are important for the prediction. And, as we have argued, we need to understand that for assessing the external validity of our prediction. To that aim, we'll introduce some more diagnostic tools. Before doing so though, let's discuss how to carry out a random forest prediction in practice, and let's illustrate that with our case study.

16.3   The Practice of Prediction with Random Forest

It turns out that predicting y with the help of a random forest is relatively straightforward in practice. There is a lot of computation that goes into bootstrapping, growing decorrelated trees, and aggregating the results. But it's the computer's work, not the data analyst's.

Moreover, there are few parameters to set when running a random forest algorithm, and there are good rules of thumb for setting each of those parameters. Recall these are called **tuning parameters**; earlier examples include the λ parameter for LASSO or the required improvement of fit for the stopping rule when growing a regression tree.

The first parameter is the number of bootstrap samples to draw. The more the better, but computational time is a constraint. Usually, a few hundred bootstrap samples are enough.

The second parameter is the number of x variables to consider for each split when growing the decorrelated trees. As we indicated above, a good rule of thumb is the square root of the number of all x variables we want to use. Thus, for example, with about 100 x variables, the number of variables to use for each split is 10. When the number of variables is small, it's good practice to use a minimum number of four of the x variables.

The third parameter to set is the stopping rule for each tree. Recall that the idea is to grow large trees, without pruning. So we should set a lenient stopping rule that allows for growing many levels. Also, we should adopt a stopping rule that takes little time to implement. Thus, a stopping rule based on improved fit in the test sample is not a good candidate because it would take a lot of time to calculate. Instead, it is good practice to set the stopping rule in terms of the minimum number of observations required for the terminal nodes, and to set a small number for it. Usual choices include 5, 10, or 20 observations.

In practice, we may embed many random forests in a search algorithm that tries out various values of these parameters and settles for the one with the best prediction in terms of cross-validated MSE. That may take a lot of time, though. Having good rules of thumb helps save time.

As we'll see later, there are other ensemble methods that are based on many trees, and some can give a better prediction than a random forest. However, we consider the random forest a good benchmark prediction model. Besides its usually good performance, the main argument for the random forest is its relative ease of use. In particular, we are unlikely to make big mistakes when running a random forest algorithm. That is because we only have three tuning parameters, and we have good rules of thumb for each of them.

> **Review Box 16.2   Random forest**
>
> - Random forest is an ensemble method combining the results of hundreds of regression trees.
> - The most important elements of the random forest are:
>   - bagging: aggregating the predictions of many trees grown on bootstrap samples of the data;
>   - each tree is grown to be large, using a simple stopping rule;
>   - decorrelating trees: when growing each tree, we use only a subset of the variables for each split.
> - In practice, carrying out prediction with a random forest is quite easy due to good software solutions with sensible default options.

CASE STUDY – Predicting Airbnb Apartment Prices with Random Forest

Random forest models

In our case study, we continue working with information on Airbnb rentals and use the dataset we started working with in Chapter 14, Section 14.5. We have illustrated the basics of growing a regression tree using the `airbnb` dataset in a single London borough. In this case study we use data from all of London to predict rental prices. The location (borough) of the apartments will be one of their features. With a wide range of locations, our predictive model has to be able to capture potential interactions between locations and other apartment features. We need a model that is expected to give a very good prediction, but we also need a model that can be implemented quickly. The random forest is a good choice to carry out the prediction with these goals.

Regarding the extended dataset, we are using the full London `airbnb` dataset. It is the same data table we used in Chapter 14, but including all observations for Greater London. Similarly to the related case study in Chapter 14, the data includes various types of apartments (houses, rooms, apartments). Unless it's necessary to distinguish among these, we'll call them apartments. The full London dataset has N = 51 646 observations. We dropped very large units (that can accommodate eight or more people), and we dropped some observations for which important variables were missing. The final dataset that we used for our analysis has 49 826 observations.

We first split the sample into two sub-samples, a holdout sample and the work (training+test) sample. We reserve 30 percent of data for the holdout set. On the work sample we will do 5-fold cross-validation: divide the work set into five 20-percent random subsamples for test sets, and use the other 80 percent as a training set.

We considered all predictor variables in the data. This is a large set of variables, so let's describe them as smaller lists. We included the number of guests the rental can accommodate ("n_accommodates"), the number of beds ("n_beds"), the type of property – apartment/house ("f_property_type"), the room type – full apartment, single room, or shared ("f_room_type"), the number of days in operation ("n_days_since"), number of bathrooms ("n_bathroom"), cancellation policy types ("f_cancellation_policy"), and bed type – couch or real bed ("f_bed_type"). We also includes dummies for the 33 London boroughs ("f_neighbourhood_cleansed"). In addition, we included information on reviews ("n_number_of_reviews," "n_review_scores_rating") and a large number of binary variables for amenities such as TV, hairdryer, and wifi. We added a flag for the case when the number of reviews ("n_number_of_reviews") is 0, as for a third of the observations there are no reviews. Note that we use prefix "n_" for quantitative variables and prefix "f_" for qualitative (factor) variables, all of which are converted into appropriate binary variables. These amenity features were parsed from the ad text as described in Chapter 14, Section 14.B1. After feature engineering, we have 94 variables in total, including a set of binary variables for the boroughs of London.

A random forest needs little tuning, just three parameters: the number of bootstrap samples, the number of variables considered for each split, and the minimum number of observations in the terminal nodes of each tree as a stopping rule. We argued that the choice of these values matters little, as long as they are in a reasonable range. To illustrate that, let's consider a few values and see how our prediction depends on them. For the number of bootstrap draws, we went with the default option of 500. For the number of variables, one rule of thumb is to pick the square root of the total number of variables, which would be around 10, so we tried 8, 10, and 12. For the minimum number of observations in the terminal nodes we choose 5, 10, and 15.

Table 16.1 shows the cross-validated test set RMSE values for the nine combinations of these tuning parameters. The lowest RMSE values is for 5 observations in the terminal nodes and 12 variables to consider at each split. We also carried out an automated search for those tuning parameters in the R package, called autotune. The cross-validated RMSE for autotune produced a cross-validated RMSE of 44.7 with 5 observations in terminal nodes and 49 variables for each split. This RMSE value is actually a little worse than the best model from among the parameter values we considered explicitly. Thus, we have chosen the tuning parameters that produced the best RMSE according to our own search not the autotune algorithm. Our benchmark random forest model is with tuning parameters of 500 bootstrap draws, 5 observations in terminal nodes, and 12 variables at each split.

The most important conclusion from this exercise is that the differences in RMSE are very small. They are within 0.8 US dollars, which is about one fiftieth of the mean RMSE values. Another way to appreciate how small these differences are is to compare them to what we would have if we left out some predictor variables from the prediction. Even when we leave out the text-parsed amenities variables, which will turn out to be not very important, the best-fitting random forest model produces an RMSE of 46.7. These small differences support our earlier claim that the random forest tends to be robust to what tuning parameter values we choose.

Table 16.1   Random forest RMSE by tuning parameters

	Variables		
Min. nodes	8	10	12
5	44.93	44.69	44.54
10	45.14	44.87	44.72
15	45.34	45.05	44.84

Note: Predictor variables described in text. Min nodes: minimum number of observations in the terminal nodes. 5-fold cross-validated RMSE shown in the cells of the table.

Source: `airbnb` dataset. London, for one night in March 2017, N=49 826 (work set, N=34 880).

16.4   Diagnostics: The Variable Importance Plot

What patterns of association between y and x the random forest uses, and how, is hard to understand. A linear regression produces coefficients that we can interpret. A single tree doesn't do that, but at least it allows us to look at the tree itself (if only with a magnifying glass). In a random forest we have many trees, each one grown in a decorrelated fashion, and each one grown to be large. There is no way we can directly look into this forest. Instead, we use diagnostic tools after we have made our prediction, using the holdout sample that we set aside (Chapter 14, Section 14.7).

Our main diagnostic tool captures which x variables matter most for the prediction: the **variable importance plot** that we introduced in Chapter 15, Section 15.7. The variable importance plot is a bar chart that shows the x variables and the average improvement of the fit (reduction in average test sample MSE) when we use that x variable for splitting the data. The variable importance plot for a single tree is based on the fit improvement averaged over all splits. The variable importance plot for a random forest is based on the fit improvement averaged over all splits and all trees.

There are two ways we can show the variable importance for a qualitative (factor) variable that has multiple categories, such as color, brand, or city. We enter such a variable in the model as a series of binary variables (dummies). By default, the variable importance plot shows the contribution of each of the binary variables. In some cases this is what we want – does the information of whether a product is red or not red help predict sales? However, often what we want is to know if color as a categorical variable helps the prediction in an important fashion. We can calculate this by grouping variables and re-calculating variable importance with color as a group of binary variables.

16.5 Diagnostics: The Partial Dependence Plot

The variable importance plot informs us about how much each x variable contributes to predicting y. It does not tell us about how they do so. More specifically, it does not tell us about the direction and shape of association with y. And, because the random forest and the underlying trees have no coefficients – unlike a linear regression – we can't directly get measures of association from the estimated model.

However, there are several diagnostic tools that can compute and visualize the patterns of association. One such tool is the **partial dependence plot** (**PDP**). The PDP is a graph with the values of the x variable on the horizontal axis and the values of average y on the vertical axis. It shows how average y differs for different values of x when all the other x values are the same. The "partial" in PDP means that it considers differences with respect to this x variable, conditional on all other x variables (differences attributed to them are "partialled out").

One way to think about the PDP is that it's a non-parametric regression, like a bin scatter or a lowess. The PDP can uncover and visualize any kind of shape, be that linear, nonlinear, monotonic, or non-monotonic. But, unlike a bin scatter or a lowess, the PDP shows the y–x relationship conditional on all other x variables. Or, viewed in another way, it's like visualizing a slope in a multiple linear regression, except it's non-parametric.

The PDP uncovers the x–average y relationship making use of an algorithm that is intuitive but requires a lot of computation. Let's start with how it works when x has a few values only. The algorithm starts by taking the original data and creating as many copies of it as there are possible values of the x variable. Then, within each copy of the data, it replaces the observed x value with the same value for all observations: the first potential x value in the first copy of the data, the second potential value in the second copy, and so on. Then, within each copy of the data, it predicts y by a random forest algorithm in the usual way, by cross-validation. Finally, it computes the average predicted y value across all observations within each of the copies of the data. The partial dependence plot shows the values of the x variables within each copy of the data against the average predicted y from that data. The process is similar for a quantitative x variable, except that a few values are selected instead of using all values.

It turns out that we can carry out this algorithm with any kind of predictive model, not just a tree or a random forest. For this reason, we say that the partial dependence plot is an example of a **model-agnostic tool**.

16.6   Diagnostics: Fit in Various Subsets

The third tool we introduce looks at how the fit of a predictive model differs for different subsets of the data, when these subsamples are defined by values of an *x* variable we use. As always, we carry out diagnostics in the holdout sample, so we look for differences in how the prediction fits various parts of the holdout data.

Learning about how good our prediction is in various subsamples can be important because it informs us about the external validity of our prediction across groups represented by the subsamples. Moreover, it informs us about how we should use our prediction when supporting a decision. If our prediction works a lot better for some kinds of observations than others, we may be explicit and use the prediction for the former types of observations only. If we are interested in the less well predicted groups as well, we know that we have to collect more information on them.

Calculating the differences of fit across subsamples is straightforward: we just calculate RMSE for each subsample separately and compare them. However, we should keep in mind that a larger RMSE may mean a different thing at different levels of the *y* variable. When *y* is larger, the same RMSE indicates less error in relative terms than when *y* is smaller. Thus, we should normalize the RMSE for comparison across subsamples – e.g., by dividing it by the within-subsample average *y*.

Review Box 16.3   Prediction diagnostics after ensemble methods

- Ensemble methods are black box models: they don't reveal the patterns of association that drive the predictions.
- Several diagnostic tools can be used to uncover information about the patterns of association that drive the prediction:
  - The variable importance plot shows the average improvement of fit when we use an *x* variable, or a group of *x* variables.
  - The partial dependence plot shows how average *y* differs for different values of *x* conditional on all other predictor variables.
  - Examining the fit in various subsamples can inform us about the external validity of the prediction.

16.A2   CASE STUDY – Predicting Airbnb Apartment Prices with Random Forest

Diagnostics: Understanding the patterns of the x–y association

For diagnostics, we use our benchmark random forest model with tuning parameters chosen previously. Let us start with variable importance, displayed in Figure 16.1. Variable importance on the horizontal axis is measured in percent. To get it, we first averaged improvement in the model fit – (MSE reduction averaged across the trees), and then divided by its sum across all variables. Even though we showed variables with at least half a percent contribution to MSE reduction, this graph is hard to read. Let us suggest two methods to generate better graphs.

One way to get a clearer picture is focusing on the most important variables only. Figure 16.2a shows the ten variables with the largest average MSE reduction. We see that the most important predictors are size and room type (whether it's private or not), and that location matters as well, such as being in the boroughs of Westminster, Kensington, and Chelsea.

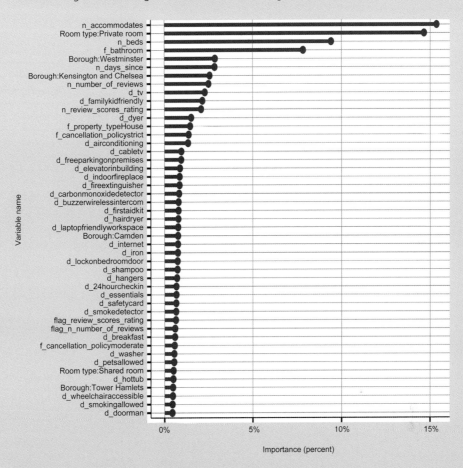

Figure 16.1 Variable importance plot

Note: Benchmark random forest model described in text. Factor variables are represented as separate binary variables. Variable importance based on predictions for the holdout set.
Source: `airbnb` dataset. London, for one night in March 2017, N=49 826 (holdout set, N=14 946).

Another way is to group qualitative (factor) variables that are entered as several binary variables. Variable importance then is a sum of gains (in terms of MSE reduction) by splits involving the factor variable. For instance, rather than considering splits by the borough binary variable Westminster, we now consider all the splits by any values of the neighborhood variable. Figure 16.2b has these factor variables grouped. The variables that matter the most for the prediction are the type of room, the number of people it can accommodate, the neighborhood, the number of beds, and whether it has a bathroom.

Next, we turn to examining the shape of the association between average y and some of the x variables, conditional on the rest. We picked two important variables: the number of guests to accommodate (Figure 16.3a) and the type of room (Figure 16.3b). We created partial dependence plots (PDPs) for each. The plots suggest a pretty linear relationship between predicted price and number of guests. For room types, entire apartment is the most expensive. Interestingly, shared room (a larger place but may be shared with others) is more expensive than private room (no room-mates, but may be a smaller room).

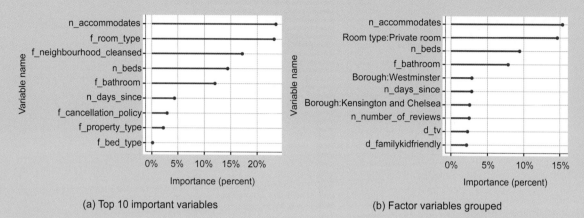

(a) Top 10 important variables   (b) Factor variables grouped

Figure 16.2   Modified variable importance plots

Note: Benchmark random forest model described in text. Factor variables are represented as separate binary variables. Variable importance based on predictions for the holdout set.
Source: airbnb dataset. London, for one night in March 2017, N=49 826 (holdout set, N=14 946).

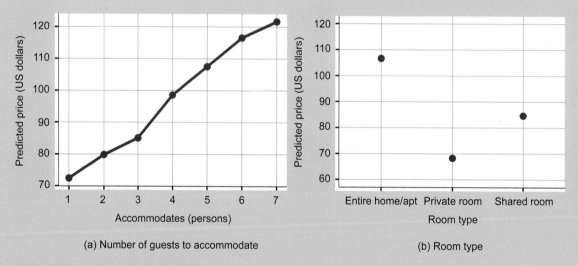

(a) Number of guests to accommodate   (b) Room type

Figure 16.3   Partial dependence plots

Note: Vertical axis is predicted average price. Benchmark random forest model described in text. Partial dependence plot is based on predictions for the holdout set.
Source: airbnb dataset. London, for one night in March 2017, N=49 826 (holdout set, N=14 946).

To further investigate the performance of our random forest model, we look at subsamples by three *x* variables in Table 16.2. First, we divided the sample into two groups based on how many guests the apartment can accommodate: smaller apartments with three or fewer guests, and larger apartments with more than three guests. We calculated the RMSE for both groups to see whether our prediction is equally good in the two groups. But this is not necessarily a meaningful measure: RMSE is based on price differences and is hence by definition lower when prices are lower. Instead, we can compare RMSE values relative to the corresponding mean predicted y. Indeed, when we compare RMSE divided by mean price, we see no difference.

We compared the predictive performance of our model in six boroughs in similar fashion: the three richest boroughs and the three poorest ones. There is some difference, but nothing major – the relative RMSE values suggest a fairly balanced model performance.

Where we see a difference is by property type: prices of houses are harder to predict than prices of apartments, indicating that there may be more unobserved features there. Thus the conclusion of this diagnostic exercise is that the prediction errors are similar across apartment size and boroughs, but house prices are harder to predict than the prices of apartments.

Table 16.2 Performance across subsamples

	RMSE	Mean price	RMSE/price
Apartment size			
Large apt	62.11	144.6	0.43
Small apt	28.53	62.3	0.46
Type			
Apartment	42.32	92.8	0.46
House	42.47	76.3	0.56
Borough			
Kensington and Chelsea	65.11	146.3	0.45
Westminster	62.39	131.0	0.48
Camden	50.23	108.5	0.46
Hackney	33.99	78.2	0.43
Tower Hamlets	34.29	72.0	0.48
Newham	31.94	63.3	0.50
All	42.36	88.8	0.48

Note: Benchmark random forest model described in text. Predictions are for the holdout set. Prices in US dollars.

Source: `airbnb` dataset. London, for one night in March 2017, N=49 826 (holdout set, N=14 946).

16.7   An Introduction to Boosting and the GBM Model

After discussing the idea and practice of predicting a quantitative y with random forest, we briefly discuss **boosting**, an alternative ensemble method. Whereas bagging in general, and the random forest in particular, aims at growing independent trees, boosting grows trees that build on each other. Then, similarly to bagging, it combines all those trees to make a prediction.

The basic idea of boosting is to grow trees sequentially, using information from the previous tree to grow a better tree the next time. The information used from the previous tree is which observations were harder to predict. The new tree then puts more emphasis on fitting those observations. Typically, this is done by taking the residuals from the previous prediction and fitting a model on those residuals instead of the original *y* variable. As an additional twist, the prediction after having grown this next tree is not from the new tree only, but a combination of the new tree and the previous tree. Then, in the following step, the algorithm grows a yet newer tree building on that combined prediction, taking its residuals, and so on. The algorithm stops according to a stopping rule, such as the total number of trees grown.

The final ingredient in boosting is aggregation. Instead of settling for the last tree that was built after improving sequentially on all previous trees, the approach takes all previous trees as well to make the final prediction. That's very much in the spirit of ensemble methods. Instead of using the results from one tree, we combine results from many trees even if they are known to be imperfect. What's new is that we don't want those many trees to be independent of each other.

One particular method that uses this approach is called the **gradient boosting machine**, or **GBM**. The gradient part of its name refers to a search algorithm that it uses to find a better fit. The method also builds in a process that ensures that, at every step, the new model doesn't differ very much from the previous one.

The GBM, similarly to other boosting methods, has more tuning parameters than random forest. They determine the complexity of trees, the number of trees, how we combine the trees to form the new prediction at each step, and how large each tree should be. We can build a search algorithm to find the parameter combination that provides the best fit (using cross-validation), but we need to specify a range for each parameter in which the algorithm should search. That can take a lot of time, and nothing guarantees that there is no better fitting model with parameters outside the range that we specified. Thus, more expertise is required to build GBM models.

Thus, our advice is to experiment with boosting models only after learning more about them. Luckily, there are many available resources to do so, and we list some of those at the end of the chapter. The list of good descriptions of the models, and, indeed, the list of models itself, is growing fast, so interested readers should do their own search.

Review Box 16.4   Boosting

- Boosting is an ensemble method based on regression trees.
- Boosting is based on combining predictions of many trees that are built sequentially, each tree improving on the previous one.
- GBM (gradient boosting machine) is a popular boosting method.
- Finding the appropriate tuning parameters is more important, and more difficult, for boosting methods than for the random forest.

16.A3   CASE STUDY – Predicting Airbnb Apartment Prices with Random Forest

Comparing predictions from RF, GBM, a single CART, and linear regression estimated by OLS and LASSO

The main task of our case study in this chapter is to build a model to predict property rental prices. This could be useful, for instance, in case we want to price new properties we manage. Eventually, we would like to use a single model – the best one. For a loss function, we used mean squared error (MSE or RMSE). To figure out which model to use, we ran a horse race for all the models we have covered in Chapter 14, Sections B2 and B3, as well as earlier in this chapter.

We ran several models including linear regression using all variables, a LASSO using all variables and many interactions, a single regression tree with CART, two random forest models (our benchmark model plus the autotuned version), and two GBMs.

The LASSO model started off with the OLS model with all variables and kept 81 coefficients. For the random forest models, we repeated the RMSE values shown earlier. For GBM1, we only tried a few parameters: complexity of tree (1, 5, 9); number of trees (50, 100,..., 500), while others were fixed: learning rate = 0.1, minimum samples = 20. For GBM2, we tried 1200 different combinations.

For all models, we computed a cross-validated RMSE. The results are shown in Table 16.3.

Table 16.3 Predictive performance of different models

Model	RMSE
Linear regression (OLS)	48.1
Linear regression (LASSO)	46.8
Regression Tree (CART)	50.4
Random forest (basic tuning)	44.5
Random forest (atotuned)	44.7
GBM (basic tuning)	44.6
GBM (broad tuning)	44.4

Note: Model descriptions in text. 5-fold cross-validation for all models. Some results may be package dependent.

Source: `airbnb` dataset. London, for one night in March 2017, N=49 826 (work set, N=34 880).

GBM and Random Forest performed about equally well, with tuning making just a very small difference. These models are followed by linear regression with LASSO. The last contender is the single regression tree. The relatively good performance of the OLS regression without any nonlinear functional forms and interactions suggests that those are not very important for the prediction. Indeed, we have seen when we examined the partial dependence plot for the random forest model that the number of guests is practically linearly related to price. At the same time, the more sophisticated models that do take those complicated patterns into account, such as LASSO and the ensemble models, do perform better.

As suggested in Chapter 14, Section 14.7, we finally take the best model, estimate it on the work set, and evaluate it on the holdout set. That's GBM with broad tuning; its holdout set RMSE is 42.1: we can expect to make an error of 42 dollars when using our model on the live data if we can assume high external validity. The holdout set RMSE here is very close to the cross-validated RMSE. It's actually a little smaller, which can happen, due to differences in sample sizes used to estimate and evaluate the models during cross-validation and for holdout set predictions.

This concludes our case study. Our task was to build a model for predicting Airbnb rental prices for one night in Greater London, using apartment location and features as predictors. The GBM model won the contest in terms of best fit, if just marginally beating random forest. The random forest model worked well and was faster (we'll return to this issue in the next section). Perhaps most importantly, the random forest was relatively easy to implement, especially relative to the GBM models. Moreover, parameter tuning mattered only marginally for the random forest, while it mattered more for GBM.

If we are interested in getting the lowest expected error, we would choose the GBM model. However, the random forest is an excellent alternative if we want to do something that is close to be the best and a lot easier to implement.

16.8 A Review of Different Approaches to Predict a Quantitative y

In Chapters 13 through 16, we introduced and discussed several methods that have the same goal: predicting a quantitative y variable with the help of x variables. We focused on five such models. We started with linear regression estimated by OLS, then discussed linear regression with LASSO. After these we turned to tree-based methods, starting with a single tree (with pruning) and, in this chapter, random forest and boosting (GBM).

These models differ along a lot of dimensions. In Table 16.4 we list several of those dimensions and rate the five models along them. Our rating is admittedly oversimplified; however, it should serve as a rough guide that works in many, but probably not all, cases.

Table 16.4 Models summary

	OLS	LASSO	CART	RF	GBM
Performance (RMSE)	48.1	46.8	50.4	44.5	44.4
Speed (in min)	0.07	0.3	0.4	19	756
Solution	formula	algo	algo	algo	algo
Choice of tuning parameters	n.a.	easy	easy	easy	difficult
Interpretation	easy	easy	easy	difficult	difficult
FE: Variable selection	hand	algo	algo	algo	algo
FE: Nonlinear patterns	hand	hand	algo	algo	algo
FE: Interactions	hand	hand	algo	algo	algo

Note: Speed is measured as run time for the Airbnb case study on a good but not great laptop. RF (random forest) results are for the benchmark model (basic tuning). GBM results are for the broadly tuned model. (The autotuned RF model runs for 46 minutes; the basic tuned GBM model runs for 20 minutes.) FE is feature engineering.

First, let's repeat the most important conclusion of the case study: ensemble tree methods give better predictions than linear regression methods and a single tree. Of these, GBM with broad tuning gives a better prediction than random forest, but the random forest prediction is almost as good.

In terms of human input for feature engineering, tree-based methods are a lot easier to use. Regression trees approximate the kind of functions and their nonlinearities, and they find the most important interactions. In contrast, in a linear regression we need to define functional forms and interactions from the original x variables. To estimate a linear regression with OLS, we need to do that by hand, and to examine several regression models, we need to define all those models by hand, even though we didn't do that for the baseline OLS model only for the LASSO. Tree-based models save us from all that work. Perhaps as importantly, they also save us from all the potential mistakes we can make when deciding how to define functional forms and what interactions to consider. Of the ensemble methods, random forest is easier to implement than GBM, because it has fewer tuning parameters to set and the results are more robust to those settings.

The advantages of ensemble tree methods come at the cost of computational time and ease of interpretation. The first one is not really an issue for datasets of moderate size: in our Airbnb case study with close to 50 000 observations (of which we allocated 70 percent to training and cross-validation sets), the difference between linear regression with OLS and Random Forest is a few seconds versus 20 minutes, 46 minutes if autotuned. At the same time, GBM with broad tuning took over 12 hours to run. Thus, machine learning with just some tuning can be used with ease on personal computers, while heavy tuning is rather time consuming. Of the two ensemble methods, random forest takes less time, especially without autotuning.

The most important disadvantage of the ensemble methods is that they make it hard to interpret the results. In themselves, neither the random forest nor the GBM reveals anything about the patterns of association between y and x that form the basis of their predictions. For that reason, these models are often referred to as **black box** models, even more than regression trees. As we argued, that's a problem particularly because it makes it difficult to assess external validity. In the end, we want to predict y in the live data, not the original data. Our prediction using the original data has higher external validity, the closer the patterns of association between y and x are in the two. To assess that, we need to know a lot about those patterns in our original data, and the population, or general pattern, it represents.

For this reason, and perhaps because of a general fear of the unknown, people tend not to trust black box models. Usually, we make predictions to support business or policy decisions, and thus decision makers need to trust in our results. Decision makers would certainly ask questions about the patterns of association behind a prediction (e.g., how apartment size is related to price, which neighborhoods are more expensive). Sometimes, decision makers have a legal obligation to be able to argue how certain predictions were made. In such cases a linear regression has a big advantage. This aspect is a barrier to using black box models in business and policy.

We covered a few diagnostic tools in this chapter (variable importance plot, partial dependence plot, subsample results) that can help uncover some aspects of the patterns of association behind a black box predictive model. There are many more tools that may be helpful, and many data scientists are working on developing yet more tools. In the end, data analysts may end up spending more time on using diagnostic tools to understand what drives their predictions from black box models than developing and running those models themselves to make the predictions. However, many of those diagnostic tools take a lot of time to run. For example, the partial dependence plot needs to re-run the entire estimation procedure for specific values of each variable of interest. Here the time requirements of ensemble methods, especially GBM, may be an important obstacle.

Another approach is to use two predictive models: one that we can interpret and a black box model that tells us what a good prediction should look like. For example, we may use random forest as a benchmark, to see what RMSE we can achieve with a really good model. Then, we can develop a linear regression model by hand, and try to get as close as possible to that benchmark RMSE. If the gap in terms of performance is large, we should probably abandon our linear regression and opt for the random forest model, because it uses patterns that our linear regression doesn't include. Then, we need to work hard on diagnostics to interpret the patterns our random forest uses. If, however, the gap in performance is small, we may be more confident that the linear regression shows the same patterns of association that the random forest uses to make its prediction. In this case, we can use the coefficient estimates of our linear regression to interpret the results of our prediction.

In the end, our prediction will have error. With a good choice of model, we can minimize the role of model error in total prediction error (see the error components in Chapter 13, Section 13.3). Choosing a good model may help reduce estimation error, too, but that's more strongly determined by the number of observations. Thus, with bigger data we can achieve a better prediction even with a less good model. Similarly, it is our data, not our method, that determines the third component, irreducible error. Recall that irreducible error is the part that we couldn't reduce with the best possible prediction model using infinitely many observations. It is constrained by the variables we have in our data. Any predictive model can only use the x variables we have in our data, the way they are measured. Thus, to reduce "irreducible" error, we need to measure more x variables or, perhaps, measure them in better ways. Thus, while choosing a good prediction model is obviously important, we should also work on the size, content, and quality of our data if possible.

16.9   Main Takeaways

Random forest is a prediction method that uses several regression trees.

- Ensemble methods that combine predictions from many imperfect models can produce very good predictions.
- Random forest is the most widely used ensemble method based on regression trees; boosting is a more complicated but often better alternative.
- Both random forest and boosting are black box methods. We need to do additional diagnostics to uncover how the x variables contribute to our prediction.

PRACTICE QUESTIONS

1. What's an ensemble prediction method based on trees, and what's the basic idea behind it?
2. What does the wisdom of crowds mean in the context of prediction, and when is it more likely to work?
3. What's bagging?
4. The random forest method combines bagging with decorrelating trees. What's the purpose of the second and how does it work?
5. What's the variable importance plot, and how is it created from a random forest prediction?
6. Let us compare two predictions, one with random forest and one with a single tree. Which model do you expect to produce a larger cross-validated RMSE and why?
7. After a prediction with random forest, do you expect a larger or smaller RMSE in the holdout sample than the cross-validated RMSE? Why?
8. What do we mean when we say that the random forest is a black box model and why is it a problem?
9. Is it possible to arrive at a better prediction using more observations but a less sophisticated model? Why or why not?
10. Is it possible to arrive at a better prediction using more and better measured x variables but a less sophisticated model? Why or why not?

11. Comparing a linear regression estimated with OLS and a random forest, which one is likely to better predict a quantitative *y* variable in the live data if the live data is similar to the original data? What if it is very different from it?

12. After predicting rental prices of apartments, the variable importance plot shows a higher percentage for the neighborhood variables than for the variables that show what amenities the apartment has. What does this mean?

13. After predicting rental prices of apartments, the partial dependence plot shows a positive and linear slope for the number of persons the apartment can accommodate. What does this mean?

14. When predicting the price of used cars of a certain type and make using data from various cities, we see that the cross-validated RMSE of a linear regression estimated with OLS is 1% higher than the cross-validated RMSE of a random forest. Which model would you use for prediction, and what would you use to understand the patterns of association that drive your prediction?

15. What would be your answer to the previous question if the difference was not 1% but 10%?

DATA EXERCISES

Easier and/or shorter exercises are denoted by [*]; harder and/or longer exercises are denoted by [**].

1. Use the `airbnb` dataset we used in our case study. Consider the variable importance plot we showed for our benchmark random forest model. For diagnostic purposes, repeat it for one of the random forest models with different tuning parameters and discuss any difference you may see. [*]

2. Use the `airbnb` dataset we used in our case study. Pick a borough in London (such as Hackney); this will be the holdout set. Build a prediction model for all London except for the borough you picked. Use the model on the holdout set (the borough you picked) and evaluate. Discuss your results and compare them to those of the case study. [**]

3. Visit the website we got the `airbnb` dataset from: `http://insideairbnb.com/get-the-data` `.html` and download data from another city. Build a prediction model similarly to how we did in our case study for London. Discuss your modeling decisions and compare your results to those of the case study. [**]

4. Use all observations from the `used-cars` dataset from previous chapters. Take a 30 percent random holdout sample, and build a random forest prediction model by 5-fold cross-validation using the rest. Then build a linear regression prediction with LASSO using the same work sample and cross-validation. Report the cross-validated RMSE from the two predictions. Discuss your modeling decisions and your results. [**]

5. Do a hotel price prediction exercise for hotels. Use all observations from the `hotels-europe` dataset from previous chapters. Filter for a single date. Take a 30 percent random holdout sample, and build a random forest prediction model by 5-fold cross-validation using the rest. Report the cross-validated RMSE and the holdout set RMSE and interpret them. Then create two versions of the variable importance plot, one with each city as a separate binary variable and one with cities as a group of variables. Discuss your modeling decisions and your results. [**]

REFERENCES AND FURTHER READING

A great summary essay on machine learning used for policy problems is Athey (2017).

An excellent book on understanding machine learning models is Molnar (2019). A great technical discussion on partial dependence plots is Greenwell (2019). On building models, a nice advanced book is Kuhn & Johnson (2019), also at http://appliedpredictivemodeling.com/.

All computations in this chapter are run in R using the Ranger and Caret packages. We highly recommend readers who use R to study the Caret package developed by Max Kuhn (2019). On benchmarking and comparing machine learning software implementations, a good source is Pafka (2019).

17 Probability Prediction and Classification

How to predict the probability of a binary variable ($y = 1$ versus $y = 0$), and how to carry out a classification

---

Motivation

Predicting whether people will repay their loans or default on them is important to a bank that sells such loans. Should the bank predict the default probability for applicants? Or, rather, should it classify applicants into prospective defaulters and prospective repayers? And how are the two kinds of predictions related? In particular, can the bank use probability predictions to classify applicants into defaulters and repayers, in a way that takes into account the bank's costs when a default happens and its costs when it forgoes a good applicant?

Many companies have relationships with other companies, as suppliers or clients. Whether those other companies stay in business in the future is an important question for them. You have rich data on many companies across the years that allows you to see which companies stayed in business and which companies exited, and relate that to various features of the companies. How should you use that data to predict the probability of exit for each company? How should you predict which companies will exit and which will stay in business in the future?

In the previous chapters we discussed the logic of predictive analytics and its most important steps, and we introduced specific methods to predict a quantitative y variable. But sometimes our y variable is not quantitative. The most important case is when y is binary: $y = 1$ or $y = 0$. How can we predict such a variable?

This chapter introduces the framework and methods of probability prediction and classification analysis for binary y variables. Probability prediction means predicting the probability that $y = 1$, with the help of the predictor variables. Classification means predicting the binary y variable itself, with the help of the predictor variables: putting each observation in one of the y categories, also called classes. We build on what we know about probability models and the basics of probability prediction from Chapter 11. In this chapter, we put that into the framework of predictive analytics to arrive at the best probability model for prediction purposes and to evaluate its performance. We then discuss how we can turn probability predictions into classification with the help of a classification threshold and how we should use a loss function to find the optimal threshold. We discuss how to evaluate a classification making use of a confusion table and expected loss. We introduce the ROC curve, which illustrates the trade-off of selecting different classification threshold values. We discuss how we can use random forest based on classification trees. Finally, we note the potential issues with the probability prediction and classification of rare events.

We use the case study **Predicting firm exit: probability and classification** in this chapter. The goal is to predict corporate exit: firms going out of business. We use the `bisnode-firms` dataset, which covers all firms in specific industries in a European country. We use this case study to illustrate all steps of probability prediction and classification.

Learning outcomes

After working through this chapter, you should be able to:

- understand situations that call for probability prediction versus classification;
- carry out probability predictions with the help of logit and random forest models and cross-validation;
- convert predicted probabilities into classification using a threshold value, create confusion tables, and understand the various measures computed from confusion tables;
- understand what ROC curves show and how the area under the ROC curve can be used in model selection;
- find the optimal classification threshold with the help of a loss function, and find the best model for classification by cross-validation of probability models and optimal classification thresholds.

17.1   Predicting a Binary *y*: Probability Prediction and Classification

In Chapter 11 we introduced probability models that have a binary *y* variable: $y = 1$ or $y = 0$. A binary *y* variable often denotes whether an event happens or not, or whether an observation belongs to a specific category or not. Probability models aim to uncover the patterns of association between the probability of $y = 1$ and the *x* variables.

In Chapter 4, Section 4.3, we introduced the concept of conditional probability that summarizes such patterns: $Pr[y = 1|x]$. In Chapter 11 we discussed the linear probability model, which is nothing other than linear regression with a binary *y*, and we introduced two nonlinear alternatives, the logit and the probit. We have seen that the linear probability model is usually fine when we are interested in the average patterns of association between the probability of $y = 1$ and the *x* variables. However, the logit and the probit tend to be better when our goal is prediction. The kinds of prediction we discussed in Chapter 11 are **probability predictions**: their aim is predicting the probability that $y = 1$, conditional on the *x* variables.

As an example, consider a bank that sells unsecured loans to people and wants to know how likely an applicant is to repay their loan ($y = 1$) instead of defaulting ($y = 0$). This is a probability to predict. Observing many features of the applicants may help, such as their age, income, occupation, and credit history (these are the *x* variables). With data on past customers, some of whom defaulted on their loans and some who repaid their loans, we can build a model that predicts the probability of default.

For many decisions, predicting the conditional probability is the important thing. One example is planning for losses because of defaults on personal loans. To that end the bank needs to have a good idea about the proportion of its customers who will repay versus default in the future. Having a good prediction $Pr[y = 1|x]$ from the past can help the bank know what repayment proportion to expect in the future, by applying that prediction to its current customers (whose *x* variables it observes).

For other decisions, however, the probability is not really what we care about. Rather, we want each observation to be classified into one of the possible y values or **classes**. That's **classification**: predicting whether $y = 1$ or $y = 0$.

When the bank wants to decide to which applicants to extend a loan and to which applicants to deny a loan, it needs to classify applicants into prospective repayers ($\hat{y} = 1$) and prospective defaulters ($\hat{y} = 0$). It may use data from the past to see which kinds of customers are likely repayers and which are likely defaulters, based on their x features, and it would give loans only to applicants that it classifies to be prospective repayers not defaulters.

We can think of classification as an extra step after predicting probabilities. Observations with a high predicted probability are to be classified as $\hat{y} = 1$; observations with a low predicted probability are to be classified as $\hat{y} = 0$. One topic of this chapter will be how to make that extra step, which is really the question of what threshold value to use. A related question that we'll discuss is how to evaluate the results of such a classification.

Review Box 17.1 Probability prediction and classification

With a binary y variable, we can make two kinds of predictions:

- Probability prediction: predicting the probability of $y = 1$ for each observation, $\hat{y}^P$, which is the shorthand notation for $\hat{P}[y = 1|x]$.
- Classification: predicting whether $\hat{y} = 0$ or $\hat{y} = 1$ for each observation.

17.A1   CASE STUDY – Predicting Firm Exit: Probability and Classification

Question, data, and feature engineering

In this case study, our aim is to predict corporate exit: a company going out of business, or, as is sometimes said, exiting.

Some business questions need the predicted probability of exit. When a company is thinking about which supplier to select for a long-term relationship, the probability that each candidate will be around in the future is an important factor to include in its decision. Other business questions also need classification. When a bank wants to decide whether to approve a loan application from a firm, it wants to decide whether that firm is going to be in business by the time it needs to repay its loan. Similarly, when the owner of an office building wants to decide whether to lease space to a company for a fixed term, it would like to know whether the company will still be in business at the end of that term.

In this case study, called **Predicting firm exit: probability and classification**, we use a lot of information on a set of firms in a European country to predict the probability of firm exit and to classify firms into prospective exiting firms and prospective staying in business firms, from the `bisnode-firms` dataset. The data was collected, maintained, and cleaned by Bisnode, a major European business information company.

Our original dataset covers the entire population of companies between 2005 and 2016 for a few industries in manufacturing (Electronic and optical products, Electrical equipment, Machinery and equipment, Motor vehicles, Other transport equipment, Repair and installation of machinery) and services (Accommodation and Food and beverage service activities). In the data, there are some firms who changed their main classification over time. Large firms are excluded for data protection (above 100 million euros in annual revenues).

The dataset is made up of several data tables, which makes it a little complicated to use. Data tables included are presented in Table 17.1.

Table 17.1   Data tables for firm-level data

Data table	Unit of observations	Important variables
Financial data	firm–year	revenue, material cost, EBITDA, assets,
Managers	person–time interval–firm	CEO age, gender
Employment	firm–year	average wages
Corporate registry	firm	city of headquarters, year of firm birth
Industry classification	firm	NACE industrial classification

Source: `bisnode-firms` dataset.

We combined these tidy data tables into a single workfile. This workfile is an xt panel at the company–year level (rows are identified by company id and year), following each company during their active operation. Many companies entered the dataset during the 2005–2016 period, and many exited. Important variables include sales, assets, manager age, and ownership type. We know when the firm was established and when it exited (the last year it was in business).

In this case study, we focus on a cross-section of companies in 2012, and we'll ask whether they stayed in business in subsequent years.

Let us start with label engineering: defining our y variable. In the data, going out of business (exit) is not directly measured. In this case study, we say that a firm went out of business if it was operational in 2012 but not in 2014. The y variable is hence a binary variable called exit. It is 1 if the firm exited within 2 years and 0 otherwise.

The second task is sample design: making decisions regarding which firms to keep in the data. That decision determines for what kinds of firms we'll predict exit. We focus on the small and medium enterprise (SME) sector, captured by firms' sales. We only keep firms below 10 million euros of annual sales. We also drop firms that seem to be non-operational in 2012: those with sales below 1000 euros. There are about a thousand firms established in 2012, and we keep them in the data. These decisions make it clear for what kinds of firms our predictions will be valid, but they are arbitrary. You are invited to replicate the analysis for a different set of firms as a data exercise.

As a result of our sample design, we have 19 036 firms in the full cleaned original dataset. These are firms that reported sales between 1 thousand and 10 million euros in 2012. After these sample design steps, we find that 3848, or 20% of firms will have exited within two years.

The third task is feature engineering: selecting our x variables, cleaning them, and putting them in appropriate form for the predictive models. The variables can be organized into four groups: size, management, financial variables, and other characteristics.

Part of feature engineering is deciding on functional forms. That turns out to be tricky for the financial variables: there is a range of possibilities for potential extreme values, including error (as people filled in the forms), and genuinely unusual values. There are a dozen variables with potential extreme values, and we decided to do feature engineering driven by a mix of domain knowledge and patterns we see in the data. Our focus was making decisions on functional form, and we created several new variables based on a single existing one.

First, there are variables that should not be negative in a financial account (such as inventories, current liabilities, or subscribed capital). In these cases, we replaced negative values with zero and added a binary variable to flag error. Second, for all our variables, we created ratios: balance sheet variables were expressed as ratios to the size of the balance sheet (total assets), while profit and loss items were scaled by total sales. This helps not only interpretation but also finding extreme values.

Table 17.2	Firm exit predictor variables	
Group	**N vars**	**Description**
Firm	5	Age of firm, squared age, a dummy if newly established, industry categories, location regions for its headquarters, and dummy if located in a big city.
Financial 1	16	Winsorized financial variables: sales, fixed, liquid, current, intangible assets, current liabilities, inventories, equity shares, subscribed capital, sales revenues, income before tax, extra income, material, personal and extra expenditure, extra profit.
Financial 2	0	Flags (extreme, low, high, zero – when applicable) and polynomials: quadratic terms are created for profit and loss, extra profit and loss, income before tax, and share equity.
Growth	1	Sales growth is captured by a winsorized growth variable, its quadratic term and flags for extreme low and high values.
HR	5	For the CEO: female dummy, winsorized age and flags, flag for missing information; foreign management dummy; labor cost, and flag for missing labor cost information.
Data Quality	3	Variables related to the data quality of the financial information, flag for a problem, and the length of the year that the balance sheet covers.
Interactions	0	Interactions with sales growth, firm size, and industry.

Note: N vars means the number of original variables. Flags denoting specific values and polynomial terms are not original variables.
Source: `bisnode-firms` dataset. N=19 036.

To capture extreme values (but not obvious errors), we also made use of a method called **winsorization**. This is a process where, for each variable, we identify a threshold value, and replace values outside that threshold with the threshold value itself and add a flag variable. A frequent use of winsorization is an automatic approach, where the lowest and highest 1 percent or 5 percent is replaced and flagged. Instead, we picked thresholds by domain knowledge as well as by looking at non-parametric regressions. For instance, some firms have extremely high or extremely low profits, often a signal of substantive change happening. Thus, profit to sales ratio above 1 or below -1 were winsorized.

Finally, for some variables we also added quadratic terms to capture nonlinearity.

Zero value for financial variables is another potential signal – often it is a sign of very little activity. Hence, we added a binary variable to flag zero values. For instance, having no fixed assets is a different piece of information from having fixed assets with a low value, and exactly zero profit could be a signal, too. Thus, we have a set of flags for zeros for each financial variable.

As a result, we have several groups of predictor variables as shown in Table 17.2.

17.2   The Practice of Predicting Probabilities

As a starting point, let's discuss how to carry out probability predictions. When our aim is to predict probabilities, this is the process to follow. When our goal is classification, this can be our first step before turning probabilities into 1 or 0 values.

It turns out that we know all the ingredients to carry out probability predictions. We have discussed the models to use and the measures of fit in Chapter 11. We have discussed the process of carrying out predictions in Chapters 13 and 14. All we need to do is to put those together.

In Chapter 11 we introduced the $y^P = P[y = 1|x]$ notation for conditional probabilities. We also introduced the **logit** as a good probability model for prediction. In addition, we argued that another model, the probit, tends to give very similar predictions to the logit. For historical reasons, and because estimating the logit tends to take a little less computer time, data analysts making predictions prefer the logit. We'll keep to that tradition. The logit is a nonlinear twist to a linear regression: the linear combination of the x variables with their β coefficients are fed into a link function called Λ:

$$y^P = \Lambda(\beta_0 + \beta_1 x_1 + \beta_2 x_2 + \cdots) \tag{17.1}$$

The predicted probabilities from the logit model are

$$\hat{y}^P_{logit} = \Lambda(\hat{\beta}_0 + \hat{\beta}_1 x_1 + \hat{\beta}_2 x_2 + \cdots) \tag{17.2}$$

One result of the Λ transformation is that the predicted probabilities are always greater than zero and less than one.

To carry out an actual prediction we need to build models, select the best model, make the prediction using that model, and evaluate its performance. When predicting probabilities, the models to consider are logit models. They take the place of the linear regressions that we considered in Chapters 13 and 14. Just like with predictions using linear regression, we can build various logit models after extensive feature engineering and considering functional forms and interactions. That is a lot of work taking a lot of the data analyst's time. Some of that work is unavoidable, including creating binary variables from qualitative ones with multiple categories, and checking missing values and extreme values and deciding what to do about them. But some of the extensive model building time can be saved by deploying an algorithm.

Just as with predictions using linear regression, we can specify a logit model with a large number of variables including flexible functional forms and many interactions, and use LASSO to select the ones that should remain there (and estimate its coefficients). The logit LASSO is a little different from the one used for linear regression, but it exists, and it is available for the statistical software we use.

As usual, we should select a holdout sample of, say, 20 percent of the observations in the original data for diagnostics, and use the rest for model building and model selection. And, as usual, we should use k-fold cross-validation to select our preferred model.

The measure of fit to use in model selection can remain the same: **mean squared error** (MSE) or its square root, the **root mean squared error** (RMSE). Recall from Chapter 11, Section 11.5, that the MSE is called the **Brier score** with respect to probability predictions. But it's the same thing. So for a symmetric convex loss function, the Brier score is a good choice. If we happen to know the shape of the **loss function**, or we want to use another approximation with different features such as asymmetry, we would use that loss function for evaluating the fit in the test samples. The result of cross-validation is picking the model that delivers the smallest average Brier score (MSE), or other loss, averaged over the test samples.

Once we pick the best model, we should estimate it on the entire work set, make a prediction using the holdout sample, and evaluate its performance using the holdout sample. That amounts to comparing the probability predictions to the values of the original y variable in the holdout sample. The original y variable is either zero or one; the prediction from a logit is always some number between zero and one (but never actually zero or one). What we look for is how close the predicted probabilities are to the actual zero or one values. We covered several tools for this in Chapter 11, one of which is the Brier score (MSE) we discussed earlier.

Another measure is calibration. **Calibration**, as we discussed it in Chapter 11, Section 11.7, is about whether a probability prediction is biased or unbiased. Bias means the difference between the actual proportion of $y = 1$ and the predicted probability of $y = 1$. Calibration looks at the bias for each and every value of the predicted probability. A calibration curve is a visualization of this measure: it plots the proportion of observations with $y = 1$ on the vertical axis for various values of the predicted probabilities on the horizontal axis. The calibration curve of a well-calibrated prediction is the 45 degree line, or at least very close to it. We can use other tools for evaluating probability predictions, too, such as comparing the distribution of predicted probabilities across observations with $y = 1$ versus $y = 0$, using visualizations such as the histogram, the box plot, or the violin plot.

17.A2   CASE STUDY – Predicting Firm Exit: Probability and Classification

Probability prediction and model selection

Next in our case study we carry out a probability prediction by logit, select the best logit model by cross-validation, and evaluate the prediction from that model using the holdout. The work sample has 15 229 observations (3056 exits) and the holdout has 3807 firms (792 exits).

Our first task is to build a predictive model of the probability of a firm's exit from business.

We consider five logit models. The models differ in the way they approximate nonlinearity and the numbers and kinds of variables and interactions they include. We also consider LASSO, with flexible functional forms (many dummies for tail values) and a large set of potential interactions.

First, we only pick variables that could be important based on our domain knowledge. For the logit M1 model, the basic variables are: sales, sales growth, profit and loss, and industry categories (with squared sales and seven industry dummies, the model also includes fixed assets, equity, current liability and its flags, age, foreign management dummy (nine variables and 19 coefficients). For additional models we include financial and firm variable groups followed by growth, HR, and data quality. For the last logit model and the logit LASSO model, we also include interactions. Table 17.3 summarizes our six models.

Table 17.3   Probability model specifications: number of variables in models

	Hand-picked	Firm	Financial 1	Financial 2	Growth	HR	Data quality	Interactions
Logit M1	x							
Logit M2	x	x						
Logit M3		x	x		x			
Logit M4		x	x	x	x	x	x	
Logit M5		x	x	x	x	x	x	x
Logit LASSO		x	x	x	x	x	x	x

Note: See model variable description in text. Financial 2 includes all the flags.
Source: bisnode-firms dataset. N=19 036.

Table 17.4   Simple logit model coefficients

Variable	Coefficient	Marginal difference
Age	-0.035	−0.005
Current liabilities	0.171	0.023
Curr. liab. flag error	0.318	0.043
Curr. liab. flag high	0.135	0.018
Change in log sales	-0.482	−0.065
Fixed assets	-0.811	−0.109
Foreign management	0.216	0.029
Electrical equipment	0.145	0.018
Machinery and equipment	0.033	0.004
Motor vehicles	0.406	0.052
Other transport equipment	-0.033	−0.004
Repair and installation	-0.158	−0.018
Accommodation services	0.129	0.015
Food & beverage services	0.464	0.061
Profit loss last year	-0.450	−0.060
Log sales	-0.180	−0.024
Log sales sq	0.015	0.002
Share equity	-0.388	−0.052

Note: Logit Model 2 on the full sample. Logit coefficients and corresponding marginal differences. Reference industry category: electronic and optical products.
Source: bisnode-firms dataset, 2012. N=19 036.

First, let us have a look at some important patterns, by displaying coefficients and marginal differences (as introduced in Chapter 11, Section 11.4) based on the logit M4 model. In Table 17.4, we can see that some predictors are correlated as expected: older, larger, better capitalized firms and those that have growing sales are less likely to exit, while those with high current liabilities or those operating in the food and beverage services business (e.g., restaurants) are more likely to exit. Interestingly, foreign management (once we have taken into account financial variables) is positively correlated with exit.

Our set of models includes a LASSO for logit. We start with a logit M5 model that includes all our variables and interactions, and ask the LASSO algorithm to select variables (and shrink coefficients) for a better predictive model. The LASSO produces a model that includes most but not all variables, reducing the number of predictors from 154 to 143. In particular, it drops some interactions and some flags on financial variables.

Now let us look at the predictive performance of our models. For our predictive purpose, we take a 20% random sample of the data for holdout: the remaining 80% is our work set. The work set will be divided into training and test sets five times as we are doing 5-fold cross-validation. We evaluate each model by its cross-validated average RMSE. Table 17.5 presents results and also lists the number of variables.

Table 17.5   Cross-validated RMSE of logit models

	N Vars	N coeffs	CV RMSE
Logit M1	4	12	0.374
Logit M2	9	19	0.366
Logit M3	22	36	0.364
Logit M4	30	80	0.362
Logit M5	30	154	0.363
Logit LASSO	30	143	0.362

Note: See model details in text. Models may include additional terms as polynomials or interactions. 5-fold cross-validated average RMSE.

Source: `bisnode-firms` dataset, 2012. N=19 036 (work set, N=15 229).

The logit M4, logit M5, and the logit LASSO models seem to work comparably well. Based on the cross-validated RMSE (0.362), we will consider the logit M4 model as our benchmark model. It has all the variables including flags but does not have interactions. We evaluate its performance using data from the holdout sample. In particular, we estimate the model coefficients on the entire work set and use those coefficients to predict the probability of exit on the holdout set.

Figure 17.1 shows the calibration curve for these predictions. We grouped predicted probabilities from the logit M4 model into 10 bins, and plotted the average predicted probability for each bin with the proportion of $y = 1$ cases for those observations. The calibration curve shows that the model is quite well calibrated.

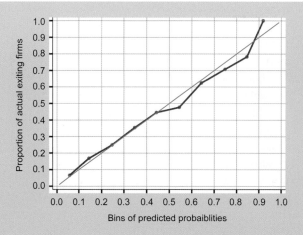

Figure 17.1 Calibration curve

Note: Logit M4 model, estimated on work set, prediction evaluated on holdout set. 20 bins.
Source: `bisnode-firms` dataset. N=19 036 (holdout set, N=3807).

17.3 Classification and the Confusion Table

As introduced earlier, classification assigns each observation to one of the two y values, also called one of the two classes of y. In effect, classification is a process that converts probabilities to predicted zero–one variables. Predicted probabilities are turned into classifications by applying a **classification threshold**. Observations with predicted probabilities at or below the threshold are assigned to $\hat{y} = 0$; observations with predicted probabilities above the threshold are assigned to $\hat{y} = 1$.

The starting point is predicting probabilities in the best possible way; the next step is turning them into classifications. There is one decision here: the threshold value. An intuitive threshold is 0.5: $\hat{y} = 0$ if $\hat{y}^P \leq 0.5$, $\hat{y} = 1$ if $\hat{y}^P > 0.5$. This rule is intuitive because it instructs us to assign membership to the class that is more likely.

However intuitive the 0.5 rule is, it may not be optimal for all classifications. Consider, for example, relatively rare events, so that $y = 1$ for 10 percent of the observations. An unbiased probability prediction has an average predicted probability of 0.1 in this case. Depending on the refinement of our prediction (Chapter 11, Section 11.7), we may have predicted probabilities in the close neighborhood of that average of 0.1, or we may have a lot of spread around it. However, even with a reasonably good model with a reasonably good refinement, we may end up with all of our predicted probabilities below 0.5. Using the 0.5 threshold would then classify every observation into the $y = 0$ class. But, from a classification point of view, that's as useful as not estimating a model at all but simply saying that we classify all observations as 0. We should be able to do better than that with the probability predictions we have. For example, we could choose a threshold value so that we classify the top 10 percent of the observations as $\hat{y} = 1$. That sounds like an intuitive choice, too, because that would yield 10 percent of the observations classified as 1. But is this intuition good enough to produce the best threshold for classification? Not necessarily, it turns out.

The threshold that we apply is our choice. This choice should be guided by what we intend to do with the classification, and the consequences of that classification for the decisions we truly care about. In the framework of predictive analytics, those consequences are formalized by loss functions (Chapter 13, Section 13.4). We'll discuss the role of a loss function in choosing a threshold value later, in Section 17.5. Before doing so, let's introduce some more terminology that helps in thinking about classification.

To think about how the results of classification can be right or wrong, data analysts often draw a **confusion table**, also known as a **confusion matrix**. In the case of a binary y variable, the confusion table is a 2×2 table. The rows show predicted y values, the columns show actual y values. Of the four combinations, two denote correct classifications and two denote false classifications. The cells of a confusion table show numbers of observations that belong to each of the four combinations. When we calculate the confusion table for a test sample, these are numbers of observations in the test sample. When we calculate the confusion table for the holdout sample, these are numbers of observations in the holdout sample.

Table 17.6 shows the confusion table for binary y. In the context of a confusion table, values of 0 are called **negatives**, values of 1 are called **positives**, correct classifications are called **true classifications**, and true y values are called **actual values**. **False positive** and **false negative** cases are called **misclassification**.

Table 17.6 The confusion table for binary y

	$y_j = 0$ **Actual negative**	$y_j = 1$ **Actual positive**	**Total**
$\hat{y}_j = 0$ **Predicted negative**	TN (*true negative*)	FN (*false negative*)	TN + FN (*all classified negative*)
$\hat{y}_j = 1$ **Predicted positive**	FP (*false positive*)	TP (*true positive*)	FP + TP (*all classified positive*)
Total	TN + FP (*all actual negative*)	FN + TP (*all actual positive*)	N = TN + FN + FP + TP (*all observations*)

The confusion table can help us specify the loss function and the threshold value for predicted probabilities or, at least, think about them. It also helps understand various measures of fit for classification. The most intuitive measure is the proportion of correctly classified observations: it's the number of true positives (*TP*) plus true negatives (*TN*) divided by the total number of observations (*N*). That is called the **accuracy** of the classification:

$$accuracy = \frac{TP + TN}{N} \tag{17.3}$$

Let us introduce two more measures of correct classification first, using the confusion table. These are the proportions of correct classifications among observations with the same actual y value. The first one is called **sensitivity**: the proportion of true positives among all actual positives:

$$sensitivity = P[\hat{y} = 1 | y = 1] = \frac{TP}{TP + FN} \tag{17.4}$$

The second measure is **specificity**: the proportion of true negatives among all actual negatives:

$$specificity = P[\hat{y} = 0 | y = 0] = \frac{TN}{TN + FP} \tag{17.5}$$

Whenever we have a confusion table, we can calculate these measures. In turn, for a classification table, we need a classification threshold chosen by the analyst. Different thresholds lead to different values for accuracy, sensitivity, and specificity. In fact, there is a trade-off between specificity and sensitivity, and we discuss that in the next section.

Review Box 17.2   The confusion table

- The confusion table shows the number of observations by their predicted class ($\hat{y} = 0$ or $\hat{y} = 1$) and actual class ($y = 0$ or $y = 1$).
- In the table, correctly classified observations are called true positives (*TP*; $\hat{y} = 1, y = 1$) and true negatives (*TN*; $\hat{y} = 0, y = 0$).
- Incorrectly classified observations are called false positives (*FP*; $\hat{y} = 1, y = 0$) and false negatives (*FN*; $\hat{y} = 0, y = 1$).

17.4   Illustrating the Trade-Off between Different Classification Thresholds: The ROC Curve

The **ROC curve** is a widely used tool that graphically presents the trade-offs between false positives and false negatives that arise when we apply different classification thresholds to the probability predictions from an estimated model. The name is an abbreviation of Receiver Operating Characteristic curve, and it comes from engineering. The ROC curve has false positive rate (one minus specificity) on its horizontal axis, showing the proportion of false positives among actual negatives. The vertical axis is true positive rate (sensitivity), showing the proportion of true positives among actual positives.

The main idea behind the ROC curve is to illustrate that choosing a threshold value creates a trade-off between how well a probability prediction leads to correct classification of $y = 1$ observations versus $y = 0$ observations. But this trade-off should be less severe for better probability predictions. The curve shows this across all possible threshold values. The ROC curve doesn't show the threshold values themselves. But a higher threshold means fewer positives and thus fewer false positives and/or fewer true positives. Conversely, a lower threshold means more positives and thus more false positives and/or more true positives. Therefore, starting with a threshold value of one and decreasing it bit by bit, we move to the right on the horizontal axis and upwards on the vertical axis. But true positives and false positives do not necessarily increase at the same rate. In fact, the idea behind the ROC curve is to see how one increases relative to the other.

To see how the ROC curve works, consider what happens when we look at lower and lower threshold values of the predicted probability to classify observations as positive ($\hat{y} = 1$). When the threshold value is one, no observation is classified as positive, so the proportion of false positives to all actual negatives is zero. That means one minus specificity is zero, and we are at the zero point of the horizontal axis. Similarly, because at a threshold value of one no observation is classified as positive, the proportion of true positives to all actual positives is zero, too. That means sensitivity is zero, and we are at the zero point of the vertical axis. That's the bottom left corner of the ROC curve.

If the classification were totally random, the proportion of true positives and false positives would increase at the same rate as we decreased the threshold. That would be moving North-East along the 45 degree line. Random classification would result from a probability prediction that is completely non-informative, such as assigning a completely random number as the predicted probability to the various observations regardless of the values of their x variables.

However, if the predicted probabilities capture meaningful patterns of association between x and y, and thus our predictions are better than random, we expect true positives to increase more than false positives as we decrease the threshold. That would move the curve above the 45 degree line. In fact, the better the prediction, the more true positives we expect for any level of false positives. Thus, the better the prediction, the higher the ROC curve should be compared to the 45 degree line. We show an example of the ROC curve in our case study below.

The better the predictions, the further away the ROC curve is from the 45 degree line and the closer it is to the upper edge of the box. That idea is captured in a single measure, the **area under the ROC curve**, often abbreviated as **AUC**, for "area under the curve." A perfect prediction would give an area of 1. The ROC curve for a completely random prediction would be the 45 degree line, yielding an area under the ROC curve of 1/2. Real-life predictions yield an area under the ROC curve between 1/2 and 1 – the higher, the better.

Thus the AUC can be used as a model selection criterion for probability predictions. It is thus an alternative to MSE (which is equal to the Brier score), or its square root, RMSE.

Review Box 17.3 The ROC curve and the area under the ROC curve (AUC)

- The ROC curve illustrates the trade-off between false positives and false negatives for when various thresholds are used to turn probability predictions from an estimated model into classification.
- The ROC curve shows the proportion of false positives among all $y = 0$ observations (one minus specificity) and the proportion of true positives among all $y = 1$ observations (sensitivity); the threshold values are not shown on the graph.
- The ROC curve of a completely random probability prediction is the 45 degree line.
- The ROC curve of a perfect probability prediction would jump from zero to one and stay at one (running along the upper edge of the box).
- The area under the ROC curve (also called AUC) summarizes how good a probability prediction is; it would be one for a perfect prediction and 0.5 for a completely random prediction.

17.A3   CASE STUDY – Predicting Firm Exit: Probability and Classification

ROC curve, model selection by AUC, and classification diagnostics by the confusion table

Previously, as part of cross-validation, we estimated the logit M4 model on the five training sets. To illustrate the ROC curve, we picked one of these, predicted the probabilities using the corresponding test set, and drew the ROC curve. In fact, we drew two versions. The first version, Figure 17.2a, shows values of the ROC curve for selected threshold values, between 0.05 and 0.75, by steps of 0.05. It also uses color coding to denote the approximate values of the corresponding thresholds, which are not shown directly on the ROC curve. The second version, Figure 17.2b, is similar to how the ROC curve is usually shown. It fills in for threshold values in-between, but it has no reference to the corresponding threshold values.

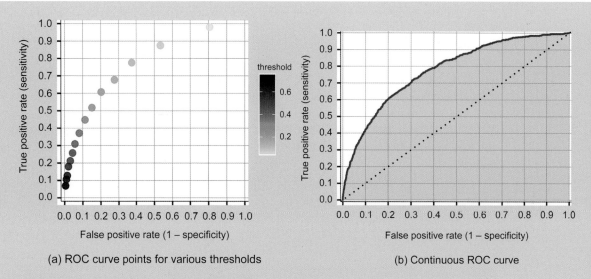

(a) ROC curve points for various thresholds   (b) Continuous ROC curve

Figure 17.2   ROC curve for predicting firm exit

Note: ROC curve based on the logit M4 model, estimated on one of the training sets; predictions on the corresponding test set.
Source: `bisnode-firms` dataset. N=19 036 (work set, N=15 229).

The shaded area below the ROC curve is the area under the curve. Table 17.7 below shows the 5-fold cross-validated RMSE and AUC (the average of the five folds). The logit M4 model has the lowest RMSE and highest AUC, followed by M3 (AUC) or LASSO (RMSE). The order suggested by RMSE and AUC is very similar but not exactly the same. That's a rather typical outcome.

Table 17.7   RMSE and AUC for various models of firm exit

Model	RMSE	AUC
Logit M1	0.374	0.738
Logit M2	0.366	0.771
Logit M3	0.364	0.777
Logit M4	0.362	0.782
Logit M5	0.363	0.777
Logit LASSO	0.362	0.768

Note: Models are described in the text. Five-fold cross-validated RMSE and AUC (area under the ROC curve) values.
Source: `bisnode-firms` dataset. N=19 036 (work set, N=15 229,).

Having picked the best model for predicting probabilities, we illustrate classification using the holdout set. We show the confusion table for two possible thresholds: 0.5 and 0.2. Recall that the proportion of exiting firms is about 20 percent in the data so the second threshold classifies firms as "likely to exit" ($\hat{y} = 1$) whenever the predicted probability is greater than the sample proportion. Table 17.8 shows the confusion tables for both of these thresholds.

Table 17.8 Confusion tables with thresholds 0.5 and 0.2

	Threshold: 0.5			Threshold: 0.2		
	Actual stay	Actual exit	Total	Actual stay	Actual exit	Total
Predicted stay	75%	15%	90%	57%	7%	64%
Predicted exit	4%	6%	10%	22%	14%	36%
Total	79%	21%	100%	79%	21%	100%

Note: Percentage of observations in cells. Firm exit predictions based on the logit M4 model. Classification on the holdout sample; two confusion tables next to each other.

Source: `bisnode-firms` dataset. N=19 036 (holdout set, N=3807).

Having a higher threshold leads to fewer predicted exits: 10% when the threshold is 0.5 versus 36% for threshold 0.2. With a higher threshold, we also have fewer false positives (4% versus 22%) but more false negatives (15% versus 7%). Perhaps surprisingly, the 0.5 threshold leads to a higher accuracy rate than the 0.2 threshold ($75\% + 6\% = 81\%$ versus $57\% + 14\% = 71\%$) even though the 0.2 threshold is very close to the actual proportion of exiting firms.

Table 17.9 shows the same information using measures we introduced earlier: accuracy, sensitivity, and specificity. Indeed, the 0.2 threshold results in worse accuracy and lower specificity, but it results in higher sensitivity. To practice reading ROC curves, you are invited to find the corresponding points on Figures 17.2b, and you can also verify the corresponding thresholds, at least approximately, on Figure 17.2a.

Table 17.9 Accuracy, sensitivity, and specificity for threshold values 0.5 and 0.2 (in percent)

	Threshold: 0.5	Threshold: 0.2
Accuracy	81%	71%
Sensitivity	28%	68%
Specificity	95%	72%

Note: Firm exit predictions based on the Logit M4 model. Classification on the holdout sample based on two thresholds.

Source: `bisnode-firms` dataset. N=19 036 (holdout set, N=3807).

17.5 Loss Function and Finding the Optimal Classification Threshold

As we discussed in Section 17.3, we need a threshold value to convert predicted probability into classification. We have seen that different thresholds lead to different frequencies of false positives and **false negatives**.

The goal of classification is to use the predicted probabilities and find the value of the classification threshold that is best for the purpose of answering the question of the analysis. We need a loss function to do that. Similarly to any loss function (Chapter 13, Section 13.4), a **classification loss function** quantifies the consequences of decisions that are driven by the prediction. As we have seen, when classifying observations into classes of a binary y variable, we can be wrong in two ways: making a false negative classification (FN) or making a **false positive** classification (FP). A loss function would have only two values here: a loss due to false negatives and a loss due to false positives.

The expected loss of a classification is the probability of false negatives multiplied by the loss due to a false negative plus the probability of false positives multiplied by the loss due to a false positive. When estimated from the data, those probabilities are relative frequencies: the proportion of false negatives and the proportion of false positives.

$$E[loss] = P[FN] \times loss(FN) + P[FP] \times loss(FP) \tag{17.6}$$

$$= \frac{FN}{N} \times loss(FN) + \frac{FP}{N} \times loss(FP). \tag{17.7}$$

With predicted probabilities, we need to find the threshold value for classification that results in the smallest expected loss. That is the best threshold we can have, also called the **optimal classification threshold**.

It turns out that, under ideal circumstances, we can compute the optimal classification threshold from the relative magnitude of the two losses. It is simply

$$optimal\ classification\ threshold = \frac{loss(FP)}{loss(FP) + loss(FN)} \tag{17.8}$$

Thus, for example, if the two losses were equal, this value would be 0.5; if the loss due to false positives were three times larger, the value would be 0.75. But this calculation is true only under ideal circumstances. More precisely, it is true if the model that predicts the probabilities is the best one, in the sense that it uses the x variables in the best possible way to predict the probabilities. While we try to find the best model using cross-validation, we can never be sure to have found it.

A more robust, although more cumbersome, solution is to find the optimal classification threshold using the data. That means looking for the classification threshold that gives us the smallest expected loss, by cross-validation. This then becomes a search problem. The problem is straightforward in principle, because the classification threshold has a value that is somewhere between zero and one. It takes time and computing power though. Based on the probability predictions, the search algorithm needs to try various values between zero and one for the classification threshold, calculate the expected loss for each, and pick the one that produces the smallest expected loss. We should find the best classification (model + threshold) through the same k-fold cross-validation. This procedure is more robust than applying the simple formula for the optimal threshold because it allows for the model to be imperfect, and it finds the threshold value that would lead to the smallest expected loss with that imperfect model.

Note a technical detail about this search problem. Some software routines that search for the optimal classification threshold don't look for the smallest expected loss. Instead, they search for the threshold that maximizes a different function, sometimes called the probability cost function or the cost-sensitive Youden index. But that's just a technical detail as the classification threshold that maximizes this different function is the same one that minimizes expected loss. We show that formally in Under the Hood section 17.U2.

Finding the optimal classification threshold by cross-validation is more robust, because it allows for the underlying probability model to be imperfect in capturing how the x variables are related to the probability of $y = 1$. So we advise using that approach when there is enough time and computing power. Nevertheless, we can usually be close to correct by choosing the formula value for the optimal classification threshold. Our case study will illustrate these points.

Note that, whether we apply the formula or search for the optimal threshold by cross-validation, what matters is not the levels of the losses ($loss(FN)$ and $loss(FP)$) but their relative magnitudes.

Intuitively, that's because with different thresholds we end up with a different relative proportion of false negatives and false positives, and the best classification has their proportion in line with the relative losses they cause. Because it's the relative magnitudes that matter, data analysts often set one of the two loss amounts to one.

Finally, we should remember that classification makes sense only when we have a loss function. Without a loss function, there is no optimal classification threshold and so we can't find it. We could select a threshold value based on some other criterion, but, in fact, that threshold value would be optimal only with some loss function. Thus, implicitly, we impose a loss function anytime we impose a classification threshold even if we didn't say what loss function would make it optimal. For this reason, when we do not have a loss function, the transparent choice is to select the best model to predict the probabilities according to some probability-model criterion (such as MSE).

Review Box 17.4 Classification and optimal threshold selection

- A loss function for classification attaches loss values for incorrect predictions (*FP* and *FN*).
- The best classification produces the lowest expected loss: $E[loss] = P[FN] \times loss(FN) + P[FP] \times loss(FP)$.
- Based on predicted probabilities, the best classification is achieved with the optimal classification threshold, which minimizes expected loss.
- One way to find the optimal threshold is to use the formula $\dfrac{loss(FP)}{loss(FP) + loss(FN)}$.
- Another method of finding the optimal threshold is a search algorithm, which selects the probability model and the optimal classification threshold together.

17.A4 CASE STUDY – Predicting Firm Exit: Probability and Classification

Classification from predicted probabilities

In this section, we consider the case when we do have a loss function and look to find the threshold that gets the lowest expected loss.

Let's assume that we are advising a bank that decides to give a loan of 10 thousand euros to a company based on our model's recommendation. The "positive" event is exit, which leads to non-repayment. The "negative" event is staying in business, which leads to repayment. Let's assume that the bank loses all 10 thousand euros if it extends the loan but the firm exits. This would happen if our classification told the bank that the company would not exit but it did in fact exit: a false negative. The other mistake is having our classification say the company would exit, making the bank deny the loan when the company stayed in business in fact (a false positive). This is a loss because the bank loses the profit opportunity, and let's assume that this loss is 1 thousand euros. With correct decisions, there is no loss. Table 17.10 shows the values of this loss function.

Table 17.10   Loss function for classification

	Actual negative	Actual positive
Predicted negative	0	10
Predicted positive	1	0

According to the formula, the optimal classification threshold is $1/11 = 0.091$. We also used the more robust way to find the optimal threshold by a search algorithm. Consider our M4 logit model, its predicted probabilities, and the loss function in Table 17.10. We run the optimal threshold selection algorithm on the work set, with 5-fold cross-validation. The selected threshold is 0.082 with expected loss of 0.619. Figure 17.3 shows all expected loss values for the grid of possible threshold values from 0 to 1, for a single test set. (The expected loss value turns out to be 0.60 on this single test set; it's cross-validated average is 0.619.)

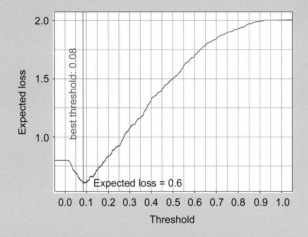

Figure 17.3   Threshold–loss curve

Note: Firm exit predictions based on the M4 logit model. Selection of the optimal classification threshold with loss function in Table 17.10 with 5-fold cross-validation on the work set. The graph is based on a single test set, fold5.
Source: `bisnode-firms` dataset, 2012. N=19 036 (work set, N=15 229).

Indeed, the formula and the search algorithm give approximately the same threshold value. That is reassuring. Figure 17.3 also shows that the expected loss would be quite similar if, instead, we chose a threshold value that is a little smaller or a little larger, because the expected loss is similar, around 0.09. Thus, even if we had chosen a slightly different threshold value, say, 0.08 or 0.1, our expected loss would have remained very similar.

As we described in Section 17.5, to find the best classification via the search algorithm, we need to estimate each probability model and find its corresponding optimal threshold in cross-validation, and we need to calculate the cross-validated expected loss. The best classification is given by the model, and its corresponding optimal threshold that produces the smallest expected loss.

Table 17.11 summarizes our results, repeating the cross-validated RMSE values. To describe the process in a little more detail, we started with the work set and carried out 5-fold cross-validation. For example, for fold 1, we estimated the probability model on the training set 1, used the model to predict the probabilities on test set 1, and searched for the optimal classification threshold on test set 1. In practice, we used an algorithm that searches for that optimal classification threshold by maximizing the cost-sensitive Youden index. However, as we explained, the result of this maximization is the same as if we had searched for the threshold that minimizes expected loss. We repeated this for all five folds, and took the average of these five estimated thresholds and the five expected losses.

Table 17.11   Cross-validated ranking of classifications (models and optimal classification thresholds)

	RMSE	Optimal threshold	Expected loss
Logit M1	0.374	0.089	0.722
Logit M2	0.366	0.096	0.660
Logit M3	0.364	0.092	0.630
Logit M4	0.362	0.082	0.619
Logit M5	0.363	0.091	0.637
Logit LASSO	0.362	0.104	0.665

Note: Models are described in the text. RMSE, optimal threshold selection, and expected loss are results of 5-fold cross-validation (averages).

Source: `bisnode-firms` dataset, 2012. N=19 036 (work set, N=15 229).

The optimal classification threshold turns out to be similar, but not exactly the same, for the six models. The model that has the smallest RMSE (M4) turns out to be the same one that has the smallest expected loss. In general, we expect best thresholds to be close, but not necessarily the same. The variation illustrates why optimal threshold selection may help finding the best probability model when our goal is classification.

17.6   Probability Prediction and Classification with Random Forest

In Chapters 15 and 16, we considered quantitative outcomes and their prediction with a single regression tree grown with the CART algorithm and a random forest based on many such regression trees. Recall that the main advantage of tree-based methods is that they can automatically capture important nonlinearities and interactions. Single regression trees are not used in actual prediction because they tend to severely overfit the data. However, ensemble methods that combine multiple regression trees grown on the same data can give excellent predictions. Of them, we focused on the random forest method, which is relatively easy to implement and tends to give very good predictions. Its disadvantage is its black box nature: we need to carry out extensive diagnostic evaluation to understand how the specific x variables contribute to the prediction, which is important for assessing the external validity of a prediction. Thus, when our goal is to predict a quantitative y variable, random forest is an excellent method to choose, with the caveat that we would need to carry out diagnostics afterwards.

We can use the same methods to predict a binary y variable. Not much changes from predicting probabilities, but, as we'll see, there is some new terminology, and we have to be a little more careful when we carry out a classification. A tree with a binary y variable is called a **classification tree**.

It turns out that the classification tree and the regression tree are essentially the same thing, and the CART algorithm to grow them is the same, too. (See Chapter 15, Section 15.2, for how a regression tree is grown.) The process is based on binary splitting; the algorithm is greedy and top-down, based on the improvement of each step to the fit. In a regression tree, the measure of fit is MSE. In a classification tree, the measure of fit is called **Gini impurity**. It turns out, however, that the MSE and Gini impurity measures of fit are essentially the same for binary y variables and thus lead to the exact same splitting decisions. We show the details in Under the Hood section 17.U1.

The terminal nodes of a classification tree consist of observations, some of which have $y = 1$ and some $y = 0$. The proportion of $y = 1$ observations in the terminal node is the probability prediction generated by the classification tree. To these probabilities, a classification tree applies a classification threshold to classify observations into $\hat{y} = 1$ or $\hat{y} = 0$.

Importantly, as with any classification, the selection of the classification threshold should be based on a loss function. We should use one of the two approaches we described in Section 17.5: apply the formula using relative losses $(loss(FP)/(loss(FP) + loss(FN)))$ or find the optimal classification threshold via a search algorithm. The first approach is easier, it's the correct one when the model is the best possible model, and it's usually fine at other times, too. The second approach is more robust in that it finds the optimal threshold for the model whether it's the best possible model or not, but it requires more work. In our case studies we use the second approach, but the first one is good practice, too.

Note that many software implementations of classification trees don't follow these good practices. Instead, they apply a default classification threshold of 0.5 calling it "the majority rule." We strongly advise against using this default option. The 0.5 threshold is optimal only if the losses due to a **false positive** and a **false negative** are equal $(loss(FP) = loss(FN))$. It can lead to bad classification results otherwise. Most default options for trees and random forest are fine; this one is an important exception.

A single classification tree is almost never used for classification in practice, just as a single regression tree is almost never used for predicting a quantitative variable. Instead, ensemble methods with many trees are used here, too. Of them, we advise using the random forest method that we introduced in Chapter 16 for predicting a quantitative y variable. The approach is the same here: we build many decorrelated trees on bootstrapped datasets and aggregate them. However, with a binary y variable, there are two versions of the random forest that can be used, depending on what actually is aggregated from the individual trees.

The first version of the random forest predicts probabilities. It is sometimes called a **probability random forest**. It aggregates the probability predictions of each tree by averaging them across all trees. The model's predicted probabilities are simply these averages. If our goal is predicting probabilities, this is the version to use. But we can use it for classification, too, by simply applying the optimal classification threshold to the predicted probabilities.

The second version carries out the classification at the end of each individual tree and then aggregates those classifications to arrive at the final classification by the random forest. This is sometimes called the **classification random forest**. When our goal is predicting probabilities, this is not a good approach. When our goal is classification, we can use either version, and their results tend to be very similar – with the caveat that we have to find the optimal classification threshold using a loss function.

The random forest is a good model to use for probability prediction or classification. It is a black box model so we need to do extra work to evaluate how each x variable contributes to the prediction. But it tends to be among the best models to combine the x variables for the prediction, and it requires less work for model building from data analysts than, for example, logit models.

> **Review Box 17.5 The classification tree and random forest for probability prediction and classification**
>
> - The classification tree is similar to a regression tree. Its terminal nodes are predicted class probabilities that can be turned into classifications.
> - A probability random forest aggregates probability predictions from each tree to arrive at predicted probabilities.
> - A classification random forest aggregates classifications from each tree to arrive at a classification.
> - For classification purposes, we should always set the threshold value based on a loss function instead of using an ad-hoc value.

17.A5   CASE STUDY – Predicting Firm Exit: Probability and Classification

Probability prediction and classification with random forest

In this section, we use random forest to predict class probabilities and make classification decisions.

We start with a single classification tree. As we make consecutive splits, the eventual outcome will be a tree with predicted probabilities at each terminal node. The tree in Figure 17.4 is a small tree we built for illustration purposes with only three variables: firm size (sales_mil), annual profit or loss, and a binary variable for having a foreign management. It shows the share of exiting firms, which will be the predicted probability. In this illustration, very small firms with large losses have a higher predicted probability of exit, while the predicted probability is much smaller for larger firms.

We built a probability random forest model to predict probabilities. We used the same variables as in model M4, except we didn't do any feature engineering. We didn't enter polynomials, add flag variables to extreme values, or winsorize values above or below certain thresholds. The main advantage of the tree-based models is that they are supposed to find good ways to approximate the most important nonlinearities and interactions. We used the default options of growing 500 trees, and a simple tuning ending up with 15 observations as the minimum per terminal node, and 5 variables used for each split; and we used 5-fold cross-validation with the Gini impurity index (which, as we know, is the same as using MSE or the Brier score).

The random forest outperformed the logit models in terms of predicting probabilities, with a cross-validated RMSE of 0.358 and AUC of 0.808. We used predicted probabilities to find the optimal threshold by cross-validation (0.098), and used this value to make the classification. The cross-validated expected loss was smaller (0.587) than for the best logit model in terms of expected loss, the logit M4 (0.619). We'll return to ranking models at the end of our case study. For the random forest, we re-estimate the model on the work set and do the prediction on the holdout set. Holdout RMSE is 0.358 and holdout AUC is 0.808.

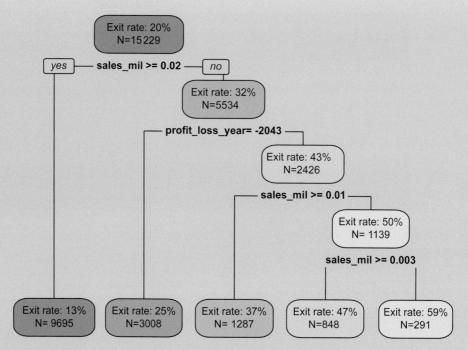

Figure 17.4   Classification tree

Note: Simple classification tree grown by CART, with three variables.
Source: `bisnode-firms` dataset. N=19 036 (work set, N=15 229).

To evaluate the result we can take the holdout set and look at the classification results in the appropriate confusion table, in Table 17.12.

Table 17.12 Confusion table for random forest classification		
	Actual stay	**Actual exit**
Predicted stay	33.6%	1.3%
Predicted exit	45.4%	19.7%

Note: Probabilities are predicted by random forest; optimal classification threshold, selected by cross-validation, is 0.098. Confusion table computed for the holdout set, based on the probability prediction model using the entire work set.
Source: `bisnode-firms` dataset, 2012. N=19 036 (holdout set, N=3807).

With our loss function and the confusion table, we can directly calculate the expected loss on the holdout set as: $(10 * 0.013 + 0.454) = 0.587$. If external validity is high, this means that we can expect to make a loss of 587 euros per classification on the live data. This is what will have to be offset by revenues we get for the project. Note that this low loss value is achieved by minimizing false negatives (predicted stay, actual exit) at the cost of allowing for many false positives (predicted exit, actual stay). This is the result of the strong asymmetry of the loss function.

Let us emphasize again that using the optimal threshold is important. Had we used a 0.5 threshold, the expected loss would have been 1540 vs. 587 euros for the best threshold model. This is 2.6 times the loss from the optimal threshold.

Having tried out several models, we can finally compare their performance in predicting probabilities and in classifying observations. Table 17.13 compares the random forest and the most important models we have seen earlier, focusing on our various measures of performance – all coming from 5-fold cross-validation on the work set.

Table 17.13 Summary of model performance measures

	N predictors	N coefficients	CV RMSE	CV AUC	CV threshold	Expected loss
Logit M1	11	12	0.374	0.736	0.089	0.722
Logit M4	36	79	0.362	0.784	0.082	0.619
Logit LASSO	36	143	0.362	0.768	0.106	0.642
RF probability	36	n.a.	0.354	0.808	0.098	0.587

Note: 5-fold cross-validation averages. Optimal classification threshold is selected by 5-fold cross-validation, for each model. AUC is area under the ROC curve.

Source: `bisnode-firms` dataset, 2012. N=19 036 (work set, N=15 229; holdout set, N=3807).

The best model is the random forest model, both for probability prediction and classification. It is followed by the M4, M5, and LASSO logit models, which are very similar in all fit measures, with somewhat different ranking within them. The worst model is the simple logit model M1. The optimal classification threshold selected for the different models is somewhat different, ranging from 0.082 for logit M4 to 0.106 for LASSO. All threshold values are close to what the formula would suggest ($1/11 = 0.091$).

To appreciate the differences in the classification performance of the different models, let's return to the example behind our loss function. Suppose that the bank extends loans of 10 000 euros and earns 1000 euros for loans that are repaid. The classification tells the bank whether to extend the loan (if the firm is predicted not to exit, the negative) or deny the loan (if the firm is predicted to exit, the positive). We have our loss function: a false negative yields a loss of 10 000 euros, while a false positive yields a loss of 1 000 euros. Our simplest logit M1 model classifies with the expected loss of −722 euros per firm, the random forest model results in an expected loss of −587 euros. So building a better model yields 139 euros higher profit per firm. If the bank reviews 1000 applying firms, this translates into an increase of 139 000 euros in profits due to better decisions.

Often, government agencies, such as industry regulators, legally oblige companies to produce predictions in which the role of each predictor variable is clearly understood. To comply with such regulations, it is often better to use an interpretable model, such as a logit, instead of a black box model, such as a random forest. Here, logit M4 model gives the best classification. Comparing the expected loss from logit M4 with the expected loss from the simplest model, logit M1, the increase in expected profits is 103 000 euros.

Having a good estimate for the increase in expected profit due to better models matters because this is the number we can compare to model development costs (such as adding more financial variables and training and selecting models).

Finally, let us discuss the external validity of these results. The starting point of this analysis was a single cross-section: taking financial variable values for 2012 and predicting 2-year exit probability. A check on external validity would be to see how the very same model works for predicting exit for another period, say 2013–2015. You are invited to carry this out as a data exercise.

This concludes our case study. We have used a rich but complex dataset to predict exit of firms. We have specified various logit models, a LASSO logit model, and random forest, to predict the probability of exit. We then specified a decision situation with losses due to bad decisions, and we used the loss function together with the predicted probabilities to classify firms into those that would likely exit and those that would likely stay in business. In this case study we searched for the optimal classification threshold for each model by cross-validation; we leave the simpler but less robust method of using a formula as a data exercise. We found that the random forest is best both in predicting the probability of exit and classifying firms that are likely to exit.

17.7   Class Imbalance

Before taking stock, let us make a small detour and discuss a practical issue of working with binary outcomes.

A potential issue may arise for some datasets with respect to the relative frequency of the classes. **Class imbalance** refers to the situation when one of the two "classes" of our y variable ($y = 1$ or $y = 0$) is a lot more frequent than the other one. In other words, the event is very rare or very frequent. Sometimes, such events are called tail events: events that happen only when some underlying thing has a very extreme ("tail") value.

What constitutes an imbalance as opposed to a balance doesn't have a clear-cut definition. For sure we have imbalance if $P[y = 1] = 0.999$ or $P[y = 1] = 0.001$; and we are likely to have imbalance for $P[y = 1] = 0.01$. The size of the dataset matters: in a larger dataset we can identify rare patterns better. For 10 thousand observations, 1% means 100 observations with, say, $y = 1$, but when we have millions of observations, we have tens of thousands of these.

Class imbalance turns out to be pretty frequent in real-life prediction. For instance, data on fraudulent consumers typically has very few fraudsters, and, at the level of transactions, fraud is even less frequent. Large losses on one's portfolio are rare but extremely important events. Serious sport injuries matter a great deal to the player who suffers them as well as to their employing team, but – in most sports – serious injuries fortunately happen rarely.

The problem with class imbalance is that the methods that we use for probability prediction and classification are not good at handling it. That is true both for the models to predict probabilities and for the measures of fit we use for model selection. For example, the functional form assumptions behind the logit model tend to matter more, the closer the probabilities are to zero or one. And those functional form assumptions, like any such assumption, are unlikely to be true in real-life situations. Cross-validation can be less effective at avoiding overfitting with very rare or very frequent events if the dataset is not very large. Usual measures of fit can be less good at differentiating models.

What can we do when we have class imbalance? First, we should acknowledge that such a feature of our data will hamper our prediction efforts: it is very hard to identify reasons behind rare events. Second, there are some technical solutions that can yield better predictive models.

A frequent solution is **class rebalancing**, which reduces class imbalance: making the event not as extremely rare (or frequent) in the data as it is in real life. Suppose $y = 1$ is rare in our dataset. One way to do class rebalancing is called **downsampling**: randomly delete observations with the very frequent $y = 0$ value from our data. Another option is to resample observations with $y = 1$. There are more complicated methods such as Synthetic Minority Over-Sampling Technique or **SMOTE** that does balancing automatically.

Class rebalancing approaches will eventually result in a higher proportion of observations in the rare class than its true proportion. Importantly, we should do it on the training set only. Model selection and calculating expected performance should be done on unmodified sets. This comes from the approach of having test and holdout sets as close as possible to how live data would look.

Alternatively, sometimes, we can address class imbalance during data collection. If possible, we can collect the data paying attention to class balance and sample more observations with the rare y value in the data collection phase.

17.8 The Process of Prediction with a Binary Target Variable

Let us review the process and the use of various tools for prediction problems with a binary target variable and draw a few methodological conclusions.

First, we need to decide whether the goal of the prediction is predicting probabilities ($\hat{y}^P$ between 0 and 1) or classification ($\hat{y} = 0$ or $\hat{y} = 1$). Sometimes the predicted probabilities, or the ranking of them (who is more likely to default on a loan?), is what a decision needs. Other times, the decision needs classification (is this client going to default on a loan?).

Second, whatever the ultimate goal, the primary outcome of prediction with a binary target variable is the set of predicted probabilities, which are functions of the x variables.

Third, when our goal is probability prediction, we should find the best model that predicts probabilities by cross-validation. The most widely used selection criteria are RMSE (or its square, MSE, which equals the Brier score) or the area under the ROC curve (often abbreviated as AUC).

Fourth, when our goal is classification, we should apply an optimal classification threshold to convert the predicted probabilities into predicted class. We can find the optimal classification threshold only if we have a loss function: the loss due to a **false positive** classification and the loss due to a false negative classification (in fact we only need their relative magnitudes).

Fifth, to find the optimal classification threshold, we have to do one of two things. First, we can use the formula that derives the threshold value from the relative losses. This approach requires that we have found the best possible model to predict the probability of $y = 1$ using the x variables, which we can't be sure of in real life. The second approach is more robust in that it doesn't require finding the best possible model. It searches for the optimal classification threshold by cross-validation, together with finding the best model that predicts the probabilities. The most widely used selection criterion is expected loss (or an equivalent criterion called the cost-sensitive Youden index).

If we are unable, or unwilling, to specify a loss function, we can predict probabilities, and we should select the best model for predicting probabilities using a selection criterion for probability prediction

(RMSE or AUC). Nothing guarantees that this same model would also give the best classification with a particular loss function. But it's usually a pretty good choice. The best probability predictions can later be used to achieve good, if not necessarily the best, classification with various classification thresholds corresponding to various loss functions.

17.9   Main Takeaways

With a binary target variable, we can carry out two kinds of prediction: probability prediction (the probability that an observation has $y = 1$) and classification (whether an observation has $y = 1$ or $y = 0$).

- Predicting the probability that $y = 1$ is very similar to predicting the expected value of y, but it may require a different model.
- We can classify by using a threshold value for predicted probabilities.
- We need a loss function for finding the optimal classification threshold value and classify accordingly.

PRACTICE QUESTIONS

1. What's the difference between probability prediction and classification? Give an example of a decision for which one is needed and another example for which the other one is needed.
2. What's the expected loss of a classification? Give an example.
3. When you consider higher and higher thresholds of predicted probabilities for classification, the number of false positives and false negatives changes. How and why?
4. Draw a confusion table and explain what's in its four cells.
5. What are accuracy (percent correctly predicted), sensitivity, and specificity, and how do you calculate them from a confusion table?
6. Accuracy, also known as percent correctly predicted, is an intuitive but imperfect measure of goodness of fit for a classification. Give an example where it's not an informative measure.
7. Does a well-calibrated probability prediction yield a classification without error? Why or why not? Give an example.
8. How does the ROC curve represent classifications with different probability thresholds?
9. Draw two examples of the ROC curve, one representing a better prediction than the other, and explain why it's better.
10. You want to classify incoming customer complaint emails into urgent ($y = 1$) and not urgent ($y = 0$). Based on the consequences of that classification, you calculate that the loss of false positives is 2 euros; the loss of false negatives is 5 euros. What do these numbers mean? What's the theoretically optimal classification threshold, and what does that mean?
11. In the previous example, you produce a good probability prediction, and you want to use that for classification. Suppose that you chose a higher classification threshold than optimal. What would be the consequence for the expected loss, the rate of false positives, and the rate of false negatives? Why?
12. Again using the previous example, one threshold gives you a 0.4 probability of false positives and a 0.4 probability of false negatives. Another threshold gives you a 0.2 probability of false

positives and a 0.5 probability of false negatives. Which of the two would produce a better classification and why?

13. You want to classify loan applicants into two classes: those that would default on their loans ($y = 1$) and those that repay their loan ($y = 0$). Draw a confusion table and explain its four elements using the example.

14. Using the example of loan applicants who either default on their loans or repay them, carry out a probability prediction and draw a ROC curve. Explain what's measured on the two axes of the ROC curve in this example and what's a point on the ROC curve.

15. Again using the previous example, explain how you would carry out a classification exercise if you knew the loss values of false positives and false negatives. Describe each step of the analysis.

DATA EXERCISES

Easier and/or shorter exercises are denoted by [*]; harder and/or longer exercises are denoted by [**].

1. Use the same `bisnode-firms` dataset and the same year (cross-section of 2012) that we used in the case study, but do not drop any of the firms because of too little or too much sales during sample design. Carry out the probability prediction exercise on this larger original dataset without a loss function, the same way as in the case study (same holdout sample selection, same cross-validation, same logit models). Evaluate your prediction with the help of the ROC curve using a randomly selected holdout sample. Compare the area under the ROC curve with the corresponding measure in the case study above. Discuss your findings. [**]

2. Use the same `bisnode-firms` dataset and the same data (cross-section of 2012, same sample design) that we used in the case study. Carry out the classification exercise with a loss function that is different from what we used in the case study. Consider a random forest of classification trees and find the optimal classification threshold using expected loss (cross-validated). Compute the confusion table on the holdout sample and compare it to what we had in our case study. Discuss your findings. [*]

3. Use the same `bisnode-firms` dataset and the same data (cross-section of 2012, same sample design) that we used in the case study. Carry out the random forest prediction process and then run similar diagnostics to what we have done in Chapter 16: variable importance plot and heterogeneity of prediction fit by type of firm. Discuss your findings. [*]

4. Use the same `bisnode-firms` dataset that we used in the case study, but pick a different year. Carry out the prediction exercise without a loss function, using the same logit models as in the case study, and pick the best one by the cross-validated Brier score. Evaluate your prediction using a randomly selected holdout sample. Discuss your findings. [**]

5. Find data on probabilistic weather predictions of a binary event such as rain or snow the next day, together with data on actual events (rain or snow). Create a calibration curve (join predicted values into bins if necessary), and discuss what you see. [*]

REFERENCES AND FURTHER READING

On LASSO for logit, an advanced but thorough discussion is in Chapter 3 on Generalized Linear Models of Hastie et al. (2015).

On building the logit prediction model to better adjust for the loss function, see the advanced paper Elliott & Lieli (2013).

On loss sensitive classification, an important technical paper is Drummond & Holte (2000).

The facts that MSE and the Gini impurity are essentially the same thing, and several other measures of fit are also closely related to each other, were shown in detail by Rogozhnikov (2016).

Regarding class imbalance and SMOTE, a classic paper is Chawla et al. (2002).

17.U1   UNDER THE HOOD: THE GINI NODE IMPURITY MEASURE AND MSE

For historical reasons, classification trees make the splitting decision based on how it improves the fit as measured by Gini impurity. To define it, let's consider a split, for node m, and let $\hat{p}_m$ represent the share of observations with $y = 1$ (and $1 - \hat{p}_m$ represent share of observations with $y = 0$). To be more precise, let n_m denote the number of observations in node m, let the number of observations with $y = 0$ be n_{0m}, and let the number of observations with $y = 1$ be n_{1m}, so that

$$\hat{p}_m = \frac{n_{1m}}{n_m} \tag{17.9}$$

$$1 - \hat{p}_m = \frac{n_{0m}}{n_m} \tag{17.10}$$

Then, the Gini index of node impurity is

$$Gini_m = 2\hat{p}_m(1 - \hat{p}_m) = 2\frac{n_{1m}}{n_m}\frac{n_{0m}}{n_m} \tag{17.11}$$

The index is zero if all observations have either $y = 0$ or all have $y = 1$ ($\hat{p}_m = 0$ or $\hat{p}_m = 1$). The closer $\hat{p}_m$ to 0.5, the larger the value of the index. Thus, a small value implies that the node is made up entirely of a single class.

Recall that the MSE is defined as the mean of the squared difference between the predicted and actual values. Here, the predicted values are the predicted probabilities. Among the observations in node m, the predicted probability of $y = 1$ is simply the fraction of observations with $y = 1$. According to our notation, that's n_{1m}/n_m. Thus, among the observations in node m, the MSE is

$$MSE_m = \frac{1}{n_m}\sum\left(\frac{n_{1m}}{n_m} - y_i\right)^2 \tag{17.12}$$

For the derivations, lets' skip the m subscript; all that we'll do will be relevant for node m.

Let's expand on the MSE formula. Recognizing that some y_i values are zero and others are one, we can write out the sum in two parts, one for the sum of ones, and the other for the sum of zeros.

$$MSE = \frac{1}{n}\left(\sum_1\left(\frac{n_1}{n} - 1\right)^2 + \sum_0\left(\frac{n_1}{n}\right)^2\right) \tag{17.13}$$

$$= \frac{1}{n}\left(\sum_1\left(\frac{-n_0}{n}\right)^2 + \sum_0\left(\frac{n_1}{n}\right)^2\right) \tag{17.14}$$

$$= \frac{1}{n}\left(\sum_1 \frac{n_0^2}{n^2} + \sum_0 \frac{n_1^2}{n^2}\right) \tag{17.15}$$

$$= \frac{1}{n}\left(n_1 \frac{n_0^2}{n^2} + n_0 \frac{n_1^2}{n^2}\right) \tag{17.16}$$

$$= \frac{n_1 n_0^2}{n^3} + \frac{n_0 n_1^2}{n^3} \tag{17.17}$$

$$= \frac{n_1 n_0^2 + n_0 n_1^2}{n^3} = \frac{(n_1 + n_0)n_1 n_0}{n^3} \tag{17.18}$$

$$= \frac{n_1 n_0}{n^2} \tag{17.19}$$

where the last equation follows from $n = (n_1 + n_0)$.

But that's almost the same as the Gini node impurity index, because that index (without the m subscript) is

$$Gini = 2\frac{n_1}{n}\frac{n_0}{n} = 2\frac{n_1 n_0}{n^2} \tag{17.20}$$

The difference is that the Gini index is multiplied by 2. That multiplication doesn't matter for finding the minimum value, so using the Gini index of node impurity or using MSE to find the best fit leads to the same result.

17.U2 UNDER THE HOOD: ON THE METHOD OF FINDING AN OPTIMAL THRESHOLD

In this section we show that the optimal threshold found by minimizing expected loss is the same optimal threshold that we would find if, instead, we searched for the maximum of the cost-sensitive Youden index.

Let's start by stating the two criteria. The first one is expected loss, $E[loss]$. We want the threshold value that minimizes this criterion. The second one is the cost-sensitive Youden index, in which both the prevalence rate and the relative losses are entered. This we denote with letter J, and we want the threshold value that maximizes this criterion. We will show that the two problems lead to the same selection of the threshold value.

$$E[loss] = fp \times loss(FP) + fn \times loss(FN)$$

$$J = sensitivity + specificity \times \frac{1 - prevalence}{relcost \times prevalence}$$

In the expected loss formula, $fp = \frac{FP}{N}$ and $fn = \frac{FN}{N}$ where $N = TP + FP + TN + FN$ is the total number of observations. J is the modified Youden index, and $relcost = \frac{loss(FN)}{loss(FP)}$ is the relative cost of a false negative to positive classification. $prevalence = \frac{TP+FN}{N}$ is the share of $y = 1$ observations, and, for future reference, $1 - prevalence = \frac{TN+FP}{N}$ is the share of $y = 0$ observations.

First rearrange the expected loss formula as

$$E[loss] = loss(FP) \times (fp + fn \times relcost)$$

This is minimized when $(fp + fn \times relcost)$ is minimized because the threshold selection doesn't affect $loss(FP)$.

Then realize that the sensitivity and the specificity we have in the modified Youden formula can be rewritten as

$$sensitivity = \frac{TP}{TP+FN} = 1 - \frac{FN}{TP+FN} = 1 - \frac{1}{N}\frac{FN}{\frac{TP+FN}{N}}$$

$$= 1 - \frac{1}{N}\frac{FN}{prevalence} = 1 - \frac{1}{prevalence}\frac{FN}{N}$$

$$= 1 - \frac{1}{prevalence}fn$$

$$specificity = \frac{TN}{TN+FP} = 1 - \frac{FP}{TN+FP} = 1 - \frac{1}{N}\frac{FP}{\frac{TN+FP}{N}}$$

$$= 1 - \frac{1}{N}\frac{FP}{1-prevalence} = 1 - \frac{1}{1-prevalence}\frac{FP}{N}$$

$$= 1 - \frac{1}{1-prevalence}fp$$

so that the modified Youden formula simplifies to

$$J = \left(1 - \frac{1}{prevalence}fn\right) + \left(1 - \frac{1}{1-prevalence}fp\right)\frac{1-prevalence}{relcost \times prevalence}$$

$$= \left(1 + \frac{1-prevalence}{relcost \times prevalence}\right) + \frac{relcost}{prevalence}(-fn \times relcost - fp)$$

This is maximized if $(-fn \times relcost - fp)$ is maximized, because the term in the first parentheses is not affected by the threshold choice, and, similarly, the factor $\frac{relcost}{thefactor\ prevalence}$ that multiplies the second parentheses is not affected by the threshold choice, either. But this is maximized when its negative is minimized, and its negative is nothing other than $(fn \times relcost + fp)$. And this is exactly where expected loss is minimized.

18 Forecasting from Time Series Data

How to use time series data for predictions with the help of trends, seasonality, serial correlation, and predicted values of other variables

Motivation

Your task is to predict the number of daily tickets sold for next year in a swimming pool in a large city. The swimming pool sells tickets through its sales terminal that records all transactions. You aggregate that data to daily frequency. How should you use the information on daily sales to produce your forecast? In particular, how should you model trend, and how should you model seasonality by months of the year and days of the week to produce the best prediction?

Your task is to predict how home prices will move in a particular city in the next months. You have monthly data on the home price index of the city, and you can collect monthly data on other variables that may be correlated with how home prices move. How should you use that data to forecast changes in home prices for the next few months? In particular, how should you use those other variables to help that forecast even though you don't know their future values?

In the previous chapters we discussed the logic and practice of prediction without specifying whether the data we use is cross-sectional or time series. At the same time, our case studies used cross-sectional data and applied the estimated patterns of association in such data to predict a target variable in some future live data. Sometimes our prediction problem requires using time series data. The fundamental logic of prediction is the same whatever kind of data we use. But prediction using time series data can have specific issues that require specific solutions.

This chapter discusses forecasting: prediction from time series data for one or more time periods in the future. The focus of this chapter is forecasting future values of one variable, by making use of past values of the same variable, and possibly other variables, too. We build on what we learned about time series regressions in Chapter 12. We start with forecasts with a long horizon, which means many time periods into the future. Such forecasts use information on trends, seasonality, and other long-term features of the time series. We then turn to short-horizon forecasts that forecast y for a few time periods ahead. These forecasts make use of serial correlation of the time series of y besides those long-term features. We introduce autoregression (AR) and ARIMA models, which capture the patterns of serial correlation and can use it for short-horizon forecasting. We then turn to using other variables in forecasting, and introduce vector autoregression (VAR) models that help in forecasting future values of those x variables that we can use to forecast y. We discuss how to carry out cross-validation in forecasting and the specific challenges and opportunities the time series nature of our data provide for assessing external validity.

We use two case studies in this chapter. The first one is **Forecasting daily ticket volumes for a swimming pool**, and it uses the `swim-transactions` dataset. This case study illustrates the use of trend, and, especially, of seasonality, in forecasting for many time periods ahead. The second one is **Forecasting a home price index**, which uses the monthly time series `case-shiller-la` dataset. This case study illustrates how we can apply ARIMA models of serial correlation in the target variable, and VAR models that include other variables, too, in forecasts for a few time periods ahead.

Learning outcomes

After working through this chapter, you should be able to:

- build time series regression models to make forecasts for long time horizons by capturing trends, seasonality, and predictable events;
- build time series regression models to make forecasts for short time horizons by capturing the patterns of serial correlation with the help of ARIMA;
- build vector autoregression (VAR) models to use the predicted values of x variables in forecasting y;
- use cross-validation for time series to select the best forecasting model.

18.1   Forecasting: Prediction Using Time Series Data

Forecasting is a special case of prediction that uses time series data to predict the future values of a y variable. Typically, we use data on y available through time period T to forecast its values for later time periods. We want to make the forecast using data up to time period T, and we want to predict the value of the target variable for multiple time periods ahead, for $T+1$, $T+2$, ... Thus, we use data

$$y_1, y_2, ..., y_T \qquad (18.1)$$

to make forecasts

$$\hat{y}_{T+1}, \hat{y}_{T+2}, ..., \hat{y}_{T+H} \qquad (18.2)$$

We use the term **forecast horizon** for the length of the time period we want to forecast for; in the formula above, that's H. When we forecast for a few time periods, so that H is a small number, we say that we forecast for a short horizon. When H is a large number, we say that we forecast for a long horizon.

Note that the forecast horizon is defined in terms of the number of time periods for which we prepare our forecast and not some objective length of time. Thus, it depends on the frequency of the time series (we introduced time series frequency in Chapter 2, Section 2.3). For example, forecasting for three months ahead would be a long-horizon forecast for hourly time series data, while it would be a short-horizon forecast for monthly time series data.

Sometimes we use other variables besides past values of y to make the forecast. Typically, we know the values of those other variables to time T, just like the values of the y time series:

$$x_1, x_2, ..., x_T \qquad (18.3)$$

We covered several important features of time series data in Chapter 12. Time series observations have a natural order and frequency (daily, monthly, and so on). The most important features of time series variables are potential trends, seasonality, random walk-like characteristics, and serial correlation. Discussing forecasting needs this separate chapter because those features raise specific issues related to model building, cross-validation, and holdout sample evaluation.

> ### Review Box 18.1   The basics of forecasting
>
> - Forecasting is a special case of prediction.
> - Forecasting makes use of time series data on y, and possibly other variables x.
> - The original data used for forecasting is a time series from 1 through T, such as $y_1, y_2, ..., y_T$
> - The forecast is prepared for time periods after the original data ends, such as $\hat{y}_{T+1}, \hat{y}_{T+2}, ..., \hat{y}_{T+H}$.
> - The length of the live time series data (here H) is the forecast horizon.
> - Short-horizon forecasts are carried out for a few observations after the original time series; long-horizon forecasts are carried out for many observations.

18.2   Holdout, Training, and Test Samples in Time Series Data

We discussed in Chapters 13 through 17 that we should build models on training samples, select the best predictor model using k-fold cross-validation, and evaluate the final predictive model using a holdout sample. So far, the holdout sample has been a random subsample of the original data, and the training and test samples have been randomly selected, too, using the remainder of the original data.

However, when forecasting from time series, things are more complicated. Typically, in time series data, it usually matters whether an observation is before another one and whether two observations are close to each other. True, we may have time series variables whose values aren't related to each other across time and whose ordering doesn't matter: percentage returns to company stocks were an example for that in Chapter 12, Section 12.A1. But that's rare. In most forecasting analyses when creating holdout, test, and training sets, we need to take into account the characteristics of time series variables. If we were to select them in a random fashion, we would remove observations from their neighborhoods, and we would put them together without paying attention to how far they were from each other in the original time series data.

Instead, therefore, it is good practice to take uninterrupted time series segments as samples. Thus we would select a holdout time series, and divide the rest between training and test time series. From a holdout set, we want to know how our forecast performs on the live data. Thus, it makes sense for the holdout time series to be as close to the live data as possible: at the end of our original time series data. By the same intuition, we may want our test time series to follow our training time series, although we'll see that that's not always the best choice.

The length of the holdout and test sets should depend on the forecasting horizon. Again, the principle is that we want our holdout and test samples to tell us what to expect in the live data forecasting situation. Therefore, it makes sense for these samples to be as long as the length of the forecasting horizon. If we want to forecast for six time periods, we want the holdout set to be a time series of the last six observations in the original data, and we want the test samples to be time series with six consecutive observations. If we want to forecast for the next year using daily data, we want both the holdout and the test sets to cover an entire year.

In fact, there are several ways to select training and test samples for cross-validation in time series data. We discuss two approaches here, which have their advantages and disadvantages. Each approach starts with setting aside the last time periods as a holdout set. Then, each selects non-overlapping time series for the test sets. The two approaches differ in the training sets.

The first approach is inserting test sets. It uses all remaining observations for the training sets, allowing for the training time series to continue after a test time series. The advantage of this approach is that it uses all observations in the work set for each fold (training + test set combination). Its disadvantage is that it disrupts the training time series. Thus, this approach is recommended when we don't want to make use of previous observations for the forecast. That's the case for long-horizon forecasts, with many time periods to predict for.

The second approach is rolling windows. For each test set, it uses only the observations before the test set for the training set. In order to make the training time series have the same length, we start the training time series later for later test sets. The advantage of this approach is that it doesn't disrupt the training time series, and yet it produces training sets of the same size across folds. Its disadvantage is that it doesn't use all observations in the work set for each fold (training + test set combination). This approach is recommended when we do want to make use of previous observations for the forecast, typically when we have a short forecast horizon.

Figures 18.1 and 18.2 show stylized examples for the two approaches. Our two case studies will illustrate both approaches.

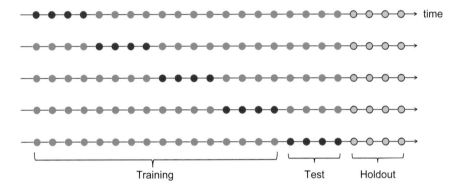

Figure 18.1   Time series forecast cross-validation with inserted test sets

Note: Colors denoting sets: green: training set, dark blue: test set, yellow: holdout set.

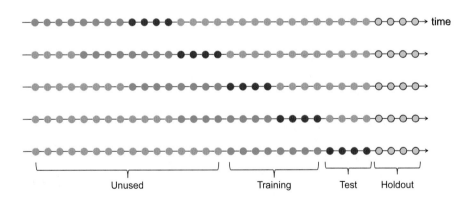

Figure 18.2   Time series forecast cross-validation with rolling windows

Note: Colors denoting sets: green: training set, dark blue: test set, yellow: holdout set; gray: observations not used.

With the appropriate holdout and test samples selected, we can evaluate the forecasts as usual, by computing MSE or its square root, RMSE. One thing to keep in mind when calculating these measures here is that they are now averages over time. For example, when forecasting for one year using monthly data, the MSE is an average of the forecast errors over 12 months. When forecasting for one year using daily data, the MSE is an average of the forecast errors over 365 days. By doing so, we give equal weight to how good our forecast is at different time periods (one day ahead versus 365 days ahead). That is consistent with a loss function that assigns the same loss to the different forecast time periods. If, instead, our forecast were to be used in a decision for which closer time periods matter more than time periods further out, we should use a modified loss function that gives larger weights to shorter horizon errors. In contrast, if our forecast were to be used in a decision for which longer horizons matter more, we would put more weight on longer horizon errors.

Review Box 18.2   Training, test, and holdout samples in forecasting

Consider a forecast for horizon H (e.g., 12 months, or 365 days).

- For the holdout set, reserve the last H time periods in the original data and use the rest as the work set.
- From the work set, select k test sets as non-overlapping, uninterrupted time series of length H.
- For each test set, select the corresponding training set in one of the following two ways:
  - Inserted test sets (for forecasts that don't use serial correlation): select all other observations, including those after the test set.
  - Rolling window training–test sets (for forecasts that use serial correlation): select the time series preceding the test set, in such a way that all training sets are of equal length.

18.3   Long-Horizon Forecasting: Seasonality and Predictable Events

When forecasting for a long time horizon (many periods ahead), we want to make use of features in the data that matter in the long run. The most important of such features are trend, seasonality, and the random walk property; we discussed each of these in Chapter 12, Sections 12.2 and 12.3. A time series has a trend if it tends to change in one direction. Seasonality means regularly occurring differences. A time series follows a random walk or a more general unit-root process if its change is completely random so its spread increases with time.

In Chapter 12, our goal was to use time series data to uncover patterns of association between y and x. For such analyses, these features created challenges, potentially leading to spurious association or biased standard error estimates. Thus, we discussed models that would address these features to eliminate, or mitigate, their influences. But here our goal is different: we want to predict future values of y. For forecasts, some of those features turn out to be great help.

The most helpful of such features is seasonality. That is especially true for forecasts with a daily or higher frequency such as hours or minutes. While we tend to think of seasonality as regular differences across seasons of the year, regular differences related to days of the week or hours of the day can be just as important for time series of high frequency. Besides such regular cycles, there may be specific time periods that tend to be different in regularly recurring ways, such as holidays.

For example, traffic at internet sites tends to have regular differences between hours of the day and between days of the week, and perhaps between months of the year, too. In addition, specific days of the year may see exceptionally high traffic (e.g., for web stores, "cyber Monday," the Monday after Thanksgiving weekend in the USA) or exceptionally low traffic (e.g., widely observed holidays for work-related websites such as data repositories).

The simplest way to model seasonality in regressions is to include seasonal binary variables, also known as season dummies (Chapter 12, Section 12.2) for months, days of the week, holidays, hours of the day, and so on. A regression-based prediction with y_t on the left-hand side and season dummies representing S number of seasons on the right-hand side is

$$\hat{y}_t = \hat{\beta}_0 + \sum_{s=1}^{S-1} \hat{\beta}_s season_{st} \tag{18.4}$$

Here $season_{st}$ is one if time period t is in season s, and it's zero otherwise. As usual, we include one fewer season dummies than the number of seasons (11 dummies for the 12 months, 6 dummies for the 7 days of the week, and so on). Here $\hat{\beta}_0$ is predicted y for the reference season (month, day), and $\hat{\beta}_0 + \hat{\beta}_s$ is predicted y for season s.

This is of course quite a restricted model, predicting the same y for all time periods in the same season. For example, with daily data and day-of-week dummies, this model predicts the same y for all Mondays, the same y for all Tuesdays, and so on. For models with both month dummies and day-of-week dummies, we would make predicted y differ between Mondays and Tuesdays by the same amount in every month, except at different levels.

But the same modeling framework allows for using more complicated seasonal patterns in fore-casting. In particular, we can allow for the differences at various levels of seasonality to differ: day-of-the-week differences to be different in various months, for example. To capture such differ-ence, we need to interact the dummies of different levels: month dummies with day-of-the-week dummies, day-of-the-week dummies with hour-of-day dummies, and so on.

Another kind of seasonality is regularly recurring specific time periods, such as holidays, or days or hours of specific events that are scheduled on known dates and times (e.g., scheduled web main-tenance, scheduled sports events). We can model such specific time periods similarly to regular seasonality, by including dummy variables in the regression.

The important thing to keep in mind here is that we can use patterns for prediction only if we can identify those patterns not only in the original data but in the live data, too. That is true for specific events as well: we can use them in prediction only if we know when they would happen ahead of time. Thus, for example, we can't use the effects of unpredictable events on y, such as pandemics, natural disasters or political crises, for prediction. We may be able to identify observations that are affected by such events in the original data, but we won't be able to tell which, if any, observations would be affected by such events in the live data. Therefore, we shouldn't include variables that denote unpredictable events in our model. Instead, we should treat variation in y due to such events as irreducible prediction error (Chapter 13, Section 13.3). Examples for predictable events that we can have in a forecast include holidays or events that are scheduled well in advance.

18.4   Long-Horizon Forecasting: Trends

Trends are also potentially important in any forecast, especially long-horizon (many periods ahead) forecasts. Recall from Chapter 12, Section 12.2, that a variable has trend if it has a tendency to increase or decrease. When our goal is prediction, we may model a trend in two ways: estimating the average change or fitting a trend line.

The first way to model a trend starts by transforming the y variable into changes ($\Delta y_t = y_t - y_{t-1}$) – we covered this approach in Chapter 12, Section 12.2. We may transform y into relative changes, too, which can be approximated by log changes ($\Delta \ln(y)_t = \ln(y)_t - \ln(y)_{t-1}$). Then we estimate a linear trend as

$$\widehat{\Delta y} = \hat{a} \tag{18.5}$$

where we omitted the t subscript after $\widehat{\Delta y}$ because the change is predicted to be the same ($\hat{a}$) wherever we are in the time series (whatever the value of t is).

That's a prediction of how y changes from one time period to the next one. It's not a prediction of y in any particular time period. To get that, we need to add the predicted change to some baseline level. And that baseline level is the last observation in our original data: y_T. Thus,

$$\hat{y}_{T+1} = y_T + \widehat{\Delta y} \tag{18.6}$$

$$\hat{y}_{T+2} = \hat{y}_{T+1} + \widehat{\Delta y} = y_T + 2 \times \widehat{\Delta y} \tag{18.7}$$

$$\dots$$

$$\hat{y}_{T+H} = y_T + H \times \widehat{\Delta y} \tag{18.8}$$

This is extra work indeed, but it's quite intuitive. To predict y when our model predicts Δy, we add the predicted Δy to the last observation in the data we have, then we add the predicted Δy to that prediction, and so on.

The second way of modeling trend involves fitting a **trend line** on the level of the variable. The trend line is a function of time itself. The simplest trend line is linear in time, with an intercept and a slope multiplying the time variable:

$$\hat{y}_t = \hat{a} + \hat{\delta}t \tag{18.9}$$

Here $\hat{a}$ is predicted y when $t = 0$, and $\hat{\delta}$ tells us how much predicted y changes if t is increased by one unit. To get the value of predicted y, we simply use the estimated $\hat{a}$ and $\hat{\delta}$ coefficients and the value of t. This model captures a linear trend, but we can generalize it to capture potential nonlinear trends, by including polynomials or piecewise linear splines, or even more complex functions.

There is an important difference between models that capture trend as changes and models that capture trend by fitting a trend line. When we model changes, we assume that y continues from the last observation and increases by the same amount each time. If the last observation in our data happens to be an unusually large or small y value, a trend modeled as change would continue from that unusual value. In contrast, with a trend line, we assume that y remains close to the trend line. If the last observation was an unusual value, that would not matter much for the forecast, because the forecast would be the trend line. Neither approach is inherently better than the other. When y is a random walk with a drift (see Chapter 12, Section 12.3), modeling the trend as a change is the right solution. In general we should let our model selection tools decide on whether changes or trend lines give a better forecast.

When we have trend in the y variable, the role of estimation error increases for forecasts that are further ahead in the future. When we model the trend as a change, any estimation error will compound as we add the estimated changes to get forecasts further ahead. When we estimate a trend line, its estimation error will have a more severe consequence further ahead, because an estimation error in the slope of the trend line leads to larger prediction errors further ahead.

Note that if y follows a random walk (with or without a drift), the prediction error tends to grow as we forecast further ahead even more than suggested by a trend. That's because the irreducible component of the prediction error grows, too, for a random walk. Indeed, random walks are said to be unpredictable after too many steps. What that really means is that the irreducible prediction error becomes very large, and thus the prediction interval becomes very wide.

Thus, when producing long-term forecasts, seasonality is our friend if we can model it as stable differences – e.g., as regressions of y_t on season dummies, including, possibly, interactions between different kinds of seasonality. Trends are more problematic because they lead to less and less precise predictions for forecasts further ahead, due to increasing estimation and model errors. Random walks are the most problematic to forecast for the long horizon, because not only their estimation error but also their irreducible error grows for time periods further ahead.

> **Review Box 18.3   Forecasting for the long run using seasonality and trends**
>
> - Seasonal differences and differences related to predictable events can be a great help in forecasting.
> - We can model trend as a change, e.g., $\widehat{\Delta y} = \hat{a}$. Then we forecast y values by adding predicted changes to the last observation in the original time series (to y_T).
> - Alternatively, we can model trend as trend line, e.g., $\hat{y}_t = \hat{a} + \hat{\delta}t$.
> - An estimated trend leads to larger prediction error further ahead.

18.A1   CASE STUDY – Forecasting Daily Ticket Volumes for a Swimming Pool

Question and data

Our first case study is forecasting swimming pool ticket sales in an outdoor swimming pool in Albuquerque (ABQ, in short), the largest city in New Mexico, USA. In particular, we want to predict the number of tickets sold (ticket volume) for each day for one year in the future. We use the swim-transactions dataset in this case study.

The data is transaction level ticket sales for each swimming pool in the city, available because of the open data policy of the city. This is Big Data: an admin (transaction) data with a lot of observations (over 1.5 million transactions), and it is collected automatically from point of sales or POS terminals (i.e., ticketing systems operating at the pool). The raw data is from January 1999 to November 2017; we use the data from January 1, 2010 to December 31, 2016. For each transaction, we know the number of tickets sold, the date and time of the transaction, the name of the swimming pool, the type of the ticket (such as adult or senior), and a special category used for discounts and events.

For this case study we selected one large outdoor swimming pool, called Sunport. You are invited to replicate this prediction analysis for other pools as a data exercise.

Like most Big Data, transaction data is not collected for the purpose of analysis (see Chapter 1, Section 1.5). We identified two main problems, and asked the data managers at the city to help with their domain knowledge. First, some values are negative for the number of tickets sold. The managers of the dataset informed us that negative amounts are likely to be corrections to entries made earlier; some of those entries had to be corrected because they were errors, and others because they were free tickets for attending specific events. Importantly, this adjustment could happen on the same day of the event or at a later day.

The second problem is that in a few cases (about one percent of the entries), the number of tickets is extremely large, with the largest number being 2762 tickets sold at once (at a single pool at a single point in time). The data managers informed us that the headcount is added at the end of the day, end of the weekend, or end of the week for large events, and such events typically include many spectators.

Hence, we focused on ticket types that reflect normal business: adult, senior, teen, child, and toddler issued under normal circumstances. Out of the 114 thousand transactions, we dropped 9 thousand transactions with this decision. Most of these are spectator tickets, but they also include military tickets. Most transactions have a few tickets – the average is 1.4. However, some transactions involve groups with dozens of tickets at once. Negative values and large positive values among these ticket types imply corrections, so we kept them.

We aggregated the transaction-level data into daily frequency. The y variable in this data is the number of tickets sold; we'll also refer to it as ticket volume or simply volume. Our daily time series data has 2522 observations spanning 7 years. In each year, there are a few days, for which the swimming pool is closed. Thus, our data is a time series with daily frequency and with a few gaps. We divided this data into a work set with years 2010 to 2015 and a holdout set with year 2016.

To get a feel for the strength of trends and seasonality, let us first look at the graphs of daily sales, first for just one year, 2015, in Figure 18.3a, then for the other five years in our work set 18.3b. The figures suggest that there is strong seasonal variation in daily volumes, but there is no visible trend.

While the plotted time series show the importance of monthly seasonality within years, they are not ideal to capture the magnitude of those seasonal differences. Moreover, they are not good at showing within-week seasonality. To capture those differences, we created box plots by months of the year and by days of the week. Figures 18.4a and 18.4b show the results.

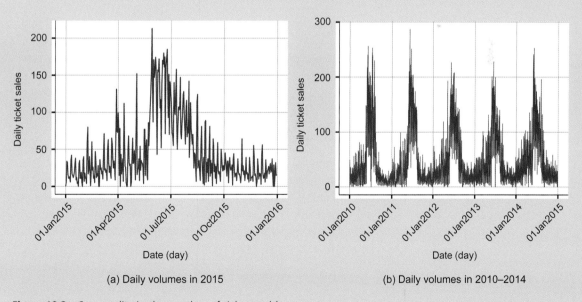

(a) Daily volumes in 2015   (b) Daily volumes in 2010–2014

Figure 18.3   Seasonality in the number of tickets sold

Source: `swim-transactions` dataset. Daily time series, 2010 to 2016, N=2522 (work set 2010–2015, N=2162).

The figures show strong monthly seasonality, with a lot more visitors in the summer, especially in June and July, and a lot fewer visitors in other months, especially in October through February. Daily seasonality is also important. Weekends are typically busier than weekdays, and Fridays tend to have especially low volumes (as some events are scheduled for Friday).

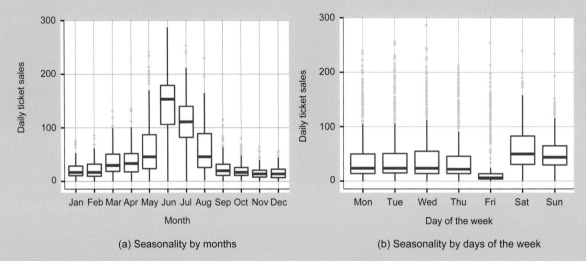

(a) Seasonality by months   (b) Seasonality by days of the week

Figure 18.4   Monthly and daily seasonality in the number of tickets sold

Note: Box plots.
Source: `swim-transactions` dataset. Daily time series, 2010 to 2016, N=2522 (work set 2010–2015, N=2162).

Because seasonal differences are strong both across months and across days, we should ask whether these two levels of seasonality are related. In other words, are day-of-the-week differences the same in different months or different? A heatmap is a useful tool to explore patterns of association along two dimensions, such as seasonality by month and day. A **heatmap** is a three-dimensional figure shown in two dimensions, with the third dimension visualized by colors, with darker colors meaning higher values. Here the horizontal axis is days of the week, the vertical axis is months of the year, and the color shows daily ticket volumes averaged over the years.

Figure 18.5 shows average daily volumes for the 2010–2015 period by day of the week and months. The bottom left cell is looking at all Mondays in January and taking the average of tickets sold; the top right cell is looking at Sundays in December.

The most important message from the heatmap is that day-of-the-week differences are different in summer months than in other months. The low volumes on Fridays are present for the school year but not for summer months, and volumes on Sundays are more similar across months than other days.

After sample design, let's turn to model building. We specified four models. The simplest one, M1 has a trend and monthly binary variables, M2 adds day-of-the-week binary variables, M3 adds holidays as a set of binary variables for each holiday. Model M4 also has day-of-the-week binary variables interacted with a binary variable for school holidays, as another kind of seasonality. M5 also has weekend dummy times monthly binary variables to capture the interaction of monthly and daily seasonality that we documented. Finally, we specified model M6, which is same as Model 4, except it has y in logs.

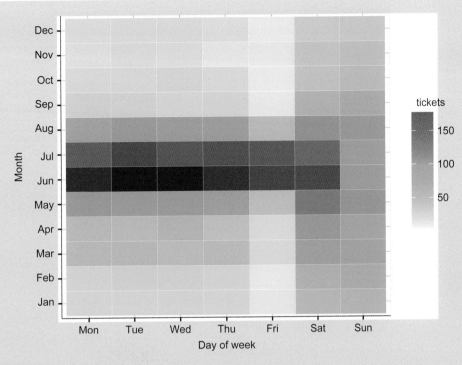

Figure 18.5 Heatmap for ABQ Sunport swimming pool data

Note: 2010–2015 average values.
Source: `swim-transactions` dataset. Daily time series, 2010 to 2016, N=2522 (work set 2010–2015, N=2162).

Our Model 7 is the result of a model-building algorithm called **Prophet**. Prophet is a time series prediction tool that builds and tests models in an automated fashion, allowing for a lot of flexibility in the modeling choices. In particular, Prophet is an algorithm that automatically builds a regression model with trend and seasonality. It assumes that trend, seasonality, and irregular events, as groups of variables may be added linearly. The model is able to find change points for trends and interactions between trend and seasonality. We used Prophet to build a model using information on year, month, and day or the week, without specifying school holidays. Thus, M7 uses less information but allows for more flexible functional forms than models M3 through M6. You are invited to use Prophet for prediction adding the holidays as a data exercise.

To select the best of these models, we carried out 6-fold cross-validation. The test sets were 2010,..., 2015, and the corresponding training sets included all other years in the work set, both preceding and following the test set (the inserted test sets approach, see Section 18.2). Table 18.1 summarizes the models and shows the cross-validated RMSE for each. According to the results, our best forecasting model is M5: it includes a linear trend, dummies for months, school holidays and days of the week, and it includes the interaction of days of the week with school holidays and, separately, with months. By their cross-validated RMSE, the close second best is M4 (the one without the day-of-the-week and month interactions). Apparently, M3 and M4 slightly underfit the test data and so does Prophet, because school holidays are important. Comparing models M2 and M7 that use the same information, Prophet (M7) gives a better prediction.

Table 18.1   Model features and RMSE

	trend	months	days	holidays	school*days	days*months	RMSE
M1	X	X					32.35
M2	X	X	X				31.45
M3	X	X	X	X			31.45
M4	X	X	X	X	X		27.61
M5	X	X	X	X	X	X	26.90
M6 (log)	X	X	X	X	X		30.99
M7 (Prophet)	X	X	X		N/A	N/A	29.47

Note: Trend is linear trend, days is day-of-the-week, holidays: national US holidays, school*days is school holiday (mid-May to mid-August and late December) interacted with days of week. RMSE is cross-validated.

Source: `swim-transactions` dataset. Daily time series, 2010–2016, N=2522 (work set 2010–2015, N=2162).

To evaluate the actual fit of our winning model, we estimated model M5 on the entire work set and applied its prediction to the holdout set. The RMSE on the holdout set is RMSE=24.57. This is actually smaller than the cross-validated RMSE across the test sets, which is good news, as it suggests that the patterns of association behind our prediction remained stable for the test set (see more about this later, in Section 18.9). Figure 18.6 shows the time series of our forecast together with the time series of actual ticket volumes in 2016.

The figure shows that our forecast captures the shape of monthly and daily seasonality in the holdout set, which suggests, again, that those patterns are quite stable. At the same time, it also shows that our forecast doesn't typically capture especially high or especially low volumes. To see it more clearly, Figure 18.7a shows actual versus predicted ticket volumes for August 2016.

As a final diagnostic step, Figure 18.7b shows RMSE on the holdout set for each month in 2016. This figure suggests that our model performs similarly across months, which is a good sign, except that it makes larger errors in December – possibly related to variations in the daily schedule during the Christmas break. That shows a problem: to produce better forecasts for Decembers, we may need to incorporate the precise days of the Christmas break into our model.

This concludes our case study. The goal of the case study was to predict daily ticket volumes for a particular open-air swimming pool. We used administrative transaction-level data for seven years, which we aggregated to daily data after some cleaning. From this data we reserved the last year as our holdout set and used the rest as our work set. From the work set, we selected complete years as test sets and all other observations as the corresponding training sets, including those following the corresponding test set.

We specified various models to capture trend and seasonality. For seasonality, we included months, days of the week, and school holidays, and we interacted these for some of our more complicated models. We also specified a model for log volumes instead of volumes as the target variable, and we used the Prophet tool for automatic model building. In the end, we found that our hand-built model with interacted seasonality and school holidays was the best. From among the models that didn't include school holidays, the Prophet-built model was the best. Finally, we evaluated the best prediction on our holdout set and found that it captured the patterns of seasonality reasonably well, but it pointed to a problem with predicting ticket volumes in December.

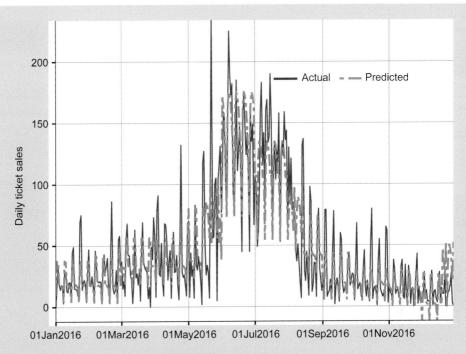

Figure 18.6 Daily swimming pool ticket volume forecasts

Note: Predictive model M5, see text for details.
Source: `swim-transactions` dataset. Daily time series, 2010–2016, N=2522 (holdout set is 2016, N=366).

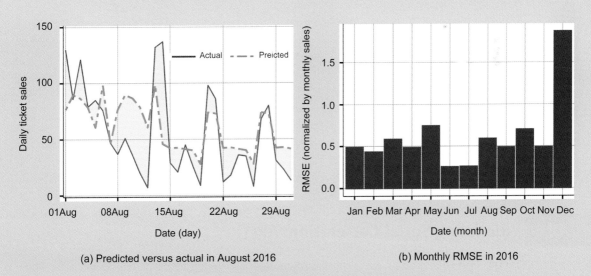

(a) Predicted versus actual in August 2016   (b) Monthly RMSE in 2016

Figure 18.7 Prediction diagnostics on the holdout set (2016)

Note: Holdout predictions, Model M5.
Source: `swim-transactions` dataset. Daily time series, 2010 to 2016, N=2522 (holdout set is 2016, N=366).

What can we conclude from our results? First, we found that seasonality is indeed a very important pattern for long-horizon forecasts, including predictable special time periods (in this case school holidays). Second, we found that the best model captured the interaction between different levels of seasonality and holidays. Third, from among the models that didn't use holidays, the model selected by the automated Prophet tool was the best, but it was not the overall best model because of the importance of holidays. Fourth, we found that our best prediction gave a reasonably good fit on the holdout time series, suggesting that the seasonal patterns behind the prediction remained stable. Finally, we used diagnostic tools to identify a weakness of our prediction model (bad fit in December) that could motivate building a better model.

18.5   Forecasting for a Short Horizon Using the Patterns of Serial Correlation

When the forecast horizon is short (i.e., we forecast few periods ahead), short-run characteristics of time series can help in the forecast besides seasonality and trend. These are dependence of the values of y between neighboring time periods, and dependence with contemporaneous or lagged values of some x variables. In this section, and the next few sections, we continue focusing on time series data with a single y variable. We'll discuss how to use other variables in subsequent sections.

Recall from Chapter 12, Section 12.6, that the correlation across time between observations of the same y variable is called **serial correlation**, or **autocorrelation**. With positive serial correlation we expect a higher than average value of y_t if its value was higher than average in earlier time periods ($y_{t-1}, y_{t-2}, \ldots$). With negative serial correlation, we expect a lower than average value of y_t if its value was higher than average in earlier time periods.

That feature of time series variables becomes very helpful for short-horizon forecasts. With serial correlation, we can get a better forecast $\hat{y}_{T+1}$ if we take that serial correlation into account, because we know the value of the previous observation, y_T. The same is true for $\hat{y}_{T+2}$, although typically to a smaller extent. In time series, the further away observations are, the weaker the serial correlation. Thus, serial correlation tends to help more, the closer the forecast time period to our last observation.

Besides serial correlation, seasonality and trends may also matter in the short run. So we should take them into account when building our forecasting model. Note the asymmetry here: serial correlation matters for short-horizon forecasts only, while trend and seasonality matter for both short-horizon forecasts and long-horizon forecasts.

In order to use serial correlation for forecasting, we need to build it into our model and estimate it. We discuss such models in the next two sections.

18.6   Modeling Serial Correlation: AR(1)

Autoregressive models, abbreviated as **AR models**, aim to capture the patterns of serial correlation in a variable in time series data. AR models are linear regressions in which the value of a variable y at time t is regressed on its lags, that is its past values, $y_{t-1}, y_{t-2}, \ldots$ The simplest autoregressive model includes one lag only, and is called **AR(1)**:

$$y_t^E = \beta_0 + \beta_1 y_{t-1} \tag{18.10}$$

Here β_0 means average y in time periods when y was zero in the previous time period; β_1 measures how much higher y is on average if it was one unit higher in the previous time period. And β_1 is also the coefficient of first-order serial correlation. That's because the slope coefficient of a simple linear regression is equal to the correlation coefficient between the left-hand-side variable and the right-hand-side variable if the standard deviation of the two variables is the same (Chapter 7, Section 4.U1). And here those standard deviations are the same because the variables themselves are the same, only one is a lagged observation. Thus, β_1 is the serial correlation coefficient. As all correlation coefficients, it's less than one and greater than negative one (negative values indicate negative serial correlation).

For a one-period-ahead forecast from an AR(1) model with estimated coefficients $\hat{\beta}_0$ and $\hat{\beta}_1$, we plug in the value of y observed at T:

$$\hat{y}_{T+1} = \hat{\beta}_0 + \hat{\beta}_1 y_T \tag{18.11}$$

Forecasting to $T + 2$ would need y_{T+1} in the formula. But when making the forecast, our last observation is y_T. Therefore, instead of y_{T+1}, we need to use its predicted value, $\hat{y}_{T+1}$:

$$\hat{y}_{T+2} = \hat{\beta}_0 + \hat{\beta}_1 \hat{y}_{T+1} = \hat{\beta}_0 + \hat{\beta}_1(\hat{\beta}_0 + \hat{\beta}_1 y_T) = \hat{\beta}_0(1 + \hat{\beta}_1) + \hat{\beta}_1^2 y_T \tag{18.12}$$

And so forth with longer time horizons. Because β_1 is less than one (in absolute value), its square is smaller, and higher powers are even smaller. Thus, the contribution of $\hat{\beta}_1$ gets smaller and smaller as we predict further ahead, to reach practically zero after a while. We see in this model what's true in general: serial correlation tends not to add to forecasts far ahead in time.

We can specify an AR(1) model when y is in changes not levels, too ($\Delta y_t = y_t - y_{t-1}$). Then, to make a forecast, we need to add the predicted changes to the last y_T value we have, as we have seen in Section 18.4.

When using an AR(1) model for prediction, the prediction error is bound to be larger, the longer the forecast horizon. That's true whether we have the original AR model estimated in changes of y or levels of y. This is because at longer horizons we use variables in the model that are forecasts themselves (e.g., $\hat{y}_{T+1}$ when forecasting $\hat{y}_{T+2}$). Hence, when substituting for those predicted values, we use the estimated coefficients, which have estimation error.

18.7 Modeling Serial Correlation: ARIMA

The AR(1) model captures a specific kind of serial correlation. It estimates that serial correlation between adjacent observations is $\hat{\beta}_1$, serial correlation between observations that are two time periods apart is $\hat{\beta}_1^2$, and so on. But real-life time series variables may have other patterns of serial correlation.

In this section we briefly introduce **ARIMA** models that are generalizations of the AR(1) model and can approximate any pattern of serial correlation. We have a more detailed introduction, with formulae, in Under the Hood section 18.U1.

ARIMA models are put together from three parts: AR, I, and MA. AR stands for autoregression, I stands for being integrated, and MA stands for moving average. In this section, we summarize the key ideas, and Under the Hood section 18.U1 offers a detailed and formal discussion.

The first part of ARIMA is **AR**: an autoregressive model. In the previous section we discussed AR(1), which is a regression whose right-hand-side variable is the first lag of the left-hand-side variable. But we can include further lags on the right-hand side of the regression. The result is an AR(p), which predicts y_t using up to p of its own lags. Forecasting from AR(p) models is a generalization of forecasting from AR(1) models. The main difference is that the estimated coefficients in those additional lags play a role.

The last part of an ARIMA model is an **MA** model. MA models capture serial correlation in y in a way that is different from AR models. While AR models are good when serial correlation becomes smaller for longer lags in a gradual fashion, MA models are good when the serial correlation drops suddenly to zero after some lags. The letter q in the notation MA(q) refers to details in the model that also capture the number of lags after which serial correlation drops.

Putting together AR and MA models yield **ARMA** models. They have both an AR part with one or more lagged y variables on the right-hand side and an MA part. An ARMA(p,q) model has p lags for the AR model and captures q lags of serial correlation in the MA model.

The middle part of an ARIMA model is the letter I in the middle. That stands for whether the ARMA model is written in terms of y itself or its change, Δy. The general notation of the parameters of an ARIMA model is ARIMA(p,d,q): p is for AR, q is for MA, and d is for I. The technical term for I is "integrated." If the model is meant to capture serial correlation in y, it's not integrated and thus $d = 0$. If the model is meant to capture serial correlation in its change (Δy), it's said to be integrated and thus $d = 1$. In principle, we could have $d = 2$ for the change of the change, and so on, but those are rare in practice. Thus, most ARIMA(p,d,q) models are either ARIMA(p,0,q) models or ARIMA(p,1,q) models. An ARIMA(p,0,q) is an ARMA(p,q) model written in terms of y; an ARIMA(p,1,q) model is an ARMA(p,q) model written in terms of Δy. For example, an AR(1) model written out in terms of y is an ARIMA(1,0,0) model; an AR(1) model written out in terms of Δy is, instead, an ARIMA(1,1,0) model.

For a prediction purpose, the principles of selecting the best ARIMA(p,d,q) model are no different from the principles of selecting any other model. We can specify models that are different in terms of the p, d, and q, and examine their cross-validated RMSE. In practice, when we specify an ARIMA model, the first thing to decide on is whether to specify the model in terms of changes or levels of y: whether $d = 0$ or $d = 1$. Then we decide on whether and how we want to model trend and seasonality, and the last question is to decide on the p and q parameters of the ARIMA part. The larger p and/or q, the more complex the model as it has more coefficients to estimate. As usual, model complexity presents a trade-off between underfitting and overfitting the data.

Besides specifying and cross-validating ARIMA models by hand, we can make use of a search algorithm for p, d, and q. Such a search algorithm is called **auto-arima**. See more details about auto-arima in Under the Hood section 18.U2.

Review Box 18.4   Forecasts using serial correlation and ARIMA models

- In the short run (forecasting few periods ahead), serial correlation in y can be a great help in forecasting. In the long run, serial correlation tends not to help.
- ARIMA models capture complicated patterns of serial correlation in flexible ways and can therefore produce better forecasts at short horizons.
- ARIMA models are characterized by three parameters, p, d, and q, denoting an AR(p) part, an MA(q) part, and they may be specified in terms of y (then $d = 0$) or Δy (then $d = 1$).

18.B1   CASE STUDY – Forecasting a Home Price Index

Question, data, forecasting from *y* only, with ARIMA models

The second case study in this chapter, **Forecasting a home price index**, aims to forecast the home price index for the city of Los Angeles in California, USA. We use the `case-shiller-la` dataset. The data is a monthly time series of the S&P/Case–Shiller Greater Los Angeles Home Price Index between 2000 and 2017. With 18 years of monthly data, we have 216 observations.

A price index shows average market prices relative to a benchmark period. Here prices are compared to January 2000. The value of the price index in January 2000 is 100. In January 2017, its value was 254 meaning that home prices were 154% higher, on average, than in January 2000. Note that the data includes both the price index and its seasonally adjusted version. We work with the price index itself not its seasonally adjusted version, because forecasting the index itself is what can be relevant in decision making.

The goal of this case study is to forecast the price index for one year. With the monthly data at hand, this would be a 12-period forecast horizon, in which we are interested in the price index at time $T + 1$, $T + 2$, ..., $T + 12$. This is a relatively short horizon forecast, where serial correlation may matter as much as seasonality, especially for the first few months.

The time series of the index on the entire 2000–2017 time period is shown in Figure 18.8.

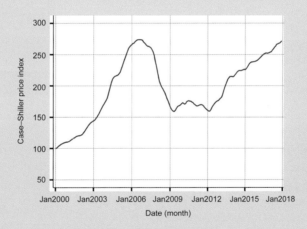

Figure 18.8   The Case–Shiller home price index, Los Angeles

Source: `case-shiller-la` dataset. Monthly time series, 2000–2017, N=216.

Looking at the time series we see no visible evidence of seasonality. Overall, there is positive trend in the data with a major downturn in 2007–2009. The trend appears exponential prior to the downturn, corresponding to the home price bubble of the 2000s. After the downturn, prices remained stagnant between 2009 and 2012, increased steeply in 2012 and 2013, and continued to increase in a linear fashion at a lower rate afterwards. The price index increased substantially from the beginning of the time period to its end, meaning that it had a positive trend overall. However, the trend is not linear, nor exponential, and there is no simple line that would appropriately describe its path.

Recall that our goal is to forecast the home price index for 12 months. To evaluate a 12-period forecast we need a 12-month long holdout time series and 12-month long test time series. We take the 12 months in 2017 as our holdout set and use 2000 to 2016 as work set. In our last section we look at year 2018 as our holdout set as an alternative.

In the work set time series of 2000–2016, we created four rolling window training–test splits from the rest of the time series. In particular, we took one-year test sets of 2013, 2014, 2015, 2016. The training sets are always 13 years before the test set; for example, it is 2000 to 2012 for the 2013 test set, and 2003 to 2015 for the 2016 test set. This rolling windows training–test split is in the spirit of Figure 18.2 in Section 18.2. We calculated cross-validated RMSE the usual way: we calculated MSE in each test set, took their average across the test sets, and took its square root. We considered several models and tested them with 4-fold cross-validation.

We considered six models. The target variable is p, the price index itself, for models M1 through M4. For model M5 the target variable is Δp; for model M6 it's ln p. We include trend in M1 and M4 as a trend line, and we include a constant in M5, which also captures a trend as its target variable is Δp. We include season dummies in all models except for M2. M1 and M5 are benchmark models that don't use the patterns of serial correlation for forecasting; all other models include an ARIMA part to fit the patterns of serial correlation. To capture the best-fitting ARIMA model for each specification, we used the auto-arima algorithm to select ARIMA(p,d,q) parameters for different models.

The summary of models and cross-validated RMSE results are shown in Table 18.2. The results suggest that M4 is the best model. M4 has the price index as its target variable, it includes a trend line, season dummies, and it makes use of the patterns of serial correlation with an ARIMA(2,0,0), which is nothing else than a simple AR(2).

Table 18.2   Home price index prediction from ARIMA models

id	target	ARIMA	trend	season	AR	I	MA	RMSE
M1	p	NO	X	X				31.9
M2	p	YES			1	1	2	9.5
M3	p	YES		X	1	1	0	4.1
M4	p	YES	X	X	2	0	0	2.2
M5	dp	NO	X	X				18.8
M6	lnp	YES		X	0	2	0	7.2

Note: Case–Shiller home price index for Los Angeles. 4-fold cross-validated RMSE. ARIMA features chosen by auto-arima.

Source: `case-shiller-la` dataset. Monthly time series, 2000–2017, N=216 (work set is 2000–2016, N=204).

Having chosen the best forecasting ARIMA model, we can evaluate its performance on the holdout set. Here we use year 2017 as our holdout set. The holdout set fit turns out to be very good. It has $RMSE = 1.3$, which is one third of the average test set RMSE. Figure 18.9a shows the predicted time series for 2017 together with the actual time series of the price index. Figure 18.9b shows the interval prediction (Chapter 13, Section 13.2). The 80% prediction interval has a fan shape, corresponding to the fact that the prediction error gets larger for forecasts at later time periods.

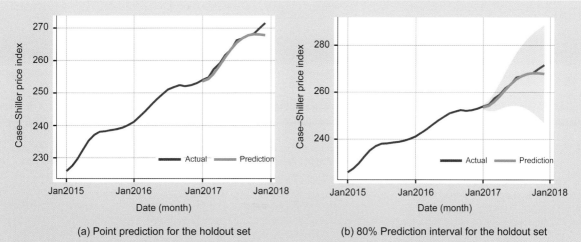

(a) Point prediction for the holdout set   (b) 80% Prediction interval for the holdout set

Figure 18.9   Predicted vs. actual home price index, Los Angeles in 2017

Note: Best ARIMA model trained and cross-validated on work set, prediction for the holdout set.
Source: `case-shiller-la` dataset. N=216 (work set is 2000–2016, N=204, holdout set is 2017, N=12).

     The point predictions fit the holdout time series very well. They are very close to the actual price index time series until the last time periods. In the last months of the holdout set, the prediction is lower than the actual price index, because, in 2017, the price index didn't decrease from its trend as much as it did at the end of the years in the work set. At the same time, the prediction interval becomes very wide after a few months. That reflects that patterns of the home price index time series changed considerably during the 17 years used as the work set, and thus the forecast is uncertain. The point predictions turn out to fit this holdout set very well, but prediction interval suggests that we should not expect the same to happen in other years.

18.8   VAR: Vector Autoregressions

The time series models considered so far use past values of y, and season dummy variables. They do not make use of other variables. Yet we can often produce better forecasts with the help of other variables, at least for short forecast horizons. The main problem when producing forecasts of y with the help of an x variable is that we need forecasts of the x variable as well. For example, when we want to use x_{T+1} to forecast y_{T+2}, we don't know the value of x_{T+1}. Instead, we need to forecast it, and for that, we need a model.

     Vector autoregression, abbreviated as **VAR**, is a method that incorporates other variables in time series regressions and can use those other variables for forecasting y. A VAR is a set of time series regressions. A VAR has as many regression equations as there are variables, with each variable as a dependent variable in one of the regressions. The right-hand side of each regression has the lags of all of the variables. Thus, all regressions have the same right-hand-side variables.

     The simplest VAR model has y and one x variable, and it includes one lag of each. Because it has one lag, this is called a VAR(1) model. To estimate such a model, we need time series data that includes the same number of observations and the same frequency for the x and y variables. This simple VAR model is a set of two time series regressions, with the lags of both variables on the right-hand side of each equation:

$$y_t^E = \beta_{10} + \beta_{11}y_{t-1} + \beta_{12}x_{t-1} \tag{18.13}$$

$$x_t^E = \beta_{20} + \beta_{21}y_{t-1} + \beta_{22}x_{t-1} \tag{18.14}$$

Here the β_{10}, β_{11}, and β_{12} are the coefficients in the first VAR regression; the β_{20}, β_{21}, and β_{22} are the coefficients in the second VAR regression.

For a one-period-ahead forecast of our target variable y, we don't actually need the coefficients from the second regression – only from the first one:

$$\hat{y}_{T+1} = \hat{\beta}_{10} + \hat{\beta}_{11}y_T + \hat{\beta}_{12}x_T \tag{18.15}$$

However, for forecasting y further ahead, we do need all coefficient estimates. That is because such forecasts use forecast values of x as well as y. A two-period-ahead forecast of y from a VAR(1) is

$$\hat{y}_{T+2} = \hat{\beta}_{10} + \hat{\beta}_{11}\hat{y}_{T+1} + \hat{\beta}_{12}\hat{x}_{T+1} \tag{18.16}$$

where $\hat{y}_{T+1} = \hat{\beta}_{10} + \hat{\beta}_{11}y_T + \hat{\beta}_{12}x_T$, and $\hat{x}_{T+1} = \hat{\beta}_{20} + \hat{\beta}_{21}y_T + \hat{\beta}_{22}x_T$. Forecasts for $T+3$, $T+4$, ..., are analogous.

As we can see, when making forecasts for more than one time period ahead, VAR models use forecasts of both the y and x variables. That means that they use the estimated coefficients from all of their equations to help such forecasts. That's the only way to make use of x variables: we don't know their future values, so we need to forecast those future values if we want to use them to forecast y. But that also means that many coefficients go into the y forecast, making the model more complex and resulting in larger estimation error and model error. In exchange, by using x variables, we can hope to reduce the otherwise irreducible error component of forecasts (recall that "irreducible" means we can't reduce it without using other information).

A VAR can have mode lags on the right-hand side: a VAR(2) has two lags of all variables on the right-hand side of each of its equations, a VAR(3) has three lags, and so on. And, of course, a VAR can have two or more variables, and, thus, two or more equations. There are four important characteristics of a VAR:

- A VAR has a regression for each of the variables.
- The right-hand side of each equation has all variables.
- Right-hand-side variables are in lags only.
- All right-hand-side variables in all regressions have the same number of lags.

When building a VAR model, first we decide what other variable or variables to include. We want variables that make a big difference in forecasting y, in the sense that their inclusion would lead to a great reduction of the otherwise irreducible prediction error. But we have to be economical with our choice. Including an additional variable into a VAR can increase its complexity a lot, and we want to avoid specifying too complex a model.

The second decision we always need to consider with time series regressions is whether to include the variables in levels or changes (or relative changes, possibly approximated by log changes). This decision should be based on whether the variables follow random walks: if they do, we should take changes (or relative changes). We have more than one variable in a VAR model, and some may follow a random walk while others may not. It is nevertheless good practice to include all variables in the same way: all in levels or all in changes.

The third decision is how many lags to include. Recall that this is a single choice with VAR models: we include the same number of lags of all variables in all equations. The more variables we include, and/or the more lags we include, the more complex the VAR model. The simple VAR(1) model with two variables that we wrote out earlier has six coefficients to estimate. A VAR(2) with two variables has two lags, and it would add two coefficients to each equation, resulting in ten coefficients altogether. A VAR(1) with three variables would have 12 coefficients (four in each of its three equations). A VAR(2) with three variables would have 21 coefficients. And so on. The trade-off with model complexity is the same as always: a more complex model may avoid underfitting the data, but it is more likely to overfit the data. In practice, we should select the number of lags by cross-validation – by comparing the cross-validated RMSE of VAR models that differ in the numbers of lags.

Review Box 18.5 VAR: vector autoregression

- VAR models are a set of time series regressions with more than one variable.
- VAR models have a regression for each variable; the lagged values of all variables are entered on the right-hand side of each equation, with the same number of lags everywhere.
- A VAR(1) model with two variables y and x is
  - $y_t^E = \beta_{10} + \beta_{11} y_{t-1} + \beta_{12} x_{t-1}$
  - $x_t^E = \beta_{20} + \beta_{21} y_{t-1} + \beta_{22} x_{t-1}$
- As with any time series regression, VAR models can have their variables in levels (logs) or changes (log changes) and can include trend lines and season dummies.
- We can use x variables to help predict y with the help of VAR models. For time periods further ahead, VAR models use predicted values of the x variables when predicting y.

18.B2 CASE STUDY – Forecasting a Home Price Index

Using other variables in the forecast with VAR

We specified VAR models with two additional variables for our case study. The first additional variable is the monthly unemployment rate: the number of unemployed divided by the number of people in the labor force (employed+unemployed). The unemployment rate may be thought of as an indicator for the business cycle. During economic booms the unemployment rate is low; during economic downturns the unemployment rate tends to be high. Unemployment rate is available for the entire state of California not for the city of Los Angeles, so we use that.

The second additional variable we include is total employment: the number of people who work for pay. Besides being another indicator of the business cycle, total employment is also an indicator of population: total employment can increase both due to the business cycle and population growth. We use total employment (in thousand people) instead of population itself because the latter is available at a yearly frequency only, while total employment is available at a monthly frequency. Similarly to the unemployment rate, we use total employment for the entire state of California.

Home prices, the business cycle, and population growth affect each other in complicated ways. For example, boom times may attract more population and raise home prices, a growing population in itself may increase home prices, and changes in home prices may affect immigration and thus population growth. Our goal is not to disentangle those relationships. Instead, we want to use the unemployment rate and total employment variables to help predict home prices. Thus, what we need is stability: the patterns of association between these variables should remain the same.

Figures 18.10a–d show the time series of unemployment rate, its month-to-month change, and total employment, and its month-to-month log change. The unemployment rate shows large swings with the business cycle. Total employment shows similar cyclical features but it also has a strong positive trend. There is strong seasonality in both time series.

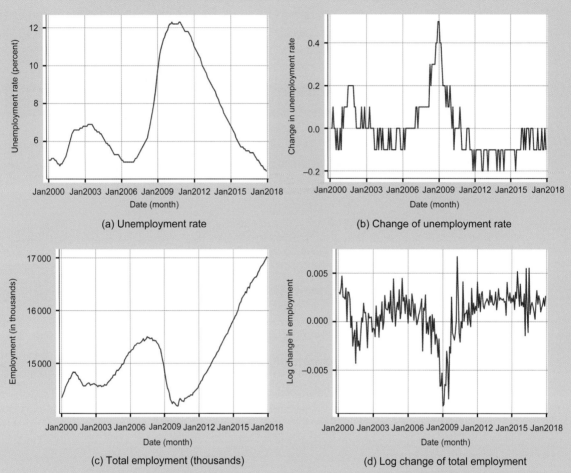

Figure 18.10   Time series of the two new variables: unemployment rate and total employment

Source: `case-shiller-la` dataset. Monthly time series, 2000 to 2017. N=216.

We include the y variable, price index, in changes (Δp) in the VAR due to its trend. To conform to the fact that y is in differences, we enter the unemployment rate as a difference ($\Delta unemp$), too, and total employment as log difference ($\Delta \ln emp$) – total employment has a trend, too. The formula for our model, the VAR(1) with month dummies, is:

$$\Delta p_t^{\,E} = \beta_{10} + \beta_{11}\Delta p_{t-1} + \beta_{12}\Delta \ln emp_{t-1} + \beta_{13}\Delta unemp_{t-1} + \sum_{m=1}^{11} \theta_{1m} D_m$$

$$\Delta \ln emp_t^{\,E} = \beta_{20} + \beta_{21}\Delta p_{t-1} + \beta_{22}\Delta \ln emp_{t-1} + \beta_{23}\Delta unemp_{t-1} + \sum_{m=1}^{11} \theta_{2m} D_m \qquad (18.17)$$

$$\Delta unemp_t^{\,E} = \beta_{30} + \beta_{31}\Delta p_{t-1} + \beta_{32}\Delta \ln emp_{t-1} + \beta_{33}\Delta unemp_{t-1} + \sum_{m=1}^{11} \theta_{3m} D_m$$

where the D_m are the month dummies, of which we include 11 and leave one out for the reference category. Note that while this is the simplest VAR model with three variables and month dummies, it already has $3 \times (1 + 3 + 11) = 45$ coefficients. A more complex model would have even more coefficients. In a sense, this VAR model builds on our previous model M3, which was an ARIMA(1,1,0) with seasonality. When evaluating the fit of our VAR model, model M3 is a useful benchmark.

The cross-validated RMSE result for the VAR is $RMSE = 4.4$. This is larger than the best predicting M4 model that used the time series of the price index itself. It is smaller than the RMSE of the more natural comparison model M3 (RMSE of M3 and M4 are in Table 18.2). Thus, it turns out, that the VAR model that uses the unemployment rate and total employment overfits the data. As a result, it does not give a better prediction than the time series model that used the home price index only.

18.9 External Validity of Forecasts

As with any prediction, forecasting from time series data is using information in the original data to guess the actual y values in the live data. We build fine-tuned models and select the best from them using sophisticated modeling and cross-validation techniques, and we can evaluate model performance using the holdout set. All of that uses the original data we have. Our methods help find the best model and evaluate its performance not in training sets but in the various test sets, and, thus, they can find the best model that fits the population, or general pattern, our original data represents.

That's all very well, but what we care about is how our forecasts will perform on the live data. As usual (see Chapter 13, Section 13.11), if external validity is high, the best predictive model in the population, or general pattern represented by the original data is also the best predictive model in the live data. And that happens if things are stable. More precisely, that happens when the forecast is stable, which means stability of all of the patterns of association that are used in the forecast. Thus, for high external validity we need those patterns to be stable.

Here, too, forecasting from time series introduces additional challenges but also provides some new opportunities. The additional challenge is due to the fact that now the prediction is not for one point in time in the future but many different points in time: $T+1$, $T+2$, all the way to $T+H$. This is an additional challenge because we can expect different degrees of external validity at different future time periods. The patterns in the original data and the live data may be very close to each other in time period $T+1$, but they may be less close in time period $T+H$. When evaluating forecasts, we usually take an MSE that is averaged over the forecast horizons. We do that to select and evaluate models that are good over the entire forecast horizon we care about. But that's all in the original data. How different the patterns are close versus far off may itself change in the future. And that's something that we can't take into account when building, selecting, or evaluating our forecasting models.

At the same time, evaluating forecasts in time series data provides additional opportunities to assess external validity. Following good practice, the training–test split of the data for cross-validation is not random: it results in uninterrupted test time series. We can use this feature of time series cross-validation to get some insight into how stable our forecasts are. For example, we may find that the same model is the best in all test sets, and it produces similar RMSE in those test sets. This would be reassuring, supporting the stability of our forecasts across time. Of course, this wouldn't in itself prove that things will remain stable for the live data, too. But it would be a good sign. Or, in contrast, we may find that the best model is different in the different test sets, and/or the fit is very different in the different test sets. Such findings would raise concerns with the stability of our forecasts. If the best model is different across test sets, or the fit of a single model varies widely across test sets, we should be worried. These are signs of instability, signaling low external validity of our forecast.

Review Box 18.6   External validity of forecasts

- External validity of forecasts may vary across observations within the same live time series: it's likely higher for forecasts for the near future and lower for forecasts further ahead.
- Comparing the fit of forecasts across different test time series can give useful information about stability and thus external validity.

18.B3   CASE STUDY – Forecasting a Home Price Index

External validity

To investigate the potential external validity of the predictions from our models, let's look at their RMSE for the four folds. Table 18.3 shows the results. First, the winning model M4 has the lowest RMSE in three of the four folds, and it has the second lowest RMSE in fold 2. Second, the RMSE of model M4 is quite stable across the folds. Note that the other models are less stable in this respect. Thus, the evidence across test time series suggests that patterns of association behind our chosen prediction are quite stable, and, thus the external validity of our prediction may be high. Moreover, our selected model did a very good job at predicting the home price index on the holdout set of 2017. That suggests that the stability of our prediction extended to the holdout set, too.

Table 18.3   Home price index model fit on test sets

	Fold1	Fold2	Fold3	Fold4	Average
M1	14.90	17.58	34.44	48.58	31.9
M2	14.83	8.39	6.23	5.52	9.5
M3	6.68	1.39	3.29	3.22	4.1
M4	2.22	1.96	2.88	1.20	2.2
M5	33.94	9.79	10.44	7.39	18.8
M6	2.49	4.95	9.22	9.54	7.2
M7 (var)	13.30	5.85	3.52	4.28	7.8

Note: Case–Shiller home price index for Los Angeles. RMSE in each test set for each model (rolling windows, four folds).

Source: `case-shiller-la` dataset. Monthly time series, 2000–2017, N=216 (work set is 2000–2016, N=204).

Yet stability across our four test years and one holdout year doesn't necessarily mean stability in future years, too. Unfortunately, in most cases we don't know how things might change in the future. But here we could do something more.

This case study was prepared in the spring of 2018. We used data available at that time, running till the end of 2017. In the fall of 2019, we revisited the case study, with an additional year of data available, and we used data from 2018 as an alternative holdout sample to see how our prediction works there.

Figure 18.11 repeats the prediction exercise with the best M4 model, with 2018 being the holdout set.

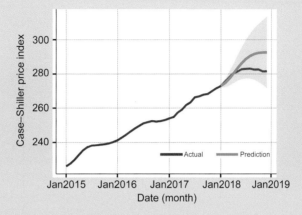

Figure 18.11 Prediction on new holdout

Note: Model M4 estimated on the 2000–2017 time series and predicted for the holdout set of 2018. Years 2015 through 2018 shown on graph.
Source: `case-shiller-la` dataset. 2000–2018, N=228 (work set is 2000–2017, N=216, holdout set is 2018, N=12).

These results are very different from what we had when we looked at year 2017 as the holdout set (Figures 18.9a and 18.9b). The prediction for 2018 turned out to be not so good. To be more precise, our prediction was still very good for the first few months. But then the actual price index stopped increasing, and, at the end of the year, even dropped a little. Yet our model predicted increase throughout the year plateauing in the last few months only.

What happened? Looking at the time series of the home price index in years 2013 through 2018 helps answer this question. The four years of 2013–2016 were our test sets for model selection; year 2017 was the original holdout set, year 2018 is the new holdout set. The time series looked quite similar during all years that we used as test sets: close-to-linear increase that slowed down in the last months, picking up its trend again at the beginning of the following year. We have selected the model that performed best on these test years, and we have seen its good performance in 2017, too. But 2018 turned out to be different from the previous few years. The price index slowed down earlier in the year, and eventually it stopped increasing altogether.

Our model couldn't fit this pattern, because this pattern was new. Thus, even though all indicators of our prediction using data up to 2017 suggested high external validity, external validity turned out to be not so high for 2018. Indeed, the stability of the patterns of a time series within a time period is no proof of stability beyond that time period. Note that this forecast is still within the prediction interval. That's a strong argument for showing prediction intervals together with point predictions. Here the rather wide prediction interval is a sign that forecast errors of this magnitude may happen.

This concludes our case study. Our goal was to predict the home price index in Los Angeles for 12 months, using monthly data starting with 2000. We have specified several models using trend, seasonality, and patterns of serial correlation of the price index. Of them, we found a best predicting model that was relatively simple and performed well across all folds. We also found that using two other variables, the unemployment rate and total employment, didn't help predicting the home price index. When evaluating the prediction of the selected best model on the holdout set, we found that it performed very well. However, we found that the prediction interval around the forecast was very wide, suggesting that the forecast error may be much larger than what we saw in our holdout year. Indeed, when we revisited the case study later and used a later year as a holdout set, we found that the prediction performed substantially worse. We concluded that the external validity of our prediction may be lower than what the stability of the prediction suggested in the test sets and the first holdout set, and the rather wide prediction interval was justified by the large uncertainty of our forecast.

On the methods side, this case study illustrated the use of cross-validation with uninterrupted time series as test sets and equal-length time series preceding those test sets as training sets. It also illustrated the use of auto-arima, a tool for model building and selection for time series forecasts. We have also built and estimated a VAR model with two other variables, although it appeared to overfit the data, giving worse cross-validated RMSE than the models that used the time series of the target variable only. We have used the stability of forecasts across test sets and on the holdout set to assess the stability of the forecast and thus its potential external validity. However, when we looked at an additional year, we have seen that stability across years in the data doesn't necessarily mean stability for future years. Finally, we have seen that presenting the prediction interval can be a good way to convey the large uncertainty of a forecast.

18.10   Main Takeaways

Forecasts use time series data to predict y for one or more time periods ahead.

- For long-horizon forecasts, trend and seasonality are the most important features.
- For short-horizon forecasts, serial correlation can be important, too.
- When using x variables to help forecast y, we need to forecast the values of x, too, and use those in forecasting y.

PRACTICE QUESTIONS

1. Give an example for a long-horizon forecast and an example for a short-horizon forecast.
2. How do you forecast y for two periods ahead, using a model that gives prediction for Δy? Explain each step; you may write out a specific model and use it in your answer.
3. Give an example of forecasting when external validity is likely to be low, and another example when external validity is likely to be high.

4. What are ARIMA models good for, and what are the abbreviations in the name?
5. How can we produce a two-period-ahead forecast from an AR(1) model? Write down the formula and explain it.
6. Write down a VAR(1) model with two variables, y and x. Explain how you would use the estimated coefficients of this model to forecast $\hat{y}_{T+1}$ and $\hat{y}_{T+2}$.
7. How can you use the results of time series cross-validation to assess the external validity of your forecast?
8. Using time series data on monthly sales of pre-packaged ice cream from 15 years, you want to forecast sales for the next 12 months. Ice-cream sales are trending upwards, in an exponential way, and they exhibit monthly seasonality. Write down a model that may make sense to use for forecasting and explain why it makes sense.
9. In the ice-cream sales example above, describe how you would evaluate your forecasts.
10. In the ice-cream sales example you may want to use another variable to help your forecast. Give an example for such a variable and explain why it may make sense to include it. Write down a model that you could use for this forecast.
11. You want to forecast weekly sales in a movie theater for four weeks. Describe a model that would make use of serial correlation, seasonality, and holidays. What kind of data would you need to carry out that forecast?
12. Using the movie theater weekly sales example, explain step by step how you would carry out model selection and prediction if you had data from 200 previous weeks.
13. You want to forecast the monthly industrial price index for 6 months, using time series data for 240 months. Describe the two ways of splitting the original data into evaluation, training, and test sets. Which one would you choose here and why?
14. Using the industrial price index forecasting example, specify three ARIMA models of increasing complexity. Explain how you would choose the best forecasting model from them and how you would evaluate it.
15. In the industrial price index example, give an example for how you could reduce each of the three components of the forecast error.

DATA EXERCISES

Easier and/or shorter exercises are denoted by [*]; harder and/or longer exercises are denoted by [**].

1. Use the daily time series based on the `swim-transactions` dataset that we employed in the **Forecasting daily ticket volumes for a swimming pool** case study. Specify a model that includes month dummies and a school holiday dummy, both interacted with day-of-the-week. Evaluate the forecast performance of this model using the same cross-validation that we had in the case study and compare your results to what we had for the other models. Discuss your findings. [*]
2. Use the daily time series based on the `swim-transactions` dataset that we employed in the **Forecasting daily ticket volumes for a swimming pool** case study. Specify models that are similar to what we had in the case study, except enter the y variable in logs. When making your forecasts of y apply the appropriate transformation (Chapter 14, Section 14.5). Find the best

predicting model using appropriate cross-validation, evaluate its performance on the holdout data, and compare your results to what we had in the case study. Discuss your findings. [**]

3. Use the daily time series based on the `swim-transactions` dataset that we employed in the **Forecasting daily ticket volumes for a swimming pool** case study. Pick a different swimming pool. Aggregate the data into daily time series, dropping observations if you think it necessary. Document and argue for your decisions. Then, using the daily time series data, carry out the same forecasting exercise that we did in the case study, including the various models of seasonality. Compare your results to what we had and discuss your findings. [**]

4. Use the `case-shiller-la` dataset that we used in the **Forecasting a home price index** case study. Specify the same ARIMA models that we employed in the case study and evaluate their performance randomly selected test sets for cross-validation instead of the time series cross-validation we applied. Compare your results and discuss your findings. [*]

5. Use the home price index for a different city of your choice and carry out the same forecasting exercise that we did in the **Forecasting a home price index** case study. Compare your results to what we had for Los Angeles and discuss your findings. [**]

REFERENCES AND FURTHER READING

For a more advanced textbook on modeling time series data and forecasting, a very good choice is Hyndman & Athanasopoulos (2019) available at `https://otexts.org/fpp3/`. It is also the reference for auto-arima.

The reference paper for Prophet is Taylor & Letham (2018). The package has a Github site `https://facebook.github.io/prophet/` where well-structured documentation can be read.

18.U1   UNDER THE HOOD: DETAILS OF THE ARIMA MODEL

An ARIMA(p,d,q) model can capture the patterns of serial correlation in a y variable in a flexible way. The middle part, d, stands for whether the model aims to capture serial correlation in y itself (then d is 0), or in its change, Δy (then d is 1).

We'll introduce the ARIMA model with several formulae. The novel thing in these formulae is the innovation term. The innovation term is the difference between the value of variable y at time t and its expected value (y_t^E). Thus, y_t is y_t^E plus the innovation term e_t:

$$y_t = y_t^E + e_t \tag{18.18}$$

The content of the innovation term is quite simple: what's new in y_t on top of what was expected of it. It's called an innovation term because y^E is based on previous y observations. Thus, today's y value is what we expected of it based on what we knew yesterday, plus what's new today: the innovation.

Note that we have already seen this innovation term in a specific example, the random walk, in Chapter 12, Section 12.3. There, we defined the random walk as a variable that changes completely randomly, so that its value at time t is equal to its previous value plus a random term: $y_t = y_{t-1} + e_t$. That random term e_t is the innovation; for the random walk, $y_t^E = y_{t-1}$.

Let's start with the formula for an AR(p) model in y; it's an ARIMA(p,0,0). Its formula is easy, since AR(p) is a model for the expected value of y, so that y itself is the AR(p) part plus the innovation:

$$y_t = \beta_0 + \beta_1 y_{t-1} + \cdots + \beta_p y_{t-p} + e_t \tag{18.19}$$

Next, let's look at an AR(p) model that is specified not in terms of the levels of y but its changes. It's an ARIMA(p,1,0) model:

$$\Delta y_t = \beta_0 + \beta_1 \Delta y_{t-1} + \cdots + \beta_p \Delta y_{t-p} + e_t \tag{18.20}$$

We kept the notation to be the same as in the ARIMA(p,0,0) formula, but the interpretation of the coefficients and the innovation term are different here: for example, β_0 captures the trend, and e_t captures how the change in y is different from what we would expect from it based on the AR(p) part of the model.

The trickier part is the MA model. An MA(1) model is a linear combination of two consecutive innovations:

$$y_t = e_t + \theta e_{t-1} \tag{18.21}$$

Note that this is not a regression model. Thus, we can't interpret θ as a regression coefficient. Instead, it is the moving average coefficient: the current value of y is the linear combination of this period's innovation and last period's innovation, and θ is what multiplies last period's innovation. In MA(1) models, $|\theta| < 1$. Also note that, despite the name moving average, this is not an average because the coefficients on e_t and e_{t-1} don't add up to one. Instead, it's a slightly more general thing than an average: it's a linear combination. Finally, because this is not a regression, we need some other technique than OLS to estimate θ. Indeed, it's usually estimated via maximum likelihood (see Chapter 11, Section 11.12).

The MA(q) model (an ARIMA(0,0,q)) is a generalization of the MA(1):

$$y_t = e_t + \theta_1 e_{t-1} + \cdots + \theta_q e_{t-q} \tag{18.22}$$

And, similarly to an AR model, we can specify an MA model for the changes in y, which would be an ARIMA(0,1,q).

MA models are best thought of as models of specific patterns of serial correlation. An MA(1) model implies that the first-order serial correlation is $Corr(y_t, y_{t-1}) = \theta/(1 + \theta^2)$. That's a little complicated, but the important thing here is that it has θ in it and nothing else. The first-order serial correlation is zero if θ is zero, it's positive if θ is positive, and it's negative if θ is negative. Moreover, because θ is less one (in absolute value), the first-order serial correlation is stronger, the larger θ is (in absolute value). Even more importantly, if y_t is an MA(1), its second-order serial correlation is zero, and so are all other serial correlations: $Corr(y_t, y_{t-2}) = 0$, $Corr(y_t, y_{t-3}) = 0$, ... This is in contrast to an AR(1) model, which implies serial correlations that decrease with the distance but don't drop to zero. Thus, the AR and MA models can capture patterns of serial correlation that are very different. That's the idea behind combining them: with the combination of AR and MA modeling, we can capture patterns of serial correlations in a flexible way.

Putting these together, an AR(p) and an MA(q) yield an ARIMA(p,0,q) model:

$$y_t = \beta_0 + \beta_1 y_{t-1} + \cdots + \beta_p y_{t-p} + e_t + \theta_1 e_{t-1} + \cdots + \theta_q e_{t-q} \tag{18.23}$$

The analogous model when y is in changes is an ARIMA(p,1,q):

$$\Delta y_t = \beta_0 + \beta_1 \Delta y_{t-1} + \cdots + \beta_p \Delta y_{t-p} + e_t + \theta_1 e_{t-1} + \cdots + \theta_q e_{t-q} \tag{18.24}$$

Forecasting from ARIMA models is a generalization of forecasting from AR(1) models, with two differences. The first difference is that, with more than one AR term, the estimated coefficients in those additional lags play a role. The second difference is in using the MA terms. In essence, the innovations are estimated from the model as differences from actual y values and what's implied for them by the model, and the values of the estimated innovations are used for the forecasting. However, the innovation forecasts themselves are all zero because we forecaesst future y values using our model, so we do not predict any difference in actual y and the predicted y that would be needed for the MA part. Thus, after forecasting several periods ahead, the MA terms don't play a role anymore. In contrast, the AR terms may still matter, as they use the predicted values of y. That is, at least, in principle; in practice, even the AR part of the ARIMA models doesn't matter much after a few time periods because the estimated serial correlation becomes practically zero.

18.U2   UNDER THE HOOD: AUTO-ARIMA

ARIMA(p,d,q) models have a set of parameters that may be selected in various ways. One such option is using auto-arima algorithms, which select and estimate p, d, q. We used the algorithm in the R package ARIMA developed by Hyndman & Athanasopoulos (2019). The algorithm first looks at serial correlation and first differentiates (once or twice) if unit root cannot be rejected. This determines $d = 0,1,2$. After that, a step-wise search is used to pick p and q. In particular, it starts by trying out the most common models: ARIMA(0,d,0), ARIMA(2,d,2), ARIMA(1,d,0), and ARIMA(0,d,1), and the best model is picked by the AIC using the entire work set (see Chapter 13, Section 13.8).

PART IV Causal analysis

19 A Framework for Causal Analysis

How to think about the effect of an intervention and when we can uncover an effect using actual data

---

Motivation

You work for a company that wants to quantify the benefits of its online advertising: how many people buy its product because they see an ad posted online. How can you translate this question into something you can uncover using actual data? What kind of data do you need to get a good answer to this question? What would be the most important issues to consider with that data?

You believe that eating a lot of fruit and vegetables helps you remain healthy. But your friend is skeptical. What kind of evidence could tell who is right: whether there are positive effects and how strong those effects are? More specifically, can you use available data on people's eating habits and health to uncover those effects? What are the most important problems with using such data to answer your question, and can you do anything about them?

In Part IV of our textbook we focus on whether and how patterns of associations between x and y uncover the effect of x on y. As we'll see, defining what we mean by an effect requires some thinking, and the definition of the effect guides our analysis. And, as we'll also see, uncovering such effects can be difficult. Moreover, what kind of data we have determines whether, and how, we can uncover the effect.

A change in focus brings about changes in language. When our goal was to uncover patterns of association, we talked about comparisons and differences and avoided words such as "effect" or "leads to." In this part of the textbook, we will be more ambitious: the goal will be to uncover effects. The same cautious language will continue to be useful. But, when we can, we will also use the more ambitious language of effects when it's appropriate.

We start by introducing the conceptual framework for causal analysis. For most cases, we focus on the effects of interventions: business or policy decisions that may affect people, firms, etc. The conceptual framework addresses two broad questions: how we define the effect of an intervention, and what are the most important features of the data that are needed to uncover that effect.

The chapter starts by introducing the potential outcomes framework to define subjects, interventions, outcomes, and effect. We define the individual treatment effect, the average treatment effect, and the average treatment effect on the treated. We then show how these effects can be understood using the closely related definition of ceteris paribus comparisons. We close the conceptual part by introducing causal maps, which visualize data analysts' assumptions about the relationships between several variables. We start our discussion of how to uncover an average treatment effect using actual data by focusing on the sources of variation in the causal variable, and we distinguish exogenous and endogenous sources. We define random assignment and show how it helps uncover the average effect. We then turn to issues with identifying effects in observational data. We define confounders, and we discuss that, in principle, we could identify average effects by conditioning on them. We then briefly discuss additional issues about variables we should not condition on, and the consequences of the typical mismatch between latent variables we think about and variables we can measure in real data. Finally, we discuss internal validity and external validity in causal analysis.

The case study we discuss in this chapter is **Food and health**. It asks whether, and to what extent, eating more fruit and vegetables leads to lower blood pressure and, thus, lower risk of heart disease. It uses the `food-health` dataset. This case study illustrates how we should approach estimating an effect from observational data, including how to think about sources of variation in the causal variable, what variables to condition on, and what variables not to condition on.

Learning outcomes

After working through this chapter, you should be able to:

- define subjects, interventions, and potential outcomes for a causal question;
- define individual treatment effects and the average treatment effect in the framework of potential outcomes;
- understand effects as ceteris paribus comparisons;
- assess potential sources of variation in a causal variable and whether they are exogenous or endogenous;
- understand why and how random assignment helps identify the average treatment effect;
- understand what kinds of variables we need to condition on and what kinds of variables we should not condition on, when our aim is to uncover an average effect using observational data;
- create and understand causal maps that visualize the analyst's assumptions about the causal relationships between variables;
- assess the internal and external validity of the results of a causal analysis.

19.1 Intervention, Treatment, Subjects, Outcomes

When analyzing cause and effect, or just thinking about them, we should start with a precise understanding of three things: what the **causal variable** is, what the **outcome variable** is, and who or what the **subjects** are. In this section we clarify these concepts and show how to use them to define, and understand an effect we want to uncover.

In most cases of business, economics, and policy the causal variable represents an **intervention**. Data analysts use the term intervention to describe decisions and actions that aim to change the behavior or situation of people, firms, and other subjects. Interventions in business environments include advertising, changing prices, changing product display, or implementing business practices or processes. Policy interventions include implementing laws and regulations, changing taxes or benefits, or introducing specific programs aiming at improving the situation of some people. Borrowing language from the medical literature, interventions are also called **treatment** in data analysis.

The subjects of an intervention are those that may be affected, or, if not affected by the particular intervention, could have been affected, at least in principle. People, firms, or other subjects that are targeted directly by an intervention are called **treated subjects**, or **treated units**. In contrast, **untreated subjects**, or **untreated units**, are not the direct targets of the intervention. As we shall see, uncovering the effect of an intervention requires comparing the outcomes of treated subjects and untreated subjects. Thus, for causal analysis, untreated subjects are just as important as treated subjects.

For an example, consider a company that wants to place online advertising to induce its viewers to buy a product. Potential buyers either see the ad or don't see the ad. If potential buyers see the ad, they may click on a link to visit a website, and may or may not make a purchase. Of course people may purchase the product without seeing the ad, too. The intervention, or treatment, is presenting the advertisement to some people. The subjects are people who are potential buyers of the product. Treated subjects are people who are presented with the online advertising. Untreated people are not presented with the ad.

Outcome variables, or simply outcomes, are variables that may be affected by the intervention. Some outcome variables may be explicitly targeted by the intervention: the goal of the intervention is to induce a change in them. Other outcome variables may be unintentionally affected by the intervention. In line with the notation we have used throughout this textbook, we'll denote the outcome variable by the letter y.

Causal variables or **treatment variables** are the variables that indicate the intervention. In the simplest case the causal variable is binary indicating whether a subject is treated or not. Other times the causal variable has more values, indicating not only whether a subject is treated or not but different kinds of treatment or different levels of the treatment. We shall denote the treatment variable by the letter x.

In our online advertising example, the outcome is a **binary variable** of whether a person purchases the product. The causal variable is binary, too, indicating whether a person is presented with the ad or not.

Or consider a different example: the effect of the price a company charges for its product on how much it sells of this product. The intervention is the price charged. The causal variable is quantitative (price); the outcome is sales, another **quantitative variable**. Intuitively, the subjects are customers, here, too. However, both the treatment and the outcome may be defined not at the level of individual customers but at the level of markets. Different markets may be different geographic areas or different time periods, such as weeks or months.

Having a clear definition for the intervention, subjects, and outcome is essential to understanding a situation. Technically it's not required, but it's very useful to have an idea why the intervention may affect an outcome for the subjects. This is called the **mechanism** or **pathway** by which an intervention exerts an effect on a particular outcome variable. We can often think of variables that can describe mechanisms; these are called **mechanism variables** or **mediator variables**.

The mechanism is relatively simple in our advertising example: through seeing an ad, people may be induced to think that they need to buy that particular product. Notice, however, that the mechanism may take time. Seeing the ad may have an effect right away: people see the ad and make a purchase. But it may have a delayed effect, too: people see the ad and make a purchase later, after some more thinking, talking, and searching. A mechanism variable (mediator) that measures the immediate mechanism would be the binary variable of whether the subject clicks on the link. But it's not the only mechanism variable, as it wouldn't measure other potential ways people may make a purchase after they see the ad.

Thinking through the potential mechanisms is useful because it may have consequences for our analysis. Sometimes, there are mechanisms that we want to focus on while excluding other mechanisms. And, sometimes, the mechanism highlights the possibility of delayed effects, so we should measure the outcome variable with a delay. In our example, thinking about the mechanisms helps in the data collection: if we can, we should include purchases not only right after presenting the ad but also some time later.

Review Box 19.1   The most important elements of a precise causal question

- What is the intervention?
- Who/what are the subjects?
- What's the outcome (y) variable?
- What's the causal (x) variable that represents the intervention? Is it binary or quantitative?
- What is/are the potential mechanisms?

19.2   Potential Outcomes

After defining the intervention, subjects, outcomes, and mechanisms, we turn to what we mean by an effect. In this section we introduce the **potential outcomes framework**, which will help understand that. We focus on interventions that can be represented by a **binary causal variable:** subjects may be either treated or untreated. We will discuss how we should think about **non-binary causal variables** later, in a separate section. The outcome may be anything, including binary or quantitative variables.

The basic idea of the potential outcomes framework is that we can always think about two **potential outcomes** for each subject: what their outcomes would be if they were treated (their **potential treated outcome**), and what their outcomes would be if they were untreated (their **potential untreated outcome**).

Some notation will help in the future, so let's denote these potential outcomes with superscript 1 (treated) and 0 (untreated). Then, for each subject i:

$$y_i^1 = \text{potential treated outcome}$$
$$y_i^0 = \text{potential untreated outcome}$$

Of these two potential outcomes, each subject will experience only one: that one is their **observable outcome**. The observable outcome of a subject that ends up being treated is their treated outcome. The observable outcome of a subject that ends up not being treated is their untreated outcome.

$$y_i = \text{ observable outcome}$$
$$y_i = y_i^1 \text{ for subjects that end up being treated}$$
$$y_i = y_i^0 \text{ for subjects that end up being not treated}$$

The other potential outcome of a subject, the one that remains unobserved, is called their **counterfactual outcome**. Counterfactual outcomes are what could have been observed had the subject experienced what did not happen. This situation didn't happen, it is against the facts, or, to use a fancier word, it is counterfactual. The counterfactual outcome of a subject that ends up being treated is their untreated outcome. The counterfactual outcome of a subject that ends up not being treated is their treated outcome.

In our online advertising example, the potential treated outcome of a subject is whether they would make a purchase if they saw the ad. Their potential untreated outcome is whether they would make a purchase if they didn't see the ad. Their actual purchase decision is their observable outcome. For individuals who see the ad, the observable outcome is their potential treated outcome; for individuals who don't see the ad, the observable outcome is their potential untreated outcome. The outcome variable is binary: each potential, observable, or counterfactual outcome is either zero (no purchase) or one (purchase).

One way to think about potential outcomes and observable outcomes is that each subject has two potential outcomes before the intervention, both unobserved. Then each subject gets **assigned** to be treated or untreated. The intervention reveals one of their potential outcomes, the one that conforms to their assignment. Their other potential outcome remains unobserved – this is their counterfactual outcome.

As we'll see, the potential outcomes framework is very useful not only for defining the effect we want to uncover, but also for thinking about what kind of data we need to uncover it.

Review Box 19.2   Potential outcomes, individual treatment effects

- Each subject is characterized by two potential outcomes:
  - a potential treated outcome (y_i^1), and
  - a potential untreated outcome (y_i^0).
- Each subject is either assigned to be treated or assigned to be untreated.
- For each subject, only one of the potential outcomes is observed, the other potential outcome is counterfactual.
- If a subject is assigned to be treated, their observable outcome is their potential treated outcome, and their counterfactual outcome is their potential untreated outcome.
- If a subject is assigned to be untreated, their observable outcome is their potential untreated outcome, and their counterfactual outcome is their potential treated outcome.

19.3   The Individual Treatment Effect

Defining what we mean by the **effect of an intervention** is straightforward in the framework of potential outcomes. To be more precise, it is straightforward to define what we mean by the effect for a single subject.

The **individual treatment effect** of the intervention for a particular subject is the difference between their two potential outcomes: the value of the potential treated outcome for the subject minus the value of the potential untreated outcome. As a formula, the effect for subject i is

$$te_i = y_i^1 - y_i^0 \qquad (19.1)$$

The individual treatment effect may be zero: whether the subject is treated or not, their outcome would be the same. The individual treatment effect may be positive: if the subject were treated their outcome would be larger than if they were untreated. Or, the individual treatment effect may be negative: if the subject were treated their outcome would be smaller than if they were untreated.

With a binary outcome, which takes the value zero or one, the individual treatment effect may have one of three values: positive one, zero, or negative one. The individual treatment effect is one if the potential treated outcome is one and the potential untreated outcome is zero. The individual treatment effect is negative one if the potential treated outcome is zero and the potential untreated outcome is one. The individual treatment effect may be zero in two cases: if both the potential treated outcome and the potential untreated outcome is one, or if both are zero.

In our online advertising example, the outcome is binary: making a purchase ($y = 1$) or not making a purchase ($y = 0$). The individual treatment effect is the difference between whether a subject would make a purchase if they saw the ad minus whether they would make a purchase if they didn't. Thus the individual treatment effect is either one, zero, or negative one. The treatment effect is a positive one if seeing the ad makes the individual purchase the product that they would not have purchased otherwise. The treatment effect is zero if seeing the ad makes no difference for the purchase decision of the individual: they would either purchase the product anyway or would not purchase it anyway. The treatment effect is negative one if seeing the ad makes the individual not purchase the product that they would have purchased otherwise. While a negative effect seems unreasonable, we cannot rule it out in principle.

For a non-binary outcome, consider a slightly different example, with the same online advertising intervention, but with a new outcome of how much a subject spends on the products of the company. The potential outcomes here are how much the individual spends if they are presented with the ad (potential treated outcome), and how much they spend if they aren't presented with the ad (potential untreated outcome). The effect is the difference between the two. As the outcome is quantitative here (spending), the effect may take many values, positive, negative, zero, large, or small.

As with potential outcomes in general, individual treatment effects help us think about cause and effect. Unfortunately, however, the individual treatment effect is never observable, so we can't measure it. It's unobservable for the fundamental reason that only one of the two potential outcomes is observable, while the other one is counterfactual. For treated subjects, there is no way to know what their potential untreated outcomes would have been. For untreated subjects, there is no way to know what the potential treated outcomes would have been.

Thus, for example, we cannot hope to learn whether presenting an online ad to a specific person would make that person buy the product. If the person is presented with the ad, all we can learn is whether they make a purchase if presented with the ad: their potential treated outcome. We don't know what the person would have done if they weren't presented with the ad. Similarly, if the person is not presented with the ad, we can learn what they do then, but we don't know what they would have done if they saw the ad.

19.4   Heterogeneous Treatment Effects

The fact that we can't observe individual treatment effects has important consequences. Quite naturally, individual treatment effects may differ across subjects. With a binary outcome variable, the treatment effect may be positive one for some subjects, negative one for others, and zero for yet others. With a quantitative outcome variable, individual treatment effects may vary even more. The possibility that the individual treatment effects are different across subjects is called the possibility of **heterogeneous treatment effects**. As a formula, heterogeneous treatment effects mean that the individual treatment effect may differ across subjects, so that there are subjects i and j for whom $te_i \neq te_j$.

Ideally, when trying to uncover the effects of an intervention, we would like to learn the distribution of individual treatment effects across the subjects. Knowing that distribution would allow us to answer questions such as the proportion of individuals with negative, zero, or positive treatment effects; the maximum and minimum effect in the group; the median effect (half of the subjects would experience a larger effect, half a smaller effect); or the mode of the effect (the effect the largest proportion of subjects would experience).

Unfortunately, the fact that individual treatment effects are impossible to observe means that the distribution of treatment effects is impossible to uncover. Thus, we won't be able to uncover the proportion of subjects positively affected by the intervention, the proportion negatively affected, the proportion not affected, and so on. And we won't be able to uncover statistics such as the median or mode of the distribution.

But all is not lost. It turns out that we may be able to uncover the average of the distribution of the individual treatment effects, even if we can't uncover the entire distribution or other statistics describing the distribution. And that's great news, because the average effect is an important quantity to learn. The next sections define average effects and how we may uncover them.

Review Box 19.3 The individual treatment effect

- The individual treatment effect (te_i for subject i) is the difference between the potential treated outcome and the potential untreated outcome. As a formula: $te_i = y_i^1 - y_i^0$.
- Individual treatment effects are likely heterogeneous: the same intervention likely has a different treatment effect for different subjects.

19.5 ATE: The Average Treatment Effect

The **average treatment effect**, abbreviated as **ATE**, is the average of the individual treatment effects across all subjects. Recall that the individual treatment effect is the difference between the potential treated outcome and the potential untreated outcome. So the average of individual treatment effects is the average of those differences across all subjects.

As a formula, and using expectation ($E[]$) to denote the average, the average treatment effect is

$$ATE = E[te_i] = E[y_i^1 - y_i^0] \tag{19.2}$$

For future reference, let's record the following fact: the average of the differences is equal to the difference of the averages. Thus the average treatment effect is also the difference between the average of potential treated outcomes and the average of potential untreated outcomes:

$$ATE = E[y_i^1] - E[y_i^0] \tag{19.3}$$

As with all averages, ATE makes sense for a well-defined group or population. In other words, when we want to measure ATE, or even just think about it, we need to be explicit about the subjects whose individual treatment effects are counted within the average. For example, in order to be able to think about the average effect of presenting an online ad to potential customers, we need to define who those potential customers are. If the online ad appears for those who search for certain words online, we may define the population as people who search for those words, or the larger population they represent. If the online ad appears in an online magazine, we may define the population as the readers of that magazine, or the larger population they represent.

The average effect turns out to be a natural choice if we want to condense heterogeneous treatment effects in one number. It can be viewed as the expected effect of the intervention for a subject randomly chosen from the population – when the outcome is quantitative. Moreover, the average treatment effect gives the **total effect of the intervention:** we just have to multiply it by the size of the population (total increase in purchases, total loss in house values, and so on). Totals are very informative for decision makers if they want to compare the benefits of an intervention to its costs.

When a company wants to uncover how many more purchases its advertising generates in total, knowing ATE is very helpful: all that is required is to multiply it by the size of the entire population. For example, a 0.1 percentage point increase in the purchase probability would translate to 1000 more buyers in a population of one million potential buyers.

However informative, the same average treatment effect may hide very different distributions of individual treatment effects. For example, the average treatment effect may be zero because all individual treatment effects are zero. Alternatively, the average treatment effect may be zero if the intervention has positive effects on some subjects and negative effects on other subjects, but they cancel out each other. Similarly, a positive average effect may mean that the effect is positive for all subjects. It may also mean that it is positive for some subjects and zero or even negative for other subjects, but the positive effects dominate the negative effects.

A special case when we may be able to uncover the distribution of the individual treatment effects is when they can be one of two possible values (0 or 1, 0 or −1), and the distribution is simply the share of 1 values (or −1). Such situations don't occur naturally, but only if we make additional assumptions when our outcome variable is binary: we assume that the third possible value cannot occur. In the example of the effect of online advertising on whether subjects make a purchase, the outcome is binary, so individual treatment effects can be −1, 0, or 1. If we convince ourselves that effects of −1 don't occur (nobody is induced not to purchase the product because of seeing the ad), it's just 1s and 0s. Then ATE is the proportion of 1s: the proportion of subjects who are induced to purchase the product by the ad. Here, with a binary outcome and the assumption of no negative effects, ATE actually tells us everything about the distribution of the individual treatment effects. But this is a special case.

While not conveying all the information about the distribution of the individual effects, ATE is a very useful quantity to know. Because of its usefulness and, perhaps just as importantly, because they may actually be able to measure it, data analysts tend to think of the average treatment effect when they talk about "the **effect" of an intervention**. In the remainder of the textbook, we will follow this tradition.

Review Box 19.4 The average treatment effect (ATE)

- The average treatment effect (ATE) is the average of individual treatment effects across all subjects. As a formula: $ATE = E[te_i] = E[y_i^1 - y_i^0]$.
- As with all averages, data analysts need to be clear about the population of subjects to which ATE refers.
- Data analysts often mean ATE when they refer to "the effect" of an intervention.
- The same ATE may hide different distributions of individual treatment effects.

19.6 Average Effects in Subgroups and ATET

The average treatment effect, ATE, is the average of the individual treatment effects across all subjects in the population that we defined. But sometimes we are interested in not only the overall average, but the average in specific subsets of the population. For example, we may be interested in the effect of an online ad campaign on potential customers living in various geographic areas. Or we may want to know the effect on young versus old people.

It turns out that defining average treatment effects for various groups is straightforward. All we need is to identify the group: to know whether each subject in the population belongs in the group or not. Then the average treatment effect in the group is the average of individual treatment effects to be calculated only across members of this group. Everything is the same as with the overall ATE, including the challenges of actually uncovering this average effect that we'll discuss in detail later.

Of these various averages, one will turn out to be especially important: the **average treatment effect on the treated**, abbreviated as **ATET**. ATET is the average treatment effect across all subjects that end up being treated. As we shall see, ATET sometimes equals ATE, but other times it does not. The importance of ATET versus ATE will be clear after we discuss how we may uncover such effects using observational data, in Chapter 21.

> ### Review Box 19.5 Average treatment effect in subgroups; average treatment effect on the treated (ATET)
>
> - The average of individual treatment effects can be defined for any subgroup of subjects.
> - The most important of such averages is ATET: the average treatment effect on the treated subjects.

19.7 Quantitative Causal Variables

The framework of potential outcomes and the definition of effects were both introduced for binary causal variables: whether a subject is treated or not treated. In this section we briefly discuss what potential outcomes, individual treatment effects, and average effects look like when the causal variable is not binary. Non-binary causal variables may denote several different treatments. And, often, they are **quantitative causal variables**, representing treatments that vary in their quantity, value, or intensity. Because of their ubiquity, we focus on quantitative causal variables here.

Examples of interventions that lead to quantitative causal variables include setting prices of products or services; giving various amounts of tax refunds to taxpayers; deciding on the interest rate or other monetary policy instrument; allocating varying hours of training to employees; and deciding on the budget to be spent on advertising through a social media platform.

The potential outcomes framework was developed for binary interventions. Its concepts and logic apply to quantitative causal variables, too. But things become a little more complicated.

With a quantitative causal variable, we have more than two potential outcomes, each corresponding to a specific value of the causal variable. With many potential outcomes for each subject, we can think of many individual treatment effects. In principle, we could take any two values of the causal variable and compare the corresponding potential outcomes. A more practical approach is to compare values to a benchmark value or values with a unit difference.

Consider our example of a company deciding on the price of its product and the effect of that price on sales. Suppose that the product is a beverage, the causal variable is monthly price, and the outcome is monthly quantity sold. While the subjects are the customers eventually, it's better to think of the different months as the subjects here. Potential outcomes in a specific month are the amounts of beverage that the company could sell if it charged various prices. An individual treatment effect here is how much more beverage the company would sell in a particular month if it charged a particular price, compared to how much it would sell if it charged another price. One natural comparison here is between price values that are one percent different from each other: the difference in quantity sold (in percentage terms) if the price were different by one percent, which is a price elasticity.

To get a tractable measure of those many treatment effects for each subject, data analysts often collapse them into an average. This average says how much the potential outcome is expected to increase if the causal variable is increased by one unit. An example would be the expected change in the amount of beverage the company would sell next January if it were to increase price by one percent. Let us consider three different price increases in January. Suppose that sales would decrease by 1.5% if the company increased its price by 1% from its current level; it may decrease a further 2% for an additional 1% price increase; and it may decrease yet more by 2.5% for one more 1% increase in price. These three changes average to a 2% decrease, corresponding to a 1% price increase next January. This is an average, but it's still an individual treatment effect: it corresponds to a single month (next January). For an ATE, we would have to know these average individual effects for each month and take their average.

Thus, quantitative causal variables lead to not one individual treatment effect but a series of them, which introduces one more step: calculating some sort of an average individual treatment effect before taking the average across subjects for ATE. Due to this extra step, it can be a little difficult to think about average effects of quantitative causal variables. But the idea is fundamentally the same.

In the remainder of this chapter we'll keep focusing on binary interventions. Even in the case of quantitative causal variables, we can often get an intuitive understanding of all the issues by thinking of the variable in binary terms (high versus low values).

Review Box 19.6   Quantitative causal variables

- With a quantitative causal variable, there are multiple potential outcomes, corresponding to the many values of the causal variable.
- Correspondingly, there is a series of individual treatment effects – e.g., by considering unit differences in the causal variable.
- Average individual effects are the expected increase in the potential outcome for a unit increase in the causal variable, for each subject.
- With a quantitative treatment variable, ATE is the average, across subjects, of those average individual effects.

19.A1   CASE STUDY – Food and Health

Question and data

You are what you eat, some people would say. Behind this saying is a causal statement: some kinds of food make you healthier than other kinds of food. In this case study we ask a related, but narrower question: does eating more fruit and vegetables help us avoid high blood pressure?

High blood pressure, if not controlled, can lead to severe diseases. It can damage the arteries for many years before other symptoms develop. Among the many causes of high blood pressure, diet may be an important one, especially among middle-aged people.

To focus our attention on middle-aged people, we define subjects as people between age 30 and 59. Of course, this is a somewhat arbitrary choice; you will be invited to re-do the analysis for other age groups as a data exercise.

The effect we want to uncover in this case study is whether middle-aged people have lower blood pressure because of eating more fruit and vegetables. We define x as the amount of fruit and vegetables an individual consumes in a day, in grams, on average. This is a quantitative causal variable. Blood pressure is a quantitative outcome variable. We'll describe how we measure our x and y variables in more detail when we introduce our data.

The causal variable is quantitative so we have several potential outcomes. In the data we will have x measured in grams consumed in the past two days – e.g., no fruit and vegetables at all (0 grams), one gram, and so on, all the way to extreme values (the two largest values are over 5000 grams). While these are measures corresponding to just two days in the data (see later), we take them as indicators of how much fruit and vegetables people consume in general, on average. One way to think about potential outcomes for each individual is their blood pressure if they consume zero grams, one gram, two grams, and so on.

Corresponding to the several potential outcomes, we can define several treatment effects for each individual. One treatment effect is the difference in blood pressure if consuming one gram of vegetables or fruit instead of zero, another one is the difference in blood pressure if consuming two grams instead of one gram, and so on. Instead of computing all of these, we can do two things. First, we can think in terms of an average individual effect as the average blood-pressure differences corresponding to these one-gram differences. Second, we could do this in ranges of grams to allow for nonlinearities – e.g., average blood pressure difference corresponding to one more gram of fruit and vegetables between 0 and 500 grams, between 500 and 1000 grams, and so on. The average treatment effect is then the average of these individual effects across all subjects.

The `food-health` dataset we use comes from the National Health and Nutrition Examination Survey (NHANES) in the United States. The NHANES is one of the main health studies in the USA that measure the health status of the population in great detail. It is a survey that is based on interviews and physical measurements, most of which are conducted inside sophisticated mobile examination centers and administered by trained personnel.

Blood pressure is one of the many physical health measures that are taken by qualified personnel in the mobile health units. More than one measurement is taken; we use the first reading – taken after a 60 second rest. We define y as a summary measure of blood pressure: the sum of systolic and diastolic measurement. These measures are considered normal if below 120 and 80, respectively, adding up to less than 200.

The amount of fruit and vegetables consumed is measured by an interview that asks respondents to recall everything they ate in two days. These interviews are conducted by trained dietary interviewers who translate what respondents say into food type codes and amounts in grams. While probably imperfect, this method is considered a very good way to learn about what people actually eat. It's almost certainly better than, for example, asking people about what they usually eat, or make them check items from a list of food items. By focusing on single days, this measurement creates a measurement error in eating habits, because what people eat on one or two days is an imperfect measure of what they eat in general. But this strategy makes people's reports as valid as perhaps possible without intruding into their lives.

The NHANES data is collected continuously, and it's organized into datasets, each of which covers two years. We downloaded the publicly available data for 2009 through 2013. The structure of the dataset is a little complicated. Altogether, there are 7930 30–59-year-old respondents in the data. Two of them reported an extremely high, and most likely erroneous, value for fruit and vegetables (over 5000 grams whereas the next largest values are around 3000 grams). We discarded these observations. Similarly, we discarded the observations for which blood pressure is missing. The workfile for our analysis has 7358 observations.

Let's look at the most important descriptive statistics of the outcome and causal variables in Table 19.1.

Table 19.1   Food and health – descriptive statistics

	Mean	Median	Std.Dev.	Minimum	Maximum	Observations
Blood pressure (systolic+diastolic)	194	192	24	129	300	7358
Fruit and vegetables per day, grams	260	188	274	0	2740	7358

Source: `food-health` dataset, USA, ages 30 to 59, 2009–2013.

The descriptive statistics give context to the subsequent analysis. Among other things, the statistics show that the distribution of blood pressure is fairly symmetric, and it is moderately spread (similar mean and median, standard deviation of one eighth of the mean), whereas the distribution of the amount of fruit and vegetables is skewed with a long right tail, and its spread is substantial (higher mean than median, standard deviation and mean are approximately equal).

In sum, we can conclude that the NHANES dataset has good measures of the causal and outcome variables. We have seen that those variables have considerable spread in the data, some of which may be measurement error. The dataset includes many more variables, some of which we'll describe later. It is observational data, recording what people usually do.

19.8   Ceteris Paribus: Other Things Being the Same

So far we discussed effects, individual or average, in the framework of potential outcomes. In this section we introduce the ceteris paribus definition that offers an alternative way to think about such effects. The ceteris paribus definition of an effect and the definition using potential outcomes have a lot in common, but they emphasize different things. They have their own advantages, which we'll discuss at the end of this section.

Ceteris paribus means other things being equal when making a comparison. The idea is that, when we make a comparison, something is different across the compared units, but everything else is the same. The ceteris paribus definition of the individual treatment effect is about comparing the outcomes of a treated subject and an untreated subject. It's the difference in the outcomes of the two subjects if there are no other differences between them. Or, more generally that allows for a quantitative causal variable, it's the difference in outcome if the causal variable is different but everything else is the same. This would be an individual effect in the sense that it's defined for subjects who are the same in terms of that everything else.

Admittedly, so far this is quite vague. What exactly needs to be the same and what should, or can, be different, depends on the causal question and the details of the situation. But this vagueness can be turned into an advantage for thinking in terms of ceteris paribus. It focuses our attention on what should be the same, and what could, or should, be different.

For example, when interested in the effect of online advertising on whether potential customers purchase a product of the company, we want to compare the purchase decision of a subject who sees the ad to the purchase decision of another subject who does not see it, but who is otherwise the same in all other things that matter. Such other things would include the subjects' income, preferences, or whether they saw something else on the Internet before seeing the ad that could influence their purchase decision.

Or take another example: the effect on house prices of extracting oil by fracking (hydraulic fracturing) close to residential areas. The subjects here are potentially affected neighborhoods. In the **potential outcomes framework**, the **individual treatment** effect is defined as average house prices in a neighborhood if fracking has taken place, minus average house prices if fracking didn't take place in the neighborhood. The ceteris paribus individual effect is defined as comparing two neighborhoods, one with fracking and one without fracking, and they would differ in all the differences that fracking may bring about, such as potential effects on the water base for drinking water. But, to be a ceteris paribus comparison, we want the two neighborhoods to be similar in all other factors that affect house prices independently of fracking, such as housing regulations, available land for development, or the income of the residents.

It should be quite apparent by now that the ceteris paribus approach has a lot in common with the now familiar approach of potential outcomes. The potential treated outcome minus the potential untreated outcome should show a difference only when the treatment status is different. Implicitly, that suggests that nothing else is different, which is a ceteris paribus comparison.

An advantage of the potential outcomes framework is that it forces us to think in terms of "what ifs." It emphasizes the inconvenient truth that we would like to compare potential outcomes for the same subject, but we can't do that. Since all we can do is to compare different observations, the potential outcomes framework tells us that such a comparison can uncover an effect (an ATE) if, somehow, it reproduces the infeasible comparison of potential outcomes.

An advantage of the ceteris paribus approach is that it forces us to think about other things that may be different across observations. That can be helpful when we want to make comparisons across different observations in actual data: it makes us think about variables whose values should be the same versus variables whose values could, or should, be different.

19.9 Causal Maps

After defining the intervention, outcome, subjects, and effect, we introduce causal maps, a tool that can be helpful in guiding our subsequent analysis. Defining the effect, either within the potential outcomes framework or using the ceteris paribus definition, is essential for a meaningful causal analysis. Causal maps are not essential in that sense. But they can be very helpful to clarify and summarize our assumptions about the relationship between variables to guide our subsequent analysis.

A **causal map** is a graph that connects variables (nodes) with arrows (directed edges). The arrows represent effects. Many data analysts use these, or similar, graphs, for various purposes. We focus on their most frequent use: summarizing our assumptions about how variables affect each other. Doing so helps us understand whether and how we can uncover the effect we are after.

We are interested in the effect of x on y (ATE). This is our question; thus the causal map connects x and y with an arrow, next to which we put a question mark.

The rest of the causal map has all other variables that we think affect y, x, or both, and are potentially important for how we can uncover the effect we are after. Arrows connecting variables on the map show directions of causality. Sometimes, causality can run both ways; then we have two arrows, pointing in opposite directions. Causal maps are most helpful when they show not only what (we think) affects what, but also in what direction. Thus, we put positive or negative signs next to the arrows, signifying a positive, or negative effect. When we think there is no effect, we don't draw an arrow. When we think there is an effect but we are not sure of its direction, we put a $\pm$ sign next to it.

Figure 19.1 shows a simple example. It shows our question: the effect of x on y. It also shows that we think that, besides x, variable z affects y, too. This is a general illustration so we put "$+/-$" next to the z to y arrow; in a particular application it would be $+$, $-$, or $\pm$, depending on what we assume about the sign of the effect. On this map there is no connection between x and z: we assume that they do not affect each other. There are no other variables on this map. That may reflect our assumption that no other variables affect x or y. That's unlikely to be true in real life. More plausibly, it may reflect our assumption that all those other variables don't matter for our analysis, whose goal is to uncover the effect of x on y. Whether that's a good assumption depends on the situation and the kind of data we have. This is going to be a lot clearer later when we apply this map to various examples.

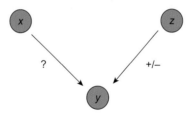

Figure 19.1   A simple causal map
Note: Question: effect of x on y. Assumption: z affects y but unrelated to x. Sign of the $z-y$ effect is either positive or negative.

Consider our example of online advertising and whether it makes viewers of an ad more likely to purchase the product of the company. Subjects are potential viewers of the online ad. Here x is whether subjects see the ad, and y is whether they make a purchase. The effect of x on y is the average treatment effect on the purchase probability across the subjects: whether, and by how much, seeing the ad makes people more likely to purchase the product. z is some other factor that makes subjects more or less likely to purchase the product, independently of whether they see the ad. Examples include taste differences, income, peer pressure. There is no connection between x and z on this graph, reflecting our assumption that who sees the ad is not related to that other factor. This may or may not be true. In fact, as we'll see soon, that latter assumption is crucial for whether and how we can uncover the effect we are after.

Mechanism variables, also called **mediator variables**, can also be included in causal maps. Figure 19.2 expands the previous simple causal map (Figure 19.1). It includes one mechanism variable for each of the effects: m_{xy} through which x affects y, and m_{zy} through which z affects y. For simplicity, we haven't added signs to the assumed causal relationships on the graph between z and m_{zy} or between m_{zy} and y.

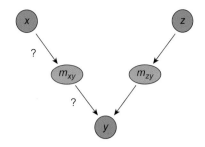

Figure 19.2   A simple causal map with mechanism variables

Note: Question: effect of x on y. Assumption: z affects y but is unrelated to x. Assumed mechanisms: x affects y through m_{xy}; z affects y through m_{zy}.

Continuing with our example of online advertising, an example for m_{xy} is whether people click on the link in the online ad that leads them to the website where they can make the purchase. We put question marks both next to the effect of seeing the ad on clicking on the sales website as well as next to the effect of clicking on the sales website on making the actual purchase. These question marks say that we want to uncover the effects through this mechanism. m_{zy} is the mechanism by which the other factor affects the purchase decision: e.g., having friends who already purchased the product (z) can influence people's decisions if they discuss the product (m_{zy}).

What we call causal maps, are related to various kinds of graphs used in data analysis. A causal map is a **directed acyclic graph**, abbreviated as **DAG**. Besides representing data analysts' assumptions about the causal relationships between the variables they care about, DAGs are also used to illustrate other steps of causal analysis. Another, somewhat older, related graph is the **path diagram**. Besides summarizing data analysts' assumptions before the analysis, path diagrams are used to present the results of the analysis. In this textbook we use these graphs for a single purpose: visualizing our assumptions about the causal relations between the variables that we think are important for our analysis.

19.10 Comparing Different Observations to Uncover Average Effects

The previous sections of this chapter discussed how we can define cause and effect and how we can visualize causal relations. These frameworks and tools are helpful to think more precisely about the effect we want to measure. In the remainder of this chapter we turn to the next question: now that we understand what we want to uncover, how can we uncover it? More specifically, how can we use the information in actual data to uncover the average treatment effect? In the remainder of this chapter we discuss concepts and tools that help guide our thinking about what we want to do. We'll turn to actual methods of data analysis in the subsequent chapters.

While effects are defined as differences between potential outcomes for the same subjects, that's impossible to measure because only one of the potential outcomes is observable for each subject. In reality, the only way we can uncover the effect of an intervention is by comparing observations in the data: the outcomes of all or some treated observations versus the outcomes of all or some untreated observations. More generally, to allow for quantitative causal variables, we compare observations that are different in the causal variable.

The effect that we can hope to uncover is the average effect of an intervention (ATE) because, as we have shown in Section 19.5, the average of the individual effects is equal to the difference of two average potential outcomes: $ATE = E[te_i] = E[y_i^1 - y_i^0] = E[y_i^1] - E[y_i^0]$. This fact does not help in itself as we still have averages of potential outcomes, not observable outcomes. But it points to the next step.

The potential treated outcome (y_i^1) is observable for subjects that end up being treated. The potential untreated outcome (y_i^0) is observable for subjects that end up not being treated. Thus, the question is whether we can uncover those average potential outcomes from the average observable outcome among treated subjects and the average observable outcome among non-treated subjects.

This question is actually two questions. The first one is whether the average of the observed outcomes for treated subjects is a good approximation to the average of the potential treated outcomes across all subjects. The second question is whether the average of the observed outcomes for untreated subjects is a good approximation to the average of the potential untreated outcomes across all subjects. Let's denote the average observable outcome among the treated subjects as $E[y_i|\ i\ is\ treated]$ and the average observable outcome among the non-treated subjects as $E[y_i|\ i\ is\ not\ treated]$. As formulae the two questions are

$$E[y_i|\ i\ is\ treated] \overset{?}{\approx} E[y_i^1] \tag{19.4}$$

$$E[y_i|\ i\ is\ not\ treated] \overset{?}{\approx} E[y_i^0] \tag{19.5}$$

If the approximations are good, the difference of average observed outcomes among treated versus untreated subjects is a good approximation to the average treatment effect (ATE).

Of course, as neither the potential treated outcomes nor the potential untreated outcomes are observable for all subjects, we can't directly assess whether these conditions are satisfied. Instead, we'll have to rely on indirect evidence. If both equalities hold, with a good enough approximation, we're there. If not, the next question is whether all is lost or if we can do something else. The following sections in this chapter will discuss these questions.

Before turning to those questions, one more remark. So far we have assumed, implicitly, that each subject is observed only once. That's true in the simplest data structure, **cross-sectional (xsec) data**, in which each observation is a different subject. Here all we can do is compare treated subjects to untreated subjects. That approach is called **between-subject comparison**. An example is data on many people, some of whom were shown an online ad the others weren't, and we have information on whether each person purchased the product.

But sometimes we have data with multiple observations on each subject (**longitudinal data**, or cross-section time series **panel data**, or simply xt data; see Chapter 1, Section 1.2). Often, in such data, many subjects are observed both when they are treated and when they are not treated. Such data may allow for a **within-subject comparison**: outcomes may be compared for the same subjects when they are treated versus untreated. In the online ad example, subjects may be observed before anyone was presented with the ad (time zero), and also after the treated subjects were presented with the ad (time one). Here we could compare purchases of treated and untreated subjects at time one: that would be a between-subject comparison. But we could also compare purchases of subjects that ended up being treated at time one to their own untreated purchases at time zero: that would be a within-subject comparison. (In fact, we can combine these two comparisons, as we'll discuss in Chapter 22.)

While a within-person comparison is closer to comparing potential outcomes for the same person, it's not the same, because we don't actually observe **counterfactual** outcomes. Take, for example, subjects who ended up being treated at some point in time. Their observable outcomes before they were treated is their untreated outcome, but it is their untreated outcome before they were treated which may be different from their (counterfactual) potential untreated outcome after they had been treated. Many things may change that make before-treatment outcomes different from after-treatment potential untreated outcomes. Trends, seasonality, or unexpected events affecting the entire market may make purchase probabilities change between the two time periods in our example, which we may then confuse with the effect of the online ad.

It turns out that panel data that allows for within-subject comparisons is often better suited to causal analysis, and we'll discuss how to use it in Chapters 22 through 24. But the fundamental problem of uncovering average effects remains the same in such data: for each subject, we can observe only one of the potential outcomes. Thus, in the remainder of this chapter, we'll keep focusing on between-subject comparisons, for simplicity.

19.11 Random Assignment

In the previous section we have seen that we can uncover the average treatment effect by comparing treated and untreated subjects if two conditions are satisfied: the average outcome among treated subjects is close enough to what the average potential treated outcome would be among all subjects, and the average outcome among untreated subjects is close enough to what the average potential untreated outcome would be among all subjects.

The condition that ensures that those two conditions are satisfied is called **random assignment**. The random assignment condition means that assignment is independent of **potential outcomes:** whichever subject ends up being treated or untreated is independent of their potential outcomes. In other words, random assignment makes the causal variable x differ across subjects for a reason that has nothing to do with what their potential outcomes would be.

The name for this condition is a little unfortunate. Random assignment here means independence of potential outcomes. It's not about how assignment was actually carried out. In particular, it doesn't necessarily mean that assignment was determined by some randomization device, such as flipping a coin, rolling a dice, or choosing a random number generated by a computer. Following practice in business, economics, and social sciences, we'll use the term random assignment in the sense of independence throughout the textbook.

Consider our example of online advertising. Assignment is random if whether a person is presented with the ad is independent of what they would do if they were presented with the ad (their potential treated outcome) and what they would do if they weren't (their potential untreated outcome). If that is true, those who saw the ad would have had a very similar likelihood to buy the product had they not seen the ad to those who didn't see the ad. And, similarly, those who didn't see the ad would have had a very similar likelihood to buy the product had they seen the ad to those who saw the ad.

If assignment is random, the difference between average observed outcomes of treated versus untreated subjects is a good estimate not only of ATE but also of ATET. That's because, in this case, ATE and ATET are equal. Random assignment makes sure that those who end up being treated are no different in terms of their potential outcomes than the entire population. Thus, the average of the individual treatment effects among subjects that ended up being treated (ATET) is equal to the average of individual treatment effects among all subjects (ATE).

So random assignment ensures that we can uncover ATE and ATET. But random assignment is a theoretical condition. It's about the independence of two things, one of which is unobserved: being treated versus untreated is observed, but potential outcomes are unobserved. There is no direct way to assess whether random assignment holds in any particular situation. How can we tell in real data whether it holds? And is there anything we can do when assignment isn't random? The next sections will address these questions.

> **Review Box 19.7   The random assignment condition**
>
> - Random assignment of the causal variable means that the causal variable is independent of potential outcomes.
> - With random assignment,
>   - treated and untreated subjects are similar in their average potential outcomes;
>   - ATE and ATET are the same;
>   - the difference in average y between treated and untreated subjects is a good estimate of ATE (and ATET).

19.12   Sources of Variation in the Causal Variable

A good starting point for actual analysis is to understand what may be behind the variation in the causal variable, x, in the data. As we discussed in Chapter 4, Section 4.8, the **sources of variation** in a variable are the reasons why different observations have different values. As we shall see, the sources of variation in the causal variable determine whether we can assume random assignment and what we can do when we can't assume random assignment.

Assessing the sources of variation in x is a thinking process. But it's not purely abstract thinking: it's about what could make the value of x different for the different observations in the data. Understanding the sources of variation in the causal variable requires knowing our data: how the data was born, what the observations are, what the causal variable measures. It also requires **domain knowledge**: an understanding of the situation, including the potential mechanisms that can affect the causal variable and the outcome variable.

The most important question about the sources of variation in x is whether and how they are related to y. A particular source of variation that is also related to y is an **endogenous source of variation** in the causal variable. A source of variation that affects x but is independent of y is an **exogenous source of variation** in the causal variable.

Visualizing all potential sources of variation in x on a **causal map** helps understand these concepts. Figure 19.3 shows a simple example. The question is the causal effect of x on y. x has two sources of variation, z_1 and z_2. The fact that z_1 and z_2 are sources of variation in x is visualized as arrows from them towards x. z_1 is an exogenous source: it affects x, but it's unrelated to y. z_2 is an endogenous source: it affects both x and y.

In our example of the effect of prices on sales, an exogenous source of variation in price is an autonomous decision by the company's managers (z_1). An endogenous source of variation may be the strength of competition on the market (z_2). Stronger competition would reduce sales (effect on y), and it would push the company to charge a lower price (effect on x).

Random assignment and exogeneity in the source of variation are close concepts. When assignment is random, there are only exogenous sources of variation in x. When assignment of x is not random, there are endogenous sources of variation, but there may be exogenous sources of variation, too.

Focusing on sources of variation in x, and whether each source is exogenous versus endogenous, is a useful starting point in causal analysis. Here we start thinking about what can make x vary in the data we have, and then we assess whether each source is related to y. However, we could also do this the

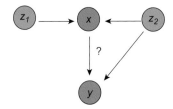

Figure 19.3 An exogenous and an endogenous source of variation in x

Note: Question: effect of x on y. Assumptions: z_1 is an exogenous source of variation in x; z_2 is an endogenous source of variation in x.

other way around: start thinking about what can make y vary in the data, and then assess whether each source is related to x. In principle, the two approaches are equally fine to find endogenous sources of variation in x. Indeed, the second approach seems more intuitive from the point of view of ceteris paribus comparisons (Section 19.8).

Nevertheless, we advise following the first approach and focusing on sources of variation in x for two reasons. First, it tends to be easier in practice: in most cases, y is related to a myriad of things, and listing all of those can be a hopeless enterprise. But we don't need all of those items: only the ones that are also related to x. And, usually, there are fewer things that affect x than y. Second, this approach makes us think about exogenous as well as endogenous sources of variation in x. And exogenous sources are important, too. In fact, as we'll see, exogenous variation in x is necessary to uncover the effect even in the presence of endogenous sources.

We can summarize this approach the following way. For the question of the effect of x on y, we need to assess all things that may make x vary across observations, and then divide them into good ones (exogenous) and bad ones (endogenous). To uncover the effect we'll need to keep the good ones and get rid of the bad ones. The next section gives a bird's eye view of the possible options to do that.

> **Review Box 19.8 Exogenous and endogenous sources of variation in the causal variable**
>
> - Exogenous sources of variation in x affect x but are not related to y.
> - Endogenous sources of variation in x affect x and are also related to y.
> - To estimate the effect of x on y, we need exogenous variation in x only.

19.A2 CASE STUDY – Food and Health

Sources of variation in food and causal map

We use observational data to uncover the effect of the amount of fruit and vegetables people consume on their blood pressure. Our x variable is how much fruit and vegetables people consume on average, in grams. Our y variable is their blood pressure. Our question is the average effect of consuming more fruit and vegetables on blood pressure. Due to the observational nature of the data, we have several sources of variation in x that we need to consider.

To summarize our assumptions about the most important causal relations in the situation, we prepared a causal map, shown here as Figure 19.4.

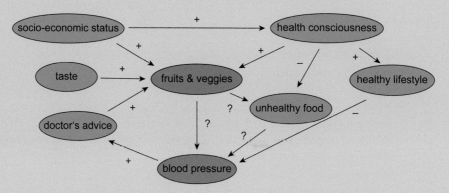

Figure 19.4   Causal map for the effect of consuming fruit and vegetables on blood pressure

Note: Question: effect of consuming fruit and vegetables on blood pressure.

The map shows the effect of interest: how consumption of fruit and vegetables affects blood pressure. We have drawn a **direct effect**, and also an effect through the mechanism of unhealthy food. The first effect represents the potential of nutritional benefits, including micro-nutrients, fiber, and so on, contained in fruit and vegetables, all of which may prevent high blood pressure. The second effect describes the possibility that, by eating more fruit and vegetables, people may eat less unhealthy food. Unhealthy food may lead to higher blood pressure. Thus, even if eating more fruit and vegetables didn't improve blood pressure directly, it may benefit blood pressure indirectly, by making people eat less unhealthy food. Either way, the effect is good. That's why we put question marks next to both the direct and **indirect effects:** we want to include both.

We put four sources of variation in eating more fruit and vegetables. Of the four, we assume that one is exogenous: taste. Here we assume that some people like fruit and vegetables more than others, and that has nothing to do with whatever else may affect their blood pressure. The other three are endogenous sources of variation. Socio-economic status describes people's income, wealth, education, and other things that matter for succeeding in society. We assume that it affects eating fruit and vegetables directly, in a positive sense, because they tend to be more expensive than most other food, hence people with higher income can afford to eat more of them. Socio-economic status is an endogenous source of variation because it is related to blood pressure through other channels such as engaging in more healthy behaviors.

The second source of endogenous variation on this map is health consciousness. We assume that people who are more health conscious tend to eat more fruit and vegetables. But they tend to lead a healthy lifestyle besides what they eat, too. For example, they are more likely to exercise regularly, less likely to smoke, and so on. And, through those other elements of healthy lifestyle, health consciousness affects blood pressure besides its effect through eating more fruit and vegetables. On our map, socio-economic status affects health consciousness, as more educated and more affluent people tend to lead healthier lives. It is through this effect that socio-economic status affects blood pressure besides its effect through fruit and vegetables.

The third endogenous source is the doctor's advice. It is actually a mechanism of **reverse causality**, by which blood pressure affects eating fruit and vegetables. The assumption here is that people with high blood pressure tend to get advice from their doctors to eat more fruit and vegetables, and some of them take that advice and do so.

Note one more of our assumptions on this map: health consciousness makes people eat less unhealthy food, which may affect blood pressure. Thus, eating less unhealthy food is a mechanism through which eating more fruit and vegetables may affect blood pressure, but it's also affected by health consciousness, which is an endogenous source of variation in eating fruit and vegetables.

19.13 Experimenting versus Conditioning

The two main approaches that data analysts may follow to uncover the average effect of an intervention are experiments and conditioning. The first approach uses **experimental data**, which has controlled variation in the causal variable x. Ideally, that makes all variation in x exogenous. The second approach uses **observational data**. In typical observational data, x has multiple sources of variation, some of which are likely endogenous. With observational data, most often, data analysts try to condition on the endogenous sources of variation in x, so that they compare observations that are different in x only because of exogenous sources. In this section we give a short summary of these approaches. In the following sections we'll discuss more details of both approaches.

The first, and more promising, approach, at least in principle, is carrying out a **controlled experiment**. The controlled experiment is the classic scientific method to uncover an average effect because it can achieve random assignment of the causal variable x. Its basic idea is to make x differ across observations solely because an experimenter made them different. For binary x, that means that the experimenter assigns treatment: they decide on which subject gets into the treated group and which subject gets into the non-treated group. Figure 19.5 shows a simple causal map with experimentally controlled variation in x.

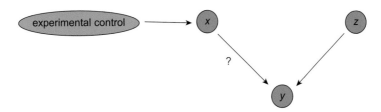

Figure 19.5   Controlled experimental variation in x

Note: Question: effect of x on y. Experimental control is the only source of variation in x. Other variables, summarized by z, may affect y but are unrelated to x.

If assignment is done well and some other conditions are satisfied, controlled experiments achieve **random assignment**. The next chapter (Chapter 20) will discuss how to carry out controlled experiments in practice. Among other topics, it will discuss how to assign treatment, how to ensure other important conditions are met, and what we can do when they aren't.

Note that random assignment, as we defined in Section 19.11, is about independence of **potential outcomes**. It's not necessarily about assigning treatment by some randomization device, such us rolling dice or generating random numbers by a computer. Controlled variation can achieve such an independence in various ways. Using some randomization device may be one of those ways, although it is the most commonly used way in business and policy experiments.

Unfortunately, controlled experiments are often impossible to carry out, for practical or ethical reasons. Even when they are possible, their results may be difficult to generalize to situations we truly care about. Sometimes, in order to control for everything, analysts may have to create experimental situations that are far from the real-life situations that they care about. We'll return to this issue later in this chapter when we discuss internal validity and external validity.

When controlled experiments are impossible, impractical, or would produce uninformative results, data analysts have to resort to using observational data.

In fortunate circumstances, data analysts may assume that variation in x in observational data is exogenous, just as if it came from a controlled experiment. Such circumstances constitute a **natural experiment**. In contrast to controlled experiments, natural experiments do not have experimenters who assign treatment in a controlled way. Instead, data analysts assume that assignment in a natural experiment took place as if it were a well-designed controlled experiment.

As an example for a natural experiment, think of the effect of land transportation costs on sales in distant markets (y) by companies. Suppose that an earthquake just destroyed some railways and highways but not others. Some companies had their products shipped on affected railways or highways and, as a result, had to re-configure their shipping routes and experienced an increase in their costs. At the same time, other companies had their products shipped using unaffected routes and didn't have a cost change. We can think of this as if nature assigned treatment: some companies' shipment costs are affected by the earthquake (treated companies) while other companies' shipment costs are not (untreated companies). This is a natural experiment if it is the case that whichever company was hit (treated) is independent of what their sales would have been in distant markets without the earthquake (their y^0), and symmetrically, if untreated companies would have had similar sales in distant markets to treated ones if they, too, were affected by the earthquake (their y^1). That amounts to assuming random assignment. If the assumption is true, we can uncover the effect of shipment costs on sales in distant markets using data on these companies. (That is, of course, if the earthquake affected shipping costs but nothing else. Otherwise, many other things would change, and we wouldn't be able to attribute any sales differences to changes in shipping costs only.)

Most often, though, we should not assume random assignment of the causal variable when our data is observational. That calls for the second approach: **conditioning on endogenous sources of variation** in the causal variable. Conditioning, as we discussed it in Chapter 4, Section 4.2,, is the way data analysts compare values of one variable across observations, while considering values of another variable. Here conditioning means further conditioning on the values of variable z when comparing the values of y by values of x. In the context of causal analysis, we'll use the term conditioning as a shorthand for this kind of further conditioning.

The idea is letting exogenous sources vary while, at the same time, not letting endogenous sources vary. That means comparing observations that are different in terms of exogenous sources of variation in x, while having similar values for the variables that are endogenous sources of variation. In essence, such conditioning aims at isolating exogenous sources of variation in x: comparing observations that are different in x only for exogenous reasons. In the next few sections of this chapter we discuss the most important principles of conditioning on endogenous sources of variation in x; we will start discussing how to do that in practice in Chapter 21.

> **Review Box 19.9 Experimenting versus conditioning**
>
> - In controlled experiments, data analysts assign treatment and make sure it is random.
> - In natural experiments, data analysts don't control assignment; instead they use observational data but assume that assignment is as if it were random.
> - In observational data, data analysts aim to isolate exogenous variation in the causal variable. Most often, they try to do that by conditioning on endogenous sources of variation.

19.14 Confounders in Observational Data

In the previous section we saw that, typically, data analysts need to condition on other variables if they want to uncover the average effect of an intervention using observational data. Those other variables are endogenous sources of variation in the causal variable (x): they affect x and are related to y at the same time. In this section we discuss such variables in more detail.

First, some more language. Variables that are endogenous sources of variation in a causal variable are also called **confounder variables**, or simply confounders. The name comes from the fact that their presence confounds the association between x and y on top of what's due to the effect of x on y. Thus, for example, z_2 in Figure 19.3 is a confounder. It makes x and y related on top of the direct effect of x on y. One way to see this is assuming that x has no effect on y. Thus, there is no effect from x to y that would make them correlated. But z_2 makes them correlated, because it affects both. Observations with different values of z_2 may have different values of both x and y, and, as a result, when x is different y tends to be different, too.

When analyzing interventions in business, economics, and policy, most confounder variables involve some kind of **selection**. Of the various kinds of selection, **self-selection** is the most common. Self-selection describes the situation when subjects themselves decide on whether they are treated or not (with binary x), or what level of the causal variable they get (with quantitative x), and that decision is related to the outcome y as well, perhaps through other mechanisms. Other kinds of selection are the results of decisions of other people that would affect both x and y.

For example, we may want to uncover the effect of online advertising of running shoes (x) on sales of running shoes (y). The ad was placed on websites that are related to running. We use observational data on people, some of whom saw the ad on running-related sites, while others didn't see the ad. We have self-selection here into seeing the ad (x), because people who are more into running are more likely to spend time on sites that advertise running shoes than other people. But people who are more into running would be more likely to buy running shoes, regardless of the ad. Thus, people self-select into seeing the ad, which means that their own decisions lead to whether they see the ad or not, and these decisions are related to their propensity to buy the product. This would be an endogenous source of variation in the treatment variable (x).

More generally, we can distinguish three types of confounder variables. We visualize each type on a causal map (Figure 19.6), and we use the same example to help understand them. The first, and most frequent type is the **common cause confounder**. Here a confounder variable affects both x and y. The second type is a **mechanism of reverse causality**. Reverse causality means y affecting x instead of x affecting y. Here the confounder is a mechanism of reverse causality if y affects the confounder variable that, in turn, affects x. The third type of confounder is an **unwanted mechanism**

confounder: a mechanism through which *x* affects *y*, but one that we want to exclude. This third type is not actually a source of variation in *x*, but we want to condition on it nevertheless. Figure 19.6 shows simple causal maps for each of the three types of confounders.

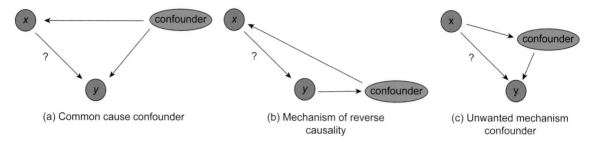

(a) Common cause confounder   (b) Mechanism of reverse causality   (c) Unwanted mechanism confounder

Figure 19.6 Three types of confounders

Note: Question: effect of *x* on *y*. Simple examples of confounder variables.

Consider our example of the effect of fracking on house prices in the neighborhood. Confounders in this example are variables that affect which neighborhood is subject to fracking and are also related to house prices for other reasons. **Common cause confounders** may be income and wealth of the residents in the neighborhood: more affluent residents may have more political power to avoid fracking in their backyard (effect on *x*), and they would live in more expensive houses (effect on *y*). A **reverse causality mechanism** would be hard to find in this example: it would mean that house prices themselves, not the affluence of residents or the location of the neighborhood, would affect whether fracking takes place. For an **unwanted mechanism confounder**, consider a more specific example with data on house prices that come from actual house sales. That's not a random sample of all houses, and fracking in the neighborhood may affect what kinds of houses are sold and thus the composition of that sample. That may result in a difference in measured house prices through this mechanism. But that's not a mechanism that we want to include: we are interested in the effect on house prices in the entire neighborhood, not on house prices in a non-random sample whose composition may be affected by fracking. This last confounder is due to self-selection, illustrating the fact that confounder variables are often due to selection.

> ### Review Box 19.10 Confounders: endogenous sources of variation to condition on
>
> When trying to uncover the effect of *x* on *y* using observational data:
>
> - confounders are variables that are endogenous sources of variation in *x*;
> - confounders make *x* and *y* related even if *x* has no effect on *y*.
>
> We can distinguish three types of confounders:
>
> 1. Common cause. The confounder affects both *x* and *y*.
> 2. Mechanism of reverse causality. *y* affects the confounder, and the confounder affects *x*.
> 3. Unwanted mechanism. *x* affects the confounder, and the confounder affects *y*. It's a mechanism through which *x* affects *y*; however, it's something we don't want to include.

From Latent Variables to Measured Variables

Without a controlled experiment, or a natural experiment, data analysts need to condition on all endogenous sources of variation in x. With between-person comparisons, that conditioning requires measuring all confounders: all variables that are endogenous sources of variation. Naturally, to do so, those confounders need to be measured in the data. So far, we didn't discuss this issue.

To start with, it is best to think about endogenous sources of variation as **latent variables**: variables that exist in our thinking but not necessarily in the data (see Chapter 4, Section 4.7). Doing so allows us to think about what may affect x and y in the situation that is represented by our data, without constraining our thinking to what's actually in our data. The result of that thinking may be a causal map that represents our assumptions about causal relationships between latent variables that are the endogenous, and exogenous, sources of variation in x. However, in order to move towards actual analysis, we need to relate those latent variables to observed variables in the actual data.

The most important feature of most real-life datasets is that they rarely contain the actual variables that correspond to all of those latent variables. As a result, we often have to omit some potentially important confounders from the ones we condition on when estimating the effect we are after. The result is an **omitted variable bias** in our estimated effect: there are some confounder variables that we don't condition on, and this makes the association of x and y in our data different from the actual effect of x on y. We'll discuss omitted variable bias in more detail in Chapter 21, Section 21.3.

If all that wasn't enough, we tend to have one more problem. Even when latent variables have corresponding observed variables in the data, those observed variables tend to be incomplete and imperfect measures. The number of firms present in a market is a good but imperfect measure of the strength of the competition; how frequently people report to have exercised last week is a good but imperfect measure of how much they exercise in general. Conditioning on an imperfect measure captures some, but not all, differences in the underlying latent variable. Observations with the same imperfect measure (same number of firms on a market, same reported frequency of exercising last week) may still be different in the latent variable (strength of competition on a market, how much they exercise in general). Thus, conditioning on imperfect measures of latent confounders likely leads to a biased estimate of the effect we are after.

If typical datasets don't have variables for all confounders, and if the variables they have are imperfect measures, does it make sense to condition on those measured variables at all?

The answer is yes, most of the time. Conditioning on a few imperfect observed confounders in observational data can be informative, even if it doesn't let us uncover the effect we are after. We'll discuss why and what we can learn from it in more detail in Chapter 21.

Review Box 19.11 From latent variables to measured variables

- Confounders that we want to condition on are most often latent variables.
- Real data rarely includes variables that measure all of the confounders.
- Moreover, the variables in real data are often imperfect measures of the latent variables that we want to consider.
- Failing to condition on some of the confounders, or conditioning on imperfect measures of them, leads to a biased estimate of the effect.

19.16   Bad Conditioners: Variables Not to Condition On

Without experimental control or a natural experiment, we should condition on all potential confounder variables to uncover the effect of *x* on *y*. But we can never be sure that we have considered all potential confounders. It is always possible that we missed some from our list or causal map. That may happen even if we would have corresponding variables in the data. So, when we have actual data at hand, does this mean that, to be on the safe side, we should condition on all available variables in our data?

The answer is no. There are variables that we should not condition on when trying to estimate the effect of *x* on *y*. We'll call these **bad conditioning variables**, or **bad conditioners** for short; another name used by data analysts is **bad control variables**. We distinguish three types of such variables.

First, we should not condition on a variable that is an **exogenous source of variation** in the causal variable *x*. Second, we should not condition on a variable that is part of the **mechanism** by which *x* affects *y* – that is of course if we want to include that mechanism in the effect we want to uncover (in contrast with an unwanted mechanism confounder, see Section 19.14). Third, we should not condition on a variable that is a **common effect**, or **common consequence**, of both *x* and *y*; such a variable is called a **collider variable**. Of the three, the first two are quite straightforward, at least in principle, while the third one is more difficult.

Figure 19.7 shows the causal graphs for each of the three types of bad conditioning variables.

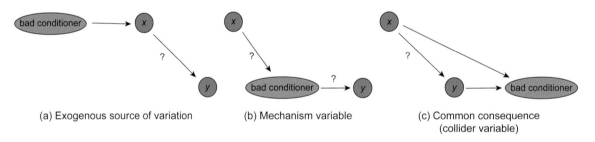

(a) Exogenous source of variation   (b) Mechanism variable   (c) Common consequence (collider variable)

Figure 19.7   The three types of bad conditioning variables

Consider our online advertising example to illustrate bad conditioning variables. Suppose that the product in question is running shoes, and the ad is placed on a runners' magazine website. Suppose, moreover, that we have data on people who are regular visitors to that website (e.g., because they are subscribers), when they visited, and whether they purchased running shoes through the website that is used by the company for its sales. Here, whether a person actually sees and notices the advertising they are presented with is a mechanism variable. Thus, even if we had a variable in our data measuring who noticed the ad and who didn't, we should not condition on it when trying to uncover the effect of the ad on the purchase probability. In the same example, we may decide to show the ad on the running magazine website on some days but not on other days. If we can do this correctly, we can make sure that this variation is exogenous: people who tend to visit the website on days when the ad is shown wouldn't be more or less likely to purchase running shoes (they have the same potential outcomes, on average). Thus, the day when the ad was shown is a source of exogenous variation in *x*, and we shouldn't condition on it. It's hard to think of a common consequence in this example, but we'll discuss one with the fracking example in the next paragraph, and we'll see it come back in our case study.

Finally, let's note that, sometimes, the same variable may be both a confounder and a bad conditioning variable. Consider our fracking and house prices example, and suppose that we have data from a survey that measured how satisfied residents were with their municipal government. That variable may reflect how much the municipal government represents the preferences of this particular neighborhood. That may be be a **common cause confounder**, as it may affect whether the municipality allows for fracking in the neighborhood (effect on x) as well as other municipal decisions that may affect house prices in the neighborhood (effect on y). But it may also reflect people's subjective views on top of how the municipality represents them. And that may be a common effect and thus a **bad conditioning variable**, because residents of the neighborhood may have a less positive view of their municipality if it allows fracking (effect of x), and they may also have a less positive view of their municipal government if they see their house prices deteriorate for other reasons that they don't fully understand (effect of y).

Data analysts don't have a single best solution when a variable in the data is both a confounder and a bad conditioning variable. But that's the life of a data analyst: single best solutions don't always exist. Then the only available option is trying both solutions: trying to uncover the effect not conditioning on the variable, and then doing the same conditioning on the variable. With luck, the two will give similar results. If not, the truth may be in-between – provided, of course, that this is the only problem to take care of.

Review Box 19.12   Bad conditioning variables

- Bad conditioning variables (or bad conditioners) are variables that we should not condition on when analyzing the effect of x on y.
- There are three types of bad conditioning variables:
  - Exogenous sources of variation in x.
  - Variables of a mechanism we are interested in.
  - Common consequences of x and y (collider variables).
- Sometimes the same variable in the data is both a confounder and a bad conditioning variable. The only option then is to try to uncover the effect with and without conditioning on it and see how different the results are.

19.A3   CASE STUDY – Food and Health

Variables to condition on

We have described our assumptions about the sources of variation in eating more fruit and vegetables on the causal map in Figure 19.4. Using that map, we first discuss what it is that we should condition on in our observational data. Except for our causal variable (fruit and vegetables) and our outcome variable (blood pressure), those variables are latent variables that we need to relate to observable variables in our data. So, when considering actual variables in our data, we have to think about whether and how well they may measure the latent variables we have in mind.

The variables to condition on are the endogenous sources of variation in eating fruit and vegetables. In other words, these are confounder variables. In Section 19.A2 we identified three of them: doctor's advice, socio-economic status, and health consciousness. The latter two affect blood pressure through various mechanisms.

Doctor's advice on eating more fruit and vegetables, due to high blood pressure, is a mechanism of reverse causality, and thus a confounder. Unfortunately, our data doesn't have that specific variable. Thus, we'll have to keep in mind that it's something that we would like to condition on but we can't.

Taste is an exogenous source of variation, so we shouldn't condition on it (it would be a bad conditioner). We don't have direct measures of taste in the data, and it's actually pretty hard even to imagine how we would measure such a thing. But that's all right, because we wouldn't want to condition on it anyway.

Socio-economic status is a common cause confounder. But socio-economic status is a latent variable. We have several variables in the data that are measures of it: household income per capita and education of the respondent. These are good but incomplete measures of socio-economic status: people with the same reported household income per capita and same education may have different socio-economic status (e.g., more or less wealth, higher or lower education of their spouses who also affect what they eat and how healthy a lifestyle they lead, and so on).

Similarly, health consciousness is a common cause confounder and a latent variable. In fact, its effect on blood pressure is not direct but through healthy lifestyle, which is a summary term for what people do and don't do that affects their health, such as exercising and smoking. We can't condition on health consciousness because it's not in our data, or, in fact, in any data. In principle, that wouldn't be a problem if we could condition on all elements of healthy lifestyle. Our data does contain some of those elements, such as whether people exercise and whether and how much they smoke. These are important elements of healthy lifestyle, but there are many other behaviors, too. Thus, these two variables are incomplete measures of the latent variable of health consciousness that we wanted to condition on.

Finally, let's consider eating less food that is unhealthy. That's part of the mechanism of eating more fruit and vegetables, and it's something that we want to include in the effect we want to measure. Thus, we should not condition on it. At the same time, it's also a mechanism through which health consciousness may affect blood pressure, which is a confounder. This would make us want to condition on unhealthy food. This is one of those cases when a variable is both a confounder and a bad conditioning variable. There is no single best solution here. Instead, we would want to estimate the effect both with and without conditioning on unhealthy food. The additional complication is we don't have an "unhealthy food" variable in the data. Instead, we should seek corresponding measured variables in the data. Our data has a detailed list of what and how much people eat, which we could just group into an unhealthy food group, just like we grouped all fruit and vegetables together. Unfortunately, though, what food items are unhealthy is not straightforward to decide. The effects of food items on health are very difficult to establish (as we saw in this case study), and conventional wisdom keeps changing (is red meat unhealthy? how about chocolate?). For illustration purposes, we have included a single food item, potato chips. You are invited to investigate other items and create a summary measure of unhealthy food as a data exercise.

Let's now look at the association between the amount of fruit and vegetables and blood pressure. Figure 19.8a shows a scatterplot with a regression line; Figure 19.8b shows the same regression line without the scatterplot with a different scale of the y axis to zoom in on its slope.

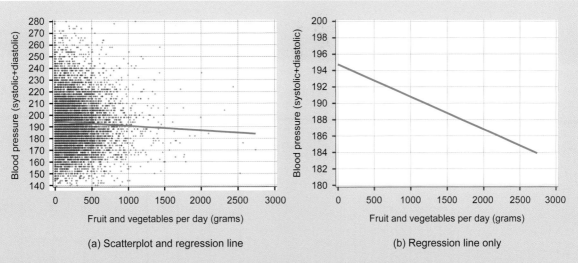

(a) Scatterplot and regression line   (b) Regression line only

Figure 19.8 The amount of fruit and vegetables consumed per day and blood pressure

Note: Blood pressure is sum of systolic and diastolic measures. Fruit and vegetables is the amount consumed per day (g)
Source: food-health dataset, USA, ages 30–59, 2009–2013. N=7358.

The association is negative: people aged 30–59 who eat more fruit and vegetables tend to have lower blood pressure. The slope of the line represents our estimate of the average effect. It's −0.0040 (95% CI is [−0.0020, −0.0060]), which means that people who eat 100 more grams of fruit and vegetables have 0.4 lower blood pressure in the data, on average. To understand the magnitude, this means that one standard deviation difference in food and vegetables corresponds to 1 point or 0.5% difference in blood pressure. This is a small magnitude. If it were close to the true average treatment effect, it would suggest that people can't lower their blood pressure very much by simply eating more fruit and vegetables. The scatterplot also helps put the magnitude into perspective. This average association is an estimate of an average effect of a quantitative treatment. It's meant to be an average in two ways, both across subjects and across levels of the treatment variable (amount of fruit and vegetables). Among the data exercises you'll be asked to estimate regressions that may accommodate nonlinear associations to see if the second kind of averaging hides important differences by the level of fruit-and-vegetable consumption.

We know that this is a biased estimate of the true average treatment effect. We know this because we want to uncover the association conditional on the confounders. And we know that we can't do that to the full extent using the data we have. But we can condition at least on the measured variables corresponding to them, however incomplete and imperfect those measures are.

How to do that well, and how to interpret the results after conditioning on them, is the subject of Chapter 21. We shall return to this case study there, to carry out the analysis as a data exercise. Here we only show some regression results that tell us that some variables indeed seem important: household income and the frequency of exercising are related to how much fruit and vegetables people eat. Figure 19.9a shows the relationship regarding log income (with a slope coefficient of 41.2 (95% CI is 34.9, 47.8)), and Figure 19.9b compares consumption of fruit and vegetables by how many days per week the person exercises (the slope coefficient is 21.2 (95% CI is [16.8, 25.5])). These figures show that income and the frequency of exercising are important sources of variation in fruit and vegetables consumption; thus they are potential confounders to condition on.

In Figure 19.10a, we also show that the amount consumed of a less healthy food item, potato chips is negatively related to the amount of fruit and vegetables consumed (the slope coefficient is −0.61 (95% CI is [−0.878, −0.35])). Recall that unhealthy food consumption may be a mechanism of the causal effect we are after: we want to condition on it only if we are interested in the effect through other mechanisms only.

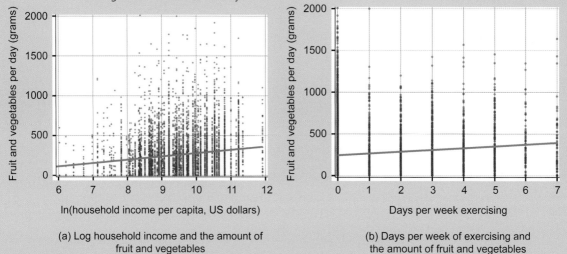

(a) Log household income and the amount of fruit and vegetables

(b) Days per week of exercising and the amount of fruit and vegetables

Figure 19.9   Two sources of variation in eating fruit and vegatables

Note: Scatterplots and the estimated regression lines.
Source: food-health dataset. USA, ages 30–59, 2009–2013. N=7358.

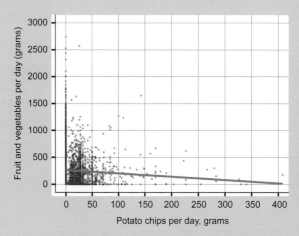

(a) The amount of potato chips and fruit and vegetables

Figure 19.10   Consumption of an unhealthy food item: a potential bad conditioning variable

Note: Scatterplots and the estimated regression lines.
Source: food-health dataset. USA, ages 30–59, 2009–2013. N=7358.

What is the takeaway from this exercise? Our question was the effect of eating more fruit and vegetables on blood pressure. We found a small (yet statistically significant) unconditional difference. However, with the observational data we couldn't answer our question, because we realized that there is a lot of endogenous variation in eating fruit and vegetables, and we can't condition on it all. In other words, we realized that comparing blood pressure across people who eat different amounts of fruit and vegetables can't tell us the effect, because people eating different amounts of fruit and vegetables tend to be different in a lot of other things that may matter for their blood pressure. Unfortunately our data doesn't have all those other things as variables, so what we can do is limited. That is despite this data being among the best and richest data we could have about the eating habits and health of people.

In a sense, the substantive conclusion of this case study is quite dispiriting. Not only couldn't we answer our question, but we also realized that it would be very difficult to answer it with any observational data.

On a more positive note, this case study shows why controlled experiments are important to carry out. Carrying out such experiments would be difficult and costly in this case, and they would have their own issues. Even with those inevitable imperfections, controlled experiments have the potential to provide effect estimates that could advance our knowledge of the effects of eating on health.

In terms of methods, this case study illustrated that thinking systematically about sources of variation in the causal variable is very important, and it's not that easy. The causal map we drew was helpful in guiding that thinking. We also saw that knowing our data is important to understand whether we can measure the variables we want to measure, and how we can measure them.

At a more abstract level, this case study illustrates that it can be difficult to measure certain things (what people usually eat), and it is very rare for real-life data to include measures of the many variables that are endogenous sources of variation in our causal variable (the many behaviors that constitute a healthy lifestyle, and the individual histories of such behaviors). As a result, it is very difficult to learn about cause and effect using observational data.

We haven't yet discussed any particular statistical methods that would allow us to condition on confounders. However, this case study illustrates a situation in which no matter what method we use, we would have no chance to get a good estimate of the effect. That's because the data doesn't have all the things we would like to condition on. And that's even though this data is among the richest kind of data available, with among the best measured variables available. Answering a causal question is difficult here both because doing so using observational data requires a lot of things to measure, and because measuring some things is inherently difficult.

19.17 External Validity, Internal Validity

The last concepts we discuss in this introductory chapter are internal validity and external validity of causal analysis. Causal analysis aims to uncover the effect of an intervention that happened in the past. Usually, we are interested in that effect because it helps predict the effect of a future intervention. Thus, the question is how close that future effect is to the effect of that past intervention as we estimate it using the data that we have. Internal validity and external validity break this question into two parts.

Internal validity of the result of a causal analysis describes the extent to which the estimated effect shows the true average treatment effect among the subjects in the data. With appropriate **confidence intervals**, the effect in the data also shows the effect in the **population**, or **general**

pattern, the data represents. We say that the internal validity of the causal analysis is high if the effect estimate is close to the true average treatment effect among the subjects. The estimated effect of online advertising on the likelihood of purchasing a product has high internal validity if it is close to how subjects in the data would change their purchase behavior due to the ad, on average. A well-designed **controlled experiment** would have high internal validity.

In contrast, internal validity is low if the estimate is far from the true average treatment effect among the subjects in the data. That occurs when we have endogenous variation in x that we didn't condition on. The estimated effect of online advertising on the likelihood of purchasing running shoes has low internal validity if the analyzed data is observational, and we simply compare people who visited a runners' magazine website where the ad was shown to people who didn't visit that website and thus couldn't see the ad. That's endogenous variation in x because visitors to the website would not only have a higher chance to see the ad, but they would also be more likely to buy running shoes independently of the ad. Low internal validity here means that the difference in the likelihood of purchase between the two groups is far from the average treatment effect of advertising among the people in the data.

We have discussed **external validity** multiple times in this textbook, first in Chapter 5, Section 5.8. External validity is the extent to which we can generalize the results of the analysis of the particular data we have, and the population and general patterns it represents, to the situation we are interested in. With good data and careful analysis, we may uncover the effect of an intervention with high internal validity. But that data includes a particular set of subjects under particular circumstances. Thus, it may be different from the kinds of subjects and the circumstances we are truly interested in. That could result in high external validity, or it could result in low external validity, depending on the details.

External validity of the estimated effect of a well-designed advertising experiment is high if the subjects of the experiment are similar to the people we want to target, and the circumstances of their decisions are similar to the circumstances of the future situation we care about. Its external validity is low otherwise. For example, external validity of the estimated effect of online advertising may be low if the experiment was run with subscribers to a particular website, and we want to know the effect for people who are not subscribers of that website. Or, external validity may be low because the experiment was run outside a holiday season, and we want to know what effect to expect during the holiday season.

Internal validity and external validity add up to answer the question of whether, and to what extent, we can take the results of our analysis to inform us about the effect of a decision to be made in the future. We need both to be high.

In principle, whether internal validity is high or low has nothing to do with whether external validity is high or low. Results of well-designed experiments have high internal validity; they may or may not have high external validity. Results from an observational study may have low internal validity due to confounders that are not accounted for. In principle, such an analysis may have high external validity nevertheless, in the sense that we could expect a similar treated–untreated difference among the subjects and under the circumstances we care about – even though those differences are bad estimates of the effect and thus won't tell us the effect of a future intervention.

In practice, however, there may be a trade-off between internal and external validity. Often, high internal validity can be achieved by designing an experiment that controls for many things, including random assignment. However, by doing so, such an experiment may include a subject pool or a situation that is different from the subjects or the situation we truly care about. In contrast, data that is collected to represent customers, workers, or firms, recording what they do under their usual circumstances, may show patterns of association with higher external validity, but, as it is observational data, causal conclusions drawn from it tend to have lower internal validity.

Review Box 19.13   Internal validity and external validity of effect estimates

- When estimating an effect using a dataset, we need to think about its internal validity and external validity.
- Internal validity of an effect estimate is high if it is close to the true average treatment effect among the subjects in the data.
- External validity of an effect estimate is high if conclusions from the data are close to what would be true in the future decision situation we care about.
- To predict the effect of a future intervention, we need both internal validity and external validity to be high.

19.18   Constructive Skepticism

We close this introductory chapter with some general advice for causal analysis. We think that the best attitude is **constructive skepticism** with respect to the results of causal analysis. Skepticism is in order for the results of controlled experiments: the experimental situation may be different from the situation we care about. Skepticism is in order for the results of natural experiments: the variation in the causal variable may not be exogenous as assumed. And, perhaps most importantly, skepticism is in order for results from observational data, because analyzing such data needs conditioning on all potential confounders, which is rarely feasible.

On the other hand, skepticism should not mean nihilism. Every analysis is imperfect, but each may be useful at the same time. Moreover, it is sometimes possible for an analysis to have both reasonably high internal validity and reasonably high external validity. Well-designed controlled experiments have high internal validity and may be informative about other situations even if their external validity is imperfect. Truly credible natural experiments are rare, but they can have both high internal and external validity. Finally, results from observational data with high external validity for patterns of association may have lower internal validity for causal interpretation, but they may be useful to put bounds on that true effect, such as its maximum magnitude.

An important skill of data analysts is to form a well-grounded assessment of the internal and external validity of an analysis. That requires a combination of statistical knowledge, experience, knowing one's data, and domain knowledge.

Moreover, we rarely try to uncover an effect that is completely unrelated to effects that people have examined before us. If we are lucky, we have access to the results of many studies trying to estimate the same effect, or an effect that is closely related. But reading the literature of past studies requires the same constructive skepticism. Every study is imperfect. Some are closer to ideal than others, but rarely does one single study settle a question for good. In addition, even those that are further away from the ideal may produce informative results. Moreover, different studies may be imperfect in different ways. In general, we should put more confidence in average effect estimates that are similar across many studies of reasonable credibility than in results that are different. Moreover, a single analysis rarely tells the absolute truth. Thus, we should take with a pinch of salt the results of a single analysis that are radically different from the rest.

Yes, uncovering an effect is difficult, and it sometimes seems impossible. So let's close this chapter on a more uplifting note. It's about a success story of learning something important from many imperfect studies. The harmful effects of tobacco smoking on health were established through a series of studies across time and countries. Studies on people were all from observational data, conditioning on many potential confounders. While the results of each study could be questioned on the grounds of selection and other omitted confounders, they were subject to different problems. Yet all produced very similar results in terms of estimated magnitudes of the association, including the fact that more intense and longer smoking was associated with more severe consequences. In addition, similar results were obtained on very different human populations. Moreover, controlled experiments showed harmful effects with cells or animals as subjects. Controlled experiments were never carried out with human subjects. Nevertheless, taken together, the evidence is overwhelming in showing a negative average effect, telling us that smoking is harmful.

19.19 Main Takeaways

To think about, and then estimate, the effect of an intervention, we need to think in terms of potential outcomes.

- Data analysis aims to uncover the average effect of an intervention.
- An exogenous source of variation in x is good: it helps uncover the average effect; an endogenous source of variation in x is bad: it confounds the effect estimate with other effects.
- Random assignment means that x is independent of potential outcomes; it makes sure that the source of variation in x is exogenous.
- Without random assignment, we need to isolate the exogenous sources of variation in x, usually by conditioning on endogenous sources of variation.

PRACTICE QUESTIONS

1. With an intervention and an outcome variable in mind, define potential outcomes and observed outcome for a subject of the intervention. What's an observed outcome and what's a counterfactual outcome here? Give an example.
2. What's the individual treatment effect? Are treatment effects likely to be heterogeneous in real life? Give an example.
3. What's the average treatment effect and how is it related to the average potential outcomes?
4. What is self-selection? Does it affect whether variation in a causal variable is exogenous or endogenous? Give an example.
5. Why and how can controlled experiments uncover average treatment effects?
6. What are natural experiments? Give an example.
7. You may attempt to uncover the average treatment effect by conditioning on all confounders. Does such an approach tend to work in practice? Why or why not? Give an example.
8. Draw a causal map for the sources of variation in attending a business analytics program. The question is the effect on earnings five years in the future. The data is observational with people from the program and other people.

9. You want to estimate the effect of foreign ownership on the quality of management of manufacturing firms. Your colleague tells you to condition on the skills and experience of senior management. Is that a good idea? Why or why not?

10. A government program aims at making firms innovate more by giving them financial support. Firms can apply to this program and receive support if they are selected by the program officers. You want to know whether, and to what extent, this program makes firms innovate more, on average. You use data on a random cross-sectional sample of firms, with a variable on whether they received support from the program and their innovation activities one year later. What's the intervention, what are the subjects, what could be a meaningful outcome variable, and how do you define individual treatment effects in this example? What's the average treatment effect? Give two examples with different distributions of individual treatment effects but the same average treatment effect.

11. You are interested in whether regular consumption of high-dose vitamin C pills makes people less likely to catch the common cold. What's the intervention, what are the subjects? If the outcome is binary (e.g., whether they caught the common cold last year), what's the individual treatment effect and what values can it take? What values can the average treatment effect take? Give two examples with different distributions of the individual treatment effects but the same average treatment effect.

12. You want to know whether and to what extent increasing the interest rate, the most widely used monetary policy tool of central banks, makes inflation lower in your country. What's the intervention, what are the subjects, what could be a meaningful outcome variable, and how do you define individual treatment effects in this example? What's the average treatment effect?

13. You want to know whether and to what extent restricting traffic of trucks and cars in your neighborhood makes home prices increase or decrease. What's the intervention, what are the subjects, what could be a meaningful outcome variable, and how do you define individual treatment effects in this example? What's the average treatment effect? Give two examples with different distributions of individual treatment effects but the same average treatment effect.

14. Consider the previous question about the effect of restricting traffic on home prices. You have data from a cross-sectional random sample of homes from your city. The data contains home prices as evaluated by their owners and the volume of truck and car traffic. No actual intervention took place (yet): the volume of traffic varies across space for other reasons. You run a regression of prices on traffic and find a statistically significant negative slope coefficient: homes in neighborhoods with more traffic are sold for lower prices. Can you conclude that a restriction of traffic would increase home prices in your neighborhood on average? Why or why not?

15. According to a recent study widely reported in news media, people who go to museums, the theater and the opera live longer. Create a causal map, and discuss whether you think this means that going to museums, the theater, and the opera makes people live longer.

DATA EXERCISES

Easier and/or shorter exercises are denoted by [*]; harder and/or longer exercises are denoted by [**].

1. Use the `food-health` dataset, and estimate a regression of blood pressure on the amount of fruit and vegetables among smokers and non-smokers. Compare the results and explain why it may be different. [*]

2. Use the `food-health` dataset and the same sample we used in our case study. Estimate first a non-parametric regression then a piecewise linear spline regression to uncover potential nonlinearities in the association between blood pressure and the amount of fruit and vegetables consumed. Compare your results to those in the case study and interpret them. [*]

3. Use the `food-health` dataset and construct a measure of the amount of unhealthy food consumed, using some of the food items in the data. Explain your choices. Investigate the association of unhealthy food consumed with blood pressure and then with the amount of fruit and vegetables. Discuss whether and why you would, or wouldn't, want to condition on your measure of unhealthy food consumption when estimating the effect of fruit and vegetables consumption on blood pressure. [*]

4. Consider our case study on **Does smoking pose a health risk?**, in Chapter 11. Define the effect of current smoking on staying healthy as we measure it in the case study. Write down the sources of variation in smoking, draw a causal map, and explain what's what on the map. The data contains variables on income, exercising, and education. Can you use these variables to measure some of the confounders you want to condition on? Can you measure them perfectly? Discuss what your findings imply for whether and how much we can estimate the effect of smoking on staying healthy using this data. Are the results here in line with what's found in the literature on the potential effects of smoking? What is your conclusion about the effects? [**].

5. Consider our case study on **Electricity consumption and temperature**, in Chapter 12. Define the effect of temperature on electricity consumption with the data we use in mind. Write down the sources of variation in temperature, draw a causal map, and explain what's what on the map. Do the estimates with or without the month dummies measure the effect of temperature using this data? [*]

REFERENCES AND FURTHER READING

There are several textbooks on causal data analysis that are more detailed and/or more technical than ours. Of them, we especially recommend Angrist & Pischke (2015), Angrist & Pischke (2018), and Imbens & Rubin (2015).

This chapter used a great deal of background material. The story on fracking and house prices is built on Muehlenbachs et al. (2015).

On the difficulty of measuring the causal effect of online ads, see Gordon et al. (2019). The example on transport routes and earthquakes comes from a study on Chile by Volpe Martincus & Blyde (2013).

The case study on diet and blood pressure was inspired by Oster (2018), who discussed why news reports based on correlations in observational data may not serve well as health advice.

Pollan (2009) offers a longer but very informative discussion about whether and how we can (or can't) uncover the effects of specific foods on health. On a related topic see Gladwell (2019) – a podcast with a story about efforts to understand the causal effect of diet in the 1970s.

On the effects of tobacco smoking, see the classic review paper Cornfield et al. (1959).

20 Designing and Analyzing Experiments

How to design and implement an experiment, how to estimate an effect from experimental data, and how to evaluate the validity of the estimated effect

Motivation

Your task is to help the admissions staff at a university design the online advertising for a graduate program. They have several competing ideas about how the online ad should look. How would you design an experiment that could tell which idea would work best? In particular, how many subjects would you need, and how would you assign them into groups, reach the subjects, and measure the outcome? Once you have the data, how would you examine data quality, estimate the effect of showing one version versus another version, and how would you use these results to answer the original question?

You work for a large company that is considering saving costs on office rentals by letting some of its employees work from home. The management is worried about potential negative effects on employee performance and attrition. How would you design an experiment that could inform the management about these effects? What important issues may come up with implementing the experiment, and how would you address those issues? Once the data is collected from the experiment, how would you assess its quality, estimate the effects, and evaluate the internal and external validity of the results?

The ideal condition of random assignment means that treatment assignment is independent of potential outcomes. In principle, random assignment helps data analysts uncover the average effect of an intervention. Controlled experiments have the potential to ensure random assignment. To achieve this, they need to be designed and implemented in appropriate ways. Then, when working with experimental data, data analysts need to look for potential problems with random assignment, address those problems when possible, estimate the effect they are after, and generalize it to the decision situation they care about.

This chapter discusses the most important questions about designing and implementing experiments and analyzing data from experiments to estimate an average effect. The first part of the chapter focuses on design; the second part focuses on analysis. We start by discussing different kinds of controlled experiments, such as field experiments, A/B testing, and survey experiments. We discuss how to carry out random assignment in practice, why and how to check covariate balance, and how to actually estimate the effect and carry out statistical inference using the estimate. We introduce imperfect compliance and its consequences, as well as spillovers and other potential threats to internal validity. Among the more advanced topics, we introduce the local average treatment effect and how to calculate the number of subjects that we would need for our experiment. We conclude the chapter by discussing how we can think about external validity in the context of controlled experiments, and whether and how we can use data to help assess external validity.

The main case study in this chapter is the **Working from home and employee performance** case study, using the `working-from-home` dataset. This case study illustrates the design, implementation, and analysis of a controlled field experiment, and it also illustrates how to use the results of a controlled experiment in an actual business decision. We also discuss a smaller case study of an A/B test that we ourselves implemented: **Fine tuning social media advertising**.

Learning outcomes

After working through this chapter: you should be able to:

- design the most important features of experiments to analyze the effects of an intervention;
- understand the main issues that may arise with experimental data, such as problems with assignment, imperfect compliance, spillovers, missing data, and so on;
- analyze experimental data to estimate effects;
- assess the internal validity of effect estimates from experimental data by evaluating covariate balance and missing data, and by thinking about other potential problems;
- think about the external validity of effect estimates, including potential problems with the composition of subjects or the circumstances in the controlled experiment.

20.1 Randomized Experiments and Potential Outcomes

As we discussed in Chapter 19, the goal of causal analysis is to uncover the average effect of an intervention. We have seen that, with **random assignment** of the causal variable x, the difference in average outcomes y between observations with different values of x gives a good estimate of the average effect of x on y (Chapter 19, Section 19.11).

Random assignment means that the causal variable x is independent of potential outcomes. In other words, random assignment means that the distribution of potential outcomes are very similar across groups with different x values. Viewed from the perspective of the sources of variation in x, random assignment means that x has exogenous sources of variation only.

The best way to make sure that assignment is random is by carrying out a controlled experiment. In a controlled experiment, the experimenter assigns subjects into two groups, treated and untreated – or, in the case of quantitative and other kinds of multi-valued causal variables, to each value of the causal variable. As assignment is under their control, experimenters can choose a rule that makes sure that assignment is independent of everything that may matter for the outcome. We'll return to how to ensure that in practice in Section 20.4.

The role of experiments has grown in business, economics, and policy analysis recently, from very limited to quite important. Experiments are frequently used to help decisions such as designing websites and online advertisements, choosing a product display or product features, designing incentive systems for employees, or carrying out public health interventions.

At the same time, implementing controlled experiments can be difficult. In this chapter we review some of the most important issues that may arise, together with how to handle those issues.

Understanding these issues is important not only for carrying out experiments by ourselves, but also to appreciate the validity of results from experiments carried out by other people. As with all kinds of data, analysts can assess the quality of experimental data only if they have a good understanding of how it was born.

20.2 Field Experiments, A/B Testing, Survey Experiments

Before discussing how to design experiments, we first introduce the kinds of controlled experiments carried out in business, economics, and public policy. Experiments aim to uncover the expected effects of an intervention to inform future interventions. Thus, the closer the situation of the experiment is to the future intervention situation, the better. This is of course the issue of external validity of the experiment, a concept that we have discussed many times in the previous chapters – e.g., in Chapter 19, Section 19.17.

An experiment should be similar to the truly relevant decision situation in many aspects. The intervention itself should be the same, and the examined outcomes should be as close as possible. The subjects of the experiment should be representative of the subjects of the decision situation. And there are usually many other circumstances that should be similar. Sometimes this is expressed as the need to carry out experiments in the "natural environment" of future interventions.

Experiments that aim to be as similar as possible to real-world decision situations are called **field experiments**. Some of the first field experiments in business examined questions related to agriculture and forestry, which may explain the name. In economics and other social sciences, field experiments are often contrasted with **lab experiments** that are carried out in an artificial environment, usually a computer lab. They are different because their goals are different. Typical lab experiments aim to answer general questions such as how people think about risk and uncertainty, or what makes them care about other people. In contrast, typical field experiments aim to answer narrower questions of the expected effects of specific interventions.

A/B tests, also known as split tests, are a frequent form of experiment. Most often they are carried out to evaluate different versions of the same product, such as an online presentation of an advertisement or a website. In an A/B test, two or more versions are presented to different groups of potential customers to see which version results in better outcomes (more purchases, more donations, more clicks). The name comes from comparing a "version A" with a "version B." Typical A/B tests are carried out online.

A/B tests are specific kinds of field experiments: they aim to uncover the effects of design choices in their relevant situations. We discuss A/B tests explicitly because they emerged largely independently of other field experiments. A typical A/B test is easier to carry out than most field experiments, and it tends to be inexpensive to scale up, which means that it can yield a large number of observations. Perhaps most importantly, an A/B test tends to be more straightforward to design than other field experiments. For example, many thousands of potential customers can be shown the same product with different features, or many thousands of potential donors can be presented with different versions of the same website that asks for donations for a political campaign. Which subject sees which version can be controlled by allocating versions by the IP address of origin.

Another type of experiment that may yield interesting insight is the **survey experiment**. These are embedded in surveys (a data collection method that asks standardized questions, see Chapter 1, Section 1.6). In a survey experiment, different groups of respondents are presented with different content, and their reactions are recorded. Design differences in products or policies may be examined in surveys, similarly to A/B testing, but here outcomes are what people say they would do.

Survey experiments are carried out within a survey, which is different from the real-world situation of interventions. Thus, they typically lead to results with lower external validity than that of well-designed field experiments. (This does not count survey experiments whose goal is improving surveys themselves, but those are quite specific examples.) Most importantly, the outcome variables in a typical survey experiment are different from real-world outcomes: they are about what people say they would do, which may be different from what they would actually do in the corresponding real-world situation. In some cases that may be a big issue; for example stated intentions to purchase a product may be very different from actual purchases, or stated intentions to donate to a charity may be very different from actual donations. In other cases it may be a lesser issue: voting intentions stated on a survey may be similar to actual voting.

Typical survey experiments are a lot cheaper to carry out than field experiments, and they tend to yield larger numbers of observations. They are sometimes used as a first check on whether an intervention might have any effect. If there is little difference in the stated intentions of people when presented with the alternatives, their actual decisions are unlikely to be very different, either.

Field experiments, A/B testing, and survey experiments differ in the details of design and implementation. But they share the basic logic of experimental design and many of its potential issues. Moreover, if well implemented, data from them may be analyzed in very similar ways. In the remainder of this chapter we shall discuss the most important aspects of designing experiments, together with how to analyze experimental data to uncover average effects.

Review Box 20.1   Types of experiments in business, economics, and public policy

- Field experiments make the experimental situation as close to the "natural environment" of the interventions as possible.
- A/B tests are specific field experiments. They evaluate design choices of products or online ads or websites, by presenting alternatives online.
- Survey experiments present different content to different respondents and record their answers to survey questions.

20.A1   CASE STUDY – Working from Home and Employee Performance

Question and field experiment

Employee retention and employee performance are highly important concerns for firms. But firms also care about the costs of employment, such as renting sufficient office space. At the same time, employees more and more often look for flexibility in working hours. One way to keep office costs down is to let some employees work fully or partially from home. That may benefit employees by making work hours flexible and decreasing commuting time. However, letting employees work from home also means less control over their work. That, in turn, may decrease the performance of employees.

This case study aims to uncover the effect of working from home on employee retention and employee performance and uses the `working-from-home` dataset.

The study analyzes the employees of one company, a large travel agency in China. The experiment took place in its call center in Shanghai that dealt with booking hotels and airfare. The average commuting time for employees was 80 minutes per day. When in the office, the employees tended to work in office cubicles. About half of the subjects were order takers whose job was to answer calls from customers and administer those calls. This group is of particular interest because their performance is relatively easy to measure by counting the number of phone calls they processed.

This is a field experiment. The intervention is making employees work from home four days a week. The subjects are employees of the firm. We consider two outcome variables: whether an employee quit the company within eight months, and how many phone calls they take, which is a measure of performance.

The company wanted to learn about the effect of this intervention because it considered letting some of its employees work from home in the future. If the uncovered effects were negative, showing that working from home led to more attrition and lower performance, the company would weigh these negative consequences against the cost savings it could achieve by renting less office space. In contrast, if the uncovered effects were positive, meaning less attrition and better performance, the company would not have to worry about these consequences when letting people work from home.

20.B1 CASE STUDY – Fine Tuning Social Media Advertising

Question and A/B testing

Universities use promotion on social media more and more to recruit students, especially in fee-paying programs. To grab attention, program managers often place a short advertisement that features the rank of the program. But there are various ways to present the rank of a program, including its ranking worldwide or regionally. The question of this case study is which kind of ranking gets people interested more when included in a social media advertisement.

At the Central European University, we decided to run an A/B test to see whether the worldwide ranking or the regional ranking generates more interest in the social media ad. We summarize the steps of designing and analyzing that experiment and highlight some of the problems that arise when doing so.

First, let's define the setup and the effect. Subjects are users of social media living in one of the countries of the region and satisfying some other criteria (age, undergraduate degree). The intervention is showing version A of the ad (worldwide ranking) versus showing version B (regional ranking); all subjects are presented one of the two versions. In the social media ad lingo, one occasion when a user is shown the ad is called an impression. There are two outcome variables: click and action. Click is whether the subject clicks on the ad and arrives at the landing page of the program. Action is whether the subject left their name and email address at the landing page for follow-up. For each outcome, there are two potential outcomes, one if the subject were to see version A (y_i^A), and one if the subject were to see version B (y_i^B). The individual treatment effect is the difference $te_i = y_i^A - y_i^B$. As discussed in Chapter 19, Section 19.5, with a binary outcome variable, the individual treatment effect can be -1, 0, or 1. Here we have two treatment effects, one for click and one for action, and both of these effects are likely heterogeneous.

While simple in principle, designing and implementing an A/B test can be complicated in practice, requiring many steps and attention to each step. In our case, these included, among other things, designing version A and version B of the ad, designing a landing page, and deciding on the size of the experiment. We'll return to how we selected the size of the experiment, and we'll present its results in the second part of this case study.

20.3 The Experimental Setup: Definitions

Before moving to other issues, let's define the setup of experiments, introducing the necessary terminology. The result of assignment is two or more groups of subjects. With a binary intervention, subjects are assigned either to be treated or not to be treated. The first group is called the **treatment group** or the **treated group**. The second group is called the **non-treatment group**, the **untreated group**, the **control group**, or the **comparison group**. The names control group and comparison group are used often because their average outcomes are to be compared to the average outcomes of the treatment group. Of course, the rationale behind this comparison is that their average outcome is meant to show the average counterfactual outcome of the treatment group: what the average outcome for the treatment group would be if its members weren't in the treatment group.

Some experiments include assignments to more than one intervention. For example, before changing the design of a product, the company may want to see how its customers react to various alternative designs. The different interventions are also called the **arms** of the experiment. Experiments with more than one intervention are called **multi-arm experiments**. A typical multi-arm experiment includes several treated groups and one untreated group, and outcomes in each treated group are compared to outcomes in the untreated group.

Experiments that aim to uncover the effect of a quantitative causal variable are multi-arm experiments: typically, they select a few groups and assign different values of the causal variable to each group. For example, a retailer may experiment with different percentages of discount to estimate their effect on sales. In the end, the data from the experiment should be analyzed in a way that makes sense for a quantitative causal variable. However, from the point of view of experimental design and implementation, these are just like any other multi-arm experiment.

20.4 Random Assignment in Practice

Whatever type of experiment we carry out, its subjects need to be randomly assigned to the treatment group. As we defined it in Chapter 19, Section 19.11, random assignment means independence of potential outcomes, which also means independence of all variables that may be related to the outcome variable apart from the intervention itself. But how can we achieve that in practice?

The solution is to implement an **assignment rule**. This has two stages: designing the rule and implementing it. A well-designed rule that is badly implemented is as bad as a badly designed rule. In fact the best designs make sure that there is little room for implementation to go wrong.

The textbook rules for random assignment are flipping a coin or rolling dice. The most common rules in practice use random numbers generated by computers. For example, such random numbers may determine the order of subjects on a list, from which the first half could be assigned to one group, and the second half to the other group.

Random numbers generated by computers are a sequence of numbers that is the same if starting from the same value. Their most important feature is a lack of any recognizable pattern. Sometimes they are called "pseudo-random" sequences. Setting the "seed" (a starting number) makes sure that any such series can be fully reproduced. That's an advantage because it lets us, or others, replicate the assignment. The most important feature of these pseudo-random numbers is their lack of any pattern. That ensures that they are independent of any variable we may care about, including potential outcomes.

In fact, there are assignment rules that ensure independence of potential outcomes even though they are even further away from "true randomness." A good example is based on even versus odd numbers, for people's birth dates, firms' registration numbers, or zip codes. Other examples are alternating assignments: after ordering subjects in any way, the first one is assigned to one group, the second one to the other group, and so on.

Attentive readers may recognize the analogy of random assignment rules to random sampling that we discussed in Chapter 1 Section 1.8. There the requirement was that selection into the sample should be independent of all variables. Here it is the assignment to groups that needs to be independent of all variables. The actual methods used to achieve independence are very similar.

Implementation of random assignment may be an issue when other people, not the experimenter, carry out the actual assignment. A typical worry is that they may assign subjects to the treated group if they think they would benefit more from the intervention. For example, in a training intervention for young unemployed subjects, trainers may feel tempted to include subjects whom they think would benefit from the training even if they were originally assigned to the untreated group. Good experimental design makes sure that such things don't happen, by supervising assignment or using assignment rules that can be checked later. For example, assignment by birthdays can be checked later, while the results of coin flips may be difficult to check later.

Besides how to carry out random assignment in practice, experimenters need to decide on many other elements of the design. Many of those elements are specific to the particular experiment, and some of them address challenges that we'll discuss later, in Section 20.11.

Finally, note the the ambiguous use of the word randomization. In the framework of potential outcomes, random assignment means independence; it does not mean what leads to that independence (see Chapter 19, Section 19.11). One way to achieve that, at least with many subjects, is using an appropriate assignment rule, as we described it in this section. That's the way experiments in business, economics, policy, and other social sciences proceed. However, in other disciplines, experimenters often control variation in other ways, for example, by making the subjects of their experiments identical in all relevant ways.

> **Review Box 20.2   Random assignment in practice**
>
> - Random assignment means that treatment is independent of potential outcomes.
> - In experiments in business, economics, policy, and other social sciences, random assignment is achieved by an assignment rule.
> - A good assignment rule makes sure assignment is independent of everything that may affect the outcome.
> - The most frequently used assignment rules are based on computer-generated random numbers, but other rules may also be appropriate.

20.5   Number of Subjects and Proportion Treated

In this section, we discuss two decisions that are relevant for all experiments: the number of subjects and the proportion of subjects assigned to treatment.

These decisions matter because they affect the precision of the effect estimate. More precision means a smaller standard error and a narrower confidence interval. It also means that we are more likely to detect a nonzero average effect by hypothesis testing. Recall from Chapter 6, testing amounts to see if there is enough evidence in the data to reject a null hypothesis. A null hypothesis is a statement about the true value of a statistic: its value in the population, or general pattern, represented by the data. In this case the null hypothesis would be a zero effect. In practice, testing whether there is a nonzero effect means comparing the mean outcome in the treated group and the untreated group, with the help of a t-test (Chapter 6, Section 6.3).

When making a decision of whether to reject the null or not, we want to avoid both a false positive and a false negative: we don't want to reject the null of no effect when there is no effect in the general pattern represented by our data, but we do want to reject the null of no effect when there is an effect in the general pattern. The likelihood of a false positive is captured by the level of significance; the likelihood of avoiding the false negative is captured by the **level of power**. A more precise effect estimate helps avoid both the false positive and the false negative (see Chapter 6, Section 6.4).

To determine the precision we need, we fix a level of significance, usually at 5%, and we want as high a power as possible. We can put a number of how high a power we want, too; usual choices are 80% or 90%. The number we put on power is not straightforward to interpret so we recommend to go with these customary levels. In any case, a low level of significance and a high power both require as precise an effect estimate as possible, and that's the goal we want to achieve.

Let's start with the question of what proportion of the subjects should be assigned to the treatment group. The answer to this question turns out to be quite simple. Given the number of subjects in the experiment, the proportion of treated subjects that makes estimates the most precise is 50 percent. Intuitively, that's because this is the way to get the most information from the data. If we increased the proportion of one group at the expense of the other group, the precision gain from more observations in the first group would not outweigh the the loss from fewer observations in the other group.

Answering the second question, how many subjects to include in the experiment, needs more work. Here we need to balance precision of the effect estimate with the costs of carrying out an experiment. On the one hand, the more subjects, the more precise the effect estimate. On the other hand, having more subjects tends to require higher costs and more time. Thus, the question is how many subjects are many enough to detect an effect, so we can keep costs at minimum.

The exercise to determine the minimum number of subjects to detect an effect is called **power calculation** or **sample size calculation**. The minimum number of subjects depends on the magnitude of the effect to detect. The larger the effect, the fewer subjects are enough to detect it (to reject the null hypothesis of zero effect).

In the typical case, we would want to know the minimum number of observations for a 5% level of significance and a power of 80%. To calculate this number, we need some more input. When the outcome is binary, we are after a difference in two proportions, and we need to assume the proportions in the two groups, not just their difference. When the outcome is a quantitative variable, we need to assume the difference in the means in the two groups and the standard deviation among all subjects.

Standard statistical software has built-in power calculators (sample size calculators): we simply type in the required inputs and get a minimum number of subjects as a response. There are online resources that do the same. Typically, these calculators have meaningful default settings for the level of significance (e.g., 5%) and the power (e.g., 80%), and they give back the number of subjects we need. We show the underlying formula behind those calculations in Under the Hood section 20.U2.

> **Review Box 20.3 Choosing the number of subjects and the proportion of the treatment group**
>
> - Deciding on the number of subjects to include and the proportion of the treatment group both affect the precision of the effect estimate.
> - Assigning 50 percent of subjects to treatment leads to the highest precision.
> - Choosing the number of subjects balances the need for precision with the costs of the experiment.
> - Sample size calculation (also known as power calculation) helps deciding on the minimum number of subjects for a precise enough estimate that can detect a true effect of a given magnitude.

20.6 Random Assignment and Covariate Balance

So far we have discussed how to design and implement a controlled experiment. In the remaining sections of this chapter, we discuss how to analyze data that comes from a controlled experiment. We start with random assignment, where the question is the following. A data analyst wants to uncover the effect of x on y using data that comes from an experiment. In this experimental data, values of x were supposed to have been assigned randomly. Is there a way to check whether assignment was indeed random?

There are two reasons for such a check. First, the process of random assignment may have been imperfect. Something might always go wrong, and it isn't always easy for a process to catch that. Second, even with a perfect process, a random rule leads to independence of potential outcomes in expectation. However, with some tiny probability, the actual assignment may lead to groups that differ in potential outcomes. With many subjects that happens with practically zero likelihood, but, it may happen with a small but non-negligible likelihood when there are only a few subjects. As usual, there is no strict rule for what's many and what's few: hundreds of subjects is usually many enough, and a dozen or two are usually too few.

Random assignment should make the distribution of potential outcomes the same in the treatment group and in the non-treatment group. For multi-arm experiments, the distribution of potential outcomes should be the same across all arms, too. Of course, potential outcomes are unobserved, so we can't examine their distributions across the experimental groups. Instead, we can check the distribution of variables that are measured in our data.

In particular, we should check the distributions of variables that affect the outcome independent of treatment. If they are related to x, these variables would be sources of endogenous variation in x. If they are not related to x, they are not sources of variation in x, so they can't make trouble. Variables of this kind are called **covariates**: they may "co-vary," or vary together with the outcome, independent of treatment. In fact, we used the name covariate for other variables to include in a multiple regression, in Chapter 10, Section 10.4. The use of the term is very similar here. Indeed, as we'll see in Section 20.9, we typically estimate the average treatment effect by a regression, in which we may include these variables as covariates together with the treatment variable. **Covariate balance** is the term used for having the same distribution of those covariates in the treatment group and in the non-treatment group.

But what are these covariates in our data that need to be balanced? We should not expect balance for variables that measure the mechanisms by which the intervention affects the outcome. In contrast, we need balance in terms of all variables that are not affected by the intervention but may be related to the outcome, such as some stable features of the subjects (examples include gender, age, education of people, sector, ownership of firms, and so on), or the outcome variable measured before the intervention. In short, potential confounders are covariates to check; bad conditioning variables shouldn't be checked (see Chapter 19).

While balance means similar distributions in principle, in practice data analysts usually compare averages of the variables. With a binary treatment, the average of all variables should be the same in the two groups. With multiple arms, we need them to be the same across all arms. When the averages are very similar, we say the variables are balanced. There are two ways to compare the average values of the covariates.

The first approach is carrying out hypothesis tests. The statistic to test is the difference between the average of a variable in the treatment group and its average in the non-treatment group. As a base rule, we should publish the p-value of the tests. We may keep the usual 5% level of significance, but that turns out to be very conservative in most cases. That is because, in most cases, there are many null hypotheses to test: all the between-group difference in the averages of each variable should be zero. And this is a typical case of testing multiple hypotheses.

As we briefly discussed in Chapter 6, Section 6.8, testing multiple hypotheses is a perilous task. In particular, looking at the results of individual tests would be very misleading here. Yet that's what we do when we look at the p-value for each variable separately. In brief, the issue is that the usual critical value of a test allows for a specific likelihood of a false positive when that test is carried out in isolation. With the typical 5% level of significance that means that, with a 5% chance, the test will lead to rejecting the null that the two means are equal, even if they are equal in the population represented by the data. However, with many such tests carried out, one or more of those 5%-chance events will occur with high likelihood. Thus, in a series of such tests, the results of some of them would suggest that the two groups are different even if they are not different in fact.

The takeaway message is that when testing balance for many variables, it's fine to have one or two "significant" differences among the many covariates whose averages are compared between the two groups. It's having many such differences that is a problem.

The second approach is to look at the magnitude of the differences – this is especially important for Big Data, when millions of observations may make all differences yield a very small p-value. Often the magnitude is judged to be large or small by eyeballing. A more systematic approach is to compare the treatment–control difference in each variable to its standard deviation. We suggest that a difference that is one tenth of the standard deviation (10%) can be considered small. A difference that is larger than one fifth (20%) of a standard deviation is often considered large enough to warrant attention.

What conclusions should data analysts draw after checking balance? We distinguish three possibilities. First, all may be fine – that is, all differences are judged small or insignificant. Then data analysts can conclude that there is no evidence against random assignment and proceed with the analysis.

Second, there may be larger and/or statistically significant differences in terms of a few variables. Here data analysts may go ahead with the analysis as if everything was fine, but they should keep those differences in mind. As we'll discuss later, in Section 20.8, we can condition on those troublesome-looking variables and see if that makes any difference in estimating the effect we are after.

Third, large differences in many variables indicate a problem. In this case we should stop and step back to try to understand what went wrong. Maybe random assignment was not designed well. Maybe it wasn't implemented well. Maybe random assignment was fine, but there was some error in data collection. Or, maybe, we, data analysts, made some mistakes when preparing or analyzing the data. If we are lucky, we can undo the errors and arrive at balanced data. If we aren't lucky, we can't do much. In that case we should treat our data as observational as opposed to experimental data and approach it as we'll discuss in Chapter 21.

Review Box 20.4   Covariate balance

- Covariate balance means that the covariates (variables that may affect y) have the same distribution in the treatment group and in the non-treatment group.
- In practice, we check whether the average of covariates is similar in the two groups.
- The results of checking covariate balance can be:
  1. all covariates are balanced, no evidence against random assignment: we can go ahead with the analysis;
  2. some covariates are unbalanced, weak evidence against random assignment: we should keep this in mind during the analysis;
  3. many covariates are unbalanced, strong evidence against random assignment: we should go back and check what went wrong, and if we can't undo it, we need to treat the data as observational as opposed to experimental.

20.A2   CASE STUDY – Working from Home and Employee Performance

Random assignment and covariate balance

The selection of subjects started with identifying eligible employees. In 2010, 994 employees worked in the airfare and hotels booking department of the Shanghai office. About half of them (503) volunteered for the experiment. Of those, 249 qualified for the experiment (they had worked for more than six months at the company and had broadband internet access and an independent workspace at home).

These 249 employees were the subjects of the experiment. Of them, 131 were assigned to work from home four days a week, and the remaining 118 employees were assigned to continue to work in the office. This is close to a 50–50% split.

The assignment rule was based on birthdays: those with an even birth date were assigned to work from home, while those with an odd birth date were assigned to work from the office. A public lottery draw decided whether even or odd numbers would be assigned to work from home. The assignment was thus fully controlled, and the rule had nothing to do with what performance would be, besides the assignment to work from home. Thus we can safely consider the assignment rule random.

The experiment was accompanied by a detailed data collection on the employees that volunteered for the experiment. Variables measured included measures of performance before the experiment, salaries, and information on their personal characteristics and living conditions. Some of these variables were used to establish eligibility for the experiment, including tenure at the company, adequate work space at home, and internet availability at home.

These variables can be used to examine balance. The published study of the experiment includes a table with the averages of many such variables in the treatment and non-treatment groups. Table 20.1 reconstructs those averages, and it adds the standard deviations to appreciate the magnitudes of the differences, and p-values of hypothesis tests of whether each difference is zero.

The two groups are rather similar in terms of the average of most variables. Let's start with the first approach: testing the hypothesis that each difference is zero. There are two p-values below 0.05: number of children and access to the internet. There is another difference, being married, which is significant at the 10% level. To be more precise, these are significant at 5% and 10% if we considered each test in isolation. However, as we warned, that would be a misleading conclusion. There are 20 tests carried out here. With 20 tests, it is quite likely to have one or two p-values below 5% and 10% even if the balance is perfect. Thus, based on the hypothesis tests, there is no strong evidence against random assignment.

Looking at the magnitudes of the differences, we can conclude that most of them are small. Perhaps most importantly, the two groups are virtually identical in terms of their performance score measured before the experiment (the "prior performance z-score"). Another reassuring fact is that the statistically significant difference in internet access is really small: a 97% versus 99% difference.

But there are some larger differences: 22% in the treatment group are married compared to 32% in the non-treatment group, and 11% in the treatment group have children, compared to 24% in the non-treatment group. Not very surprisingly, these differences were found to be statistically significantly different from zero at the 10% and 5% level, respectively. Also not surprisingly these differences are also large once we compare them to the respective standard deviations. Both are over the one-fifth threshold used by data analysts. The remaining 18 differences are smaller than the one-fifth standard deviation threshold.

What can we conclude from all this? We are in what we described above as the second case: most variables appear well balanced across the two groups, but we found a few larger deviations. We will carry on with the analysis but we'll keep in mind that being married, having children and, perhaps, having access to the internet, differ across the two groups. We'll address these differences directly later.

	Treatment mean	Control mean	Std.dev.	p-value of test of equal means

Table 20.1 Covariate balance

	Treatment mean	Control mean	Std.dev.	p-value of test of equal means
Number of observations	131	118	249	
Prior performance z-score	−0.03	−0.04	0.58	0.87
Age	24	24	4	0.85
Male	0.47	0.47	0.50	0.99
Secondary technical school	0.46	0.47	0.50	0.80
High school	0.18	0.14	0.36	0.38
Tertiary	0.35	0.36	0.48	0.94
University	0.02	0.03	0.15	0.91
Prior experience (months)	19	17	26	0.48
Tenure (months)	26	28	22	0.45
Married	0.22	0.32	0.44	0.07
Children	0.11	0.24	0.38	0.01
Age of youngest child	4.60	3.00	3.35	0.14
Rent apartment	0.24	0.20	0.42	0.44
Cost of commute (yuan)	7.89	8.34	6.96	0.63
Own bedroom	0.99	1.00	0.06	0.13
Internet	0.97	0.99	0.14	0.00
Base wage (yuan monthly)	1540	1563	161	0.23
Bonus (yuan monthly)	1031	1093	625	0.43
Gross wage (yuan monthly)	2950	3003	790	0.59
Proportion of order takers	0.52	0.56	0.50	0.53

Note: Differences in pre-treatment variables between the treatment group and the non-treatment group.

Source: working-from-home dataset.

20.7 | Imperfect Compliance and Intent-to-Treat

So far, we assumed that subjects assigned to treatment all end up being treated, and subjects assigned to the non-treatment group all end up being untreated. In other words, subjects' actual treatment is fully determined by their group assignment. But that is not always the case in real-life experiments.

The actual intervention may not reach all subjects that were assigned to it. Conversely, it may reach some subjects that were not assigned to it. For example, some of the unemployed subjects who were assigned to participate in a training program may decide not to participate or drop out early. At the same time, some of the subjects who were assigned not to participate may show up at training and may be allowed to participate.

These are issues with **compliance** in the experiment. The extent of compliance indicates the extent to which subjects that were assigned to be treated end up being treated, and the extent to which subjects that are assigned to be untreated end up being untreated.

Compliance is perfect if assignment and actual treatment are the same: all subjects assigned to treatment end up being treated and all subjects assigned to be untreated end up being untreated, as planned. Alternatively, **compliance is imperfect** if there is some **non-compliance**: some subjects assigned to treatment end up being untreated, and/or some subjects assigned to be untreated end up being treated.

The term compliance comes from pharmaceutical applications, in which some of the people assigned to take a medication may not comply and don't take the medication as prescribed, while some of the people assigned not to take the medication may not comply and end up taking the medication. The term is a little misleading as it suggests that all of that is determined by the decisions of the subjects. But we use non-compliance in a broader sense, including all cases when assignment and actual treatment differ, for whatever reason. For example, we have non-compliance if some subjects assigned to participate in a training program end up not participating because the training is not implemented on all sites where it was supposed to be implemented.

With imperfect compliance, we distinguish two kinds of average treatment effects. One is the average treatment effect (ATE), the effect of the treatment itself. The other one is the effect of being assigned to the treatment. The average effect of being assigned to treatment is called the **average intent-to-treat effect**, sometimes abbreviated as **AITTE**.

When assignment is random, we can get a good estimate of the AITTE by comparing the average observed outcomes among subjects assigned to treatment and subjects assigned to non-treatment even if compliance is imperfect. However, with imperfect compliance, we can't get a good estimate of the average treatment effect even if assignment to treatment is random. The reason is that compliance itself is rarely random. Compliance is often a decision made by the subjects or the administrators of the intervention, which leads to selection related to potential outcomes. As a result, subjects that comply are likely to be different from subjects that don't comply in terms of their potential outcomes.

While ATE would be interesting to uncover in all cases, AITTE turns out to be more important in some cases. We analyze the results of an experiment because we want to predict the effect of a future intervention. That future intervention may lead to imperfect compliance just as we had in the experiment. Then, the effect of that future intervention would be an average intent-to-treat effect, too. For example, when we want to predict the effect of a training program for unemployed people, some assigned to the treatment may not complete the training in the experiment (non-compliance). But we may expect the same for a future implementation of the training program. Thus, the effect of implementing such a program should include the fact that not everybody completes it. And that's an average intent-to-treat effect.

Moreover, with some more assumptions, we can actually get an average treatment effect even under imperfect compliance, if not for all subjects but only for a subset of them. The **local average treatment effect**, or **LATE**, is the average effect on the subjects who would comply with the assignment. Estimating the LATE turns out to be relatively straightforward once we have estimated the average intent-to-treat effect (AITTE).

We describe the idea in a nutshell here; Under the Hood section 20.U1, includes a more detailed and formal introduction. Suppose that assignment is random and compliance is imperfect, in a one-sided way: one half of the subjects who were assigned to treatment don't get treated, but all subjects assigned to non-treatment remain untreated. Because assignment is random we can get a good estimate of the average intent-to-treat effect (AITTE).

The crucial assumption is that, without the treatment, the assignment itself had no effect. Then, if AITTE is not zero, it's because of the effect of the treatment on the subjects who were actually treated. Thus, AITTE is the average of the zero effect on those who remained untreated and the nonzero effect on those who ended up being treated. In our example, this second group is half of all of those assigned to treatment. Thus, the average effect of the treatment on them (which is the LATE) is twice the AITTE. All is analogous with different proportions of non-compliance; e.g., when 90% comply and 10% don't, we inflate AITTE by a smaller fraction, 1/0.9.

In short, LATE is scaled-up from AITTE, in which the scaling factor is the inverse of the proportion of those that comply. Things are a bit more complicated with non-compliance in the other group, too, but the idea is the same: we can get LATE by scaling up AITTE. Under the Hood section 20.U1 provides more detail.

Review Box 20.5 Imperfect compliance

- Compliance is perfect when all subjects in the treatment group end up being treated, and all subjects in the non-treatment group end up being untreated.
- Compliance is imperfect if not all subjects in the treatment group end up being treated, and/or not all subjects in the non-treatment group end up being untreated.
- With imperfect compliance and random assignment, the difference of average outcomes between the treatment group and the non-treatment group identifies the average intent-to-treat effect (AITTE): the average effect of being assigned to the treatment group.
- With imperfect compliance, we can't get a good estimate of the the average treatment effect (ATE), because non-compliance is rarely random.
- Even when compliance is imperfect, we can get a good estimate of the the local average treatment effect (LATE), the average effect on the subjects who would comply with the assignment.

20.A3   CASE STUDY – Working from Home and Employee Performance

Compliance

When volunteering for the experiment, employees agreed to work from home if assigned to the treatment group, and they agreed to work from the office if assigned to the non-treatment group. The company enforced these assignments through the duration of the experiment (eight months). However, a small fraction (less than 20%) of employees in the treatment group had to be re-assigned to work in the office because of changes in their circumstances (failure to establish internet connection, loss of private work space, and so on). At the same time, all employees assigned to the non-treatment group worked from the office through the duration of the experiment.

We can conclude that compliance in this experiment was imperfect. A little over 80 percent of the group assigned to treatment was in fact treated through the entire duration of the experiment. This non-compliance was one-sided: imperfect in the treatment group and perfect in the non-treatment group. Because of imperfect compliance, comparing average outcomes between the treatment group and the non-treatment group yielded good estimates of the average intent-to-treat effect (AITTE).

At the same time, the degree of non-compliance was small. Thus the average intent-to-treat effect was likely not much smaller than the average treatment effect. And, in any case, the AITTE is closer to what to expect from a future intervention. Were the company to let some of its employees work from home as in the experiment, some employees would not be able to do so even if they wanted due to changes in their circumstances.

20.8   Estimation and Statistical Inference

Random assignment ensures that the difference between the average outcome in the treatment group and the non-treatment group is a good estimate of the average treatment effect if compliance is perfect – or the average intent-to-treat effect if compliance is imperfect. But how should we carry out such comparisons in practice? And how should we estimate the confidence interval around the estimated average treatment effect?

The obvious approach is to calculate the average outcome in each group and take their difference. But creating a confidence interval around it, or testing the hypothesis that it is zero, would require further steps. To make things easier in practice, data analysts estimate this difference using a simple linear regression.

The regression approach uncovers the exact same difference as comparing means. The regression has outcome variable y on the left-hand side, and the binary assignment variable x on the right-hand side. This x variable is one for subjects in the treatment group and zero for subjects in the non-treatment group.

$$y^E = \alpha + \beta x \qquad (20.1)$$

Here α is average y in the non-treatment group, and β is the difference in average y between the treatment group and the non-treatment group. Thus β estimates the treatment effect if compliance is perfect. If compliance is imperfect it estimates the average intent-to-treat effect. This is a regression, so standard statistical software estimates the standard error of β, which we can use to form a confidence interval, and we also get the p-value of the test that $H_0: \beta = 0$.

We can interpret the confidence interval and the p-value in the usual way. A 95% CI around β tells us the interval in which we should expect, with 95% confidence, the average effect to be in the population represented by the subjects in the experiment. The p-value would tell us the highest level of significance at which we could reject the hypothesis that there is no effect in the population represented by the subjects in the experiment.

Review Box 20.6   Estimating the average treatment effect or the average intent-to-treat effect

- The average effect of an experiment is best estimated by the regression

$$y^E = \alpha + \beta x \qquad (20.2)$$

- The estimate of β is the difference in the average outcome (y) between the treatment group ($x = 1$) and the non-treatment group ($x = 0$).
- β is a good approximation of ATE if assignment is random and compliance is perfect.
- β is a good approximation of AITTE if assignment is random and compliance is imperfect.

20.B2   CASE STUDY – Fine Tuning Social Media Advertising

Size of the experiment, results, and conclusion

An important task in the social media experiment was to determine the size of the experiment: how many impressions to show. Recall that an impression is an occasion when a user is shown the ad. The social media company charges by impressions, so the task was to determine the number of impressions. We know that we need to divide the subjects equally between group A (who are shown the ad with the global ranking) and group B (who are shown the ad with the regional ranking). Then, the question is how many subjects we need for this experiment to detect a difference in outcomes brought about by design A versus design B.

To determine the minimum number of subjects, we need to make assumptions about the expected outcomes in the two groups. We have two outcomes: click and action. We assumed that, of the subjects (impressions), around 1% click on the ad – this is called the **click through rate**. Moreover, we assumed that of the subjects who click on the ad, about 5% take an action – this is called the **conversion rate** – the rate at which clicks are converted to actions. That means that we need 100 impressions for a click, and 2000 impressions for an action.

We then asked the following question: how many impressions do we need if we want to detect a 20% difference in actions between group A and group B? To be more precise, we want the number of subjects needed for a t-test to reject the null of equal means at a 5% significance level if the mean (the proportion of actions) in one group is 0.0005, and it's 20% higher in the other group, which is 0.0006. We also set power to the customary 80% level. The minimum number of subjects was determined to be 1.7 million.

In reality, the social media site doesn't ask for the number of impressions. Instead, it gives an approximate price per impression and shows them to people using an algorithm. We allocated a budget that would be approximately enough to target 2 million impressions, which is a slightly larger number than we calculated (1.7 million).

Table 20.2 shows the results of the experiment. The first two columns show the allocated amount of money and the targeted number of impressions for versions A and B. The following columns show the results: the number of clicks and the number of actions taken. The last column shows the implied cost of an action (the allocated amount of money divided by the number of actions). The table shows the percent differences of clicks and of actions, together with the p-values of these differences. Each p-value is simply the result of testing the null hypothesis that the corresponding difference is zero, given with the number of observations in the data (2 million).

In terms of clicks, there is a small difference of 6% in favor of version A. This difference is statistically significant at the 5% level, but not at the 1% level. The difference between the number of actions is large in relative terms – more than 50% in favor of version A. This means that the implied costs per action are lower for version A. However, the number of actions is very small. As a result, the difference is not statistically significant even at the 5% level. Thus, we cannot reject the hypothesis that the two numbers are equal.

We targeted a large enough number of impressions that would result in statistically significant test results for large enough differences. Yet the results are not statistically significant.

Table 20.2 Social media campaign results					
	Cost (dollars)	Target no. of impressions	No. of clicks	No. of actions	Cost per action (dollars)
A	1000	1 million	3323	32	31.25
B	1000	1 million	3128	21	47.62
Percent difference			6.23%	52.4%	
p-value			0.015	0.131	

Source: Summary data from the social media campaign.

Why? It turned out that the assumptions we used to determine the target number of impressions were very optimistic. In reality, the click through rate was closer to 0.3% instead of 1%, and the conversion rate was less than 1% instead of 5%. The probability of action (averaged over groups A and B) was less than 0.00003, little more than one-twentieth of the assumed 0.0005. With these rates, detecting a 20% difference would have required more than 30 million impressions, not 1.7 million.

Are the results of this experiment then completely uninformative? No. The most important result is that the click through rate, and especially the conversion rate, are low, regardless of the design choice. The experiment provided quite good estimates for them: 0.3% and 1%. These results should inform the decision as to whether the organization wanted to do the campaign with such low rates at all, spending on average 40 dollars per action. If the answer is yes, we would have to decide on version A versus version B. How should the results of the experiment contribute to that decision? Version A looks better in the data, but we can't be certain enough that it is better indeed and that what we see is not just random variation. If we had an ongoing ad with version B, this evidence would not be enough to replace it with version A. If, on the other hand, we wanted to start an ad and had to make a choice, we would go with version A.

On the method side, there are three main takeaways. First, it is actually easy to run an A/B test, and the analysis is relatively simple. However, deciding on the size of an A/B test can be hard, requiring several assumptions that may not turn out to be true: the click through and conversion rates were much lower than expected in this case study. Indeed, very large sample sizes will often be needed, as online actions are rare. Finally, the design part could actually be hard, as there are many decisions to make, and many of them are technical decisions regarding the implementation, which we haven't discussed here. It is advised to run a pilot study (as introduced in Chapter 1, Section 1.10), which we did, and it was indeed very useful to catch errors in implementation.

20.9   Including Covariates in a Regression

Another advantage of estimating average effects via regressions is that we can include other variables in its right-hand side. Recall from Chapter 10 that the coefficient of a right-hand-side variable in a multiple regression with other right-hand-side variables is an approximate way of conditioning on those other variables: comparing observations that are different in x but similar in the variables in the regression. The variables we would want to include in the regression are the covariates that we discussed earlier in Section 20.6: variables that are related to y and would be confounders if they were related to x too. The covariates should not include bad conditioning variables, such as variables of mechanisms.

A regression with outcome y, treatment variable x, and covariates $z_1, z_2, \ldots$ can be formulated in the following way:

$$y^E = \beta_0 + \beta_1 x + \beta_2 z_1 + \beta_3 z_2 + \cdots \tag{20.3}$$

The coefficient of interest is β_1. With a binary treatment variable ($x = 1$ if in the treatment group, $x = 0$ if in the non-treatment group) β_1 shows the average difference in outcome y between the treatment group and non-treatment group observations that are similar in the z covariates.

With random assignment there is no need to condition on those covariates. Thus, there is no need to include those covariate variables in a regression for getting an unbiased estimate of the average effect (or average intent-to-treat effect with non-compliance). Nevertheless, data analysts often estimate the effects with multiple regressions that include covariates. They do that for two reasons.

First, including covariates can make sure that minor problems with covariate balance don't affect the effect estimate. As we discussed earlier in this chapter, checking balance is a tool to see if assignment was in fact random.

Including the covariates in the regression is an indirect way to check balance. With balanced groups, the estimated effects should be the same whether we include those covariates or not. That should be true even if the covariates have nonzero slope coefficients. If they are not related to the treatment variable x, the coefficient estimate of x should remain the same (see, for example, Chapter 10, Section 10.2). If that is what we find, all is fine. If, however, we find a substantial difference in the coefficient estimates of x with and without the covariates, we should not assume random assignment of x.

The second reason why data analysts often include covariates in the regression is to get a more precise estimate of the average treatment effect. A more precise estimate means a smaller standard error of the slope coefficient β_1 and thus a narrower confidence interval. This standard error is smaller if the covariates explain a lot of the variation of the outcome y but are not related to the treatment variable x. We have seen this in Chapter 10, Section 10.5.

Review Box 20.7   Including covariates in the regression

- When assignment is random, there is no need to include covariates in the regression to estimate ATE (or AITTE if compliance is imperfect).
- When assignment is random, including covariates in the regression may lead to smaller SE and thus narrower CI.
- When we aren't sure if assignment is random, because covariate balance is not perfect, we can check if those imbalances make a difference by comparing the estimated effect with or without including the covariates.

20.A4   CASE STUDY – Working from Home and Employee Performance

Estimating effects and including covariates

We consider two outcomes: employee retention and employee performance. As we discussed earlier, employee retention is measured by whether an employee quit the firm within eight months of the experiment. This measure is available for all 249 subjects in the experiment. If working from home increases employee retention, it should decrease the probability of quitting.

Performance is best measured for a group of the subjects who worked as order takers. Recall that about half of the 249 subjects were order takers whose job was to answer calls from customers and administer those calls. Performance of other subjects is a little less straightforward to measure so we don't examine that here. We measure the performance of these 134 order takers by the number of telephone calls they take. Workers who quit the company or were on leave have zero calls for those days in the data.

The outcome variable for quits is binary: $y = 1$ for subjects who quit the firm within eight months after the start of the experiment, and $y = 0$ for those who didn't. In the treatment group, 16% quit, compared to 35% in the non-treatment group. The difference is 19 percentage points. These 16% and 35% quit rates are conditional probabilities (see Chapter 4, Section 4.3). The 19 percentage-point difference is large. It implies that working from home reduced the proportion of job-quitters by more than a half. Viewed from another angle, it implies that working from home increases worker retention by around 30% (from 65% to 84%). The next figure (Figure 20.1) shows stacked bars that help appreciate the magnitude of the difference viewed from both angles.

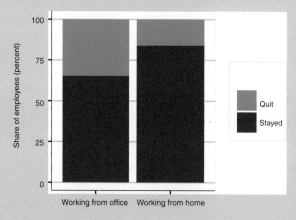

Figure 20.1 Employee retention, working from home vs working from office

Note: Treatment group: working from home; non-treatment group: working from the office. Stayed: remained employed for eight months; quit: quit the company within eight months.
Source: `working-from-home` dataset. N=249.

The outcome variable for performance among order takers is the number of phone calls taken, measured in thousands. The mean in the treatment group is 14 thousand; the mean in the non-treatment group is 10 thousand. The difference is 4 thousand calls.

Table 20.3 shows the corresponding two regression outputs: the left-hand-side variable is the outcome variable, and the right-hand-side variable is the treatment group variable. The regression table shows the same effect estimates as the ones we calculated. The probability of quitting is lower by 19 percentage points in the treatment group. This is a large effect, as it's more than half of the 35% probability in the non-treatment group. Order takers in the treatment group worked 4 thousand more phone calls on average, which is more than a third more than the 10 thousand calls in the non-treatment group.

Table 20.3 Effect estimates: probability of quitting and number of calls

Variables	(1) Quit job	(2) Phone calls (thousand)
Treatment group	−0.19**	4.04**
	(0.055)	(0.99)
Constant	0.35**	10.06**
	(0.044)	(0.75)
Observations	249	134
R-squared	0.047	0.113

Note: Linear regression estimates. Robust standard error estimates in parentheses.
**$p<0.01$, * $p<0.05$.

Source: working-from-home dataset.

Part of the effect on the number of calls comes from the first effect, the lower quit rate: employees in the treatment group stayed with the firm longer, on average, and thus could work more phone calls. Further analysis shows that that's not the whole story: even if we compare employees who stayed with the firm, those who were assigned to stay at home placed more calls per day. You are invited to verify this as a data exercise.

Recall that we have one-sided non-compliance here that isn't too strong. Thus, our estimates are average intent-to-treat effect estimates. They show that being assigned to working from home leads to a decrease of the likelihood of quitting by more than a half, and, among order takers, an increase in the number of calls by one third. About 20% of the subjects assigned to work from home ended up working in the office, while everyone assigned to working in the office did so. Thus, the average treatment effects are likely larger than the average intent-to-treat effects we estimated, but the differences should be small. Thus, with some sloppiness, we can call these estimates the effects of working from home.

We can use the standard error estimates to construct confidence intervals. The 95% CI for the effect on the quit rate is [−0.30, −0.08]: we can be 95% confident that working from home makes employees similar to those in the experiment between 8 and 30 percentage points less likely to quit the company (or any company represented by it). The 95% CI for the performance effect is [2.08, 6.0]: we can be 95% confident that working from home makes employees similar to those in the experiment make 2 to 6 thousand more phone calls in 8 months.

Both of these confidence intervals exclude zero. Formal tests also show that the estimates are statistically significantly different from zero, with p-values less than 0.01. Thus we can safely conclude that working from home has a positive effect on the retention and performance of employees similar to those in the experiment.

Recall that when we checked for balance, we found three variables that were problematic: being married and having children were both substantially different and statistically significantly different between treated and non-treated, and the difference in having internet access, while small, was also statistically significant.

Let's see what happens to the effect estimates, and their standard errors, when we include these three variables in the regression. Table 20.4 shows the results of the two regression outputs corresponding to the two outcome variables, quitting and the number of phone calls (the second one for order taker employees only).

Table 20.4   Effect estimates conditioning on the three unbalanced covariates

Variables	(1) Quit job	(2) Phone calls (thousand)
Treatment group	−0.19**	4.06**
	(0.056)	(0.96)
Married	−0.13	−5.44*
	(0.074)	(2.17)
Children	0.11	3.87
	(0.097)	(2.41)
Internet at home	0.18**	
	(0.036)	
Constant	0.19**	10.65**
	(0.056)	(0.76)
Observations	249	134
R-squared	0.055	0.168

Note: Linear regression estimates. There is no coefficient estimated for internet at home in column (2) because all order takers had internet access. Robust standard error estimates in parentheses.
** $p<0.01$, * $p<0.05$.
Source: working-from-home dataset.

The effect estimates are essentially the same as when we didn't condition on these three variables (see Table 20.3): a 19 percentage points lower quit rate and 4 thousand more phone calls. The standard errors, too, are very similar. Including these covariates made little difference in the estimated effect. As a data exercise, you are invited to include more variables to see if their inclusion makes a difference to the standard error estimates.

From these results, we can conclude that the fact that a few covariates weren't perfectly balanced makes no difference for the effect estimates. The conclusions we drew earlier hold: working from home increased employee retention significantly, and, among order takers, it increased employee performance, too.

20.10   Spillovers

Everything that we have discussed so far in this chapter hinges on the hidden assumption that there are no spillovers. **Spillovers**, also called **extraneous effects**, refer to effects of the intervention on other subjects. When there are spillovers, the fact that a particular subject is in the treatment group has an effect on the outcomes of some of the other subjects. In some situations we may safely assume that there are no spillovers. But, in other situations, we can't dismiss the possibility of spillovers.

There are many examples where spillovers may occur. Public health interventions to treat infectious diseases may affect other people who are in contact with, and can be infected by, the subjects of the experiment. Information interventions that make subjects aware of some things may affect other people they talk to, and make them aware of those things, too. These are examples of **positive spillovers**.

But **negative spillovers** are also a possibility. For example, interventions that help some people find jobs may hinder other people's chances as the intervention may increase competition for jobs.

Spillovers, when they occur, have severe consequences. Average, and total, effects may be larger or smaller than what we would get without the spillovers, depending on whether the spillovers are positive or negative. For example, vaccination has positive spillover, and its total effect is stronger than the sum of the individual effects on the treated subjects. In contrast, with a negative spillover, the total effect is weaker than the sum of the effects on the treatment group.

Another potential consequence of spillovers is that they may also lead to biased estimates of the average effect on the subjects in the treatment group. That happens when the spillover affects members of the non-treatment group. In such a case, the average outcome of the untreated subjects is not a good approximation to the potential untreated outcome of the treated subjects. With positive spillovers affecting the non-treatment group, their average outcome is better than it would be if the intervention didn't take place. With negative spillovers affecting the non-treatment group, their observed outcomes are worse than it would be if the intervention didn't take place.

When spillovers are likely, good experimental design takes them into account. To avoid the effect of spillovers on effect estimates, it is good practice to create treatment groups and non-treatment groups in a way that minimizes contact between them. For example, in an experiment of a vaccination intervention in a rural area, experimenters may randomly assign entire villages to treatment or non-treatment groups instead of assigning individuals or households. Spillovers are much more likely within a village then across villages, thus this design decreases the chances of spillovers to members of the non-treatment group. It can also help estimate the spillover effects themselves if not everybody in the village is treated.

Whether spillovers are likely in a particular experiment is difficult to tell in advance. However, we often know something about their likelihood from domain knowledge, and, perhaps, the evidence from past experiments. For example, and not surprisingly, vaccinations against highly infectious diseases tend to have strong positive spillovers. Perhaps more surprisingly, increasing the job finding prospects of some people doesn't tend to decrease the chances of other people.

Review Box 20.8   Spillovers

- Spillovers, or extraneous effects, affect other subjects when a particular subject is treated.
- With spillovers, the total effect of an intervention includes the effects on all subjects.
- When spillovers affect members of the comparison group, estimates of the average effect for the treated subjects are biased.
- When spillovers are a possibility, good experimental design takes them into account – for example, by randomized assignment across groups as opposed to individuals.

20.11   Additional Threats to Internal Validity

In this section, we discuss threats to internal validity: things that can make the estimated effect in an intervention a bad estimate of the true effect. In Chapter 19, Section 19.17, we defined internal validity in the context of causal analysis in general. In the context of experiments, **internal validity** means the extent to which the estimated effect shows the true average effect among the subjects of the experiment.

So far we have argued that the difference in average outcomes between the treatment and the non-treatment groups provides a good estimate of the average treatment effect if assignment is random, compliance is perfect, and there are no spillovers. When compliance is imperfect but assignment is random and there are no spillovers, the same comparison gives a good estimate of the average intent-to-treat effect. In short, random assignment leads to high internal validity of an effect estimate. All of this is true unless other things go wrong. Unfortunately, there are some additional things that may go wrong.

A frequent issue is **missing outcome values**. Outcomes are often missing due to **attrition**: as time passes, some of the subjects become unavailable for measurement. Subjects with missing outcome values cannot be included in the averages we compute or the regressions we run. Outcome values may be missing for two main reasons: due to problems with the data collection, or due to fundamental reasons.

Issues with data collection arise often when the outcome is measured in surveys, due to nonresponse (see Chapter 1, Section 1.8). For example, in an experiment to help unemployed people find long-term jobs, an outcome may be how satisfied people are with the service they received, measured in a survey. Nonresponse to this survey may be a problem. The second reason, missing outcome variable for fundamental reasons, occurs when the outcome is observed only under some conditions, and some subjects don't meet that condition. In the same example of the experiment to help unemployed people find long-term jobs, an outcome is how long people stay in their job, but this is not observed for subjects who don't find a job.

Missing data is a problem for internal validity if observations with missing data are different in terms of potential outcomes. In other words, it's a problem when the outcome variable is not missing at random. **Missing at random** would mean that whether the value of the outcome variable is missing is independent of potential outcomes. Analogously to random assignment, this definition of randomness is also about independence. If the outcome variable is missing at random, it does not affect internal validity.

It is difficult to uncover whether outcome values are missing at random or not. As usual, two approaches may help. The first is checking whether observations with missing outcome values are similar to observations with observed outcome values. That's analogous to checking covariate balance. A related check is whether outcome values are missing at the same rate in the treatment group and the non-treatment group. Different rates do not necessarily imply that missing is related to potential outcomes. Nevertheless, such a difference would imply that there is something systematic about missing values, which should be investigated.

The second approach is to understand the reasons for missing data. For example, subjects in the non-treatment groups may be harder to follow if their outcomes are worse. That would lead to missing outcome values in a systematic, non-random, way. Other examples include when the reasons are fundamental as opposed to data problems; in such cases missing outcome values are almost always not missing at random.

What can data analysts do when they can't conclude that outcomes are missing at random? The first thing to consider is the scale of the problem. It's probably fine to ignore the problem and use observations with non-missing values only when less than 10 percent of observations have missing outcomes. If we can't ignore it, the next thing to consider is the likely cause for missing outcomes, and how that may be related to potential outcomes. Doing so can help assess in which direction the effect estimates are biased and, perhaps, undo some of that bias by including covariates in the regression. The third option is to create upper and lower bounds to the effect estimates by making assumptions about the outcome values for the missing observations. How to create such bounds is beyond the scope of this textbook.

Besides missing data, some experiments may be subject to other kinds of issues that threaten internal validity. An experiment may affect the outcomes of its subjects for reasons other than the intervention we want to examine. We distinguish three kinds of issues here, by whether they affect treated subjects, whether they affect untreated subjects, or whether they affect both.

Being part of the treatment group may affect some outcomes through mechanisms that we don't want to consider. Perhaps the best known of these is the **placebo effect**. A placebo effect occurs if the knowledge of being treated affects behavior itself. This is a frequent concern in medical experiments, when the act of taking a pill, interacting with a doctor, or undergoing a procedure may affect the health, or reported health, of people, regardless of the physiological effects of those interventions. But it may arise in a business context as well, for example when treated subjects within a company feel they receive more attention from their supervisors. A placebo effect affects the behavior of the treated group.

In contrast, some interventions may affect the behavior of subjects in the non-treatment group. People may volunteer for an experiment in the hope of being selected into the treatment group. If, instead, they are selected into the non-treatment group, they may do things differently and have different outcomes than if the experiment didn't take place at all (their potential untreated outcome).

Lastly, both treated and non-treated subjects may change their behavior just because of being part of an experiment. Or subjects may change their behavior because of more data being collected on them – for example, by a more intrusive measurement of what they do on the job. Careful experimental design should mitigate the effects of such issues.

Designing experiments with high internal validity is hard. There are many potential issues that need to be avoided or minimized. For that reason experiments are best carried out by teams of people with varying expertise, including expertise on designing experiments and domain knowledge.

Review Box 20.9   Threats to internal validity

Internal validity of experimental estimates of an average effect (ATE or AITTE) may be low due to:

- non-random assignment;
- spillovers;
- effects on treatment group subjects due to their knowledge of being in the treatment group (placebo effects);
- effects on non-treatment group subjects due to their knowledge of being assigned to the non-treatment group;
- effects on all subjects due to their knowledge of being part of an experiment.

20.A5   CASE STUDY – Working from Home and Employee Performance

Internal validity

In this experiment, assignment was random. Compliance was imperfect, but only in the treatment group, and even here more than 80% of the subjects complied with the treatment. Spillovers are unlikely to be important in this experiment: whether some of the subjects work from home or in the office is unlikely to affect the retention and performance of other subjects.

There are no missing values of the outcome variable in this data. All subjects of the experiment were followed as long as they remained employed with the company. As a result, which employees quit and which stayed on the job is observed for all employees. At the same time, employee performance, including the number of phone calls for order takers, can be measured only for the subjects who stayed in the job. That is a case of missing data because of a fundamental reason as opposed to data problems. We don't know how many phone calls employees would have placed, had they stayed employed with the company. In practice, we imputed zero phone calls for the weeks an employee was not working – e.g., because they quit the company. But it would be good to know how many phone calls quitters would have made. The estimated effect of working from home is 4000 more phone calls among order takers. But the treatment also decreased quits. Thus, with zero calls imputed for quitters, it is possible that the effect on the number of phone calls is positive simply because the treatment group has fewer zeros.

Is this an issue for measuring the effect of the intervention? From the point of view of the company, not necessarily. Either way the company benefits. This viewpoint is reflected in the way we handled missing values, imputing zeros for them. Yet it would be good to know if working from home improved performance on top of improving worker retention. You are invited to examine this, as a data exercise, by comparing the number of phone calls among employees who worked with the firm throughout. Note that this comparison includes workers who remained with the company, thus treating quitters as missing observations. Due to the fundamentally non-random reasons for missing values, the estimated effect on performance among workers who stayed with the company is likely different from the true effect.

Other threats to internal validity may be relevant, too, here. In principle, it is possible that the retention rate and average performance in the treatment group were better not because working from home made them better but because of other aspects of the experiment. Some employees in the treatment group may have been grateful to the company for the opportunity and worked better as a result. Some employees in the control group may have quit or worked less because they were disappointed by not being selected to work from home.

To assess the role of attitudes among treated subjects, the experimenters asked members of the treatment group how working from home improved their performance. Among the possible answers presented to the respondents was feeling positive toward the company for letting the employee work from home: 12% chose this answer. The more popular answers were related to the work environment itself (convenience, quiet environment). Thus, while a positive attitude may have played some role, it was not the most important reason for better performance.

To examine the role of potential disappointment in the control group, the analysts of the experiment compared the outcomes in the treatment group to other groups of employees. The most important such group was employees at another call center, in a different city, doing the same tasks as the Shanghai office, and who had characteristics that would have made them eligible for the experiment. The analysts found that performance changed more positively in the treatment group than in this other comparison group in the same way as compared to the control group.

Thus, lower performance in the control group was unlikely to be caused by negative attitudes towards the company.

These are good examples of how data analysts can assess potential issues with internal validity. Doing so strengthens the credibility of the conclusions of the main analysis. Here, that conclusion is that those potential threats to internal validity are not important. Thus, it was working from home that made employees less likely to quit and increase their work output, on average.

20.12 External Validity, and How to Use the Results in Decision Making

After discussing issues with internal validity, the last question to discuss is external validity: the extent to which the conclusions from an experiment can be applied to the situation we really care about. Usually, that situation is an intervention to be implemented in the future, under real-life circumstances.

To make sure that the results of the experiment help actual decision making, data analysts need to address two challenges to external validity. The first challenge is the usual one: whether the general pattern is the same across space, time, and subject pool. For example, an experiment with employees at a Chinese travel agency in 2010 may or may not be informative about how employees in another country or industry, in another year, would react to the same intervention. Or the estimated effect of price discounts on sales of a retailer may be different at other locations and other times.

The second challenge is specific to experiments. Good field experiments attempt to create experimental situations that are as close as possible to the situation relevant for decision making. The more they succeed, the better for external validity. However, in order to ensure high internal validity, experiments are often carried out in controlled circumstances. And those circumstances may differ from the circumstances of future interventions in important ways.

One such difference is random assignment itself. As we have seen, random assignment is essential for high internal validity. With random assignment, the estimated average effect shows what to expect when the intervention is implemented for all subjects. That is fine for external validity if, eventually, the subjects represent the target population that will become treated. An example is evaluating the effect of discounts on sales with an experiment that offered discounts to a randomly chosen subset of shoppers, informing the decision of whether to offer discounts to all shoppers eventually.

However, average effects estimated from an experiment with random assignment may be different from what to expect from a future intervention if that lets subjects choose to opt out or opt in. The experimental effect estimates may actually underestimate those effects. That happens when subjects who would benefit more are more likely to opt in when the intervention is implemented in real life. For example, when participating in training is optional, subjects with the highest motivation may be more likely to participate, and, at the same time, they would make the best use of what they learn there. The effect on them is larger than a random subset of the population. In other cases, the experimental effect estimates may overestimate the expected effect of a future intervention. That happens if subjects who would be the worst off without an intervention opt in, and they tend to benefit less from it. That may be a concern, for example, when program administrators encourage the most disadvantaged subjects to participate in a program that trains unemployed people.

Other features of a controlled experiment may also make the effect estimates different from the expected effects of a future intervention. In order to focus on the effect of the intervention, experiments often create situations that exclude the effect of other things on the outcome. However, when implemented in real life, those other things would matter, too, potentially modifying the effect of the intervention. This is a frequent worry with pharmaceutical experiments, in which the effects of drugs are examined in isolation whereas in real life most patients take multiple drugs at the same time. A similar example may be estimating the effect of various advertising tools in isolation (say, on social media, with online search, with online retailers, and so on) whereas in real life a mix of them would be implemented.

Data analysts need to think about such potential issues with external validity, both when designing an experiment and when concluding from the results of an experiment. For example, they may build in interactions of various interventions into the experimental treatment. Or they may allow subjects to choose within an experiment, randomizing not participation but the opportunity to participate. Moreover, data analysts may draw conclusions from an experiment making use of the results of other analyses, too. For example, they may have access to the results of many experiments carried out under different circumstances. Or they may collect data not only from the experiment with random assignment but also in a similar situation without random assignment and allowing selection. An example of the last of these is the **Working from home and employee performance** case study, that examined how outcomes change after employees are offered the choice to work from home, allowing for self-selection.

We can conclude that designing and analyzing experiments is not easy. External validity of any analysis is bound to be imperfect. Careful design and the analysis of data from multiple sources may help mitigate some of the issues. And, even with such imperfections, well-designed and well-implemented experiments can be very informative about what to expect from a future intervention.

20.A6 CASE STUDY – Working from Home and Employee Performance

External validity and business decision

The management of the company wanted to learn whether and how much the company can benefit from letting employees work from home four days a week. Before the experiment it expected substantial savings on office space, but it was worried that employee performance may decline because of the lack of control. The results of the experiment convinced the management that, instead, working from home substantially increased the retention of employees and increased their performance, on average. These results were unexpected for the management and convinced them that letting employees work from home was a good business decision.

However, the positive average effects may have hidden very heterogeneous individual effects. Recall that it is impossible to know individual treatment effects because we don't know the counterfactual outcomes. Instead, the analysts examined variation in individual performance during the experiment compared to their performance before the experiment. Doing so, they uncovered substantial variation in the treatment group. Some employees increased their performance a lot when working from home, others increased their performance only a little, and yet others decreased their performance. This large variation suggests that maybe not everybody worked better from home. So making everyone work from home was perhaps not a good idea.

Instead, the management decided to allow employees to choose whether they wanted to work four days a week from home and one day in the office (as in the experiment), or work in the office all five days. The employees who were allowed to choose included the subjects of the experiment, too. About half of the treatment group chose to go back to the office. These switchers tended to have lower performance from home when compared to their performance before the experiment. Similarly, about half of the non-treatment group chose to work from home. Of the employees who did not volunteer for the experiment, 10 percent chose to work from home. These patterns of switching suggest that employees learned about whether working from home is good for them, either from their own experience (the treatment group) or the experience of their peers (the other employees).

Analyzing the performance of all employees revealed that those who chose to work from home increased their performance by more than the estimated average effect in the experiment. This suggests that self-selection into working from home resulted in even larger gains for the company than what was expected after the experiment. The experiment carried out random assignment to overcome self-selection that may bias the effect estimates. However, the same self-selection turned out to be important when the policy was implemented.

What have we learned from this experiment? Most importantly, a company saved costs and improved worker retention and performance because of the results of a well-designed and well-implemented experiment. The results of the experiment were surprising to the management, showing that experiments can lead to new insights. On the substance, we learned that many, but not all, employees work better from home, at least in the jobs covered in the experiment.

On the methods side, we have seen that many details need to be addressed in a field experiment. Besides making sure that assignment was random, the experimenters had to keep track of all subjects using admin data of the firm and additional surveys. Using this data, we could estimate the effect of the intervention on outcomes and check covariate balance. The careful data collection helped minimize the prevalence of missing values and provided ways to address several potential issues with internal validity. Moreover, the analysts didn't stop at establishing internally valid effect estimates. Instead, they went on to describe how the management could use the results in their business decisions and what the effects of those decisions were.

Review Box 20.10   External validity of experiments

- External validity of an experiment is high if its conclusions hold for the decision situation we are interested in.
- The usual threats to external validity are relevant here, too: the conclusions may differ for different time periods, locations, and kinds of subjects.
- In addition, the experimental situation may include features that ensure higher control and thus higher internal validity but make it different from the situation we are interested in.

20.13   Main Takeaways

Designing and implementing good experiments is hard: it needs thinking, experience, and a lot of work.

- If implemented well, controlled experiments with random assignment allow to estimate the average treatment effect.
- Experiments need to have both high internal validity and high external validity to help decisions.

PRACTICE QUESTIONS

1. What's A/B testing? What's a field experiment? What's a survey experiment? Give an example for each.
2. With a binary treatment variable in mind, list two examples for rules that lead to random assignment in practice and two examples for rules that don't. What's wrong with the latter two rules?
3. When do we say that the covariates in experimental data are balanced? How can we check that?
4. When do we say that compliance in an experiment is perfect? What's a one-sided non-compliance?
5. What's the average intent-to-treat effect? When is it the same as the average treatment effect and when is it different?
6. When do we say that the estimated effect of an intervention has high internal validity? Give an example for high internal validity and one for low internal validity.
7. What do you expect to happen to the slope coefficient estimate on the treatment variable in a regression if you include covariates and assignment is random (and compliance perfect)? Why?
8. What do you expect to happen to the slope coefficient estimate of the treatment variable in a regression if you include covariates and assignment is *not* random? Why?
9. When do we say that an intervention has spillovers? Give two examples.
10. When do we say that the estimated effect of an intervention has high external validity? Give an example for high external validity and one for low external validity.
11. Design an experiment that could tell the expected effect of substituting lectures in Data Analysis with online lectures. Be specific about the subject pool, the outcome, the intervention, assignment, how you would measure the outcome, and so on. Would your design be robust to potential spillovers?
12. Design an experiment that could show the expected effect of extra tutoring in Data Analysis. Be specific about the subject pool, the outcome, the intervention, assignment, how you would measure the outcome, and so on. Should you be concerned about non-compliance?
13. You are asked by the admissions officer of your university to help design a webpage for the admissions website. Experts in the area came up with various competing ideas of what the website should look like. Your task is to evaluate those ideas. How would you design an experiment that could do that?
14. The management of the company you work for is thinking about introducing free coffee and free lunch sandwiches for all employees. (The company has many offices.) Design an experiment that could assess the effect of this on the morale and retention of employees. Should you worry about spillovers in your experiment? If yes, in what way would it affect your estimates and could you do anything about it? If not, why not?
15. Design an experiment to evaluate the effect of nicotine patches on quitting cigarette smoking. Be explicit about who the subjects of the experiment would be and how you would recruit them. Define the outcome variable and discuss how you would measure it. Would you have to

worry about non-compliance? If yes, how would you address this? What if you can't address it? Would you have to worry about placebo effects, when the treatment group may change their behavior simply because of being part of the intervention? If yes, how would you address this? Finally, would you have to worry about missing outcome data at the end of the experiment? If yes, how would you address it?

DATA EXERCISES

Easier and/or shorter exercises are denoted by [*]; harder and/or longer exercises are denoted by [**].

1. Use the data of the **Working from home and employee performance** case study. Estimate the effect on phone calls among employees who didn't quit. Compare these to the estimates in Table 20.3. Interpret both coefficients, and explain what their difference means. [*]
2. Use the data of the **Working from home and employee performance** case study. First, estimate the effect on phone calls (among order takers) but include the number of phone calls in the pre-treatment period. Second, in addition, include all of the variables in Table 20.1 except the age of the youngest child (that is defined only for those with children). Compare the effect estimates and their standard errors, and explain what you find. [*]
3. Consider the formula for sample size calculation in Under the Hood section 20.U2, and calculate the expected number of ads in our **Fine tuning social media advertising** case study. Calculate the expected number by altering assumptions. [*]
4. Think about a simple problem with two alternative solutions, A and B. Design and carry out an online A/B testing experiment (or at least a pilot version). Describe the process, the choices you had to make, and the result. [**]
5. The study "Put Your Money Where Your Butt Is: A Commitment Contract for Smoking Cessation" evaluates a field experiment carried out in the Philippines to see what helps people quit smoking. The experiment had a randomized control group and two treatment arms: nasty pictures ("cue cards") and, more importantly, a "commitment device": treated people were encouraged to set aside money that they would get back at the end of the experiment, but only if they passed a urine test showing that they quit smoking. Find the study (the World Bank discussion paper is ungated), and summarize the experiment in less than one page. Find the data (Stata file cares1yr_preanalysis. data available at ICPSR). Estimate the intent-to-treat effect at the 1-year horizon without covariates and assuming missing outcomes at random; then with covariates (latter is in col (4) in table 4; variables for the two treatment arms are "cues" and "treament"; outcome is passedtest_1yr). Discuss what you find. [**]

REFERENCES AND FURTHER READING

The case study on the effects of working from home is based on Bloom et al. (2015).

On experiments, useful readings include Jadad & Enkin (2009), Gerber & Green (2013) and the practical tool collection in Duflo et al. (2008). Cai & Szeidl (2017) assess the role of relationships between small businesses in China and illustrate many issues in designing experiments. Bandiera et al. (2011) is a nice review article that discusses field experiments within firms. Banerjee & Duflo (2011) is an excellent popular book that discusses field experiments in economic and social policy in developing countries. On an experiment regarding smoking, see Giné et al. (2010). Luca & Bazerman (2020) discuss how internet companies use experiments.

We already mentioned Salsburg (2001), it is a wonderful book on the history of statistics, including a great discussion on how the idea of random assignment in experiments emerged.

20.U1   UNDER THE HOOD: LATE: THE LOCAL AVERAGE TREATMENT EFFECT

With random assignment but imperfect compliance, we can uncover the average intent-to-treat effect (AITTE) for all subjects but not the average treatment effect (ATE) for all subjects. However, as we discussed in Section 20.7, we can uncover the average treatment effect on those who would comply with the assignment. That effect is called the local average treatment effect, or LATE.

Some notation. Let the outcome be y, assignment to treatment w ($w = 1$ if assigned to the treatment group, $w = 0$ if assigned to the non-treatment group), and let actual treatment be x ($x = 1$ if ends up being treated, $x = 0$ if not). Let's allow for both kinds of non-compliance: some subjects assigned to treatment ($w = 1$) comply and end up being treated ($x = 1$) but some don't ($x = 0$); some subjects assigned to non-treatment ($w = 0$) comply and end up being untreated ($x = 0$) but others don't ($x = 1$). And let p be the proportion treated among subjects assigned to treatment (those that comply), and let q be the proportion of those that are treated among subjects assigned to non-treatment (here these don't comply). As formulae:

$$p = Pr[x = 1 | w = 1] \tag{20.4}$$

$$q = Pr[x = 1 | w = 0] \tag{20.5}$$

The average intent-to-treat effect (AITTE) is the average effect of being assigned to treatment, with this average defined across all subjects. Because assignment is random, we can get a good estimate of the AITTE by comparing the average observed outcomes among subjects assigned to treatment ($w = 1$) and subjects assigned to non-treatment ($w = 0$):

$$AITTE \approx E[y | w = 1] - E[y | w = 0] \tag{20.6}$$

From this AITTE estimate we can get a LATE estimate by scaling it up with the difference in compliance rate between the two groups:

$$LATE = \frac{AITTE}{p - q} \approx \frac{E[y | w = 1] - E[y | w = 0]}{Pr[x = 1 | w = 1] - Pr[x = 1 | w = 0]} \tag{20.7}$$

This general formula gives back the simpler case we discussed in Section 20.7 with one-sided non-compliance. Using our notation there we had $p = 0.5$ and $q = 0$ so $LATE = \frac{AITTE}{0.5} = 2 \times AITTE$.

20.U2   UNDER THE HOOD: THE FORMULA FOR SAMPLE SIZE CALCULATION

In this section we show the most widely used formula for the minimum number of observations to achieve a pre-determined level of significance and a pre-determined level of power. In particular, we show the formula that we need to discover an average outcome difference of a particular magnitude between the treatment group and the control group.

Let's use the following notation. Let the mean outcome in the treated group be m_1, and let the mean outcome in the untreated group be m_0. The standard deviation of the outcome variable is σ. We want to test the following null hypothesis against the following alternative hypothesis:

$$H_0: m_1 - m_0 = 0 \tag{20.8}$$

$$H_A: m_1 - m_0 \neq 0 \tag{20.9}$$

Let's pick a 5% level of significance: we tolerate a 5% chance of a false positive. Let's pick the usual level of power, 80%: we want to avoid a false negative with at least an 80% chance – in other words, we allow for 20% or less chance for a false negative. To be more precise, we can make sure the power is 80% against a specific alternative instead of the general one we specified above in H_A. The specific alternative is that, instead of zero, the difference is exactly what we assume for it, $m_1 - m_0$.

We set the number of treated and untreated observations to be the same ($n_0 = n_1$) and the total number of observations is $n = n_0 + n_1$.

Then the number of observations (n) we need can be computed using the two means (m_1 and m_0) and the standard deviation (σ) by the following formula:

$$n = 4\sigma^2 \times \left(\frac{1.96 + 0.84}{m_1 - m_0}\right)^2 \tag{20.10}$$

In this formula, 1.96 corresponds to the 5% level of significance we set (the inverse normal distribution of 0.025 is 1.96, and 0.025 is half of the 5% on each side of the two-sided alternative), and 0.84 corresponds to the 80% level of power we set (the inverse normal distribution of 0.2 is 0.84).

More generally, we can have any level of significance α and any level of power β; the corresponding values of the inverse normal distribution are denoted by $t_{\alpha/2}$ and $t_{1-\beta}$. The formula for n is then

$$n = 4\sigma^2 \times \left(\frac{t_{\alpha/2} + t_{1-\beta}}{m_1 - m_0}\right)^2 \tag{20.11}$$

Finally, let's look at the case when the outcome variable is binary so that its average is a proportion. Let's call the proportion of 1s among treated observations r_1, and let's call the proportion of 1s among untreated observations r_0. Then we look at the hypotheses

$$H_0: r_1 - r_0 = 0 \tag{20.12}$$

$$H_A: r_1 - r_0 \neq 0 \tag{20.13}$$

Here, the problem becomes simpler, because we can easily derive the standard deviation (σ in the formula). The overall proportion of 1s is $r = r_1/2 + r_0/2$, and $\sigma = \sqrt{r(1 - r)}$. For a 5% level of significance and an 80% power, the formula is

$$n = 4r(1 - r)\left(\frac{1.96 + 0.84}{r_1 - r_0}\right)^2 \tag{20.14}$$

You are invited to verify that this formula gives approximately 1.7 million for the required number of observations with the initial assumptions in our **Fine tuning social media advertising** case study ($r_1 = 0.0006$, $r_0 = 0.0005$).

21 Regression and Matching with Observational Data

How to use regression analysis and matching to condition on confounder variables in practice

Motivation

Many firms are owned by their founder or family members of their founder. You want to uncover whether such founder/family-owned firms are as well managed as other kinds of firms and, if there is a difference, how much of that is due to their ownership as opposed to something else. You have cross-sectional observational data on firms and their management practices, and you estimate a difference using simple regression. But is that difference due to founder/family ownership? In particular, can you use multiple regression to get a good estimate of the effect of founder/family ownership? If not, can you tell whether your estimate is larger or smaller than the true effect?

You want to estimate the effect of foreign ownership of football (soccer) clubs in Europe on their performance. You have data on all football clubs from many European countries. But foreign ownership is more prevalent in some kinds of clubs than in others, depending on the country, the division, and the size of the city of the clubs. In particular, not all countries allow foreign ownership of football clubs, and foreign ownership tends to be more prevalent in upper division clubs in larger cities. Do these issues pose a problem for your analysis? If yes, how should you address them?

In Chapter 19 we discussed that, in principle, data analysts can uncover the effect of an intervention using observational data by conditioning on confounders. We also emphasized the practical difficulties of this approach, stemming from the fact that real-life data rarely includes variables that are good measures of all potential confounders. But we argued that even though the ideal is rarely attainable, conditioning on confounder variables in the data can help understand what the true effect may be.

In this chapter we discuss how to condition on potential confounder variables in practice, and how to make sense of the results when our question is causal. We start with our old friend, the multiple linear regression (introduced in Chapter 10), and discuss how to select the variables to condition on and how to decide on their functional form. We then turn to matching, which is an intuitive alternative that turns out to be quite complicated to carry out in practice. Matching can detect a lack of common support (when some values of confounders appear only among treated or untreated observations). However, with common support, regression and matching, when applied according to good practice, tend to give similar results. We also give a very brief introduction to other methods: instrumental variables and regression-discontinuity. These methods can give good effect estimates even when we don't have all confounders in our data, but they can only be applied in specific circumstances.

This chapter reviews methods that can be used for all kinds of observational data, including cross-sectional data, time series data, and panel data. However, data with a time series dimension, especially panel data, offers additional opportunities, which call for more specific methods. We'll discuss those in Chapters 22, 23, and 24.

The case study in this chapter, **Founder/family ownership and quality of management**, investigates whether the fact that a company is owned by its founder or their family affects the quality of management. The case study uses the `wms-management-survey` dataset, which is cross-sectional observational data from the World Management Survey that we described in Chapter 1 and used in Chapter 4. It illustrates how to think about confounders and what's measured from among them in the data, how to estimate effects by regression and matching, and how to think about whether and how our estimate may be biased relative to the true effect.

Learning outcomes

After working through this chapter, you should be able to:

- formulate a thought experiment that would uncover the effect of a causal variable;
- think about the sources of variation in the causal variable in the data, whether they are exogenous or endogenous sources;
- estimate the effect using multiple linear regression, by selecting the appropriate right-hand-side variables and their functional form;
- understand analyses using exact matching and matching on the propensity score, and understand the potential issues with such estimates;
- think about how to sign the bias of an effect estimate that is due to the fact that not all endogenous sources of variation are conditioned on;
- understand the idea of instrumental variables and regression-discontinuity, and identify situations in which they may be applied.

21.1 Thought Experiments

Data analysts turn to observational data to answer causal questions when they can't run an appropriate experiment. Often there is not enough time or resources to carry out an experiment. Sometimes an experiment would require controlling for too many things that would make external validity too low. Sometimes an experiment would be impossible to run due to ethical concerns.

Even in such cases, with no actual experiment to run, it is good practice to think about an experiment that could help uncover the effect we are after. These are called **thought experiments**: experiments that are designed but not carried out.

It is good practice to think through a thought experiment when doing causal analysis on observational data, for several reasons.

First, a thought experiment can clarify the details of the intervention: the subjects, the treatment variable, the outcome we want to examine, and how it compares to the causal variable in the data. This helps understand what we mean by being treated and untreated and thus what the counterfactual outcome could be.

Second, it can help understand the mechanisms through which the causal variable may affect the outcome. Understanding what mechanisms may play a role is important for various reasons, including identifying the variables that we should not condition on.

Third, a thought experiment helps understand how the ideal situation compares to what we have: how a hypothetical random assignment compares to the sources of variation in the causal variable in our data.

Review Box 21.1   Thought experiment

- A thought experiment is an experiment that is designed in some detail but not carried out.
- Thought experiments help data analysts to:
  - clarify the subjects, the intervention, the outcome, and the counterfactual outcome;
  - clarify the mechanism(s) of interest;
  - contrast random assignment with the actual sources of variation in the causal variable in their data.

21.A1   CASE STUDY – Founder/Family Ownership and Quality of Management

Question, thought experiment, data

In this case study we investigate whether the fact that a company is owned by its founder, or their family members, has an effect on the quality of management. In other words, we want to know whether founder/family-owned companies are better or worse managed than other firms, on average, because of their ownership.

This is a causal question, and we are after an average effect. Let's think through a **thought experiment**. The subjects of this thought experiment are companies. The intervention is a change in company ownership. For this, we need a subject pool with the same ownership, and we need to randomly assign some of them to change their ownership.

In fact, we should be more precise about the intervention and how it affects ownership. To change ownership, the owners would sell their stake to other investors – either directly, or indirectly by listing their company on a stock exchange. Thus, the effect of the intervention would be a form of ownership that can be the result of such sales.

In real life, founder/family-owned firms can and do sell their shares to other investors, whereas other forms of ownership rarely change to founder/family ownership. So the intervention works in one direction, from founder/family ownership to other ownership, but not the other. Moreover, this thought experiment puts a restriction on the form of ownership after the intervention: some types of ownership are unlikely to emerge, such as ownership by the government or municipalities. We should keep this in mind when working with observational data that includes companies with such forms of ownership.

Therefore, in the thought experiment, we would take all founder/family-owned companies, randomly choose half of them, and make them sell their stakes to whoever might want them. (This is a thought experiment so we may as well assume perfect compliance: treated companies receive offers that they don't refuse.) As a result of the intervention, untreated companies remain in founder/family ownership, while treated companies have other forms of ownership, such as other private individuals, dispersed shareholders, and private equity.

With enough time elapsed after the intervention, such as one or two years, we would measure the quality of management among treated and untreated firms. The difference between their average quality scores would show the average effect of giving up founder/family ownership.

Note that the intervention in this thought experiment is the opposite of what the original question would imply. The question is about the effect of founder/family ownership, while the intervention is changing ownership from founder/family to something else. This is an additional step of thinking, which, although pretty straightforward, can lead to confusion. To avoid that, we'll focus on the opposite of the effect identified in our thought experiment: remaining founder/family-owned. Thus, we will examine the effect of founder/family ownership on the quality of management, and by that we'll mean the average effect of founder/family firms not selling their shares to other investors.

We use the `wms-management-survey` dataset which is cross-sectional observational data from the World Management Survey. The World Management Survey is an international project that collects data on management practices from many companies and organizations across various industries and countries. We discussed the details of this survey, along with the quality of its data, in the case study **Management quality and firm size: data collection** in Chapter 1, and we used a subset of this data in the case study **Management quality and firm size: describing patterns of association** in Chapter 4.

The data we use in this case study was collected between 2004 and 2015. It is a cross-section of 10 282 firms in manufacturing from 24 countries. Thus, this is observational cross-sectional data. As we described in Chapter 1, Section 1.8, the survey aimed to get a representative sample of firms of medium size within the included countries. The countries themselves are not a representative sample of the world: they are mostly rich countries, including the USA and countries from Western Europe, complemented by large Latin American countries and India.

The outcome variable is the management score. Recall from Chapter 1 that this score is the average of 18 scores that measure the quality of specific management practices. Each score is measured on a 1 through 5 scale, with 1 for worst practice and 5 for best practice.

The causal variable is founder/family ownership. The ownership variable in the data is quite detailed, with 11 categories. From the many categories we created a binary variable that is 1 if the firm is founder-owned or family-owned and 0 otherwise. As we argued in the thought experiment, we are interested in ownership categories that could be the result of founders or their families selling their shares. Thus we dropped observations that were owned by the government. We also dropped observations with missing ownership data and with "other" ownership type.

The result is a cross-sectional data file with 9569 companies in manufacturing, from 24 countries. Of these, 4353 are owned by their founder or family (45%).

21.2 Variables to Condition on, Variables Not to Condition On

After defining the causal variable and the outcome variable and describing an appropriate thought experiment, we should turn to the sources of variation in the causal variable. Recall from Chapter 19, Section 19.12, that we distinguish two types of variation in the causal variable x. Exogenous sources are variables that are independent of potential outcomes, while endogenous sources are variables that are related to potential outcomes.

Eventually, the goal of our analysis will be to use exogenous sources in x. In observational data, one way to ensure that, at least in principle, is conditioning on all endogenous sources of variation – these are the confounders. (Under rare circumstances, we may have other ways to ensure that, see later in Sections 21.9 and 21.10.) Taking stock of all potential sources of variation in x and thinking about whether each is endogenous or exogenous are the necessary first steps towards that goal.

As we discussed in Chapter 19, Section 19.12, this is still a thinking exercise, without examining the variables in our data. But this thinking should be based on an understanding of where the data came from and domain knowledge about the potential mechanisms that may drive variation in the causal variable.

In Chapter 19, Section 19.13, we distinguished three types of variables that are endogenous sources of variation, which we should condition on. These confounder variables are:

- Common cause: the variable affects x and y.
- Mechanism of reverse causality: y affects x through this variable.
- Unwanted mechanism: x affects y through this variable, but we don't want to consider it when estimating the effect of x on y.

In Chapter 19, Section 19.16, we listed three kinds of **bad conditioners**: variables that data analysts should not condition on when attempting to uncover the effect of x on y:

- An exogenous source of variation in x.
- A mechanism that we want to include in the effect to be uncovered.
- Common consequence: both x and y affect the variable.

The result of the thinking exercise is a list of the exogenous and endogenous sources of variation in the causal variable. We may visualize that by drawing a causal map (Chapter 19, Section 19.9). This list, or causal map, describes our assumptions of the causal relations between latent variables: variables that we can think about, but which may or may not be measured in our data.

The next step is to relate those variables to variables in our data. These are the variables we can condition on. Typical real-life observational data doesn't have good measures of all of the variables we want to condition on. This is in contrast to the ideal of ceteris paribus comparison. While imperfect, conditioning on what we can observe can still give us valuable results. In the next sections we discuss how to do that in practice and how to interpret the results.

21.A2   CASE STUDY – Founder/Family Ownership and Quality of Management

Sources of variation in ownership, causal map, observable variables to condition on

The causal variable (x) in our case study is the binary founder/family ownership variable: 1 if owned by the founder or their family and 0 otherwise. In order to decide on which z variables to condition on in this observational cross-sectional data, let's first think about sources of variation in x.

One source of variation in ownership is whether the firm started as founder/family-owned to begin with. Alternative ways to start a firm include spin-offs, joint ventures, or affiliates of other firms, including multinationals. But what could explain how a firm starts? Let's focus on the product the firm wants to sell and the technology needed to produce that. Some technologies require a lot more investment than others, and firms with such expensive projects are more likely to include outside investors from the start. The technology that the firm uses is thus a source of variation in ownership. It's likely to be an endogenous source: different kinds of production technologies make different management practice more or less favourable, but the sign of the association is not obvious.

Whether firms start as founder-owned or involve outside owners from the beginning may also depend on cultural and institutional factors in a society. This may be an especially important source of variation in data collected from many countries, or within countries in which values and institutions vary. The same cultural and institutional factors may affect the quality of management practices. Thus they are likely endogenous sources of variation in ownership, too. In particular, some traditional cultural and institutional factors (such as the role of trust in society) make founder/family ownership more likely but, at the same time, they may lead to a lower quality of management.

Besides how firms started, the other broad set of variables that affect current ownership is what happened between the time they started and the time we observed them in the data. Many firms start as founder-owned; then some remain in the ownership of their founders or their families, while other are sold to other investors. Whether founder/family shares are sold to other investors depends on supply (whether owners want to sell) and demand (whether investors want to buy). Thus it is a good starting point to think about potential supply and demand factors that may affect observed ownership.

Some of those supply factors are likely **exogenous sources of variation**. For example, life events and changes in family circumstances, such as the number and gender of the children of the founder, affect family ownership in the next generation, but they are unlikely to affect the quality of management through other mechanisms.

In contrast, cultural norms are **endogenous sources of variation** in the willingness to sell family ownership. Founders and their families may be more likely to want to keep their ownership in more traditional societies. At the same time, firms in such societies may be slower to adopt better management practices. This is another example of how cultural values in a society can be endogenous sources of variation in ownership. Institutions, such as urban financial centers, would also help facilitate take-overs as well as educate managers.

Most of the demand factors are likely endogenous, too. One endogenous demand factor is strong competition on the product market. Stronger competition may lead to a higher quality of management and, at the same time, may make a firm a more desirable target for takeover by a competitor. Another endogenous source may be firm size: larger firms tend to be better managed, as we have seen in the case study **Management quality and firm size: describing patterns of association** in Chapter 4. In fact, firm size may be an effect of management quality: better managed firms may be more successful and grow larger. But size may be a demand factor, too, as investors may be more interested in buying larger firms. Thus, it is likely an endogenous source of variation in ownership. Similarly, the age of the firm is related to demand factors: the older the firm, the more time outside investors had to acquire it. It's also an endogenous source of variation:

better managed firms tend to be more likely to stay in business for a longer time. Thus, firm size and age may be mechanisms of reverse causality.

Based on these thoughts, we identify the following sources of variation in founder/family ownership:

- Family circumstances may affect whether a company remains in founder/family ownership, such as whether the founder has children, their number, gender, and so on. This is an exogenous source of variation.
- How complex is the technology the firm uses. Some kinds of technologies make founder/family ownership more likely; they may negatively or positively affect the quality of management.
- Cultural and and institutional factors in the society. The factors that positively affect founder/- family ownership may likely negatively affect the quality of management.
- Competition. Negatively affects founder/family ownership, positively affects the quality of management.
- Firm size and age may be mechanisms of reverse causality (better managed firms may stay in business and grow larger and may, in turn, attract outside investors).

We summarize these assumptions in the causal map shown in Figure 21.1.

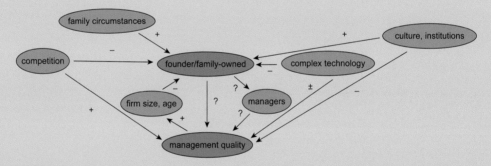

Figure 21.1   Founder/family ownership: sources of variation in observational data. Causal map

Most of these are latent variables. Which, if any, of the variables in the data can measure these latent variables? The few variables we have are the following: employment, age of firm, proportion of employees with college education (except for management), whether the firm faces moderate or strong competition in the market of its main product, in which industry the firm operates (standard industrial sector classification within manufacturing, with 2 digits), and the country in which the firm operates.

Of these, industry can be used as a measure of how complex a technology the firm uses and how competitive the product market is. Our data has 20 industry groups, such as "food and related products" and "electronic and other electrical equipment." These are rather broad categories, so industry is a useful but imperfect measure of product market and technology. Another useful but imperfect measure of the complexity of technology is the share of college-educated workforce. The number of competitors on the product market is also a useful but imperfect measure of the strength of competition.

The country where the firm is located is a measure of cultural and and institutional factors in the society. If countries were homogeneous culturally and institutionally, conditioning on country would take care of these confounders. Instead, it's an imperfect measure because there are differences even within some countries, especially within large and diverse ones.

The number of employees is a good but imperfect measure of firm size (sales or assets would add more information). Age of the firm turns out to be missing for 14 percent of the observations. We specified three binary variables to measure age: whether the firm is young (less than 30 years old), whether it is old (older than 80 years), and whether age is missing – middle age (30 to 80 years old) is the reference category.

Finally, let's discuss two variables in the data that are likely cases of bad conditioning variables. First, measures of the knowledge and skills of senior management, such as their level of education, may be mechanism variables: one of the ways owners can affect the quality of management is by hiring senior managers. Second, the share of exports in sales may also be a bad conditioning variable. Exporting is a decision made by the management of the firm so it may depend on who the owners are. At the same time, better managed firms tend to be more productive and are more likely to be exporters. So exporting may be a common consequence variable, something we shouldn't condition on.

21.3 Conditioning on Confounders by Regression

After reviewing the principles of what variables we should consider for conditioning when estimating an effect using observational data, let's turn to how we can actually do it. We start with our old friend, the linear regression.

Recall that multiple linear regression analysis offers to condition on selected variables (Chapter 10). In a causal analysis, we would like to use the multiple regression to estimate the effect of x on y, conditioning on observable confounder variables (z_1, z_2, ...):

$$y^E = \beta_0 + \beta_1 x + \beta_2 z_1 + \beta_3 z_2 + \cdots \tag{21.1}$$

As we know, here β_1 approximates the average difference in y between observations that are different in x but have the same values for z_1, z_2, ... This interpretation of β_1 is always true regardless of whether those z variables capture all endogenous variation in x.

If the z_1, z_2, ... variables capture all **endogenous sources of variation**, we say that x is **exogenous in the regression**. That means that, conditional on the z_1, z_2, ... variables in the regression, the variation in x is exogenous. In this case, the OLS estimate of β_1 in the regression is a good estimate of the average effect of x on y.

Unfortunately, as we know, that's very unlikely to happen in **observational data**. Instead, the z_1, z_2, ... variables tend to capture only some, but not all, of the endogenous sources of variation in x. In this case we say that x is **endogenous in the regression**. When x is endogenous in the regression, the OLS estimate of β_1 is a not good estimate of the average effect of x on y. Instead, it's a biased estimate of that effect.

That bias is called the **omitted variables bias**. The omitted variables bias is the difference between the true average effect of x on y and what estimate we can get for the β_1 coefficient on x by OLS from the regression. When x is exogenous in the regression, the omitted variable bias is zero. When x is endogenous in the regression, the omitted variables bias is not zero, and the bias occurs because we omit some confounders (therefore its name). As we discussed in Chapter 10, Section 10.3, the bias depends on how the omitted variables are related to x and y. There we derived its formula for a simple case; here we review the intuition.

Omitted variables bias is positive (the estimate is greater than the true effect) when the omitted confounder variables tend to be associated in the same direction with x as with y. It is negative when the omitted confounders tend to be associated in the opposite direction with x and y. In these cases, we say that we can **sign the omitted variable bias**. In other cases we may not be so lucky: some omitted confounders likely affect x and y in the same direction, others affect them in opposite directions, and no group dominates the other. In such cases we can't sign the omitted variable bias.

Indeed, signing the omitted variable bias is often the most important conclusion of a causal analysis using observational data. We can rarely get an unbiased effect estimate from such data. However, it's sometimes possible to arrive at an estimate that is arguably biased in a specific direction. That way we can conclude that the true effect is likely larger, or smaller, than our estimate.

For an example, recall our **Food and health** case study in Chapter 19, in which we wanted to uncover the effect of eating a lot of fruit and vegetables on maintaining normal blood pressure. Among the potential confounders we identified health consciousness, which likely affects how much fruit and vegetables people eat, together with other healthy behaviors that may in themselves affect blood pressure.

Assume for now that health consciousness is the only endogenous source of variation in eating fruit and vegetables that we need to worry about. But our data doesn't contain health consciousness at all, and it contains only a few, roughly measured variables on healthy behaviors, such as people's reports on whether they smoke or how many days a week they exercise. A lot of other behaviors remain unmeasured, such as healthy sleeping habits or the ability to manage emotional stress. Those are omitted variables that may negatively affect blood pressure but may, at the same time, be positively related to fruit and vegetable consumption because of the level of health consciousness. This would result in a negative omitted variable bias. In other words, this would make the estimated effect show a stronger negative effect than the true effect.

Continuing with the same example, recall that the doctor's advice may be another confounder, a mechanism of reverse causality. After diagnosing high blood pressure, doctors may advise people to eat more fruit and vegetables, introducing a positive correlation between blood pressure and the amount of fruit and vegetables consumed. This would introduce a positive omitted variable bias in the effect estimate: it would make the estimate less negative (or maybe even zero or positive) than it truly is. If both this and the previous bias are present, we can't sign it: it may be positive, zero, or negative. If, however, we convince ourselves that the first, negative bias is stronger, we can sign the overall bias to be negative.

Before moving on to discuss other questions, let's note that most data analysts use a slightly different notation for regression analysis when their goal is estimating the effect of x on y. Our standard notation for a regression is a shorthand for the conditional expected value: $y^E = E[y|\ldots]$. However, as we mentioned in Chapter 7, Section 7.2, an alternative notation includes an error term: $y = f(x) + e$.

With causal analysis, a variant of that notation can be helpful. In this notation the error term is called unobserved heterogeneity and is denoted by u not e. We discuss this notation and how it can be derived from potential outcomes in Under the Hood section 21.U1. Nevertheless, we won't use that notation in this textbook because it can be confusing, and we can explain all advantages and disadvantages of regression analysis without this notation. Instead, we'll continue using our notation of the regression as the conditional expectation.

> **Review Box 21.2 Conditioning on confounders in a regression**
>
> - When estimating a regression
>
> $$y^E = \alpha + \beta_1 x + \beta_2 z_1 + \beta_3 z_2 + \cdots \qquad (21.2)$$
>
> with the goal of uncovering the effect of x on y:
>   - x is exogenous in the regression if it has only exogenous sources of variation once z_1, z_2, ... are included;
>   - x is endogenous in the regression if it has any endogenous sources of variation even when z_1, z_2, ... are included.
> - When x is endogenous, the regression produces a biased estimate of the average effect of x on y: this is omitted variables bias.
> - Even a biased effect may be informative if we can sign the omitted variables bias.
>   - The omitted variables bias is positive if the omitted confounders tend to be correlated with x and y in the same direction.
>   - The omitted variables bias is negative if the omitted confounders tend to be correlated with x and y in opposite directions.
>   - We can't sign the omitted variables bias if some omitted confounders likely affect x and y in the same direction, others affect them in the opposite direction, and no group dominates the other.

21.4 Selection of Variables and Functional Form in a Regression for Causal Analysis

Perhaps the most important practical question when estimating an effect by regression is **variable selection**: what other variables to include together with the causal variables. This question, in turn, has two parts. The first question is whether we should include all of the observed confounders in the data or only some of them, and which ones. The second part of the question is how to enter those variables, in what functional form, including potential interactions. Recall from Chapter 8 that we can take logs, create piecewise linear splines, or create polynomials from the original variables to better approximate nonlinear patterns of association. Moreover, we can include interactions (Chapter 10, Section 10.10) that allow for different slopes among observations with different values of another variable.

The general principle is that variable selection matters to the extent that our choices affect the effect estimate: the coefficient estimate on the causal variable x. Regressions are equally good for us if they give very similar estimates of the coefficient on x, even if they are different in terms of what else they include. From among them we should prefer the simplest model, with the fewest variables, the simplest functional forms, and the fewest interactions.

Things are different if the regressions with different sets of other variables give substantially different coefficient estimates on x. Among them we should usually choose the one that includes more variables. This means the regression that includes more of the observed confounders, or uses more flexible functional forms, or more interactions. Of course, this advice does not extend to bad conditioning variables, such as mechanisms, exogenous sources of variation, or common consequences (see Section 21.2). We should not include bad conditioning variables regardless of what their inclusion does to the estimated effect of x. Another important caveat is that sometimes having many variables in the regression that don't matter can make the effect estimates imprecise, with a large standard error and a wide confidence interval (recall the degrees of freedom argument in Chapter 10, Section 10.5).

Thus, in principle, we should start by including all potential confounder variables in the data and then look at simpler versions with fewer confounders. If the simpler and more complex versions give us similar effect estimates, we should opt for the simpler one. However, following this turns out to be difficult in practice for choosing functional forms and interactions. The general principle is still true: more flexible forms and more interactions are better if they make a difference to the effect estimate, and we should opt for the simplest version if they don't make a difference. But there is no obvious starting point here, as including all possible interactions, or high-order polynomials, would be impossible. Arriving at such a specification is part of feature engineering (Chapter 14). Feature engineering is a time-consuming exercise and requires many decisions. Is it worth the effort?

Most often, the answer is no: when all we care about is the coefficient on the causal variable, the functional form of the included confounders doesn't matter in most cases. But it may matter sometimes. The trouble is that we don't know if our case is one where it matters or one where it doesn't matter.

Thus, we advise considering flexible functional forms and interactions with respect to the most important confounders but not the rest, and starting with a regression that includes them. Then, we should compare the effect estimates from this more complex model to the effect estimates from a simpler model with simple functional forms and without interactions, and choose the more complex model only if it gives a different effect estimate.

21.A3   CASE STUDY – Founder/Family Ownership and Quality of Management

Multiple regression analysis

The y variable is the management score: it measures the quality of management on a 1–5 scale, with 1 being the worst possible quality and 5 the best possible quality. This score is the average of the 18 scores of management practices (see Chapter 1, Section 1.C1, for more details). The range of y in the data is 1 to 4.9, its average is 2.88, standard deviation 0.64.

The causal variable, x, is binary, denoting whether the firm is owned by its founder or their family. Some 45% of the firms are founder/family-owned in the data.

When comparing founder/family-owned firms with the other firms in the data, we find that the average management score is 2.68 among founder/family-owned firms and 3.05 among the other firms. This is a difference of −0.37. It is a relatively large difference, more than half of the standard deviation of the outcome variable.

Of course, we know that this difference is the result of many things, of which the effect of ownership is only one. Recall from our thought experiment that the effect we are after is the management score difference due to the fact that the firm remained founder/family-owned instead of changing to have another ownership structure. In this cross-sectional observational data, there are many sources of endogenous variation in ownership. To address some of that endogeneity, based on our previous arguments, we want to condition on the following variables in our data:

- industry of the firm (SIC: standard industrial classification, 20 categories);
- country the firm operates in (24 countries);
- proportion of non-management employees with college education;
- strength of competition in the market for its main product;
- age of firm;
- number of employees.

We entered the proportion of college-educated workforce in a quadratic form. Of the four categories of degree of competition, we created three by merging the "0 competitors" category (54 firms, less than 1% of all firms) with the "1–4 competitors" category (1954 firms, 23%). We created four categories regarding age of firm: below 30 years, 30 to 80, 81 or older, plus unknown). We measure employment in logs.

We dropped observations for which any of these variables had missing values (except for the age of the firm, which was missing in 14% of the cases; we created a separate variable for this). In addition, we dropped the few firms with less than 50 employees or with more than 5000 employees (227 firms). The final data table, our workfile, has 8439 observations.

We estimated two versions of the regression with confounders. In the first version there are no interactions between them. This has 50 right-hand-side variables on top of the causal variable: 19 binary indicators for industry, 23 for country, 2 for competition, 2 for quadratic variables for the share of college-educated workers, 3 for the categories of firm age, and log employment. The second version includes many interactions: country interacted with industry, country interacted with all other confounders, and industry interacted with all other confounders. The rationale behind these interactions is that the association between the confounders and the causal variable and/or the outcome variable may differ by country (e.g., higher education may mean different things in different countries) or by industry (e.g., the number of competitors may mean different levels of competition in different industries). On top of the causal variable, there are 745 right-hand-side variables in the regression with interactions (the number of potential combinations is higher but many don't exist in the data).

Table 21.1 shows the results. Column (1) shows the regression results without conditioning on any of the confounders. Column (2) includes all confounders without interactions, and column (3) has all the interactions with country and industry. The table shows the estimate of the coefficient of interest together with other useful information. It does not show the coefficients on all other variables.

Without conditioning on other variables (column 1), the effect estimate is -0.37, reproducing the average management score difference between founder/family-owned firms and other firms (95% confidence interval is $[-0.39, -0.35]$). This difference is large: it's more than half of the standard deviation of the management score (0.64). This difference may be due to many reasons, ownership being only one of them.

	(1)	(2)	(3)
Table 21.1 Estimates of the effect of founder/family ownership on the quality of management. Multiple regression results			
Variables	**No confounders**	**With confounders**	**With confounders interacted**
Founder/family owned	−0.37**	−0.19**	−0.19**
	(0.01)	(0.01)	(0.01)
Constant	3.05**	1.75**	1.46**
	(0.01)	(0.05)	(0.22)
Observations	8440	8439	8439
R-squared	0.08	0.29	0.37

Note: Outcome variable: management quality score. Robust standard error estimates in parentheses.
** $p<0.01$, * $p<0.05$.

Source: wms-management-survey dataset.

The magnitude of the ownership difference decreases to −0.19 in column (2) if we condition on the confounder variables measured in the data. The estimate remains the same −0.19 if we include all the interactions as well (column 3). This is about 30% of the standard deviation of the management quality variable. The 95% CI is [−0.21, −0.17]. Including the many interactions improved the fit of the regression (the R-squared increased from 0.29 to 0.37), but it made no difference to the effect estimate. According to these estimates, the quality of management is lower, on average, by about 30% of a standard deviation, in founder/family-owned firms than other firms of the same country, industry, size, age, with the same proportion of college-educated workers, and with a similar number of competitors.

Thus, the regression that allows for many interactions produced a very similar effect estimate. So ours appears to be one of those frequent cases when the regression with many interactions produces a result that is very similar to what we get from the regression without any of those interactions. But we didn't know that before estimating the regressions with the interactions.

Instead, far more important was to condition on the confounders: the effect estimate without conditioning them is −0.37; the effect estimate conditional on them is −0.19. But what do all these numbers mean?

If all potential confounders were captured by the included right-hand-side variables, we could put the expected effect of changing ownership between our estimates of −0.21 and −0.17 in the population, or general pattern, represented by our data (this is our 95% CI). But our data is very far from the ideal situation of including good measures of all potential confounders. Then, you may ask, can this estimate say anything about what causal effect of ownership to expect in this situation?

Not really if we were completely agnostic about what confounders we may have left out. If we cannot make any additional assumptions, the bias can go either way, and we should remain rather skeptical about our estimate of about −0.2 measuring causal effect.

However, the estimates are informative if we are willing to make some assumptions. In particular, we may be able sign the bias if we assume how the omitted confounders are related to our x and y. In our case, we could argue that most of the omitted confounders are correlated with founder/family ownership and the quality of management in opposite directions. For example, factors like being in a large city may make outside investors more interested in buying a firm (and leading to fewer founder/family-owned firms in a cross-section) but also making the quality of its management better.

If we are right about these assumptions, the estimated effect of founder/family ownership is biased in the negative direction. Thus the true effect is probably weaker (less negative). In other words, we should expect less improvement in management quality after transferring ownership of currently founder/family-owned firms than what's suggested by our estimates. Remember that having added confounders such as industry and country has already led to a decrease in the estimated effect magnitudes (they became weaker, from -0.37 to about -0.2). If other omitted confounders behaved the way that confounders we had in the data do, we would see a similar pattern: an even smaller coefficient estimate (in absolute value).

Thus, we have some domain knowledge and some data evidence to suggest that there could indeed be additional confounders omitted from our model, and that including these variables would further reduce the estimated effect. By how much, we can't know.

21.5   Matching

As we have emphasized many times, linear regression is an approximation. It approximates the difference in average y between observations with different x but the same values for the other right-hand-side variables z_1, z_2, ... (Linear regressions that are saturated models are not approximations; see Chapter 11, Under the Hood section 11.U1.) But most often the linear regressions we estimate are not saturated models.) But why do we need an approximation when we want to compare observations with the same z_1, z_2, ... values? Why can't we just take those variables and find observations with the exact same values?

That's the idea behind the method we introduce in this section: **matching**. Matching aims to compare the outcomes between observations that have the same values of all of the other variables and different values of the x variable. While matching can be applied with multi-valued treatments as well, we discuss matching with a binary causal variable: $x = 0$ *or* 1. As we'll see, matching is an intuitively attractive method, but many issues arise when we implement it. Therefore, we introduce several versions of matching.

The ideal way of matching, called **exact matching**, is not an approximation. It matches observations that have the exact same values for all of the other variables. Perhaps the best way to understand, and implement, exact matching is considering it as a data aggregation procedure.

For exact matching, we create an aggregate data table from the original data. The observations of this aggregate data table are different value-combinations of the observed confounder variables.

Consider the following example. Our goal is to estimate the effect of foreign ownership of football (soccer) clubs in Europe on their performance. We use cross-sectional data on all clubs in all European countries that play in the first or second division of their country. As confounder variables, we want to condition on country, division, and the size of the home city of the club. To estimate the effect by matching, we would like to match football teams with foreign versus domestic ownership in the same country, division, and in a city of the same size.

Suppose that we have 20 countries, two divisions, and five city size categories in the data. Then the aggregate data table for exact matching would have $20 \times 2 \times 5 = 200$ observations. Let's call the observations in this aggregate data table *cells*.

With $z_1, z_2, \ldots$ variables, each cell would have a particular value-combination $z_1 = z_1^*, z_2 = z_2^*, \ldots$ Within each cell, we compute the average y for all treated observations and the average y for all untreated observations, and we take their difference:

$$E[y|x = 1, z_1 = z_1^*, z_2 = z_2^*, \ldots] - E[y|x = 0, z_1 = z_1^*, z_2 = z_2^*, \ldots] \tag{21.3}$$

In our example of 20 countries, 2 divisions, and 5 city size categories, this would mean taking the difference between the average performance of football teams with foreign owners (the treated ones) versus domestic owners (the untreated ones) within each of the 200 cells. We also count the number of treated and untreated observations in each cell, as well as their sum (all observations in the cell).

The exact matching estimate of ATE, the average treatment effect, is the average of these differences weighted by the number of observations in the cells. If, instead, we were to use the the number of treated observations in the cells as weights, we would get an estimate of the **average treatment effect on the treated**, ATET (Chapter 19, Section 19.6).

For ATE, the average is weighted by the number of observations, because we want to calculate the average in the original data, and the population it represents. For ATET, the average is weighted by the number of treated observations, because we want to calculate the average among the treated observations in the original data, and the population they represent.

As we noted earlier, this is not an approximation, unlike a linear regression. Unfortunately, however, exact matching is rarely feasible. The rare cases when it is feasible are datasets with a massive number of observations and relatively few confounder variables to condition on. More frequently, we have many variables to condition on relative to the number of observations. In these more frequent cases, we are unlikely to find exact matches for all z values. In practice, that means that, in some of the cells defined by value-combinations of the observed confounder variables, we may have $x = 1$ observations only, and in others, $x = 0$ observations only. Both may be a problem for estimating ATE. For estimating ATET, we need $x = 0$ observations in all cells in which we have $x = 1$ observations; having $x = 0$ alone in cells is not a problem.

Sometimes that's a substantive issue: the $x = 1$ and $x = 0$ observations may differ so much that some values of some confounder variables exist only in one of the two groups in the population, or general pattern, represented by the data. Consider our example, of examining the effect of foreign ownership of football clubs on the performance of the teams in cross-country data. It is possible that some countries in the data do not have foreign-owned football clubs – indeed, foreign ownership of football clubs is prohibited in some European countries, including Germany. That would make exact matching impossible in those countries. Exact matching is not feasible here because of how the general pattern is. Thus it is not something that data analysis should or could solve. We'll explore the consequences of such impossible matches in Section 21.6.

Other times, though, it's an issue with the data, or more precisely, the sample. Such matches may very well exist in the population, or general pattern; however, we don't have them in the particular data we analyze. It would be conceivable to have both foreign-owned and domestically owned clubs of a certain city size in the first division of a country, but our data may have only a handful clubs in that particular city size in that particular country, all owned domestically. Exact matching is not feasible here, but that's not because of the population or the general pattern. Instead, it's a data problem.

The failure to find exact matches due to data problems turns out to be a common issue. Consider the case with just five confounder variables, each with five possible values. This is few variables: in most cases we would want to condition on far more variables. But these five would result in $5^5 = 3125$ value-combinations and thus 3125 cells. Even in large datasets, there is a high likelihood that we can't find exact matches for many observations.

Coarsened exact matching is one solution to this problem based on grouping (coarsening) variables. Coarsening qualitative variables means combining categories into fewer, broader ones (e.g., groups of countries, less refined industry categories). Coarsening quantitative variables means creating bins (e.g., bins for age or size). Fewer binary variables and fewer bins of quantitative variables make exact matches more likely by reducing the number of variables. Coarsening may be done by the data analyst using domain knowledge (i.e., combining leather and textile industries) or by an algorithm.

Coarsening creates a trade-off: it makes exact matches more likely, but it makes the observed confounder variables even less perfect measures of the latent concepts, thus making the effect estimates more biased. If we match by groups of countries instead of countries, there will remain more within-group variation of the causal variable that is endogenous. Coarsening amounts to not conditioning on some variation in the confounders.

In Section 21.7, we shall introduce another, more widely used approach to address the technical problems with exact matching. But, before doing so, we discuss a few additional questions: what it means if we don't have matches for substantive reasons (and what to do with them), and how that affects the kind of average effect we can uncover.

Review Box 21.3 Exact matching

- Exact matching compares units that are the same in terms of relevant z variables, but differ in the causal variable x.
- Exact matching is often only possible for a subset of units.
- Coarsened exact matching creates fewer values for the z variables, thus allowing for a greater share of units to be matched.

21.6 Common Support

Exact matching may fail because of lack of data – many confounders with few observations. Exact matching may also fail for a substantive reason related to the range of values variables cover. It turns out that this is the more serious issue for the estimation strategy.

When exact matching fails for a substantive reason, that means there is a lack of **common support**. Support is the word used in mathematics for the set of values a variable, or several variables, can take. Common support means that the confounder variables can take the same values among treated and untreated observations. With common support, we have both treated and untreated observations for all values of the confounder variables in the population.

Importantly, common support refers to the population, or general pattern, our data represents. It's about what values the variables can take, not about what values they end up taking in a particular dataset. Even with common support, we may end up having only treated or only untreated observations for some confounder values in the particular data.

When we don't have common support, we can't estimate the effect for all subjects in the data. And we shouldn't. Instead, we can, and should, estimate the effect of x on the part of the dataset with common support.

Consider our example when we could not find foreign-owned football clubs in some countries, due to legal restrictions. That's a lack of common support: some countries appear only among domestically owned clubs and not among foreign-owned clubs. Lack of common support means that this is true not only in our data; it's a characteristic of the general pattern. If this is indeed the case, we can't hope to estimate the effect of foreign club ownership in those countries. Instead, to estimate a causal effect that is true in the population or the general pattern, we need to exclude these countries from our analysis.

These examples suggest that what we mean by "average" in the average effect may be far from being obvious. Thus, we should be explicit about the population of subjects when we try to estimate an average effect. To manage this problem, we will offer two options, an advanced method for matching, and proposing an extra step to add for regression analysis.

Review Box 21.4   Common support

- Common support means that the set of the values of the confounder variables is the same for treated and untreated observations in the population.
- Lack of common support makes comparisons impossible for some values of the confounder variables.
- Average effects can be measured for the population with common support.

21.7   Matching on the Propensity Score

The most popular approach when exact matching is not feasible for data reasons is called **matching on the propensity score** (also called propensity score matching).

The idea is to create a single quantitative variable from the many observed confounder variables. Matching is then done by finding similar observations in terms of this single quantitative variable. This single quantitative variable is the **propensity score**. It is a conditional probability: the probability of an observation having $x = 1$ as opposed to $x = 0$, conditional on all the measured confounder variables z_1, z_2, ... As a result, the propensity score is a single quantitative variable that combines all confounder variables. (On conditional probabilities, see Chapter 4, Section 4.3, and on models for conditional probabilities, see Chapter 11.)

The propensity score is not something we know. It is something we need to estimate. That means estimating, or, more precisely, predicting, the probability of $x = 1$ for each and every observation in the data, based on what values they have for the z variables. The usual procedure is to estimate a probability model, most often a logit, for the probability of $x = 1$, as a function of the confounder variables. Using the notation we introduced in Chapter 11, Section 11.3, with a **logit** model used, and denoting the propensity score as *pscore*,

$$pscore = P[x = 1 | z_1, z_2, \ldots] = x^P = \Lambda(\gamma_0 + \gamma_1 z_1 + \gamma_2 z_2 + \ldots) \qquad (21.4)$$

With an estimated value of *pscore* for the observations in the data, we can match $x = 1$ and $x = 0$ observations that are close to each other in terms of their *pscore*. The most widely used matching procedure is called the **nearest neighbor matching on the propensity score**. This procedure takes each $x = 1$ observation and matches it to the $x = 0$ observation with the nearest value of the propensity score. Once a match is found, we take the difference of y between the $x = 1$ and the $x = 0$ observation. If more $x = 0$ observations are matched to this $x = 1$ observation, we subtract the average of y for the $x = 0$ observations from the y value for the $x = 1$ observation. This matching and then difference taking is repeated for all $x = 1$ observations. The estimated effect of x on y is then the average of those differences. When unweighted, this is an estimate of the **average treatment**

effect on the treated (ATET), because each difference within the average is computed for each and every observation with $x = 1$. If the weights include the number of $x = 0$ observations, too, it's an estimate of the **average treatment effect** (ATE).

Why matching on the propensity score works is not straightforward. By "working" we mean that if exact matching would give a good estimate of the effect, had it been feasible, then matching on the propensity score would give an equally good estimate of the same effect, too. The essence of the idea is that, if all confounders are included, the propensity score incorporates all endogenous sources of variation in the causal variable. Moreover, it incorporates them in the way that truly matters for **endogeneity**: how they are related to x.

In practice, though, what model to specify for the propensity score is the data analysts' choice. That is a complex choice, including choosing the type of model (logit, probit, or something else?), the confounder variables to enter, and their functional form. Once the propensity score is estimated for all observations, there are additional decisions to be made for how matching should be performed. These are many decisions to make, indeed, without obvious best choices.

While it involves many steps, estimating effects by matching on the propensity score is quite straightforward in practice. Software packages will perform all the steps of matching on the propensity score, including estimating a probability model, predicting the propensity scores, performing the matching, and estimating the average effect by averaging the differences across matches. They also estimate appropriate standard errors. Importantly, these commands tend to have sensible default options so novice data analysts can carry out meaningful matching. Nevertheless, understanding the details of matching on the propensity score requires more knowledge than our textbook can provide. Thus, we advise to use this method mostly to complement regression analysis.

> **Review Box 21.5   Matching on the propensity score**
>
> - The propensity score is the probability of being treated conditional on the confounder variables in the data: $P[x = 1 | z_1, z_2, \ldots]$.
> - In practice we predict the propensity score for each observation in the data from a probability model, such as logit.
> - To each treated observation, nearest neighbor matching, on the propensity score procedure, assigns the untreated observation that has the nearest value of the propensity score.
> - Estimated ATE or ATET is the average of the outcome differences in all matched pairs (different weights for ATE vs. ATET).

21.A4   CASE STUDY – Founder/Family Ownership and Quality of Management

Matching

Let's continue our case study by estimating the effect of founder/family ownership on the quality of management by matching. We'll define ATE in this context and compare it, conceptually, to ATET. Then we'll attempt (and fail) to estimate both by exact matching. Finally, we'll estimate them by matching on the propensity score.

Recall that the outcome variable is the management score; its range in the data is 1 to 5, its average is 2.88, standard deviation 0.64. The causal variable is whether the firm is owned by its founder or their family. Some 45% of the firms are founder/family-owned in the data. The raw difference in the average management score was −0.37, which is more than one half of the standard deviation. In a linear regression that conditioned on the observable confounder variables in the data, we estimated an average difference of −0.19. Whether we included a large set of interactions in this estimate did not matter.

Let's estimate the same difference by matching, first by exact matching. Matching starts with the same observable confounder variables as the regression. For exact matching we created bins from the quantitative variables. The variables are the proportion of non-management employees who have a college degree (we created four bins), age of the firm (4 bins), level of competition (3 categories), employment (we created 10 bins), standard industrial classification (20 industries), and country (24 of them). In principle, this results in over 100 000 possible value-combinations, which would result in an aggregate data file with 100 000 cells. In the data, we have only about 7000 of them, because many of the possible value-combinations don't appear. Still, this is a lot of cells for the 8439 firms we have in the data.

Indeed, we don't have exact matches for most firms in the data. From the 8439 firms, only 1207 are in cells, in which we have both founder/family-owned and other ownership firms. The remaining 7232 firms are in cells with only one of the two ownership types. And that's an obvious problem for estimating ATE, or ATET, by exact matching.

The lack of exact matches is most likely due to problems with the data as opposed to problems with common support. For example, there is one firm in the data from Australia, in the food industry, without college-degree employees, with 0–4 competitors, medium age, in the third employment bin, and it's a founder/family-owned firm. There is nothing in the general pattern that would prevent firms with other ownership modes having the exact same features. Indeed, the data includes a very similar firm that differs from the previous one only in that it's a little larger, in the fourth employment bin, and its ownership is different. Indeed, as we'll see later in Section 21.A4, the support of all observed confounder variables is common across treated and untreated observations in this data; lack of exact matches in these detailed cells is very likely a data problem.

So we have a small minority of firms that we can match exactly, due to data problems. That makes any ATE or ATET estimate uninformative: they would be average differences estimated for a subsample of the observations only, and not a random subsample. For the sake of interest, we estimated them for the 1207 observations with exact matches (out of the total of 8439 observations). The ATE estimate for those we could match is −0.16; the ATET estimate is −0.15. These estimates happen to be close to each other and to the regression estimate. But they refer to a non-random subsample of the data and hence exact matching is not a solution in this case. This means, in a presentation or paper, we would not even report these numbers.

Coarsening the variables may help. For example, we may create coarser industry categories (e.g., by joining food and tobacco, or lumber and furniture). You are invited, as a data exercise, to see whether exact matching with coarser categories leads to matches for all, or almost all, founder/family-owned firms in the data.

We estimated the effect of founder/family ownership by matching on the propensity score using the same potential confounder variables as with exact matching and regression. Here we used them in the same form as for the linear regression above. Using these variables we estimated (predicted) the propensity score by logit and then matched each "treated" (founder/family-owned) firm with its nearest neighbor "non-treated" (other-owned) firm in terms of the estimated propensity score. The average effect estimate is the average of the differences of the matches.

In fact we didn't carry out these steps one by one. Instead, we used the statistical software to perform the entire procedure, estimating the average effect by nearest neighbor matching on the propensity score, together with appropriate standard errors.

Table 21.2 Estimates of the effect of founder/family ownership on the quality of management. Results from nearest neighbor matching on the propensity score

	(1) All confounders	(2) All confounders interacted with industry and country
ATE estimate	-0.18**	-0.18**
	(0.02)	(0.03)
ATET estimate	-0.20**	-0.21**
	(0.02)	(0.03)
Observations used by logit	8439	8223
Number of matched observations	5751	5528
Propensity score model	Logit	Logit

Note: Outcome variable: management quality score. Robust standard error estimates in parentheses.
** $p < 0.01$, * $p < 0.05$.

Source: `wms-management-survey` dataset.

Using matching on the propensity score with all observable confounder variables (Table 21.2 column 1) gives a very similar estimate to the regression estimate: -0.18. With matching we can estimate ATET, too, and it's similar, too: -0.20. The estimates have slightly larger standard errors, due to the fact that matching on the propensity score is a more flexible model. Note that logit uses fewer observations in column (2). That's because of a technical feature of the logit: it drops observations if their x variables perfectly predict the outcome, which is more likely to happen with many interactions. The number of matched observations is a lot smaller in both models, because most untreated observations end up being not matched. The effect estimates are very similar in absolute terms (column 2), but they have larger standard error, so the estimates from column (1) are within their 95% confidence intervals.

21.8 Comparing Linear Regression and Matching

In this section we compare regression analysis and matching. Both aim at the same thing: comparing average y for $x = 1$ versus $x = 0$ observations conditional on variables $z_1, z_2, \dots$ But they do that in different ways. Do those differences matter for their effect estimates? When, how, and why?

One difference between regression and matching is the way they uncover and deal with the lack of common support. Exact matching automatically drops observations without common support: they would not be matched. Unfortunately, as we have seen, exact matching drops observations with common support, too, if they have no match due to data problems. We want to avoid this second problem, hence the alternative matching procedure on the propensity score.

Matching on the propensity score, too, detects the lack of common support. It does so by producing propensity scores that are very close to zero or very close to one and thus would not be matched by nearest neighbor matching. Thus, the various kinds of matching methods detect and deal with the lack of common support: they estimate effects on the part of the data with common support only.

In contrast, a linear regression doesn't detect the lack of common support. It uses all data to produce its coefficients. This would include observations without common support. And that turns out to be a problem because lack of common support may cause a linear regression to estimate a biased average effect of x on y. To be more precise, ATE and ATET should be defined as average effects among the subjects for whom the data has common support. However, when all the data is used to estimate them, including the part without common support, the estimated regression line is affected by observations that should not be included.

Thus, when estimating average effects by regression, we need to make sure that the support is common before the estimation. That requires an extra step of data analysis: checking the balance, and potentially dropping observations to get closer to common support. In our example of foreign ownership of football clubs in Europe, we should drop countries from the data that don't allow for foreign club ownership. Exact matching would drop those clubs automatically; matching on the propensity score would also drop them as they would have lower propensity scores than the treated observations; for regression analysis, we would need to drop them before starting the analysis. As a result, one way to think about matching is to check common support before running regressions. Matching can be a solution in its own right, it can be used as a robustness check complementing regression estimates, or it can be used as a step before estimation to restrict the sample.

When the lack of common support is not a problem, nearest neighbor matching on the propensity score and regression tend to give similar results. In the rare cases when the results are different, it signals some problem. Often, a few observations or specific groups are responsible for such differences. That requires further analysis – e.g., by specifying models that include more interactions.

The reason why matching and regression tend to give very similar results is that they are all based on the same idea: conditioning on the observable confounder variables in the data. Whatever method we use, in the end we can only condition on what we observe in the data. The confounders that we don't have in the data will remain omitted, causing an omitted variable bias, whatever method we use. That highlights an important lesson: the data we can use to estimate an effect tends to be more important than the particular method we use.

Review Box 21.6   Regression and matching

- Without common support, a linear regression can give a biased estimate of the average effect, but matching automatically guarantees common support.
- With common support, matching and regression tend to give very similar estimates of the average effect.

21.A5   CASE STUDY – Founder/Family Ownership and Quality of Management

Regression versus matching, common support, conclusion

We found that the quality of management is lower, on average, in founder/family-owned firms in our data, by more than half of a standard deviation. Using linear regression to condition on observable confounders, we estimated that founder/family-owned firms have lower management quality by 30 percent of a standard deviation compared to other firms in the same industry, country, of similar size, age, facing similar numbers of competitors and having a similarly educated workforce. We couldn't use exact matching because we found no match for the majority of the sample. When we used nearest neighbor matching on the propensity score, we estimated an average difference conditional on those features that was very similar to the regression estimates. The matching estimate of ATET was also very similar to the estimated ATE.

Regression estimates don't automatically check for common support, so we need to do that separately. We checked the most important statistics of the distributions of each included confounder variable among founder/family-owned firms and firms with other ownership. For binary variables, the statistic to examine is the proportion of observations with value 1 among founder/family-owned firms and among other-owned firms (e.g., the proportion of the two kinds of firms in Argentina). Common support requires that these proportions are never zero: we have them both among founder/family-owned firms and other-owned firms. That turns out to be true for all binary confounder variables in our case. For the two quantitative variables, such as the share of college educated in the workforce and employment, we examined the minimum, the 5th percentile, the 95th percentile, and the maximum values to see if their range is the same among the $x = 1$ and the $x = 0$ observations. That also turns out to be true in this data.

Thus we can conclude that the common support assumption is fine in our data with respect to the confounder variables we conditioned on (both in the regression and the propensity score). This fact is an important reason for why we obtained such similar results from regression and from matching on the propensity score. Note that exact matching was unable to match the majority of the observations, highlighting the shortcomings of exact matching.

This concludes our case study, What did we learn about the effect of founder/family ownership on management quality from it?

We wanted to uncover the effect of founder/family ownership on the quality of management. By that effect we meant how management quality would change if a founder/family-owned firm stayed founder/family-owned instead of becoming owned by other private owners. In our data, the quality of management in founder/family-owned firms is substantially lower, by more than one half of a standard deviation, than in other firms, on average. When comparing firms from the same countries, industries, of similar age and size, with similarly educated workers, facing similar levels of competition, the difference is smaller, the quality of management is lower in founder/family-owned firms, on average, by 30% of a standard deviation. The 95% confidence interval around this estimate is tight, implying that the average difference, conditional on these other variables, is likely similar in the population, or general pattern, represented by our data.

Conditioning on the observed confounders in the data made a big difference in the effect estimate. The conditional difference is about half as large as the unconditional difference. However, there is obviously a lot more that we should have conditioned on. Most of the confounders we included on our causal map (Figure 21.1) are not measured in our data or are measured very imperfectly. Thus, our effect estimate is still likely different from the true average effect of founder/family ownership.

What does all that mean for our question? Did we uncover anything informative about the effect of founder/family ownership on the quality of management? If we are very strict, no: the effect estimate is biased even after conditioning on the observed confounders. At the same time, we argued that we can use the results as a bound: the true effect is likely smaller than its estimate. Moreover, even if we remain skeptical about the way our estimate is biased, we learned a lot about what kind of data we would need to uncover the effect. And we shall bear in mind that it would be rather difficult to have experimental evidence for our research question.

What do we learn from this case study about the methods covered in this chapter? Perhaps most importantly, we found that linear regression and matching on the propensity score gave very similar results when we conditioned on the same set of variables. The similarity of these results is, in part, due to the common support in terms of the conditioning variables. We also found that allowing for many interactions didn't lead to any difference in the regression estimate of the effect. Including many interactions made some difference to the propensity score estimates of the effects, but those differences were small and statistically not significant due to large standard errors. In this respect, the linear regression estimates appear more stable. We also found that exact matching was infeasible for the majority of our observations, most likely due to data issues.

The main conclusion from this case study is that, if we want to uncover the effect of ownership, different methods won't help much. Instead, we need even better data, with more and better-measured confounder variables. Or, we need to identify and isolate exogenous variation in ownership in some other way.

21.9   Instrumental Variables

In the last two sections of this chapter we briefly introduce two ways to isolate exogenous variation in x to uncover its effect on y: instrumental variables and regression-discontinuity. Instead of trying to condition on all confounders, these methods offer direct ways to make sure that we use only the exogenous part of variation in x for estimating its effect. These methods can be used under specific circumstances. An important aspect of learning these methods is identifying situations, in which we can use them.

In this section we introduce **instrumental variables**, often abbreviated as **IV**, a powerful method that can uncover the effect of x on y even if x has endogenous sources of variation besides exogenous sources. The power of the method lies in the fact that we don't have to observe all, or any, variables that are endogenous sources. But we have to observe at least one variable that is an exogenous source of variation in x. Figure 21.2 is the causal graph that describes this situation.

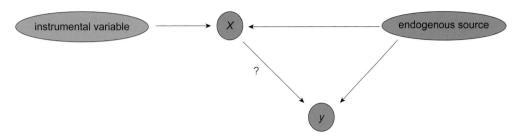

Figure 21.2 Instrumental variable that helps uncover the effect of x on y

Note: The question is the effect of x on y; there is an exogenous instrumental variable and another variable that is an endogenous source of variation in x.

Let's start with the main idea. Suppose that we observe a variable that is an exogenous source of variation in x. This is going to be our instrumental variable, or IV, or simply **instrument**. This IV affects x, but it is not related to y in any other way. In other words, this IV is not related to potential outcomes. But it may be related to observed y through x because it affects x, and x may affect y. Then, if we see that y is different across observations that are different in the IV, we know that it's because x affects y.

The essence of the trick is comparing observations that are different in the instrumental variable. It wouldn't be a good idea to compare observations that are different in x because some of its sources of variation are endogenous. But the same is not true for the instrumental variable: that is an exogenous source. Therefore, we can get a good estimate of its average effect by comparing observations that are different in its value. Moreover, this instrumental variable affects y only through x. Therefore, if it affects y, we know that it's because x affects y. The name instrumental variable comes from the fact that we use that variable not to learn about its effect but the effect of another variable, x.

One example is using the gender mix of the first two children in a family as an instrumental variable to uncover the effect of having a third child (x) on the likelihood of whether the mother will work for pay or not (y). This example uses the influential paper of Angrist and Evans, see reference at the end of the chapter. Here the instrument is whether the first two children are of the same gender. The gender of children is random. By that we mean that it's independent of whether women would work under any circumstance (potential outcomes). At the same time, it turns out that in many societies parents tend to prefer having both boys and girls so having two boys or two girls makes it more likely to have a third child than having one boy and one girl. Therefore, the instrumental variable affects x on average.

Whether women with two children give birth to a third child depends on many things, many of which are likely endogenous. For example, whether they live in a stable relationship may affect both whether they would want to have a third child and whether they would want to work for pay in the future. So comparing the employment rate of women with three children versus two children would not give a good estimate of the effect we are after. But the gender mix of the two children is exogenous so that it gives an opportunity to measure the effect.

But how actually does IV estimation work? Intuitively, it's best understood in three steps. In the first step we estimate the effect of the IV on the causal variable (x). This is done by regressing x on the IV, a regression also called the **first stage of IV**. This regression gives a good estimate of the effect of the IV on x because it is exogenous in this regression. The second step is to estimate the effect of the IV on y. That's also done with a regression, with dependent variable y here. The instrument is exogenous in this regression, too, yielding a good effect estimate again. This is called the **reduced form of IV**.

The third, and final, step combines the results of the first two steps to convert the effect of the IV on y into the effect of x on y that we are interested in. In a sense that amounts to re-scaling the estimated effect of the IV on y, with the effect of the IV on x as a scaling factor.

Let's denote the IV estimator for effect of x on y as β_{IV}. It is calculated as follows (we use hats in the notation to emphasize that the coefficients are estimated from the data):

$$\hat{x}^E = \hat{\pi}_0 + \hat{\pi}_1 IV \tag{21.5}$$

$$\hat{y}^E = \hat{\varphi}_0 + \hat{\varphi}_1 IV \tag{21.6}$$

$$\hat{\beta}_{IV} = \hat{\varphi}_1 / \hat{\pi}_1 \tag{21.7}$$

Consider our example of the effect of a third child on mothers' employment in the future. Using actual numbers from the USA from 1990, $\hat{\pi}_1 = 0.06$ (the proportion of women who give birth to a third child is 6 percentage points higher if the first two children have the same gender); $\hat{\varphi}_1 = -0.008$ (the proportion of women who work for pay is 0.8 percentage point lower if the first two children have the same gender). Then the IV estimate is $\hat{\beta}_{IV} = -0.13$ ($-0.008/0.06$): having a third child makes women less likely to work by 13 percentage points.

Another way of calculating the same IV estimator is called **two-stage least squares**, sometimes abbreviated as **2SLS**. This starts with the same first stage (x regressed on the instrument), but it keeps not the slope coefficient of that regression but the predicted value $\hat{x}$. Then the second stage is the regression of y on this $\hat{x}$. When estimated by OLS, the slope coefficient estimate on $\hat{x}$ is $\hat{\beta}_{IV}$: the IV estimate of the effect of x on y. This is the same $\hat{\beta}_{IV}$ as before. The intuition here is that regressing y on $\hat{x}$ instead of x solves the problem of endogeneity in x because the variation in $\hat{x}$ is only due to variation in the IV, which is exogenous.

The **exogeneity of the instrument** is the crucial assumption. It means that the instrument is independent of the potential outcomes, where the potential outcomes are defined as potential values of y for different x values for the same subject. In our example, the instrument is exogenous if the gender of the first two children is unrelated to how much mothers would work for any other reason other than the effect of a third child. Or, formulated in terms of potential outcomes, the gender of the first two children is independent of how much mothers would work if they had a third child or if they didn't. If this assumption holds, and we still see a difference in how much mothers work by the gender of their first two children (the reduced form regression), it must be because of the effect of the gender of the first two children on whether they have a third child, and the effect of having that third child on how much they work.

Whether the instrument is exogenous or not is an assumption – something we can't directly test using our data. All we can do is think and use some indirect evidence. In our example the gender of children is known to depend on biological mechanisms that people can't predict or affect (as of now). So its variation is very likely random. Moreover, it can be shown that whether the first two children are of the same gender or of different gender is independent of many observed variables that may affect women's employment such as their age, education, or other demographic features.

It turns out that the **LATE** that we introduced in Chapter 20, Section 20.14 is an example of an instrumental variable method. Using the terminology here, let's think about random assignment in the experiment as a binary instrumental variable. $IV = 1$ if the subject is assigned to the treatment group and $IV = 0$ if assigned to the non-treatment group. x is actual treatment: $x = 1$ if treated and $x = 0$ if untreated. IV and x are different if compliance is imperfect. The reduced form is the regression that estimates the average intent-to-treat effect, and LATE is the IV regression. Under the Hood section 21.U2 contains more detail.

The method of instrumental variables is often used in academic research in economics and policy. It is less often used in more applied business and policy research, because it requires observing a variable that is an exogenous source of variation in the causal variable, which is a rare situation. When it occurs, though, it offers an opportunity to estimate an effect even in observational data.

21.10 Regression-Discontinuity

The other method that offers to isolate exogenous variation in the causal variable is called **regression-discontinuity design**, or shortly regression-discontinuity, abbreviated as **RD**. RD is applicable under even more specific circumstances than IV.

Consider a binary causal variable: $x = 1$ if the subject is treated, $x = 0$ if the subject is untreated. RD is applicable if whether a subject is treated or untreated is determined by a clear rule based on a quantitative variable, called the **running variable**. More specifically, RD requires that treatment is determined by a threshold of the running variable: all subjects are treated on one side of the threshold, and no subject is treated on the other side.

One example is a compulsory job search program for young unemployed people if they are below, say, 25 years of age, which is not available to anybody of age 25 or older. Another example is a tax break given to small enterprises to recover their innovation expenditures if they have, say, 200 or fewer employees, with no enterprise eligible for the tax break if they have more than 200 employees.

RD then compares the average outcome of the subjects right around the threshold of the running variable: subjects who are just below the threshold versus subjects who are just above the threshold. In our examples, this could be comparing the job finding rate of 24-year-old unemployed people versus 25-year-old unemployed people; or the average innovation activities of firms with 196–200 employees versus firms with 201–205 employees.

The basic idea behind RD is that subjects right on the two sides of the threshold are very similar in everything measured or unmeasured, except for the fact that they are treated or not treated. If that is true, comparing their outcomes is just like comparing outcomes of randomly assigned treated and untreated subjects.

The basic RD method requires that all subjects are treated on one side of the threshold, and no subject is treated on the other side. A variant on the RD method allows for a more fuzzy setup, with having both treated and untreated subjects on both sides, as long as their rate is different. One example would be our job search program that was available but not compulsory under age 25 but not available over age 25 – here there would be treated and untreated below age 25, but only untreated above age 25, a clear difference in the rate of treatment.

The RD method has three important caveats besides the fact that it's applicable only if there is a threshold that determines treatment. The first one is that only the intervention in question should depend on the threshold value of the running variable. In other words, nothing else should be determined by this threshold that may, in any ways, be related to the outcome. In our compulsory job search example, that means that nothing else should change with reaching age 25 that should affect the unemployed people. Often, this is ensured by having a fairly arbitrary threshold. An example that would violate this condition would be a rule that would make some kinds of social assistance available to people only below, or, for that matter, only above, 25 years of age.

The second additional caveat is that the subjects should not be able to manipulate the running variable. Otherwise those who would expect more benefit from the treatment may change their running variable to be on the "right" side of the threshold, making subjects on the two sides different. That may happen, for example, in our tax break example: firms that want to make use of the tax break may stay smaller than 200 employees in order to qualify. Similar manipulation is less likely to happen in the job search help example, because people can't manipulate their age.

The third caveat with the RD method is that, even under ideal circumstances, what it can help estimate is the average effect of the treatment for subjects who are around the threshold value of the running variable: the effect of the job search program on unemployed people around age 25; the effect of tax incentives on innovation for firms of around 200 employees. However, treatment effects are likely heterogeneous (Chapter 19, Section 19.4), so the average effect among subjects around the threshold may be different from the overall average treatment effect for all subjects.

Thus, the RD method is applicable under very specific situations, and its results need to be interpreted carefully. That's why it is used relatively rarely outside academic research. Nevertheless, when applicable, the RD method offers an excellent opportunity to get a good estimate of the effect for a clearly identified subset of the subjects.

21.11   Main Takeaways

We need exogenous variation in x to uncover its effect on y, but that's hard to achieve with cross-sectional observational data.

- We can rarely condition on all confounders, so our effect estimates are almost always biased. But we may decrease this bias and we may be able to sign it.
- Linear regression, exact or coarsened exact matching, and matching on the propensity score, are alternative ways to condition on observable confounders. With common support, regression and matching tend to give similar results.
- With a little experience and a lot of luck, we may find another, more direct way to isolate exogenous variation in x in the data.

PRACTICE QUESTIONS

1. What's a thought experiment? Give an example and explain why that is useful before analyzing the effect of an intervention using observational data.
2. When do we say that a causal variable is endogenous in a regression? Give an example.
3. What's matching on the propensity score, and when can it identify the effect of x on y with high internal validity?
4. You try to estimate the effect of an intervention by exact matching, but you find that many treated observations have no matching untreated observations. Give an example when that's evidence for the lack of common support. Give another example when it isn't.
5. True or false? Matching on the propensity score is a better method than regression because it gives an estimate that is closer to the true effect.

6. Draw a causal map for the sources of variation in foreign ownership in observational data on manufacturing firms from a single country. The question is the effect on the quality of management.

7. You want to estimate the effect of graduating from your program on salaries five years later using observational data on students from many similar programs. Would you condition on GPA (grade point average) at the end of the program? Why or why not?

8. You want to estimate the effect of foreign aid on corruption using cross-sectional cross-country data. List one endogenous and one exogenous source of variation.

9. You want to estimate the effect of gasoline tax on CO_2 emission using cross-sectional cross-country data. List one endogenous and one exogenous source of variation.

10. Consider the **Food and health** case study in Chapter 19 and the effect of fruit and vegetable consumption on blood pressure. Write down a regression, interpret its slope coefficient, and sign its bias due to the omission of income.

11. Consider the **Does smoking pose a health risk?** case study in Chapter 11. Explain how you would estimate this effect using propensity score matching (use a linear probability model for staying healthy).

12. Consider the **Electricity consumption and temperature** case study in Chapter 12, and the effect of cooling degrees. Are the coefficient estimates in Table 12.6 column (1) good estimates of the contemporaneous and lagged effects? Why or why not?

13. Using observational data on high-school students, you want to estimate the effect of smartphone usage on their grades. List two variables that you would want to condition on and a variable that you wouldn't, and explain why.

14. Whether the founder of a company has children can affect whether the company will remain in founder/family ownership. Could this be a good instrumental variable when estimating the effect of founder/family ownership on the quality of management?

15. You want to estimate whether increasing the pension people receive affects the age at which they retire. By a law passed in the past, people born before 1950 are eligible for higher pensions than people born later. How should you carry out a regression-discontinuity estimation?

DATA EXERCISES

Easier and/or shorter exercises are denoted by [*]; harder and/or longer exercises are denoted by [**].

1. What's the effect of founder/family management (i.e., whether the top management of the firm is founder or family, regardless of its ownership) on the quality of management among founder/family-owned firms? Describe a thought experiment, discuss endogenous and exogenous sources of variation using cross-sectional data on firms from various countries (you may draw a causal map), and try to estimate the effect by multiple regression and matching on the propensity score conditioning on observable confounders using the `wms-management-survey` dataset from earlier chapters. Discuss your decisions along the way and your results. [**]

2. What's the effect of immunization of children on their survival chances? Describe a thought experiment, and discuss endogenous and exogenous sources of variation using cross-sectional cross-country data (you may draw a causal map). Try to estimate the effect by multiple regression and matching on the propensity score conditioning on observable confounders using countries

from one year in the `world-bank-immunization` dataset from Chapter 2. Discuss your decisions along the way and your results. [**]

3. What's the effect of smoking on staying healthy among middle-aged people? Describe a thought experiment, discuss endogenous and exogenous sources of variation using individual data from many countries (you may draw a causal map), and try to estimate the effect by multiple regression and matching on the propensity score conditioning on observable confounders using the `share-health` dataset from Chapter 11. Discuss your decisions along the way and your results. [**]

4. What's the effect of exercising on staying healthy among middle-aged people? Describe a thought experiment, discuss endogenous and exogenous sources of variation using individual data from many countries (you may draw a causal map), and try to estimate the effect by multiple regression and matching on the propensity score conditioning on observable confounders using the `share-health` dataset. Discuss your decisions along the way and your results. [**]

5. What's the effect of eating vegetables on blood pressure among middle-aged people? Describe a thought experiment, discuss endogenous and exogenous sources of variation using individual data from a single country (you may draw a causal map), and try to estimate the effect by multiple regression and matching on the propensity score conditioning on observable confounders using the `food-health` dataset from Chapter 19. Discuss your decisions along the way and your results. [**]

REFERENCES AND FURTHER READING

The example of instrumental variables is from the very nice and influential paper Angrist & Evans (1998). In Section 21.9 we referenced Tables 4 and 5.

A very useful summary on matching methods is Imbens (2015). On the method of coarsened exact matching, see Iacus et al. (2009). They provide a description of their automatic coarsening algorithm. On a variety of econometric tools for understanding causal effects, you may consult the excellent textbook Angrist & Pischke (2015).

Regarding our case study, there is interesting new literature on ownership and management practices including Bandiera et al. (2018) and Lemos & Scur (2019), who use an extended version of data we use. On the role of culture and institutions, see for instance Ostrom (2005). A great paper discussing an experiment on improving management quality is Bloom et al. (2012).

On the foreign ownership of football teams a useful review is Rohde & Breuer (2017).

21.U1 UNDER THE HOOD: UNOBSERVED HETEROGENEITY AND ENDOGENOUS X IN A REGRESSION

In Section 21.3 we introduced an alternative notation for the regression equation. That notation differs from our usual notation in two ways. First, the slope coefficient in that notation denotes not the conditional mean but the effect we are after. Second, the equation contains an additional term, u, that we call unobserved heterogeneity.

Heterogeneity in y means that its values differ across observations. If x does indeed affect y, then one reason for a difference in y would be differences in x. Typically, though, y differs across observations for many other reasons, too. In a simple regression of y on x, all those other reasons are called

unobserved heterogeneity. Heterogeneity in y means that observations differ in the value of y; it is unobserved because the reasons for such differences are not captured by the regression that includes only x as a right-hand-side variable.

A commonly used formula for the linear regression includes this unobserved heterogeneity. It's u in the formula below. To emphasize heterogeneity, we put an i subscript to the variables that vary across observations.

$$y_i = a + \beta x_i + u_i \tag{21.8}$$

Unobserved heterogeneity in this regression is intimately related to potential outcomes. It can be thought of as a sum of two components: how subjects differ in y on top of the effect of x, and how subjects differ in y due to differences in the effect of x on them.

To see this, consider binary interventions, with $x = 1$ or $x = 0$. The potential untreated outcome of subject i is y_i^0. The potential treated outcome for subject i is y_i^1. The observed outcome for individual i is their potential untreated outcomes if untreated ($x_i = 0$) or their potential treated outcomes if treated ($x_i = 1$). We can summarize this in a single formula, multiplying each potential outcome by zero or one, depending on whether the individual is treated. Then we can further manipulate this formula to get the individual treatment effect (te_i) in there:

$$y_i = y_i^0(1 - x_i) + y_i^1 x_i = y_i^0 + (y_i^1 - y_i^0)x_i = y_i^0 + te_i x_i \tag{21.9}$$

Now let's introduce some more notation:

$$y_i^0 = E[y_i^0] + (y_i^0 - E[y_i^0]) = \bar{a} + a_i \tag{21.10}$$
$$te_i = E[te_i] + (te_i - E[te_i]) = \bar{\beta} + \beta_i \tag{21.11}$$

Then

$$y_i = \bar{a} + a_i + (\bar{\beta} + \beta_i)x_i \tag{21.12}$$
$$= \bar{a} + \bar{\beta}x_i + (a_i + \beta_i x_i) \tag{21.13}$$
$$= \bar{a} + \bar{\beta}x_i + u_i \tag{21.14}$$

where

$$u_i = a_i + \beta_i x_i = (y_i^0 - E[y_i^0]) + (te_i - E[te_i])x_i \tag{21.15}$$

is the unobserved heterogeneity of observed outcome y_i in the regression.

What we did was re-write the observed individual outcome as the sum of the mean potential untreated outcome and the average treatment effect multiplied by the treatment variable, plus everything else that remained. That everything else is the unobserved heterogeneity in the regression. It's what makes the individual observed outcome different from the mean potential untreated outcome if untreated, or the mean potential treated outcome if treated (the mean treated potential outcome equals the mean potential untreated outcome plus the treatment effect).

Thus, unobserved heterogeneity in the outcome variable has two components: individual heterogeneity in the potential untreated outcome, and individual heterogeneity in the treatment effect. If i is untreated, it's how its potential untreated outcome differs from the average: $u_i = y_i^0 - E[y_i^0]$. If i is treated, it's how its potential treated outcome differs from the average: $u_i = (y_i^0 - E[y_i^0]) + (te_i - E[te_i]) = (y_i^0 - E[y_i^0]) + ((y_i^1 - y_i^0) - E[y_i^1 - y_i^0]) = y_i^1 - E[y_i^1]$.

Whether x is exogenous or endogenous in the regression can be understood by its relationship to unobserved heterogeneity. x is exogenous if it's independent of potential outcomes. That means that it's independent of unobserved heterogeneity in the regression: it's independent of what makes the potential untreated outcome vary among subjects, and it's independent of what makes the potential treated outcome vary among subjects. In contrast, x is endogenous if it's related to unobserved heterogeneity.

When x is exogenous in the regression, estimating β by OLS leads to a good estimate of the average treatment effect. In contrast, when x is endogenous in the regression, estimating β by OLS leads to a biased estimate of the average treatment effect. That endogeneity can be expressed formally as the correlation between x and u in this regression. When x and u are correlated, x is endogenous in the regression. Its bias is the omitted variables bias. And, it turns out, that the direction of the bias is the same as the sign of the correlation between x and u. Our ability to relate the omitted variables bias to the correlation between x and u helps technical derivations of the bias, although it doesn't add to the intuition behind it. To sign the omitted variable bias, we still need to think through the omitted confounder variables, which do not appear explicitly in the formula, only as part of u.

It is straightforward to extend this setup to include covariates $z_1, z_2, \ldots$, together with x in the regression:

$$y_i = \beta_0 + \beta_1 x_i + \beta_2 z_{1i} + \beta_3 z_{2i} + \cdots + u_i \tag{21.16}$$

If x is exogenous in this regression, it's not correlated with u, and the OLS estimate of β_1 is a good estimate of the average treatment effect. If x is endogenous in this regression, it's correlated with u, and the OLS estimate of β_1 is a biased estimate of the average treatment effect.

Finally, we have to note a confusing aspect of this notation that leads to frequent misunderstanding. Unobserved heterogeneity is conceptually different from the regression residual, and the two may or may not be equal in practice. The regression residual is the difference in y from its predicted value after the regression is estimated on data. With a simple linear regression, a residual is $y - (\hat{a} + \hat{\beta}x)$. Unobserved heterogeneity captures differences in y on top of the average effect of x on y. The two are the same if the estimated slope coefficient of the regression equals the effect of x. But they are different otherwise. One consequence of this is that examining the correlation between the regression residual and x cannot tell anything about the correlation of unobserved heterogeneity and x, which would help determine the omitted variables bias. Indeed, the correlation between x and the residual of a regression estimated by OLS is always zero, which is a consequence of the OLS estimation procedure.

21.U2   UNDER THE HOOD: LATE IS IV

As we discussed briefly in Section 21.9, the LATE that we introduced in Chapter 20, Under the Hood section 20.U1, turns out to be an example of the IV method. Here we show that in more detail.

LATE stands for local average treatment effect. We introduced it in the context of randomized assignment of a binary treatment variable with imperfect compliance. Let the treatment variable be x: $x = 1$ if treated and $x = 0$ if untreated. Using the notation we introduced in Under the Hood section 20.U1, $w = 1$ if the subject is assigned to the treatment group and $w = 0$ if assigned to the non-treatment group. Compliance is imperfect, which makes z and x different for some subjects. In particular, some subjects that are assigned to treatment ($w = 1$) may end up without treatment ($x = 0$), and/or some subjects that are assigned to the non-treatment group ($w = 0$) may end up being treated ($x = 1$).

Recall the definition of LATE from Chapter 20, formula (20.7):

$$LATE = \frac{E[y|w = 1] - E[y|w = 0]}{Pr[x = 1|w = 1] - Pr[x = 0|w = 0]} \tag{21.17}$$

This formula is an IV formula. To see that, let's recall the IV estimator formula from Section 21.9, but let's rename the IV variable as w:

$$\hat{x}^E = \hat{\pi}_0 + \hat{\pi}_1 w \tag{21.18}$$

$$\hat{y}^E = \hat{\varphi}_0 + \hat{\varphi}_1 w \tag{21.19}$$

$$\hat{\beta}_{IV} = \hat{\varphi}_1 / \hat{\pi}_1 \tag{21.20}$$

Since x is a binary variable, the slope coefficient on w estimates the difference in the probability of $x = 1$ for observations with $w = 1$ versus $w = 0$:

$$\pi_1 = Pr[x = 1 | w = 1] - Pr[x = 0 | w = 0] \tag{21.21}$$

In the second equation, with y as the left-hand-side variable, the slope coefficient on w estimates the difference in the expected value of y for observations with $w = 1$ versus $w = 0$:

$$\varphi_1 = E[y | w = 1] - E[y | w = 0] \tag{21.22}$$

As a result, the IV estimator, which is the ratio of the estimates of these two coefficients, is the estimator for the LATE.

Applying the IV terminology to LATE, random assignment (w) is the exogenous instrumental variable, actual treatment (x) is the endogenous causal variable, the equation of x on w is the first stage (it gives an estimate of $Pr[x = 1 | w = 1] - Pr[x = 0 | w = 0]$), and the equation of y on w is the reduced form (it gives an estimate of $E[y | w = 1] - E[y | w = 0]$).

The IV is exogenous here: it's random assignment. Thus, we can get a good estimate of its average effect. The reduced form – the regression of y on w – gives that effect: it's the effect of assignment on the outcome variable. Thus, it's the average intent-to-treat effect: $AITTE = E[y | w = 1] - E[y | w = 0]$. As non-compliance is almost surely non-random (likely related to potential outcomes), and thus x is endogenous, comparing the treated and the non-treated would give a biased estimate of the average treatment effect. At the same time, we can get a good estimate of LATE using the IV formula.

The analogy between LATE and IV helps in interpreting the IV estimates in other contexts, too. Recall that LATE gives a good estimate of the average treatment effect among subjects who comply with the assignment: they get treated if assigned to treatment and they don't get treated if assigned to non-treatment. The same is true for an IV estimator: it gives a good estimate of the effect of the endogenous causal variable (x) among observations whose x is affected by the exogenous instrument IV.

22 Difference-in-Differences

How to carry out difference-in-differences analysis with panel data or pooled cross-sectional data, and when to interpret its results as the effect of an intervention

Motivation

You want to uncover the effect of flexible work hours on employee retention: whether by giving employees more freedom to choose their work hours makes them more likely to stay with their employer. You can use observational data on firms from two years, and some firms introduced flexible work hours between those two years. How can you use this data to estimate the effect you are after?

You work for a competition authority, and you are tasked with evaluating the effect of a merger between two companies that took place a few years ago on the prices their customers face. You have transaction-level data from a few years both before and after the merger took place. You can define several markets from this data, and you find that the two companies were present in some of those markets but weren't present in others. How can you use this data to estimate the effect of the merger on prices? In particular, could you use data aggregated to market level and compare prices before and after the merger? And, can you use the data to assess whether such a comparison leads to a good estimate of the average effect of the merger?

In the previous chapters we argued that it's very difficult to estimate the effect of x on y in observational data by conditioning on all endogenous sources of variation in x. It turns out that there is more hope for that when our observational data allows for within-subject comparison as well as between-subject comparison. The data we need for such comparisons is cross-section time series (xt) panel data. We start with xt data with two time periods, in which subjects are observed twice. We will consider what we can do when we have more observations per subject in the following chapters.

This chapter introduces difference-in-differences analysis, or diff-in-diffs for short, and its use in understanding the effect of an intervention. We explain how to use (xt) panel data covering two time periods to carry out diff-in-diffs by comparing average changes from before an intervention to after it, and how to implement this in a simple regression. We discuss the parallel trends assumption that's needed for the results to show average effects. Finally, we discuss some generalizations of the method to include observed confounder variables, to estimate the effect of a quantitative causal variable, or to use pooled cross-sectional data instead of an xt panel, with different subjects before and after the intervention.

The case study in this chapter, **How does a merger between airlines affect prices?**, examines the effect of a merger between two major US airlines on the prices paid by customers. It uses the `airline-tickets-usa` dataset. This case study illustrates the use of basic diff-in-diffs analysis and its various generalizations. It also shows how we can use a big and complex dataset and transform it into a simple data table, to which we can apply the methods we learned.

Learning outcomes

After working through this chapter, you should be able to:

- identify situations in which difference-in-differences analysis may be applied to uncover the average effect of an intervention;
- carry out difference-in-differences analysis using panel data within the framework of linear regression and interpret its results;
- understand when difference-in-differences analysis can give a good estimate of an effect, and what kind of evidence can help assess whether those conditions hold;
- carry out difference-in-differences analysis using pooled cross-sections, interpret its results, and understand the potential role of selection.

22.1 Conditioning on Pre-intervention Outcomes

In Chapter 19, we discussed how we should think about the challenges of uncovering the effect of an intervention using observational data, and what methods we may apply. In Chapter 21, we discussed what to do with observational cross-sectional data. Here we move on to discuss difference-in-differences analysis, or diff-in-diffs for short, which requires cross-section time series (xt) panel data: repeated observations on many subjects. This is still observational data, but it has something that typical cross-sectional data doesn't have: the outcome variable is observed not only after the intervention but also before it.

We will define the method in the next section. Here we discuss why observing the outcome variable before the intervention helps uncover the effect and, thus, why diff-in-diffs has a better chance at uncovering effects than methods that use cross-sectional data with outcomes observed only after the intervention. In doing so, we briefly review the argument for conditioning on confounders.

Let's focus on the simple case with binary treatment, and let's use the language of potential outcomes. Some subjects are treated ($x = 1$), others are untreated ($x = 0$), and we want to uncover the effect of the treatment (the intervention) on outcome y. Before the intervention, all subjects were untreated. Some became treated after the intervention, others didn't.

The challenge with observational data is that the treated and untreated groups tend to be different in terms of their potential outcomes (see Chapters 19 and 21). And that's a problem, because the only way to estimate an effect is by comparing the observed outcomes of treated subjects to the observed outcomes of untreated subjects. And, with observational data, the outcomes of the untreated subjects don't usually tell us what the outcomes of the treated would have been had they not been treated (their potential untreated outcomes). Similarly, the observed outcomes of the treated subjects don't usually tell us what the outcomes of the untreated would have been had they been treated (their potential treated outcomes).

The reason is endogenous sources of variation in x. The variables behind such endogenous variation are the confounders. In principle, we could ensure that all variation in x is exogenous if we conditioned on all confounders. But conditioning on all confounders is rarely possible in real life because typical data doesn't include all confounders. Instead, real-life data has observed variables that are imperfect measures of only some of the confounders. However, if we found a variable that captured a lot of the endogenous variation, we could get close to estimating the effect we are after.

The pre-intervention observation of the outcome variable may be such a variable. The **pre-intervention outcome** is the untreated outcome at the time before the intervention. If we condition on the pre-intervention outcome, it amounts to comparing subjects that are similar in their potential untreated outcomes, at least as measured before the intervention. Of course, that's not the same thing as conditioning on their potential untreated outcomes after the intervention, which we would like to do. But it can be a good approximation if subjects that are similar in their pre-intervention outcomes are similar in their potential untreated outcomes after the intervention, too. And that could get us half of what we would want to condition on: potential untreated outcomes after the intervention. The other half would be conditioning on potential treated outcomes after the intervention, and we'll return to this later.

Let's discuss an example to show why this approach is needed, and how it can help. For example, we may want to uncover whether firms can retain more employees by giving them more freedom to choose their work hours. The subjects are firms, the outcome is a measure of employee retention, say, whether employees stay with the firm for two years or more after they are hired. Suppose that we have observational data that includes firms that introduced flexible work hours recently as well as firms that didn't. Simply comparing the retention rate of the two kinds of firms would give a biased estimate of the effect, because the firms that introduced flexible work hours are likely different from the firms that didn't. For example, it may be the case that firms that have to compete more for their employees are more likely to introduce flexible work hours. But such firms likely have a lower employee retention rate than other firms. This self-selection induces a negative omitted variables bias: firms that introduce flexible work hours would have lower retention rates because of self-selection, making a true positive effect look smaller or even negative.

Now suppose that we have a variable on retention rates from an earlier year, too, before the firms in the data introduced flexible work hours. That is a pre-intervention outcome. Conditioning on it would go a long way in solving the self-selection problem. Such a conditioning would amount to comparing firms with similar initial retention rates, removing the differences between firms in terms of their difficulty of retaining their employees – at least to the extent that initial retention rates capture such differences. Then, if we see that firms that introduced flexible hours achieved higher retention rates than firms that didn't introduce flexible work hours but were similar in initial retention rates, we could be more confident that this shows the effect of the intervention than comparing all firms regardless of their initial retention rates.

Data that include pre-intervention outcomes allow us to condition on them and thus get better effect estimates. One way to do this is to include the pre-intervention outcome variable as a right-hand-side variable of a regression or as a variable used for matching. However, a simpler and more intuitive way to use it is to examine the change in the outcome, from before the intervention to after the intervention.

In the following sections of this chapter we'll discuss how we can estimate an effect by examining the change in the outcome variable and when this leads to a good estimate of the effect. We'll start with a formal definition of difference-in-differences analysis.

22.2   Basic Difference-in-Differences Analysis: Comparing Average Changes

Difference-in-differences analysis, often abbreviated as **diff-in-diffs**, is perhaps the most widely used method to evaluate the effects of business and policy interventions with observational data.

In this section we introduce the simplest version, basic diff-in-diffs analysis, with the aim of uncovering the effect of a binary causal variable $x = 0$ *or* 1 on outcome variable y.

Basic diff-in-diffs is a simple method to uncover the effect of an intervention. It amounts to comparing the average change in y among treated subjects and the average change in y among untreated subjects, from before the intervention to after the intervention. For basic diff-in-diffs, all subjects need to be observed twice, once before the intervention and once after the intervention. These values are called before values, or baseline values, and after values, or endline values. Basic diff-in-diffs analysis needs cross-section time series (xt) panel data with two time periods for each subject, which is a balanced two-period panel (we discussed these concepts in Chapter 1, Section 1.2).

Let's return to our example of uncovering the effect of flexible work hours on employee retention. To carry out diff-in-diffs analysis, we would need data on many firms, some of which introduced flexible work hours, while others didn't: these would be the treated and untreated subjects. For each firm, we would need an observation on the retention rate both before and after the year the treated firms introduced flexible work hours.

With the usual Δ notation, the change in outcome y for subject i is

$$\Delta y_i = y_{i,after} - y_{i,before} \tag{22.1}$$

Let's denote the **diff-in-diffs estimator** of the effect of x on y as $\beta_{diff-in-diffs}$. It is the difference of average changes between treated and untreated subjects. Its value estimated from data is $\hat{\beta}$ diff-in-diffs. Denoting the average change among the treated subjects as $\Delta \bar{y}_{treated}$ and the average change among the untreated subjects as $\Delta \bar{y}_{untreated}$ in the data, the diff-in-diffs is

$$\hat{\beta}_{diff-in-diffs} = \Delta \bar{y}_{treated} - \Delta \bar{y}_{untreated} \tag{22.2}$$

Table 22.1 shows how these things are related: it shows the four averages, their differences, and the difference of their differences. For the change we use the delta notation. The difference-in-differences is in the lower right corner of the table.

Table 22.1 The difference-in-differences setup

	Untreated	Treated	Diff: Treated–Untreated
Before	$\bar{y}_{untreated,before}$	$\bar{y}_{treated,before}$	$\bar{y}_{treated,before} - \bar{y}_{untreated,before}$
After	$\bar{y}_{untreated,after}$	$\bar{y}_{treated,after}$	$\bar{y}_{treated,after} - \bar{y}_{untreated,after}$
Diff: After – Before	$\Delta \bar{y}_{untreated}$	$\Delta \bar{y}_{treated}$	$\Delta \bar{y}_{treated} - \Delta \bar{y}_{untreated}$

We usually calculate this difference by running a regression with Δy as the dependent variable and *treated* as the explanatory binary variable:

$$\Delta y^E = \alpha + \beta \, treated \tag{22.3}$$

In this diff-in-diffs regression, the estimated $\hat{\alpha}$ is the average change in y among untreated subjects in the data. In Table 22.1, this is $\Delta \bar{y}_{untreated}$, in the bottom left cell.

The diff-in-diffs estimate of the effect of the intervention is $\hat{\beta}$: it is the difference between the average change in y among treated subjects (*treated* = 1) and untreated subjects (*treated* = 0) in the data. Thus, it is the exact same thing as the diff-in-diffs estimate $\hat{\beta} = \hat{\beta}_{diff-in-diffs}$. In Table 22.1, this is the bottom right cell.

But what kind of an effect can diff-in-diffs uncover? Before the intervention, all subjects were untreated. Some became treated after the intervention; others didn't. We compare the change in their outcome to the change among subjects that remained untreated. What this comparison reveals depends on how the outcomes would have changed, on average, if things turned out differently.

Diff-in-diffs gives a good estimate of the average treatment effect on the treated (ATET) if the average change among untreated subjects is a good counterfactual to the average change among treated subjects. That happens if the outcome of the treated subjects would have changed, on average, in the same way as it changed among the untreated subjects, had the intervention not taken place.

In addition, diff-in-diffs gives a good estimate of the overall average treatment effect (ATE) under two conditions. First, the previously described condition for the ATET is satisfied. Second, if the average change among treated subjects is a good counterfactual to the average change among untreated subjects. This second condition is met if the outcome of the untreated subjects would have changed, on average, the same way as the outcome would have changed for the treated subjects, had they, too, been treated.

It turns out that, most of the time, diff-in-diffs analysis focuses on estimating ATET. For that, it is the first condition that is required: changes among the untreated should be a good counterfactual to changes among the treated. Figure 22.1 shows this idea. It has two lines to show how average outcomes change: one for untreated subjects and one for treated subjects. The graph shows a third line, too, which is dashed here. One way to look at this third, dashed line is that it's simply a shifted version of the untreated line, so we can see the difference between the change among the treated and untreated. The other way to look at this line is that it is an assumption about the counterfactual change for the treated subjects: how their outcomes would have changed, on average, had they not been treated.

The figure also shows how the changes are related to the coefficients of the regression. α is the average change among untreated subjects; $\alpha + \beta$ is the average change among treated subjects; β is the difference between the two.

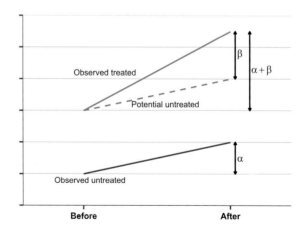

Figure 22.1   Difference-in-differences: illustration of average outcomes and their changes

It is good practice to estimate diff-in-diffs by a regression. One advantage is that it produces standard error estimates. As usual, we should get the software to estimate robust standard errors, which are fine whether there is heteroskedasticity or homoskedasticity. Another advantage, which we'll discuss later, is that it allows for including other right-hand-side variables to condition on confounders. But perhaps the greatest advantage is that this regression formula is also the starting point for generalized versions of diff-in-diffs. In this and the subsequent chapter, we'll discuss many such generalizations that use quantitative causal variables and/or more time periods.

Finally, a note on weights. Basic diff-in-diffs compares averages. In some cases we need weighted averages instead of simple ones. A typical case for the need to use weighted averages is when the subjects in the data are more aggregated than the subjects for which we would like to learn the effects. We may have firm-level data to estimate an effect on employees; or we may have country-level data to estimate an effect on people. As we said, it's best to estimate diff-in-diffs via regression. If needed, we can use weights in the regression, as we discussed in Chapter 8, Section 8.13.

For example, we may want to use weights when we want to uncover the effect of introducing flexible work hours on employee retention. The diff-in-diffs estimator of the effect would compare the average change in the fraction of retention rates between the treated firms and the untreated firms. This is firm-level data, yet our question is at the level of employees. Thus, if we want a diff-in-diffs estimate of the effect on employees, we would estimate a regression that uses the number of employees as weights. These weights make firms with more employees more important when calculating average changes.

Review Box 22.1   Basic difference-in-differences analysis

- Basic difference-in-differences analysis estimates the average effect of an intervention on outcome y:
  - by comparing the average change in y;
  - from a time period before the intervention to a time period after the intervention;
  - between subjects that are affected by the intervention and subjects that are not affected.
- The data needs to have observations of the outcome for each subject from both time periods.

In formulae:
$$\hat{\beta}_{diff\text{-}in\text{-}diffs} = \left(\bar{y}_{treated,after} - \bar{y}_{treated,before}\right) - \left(\bar{y}_{untreated,after} - \bar{y}_{untreated,before}\right)$$

In a regression:
$$\Delta y^E = \alpha + \beta\, treated$$

22.A1   CASE STUDY – How Does a Merger between Airlines Affect Prices?

Question, data, and basic diff-in-diffs analysis

The question of this case study is the effect of the merger of two firms on the markets they serve. Mergers of two firms can have various effects on the performance of the firms and the welfare of their customers. When firms merge, the new firm may become more efficient and produce the same products or services at lower costs or higher quality. That can increase the incomes of their shareholders and benefit their customers at the same time, to the extent that the efficiency gains are passed on to customers.

However, mergers can have negative effects on their customers, too. When two firms in the same market merge, the new firm has increased market power. With higher market power, this new firm thus may charge higher prices without losing as many customers as before. That would harm customers, because they would have to pay more for the same product or service. Market power, and thus mergers, may decrease the quality of service, too. In this case study we focus on the effect on prices.

In fact, competition authorities examine the expected effects of such mergers before they take place and allow them only if they conclude that such harmful effects are unlikely. Such examinations are called ex-ante merger analysis. The particular merger we examine was allowed to take place. Our question is what actually happened after the merger took place. Such an analysis is called ex-post merger analysis. Ex-post merger analyses are important because they are the only way we can actually learn about an effect: we can uncover what tends to happen only by analyzing the effects of mergers that actually took place. Information learned this way is helpful for future ex-ante merger analyses and thus decisions on future mergers.

American Airlines, one of the biggest passenger airline carriers in the United States, filed for bankruptcy in November 2011. US Airways, a competitor, announced its intent to take over American Airlines in 2012. After years of legal and regulatory deliberations, the merger was allowed in April 2015. The reservation systems of American and US Airways were merged in the second half of 2015. The question of the case study is the effect of this merger on airline prices.

Our data comes from a very large database maintained by the US Department of Transportation (DB1B data). It is a 10 percent sample of all tickets sold on the US market taken in each quarter, starting with 2010. The unit of observation in the data is an airline ticket. For confidentiality reasons, the date of each flight is unknown in the data – only the quarter is known. The variables include the airports visited including the origin and all subsequent airports, ticket price, number of passengers and airline.

The data we use is another example of Big Data. It comes from automatic ticketing system, it is complicated in nature, and it is very large. For a single quarter, the raw data on tickets has about 3–3.5 million observations. The total data used for the case study has the size of around 15 GB. Before discussing the difference-in-differences setup we define markets and make some sample design choices.

Defining the market in this setup is not straightforward. Consider two ways to fly from New York JFK to Los Angeles LAX: one nonstop, one with one stop in Chicago ORD (O'Hare). If the passenger's only goal is to get to Los Angeles, these two routes are close substitutes and can be considered in the same market. If, however, the passenger's goal is to visit their aunt in Chicago first and get to Los Angeles afterwards, the two routes are not substitutes and should not be considered in the same market. The data doesn't have any information that may help tell the two kinds of customers apart: it lumps all JFK–Chicago ORD–LAX tickets together, whether the arrival and departure in Chicago is on the same day or not. For this case study, we made the decision that the first kind of passenger is more frequent and thus considered routes with the same origin and the same final destination as one market.

Another question is one-way tickets versus return tickets. One-way tickets in the data have different first and last airports of their route. Return tickets have the same origin airport and last airport. More than one third of the tickets are return tickets. For return tickets, the final destination is not always straightforward to obtain. For this case study we made the decision to consider return tickets where the final destination is reasonably clear and drop the other return tickets.

In particular, we defined markets the following way. For one-way tickets we considered a market defined by the origin and the final destination, which is the last airport here. For return tickets, we selected routes with a clear middle airport only: routes with an odd number of airports. We dropped all other return routes. This affected many routes but less than 10 percent of the passengers. Two thirds of the routes we kept were symmetric and are almost surely return routes with the center as the destination. Asymmetric routes have different airports between the origin and the designated destination and may have a different destination in fact, but this is the less likely case and thus we decided to keep them. When interpreting the results of our analysis, we'll return to the question of market definition and whether and how that may affect the results.

In short, therefore, markets are defined by their origin airport and their destination airport, and whether they are one-way or return routes. An example for a market is origin New York JFK, destination Los Angeles LAX, one-way. This includes all non-stop flights as well as flights that stop once or twice in-between. The JFK–LAX–JFK return route is a different market, and this, too, includes flights that are non-stop between JFK and LAX as well as those with one or two stops in-between.

For 2011, there are 460 public airports in the USA that are included in the data. That means $460 \times 459 = 211\,140$ theoretical possibilities for markets, both one-way and return. Of these $422\,280$ possibilities, there are passengers flying in $141\,712$ actual markets in our data in any year.

In our data (a 10 percent representative sample of all domestic flights and their passengers), we see that most of these markets have very few passengers and a few markets have many passengers: in 2011, the median number of passengers was 7 and the mean was 170. The JFK–LAX one-way market had 31 thousand passengers in 2011, the JFK–LAX–JFK market had 38 thousand. Thus, the distribution of passengers across markets is extremely skewed.

Both small and large markets are important for the welfare of customers, but airline competition may play out very differently in them. Thus, besides its overall effect, we examined the effect of the merger in small and large markets separately. We defined small markets as those with less than 5000 passengers in a year in the data (that's about 140 passengers per day in the total represented by our data). The median number of passengers is 7 in small markets and 8000 in large markets; the means are 100 and 10 000, respectively. More than 99% of the markets are small according to this definition, with around 60% of the passengers.

Having defined our data table for the analysis, we can now introduce the difference-in-differences setup. For the difference-in-differences analysis we defined the "before" time period as year 2011 and the "after" time period as year 2016 (recall that the merger was announced in 2012 and completed in 2015).

This resulted in an unbalanced panel. There are around 140 000 markets in both 2011 and 2016; of these, 113 000 are in both years and the remaining less than 30 000 are only in one of the years. Not surprisingly, the markets that are in only one of the years are a lot smaller, with 10 passengers on average compared to 240 in the other markets. In fact, these one-year-only markets have around 1% of the passengers in a given year.

To carry out basic diff-in-diffs analysis we need a balanced panel. While our panel data is unbalanced, we can make it balanced by dropping markets that are not in the 2011 and 2016 data. This balanced panel includes almost all passengers, and covers 113 thousand (112 632) markets.

We defined a market as treated if both American Airlines and US Airways were present in it in the baseline time period, in year 2011. It is these markets where a merger would increase the market power of the new firm. In contrast, we defined untreated markets as those that had neither American nor US Airways present in the before time period. Whether a market is treated or untreated is determined by their baseline features here.

This definition of treated and untreated markets left some markets neither treated nor untreated: those with only American or only US Airways present in 2011. For the main analysis we dropped these from the data. It is possible that the merger affected these markets as well. In a data exercise you'll be invited to examine if including these markets among the treated ones leads to different conclusions.

Of the 113 thousand markets in our balanced panel data, 12 thousand are treated (14 million passengers per year in the data), 72 thousand are untreated (4 million passengers), and 29 thousand are neither treated nor untreated (6 million passengers). Evidently, the treated markets are larger, on average, than the untreated markets (1200 passengers versus 50 passengers on average). We shall return to this issue in the subsequent sections of this chapter.

The outcome variable is the average price of an airline ticket on a market. Its distribution is somewhat skewed, having a long right tail with large values but similar median and mean. We took its natural log, mostly for substantial reasons, to measure price differences in relative terms. For some markets, the data shows zero average price, which are likely errors. These markets are very small, with 1.1 passengers on average, and we dropped them from the data, resulting in $N = 112\ 623$ markets.

To uncover the effect of the merger on prices by basic diff-in-diffs, we estimated a regression. The left-hand-side variable was the change in log prices; the right-hand-side variable was a binary indicator for whether both AA and US were present on the market before the merger, and we used the number of passengers as weights. We estimated the effect for all markets and then separately for small markets (less than 5000 passengers in 2011) and large markets. The formula for the regression is below; the results are in Table 22.2:

$$(\Delta \ln p)^E = \alpha + \beta AAUS_{before} \tag{22.4}$$

The estimated intercept in column (1) shows that prices increased by 16%, on average, in untreated markets between 2011 and 2016. The 95% confidence interval is [14%, 18%]. When looking across small markets (column 2) and large markets (column 3) we see that prices increased a lot more in large markets, by 24% compared to the 14% increase in small markets. Note that prices are not adjusted for inflation here so some of the price increase is sort of natural. Still, prices increased by a lot more on large markets.

However, compared to untreated markets, prices on treated markets increased by 18% less, on average (column 1); 95% CI [−20%, −16%]. This means that on treated markets, prices actually dropped a little (−2%).

Table 22.2 Basic difference-in-differences estimate of the effect of the AA–US merger on log prices

Variables	(1) All markets	(2) Small markets	(3) Large markets
$AAUS_{before}$	−0.18**	−0.16**	−0.26**
	(0.01)	(0.01)	(0.03)
Constant	0.16**	0.14**	0.24**
	(0.01)	(0.01)	(0.02)
Observations	112 632	111 745	887
R-squared	0.05	0.04	0.09

Note: Dependent variable: change in ln average market price. Observations: markets in the United States (origin–final destination airport pairs separately for one-way and return routes). Before period: 2011. After period: 2016. $AAUS_{before}$: binary variable for both AA and US on market in 2011. Weighted by the number of passengers at baseline. Robust standard error estimates in parentheses. ** $p < 0.01$, * $p < 0.05$.

Source: `airline-tickets-usa` dataset.

Note that we could get the same estimates from a diff-in-diffs table with the average outcome values for treated and untreated markets before and after, similar to Table 22.1 above. We show that in Table 22.3 for all markets.

Table 22.3 Difference-in-differences table for the effect of AA–US merger on log prices

	(1) Untreated	(2) Treated	(3) Difference: Treated − Untreated
Before	4.92	4.96	+0.04
After	5.08	4.94	−0.14
Difference: After − Before	+0.16	−0.02	−0.18

Note: See notes to Table 22.2. Average log price, weighted by the number of passengers at baseline.

Source: `airline-tickets-usa` dataset. N=112 632 markets.

The average values in the table don't mean much as they are averages of log prices, but their differences show relative differences. The bottom left number shows the average change on untreated markets: this is equal to the regression intercept. And the bottom right number is the diff-in-diffs estimate of the effect: it's equal to the regression coefficient on the treated variable.

So we found diff-in-diffs estimates for the effect of the merger on average price to be −18% across all markets, −16% on small markets, and −26% on large markets.

But are these good estimates of the effect of the merger? We'll address this question in the next section.

22.3 The Parallel Trends Assumption

Diff-in-diffs gives a good estimate of the average treatment effect on the treated subjects (ATET) under one assumption: without the treatment, the outcome in the treatment group would have changed in the same way as it did in the non-treatment group. This is called the **parallel trends assumption**. The "trends" here mean the average change in the potential outcomes in the two groups.

The parallel trends assumption says that without the intervention, these changes would be the same: the trends would be parallel. This is the assumption on our Figure 22.1 above: the dashed green line is parallel to the blue line. If the assumption holds and we nevertheless see a difference in the average change in actual outcomes between treated and untreated, that difference must be caused by the intervention.

The parallel trends assumption is about how potential untreated outcomes would change: the change in average potential untreated outcomes is assumed to be the same in the treated group and the untreated group. The first potential outcome change is counterfactual; the second one is observed.

In principle, we could add one more parallel trends assumption: that potential treated outcomes would have changed the same, on average, among untreated subjects, as they did among treated subjects. With the two assumptions together, diff-in-diffs would give a good estimate of the average treatment effect (ATE). We usually don't make this second assumption, for two reasons. First, ATET is often the more interesting thing to estimate: what the effect was on those that experienced the intervention (the introduction of flexible working hours among firms that did introduce them; the effect of a merger on markets in which the merger took place). Second, as we'll see, sometimes we have data to examine how the outcome changed in earlier periods, which can help assess the first assumption (how potential untreated outcomes change), but not the second one.

Note that the parallel trends assumption is analogous to the random assignment, yet it is not the same. Random assignment amounts to assuming that the average of potential untreated outcomes is the same in the treated group and the untreated group. Random assignment is an assumption about levels. The parallel trends assumption is about changes. In fact, we can think of the parallel trends assumption as random assignment of changes in potential outcomes. The parallel trends assumption is less strict: it allows for level differences in average potential outcomes, as long as the changes are the same.

The parallel trends assumption is an assumption that is impossible to verify or falsify by analyzing our data because it is based on comparing actual and counterfactual outcomes. We can't know how outcomes would have changed on average in the treated group without the intervention. That's a counterfactual outcome.

At the same time, we can look for indirect evidence in our data to support or contradict the parallel trends assumption. The most widely examined indirect evidence is whether **pre-intervention trends**, or briefly **pre-trends**, in average outcomes are similar across treated and untreated subjects. In practice that means examining whether the time series lines, or curves, of average outcomes before the intervention are parallel between treated and untreated subjects. Such an examination is possible with data from more time periods than used for the diff-in-diffs analysis: instead of a single baseline time period, we need observed outcomes from more time periods prior to the intervention to examine its time series.

Review Box 22.2 The parallel trends assumption

- The parallel trends assumption: without the intervention, outcomes would have changed the same way, on average, in the treatment group and the non-treatment group.
- If the assumption is true, diff-in-diffs gives a good estimate of ATET.

- If, in addition, the average of outcomes in the non-treatment group would have changed the same way, had they been treated, as it changed in the treatment group, diff-in-diffs gives a good estimate of ATE, too.
- The parallel trends assumption cannot be verified or falsified directly.
- We can get indirect evidence on parallel trends by examining pre-intervention trends.

22.A2 CASE STUDY – How Does a Merger between Airlines Affect Prices?

Pre-intervention trends

In our case study, the parallel trends assumption posits that, without the merger, on average, the market prices would have changed on treated markets (both AA and US present before the merger) the same way they changed on untreated markets (neither AA nor US present before the merger).

This is an assumption that is impossible to assess directly, but examining pre-intervention trends could provide valuable information. We used the original year-quarter-level data and calculated average price for the treated and untreated markets in each quarter.

Ideally, we would have a long time series prior to the merger. Recall that the date of the intervention is ambiguous: the merger was announced in early 2012 but it took place in mid-2015. Unfortunately, our data starts in 2010 Q2. That gives only a few quarters before the announcement of the merger. It gives a few more until the merger took place in practice. Figure 22.2 shows the two time series of the log of average prices. We drew vertical lines for the two dates of interest: 2012 Q1 when the merger was announced and 2015 Q3 when the merger took place in practice.

The average price was lower in treated markets through the entire time period, but that's fine with diff-in-diffs. Both of the two lines increase before 2015, with some ups and downs that are similar, and some that are different. The treated average appears to have increased a little less. Then, right around the time the merger was finalized, the average prices started to decline considerably in both treated and untreated markets, but more so in treated markets.

Are pre-intervention trends parallel, then? Not exactly. And, by and large, untreated prices increased less until 2015 than treated prices. At the same time the two lines are a lot more similar before 2015 than after. Thus, although the evidence is not very strong, we may conclude that the trends before the intervention were not very different, and, especially, not as different as when they started to diverge after the treatment.

To gain more evidence, we have examined pre-intervention trends separately for small and large markets, too. Figures 22.3a and 22.3b show the results.

The pre-intervention lines for small markets have a similar shape to all markets, with larger differences between treated and untreated markets and larger increases and decreases (the scales of the y axes are different). Average prices tend to move together before 2015, with

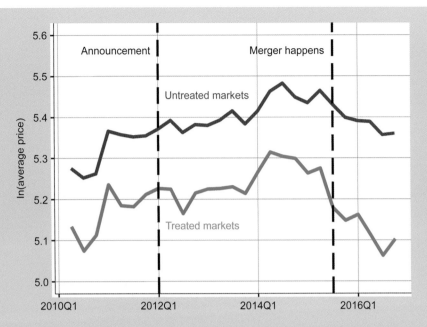

Figure 22.2   Pre-intervention trends in log price

Note: Airline markets in the United States (origin–final destination airport-pairs separately for one-way and return routes). Treated: both AA and US in market in 2011; untreated: neither in market. Weighted averages by the number of passengers.
Source: `airline-tickets-usa` dataset. N=112 632 markets.

slightly less increase in treated markets. But those differences are nothing compared to the differences in the decline in prices after 2015.

The figure for large markets is very different. Prices tend to be higher in treated markets, and the lines are flatter. We see some differences in trends on large markets. Prices increased before 2015, but more so in untreated markets. Then, starting from the beginning of 2015, prices in treated large markets started to decrease while prices in untreated large markets remained flat. Here, too, prices in treated markets already tended to decrease relative to untreated markets (they increased less) before the merger was completed. But, again, the additional decrease in prices in treated markets after the merger was larger.

What can we conclude from this analysis about parallel trends? The evidence shows that pre-intervention trends in average log prices were somewhat different between treated and untreated markets. However, those pre-treatment differences were smaller than the differences after the merger took place in 2015. Thus, the evidence doesn't exactly support the parallel trends assumption. But it suggests that our estimates are informative about ATE: the effect of how the merger affected prices in markets where both airlines were present. Perhaps the effect wasn't as negative as we estimated, as prices in treated markets decreased somewhat relative to untreated markets even before the merger. But those different pre-trends can't explain all the negative effect estimates.

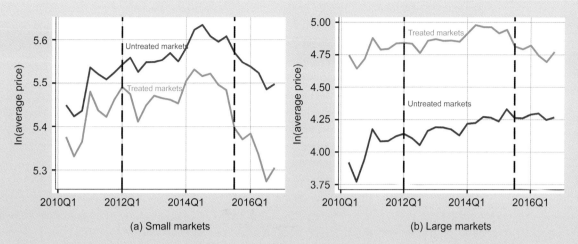

Figure 22.3 Pre-intervention trends in log price: small versus large markets

Note: Airline markets in the United States (origin–final destination airport-pairs separately for one-way and return routes). Treated: both AA and US in market in 2011; untreated: neither in market. Weighted averages by the number of passengers. **Source:** `airline-tickets-usa` dataset. N=112 632 markets.

22.4 Conditioning on Additional Confounders in Diff-in-Diffs Regressions

If the parallel trends assumption is not true, we have a problem. It's the usual problem of endogeneity: treatment is endogenous, so the untreated subjects do not show what would have happened to the treated subjects without the intervention. In the context of diff-in-diffs, endogeneity means correlation with the change of potential outcomes: treated and untreated subjects are different in how potential outcomes would change among them, on average.

The usual indirect strategy to mitigate the problem is conditioning on potential confounders. As we discussed in Chapter 21, first we should think about the potential sources of variation in the treatment variable, and whether those sources are exogenous or endogenous. In the context of diff-in-diffs analysis, that means thinking about whether they are related to how potential outcomes change. After establishing endogenous sources, we should find variables in the data that can measure them.

Conditioning on confounders in a diff-in-diffs regression is straightforward, except for one additional issue. The fact that we observe observations both before and after the intervention introduces new opportunities for such conditioning, but it also raises some specific questions.

With outcome y, binary variable *treatment*, and observed potential confounder variables z_1, z_2, ... in the data, the general form of the diff-in-diffs regression with additional right-hand-side variables is

$$\Delta y^E = a + \beta \, treatment + \gamma_1 z_1 + \gamma_2 z_2 + \cdots ; \tag{22.5}$$

β can be interpreted as the difference in expected change in y between treated and untreated subjects with the same values for the z variables. As usual, if those z variables include all potential confounders and measure them perfectly, and there is no reverse causality, β is a good estimator for the average treatment effect. In the diff-in-diffs framework, those conditions ensure that the parallel trends assumption holds, conditional on the z variables. More realistically, these z variables capture some, but not all, of the endogenous variation in *treatment*. Then we are in the usual situation of observational analysis: we need to think about the remaining bias, and, if possible, sign it and address its magnitude (see Chapter 21, Section 21.3).

The additional issue here is timing: we have observations from both before and after the intervention. Thus, these z variables may be measured before the intervention (baseline values), after the intervention (endline values), or they may actually measure the change between baseline and endline. Some variables don't change during the time of the intervention. But other variables do change. For observed confounder variables that change during the intervention, should we include their baseline value, their change, or their endline value?

To answer this question, we need to think about which version of the variable is more likely to be a confounder and which version may be a bad conditioning variable (see Chapter 21, Section 21.2). In particular, endline values may be bad conditioning variables if they are parts of the effect (mechanism variable) or are caused by the treatment and the outcome at the same time (common consequence variable). Baseline values are safe from this point of view because their value is determined before the treatment. Changes may be affected by the treatment, too, but sometimes it is the change in a variable that is the confounder, not its baseline level. So changes may be confounders to include, or they may be bad conditioning variables – if we are unlucky, they are both.

To summarize, we should condition on either the baseline value or the change in a potential confounder variable, depending how it affects the treatment, but we should not condition on its endline value.

Think of our example of the effect of flexible work hours on the retention of employees. We have data on many companies for two years, none of them allowing for flexible work hours at baseline and some of them introducing flexible work hours between the two years (these are the treated companies). The outcome is the retention rate of employees at the company. The parallel trends assumption is about whether the retention rate would have changed in the same way among the treated companies, had they not introduced flexible work hours, as it changed among the untreated companies. In other words, what we are interested in is whether variation in treatment is exogenous: whether companies that introduced flexible work hours were similar to companies that didn't introduce flexible hours in regard to how the retention rate would have changed.

Variables that are endogenous sources of variation would include common cause confounders: things that affect changes in the retention rate and make companies introduce flexible work hours. An example for baseline variables that are endogenous sources is the retention rate itself. Companies that have experienced low retention rates may be more likely to introduce flexible work hours and/or other measures to retain their employees. Yet, at the same time, companies with low retention rates may be more likely to experience an increase in their retention rates simply because of mean reversion. Mean reversion is the phenomenon that, in a random sequence of values of a variable, larger-than-usual values tend to be followed by less large values that are closer to the mean (see Chapter 7, Section 7.11). This also implies that we can expect an increase after a small value and a decrease after a large value. To avoid this, we should include the baseline value of the retention rate in the right-hand side of the diff-in-diffs regression.

An example for an endogenous source that is a change between the two years is other policies that companies implemented between the two years to retain their employees. These may include increasing salaries, increasing paid leave, or introducing free coffee or fruit at the workplace. If companies that introduce flexible work hours are more likely to introduce these changes as well, they are endogenous sources of variation in treatment.

In contrast, for an example of a change variable that is a bad conditioning variable in this example, consider employee satisfaction. The satisfaction of employees is a mechanism toward their retention: more satisfied employees are more likely to stay. Thus, we shouldn't condition on the change in employee satisfaction, even if we had a measure for it.

Review Box 22.3   Conditioning on potentially endogenous sources of variation in a diff-in-diffs regression

- In a diff-in-diffs regression using panel data with two time periods, we should condition on the baseline values of potential confounders or their change, depending on our assumptions about how the confounders affect, or are related to, the treatment variable.
- Conditioning on the baseline value:

$$\Delta y^E = \alpha + \beta \, treated + \gamma z_{baseline}$$

- Conditioning on the change:

$$\Delta y^E = \alpha + \beta \, treated + \gamma \Delta z$$

22.A3   CASE STUDY – How Does a Merger between Airlines Affect Prices?

Conditioning on potentially endogenous sources of variation

What are the sources of variation in the causal variable? In other words, why were both AA and US present in some markets before the intervention and why weren't they present in other markets? This is a question about baseline features of markets, so we should worry about confounders at the baseline.

The size of the market is one potential source of variation, and there are many small markets and fewer large markets. Both airlines are more likely to be present in larger markets; that's indeed the case in our data. At the same time, larger markets may be more expensive if demand is higher there because the origin or destination city is larger or richer. Thus market size is a likely confounder.

The competition structure of the market is also a likely confounder. Our two airlines are more likely to be present in markets that are more competitive, almost by definition, as a market tends to be more competitive the more airlines share it. At the same time more competitive markets tend to have lower prices, and they may experience smaller price increases or larger price decreases. Thus not conditioning on how competitive the market is makes our effect estimates biased in the negative direction.

Finally, various features of the routes are potential sources of variation in the treatment variable, and many of them may be endogenous. The origin or destination airport of some markets may have been hubs for American or US Airways in 2011. Many features make a city a hub: they tend to be large airports in large cities and are spread across the country following some planning in the past. Some of those features are likely irrelevant today; others are likely more relevant.

Another feature of routes is the number of stops. It's a potential source of variation in the treatment variable: larger airlines, such as American, are more likely to service routes with more stops than smaller airlines, because they are more likely to have flights connecting such stops. But the number of stops may affect prices, too, in two opposite directions. First, with the same final destination, flights with more stops should be cheaper, because they are less convenient for passengers. At the same time, more stops may mean longer flights, and those are usually more expensive. Thus this is a potential confounder, but the direction in which it may affect the effect estimate is unclear.

Whether the market is a one-way route or a return route is another potential confounder. Large airlines, such as American, tend to price their tickets by offering one-way tickets for the same price as return tickets, while many small "low-cost" airlines offer return prices that are simply the sum of two one-way prices. Thus American's share is larger in return markets than in one-way markets. At the same time, return tickets are more expensive.

Our data has few variables. The number of passengers is a good measure of market size, a potential confounder. How competitive a market is may be measured in various imperfect ways: our data has the share of the largest carrier. Finally, we know the number of stops and whether the market is a return route. The number of stops and whether it is a return route market are features of the markets that don't change over time. The other two variables, number of passengers and share of the largest carrier, are entered at their baseline value. We took the log of the number of passengers both for substantive and statistical reasons (relative differences are more intuitive, and the distribution is very skewed).

The equation for the estimate regression is

$$(\Delta \ln p)^E = \beta_0 + \beta_1 AAUS_{before} + \beta_2 \ln passengers_{before}$$
$$+ \beta_3 return + \beta_4 stops + \beta_5 sharelargest_{before} \tag{22.6}$$

The results of the regressions are in Table 22.4.

Conditioning on the measured potential confounders did make a difference. All estimated effects are smaller in magnitude, by one third to one half. They are still negative and quite large in magnitude.

Are these good estimates of the effect of the merger? As usual with conditioning on observed confounders, we can never know. There may be confounder variables that are not in our data, such as unmeasured features of the routes themselves. And some of the measures we have may be imperfect, such as the share of the largest carrier to capture the strength of competition.

At the same time, conditioning on these confounders led to estimates that are in line with what we would have expected for the true effects after we analyzed pre-trends. The evidence we found there suggested that the true effect was likely negative indeed, but perhaps not as large as the basic diff-in-diffs estimates suggested. And that's exactly how the estimates change after conditioning on the observable confounders.

Thus, the true effect may be close to what we estimated, or may even be smaller negative number. But there is nothing in this data that would suggest that the merger led to an increase in prices. If customers were not harmed by effects on service quality, these results support the decision of the competition authority that allowed the merger.

	(1)	(2)	(3)
Variables	**All markets**	**Small markets**	**Large markets**
$AAUS_{before}$	−0.11**	−0.10**	−0.13**
	(0.01)	(0.01)	(0.03)
ln no. passengers$_{before}$	−0.00	0.00	0.06**
	(0.00)	(0.00)	(0.02)
Return route	0.19**	0.20**	0.17**
	(0.01)	(0.01)	(0.03)
Number of stops	−0.03**	0.00	−0.07**
	(0.01)	(0.01)	(0.02)
Share of largest carrier	0.26**	0.21**	0.43**
	(0.02)	(0.02)	(0.07)
Constant	−0.15**	−0.17**	−0.74**
	(0.03)	(0.02)	(0.21)
Observations	112 632	111 745	887
R-squared	0.14	0.11	0.23

Table 22.4 Difference-in-differences estimates of the effect of AA–US merger on log prices, conditioning on confounder variables

Note: Dependent variable: change in ln average market price. Observations: markets in the United States (origin–final destination airport pairs separately for one-way and return routes). Before period: 2011. After period: 2016. AAUSbefore: binary variable for both AA and US on market in 2011. Weighted by the number of passengers at baseline. Robust standard error estimates in parentheses. ** $p < 0.01$, * $p < 0.05$.

Source: `airline-tickets-usa` dataset.

22.5 Quantitative Causal Variable

We can generalize basic diff-in-diffs analysis to a quantitative x variable from the original setup of a binary *treatment* variable. That generalization is straightforward in the framework of regression.

Just like in basic diff-in-diffs we need two observations for each unit, one before the intervention (baseline) and one after the intervention (endline). In other words we need balanced cross-section time series (xt) panel data with two time series observations for each cross-sectional unit.

With outcome y, change in outcome Δy, and quantitative causal variable x, the regression formula looks the same as with a binary x variable. However, the interpretation of the coefficients is slightly different.

The causal variable may be defined by baseline features of the subjects or by a change in some features. To highlight the difference between the two cases we'll denote the causal variable in the first case as x and in the second case as Δx.

First, let's consider a quantitative causal variable determined by baseline features: $x_{baseline}$.

$$\Delta y^E = \alpha + \beta x_{baseline} \tag{22.7}$$

α shows how y is expected to change when $x_{baseline}$ is zero. β can be interpreted as the difference in the expected change in y between subjects that are different in $x_{baseline}$ by one unit at baseline. In other words, comparing two subjects that are different in x at baseline by one unit, we can expect y to change by β more units for the subject with the larger x value.

Second, let's consider the case with a quantitative causal variable that is a change Δx:

$$\Delta y^E = \alpha + \beta \Delta x \qquad (22.8)$$

Here α shows how y is expected to change when x does not change. β shows the difference in the expected change in y between subjects with different change in x. In other words, comparing two subjects that are different in how much x changes, by one unit, we can expect y to change by β more units for the subject with the larger change in x.

Review Box 22.4   Difference-in-differences analysis with quantitative x

- With a quantitative causal variable x measured at baseline, the diff-in-diffs regression is

$$\Delta y^E = \alpha + \beta x_{baseline}$$

  Here β shows the expected difference in how y changes for subjects with a unit larger level of x at baseline.
- With a quantitative causal variable Δx, which is the change in x, the diff-in-diffs regression is

$$\Delta y^E = \alpha + \beta \Delta x$$

  Here β shows the expected difference in how y changes for subjects with a unit larger change in x.

22.A4   CASE STUDY – How Does a Merger between Airlines Affect Prices?

Quantitative causal variable

With basic diff-and-diffs, we defined two kinds of markets: treated ones were those with a presence of the two airlines, and untreated ones were without them. The idea was that markets where the two airlines were present were affected by the merger, while markets with neither of them weren't. But, presumably, markets in which the two airlines had a small share were less affected than markets in which they had a larger share. To capture this idea, we can define the causal variable as their combined market share at baseline.

This share variable is between zero and one. The share is zero in 72 000 of the 113 000 markets, covering 3 million of the 24 million passengers in the data for 2011. The share is one, or 100%, in 4000 markets with only 34 000 passengers. Both the zero share and the 100% share markets tend to be small in terms of passengers. The 37 000 markets with in-between shares include most of the large markets, comprising 20 million passengers in the data.

Figure 22.4 visualizes the heterogeneity of markets in terms of the market share of the two airlines at baseline. It's a histogram showing the distribution of markets, weighted by the number of passengers, at baseline. Thus, in effect, it shows how passengers were distributed across markets with different market shares of the merged companies, before the merger took place. The main message of the figures is that markets vary a lot in terms of the market share of the two airlines.

We estimated a diff-in-diffs regression with the baseline share of AA+US as the causal variable, which is a quantitative variable. We conditioned on the same confounders as earlier, and used the number of passengers at baseline as weights. The regression formula is the following:

$$(\Delta \ln p)^E = \beta_0 + \beta_1 AAUSshare_{baseline} + \beta_2 \ln passengers_{baseline}$$
$$+ \beta_3 return + \beta_4 stops + \beta_5 sharelargest_{baseline} \quad\quad (22.9)$$

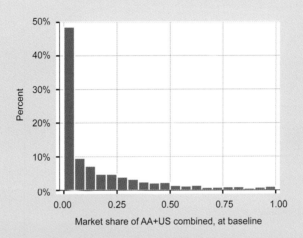

Figure 22.4   Market share of AA+US at baseline

Note: Airline markets in the United States (origin–final destination airport-pairs separately for one-way and return routes). Baseline is year 2011. The histogram is weighted by the number of passengers at baseline.
Source: `airline-tickets-usa` dataset. N=112 632 markets.

The results of the regressions are in Table 22.5. The interpretation of the coefficient on the AA+US share variable is a little different from the interpretation of the binary treatment variable earlier. Considering all markets, let us compare markets where the number of passengers and the market share of the largest carrier were the same in 2011 and that are similar in whether they are return routes and how many stops they have. Prices decreased by 27% more, on average, in markets where the pre-merger share of AA and US was 100% instead of 0%. Or, to emphasize the fact that we have fine-grained share here, we can also say that prices decreased by 2.7% more, on average, in markets where the pre-merger share of AA and US was 10% more.

All estimates are similar in direction, but they are substantially stronger than we had with a binary definition of treatment, in Table 22.4. Why?

The difference comes from the fact that here we distinguish between markets where the two airlines were present with a lower market share and markets where they were present with a higher market share. If diff-in-diffs estimates reflect the pricing behavior of the merged airline, we would expect stronger effects in markets with larger shares. And that's exactly what we find.

Thus the results support the interpretation that markets more affected by the merger saw average prices decline more because the new merged company sold tickets at lower prices on average.

And this interpretation is in line with the causal interpretation of the results: the merger led to lower prices.

Table 22.5   Difference-in-differences estimates of the effect of AA–US merger on average log prices. Treatment is the combined market share of the two airlines at baseline

Variables	(1) All markets	(2) Small markets	(3) Large markets
Market share before	−0.27**	−0.17**	−0.42**
	(0.02)	(0.02)	(0.05)
ln no. passengers before	−0.01**	−0.01**	0.05*
	(0.00)	(0.00)	(0.02)
Return route	0.21**	0.21**	0.19**
	(0.01)	(0.01)	(0.02)
Number of stops	−0.03**	0.00	−0.07**
	(0.01)	(0.01)	(0.02)
Share of largest carrier	0.31**	0.26**	0.47**
	(0.02)	(0.02)	(0.05)
Constant	−0.12**	−0.15**	−0.72**
	(0.03)	(0.02)	(0.20)
Observations	112 632	111 745	887
R-squared	0.15	0.11	0.30

Note: Dependent variable: change in ln average market price. Observations: markets in the United States (origin–final destination airport pairs separately for one-way and return routes). Before period: 2011. After period: 2016. AAUSbefore: binary variable for both AA and US on market in 2011. Weighted by the number of passengers at baseline. Robust standard error estimates in parentheses. ** $p < 0.01$, * $p < 0.05$.

Source: `airline-tickets-usa` dataset.

22.6   Difference-in-Differences with Pooled Cross-Sections

Basic difference-in-differences analysis requires balanced panel data: observations for every subject from both before and after the intervention. Sometimes our data has observations on different subjects in the before period and the after period. In our case study example of airline markets, that would mean prices observed for different markets before and after the airline merger took place. Instead of a panel, this is **pooled cross-sectional data**. In this section we discuss diff-in-diffs analysis with pooled cross-sectional data.

When we have unbalanced panel data, basic diff-in-diffs requires keeping only the balanced part of the data and dropping the subjects that are observed once only. The version of diff-in-diffs considered in this section does not require a balanced panel. Thus, this method allows us to make use of more observations in an unbalanced panel.

Difference-in-differences with pooled cross-sections can be computed by measuring the average outcomes in the treatment group and the non-treatment group, both before and after the intervention. The formula is the same as earlier, except that instead of treated and untreated, we use treatment group and non-treatment group to denote the two groups. The reason for this is that observations in the treatment group before the intervention are not really treated. Instead, they share the features of the observations that become treated after the intervention, so that they would be treated, too, had they been observed then:

$$\beta_{diff\text{-}in\text{-}diffs} = (\bar{y}_{treatment, after} - \bar{y}_{treatment, before})$$
$$- (\bar{y}_{non\text{-}treatment, after}) - \bar{y}_{non\text{-}treatment, before}) \qquad (22.10)$$

For example, we may want to analyze the effect of extracting natural gas by hydraulic fracturing (fracking) on the price of nearby houses. Our data may come from a single county with observations on house transactions: houses that are bought and sold. Fracking starts in this county at a point in time; some of the transactions took place before that, others after. Typically, the houses that are bought and sold before fracking starts are different from the houses bought and sold after it started. So the data is pooled cross-sections.

In this example, some of the houses are near the fracking site while others are far away. Houses in the treatment group are those that are near the fracking site whether they are observed before fracking started or after.

This difference-in-differences is impossible to represent as a regression on changes within subjects as we cannot compute the change in the outcome, Δy_i, for the same subjects. Instead, we can represent this difference-in-differences in a regression using all subjects as separate cross-sectional observations.

Let's denote the outcome variable by y, as usual. However, here y itself is on the left-hand side and not its change. On the right-hand side, we'll have two binary variables, plus their interaction. The first binary variable, *treatment*, shows whether the observation belongs to the treatment group. The second binary variable, *after*, shows whether the observation is observed in the after period. The pooled xsec diff-in-diffs regression is

$$y^E = \alpha + \beta\ treatment + \gamma\ after + \delta\ treatment \times after \qquad (22.11)$$

The intercept α shows average outcome for observations in the non-treatment group before the intervention. The slope coefficient on *treatment*, β, shows the average outcome difference between the treatment group and the non-treatment group before the intervention. The slope coefficient on *after*, γ, shows the average outcome difference between the time periods in the non-treatment group.

Finally, it is the coefficient of the interaction term, δ, that is the difference-in-differences estimate: it shows how much larger the after–before difference of average outcomes is in the treatment group than in the non-treatment group.

When we have a balanced panel, we can estimate this pooled xsec diff-in-diffs regression, and we get back the same results as with the basic diff-in-diffs regression that has the change in y on its left-hand side. One way to see this is taking a difference of the entire equation: substituting in one for *after*, then zero for *after*, and subtracting the second equation from the first. That would result in Δy^E on the left-hand side, γ for the intercept, and the only remaining right-hand-side variable would be *treatment* × *after*, multiplied by the coefficient δ. α would drop out, and so would $\beta \times$ *treatment*, because they are both the same whether *after* is one or zero.

Just as with basic difference-in-differences analysis, parallel trends are required for the difference-in-differences estimate to identify the effect of the intervention. To evaluate whether this assumption is true, we have to address a new problem in addition to the usual concerns: the subjects observed before the intervention in the treatment group represent the counterfactual average of the subjects observed after the intervention in the treatment group.

This additional problem is one of selection. It may be that the intervention changed what kind of subjects we can observe after the intervention as compared to before the intervention. This may be an issue: if the two sets of observations are different, the before-intervention average outcome of observed subjects is not a good measure of what that average would have been for subjects observed after the intervention.

For example, we have to worry about selection when we use diff-in-diffs to estimate the effect of fracking on house prices using data with observations that includes different houses before and after the intervention. This is because fracking itself may affect the composition of houses that are bought and sold, and thus it affects the selection of all houses into the sample of houses whose prices we can observe. This effect is an unwanted mechanism confounder (see Chapter 19, Section 19.14), which could bias our effect estimates.

Finally, let's discuss how we can condition on observed confounder variables in a pooled cross-sectional diff-in-diffs regression. We don't want to include values of potential confounders from the after period (see Section 22.4), and we can't include the changes because we have a pooled cross-section. But we can include the baseline values.

However, it's a little more cumbersome to condition on baseline value confounders in pooled xsec diff-in-diffs regressions. To be more precise, it's cumbersome to include them in a way that is analogous to their inclusion in panel diff-in-diffs regressions (Section 22.4). There we estimated how change in the outcome differed across treated and untreated groups, conditional on the confounders. Here we have the level of the outcome on the left-hand side. What we want is how the after versus before difference in the outcome is different in the treatment group and the non-treatment group, conditional on the baseline values of the confounders. But simply including the baseline values of the confounders in the pooled xsec diff-in-diffs equation wouldn't do that. (To see the technical side of this, take the difference of the pooled xsec diff-in-diffs regression with baseline values of confounder variables; they would drop out.) Instead, we also need to include their values interacted with the *after* dummy.

Review Box 22.5 Difference-in-differences analysis with pooled cross-sections

- Difference-in-differences with pooled cross-sections can be computed by measuring average outcomes in the two groups in the two time periods. The formula is the same as with basic diff-in-diffs:

$$\beta_{\text{diff-in-diffs}} = \left(\bar{y}_{\text{treatment, after}} - \bar{y}_{\text{treatment, before}}\right)$$
$$- \left(\bar{y}_{\text{non-treatment, after}} - \bar{y}_{\text{non-treatment, before}}\right)$$

- However, with pooled cross-sections the averages are computed using different observations in the before and the after time period.
- The regression equivalent includes observations from both before and after, and they need not be a balanced panel:

$$y^E = \alpha + \beta \, treatment + \gamma \, after + \delta \, treatment \times after$$

where δ is the difference-in-differences estimator.

- Confounder variables are best included in this regression as their baseline values, also interacted with the *after* dummy.
- In addition to the usual concerns, here we also need to pay attention to selection into measurement (what kinds of subjects are observed before vs. after).

22.A5   **CASE STUDY – How Does a Merger between Airlines Affect Prices?**

Using the entire unbalanced panel and diff-in-diffs with pooled cross-sections

Recall that our data is an unbalanced panel: not all markets that are observed at baseline are observed at endline, and vice versa: not all markets observed at endline are observed at baseline. If we want to include those markets in the analysis, we can apply diff-in-diffs on pooled cross-sections.

It turns out that it is impossible to include the entire unbalanced panel in this estimation. That's because the treatment variable (as well as the weights) are defined in the baseline time period for all markets. A market is considered treated if both AA and US were present there in 2011, and we used the number of passengers in 2011 as weights. As a result, markets that were not observed at baseline have neither a treatment variable nor appropriate weights. Therefore, when extending our data to the unbalanced panel, this analysis includes markets that have observations from the baseline time period only, but it does not include markets that have observations from the endline time period only.

There are 22 851 markets that are observed in the after time period only; we don't use them in the analysis. They comprise about half a million passengers in the data. There are 28 665 markets that are observed in the before time period only; these are the markets that we include here but we didn't include in the previous analysis. They comprise only a hundred thousand passengers. The difference between this new, unbalanced panel and the original balanced panel is very small in terms of passengers. The pooled cross-sectional sample used for the estimation has 24 850 observations.

The regressions we estimate – again for all markets, both small and large markets – have the following form:

$$(\ln p)^E = \alpha + \beta\, AAUS_{before} + \gamma\, after + \delta\, AAUS_{before} \times after \qquad (22.12)$$

We don't show the results of this regression; the diff-in-diffs coefficient estimates (on $AAUS_{before} \times after$) are practically the same as the diff-in-diffs coefficients in Table 22.2. That's not surprising, because all regressions are weighted by the (baseline) number of passengers, and the additional observations we include here have very few passengers in comparison to the entire data.

Perhaps more interesting to see is what happens when we include the observed confounders: the log number of passengers at baseline, the share of the largest carrier on the market (at baseline), whether the market is a return route, and the number of stops on the route. Following the advice we gave in Section 22.6, we include these variables directly as well as their interactions with the binary *after* variable.

The regression estimates are in Table 22.6. The diff-in-diffs coefficient estimates (on $AAUS_{before} \times after$) are, again, practically the same as the corresponding diff-in-diffs coefficients in Table 22.4. This shows that the way we conditioned on the observed confounder variables did indeed work the same way it did with the panel diff-in-diffs regressions. As a data exercise, you can re-estimate these pooled xsec diff-in-diffs regressions restricted on the balanced panel to see if you get the exact same results as with the panel diff-in-diffs. You can also check that simply conditioning on the confounder variables, without interacting them with the *after* variable, wouldn't result in the diff-in-diffs estimate.

Table 22.6   Difference-in-differences estimates of the effect of AA–US merger on log prices. Pooled cross-sections

Variables	(1) All markets	(2) Small markets	(3) Large markets
$AAUS_{before} \times after$	−0.11**	−0.10**	−0.14**
	(0.01)	(0.01)	(0.03)
$AAUS_{before}$	0.43**	0.29**	0.69**
	(0.02)	(0.01)	(0.05)
after	−0.19**	−0.14**	−0.82**
	(0.04)	(0.03)	(0.22)
ln no. passengers before	−0.37**	−0.29**	−0.54**
	(0.01)	(0.00)	(0.05)
Return route	0.84**	0.84**	0.95**
	(0.02)	(0.01)	(0.05)
Number of stops	0.07**	0.14**	0.03
	(0.02)	(0.01)	(0.04)
Share of largest carrier	−1.45**	−1.40**	−1.69**
	(0.05)	(0.03)	(0.13)
ln no. passengers before $\times$ *after*	−0.00	−0.00	0.06*
	(0.00)	(0.00)	(0.02)
Return route $\times$ *after*	0.20**	0.20**	0.19**
	(0.01)	(0.01)	(0.03)
Number of stops $\times$ *after*	0.01	−0.00	0.01
	(0.02)	(0.02)	(0.05)
Share of largest carrier $\times$ *after*	0.30**	0.23**	0.44**
	(0.02)	(0.02)	(0.07)
Constant	7.85**	7.33**	9.23**
	(0.06)	(0.03)	(0.40)
Observations	254 178	252 404	1 774
R-squared	0.68	0.68	0.56

Note: Dependent variable: change in ln average market price. Observations: markets in the United States (origin–final destination airport pairs separately for one-way and return routes). Before period: 2011. After period: 2016. Unbalanced panel, also including markets observed at baseline only. AAUSbefore: binary variable for both AA and US on market in 2011. Weighted by the number of passengers at baseline. Robust standard error estimates in parentheses.
** $p < 0.01$, * $p < 0.05$.

Source: `airline-tickets-usa` dataset.

This concludes our case study. What did we learn from it? On the substance side, we estimated that the merger led to a decrease in prices. When we examined pre-trends, we couldn't conclude that prices changed the same way before the merger on affected markets and unaffected markets, but the divergence in prices after the merger was a lot stronger. Thus, we concluded that maybe the true effect of the merger was smaller than our estimate, but it was likely negative. Our other results supported the same conclusion: including baseline confounder variables led to smaller negative estimates, but when we replaced the binary treatment variable with the pre-treatment share of the two airlines, we obtained stronger negative effect estimates.

Thus, we can safely conclude that this merger didn't lead to an increase in prices. However, our analysis has important limitations. First, we have no data on the quality of service, so we can't tell whether it has improved, remained the same, or deteriorated as a result of the merger. Second, our results are about the short run; we would need data from additional years after the merger to assess longer-run effects, and we would need a method to estimate such effects. We'll discuss these in the next chapter.

On the methods side, this case study illustrated how we can use publicly available Big Data to uncover the effect of an intervention. To do so, we aggregated the data to market level. An important task in that process was defining markets. Then we used our knowledge of the intervention to define the before and after time periods, and we carried out a basic diff-in-diffs analysis using the balanced panel. We then went back to the data with more time periods to investigate pre-trends. The results of that investigation weren't straightforward to interpret, but they supported the estimated negative effect nevertheless. In particular, examining pre-trends didn't exactly support the parallel trends assumption, but it clearly showed that the differences between how prices moved on treated versus untreated markets became much larger after the intervention.

The case study also showed how to include baseline values of confounders in a diff-in-diffs regression, and how to estimate diff-in-diffs replacing the binary treatment variable with a quantitative variable that is a more refined measure of the exposure to the potential effects of the merger. Finally, we illustrated how to estimate diff-in-diffs regressions using pooled xsec data, and how to include baseline values of observable confounder variables in them.

This case study was long and complicated. It included many steps and required many decisions along the way. Once we arrived at a balanced panel, carrying out the actual diff-in-diffs analysis was not hard. It was harder to get the original data in a format that was appropriate for that analysis. Even that wasn't super hard, but it was long. It required time, domain knowledge (some basic things about how the airline industry works), programming, common sense, and a constant focus on the eventual goal of the analysis. We believe that it was a good demonstration of what most data analysts experience in real life: most of the time is spent on data wrangling and thinking about the decisions along the way. Less time is needed for the actual analysis. At the same time, we had to put in more effort and thought, again, to present and interpret the results of the analysis and answer the original question on the basis of those results.

22.7 Main Takeaways

Difference-in-differences (diff-in-diffs) estimates the effect of an intervention by comparing how the outcome variable changes among treated subjects versus untreated subjects.

- Diff-in-diffs uses observational panel data and has a better chance to estimate the effect of an intervention than using cross-sectional data, because it conditions on pre-intervention outcomes.
- Diff-in-diffs gives a good estimate of the effect if the parallel trends assumption holds.

- We can't test the parallel trends assumption directly, but examining pre-intervention trends can give indirect evidence.

PRACTICE QUESTIONS

1. Your data is a balanced two-period xt panel. Write down the 2×2 table for basic diff-in-diffs with averages of the outcome variable and their differences. Then write down the regression for basic diff-in-diffs. What in the table corresponds to which coefficient in the regression?

2. What's the parallel trends assumption, and how does it compare to the assumption of random assignment? Does one imply the other?

3. Why does the parallel trends assumption make sure that basic diff-in-diffs gives a good estimate of the effect of an intervention?

4. Can you tell whether the parallel trends assumption holds in a particular case? If yes, how? If not, can you examine evidence to support or contradict it?

5. Write down the regression equation for diff-in-diffs on pooled cross-sections and interpret its coefficients.

6. Selection into the "after" time period may be an issue with diff-in-diffs on pooled cross-sections. Why? Give an example.

7. In our airline merger case study, we used the share of AA+US at baseline as a quantitative causal variable. What's the argument for using the baseline share and not the change in this share instead?

8. Some states in the USA increased the minimum wage, in the same year, while others didn't. You want to learn the effect of whether and to what extent an increase in the minimum wage affects employment among teenagers. Consider two strategies to estimate this effect. The first one is estimating a regression using cross-sectional data on employment after the minimum wage increase took place. The second one is a difference-in-differences estimation. What kind of data would you need for each strategy? When would each strategy measure the effect of the intervention with high internal validity? Which strategy would you prefer and why?

9. A city with a historic downtown area decided to restrict the entry of cars and trucks into the downtown area. You would like to know the effect of this policy on the prices of apartments in downtown. What kind of data do you need to estimate the effect by difference-in-differences analysis? Write down the regression equation you would use to estimate the effect and interpret its coefficients. When can this regression identify the causal effect with high internal validity?

10. Children in a country are eligible for no-cost preschool starting from age four years. A few municipalities in the country extended the coverage, in the same year, to include children starting from age two years. Other municipalities did not. First, explain in words how you would use a diff-in-diffs method to estimate the effect of this policy intervention on the likelihood of whether mothers with children of age three years work for pay. What kind of data do you need to estimate the effect by difference-in-differences analysis? Write down the regression equation you would use to estimate the effect, and interpret its coefficients.

11. Some countries introduced a carbon tax on gasoline sales, in the same year, while other countries did not. How would you estimate the effect of this policy intervention on CO_2 emission? Under what condition(s) can this method identify the effect with high internal

validity? What evidence would you use, and how would you establish if the condition(s) you described are met in this case?

12. In a diff-in-diffs regression on two-period panel data on firms, the change in spending on innovation is regressed on whether the firm received a tax break for such spending. Firms were eligible for such tax breaks if they had less than 1000 employees. Write down the regression, and interpret its coefficients. When can you interpret the result as the effect of the tax breaks?

13. You carry out a diff-in-diffs regression on a pooled cross-section of firms from two years. The outcome is spending on innovation; the treatment is whether the firm was eligible for a tax break for such spending, which was introduced in-between the two years in your data. Firms were eligible for such tax breaks if they had less than 1000 employees. Write down the regression and interpret its coefficients. Are there additional issues here with internal validity compared to what you would have with a two-period panel of firms?

14. Tariffs on imported wines were increased in a country that itself also produces wine. The data is a pooled cross-section of two random samples collected in a large retail chain, from before and after the tariff increase, of sales of wine brands both imported and domestic. Write down the diff-in-diffs regression to measure the effect of the tariff increase on sales, and interpret its coefficients. Would you use weights here? Why or why not?

15. A new low-cost airline enters some air travel markets in a large country. You have market-level data from the entire country on the number of passengers by airlines from both before and after the entry. How would you estimate the effect of the entry of the new airline on the number of passengers carried by the other airlines? When would that strategy give a good estimate of the effect?

DATA EXERCISES

Easier and/or shorter exercises are denoted by [*]; harder and/or longer exercises are denoted by [**].

1. Use the same `airline-tickets-usa` dataset that we used in the case study, with the same two years, 2011 and 2016. Apply diff-in-diffs to estimate the effect of the merger in three kinds of markets, defined by how expensive they were prior to the merger. Re-do Tables 22.2 and 22.4, discuss the differences (if any), and explain why you see what you see. [*]

2. Use the same `airline-tickets-usa` dataset that we used in the case study, with the same two years, 2011 and 2016. Re-do the analysis with an alternative treatment definition: markets that had either AA or US (or both) present at baseline. In particular, re-do Tables 22.2 and 22.4, discuss the differences (if any), and explain why you see what you see. [*]

3. Use the `airline-tickets-usa` dataset, but define markets differently from the way we did for our case study. In particular, define markets as routes that have the same originating airport. Re-do Tables 22.2 and 22.4, discuss the differences (if any), and explain why you see what you see. Finally, argue for one of the two market definitions to use in the analysis. [**]

4. Use the same `airline-tickets-usa` dataset that we used in the case study, with the same two years, 2011 and 2016. Re-do the basic diff-in-diffs analysis and the diff-in-diffs on pooled cross-sections of our case study, but display more decimal digits for the results (Tables 22.2 and 22.6). See if there are differences there. Then re-do the diff-in-diffs on pooled cross-sections

restricting the data to the balanced panel, and see if those results are different at more decimal digits. Discuss what you see. [*]

5. Use the same `airline-tickets-usa` dataset that we used in the case study, with the same two years, 2011 and 2016. Investigate the effect of market concentration on prices. Define market concentration as the share of the largest carrier on the market. First estimate cross-sectional regressions for both 2011 and 2016 with log average price on the left-hand side, and then estimate generalized diff-in-diffs regression with the change in log average price on the market share of the largest carrier at baseline. Condition on other variables, such as the number of passengers (whether baseline value or change; argue for your choice). Interpret and discuss your results. What can you learn from this exercise about the effect of market concentration on prices? [**]

REFERENCES AND FURTHER READING

Difference-in-differences is a classic tool in economics and is widely discussed. Expositions include textbooks like Angrist & Pischke (2015). The idea was popularized by Card & Krueger (1994), an influential paper that looked at the employment effect of raising the minimum wage in the US state of New Jersey in 1992. The example of fracking comes from Muehlenbachs et al. (2015).

The case study was inspired by a larger literature studying mergers. Some examples examining the airline industry that use, among other tools, difference-in-differences, are Chen & Gayle (2019), Shen (2017), and Das (2019). More information on the data is available at US Bureau of Transportation Statistics website (`www.transtats.bts.gov/DatabaseInfo.asp?DB_ID=125`).

23 Methods for Panel Data

When, why, and how to carry out regression analysis using panel data with multiple time periods

Motivation

You want to know how the industrial production of your country is affected by changes in the import demand of your country's largest trading partner. You have time series data on the industrial production of your country and total imports of its trading partner. How should you estimate this effect? Is there a way to get a reasonably precise effect estimate when your time series is not very long? In particular, can you use similar time series from similar countries to get a good and more precise estimate of the effect for your country?

You want to quantify the effects of immunization against measles. Among other potential effects, you want to know whether, and to what extent, immunization saves the lives of young children. You have access to data on immunization rates and child mortality from many countries from many years. How should you use this data to get a good estimate of the effect?

This chapter introduces the most widely used regression methods to uncover the effect of an intervention when observational time series (tseries) data or cross-section time series (xt) panel data is available with more than two time periods. We discuss the potential advantages of having more time periods in allowing within-subject comparisons, assessing pre-intervention trends, and tracing out effects through time. We then review time series regressions, and discuss what kind of average effect they can estimate, under what conditions, and how adding lags and leads can help uncover delayed effects and reverse effects. Then we discuss when we can pool several similar time series to get a more precise estimate of the effect. This is xt panel data with few cross-sectional units, and we discuss how to use such data to estimate an effect for a single cross-sectional unit.

In the second, and larger, part of the chapter, we turn to xt panel data with many cross-sectional units and more than two time periods, to estimate an average effect across the cross-sectional units. We introduce two methods: panel fixed-effects regressions (FE regressions) and panel regressions in first differences (FD regressions). Both can be viewed as generalizations of the diff-in-diffs method we covered in Chapter 22. We explain when estimates from each kind of regression give a good estimate of the average effect, and show how adding lags and leads can help uncover delayed effects, differences in pre-trends, and reverse effects. We discuss adding binary time variables to deal with aggregate trends of any form in FE or FD regressions, and how we can treat unit-specific linear trends in FD regressions. We discuss clustered standard error estimation that helps address serial correlation and heteroskedasticity at the same time. We briefly discuss how to analyze unbalanced panel data, and close the chapter by comparing FE and FD regressions.

This chapter includes two case studies. The first one, **Import demand and industrial production**, aims to uncover the effect of US import demand on the industrial production of Thailand with the `asia-industry` dataset. To get more precise estimates, it also combines Thai data with time series data from other countries. The second case study, **Immunization against measles and saving children**, examines the effect of increased vaccination rates of infants on their chances of survival. In this case study we employ a country–year panel from the `worldbank-immunization` dataset to illustrate FE and FD panel regressions.

Learning outcomes

After working through this chapter, you should be able to:

- understand when and why to do pooled time series regressions to estimate effects, carry them out, and interpret their results;
- carry out fixed-effects (FE) regression analysis on xt panel data and interpret its results;
- carry out first-differenced (FD) regression analysis on xt panel data and interpret its results;
- assess the extent to which the results of FE and FD regressions give good estimates of the average effect of a causal variable.

23.1   Multiple Time Periods Can Be Helpful

In the previous chapter (Chapter 22), we introduced diff-in-diffs, a method to estimate the average effect of an intervention using observational panel data with two time periods. **Diff-in-diffs** gives a good effect estimate of the average effect on the treated units if the parallel trends assumption holds: outcome y changed, on average, among untreated units the same way as it would have changed among treated units without the intervention. This is a less strict assumption than random assignment, as the average level of actual untreated y and counterfactual untreated y may be different with diff-in-diffs – only their change must be the same. We can't directly evaluate this assumption as it is about a counterfactual change. But, as we have seen, examining pre-intervention trends in y can help assess its validity (Chapter 22, Section 22.3). To do so we need more than two time periods: we need many of them before the intervention.

Diff-in-diffs estimates the effect at a single point in time: in the after, or endline, time period. When exactly we measure the effect is not important if the effect is immediate and stays the same. But that's rare. In most real-life situations, the effect may kick in after some delay, it may take some time to build up fully, and it may be more or less persistent, sometimes fading away in the longer run. In such cases, having a single endline time period is not enough to tell the full story. To be able to estimate how an effect plays out in time, we need more time periods.

Consider our diff-in-diffs case study in Chapter 22, Section 22.A1, in which we wanted to uncover the effect of the merger between two airline companies on prices. To estimate the effect we compared treated and untreated markets across two years, 2011 and 2016. In fact, we had access to more years. We used data from those years to examine pre-intervention trends (Chapter 22, Section 22.A2). We used the several years in the data to pick the before and after time periods carefully: the merger was first discussed in 2012, and it was completed in 2015, so we took the entire year of 2011 as the "before" time period, and the entire year of 2016 as the "after" time period. The 2016 data allowed us to estimate a short-term effect, one year after the merger was completed. We would have had to use additional years to estimate more delayed effects.

Another case when we need data from multiple time periods is when an intervention is scattered through time: some subjects become treated at one point, some other subjects at another point, and so on. For example, when assessing the effect of the opening of large malls in small towns on the survival of small downtown shops, two-period diff-in-diffs can be applied if the the mall openings were concentrated around the same time. In contrast, if malls opened in different years in different towns, scattered over a decade or more, the situation is unsuited for two-period diff-in-diffs. Instead, we would need data from small towns with many time periods, and we would need a more general method.

In this chapter, we introduce such more general methods. When using data from a single subject and multiple time periods, we use time series regression methods (see Chapter 12). When using xt panel data with multiple time periods from many cross-sectional units, we need new kinds of regressions. In the end, the xt panel regressions and pooled time series will look similar. However, they are used for different purposes and different kinds of data. Pooled time should be used when our question regards a single subject, and we have few similar subjects in the data. In contrast, xt panel regressions are designed to estimate average effects for many subjects.

23.2 Estimating Effects Using Observational Time Series

Let's start with estimating an effect from a single time series. This kind of data allows for **within-subject comparisons** only. The effect we can estimate from a single time series is an average effect across time for the same subject. This approach is useful when we care about a single country or shop, or the intervention happens at one place only.

Recall from Chapter 12 that we can have a **time series regression** specified in levels as well as changes. In either case we write out the t index to all variables. This notation is more complicated than what we had with cross-sectional data (y^E without any index). One reason to use this more complicated notation is to make clear that we have time series observations that call for special care. The other reason is to clarify which variable is measured at which time period. Here we have changes in x related to changes in y at the same time period. With lags and leads, which we'll discuss later, we'll look at different time periods within the regression, too.

When specified in levels, the time series regression is

$$y_t^E = \alpha + \beta x_t \tag{23.1}$$

where α is the average y when $x = 0$; β shows how much larger y is, on average, when x is larger by one unit.

Alternatively, we can specify a time series regression in terms of changes in y and changes in x:

$$\Delta y_t^E = \alpha + \beta \Delta x_t \tag{23.2}$$

Once again, Δ denotes change – e.g., $\Delta y_t = y_t - y_{t-1}$. The regression coefficients have a different interpretation than in a regression in levels. When the left-hand-side variable is Δy, α estimates the trend: the average change in y when x doesn't change. β shows how much y changes, on average, and in addition to the trend, when x increases, or decreases, by one unit.

When our goal is to estimate the effect of x on y, it usually makes more sense to specify the time series regression in changes. That way we can avoid estimating spurious effects due to trends and random walks (Chapter 12, Section 12.5). This is different from how we should proceed when our goal is prediction: there, whether we should have a model in levels or changes should be determined by the predictive performance of the different models (Chapter 18). From now on, we focus on time series regressions specified in changes.

The regression formula can be applied whether x is binary or quantitative, and the interpretation we have just given is always correct. When x is binary, its change can be $+1$ (changed from untreated to treated), -1 (changed from treated to untreated), or 0 (remained untreated or remained treated). Of the four possible treated–untreated transitions, the estimate of β combines two (increase or decrease), and compares it to the combination of the other two (two ways to remain the same).

When does $\hat{\beta}$ in this regression give a good estimate of the effect of a change in x on y? We can apply what we learned in Chapter 19, Section 19.12: variation in Δx should be exogenous. In other words, whatever makes x change at time t should be independent of all other things that would make y change at time t. Here this is a within-subject criterion: changes in x and y are for the same subject. This criterion is also a version of the parallel trends assumption for diff-in-diffs (Chapter 22, Section 22.3). The reformulated parallel trends assumption for within-subject comparisons with a binary x variable is the following: in time periods when the treatment status changed ($\Delta x_t \neq 0$), y would have changed the same way, on average, had the treatment status remained the same, as it changed in time periods when the treatment status did remain the same.

Consider the example of a company selling gasoline that wants to uncover how much the gasoline it sells in a specific market is affected by the price it charges. The company may have weekly data on the price it charged for gasoline (x) and the amount of gasoline it sold (y). A regression of change in log quantity, $\Delta \ln(y)$, on the change in log price, $\Delta \ln(x)$, gives a good estimate of this effect if variation in $\Delta \ln(x)$ is exogenous. That would be the case if prices had the tendency to change when nothing else changes that would affect demand for gasoline. But that's unlikely: the price this company charges likely changes in similar directions, and by similar magnitudes, to the price its competitors charge, due to common costs, such as changes in the wholesale price of gasoline. And what price the competitors charge affects the quantity this company sells. Thus, the prices of competitors are confounders. However, the price variable may be exogenous if measured relative to the competitors, or if we include the prices of competitors in the regression. The requirement of exogenous variation is about within-subject variation: why the company changes its price (relative to its competitors) differently in different time periods should be independent of what other things may affect the quantity it sells.

As we discussed in Chapter 12, time series data tend to have their specific issues, of which the most important are **trends** and **seasonality**. These present additional threats to exogeneity: trends or seasonality shared by x and y would lead to spurious effect estimates. With x and y already specified as changes, trends are unlikely to cause a problem. To address seasonality, adding season dummies is usually a good solution. Thus, while trends and seasonality are additional threats to internal validity of a causal estimate from time series data, we have tools to handle them.

Before we move on, let's recall the way we should estimate standard errors in time series regressions. Recall from Chapter 12, Section 12.6, that it's serial correlation that we need to worry about here: observations of the left-hand-side variable (conditional on the right-hand-side variables) are correlated across time. **Serial correlation** matters because it may lead to biased standard error estimates. We recommended two ways to address this problem: estimate **Newey–West standard errors** or include the lag of the dependent variable in the regression. Later in this chapter, when we discuss regressions using panel data with time series on a lot of subjects, we'll consider a third solution, too.

> ### Review Box 23.1 Time series regressions to estimate effects
>
> - A time series regression can be specified in levels, with y_t regressed on x_t. However, we suggest to estimate time series regressions not in levels but in changes.
> - A time series regression in changes, such as $\Delta y_t^E = a + \beta \Delta x_t$, can uncover the effect of a change in x on how y changes within the same time period.
> - A time series regression can uncover an average effect across the span of the times series for the single subject.
> - For β to uncover the effect, Δx needs to be exogenous: time periods with different changes in x would have experienced the same change in y, had x changed the same way for them.

23.3 Lags to Estimate the Time Path of Effects

One advantage of using data with multiple time periods is that we can estimate the time path of effects, such as immediate effects, effects in the near future, and **long-run effects**. To capture those in a **time series regression**, we need to include appropriate **lags** of Δx. We have introduced the use of lagged right-hand-side variables in a time series regression in Chapter 12, Section 12.8. Here we review this question when our goal is to estimate an effect.

With lags, we can estimate effects within the same time period (β_0 below), effects one time period later (β_1), and so on – provided, as usual, that x changes in an exogenous fashion. The time series regression that can estimate effects for up to K time periods has K lags of Δx:

$$\Delta y_t^E = a + \beta_0 \Delta x_t + \beta_1 \Delta x_{t-1} + \cdots + \beta_K \Delta x_{t-K} \tag{23.3}$$

Then, by adding up the coefficients on all lags, we can estimate the long-run effect on y of a one-unit change in x. Or, as we introduced in Chapter 12, Section 12.8, we can modify the right-hand-side variables to get a direct estimate of the long-run effect. With K lags of Δx, that is

$$\Delta y_t^E = a + \beta_{cumul} \Delta x_{t-K} + \delta_0 \Delta(\Delta x_t) + \cdots + \delta_{K-1}\Delta(\Delta x_{t-(K-1)}) \tag{23.4}$$

where $\beta_{cumul} = \beta_0 + \beta_1 + \cdots + \beta_K$ above. β_{cumul} shows the **cumulative effect**: the total change in y within K time periods after a unit change in x, on average. When variation in Δx is exogenous, β_{cumul} shows the total effect of Δx_t on Δy over the long run. We do not interpret the coefficients on the other variables here; in fact, we usually don't show them in the regression output.

23.4 Leads to Examine Pre-trends and Reverse Effects

Exogeneity of Δx_t is key in estimating an effect in a time series regression. Unfortunately, as always, the exogeneity assumption is impossible to assess directly, as it is about how y would have changed in time periods with different x changes if x had changed the same way instead. While we can't tell how y would have changed, we can examine how y did change in the previous time period, or several time periods earlier. To do so, we need to include **lead terms** of Δx in the regression. The simplest such regression in differences with no lags but L leads is the following:

$$\Delta y_t^E = a + \beta \Delta x_t + \gamma_1 \Delta x_{t+1} + \cdots + \gamma_L \Delta x_{t+L} \tag{23.5}$$

The lead terms are Δx_{t+1} through Δx_{t+L}. Their coefficients, γ_1 through γ_L, show how y tends to change one through L time periods before x changes. They show that, because Δy_t is one time period before

Δx_{t+1}, two time periods before Δx_{t+2}, ... Thus $\gamma_1 = \cdots \gamma_L = 0$ would show that, regardless of how x changes, y tends to change the same way one through L time periods earlier. That would support the version of the parallel trends assumption we need here: it's analogous to examining **pre-intervention trends**, or **pre-trends** in diff-in-diffs regressions (Chapter 22, Section 22.3).

A specific case of endogenous change in x would be a **reverse effect**: y affecting x instead of, or besides, x affecting y (we introduced **reverse causality** in Chapter 19, Section.19.14). With observations from multiple time periods, we can actually capture this reverse effect. The idea is that we can estimate the reverse effects if it takes time. In that case, as a result of the reverse effect, a change in x would tend to follow a change in y. If that happens within one time period, Δy_t, a change in y at t, is associated with Δx_{t+1}, a change in x one time period later. And the coefficient on it would capture that reverse effect.

Consider our example of the gasoline retailer and the time series regression to uncover the effect of price on quantity sold. The retailer may reduce its price when it sees its sales go down more than expected. This would be a reverse effect: when we want to uncover the effect of changing price on sales, here a change in sales affects price. That may be interesting to uncover in itself. Moreover, that may bias our effect estimate if the drop in sales that prompts the retailer to reduce its price would in itself affect further changes in sales. But we can capture this reverse effect because it takes time: the negative change in sales would precede a negative change in price. That would be captured in our regression by including the **lead term** on the price change (Δx_{t+1}). If the lead term's coefficient is zero, we don't need to worry about a reverse effect, just as we wouldn't need to worry about pre-existing trends. If its coefficient is not zero, we have conditioned on it in this regression, just like we would condition on an observable confounder variable. If conditioning on the lead term captures the entire reverse effect, the remaining variation in Δx_t could be exogenous. If it captures part of it only, we can get closer to an unbiased estimate.

Thus, including one or more lead terms in the regression can have multiple benefits. It can check pre-trends as well as a reverse effect. When the coefficients on the lead terms are zero, we have evidence for exogenous variation in the causal variables. When they are not zero, we do have issues with exogeneity. But, by conditioning on the lead term, we get closer to exogeneity.

Review Box 23.2   Lags and leads in time series regressions to estimate delayed effects

- A time series regression, in differences, with K lags and L leads, has the form

$$\Delta y_t^E = \alpha + \beta_0 \Delta x_t + \beta_1 \Delta x_{(t-1)} + \cdots + \beta_K \Delta x_{(t-K)} + \gamma_1 \Delta x_{(t+1)} + \cdots + \gamma_L \Delta x_{(t+L)} \quad (23.6)$$

- The lag terms help capture delayed effects.
- The lead terms help capture differences in pre-trends and reverse effects.

23.5   Pooled Time Series to Estimate the Effect for One Unit

Despite the advantages of estimating effects from time series, single time series are rarely used to estimate effects in practice. That is primarily because time series are rarely long enough. In addition, often there isn't enough variation in Δx, especially if we condition on trend, seasonality, and confounder variables. These issues tend to result in imprecise estimates that can change with small changes in the data and produce wide confidence intervals.

In our example of gasoline price and quantity, the price the company charges may change very similarly to the price changes of its competitors, most of the time. As a result, a relative price measure may change very little most of the time. With weekly data spanning, say, 10 years, the time series would have over 500 observations. In effect, though, the number of observations with large changes in the relative price may be a lot smaller. Suppose that the company changes its price together with its competitors 9 out of 10 times, and only once would it change its price differently for some reason. In practice, that would mean that we have around 50 such changes in our data. In effect, that means that we would have 50 observations we can use in the time series to estimate the effect of relative price changes. That is better than nothing, but it is far from 500. Most likely, we would end up with a very wide confidence interval for an effect estimate, which may offer limited help for decision making.

Unfortunately, even long time series tend to be less helpful than we may think. The economic and social environment keeps changing. As a result, observations from the distant past are not very helpful for uncovering an effect that's relevant for future decisions. This puts further limits on the number of observations we can use for estimation. For example, in our gasoline price and sales example, the gasoline retailer may have data on weekly observations from 50 years back, resulting in over 2500 observations not 500. However, 50, or even 20 years ago, the demand for gasoline may have been very different, and the structure of competition may have been very different, too. Thus, an average effect estimate that includes observations from the distant past tends to be less informative about what to expect now and in the future.

One solution to having too few observations in a time series is to combine time series from several subjects (cross-sectional units). The result is a data table with **pooled time series**. Each cross-sectional unit is denoted by index i; each time period by t. For example, when trying to estimate the effect of increasing the price of gasoline on gasoline sales for a particular market, we may pool time series data on prices and sales from about a dozen markets. This is cross-section time series **(xt) panel data**. But it has only a few cross-sectional units.

This solution can help if we are interested in the effect for a single subject. Here we pool those additional subjects to get a more precise effect estimate for the subject of interest. This solution is good if the estimates for the additional subjects would be good approximations to the effect for the subject we are interested in.

The simplest pooled time series regression estimates a single intercept and a single slope. Most often, though, we include separate intercepts for each i. Doing so allows for trends to be different across i.

$$\Delta y_{it}^E = a_i + \beta \Delta x_{it} \tag{23.7}$$

Here β shows the average change in y, across time and units i, when x increases by one unit. This estimate is conditional on i-specific trends: even if different subjects had different trends, this would not affect our estimate. We can freely add **lags**, **leads**, and other variables to this regression, just as in the case of a single time series. We should also estimate standard errors that are robust to serial correlation. Here that would require including a lagged left-hand-side variable ($\Delta y_{i(t-1)}$): **Newey–West standard** error estimates are complicated to estimate with pooled time series.

An important question is how to select the subjects to pool if we want to estimate the effect for a single subject. We want those other subjects to be as similar to the subject of interest as possible, in terms of the average effect we are after. While we don't know the effect for the different subjects, we can estimate them, using the same time series regressions. It is good practice to use those estimates, together with **domain knowledge**, to select the other time series to pool. Our case study provides an example for this solution.

> **Review Box 23.3 Pooled time series to estimate effects for one unit**
>
> - When interested in the effect of x on y for a single unit, we can pool additional time series from similar units to obtain more precise estimates.
> - It is good practice to allow for different intercepts for the different units while estimating a single slope coefficient to estimate an average effect.

23.A1 CASE STUDY – Import Demand and Industrial Production

Question, data, single time series estimates, pooled time series estimates

In this case study we ask how the import demand of the USA affects industrial production in Thailand. This is a causal question, although it's not after the effect of an explicit intervention. There is no one person or committee or institution that would choose the level of import demand, and thus no such decision is informed by learning this effect. Instead, this question asks what happens in a mid-sized open economy when something changes in the big country that is its major trading partner. If something happens to the US economy that affects its import demand, it would probably affect the industrial production of smaller countries because a good part of those countries' production is for the US market. As part of global supply chains, exports from Thailand also end up as imports in the USA indirectly, often through China. This is one of the mechanisms by which US import demand may affect Thai industrial production. How large the overall effect is can be important for economic policy makers in Thailand, to plan ahead for changing circumstances and prepare predictions under various scenarios.

The causal variable x is total imports into the USA. It is an approximation of import demand of the USA. In principle, it's an imperfect proxy of demand because it may be affected by things that happen in Thailand, on top of changes in US demand itself. But Thailand is such a small part of US imports that the observed variation in US imports is practically independent of Thai events. The outcome variable y is industrial production in Thailand. To answer our question we need data with many observations about x and y. There is only one Thailand, so we need time series data to have many observations.

We use the `asia-industry` dataset for this case study. It consists of monthly time series of industrial production from four countries, and total import in the USA. The data comes from the World Bank's Global Economic Monitor database. The Thai industrial production data covers about twenty years, starts from February 1998 and goes up to April 2018.

Both time series have a positive trend, at least in their first half (Figure 23.1). The trend in Thai industrial production halts at the end of 2008, with a sharp decline as the global crisis of 2008–2009 unfolds. It rebounds by 2010 and stays relatively flat afterwards, except for a one-time large decline in the end of 2011. It is not a data error, but the impact of a natural event – a massive flooding undermined production. The positive trend in US imports stops, too, at the end of 2008, with a large drop that lasts until 2010, and it flattens out afterwards. Let's note three facts: there is trend in both series, at least for some time; there is one extreme event that we see both in US imports and Thai industrial production; and the time series look different before that extreme event and after. Both time series are seasonally adjusted by the data provider. As a result, we do not have to worry about seasonality.

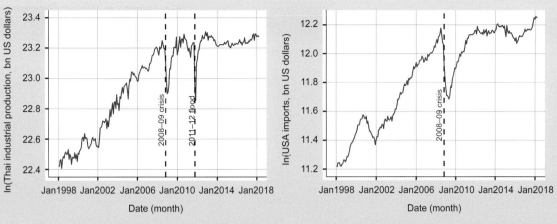

(a) Industrial production in Thailand, in logs, monthly time series   (b) US total imports, in logs, monthly time series

Figure 23.1   Thai industrial production and US total imports: individual time series

Source: `asia-industry` dataset. Monthly data, seasonally adjusted, February 1998–April 2018. N=243.

Based on the features of the time series, we specified the following time series regression to estimate the effect of US import demand on Thai industrial production:

$$\Delta \ln(ipTHA)_t = a + \beta_0 \Delta \ln(impUSA)_t + \beta_1 \Delta \ln(impUSA)_{t-1} + \cdots$$
$$+ \beta_4 \Delta \ln(impUSA)_{t-4} + \varphi \Delta \ln(ipTHA)_{t-1} \qquad (23.8)$$

The variables are in (log) differences in equation (23.8), to make sure that trends don't confound the effect estimates. We allowed for four lags so that a one-time change in US imports can have an effect on how Thai industrial production changes through four months. We included a lagged dependent variable to take care of serial correlation. We didn't include season dummies because both series are already seasonally adjusted. We included all time periods, even the crisis of 2010. We have positive and negative changes in US imports in the data, but we estimate an average effect through its increases and decreases. You are invited to try alternative specifications to see how the results change.

Column (1) of Table 23.1 shows the results of this regression. It doesn't show each of the $\hat{\beta}$ estimates. Instead, it shows the estimated **cumulative coefficient**. The estimate shows that, after a one percent increase in US imports, Thai industrial production increases by 0.4 percent, on average, accumulated over the next four months. If we assume that variation in the change of total US imports is exogenous with respect to the change in Thai industrial production, this is the estimate of the average effect through this 20-year period. The standard errors are relatively large so the 95% confidence interval of this estimate is quite wide, [0.02,0.78], allowing for a practically zero effect and a large effect of an elasticity close to 0.8.

To gain more precise effect estimates, we pooled three additional time series: the industrial production of Malaysia, the Philippines, and Singapore. Columns (2) through (4) show the individual time series estimates of the same cumulative effect for the three other countries. Column (5) shows the estimates from the pooled regression, in which each country has its own intercept, as in equation (23.7).

Table 23.1 US imports and industrial production in Thailand and three other countries

Variables	(1) Thailand	(2) Malaysia	(3) Philippines	(4) Singapore	(5) Pooled
USA imports log change, cumulative coeff.	0.400* (0.190)	0.358** (0.112)	0.556** (0.185)	0.367 (0.289)	0.437** (0.103)
Industrial production log change, lag	−0.119 (0.065)	−0.460** (0.059)	−0.242** (0.064)	−0.376** (0.061)	−0.315** (0.031)
Malaysia					0.000 (0.004)
Philippines					−0.001 (0.004)
Singapore					0.002 (0.004)
Constant	0.002 (0.003)	0.004* (0.002)	0.001 (0.003)	0.005 (0.004)	0.003 (0.003)
Observations	238	238	238	238	952
R-squared	0.070	0.231	0.140	0.183	0.123

Note: Time series regression estimates; dependent variable is change of log industrial production in each country; four lags of the change in log US imports. Standard error estimates in parentheses. ** $p < 0.01$, * $p < 0.05$.

Source: `asia-industry` dataset, monthly time series, seasonally adjusted, February 1998–April 2018. N=243.

The effect estimates vary somewhat across countries, but they are pretty similar to the Thai estimate. Together with the fact that they are all open economies in the same geographic area, this suggests that pooling these countries makes sense. The pooled regression estimate is very similar to the Thai estimate, but its standard error is about half as large. The resulting 95% confidence interval is [0.24, 0.64].

But is this a good estimate of the effect we are after? Yes, if the change in US imports is exogenous – i.e., that changes in US imports are independent of things that would make industrial production change in Thailand and the other Asian countries. As a start, reverse effects are unlikely: Thailand and the other countries are probably too small to affect the total volume of US imports.

There may be other kinds of omitted confounders, such as financial market events, technology shocks, and innovations, that affect the US economy and thus US imports and, independently, industrial production in these Asian countries. In contrast, changes in the world economy that affect industrial production in Asian countries through US import demand are fine. One such mechanism could be an increased worldwide demand for natural rubber that would increase US rubber imports from Thailand, too. Our time series starts with 1998, after the Asian crisis of 1997, so that's not affecting our estimates. But the crisis of 2008–2009 does. The crisis may have affected industrial production through various channels besides import demand, for example, through the role of financial markets (a confounder). As a data exercise, you'll be invited to estimate the effect without the crisis months. You will also be asked to include lead terms to check for other potential violations of parallel trends. Both of these produce results that are similar to, or only slightly smaller than, the main results. This supports – although, of course, doesn't prove – the exogeneity of US imports.

What have we learned from this case study? From a substantive point of view, we have an estimate that may be confounded by omitted unmeasured variables, but our domain knowledge supports evidence for a causal effect. Taking it as a good approximation to the expected effect, we can conclude that the industrial production of Thailand is quite responsive to import demand from the USA. A 1% increase (decrease) in US import demand is expected to be followed by a 0.4% increase (decrease) in Thai industrial production within the following four months. With pooling Thai data with similar countries, we could narrow down the confidence interval to 0.24%–0.64%, so that we may expect an impact within this range for countries like Thailand. There is no clear evidence of causality, but with these results and some domain knowledge about southeast Asian economies, we have some confidence in fluctuations in US demand causing fluctuations in Thai output. Importantly, US demand does not only directly affect Thai imports. The USA imports a great deal from China and Japan, which are both export destinations of Thailand and other southeast Asian economies. This indirect link is a mechanism of causal effect.

From a methods point of view, we learned that we can estimate the effect of economic events in a large country on its smaller trading partners. We relied on the realistic assumption of no reverse causality based on the relative size (about 1 : 50) of the two economies. Other confounders may be a threat to exogeneity, but our domain knowledge suggests that should play a limited role. We also emphasized the role of mechanisms: US demand indirectly affecting Thai exports. We have also made good use of all that we learned about time series regressions in Chapter 12 to specify a regression that is not affected by spurious effects and to get good standard error estimates. Finally, we have seen that pooling a few time series from similar cross-sectional units can give meaningful, and substantially more precise, estimates even if we are interested in the effect for one cross-sectional unit only.

23.6 Panel Regression with Fixed Effects

In the previous section, we pooled time series from a few subjects to estimate the expected effect of a causal variable x on outcome y in one of the subjects. In the remainder of the chapter we consider a different situation, in which the question is the effect of x on y averaged across many subjects. This is the same kind of question that a diff-in-diffs analysis can answer (see Chapter 22). Here we discuss what we can do when we have more than two time periods for each subject in the data.

The **pooled time series** is a useful starting point. One way to view panel data with multiple time periods is as if they were pooled time series. We can specify the regression in levels or changes, we can include leads and lags, and we should worry about trends, serial correlation, and seasonality. However, in typical multi-period panel data, we have many subjects (cross-sectional units) observed only a few times. This means that time series properties are less important, while differences across subjects are more important. Thus, it makes sense to discuss regression models in this context differently from the pooled time series setup.

The first regression model that we discuss for multi-period panel data is the **fixed-effects regression** (**FE regression**). Fixed effects are separate intercepts in the regression for different cross-sectional units. In FE regressions we have y and x (in levels, not changes), and xsec FE: a separate intercept for each cross-sectional unit. The simplest linear panel regression with cross-sectional fixed effects is

$$y_{it}^E = a_i + \beta x_{it} \tag{23.9}$$

The fixed effects are denoted by a_i. These mean that the intercept is allowed to be different for different cross-sectional units.

Why do we include the fixed effects? In other words, why do we include separate intercepts for each cross-sectional unit instead of including a common intercept? The reason is the following. Suppose that subjects tend to have higher values of y on average due to some unobserved **confounder variable** that also affects x. Suppose, moreover, that the confounder affects x or y in the same way at all times. Then, with a common intercept a, we would have a usual linear regression as in cross-sectional data, and the coefficient β would be estimated with **omitted variables bias**. However, with the inclusion of the fixed effects, we can avoid, or mitigate, that bias. That's because including fixed effects means conditioning on all variables that don't change through time. We provide an argument in the following paragraphs, and we'll also return to this question later, in Section 23.12.

Technically, the inclusion of the cross-sectional **fixed effects** acts as a transformation of the y and x variables into differences from their cross-sectional means: $y_{it} - \bar{y}_i$ and $x_{it} - \bar{x}_i$, where $\bar{y}_i$ and $\bar{x}_i$ are average values of y and x across all time periods within cross-sectional unit i. Indeed, it can be shown that the β in the model $y_{it}^E = a_i + \beta x_{it}$ is exactly the same as the β in the model $(y_{it} - \bar{y}_i)^E = a + \beta(x_{it} - \bar{x}_i)$.

As a result, in the FE regression, β shows how much larger y is, on average, compared to its mean within the cross-sectional unit, where and when x is higher by one unit compared to its mean within the cross-sectional unit. Or, to say it differently: compare two observations that are different in terms of the value of x compared to its i-specific mean. On average, y is larger, compared to its i-specific mean, by β, for the observation with the larger x value, compared to its i-specific mean. That's a **within-subject comparison**, and it's not affected by whether one subject has larger average y or x. That's why it's not affected by whether an unobserved confounder affects y or x in the same way in all time periods (and thus their average values).

Consider an example related to the case study we started in Chapter 19. There the question was the effect of eating more fruit and vegetables on blood pressure, and we saw, among other things, that family income is related to both blood pressure and how much fruit and vegetables people eat. Now consider a related question: how family income affects people's fruit and vegetable consumption. Instead of the cross-section, suppose that we have **xt panel data**: people are followed for 10 years, and their income and fruit and vegetable consumption is measured every year.

In a fixed effects regression, we would be able to estimate how much more fruit and vegetables people eat (compared to their 10-year average) when their income is higher than their average 10-year income. That comparison is free from the effect of confounders that may be related to average income and average fruit and vegetable consumption over those 10 years. For example, some personality traits, such as being future-oriented, tend to lead to higher incomes and may affect lifestyle choices, including eating more fruit and vegetables. Thus, when simply comparing people with more income, differences between them confound the effect of income itself and personality differences. However, with fixed effects in the regression, personality differences between people don't play a role, because we compare years when incomes are different from their within-family averages.

Before moving on let's note two technical issues about FE panel regression. First, the R-squared of FE regressions can be misleading. In fact, there are two ways to compute an **R-squared** for a FE regression. The first way, which makes more sense, treats the FE regression as a regression of mean-differenced variables: $y_{it} - \bar{y}_i$ regressed on $x_{it} - \bar{x}_i$. This is a within-subject comparison, and thus this R-squared is sometimes called **within R-squared**. But there is another way to compute the R-squared, because an FE regression can also be viewed as a regression with many **binary variables** for each cross-sectional unit (denoted by a_i in equation (23.9)). Running the regression with many fixed effects will lead to an R-squared calculation that includes those binary variables. This second way of calculating R-squared can lead to much higher values. Statistical software often reports this second version, but it's very misleading, as it doesn't tell us how much of the variation in y is explained by x. Instead, it tells us how much of the variation in y is explained by x as well as by the i-specific intercepts. For that reason, we should always be precise about what kind of R-squared we present with FE regression results. Moreover, we suggest presenting the within R-squared as that's the more informative statistic.

The other issue is that we do not present a regression intercept with FE regressions. There are as many a_i intercepts as the number of cross-sectional units. Some software calculate the average of those intercepts and presents that in regression tables. Such an average intercept makes sense, but its interpretation is different from the usual interpretation of a single intercept, and its presentation may erroneously suggest that the regression has a single intercept as opposed to fixed effects.

23.7 Aggregate Trend

Trends are a potential problem in time series regressions as well as in panel regressions. Luckily, xt panel data allows for a flexible way to condition on aggregate trends of any form.

An **aggregate trend** is a trend in y or x that is shared across all cross-sectional units in the data. The term trend is used broadly here: aggregate trends may include cycles, too. Examples include global economic conditions for cross-country panel data, or industry conditions for panel data of firms in an industry.

With **xt panel data**, we can condition on an aggregate trend, whatever form it has, including nonlinear trends or even ups and downs. To do so, we need to include **time dummies**: binary variables for each time period. These are sometimes called **time fixed effects**, but we prefer the time dummy name to avoid confusion with the individual intercepts in the FE regression. A FE panel regression with time dummies can be written with separate intercepts (θ_t) for each time period:

$$y_{it}^E = a_i + \theta_t + \beta x_{it} \tag{23.10}$$

The notation shows the symmetry between cross-sectional FE and time FE – as time dummies are called sometimes. Note that, just like with any series of dummy variables, we would need to leave out a reference time period.

The interpretation of the slope coefficient is more complicated in such regressions. β shows how much larger y is, on average, compared to its mean within the cross-sectional units as well as its mean across units in the actual time period, where and when x is higher by one unit compared to its mean within the cross-sectional unit and its mean across units in the actual time period. Or, to say it differently, β shows how much larger y is, on average, compared to its mean within the cross-sectional units when x is higher by one unit compared to its mean, conditional on the aggregate trend both in x and y.

Consider our example of the effect of family income on fruit and vegetables consumption. Including year dummies would capture the aggregate trend, which may be important to condition on. Average family income tends to increase due to economic growth, fruit and vegetables consumption tends to increase due to changing attitudes, and these two trends together would result in a spurious association if we didn't condition on them. Having year dummies allows for the trend to have any form.

Review Box 23.4   Fixed-effects regression

- The fixed-effects (FE) regression without covariates, using xt panel data with more than two time periods, is

$$y_{it}^{E} = a_i + \theta_t + \beta x_{it} \qquad (23.11)$$

- Both x and y are in levels (as opposed to first differences).
- a_i are the cross-sectional FE; θ_t are the coefficients on time dummies, also known as time FE.
- β shows how much larger y is, on average, compared to its mean within the cross-sectional units and its mean within the time period, where and when x is higher by one unit compared to its mean within the cross-sectional unit and its mean within the time period. (It's also correct to say aggregate trend instead of "mean within the time period." Also, it's correct to say long-run mean within i instead of "mean within the cross-sectional units" if the panel is long enough.)
- The cross-sectional FE regression can get us closer to estimating the effect of x on y by conditioning on confounders that don't change; with time dummies we can condition on aggregate trends of any shape.

23.B1 CASE STUDY – Immunization against Measles and Saving Children

Question, data, and FE regressions

In this case study, we want to uncover the effect of vaccination against measles on the survival chances of young children. The causal variable is the vaccination rate. It's not a direct policy variable, but it's the result of policy decisions, including whether to make vaccination against measles compulsory, how to enforce that, and how to make sure vaccination is available to all children. The effect on child survival is only one of the effects of vaccination, although an important one. Understanding this effect helps assess the benefits of policies that can increase the vaccination rate.

Measles is a contagious disease that leads to high fever, cough, and rashes. It may lead to death, too, especially among children that are malnourished or have a weakened immune system. Measles is caused by an airborne virus, and there is no known treatment for the disease. However, there is a vaccine that is known to prevent it with high efficacy. The recommendation is to administer the vaccine first at 12 months of age, and repeat it at 5 years of age. In most rich countries, the vaccine is part of compulsory immunization and covers the large majority of the population. In poorer countries, the measles vaccine is often administered together with other medications and nutritional supplements.

Figure 23.2a shows the rate of immunization against measles in the seven regions of the World, among children of age 12 to 23 months old. We labeled two regions, South Asia and sub-Saharan Africa, where the immunization rate was especially low in 1998. Both regions experienced a large increase in immunization against measles. By 2017, the end of our time series, South Asia approached the other five regions. But the increase stopped in 2010 in sub-Saharan Africa, where the immunization rate has stagnated at around 70% since.

The other panel, Figure 23.2b, shows the survival rate of children aged zero to five in the same seven regions. Here we see stable and constant improvement in all regions, including sub-Saharan Africa that started below 85% and South Asia that started at 90%. By 2017, child survival rate was above 90% in all regions.

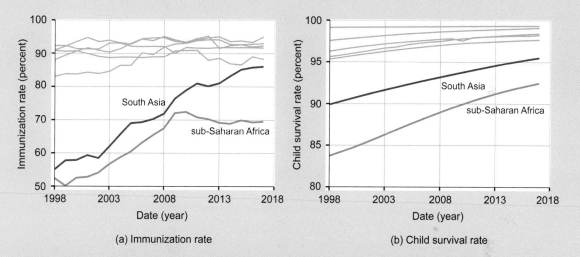

(a) Immunization rate   (b) Child survival rate

Figure 23.2 Immunization against measles and child survival rate in seven regions of the world

Note: Immunization rate: percentage of children of age 12 to 23 months who received vaccination against measles. Child survival rate: 100% minus the percentage of children of age 0 to 5 years who died in the given year.
Source: `worldbank-immunization` dataset. Annual data, 1998–2017, aggregated to seven geographical regions. N=140.

Immunization against measles may increase the child survival rate both directly, and indirectly through a spillover by decreased contagion. The direct effect is preventing measles for the children who receive immunization, while the spillover effect is decreasing the likelihood of transmitting measles to non-immunized children. Decreasing the chances of measles increases survival chances among weak and malnourished children. The direct effect may be reinforced by the medications and nutrients that children tend to receive together with immunization in poor countries. Note that the direct effect implies a pattern through time: immunization is administered when children are one year old, and their survival chances are included in our survival measure (age 0–5 years) for four more years but not longer. The spillover effect may also work for longer horizons, by decreasing contagion. In addition, the other medications and dietary supplements that are administered with the measles vaccine in poor countries may also have effects of their own. Our data allow for estimating these effects combined, not separately.

What is a meaningful thought experiment to measure the effect of measles immunization on child survival? Since the mechanisms include spillover effects, it would be best to randomize not across individuals, but communities (see Chapter 20, Section 20.10). Also note that we are interested in the effect of an increase in immunization rate, a quantitative causal variable. Thus, one meaningful thought experiment would be to consider communities with possibly different levels of immunization, and randomly select some of them to receive an increase in immunization, others to receive a large increase, yet others no increase. Then, we would measure child mortality in those communities for several years. The average effect is the difference in child survival between groups of communities that were assigned different increases in the immunization rate, normalized by the size of the increase and averaged over the groups. This thought experiment is clearly infeasible: nobody would assign immunization rates, or policies that affect immunization rates, randomly across communities.

Instead, we attempt to estimate this average effect using observational panel data. The data is at the level of countries: it satisfies the criterion of the thought experiment of including communities not individuals. We could probably do better using a larger number of smaller communities, as that would yield more data and more variation in x, but here it's cross-country data we have. Finally, we need data that spans many years, to allow for effects to be measured years later.

The data we use is a country–year panel collected from the World Development Indicators maintained by the World Bank, which covers almost all countries for many years. We kept years 1998 through 2017 and all countries in the data. We use five variables. The outcome variable is the child survival rate: the percent of children of age 0 to 5 who survive to age 5. We calculated it from the child mortality rate (percent of deaths among 0–5-year-old children), and we denote it as *surv*. The causal variable is the immunization rate against measles: the proportion of 12–23-month-old children who received the measles vaccine. We denote this variable as *imm*. In addition, we use two other variables: population in millions (*population*), and GDP per capita (*GDPpc*, measured in constant 2011 US dollars using purchasing power parity conversion rates).

Our data covers 192 countries through 20 years. Of these, 172 have observations for all variables for all 20 years, and we use this balanced panel for our analysis. The result is a data table with 3440 observations (172 × 20).

We have estimated two FE regressions to uncover the effect of immunization against measles on child survival. Both versions have both country FE and year dummies. The first regression has nothing else; the second regression includes the potential confounders log GDP per capita and log population. The 172 countries in the data have valid observations for GDP per capita and population through all 20 years. Thus, this is a balanced panel. We use population as the weight in all regressions, because our question is about the effect on individual children. Standard errors estimated in an appropriate way, the details of which we'll discuss in Section 23.8. Table 23.2 shows the results.

The slope parameter estimate on immunization is 0.077 without conditioning on any confounders in the data (column (1)), and it drops to 0.038 when we condition on GDP per capita and population (column (2)). For this second estimate, the 95% confidence interval is $[0.016, 0.060]$. This coefficient estimate means that when we compare years with the same GDP and population, in years when the immunization rate is higher by 10 percentage points than its average rate within a country, child survival tends to be 0.38 percentage points higher than its average within the country, conditional on aggregate trends in the world. We can expect it to be 0.16 to 0.6 percentage points higher in the general pattern represented by our data.

	(1)	(2)
Table 23.2 The effect of measles immunization on child survival. FE regressions		
Variables	Survival rate	Survival rate
Immunization rate	0.077**	0.038**
	(0.010)	(0.011)
ln GDP per capita		1.593**
		(0.399)
ln population		12.049**
		(1.648)
Year dummies	Yes	Yes
Observations	3440	3440
R-squared	0.717	0.848
Number of countries	172	172

Note: Within R-squared presented for FE regressions. Appropriate standard error estimates in parentheses. ** $p < 0.01$, * $p < 0.05$.

Source: `worldbank-immunization` dataset; balanced yearly panel, years 1998–2017 in 172 countries.

23.8 Clustered Standard Errors

With more than two time periods, we have to worry about serial correlation when estimating the right standard errors. Recall that we suggested estimating Newey–West standard errors for single time series or including the lagged dependent variable for single or pooled time series. We have to do something with serial correlation here, too. However, in **xt panel data** with many cross-sectional units we have a simpler, and potentially more powerful, solution: **clustered standard errors**.

Standard errors clustered at the level of cross-sectional units treat cross-sectional units as independent but time series observations as non-independent. The basic idea is that the clustered standard error estimation uses the many cross-sectional observations to estimate the patterns of serial correlation that are shared by all cross-sectional units. For example, it estimates and uses the correlation coefficient between the first time series observation and the seventh time series observation separately from the correlation coefficient between the second time series observation and the eighth time series observation, because we have the cross-sectional observations to do so. For this to work well, clustered standard errors need many cross-sectional units. How many is enough depends on the details. But 30 or more can be a general rule of thumb.

Clustered standard errors are robust in two aspects. They are fine in the presence of any kind of serial correlation, and they are also fine without any serial correlation. They are also fine in the presence of heteroskedasticity as well as homoskedasticity.

The standard errors in the **FE regressions** presented in Table 23.2 in the case study are estimated in the appropriate way: they are all clustered at the country level. This means that they are robust to both

serial correlation and **heteroskedasticity**. Table 23.3 repeats the results for the FE regression that include log GDP per capita and log population, as covariates. The coefficient estimates are the same as in Table 23.2 and the standard errors in column (1) are also the same since they are the appropriate clustered standard errors. However, in column (2) below, we have the biased simple standard errors, which would be the default option for most statistical software. The simple SE estimate is much smaller, by more than a factor of five, which would imply a misleadingly narrow confidence interval.

Table 23.3 Clustered SE versus biased simple SE in a FE panel regression

Variables	(1) Clustered SE	(2) Simple SE
Immunization rate	0.038**	0.038**
	(0.011)	(0.002)
ln GDP per capita	1.593**	1.593**
	(0.399)	(0.071)
ln population	12.049**	12.049**
	(1.648)	(0.227)
Observations	3440	3440
R-squared	0.848	0.848
Number of countries	172	172

Note: Measles immunization and child survival, FE panel regression estimates. Within R-squared presented for FE regressions. Standard error estimates in parentheses. ** $p<0.01$, * $p<0.05$.

Source: worldbank-immunization dataset; balanced yearly panel, years 1998–2017 in 172 countries.

We should avoid estimating simple standard errors in xt panel regressions. Sometimes, including a lagged dependent variable does the trick, as we recommended in Section 23.5. That's recommended when the time series is long (more than 20 time periods); otherwise, it may raise other complications that are beyond the scope of this textbook. In typical xt panel data, with many cross-sectional observations, the best choice is to estimate clustered SE.

Review Box 23.5 Clustered SE in panel regressions

• When estimating regressions using xt panel data with more than two time periods, the standard errors need to be clustered at the level of the cross-sectional units.
• Clustered standard errors are robust to serial correlation as well as heteroskedasticity.

23.9 Panel Regression in First Differences

Just as with time series regressions, we can specify xt panel regressions in changes as well as levels. When using cross-section time series (xt) panel data with many cross-sectional units, data analysts call such a regression a **panel regression in first differences**, or **FD regression**. As before, the formula for changes is Δ, so that, for example, $\Delta y_{it} = y_{it} - y_{i(t-1)}$. The simplest FD panel regression has no other variables and has a common intercept across all i. The formula is similar to the pooled time series regression in equation (23.7), except that here we have a common intercept, and it is used on xt panel data for many cross-sectional units:

$$\Delta y_{it}^E = \alpha + \beta \Delta x_{it} \tag{23.12}$$

In equation (23.12), as for panel regressions in general, we write out the *it* index to all variables. Here, Δy_{it}^E means how y is expected to change from $t-1$ to t for cross-sectional unit i given how x changes between $t-1$ and t for i and given the coefficients α and β.

Let's turn to the interpretation of the coefficients of this FD regression. α shows the average change in y where and when x does not change. It is an average across both cross-sectional units and time periods.

β shows the difference in the average change of y for units that experience a change in x during the same period. In more detail: comparing different cross-sectional units for the same time, or comparing different time periods for the same unit, β shows how much more y changes, on average, where and when x increases by one unit.

This somewhat awkward "where and when" highlights the fact that β approximates the average pattern of association across both time and the cross-section. As always, the linear specification is best thought of as an approximation to the average pattern of association if the pattern itself may be different for different values of x (nonlinearity), different cross-sectional units (cross-sectional heterogeneity of the association), and/or across different time periods (changing patterns of association).

Let's focus on a simple example to see what we can estimate with the help of an FD model. In this example, x is binary, and it changes from 0 to 1 only. It does so at different times in different cross-sectional units. We have three kinds of cross-sectional units in this case: some start untreated and become treated, some start untreated and remain untreated, and some start treated and remain treated. Examples include a panel of firms that introduced flexible work hours in different years; a panel of countries that introduced bans on smoking in public spaces in different years; a panel of small towns where a large supermarket chain opened a store in different months.

In this example, β shows how y changes, on average, in the time period when x becomes one. Thus, it can estimate the immediate effect of treatment (if Δx is exogenous). If, for example, the effect takes place with a delay, $\hat{\beta}$ would be zero, whatever the size of the eventual effect. Similarly, if the effect takes place gradually, first increasing y a little, and then more, $\hat{\beta}$ would capture that first small increase only. We'll show how to include lags in FD models to capture delayed effects in the next section.

Review Box 23.6   Panel regressions in first differences (FD)

- Simple FD regression using xt panel data:

$$\Delta y_{it}^E = \alpha + \beta \Delta x_{it} \tag{23.13}$$

- β shows how much more y changes, on average, for observations with a one unit higher increase in x. It's an average both across different cross-sectional units and different time periods.
- When Δx_{it} is exogenous, β shows the average effect of a change in x within the same time period.

23.10 Lags and Leads in FD Panel Regressions

Often, we want to estimate not only immediate effects but longer-run effects, too. Multiple time periods allow us to capture the time path of the effects by including lags of Δx in the regression. The linear panel regression in first differences with K lags can be written the following way:

$$\Delta y_{it}^E = a + \beta_0 \Delta x_{it} + \beta_1 \Delta x_{i(t-1)} + \cdots + \beta_K \Delta x_{i(t-K)} \qquad (23.14)$$

Again, a shows the trend in y: average change in y when x does not change and did not change in the previous K time periods either. β_0 is the contemporaneous slope. Here it shows how much more y changes, on average, for observations with a larger change in x in the same time period but the same change in all K preceding time periods. β_k is the slope on lag number k ($k = 1, 2, \ldots, K$). It shows how much more y changes, on average, for observations with a one unit higher increase in x in the kth preceding time period but with the same change of x in the current time period as well as all K preceding time periods except for the kth.

When can we give β coefficients a **causal interpretation**? More precisely, when are the β coefficients good estimates of the average treatment effect? When the relevant version of the parallel trends condition holds: if the current and all lagged x variables (x_1, x_2, $\ldots$, x_K) changed the same way, y would have changed the same way, too, on average. Note that this is a general version of the parallel trends assumption, and, if it holds, the estimated effects are good approximations of ATE.

If the causal interpretation is correct, the slope on the contemporaneous change in x (β_0) shows the immediate effect of Δx within the same time period. The slope on the once lagged change in x (β_1) shows the effect of Δx one time period after its change. The slope on the twice lagged change in x (β_2) shows the effect of Δx two time periods after its change. And so on: the slope on the K-lagged change in x (β_K) shows the effect Δx K time periods after its change.

With a causal interpretation of a regression with lags, the most important effect to learn is the cumulative effect, or long-run effect of the change of x. That is the sum of the immediate effect and all lagged effects:

$$\beta_{cumul} = \beta_0 + \beta_1 + \cdots + \beta_K \qquad (23.15)$$

As with single time series, we can make the software give us the cumulative coefficient directly, without us having to add up numbers, also giving us the appropriate standard error that we can use to create a confidence interval around the cumulative effect. As in time series (equation (23.4)), the trick in a regression with K lags is to include the Kth lag and the differences of the previous lags: the cumulative coefficient is then the one on the Kth lag. When variables are in first differences, the Kth lag is in difference, and the previous lags are differences of the difference. The formula for panel regression is

$$\Delta y_{it}^E = a + \beta_0 \Delta x_{it} + \beta_1 \Delta x_{i(t-1)} + \cdots + \beta_K \Delta x_{i(t-K)}$$
$$= a + \beta_{cumul} \Delta x_{i(t-K)} + \gamma_0 \Delta(\Delta x_{it}) + \gamma_1 \Delta(\Delta x_{i(t-1)})$$
$$+ \cdots + \gamma_{K-1} \Delta(\Delta x_{i(t-K+1)})$$
$$\text{with} \quad \beta_{cumul} = \beta_0 + \beta_1 + \cdots + \beta_K \qquad (23.16)$$

Data with multiple time periods allows us to examine pre-intervention trends, or pre-trends, too: what happened to y before an intervention, or more generally, before a change in the causal variable x. It's the same concept as with diff-in-diffs. Recall from Chapter 22, Section 22.3, that examining pre-intervention trends can help assess the parallel trends assumption: whether the outcome would have changed among treated subjects without the intervention as it changed among untreated subjects.

We can also add lead terms to an FD regression to examine pre-trends and capture reverse effects, just like with single time series (presented in equation (23.6)). An FD panel regression with K lags and L leads looks like this:

$$\Delta y_{it}^E = a + \beta_0 \Delta x_{it} + \beta_1 \Delta x_{i(t-1)} + \cdots + \beta_K \Delta x_{i(t-K)} + \gamma_1 \Delta x_{i(t+1)} + \cdots + \gamma_L \Delta x_{i(t+L)} \qquad (23.17)$$

The γ coefficients on the lead terms are zero if, prior to time periods when x may change, y tends to change the same way regardless of whether and how much x actually changes. That would be evidence for similar pre-trends, as well as no reverse effect. Of course, zero coefficients on the lead terms are not decisive evidence for exogeneity in themselves, as other confounders may play a role. But they are important evidence. When the coefficients are not zero, including those lead terms can mitigate the bias in the effect estimates.

Review Box 23.7   Lags and leads in FD panel regressions

- Panel regression in first differences with K lags:

$$\Delta y_{it}^E = \alpha + \beta_0 \Delta x_{it} + \beta_1 \Delta x_{i(t-1)} + \cdots + \beta_K \Delta x_{i(t-K)} \qquad (23.18)$$

- The cumulative coefficient is

$$\beta_{cumul} = \beta_0 + \beta_1 + \cdots + \beta_K \qquad (23.19)$$

- β_{cumul} shows how much more y tends to increase in total within the next K time periods, after a one-time increase of x by one more unit.
- When Δx is exogenous (contemporaneous and lagged), β_{cumul} shows the effect of a one-unit change of Δx on Δy, on average, over K time periods.
- We can estimate differences in pre-trends across cross-sectional units, and potential reverse effects, by including lead terms in the regression: $\Delta x_{i(t+1)}, \Delta x_{i(t+2)}, \dots$

23.B2   CASE STUDY – Immunization against Measles and Saving Children

FD regressions

Let's estimate the effect of the immunization rate on the child survival rate with FD panel regressions. We start with the simplest FD regression, with left-hand-side variable $\Delta surv$ (year-to-year change in the survival rate of children below age 5, in percentage points), and right-hand-side variable Δimm (year-to-year change in the immunization rate of children of age 1 to 2 years, in percentage points). Then we estimate FD regressions with lags and leads. Similarly to the FE regressions above, we use population as the weight in all regressions, because our question is about the effect on individual children.

Table 23.4 shows the results of four FD regressions. In each regression, the left-hand-side variable is the change in child survival rate in percentage points. In the first regression we include the contemporaneous change in the immunization rate; in the second one we include its five lags, too; in the third one we have the same five lags but use the transformation to get a direct estimate of the cumulative effect. The fourth regression adds three lead terms in the change of immunization rate.

First, note the numbers of observations. In column (1) we have 3268 observations: with 20 years of data for 172 countries, we have $172 \times 19 = 3268$ year-to-year changes. In columns (2) and (3) we include 5 lags, and that uses up the first five observations of Δimm in each country. As a result, we have $172 \times 14 = 2408$ observations in total. In column (4) the last three years are used up by the lead terms, reducing the number of observations to $172 \times 11 = 1892$.

Table 23.4 The immediate and lagged effect of measles immunization on child survival

Variables	(1) Δ surv	(2) Δ surv	(3) Δ surv	(4) Δ surv
Δ*imm*	0.009**	0.010**		
	(0.002)	(0.002)		
Δ*imm* lag 1		0.010**		
		(0.002)		
Δ*imm* lag 2		0.011**		
		(0.002)		
Δ*imm* lag 3		0.009**		
		(0.002)		
Δ*imm* lag 4		0.007**		
		(0.002)		
Δ*imm* lag 5		0.006**		
		(0.002)		
Δ*imm* lead 1				0.008**
				(0.002)
Δ*imm* lead 2				0.007**
				(0.002)
Δ*imm* lead 3				0.005
				(0.003)
Δ*imm* cumul			0.053**	0.054**
			(0.010)	(0.008)
Constant	0.188**	0.136**	0.136**	0.125**
	(0.024)	(0.018)	(0.018)	(0.018)
Observations	3268	2408	2408	1892
R-squared	0.013	0.078	0.078	0.093

Note: FD panel regression estimates. The regressions that show the cumulative effect estimates include lags of the further differenced right-hand-side variable. Clustered standard error estimates in parentheses.
** $p < 0.01$, * $p < 0.05$.
Source: worldbank-immunization dataset. balanced yearly panel, years 1998–2017 in 172 countries.

Focusing on the coefficients of interest, column (1) shows that child survival tends to increase by 0.09 percentage points more when immunization against measles increase by 10 percentage points more. Column (2) shows lagged associations: that lives tend to be saved in the years following an increase in immunization. (The fourth and fifth lag coefficients are smaller; further lags would have even smaller coefficients.) The coefficient of the fifth lag in column (3) shows the cumulative association: within five years of an increase in immunization by 10 percentage points, child survival tends to increase by approximately 0.53 percentage points, 95% CI is [0.035,0.071]. (You may check that the cumulative coefficient is indeed equal to the sum of all coefficients in column (2).)

The estimate of the cumulative coefficient is virtually the same in column (4) despite including the lead terms. At the same time, some of the coefficients on the lead terms are positive, indicating positive pre-trends: immunization rates tend to increase after child survival rates have already increased. These pre-trends are weaker than the cumulative effect estimates, and conditioning on them doesn't change the results, but their existence raises the possibility that the true effect of immunization is smaller than our estimate here.

But how close is our estimated coefficient of approximately 0.05 to the actual average effect? The time path of the lagged effects supports the causal interpretation, but the positive pre-trends are a problem. We'll investigate this question further later, after we introduce a few tools to address trends in FD regressions.

23.11 Aggregate Trend and Individual Trends in FD Models

In contrast with the simple **FE regressions**, simple **FD regressions** capture aggregate trends, at least linear **aggregate trends**: the intercept in an FD regression is the estimate of the average change in y. However, similarly to FE regressions, we can add time dummies to FD regressions, too. Those time dummies can capture nonlinear aggregate trends.

The formula of a FD regression with K lags and time dummies (time FE) is the following:

$$\Delta y_{it}^E = \theta_t + \beta_0 \Delta x_{it} + \beta_1 \Delta x_{i(t-1)} + \cdots + \beta_K \Delta x_{i(t-K)} \tag{23.20}$$

In equation (23.20), θ_t denotes the coefficients of the time dummies, or, in other words, the time-specific intercepts also known as **time fixed effects**. They capture potential nonlinearities in the aggregate trend: average changes in y across cross-sectional units that may be different from one time period to another time period.

While time dummies capture an aggregate trend in a completely flexible way, that does not necessarily solve all problems with trends. Besides an aggregate trend, cross-sectional units in the data may have their own trends, too. Here we don't have the opportunity to estimate flexible trends, because we have only one observation for each time period for each unit. But we can capture individual linear trends. The way to do this is similar to what we did with **pooled time series**: allow the intercept to be different across cross-sectional units. The formula for an FD regression with K lags, time dummies, and individual-specific intercepts to capture individual trends is

$$\Delta y_{it}^E = a_i + \theta_t + \beta_0 \Delta x_{it} + \beta_1 \Delta x_{i(t-1)} + \cdots + \beta_K \Delta x_{i(t-K)} \tag{23.21}$$

The new thing in the equation is a_i. It measures the average change in y in cross-sectional unit i across all time periods, as a deviation from the flexibly estimated aggregate trend θ_t, and when x does not change (and didn't change for the past K time periods). In effect, the a_i denote separate intercepts for each cross-sectional unit i. This is the same idea as allowing for individual-specific intercepts in pooled time series regressions, see Section 23.5.

Note that with both the time dummies and subject-specific intercepts, there are too many coefficients to estimate. Thus, in practice, when the software estimates such a regression, it leaves out one of the time dummies and one of the individual intercepts. But that's a technical detail. The important thing is that the inclusion of these intercepts changes the interpretation of the coefficients of interest (here the β coefficients) by conditioning on aggregate trends of any form and linear individual-specific trends. In other words, we examine changes in a way that compares observations that are deviations from the aggregate trend and the individual linear trend as well.

Review Box 23.8   Aggregate trends and individual trends in FD panel regressions

- FD panel regressions take care of aggregate linear trends automatically, by estimating associations of changes not levels.
- We can capture aggregate trends of any form by adding time dummies to FD regressions.
- We can capture individual linear trends by adding individual-specific intercepts to FD regressions.

23.B3   CASE STUDY – Immunization against Measles and Saving Children

Aggregate trends, confounders, individual trends

We re-estimated the FD panel regressions including year dummies, potential confounders, and country-specific intercepts. Recall that year dummies in FD regressions can take care of aggregate trends that are not linear, confounders can capture time-varying measured confounder variables, and country-specific intercepts can take care of country-specific linear trends.

The focus of this case study is the effect of immunization on child survival. Thus we show the cumulative coefficient that is our estimate of the long-run effect. Table 23.5 also shows what other variables the regressions include, but it does not show the estimates themselves.

Table 23.5   The effect of measles immunization on child survival. FD panel regression estimates with year dummies, confounders, and country-specific trends

Variables	(1) Δ *surv*	(2) Δ *surv*	(3) Δ *surv*
Δimm cumulative	0.052**	0.030**	0.011**
	(0.010)	(0.009)	(0.003)
Year dummies	Yes	Yes	Yes
Confounder variables	No	Yes	Yes
Country-specific trends	No	No	Yes
Observations	2408	2408	2408
R-squared	0.088	0.212	0.331

Note: FD panel regressions with 5 lags of all right-hand-side variables. The table shows the cumulative coefficient on the change of immunization over the 5 lags. Clustered standard error estimates in parentheses. ** $p < 0.01$, * $p < 0.05$.
Source: `worldbank-immunization` dataset; balanced yearly panel, years 1998–2017 in 172 countries.

Column (1) adds year dummies to the regression that we presented in column (3) in Table 23.4 earlier. Recall that the cumulative coefficient there was 0.053; here it is 0.052. Thus conditioning on the aggregate trend in a flexible way led to the same effect estimate as conditioning on linear aggregate trend only.

Column (2) shows that including the potential confounders of changes in GDP per capita and population makes a significant difference to the effect estimate. It's now 0.030, with 95% CI [0.012, 0.048]. We don't show the coefficients of the included confounders here: for GDP, they are mostly positive and their sum is statistically significant; for population they are strong and positive and statistically significant. Thus, it was omitting population growth, and, to a smaller extent, GDP growth, that made the estimates in column (1) larger than the estimates in column (2).

Note that the estimate of the cumulative coefficient is similar to the FE estimate (0.038) that also conditioned on year dummies and the confounder variables (column (2) in Table 23.2). This is in line with the fact that FE regressions tend to approximate long-run associations.

Finally, column (3) includes the country-specific linear trends (country-specific intercepts in the FD regression), along with the year dummies and the confounders. Including country-specific linear trends leads to a large drop in the cumulative coefficient. It's now 0.011, but the SE is smaller, too, so that the 95% CI is [0.005, 0.017]. We don't show the estimates on the population and GDP; they are not statistically significantly different from zero. In fact, we get the same estimate on the cumulative coefficient on immunization whether we include those confounders or not. This shows that including country-specific trends captures all observed confounders.

To interpret this coefficient: a 10 percent increase in the immunization rate tends to be followed by a 0.1 percentage point increase in the child survival rate within five years in the data relative to its country-specific trend; the corresponding expected increase in child survival is 0.05 to 0.17 percentage points in the general pattern represented by the data.

This concludes our case study. What have we learned from this analysis about the effect of measles vaccination on saving children's lives? To answer this question, let's consider our best estimate, the one that conditions not only on observable confounders but country-specific trends as well (Table 23.5, column (3)). This is the estimate that we think is closest to the true effect. It says that, when ten percentage points more children receive immunization against measles, the child survival rate tends to increase by 0.05 to 0.17 percentage points relative to its country-specific trend. Or, when ten percentage points fewer children receive immunization against measles, the child survival rate tends to drop by 0.05 to 0.17 percentage points relative to its country-specific trend.

Is this the expected effect of immunization on child survival? We can't be certain. The FD panel regression model that we used to estimate it conditions on many things, the most important of which turned out to be country-specific trends. While we can't be certain that this ensures that the parallel trends assumption holds, the evidence in the data doesn't show that it's violated: including confounders in that regression made no difference, and there was no difference in the pre-trends. So, this estimate may be a good approximation to what the true effect is. Thus, while maintaining that with this observational data we can't be sure, we can say that it appears that immunization against measles indeed saves children.

What have we learned about FE and FD regressions from this case study? We have seen how we can use multiple lags in an FD regression to estimate cumulative associations. The case study illustrated that we can use FE regressions to estimate the same long-term association in a simpler way. We were able to condition on aggregate trend in a flexible way and include observed confounder variables in our FE and FD regressions.

At the same time, we have seen that the FD model can easily include country-specific intercepts to handle country-specific trends, which can make a big difference. When relevant, this suggests that the parallel trends assumption wasn't true without conditioning on these trends. Whether conditioning on them makes the assumption true remains a question, but it certainly gets us closer to satisfying it. Moreover, we could use evidence in the data, such as examining pre-trends with this regression, to get some evidence about the parallel trends assumption. In this example the evidence supported it, so we concluded, with the caveat that we can't be sure about it, that the estimate from the FD regression with additional xsec fixed-effects may be a good approximation to the true effect.

23.12 Panel Regressions and Causality

In Chapter 21, we argued that it's difficult to estimate the effect of x on y by conditioning on all confounders, because typical data don't include all potential confounder variables.

However, as we argued in Section 23.6, including cross-sectional fixed effects amounts to conditioning on some kinds of unobserved confounders. To be more precise, it amounts to conditioning on all confounders, observed or unobserved, that don't change, as long as those confounders affect only the the individual-specific average values of x and y. Moreover, this is true not only for FE regressions but for FD regressions, too. All of this sounds a little complicated, but we'll devote the next section to an explanation.

Suppose that the following regression would give a good estimate of the effect of x on y by conditioning on z:

$$y_{it}^E = a + \beta x_{it} + \gamma z_i \qquad (23.22)$$

Importantly, here z_i differs across i but is the same for all t: it doesn't change. That is in contrast to y_{it} and x_{it}, both of which differ not only across i but also across t.

Suppose, moreover, that we don't observe z_i in the data. Recall our example of the effect of family income on fruit and vegetable consumption. Both may be affected by personality traits, such as how future-oriented people are. But those personality traits are unobserved in the data. Thus, regressing fruit and vegetable consumption on income confounds the effect of income and the effect of unobserved personality traits. Suppose, however, that personality traits don't change, at least not during the years we observe people in the data. That would be an example of a confounder that doesn't change.

Now consider the FE regression. One way to understand the FE regression is that it transforms variables into mean differences: their differences from the average value of each i across time. That's nothing other than than the difference between the next two equations:

$$y_{it}^E = a + \beta x_{it} + \gamma z_i \qquad (23.23)$$
$$\bar{y}_i^E = a + \beta \bar{x}_i + \gamma z_i \qquad (23.24)$$

When we take the difference of these two equations, γz_i drops out because z_i doesn't change, and so its average value within i is simply its value: $z_i = \bar{z}_i$. So

$$(y_{it} - \bar{y}_i)^E = \beta(x_{it} - \bar{x}_i) \qquad (23.25)$$

But the same is true for FD regressions, which are differences between two time periods. Let's write out the original regression for times t and $t-1$, and take their difference:

$$y_{it}^E = a + \beta x_{it} + \gamma z_i \qquad (23.26)$$

$$y^E_{i(t-1)} = \alpha + \beta x_{i(t-1)} + \gamma z_i \qquad (23.27)$$

$$\Delta y^E_{it} = \beta \Delta x_{it} \qquad (23.28)$$

Thus, FE regressions and FD regressions can estimate the effect of x on y without the bias due to confounders that don't change.

Confounders that do change may still matter, though. Moreover, even confounders that don't change may matter if they affect not simply the levels of x and y but their changes. That's in fact part of the parallel trends assumption: there should be nothing out there that would make y change differently for subjects that are different in x on top of the effect of x itself.

As a counterexample, consider family income and fruit and vegetable consumption. Suppose that personality traits affect not only the average income and average fruit and vegetable consumption of families but also their change. For example, the income of more future-oriented people may grow faster, and such people may also be quicker at incorporating new advice into their diet. That would lead to a biased effect of income both in an FE and an FD regression: fruit and vegetable consumption as well as income would increase more among families with more future-oriented members than among families with less future-oriented members, even if income had no effect itself. That would be the usual violation of the parallel trends assumption: y would change differently among subjects who are different in x, even if x had no effect.

To summarize, FE and FD regressions can lead to unbiased estimates of the effect of x on y even if there are unmeasured confounders, as long as those confounders don't change and affect only the levels of x and y not their changes. Conditioning on individual trends can lead to unbiased effect estimates with confounders that don't change themselves but affect changes in x and y. Confounders that change through time need to be observed and included in the FE or FD regression. We have seen that conditioning on individual trends is feasible with FD regressions: we need to include i-specific intercepts. There are more advanced models that allow for conditioning on individual trends in FE regressions, too, but those are beyond the scope of this textbook.

23.13 First Differences or Fixed Effects?

The FE and FD panel regressions are alternative methods to estimate the average long-run effect of x on y using xt panel data with multiple time periods. Which one should we use, when, and why?

In a sense, FE and FD regressions are similar because both condition on confounders that affect the level of y and x and don't change through time. FE regressions do that by comparing values of y and x to their cross-sectional means. FD regressions do something similar by comparing values of y and x to their values in the previous time period. Confounders that affect the change in y or x still matter for both FE and FD regressions, whether the confounders themselves change through time or not.

At the same time, FE and FD regressions have their differences. Each has its advantages and disadvantages. Let's start with FD.

The main advantage of **FD regressions** is the transparent way they estimate how y tends to change when x changes, both in the same time period and in each time period afterwards. The coefficient on the contemporaneous term (Δx_{it}) shows how y changes in the same time period; the coefficient on the first lag ($\Delta x_{i(t-1)}$) shows how y changes one time period later, and so on.

But this is also the disadvantage of the FD regression: it won't estimate associations, or effects, in time periods that are not included among the lags. With a contemporaneous term (Δx_{it}) only, we can hope to estimate immediate effects only; by including one lag, we can hope to estimate effects that are immediate and delayed by one time period only, and so on. Thus, to be able to estimate long-run effects with an FD regression, we need to include enough lags. But having many lags makes the number of observations small, leading to less precise estimates.

In principle, another advantage of FD regressions is that they condition on a linear aggregate trend simply by having both y and x as changes in the regression. However, this advantage is not very important in practice. That's because it is good practice to include time dummies in both the FE and FD regressions anyway, and those take care of an aggregate trend of any form in either kind of regression.

A more important advantage of FD regressions is that they offer a straightforward way to condition on linear trends that differ from cross-sectional unit to cross-sectional unit, by including xsec FE in the FD regression.

In contrast, FE regressions are a simple method of estimating long-run effects. We don't have to think about lags; we don't have to transform variables in funny ways – we simply get an estimate of the long-run effect. To be more precise, we get an estimate of the average of short-term and long-term effects. When the long-term effects kick in fast, that's a good approximation of the long-term effects themselves. A further advantage is that gaps in the data – missing observations for some years for some units – are much less of a problem for FE models, as FD models would lose two observations for every missing value.

When we are interested in how an effect plays out over time, FE regressions are a less intuitive choice. We can include lags and leads in an FE regression, too, to learn about the time path of the effect and pre-trends. It's not as intuitive as using the FD regression, but it can give a good approximation. It turns out that we can make FE regressions condition on unit-specific trends, too. That's more cumbersome than with FD regressions, and it has some limitations. We haven't discussed that method in this textbook.

To summarize, if we are interested in how the effect plays out over time, FD regressions are the good choice. If we are interested in long-run effects, we can choose either. FD regressions are still more intuitive, but it's more cumbersome to estimate long-run effects in their framework. FE regressions are simpler to estimate, although they are less intuitive, and conditioning on unit-specific trends is more difficult with them.

As usual, when there is no clear ranking between methods, it is good practice to carry out the analysis both ways. Thus, when interested in long-run effects, it's good practice to estimate both appropriate FE and FD regressions. If they point to the same conclusions, it's a sign of robustness. If not, we should understand why they differ. Maybe the FD regression didn't include enough lags; maybe the FE estimate is affected by the slow buildup of the effect; maybe losing observations in FD due to lags is important; or maybe the way the two models condition on observed confounders or unit-specific trends is different. Once we understand the difference in the results, we can make a conscious choice and estimate the effect using the better regression.

Review Box 23.9   First differences (FD) or fixed effects (FE)?

FD regressions:

- can uncover immediate associations without including lags;
- can uncover long-run associations by including sufficient numbers of lagged right-hand-side variables and calculating the cumulative slope coefficient;
- take care of linear aggregate trends without including anything else;

- can take care of nonlinear aggregate trends by including time dummies;
- can take care of cross-sectional unit-specific linear trends by including cross-sectional FE.

FE regressions:

- can uncover long-run associations without including lags;
- can uncover the time path of associations by including lags;
- can take care of average nonlinear aggregate trends by including time dummies;
- can take care of cross-sectional unit-specific linear trends in a cumbersome way.

Summary advice:

- FD is a better choice if interested in the time path of effects;
- for long-run effect estimates, both FE and FD may be a good choice, with appropriate modifications.

23.14 **Dealing with Unbalanced Panels**

Before concluding our chapter, let's discuss the potential problems that can arise with unbalanced panel data when our goal is estimating the effect of an intervention. We discussed problems with unbalanced panel data with two time periods in Chapter 22, Section 22.6.

Recall that, in **balanced xt panel data**, all subjects (cross-sectional units) are observed at the same time periods. The time series have the same length for each subject, and there are no gaps in them, or all units have the same gaps (e.g., holidays). In contrast, in **unbalanced xt panel data**, not all cross-sectional units are observed at the same time periods (see Chapter 1, Section 1.2).

As with any kind of missing data, this raises two problems (see Chapter 2, Section 2.8). The first, and usually less severe, problem is that we have fewer observations for some units, resulting in wider confidence intervals. The second, but potentially more severe, problem is that data may not be missing at random.

If we have unbalanced panel due to data **missing at random**, we don't have to worry about biased estimation. In contrast, with non-random missing data, we have selection bias in terms of the length of observed event times: subjects for whom we observe more observations before or after the treatment may be different in terms of their potential outcomes.

Consider our **Immunization against measles and saving children** case study using country-year panel data. An example for an unbalanced panel data would have some countries with fewer years in the data. In this case the cause would be almost surely non-random: countries with fewer observations on immunization and mortality tend to have years, in which standard data collection practices were not yet implemented or were disrupted by some crisis. In the latter case, disruption by crisis, we could expect immunization and mortality to be different, even compared to their average values within the country. Thus, by omitting those years, we would look at immunization and mortality rates in other, non-crisis years. However, the evolution of mortality and immunization before or after such a crisis may be affected by the crisis itself, thus introducing an omitted variables bias into FD or FE estimates. As a data exercise, you are invited to check if the results of our case study are different when using the unbalanced panel for the 20 years of our analysis. (The results are the same, because there are very few missing data points.)

What can we do when we have unbalanced data and we worry that it's due to non-random missing data points?

The most widely used solution is to analyze a balanced panel subset of the data. This can be achieved in two ways: including only time periods that are observed for all cross-sectional units, or including only cross-sectional units with the same number of time periods observed.

The first choice, restricting the time periods, is an appropriate solution if the time periods we exclude wouldn't matter, either because they would be similar to the ones we included, or we are not interested in them, or, more realistically, we can accept that we can't estimate them (such as very long-run effects). In fact, this is what we did in our **Immunization against measles and saving children** case study. The data starts in 1980, but only 64 of the 192 countries had non-**missing values** for immunization and child mortality from 1980 onward. Instead, we considered only the 20 years starting with 1998, for which 186 of the 192 countries had non-missing values for immunization and child mortality.

The second choice, restricting the set of cross-sectional units, has similar consequences. By doing so, we acknowledge that we can generalize the results of the analysis to subjects that are represented by the data. At the very least, we should have a good idea what kinds of subjects a restricted set represents. A good way to achieve that is to select subjects based on some observable characteristics so we have a clearer idea of what they represent, such as excluding countries based on income level, firms based on size, or employees based on tenure. That clarifies what our balanced data represents, but it doesn't make it represent other kinds of subjects.

An alternative to using the balanced panel only is to work with the entire unbalanced dataset. That is the good solution when our panel data is unbalanced due to missing values at random. It may also make sense if the proportion of missing observations is large and we want all cross-sectional units represented.

As usual, there is rarely a single best solution, and the good solutions may vary from case to case. In any case, it's good practice to check if the conclusions of the analysis are robust across alternative solutions that make sense. And, most importantly, it's good practice to make conscious decisions, based on domain knowledge and knowing the data, and to document those decisions in a transparent way.

23.15 Main Takeaways

Panel data methods help us get a step closer to causality.

- Data with multiple time periods can help uncover short- and long-run effects and examine pre-trends.
- When interested in the effects on a single cross-sectional unit, we may analyze a single time series or pool several time series of similar units.
- With panel data having multiple time periods, we should use an FD regression to uncover the development of the effect over time, and an FD or an FE regression to uncover the long-run effect.

PRACTICE QUESTIONS

1. Write down a time series regression in first differences and one lag of the causal variable, and interpret its coefficients.
2. Write down a panel regression in first differences with a causal variable and its lag. Interpret all coefficients.

3. What are clustered standard errors good for in a panel regression? When should we use them?

4. What are lead terms in an FD regression, and what are they good for?

5. How can you condition on an aggregate linear trend in an FD regression? How about an aggregate non linear trend?

6. How can you condition on an aggregate trend in an FE regression? Does that take care of a nonlinear trend, too?

7. What are time fixed effects in a panel regression? What kinds of problems do they solve, and what kinds of problems do they not solve?

8. An FE regression to estimate the effect of an intervention using multi-period panel data gives different estimates when you include time dummies and when you don't. Which result would you prefer and why?

9. You want to estimate the effect of a change in the exchange rate on inflation in a small open economy, using monthly time series data. Write down a regression that will allow you to estimate immediate and delayed effects as well. Define the coefficient of cumulative association and interpret it.

10. You want to estimate the impact of whether a company offers flexible work hours on the proportion of employees it retains. You have panel data with many companies from several years; no firm had flexible work hours in the beginning. Write down an FD regression to estimate this effect and interpret its coefficients.

11. In the same example, when does the coefficient on the causal variable estimate the effect, and what exactly can it estimate?

12. Using cross-country yearly panel data, the year-on-year change of log CO_2 emission is regressed on the year-on-year change of log GDP. The slope coefficient is 0.6. What is the proper interpretation of this coefficient without further assumptions? When can you interpret it as an effect, and what is the interpretation then?

13. You want to estimate the effect of a merger between mobile telephone providers on the price they charge. You have data from several countries for several years. Such a merger took place in some countries in some years. Your outcome variable is an average combined price of mobile services in each country in each year. Write down an FE panel regression that could estimate the effect and interpret the coefficient on the causal variable. When does this give a good estimate of the effect you are after?

14. The goal is to learn how gasoline sales change at a gas station if they change their price relative to the price of local competitors. You have time series data on weekly quantity sold at all the gas stations, weekly price, and weekly price of the local competitors averaged. From the two price variables, you create a relative price: the price charged by the gas station divided by the price charged by local competitors. Write down a time series regression in log changes that can estimate the effect and interpret its coefficients. When can you interpret your slope estimate as an effect, and what is its interpretation then?

15. You are interested in learning if higher income makes people spend more on computers. You have a panel dataset of individuals followed between 2005 and 2015; one observation is a person–year. For each person–year, you know the annual income and the annual spending on computers (laptops, software, services). The data is from a web survey, and it is an unbalanced panel. What regression would you use to uncover the effect you are after? Describe a problem that the unbalanced nature of the panel may cause and how you would handle it.

DATA EXERCISES

Easier and/or shorter exercises are denoted by [*]; harder and/or longer exercises are denoted by [**].

1. Answer the same question as in our case study **Import demand and industrial production** (how the import demand of the USA affects industrial production in Thailand) using the same `asia-industry` dataset, but carry out a few robustness checks. Include season dummies, exclude five months after September 2008 with the largest drops, and include lead terms. Discuss your findings and compare them with the case study results. [*]

2. Repeat the exercise in our case study **Import demand and industrial production** for a different country using the World Bank's World Development Indicators database. You may choose a country in Central or South America, or a small European country, and total imports from Germany instead of the USA. Document all the key decisions you had to take. [**]

3. Use the same `worldbank-immunization` dataset to estimate the effect of immunization on child survival employing FD regressions with seven lags instead of the five lags we had in the case study. Estimate the FD regressions, present the results analogous to the ones in Tables 23.4 and 23.5, and discuss what you find. [*]

4. Use the same `worldbank-immunization` dataset to estimate the effect of immunization on child survival, employing FD regressions. Carry out two robustness checks. First, use all observations in an unbalanced panel. Second, drop the observations with extreme changes in the immunization rate. For each modified sample, re-estimate the FE and FD models, present results analogous to the ones in Tables 23.4 and 23.5, and discuss what you find. [*]

5. Use the `airline-tickets-usa` dataset that we used in the case study in Chapter 22, but, instead of aggregating the quarterly data to years and keeping two years only, keep the quarterly data, and keep all quarters. Define a binary treatment variable that is one for observations where the merged new airlines company operated, and zero otherwise (all markets would have zero value before the time of the merger). You can choose the time of the merger as the last quarter of 2015. Estimate an FE regression and interpret its coefficient. You may consider including quarter dummies, year dummies, and observable confounders, and you may or may not use weights (average before-merger passenger number is a good candidate for weight). Argue for your modeling choices and discuss your findings. Do you arrive at the same conclusion as we did in Chapter 22, Section 22.A3 [**]

REFERENCES AND FURTHER READING

There are several very good advanced textbooks and handbooks on the analysis of panel data. Of them, we recommend Baltagi (2013), Matyas & Sevestre (2008), and Wooldridge (2001).

24 Appropriate Control Groups for Panel Data

How to estimate the counterfactual using pre-intervention outcomes in comparative case studies and event studies

Motivation

A country experienced a major natural disaster in the recent past. You want to estimate the effect on total GDP in the year of the disaster, and the following few years. You have data on GDP and other macro variables for the country and several other countries for several years before and after the disaster. It's straightforward to show how total GDP changed after the disaster. But how should you use this data to estimate the counterfactual: how total GDP would have changed in the country without the natural disaster?

Success in team sports depends on many things, and the work of the coach, or manager, is likely one of them. When a team performs below expectations, replacing the manager is one of the options teams can consider. You want to estimate the expected effect of replacing a manager in professional football (soccer). You have data on all games for several seasons from the league you are interested in, and you have data on the managers working for the teams in this league. How would you use this data to estimate the effect of manager replacement on team performance? In particular, how would you estimate the counterfactual: how the performance of low-performing teams would have changed if the manager hadn't been replaced?

When using xt panel data to estimate the effect of an intervention by diff-in-diffs or FD or FE methods, we compared all treated subjects to all untreated subjects in the data we had. But there may be reasons to select only some of the untreated subjects to form a control group. The control group should help in getting a good estimate of the counterfactual non-treated outcome: what would have become of outcome y for the treated observation, or observations, if they hadn't been treated.

This chapter discusses how data analysts can select a subset of the $x = 0$ observations in their data that are the best to learn about the counterfactual, and when that needs to be a conscious choice instead of using all available observations in the data. We introduce two methods. The first one is the synthetic control method, which creates a single counterfactual to an intervention that affects a single subject. The second one is the event study method, which helps trace the time path of the effect on many subjects that experience an intervention at different time points. Event studies are FD or FE panel regressions with a twist. Besides introducing the method, we discuss whether and how we can choose an appropriate control group and how we can include them in event study regressions.

This chapter includes two case studies. First, in **Estimating the effect of the 2010 Haiti earthquake on GDP**, using the `haiti-earthquake` dataset, we use the synthetic control method to quantify the impact of the natural disaster that hit the country. Second, we come back to football managers, whom we briefly examined in Chapter 2. In the case study **Estimating the impact of replacing football team managers**, we apply an event study method to analyze the effect of replacing a manager, after low performance in the middle of a season, on subsequent team performance, using the `football` dataset.

Learning outcomes
After working through this chapter, you should be able to:

- identify comparative case study situations that permit synthetic control analysis;
- estimate the effect of a single intervention using the synthetic control method;
- identify situations that permit event study analysis using xt panel data;
- carry out an event study analysis using xt panel data after selecting an appropriate control group.

24.1 When and Why to Select a Control Group in xt Panel Data

With observational xt panel data, we can use diff-in-diffs or FD or FE regression to estimate the effect of an intervention (Chapters 22 and 23). Typically, we use all observations in the data for these methods. When estimating the effect of a binary treatment variable, this means that we use all observations with $x = 0$ to learn about the counterfactual. Most of the time, those other observations include cross-sectional subjects that were never treated as well as time periods of treated subjects (those that were treated at some point) in which they weren't treated.

Whether that's a good choice depends on whether the parallel trends assumption holds for all those other observations. Recall that this assumption postulates that the change of outcome y among untreated observations is the same, on average, as what the average change in y would have been among treated observations, had they not been treated (see Chapter 22, Section 22.3, and Chapter 23, Sections 23.6 and 23.9).

Sometimes the parallel trends assumption holds when considering all $x = 0$ observations in the data. Other times, though, it holds only for some of the $x = 0$ observations in our data. In this second case, we should keep only some of the $x = 0$ observations, for which the parallel trends assumption holds. But how can we know whether the assumption holds for all, or only some of the observations, and, in the second case, how can we select the observations for which it holds?

In this chapter we consider situations in which data analysts can select a subset of the $x = 0$ observations in their data that has a better chance of satisfying the parallel trends assumption. This amounts to selecting the **control group**: a group of untreated observations that we use to learn about the counterfactual average outcome of the treatment group. We start with the conceptually most straightforward case, with a single cross-sectional subject treated in a single time period.

24.2 Comparative Case Studies

The first method we introduce in this chapter can help answer a very specific question: what was the effect of an intervention (binary x) on y that happened in a specific subject i (country, region, firm)? Such situations are called **comparative case studies**. In social science, "case study" often means examining one event. They are comparative because we want to know not only what happened there after the intervention but also the counterfactual: what would have happened without the intervention. To say something about the counterfactual, we need a control group of other observations.

Take the example of one of the best-known comparative case studies. The state of California introduced taxes on tobacco and restricted tobacco use in indoor places in 1988. The study investigated the effect of these policies on cigarette sales. Cigarette sales decreased substantially after 1988 in California. But the trend was negative even before 1988. How much of the negative trend after 1988 was due to the policies introduced in 1988, and how much of it would have happened anyway?

The best way to answer such a question is to estimate an explicit counterfactual: the value of y that we think we would have observed had the intervention not taken place. Thus, for this comparison, we would have two time series for the time periods after the intervention: one for the observed y, and one for the counterfactual y. Comparing these two can answer our question. But what's the best way to construct that second, counterfactual time series?

24.3 The Synthetic Control Method

The idea of this method is to construct a single control subject that gives us the counterfactual time series of y. The constructed subject is called a **synthetic control**. It's a control because it serves to estimate the counterfactual – it's a control group with one element. It's synthetic, because it is not an actual observed subject. Instead, it is one that is constructed from multiple observed subjects. Those other subjects are called the **donors**; their set is called the **donor pool**.

The synthetic control is created using information before the intervention. It's created so that it's as similar to the treated subject as possible before the intervention. Then we compare the outcomes after the intervention between the treated subject and the synthetic control. This comparison is the estimate of the effect.

To be more precise, the synthetic control method uses panel data with multiple time periods. This data includes observations on the treated subject as well as observations on the donor pool. The donor pool comprises the subjects that the analyst chooses for the method to consider. From the subjects in the donor pool, the method creates a single synthetic subject. That single synthetic subject is a weighted average of the subjects in the donor pool.

The method relies on an optimization algorithm to calculate the weights making sure that the values of the outcome variable and the observed confounder variables before the event are similar between the treated subject and the synthetic control. Which variables we want to include here is our choice. But it's always about their pre-intervention values. We usually want the average pre-intervention values of the outcome and the confounders to be similar between the treated subject and the synthetic control. Most of the time it's impossible to create a synthetic control such that all average pre-intervention values of the outcome and the confounders are the same. Instead, the method creates a synthetic control for which those values are as close to the values for the treated subject as possible.

In practice, the method tends to put zero weight on many subjects in the donor pool and picks only a few with a positive weight. As a result, the synthetic control is an average of a few subjects in the donor pool, and it is as similar to the treated subject as possible in terms of the pre-intervention values of the outcome and the observed confounders.

For example, in the California tobacco control example, the donor pool may consist of all other states in the USA, the outcome variable would be cigarette sales, and the observed confounder variables may include GDP per capita, cigarette price, or per capita beer consumption, as well as cigarette sales before 1988. Of the many states, the method puts nonzero weight on only a handful of states. Thus, synthetic California is made up of a little bit of each of those handful of states, such as Colorado and Connecticut.

Recall that the parallel trends assumption is not testable, but we usually assess it by comparing pre-trends: average y among treated and untreated subjects before the intervention. The synthetic control method is designed to make the pre-intervention value of y as close as possible between the treated subject and the synthetic control. Thus, if done well, the method results in pre-trends that are very close. Of course, this does not guarantee that the parallel trends assumption also holds. But that's about the best we can do with observational data.

For the synthetic control method, data analysts need to choose the donor pool and the variables whose pre-treatment values they want to make as similar as possible. They also need to set the time period for which the before-intervention values are considered. A different donor pool, a shorter or longer before-intervention time period, or different variables, may all result in different synthetic controls and different effect estimates.

The synthetic control method has the advantage that data analysts have to make those decisions in an explicit way, and those decisions become natural parts of the description of the analysis. Once these calls are made, the method does not rely on the analyst's selection of control units. Thus, the synthetic control method offers a transparent way to estimate the effect of a single event using observational data.

Review Box 24.1   Synthetic control method to estimate the effect of a single event

- A comparative case study uncovers the effect of a single event, or intervention, on variable y for a single subject, by asking how the outcome would have changed without the event.
- The synthetic control method estimates the effect in a comparative case study framework.
- The synthetic control method creates a single control subject from a donor pool of many untreated subjects,
  - as a weighted average of the subjects in the donor pool;
  - by assigning weights to each subject in the donor pool;
  - making sure that the pre-intervention values of y and observed confounder variables are similar.
- The effect is estimated by comparing the observed y in the treated subject with the y value constructed from the synthetic control.
- Data analysts need to choose the donor pool, the pre-intervention variables, and the length of the pre-intervention time period. Then, the donors to the control group and their weights are selected by the algorithm.

24.A1   CASE STUDY – Estimating the Effect of the 2010 Haiti Earthquake on GDP

Question, data, synthetic control

In January 2010, a strong earthquake hit the Caribbean island country Haiti, with an epicenter very close to the country's capital. Over 100 000 people died in the earthquake. Haiti is a mid-sized country (almost 10 million inhabitants in 2009) with a high population density, comprising half of an island in the Caribbean. It is a poor country, with a total GDP of 7 billion US dollars in 2009, or a GDP per capita of 710 US dollars at market exchange rate.

The question of this case study is the effect of the 2010 earthquake in Haiti on the total GDP of Haiti. This is a comparative case study: its goal is to estimate the effect of one intervention in one country. This case study follows a published study; see the references at the end of this chapter. We use the data made available by the authors of the study, and we use their specification of the synthetic control method.

The earthquake could affect total GDP through various mechanisms. Beyond the death toll, it led to a decrease in the population of Haiti by causing many survivors to emigrate. It destroyed infrastructure, which made economic, and any other, activity difficult. It also led to diseases and malnutrition of many survivors, decreasing their productivity in addition to all other consequences.

The real question of the analysis is not whether the earthquake decreased total GDP in Haiti: it certainly did. Instead, one question is the magnitude of the negative effect. The other question is how much of the negative effect was permanent: has Haiti returned to the level or growth of GDP it could have had without the earthquake?

The outcome variable, y, is total GDP, at constant US prices of 2010. The post-intervention time is 2010 through 2015.

To start, let's plot the time series of y in Haiti. Figure 24.1 shows the time series from 2004 through 2015; we have marked 2010, the year of the earthquake, with a vertical line. The graph shows a substantial drop in 2010, from 7 billion to 6.6 billion US dollars, and some growth in total GDP in subsequent years.

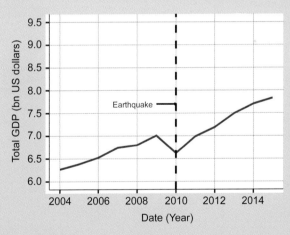

Figure 24.1   Total GDP in Haiti

Note: Total GDP, US dollars, constant prices of 2010, in billions.
Source: `haiti-earthquake` dataset.

While the time series of GDP in Haiti tells us what happened to y after the earthquake, it doesn't tell us what would have happened to it without the earthquake. In other words, we don't know the counterfactual. Figure 24.1 suggests a substantial drop in the year of the earthquake that appears persistent, but we don't know what to compare it to. Should it be to the level in 2009? Should it be to a trend line that's a continuation of the positive trend before 2009? If yes, how should we continue it? To learn how much of the drop in Haitian GDP was due to the earthquake, and how persistent that drop was, we need a time series of counterfactual GDP.

The synthetic control method offers to estimate that counterfactual. It is an algorithm that creates a synthetic control subject as the weighted average of the donor pool. The counterfactual outcome is the outcome of this synthetic control subject: the average outcome variables of the donor subjects, using the previously calculated weights. In Section 24.2 we described the decisions we have to make for the method. The decisions that we made following the study we reference below are as follows.

The donor pool is 22 countries that have GDP per capita below USD 4000 in 2009 (PPP) and data available for all variables we use, from 2004 through 2015. These 22 countries are Bangladesh, Benin, Burkina Faso, Burundi, Cambodia, Cameroon, Kenya, Kyrgyz Republic, Liberia, Madagascar, Mali, Moldova, Mozambique, Nepal, Nicaragua, Rwanda, Senegal, Sierra Leone, Sudan, Tanzania, Togo, and Uganda.

The pre-intervention time period is 2004 through 2009. The set of confounder variables comprises key geographical and macro-economic variables: land size, population, GDP per capita, exports, imports, consumption, gross capital formation, and inflation. All variables are at yearly frequency; the method will consider their average across the pre-intervention years. Instead of its pre-intervention average, we include the value of total GDP (our y variable) in three selected pre-intervention years (2005, 2007, and 2009).

The synthetic control method chose 5 of the 21 countries to have nonzero weight: Burundi (23%), Cameroon (21%), Moldova (9%), and Togo (47%), plus Liberia with 0.2%. The next figures show the results, in two ways. First, Figure 24.2a shows the time series of total GDP in Haiti and the synthetic control country. Second, Figure 24.2b shows the log difference between those two, to approximate the percent loss of GDP.

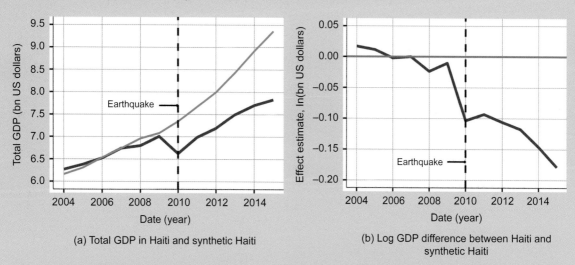

(a) Total GDP in Haiti and synthetic Haiti

(b) Log GDP difference between Haiti and synthetic Haiti

Figure 24.2   The effect of the 2010 earthquake on the total GDP of Haiti. Synthetic control estimate

Note: Total GDP, constant USD prices of 2010, in billions. Synthetic Haiti: synthetic control country (23% Burundi, 21% Cameroon, 0.2% Liberia, 9% Moldova, 47% Togo).

Source: `haiti-earthquake` dataset.

Both Figures 24.2a and 24.2b are informative, and it's best to examine the two together. The left panel gives more context, while the right panel is better able to tell the story in numbers.

According to the results, the 2010 earthquake had a severe and permanent negative effect on Haitian GDP. In 2010, Haitian GDP dropped to about 10 percent below what it would have been without the earthquake. That initial drop proved to be permanent: Haitian GDP remained 10 percent below the synthetic control GDP for the next two years. Then, GDP increased, but the gap with counterfactual GDP widened further.

Note that, even though our method aimed to create a synthetic control that matches the pre-trend in GDP, it didn't achieve that perfectly. Total GDP in Haiti grew a little less than in the synthetic control even before the earthquake. But that difference in pre-trends is tiny compared to what happened in 2010. Thus, the 10% decline in GDP is likely due to the earthquake itself. It's more difficult to tell to what extent the further decline after 2013 is the result of the earthquake. Even without that further decline, though, the decline due to the earthquake appears to have been permanent. The synthetic control method thus helped us create a counterfactual and quantify the impact of the earthquake.

How robust are the conclusions of this analysis? The counterfactual time series of GDP is as good as the countries the method chooses. Here the countries with substantial weights are Togo, Burundi, and Cameroon, all African countries, chosen because of their pre-2010 level of GDP and other macroeconomic variables. They are different, in many ways, from Haiti. They are on a different continent, they have different economic structures, and their export markets are different, too. Note that the synthetic control included not a single Central American or Caribbean country, and the donor pool contained only one because the others had either too high GDP or had no appropriate data available. Indeed, this problem is quite general when we want to create counterfactuals from other countries. There are just so many countries on Earth to choose from, and all are different in many ways.

This concludes our case study. It illustrates how we can carry out a synthetic control analysis to estimate the effect of a single event for a single country. The donor pool was selected according to a simple criterion, and we created the synthetic control country using pre-intervention values of those variables. The algorithm gave positive weights to a few of the donor countries and zero weight to the rest. We showed the effect estimates by comparing the time series of Haitian GDP to the time series of the GDP estimate of the synthetic control. This case study illustrates both the strength and the limitations of the synthetic control method.

24.4 Event Studies

After considering comparative case studies with a single intervention affecting a single subject, we turn to interventions with more than one treated subject. We continue to consider binary causal variables that can change from 0 to 1 but not the other way around. Some subjects become treated at one point in time; others may remain untreated. Importantly, different subjects may become treated in different time periods.

In Chapters 22 and 23, we discussed methods that we can use to estimate the effect of such interventions: diff-in-diffs and its generalizations, FD and FE regressions. In this section we introduce the event study method, which is best viewed as a twist to those methods.

The event study method is not really a separate method. It means reorganizing the data, and then using the familiar FD or FE regression, with lags and leads. Recall that, in xt panel data, each observation is identified by which subject it belongs to (index i), and which time period it belongs to (index t). t denotes natural time: the year, the month, the day, of the observation. With different subjects becoming treated at different times, x_{it} turns from zero to one at different values of t.

The essence of the **event study method** is to re-define time in the data. Instead of natural time, we define and use **event time**: time around the intervention. Pre-intervention time periods are labeled with negative numbers: -1 stands for one time period before the intervention, -2 for two periods before, and so on. The time period when the intervention happens is usually labeled as event time zero, and time periods following that are labeled with positive numbers: $+1$ for one time period after the intervention, $+2$ two periods after, and so on. However, sometimes the event happens between two observations. In this case, some data analysts define time zero as the first time period after the intervention, $+1$ as the second time period, and so on. This can be a little confusing, but it has the advantage of keeping the frequency at one unit. The alternative solution, preferred by other data analysts, is to skip zero, and have $+1$ follow -1. This has the advantage of being clear about before and after, but it leads to a jump in the event time, which can lead to problems when using statistical software. In the end, it's the data analyst's choice whether to include zero as an event time period and give it some meaning, or make event time jump from -1 to $+1$.

Let's start with a simple case, in which all subjects become treated at some point. Here we don't have a control group of subjects that never become treated. Defining event time for subjects that become treated at one point is straightforward. It would be less straightforward with a control group of subjects who don't become treated; we'll discuss that in subsequent sections.

Without a control group, we do within-subject comparisons, analogously to a single after–before diff instead of a diff-in-diffs. In this case the event study estimates describe the patterns of pre-intervention changes and post-intervention changes in the outcome variable. If we see no changes right before a subject becomes treated, or those changes are similar to the usual trend or seasonality, we may conclude that those pre-intervention changes are a good counterfactual: without the intervention the outcome would have changed similarly. However, when we estimate significant pre-intervention changes, we have a problem: subjects were selected into the treatment after their outcomes changed in specific ways. Thus, even without the intervention, their subsequent outcomes may have changed differently, and the pre-intervention changes are not a good counterfactual. Thus, uncovering what tends to happen before as well as after the intervention can be useful.

To estimate the effect of the intervention, we need to specify an xt panel regression in first differences (FD) or fixed effects (FE). Let's write down an FD **event study regression** without confounder variables. Using data with only observations that become treated (for a time period between s_{min} and s_{max}), it is

$$\Delta y_{it}^E = a + \sum_{0}^{s_{max}} \beta_s D_{is} + \sum_{s_{min}}^{1} \gamma_s D_{i(-s)} \tag{24.1}$$

In this regression, the D_{is} variables are binary indicators for each event time period s (D stands for dummies). So, for example, $D_{i1} = 1$ if the observation is for subject i and event time 1. Just as with any other xt panel regression, we can add other right-hand-side variables if we want to.

β_0 shows the average change in the year of the intervention, β_1 shows the average change one year after, and so on, with $\beta_{s_{max}}$ showing the change s_{max} years after. γ_1 shows the average change one year before the intervention, and γ_s shows the average change s_{min} years before. s_{max} and s_{min} are the choices of the data analyst. a shows the average change across all other years: those after s_{max} and those before s_{min}. Data analysts may choose to cover all event time periods with the D dummies, in which case we wouldn't have an intercept in the regression (or leave one event time period out for a reference).

Just as with any FD regression, we can include covariates here, as well as their lags. For simplicity, we continue examining regressions without covariates. All interpretations would be similar with covariates, except we would condition on their values if we included them.

As an example, consider the effect of receiving an environmental certification, such as the ISO 14001, on toxic emissions by chemical firms. Firms choose whether and when to apply for a certification, so there is self-selection here. Suppose that we have yearly balanced panel data (say, for the 2009–2018 period) on the emission levels of many companies, none of which were certified in the beginning, but all became certified in one year or another within this time window. Let's define the event time as zero in the year when the firm got certified, negative before that, and positive after that. Suppose all firms in the data got certified between 2012 and 2016. Here we have seven pre-intervention years observed if certified in 2016, and fewer years if certified earlier. We have six post-intervention years observed if certified in 2012, and fewer years if certified later.

Suppose that we want to estimate the (log) change in emissions one year before the certification, in the year of the certification, and one to two years after the certification. The regression that can estimate those would have four dummies: three for event times 0 to 2, and one for event time -1:
$(\Delta \ln y_{it})^E = a + \beta_0 D_{i0} + \beta_1 D_{i1} + \beta_2 D_{i2} + \gamma_1 D_{i(-1)}$. Here $s_{max} = 2$ and $s_{min} = 1$.

In this example, a shows the trend: the average change in all other event time periods. β_0 shows the change in toxic emissions (in log points) in the year when companies got certified, on average, in addition to the trend (a); β_1 shows the average change one year after certification in addition to trend, β_2 two years after, and γ_1 shows the average change one year before certification in addition to trend. This specification makes sense if the change in toxic emissions deviates from its trend only in the -1 year to $+2$ year window around the certification.

Note that we would get the exact same results in this example if we left natural time as it was, without transforming it into event time, and we specified an FD regression with a contemporaneous term, two lags, and a lead. And that's true for all event studies: we can get the exact same estimates from an appropriately specified regression using xt panel data with natural time. So what's the difference, and when and why would we want to use this event time transformation?

One advantage is that the notation in event study regressions is more intuitive. Negative indices on the D binary indicators refer to changes before the intervention; positive indices refer to changes after the intervention. In contrast, when leaving time in natural units, changes before the intervention are captured by lead terms, while changes after the intervention are captured by lag terms. This is a minor advantage for experienced data analysts, but may be a great help for the audience to understand the results of the analysis.

Second, an apparent disadvantage is that the event time is not straightforward to define for subjects that never become treated. However, as we'll see, we can turn this into an important advantage: defining event time for untreated subjects forces us to think about the control group in an explicit way. It leads to conscious and transparent decisions about which untreated subjects to include in the control group and how.

Third, a disadvantage of the event study transformation is that it becomes more cumbersome to include variables that are related to natural time, such as time dummies for aggregate trends (Chapter 8).

With these advantages and disadvantages, the event time transformation is not always the best choice. We'll return to when to go for it after we discuss control group selection. But first, we illustrate the method using treated subjects only in our case study.

> **Review Box 24.2 Event studies**
>
> - Event studies are a method to analyze the effect of an intervention (binary causal variable, or treatment) using xt panel data with subjects, some of which become treated during the time period covered in the data.
> - Event studies re-define time around the intervention: this is called event time.
> - Event studies provide a straightforward way to describe pre-intervention changes and post-intervention changes among treated subjects.

24.B1 CASE STUDY – Estimating the Impact of Replacing Football Team Managers

Question, data, event study with treated teams only

In this case study we explore the extent to which replacing the manager of an underperforming football (soccer) team leads to better team performance. Football managers are best thought of as coaches with a broad responsibility. When a professional football team performs below expectation, one of the options the team can consider is replacing its manager. The expected effect of manager replacement is obviously interesting for the teams themselves, but it also helps sports bettors and fans to form expectations about team performance.

Besides football, or sports more generally, this question is relevant for all organizations with a person in a managerial role with high potential impact on the performance of the organization, including for-profit companies, non-governmental organizations, and governments and municipalities. Analyzing sports is helpful because we have good measures of performance. For sports fans, it's also interesting in its own right.

Here is a thought experiment that helps clarify the intervention and what we mean by an effect. Take many teams that have performed below expectations for some time, say six games, during the season. Replace the manager in half of them with a new manager who is available. Record the performance of the teams for some time again, say 12 games. The average treated outcome is the average performance among teams whose managers were replaced. The average untreated outcome is the average performance among teams whose managers weren't replaced. The difference between these averages shows the average effect of replacing a manager.

Note a few details in this thought experiment. First, the subjects are not random teams: they are teams that have underperformed for some time. Second, new managers must come from somewhere: they should be available to replace the managers that left. And third, manager replacement takes place during the season, not at the end of the season. The first choice makes our thought experiment in line with our question: it's about replacing a manager due to inadequate team performance not for some other reason. Second, we need to keep in mind that the replacements should come from a pool that is relatively limited, and this is a constraint that may make the effect less positive. The third choice is for making the intervention more specific and linking our thought experiment to our measurement strategy. When managers are replaced between seasons, many other things may change, including, most importantly, the players themselves. Focusing on replacement within seasons isolates the intervention from other potential changes.

Before jumping into the analysis, let's think about what effects we can expect and why. We may expect a positive effect: the new manager shakes up the team, gives confidence, thus performance improves compared to what it would be without replacing the manager. But we may also expect a negative effect, or no effect, in the short run, even if the effect is positive in the longer run, because that positive effect may take time to build. Alternatively, replacing the manager may have no effect on team performance, neither in the short run nor in the long run. In this case, performance after replacing a manager would be the same as what it would have been, had the manager not been replaced. A version of this case is mean reversion: after a run of bad luck, things go back to normal, which would seem like an improvement, whether the manager is replaced or not. A manager that is replaced even though that had no real effect would be a little like a sacrifice to bring good weather. Some sports analysts call this possibility ritual scapegoating. But note that all, or some, of the effects we listed may happen simultaneously. In particular, mean reversion and a positive long-term effect may exist at the same time. In this complex case, we would expect team performance to increase even without replacing the manager, but replacing the manager improves it even more in the long run.

Our data is observational, without randomized interventions. So the most important question is the sources of variation in the causal variable: why is it that some teams replace their managers in the middle of a season, while others don't? And are those sources endogenous or exogenous?

Performance below expectations is an important source of variation in whether a manager is replaced. It's also endogenous, as past performance is likely related to future performance – for example, through mean reversion. Another source is whether a suitable manager replacement is available when the team wants to replace its manager. This may be an exogenous source. Conflicts between managers and others in the management team may also be a source of variation, and it's likely an endogenous source. Thus, of the various sources of variation, most are likely endogenous. But there may be exogenous sources as well, which is encouraging, because it makes estimating the effect of manager replacement possible, at least in principle.

We use the `football` dataset in this case study. It comes from the English Premier League (EPL), one of the top professional football (soccer) leagues in the world. Our data includes all games in 11 seasons (2008/9 through 2018/9) and who the team manager was at each game. We constructed this data from two tidy data tables, one on team–games and one on managers; we explained the source and construction of this data in the **Identifying successful football managers** case study in Chapter 2. (Note that in each season there are 20 teams, and teams from the second division replace the bottom three performers after each season. Within each season, each team plays with every other team twice.)

One row in the data table we use for this case study is a team–game observation: one team playing one game. Thus, each game is featured twice in this data table, once for each of the two teams. There are 8360 observations in the data, 760 in each season (38 games for each of the 20 teams in a season). The number of team–seasons is 220: each of the 11 seasons had 20 teams. There are 36 teams altogether in this data; 7 played in each of the 11 seasons in the EPL, 2 played in only one of the 11 seasons, and the rest played in more than one but less than 11 seasons. The most important variables are the team and season identifiers, the game number for the team (starting with one at the beginning of each season and ending with 38), the identifier of the manager, and the points the team achieved (0 for loss, 1 for draw, 3 for win).

In our data, about one quarter of the games end with a draw (1 pt), while the rest are won by one of the teams. This implies an average point per week rate of 1.38.

We created a binary variable that denotes a manager change within the season. There are 94 manager changes in the data. To be able to analyze pre-intervention changes and post-intervention changes in performance, we need manager changes with enough games the team played both before and after it. We decided to analyze 12 games before and 12 games after the change, within the same season. Thus, we selected only changes that occurred between game 13 and game 26 of the 38 games each team played in each season, and we didn't select games that were preceded or followed by another manager change within 12 games. This resulted in 33 of the 94 manager changes meeting the analysis criteria; these 33 manager changes are the interventions we analyze. Figure 24.3 shows the number of interventions by game in the season in our data. There are no interventions before the 13th game and after the 26th game, because we defined interventions having at least 12 games before and 12 games after the manager change. The number of interventions between the 13th and the 26th game is distributed relatively evenly.

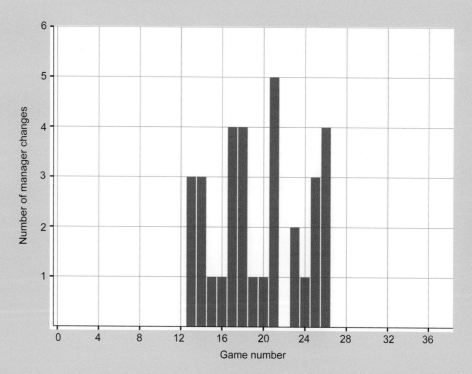

Figure 24.3   The numbers of manager changes by game number

Note: The numbers of interventions by game week. Interventions are manager changes with 12 games before and after in the season without another manager change.
Source: `football` dataset. English Premier League, 11 seasons from 2008–2009 to 2018–2019. N=33 manager changes.

With the interventions selected, let's define the event time variable. We set event time for +1, +2, ..., +12, for the games with the new manager and −1, −2, ..., −12, for games before the new manager took over. Note that we decided not to have zero here, because manager changes happen between games.

We examine points, our performance measure, for 1 to 12 games before the intervention and 1 to 12 games after the intervention. The way we defined interventions makes sure that we have observations for all of these 24 event time periods for all interventions: a balanced panel in terms of event time.

Figure 24.4 shows those averages (over the 33 cases) by event time. It adds four lines for averages of 6 games: −12 to −7, −6 to −1, +1 to +6, and +7 to +12. The graph includes a vertical dashed line at zero where there are no data points.

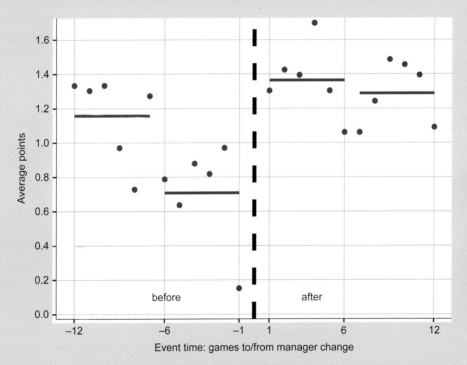

Figure 24.4 Average points before and after manager replacement

Note: Average points (wins 3 pts, draws 1 pt, losses 0 pt; over 33 events) before and after manager change by event time (games before/after the manager change). Six-week average lines added.
Source: `football` dataset. English Premier League, 11 seasons, balanced panel of 12 games before and after the 33 manager changes. N=792 team-games.

The figure shows three important patterns in pre-intervention outcomes. First, teams that ended up replacing their manager had lower points than average already 7 to 12 to games before the event: an average of 1.16 points compared to the overall average of 1.38 points. Second, they then experienced a drop to an average of 0.71 points for the next six games. And, third, even among those six games, they achieved only 0.15 points in the game immediately preceding the manager change. This pattern suggests that managers tend to be changed for below-average performing teams sliding into even worse performance, and the change itself happens after a lost game (or, exceptionally, a draw). When thinking about a control group to estimate a counterfactual, we need to keep these patterns in mind.

It turns out that this phenomenon, the drop in average outcome before the intervention, is a common feature of interventions. It's also called the **pre-intervention dip** or **Ashenfelter's dip** after the economist who first discovered it and understood its importance.

After the manager change, performance tends to bounce back to close to the overall league average (1.38), or slightly below that, and stays around that level for at least 12 games (1.36 points in the first 6 games; 1.29 points for the next six games).

So we see a substantial increase in average performance after managers are replaced. But the pre-intervention changes are substantial, too, suggesting strong selection into which team replaces a manager and when. That is of course not surprising. But it also means that we can't get a good estimate of the effect of manager replacement by analyzing this sample, consisting only of teams that replaced their managers.

The question, of course, is the counterfactual: how average performance would have changed if the managers weren't replaced. To answer this question, we need to select an appropriate control group.

24.5 Selecting a Control Group in Event Studies

Examining pre-intervention trends in y using the event study approach can reveal important pre-intervention changes. To have a chance of satisfying the parallel trends assumption, we need a control group with similar pre-intervention changes in y. But the observations that could make up the control group don't have an intervention. How can we find subjects with pre-intervention changes that are similar to what we see in the treated group, if those subjects didn't experience an intervention?

In the comparative case studies, the answer is straightforward: examine what happened to potential control subjects before the point in calendar time when the intervention happened in the treated subject (1988 in the California tobacco tax example, 2010 in the Haiti earthquake). However, with many subjects becoming treated at different times, that would be cumbersome.

Instead, therefore, many data analysts select the control group by focusing on the average patterns of pre-intervention outcome changes in the treatment group, and possibly other variables. In effect, this means defining **pseudo-interventions**: points in time for untreated subjects that are preceded by changes in y that are, on average, similar to actual pre-intervention changes among treated subjects.

Let's go back to our example of chemical firms receiving an environmental certification, and the effect of this certification on subsequent toxic release. Suppose that we see that firms that become treated are larger than average, and they had a more negative pre-treatment trend. That more negative pre-treatment trend means that they reduced their toxic release more than average through the entire pre-treatment time period. Suppose, moreover, that these firms reduced their toxic release even more in the year before they got certified. An appropriate control group would consist of firms with a similar pattern of pre-treatment emissions beside being from the same industry and of the same size.

This approach to selecting a control group is similar, in spirit, to the synthetic control method: the control group is defined to provide similar pre-intervention patterns. We use no data after the intervention to define the control group.

With the appropriate control group, and a pseudo-intervention time for each control subject, we can define event time for them just as we did for treated subjects. Then we can estimate an event-time regression to estimate average changes in y before and after the intervention, separately for treated and untreated subjects. Building on the event study regression we specified for treated subjects only, we would add an interaction term to the dummy variables of pre-intervention and post-intervention time periods:

$$\Delta y_{it}^E = a + \sum_0^{s_{max}} \beta_s D_{is} + \sum_{s_{min}}^1 \gamma_s D_{i(-s)} \tag{24.2}$$

$$+ \eta treated_i + \sum_0^{s_{max}} \delta_s treated_i \times D_{is} + \sum_{s_{min}}^1 \varphi_s treated_i \times D_{i(-s)}$$

In this regression, the β coefficients show the average post-intervention changes among untreated subjects – for them, these are the average changes after their designated pseudo-interventions. The effect estimates are the δ coefficients: they show the average difference in post-intervention changes between treated and untreated subjects, corresponding to the time period of the treatment (δ_0), the first time period after the treatment (δ_1), and so on.

a is the trend among untreated subjects, while η is the difference between the trends among treated and untreated subjects. If the control group was selected appropriately, the trend before the intervention will be the same in the two groups. If, in addition, the post-treatment dummies cover all time periods in which the changes are different, the overall trends should be very similar in the remaining event time periods. Thus, η should be close to zero. The γ coefficients show differences in pre-intervention changes from trend among untreated subjects (their pre-pseudo-intervention changes), and the φ coefficients show how those differ for treated subjects. Again, the φ coefficients should be close to zero if the control group selection was successful, in the sense that it has similar changes before the pseudo-interventions as the actual pre-intervention changes among treated subjects, on average.

Review Box 24.3 Selecting a control group for event studies

- Selecting a control group of untreated subjects is necessary to estimate the counterfactual: what would have happened to treated subjects without the treatment.
- In event studies, we define the control group by defining pseudo-interventions.
- Pseudo-interventions are event time periods for untreated subjects that are preceded by changes in outcomes that are similar, on average, to pre-intervention changes in outcomes among treated subjects.

24.B2 | CASE STUDY – Estimating the Impact of Replacing Football Team Managers

Event study analysis with a control group of pseudo-interventions

In the first part of our case study we identified 33 manager changes in the data that were preceded and followed by 12 games with the same manager in the same season. We defined event time around the changes: -12 to -1 before, and $+1$ to $+12$ after, leaving out zero. We plotted average performance (points) for each event time separately, and in six-game intervals, in Figure 24.4. We identified three important patterns in pre-intervention performance: points were slightly lower than average 7–12 games earlier (1.16 instead of 1.38); this was followed by a strong dip so that points 1–6 games earlier were substantially lower (to 0.71); the game before the manager change was a loss for almost all teams (point average 0.15).

We saw a large increase in average performance after the manager change, back to the overall average. Because of the strong pre-intervention patterns in performance, we can't simply attribute these post-intervention changes to the manager change. Instead, we need an explicit estimate of the counterfactual: how would post-intervention performance have changed if the manager hadn't been replaced.

To have a counterfactual estimate, we need a control group. A good control group would consist of 24-game intervals within a season for teams that didn't replace their managers during this time. The middle of these 24-game intervals would be the time of the pseudo-intervention. For this control group to have the potential to give a good counterfactual estimate, it needs to exhibit the same average patterns before the pseudo-intervention as the average pre-intervention patterns we documented for manager changes. Those patterns were lower than average points 12 to 7 games preceding the intervention, even lower average points 1 to 6 games before the intervention, and a lost game (or, rarely, a draw) just before the intervention.

To define such a control group, we searched for 24-game intervals for teams in seasons without any manager change. In particular, we searched for games that were preceded and followed by 12 games or more in the season and met three criteria. Average points per game for 7 to 12 games before them was between 5 and 8 points over 6 games (average points per game: 0.83–1.33); the dip for the 1 to 6 games before was between a total dip of 1 to 8 points over 6 games (average points per game: 0.17 to 1.33); and the game before had zero points (i.e., the team lost).

These criteria made sure that the six-game averages were almost exactly the same as the corresponding six-game pre-intervention averages in the treatment group. This selection resulted in 132 candidates for the pseudo-interventions and the 24-game-window around them. Some of them had overlaps with each other, for the same team in the same season. When there was more than one candidate game within the same season for the same team, we selected the first one in the season. The result was 67 pseudo-interventions, each with 12 games before and after them with the same manager.

We made many choices when we selected this control group. The results of these choices were a close replication of the pre-intervention patterns, averaged within the control group of teams that did not replace their managers. We could have made different choices, and some alternative choices could have achieved similar results in terms of pre-intervention patterns. But the choices we made were transparent. You are invited to check the robustness of the results to different choices when selecting the control group.

Figure 24.5 shows the results. It is similar to Figure 24.4 but here we add the average points for the control group by their event time (games before and after the pseudo-intervention).

The figure shows that the pre-intervention patterns are very similar in the two groups, on average. That's by construction: we selected pseudo-interventions to make this happen. The only notable discrepancy we see is a larger spread of the point averages by event time around the six-game averages in the control group (the dots around the lines). That's especially visible for game −3, where the average points value is 1.2 in the control group and 0.8 in the treatment group.

Looking at post-intervention changes, the treatment and control averages are very similar, again. Pre-intervention averages are similar by construction. But nothing in the definition of the control group used data from after the intervention, or pseudo-intervention. The post-pseudo-intervention averages are our estimates of the counterfactual: how team performance would have changed if the manager had not been replaced. According to our results, they would have changed the same way.

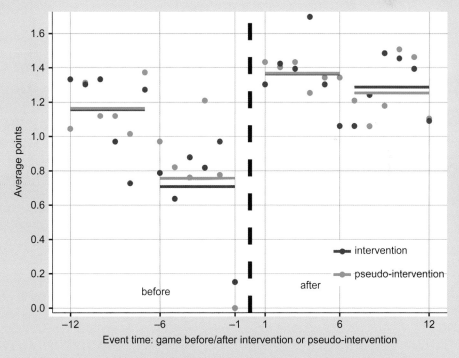

Figure 24.5   Average points before and after manager change and pseudo-intervention

Note: Average points (wins 3 pts, draws 1 pt, losses 0 pt) by event time (games before/after the management change). Six-week average lines added. Interventions: blue dots and lines. Pseudo-interventions: green dots and lines.
Source: `football` dataset. English Premier League, 11 seasons, balanced panel of 12 games before and after 33 manager changes and 67 pseudo-interventions. N=2400 team-games.

We can estimate the same results in a regression. Regression estimates complement the visualization by giving numeric estimates together with standard errors. To produce simple and easy-to-interpret results, we aggregated event time into six-game intervals. Each intervention and pseudo-intervention is preceded by two of those six-game intervals, and followed by another two of those six-game intervals. Thus, for each intervention and pseudo-intervention, we have four observations.

This is a balanced xt panel dataset, with 100 team–season observations (33 interventions and 67 pseudo-interventions), each observed 4 times. We specified an FD regression for this data. Here the change in points is the change between the six-game averages. For each team–season observation we have three changes in the data. The FD regression approach implies that differences between average team performance don't matter; it's the changes that are compared across teams (Chapter 23).

First we estimated a regression separately for the actual manager changes: $33 \times 3 = 99$ observations (three first differences from the four time periods). Then we estimated an analogous regression for the pseudo-interventions: $67 \times 3 = 201$ observations. The third regression combines them, including the interaction with treatment. The regression includes the following binary variables: *treat* for team–season with actual manager changes (the treatment group), $post_{1-6}$ for 1 to 6 games after the intervention, or pseudo-intervention, and $post_{7-12}$ for 7 to 12 games after the intervention, or pseudo-intervention. The formula for this combined regression is

$$\Delta y^E = \beta_0 + \beta_1 post_{1-6} + \beta_2 post_{7-12} + \beta_3 treat + \beta_4 treat \times post_{1-6} + \beta_5 treat \times post_{7-12} \quad (24.3)$$

Here the intercept, β_0, shows the average change in points in the reference time period, from 7–12 games before to 1–6 games before, for pseudo-interventions. β_1 shows the average change in points from 1–6 games before to 1–6 games after, in addition to β_0. β_2 shows the average change in points from 1–6 games after to 7–12 games after, again, in addition to β_0. Thus, the change from 1–6 games before the pseudo-intervention to 1–6 games after it is $\beta_1 + \beta_0$.

β_3 shows the difference between the treatment and control group in terms of average point change from 7–12 games before to 1–6 before. If we selected the control group well, this should be close to zero.

The effect estimates are β_4 and β_5. They show the difference between treated and control in average point changes from the six-game-interval before to the six-game-interval after, and the change from the six-game-interval after to the next six-game interval.

Table 24.1 shows the results of the regressions. The first column shows the estimates for the treatment group, the second column for the control group, and the third column for the two together. When estimating the regressions separately for the control group (column 2), the estimates are identical to the corresponding coefficients in the regression that combines treated observations (column 3). Treatment group estimates (column 1) are identical to the sums of the coefficients on the corresponding variables and their interaction with the treated variable. Standard errors are clustered at the season–team level to allow for serial correlation.

Table 24.1 The effect of replacing managers: FD regressions with changes between six-game-average points

Variables	(1) Treatment	(2) Control	(3) Treatment + control
post 1 − 6	1.11**	1.06**	1.06**
	(0.19)	(0.09)	(0.09)
post 7 − 12	0.37*	0.34**	0.34**
	(0.16)	(0.09)	(0.09)
treated			−0.00
			(0.10)
treated × *post* 1−6			0.04
			(0.20)
treated × *post* 7−12			0.04
			(0.18)
Constant	−0.45**	−0.45**	−0.45**
	(0.10)	(0.03)	(0.03)
Observations	99	201	300
R-squared	0.33	0.42	0.39

Note: Treatment: manager change within the season; control: pseudo-intervention; see text for more detailed definitions. Clustered standard error estimates in parentheses. ** $p <0.01$, * $p <0.05$.

Source: `football` dataset. English Premier League, 11 seasons, balanced panel of 12 games before and after 33 manager changes and 67 pseudo-interventions.

The coefficients in column (1) show that average points dropped by 0.45 between 7–12 and 1–6 games before manager change in the treated group (the constant), it increased by 0.66 (−0.45 + 1.11) for the first six games after the change, and it decreased from the first six games to the next six games after the intervention by 0.08 (−0.45 + 0.37). Column (2) shows that the corresponding changes were very similar in the control group around the pseudo-intervention: −0.45, −0.45 + 1.06 = +0.61, −0.45 + 0.34 = −0.11. To better see these calculations, you are invited to compare them to the numbers shown in Figure 24.5.

The post-intervention changes are very similar in the treatment and control groups. The coefficient estimates are close if estimated separately (columns 1 and 2), and the interaction terms, which show their differences explicitly, are small (column 3). These results are, of course, the same as we have seen in Figure 24.5.

What can we conclude for our question: the effect of replacing a manager within the season? Our results suggest that game performance is expected to improve after changing manager: comparing six games before and after the intervention, we found a large improvement. However, we found the exact same average improvement among teams that experienced a similar pattern of declining performance but didn't replace their manager.

Does this mean that replacing the manager has no effect on team performance? If the control group gives a good counterfactual estimate, the answer is yes: replacing the team manager doesn't improve team performance, on average. That would still allow for a few replacements to produce positive, above average effects, but then also some replacements would produce below-average, here negative, effects.

But this is not a controlled experiment. We estimated the counterfactual from pseudo-interventions from observational data: teams that experienced similar average decline in their performance but didn't replace their managers. Why they didn't replace their manager, we don't know. Maybe they did something else to improve performance. Maybe they expected performance to bounce back, because they knew it wasn't because of the manager. (For instance, a losing streak was understood to come from playing top teams in a row.) These would be endogenous sources of variation in manager replacement, and they would lead to our control group not giving a good estimate of the counterfactual. But some of the reasons why such teams didn't replace their managers may be due to exogenous reasons, such as the unavailability of a suitable replacement, or random decisions on team boards. Ideally, it would be great to condition on the endogenous sources of variation, or, even better, focus on the exogenous sources, as instrumental variables (Chapter 21, Section 21.9).

In any case, our results don't provide any evidence supporting the notion that team performance is expected to improve after replacing a manager in the middle of a season. That may be because our counterfactual isn't good, and we would need better data to get a better control group. However, the results are informative even if they aren't good estimates of the average effect of replacing managers. In particular, they point to the importance of mean reversion. Bad periods are often followed by average ones, which are a lot better. As bad periods often yield managerial change, this could be seen as a causal effect, even if all changes are caused by other things. Any attempt to estimate the true effect of manager change has to address mean reversion.

What did we learn from this case study about the event study approach? We saw how we can use it to study the causal effect of interventions affecting several subjects at different time periods. We showed how to create event time and present pre-intervention changes and post-intervention changes with the help of the event time. Finally, we discussed how to select a control group, by defining pseudo-interventions that follow the same average changes as the pre-intervention changes for treated subjects. It is worth noting that both the synthetic control and the event study methods are related to matching: we use some algorithm to find control subjects. In the matching methods we saw in Chapter 21, we sought control subject(s) for each treated subject. For the event study here, we took a related but different route, and found a group of control subjects that are on average similar to the treated subjects.

Finally, note that we made many decisions during this analysis. Some of those were arbitrary to some extent, in the sense that we could have made other decisions that would have been equally sensible. In particular, we could have defined a different window around interventions and pseudo-interventions instead of 12 games before and after. We could have looked at different aggregates of event time, instead of the six-game averages. We could have chosen averages for each game before the intervention to be similar in the control group. We could have chosen different ranges to select our control group. But we made all of those decisions in a transparent way. We should carry out a thorough robustness check to see if we get the same main result of zero post-intervention differences with different, but equally sensible, decisions. We leave this as a data exercise.

24.6	## Main Takeaways

When estimating the effect of an intervention using xt panel data, sometimes it's better to select a subset of non-treated observations to serve as a control group.

- To estimate the effect of an intervention for a single subject, we can estimate the counterfactual using the synthetic control method.
- With an intervention affecting many subjects at different times, we can carry out an event study with the help of a control group of comparable pseudo-interventions.

PRACTICE QUESTIONS

1. What's a comparative case study? Give an example.
2. What's the donor pool for the synthetic control method? In a typical case, are all members of the donor pool used to construct the synthetic control? Give an example.
3. What kind of causal variables in what kind of data can be used in an event study method? Give an example.
4. What's the difference between natural time and event time in xt panel data? Give an example.
5. What's a pseudo-intervention in an event study, and what do we use pseudo-interventions for? Give an example.
6. A control group of pseudo-interventions has similar pre-intervention average changes in the outcome variable as the intervention group. Is this a good thing? Why or why not? Does this make the effect estimate good? Why or why not?
7. What's mean reversion, and why does it make effect estimation hard? Give an example.
8. Consider our Haiti earthquake case study. We know that total GDP fell by 0.4 billion US dollars in the year of the earthquake. Why can't we say that the effect of the earthquake was a 0.4 billion dollar decrease? Why do we need a (synthetic) control to measure the effect instead?
9. Consider our Haiti earthquake case study. With the results of the synthetic control method, how would you estimate the effect for 2011 if you knew the GDP of Haiti, Burundi, Cameroon, Liberia, Moldova, and Togo in 2011?
10. Consider our Haiti earthquake case study, and Figure 24.2. Explain how the left and right panels of the figure are related.
11. Suppose that you want to estimate the effect of the German unification in 1990 on the GDP of West Germany. Explain how you would set up a synthetic control method to do that.
12. Consider our football manager replacement case study. Explain why mean reversion is a problem there, what we did about it, and whether our solution solved the problem.
13. Suppose that you want to estimate the effect of shortening the work week to four days on employee performance in a large company with several offices. All offices introduced the four-day work week within the same year, but in different months. You have monthly data on employee performance in all offices. Describe an event study that could estimate the effect, and discuss whether you think it would give a good estimate.
14. Suppose that you want to estimate the effect of retirement on food expenditures, using panel data on many people who worked at baseline and retired at some point. Define event time for

this data, write down a regression (in first differences without a control group) that can estimate pre-intervention changes and post-intervention changes, and interpret its coefficients.

15. Consider our case study **How does a merger between airlines affect prices?** in Chapter 22. To estimate the effect of the merger, we used data on all markets before and after the merger took place. Alternatively, we could have used only some of the markets in the control group. Explain when and why that would make sense, and give a simple example of doing it.

DATA EXERCISES

Easier and/or shorter exercises are denoted by [*]; harder and/or longer exercises are denoted by [**].

1. Use the same `haiti-earthquake` dataset that we used in the **Estimating the effect of the 2010 Haiti earthquake on GDP** case study. Carry out robustness checks: estimate the effect with at least three other specifications, using a shorter time period before the intervention, using a narrower set of donor pool countries, and using different variables. Visualize your estimates similarly to Figure 24.2b. Compare your results to the findings in the case study, and discuss your results. [*]

2. Use the same `haiti-earthquake` dataset that we used in the **Estimating the effect of the 2010 Haiti earthquake on GDP** case study. Estimate the effect of the earthquake on total population and GDP per capita. Visualize your estimates similarly to Figure 24.2b. Discuss your results. [**]

3. Use the data provided by Abadie et al. (2015) and replicate their estimate of the effect of German reunification on West German per capita GDP using their synthetic control method. In particular, verify the composition of the synthetic control West Germany and replicate their Figure 3. [**]

4. Use the same `football` dataset that we used in the case study **Estimating the impact of replacing football team managers**. Carry out robustness checks. Instead of examining 12 games before and after the intervention, examine a different window and consider different averages instead of six-game averages. Select the balanced panel of interventions accordingly; reproduce the equivalent of Figure 24.4; define appropriate pseudo-interventions and select a control group of them; and estimate the effect of manager replacement with the help of this control group. Reproduce Figure 24.5 and Table 24.1, interpret and discuss the results, and compare them to the results in our case study. [**]

5. Use the same `football` dataset that we used in the case study **Estimating the impact of replacing football team managers**. Estimate the effect of replacing the manager using the unbalanced panel. In particular, define treatment as the replacement of the manager whenever it happens during the season. If a team replaces its manager more than once in a season, consider the first replacement only, and drop all games after the second manager replacement. Reproduce the equivalent of Figure 24.4; define appropriate pseudo-interventions and select a control group of them; and estimate the effect of manager replacement with the help of this control group. Reproduce Figure 24.5 and Table 24.1, interpret and discuss the results, and compare them to the results in our case study. [**]

REFERENCES AND FURTHER READING

Perhaps the best-known synthetic control study is Abadie et al. (2010). This study examined the effect of the increased tobacco tax in California in 1988 on subsequent cigarette sales, the example we used in our chapter. Another important introduction to the method is Abadie et al. (2015). A nice paper using the synthetic control method is Alrababa'h et al. (2019), who study the effect of the arrival of Mohamed Salah, an Egyptian striker, at Liverpool FC, on social attitudes towards Muslims.

Our **Estimating the effect of the 2010 Haiti earthquake on GDP** case study is based on the study of Best & Burke (2019). We used the same data source and followed their approach.

Our case study of replacing football managers is related to a few papers, such as Paola & Scoppa (2012), Besters et al. (2016), and Buinsfold & ter Weel (2003).

Our example of the effect of firms adopting environmental certification was inspired by a series of studies analyzing this effect in various countries, such as Gomez & Rodriguez (2011) for Spain.

REFERENCES

Abadie, A., Diamond, A., & Hainmueller, J. (2010), "Synthetic control methods for comparative case studies: Estimating the effect of california's tobacco control program," *Journal of the American Statistical Association* **105**(490), 493–505.

Abadie, A., Diamond, A., & Hainmueller, J. (2015), "Comparative politics and the synthetic control method," *American Journal of Political Science* **59**(2), 495–510.

Agrawal, A. Goldforb, A., & Gans, J. (2018), *Prediction Machines: The Simple Economics of Artificial Intelligence*, Harvard Business Review Press.

Alrababa'h, A., Marble, W., Mousa, S., & Siegel, A. (2019), Can exposure to celebrities reduce prejudice? The effect of Mohamed Salah on Islamophobic behaviors and attitudes, IPL Working Paper Series, No. 19–04, May.

Anderson, M. L. (2008), "Multiple inference and gender difference in the effects of early intervention: A reevaluation of the Abecedarian, Perry Preschool, and Early Training Projects," *Journal of the American Statistical Association* **103**(484), 1481–1495.

Angrist, J. D. & Evans, W. N. (1998), "Children and their parents' labor supply: Evidence from exogenous variation in family size," *American Economic Review* **88**(3), 450–477.

Angrist, J. D. & Pischke, S. (2015), *Mostly Harmless Econometrics*, Princeton University Press.

Angrist, J. D. & Pischke, S. (2018), *Mastering Metrics*, Princeton University Press.

Athey, S. (2017), "Beyond prediction: Using big data for policy problems," *Science* **335**(6324), 483–485.

Athey, S. & Imbens, G. (2016), "Recursive partitioning for heterogeneous causal effects," *PNAS* **113**(27), 7353–7306.

Baltagi, B. H. (2013), *Econometrics of Panel Data*, Wiley.

Bandiera, O., Barankay, I., & Rasul, I. (2011), "Field experiments with firms," *Journal of Economic Perspectives* **25**(3), 63–82.

Bandiera, O., Lemos, R., Prat, A., & Sadun, R. (2018), "Managing the family firm: Evidence from CEOs at work," *Review of Financial Studies* **31**(5), 1605–1653.

Banerjee, A. & Duflo, E. (2012), *Poor Economics: A Radical Rethinking of the Way to Fight Global Poverty*, Public Affairs.

Bertrand, M. (2018), "Coase lecture – The glass ceiling," *Economica* **85**(338), 205–231.

Best, R. & Burke, P. J. (2019), "Macroeconomic impacts of the 2010 earthquake in Haiti," *Empirical Economics* **56**(5), 1647–1681.

Besters, L. M., van Ours, J. C., & van Tuijl, M. A. (2016), "Effectiveness of in-season manager changes in English Premier League football," *De Economist* **164**(3), 335–356.

Bethlehem, J. (2009), "The rise of survey sampling," *The Hague/Heerlen: Statistics Netherlands* (Discussion paper 09015).

Bloom, N. & Van Reenen, J. V. (2007), "Measuring and explaining management practices across firms and countries," *Quarterly Journal of Economics* **122**(4), 1351–1408.

Bloom, N., Eifert, B., Mahajan, A., McKenzie, D., & Roberts, J. (2012), " Does management matter? Evidence from India," *Quarterly Journal of Economics* **128**(1), 1–51.

Bloom, N., Lemos, R., Sadun, R., Scur, D., & Reenen, J. V. (2014), "The new empirical economics of management," *Journal of the European Economic Association* **12**, 835–876.

Bloom, N., Liang, J., Roberts, J., & Ying, Z. J. (2015), "Does working from home work? Evidence from a Chinese experiment," *Quarterly Journal of Economics* **130**(1), 165–218.

Bloom, N., Sadun, R., & Reenen, J. V. (2017), "Why do we undervalue competent management?," *Harvard Business Review*, September–October, 120–127.

Breiman, L. (2001), "Statistical Modeling: The Two Cultures," *Statistical Science* **16**(3), 199–231. doi.org/10.1214/ss/1009213726.

Breiman, L.. Friedman, J. H., Olshen, R. A., & Stone, C. J. (1984), *Classification and Regression Trees*, Wadsworth.

Brian, J. (2015), "Naming things (lecture slides)."
 URL: *http://speakerdeck.com/jennybc/how-to-name-files*

Broman, K. W. & Woo, K. H. (2018), "Data organization in spreadsheets," *American Statistician* **72**(1), 2–10.

Buinsfold, A. & ter Weel, B. (2003), "Manager to go? Performance dips reconsidered with evidence from Dutch football," *European Journal of Operational Research* **148**(2), 233–246.

Cai, J. & Szeidl, A. (2017), "Interfirm relationships and business performance," *Quarterly Journal of Economics* **133**(3), 1229–1282.

Cairo, A. (2012), *The Functional Art: An Introduction to Information Graphics and Visualization*, New Riders.

Cairo, A. (2019), *How Charts Lie*, W. W. Norton.

Cameron, A. C. & Trivedi, P. K. (2005), *Microeconometrics: Methods and Applications*, Cambridge University Press.

Card, D. & Krueger, A. B. (1994), "Minimum wages and employment: A case study of the fast-food industry in New Jersey and Pennsylvania," *American Economic Review* **84**(4), 772–793.

Cavallo, A. (2017), "Are online and offline price similar? Evidence from large multi-channel retailers," *American Economic Review* **107**(1), 283–303.

Chawla, N. V., Bowyer, K. W., Hall, L. O. & Kegelmeyer, W. P. (2002), "Smote: Synthetic minority over-sampling technique," *Journal of Artificial Intelligence Research* **16**(1), 321–357.

Chen, Y. & Gayle, P. G. (2019), "Mergers and product quality: Evidence from the airline industry," *International Journal of Industrial Organization* **62**(C), 96–135.

Cornfield, J., Haenszel, W. Hammond, E., Lilienfield, A., Shimkin, M., & Wynder, E. (1959), "Smoking and lung cancer: recent evidence and a discussion of some questions," *Journal of the National Cancer Institute* **22**, 173–203.

Das, S. (2019), "Effect of merger on market price and product quality: American and US Airways," *Review of Industrial Organization* **55**(3), 339–374.

Drummond, C. & Holte, R. C. (2000), "Explicitly representing expected cost: An alternative to ROC representation," in *Proceedings of the Sixth ACM SIGKDD International Conference on Knowledge Discovery and Data Mining, KDD '00*, Association for Computing Machinery, pp. 198–207.

Duflo, E., Glennerster, R., & Kremer, M. (2008), "Using randomization in development economics Research: A Toolkit," in T. P. Schultz & J. A. Strauss, eds., *Handbook of Development Economics*, vol. 4, Elsevier, chapter 61, pp. 3895–3962.

Elliott, G. & Lieli, R. P. (2013), "Predicting binary outcomes," *Journal of Econometrics* **174**(1), 15–26.

Eurostat (2013), *Handbook on Residential Property Prices Indices (RPPIs)*, Methodologies and Working papers, Luxembourg.

Faro, K. & Ohana, E. (2018), "The big data problem that market research must fix," *MIT Sloan Management Review*. October 4, 2018.

Fisher, R. A. (1925), *Statistical Methods for Research Workers*, Oliver and Boyd.

Franco, A., Malhotra, N., & Simonovits, G. (2014), "Publication bias in the social sciences: Unlocking the file drawer," *Science* **345**(6203), 1502–1505.

Gelman, A., Carlin, J. B., Sterin, H. S., Dunson, D. B, Vehtari, A., & Rubin, D. B. (2018), *Bayesian Data Analysis*, third ed., CRC Press.
   URL: *www.stat.columbia.edu/ gelman/book*

Gerber, A. S. & Green, D. P. (2013), *Field Experiments. Design, Analysis and Interpretation*, W. W. Norton.

Giné, X., Karlan, D., & Zinman, J. (2010), "Put your money where your butt is: A commitment contract for smoking cessation," *American Economic Journal: Applied Economics* **2**(4; October), 213–235. https://doi.org/10.1257/app.2.4.213.

Gladwell, M. (2019), "The basement tapes."
   URL: *http://revisionisthistory.com/episodes/20-the-basement-tapes*

Golbeck, A. (2017), "How one woman used regression to influence the salaries of many," *Significance* **14**, 38–41.

Gomez, A. & Rodriguez, M. A. (2011), "The effect of ISO 14001 certification on toxic emissions: An analysis of industrial facilities in the north of Spain," *Journal of Cleaner Production* **19**(9–10), 1091–1095.

Gordon, B. R., Zettelmeyer, F., Bhargava, N., & Chapsky, D. (2019), "A comparison of approaches to advertising measurement: Evidence from big field experiments at Facebook," *Marketing Science* **38**(2), 193–225.

Greenwell, B. M. (2019), "pdp: An R package for constructing partial dependence plots."
   URL: *https://bgreenwell.github.io/pdp/articles/pdp.html*

Grolemund, G. & Wickham, H. (2017), *R for Data Science*, O'Reilly Media.
   URL: *http://r4ds.had.co.nz*

Guyon, I. & Elisseeff, A. (2003), "An introduction to variable and feature selection," *Journal of Machine Learning Research* **3**, 1157–1182.

Hamilton, J. D. (1994), *Time Series Analysis*, Princeton University Press.

Hansen, B. E. (2019), *Econometrics*, University of Wisconsin.
   URL: *www.ssc.wisc.edu/bhansen/econometrics/*

Hastie, T. & Tibshirani, R. (2016), *The Elements of Statistical Learning: Data Mining, Inference, and Prediction*, second ed., Springer.

Hastie, T., Tibshirani, R., & Wainwright, M. (2015), *Statistical Learning with Sparsity: The Lasso and Generalizations*, Chapman & Hall/CRC.

Healy, K. (2019), *Data Visualization: A Practical Introduction*, Princeton University Press.
   URL: *http://vissoc.co*

Hyndman, R. & Athanasopoulos, G. (2019), *Forecasting: Principles and Practice*, third ed., OTexts.
   URL: *https://otexts.com/fpp3/*

Iacus, S. M., King, G., & Porr, G. (2009), "cem: Software for coarsened exact matching," *Journal of Statistical Software* **30**(9).

Imbens, G. W. (2015), "Matching methods in practice: Three examples," *Journal of Human Resources* **50**(2), 373–419.

Imbens, G. W. & Rubin, D. B. (2015), *Causal Inference for Statistics, Social, and Biomedical Sciences*, Cambridge University Press.

Jadad, A. R. & Enkin, M. W. (2009), *Randomized Controlled Trials: Questions, Answers and Musings*, BMJ Books.

James, G., Witten, D., Hastie, T., & Tibshirani, R. (2014), *An Introduction to Statistical Learning: With Applications in R*, Springer.
  URL: *http://faculty.marshall.usc.edu/gareth-james/ISL/*

Kish, L. (1965), *Survey Sampling*, Wiley.

Kuhn, M. (2019), "The caret package."
  URL: *https://topepo.github.io/caret/*

Kuhn, M. & Johnson, K. (2019), *Feature Engineering and Selection: A Practical Approach for Predictive Models*, Chapman and Hall/CRC.

Kuper, S. & Szymanski, S. (2012), *Socceronomics*, Harper Sport.

Lemos, R. & Scur, D. (2019), The ties that bind: implicit contracts and management practices in family-run firms, CEPR Discussion Papers 13794, CEPR Discussion Papers.

Luca, M., & Bazerman, M. H. (2020), *The Power of Experiments: Decision Making in a Data-Driven World*, MIT Press.

Manski, C. F. (2020), "The lure of incredible certitude," *Economics and Philosophy* forthcoming.

Matyas, L. & Sevestre, P., eds. (2008), *The Econometrics of Panel Data*, Springer.

Molnar, C. (2019), "Interpretable machine learning: A guide for making black box models explainable."
  URL: *https://christophm.github.io/interpretable-ml-book/*

Muehlenbachs, L., Spiller, E., & Timmins, C. (2015), "The housing market impacts of shale gas development," *American Economic Review* **105**(12), 3633–3659.

Oster, E. (2018), "Here's why its so impossible to get reliable diet advice from the news."
  URL: *https://slate.com/technology/2018/08/heres-why-its-so-impossible-to-get-reliable-diet-advice-from-the-news.html*

Ostrom, E. (2005), *Understanding Institutional Diversity*, Princeton University Press.

Pafka, S. (2019), "Simple/limited/incomplete benchmark for scalability, speed and accuracy of machine learning libraries for classification."
  URL: *http://github.com/szilard/benchm-ml*

Paola, M. D. & Scoppa, V. (2012), "The effects of managerial turnover," *Journal of Sports Economics* **13**(2), 152–168.

Pollan, M. (2009), *In Defense of Food*, Large Print Press.

Pollard, R. (2006), "Worldwide regional variations in home advantage in association football," *Journal of Sports Sciences* **24**(3), 231–240.

Preston, S. H. (1975), "The changing relation between mortality and level of economic development," *Population Studies* **29**(2), 231–248.

Rogozhnikov, A. (2016), "Occam razor vs. machine learning."
  URL: *http://arogozhnikov.github.io/2016/07/12/secret-of-ml.html*

Rohde, M. & Breuer, C. (2017), "The market for football club investors: A review of theory and empirical evidence from professional european football," *European Sport Management Quarterly* **17**(3), 265–289.

Romer, D. (2020), "In praise of confidence intervals." NBER Working Paper No. 26672.

Sally, D. & Anderson, C. (2013), *The Numbers Game: Why Everything You Know About Soccer is Wrong*, Viking/Penguin, New York.

Salsburg, D. (2001), *The Lady Tasting Tea*, Henry Holt and Co.

Shen, Y. (2017), "Market competition and market price: Evidence from United/Continental airline merger," *Economics of Transportation* **10**(C), 1–7.

Shumway, R. H. & Stoffer, D. S. (2017), *Time Series Analysis and Its Applications: With R Examples*, Springer Texts in Statistics, fourth ed., Springer.

Siegel, E. (2013), *Predictive Analytics: The Power to Predict Who Will Click, Buy, Lie, or Die*, Wiley.

Silver, N. (2012), *The Signal and the Noise: Why Most Predictions Fail – But Some Don't*, Penguin Books.

Sloan, F. A., Ostermann, J., Conover, C., Taylor, D. H., Jr., & Picone, G. (2006), *The Price of Smoking*, MIT Press.

Stigler, S. M. (1986), *The History of Statistics: The Measurement of Uncertainty before 1900*, Belknap Press.

Stigler, S. M. (2016), *The Seven Pillars of Statistical Wisdom*, Harvard University Press.

Stock, H. J. & Watson, M. W. (2015), *Introduction to Econometrics*, third ed., Pearson Education.

Takezawa, K. (2006), *Introduction to Nonparametric Regression*, Wiley.

Taleb, N. N. (2007), *The Black Swan*, Random House.

Taylor, S. J. & Letham, B. (2018), "Forecasting at scale," *The American Statistician* **72**(1), 37–45.

Tourangeau, R., Rips, L. J., & Rasinski, K. (2000), *The Psychology of Survey Response*, Cambridge University Press.

Tsay, R. S. (2010), *Analysis of Financial Time Series*, third ed., Wiley.

Tufte, E. (1997), *Visual Explanations: Images and Quantities, Evidence and Narrative*, Graphics Press.

Volpe Martincus, C. & Blyde, J. (2013), "Shaky roads and trembling exports: Assessing the trade effects of domestic infrastructure using a natural experiment," *Journal of International Economics* **90**(1), 148–161.

Wickham, H. (2014), "Tidy data," *The Journal of Statistical Software* **59**(10).
  URL: *http://vita.had.co.nz/papers/tidy-data.html*

Wilke, C. O. (2019), *Fundamentals of Data Visualization*, O'Reilly Media.
  URL: *http://serialmentor.com/dataviz*

Wooldridge, J. (2001), *Econometric Analysis of Cross Section and Panel Data*, MIT Press.

Wooldridge, J. (2012), *Introductory Econometrics: A Modern Approach*, fifth ed., Cengage Learning.

INDEX